# Chinese
# Compact Dictionary
### Chinese – English
### English – Chinese

**Berlitz Publishing**
New York · Munich · Singapore

Original edition edited by the Langenscheidt editorial staff

Compiled by LEXUS Ltd.

Inset cover photo: © Punchstock/Medioimages

© 2006 Berlitz Publishing/APA Publications GmbH & Co. Verlag KG
Singapore Branch, Singapore

Trademark Reg. U.S. Patent Office and other countries.
Marca Registrada.
Used under license from Berlitz Investment Corporation.

Berlitz Publishing
193 Morris Avenue
Springfield, NJ 07081
USA

Printed in Germany
ISBN-13: 978-981-246-947-2
ISBN-10: 981-246-947-8

10 09 08 07

2. 3. 4. 5

# Preface

Here is a new dictionary of English and Chinese, a tool with some 40,000 references for those who work with the English and Chinese languages at beginner's or intermediate level.

Focusing on modern usage, the dictionary offers coverage of everyday language, including vocabulary from areas such as computers and business.

The Chinese in this dictionary is mainland Chinese, written in simplified characters, with pinyin pronunciation. A short appendix of important Taiwanese equivalents in traditional characters has also been included.

The two sides of this dictionary, the English-Chinese and the Chinese-English, are quite different in structure and purpose. The English-Chinese is designed for productive usage, for self-expression in Chinese. The Chinese-English, which can also be accessed through a specially compiled radical index, is a decoding dictionary, a dictionary to enable the native speaker of English to understand Chinese.

Clarity of presentation has been a major objective. The editors of this book have set out to provide the means to enable you, the user of the dictionary, to get straight to the translation that fits a particular context of use. Is the *mouse* you need for your computer, for example, the same in Chinese as the *mouse* you don't want in the house? Is *flimsy* referring to furniture the same in Chinese as *flimsy* referring to an excuse? The English-Chinese dictionary is rich in sense distinctions like this – and in translation options tied to specific, identified senses.

Grammatical or function words are treated in some detail, on both the English-Chinese and the Chinese-English sides. And a large number of idiomatic phrases are given to show how the two languages correspond in context.

All in all, this is a book full of information, which will, we hope, become a valuable part of your language toolkit.

# Contents

# How to use the dictionary

To get the most out of your dictionary you should understand how and where to find the information you need. Whether you are writing a text in Chinese or want to understand a text in Chinese, the following pages should help.

## 1. How and where do I find a word?

**1.1 English headwords.** The English word list is arranged in alphabetical order.

Sometimes you might want to look up terms made up of two separate words, for example **antivirus program**, or hyphenated words, for example **absent-minded**. These words are treated as though they were a single word and their alphabetical ordering reflects this. Compound words like **bookseller**, **bookstall**, **bookstore** are also listed in alphabetical order.

The only exception to this strict alphabetical ordering is made for English phrasal verbs – words like ♦**go off**, ♦**go out**, ♦**go up**. These are positioned directly after their main verb (in this case **go**), rather than being scattered around in alphabetical positions.

**1.2 Chinese headwords.** The Chinese word list is arranged in English alphabetical order by being sorted on the romanization system, pinyin. So if you know how a word is pronounced, or how it is written in pinyin, you can look it up straightforwardly.

If, however, you are decoding a Chinese character, and have no idea how it is pronounced or written in pinyin, then you will have to make use of the Radical Index in order to find out the pinyin for the character in question. An explanation of the Radical Index is given on page 14.

**1.3 Running heads**

If you are looking for an English or a Chinese word you can use the **running heads** printed in bold in the top corner of each page. The running head on the left tells you the *first* headword or compound on the left-hand page and the one on the right tells you the *last* headword or compound on the right-hand page.

## 2. Swung dashes

**2.1** A swung dash (~) replaces the entire headword when the headword is repeated within an entry:

> **sly** jiǎohuá 狡猾; **on the ~** mìmì 秘密

Here **on the ~** means **on the sly**.

**2.2** When a headword changes form in an entry, for example if it is put in the past tense or in the plural, then the past tense or plural ending is added to the swung dash - but only if the rest of the word doesn't change:

> **fluster** *v/t* shǐ jǐnzhāng 使 紧 张; **get ~ed** jǐnzhāng 紧张
>
> **fore**: **come to the ~** tuō yǐng ér chū 脱颖而出

But:

> **horrify**: **I was horrified** wǒ bèi xiàhuàile 我 被 吓 坏 了
>
> ***come back** huílái 回 来; **it came back to me** wǒ xiǎng qǐláile 我 想 起 来 了

**2.3** Double or treble headwords are replaced by a single swung dash:

> ♦**hold on** *(wait, TELEC)* děngyíxià 等 一 下; **now ~ a minute!** biézháojí! 别 着 急 !
>
> ♦**measure up to:** **~X** dádào X de biāozhǔn 达 到 X 的 标准

## 3. What do the different typefaces mean?

**3.1** All Chinese and English headwords and the Arabic numerals differentiating between English parts of speech appear in **bold**:

> **alcoholic 1** *n* xùjiǔ zhě 酗酒者 **2** *adj* hán jiǔjīng 含 酒 精

**3.2** *italics* are used for:

a) abbreviated grammatical labels: *adj, adv, v/i, v/t* etc
b) all the indicating words which are the signposts pointing to the correct translation for your needs
c) explanations

> **mailbox** *(in street)* yóutǒng 邮 筒; *(for house, e-mail)* xìnxiāng 信 箱

**Thai 1** *adj* Tàiguó 泰国 **2** *n* (*person*) Tàiguó rén 泰国人; (*language*) Tàiguó yǔ 泰国语

**serve 1** *n* (*in tennis*) fāqiú 发球 **2** *v/t food, meal* duānshang 端上; *customer in store* zhāodài 招待; *one's country, the people* fúwù 服务

水面 **shuǐmiàn** surface (*of water*)

伤感情 **shānggǎnqíng** hurt (*emotionally*)

把 **bǎ** *measure word for knives and chairs*; 一把刀 *yìbǎ **dāo** a knife*; 一把钳子 *yìbǎ **qiánzi** a pair of pliers/pincers* ◊ (*marking an object moved for emphasis to the start of a sentence*): 我要把车修了 *wǒ yào bǎ chē xiūle* I'll have the car repaired

**3.3** All phrases (examples and idioms) are given in **secondary bold italics**:

剩 **shèng** remain, be left over; 没剩什么 ***méishèng shénme*** there is nothing left

**vent** *n* (*for air*) tōngfēng kǒng 通风孔; ***give ~ to*** *feelings, emotions* fàxiè 发泄

**3.4** The normal typeface is used for the translations.

**3.5** If a translation is given in italics, and not in the normal typeface, this means that the translation is more of an *explanation* in the other language and that an explanation has to be given because there is no real equivalent:

**stag party** *hūnqián nánzi jùhuì* 婚前男子聚会

阿姨 **āyí** auntie (*used also to address a woman of an age similar to one's parents*)

## 4. What do the various symbols and abbreviations tell you?

**4.1** A solid black lozenge is used to indicate a phrasal verb:

♦**auction off** *v/t* pāimài diào 拍卖掉

**4.2** A white lozenge is used to divide up longer entries into more easily digested chunks of related bits of text:

**a, an** ◊ (*no translation*): **~ bus** gōnggòng qìchē 公共汽车; **I'm ~ student** wǒ shì xuésheng 我是学生 ◊ (*with a measure word*) yī 一; **can I have ~ cup of coffee?** qǐng gěi wǒ yìbēi kāfēi? 请给我一杯咖啡?; ***five men and ~ woman*** wǔge nánde yíge nǚde 五个男的一个女的 ◊ (*per*): ***$50 ~ time*** yícì wǔshí měiyuán 一次五十美元

It is also used, in the Chinese-English dictionary, to split different translations when the part of speech of each translation is different:

白 **bái** white ◊ in vain ◊ family name

冷 冻 **lěngdòng** freeze ◊ frozen

**4.3** The abbreviation F tells you that the word or phrase is used colloquially rather than in formal contexts. The abbreviation V warns you that a word or phrase is vulgar or taboo. Be careful how you use these words.

**4.4** The symbol ⇩ means that a Taiwanese equivalent translation is given in the Taiwanese appendix on pages 669-671.

**4.5** A colon before an English or Chinese word or phrase means that usage is restricted to this specific example (at least as far as this dictionary's choice of vocabulary is concerned):

**accord:** *of one's own* ~ zìyuàn 自愿

通 缉 **tōngjí:** 被通缉 *bèi tōngjí* wanted

**4.6** The letters X and Y are used to indicate insertion points for other words if you are building a complete sentence in Chinese, for example:

**grateful** gǎnjī 感激; ***be ~ to X*** duì X xīncún gǎnjī 对 X 心 存感激

**pelt** 1 *v/t:* ***~ X with Y*** jiāng Y tóuxiàng X 将 Y 投向 X

Suspension points (...) are used in a similar way:

**below** 1 *prep* zài ... de xiàmian 在 ... 的下面

# 5. Does the dictionary deal with grammar too?

**5.1** All English headwords are given a part of speech label, unless, in normal modern English, the headword is only used as one part of speech and so no confusion or ambiguity is likely. In these cases no part of speech label is needed.

**abolish** fèichú 废除

> **lastly** zuìhòu 最后
>
> **glory** *n* róngyù 荣誉
>
> **own¹** *v/t* yōngyǒu 拥有

5.2 Chinese headwords are not given part of speech labels. Where their English translations can be of more than one part of speech, then these are separated by a white lozenge. For example:

> 统 计 **tǒngjì** statistics ◊ statistical
>
> 挖 掘 **wājué** excavate ◊ excavation

5.3 Where a Chinese word has a grammatical function, this is illustrated:

> 被 **bèi** quilt ◊ (*passive indicator*): 被 炒 鱿 鱼 了 ***bèi chǎo yóuyú le*** be fired; 被 淘 汰 ***bèi táotài*** be eliminated
>
> 了 **le** (*particle indicating completed action*): 雨 停 了 ***yǔtíngle*** it has stopped raining ◊ (*particle indicating change of state*): 头 发 白 了 ***tóufa báile*** his hair is going gray; 我 买 了 ***wǒ mǎi le*** I'll take it ◊ (*for emphasis*): 你 太 好 了 ***nǐ tài hǎo le*** that's very kind

# 6. **de** 的 with adjectives.

In translations of adjectives the word **de** 的 has been omitted. This should be added if you are using a Chinese adjective (especially one of more than one syllable) attributively before a noun. Usually the noun would also have to have more than one syllable:

> **faded** *color, jeans* tuìsè 退色
>
> **faded jeans** tuìsède niúzǎikù 退色 的 牛仔裤

# The pronunciation of Chinese

All Chinese characters in this dictionary are accompanied by a romanized script known as pinyin. Not all pinyin letters, or groups of letters, are pronounced as you would normally expect them to be in English. The following is a guide to the pronunciation of pinyin.

## Initial consonants

| | |
|---|---|
| b | more abrupt than English, like p in spare |
| c | like ts in bets |
| ch | like ch in church, pronounced with the tip of the tongue curled back |
| d | more abrupt than English, like t in stare |
| g | more abrupt than English, like c in scare; always hard as in go or girl |
| h | like the Scottish pronunciation of loch, with a little friction in the throat |
| j | like j in jeep, pronounced with the lips spread as in a smile |
| k | pronounced with a slight puff of air as in cop |
| p | pronounced with a slight puff of air as in pop |
| q | like ch in cheap, pronounced with the lips spread as in a smile |
| r | like r in rung, pronounced with the tip of the tongue curled back |
| sh | like sh in shirt, pronounced with the tip of the tongue curled back |
| t | pronounced with a slight puff of air as in top |
| x | like sh in sheep, pronounced with the lips spread as in a smile |
| z | like ds in beds |
| zh | like j in judge, pronounced with the tip of the tongue curled back |

## Finals

| | |
|---|---|
| a | as in father |
| ai | as in aisle |
| an | as in ran (with the a slightly longer as in ah); but: yan as in yen |
| ang | as in rang (with the a slightly longer as in ah) |
| ao | like ow in how |
| e | as in her |
| ei | as in eight |
| en | as in open |
| eng | like en in open and g |

| er | like *err* – but with the tongue curled back and the sound coming from the back of the throat |
| i | (1) as in magaz*i*ne |
| | (2) after c, ch, r, s, sh, z and zh like the i in b*i*rd |
| ia | like ya in *ya*rd |
| ian | similar to *yen* |
| iang | *i* (as in magaz*i*ne) merged with *ang* (above) – but without lengthening the *a* |
| iao | as in y*ow*l |
| ie | like ye in *ye*s |
| in | as in th*in* |
| ing | as in th*ing* |
| iong | *i* (as in magaz*i*ne) merged with *ong* (below) |
| iu | like yo in *yo*ga |
| o | as in m*o*re |
| ou | as in d*ou*gh |
| ong | *oong* with oo as in s*oo*n |
| u | (1) as in r*u*le |
| | (2) after j, q and x like the 'u' sound in French t*u* or German *ü*ber |
| ua | w followed by *a* (above) |
| uai | similar to *why* |
| uan | w followed by *an* (above) |
| uang | w followed by *ang* (above) |
| ue | u (above) followed by e as in l*e*t |
| ui | similar to *way* |
| un | like uan in tr*uan*t |
| uo | similar to *wa*r |
| ü | as in French t*u* or German *ü*ber |
| üe | ü followed by e as in g*e*t |

## Tones

**First tone**, as in 鸡 **jī** (chicken): a high, level tone with the volume held constant.

**Second tone**, as in 极 **jí** (extreme, extremely): rises sharply from middle register and increasing in volume, shorter than the first tone; like a surprised 'what?'

**Third tone**, as in 脊 **jǐ** (ridge): starts low, then falls lower before rising again to a point slightly higher than the starting point; louder at the beginning and end than in the middle; slightly longer than the first tone.

**Fourth tone**, as in 季 **jì** (season): starts high then drops sharply in pitch and volume; like saying 'right' when agreeing to an instruction.

# Abbreviations

| | | | |
|---|---|---|---|
| *adj* | adjective | NAUT | nautical |
| *adv* | adverb | *pej* | pejorative |
| ANAT | anatomy | PHOT | photography |
| BIO | biology | PHYS | physics |
| BOT | botany | POL | politics |
| *Br* | British English | *prep* | preposition |
| CHEM | chemistry | *pron* | pronoun |
| COM | commerce, | *prov* | proverbial |
| | business | PSYCH | psychology |
| COMPUT | computers, | RAD | radio |
| | IT term | RAIL | railroad |
| *conj* | conjunction | REL | religion |
| EDU | education | s.o. | someone |
| ELEC | electricity, | SP | sports |
| | electronics | sth | something |
| F | familiar, colloquial | TECH | technology |
| *fig* | figurative | TELEC | telecommunications |
| FIN | financial | THEA | theatre |
| *fml* | formal usage | TV | television |
| GRAM | grammar | V | vulgar |
| *hum* | humorous | *v/i* | intransitive verb |
| *interj* | interjection | *v/t* | transitive verb |
| LAW | law | → | see |
| MATH | mathematics | ® | registered |
| MED | medicine | | trademark |
| MIL | military | ⇩ | Taiwanese |
| MOT | motoring | | equivalent given in |
| MUS | music | | the appendix |

# How to find Chinese characters in the Chinese-English dictionary using the Radical Index

How can I look up the meaning of a Chinese character if I don't know how to pronounce it? This is a problem that the Radical Index solves.

There are two sets of tables to be used: the Radical Chart and the Radical Index. The Radical Chart is a means for leading you into the Radical Index; and the Radical Index is a means for leading you to the entry in the Chinese-English dictionary.

1. First you have to identify the radical in the Chinese character which you want to look up. Then look for this radical in the Radical Chart on pages 14-15 and find its radical number.

2. Go to the Radical Index and find the section starting with the number allocated to the radical you have just looked up. This number is printed as a heading.

3. If this is a shortish section, you will be able to see the Chinese character you want without any difficulty. If this is a long section, you can use another device to home in on the character you are looking for.

4. Count the number of strokes in the character you are looking for (not including the strokes in the radical itself). The Chinese characters are listed according to their stroke count. The number to the left of the characters gives you the stroke count (minus the radical strokes) in each block of characters. This narrows down the list of characters you will have to scan through.

5. When you have found the character you are looking for in the Radical Index, you will see its pinyin pronunciation given. You can then go to the Chinese-English dictionary - which is ordered in English alphabetical order according to the pinyin pronunciation - and use this like an ordinary dictionary.

6. Some Chinese characters can be analyzed as having more than one possible radical. When this happens, we have used the radical which has the smallest number of strokes.

7. Some radicals have variants. These are listed after the main radical in both the Radical Chart and the Radical Index.

# Radical Chart

## 1 stroke

| No. | Radical |
|---|---|
| 1 | 丶 |
| 2 | 一 |
| 3 | 丨 |
| 4 | 丿 |
| 5 | 乙, 乛, 亅, 乚 |

## 2 strokes

| No. | Radical |
|---|---|
| 6 | 亠 |
| 7 | 冫 |
| 8 | 冖 |
| 9 | 讠 |
| 10 | 二 |
| 11 | 十 |
| 12 | 厂 |
| 13 | 匚 |
| 14 | 卜 |
| 15 | 冂 |
| 16 | 门 |
| 17 | 八, 丷 |
| 18 | 人, 入 |
| 19 | 亻 |
| 20 | 勹 |
| 21 | 儿 |
| 22 | 几 |
| 23 | 厶 |
| 24 | 又, 乂 |
| 25 | 廴 |
| 26 | 卩, 卪 |
| 27 | 阝 (left) |
| 28 | 阝 (right) |
| 29 | 凵 |
| 30 | 刀, 刂 |
| 31 | 力 |

## 3 strokes

| No. | Radical |
|---|---|
| 32 | 氵 |
| 33 | 忄, 小 |
| 34 | 宀 |
| 35 | 扌 |
| 36 | |
| 37 | 广 |
| 38 | 门 |
| 39 | 辶 |
| 40 | 工 |
| 41 | 土 |
| 42 | 士 |
| 43 | 艹 |
| 44 | 大, 廾 |
| 45 | 尢 |
| 46 | 寸 |
| 47 | 弋 |
| 48 | 扌 |
| 49 | 小, 尐 |
| 50 | 口 |
| 51 | 囗 |
| 52 | 巾 |
| 53 | 山 |
| 54 | 彳 |
| 55 | 彡, 夕 |
| 56 | 夂 |
| 57 | 犭 |
| 58 | |
| 59 | 饣 |
| 60 | 彐, 彑 |

## 4 strokes

| No. | Radical |
|---|---|
| 61 | 尸 |
| 62 | 己 |
| 63 | 已 |
| 64 | 弓 |
| 65 | 女 |
| 66 | 纟 |
| 67 | 子 |
| 68 | 马 |
| 69 | 巛 |
| 70 | |
| 71 | 斗 |
| 72 | 文 |
| 73 | 方 |
| 74 | 火 |
| 75 | 心 |
| 76 | 户 |
| 77 | 礻 |
| 78 | 王 |
| 79 | 韦 |
| 80 | 木 |
| 81 | 犬 |
| 82 | 歹 |
| 83 | 车 |
| 84 | 戈 |
| 85 | 比 |
| 86 | 瓦 |
| 87 | 止 |
| 88 | 支 |
| 89 | 日 |
| 90 | 曰 |
| 91 | 贝 |

| 92 | 见 | 129 | 疋,疋 | 163 | 采身 |
| 93 | 父 | 130 | 皮 | 164 | 身 |
| 94 | 牛,牛,牛 | | | 165 | 角 |
| 95 | 手 | **6 strokes** | | | |
| 96 | 毛 | | | **8 strokes** | |
| 97 | 气 | 131 | 衣 | | |
| 98 | 夊 | 132 | 羊,羊,羊 | 166 | 青 |
| 99 | 片 | 133 | 米 | 167 | 其 |
| 100 | 斤 | 134 | 耒 | 168 | 雨 |
| 101 | 爪,爫 | 135 | 老 | 169 | 齿 |
| 102 | 月 | 136 | 耳 | 170 | 金 |
| 103 | 欠 | 137 | 西,覀 | 171 | 隹 |
| 104 | 风 | 138 | 页 | 172 | 鱼 |
| 105 | 殳 | 139 | 虍 | | |
| 106 | 聿,聿,聿 | 140 | 虫 | **9 strokes** | |
| 107 | 毋 | 141 | 缶 | | |
| 108 | 水,氺 | 142 | 舌 | 173 | 音 |
| | | 143 | 竹,⺮ | 174 | 革 |
| **5 strokes** | | 144 | 臼 | 175 | 骨 |
| | | 145 | 自 | 176 | 食 |
| 109 | 穴 | 146 | 血 | 177 | 鬼 |
| 110 | 立 | 147 | 舟 | | |
| 111 | 疒 | 148 | 羽 | **10 strokes** | |
| 112 | 衤 | 149 | 艮,艮 | | |
| 113 | 示 | 150 | 糸 | 178 | 髟 |
| 114 | 石 | | | | |
| 115 | 龙 | **7 strokes** | | **11 strokes** | |
| 116 | 业 | | | | |
| 117 | 目 | 151 | 辛 | 179 | 鹿 |
| 118 | 田 | 152 | 言 | | |
| 119 | 罒 | 153 | 麦 | **12 strokes** | |
| 120 | 皿 | 154 | 走 | | |
| 121 | 钅 | 155 | 赤 | 180 | 黑 |
| 122 | 矢 | 156 | 豆 | 181 | 鼠 |
| 123 | 禾 | 157 | 酉 | | |
| 124 | 白 | 158 | 辰 | **14 strokes** | |
| 125 | 瓜 | 159 | 里 | | |
| 126 | 鸟 | 160 | 足 | 182 | 鼻 |
| 127 | 用 | 161 | 豸 | | |
| 128 | 矛 | 162 | 谷 | | |

# Radical Index

| | | | | | | |
|---|---|---|---|---|---|---|
| 甲 | jiǎ | | 乌 | wū | | 了 le, liǎo |
| 申 | shēn | 4 | 乎 | hū | 2 | 飞 fēi |
| 且 | qiě | | 生 | shēng | | 乞 qǐ |
| 史 | shǐ | | 失 | shī | | 习 xí |
| 央 | yāng | | 乐 | lè, yuè | | 也 yě |
| 凹 | āo | | 丘 | qiū | 3 | 书 shū |
| 出 | chū | 5 | 丢 | diū | | 以 yǐ |
| 归 | guī | | 年 | nián | | 予 yǔ |
| 5 师 | shī | | 乒 | pāng | | 孔 kǒng |
| 曳 | yè | | 杀 | shā | 4 | 电 diàn |
| 6 串 | chuàn | | 后 | hòu | | 民 mín |
| 7 非 | fēi | | 向 | xiàng | | 司 sī |
| 畅 | chàng | | 兆 | zhào | 5 | 买 mǎi |
| 8 临 | lín | 6 | 卵 | luǎn | 6 | 乱 luàn |
| | | | 希 | xī | 7 | 乳 rǔ |

**4 丿**

| | | | 囱 | cōng | | 承 chéng |
|---|---|---|---|---|---|---|
| 1 九 | jiǔ | | 系 | xì, | 14 | 豫 yù |
| 乃 | nǎi | | | jì | | |
| 匕 | bǐ | 7 | 乖 | guāi | | **6 亠** |
| 2 千 | qiān | 8 | 拜 | bài | | |
| 川 | chuān | | 垂 | chuí | 1 | 亡 wáng |
| 么 | me | | 重 | zhòng, | 2 | 六 liù |
| 久 | jiǔ | | | chóng | 3 | 市 shì |
| 及 | jí | 9 | 乘 | chéng | 4 | 亥 hài |
| 3 乏 | fá | 11 | 甥 | shēng | | 交 jiāo |
| 午 | wǔ | 13 | 孵 | fū | | 亦 yì |
| 升 | shēng | | 舞 | wǔ | 5 | 亩 mǔ |
| 长 | zhǎng, | | 睪 | gāo | | 弃 qì |
| | cháng | 14 | 靠 | kào | 6 | 变 biàn |
| 币 | bì | | | | | 卒 zú |
| 反 | fǎn | | **5 乙, ㄱ, 乛, ㄥ** | | | 京 jīng |
| 丹 | dān | | | | | 氓 máng |
| 氏 | shì | | 乙 | yǐ | | 享 xiǎng |
| | | 1 | 刁 | diāo | | 夜 yè |

| | | | | | | |
|---|---|---|---|---|---|---|
| 7 | 哀 āi | 14 | 凝 níng | 5 | 词 cí | |
| | 亮 liàng | | | | 评 píng | |
| | 亭 tíng | **8 宀** | | | 识 shí | |
| 8 | 高 gāo | | | | 诉 sù | |
| | 离 lí | 2 | 冗 rǒng | | 译 yì | |
| | 衰 shuāi | 3 | 写 xiě | | 诈 zhà | |
| | 衷 zhōng | 4 | 军 jūn | | 诊 zhěn | |
| 9 | 毫 háo | 5 | 罕 hǎn | | 证 zhèng | |
| | 率 shuài | 7 | 冠 guàn, | | 诅 zǔ | |
| | 烹 pēng | | guān | | 诋 dǐ | |
| 10 | 就 jiù | | | 6 | 诧 chà | |
| | 亵 xiè | **9 讠** | | | 诚 chéng | |
| 12 | 膏 gāo | | | | 该 gāi | |
| | 裹 guǒ | 2 | 订 dìng | | 诡 guǐ | |
| | 豪 háo | | 讣 fù | | 话 huà | |
| 15 | 赢 yíng | | 讥 jī | | 诗 shī | |
| | | | 计 jì | | 试 shì | |
| **7 冫** | | | 认 rèn | | 详 xiáng | |
| | | 3 | 记 jì | | 询 xún | |
| 4 | 冰 bīng | | 让 ràng | | 诘 jié | |
| | 冲 chōng | | 讨 tǎo | | 诙 huī | |
| | 次 cì | | 训 xùn | 7 | 诞 dàn | |
| | 决 jué | | 讯 xùn | | 诲 huì | |
| 5 | 冻 dòng | | 议 yì | | 说 shuō, | |
| | 况 kuàng | 4 | 访 fǎng | | shuì | |
| | 冷 lěng | | 讽 fěng | | 诵 sòng | |
| | 冶 yě | | 讳 huì | | 诬 wū | |
| 6 | 净 jìng | | 讲 jiǎng | | 误 wù | |
| 8 | 准 zhǔn | | 诀 jué | | 诱 yòu | |
| | 凋 diāo | | 论 lùn | | 语 yǔ | |
| | 凉 liáng | | 设 shè | 8 | 调 diào, | |
| | 凌 líng | | 讼 sòng | | tiáo | |
| 9 | 凑 còu | | 许 xǔ | | 读 dú | |
| | 减 jiǎn | | 讶 yà | | 诽 fěi | |

课 kè
谅 liàng
诺 nuò
请 qǐng
谁 shuí
谈 tán
谊 yì
诿 wěi
9 谍 dié
谎 huǎng
谜 mí
谋 móu
谓 wèi
谐 xié
谚 yàn
10 谦 qiān
谤 bàng
谢 xiè
谣 yáo
11 谨 jǐn
谬 miù
12 谱 pǔ
13 遣 qiǎn
谵 zhān

**10 二**

二 èr
1 亏 kuī
2 云 yún
6 些 xiē

**11 十**

十 shí
2 支 zhī
3 古 gǔ
4 华 huá
协 xié
5 克 kè
6 卓 zhuó
卑 bēi
卖 mài
丧 sāng,
   sàng
直 zhí
卒 zú
7 南 nán
8 真 zhēn
索 suǒ
9 啬 sè
10 博 bó
韩 hán
辜 gū

**12 厂**

厂 chǎng
2 厄 è
历 lì
厅 tīng
3 厉 lì
4 厌 yàn
压 yā
6 厕 cè
7 厚 hòu

厘 lí
8 原 yuán
9 厩 jiù
厢 xiāng
10 厨 chú
厦 xià,
   shà
厥 jué
12 斯 sī
14 赝 yàn

**13 匚**

2 区 qū
巨 jù
匹 pǐ
4 匠 jiàng
5 匣 xiá
医 yī
8 匪 fěi
匿 nì

**14 卜**

卜 bǔ
3 卡 kǎ, qiǎ
外 wài
处 chù,
   chǔ
占 zhàn
4 贞 zhēn
6 卧 wò
卓 zhuó

**15 刂**

3 刊 kān
4 创 chuàng
　刚 gāng
　划 huá,
　　 huà
　列 liè
　刑 xíng
　则 zé
　刘 liú
5 别 bié
　利 lì
　判 pàn
　刨 bào
　删 shān
6 刺 cì
　到 dào
　刮 guā
　刽 guì
　剂 jì
　刻 kè
　刹 chà, shā
　刷 shuā
　制 zhì
7 剑 jiàn
　剃 tì
　削 xiāo,
　　 xuē
8 剥 bō, bāo
　剧 jù
　剖 pōu
　剔 tī
9 副 fù

10 割 gē
　剩 shèng

**16 冂**

2 内 nèi
4 肉 ròu
　同 tóng
　网 wǎng
6 周 zhōu

**17 八, 丷**

　八 bā
2 分 fēn
　公 gōng
3 兰 lán
　只 zhǐ, zhī
4 并 bìng
　共 gòng
　关 guān
　兴 xīng,
　　 xìng
5 兑 duì
　兵 bīng
6 弟 dì
　单 dān,
　　 chán
　典 diǎn
　具 jù
　卷 juǎn,
　　 juàn
7 兹 zī
　前 qián

　首 shǒu
　差 chà, cī,
　　 chā,
　　 chāi
8 兼 jiān
9 黄 huáng
　兽 shòu
10 尊 zūn

**18 人, 入**

　人 rén
　入 rù
1 个 gè
2 仓 cāng
　从 cóng
　介 jiè
　今 jīn
3 丛 cóng
　令 lìng
4 合 hé
　会 huì
　企 qǐ
　全 quán
　伞 sǎn
　众 zhòng
　尬 gà
5 含 hán
　余 yú
6 命 mìng
　舍 shě,
　　 shè
10 禽 qín
　舒 shū

| | | | | | |
|---|---|---|---|---|---|
| **19 亻** | | 休 | xiū | 佩 | pèi |
| | | 仰 | yǎng | 侨 | qiáo |
| *1* 亿 | yì | 伊 | yī | 使 | shǐ |
| *2* 仇 | chóu | 优 | yōu | 侍 | shì |
| 化 | huà | 仲 | zhòng | 侠 | xiá |
| 仅 | jǐn | *5* 伴 | bàn | 依 | yī |
| 仆 | pū, pú | 伯 | bó | 侦 | zhēn |
| 仁 | rén | 但 | dàn | 侄 | zhí |
| 仍 | réng | 低 | dī | 侏 | zhū |
| 什 | shí, | 佛 | fó | *7* 保 | bǎo |
| | shén | 估 | gū | 便 | biàn |
| *3* 代 | dài | 何 | hé | 促 | cù |
| 付 | fù | 伶 | líng | 俄 | é |
| 们 | men | 你 | nǐ | 俘 | fú |
| 他 | tā | 伸 | shēn | 侯 | hóu |
| 仙 | xiān | 伺 | cì | 俭 | jiǎn |
| 仪 | yí | 体 | tǐ | 俊 | jùn |
| 仗 | zhàng | 位 | wèi | 俐 | lì |
| 仔 | zǎi, zǐ | 佣 | yòng, | 俩 | liǎ, |
| *4* 传 | chuán | | yōng | | liǎng |
| 伐 | fá | 佑 | yòu | 俏 | qiào |
| 仿 | fǎng | 住 | zhù | 侵 | qīn |
| 份 | fèn | 作 | zuò, | 俗 | sú |
| 伏 | fú | | zuō | 侮 | wǔ |
| 伙 | huǒ | *6* 侧 | cè | 信 | xìn |
| 价 | jià | 侈 | chǐ | 修 | xiū |
| 件 | jiàn | 供 | gōng, | 俚 | lǐ |
| 伦 | lún | | gòng | 俑 | yǒng |
| 任 | rèn | 佳 | jiā | *8* 倍 | bèi |
| 伤 | shāng | 侥 | jiǎo, | 倡 | chàng |
| 似 | sì, shì | | yáo | 倒 | dǎo, |
| 伟 | wěi | 佬 | lǎo | | dào |
| 伪 | wěi | 例 | lì | 俯 | fǔ |
| 伍 | wǔ | 侣 | lǚ | 候 | hòu |

| | | | | | | |
|---|---|---|---|---|---|---|
| | 健 jiàn | | **20 勹** | | 6 | 凯 kǎi |
| | 借 jiè | | | | | 凭 píng |
| | 俱 jù | 1 | 勺 sháo | | 9 | 凰 huáng |
| | 倦 juàn | 2 | 勾 gōu | | 12 | 凳 dèng |
| | 倾 qīng | | 勿 wù | | | |
| | 倚 yǐ | | 匀 yún | | **23 厶** | |
| | 债 zhài | 3 | 包 bāo | | | |
| | 值 zhí | | 匆 cōng | | 2 | 允 yǔn |
| | 倌 guān | | 句 jù | | 3 | 台 tái |
| 9 | 偿 cháng | 4 | 匈 xiōng | | | 去 qù |
| | 假 jiǎ, | 5 | 甸 diàn | | 5 | 县 xiàn |
| | 　 jià | 7 | 匍 pú | | 6 | 参 cān |
| | 傀 kuǐ | 9 | 够 gòu | | 7 | 垒 lěi |
| | 偶 ǒu | | 匐 fú | | 8 | 能 néng |
| | 偏 piān | | | | | |
| | 停 tíng | | **21 儿** | | **24 又,乂** | |
| | 偷 tōu | | | | | |
| | 做 zuò | | 儿 ér | | | 又 yòu |
| 10 | 傲 ào | 2 | 允 yǔn | | 1 | 叉 chā |
| | 傍 bàng | 3 | 兄 xiōng | | 2 | 双 shuāng |
| | 储 chǔ | 4 | 先 xiān | | | 友 yǒu |
| | 傅 fù | | 充 chōng | | | 劝 quàn |
| | 傧 bīn | | 光 guāng | | | 支 zhī |
| 11 | 催 cuī | 5 | 克 kè | | 3 | 对 duì |
| | 傻 shǎ | | 兑 duì | | | 发 fā, fà |
| 12 | 僚 liáo | 9 | 兜 dōu | | | 圣 shèng |
| | 像 xiàng | | | | 4 | 观 guān |
| 13 | 僵 jiāng | | **22 几,凢** | | | 欢 huān |
| | 僻 pì | | | | | 戏 xì |
| 14 | 儒 rú | | 几 jǐ | | 6 | 艰 jiān |
| 15 | 儡 lěi | 1 | 凡 fán | | | 取 qǔ |
| | | 2 | 凤 fèng | | | 受 shòu |
| | | 5 | 壳 ké, qiào | | | 叔 shū |
| | | | 秃 tū | | 7 | 叙 xù |

| | | | | | | |
|---|---|---|---|---|---|---|
| 8 | 难 nán,<br>nàn | | 陀 tuó | 6 | 郊 jiāo | |
| 11 | 叠 dié | | 阻 zǔ | | 郎 láng | |
| | | 6 | 降 jiàng,<br>xiáng | | 耶 yé, yē | |
| **25 廴** | | | 陋 lòu | | 郁 yù | |
| | | | 陌 mò | | 郑 zhèng | |
| 4 | 廷 tíng | | 限 xiàn | 7 | 郡 jùn | |
| | 延 yán | 7 | 除 chú | 8 | 部 bù | |
| 6 | 建 jiàn | | 陡 dǒu | | 都 dū, dōu | |
| | | | 险 xiǎn | 11 | 鄙 bǐ | |
| **26 卩，巳** | | | 院 yuàn | | | |
| | | | 陨 yǔn | **29 凵** | | |
| 2 | 卫 wèi | 8 | 陵 líng | | | |
| 3 | 印 yìn | | 陪 péi | 2 | 凶 xiōng | |
| | 叩 kòu | | 陶 táo | 6 | 函 hán | |
| 5 | 即 jí | | 陷 xiàn | | 画 huà | |
| | 却 què | 9 | 隆 lóng | | | |
| 7 | 卸 xiè | | 随 suí | **30 刀，⺈** | | |
| 8 | 卿 qīng | | 隐 yǐn | | | |
| | | 10 | 隘 ài | | 刀 dāo | |
| **27 阝 L** | | | 隔 gé | 2 | 切 qiē | |
| | | | 隙 xì | 3 | 召 zhāo,<br>zhào | |
| 2 | 队 duì | 11 | 障 zhàng | 4 | 负 fù | |
| 4 | 防 fáng | 12 | 隧 suì | | 色 sè,<br>shǎi | |
| | 阶 jiē | | | | 危 wēi | |
| | 阳 yáng | **28 阝 R** | | | 争 zhēng | |
| | 阴 yīn | | | 5 | 龟 guī | |
| | 阵 zhèn | 2 | 邓 dèng | | 免 miǎn | |
| | 阱 jǐng | 4 | 邦 bāng | 6 | 券 quàn | |
| 5 | 阿 ā, ē | | 那 nà,<br>nèi | | 兔 tù | |
| | 陈 chén | | 邪 xié | 9 | 剪 jiǎn | |
| | 附 fù | 5 | 邻 lín | | 象 xiàng | |
| | 际 jì | | 邮 yóu | 13 | 劈 pī | |
| | 陆 lù | | | | | |

## 31 力

| | | |
|---|---|---|
| | 力 | lì |
| 2 | 办 | bàn |
| | 劝 | quàn |
| 3 | 加 | jiā |
| | 务 | wù |
| | 幼 | yòu |
| 4 | 动 | dòng |
| | 劣 | liè |
| 5 | 劫 | jié |
| | 励 | lì |
| | 男 | nán |
| | 助 | zhù |
| 6 | 劲 | jìn |
| | 努 | nǔ |
| | 势 | shì |
| 7 | 勃 | bó |
| | 勉 | miǎn |
| | 勋 | xūn |
| | 勇 | yǒng |
| 9 | 勘 | kān |
| 11 | 勤 | qín |

## 32 氵

| | | |
|---|---|---|
| 2 | 汉 | hàn |
| | 汇 | huì |
| | 汁 | zhī |
| 3 | 池 | chí |
| | 汗 | hàn |
| | 江 | jiāng |
| | 汤 | tāng |
| | 污 | wū |

| | | |
|---|---|---|
| 4 | 沧 | cāng |
| | 沉 | chén |
| | 泛 | fàn |
| | 沟 | gōu |
| | 沥 | lì |
| | 没 | méi, mò |
| | 沛 | pèi |
| | 汽 | qì |
| | 沙 | shā |
| | 汰 | tài |
| | 汪 | wāng |
| | 沃 | wò |
| | 汩 | gǔ |
| 5 | 波 | bō |
| | 泊 | bó, pō |
| | 法 | fǎ |
| | 沸 | fèi |
| | 河 | hé |
| | 沮 | jǔ |
| | 泪 | lèi |
| | 泌 | mì |
| | 沫 | mò |
| | 泥 | ní |
| | 泞 | níng |
| | 泡 | pào |
| | 泼 | pō |
| | 泣 | qì |
| | 浅 | qiǎn |
| | 泄 | xiè |
| | 泻 | xiè |
| | 沿 | yán |
| | 泳 | yǒng |
| | 油 | yóu |

| | | |
|---|---|---|
| | 泽 | zé |
| | 沾 | zhān |
| | 沼 | zhǎo |
| | 治 | zhì |
| | 注 | zhù |
| | 沱 | tuó |
| 6 | 洛 | luò |
| | 测 | cè |
| | 洞 | dòng |
| | 洪 | hóng |
| | 浑 | hún |
| | 活 | huó |
| | 济 | jǐ, jì |
| | 浇 | jiāo |
| | 洁 | jié |
| | 津 | jīn |
| | 浓 | nóng |
| | 派 | pài |
| | 洽 | qià |
| | 洒 | sǎ |
| | 洼 | wā |
| | 洗 | xǐ |
| | 洋 | yáng |
| | 洲 | zhōu |
| | 浊 | zhuó |
| | 浏 | liú |
| 7 | 涤 | dí |
| | 浮 | fú |
| | 海 | hǎi |
| | 浩 | hào |
| | 涣 | huàn |
| | 渐 | jiàn |
| | 浸 | jìn |
| | 酒 | jiǔ |

浚 jùn
浪 làng
流 liú
润 rùn
涩 sè
涉 shè
涛 tāo
涕 tì
涂 tú
涡 wō
涎 xián
消 xiāo
涌 yǒng
浴 yù
涨 zhàng, zhǎng
浣 huàn
8 淡 dàn
淀 diàn
涵 hán
涸 hé
混 hún, hùn
淋 lín
清 qīng
深 shēn
渗 shèn
淌 tǎng
淘 táo
添 tiān
淆 xiáo
涯 yá
淹 yān
液 yè

淫 yín
淤 yū
渔 yú
渊 yuān
淇 qí
渎 dú
9 渤 bó
渡 dù
溉 gài
港 gǎng
湖 hú
滑 huá
溅 jiàn
渴 kě
溃 kuì
湿 shī
湍 tuān
湾 wān
温 wēn
游 yóu
渝 yú
渣 zhā
滞 zhì
滋 zī
渲 xuàn
湄 méi
10 滨 bīn
滚 gǔn
滥 làn
漓 lí
溜 liū, liù
滤 lù
满 mǎn
漠 mò

溺 nì, niào
溶 róng
溯 sù
滩 tān
滔 tāo
溪 xī
溢 yì
源 yuán
滓 zǐ
滂 pāng
11 滴 dī
漏 lòu
漫 màn
漂 piāo
漆 qī
漱 shù
演 yǎn
潢 huáng
12 澳 ào
潮 cháo
澈 chè
澄 chéng
潦 liǎo
潜 qián
13 濒 bīn
激 jī
澡 zǎo
15 瀑 bào, pù
17 灌 guàn

**33 忄, 小**

1 忆 yì
3 忙 máng

| | | | | | | |
|---|---|---|---|---|---|---|
| 3 | 忏 chàn | | 惯 guàn | | **34 宀** | |
| 4 | 忱 chén | | 悸 jì | | | |
| | 怀 huái | | 惊 jīng | 2 | 宁 níng | |
| | 快 kuài | | 惧 jù | | 它 tā | |
| | 忧 yōu | | 情 qíng | 3 | 安 ān | |
| | 忡 chōng | | 惕 tì | | 守 shǒu | |
| | 忪 sōng | | 惋 wǎn | | 宇 yǔ | |
| | 忸 niǔ | | 惜 xī | | 宅 zhái | |
| 5 | 怖 bù | | 惘 wǎng | | 字 zì | |
| | 怪 guài | | 惚 hū | 4 | 宏 hóng | |
| | 怜 lián | | 悴 cuì | | 牢 láo | |
| | 怕 pà | 9 | 惰 duò | | 宋 sòng | |
| | 怯 qiè | | 愤 fèn | | 完 wán | |
| | 性 xìng | | 慌 huāng | | 灾 zāi | |
| | 怩 ní | | 惶 huáng | 5 | 宝 bǎo | |
| 6 | 恫 dòng, | | 慨 kǎi | | 宠 chǒng | |
| | tōng | | 愧 kuì | | 定 dìng | |
| | 恨 hèn | | 惺 xīng | | 官 guān | |
| | 恒 héng | | 愉 yú | | 审 shěn | |
| | 恍 huǎng | | 愕 è | | 实 shí | |
| | 恢 huī | 10 | 慑 shè | | 宜 yí | |
| | 恼 nǎo | | 慎 shèn | | 宙 zhòu | |
| | 恰 qià | 11 | 慷 kāng | | 宗 zōng | |
| | 恸 tòng | | 慢 màn | 6 | 宫 gōng | |
| 7 | 悔 huǐ | 12 | 懊 ào | | 客 kè | |
| | 悯 mǐn | | 懂 dǒng | | 室 shì | |
| | 悄 qiāo | | 憎 zēng | | 宪 xiàn | |
| | 悟 wù | | 憔 qiáo | | 宣 xuān | |
| | 悦 yuè | 13 | 憾 hàn | 7 | 宾 bīn | |
| | 悚 sǒng | | 懒 lǎn | | 害 hài | |
| 8 | 惭 cán | | 懈 xiè | | 家 jiā | |
| | 惨 cǎn | 14 | 懦 nuò | | 宽 kuān | |
| | 悼 dào | | | | 宵 xiāo | |
| | 惦 diàn | | | | 宴 yàn | |

宰 zǎi

8 密 mì
寄 jì
寂 jì
宿 sù, xiǔ, xiù

9 富 fù
寒 hán
寓 yù

10 寞 mò
寝 qǐn
塞 sāi, sài, sè

11 察 chá
寡 guǎ
蜜 mì
赛 sài
寨 zhài

## 35 丬

3 壮 zhuàng
妆 zhuāng
4 状 zhuàng
6 将 jiāng

## 36 广

广 guǎng
3 庆 qìng
庄 zhuāng
4 庇 bì
床 chuáng
库 kù

序 xù
应 yìng, yīng
5 底 dǐ
店 diàn
废 fèi
府 fǔ
庙 miào
庞 páng
6 庭 tíng
度 dù
7 唐 táng
席 xí
座 zuò
8 康 kāng
廊 láng
麻 má
庸 yōng
10 廓 kuò
廉 lián
11 腐 fǔ
15 鹰 yīng
16 靡 mí, mǐ

## 37 门

门 mén
1 闩 shuān
2 闪 shǎn
3 闭 bì
闯 chuǎng
4 间 jiān, jiàn

闷 mēn, mèn
闰 rùn
闲 xián
5 闹 nào
闸 zhá
6 阀 fá
阁 gé
闻 wén
7 阅 yuè
阄 jiū
8 阐 chǎn
阉 yān
9 阔 kuò
阑 lán

## 38 辶

2 边 biān
3 达 dá
过 guò
迈 mài
迄 qì
迁 qiān
巡 xún
迅 xùn
迂 yū
4 迟 chí
返 fǎn
还 huán
进 jìn
近 jìn
连 lián
违 wéi

| | |
|---|---|
| 迎 | yíng |
| 远 | yuǎn |
| 运 | yùn |
| 这 | zhè, zhèi |
| 5 迪 | dí |
| 迭 | dié |
| 迫 | pò |
| 述 | shù |
| 6 迸 | bèng, bìng |
| 迹 | jì |
| 迷 | mí |
| 逆 | nì |
| 适 | shì |
| 送 | sòng |
| 逃 | táo |
| 退 | tuì |
| 选 | xuǎn |
| 逊 | xùn |
| 追 | zhuī |
| 逅 | hòu |
| 7 递 | dì |
| 逗 | dòu |
| 逢 | féng |
| 逛 | guàng |
| 逝 | shì |
| 速 | sù |
| 通 | tōng |
| 透 | tòu |
| 途 | tú |
| 造 | zào |
| 逐 | zhú |
| 逍 | xiāo |

| | |
|---|---|
| 8 逮 | dǎi |
| 逻 | luó |
| 9 遊 | yóu |
| 逼 | bī |
| 遍 | biàn |
| 道 | dào |
| 遏 | è |
| 遗 | yí |
| 遇 | yù |
| 10 遣 | qiǎn |
| 遥 | yáo |
| 遢 | ta |
| 遛 | liū |
| 11 遭 | zāo |
| 遮 | zhē |
| 12 遵 | zūn |
| 13 避 | bì |
| 邀 | yāo |
| 邂 | xiè |
| 15 邋 | lā |

## 39 工

| | |
|---|---|
| 工 | gōng |
| 2 功 | gōng |
| 巧 | qiǎo |
| 左 | zuǒ |
| 4 攻 | gōng |
| 巫 | wū |
| 贡 | gòng |
| 6 项 | xiàng |

## 40 土

| | |
|---|---|
| 土 | tǔ |
| 3 场 | chǎng |
| 地 | dì |
| 圾 | jī |
| 在 | zài |
| 寺 | sì |
| 尘 | chén |
| 至 | zhì |
| 考 | kǎo |
| 4 坝 | bà |
| 坊 | fāng, fáng |
| 坟 | fén |
| 坏 | huài |
| 坚 | jiān |
| 均 | jūn |
| 坑 | kēng |
| 块 | kuài |
| 坍 | tān |
| 坛 | tán |
| 址 | zhǐ |
| 坠 | zhuì |
| 坐 | zuò |
| 5 垃 | lā |
| 坯 | pī |
| 坪 | píng |
| 坡 | pō |
| 坦 | tǎn |
| 坞 | wù |
| 幸 | xìng |
| 垄 | lǒng |
| 6 城 | chéng |

| | | | | | |
|---|---|---|---|---|---|
| | 垫 diàn | *4* | 声 shēng | | 苦 kǔ |
| | 垢 gòu | | 志 zhì | | 茅 máo |
| | 垮 kuǎ | *7* | 壶 hú | | 茂 mào |
| | 型 xíng | *9* | 喜 xǐ | | 苗 miáo |
| *7* | 埃 āi | *10* | 鼓 gǔ | | 苹 píng |
| | 埋 mái | *11* | 嘉 jiā | | 若 ruò |
| | 埔 pǔ | *17* | 馨 xīn | | 苔 tái |
| *8* | 堵 dǔ | | | | 英 yīng |

**42 ⺋**

| | | | | | |
|---|---|---|---|---|---|
| | 堆 duī | | | | 茁 zhuó |
| | 堕 duò | | | | 茉 mò |
| | 基 jī | *1* | 艺 yì | *6* | 草 cǎo |
| | 培 péi | *2* | 艾 ài, yì | | 茬 chá |
| | 域 yù | | 节 jié | | 茶 chá |
| *9* | 堡 bǎo | *3* | 芒 máng | | 荡 dàng |
| | 堤 dī | | 芝 zhī | | 荒 huāng |
| | 堪 kān | *4* | 芭 bā | | 荤 hūn |
| | 塔 tǎ | | 苍 cāng | | 茧 jiǎn |
| | 堰 yàn | | 芳 fāng | | 荐 jiàn |
| *10* | 塑 sù | | 芬 fēn | | 荔 lì |
| | 塌 tā | | 花 huā | | 茫 máng |
| | 塘 táng | | 芥 jiè | | 荣 róng |
| | 填 tián | | 劳 láo | | 药 yào |
| *11* | 境 jìng | | 芦 lú | | 荫 yīn |
| | 墙 qiáng | | 芹 qín | | 荨 xún |
| | 墅 shù | | 苏 sū | *7* | 荷 hé |
| | 墟 xū | | 苇 wěi | | 获 huò |
| *12* | 增 zēng | | 芯 xīn | | 莱 lái |
| *13* | 壁 bì | | 芽 yá | | 莉 lì |
| *17* | 壤 rǎng | *5* | 茄 qié, jiā | | 莲 lián |
| | | | 苯 bèn | | 莽 mǎng |

**41 士**

| | | | | | |
|---|---|---|---|---|---|
| | | | 范 fàn | | 莫 mò |
| | 士 shì | | 苟 gǒu | | 莓 méi |
| *3* | 吉 jí | | 茎 jīng | | 莺 yīng |
| | | | 苛 kē | *8* | 董 jǐn |

| 菠 bō | 蓄 xù | 尖 jiān |
|---|---|---|
| 菜 cài | 蒸 zhēng | 夸 kuā |
| 菲 fēi | 蓓 bèi | 5 奔 bēn, |
| 菇 gū | 11 蔼 ǎi | bèn |
| 菊 jú | 蔽 bì | 奋 fèn |
| 菌 jūn, jùn | 蔓 mán, | 奈 nài |
| 菱 líng | màn, | 奇 qí |
| 萝 luó | wàn | 6 奖 jiǎng |
| 萌 méng | 蔑 miè | 美 měi |
| 菩 pú | 摹 mó | 契 qì |
| 萨 sà | 慕 mù | 牵 qiān |
| 萄 táo | 蔗 zhè | 7 套 tào |
| 萎 wěi | 12 蕉 jiāo | 8 奢 shē |
| 萧 xiāo | 蔬 shū | 爽 shuǎng |
| 营 yíng | 蕨 jué | 9 奥 ào |
| 著 zhù | 蕃 fān | |
| 萦 yíng | 13 薄 bó, bò, | **44 尢** |
| 9 葱 cōng | báo | |
| 蒂 dì | 蕾 lěi | 3 异 yì |
| 董 dǒng | 薯 shǔ | 4 弄 lòng, |
| 葛 gě | 薪 xīn | nòng |
| 蒋 jiǎng | 14 藏 cáng, | 11 弊 bì |
| 葵 kuí | zàng | |
| 落 luò, là | 藉 jí | **45 尤** |
| 募 mù | 15 藕 ǒu | |
| 葡 pú | 藤 téng | 尤 yóu |
| 惹 rě | 16 蘑 mó | |
| 葬 zàng | 藻 zǎo | **46 寸** |
| 10 蓝 lán | | |
| 蒙 méng | **43 大** | |
| 墓 mù | | 寸 cùn |
| 幕 mù | 大 dà | 3 寻 xún |
| 蓬 péng | 1 太 tài | 导 dǎo |
| 蒜 suàn | 3 夺 duó | 寺 sì |
| | | 4 寿 shòu |

| | | | | | |
|---|---|---|---|---|---|
| 6 | 封 fēng | 抖 dǒu | | 拣 jiǎn | |
| | 耐 nài | 扼 è | | 拘 jū | |
| 7 | 辱 rǔ | 扶 fú | | 拉 lā | |
| | 射 shè | 抚 fǔ | | 拢 lǒng | |
| 8 | 尉 wèi | 护 hù | | 抹 mǒ | |
| | | 技 jì | | 拇 mǔ | |

**47 弋**

式 shì

**48 扌**

| | | | | | |
|---|---|---|---|---|---|
| 1 | 扎 zā, zhā, zhá | 拒 jù | | 拧 nǐng | |
| 2 | 扒 bā, pá | 抗 kàng | | 拍 pāi | |
| | 打 dǎ | 抠 kōu | | 抨 pēng | |
| | 扑 pū | 拟 nǐ | | 披 pī | |
| | 扔 rēng | 扭 niǔ | | 抬 tái | |
| 3 | 扬 yáng | 抛 pāo | | 拖 tuō | |
| | 执 zhí | 批 pī | | 拓 tuò | |
| | 扣 kòu | 抢 qiǎng | 6 | 挣 zhēng | |
| | 扩 kuò | 扰 rǎo | | 拯 zhěng | |
| | 扫 sǎo | 抒 shū | | 指 zhǐ | |
| | 托 tuō | 投 tóu | | 拽 zhuài, yè | |
| 4 | 抑 yì | 5 押 yā | | 按 àn | |
| | 找 zhǎo | 拥 yōng | | 持 chí | |
| | 折 zhé | 择 zé | | 挡 dǎng | |
| | 抓 zhuā | 招 zhāo | | 拱 gǒng | |
| | 把 bǎ | 拙 zhuō | | 挂 guà | |
| | 扳 bān | 拗 niù, ǎo, ào | | 挥 huī | |
| | 扮 bàn | 拔 bá | | 挤 jǐ | |
| | 报 bào | 拌 bàn | | 括 kuò | |
| | 抄 chāo | 抱 bào | | 挪 nuó | |
| | 扯 chě | 拨 bō | | 拼 pīn | |
| | | 拆 chāi | | 拾 shí | |
| | | 抽 chōu | | 拴 shuān | |
| | | 担 dān, dàn | | 挑 tiāo | |
| | | 抵 dǐ | | 挺 tǐng | |
| | | 拐 guǎi | | 挖 wā | |
| | | | | 挝 wō | |

| 7 | 振 zhèn |  | 推 tuī | 12 | 撰 zhuàn |
|---|---------|---|--------|----|----------|
|   | 捉 zhuō | 9 | 握 wò |   | 撞 zhuàng |
|   | 挨 āi, ái |   | 援 yuán |   | 播 bō |
|   | 捕 bǔ |   | 揍 zòu |   | 撤 chè |
|   | 挫 cuò |   | 插 chā |   | 撑 chēng |
|   | 捣 dǎo |   | 搽 chá |   | 撮 cuō |
|   | 捍 hàn |   | 搀 chān |   | 撅 juē |
|   | 换 huàn |   | 搓 cuō |   | 撵 niǎn |
|   | 捡 jiǎn |   | 搭 dā |   | 撬 qiào |
|   | 捐 juān |   | 搁 gē |   | 撒 sā, sǎ |
|   | 捆 kǔn |   | 搅 jiǎo |   | 撕 sī |
|   | 捏 niē |   | 揭 jiē | 13 | 擀 gǎn |
|   | 损 sǔn |   | 揩 kāi |   | 操 cāo |
|   | 捅 tǒng |   | 揽 lǎn |   | 撼 hàn |
|   | 挽 wǎn |   | 搂 lǒu |   | 擂 léi, lèi |
| 8 | 掩 yǎn |   | 揉 róu |   | 擅 shàn |
|   | 掷 zhì |   | 搔 sāo | 14 | 擤 xǐng |
|   | 捺 nà |   | 搜 sōu |   | 擦 cā |
|   | 措 cuò |   | 提 tí | 16 | 攒 zǎn |
|   | 掉 diào | 10 | 携 xié | 17 | 攘 rǎng |
|   | 接 jiē |   | 摇 yáo |   |   |
|   | 捷 jié |   | 摆 bǎi |   |   |
|   | 据 jù |   | 搬 bān |   | **49 小, ⺌** |
|   | 掘 jué |   | 搏 bó |   |   |
|   | 控 kòng |   | 搐 chù |   | 小 xiǎo |
|   | 掠 lüè |   | 搞 gǎo | 1 | 少 shǎo, |
|   | 描 miáo |   | 摸 mō |   | shào |
|   | 捻 niǎn |   | 摄 shè | 2 | 尔 ěr |
|   | 排 pái |   | 摊 tān | 3 | 当 dāng, |
|   | 捧 pěng |   | 搪 táng |   | dàng |
|   | 掐 qiā | 11 | 摘 zhāi | 3 | 尘 chén |
|   | 授 shòu |   | 摧 cuī |   | 尖 jiān |
|   | 探 tàn |   | 撇 piē, piě | 4 | 肖 xiāo, |
|   | 掏 tāo |   | 摔 shuāi |   | xiào |
|   |   |   |   | 5 | 尚 shàng |

| | | | | | |
|---|---|---|---|---|---|
| 6 | 尝 cháng | 吹 chuī | | 呦 yōu | |
| 7 | 党 dǎng | 呆 dāi | | 呸 pēi | |
| 8 | 常 cháng | 吨 dūn | | 和 hé, hè, | |
| | 堂 táng | 吠 fèi | | huò, hú | |
| 9 | 辉 huī | 否 fǒu | | 呜 wū | |
| | 掌 zhǎng | 告 gào | | 知 zhī | |
| | | 吼 hǒu | 6 | 哆 duō | |

**50 口**

| | | | | |
|---|---|---|---|---|
| | 口 kǒu | 君 jūn | 哈 hā | |
| 2 | 叭 bā | 吭 kēng | 哄 hǒng | |
| | 叮 dīng | 呕 ǒu | 咯 gē | |
| | 号 háo, | 启 qǐ | 咳 ké, hāi | |
| | hào | 吮 shǔn | 哪 nǎ, něi | |
| | 叫 jiào | 听 tīng | 品 pǐn | |
| | 可 kě | 吞 tūn | 哇 wā | |
| | 另 lìng | 吻 wěn | 响 xiǎng | |
| | 叹 tàn | 呀 ya | 哑 yǎ | |
| | 叶 yè | 吟 yín | 咽 yān, | |
| | 右 yòu | 员 yuán | yàn | |
| | 叨 dāo | 吱 zhī | 咬 yǎo | |
| 3 | 吃 chī | 吝 lìn | 哟 yōu | |
| | 吊 diào | 5 哎 āi | 咱 zán | |
| | 各 gè | 咕 gū | 咨 zī | |
| | 吗 ma | 呵 hē | 咧 liē, liě | |
| | 名 míng | 呼 hū | 咪 mī | |
| | 吐 tǔ | 咀 jǔ | 哝 nóng | |
| | 吸 xī | 咖 kā, gā | 虽 suī | |
| | 吓 xià, hè | 咙 lóng | 7 啊 ā, á, a | |
| | 吁 yù, xū | 鸣 míng | 唉 āi, ài | |
| | 吉 jí | 呢 ne, ní | 哺 bǔ | |
| 4 | 吧 ba | 咆 páo | 唇 chún | |
| | 吵 chǎo | 呻 shēn | 哥 gē | |
| | 呈 chéng | 味 wèi | 哼 hēng | |
| | | 咒 zhòu | 唤 huàn | |
| | | 呱 guā | 哨 shào | |

| | | | | | | |
|---|---|---|---|---|---|---|
| 7 | 唆 suō | | 喧 xuān | 14 | 嚎 háo | |
| | 哮 xiào | | 喻 yù | | 嚏 tì | |
| | 唁 yàn | | 嗒 dā | | 嚓 cā | |
| | 哲 zhé | | 喱 lí | 15 | 嚣 xiāo, | |
| | 唠 lào | | 喙 huì | | āo | |
| | 唧 jī | | 喔 ō, wol | 17 | 嚼 jiáo, | |
| | 哦 ó, ò, é | | 喜 xǐ | | jiào, | |
| 8 | 唱 chàng | 10 | 嗓 sǎng | | jué | |
| | 啡 fēi | | 嗜 shì | | 嚷 rǎng | |
| | 唬 hǔ | | 嗡 wēng | | | |
| | 哗 huā, | | 嗅 xiù | | **51 囗** | |
| | huá | | 嘟 dū | | | |
| | 啃 kěn | | 嗦 suo | 2 | 囚 qiú | |
| | 啦 la | | 嗝 gé | | 四 sì | |
| | 啮 niè | | 嗳 ài, āi | 3 | 回 huí | |
| | 啪 pā | | 嗨 hāi, | | 团 tuán | |
| | 啤 pí | | hēi | | 因 yīn | |
| | 商 shāng | | 嗬 hē | 4 | 囤 dún | |
| | 售 shòu | | 嗯 ńg, ǹg | | 困 kùn | |
| | 唾 tuò | 11 | 嘎 gā | | 围 wéi | |
| | 唯 wéi | | 嘛 má | | 园 yuán | |
| | 啸 xiào | | 嗽 sòu | 5 | 固 gù | |
| | 啄 zhuó | | 嘘 xū | | 国 guó | |
| | 喵 miāo | | 嘈 cáo | | 图 tú | |
| | 唿 hū | 12 | 嘲 cháo | 7 | 圃 pǔ | |
| | 喋 dié | | 嘶 sī | | 圆 yuán | |
| 9 | 喘 chuǎn | | 嘱 zhǔ | 8 | 圈 quān | |
| | 喊 hǎn | | 噜 lū | | | |
| | 喝 hē, hè | | 嘿 hēi | | **52 巾** | |
| | 喉 hóu | | 噢 ō | | | |
| | 喀 kā | 13 | 器 qì | | 巾 jīn | |
| | 喇 lǎ | | 噪 zào | 2 | 布 bù | |
| | 喷 pēn | | 嘴 zuǐ | | 帅 shuài | |
| | 喂 wèi | | 噱 xué, jué | 3 | 帆 fān | |

吊 diào
4 帐 zhàng
5 帚 zhǒu
　帖 tiē
6 帮 bāng
　带 dài
　帝 dì
8 帷 wéi
9 幅 fú
　帽 mào
10 幌 huǎng
12 幢 zhuàng

**53 山**

　山 shān
3 岁 suì
　屿 yǔ
4 岔 chà
　岛 dǎo
　岗 gāng
　岖 qū
5 岸 àn
　岭 lǐng
　岩 yán
　岳 yuè
6 炭 tàn
　峡 xiá
　峋 xún
7 峨 é
　峰 fēng
　峻 jùn
8 崩 bēng
　崇 chóng

　崎 qí
　崖 yá
　崭 zhǎn
9 嵌 qiàn
12 嶙 lín
18 巍 wēi

**54 彳**

3 行 xíng,
　　háng
4 彻 chè
　役 yì
5 彼 bǐ
　径 jìng
　往 wǎng,
　　wàng
　征 zhēng
6 待 dài
　很 hěn
　律 lù
　衍 yǎn
7 徒 tú
8 得 dé, de,
　　děi
　衔 xián
9 街 jiē
　循 xún
　御 yù
10 微 wēi
12 德 dé
13 衡 héng
14 徽 huī

**55 彡**

4 形 xíng
　杉 shān
5 衫 shān
6 须 xū
8 彩 cǎi
　彬 bīn
12 影 yǐng

**56 夕**

　夕 xī
3 多 duō
　岁 suì
8 梦 mèng

**57 夂**

2 冬 dōng
3 各 gè
4 条 tiáo
5 备 bèi
6 复 fù
7 夏 xià
9 惫 bèi

**58 犭**

2 犯 fàn
4 狂 kuáng
　犹 yóu
5 狗 gǒu
　狐 hú

狙 jū
狒 fèi

6 狠 hěn
狡 jiǎo
狮 shī
狭 xiá
狱 yù
独 dú
狩 shòu

7 狼 láng
狸 lí

8 猜 cāi
猎 liè
猫 māo
猛 měng
猪 zhū
猕 mí

9 猴 hóu
猾 huá
猩 xīng
猥 wěi
猬 wèi

13 獭 tà

**59 饣**

2 饥 jī
4 饭 fàn
饮 yǐn
饨 tún
饪 rèn
5 饱 bǎo
饯 jiàn
饰 shì

饲 sì

6 饼 bǐng
饵 ěr
饺 jiǎo
饶 ráo
蚀 shí

7 饿 è
馁 něi

8 馆 guǎn
馄 hún
馅 xiàn

9 馈 kuì
馊 sōu

11 馒 mán

**60 彐, 彑, 彐**

3 寻 xún
4 灵 líng
5 录 lù
帚 zhǒu
8 彗 huì

**61 尸**

尸 shī
1 尺 chǐ
2 尼 ní
3 尽 jìn
4 层 céng
局 jú
尿 niào
屁 pì
尾 wěi

5 届 jiè
居 jū
屈 qū
屉 tì

6 屏 bǐng,
píng
屎 shǐ
屋 wū

7 屑 xiè
展 zhǎn

8 屠 tú

9 屡 lǚ
属 shǔ
犀 xī

12 履 lǚ

**62 己, 已**

己 jǐ
已 yǐ
1 巴 bā
3 异 yì
导 dǎo
6 巷 xiàng

**63 弓**

弓 gōng
1 引 yǐn
3 弛 chí
4 张 zhāng
5 弧 hú
弥 mí
弦 xián

| | | | | | | | |
|---|---|---|---|---|---|---|---|
| 6 | 弯 wān | | 妻 qī | | **65 幺** | | |
| 7 | 弱 ruò | | 始 shǐ | | | | |
| 8 | 弹 tán, | | 委 wěi | | 幺 xiāng | | |
| | dàn | | 姓 xìng | | 幺 yāo | | |
| 9 | 强 qiáng | | 妾 qiè | 1 | 幻 huàn | | |
| | 粥 zhōu | 6 | 姜 jiāng | 6 | 幽 yōu | | |
| 16 | 疆 jiāng | | 娇 jiāo | | | | |
| | | | 姥 lǎo | | **66 子** | | |
| **64 女** | | | 耍 shuǎ | | | | |
| | | | 娃 wá | | 子 zǐ | | |
| | 女 nǚ | | 姨 yí | 2 | 孕 yùn | | |
| 2 | 奶 nǎi | | 姻 yīn | 3 | 存 cún | | |
| | 奴 nú | | 姿 zī | | 孙 sūn | | |
| 3 | 妇 fù | | 要 yāo | 4 | 孝 xiào | | |
| | 好 hǎo, | 7 | 娩 miǎn | | 孜 zī | | |
| | hào | | 娘 niáng | 5 | 孤 gū | | |
| | 奸 jiān | | 娱 yú | | 学 xué | | |
| | 妈 mā | | 娴 xián | | 孟 mèng | | |
| | 如 rú | 8 | 婚 hūn | 6 | 孩 hái | | |
| | 她 tā | | 婪 lán | | | | |
| | 妄 wàng | | 婆 pó | | **67 纟** | | |
| | 妃 fēi | | 婉 wǎn | | | | |
| 4 | 妒 dù | | 婴 yīng | 2 | 纠 jiū | | |
| | 妨 fáng | | 婊 biǎo | 3 | 红 hóng | | |
| | 妓 jì | 9 | 媒 méi | | 级 jí | | |
| | 妙 miào | | 嫂 sǎo | | 纪 jì | | |
| | 妥 tuǒ | | 婿 xù | | 纫 rèn | | |
| | 妖 yāo | 10 | 嫉 jí | | 纤 xiān, | | |
| | 姊 zǐ | | 嫁 jià | | qiàn | | |
| | 妞 niū | | 媳 xí | | 约 yuē | | |
| 5 | 妹 mèi | | 嫌 xián | 4 | 纯 chún | | |
| | 姑 gū | 11 | 嫩 nèn | | 纺 fǎng | | |
| | 姐 jiě | 12 | 嬉 xī | | 纷 fēn | | |
| | 姆 mǔ | 17 | 孀 shuāng | | 纲 gāng | | |

纳 nà
纽 niǔ
纱 shā
纬 wěi
纹 wén
纸 zhǐ
纵 zòng
5 绊 bàn
经 jīng
练 liàn
绍 shào
绅 shēn
细 xì
线 xiàn
织 zhī
终 zhōng
组 zǔ
绉 zhòu
6 绑 bǎng
给 gěi, jǐ
绘 huì
结 jiē
绝 jué
络 luò
绕 rào
绒 róng
统 tǒng
7 继 jì
绢 juàn
绦 tāo
绣 xiù
8 绷 bēng
绸 chóu
绰 chuò

绩 jì
绿 lù
绵 mián
绳 shéng
维 wéi
绪 xù
续 xù
缀 zhuì
综 zōng
9 编 biān
缔 dì
缎 duàn
缓 huǎn
缉 jī
缆 lǎn
缕 lǔ
缅 miǎn
缘 yuán
10 缠 chán
缝 féng, fèng
缚 fù
缤 bīn
11 缩 suō
12 缮 shàn
13 疆 jiāng

**68 马**

马 mǎ
3 驰 chí
驯 xùn
4 驳 bó
驴 lǘ

驱 qū
5 驾 jià
驹 jū
驶 shǐ
驼 tuó
驻 zhù
6 骇 hài
骄 jiāo
骆 luò
骂 mà
7 验 yàn
8 骑 qí
9 骗 piàn
骚 sāo
11 骡 luó
14 骤 zhòu

**69 巛**

巢 cháo

**70 灬**

4 杰 jié
5 点 diǎn
6 羔 gāo
烈 liè
热 rè
7 焉 yān
8 焦 jiāo
然 rán
煮 zhǔ
9 煎 jiān
照 zhào

| | | |
|---|---|---|
| 10 | 熬 | áo |
| | 熙 | xī |
| | 熊 | xióng |
| | 熏 | xūn |
| 11 | 熟 | shú, shóu |
| 12 | 燕 | yàn |

## 71 斗

| | | |
|---|---|---|
| | 斗 | dòu, dǒu |
| 7 | 斜 | xié |

## 72 文

| | | |
|---|---|---|
| | 文 | wén |
| 2 | 齐 | qí |
| 6 | 斋 | zhāi |
| | 紊 | wěn |

## 73 方

| | | |
|---|---|---|
| | 方 | fāng |
| 4 | 房 | fáng |
| | 放 | fàng |
| 5 | 施 | shī |
| 6 | 旅 | lǚ |
| | 旁 | páng |
| 7 | 旋 | xuán, xuàn |
| | 族 | zú |
| 10 | 旗 | qí |

## 74 火

| | | |
|---|---|---|
| | 火 | huǒ |
| 1 | 灭 | miè |
| 2 | 灯 | dēng |
| | 灰 | huī |
| 3 | 灿 | càn |
| | 灸 | jiǔ |
| | 灶 | zào |
| | 灼 | zhuó |
| 4 | 炒 | chǎo |
| | 炬 | jù |
| | 炉 | lú |
| | 炎 | yán |
| | 炖 | dùn |
| 5 | 烂 | làn |
| | 炼 | liàn |
| | 炮 | pào |
| | 烁 | shuò |
| | 烃 | tīng |
| | 炸 | zhà, zhá |
| | 炫 | xuàn |
| 6 | 烦 | fán |
| | 烘 | hōng |
| | 烬 | jìn |
| | 烤 | kǎo |
| | 烧 | shāo |
| | 烫 | tàng |
| | 烟 | yān |
| | 烛 | zhú |
| 7 | 焊 | hàn |
| | 焕 | huàn |
| | 烯 | xī |

| | | |
|---|---|---|
| 8 | 焚 | fén |
| | 焰 | yàn |
| 9 | 煌 | huáng |
| | 煤 | méi |
| | 煳 | hú |
| | 煨 | wēi, wèi |
| | 煸 | biān |
| 10 | 熔 | róng |
| | 煽 | shān, shàn |
| | 熄 | xī |
| 11 | 熨 | yùn |
| 12 | 燃 | rán |
| 13 | 燥 | zào |
| 15 | 爆 | bào |

## 75 心

| | | |
|---|---|---|
| | 心 | xīn |
| 1 | 必 | bì |
| 3 | 忌 | jì |
| | 忍 | rěn |
| | 忘 | wàng |
| 4 | 忽 | hū |
| | 念 | niàn |
| | 怂 | sǒng |
| | 态 | tài |
| | 忠 | zhōng |
| 5 | 怠 | dài |
| | 急 | jí |
| | 怒 | nù |
| | 思 | sī |
| | 怨 | yuàn |

| | | | | | | |
|---|---|---|---|---|---|---|
| | 怎 zěn | | **76 户** | | 玫 méi | |
| | 总 zǒng | | | | 玩 wán | |
| 6 | 恶 è, wù, ě | | 户 hù | | 现 xiàn | |
| | 恩 ēn | 4 | 房 fáng | 5 | 玻 bō | |
| | 恳 kěn | | 所 suǒ | | 珐 fà | |
| | 恐 kǒng | | 肩 jiān | | 珊 shān | |
| | 恋 liàn | | 戾 lì | | 珍 zhēn | |
| | 恕 shù | 5 | 扁 biǎn | | 玷 diàn | |
| | 息 xī | 6 | 扇 shàn | 6 | 班 bān | |
| | 恙 yàng | 8 | 雇 gù | | 珠 zhū | |
| | 恣 zì | | | 7 | 琅 láng | |
| 7 | 患 huàn | | **77 礻** | | 理 lǐ | |
| | 您 nín | | | | 球 qiú | |
| | 悉 xī | 1 | 礼 lǐ | | 琐 suǒ | |
| | 悬 xuán | 3 | 社 shè | | 望 wàng | |
| | 恿 yǒng | | 祀 sì | 8 | 斑 bān | |
| | 悠 yōu | 4 | 视 shì | | 琴 qín | |
| 8 | 悲 bēi | 5 | 祈 qí | | 琢 zhuó | |
| | 惩 chéng | | 神 shén | 9 | 瑰 guī | |
| | 惠 huì | | 祝 zhù | | 瑚 hú | |
| | 惑 huò | | 祖 zǔ | | 瑞 ruì | |
| 9 | 愁 chóu | | 祠 cí | | 瑜 yú | |
| | 慈 cí | 6 | 祥 xiáng | | 瑕 xiá | |
| | 感 gǎn | 7 | 祷 dǎo | 10 | 璃 lí | |
| | 想 xiǎng | | 祸 huò | 11 | 璜 huáng | |
| | 意 yì | 8 | 禅 chán | | | |
| | 愚 yú | 9 | 福 fú | | **79 韦** | |
| | 愈 yù | | | | | |
| 10 | 愿 yuàn | | **78 王** | | 韧 rèn | |
| 11 | 慧 huì | | | | | |
| | 慰 wèi | | 王 wáng | | **80 木** | |
| | | 1 | 玉 yù | | | |
| | | 3 | 玛 mǎ | | 木 mù | |
| | | 4 | 环 huán | 1 | 本 běn | |

术 shù
2 朵 duǒ
机 jī
朴 pǔ
权 quán
朽 xiǔ
杂 zá
3 材 cái
村 cūn
杜 dù
杆 gǎn,
　　gān
杠 gàng
极 jí
李 lǐ
杏 xìng
杨 yáng
杖 zhàng
4 杰 jié
采 cǎi
板 bǎn
杯 bēi
枫 fēng
构 gòu
柜 guì
果 guǒ
林 lín
枪 qiāng
枢 shū
松 sōng
析 xī
枕 zhěn
枝 zhī
5 柏 bǎi, bó

标 biāo
柄 bǐng
查 chá
栋 dòng
柑 gān
架 jià
枯 kū
栏 lán
柳 liǔ
某 mǒu
柠 níng
染 rǎn
柔 róu
柿 shì
树 shù
相 xiāng
栅 shān,
　　zhà
柱 zhù
柚 yòu,
　　yóu
栎 yuè, lì
6 柴 chái
档 dàng
格 gé
根 gēn
桂 guì
核 hé
桨 jiǎng
桔 jú
框 kuàng
栖 xī, qī1
桥 qiáo
桑 sāng

栓 shuān
桃 táo
桅 wéi
校 xiào,
　　jiào
样 yàng
案 àn
桩 zhuāng
桌 zhuō
桦 huà
7 梗 gěng
检 jiǎn
梨 lí
梁 liáng
梅 méi
渠 qú
梢 shāo
梳 shū
梯 tī
桶 tǒng
梧 wú
械 xiè
8 棒 bàng
棺 guān
棍 gùn
集 jí
椒 jiāo
棵 kē
椰 liáng
棱 léng,
　　líng
棉 mián
棚 péng
棋 qí

森 sēn
椭 tuǒ
椰 yē
椅 yǐ
植 zhí
椎 zhuī,
　　chuí
棕 zōng
椋 liáng
9 椽 chuán
概 gài
槐 huái
楞 lèng
楼 lóu
楔 xiē
榆 yú
楂 zhā
榄 lǎn
槌 chuí
栌 lú
桦 jǔ
10 榜 bǎng
槛 jiàn,
　　kǎn
榴 liú
模 mó, mú
榨 zhà
榛 zhēn
槟 bīng
11 槽 cáo
横 héng
樱 yīng
樟 zhāng
橄 gǎn

12 橙 chéng
橱 chú
橇 qiāo
橡 xiàng
橹 lǔ
橘 jú
13 檬 méng
檐 yán

**81 犬**

犬 quǎn
6 臭 chòu,
　　xiù
哭 kū
9 献 xiàn

**82 歹**

歹 dǎi
2 死 sǐ
5 残 cán
6 殊 shū
殉 xùn
8 殖 zhí
10 殡 bìn

**83 车**

车 chē
1 轧 yà, zhá
2 轨 guǐ
3 轩 xuān
4 轰 hōng

轮 lún
软 ruǎn
转 zhuàn,
　　zhuǎn
5 轻 qīng
轴 zhóu
6 轿 jiào
较 jiào,
　　jiǎo
7 辅 fǔ
辆 liàng
8 辈 bèi
辊 gǔn
9 毂 gū, gǔ
辐 fú
辑 jí
输 shū
10 辗 zhǎn
12 辙 zhé

**84 戈**

戈 gē
2 成 chéng
戍 shù
3 戒 jiè
我 wǒ
4 或 huò
5 威 wēi
咸 xián
栽 zali
战 zhàn
6 载 zǎi, zài
7 戚 qī

| | | | |
|---|---|---|---|
| 8 | 裁 cái | | |
| 10 | 截 jié | | |
| 11 | 戮 lù | | |
| 13 | 戴 dài | | |
| 14 | 戳 chuō | | |

**85 比**

| | |
|---|---|
| | 比 bǐ |
| 2 | 毕 bì |
| 6 | 毙 bì |

**86 瓦**

| | |
|---|---|
| | 瓦 wǎ |
| 6 | 瓷 cí |
| | 瓶 píng |

**87 止**

| | |
|---|---|
| | 止 zhǐ |
| 2 | 此 cǐ |
| 3 | 步 bù |
| 4 | 歧 qí |
| | 武 wǔ |
| | 肯 kěn |
| 5 | 歪 wāi |
| 6 | 耻 chǐ |
| 11 | 整 zhěng |

**88 支**

| | |
|---|---|
| | 敲 qiāo |

**89 日**

| | |
|---|---|
| | 日 rì |
| 1 | 旦 dàn |
| 2 | 早 zǎo |
| 3 | 旱 hàn |
| | 旷 kuàng |
| | 时 shí |
| 4 | 昂 áng |
| | 昌 chāng |
| | 昏 hūn |
| | 昆 kūn |
| | 明 míng |
| | 旺 wàng |
| | 易 yì |
| 5 | 春 chūn |
| | 昧 mèi |
| | 是 shì |
| | 显 xiǎn |
| | 星 xīng |
| | 映 yìng |
| | 昭 zhāo |
| | 昨 zuó |
| | 昵 nì |
| 6 | 晃 huàng, huǎng |
| | 晋 jìn |
| | 晒 shài |
| | 晓 xiǎo |
| | 晕 yūn, yùn |
| 7 | 晨 chén |
| | 匙 chí, shi |

| | |
|---|---|
| | 晚 wǎn |
| | 晤 wù |
| 8 | 晷 guǐ |
| | 晶 jīng |
| | 景 jǐng |
| | 量 liàng |
| | 晾 liàng |
| | 普 pǔ |
| | 晴 qíng |
| | 暑 shǔ |
| | 晰 xī |
| | 暂 zàn |
| | 智 zhì |
| | 晳 xī |
| 9 | 暗 àn |
| | 暖 nuǎn |
| | 暇 xiá |
| 10 | 暧 ài |
| 11 | 暴 bào |
| 14 | 曝 bào |
| 16 | 曦 xī |

**90 曰**

| | |
|---|---|
| 2 | 曲 qū |
| 4 | 者 zhě |
| 5 | 冒 mào |
| 8 | 替 tì |
| | 曾 céng, zēng |
| | 最 zuì |

## 91 贝

| | | |
|---|---|---|
| | 贝 | bèi |
| 3 | 财 | cái |
| 4 | 败 | bài |
| | 贯 | guàn |
| | 贬 | biǎn |
| | 贩 | fàn |
| | 购 | gòu |
| | 货 | huò |
| | 贫 | pín |
| | 贪 | tān |
| | 责 | zé |
| | 账 | zhàng |
| | 质 | zhì |
| | 贮 | zhù |
| 5 | 贷 | dài |
| | 费 | fèi |
| | 贵 | guì |
| | 贺 | hè |
| | 贱 | jiàn |
| | 贸 | mào |
| | 贴 | tiē |
| | 贻 | yí |
| 6 | 贿 | huì |
| | 赂 | lù |
| | 赃 | zāng |
| | 资 | zī |
| 7 | 赊 | shē |
| | 赈 | zhèn |
| 8 | 赐 | cì |
| | 赌 | dǔ |
| | 赋 | fù |
| | 赔 | péi |

| | | |
|---|---|---|
| | 赏 | shǎng |
| | 赎 | shú |
| 9 | 赖 | lài |
| 10 | 赚 | zuàn |
| 11 | 赘 | zhuì |
| 12 | 赞 | zàn |
| | 赠 | zèng |
| 13 | 赡 | shàn |

## 92 见

| | | |
|---|---|---|
| | 见 | jiàn |
| 4 | 规 | guī |
| | 视 | shì |
| 5 | 觉 | jué, jiào |
| | 览 | lǎn |

## 93 父

| | | |
|---|---|---|
| | 父 | fù |
| 2 | 爷 | yé |
| 4 | 斧 | fǔ |
| | 爸 | bà |
| 6 | 爹 | diē |

## 94 牛, 牜 , 牛

| | | |
|---|---|---|
| | 牛 | niú |
| 3 | 牡 | mǔ |
| 4 | 牧 | mù |
| | 物 | wù |
| | 牦 | máo |
| 5 | 牲 | shēng |
| | 牯 | gǔ |

| | | |
|---|---|---|
| 6 | 特 | tè |
| | 牺 | xī |
| 7 | 犁 | lí |
| 8 | 犊 | dú |

## 95 手

| | | |
|---|---|---|
| | 手 | shǒu |
| 6 | 拿 | ná |
| | 挛 | luán |
| | 拳 | quán |
| | 挚 | zhì |
| 8 | 掰 | bāi |
| 11 | 摩 | mó |
| 12 | 擎 | qíng |
| 15 | 攀 | pān |

## 96 毛

| | | |
|---|---|---|
| | 毛 | máo |
| 5 | 毡 | zhān |
| 8 | 毯 | tǎn |

## 97 气

| | | |
|---|---|---|
| | 气 | qì |
| 4 | 氛 | fēn |
| 5 | 氟 | fú |
| 6 | 氢 | qīng |
| | 氧 | yǎng |
| 8 | 氮 | dàn |
| | 氯 | lǜ |

| | | | | | |
|---|---|---|---|---|---|
| **98 攵** | | **100 斤** | | 肪 | fáng |
| | | | | 肥 | féi |
| 2 收 | shōu | 斤 jīn | | 肺 | fèi |
| 3 改 | gǎi | 1 斥 | chì | 肤 | fū |
| 4 放 | fàng | 4 所 | suǒ | 服 | fú |
| 5 故 | gù | 欣 | xīn | 股 | gǔ |
| 政 | zhèng | 7 断 | duàn | 朋 | péng |
| 6 敌 | dí | 8 斯 | sī | 肾 | shèn |
| 效 | xiào | 9 新 | xīn | 胁 | xié |
| 致 | zhì | | | 育 | yù |
| 7 敢 | gǎn | **101 爪, ⺥** | | 胀 | zhàng |
| 教 | jiào, | | | 肢 | zhī |
| | jiāo | 爪 zhuǎ, | | 肿 | zhǒng |
| 救 | jiù | zhǎo | | 肩 | jiān |
| 敏 | mǐn | 4 爬 | pá | 肯 | kěn |
| 赦 | shè | 采 | cǎi | 5 胞 | bāo |
| 8 敞 | chǎng | 斧 | fǔ | 背 | bèi |
| 敦 | duì, | 6 奚 | xī | 胆 | dǎn |
| | dūn | 爱 | ài | 胡 | hú |
| 敬 | jìng | 舀 | yǎo | 脉 | mò |
| 散 | sǎn, sàn | 13 爵 | jué | 胖 | pàng |
| 9 数 | shù, | | | 胚 | péi |
| | shǔ, | **102 月** | | 胜 | shèng |
| | shuò | | | 胎 | tāi |
| 11 敷 | fū | 月 yuè | | 胃 | wèi |
| 整 | zhěng | 2 肌 | jī | 胧 | lóng |
| | | 肋 | lèi | 胛 | jiǎ |
| **99 片** | | 有 | yǒu | 胫 | jìng |
| | | 3 肠 | cháng | 6 脆 | cuì |
| 片 | piān | 肚 | dǔ, dù | 胳 | gē |
| 4 版 | bǎn | 肝 | gān | 脊 | jǐ |
| 8 牌 | pái | 肛 | gāng | 胶 | jiāo |
| 牒 | dié | 肘 | zhǒu | 胯 | kuà |
| | | 4 肮 | āng | 朗 | lǎng |

脑 nǎo
脓 nóng
脐 qí
胸 xiōng
胰 yí
脏 zàng, zāng
脂 zhī
胱 guāng
胭 yān
7 脖 bó
脯 fū
脚 jiǎo
脸 liǎn
脱 tuō
豚 tún
8 朝 cháo, zhāo
腊 là
脾 pí
腔 qiāng
腆 tiǎn
腕 wàn
腋 yè
腌 yān
腱 jiàn
期 qī
9 腹 fù
腻 nì
腮 sāi
腾 téng
腿 tuǐ
腺 xiàn
腰 yāo

腭 è
10 膀 bǎng
膊 bó
膜 mó
11 膝 xī
12 膨 péng
膳 shàn
13 臂 bì
臀 tún
臊 sāo

## 103 欠

欠 qiàn
4 欧 ōu
欣 xīn
7 欲 yù
8 款 kuǎn
欺 qī
9 歇 xiē
10 歌 gē
歉 qiàn

## 104 风

风 fēng
8 飓 jù
11 飘 piāo

## 105 殳

4 殴 ōu
5 段 duàn
6 殷 yīn

9 縠 gū, gǔ
毁 huǐ
殿 diàn

## 106 聿, 肀, 聿

4 肃 sù
7 肆 sì

## 107 母

母 mǔ
2 每 měi
4 贯 guàn
毒 dú

## 108 水, 氺

水 shuǐ
1 永 yǒng
5 泵 bèng
泰 tài
泉 quán
6 浆 jiāng
10 黎 lí

## 109 穴

穴 xué
2 究 jiū
穷 qióng
3 空 kōng, kòng
帘 lián

| | | | | | | |
|---|---|---|---|---|---|---|
| 4 | 穿 chuān | 3 | 疙 gē | | 痱 fèi | |
| | 窃 qiè | | 疚 jiù | | 瘀 yū | |
| | 突 tū | | 疟 nüè | 9 | 瘩 dá, da | |
| 5 | 窍 qiào | | 疡 yáng | | 瘦 shòu | |
| | 容 róng | | 疝 shàn | | 瘟 wēn | |
| | 窄 zhǎi | 4 | 疤 bā | 10 | 瘪 biě, biē | |
| 6 | 窑 yáo | | 疮 chuāng | | 瘤 liú | |
| | 窒 zhì | | 疯 fēng | | 瘫 tān | |
| 7 | 窗 chuāng | | 疫 yì | | 瘠 jí | |
| | 窖 jiào | | 疣 yóu | 11 | 瘸 qué | |
| | 窘 jiǒng | 5 | 病 bìng | | 瘾 yǐn | |
| | 窝 wō | | 疾 jí | 12 | 癌 ái | |
| 8 | 窟 kū | | 痉 jìng | 13 | 癞 lài | |
| | 窥 kuī | | 疲 pí | | 癣 pǐ | |
| | 窦 dòu | | 疼 téng | 16 | 癫 diān | |

**110 立**

立 lì
1 产 chǎn
4 亲 qīn
竖 shù
5 竞 jìng
站 zhàn
6 竟 jìng
章 zhāng
7 童 tóng
9 端 duān
竭 jié

**111 疒**

2 疗 liáo
疖 jiē

（中栏续）
疹 zhěn
症 zhèng
疸 da, dǎn
疱 pào
痂 jiā
6 疵 cī
痕 hén
痊 quán
痒 yǎng
痔 zhì
7 痘 dòu
痪 huàn
痢 lì
痛 tòng
痣 zhì
痫 xián
8 痹 bì
痴 chī
痰 tán

**112 衤**

2 补 bǔ
初 chū
3 衬 chèn
衩 chǎ
5 被 bèi
袍 páo
袒 tǎn
袜 wà
袖 xiù
7 裤 kù
裙 qún
裕 yù
8 褂 guà
裸 luǒ
裱 biǎo
9 褐 hè

褪 tuì
褛 lǚ
10 褥 rù
褴 lán
11 褶 zhě
13 襟 jīn

## 113 示

示 shì
5 祟 suì
6 祭 jì
票 piào
8 禁 jìn, jīn

## 114 石

石 shí
3 矿 kuàng
码 mǎ
4 砍 kǎn
砂 shā
研 yán
砚 yàn
砖 zhuān
5 础 chǔ
砾 lì
砰 pēng
破 pò
砸 zá
6 硅 guī
硕 shuò
7 硫 liú
确 què

硬 yìng
8 碍 ài
碑 bēi
碘 diǎn
碉 diāo
碌 lù
碰 pèng
碎 suì
碗 wǎn
9 磁 cí
磋 cuō
碟 dié
碳 tàn
10 磅 bàng
磕 kē
碾 niǎn
11 磺 huáng
磨 mó
12 礁 jiāo

## 115 龙

龙 lóng
6 聋 lóng
龛 kān
袭 xí

## 116 业

业 yè
7 凿 záo

## 117 目

目 mù
2 盯 dīng
3 盲 máng
4 盾 dùn
看 kàn,
    kān
眉 méi
盼 pàn
省 shěng,
    xǐng
眨 zhǎ
盹 dǔn
5 眠 mián
眩 xuàn
6 眼 yǎn
7 睑 jiǎn
8 督 dū
睫 jié
睛 jīng
瞄 miáo
睦 mù
睡 shuì
10 瞒 mán
瞎 xiā
瞌 kē
11 瞥 piē
12 瞪 dèng
瞧 qiáo
瞬 shùn
瞳 tóng

## 118 田

| | |
|---|---|
| | 田 tián |
| | 由 yóu |
| 4 | 界 jiè |
| | 畏 wèi |
| 5 | 留 liú |
| | 畜 xù, chù |
| 6 | 累 lèi, lěi |
| | 略 lüè |
| 7 | 畴 chóu |
| | 番 fān |
| 8 | 畸 jī |

## 119 罒

| | |
|---|---|
| 3 | 罗 luó |
| 4 | 罚 fá |
| 5 | 罢 bà |
| 8 | 署 shǔ |
| | 罩 zhào |
| | 置 zhì |
| | 罪 zuì |

## 120 皿

| | |
|---|---|
| | 皿 mǐn |
| 4 | 盆 pén |
| | 盈 yíng |
| 5 | 盎 àng |
| | 监 jiān |
| | 盐 yán |
| | 益 yì |
| 6 | 盗 dào |

| | |
|---|---|
| | 盒 hé |
| | 盔 kuī |
| | 盘 pán |
| | 盛 shèng, chéng |
| | 盖 gài |
| 7 | 尴 gān |
| 8 | 盟 méng |
| 11 | 盥 guàn |

## 121 钅

| | |
|---|---|
| 2 | 钉 dìng |
| | 针 zhēn |
| 3 | 钓 diào |
| 4 | 钞 chāo |
| | 钝 dùn |
| | 钙 gài |
| | 钢 gāng |
| | 钩 gōu |
| | 钮 niǔ |
| | 钦 qīn |
| | 钥 yào |
| | 钟 zhōng |
| 5 | 铂 bó |
| | 铃 líng |
| | 铆 mǎo |
| | 铅 qiān |
| | 钱 qián |
| | 钳 qián |
| | 铁 tiě |
| | 铀 yóu |
| | 钻 zuān, zuàn |

| | |
|---|---|
| 6 | 铲 chǎn |
| | 铬 gè |
| | 铰 jiǎo |
| | 铝 lǚ |
| | 铭 míng |
| | 铜 tóng |
| | 银 yín |
| | 铐 kǎo |
| 7 | 锄 chú |
| | 锋 fēng |
| | 锅 guō |
| | 链 liàn |
| | 铺 pù |
| | 锐 ruì |
| | 锁 suǒ |
| | 销 xiāo |
| | 锌 xīn |
| | 锈 xiù |
| | 铸 zhù |
| | 锉 cuò |
| 8 | 锤 chuí |
| | 错 cuò |
| | 锭 dìng |
| | 键 jiàn |
| | 锦 jǐn |
| | 锯 jù |
| | 锣 luó |
| | 锚 máo |
| | 锡 xī |
| | 锥 zhuī |
| 9 | 镀 dù |
| | 锻 duàn |
| | 锹 qiāo |
| 10 | 镑 bàng |

| | | | | |
|---|---|---|---|---|
| | 镊 niè | 秘 mì, bì | **126 鸟** | |
| | 镍 niè | 秦 qín | | |
| | 镇 zhèn | 秩 zhì | 鸟 niǎo | |
| 11 | 镜 jìng | 租 zū | 2 鸡 jī | |
| 13 | 镰 lián | 6 秽 huì | 3 鸢 yuān | |
| | 镯 zhuó | 移 yí | 4 鸥 ōu | |
| 15 | 镳 biāo | 7 程 chéng | 鸦 yā | |
| 17 | 镶 xiāng | 稍 shāo | 5 鸵 tuó | |
| | | 税 shuì | 鸭 yā | |

**122 矢**

|  | | |
|---|---|---|
| 4 | 矩 jǔ |
| 6 | 矫 jiǎo |
| 7 | 短 duǎn |
| 8 | 矮 ǎi |
| 9 | 疑 yí |

| | |
|---|---|
| | 稀 xī |
| 8 | 稠 chóu |
| | 稚 zhì |
| 9 | 稳 wěn |
| 10 | 稻 dào |
| | 稿 gǎo |
| | 稽 jī |
| | 稼 jià |
| 11 | 穆 mù |
| 12 | 黏 nián |
| | 穗 suì |

| | |
|---|---|
| | 鸫 dōng |
| 6 | 鸽 gē |
| 7 | 鹅 é |
| 8 | 鹊 què |
| | 鹉 wǔ |
| 11 | 鹦 yīng |
| 12 | 鹫 jiù |
| 13 | 鹭 lù |
| 17 | 鹳 guàn |

**123 禾**

| | |
|---|---|
| 2 | 私 sī |
| | 秀 xiù |
| 3 | 秆 gǎn |
| | 季 jì |
| 4 | 科 kē |
| | 秒 miǎo |
| | 秋 qiū |
| | 香 xiāng |
| | 种 zhòng, zhǒng |
| 5 | 称 chēng, chèng, chèn |
| | 秤 chèng |
| | 积 jī |

**124 白**

| | |
|---|---|
| | 白 bái |
| 2 | 皂 zào |
| 3 | 的 de, dì, dí |
| 4 | 皇 huáng |

**125 瓜**

| | |
|---|---|
| | 瓜 guā |
| 11 | 瓢 piáo |

**127 用**

| | |
|---|---|
| | 用 yòng |
| | 甩 shuǎi |

**128 矛**

| | |
|---|---|
| | 矛 máo |

**129 疋, 𤴓**

| | |
|---|---|
| 6 | 蛋 dàn |
| 7 | 疏 shū |
| 8 | 楚 chǔ |
| 9 | 疑 yí |

## 130 皮

皮 pí
5 皱 zhòu

## 131 衣

衣 yī
5 袋 dài
6 裂 liè
裝 zhuāng
7 裔 yì

## 132 羊, 羊, 羊

羊 yáng
3 养 yǎng
4 羞 xiū
5 着 zháo,
zhe,
zhāo,
zhuó
6 善 shàn
羡 xiàn
7 群 qún
11 羹 gēng

## 133 米

米 mǐ
3 类 lèi
4 粉 fěn
料 liào
5 粗 cū

粒 lì
粘 zhān,
nián
6 粪 fèn
7 粮 liáng
8 粹 cuì
精 jīng
9 糊 hú, hù,
hū
10 糙 cāo
糕 gāo
糖 táng
11 糟 zāo
12 糨 jiàng
14 糯 nuò

## 134 耒

4 耙 pá
耕 gēng
耗 hào

## 135 老

老 lǎo

## 136 耳

耳 ěr
4 耽 dān
耸 sǒng
5 聊 liáo
职 zhí
6 联 lián

7 聘 pìn
8 聚 jù
9 聪 cōng

## 137 西, 覀

西 xī
4 栗 lì
6 粟 sù
12 覆 fù

## 138 页

页 yè
2 顶 dǐng
顷 qǐng
3 顺 shùn
4 顿 dùn
顾 gù
颂 sòng
顽 wán
预 yù
5 颈 gěng,
jǐng
领 lǐng
颅 lú
6 颊 jiá
颌 hé
7 频 pín
颓 tuí
颐 yí
颖 yǐng
8 颗 kē
9 额 é

| | | | | | | | |
|---|---|---|---|---|---|---|---|
| | 题 tí | | 蚯 qiū | 10 | 融 róng |
| | 颜 yán | 6 | 蛤 gé, há | | 鳌 áo |
| 10 | 颠 diān | | 蛮 mán | | 蟆 ma |
| 13 | 颤 chàn, | | 蛙 wā | | 螃 páng |
| | zhàn | | 蜒 yán | 11 | 螺 luó |
| 17 | 颧 quán | | 蛛 zhū | | 螫 shì, zhē |
| | | | 蜓 yán | | 螬 cáo |
| | | | 蛞 kuò | | 螳 zhāng |
| | | | 蛴 qí | | 蟀 shuài |
| | **139 虍** | 7 | 蜂 fēng | 13 | 蟹 xiè |
| | | | 蜕 tuì | | 蠓 měng |
| 2 | 虎 hǔ | | 蜗 wō | 14 | 蠕 rú |
| | 虏 lǔ | | 蜃 shèn | 15 | 蠢 chǔn |
| 3 | 虐 nüè | | 蜇 zhē | | |
| 4 | 虑 lù | | 蜊 li | | **141 缶** |
| | 虔 qián | 8 | 蝉 chán | | |
| 5 | 虚 xū | | 蜡 là | 3 | 缸 gāng |
| | | | 蝇 yíng | 4 | 缺 quē |
| | **140 虫** | | 蜘 zhī | 8 | 罂 yīng |
| | | | 蜻 qīng | 17 | 罐 guàn |
| | 虫 chóng | | 蜥 xī | | |
| 2 | 虱 shī | | 蜚 fēi | | **142 舌** |
| 3 | 虹 hóng | | 蝎 yì | | |
| | 蚂 mǎ | | 蜷 quán | | 舌 shé |
| | 虾 xiā | | 蜿 wān | 5 | 甜 tián |
| | 蚁 yǐ | | 螂 láng | 7 | 辞 cí |
| | 蚤 zǎo | | 蜢 měng | 8 | 舔 tiǎn |
| 4 | 蚕 cán | 9 | 蝶 dié | | |
| | 蚊 wén | | 蝴 hú | | **143 竹, ⺮** |
| | 蚋 ruì | | 蝗 huáng | | |
| | 蚝 háo | | 蝠 fú | | 竹 zhú |
| | 蚪 dǒu | | 蝌 kē | 3 | 竿 gān |
| | 蚓 yǐn | | 蝓 yú | 4 | 笆 bā |
| 5 | 蛆 qū | | 蝙 biān | | 笔 bǐ |
| | 蛇 shé | | | | |
| | 蚱 zhà | | | | |

| | | | | | | | |
|---|---|---|---|---|---|---|---|
| | 笋 sǔn | | 篱 lí | | | 舷 xián | |
| | 笑 xiào | | 篷 péng | | 6 | 艇 tǐng | |
| 5 | 笨 bèn | | 篓 golu | | | | |

**148 羽**

| | | | | | | |
|---|---|---|---|---|---|---|
| | 笛 dí | 11 | 簇 cù | | | 羽 yǔ |
| | 第 dì | | 簧 huáng | | 4 | 翅 chì |
| | 符 fú | 12 | 簿 bù | | | 翁 wēng |
| | 笺 jiān | 13 | 簸 bó, bò | | 6 | 翘 qiào |
| | 笼 lǒng | 14 | 籍 jí | | | 翔 xiáng |
| | 笤 tiáo | | | | 10 | 翱 áo |
| 6 | 策 cè | **144 白** | | 11 | 翼 yì |
| | 答 dá | | | | 12 | 翻 fān |
| | 等 děng | | 白 jiù | | 14 | 耀 yào |
| | 筏 fá | 7 | 舅 jiù | | | |

**149 艮, ⺬**

| | | | | | | |
|---|---|---|---|---|---|---|
| | 筋 jīn | **145 自** | | | 既 jì |
| | 筐 kuāng | | | | | |
| | 筛 shāi | | 自 zì | **150 糸** |
| | 筒 tǒng | | | | | |
| | 筑 zhù | **146 血** | | 4 | 紧 jǐn |
| | 筝 zhēng | | | | | 素 sù |
| 7 | 筹 chóu | | 血 xuè, | 6 | 絮 xù |
| | 简 jiǎn | | xiě | | | 紫 zǐ |
| | 筷 kuài | 5 | 衅 xìn | 11 | 繁 fán |
| | 签 qiān | | | | | |

**147 舟**

**151 辛**

| | | | | | | |
|---|---|---|---|---|---|---|
| 8 | 箔 bó | | 舟 zhōu | | | 辛 xīn |
| | 箍 gū | 4 | 般 bān | | 6 | 辟 pì |
| | 管 guǎn | | 舱 cāng | | 7 | 辣 là |
| | 箕 jī | | 航 háng | | 9 | 辨 biàn |
| | 算 suàn | | 舰 jiàn | | | 辩 biàn |
| 9 | 箭 jiàn | 5 | 舶 bó | | | |
| | 篓 lǒu | | 船 chuán | | | |
| | 篇 piān | | 舵 duò | | | |
| | 箱 xiāng | | | | | |
| 10 | 篡 cuàn | | | | | |
| | 篮 lán | | | | | |

| | | | | | | |
|---|---|---|---|---|---|---|
| *10* 辮 biàn | | *8* 豌 wān | | | **160** 足 | |
| *12* 瓣 bàn | | | | | | |

**152** 言

言 yán
*6* 譽 yù
*7* 誓 shì
*12* 警 jǐng

**153** 麦

麦 mài

**154** 走

走 zǒu
*3* 赶 gǎn
　 起 qǐ
*5* 超 chāo
　 趋 qū
　 越 yuè
*8* 趣 qù
　 趟 tāng

**155** 赤

赤 chì
*7* 赫 hè

**156** 豆

豆 dòu
*5* 登 dēng

**157** 酉

*3* 配 pèi
　 酌 zhuó
*4* 酗 xù
　 酝 yùn
*5* 酣 hān
　 酥 sū
*6* 酬 chóu
　 酱 jiàng
　 酷 kù
　 酪 lào
　 酯 zhǐ
*7* 酸 suān
　 酵 xiào,
　　 jiào
　 酿 niàng
*8* 醇 chún
　 醋 cù
　 醉 zuì
*9* 醒 xǐng

**158** 辰

辰 chén

**159** 里

里 lǐ
*4* 野 yě

足 zú
*2* 趴 pā
*4* 距 jù
　 跄 qiàng
　 跃 yuè
　 趾 zhǐ
*5* 跋 bá
　 跌 diē
　 践 jiàn
　 跑 pǎo
　 跚 shān
　 跛 bǒ
*6* 跺 duò
　 跟 gēn
　 跪 guì
　 跨 kuà
　 路 lù
　 跳 tiào
　 跷 qiāo
　 跤 jiāo
*7* 踉 liàng
*8* 踩 cǎi
　 踏 tà
　 踢 tī
　 踪 zōng
　 踝 huái
*9* 蹄 tí
　 踱 duó
*10* 蹈 dǎo
　 蹋 tà
　 蹒 pán
*11* 蹦 bèng

*12* 蹲 dūn
蹼 pǔ
*13* 躁 zào

## 161 豸

*3* 豹 bào
*5* 貂 diāo
*7* 貌 mào

## 162 谷

谷 gǔ

## 163 采

释 shì

## 164 身

身 shēn
*3* 躬 gōng
*4* 躯 qū
*6* 躲 duǒ
*8* 躺 tǎng

## 165 角

角 jiǎo,
jué
*6* 触 chù
解 jiě,
xiè

## 166 青

青 qīng
*6* 静 jìng

## 167 其

其 qí

## 168 雨

雨 yǔ
*3* 雪 xuě
*4* 雳 lì
*5* 雾 wù
雹 báo
雷 léi
零 líng
*6* 需 xū
霆 tíng
*7* 霉 méi
震 zhèn
*8* 霍 huò
霓 ní
*9* 霜 shuāng
霞 xiá
*13* 霸 bà
露 lù, lòu
霹 pī

## 169 齿

齿 chǐ
*5* 龄 líng

*6* 龈 yín
*9* 龋 qǔ

## 170 金

金 jīn
*5* 鉴 jiàn

## 171 隹

*2* 隼 sǔn
*3* 雀 què
*4* 雄 xióng
雅 yǎ
*5* 雏 chú
*6* 雌 cí
*8* 雕 diāo

## 172 鱼

鱼 yú
*4* 鲁 lǔ
鱿 yóu
*5* 稣 sū
*6* 鲜 xiān
*7* 鲤 lǐ
鲨 shā
*8* 鲸 jīng
鲱 fēi
*9* 鳄 è
*10* 鳍 qí
鳏 guān
*11* 鳕 xuě
鳗 mán

12 鳞 lín
鳟 zūn

### 173 音

音 yīn
4 韵 yùn

### 174 革

革 gé
2 勒 lè
4 靶 bǎ
靴 xuē
6 鞍 ān
鞋 xié
鞑 dá
7 鞘 qiào
8 鞠 jū
9 鞭 biān

### 175 骨

骨 gū
4 骰 tóu
5 骷 kū
6 骸 hái
9 髅 lóu
12 髓 suǐ

### 176 食

食 shí
7 餐 cān

### 177 鬼

鬼 guǐ
4 魂 hún
魁 kuí
5 魅 mèi
11 魔 mó

### 178 髟

4 髦 máo
6 髻 jì
8 鬃 zōng
鬈 quán
10 鬓 bìn

### 179 鹿

鹿 lù
2 麂 jǐ
8 麓 lù

### 180 黑

黑 hēi
3 墨 mò
4 默 mò
5 黝 yǒu

### 181 鼠

鼠 shǔ

### 182 鼻

鼻 bí
3 鼾 hān

# A

啊 ā (*surprise, wonderment*) oh

啊 à (*realization*) ah

阿尔巴尼亚 Ā'ěbāníyà Albania ◊ Albanian

阿富汗 Āfùhàn Afghanistan ◊ Afghan

阿根廷 Āgēntíng Argentina ◊ Argentinian

哀 āi sorrow; mourning

唉 āi alas

挨 āi be next to

唉 āi (*when someone calls your name*): 小王？ – 唉，什么事儿？ *xiǎo Wáng? – āi, shénme shìr?* Wang? – yes, what's up?

哎 āi (*dissatisfaction*): 哎，你怎么没告诉我呢？ *āi, nǐ zěnme méi gàosù wǒ ne?* well, why didn't you tell me then?

挨 ái undergo, suffer; endure

癌 ái cancer

矮 ǎi short *person*; low

嗳 ǎi (*disagreement*): 嗳，说哪儿去了 *ǎi, shuō nǎr qù le* hey, don't be silly

爱 ài love; like; be in the habit of; 做爱 *zuò'ài* make love; 有爱心 *yǒu àixīn* caring; 爱发脾气 *ài fā píqì* short-tempered

嗳 ài (*annoyance*): 嗳，我怎就忘不了他呢？ *ài, wǒ zěn jiù wàngbùliǎo tā ne?* why can't I just forget her?

碍 ài block; hinder; obstruct

爱称 àichēng diminutive, short form of a name

挨打 āidǎ get a beating

哀悼 āidào mourn; grieve

哀悼者 āidào zhě mourner

挨饿 ái'è starve

爱尔兰 Ài'ěrlán Ireland ◊ Irish

爱抚 àifǔ caress; fondle; pet

爱管事 ài guǎnshì bossy

爱国 àiguó patriotic

爱国者 àiguó zhě patriot

爱国主义 àiguó zhǔyì patriotism

哀号 āiháo howl

爱好 àihào enjoy ◊ hobby

爱护 àihù cherish; take care of

埃及 Āijí Egypt ◊ Egyptian

挨脚 āijiǎo get caught in the rain

挨近 āijìn approach

暧昧 àimèi ambiguous; dubious; 和 … 有暧昧关系 *hé … yǒu àimèi guānxì* have an affair with …

埃面子 àimiànzi be determined to save face

爱慕 àimù affection; worship ◊ be attached to; be attracted to

矮胖 ǎipàng tubby

爱情 àiqíng love

爱情生活 àiqíng shēnghuó lovelife

哀求 āiqiú implore

爱人 àirén husband; wife

哀伤 āishāng plaintive

爱上 àishàng fall in love with

唉声叹气 āishēng-tànqì sigh

哎呀 āiya! wow!; 哎呀，我的天啊！ *āiya, wǒde tiān'a!* good heavens!; 哎呀，糟了！ *āiya, zāole!* oh, no!

唉哟 āiyō! ouch!

哀乐 āiyuè lament MUS

挨着 āizhe be next to

挨着 āizhe linger; put off; procrastinate

癌症 áizhèng cancer

矮壮 ǎizhuàng stocky, thickset

矮子 ǎizi short person; dwarf

艾滋病 àizībìng Aids

阿拉伯 Ālābó Arabia ◊ Arab(ic)

阿弥陀佛 Āmítuófó Amitabha Buddha

安 ān peace ◊ peaceful ◊ fit; install, set up ◊ how (*rhetorical questions*)

鞍 ān saddle

按 àn press, push; click on ◊

according to

岸 **àn** shore

案 **àn** (legal) case; record; file

暗 **àn** dark; dim; secret

案板 **ànbǎn** worktop; workbench

暗淡 **àndàn** dim, gloomy; bleak; black; 使暗淡 **shǐ àndàn** dim the headlights

安定 **āndìng** calm ◊ secure

安放 **ānfàng** position

安抚 **ānfǔ** conciliatory ◊ pacify

昂贵 **ángguì** expensive

盎司 **àngsī** ounce

肮脏 **āngzāng** dirty; filthy

安好 **ānhǎo** be installed, be up

安家 **ānjiā** settle down; set up home

案件 **ànjiàn** case LAW

暗礁 **ànjiāo** reef; hidden danger

按揭贷款 **ànjiē dàikuǎn** mortgage

安静 **ānjìng** calm ◊ peacefully ◊ calm down; shut up ◊ silent, quiet; placid ◊ in silence

按扣 **ànkòu** snap fastener, press stud

按喇叭 **àn lǎbā** honk the horn

安乐死 **ānlèsǐ** euthanasia

安乐椅 **ānlèyǐ** easy chair

按铃 **ànlíng** ring (the bell)

安眠药 **ānmiányào** sleeping pill

按摩 **ànmó** massage

按摩技师 **ànmójìshī** chiropractor

按摩小姐 **ànmó xiǎojie** masseuse

按摩院 **ànmóyuàn** massage parlor

按摩浴缸 **ànmó yùgāng** whirlpool, jacuzzi

按钮 **ànniǔ** button (on machine)

安排 **ānpái** arrange, fix; arrange for; lay out; allocate; order ◊ arrangement

安全 **ānquán** safe ◊ safely ◊ safety; security; 处于安全状态 **chǔyú ānquán zhuàngtài** be safe

安全出口 **ānquán chūkǒu** fire escape

安全带 **ānquándài** seat belt

安全岛 **ānquándǎo** traffic island

安全感 **ānquángǎn** sense of security

安全检查 **ānquán jiǎnchá** security check

安全装置 **ānquán zhuāngzhì** safeguard

暗杀 **ànshā** assassinate ◊ assassination

岸上 **ànshang** on shore

暗杀者 **ànshā zhě** assassin

按时 **ànshí** on time

暗示 **ànshì** hint; implication ◊ imply, insinuate; point to, indicate

安慰 **ānwèi** comfort; console; soothe ◊ comfort; compensation; consolation

安心 **ānxīn** reassured

安葬 **ānzàng** bury the dead

按照 **ànzhào** according to

暗指 **ànzhǐ** imply

按住 **ànzhù** pin; hold down

安装 **ānzhuāng** fit, install ◊ installation

鞍子 **ānzi** saddle

案子 **ànzi** case

凹 **āo** concave; sunken

鳌 **áo** pincers

熬 **áo** endure; boil

傲 **ào** arrogant; obstinate

凹处 **āochù** dent; recess (in wall)

澳大利西亚 **Àodàlàxīyà** Australasia ◊ Australasian

澳大利亚 **Àodàlìyà** Australia ◊ Australian

奥地利 **Àodìlì** Austria ◊ Austrian

懊悔 **àohuǐ** remorse; regret

奥林匹克运动会 **Àolínpǐkè Yùndònghuì** Olympic Games

傲慢 **àomàn** arrogance ◊ arrogant, haughty

澳门 **Àomén** Macao ◊ Macanese

奥秘 **àomì** great mystery

懊丧 **àosàng** depressed; morose

凹凸不平 **āotū bùpíng** lumpy

鳌虾 **áoxiā** lobster

凹陷 **āoxiàn** dip; hollow ◊ sunken cheeks ◊ cave in

翱翔 **áoxiáng** hover; soar

熬夜 **áoyè** stay up late; burn the midnight oil

奥运会 **Àoyùnhuì** Olympics

阿司匹林 **āsīpǐlín** aspirin

阿姨 **āyí** auntie (used also to address a woman of one's parents' age)

# B

八 **bā** eight

疤 **bā** scar

拔 **bá** pull out, extract

靶 **bǎ** target

把 **bǎ** *measure word for knives and chairs;* 一把刀 **yìbǎ dāo** a knife; 一把钳子 **yìbǎ qiánzi** a pair of pliers / pincers ◊ *(marking an object moved for emphasis to the start of a sentence):* 我要把车修了 **wǒ yào bǎ chē xiūle** I'll have the car repaired

爸 **bà** dad, pop

霸 **bà** tyrant, despot

坝 **bà** dam

罢 **bà** stop, cease

把 **bà** handle

吧 **ba** *(to make suggestions):* 走吧 **zǒu ba** let's go ◊ *(in tag questions)* is he?; isn't he?; are you?; aren't you? etc; 你很忙吧 **nǐ hěn máng ba** you're very busy, aren't you?

爸爸 **bàba** dad, pop

靶场 **bǎchǎng** shooting range

拔出 **báchū** extract, pull out ◊ extraction

拔出插头 **báchū chātóu** unplug

霸道 **bàdào** domineering

罢工 **bàgōng** strike *(of workers)*

罢工者 **bàgōng zhě** striker

拔河 **báhé** tug of war

白 **bái** white ◊ in vain ◊ family name

百 **bǎi** hundred

柏 **bǎi** cypress

摆 **bǎi** place; lay

败 **bài** be defeated; defeat; fail

拜 **bài** congratulate

拜拜 **bàibāi** bye-bye

白斑儿 **báibānr** day shift

百倍 **bǎibèi** hundredfold

摆布 **bǎibù** manipulate ◊ manipulation; 任由 X 摆布 **rènyóu X bǎibù** be at X's mercy

白菜 **báicài** Chinese cabbage

白痴 **báichī** idiot

摆翅 **bǎichì** flutter *(of wings)*

摆动 **bǎidòng** swing; wag; wiggle

白饭 **báifàn** boiled rice

摆放 **bǎifàng** set out *goods*

拜访 **bàifǎng** call on, visit ◊ visit

白费力 **bái fèilì** waste one's time, go to a lot of trouble for nothing

百分比 **bǎifēnbǐ** percentage

百分之 **bǎifēnzhī** percent; 百分之百 **bǎifēnzhī bǎi** one hundred percent

白宫 **Báigōng** White House

百和花 **bǎihéhuā** lily

白喉 **báihóu** diphtheria

白桦 **báihuà** birch

败坏 **bàihuài** spoil

百花齐放 **Bǎihuāqífàng** Hundred Flowers Movement

白灰 **báihuī** lime

百货商店 **bǎihuò shāngdiàn** department store

摆架子 **bǎi jiàzi** put on airs; behave snobbishly

白酒 **báijiǔ** clear grain spirit

白开水 **báikāishuǐ** boiled water

百科词典 **bǎikē cídiǎn** encyclopedia; dictionary

百科全书 **bǎikēquán shū** encyclopedia

白兰地 **báilándì** brandy; cognac

白领工人 **báilǐng gōngrén** white-collar worker

败露 **bàilù** emerge

拜年 **bàinián** pay a New Year's visit; wish a happy New Year; 给李先生拜年 **gěi Lǐ xiānsheng bàinián** wish Mr Li a happy New Year

摆弄 **bǎinòng** fiddle with; fool around with; toy with; twiddle

白葡萄酒 **bái pútaojiǔ** white wine

白人 **báirén** white *person*

百日咳 **bǎirìké** whooping cough

白日梦 **báirì mèng** daydream

白肉 **báiròu** white meat; boiled pork fat

白色 **báisè** white

白手起家的人 **báishǒuqǐjiāde rén** self-made man

白糖 **báitáng** white sugar

白天 **báitiān** daytime, day ◊ in the daytime

白涂料 **bái túliào** whitewash

摆脱 **bǎituō** get rid of; free oneself from

拜托 **bàituō** request; 拜托！**bàituō!** do me a favor!

百万 **bǎiwàn** million

百万富翁 **bǎiwànfùwēng** millionaire

摆碗筷 **bǎi wǎnkuài** set the table

白皙 **báixī** fair *complexion*

掰下 **bāixià** break off

败兴者 **bàixìng zhě** spoilsport

白血病 **báixuě bìng** leukemia

百叶帘 **bǎiyè lián** venetian blind

白银 **báiyín** silver

柏油 **bǎiyóu** asphalt, tar

白字 **báizì** typo in Chinese characters

拔尖儿 **bájiānr** excellent

八角 **bājiǎo** star anise

巴基斯坦 **Bājīsītǎn** Pakistan ◊ Pakistani

芭蕾舞 **bāléiwǔ** ballet

芭蕾舞演员 **bāléiwǔ yǎnyuán** ballet dancer

拔毛 **bámáo** pluck

把门人 **bǎmén rén** bouncer, doorman

班 **bān** class; shift (*at work*) ◊ *measure word for bus, train etc*; 下一班飞机 **xià yì bān fēijī** the next flight

搬 **bān** move; shove; dislodge

斑 **bān** stain; spot; stripe ◊ striped

扳 **bān** turn; pull

板 **bǎn** board; sheet (*of metal, glass*)

版 **bǎn** edition; page (*of newspaper*)

半 **bàn** half; 十点半 **shídiǎnbàn** half past ten

瓣 **bàn** petal; segment

拌 **bàn** stir; mix; 拌色拉 **bàn sèlā** dress a salad

绊 **bàn** stumble, trip

扮 **bàn** get dressed up as; play the role of

办 **bàn** do; manage; deal with; 办签证 **bàn qiānzhèng** apply for a visa

版本 **bǎnběn** edition; version

半场 **bànchǎng** half time

伴唱 **bànchàng** backing (*singers*)

伴唱组 **bànchàng zǔ** backing group

搬出 **bānchū** move out

班船 **bānchuán** liner (*ship*)

版次 **bǎncì** impression (*of a book*)

绊倒 **bàndǎo** knock over; trip; stumble

半岛 **bàndǎo** peninsula

办到 **bàndào** manage to do

半导体 **bàndǎotǐ** semiconductor

板凳 **bǎndèng** stool

斑点 **bāndiǎn** spot

办法 **bànfǎ** method; means; way; way out; solution

邦 **bāng** nation; state

帮 **bāng** help ◊ gang; 帮 X 个忙 **bāng X ge máng** do X a favor

绑 **bǎng** bind

磅 **bàng** pound (*weight, sterling*)

棒 **bàng** stick; club ◊ great; excellent

榜 **bǎng** official announcement

棒棒冰 **bàngbàngbīng** Popsicle®

棒棒糖 **bàngbàng táng** sucker, lollipop

绑绷带 **bǎng bēngdài** bandage

半个小时 **bànge xiǎoshí** half an hour

半个月 **bàngeyuè** two weeks

绑架 **bǎngjià** kidnap ◊ kidnaping

邦交 **bāngjiāo** diplomatic relations

绑架者 **bǎngjià zhě** kidnaper

棒极了 **bàngjíle** fantastic; superb

帮忙 **bāngmáng** help

办公楼 **bàngōnglóu** office (*building*)

办公室 **bàngōngshì** office (*room*)

办公时间 **bàngōng shíjiān** office hours

绑票 **bǎngpiào** hold to ransom

棒球 **bàngqiú** baseball

棒球场 **bàngqiú chǎng** ballpark

棒球棍 **bàngqiú gùn** baseball bat

棒球帽 **bàngqiú mào** baseball cap

棒球运动员 **bàngqiú yùndòngyuán** baseball player

帮手 **bāngshǒu** helper

帮头 **bāngtóu** godfather (in mafia)

傍晚 **bàngwǎn** toward evening ◊ dusk

绑鞋带 **bǎng xiédài** do up one's shoelaces

帮凶 **bāngxiōng** accessory; accomplice

榜样 **bǎngyàng** role model; 树立好榜样 **shùlì hǎo bǎngyàng** set a good example

帮助 **bāngzhù** help, assist ◊ help, assistance

绑住 **bǎngzhù** lash down; tie up

棒子 **bàngzi** pole; stick

版画 **bǎnhuà** engraving; print

扳机 **bānjī** trigger

班级 **bānjí** school class; grade

搬家 **bānjiā** move, move house

绊脚 **bànjiǎo** stumble

绊脚石 **bànjiǎoshí** obstacle

搬进 **bānjìn** move in

半径 **bànjìng** radius

半决赛 **bànjuésài** semifinal

板栗 **bǎnlì** Chinese chestnut

办理 **bànlǐ** handle, take care of

伴侣 **bànlǚ** companion; company

斑马 **bānmǎ** zebra

伴娘 **bànniáng** bridesmaid

般配 **bānpèi** complement; 他们很般配 **tāmén hěn bānpèi** they complement each other

半票 **bànpiào** half-price ticket

搬迁 **bānqiān** relocate

搬迁公司 **bānqiān gōngsī** movers

半球 **bànqiú** hemisphere

版权 **bǎnquán** copyright

伴儿 **bànr** companionship

办事处 **bànshì chù** office, bureau

扳手 **bānshǒu** wrench (tool)

伴随 **bànsuí** pursue; accompany; follow

半天 **bántiān** half a day; a long time

版图 **bǎntú** territory

半途 **bàntú** halfway

板岩 **bǎnyán** slate

扮演 **bànyǎn** play, portray ◊ portrayal; 扮演哈姆莱特 **bànyǎn Hāmúláitè** as Hamlet

半夜 **bànyè** midnight; 半夜三更 **bànyè sāngēng** in the middle of the night

半圆形 **bànyuánxíng** semicircle ◊ semicircular

搬运 **bānyùn** carry; handle

拌匀 **bànyún** toss; mix

搬运工 ( 人 ) **bānyùn gōng(rén)** porter; stevedore; laborer

斑疹伤寒 **bānzhěn shānghán** typhus

板子 **bǎnzi** board; plate

搬走 **bānzǒu** move away

伴奏 **bànzòu** accompaniment, backing ◊ accompany MUS

伴奏组 **bànzòu zǔ** backing group

包 **bāo** bag; pack ◊ bundle; wrap; assure; hire; 包春卷 **bāo chūnjuǎn** wrap a spring roll; 一包香烟 **yībāo xiāngyān** a pack of cigarettes; 把 … 包起来 **bǎ … bāo qǐlái** bundle up

剥 **bāo** peel

雹 **báo** hail

薄 **báo** thin

宝 **bǎo** treasure ◊ precious

饱 **bǎo** full

堡 **bǎo** castle

豹 **bào** leopard

报 **bào** newspaper; report

暴 **bào** sudden; violent

爆 **bào** explode; blow up

抱 **bào** take in one's arms, hug

刨 **bào** plane (tool)

保安 **bǎo'ān** ensure public safety

报案 **bào'àn** report a case

保安部 **bǎo'ānbù** security

保安部队 **bǎo'ān bùduì** security forces

保安人员 **bǎo'ān rényuán** security guard

包办 **bāobàn** cater for

包办旅行 **bāobàn lǚxíng** package deal, package tour

雹暴 **báobào** hailstorm

宝贝 **bǎobèi** treasure; darling

包庇 **bāobì** harbor

保镖 **bǎobiāo** bodyguard

保持 **bǎochí** hold, maintain; keep, stay ◊ preservation; 保持沉默 **bǎochí chénmò** stay silent; 保持距离 **bǎochí jùlí** keep one's distance; 保持冷静 **bǎochí lěngjìng** keep one's cool; 与 X 保持联络 **yǔ X bǎochí liánluò** keep in contact with X

报仇 **bàochóu** take revenge

报酬 **bàochóu** reward; remuneration

保存 **bǎocún** conserve, preserve; embalm

报答 **bàodá** repay

保单 **bǎodān** warranty (card)

报道 **bàodào** cover; report, report on; present oneself ◊ coverage; report, story

暴跌 **bàodiē** drop; crash

暴动 **bàodòng** outbreak of violence

爆发 **bàofā** break out; erupt ◊ outbreak; eruption

暴发户 **bàofāhù** nouveau riche

报贩 **bàofàn** newsvendor

报废 **bàofèi** scrap

暴风雪 **bàofēngxuě** snowstorm

暴风雨 **bàofēngyǔ** rainstorm

报复 **bàofù** pay back *fig*; retaliate ◊ retaliation; revenge ◊ vindictive; 报复 X **bàofù X** get even with X

报告 **bàogào** report *news*; report, account ◊ presentation

饱嗝儿 **bǎogér** belch

保管 **bǎoguǎn** take care of ◊ storeman ◊ certainly

报关 **bàoguān** customs declaration

曝光 **bàoguāng** exposure; 曝光不足 **bàoguāng bù zú** underexposed

宝贵 **bǎoguì** precious; valuable

包裹 **bāoguǒ** package; parcel

包含 **bāohán** comprise; incorporate; include

饱和 **bǎohé** saturation

保护 **bǎohù** conservation; protection ◊ preserve; protect; safeguard; shelter; shield

保护地区 **bǎohù dìqū** reservation *(special area)*

保护费 **bǎohùfèi** protection money

包机 **bāojī** charter flight

报价 **bàojià** quotation ◊ quote *price*

保健 **bǎojiàn** health care

报警 **bàojǐng** raise the alarm

饱经沧桑 **bǎo jīng cāngsāng** checkered *career*

饱经风霜 **bǎo jīng fēngshuāng** weather-beaten

报警器 **bàojǐngqì** siren

暴君 **bàojūn** despot, tyrant

剥壳 **bāoké** shell

包括 **bāokuò** consist of; count, include; take in ◊ including

暴力 **bàolì** violence ◊ violent

爆裂 **bàoliè** burst

保龄球 **bǎolíng qiú** bowling; bowl; 打保龄球 **dǎ bǎolíng qiú** bowl; go bowling

保龄球道 **bǎolíng qiú dào** bowling alley

保留 **bǎoliú** keep, hang on to; hold; reserve ◊ reservation

暴露 **bàolù** reveal; expose ◊ skimpy

暴乱 **bàoluàn** disorder, unrest, riot

暴露自己 **bàolù zìjǐ** give oneself away

保密 **bǎomì** keep secret; conceal ◊ secrecy ◊ secret

爆米花 **bàomǐhuā** puffed rice; popcorn

暴民 **bàomín** mob

报名 **bàomíng** register; enrol; sign up

报名参军 **bàomíng cānjūn** enlist

保姆 **bǎomǔ** nanny; housekeeper

报幕 **bàomù** announce a program

暴怒 **bàonù** fury

暴虐 **bàonüè** oppressive, tyrannical ◊ tyranny

爆破 **bàopò** blow up; pop, burst

抱歉 **bàoqiàn** be sorry, regret

宝石 **bǎoshí** precious stone, jewel

保释 **bǎoshì** bail ◊ bail out *LAW*

报失 **bàoshī** report a loss

保释金 **bǎoshì jīn** bail

保守 **bǎoshǒu** conservative; straight

保守承诺 **bǎoshǒu chéngnuò** keep a promise

报税 **bàoshuì** make a tax declaration

宝塔 **bǎotǎ** pagoda

报摊儿 **bàotānr** newsstand

暴跳如雷 **bàotiào rúléi** go on the rampage

包围 **bāowéi** encircle; mob; lay siege to; surround; 被 X 包围 *bèi X bāowéi* be surrounded by X

保卫 **bǎowèi** defend ◊ defense

保温瓶 **bǎowēn píng** vacuum flask, thermos flask

保险 **bǎoxiǎn** insurance; safety ◊ safe ◊ be bound to

保险单 **bǎoxiǎndān** insurance policy

保险费 **bǎoxiǎnfèi** premium

保险杠 **bǎoxiǎn gàng** bumper

保险公司 **bǎoxiǎn gōngsī** insurance company

保险柜 **bǎoxiǎnguì** safe (*for valuables*)

保险金额 **bǎoxiǎn jīn'é** sum insured

保险丝 **bǎoxiǎnsī** fuse

保险丝盒 **bǎoxiǎnsī hé** fusebox

保险丝线 **bǎoxiǎnsī xiàn** fuse wire

保鲜纸 **bǎoxiān zhǐ** clingfilm

报销 **bàoxiāo** claim expenses

报销帐户 **bàoxiāo zhànghù** expense account

暴行 **bàoxíng** atrocity; brutality; outrage

保修期 **bǎoxiūqī** warranty period

保养 **bǎoyǎng** maintain ◊ maintenance

报应 **bàoyìng** just deserts; 他会得到报应 *tā huì dédào bàoyìng* he'll get his comeuppance

保佑 **bǎoyòu** bless

暴雨 **bàoyǔ** torrential rain

抱怨 **bàoyuàn** grumble, moan

暴躁 **bàozào** cranky, bad-tempered; fiery; hot-headed

爆炸 **bàozhà** blast, explosion ◊ explode, go off; blow (*of tire*); detonate

保障 **bǎozhàng** guarantee; security

保证 **bǎozhèng** assurance; security, guarantee ◊ ensure, guarantee; pledge; promise; 我向你保证 *wǒ xiàng nǐ bǎozhèng* you have my word

保证期 **bǎozhèngqī** guarantee period

报纸 **bàozhǐ** newspaper

保质 **bǎozhì** keep (*of food*)

保重 **bǎozhòng** look after oneself; 保重！*bǎozhòng!* take care (of yourself)!

保住 **bǎozhù** keep

包装 **bāozhuāng** pack; package ◊ packaging

包装材料 **bāozhuāng cáiliào** packaging

包装纸 **bāozhuāngzhǐ** wrapping paper

刨子 **bàozi** plane (*tool*)

包租 **bāozū** charter

拔起 **báqǐ** pull up

跋涉 **báshè** trudge; wade

八十 **bāshí** eighty

巴士 **bāshì** bus

把手 **bǎshou** handle

把握 **bǎwò** grasp; seize; certainty

巴西 **Bāxī** Brazil ◊ Brazilian

靶心 **bǎxīn** bull's-eye

八月 **bāyuè** August ◊ in August

巴掌 **bāzhang** palm of the hand

八字胡 **bāzì hú** mustache

BB机 **BB jī** bleeper, pager

杯 **bēi** cup; glass; 一杯茶 *yìbēi chá* a cup of tea

悲 **bēi** sad; mournful

背 **bēi** carry on one's back

卑 **bēi** low; inferior; humble

碑 **bēi** monument; gravestone

北 **běi** north ◊ northern; northerly

倍 **bèi** -fold; 价格长三倍 *jiàgé zhǎng sānbèi* treble the price; X

比 Y 大 … 倍 **X bǐ Y dà … bèi** X outnumbers Y by … times

辈 **bèi** generation; lifetime

背 **bèi** back ◊ recite; memorize

贝 **bèi** shellfish

备 **bèi** have; be equipped with; prepare

被 **bèi** quilt ◊ (*passive indicator*) 被炒鱿鱼了 **bèi chǎo yóuyú le** be fired; 被淘汰 **bèi táotài** be eliminated

悲哀 **bēi'āi** mournful; sad; distressed

背包 **bēibāo** pack; backpack, rucksack

卑鄙 **bēibǐ** cowardly; mean, nasty; sordid

卑鄙交易 **bēibǐ jiāoyì** sharp practice

卑鄙行为 **bēibǐ xíngwéi** dirty trick

北部 **běibù** north; X北部 **X běibù** north of X

被捕 **bèibǔ** be under arrest

悲惨 **bēicǎn** tragic; miserable ◊ misery

北朝鲜 **Běi Cháoxiān** North Korea ◊ North Korean

被单 **bèidān** sheet

被动 **bèidòng** passive; 被动形式 **bèidòng xíngshì** in the passive

被动语态 **bèidòng yǔtài** passive

北方 **běifāng** north ◊ northern

北方人 **běifāng rén** northerner

被告 **bèigào** accused, defendant; defense

被告席 **bèigào xí** dock (*in court*)

卑躬屈膝 **bēigōng qūxī** slimy

悲观 **bēiguān** pessimistic; dim ◊ pessimism

悲观者 **bēiguān zhě** pessimist

悲后 **bèihòu** behind ◊ behind one's back

北极 **Běijí** Arctic; North Pole

卑贱 **bēijiàn** humble, lowly

备件 **bèijiàn** spare part

北京 **Běijīng** Beijing, Peking

背景 **bèijǐng** setting, background; 以 … 为背景 **yǐ … wéi bèijǐng** set in, located in

北京烤鸭 **Běijīng kǎoyā** Peking duck

背景音乐 **bèijǐng yīnyuè** piped music

背景资料 **bèijǐng zīliào** background information

北极熊 **běijíxióng** polar bear

悲剧 **bēijù** tragedy

贝壳 **bèiké** shell

蓓蕾 **bèilěi** bud

贝类 **bèilèi** shellfish

卑劣 **bēiliè** contemptible; shoddy

北美洲 **Běi Měizhōu** North America ◊ North American

背面 **bèimiàn** back

背叛 **bèipàn** betray; break away ◊ betrayal

被迫 **bèipò** forced

被褥 **bèirù** quilt

悲伤 **bēishāng** sad ◊ grief

背书 **bèishū** endorse

背诵 **bèisòng** recite

被套 **bèitào** quilt cover

悲痛 **bēitòng** grief; mourning ◊ grieve

悲痛欲绝 **bēitòngyùjué** be prostrate with grief

备忘录 **bèiwànglù** memo

碑文 **bēiwén** inscription

背向 **bèixiàng** back onto

背心 **bèixīn** undershirt; vest; T-shirt

背阴 **bèiyīn** in the shade

备用 **bèiyòng** spare

备用车轮 **bèiyòng chēlún** spare wheel

备用磁盘 **bèiyòng cípán** backup disk

备用轮胎 **bèiyòng lúntāi** spare tire

备有 **bèiyǒu** stock

北约 **Běiyuē** NATO

北越 **Běiyuè** North Vietnam ◊ North Vietnamese

倍增 **bèizēng** double

背着 **bèizhe** carry, hump

备注 **bèizhù** remarks; notes

杯子 **bēizi** cup; glass

被子 **bèizi** cover; quilt

奔 **bēn** run fast

本 **běn** copy ◊ root, origin ◊ originally ◊ this ◊ *measure word for* books; 四本书 **sìběn shū** four books

笨 **bèn** stupid, dumb; clumsy

奔波 **bēnbō** rush around; juggle *fig*

奔驰 **bēnchí** dash, speed

笨蛋 **bèndàn** idiot; ass(hole)

本地 **běndì** local; native

本地人 **běndì rén** local (person)

绷 **bēng** tack; tighten; bounce

泵 **bèng** pump

蹦 **bèng** leap; skip; jump

蹦蹦车 **bèngbèngchē** motor rickshaw

绷床 **bēngchuáng** trampoline

绷带 **bēngdài** bandage

迸发 **bèngfā** outburst

绷紧 **bēngjǐn** tense up

崩溃 **bēngkuì** breakdown, collapse ◊ crumble; give way

绷绳 **bēngshéng** string

绷索 **bēngsuǒ** tightrope

崩塌 **bēngtā** collapse

本国 **běnguó** native

本国语 **běnguó yǔ** native language

本来 **běnlái** actual ◊ actually; to begin with, originally

本领 **běnlǐng** ability

本能 **běnnéng** instinct ◊ instinctive

奔跑 **bēnpǎo** sprint

本钱 **běnqián** capital

本人 **běnrén** personal ◊ personally, oneself

本身 **běnshēn** itself; in itself

笨手笨脚 **bènshǒu bènjiǎo** clumsy

本性 **běnxìng** nature, character

本质 **běnzhì** nature ◊ fundamental

笨重 **bènzhòng** cumbersome

笨拙 **bènzhuō** clumsy; awkward ◊ clumsiness

逼 **bī** force

鼻 **bí** nose

比 **bǐ** compare; compete with; 我比不过 **wǒ bǐ bú guò** I can't rival that; X比Y好 **X bǐ Y hǎo** X is better than Y; 他比我高 **tā bǐ wǒ gāo** he's taller than me

鄙 **bǐ** lowly; mean; my humble

笔 **bǐ** writing implement ◊ *measure word for sums of money*; 一大笔钱 **yí dà bǐ qián** a large sum of money

必 **bì** must

毕 **bì** finish

币 **bì** money; currency

避 **bì** avoid; prevent

壁 **bì** wall

臂 **bì** arm

闭 **bì** close; shut

边 **biān** side; rim

边…边… **biān … biān …**: 我们边喝／吃 **biānhē／chī biān tán** let's talk over a drink／meal; 边听边写 **biān tīng biān xiě** listen and take notes

编 **biān** weave; organize; edit; write; make up 编辫子 **biān biànzi** plait

鞭 **biān** whip

扁 **biǎn** flat

贬 **biǎn** devalue

变 **biàn** change; change into, become; 变老 **biànlǎo** get old

辨 **biàn** differentiate

辩 **biàn** discuss; argue

辫 **biàn** plait

便 **biàn** convenient ◊ defecate; shit; urinate; piss ◊ then

便秘 **biànbì** constipation

辨别 **biànbié** differentiate; distinguish

辩驳 **biànbó** dispute; refute

遍布 **biànbù** widespread

变成 **biànchéng** become

编程序 **biān chéngxù** program

辨出 **biànchū** discern

鞭打 **biāndǎ** whip, flog, lash ◊ whipping

扁担 **biǎndan** yoke, shoulder pole

便当 **biàndāng** lunch box

变得 **biàndé** become, go

贬低 **biǎndī** belittle, run down

变动 **biàndòng** alteration; swing, upheaval

扁豆 **biǎndòu** scarlet runner

编队 **biānduì** formation

蝙蝠 **biānfú** bat

便服 **biànfú** casual wear; civilian clothes

编号 **biānhào** number ◊ serial number

辩护 **biànhù** plead; defend ◊ defense; 为X辩护 *wèi X biànhù* defend X LAW; stick up for X

变化 **biànhuà** change, switch; variation ◊ vary

变化无常 **biànhuà wúcháng** fickle, volatile

辩护律师 **biànhù lǜshī** defense lawyer

辩护人 **biànhù rén** defense lawyer

辩护证人 **biànhù zhèngrén** defense witness

编辑 **biānjí** edit ◊ editor ◊ editorial; 体育／政治栏编辑 *tǐyù / zhèngzhì lán biānjí* sports / political editor

便笺 **biànjiān** pad (*for writing*)

边疆 **biānjiāng** frontier

编辑部 **biānjíbù** editorial department

边界 **biānjiè** border; boundary

边境 **biānjìng** border; frontier

遍及世界 **biànjí shìjiè** worldwide

便利 **biànlì** convenient

变量 **biànliàng** variable

编列 **biānliè** list

辩论 **biànlùn** debate

便秘 **biànmì** constipated ◊ constipation

鞭炮 **biānpào** firework; firecracker

便盆 **biànpén** chamber pot; potty (*for baby*)

变迁 **biànqiān** change

辨认 **biànrèn** make out, spot

辨认出 **biànrèn chū** recognize

变速杆 **biànsùgǎnr** gear lever, gear shift

变速器 **biànsùqì** gearbox; transmission

变态 **biàntài** abnormal; kinky ◊ metamorphosis

变态心理 **biàntài xīnlǐ** perversion

扁桃腺 **biǎntáoxiàn** tonsil

扁桃腺炎 **biǎntáoxiàn yán** tonsillitis

便条 **biàntiáo** note; compliments slip

便条本 **biàntiáo běn** notepad

便条纸 **biàntiáo zhǐ** notepaper

变通 **biàntōng** flexible

编舞 **biān wǔ** choreography; choreographer

边线 **biānxiàn** touchline; sideline; foul line

边线外 **biānxiàn wài** touch

便鞋 **biànxié** cloth shoes; slippers

变形 **biànxíng** buckle (*change shape*)

变压器 **biànyāqì** transformer

贬义 **biǎnyì** derogatory, disparaging

贬抑 **biǎnyì** pejorative

便衣 **biànyī** plain clothes; civilian clothes

变音 **biànyīn** inflection

边缘 **biānyuán** edge, border; brim; fringe; periphery; surround ◊ outlying

编造 **biānzào** make up, concoct

编织 **biānzhī** knit; weave ◊ knitting; weaving

编制 **biānzhì** compile

贬值 **biǎnzhí** depreciate; devalue ◊ depreciation; devaluation

变质 **biànzhì** spoil; deteriorate

编织物 **biānzhīwù** knitting

便装 **biànzhuāng** civilian dress

鞭子 **biānzi** whip

辫子 **biànzi** braid, plait

标 **biāo** mark, sign

表 **biǎo** table; form; meter; watch; surface; outside ◊ show, express

表达 **biǎodá** convey, express; formulate; show; 表达能力强 *biǎodá nénglì qiáng* articulate; 表达意见 *biǎodá yìjiàn* have one's say

表达法 **biǎodáfǎ** expression

表带 **biǎodài** watch strap

表弟 **biǎodì** cousin (*younger male on mother's side*)

标点 **biāodiǎn** punctuation

标点符号 **biāodiǎn fúhào** punctuation mark

表哥 **biǎogē** cousin (*elder male*)

表格 **biǎogé** form; table;

spreadsheet

裱糊 **biǎohú** paper

标记 **biāojì** sign; symbol

表姐 **biǎojiě** cousin (*elder female on mother's side*)

表决 **biǎojué** decide by vote

表决通过 **biǎojué tōngguò** pass, approve

表露 **biǎolù** show, display

表妹 **biǎomèi** cousin (*younger female on mother's side*)

表面 **biǎomiàn** surface; 表面上 **biǎomiàn shang** on the surface

标明 **biāomíng** mark

表明 **biǎomíng** indicate

表皮 **biǎopí** cuticle ◊ superficial

标签 **biāoqiān** label; nametag; sticker

标枪 **biāoqiāng** javelin

表情 **biǎoqíng** expression

表示 **biǎoshì** give, convey; show; express; mean ◊ display; expression; gesture

标题 **biāotí** heading; headline

标题点 **biāotídiǎn** bullet point

表现 **biǎoxiàn** show; behave ◊ performance; behavior

表兄 **biǎoxiōng** cousin (*elder male on mother's side*)

表演 **biǎoyǎn** act; perform; play; stage ◊ acting; performance; exhibition

表扬 **biǎoyáng** praise; pay a compliment

表演者 **biǎoyǎn zhě** entertainer; performer

标语 **biāoyǔ** slogan

标语牌 **biāoyǔpái** placard

标志 **biāozhì** mark; logo

标准 **biāozhǔn** standard; criterion

标准杆数 **biāozhǔn gānshù** par

婊子 **biǎozi** prostitute, whore

臂膀 **bìbǎng** arm

必备 **bìbèi** precondition, prerequisite

弊病 **bìbìng** disadvantage; mistake; defect

必不可少 **bìbù kěshǎo** necessary; vital

壁橱 **bìchú** cabinet

彼此 **bǐcǐ** each other

必定 **bìdìng** must; be sure to ◊ for sure; definitely

弊端 **bìduān** corrupt practices

别 **bié** other ◊ don't ◊ leave; part; 还要别的吗? **hái yào biéde ma?** anything else?; 别的东西 **biéde dōngxi** something else; 别动! **biédòng!** don't move!

别处 **biéchù** elsewhere

别具一格 **biéjùyìgé** unique

别离 **biélí** leave; part from

别人 **biérén** someone else; other people; 别人都去 **biérén dōu qù** everyone else is going

别墅 **biéshù** villa

别针 **biézhēn** safety pin

比分 **bǐfēn** score; goal; 比分是多少? **bǐfēn shì duōshǎo?** what's the score?

庇护 **bìhù** asylum; refuge; shelter

笔画 **bǐhuà** stroke (*in writing*)

壁画 **bìhuà** fresco; mural

避讳 **bìhuì** taboo

笔迹 **bǐjì** handwriting

笔记 **bǐjì** write down ◊ notes

比价 **bǐjià** price ratio ◊ compare prices

比较 **bǐjiào** compare ◊ comparison ◊ comparative ◊ comparatively; relatively; rather; 比较便宜 **bǐjiào piányi** cheaper ◊ it costs less

比较级 **bǐjiào jí** comparative (form)

笔记本 **bǐjìběn** notebook; notebook computer

毕竟 **bìjìng** after all

比基尼 **Bǐjīní** bikini

避开 **bìkāi** dodge, evade; ward off; keep out; make oneself scarce

鼻孔 **bíkǒng** nostril

壁垒 **bìlěi** rampart

避雷导线 **bìléi dǎoxiàn** lightning conductor

比例 **bǐlì** proportion; scale

鼻梁 **bíliáng** bridge (*of nose*)

比例绘图 **bǐlì huìtú** scale drawing

比利时 **Bǐlìshí** Belgium ◊ Belgian

壁炉台 **bìlútái** mantelpiece, mantelshelf

壁炉 **bìlú** fireplace; hearth

比率 **bǐlǜ** rate

闭路电视 **bìlù diànshì** closed-circuit television

笔帽 **bǐmào** cap (of pen)

避免 **bìmiǎn** avoid, avert; keep off

笔名 **bǐmíng** pen name

闭幕式 **bìmùshì** closing ceremony

宾 **bīn** guest

避难所 **bìnànsuǒ** haven; sanctuary; refuge

彬彬有礼 **bīnbīn yǒu lǐ** well-mannered

冰 **bīng** ice

兵 **bīng** soldier

柄 **bǐng** stem

饼 **bǐng** round, flat cake; pancake

病 **bìng** illness ◊ sick

并 **bìng** combine; merge ◊ and ◊ (negative intensifier): 我并不在意 **wǒ bìng bú zàiyì** I really don't mind

冰雹 **bīngbáo** hail

冰场 **bīngchǎng** ice rink

冰川 **bīngchuān** glacier

冰灯 **bīngdēng** ice-lantern

冰点 **bīngdiǎn** freezing point

冰冻 **bīngdòng** freeze

病毒 **bìngdú** virus, bug ◊ viral

病房 **bìngfáng** hospital room

并发症 **bìngfā zhèng** complications MED

冰封 **bīngfēng** frozen

饼干 **bǐnggān** cookie; cracker

冰糕 **bīnggāo** ice cream

冰棍儿 **bīnggùnr** Popsicle®

病假 **bìngjià** sick leave

并肩 **bìngjiān** side by side

病菌 **bìngjūn** germ

冰咖啡 **bīngkāfēi** iced coffee

冰块 **bīngkuài** ice cube

冰冷 **bīnglěng** ice-cold

兵力 **bīnglì** troops; armed forces; military strength

病例 **bìnglì** case MED

冰凉 **bīngliáng** frozen

病理学 **bìnglǐxué** pathology

病理学家 **bìnglǐxuéjiā** pathologist

兵马俑 **bīngmǎyǒng** terracotta army

并排 **bìngpái** side by side

并且 **bìngqiě** and; besides

冰淇淋 **bīngqílín** ice cream

冰淇淋店 **bīngqílín diàn** ice cream parlor

冰球 **bīngqiú** (ice) hockey

病人 **bìngrén** patient; sick person

病弱 **bìngruò** invalid ◊ sickly

冰山 **bīngshān** iceberg

病史 **bìngshǐ** case history, medical history

病态 **bìngtài** morbid; pathological; sick society

冰糖 **bīngtáng** candy sugar

病痛 **bìngtòng** pain; ailment

宾馆 **bīnguǎn** hotel; guest house

冰箱 **bīngxiāng** refrigerator, icebox; freezer

冰鞋 **bīngxié** ice-skate

兵役义务 **bīngyì yìwù** military service

病友 **bìngyǒu** friend made in the hospital; fellow patient

冰镇 **bīngzhèn** chilled

病症晚期 **bìngzhèng wǎnqī** terminally ill

冰柱 **bīngzhù** icicle

屏住呼吸 **bǐngzhù hūxī** hold one's breath

滨海区 **bīnhǎiqū** coastal region

殡仪馆 **bìnyíguǎn** funeral home

濒于 **bīnyú** be on the verge of

逼迫 **bīpò** push, pressure

壁球 **bìqiú** squash (game)

必然 **bìrán** inevitable ◊ inevitably

必然性 **bìrán xìng** certainty, inevitability

比如 **bǐrú** for example

比萨 **bǐsà** pizza

比赛 **bǐsài** competition; contest; match; 我和你比赛 **wǒ hé nǐ bǐsài** I'll race you; 与 X 比赛 **yǔ X bǐsài** compete against X

比赛场地 **bǐsài chǎngdì** arena

比赛项目 **bǐsài xiàngmù** event

闭上 **bìshàng** close ◊ closed

毕生 **bìshēng** lifetime ◊ all one's life

鄙视 **bǐshì** despise; scorn

匕首 **bǐshǒu** dagger

必死 **bìsǐ** mortal

壁毯 **bìtǎn** tapestry

鼻涕 **bíti** snot

笔芯 **bǐxīn** pencil lead; pen refill

必修 **bìxiū** compulsory *course*

必须 **bìxū** must, have (got) to ◊ obligatory

必需 **bìxū** necessary

必需品 **bìxū pǐn** necessity

必须要 **bìxū yào** call for

必要 **bìyào** essential, necessary

必要时 **bìyàoshí** if necessary, at a pinch

必要性 **bìyào xìng** necessity ◊ must

毕业 **bìyè** graduate ◊ graduation

毕业生 **bìyèshēng** graduate

鼻音 **bíyīn** twang

笔友 **bǐyǒu** penfriend, penpal

比喻 **bǐyù** analogy ◊ figurative

避孕 **bìyùn** birth control; contraception

避孕器 **bìyùn qì** contraceptive

避孕套 **bìyùn tào** condom

避孕药 **bìyùn yào** contraceptive (pill), the pill

逼真 **bīzhēn** true to life

笔直 **bǐzhí** straight; upright

币值 **bìzhí** currency value

壁纸 **bìzhǐ** (wall)paper

币制 **bìzhì** monetary system

鼻子 **bízi** nose

闭嘴 **bìzuǐ** be quiet; 闭嘴！ **bìzuǐ!** be quiet!, shut up!

拨 **bō** dial *telephone number*

播 **bō** sow seed; broadcast

波 **bō** wave

剥 **bō** peel

铂 **bó** platinum

伯 **bó** uncle (*father's elder brother*)

脖 **bó** neck

博 **bó** extensive; broad

驳 **bó** refute

跛 **bǒ** lame

博爱 **bó'ài** universal love; fraternity

薄饼 **bóbǐng** pancake

伯伯 **bóbó** uncle (*father's elder brother*); *used to address a man older than one's father*

菠菜 **bōcài** spinach

波长 **bōcháng** wavelength

驳斥 **bóchì** refute; disprove

拨出 **bōchū** set aside, earmark

驳船 **bóchuán** barge

驳倒 **bódǎo** refute; outargue

波动 **bōdòng** fluctuate ◊ fluctuation

搏动 **bódòng** pulsate

搏斗 **bódòu** fight, battle

波段 **bōduàn** frequency RAD

剥夺 X 的 Y **bōduó Xde Y** strip X of Y

播放 **bōfàng** transmission ◊ transmit

波状 **bōfú** wavy

伯父 **bófù** uncle (*father's elder brother*)

脖颈儿 **bógěngr** (nape of) neck

剥光衣服 **bōguāng yīfu** strip, undress

渤海湾 **Bóhǎi Wān** Bohai Gulf

拨号 **bōhào** dial

拨号盘 **bōhào pán** dial

拨号音 **bōhàoyīn** dial tone

薄荷 **bòhe** mint; peppermint

薄荷糖 **bòhetáng** peppermint candy

簸箕 **bòji** dustpan

拨款 **bōkuǎn** fund ◊ grant

波兰 **Bōlán** Poland ◊ Polish

波浪 **bōlàng** wave

拨浪鼓 **bōlànggǔ** rattle (*toy*)

博览会 **bólǎnhuì** trade fair

玻璃 **bōli** glass

玻璃杯 **bōlibēi** glass (*for drinking*)

玻璃纤维 **bōli xiānwéi** fiberglass

玻璃纸 **bōlizhǐ** cellophane

菠萝 **bōluó** pineapple

剥落 **bōluò** flake off, peel

勃鲁斯歌手 **bólǔsī gēshǒu** blues singer

勃鲁斯音乐 **bólǔsī yīnyuè** blues

勃起 **bóqǐ** erection ◊ erect

勃然大怒 **bórán dànù** fly into a rage

薄弱 **bóruò** weak; vulnerable

薄纱 **bóshā** gauze

博士 **bóshì** doctor; doctorate, PhD

播送 **bōsòng** on the air

波涛 **bōtāo** wave

薄雾 **bówù** haze, mist

博物馆 **bówùguǎn** museum

薄雾笼罩 **bówù lǒngzhào** misty

博物学家 **bówù xuéjiā** naturalist

跛行 **bǒxíng** limp

剥削 **bōxuē** exploit ◊ exploitation; rip-off

博学 **bóxué** well-read

播音 **bōyīn** broadcast ◊ broadcasting

播音员 **bōyīn yuán** radio announcer; broadcaster

播种 **bōzhǒng** sow *seeds*

驳船 **bózhuán** barge (*boat*)

脖子 **bózi** neck

补车票 **bǔ**; patch up; 补车票 **bǔ chēpiào** buy a ticket after boarding

捕 **bǔ** catch

部 **bù** department, ministry; unit

不 **bù** no; non ..., un ..., in ...; not ◊ won't ◊ (*in questions*): 疼不疼? **téng bùténg?** does it hurt?; 疼不? **téng bù?** does it hurt?

步 **bù** pace, step

部 **bù** unit

布 **bù** material, cloth

簿 **bù** book; exercise book; notebook

不安 **bù'ān** uneasy ◊ disquiet; 令人不安 **lìngrén bù'ān** disturbing, worrying; uneasy

不安分 **bù ānfèn** restless

不安全 **bù ānquán** insecure; unsafe

不安全感 **bù ānquángǎn** insecurity

不必 **búbì** unnecessary ◊ needn't

不变 **búbiàn** always, invariably ◊ unswerving

不便 **búbiàn** inconvenient

步兵 **bùbīng** infantry; infantry soldier

不必要 **bú bìyào** unnecessary

不测事件 **búcè shìjiàn** contingency

补偿 **bǔcháng** compensate for; make up for; reimburse ◊ recompense

不超过 **bù chāoguò** within; no more than

不成比例 **bù chéng bǐlì** disproportionate

不称职 **bú chènzhí** incompetent ◊ incompetence

补充 **bǔchōng** add to ◊ additional; incidental ◊ addition

不纯 **bùchún** impure

不辞辛苦 **búcí xīnkǔ** spare no effort

不错 **búcuò** not bad; excellent

不大 **búdà** small

不大可能 **bú dà kěnéng** improbable, unlikely

不丹 **Bùdān** Bhutan ◊ Bhutanese

不当 **búdàng** unsuitable

不到 **bú dào** under, less than

捕到 **bǔdào** catch

布道 **bùdào** preach; preach a sermon

不道德 **bú dàodé** immoral ◊ immorality

布道坛 **bùdàotán** pulpit

不得 **bùdé** have to, be compelled to

不得了 **bùdéliǎo** fantastic ◊ extremely ◊ no way out; 好得不得了 **hǎo dé bùdéliǎo** absolutely fantastic, out of this world; 多得不得了 **duōde bùdéliǎo** a hell of a lot

不得人心 **bùdé rénxīn** unpopular

不得入内 **bùdé rùnèi** no trespassing

补丁 **bǔdīng** darn; patch

布丁 **bùdīng** pudding

不定冠词 **búdìng guàncí** indefinite article

不定式 **búdìngshì** infinitive

不动 **búdòng** motionless

不动产 **búdòngchǎn** real estate

不动产商 **búdòngchǎn shāng** developer; real estate agent

不动产中间商 **búdòng chǎn zhōngjiān shāng** real estate agent

不断 **bùduàn** constant, continual

不对 **bú duì** be wrong ◊ incorrect

部队 **bùduì** corps; forces

不对劲儿 **bú duì jìnr** shifty; strange

步伐 **bùfá** step

不方便 **bù fāngbiàn** inconvenient ◊ inconvenience

部分 **bùfen** part, bit; component;

piece, section; patch; proportion ◊ partly

补付 **bǔfù** pay extra; pay later

不服 **bùfú** disobey

不符 **bùfú** not agree with; not comply with

不服从 **bù fúcóng** disobedience ◊ insubordinate

不服管 **bù fúguǎn** rebellious

不负责任 **búfùzérèn** irresponsible

不干涉 **bùgānshè** hands-off ◊ non-intervention

不干预 **bù gānyù** noninterference, nonintervention

布告 **bùgào** bulletin; announcement

布告板 **bùgào bǎn** bulletin board

不给 **bù gěi** withhold

不共戴天 **búgòng dàitiān** mortal *enemy*

不够 **búgòu** insufficient; 不够好 **búgòuhǎo** not good enough

不顾 **búgù** regardless of, irrespective of

不关你的事！ **bùguān nǐde shì!** mind your own business!

不管 **bùguǎn**: 我才不管呢！ **wǒ cái bùguǎn ne!** I don't give a damn!; for all I care; 不管什么 **bùguǎn shénme** no matter what, whatever; 不管他们多大 **bùguǎn tāmen duō dà** however big they are; 不管她说什么 **bùguǎn tā shuō shénme** no matter what she says

不顾后果 **búgù hòuguǒ** reckless

不规范 **bùguīfàn** irregular

不规矩 **bù guījù** unruly

不规律 **bùguīlǜ** irregular

不规则 **bùguīzé** irregular

补过 **bǔguò** make amends

不过 **búguò** however

不寒而栗 **bùhán'érlì** shake with fear

不含铅 **bù hán qiān** lead-free

不好 **bùhǎo** bad ◊ badly

不合法 **bù héfǎ** illegal, wrongful

不合格 **bù hégé** unqualified

不合逻辑 **bù hé luójí** illogical

不合群 **bù héqún** unsociable

不合适 **bù héshì** unsuitable

不和谐 **bù héxié** discord

步话机 **bùhuàjī** walkie-talkie

捕获 **bǔhuò** capture; catch

捕获物 **bǔhuò wù** catch (*of fish*)

不活跃 **bù huóyuè** inactive

簿记 **bùjì** bookkeeping

部件 **bùjiàn** unit

不间断 **bù jiānduàn** uninterrupted

不讲道德 **bù jiǎng dàodé** unscrupulous

不坚固 **bù jiāngù** unstable

不健康 **bú jiànkāng** unfit; unhealthy; sickly

不结盟 **bù jiéméng** nonaligned

不结实 **bù jiēshí** flimsy

不及格 **bù jígé** flunk

不仅 **bùjǐn** not only

捕鲸 **bǔjīng** whaling

布景 **bùjǐng** scenes, set THEA

不景气 **bù jǐngqì** recession; depression ◊ unhealthy *economy*

不经心 **bù jīngxīn** inattentive

补救 **bǔjiù** remedy

不久 **bùjiǔ** before long, soon after

不久之后 **bùjiǔ zhīhòu** soon after

布局 **bùjú** layout

不拘礼节 **bùjū lǐjié** offhand

不拘束 **bùjūshù** irrepressible

不拘形式 **bùjū xíngshì** free and easy

不可避免 **bùkě bìmiǎn** inevitable, unavoidable ◊ inevitably

不可分割 **bùkě fēngē** indivisible; inseparable

不可否认 **bùkě fǒurèn** undeniable

不可救药 **bùkě jiùyào** incorrigible

不可靠 **bù kěkào** unreliable

不可理解 **bùkě lǐjiě** incomprehensible

不可能 **bù kěnéng** impossible ◊ that can't be right; that's out of the question

不客气 **bú kèqi** impolite ◊ you're welcome

不可饶恕 **bùkě ráoshù**

unforgivable

不可思议 **bùkě sīyì** unthinkable; uncanny ◊ mysteriously

不可挽回 **bùkě wǎnhuí** irretrievable

不可信 **bù kěxìn** questionable

不可原谅 **bùkě yuánliàng** inexcusable

不可战胜 **bùkě zhànshèng** unbeatable

不快 **búkuài** unhappy; 令人不快 **lìngrén búkuài** miserable; unsavory; disagreeable

不愧于 **bú kuìyú** live up to; be worthy of

不老实 **bù lǎoshi** deceitful

布雷区 **bùléiqū** minefield

不理 **bùlǐ** brush aside; ignore

不利 **búlì** detrimental; disadvantageous; unfavorable; 对 … 不利 **duì … búlì** to the detriment of

不连贯 **bù liánguàn** incoherent

布料 **bùliào** cloth, fabric, material

不了解 **bù liáojiě** be out of touch

不礼貌 **bù lǐmào** impolite, disrespectful

不领情 **bù lǐngqíng** ungrateful

不利之处 **búlì zhīchù** disadvantage

不漏水 **búlòushuǐ** watertight

不论 **búlùn** no matter

部落 **bùluò** tribe

不落俗套 **búluò sútào** unconventional

布满 **bùmǎn** be full of; be bristling with

不满 **bùmǎn** discontent, dissatisfied; disgruntled; resentful ◊ displeasure; dissatisfaction; resentment ◊ resent

不满意 **bù mǎnyì** discontented; dissatisfied

部门 **bùmén** department; division; sector

不免 **bùmiǎn** unavoidable

不免一死 **bùmiǎnyìsǐ** mortal ◊ mortality

不明朗 **bù mínglǎng** noncommittal, vague ◊ vaguely

不能 **bùnéng** not be able to; be

unable; can't; mustn't; shouldn't; cannot be …

不能消化 **bùnéng xiāohuà** indigestible

不能抑制 **bùnéng yìzhì** irrepressible

不偏不倚 **bù piānbùyǐ** detachment, objectivity

不偏袒 **bù piāntǎn** unbiased

不偏心 **bù piānxīn** dispassionate

补票 **bǔpiào** buy a ticket after boarding

补票费 **bǔpiàofèi** excess fare

不平常 **bù píngcháng** extraordinary; unusual

不平等 **bù píngděng** unequal ◊ inequality

不平衡 **bū pínghéng** unbalanced, lop-sided

不恰当 **bú qiàdàng** improper; undeserved; unfortunate

不清楚 **bù qīngchu** unclear

不请自到 **bùqǐngzìdào** come uninvited, gatecrash

不确定 **bú quèdìng** indefinite; uncertain ◊ uncertainty

不然 **bùrán** otherwise; not so

不然的话 **bùrán dehuà** otherwise

不让步 **bú ràngbù** uncompromising

不容置疑 **bùróng zhìyí** indisputable ◊ indisputably

哺乳 **bǔrǔ** breastfeed

不如 **bùrú** not as good as … ◊ be better to …

哺乳动物 **bǔrǔ dòngwù** mammal

不少 **bùshǎo** quite a lot (of)

不慎 **búshèn** careless

不是 **búshì** not; no

捕食 **bǔshí** prey on

不适当 **búshì dàng** unduly ◊ inappropriate; inadequate

不适合 **bú shìhé** unfit; unsuitable; inappropriate

不实际 **bù shíjì** impractical

不适用 **bú shìyòng** inapplicable

部首 **bùshǒu** radical (*of Chinese character*)

不受欢迎 **bú shòu huānyíng** unpopular; undesirable

捕兽机关 bǔshòu jīguān trap

不守秩序 bù shǒu zhìxù disorderly

不受重视 bú shòu zhòngshì neglected

不舒服 bùshūfu unwell, poorly; uncomfortable

不熟练 bù shúliàn inept; unskilled

不顺眼 bú shùnyǎn eyesore

不舒适 bù shūshì uncomfortable

不熟悉 bù shúxī unfamiliar; 不熟悉 X bù shúxí X be unfamiliar with X

不太可能 bú tài kěnéng unlikely

补贴 bǔtiē allowance, grant

不通 bùtōng impassable

不同 bùtóng different; distinct; varied; various ◊ differ ◊ otherwise, differently

不同寻常 bùtóng xúncháng unusual

不同意 bù tóngyì disagree

不同见 bùtóng yìjiàn disagreement

不透明 bù tòumíng opaque

不褪色 bú tuìsè colorfast

不完美 bù wánměi imperfect

不完全 bù wánquán partial

不完整 bù wánzhěng incomplete

部位 bùwèi position

不卫生 bú wèishēng unhygienic, insanitary

不像 búxiàng unlike

不祥 bùxiáng ominous

不相符 bù xiāngfú incompatible ◊ incompatibility

不相干 bù xiānggān irrelevant

不相关 bù xiāngguān unrelated

不现实 bú xiànshí impractical; unrealistic

不显眼 bù xiǎnyǎn inconspicuous

不显著 bù xiǎnzhù dim

不小心 bùxiǎoxīn careless ◊ by accident

不懈 búxiè relentless

不谢 búxiè that's alright (when somebody says thank you)

不协调 bùxiétiáo clash; discord ◊ incongruous

不幸 búxíng poor; ill-fated;

unfortunate, unlucky; tragic; regrettable ◊ regrettably ◊ misfortune

不行 bùxíng it's not allowed; that's out ◊ impossible

步行 bùxíng walk; hike ◊ on foot

不幸的是 búxíng de shì unfortunately

不醒人事 bù xǐng rénshì unconscious; 打得 X 不醒人事 dǎde X bù xǐng rénshì knock X unconscious

不幸事故 búxíng shìgù mishap

不信任 búxìnrèn mistrust

不朽 búxiǔ immortal ◊ immortality

不锈钢 búxiùgāng stainless steel

不炫耀 bú xuànyào unpretentious

不许 bùxǔ not allowed; 不许动! bùxǔdòng! don't make a move!

不寻常 bù xúncháng uncommon

补牙 bǔyá filling (in tooth)

不言而喻 bù yán ér yù self-evident

不厌其烦 búyànqífán thorough

不要 bùyào not want; don't; 我不要，谢谢 wǒ bùyào, xièxiè not for me, thanks

不要脸 bú yào liǎn shameless

不宜食用／饮用 bùyí shíyòng／yǐnyòng be unfit to eat/drink

不一样 bù yíyàng it varies

不遗余力 búyíyúlì be unstinting in one's efforts

不一致 bù yízhì inconsistent; uneven, patchy ◊ clash

不用 búyòng: 不用，我来吧 búyòng, wǒ lái ba no, I'll do it; 不用，谢谢 búyòng, xièxiè no thank you; 不用客气 búyòngkèqì don't mention it; 不用了！búyòngle! don't bother!

不由自主 bùyóu zìzhǔ compulsive; stray

捕鱼 bǔyú fish; fishing

哺育 bǔyù feed; bring up

不育 búyù sterile

不愿 búyuàn be unwilling

不愿意 bú yuànyì disinclined

不在 **búzài** be away; be out

不赞成 **bú zànchéng** disapprove (of)

不早了 **bù zǎo le** get on ◊ it's getting late

不怎么样 **bù zěnme** not very, not particularly

不怎么样 **bù zěnme yàng** lousy ◊ not really; not much

不粘 **bùzhān** nonstick

部长 **bùzhǎng** minister POL; secretary ◊ ministerial

不扎实 **bù zhāshí** shaky

不真诚 **bù zhēnchéng** insincere

不正常 **bú zhèngcháng** abnormal

不整洁 **bù zhěngjié** unkempt

不整齐 **bù zhěngqí** disheveled

不正确 **bú zhèngquè** incorrect ◊ incorrectly

不真实 **bù zhēnshí** unreal; untrue

不只 **bùzhǐ** not only

布置 **bùzhì** arrange; fit out ◊ arrangement

不知害臊 **bùzhī hàisào** it's a disgrace

不知所措 **bù zhī suǒ cuò** in a daze, dazed ◊ overwhelm; paralyze *fig*; be at a loss

不值一读 **bùzhí yìdú** unreadable

不值一顾 **bùzhí yígù** beneath contempt

不知怎的 **bùzhī zěnde** somehow

不忠 **bù zhōng** disloyal; unfaithful; treacherous ◊ disloyalty; infidelity

不重要 **bú zhòngyào** unimportant

不中意 **bù zhōngyì** not appealing

不中用 **bù zhōngyòng** useless

步骤 **bùzhòu** procedure

补助 **bǔzhù** subsidy

不准 **bùzhǔn** forbid ◊ not allowed; not accurate

不准停车 **bùzhǔn tíngchē** no stopping

捕捉 **bǔzhuō** catch

簿子 **bùzi** notebook

不自然 **bú zìrán** labored, stilted; self-conscious

不自在 **bú zìzài** discomfort; 我跟他在一起感到不自在 **wǒ gēn tā zài yìqǐ gǎndào bú zìzài** I feel uncomfortable with him

不足 **bùzú** inadequate; unsatisfactory

不尊重 **bù zūnzhòng** disrespect

不足为奇 **bùzú wéiqí** unsurprising

不足信 **bù zúxìn** flimsy *excuse*

# C

搽 **cā** dab

擦 **cā** mop, wipe

擦掉 **cādiào** erase; rub off; wipe away; wipe off

擦干 **cāgān** (wipe) dry

擦光剂 **cāguāngjì** polish

猜 **cāi** guess

才 **cái** talent ◊ only; only if; 他昨天才到 **tā zuótiān cái dào** he only arrived yesterday; 你说了他们才能做 **nǐ shuōle tāmen cáinéngzuò** they won't do anything until you say so

裁 **cái** cut *paper, cloth*

材 **cái** timber; material

财 **cái** assets; wealth

采 **cǎi** pick; mine

踩 **cǎi** step; trample on; tread on; 踩刹车 **cǎi shāchē** apply the brake(s)

彩 **cǎi** color

菜 **cài** dish; vegetable; (non-staple) food

彩笔 **cǎibǐ** highlighter; marker

猜测 **cāicè** guess; conjecture; speculation ◊ speculate

彩色照片 **cǎicè zhàopiàn** color photograph

财产 **cáichǎn** possession; property

菜单 **càidān** menu

菜刀 **càidāo** kitchen knife

彩电 **cǎidiàn** color TV

裁定 **cáidìng** convict ◊ conviction; sentencing; 裁定 X 无罪／有罪 **cáidìng X wúzuì／yǒuzuì** find X innocent／guilty

采访 **cǎifǎng** interview

采访者 **cǎifǎng zhě** interviewer

裁缝 **cáiféng** dressmaker; tailor

财富 **cáifù** treasure; wealth

采购 **cǎigòu** purchase ◊ purchaser ◊ purchasing

采购员 **cǎigòu yuán** buyer; purchaser

彩虹 **cǎihóng** rainbow

才华 **cáihuá** brilliance; intelligence

菜花 **càihuā** cauliflower

采集 **cǎijí** collect

裁减 **cáijiǎn** reduce

裁决 **cáijué** judgment; ruling; verdict

裁军 **cáijūn** disarm ◊ disarmament

采矿 **cǎikuàng** mining

材料 **cáiliào** materials

采纳 **cǎinà** adopt ◊ adoption

才能 **cáinéng** ability

菜农 **càinóng** truck farmer

彩排 **cǎipái** dress rehearsal

裁判（员）**cáipàn (yuán)** umpire; referee; judge

裁判院 **cáipàn yuàn** tribunal

彩票 **cǎipiào** lottery ticket; raffle ticket

菜谱 **càipǔ** recipe

彩色 **cǎisè** color

彩色电视 **cǎisè diànshì** color television

彩色胶卷 **cǎisè jiāojuǎn** color film

采石场 **cǎishíchǎng** quarry (*for mining*)

踩踏板 **cǎi tàbǎn** pedal

财务 **cáiwù** finance ◊ financial

财务部 **Cáiwù Bù** Treasury Department

财务处 **cáiwùchù** accounts (department)

财务软件 **cáiwù ruǎnjiàn** accounting software

猜想 **cāixiǎng** guess

采用 **cǎiyòng** use

菜油 **càiyóu** rapeseed oil; vegetable oil

踩油门儿 **cǎi yóuménr** put one's foot down, accelerate; rev up

裁员 **cáiyuán** cut back, downsize ◊ layoff

财源 **cáiyuán** means
菜园 **càiyuán** vegetable garden
财政 **cáizhèng** finance ◊ fiscal
财政年度 **cáizhèng niándù** fiscal year
才智 **cáizhì** wisdom
擦净 **cājìng** mop up
擦亮 **cāliàng** polish
餐 **cān** meal
惭 **cán** ashamed
蚕 **cán** silkworm
惨 **cán** tragic; brutal; disastrous
惨案 **cǎn'àn** massacre
惨败 **cǎnbài** massacre; thrashing
残暴 **cánbào** cruel
餐车 **cānchē** restaurant car
蚕豆 **cándòu** broad bean
残废 **cánfèi** disabled, crippled
残废者 **cánfèi zhě** disabled person
舱 **cāng** ship's cabin; aircraft cabin; module
仓 **cāng** storehouse
苍 **cāng** dark green; blue; grey
藏 **cáng** hide
苍白 **cāngbái** pale; wan
仓促 **cāngcù** hasty
舱口 **cāngkǒu** hatch (*on ship*)
仓库 **cāngkù** depot, warehouse; storehouse; stockroom, store
苍鹭 **cānglù** heron
藏匿 **cángnì** hide ◊ secretion
仓鼠 **cāngshǔ** hamster
参观 **cānguān** tour
餐馆 **cānguǎn** restaurant
参观者 **cānguān zhě** visitor
苍蝇 **cāngying** fly (*insect*)
残骸 **cánhái** remains; wreck; wreckage; debris
残迹 **cánjì** remnant
残疾 **cánjí** disabled, handicapped ◊ disability, physical handicap
参加 **cānjiā** attend; compete; enter, go in for, take part in; sit *exam*; participate; join; join in participation; 参加考试 **cānjiā kǎoshì** sit an exam
蚕茧 **cánjiǎn** silk cocoon
参加者 **cānjiā zhě** entrant; participant; entry; turnout
餐巾 **cānjīn** napkin

残疾人士 **cánjí rénshì** disabled person, cripple
餐具 **cānjù** tableware
餐具垫 **cānjù diàn** place mat
餐具柜 **cānjùguì** sideboard
参军 **cānjūn** enlist
参考 **cānkǎo** refer to ◊ reference
参考书 **cānkǎo shū** reference book
参考书目 **cānkǎo shūmù** bibliography
残酷 **cánkù** cut-throat *competition*; savage; sick *sense of humor*; cruel
惭愧 **cánkuì** ashamed
灿烂 **cànlàn** radiant; brilliant; magnificent
残缺 **cánquē** incomplete
残忍 **cánrěn** brutal, cruel, ferocious ◊ brutally; in cold blood ◊ cruelty
参赛 **cānsài** play SP; participate (*in match, contest*)
参赛表 **cānsàibiǎo** entry form
参赛者 **cānsài zhě** participant; contestant
餐室 **cānshì** dining room
餐厅 **cāntīng** dining hall; restaurant
惨痛 **cǎntòng** painful
参议员 **cānyìyuán** senator
参议院 **cānyìyuàn** senate
参与 **cānyù** participate in; be a party to
残余 **cányú** remainder; remains
残渣 **cánzhā** residue
餐桌 **cānzhuō** dining table
餐座 **cānzuò** booth
操 **cāo** hold, grasp; do; speak
槽 **cáo** trough; tank; groove
草 **cǎo** grass; straw
操 **cào** √ fuck
草地 **cǎodì** lawn
草稿 **cǎogǎo** (rough) draft
操劳 **cāoláo** work hard; struggle
操练 **cāoliàn** drill MIL
草帽 **cǎomào** straw hat
草莓 **cǎoméi** strawberry
草皮 **cǎopí** turf
草坪 **cǎopíng** lawn; meadow; green space
草率 **cǎoshuài** careless, sloppy;

hasty

草图 cǎotú outline; sketch

操心 cāoxīn worry

槽牙 cáoyá molar

草药 cǎoyào herbal medicine

草原 cǎoyuán grasslands

嘈杂 cáozá noisy

操纵 cāozòng operate; control; manipulate; rig

操纵装置 cāozòng zhuāngzhì controls

操作 cāozuò operate ◊ operation

操作方法 cāozuò fāngfǎ mode

操作手则 cāozuò shǒuzé operating instructions

操作系统 cāozuò xìtǒng operating system

操作者 cāozuò zhě operator

擦伤 cāshāng graze, scrape

擦洗 cāxǐ scrub

擦油 cāyóu put cream on

擦子 cāzi grater

册 cè volume; (exercise) book

测 cè measure

侧 cè lateral, side

策 cè strategy

测定 cèdìng gauge

测航 cèháng navigate

策划 cèhuà intrigue

测量 cèliáng measure ◊ measurement

策略 cèlüè tactics; strategy

侧面 cèmiàn side; profile

策谋 cèmóu contrive

参差不齐 cēncī bùqí jagged

层 céng coat, layer; coating; story (of building); tier

曾 céng ever; once; formerly; 我曾喜欢过他 wǒ céng xǐhuānguò tā I used to like him

曾经 céngjīng ever; once, formerly

厕所 cèsuǒ toilet, bathroom

测验 cèyàn test

侧翼 cèyì flank

插 chā insert; stick in

差 chā difference MATH

叉 chā fork

茶 chá tea

搽 chá rub in

查 chá check; test; 查地图 chá

dìtú consult a map

察 chá inspect; examine

差 chà bad; poor quality; inferior ◊ badly ◊ lack; be short of; 差五分九点 chà wǔfēn jiǔdiǎn five (minutes) of nine; 差一刻五点 chà yíkè wǔdiǎn a quarter of 5

茶包 chábāo teabag

茶杯 chábēi teacup

茶杯碟 chábēidié saucer

差别 chābié difference; 没什么差别 méi shénme chābié it doesn't make any difference, it doesn't change anything

查查 cháchá check

叉车 chāchē forklift (truck)

茶匙 cháchí teaspoon

查出 cháchū dig up

差错 chācuò mistake; discrepancy

茶袋 chádài teabag

茶点 chádiǎn refreshments, tea and snacks

差额 chā'é balance, remainder

搽粉 cháfěn powder

茶馆 cháguǎn tea house

查号台 cháhàotái information TELEC

茶壶 cháhú teapot

插花 chāhuā arrangement

插话 chāhuà interrupt; 我插不上话 wǒ chābúshàng huà I couldn't get a word in edgewise

拆 chāi tear open; take apart; dismantle; demolish

柴 chái firewood

拆除 chāichú demolish

拆掉 chāidiào tear down

拆毁 chāihuǐ demolish ◊ demolition

拆开 chāikāi take to pieces; unravel; dismantle

差使 chāishǐ errand

拆下 chāixià unfix

拆卸 chāixiè dismantle

柴油 cháiyóu diesel

茶几 chájī coffee table

茶巾 chájīn tea cloth

差劲 chàjìn disappointing; bad; useless

差距 chājù gap; difference; distance

茶具 **chájù** tea service, tea set

察觉 **chájué** detect, discern

岔开 **chàkāi** diverge; sidetrack

察看 **chákàn** check on; look up

查明 **chámíng** determine; make sure

禅 **Chán** Zen

缠 **chán** wind round; bind; wrap; 硬缠着 X **yìng chánzhe X** impose oneself on X

蝉 **chán** cicada

产 **chǎn** give birth to; produce ◊ product; property

阐 **chǎn** explain

铲 **chǎn** shovel

颤 **chàn** tremble

颤动 **chàndòng** pulsate

颤抖 **chàndǒu** quaver; shake; shiver

产房 **chǎnfáng** labor ward

长 **cháng** long ◊ length

尝 **cháng** taste; 尝一尝 **chángyīcháng** have a taste

偿 **cháng** repay; compensate for; fulfil

常 **cháng** frequent

肠 **cháng** intestines

场 **cháng** place; space; course; court SP; field SP; round; scene; meeting place

厂 **chǎng** factory; plant

敞 **chǎng** spacious; open

唱 **chàng** sing

畅 **chàng** smooth; unimpeded

长白山 **Chángbáishān** Changbai mountain

长柄勺 **cháng bǐngsháo** ladle

常常 **chángcháng** frequently, often

长城 **Chángchéng** the Great Wall

长处 **chángchu** advantage; strength

常春藤 **chángchūnténg** ivy

长笛 **chángdí** flute

场地 **chǎngdì** site

长度 **chángdù** length

长短 **chángduǎn** length

唱反调 **chàng fǎndiào** dissent from

长方形 **chángfāng xíng** rectangle ◊ rectangular

偿付 **chángfù** settlement, payment

唱歌 **chànggē** sing (a song)

常规 **chángguī** customary; standard; routine ◊ custom, practice; rut; 常规上 … **chángguī shàng …** it is customary to …

长号 **chánghào** trombone

偿还 **chánghuán** pay back; settle

唱机 **chàngjī** record player

长江 **Chángjiāng** Yangtze River

场景 **chǎngjǐng** scene

长颈鹿 **chángjǐnglù** giraffe

长久 **chángjiǔ** long; long-time ◊ forever, always

敞开 **chǎngkāi** open

敞开天窗说亮话 **chǎngkāi tiānchuāng shuō liànghuà** get down to basics

常客 **chángkè** regular

厂矿企业 **chǎngkuàng qǐyè** industrial enterprises

场面 **chǎngmiàn** scene

长年 **chángnián** all year round

长袍 **chángpáo** gown

长跑 **chángpǎo** long-distance running

敞篷货车 **chǎngpéng huòchē** wagon

唱片 **chàngpiàn** album, record

长篇大论 **chángpiān dàlùn** monolog

唱片架 **chàngpiàn jià** record rack

长波 **chángpō** long wave

长期 **chángqī** the long term ◊ long-term ◊ permanently

常青 **chángqīng** evergreen

偿清 **chángqīng** pay off

长沙发 **cháng shāfā** couch

厂商 **chǎngshāng** commercial and industrial enterprises; factories and stores; manufacturer

长舌 **chángshé** gossip

昌盛 **chāngshèng** flourish; do well ◊ flourishing

常识 **chángshí** general knowledge

尝试 **chángshì** attempt; try; taste

常识 **chángshì** common sense

长寿 **chángshòu** long life

场所 **chǎngsuǒ** place

畅所欲言 chàngsuǒyùyán vocal

长条 chángtiáo strip

畅通 chàngtōng unobstructed

长统袜 chángtǒngwà stocking

长途 chángtú long distance

长途电话 chángtú diànhuà long-distance call

长途汽车 chángtú qìchē (long-distance) bus

肠胃 chángwèi intestines and stomach; guts

畅销 chàngxiāo in demand; selling well

畅销书 chàngxiāo shū best-seller

长袖 chángxiù long-sleeved

长袖运动服 chángxiù yùndòngfú tracksuit

肠炎 chángyán enteritis

长椅 chángyǐ bench

常用 chángyòng in common use; everyday

长于 chángyú be good at

长远 chángyuǎn long-range; long-term

厂长 chǎngzhǎng director of a factory

长征 Chángzhēng Long March

肠子 chángzi intestine

产后 chǎnhòu postnatal

忏悔 chànhuǐ repent; confess ◊ confession; penitence

搀假 chānjiǎ adulterate

产假 chǎnjià maternity leave

缠结 chánjié snarl

产科病房 chǎnkē bìngfáng maternity ward

产科医师 chǎnkē yīshī obstetrician

产量 chǎnliàng production; capacity; output; yield; turnover ◊ turn over

阐明 chǎnmíng explain; interpret

产品 chǎnpǐn produce ◊ product

铲平 chǎnpíng bulldoze, demolish

产前 chǎnqián antenatal

缠绕 chánrào wrap; wind; curl

缠人 chánrén clingy

产生 chǎnshēng produce; emerge; generate; give rise to

阐述 chǎnshù explain

铲子 chǎnzi shovel; spade

禅宗佛教 Chánzōng Fójiào Zen Buddhism

抄 chāo copy; transcribe; plagiarize

钞 chāo bank bill

超 chāo exceed; surpass; transcend ◊ super; ultra; extra

巢 cháo nest

潮 cháo tide ◊ damp

嘲 cháo ridicule; mock

朝 cháo toward; facing ◊ court; dynasty

炒 chǎo cook; stir-fry

吵 chǎo make a noise; quarrel

炒菜 chǎo cài cook ◊ stir-fried dish

炒菜锅 chǎocàiguō wok

超车 chāochē pass, overtake

超出 chāochū exceed ◊ beyond; 超出我的能力范围 chāochū wǒde nénglì fànwéi it's beyond me

朝代 cháodài dynasty

超短裙 chāoduǎnqún mini, miniskirt

炒饭 chǎofàn fried rice ◊ fry rice

超过 chāoguò exceed; outgrow; overtake, pass ◊ over

吵架 chǎojià argue ◊ argument

超级大国 chāojí dàguó superpower

超级市场 chāojí shìchǎng supermarket

潮流 cháoliú trend

炒面 chǎomiàn fried noodles ◊ fry noodles

吵闹 chǎonào carry on, make a fuss ◊ noise; scene

嘲弄 cháonòng jeer; mockery

钞票 chāopiào bank bill

超声波 chāoshēngbō ultrasound

朝圣者 cháoshèng zhě pilgrim

朝圣之行 cháoshèng zhī xíng pilgrimage

超时 chāoshí overrun

潮湿 cháoshī moist; damp

潮水 cháoshuǐ tide

超速 chāosù overdrive ◊ speed ◊ speeding

超文本 chāowénběn hypertext

抄袭 chāoxí copy

朝鲜 **Cháoxiān** Korea

朝向 **cháoxiàng** look onto, face

嘲笑 **cháoxiào** laugh at, poke fun at; taunt ◊ taunt

抄写 **chāoxiě** copy; transcribe

巢穴 **cháoxué** den; lair

超音速 **chāoyīnsù** supersonic

炒鱿鱼 **chǎo yóuyú** dismiss, fire; 被炒鱿鱼了 **bèi chǎo yóuyú le** be fired

超载 **chāozài** overload

超支 **chāozhī** overdraft ◊ overdraw; overspend; 超支八百美元 **chāozhī bābǎi měiyuán** be $800 overdrawn

超重 **chāozhòng** overload ◊ overweight

超重的行李 **chāozhòngde xíngli** excess baggage

超自然 **cháozìrán** supernatural

吵嘴 **chǎozuǐ** quarrel

查票员 **chápiào yuán** (ticket) inspector

插入 **chārù** insert; slot in ◊ insertion; 把 X 插入 Y **bǎ X chārù Y** insert X into Y

茶室 **cháshì** tearoom

插手 **chāshǒu** involvement

插头 **chātóu** pin; plug ELEC

插图 **chātú** illustration

查问 **cháwèn** questioning

插销 **chāxiāo** bolt

查询 **cháxún** enquire

茶叶 **cháyè** tea; tea leaves

差异 **chāyì** gap

诧异 **chàyì** amazed

搽用 **cháyòng** put on

查阅 **cháyuè** look up; consult

叉子 **chāzi** cross; fork

查字典 **chá zìdiǎn** look up; consult a dictionary

插嘴 **chāzuǐ** butt in, chip in

插座 **chāzuò** socket

车 **chē** vehicle; car; bus

扯 **chě** pull; bear; tell lies; talk nonsense

撤 **chè** pull back; withdraw

彻 **chè** thorough; penetrating

车把 **chēbǎ** handlebars

车床 **chēchuáng** lathe

车次 **chēcì** train number; bus number

扯蛋 **chědàn** talk nonsense

彻底 **chèdǐ** exhaustive, thorough; outright; resounding; radical; solid *support* ◊ radically; right, completely; soundly

彻底变革 **chèdǐ biàngé** revolutionize

彻底击垮 **chèdǐ jīkuǎ** undermine

车顶架 **chēdǐng jià** roof rack

车队 **chēduì** convoy, fleet (of vehicles)

撤回 **chèhuí** withdraw

车祸 **chēhuò** traffic accident

车架横梁 **chējià héngliáng** crossbar

车间 **chējiān** workshop

车库 **chēkù** garage

撤离 **chèlí** evacuate; move out; pull out

车辆 **chēliàng** vehicle

车龙 **chēlóng** traffic jam

车轮 **chēlún** wheel

沉 **chén** sink

晨 **chén** morning

陈 **chén** old; stale ◊ lay out; display

衬 **chèn** line

陈词滥调 **chéncí làndiào** platitude

衬垫 **chèndiàn** lining

沉淀物 **chéndiànwù** sediment

陈腐 **chénfǔ** conventional; hackneyed

撑 **chēng** support, hold up

称 **chēng** call; say; weigh; 称 … 的重量 **chēng … de zhòngliàng** weigh

乘 **chéng** by ◊ multiply; 二乘四 **èr chéng sì** 2 by 4

橙 **chéng** orange (*color, fruit*)

成 **chéng** achieve; become; succeed; mature

诚 **chéng** honest; sincere

城 **chéng** city; wall

呈 **chéng** submit

程 **chéng** rule; pattern

惩 **chéng** punish

澄 **chéng** clear

承 **chéng** hold; carry; undertake

秤 **chèng** scales

承包 **chéngbāo** commission;

contract

城堡 **chéngbǎo** castle; fortress

呈报 **chéngbào** declare

承包人 **chéngbāo rén** contractor

成本 **chéngběn** cost

成本加运费 **chéngběn jiā yùnfèi** cost and freight

成本价格 **chéngběn jiàgé** cost price

成比例 **chéng bǐlì** proportional

乘车 **chèngchē** ride

惩处 **chéngchǔ** punish; penalize

承担 **chéngdān** bear; undertake; 承担责任 **chéngdān zérèn** be held responsible; take responsibility

成单行 **chéngdānháng** in single file

呈递 **chéngdì** submit; hand in; hand over

程度 **chéngdù** degree, extent; measure; 在一定程度上 **zài yídìng chéngdùshang** to a certain extent; in a way

成堆 **chéngduī** in piles; loads of

承兑 **chéngduì** cash; accept *check*

惩罚 **chéngfá** discipline; penalty; punishment ◊ punish

成分 **chéngfèn** component; ingredient

撑杆跳 **chēnggān tiào** vault

撑竿跳高 **chēnggān tiàogāo** polevault

成功 **chénggōng** do well, succeed, prosper ◊ success ◊ successful; fruitful ◊ successfully; 取得成功 **qǔdé chénggōng** work out, succeed

成果 **chéngguǒ** achievement; success

称号 **chēnghào** title; designation

称呼 **chēnghu** form of address ◊ address

乘机 **chéngjī** fly (*in plane*)

成绩 **chéngjì** achievement; results

成见 **chéngjiàn** prejudice; stereotype

呈交 **chéngjiāo** put in, submit

成交！ **chéngjiāo!** it's a deal!

成吉思汗 **Chéngjísīhàn** Genghis Khan

成就 **chéngjiù** achievement

撑开 **chēngkāi** open *umbrella*

乘客 **chéngkè** passenger

诚恳 **chéngkěn** sincere

乘客座位 **chéngkè zuòwèi** passenger seat

成立 **chénglì** establish, set up ◊ foundation

成名 **chéngmíng** make a name for oneself

成年 **chéngnián** come of age ◊ adult ◊ F all year

承诺 **chéngnuò** promise; commit; pledge

尘垢 **chéngòu** grime

澄清 **chéngqīng** clarify; acquit, clear; unravel; settle (*of liquid*)

成人 **chéngrén** adult

承认 **chéngrèn** acknowledge, recognize; admit, confess; concede ◊ admission; recognition

成人片 **chéngrén piān** adult film

橙色 **chéngsè** orange (*color*)

诚实 **chéngshí** honest, truthful ◊ honesty; integrity

城市 **chéngshì** city ◊ civic

城市化 **chéngshìhuà** urbanization

成熟 **chéngshóu** ripen

承受 **chéngshòu** bear, carry; 承受压力 **chéngshòu yālì** be under pressure

成熟 **chéngshú** full-grown; grown-up; ripe; mature ◊ maturity ◊ mature; ripen

成套 **chéngtào** complete set; 成套用品 **chéngtào yòngpǐn** complete set of equipment

成为 **chéngwéi** become; turn into

呈文 **chéngwén** submission; petition

乘务员 **chéngwùyuán** conductor; ticket collector; steward; stewardess

成现 **chéngxiàn** arise; materialize

成效 **chéngxiào** effect

称心如意 **chènxīn rúyì** desirable

程序 **chéngxù** program; procedure; system; order

程序表 **chéngxùbiǎo** schedule

程序员 **chéngxùyuán** programmer

诚意 **chéngyì** honesty; sincerity

成瘾者 **chéngyǐn zhě** addict

盛有 **chéngyǒu** hold

乘游艇 **chéng yóutǐng** yachting

成员 **chéngyuán** member

成员人数 **chéngyuán rénshù** membership

成员证 **chéngyuánzhèng** membership card

成员资格 **chéngyuán zīgé** membership

称赞 **chēngzàn** praise

成长 **chéngzhǎng** grow ◊ growth

诚挚 **chéngzhì** sincere ◊ sincerely

称职 **chèngzhí** competent

橙汁 **chéngzhī** orange juice; orangeade

称重量 **chēng zhòngliàng** weigh

撑柱 **chēngzhù** stilts (*under house*)

沉着冷静 **chéngzhuó lěngjìng** imperturbable

橙子 **chéngzi** orange (*fruit*)

橙子酱 **chéngzijiàng** marmalade

沉积 **chénjī** deposit

沉浸 **chénjìn** immerse oneself in

陈旧 **chénjiù** outmoded

衬里 **chènlǐ** lining; 安衬里 **ān chènlǐ** line (*with material*)

衬料 **chènliào** lining; padding

陈列 **chénliè** display ◊ be on display

陈列柜 **chénlièguì** display cabinet

沉闷 **chénmèn** dreary; close, oppressive *weather*; dejected; reserved *character*

沉没 **chénmò** sink, go under

沉默 **chénmò** silent ◊ silence

沉默寡言 **chénmò guǎyán** silent; taciturn

沉溺 **chénnì** addiction

衬裙 **chènqún** underskirt

衬衫 **chènshān** shirt; blouse

陈述 **chénshù** set out

沉思 **chénsī** thoughtful, pensive ◊ muse

沉痛 **chéntòng** deeply distressed

尘土 **chéntǔ** dust

晨曦 **chénxī** daybreak

称心 **chènxīn** be satisfied with

沉重 **chénzhòng** heavy; serious; oppressive *weather*

沉着 **chénzhuó** level-headed, composed; self-possessed

车子 **chēzi** bicycle; car

车牌 **chēpái** license plate

车牌号码 **chēpái hàomǎ** license number

车皮 **chēpí** freight car

车票 **chēpiào** ticket

车身 **chēshēn** bodywork

车胎 **chētāi** tire

车胎爆炸 **chētāi bàozhà** blow-out

车条 **chētiáo** spoke

撤退 **chètuì** retreat; withdraw ◊ withdrawal

车厢 **chēxiāng** car (*of train*)

撤销 **chèxiāo** undo COMPUT; withdraw; cancel; get rid of ◊ withdrawal

车站 **chēzhàn** bus stop; bus station; station

车辙 **chēzhé** rut

吃 **chī** eat; take; live on; absorb; suffer; bear; 吃点儿饭怎么样？ **chī diǎnr fàn zěnmeyàng?** what about some dinner?; 吃早餐 **chī zǎocān** have breakfast

池 **chí** pool; pond

迟 **chí** late

持 **chí** hold; grasp; keep; maintain; manage

匙 **chí** spoon

尺 **chǐ** Chinese foot; rule; ruler

耻 **chǐ** shame; disgrace

齿 **chǐ** tooth

赤 **chì** red; bare

翅 **chì** wing; shark's fin

斥 **chì** scold

翅膀 **chìbǎng** wing

吃饱了 **chī bǎo le** be full up

持不同政见者 **chí bùtóng zhèngjiàn zhě** dissident

吃不消 **chībùxiāo** unbearable

吃草 **chīcǎo** graze

吃醋 **chīcù** be jealous

尺寸 **chǐcùn** dimension; measurement

迟到 **chídào** be late

赤道 **chìdào** equator

吃的 **chīde** food

尺度 **chǐdù** measure; standard; rule

迟钝 **chídùn** clumsy, awkward; stupid; backward; numb

吃饭 **chīfàn** eat, have a meal

吃个饱 **chīgebǎo** eat one's fill

齿冠 **chǐguàn** crown (*on tooth*)

吃光 **chīguāng** eat up; scoff

吃好 **chīhǎo** enjoy!

迟缓 **chíhuǎn** slow; hesitant

持家 **chíjiā** keep house, run a home

赤脚 **chìjiǎo** barefoot

赤脚医生 **chìjiǎo yīshēng** barefoot doctor

吃惊 **chījīng** be amazed; be surprised; 令人吃惊 **lìngrén chījīng** staggering

持久 **chíjiǔ** enduring

吃苦 **chīkǔ** bear hardships; suffer

吃亏 **chīkuī** be at a disadvantage ◊ disadvantaged

吃力 **chīlì** with difficulty ◊ punishing

齿轮 **chǐlún** gear

赤裸裸 **chì luǒluo** in the nude

持枪歹徒 **chíqiāng dǎitú** gunman

耻辱 **chǐrǔ** dishonor; disgrace; shame

池塘 **chítáng** pond

赤陶 **chìtáo** terracotta

持械抢劫 **chíxiè qiǎngjié** armed robbery

持续 **chíxù** continue; last; endure

持续不断 **chíxù búduàn** persistent

持续观察 **chíxù guānchá** monitor

吃药 **chīyào** take medicine

齿龈 **chǐyín** gum

持异议 **chí yìyì** dissent

持有 **chíyǒu** possess, hold ◊ possession

迟于 **chíyú** past; later than

迟早 **chízǎo** sooner or later

斥责 **chìzé** rebuke, reprimand

吃住 **chīzhù** board and lodging

尺子 **chǐzi** ruler (*for measuring*)

赤子 **chìzǐ** newborn child

赤字 **chìzì** shortfall, deficit

充 **chōng** full

冲 **chōng** push forward; charge; attack; flush; rinse

虫 **chóng** insect

重 **chóng** repeat; double ◊ again ◊ layer

宠爱 **chǒng'ài** dote on

崇拜 **chóngbài** worship

崇拜者 **chóngbài zhě** admirer; worshipper

重播 **chóngbō** repeat (broadcast)

冲刺 **chōngcì** spurt (*in race*)

充当 **chōngdāng** serve as

充电 **chōngdiàn** charge; recharge

冲掉 **chōngdiào** flush away

重迭 **chóngdié** overlap

冲动 **chōngdòng** impulse; 凭一时的冲动 **píng yìshíde chōngdòng** on the spur of the moment

宠儿 **chǒng'ér** pet, favorite

重放 **chóngfàng** replay

充分 **chōngfèn** full; ample; sufficient

冲锋 **chōngfēng** charge (*of troops*)

重逢 **chóngféng** meet again

冲锋枪 **chōngfēngqiāng** submachine gun

重复 **chóngfù** repetition; duplicate; action replay ◊ repeat; echo ◊ repetitive; 我是不是重复了？ **wǒ shìbúshì chóngfù le?** am I repeating myself?

崇高 **chónggāo** lofty; exalted

虫害 **chónghài** plague of insects

宠坏 **chǒnghuài** spoil ◊ spoilt

重婚 **chónghūn** bigamy

冲昏了头 **chōnghūn le tóu** get carried away

重获 **chónghuò** regain

冲击 **chōngjī** lunge at; lash; charge

重建 **chóngjiàn** rebuild

崇敬 **chóngjìng** revere

冲浪板 **chōnglàngbǎn** surfboard

冲浪运动 **chōnglàng yùndòng** surfing

冲浪者 **chōnglàng zhě** surfer

充满 **chōngmǎn** fill up ◊ be full of

充满怨恨 **chōngmǎn yuànhèn** bitter

充气 **chōngqì** inflate ◊ pneumatic

充任 **chōngrèn** occupy; hold the post of

重赛 **chóngsài** replay

重申 **chóngshēn** echo *views*; reiterate

重审 **chóngshěn** reopen

充实 **chōngshí** beef up ◊ full *life*

冲突 **chōngtū** clash; conflict

重温 **chóngwēn** brush up

宠物 **chǒngwù** pet (*animal*)

冲洗 **chōngxǐ** develop *photograph*; flush ◊ development

重现 **chóngxiàn** reappear

重写 **chóngxiě** rewrite

重新 **chóngxīn** again

重新安排 **chóngxīn ānpái** reorganize, rearrange ◊ reorganization

重新出现 **chóngxīn chūxiàn** resurface

重新发展 **chóngxīn fāzhǎn** redevelop

重新开始 **chóngxīn kāishǐ** go back to the drawing board; renew ◊ renewal; fresh start

重新开张 **chóngxīn kāizhāng** reopen

重新考虑 **chóngxīn kǎolǜ** reconsider

重新命名 **chóngxīn mìngmíng** rename

重新评价 **chóngxīn píngjià** revaluation

重新武装 **chóngxīn wǔzhuāng** rearm

重新装修 **chóngxīn zhuāngxiū** redecorate

充血 **chōngxuè** congestion; MED hyperemia

虫牙 **chóngyá** decayed tooth

重阳节 **Chóngyángjié** Double Ninth Festival

重印 **chóngyìn** reprint

重影 **chóngyǐng** double

充裕 **chōngyù** abundant

虫子 **chóngzi** insect; worm

充足 **chōngzú** ample; sufficient ◊ sufficiently

重组 **chóngzǔ** shake-up ◊ reshuffle; reorganize

抽 **chōu** pull out; draw

稠 **chóu** thick; dense

筹 **chóu** plan; prepare

酬 **chóu** reward; remuneration

愁 **chóu** worry

仇 **chóu** enemy; hatred

丑 **chǒu** ugly

臭 **chòu** stinking

酬报 **chóubào** reward; payment

筹备 **chóubèi** arrange

抽不开身 **chōu bù kāi shēn** tied up, busy

抽出 **chōuchū** pull out, draw

抽搐 **chōuchù** convulsion; twitch

仇敌 **chóudí** enemy

丑恶 **chǒu'è** repulsive, revolting

仇恨 **chóuhèn** hatred; enmity

筹划 **chóuhuà** map out

筹集 **chóují** raise *money*

抽奖 **chōujiǎng** raffle

丑角 **chǒujiǎo** comedian; clown

抽筋 **chōujīn** cramp

酬金 **chóujīn** fee

丑角 **chǒujué** clown

抽开 **chōukāi** pull away

抽空 **chōukòng** take time; devote time

丑陋 **chǒulòu** ugly, hideous

筹码 **chóumǎ** chip, counter

臭骂一顿 **chòumà yídùn** bawl out

愁闷 **chóumèn** worried; down

稠密 **chóumì** thick; dense

稠密度 **chóumì dù** density

臭名远扬 **chòumíng yuǎnyáng** infamous

臭名昭著 **chòumíng zhāozhù** infamous

抽泣 **chōuqì** sob

臭气 **chòuqì** stink

抽税 **chōushuì** tax; levy a tax

抽丝 **chōusī** run (*in pantyhose*)

抽屉 **chōuti** drawer

臭味儿 **chòuwèir** stink

丑闻 **chǒuwén** scandal

抽吸 **chōuxī** suction

抽象 **chōuxiàng** abstract

抽烟 **chōuyān** smoke

抽样 **chōuyàng** sampling

臭氧 **chòuyǎng** ozone

臭氧层 **chòuyǎng céng** ozone

layer

抽油烟机 chōuyóu yānjī hood (*over cooker*)

出 chū out ◊ go out; come out; give out; publish; produce; happen

初 chū beginning ◊ first

橱 chú cupboard

除 chú eliminate; remove; except; divide MATH; 除 … 外 chú … wài apart from …

锄 chú hoe

雏 chú young *bird*

储 chǔ store up

处 chǔ get along with; manage; be situated in

穿 chuān wear; pierce; penetrate; 穿衣服 chuān yīfu get dressed, dress; 穿黄色衣服 chuān huángsè yīfu dressed in yellow; 我穿不上裤子 wǒ chuān bú shàng kùzi I can't get these pants on

传 chuán pass on; spread; infect; transmit; call

船 chuán boat, ship, vessel; 在船上 zài chuánshàng be aboard

喘 chuǎn breathe heavily; 喘不过气来 chuǎn bū guò qì lái breathless, out of breath

串 chuàn string together ◊ bunch; kebab ◊ *measure word for strings, bunches of things*; 一串项链 yíchuàn xiàngliàn a necklace

传播 chuánbō spread

船舶 chuánbó shipping

喘不过气 chuǎn bū guò qì breathlessness

船舱 chuáncāng cabin

船厂 chuánchǎng dockyard

传达 chuándá pass on; transmit ◊ janitor; 请传达给我 qǐng chuándá gěi wǒ please keep me informed

穿戴 chuāndài wear; dress

传单 chuándān flyer (*leaflet*)

传导 chuándǎo conduct ELEC

传道 chuándào preach

传道人 chuándào rén preacher

传导器 chuándǎoqì transmitter

传递 chuándì pass on; convey

传动 chuándòng transmission

船队 chuánduì convoy

疮 chuāng sore

窗 chuāng window

床 chuáng bed

创 chuàng start; initiate

窗板 chuāngbǎn shutter

创办 chuàngbàn found, start

创办人 chuàngbàn rén promoter

窗玻璃 chuāng bōlí windowpane

床单 chuángdān sheet

床垫 chuángdiàn mattress

窗户 chuānghu window

创建 chuàngjiàn found, establish

创建人 chuàngjiàn rén founder

创可贴 chuàngkětiē adhesive plaster

窗口 chuāngkǒu hatch; window; contact

创立 chuànglì found, establish

窗帘 chuānglián curtain; drapes

床铺 chuángpù bunk

闯入 chuǎngrù burst into a room

创伤性 chuàngshāng xìng traumatic

床上用品 chuángshàng yòngpǐn bedclothes, linen

创始人 chuàngshǐ rén founder; originator

窗台 chuāngtái windowsill

床头 chuángtóu bedstead

穿过 chuānguò cross ◊ through

创新 chuàngxīn create ◊ revolutionary *new ideas*

创业 chuàngyè enterprise; 有创业才能 yǒu chuàngyè cáinéng entrepreneurial

创业园 chuàngyèyuán venture park

创造 chuàngzào create

创造者 chuàngzào zhě creator

床罩 chuángzhào bedspread

创作 chuàngzuò create; compose ◊ creation

传呼 chuánhū page

传唤 chuánhuàn subpoena; summon to court

传话 chuánhuà pass on a message

传呼机 chuánhūjī pager

传教 chuánjiào do missionary work

传教士 chuánjiàoshì missionary

穿孔 **chuān kǒng** puncture

窗框 **chuāngkuàng** sash

船篷 **chuánpéng** awning

传票 **chuánpiào** subpoena; summons

船票 **chuánpiào** ticket (*for ship*)

奇奇 **chuánqí** legend

喘气 **chuǎnqì** gasp (for breath); pant

传球 **chuánqiú** pass (the ball)

传染 **chuánrǎn** infect ◊ contagious

传染性 **chúanrǎn xìng** catching; infectious

船首 **chuánshǒu** prow

传授 **chuánshòu** teach

传说 **chuánshuō** legend ◊ legend has it; it is said

传送 **chuánsòng** carry (of sound)

传送带 **chuánsòng dài** conveyor belt

穿梭 **chuānsuō** shuttle

穿梭业务 **chuānsuō yèwù** shuttle service

穿梭营运 **chuānsuō yíngyùn** shuttlebus

船台 **chuántái** berth

传统 **chuántǒng** tradition ◊ traditional ◊ traditionally

穿透 **chuāntòu** penetrate

船头 **chuántóu** bow (of ship)

船桅 **chuánwéi** mast

船尾电动机 **chuánwěi diàndòngjī** outboard motor

传闻 **chuánwén** hearsay; rumor ◊ it is said

船屋 **chuánwū** houseboat

船坞 **chuánwù** dock

喘息 **chuǎnxī** gasp, pant; puff

传下来 **chuánxiàlái** hand down

船舷 **chuánxián** side of a ship

传销 **chuánxiāo** pyramid selling

传下去 **chuánxiàqù** hand on

传讯 **chuánxùn** summons

船员 **chuányuán** sailor

传阅 **chuányuè** circulate

船长 **chuánzhǎng** captain, skipper

传真 **chuánzhēn** fax; 用传真传 **yòng chuánzhēn chuán** fax, send by fax; 把 X 传真给 Y **bǎ X chuánzhēn gěi Y** fax X to Y

传真机 **chuánzhēnjī** fax machine

船主 **chuánzhǔ** shipowner

穿着 **chuānzhuó** clothing; 穿着单薄 ***chuānzhuó dānbó*** scantily clad

橼子 **chuánzi** rafter

出版 **chūbǎn** publish; come out

出版公司 **chūbǎn gōngsī** publishing company

出版社 **chūbǎnshè** publisher

出版物 **chūbǎnwù** publication

出版业 **chūbǎnyè** publishing

储备 **chǔbèi** store; reserve ◊ stock up on; stockpile

储备金 **chǔbèi jīn** reserves FIN

储备物资 **chǔbèi wùzī** stockpile

除冰 **chúbīng** de-ice

除冰器 **chúbīng qì** de-icer

储藏 **chǔcáng** store; deposit

除草剂 **chúcǎojì** weedkiller

出差错 **chū chācuò** slip up

出差 **chūchāi** go on a business trip

出产 **chūchǎn** yield; produce

出场 **chūchǎng** entrance

出丑 **chūchǒu** make a spectacle of oneself; 别当众让我出丑 ***bié dāngzhòng ràng wǒ chūchǒu*** don't show me up in public

橱窗 **chúchuāng** display window; store window ◊ in the window

初次 **chūcì** the first time

储存 **chǔcún** put aside, put by; save; bank ◊ stock; store; reserves

出错 **chūcuò** make a mistake; stumble over

处得来 **chùdelái** get on, be friendly

触电 **chùdiàn** shock

除掉 **chúdiào** eliminate

出尔反尔 **chū'ěr fǎněr** backpedal; contradict oneself

出发 **chūfā** departure ◊ leave; set off

除法 **chúfǎ** division

触发 **chùfā** trigger off

出发点 **chūfā diǎn** starting point

厨房 **chúfáng** kitchen

处方 **chǔfāng** prescribe ◊ prescription

除非 **chúfēi** only if; unless

橱柜 **chúguì** compartment

出国 chūguó go abroad
出汗 chūhàn sweat, perspire
出航 chūháng outgoing *flight*
储户 chǔhù depositor
出乎意料 chūhū yìliào unexpected ◊ strangely enough
吹 chuī blow
垂 chuí hang down; droop
锤 chuí hammer
吹风器 chuīfēngqì hairdrier
吹干 chuīgān blow-dry
吹鼓手 chuīgǔshǒu *band that plays at weddings and funerals*
吹口 chuīkǒu mouthpiece
吹口哨 chuī kǒushào whistle
垂柳 chuíliǔ weeping willow
吹灭 chuīmiè blow out *candle*
吹牛 chuīniú boast, talk big
吹牛拍马 chuīniú pāimǎ suck up; brown nose; be obsequious
吹气 chuīqì blow
吹哨 chuīshào blow
垂死 chuísǐ dying
垂下 chuíxià hang
垂涎 chuíxián lick one's lips; 令人垂涎 *lìngrén chuíxián* mouthwatering
吹嘘 chuīxū show off, brag
垂直 chuízhí perpendicular; vertical
垂直上移 chuízhí shàngyí scroll up
垂直下移 chuízhí xiàyí scroll down
锤子 chuízi hammer
初级 chūjí elementary
雏鸡 chújī baby chicken
出家 chūjiā become a monk / nun
出价 chūjià bid
触角 chùjiǎo antenna, feeler
出家人 Chūjiā rén Buddhist monk / nun
出借 chūjiè lend; loan
初级阶段 chūjí jiēduàn infancy
出境 chūjìng leave the country
处境 chǔjìng position
初级小学 chūjí xiǎoxué lower elementary school
处决 chǔjué execute, put to death
触觉 chùjué touch
出口 chūkǒu exit; export; outlet ◊

export
出口处 chūkǒuchù exit
出口商 chūkǒushāng exporter
出口物 chūkǒuwù exports
出来 chūlái come out; get out; be ◊ out
畜栏 chùlán corral
除了 chúle apart from, aside from, except; all but; besides; excluding; 除了 X 以外 *chúle X yǐwài* except for X; 除了 X 之外 *chúle X zhīwài* in addition to X
处理 chǔlǐ attend to; take care of; deal with; process *data*; treat ◊ disposal (*of waste*); treatment, processing
处理不当 chǔlǐ búdàng mishandle
处理器 chǔlǐqì processor
出路 chūlù exit, way out
出卖 chūmài sell; betray, sell out
出毛病 chū máobìng break down ◊ broken
除毛剂 chúmáojì hair remover
出名 chūmíng well-known ◊ become famous
触摸 chùmō feel; touch
春 chūn spring
纯 chún pure; neat, straight *drink*; net *price*; solid *gold*
唇 chún lip
蠢 chǔn stupid
处男 chù'nán virgin (*male*)
出纳员 chū'nàyuán cashier; teller
蠢材 chǔncái clown
纯粹 chúncuì pure; unspoilt
唇读 chúndú lipread
纯度 chúndù purity
春分 Chūnfēn Spring equinox
唇膏 chúngāo lipstick
春季 chūnjì spring, springtime
春节 Chūnjié Chinese New Year, Spring Festival
纯洁 chúnjié innocent; pure; honest
纯净 chúnjìng clean
春卷 chūnjuǎn spring roll
纯利润 chún lìrùn net profit
纯巧克力 chún qiǎokèlì plain chocolate
蠢人 chǔnrén fool

纯熟 **chúnshú** proficient; skillful

春天 **chūntiān** spring

处女 **chǔnǚ** virgin (*female*)

纯正 **chúnzhèng** pure

纯种 **chúnzhǒng** pedigree, thoroughbred

戳 **chuō** jab; prick

绰号 **chuòhào** nickname

出钱 **chūqián** chip in; fork out

出勤 **chūqín** attendance

出去 **chūqù** go out; 出去！ **chūqù!** get out!

除去 **chúqù** drop; remove; obliterate; strip

出去吃 **chūqù chī** eat out

出去一会儿 **chūqù yíhuìr** step out, go out

出让 **chūràng** part with; sell; lease out

出人意外 **chūrényìwài** surprisingly

出入境口 **chūrùjìng kǒu** terminal

出身 **chūshēn** family background

出神 **chūshén** fascinated ◊ space out

出生 **chūshēng** be born; 孩子什么时候出生 **háizi shénme shíhòu chūshēng?** when is the baby due?

畜生 **chùshēng** beast; brute

出声 **chūshēng** aloud; 别出声！ **bié chūshēng!** just be quiet!, hush!

出生地 **chūshēng dì** birthplace

出生率 **chūshēng lǜ** birthrate

出生年份 **chūshēng niánfèn** year of birth

出生日期 **chūshēng rìqī** date of birth

出生证 **chūshēng zhèng** birth certificate

出神儿 **chūshénr** go into a trance; space out

出示 **chūshì** show

出事 **chūshì** go wrong; have an accident

厨师 **chúshī** chef; cook

出事故 **chū shìgù** crash COMPUT

出售 **chūshòu** put up for sale

触手 **chùshǒu** tentacle

储水池 **chǔshuǐ chí** tank (*for water etc*)

出庭 **chūtíng** appearance (*in court*)

锄头 **chútóu** pickaxe; hoe

出席 **chūxí** be present; attend

除夕 **Chúxī** Chinese New Year's Eve

出现 **chūxiàn** appear; emerge

出血 **chūxiě** hemorrhage

除臭剂 **chúxiù jì** deodorant

除锈剂 **chúxiùjì** rust remover

储蓄 **chǔxù** save; deposit ◊ savings

初选 **chūxuǎn** primary

出血 **chūxuè** bleed

初学者 **chūxué zhě** beginner

储蓄银行 **chǔxū yínháng** savings bank

储蓄帐户 **chǔxù zhànghù** savings account

初一 **Chūyī** (Chinese) New Year's Day; Grade 1 in Junior High

出游 **chūyóu** outing, trip

出狱 **chūyù** get out of prison

处于 **chǔyú** be (*in a situation*); 处于困境 **chǔyú kùnjìng** be stranded

出院 **chūyuàn** discharge

出证 **chūzhèng** give evidence

出众 **chūzhòng** excel, shine

初中 **chūzhōng** junior high school

出皱褶 **chū zhòuzhě** wrinkle

出租 **chūzū** rent ◊ for rent

出租车 **chūzūchē** taxi, cab

出租车司机 **chūzūchē sījī** taxidriver, cab driver

出租车停车处 **chūzūchē tíngchēchù** taxi rank, cab stand

出租车站 **chūzūchē zhàn** taxi rank, cab stand

出租汽车 **chūzū qìchē** cab, taxi

出租汽车司机 **chūzū qìchē sījī** cab driver, taxi driver

磁 **cí** magnetism; china; ceramic

瓷 **cí** porcelain; china

词 **cí** term; word

慈 **cí** kind

雌 **cí** female

辞 **cí** word

祠 **cí** ancestral temple

此 **cǐ** this

刺 **cì** prick (*pain*); prickle, spine;

thorn; splinter ◊ stab

次 cì time

刺鼻 cìbí pungent

辞别 cíbié say goodbye ◊ farewell

磁带 cídài cassette; tape

磁带驱动器 cídài qūdòngqì tape drive

词典 cídiǎn dictionary

刺耳 cì'ěr ear-piercing; shrill; grating

词根 cígēn root (of word)

刺骨 cìgǔ piercing

此后 cǐhòu after this; henceforth

伺候 cìhòu attend to; wait on; serve

词汇 cíhuì vocabulary

词汇表 cíhuì biǎo vocabulary; glossary

刺激 cìjī stimulate; irritate

此路不通 cǐ lù bù tōng dead end

磁盘 cípán disk

磁盘带动机 cípán dàijī disk drive

瓷漆 cíqī enamel

瓷器 cíqì porcelain; china

瓷器厂 cíqìchǎng porcelain factory

慈善 císhàn benevolent; charitable

慈善机构 císhàng jīgòu charity (organization)

慈善家 císhànjiā philanthropist

磁石 císhí magnet

次数 cìshù number of times; frequency

刺探 cìtàn pry into

祠堂 cítáng ancestral temple

刺痛 cìtòng smart

刺透 cìtòu pierce

辞退 cítuì dismiss, fire

此外 cǐwài besides; also

词尾 cíwěi ending (of word)

刺猬 cìwei hedgehog

慈祥 cíxiáng kind; loving

雌性 cíxìng female

词性 cíxìng part of speech

磁性 cíxìng magnetism ◊ magnetic

雌性动植物 cíxìng dòngzhíwù female

刺绣 cìxiù embroider ◊ embroidery

刺绣品 cìxiùpǐn embroidery

次序 cìxù order

次序颠倒 cìxù diāndǎo out of order

次要 cìyào minor, secondary; peripheral

赐予 cìyǔ bestow

词藻华丽 cízǎo huálì flowery

辞职 cízhí quit; resign ◊ resignation

此致 cǐzhì yours truly; best regards

瓷砖 cízhuān tile

葱 cōng scallion; green onion; Chinese onion

匆 cōng hasty; urgent

从 cóng bushes

从 cóng from; 从十八世纪起 cóng shíbā shìjì qǐ from the 18th century; 从他来中国以后 … cóng tā lái Zhōngguó yǐhòu … ever since he came to China … ; 我从没去过北京 wǒ cóng méi qùguò Běijīng I've never been to Beijing; 从 … 以来 cóng … yǐlái since …; 从明天开始 cóng míngtiān kāishǐ (starting) from tomorrow; 从五月一日起生效 cóng wǔyuè yīrì qǐ shēngxiào effective May 1; 从现在开始 cóng xiànzài kāishǐ from now on; 从星期一到星期三 cóng xīngqīyī dào xīngqīsān from Monday to Wednesday; 从Y中减去X cóng Y zhōng jiǎnqù X deduct X from Y

从不 cóng bù never

从 … 下来 cóng … xiàlái get off

从此 cóngcǐ from now on; henceforth

匆匆 cōngcōng hurried

从句 cóngjù clause

从来 cónglái ever

从来不 cónglái bù never; 她从来不工作 tā cónglái bù gōngzuò she never does a stroke

从来没 cónglái méi (has) never; 他从来没去过那儿 tā cónglái méi qùguò nàr he has never been there

丛林 cónglín jungle

匆忙 **cōngmáng** hasty ◊ in a hurry; 匆忙做 … **cōngmáng zuò** … do … in a rush; 匆忙写 **cōngmáng xiě** dash off

聪敏 **cōngmǐn** smart

聪明 **cōngmíng** intelligent, bright, clever ◊ intelligence

从前 **cóngqián** earlier; in the past; once upon a time

从容 **cóngróng** calm; leisurely

从事 **cóngshì** engage in; deal with

从事间谍活动 **cóngshì jiàndié huódòng** spy

从头到尾 **cóngtóu dàowěi** from beginning to end; from top to toe; through

从头至尾 **cóngtóu zhìwěi** overall

从中 **cóngzhōng** from among; between; out of

从中获利 **cóngzhōng huòlì** cash in on

凑合 **còuhe** rough it; make the best of ◊ so-so, average

凑巧 **còuqiǎo** luckily; by chance

粗 **cū** thick; coarse; rough

醋 **cù** vinegar

促 **cù** urge

篡改 **cuàngǎi** fiddle, falsify

粗暴 **cūbào** rough; gruff; 粗暴地 对待 **cūbàode duìdài** manhandle

粗笨 **cūbèn** crude; awkward

粗糙 **cūcāo** coarse; rough

促成 **cùchéng** contribute to; shape

促动 **cùdòng** motivate

粗话 **cūhuà** bad language

催 **cuī** rush; drive; urge

摧 **cuī** break; destroy

脆 **cuì** fragile; brittle; crisp

催促 **cuīcù** hurry up; press for

催化转化器 **cuīhuà zhuǎnhuà qì** catalytic converter

摧毁 **cuīhuǐ** destroy; devastate

摧毁性 **cuīhuǐ xìng** devastating

催泪气 **cuīlèi qì** tear gas

催眠疗法 **cuīmián liáofǎ** hypnotherapy

催眠曲 **cuīmián qǔ** lullaby

催眠术 **cuīmiánshù** hypnosis

脆弱 **cuìruò** weak; frail

催账单 **cuīzhàng dān** reminder

促进 **cùjìn** advance, further; stimulate ◊ boost

醋栗 **cùlì** gooseberry

粗鲁 **cūlǔ** crude, vulgar; ignorant; fresh, impertinent; rude; 他 待她 很粗鲁 **tā dài tā hěn cūlǔ** he was very unpleasant to her

粗略 **cūlüè** rough; cursory

粗面 **cūmiàn** matt

村 **cūn** village

存 **cún** exist; survive; store; save

寸 **cùn** Chinese inch

存储 **cúnchǔ** deposit

存储力 **cúnchǔlì** memory COMPUT

存储芯片 **cúnchǔqì** memory chip

存储容量 **cúnchǔ róngliàng** storage capacity COMPUT

存放 **cúnfàng** keep, store; check (in checkroom)

存放行李处 **cúnfàng xíngli chù** baggage check

存根 **cúngēn** stub

存活 **cúnhuó** survive

存货 **cúnhuò** stock

存款 **cúnkuǎn** savings ◊ deposit

村里人 **cūnlǐ rén** villager

存盘 **cúnpán** save; saving

存入 **cúnrù** pay in; deposit; 存入 帐户 **cúnrù zhànghù** credit an amount to an account

村舍 **cūnshè** cottage

存为 **cúnwéi** save as COMPUT

存在 **cúnzài** exist ◊ existence

存折 **cúnzhé** bank book

村庄 **cūnzhuāng** village

错 **cuò** wrong ◊ mistake; fault; 是 你的 / 我的 错 **nǐde / wǒde cuò** it's your / my fault; 不错 **bú cuò** not bad; excellent; 错了 **cuòle** that's wrong; you're wrong

撮 **cuō** group, clump

搓 **cuō** rub; twist

挫 **cuò** foil, thwart

锉 **cuò** file

挫败 **cuòbài** foil, thwart

措词 **cuòcí** phrase ◊ wording

锉刀 **cuòdāo** file (for wood, nails)

错过 **cuòguò** miss

错觉 **cuòjué** misconception; illusion

错开 **cuòkāi** stagger

磋商 **cuōshāng** consult

挫伤 **cuòshāng** bruise

措施 **cuòshī** step, measure

错视 **cuòshì** optical illusion

错误 **cuòwù** error, mistake ◊ wrong; false ◊ wrongly; 犯错误 **fàn cuòwù** make a mistake; go wrong; 使 ... 犯错误 **shǐ ... fàn cuòwù** trip up; 错误地 **cuòwùde** by mistake

错印 **cuòyìn** misprint

挫折 **cuòzhé** setback; failure; rebuff

错综复杂 **cuòzōng-fùzá** complicated

粗砂 **cūshā** grit

粗石 **cūshí** rubble

促使 **cùshǐ** impel; spur; cause to happen

粗饲料 **cū sìliào** roughage

粗俗 **cūsú** coarse, vulgar; gross; tasteless

粗体 **cūtǐ** bold

粗心 **cūxīn** careless, slipshod; thoughtless

粗心大意 **cūxīn dàyì** negligent

簇叶丛生 **cùyè cóngshēng** overgrown

粗硬 **cūyìng** coarse

促孕药 **cùyùnyào** fertility drug

粗壮 **cūzhuàng** stocky

# D

答 **dā** reply, answer

搭 **dā** pitch; put up; take

打 **dá** dozen

达 **dá** arrive at, reach

答 **dá** reply, answer

打 **dǎ** hit, beat; play; make; do; get ◊ beating

大 **dà** big, large; great

答案 **dá'àn** answer

打败 **dǎbài** thrash; defeat ◊ thrashing; defeat; 被打败 **bèi dǎbài** get a thrashing

大白菜 **dàbáicài** Chinese cabbage

打扮 **dǎbàn** dress up; put on make-up; get dolled up ◊ style; dress; make-up

打包 **dǎbāo** package; pack; bale

大杯 **dàbēi** mug

大便 **dàbiàn** defecate; shit F ◊ feces; shit F

搭便车 **dā biànchē** ride, lift ◊ hitch a ride; get a lift

大鼻子 **dà bízi** *pej* Westerner; Caucasian (*literally*: big nose)

大伯子 **dàbózi** brother-in-law (*husband's older brother*)

大步 **dàbù** stride

打补丁 **dǎ bǔdīng** patch

大不列颠 **Dà Bùlièdiān** Great Britain ◊ British

打不碎 **dǎ bú suì** unbreakable

大步走 **dàbù zǒu** stride

打草图 **dǎ cǎotú** outline

大草原 **dàcǎoyuán** prairie

大吵大闹 **dàchǎo dà'nào** make a scene

搭车 **dāchē** thumb a ride; take a cab

搭乘 **dāchéng** fly

达成交易 **dáchéng jiāoyì** clinch a deal

达成协议 **dáchéng xiéyì** reach agreement on

大吃 **dàchī** big eater; food freak ◊ tuck away; gorge oneself

大吃大喝 **dàchīdàhē** eat, drink and be merry

大吃一惊 **dàchīyìjīng** stun; be flabbergasted

大锤 **dàchuí** sledge hammer

大吹大擂 **dàchuī dàléi** hype

大葱 **dàcōngī** leek; Chinese onion

大错 **dàcuò** blunder; big mistake

大胆 **dàdǎn** bold, daring

大胆地说 **dàdǎn de shuō** speak out

搭档 **dādàng** partner

搭档关系 **dādàng guānxi** partnership

达到 **dádào** come to; reach, attain; accomplish

大道 **dàdào** avenue; main road

达到顶峰 **dádào dǐngfēng** peak

打电话 **dǎ diànhuà** call, phone; make a call ◊ (tele)phone; 给 X 打电话 **gěi X dǎ diànhuà** give X a call

打电话给 **dǎ diànhuà gěi** call

打电话来 **dǎ diànhuà lái** call in

大调 **dàdiào** major MUS

大跌 **dàdiē** plummet

打动 **dǎdòng** touch, move

大豆 **dàdòu** soybean

打赌 **dǎdǔ** bet

打断 **dǎduàn** interrupt

打盹儿 **dǎdǔnr** doze; have a nap

大多数 **dà duōshù** bulk, majority; most

大都市 **dà dūshì** metropolis ◊ metropolitan

大肚子 **dà dùzi** paunch ◊ pregnant

打发 **dǎfa** idle away

大发雷霆 **dà fā léitíng** fly off the handle

大方 **dàfang** generous; liberal ◊ generosity

大方的举动 **dàfang de jùdòng**

带 **dài** bring; take ◊ belt; area; 我能带个朋友来吗? **wǒ néng dàige péngyǒu láima?** can I bring a friend?

大发脾气 **dàfā píqì** blow up, get really angry

大风 **dàfēng** gale

答复 **dáfù** answer; respond ◊ answer; response

大概 **dàgài** about, roughly ◊ rough, approximate

大纲 **dàgāng** syllabus

大钢琴 **dàgāngqín** grand piano

打嗝 **dǎgé** belch, burp

大哥 **dàgē** eldest brother; *a term of address for a man of similar age to oneself*

大哥大 **dàgēdà** cell phone

嗝儿 **dàgér** hiccup ◊ have the hiccups

大公无私 **dàgōng wúsī** selfless

搭钩 **dāgōu** buckle

打勾 **dǎgōu** check ◊ check(mark), tick

打鼓 **dǎgǔ** beat a drum; play drums

大褂 **dàguà** gown

达观 **dáguān** resilient

达官贵人 **dáguān guìrén** dignitary

打官司 **dǎ guānsī** sue; 和 X 打官司 **hé X dǎ guānsī** take X to court

大规模 **dàguīmó** wholesale, indiscriminate; large-scale

大姑姐 **dàgūjiě** sister-in-law (*husband's elder sister*)

大海 **dàhǎi** sea

打鼾 **dǎ hān** snore

大喊 **dàhǎn** call, call out; shout, shout out

大汗淋漓 **dàhàn línlí** covered in sweat

打哈欠 **dǎ hāqian** yawn

打呵欠 **dǎ hēqian** yawn

打滑 **dǎhuá** skid

大黄蜂 **dàhuángfēng** hornet

大会 **dàhuì** convention

打昏 **dǎhūn** stun

打火机 **dǎhuǒjī** (cigarette) lighter

打火钥匙 **dǎhuǒ yàoshi** ignition key

呆 **dāi** slow-witted; dull; blank ◊ F stay

待 **dāi** wait

带 **dài** bring; take ◊ belt; area

代 **dài** replace ◊ era; generation

袋 **dài** bag; pack

戴 **dài** put on; wear

贷 **dài** loan ◊ borrow, lend

待 **dài** await, wait for

呆板 **dāibǎn** mechanical ◊ mechanically

代表 **dàibiǎo** represent ◊ representative

代表大会 **dàibiǎo dàhuì** congress

代表人 **dàibiǎo rén** representative

代表团 **dàibiǎotuán** delegation

代表我／他 **dàibiǎo wǒ/tā** on my/his behalf

逮捕 **dàibǔ** arrest

代词 **dàicí** pronoun

贷方 **dàifāng** credit

大夫 **dàifu** doctor, physician

急工 **dàigōng** go-slow

代沟 **dàigōu** generation gap

待会 X **dāihuir** in a minute

代价 **dàijià** cost

代价惨重 **dàijià cǎnzhòng** costly

带菌者 **dàijùn zhě** carrier (*of disease*)

贷款 **dàikuǎn** loan

带来 **dàilái** bring; bring about

代理 **dàilǐ** represent; act for

代理处 **dàilǐ chù** agency

带领 **dàilǐng** lead; guide

代理权 **dàilǐ quán** proxy

代理人 **dàilǐ rén** agent; representative

代理商 **dàilǐ shāng** rep, representative; agent

急慢 **dàimàn** snub

代母 **dàimǔ** surrogate mother; godmother

带球 **dàiqiú** dribble SP

戴上帽子 **dàishang màozi** put one's hat on

待售 **dàishòu** for sale

代替 **dàitì** stand in for; substitute

代替人 **dàitìrén** replacement

歹徒 **dǎitú** mobster, gangster

带血 **dàixuè** bloody, blood-stained

呆一会儿 **dāi yíhuìr** stick around

代用品 **dàiyòngpǐn** makeshift

待遇 **dàiyù** perk; package; treatment

呆在 **dāizài** stay, remain; 呆在家里 **dāi zài jiālǐ** stay at home; 呆在一起 **dāi zài yìqǐ** stay together, stick together

带着 **dàizhe** carry; leave on

呆滞 **dāizhì** glazed *expression*

带状疱疹 **dàizhuàng pàozhěn** shingles

带子 **dàizi** belt; tape; strip

袋子 **dàizi** bag

打击 **dǎjī** blow ◊ hit; deal a blow to

打架 **dǎjià** fight

大家 **dàjiā** everyone; all of us

大剪刀 **dàjiǎndāo** shears

打搅 **dǎjiǎo** bother, disturb; 请勿打搅 **qǐngwù dǎjiǎo** please do not disturb

大叫 **dàjiào** shout, bawl, yell

打交道 **dǎ jiāodào** have dealings with

大教堂 **dà jiàotáng** cathedral

打结 **dǎjié** knot, tie

大姐 **dàjiě** eldest sister

大惊小怪 **dàjīng xiǎoguài** fuss

大祭司 **dà jìsī** high priest

搭救 **dājiù** save, rescue

打击乐 **dǎjīyuè** percussion

打击乐器 **dǎjī yuèqì** percussion instrument

大咀大嚼 **dàjǔdàjué** munch

打开 **dǎkāi** open; turn on; switch on ◊ wide-open

打开包裹 **dǎkāi bāoguǒ** unpack

打瞌睡 **dǎ kēshuì** doze off; snooze

打孔 **dǎ kǒng** punch *hole* ◊ perforated

打孔机 **dǎkǒngjī** punch *(tool)*

大口袋 **dà kǒudài** sack

大块 **dàkuài** chunk

打烂 **dǎlàn** break down

打雷 **dǎléi** thunder

打量 **dǎliang** look over; size up

大梁 **dàliáng** girder

大量 **dàliàng** generous; great; heavy; plentiful ◊ wealth of; loads of

大量买进 **dàliàng mǎijìn** buy up

大量生产 **dàliàng shēngchǎn** mass-produce ◊ mass-production

打猎 **dǎliè** hunt

打临时工 **dǎ línshígōng** (work as a) temp

大理石 **dàlǐshí** marble

大陆 **dàlù** continent, mainland; mainland China

大路 **dàlù** main road

打乱 **dǎluàn** disrupt; screw up

大麻 **dàmá** hemp; marijuana

大马哈鱼 **dàmǎhāyú** salmon

大麦 **dàmài** barley

大门 **dàmén** (entrance) door; gate

打磨机 **dǎmójī** sander

大模型 **dàmóxíng** mock-up

大牧场 **dà mùchǎng** ranch

单 **dān** simple; only; single; odd *number* ◊ list; sheet; bill

担 **dān** carry on one's shoulder; undertake

丹 **dān** red

胆 **dǎn** gall bladder; courage, guts

蛋 **dàn** egg

氮 **dàn** nitrogen

淡 **dàn** faint; weak; bland *taste*; pale *color*; light; 淡粉 **dànfěn** pale pink

诞 **dàn** birth

但 **dàn** but; only

旦 **dàn** dawn

担 **dàn** burden

弹 **dàn** bullet; bomb; pellet

大男人主义者 **dà nánrén zhǔyì zhě** chauvinist

大男子气 **dànánziqì** macho

大闹一场 **dànào yìchǎng** kick up a stink

蛋白 **dànbái** white *(of egg)*

蛋白质 **dànbáizhì** protein

担保 **dānbǎo** guarantee; vouch for; sponsor ◊ sponsorship

担保人 **dānbǎo rén** guarantor; sponsor

单薄 **dānbó** scanty

蛋炒饭 **dànchǎofàn** egg fried rice

诞辰 **dànchén** birthday

单程 **dānchéng** one-way

单程票 **dānchéng piào** one-way ticket

单纯 dānchún simple; pure; alone

单词 dāncí word

单打 dāndǎ singles (*in tennis*)

弹道导弹 dàndào dǎodàn ballistic missile

单调 dāndiào monotonous; dull; drab

单调乏味 dāndiào fáwèi monotonous

单独 dāndú alone; independently of; in isolation

单方面 dān fāngmiàn unilateral

当 dāng work as; equal; should ◊ when; just at; 当 … 的时候 dāng … de shíhòu when …; 把 X 当成 Y bǎ X dāngchéng Y confuse X with Y

党 dǎng party

挡 dǎng block, obstruct ◊ gear

档 dàng shelf; file

荡 dàng shake; swing

当 dàng right; proper ◊ pawn; equal; treat as; think

胆敢 dǎngǎn dare

档案 dàng'àn file; records; archives

档案室 dàng'ànshì archives

档案箱 dàng'ànxiāng file cabinet

蛋糕 dàngāo cake

当场 dāngchǎng immediately, on the spot; 当场抓获 *dāngchǎng zhuāhuò* caught in the very act

当代 dāngdài contemporary ◊ the present era

党代会 dǎngdàihuì party conference

当地 dāngdì local

当地人 dāngdì rén native; local

当地时间 dāngdì shíjiān local time

当地特产 dāngdì tèchǎn local produce

耽搁 dāngé detain, hold up

挡风玻璃 dǎngfēng bōlí windshield

当今 dāngjīn nowadays

当局 dāngjú the authorities

挡路 dǎnglù be in the way

当铺 dàngpù pawnshop

当前 dāngqián present

荡秋千 dàng qiūqiān swing; rock

当权 dāngquán ruling

当权派 dāngquánpài the Establishment

当权者 dāngquán zhě the authorities; decision-maker

当然 dāngrán of course, naturally; 当然可以 *dāngrán kěyǐ* by all means

当时 dāngshí at that time; then

当天 dàngtiān on the same day

胆固醇 dǎngùchún cholesterol

党委 dǎngwěi party committee

当心 dāngxīn be careful

当演员 dāng yǎnyuán go on the stage

党员 dǎngyuán party member

当中 dāngzhōng in the middle

当众 dāngzhòng in public, publicly

党中央 Dǎng-Zhōngyāng Communist Party Central Committee

挡住 dǎngzhù block out

淡化 dànhuà play down

蛋黄 dànhuáng yolk

单簧管 dānhuángguǎn clarinet

淡季 dànjì low season, off-season

担架 dānjià stretcher

单价 dānjià unit cost; unit price

单脚跳 dānjiǎotiào hop

胆结石 dǎnjiéshí gallstone

蛋壳 dànké eggshell

胆量 dǎnliàng guts, nerve

丹麦 Dānmài Denmark ◊ Danish

胆囊 dǎnnáng gall bladder

单排扣 dānpáikòu single-breasted

单枪匹马 dānqiāng pīmǎ single-handed

胆怯 dǎnqiè cowardly

单亲 dānqīn single parent

单亲家庭 dānqīn jiātíng single parent family

单曲唱片 dānqǔ chàngpiàn single (*record*)

单人 dānrén solo

担任 dānrèn take on; act as

单人床 dānrénchuáng single bed

单人房间 dānrén fángjiān single room

单人沙发 dānrén shāfā armchair

单色 dānsè plain, self-colored
淡色 dànsè tint
单身 dānshēn single, unmarried
诞生 dànshēng be born ◊ birth
单身汉 dānshēn hàn bachelor
单身母亲 dānshēn mǔqīn single mother
单身女子 dānshēn nǚzi single woman
但是 dànshì but; nevertheless
单数 dānshù singular
淡水 dànshuǐ fresh water
单体 dāntǐ module
单体设计 dāntǐ shèjì modular
弹头 dàntóu warhead
大怒 dànù be fuming
淡忘 dànwàng gradually forget
单位 dānwèi unit; work unit
耽误 dānwù delay, hold up
胆小 dǎnxiǎo cowardice ◊ cowardly
胆小鬼 dǎnxiǎo guǐ coward
担心 dānxīn be afraid of; worry ◊ apprehensive; worried; 令人担心 lìngrén dānxīn worrying
单行道 dānxíng dào one-way street
弹药 dànyào ammunition
单一 dānyī isolated
担忧 dānyōu worry, concern; disturb, trouble ◊ worried ◊ worry
单元 dānyuán unit
但愿 dànyuàn hopefully
单张 dānzhāng leaflet
胆汁 dǎnzhī bile
胆子 dǎnzi courage
担子 dànzi burden
胆子大 dǎnzi dà brave
胆子小 dǎnzi xiǎo cowardly
刀 dāo knife
岛 dǎo island
捣 dǎo pound; thresh; attack
导 dǎo guide; lead; conduct
倒 dǎo fall; fall down; trip over; close down ◊ change; exchange
道 dào way; road; path; Tao ◊ say
倒 dào empty; pour; tip over; rewind; reverse ◊ upside-down ◊ however; actually; maybe
到 dào arrive; reach ◊ to; up to; 到时间了 dào shíjiān le time is up;

到我那儿去 dào wǒ nàr qù go to my place
盗 dào steal ◊ thief
悼 dào mourn
稻 dào paddy; rice
盗版 dàobǎn pirate ◊ pirate copy
倒闭 dàobì go bankrupt, go bust
倒彩 dàocǎi catcall; boo
稻草人 dàocǎorén scarecrow
到场 dàochǎng appear
倒车 dàochē back, reverse car
倒出 dàochū pour out
到处 dàochù everywhere
悼词 dàocí lament
到此为止 dàocǐ wéizhǐ as yet
到达 dàodá arrival; arrivals ◊ arrive; come in; come to; get in; get to, reach ◊ in, arrived
导弹 dǎodàn (guided) missile
捣蛋 dǎodàn get up to mischief
倒档 dàodǎng reverse gear
道德 dàodé morals, ethics
道德高尚 dàodé gāoshàng virtuous
道德经 Dàodéjīng Tao Te Ching
到底 dàodǐ ever; at last; after all ◊ to the end
祷告 dǎogào prayer; 道高一尺，魔高一丈 dàogāo yìchǐ, mógāo yízhàng prov magic works better than doctrine
稻谷 dàogǔ rice (as crop)
倒光 dàoguāng drain
导火线 dǎohuǒ xiàn fuse; catalyst
到家 dàojiā get in; get home
道家 Dàojiā Taoism, Taoist philosophy
道具 dàojù prop
倒空 dàokōng empty
到来 dàolái arrive, show up ◊ appearance
道理 dàolǐ sense; reason; principle; truth
道路 dàolù road
捣乱 dǎoluàn cause trouble; create unrest
捣乱分子 dǎoluàn fènzǐ

undesirable element

搗乱者 **dǎoluàn zhě** troublemaker

倒霉 **dǎoméi** have bad luck ◊ unfortunate

悼念 **dàoniàn** mourn

到期 **dàoqī** become due; mature; expire; be up

道歉 **dàoqiàn** apologize ◊ apology

盗窃 **dàoqiè** steal; burglarize ◊ break-in, burglary

道士 **Dàoshì** Taoist priest

倒数第二 **dàoshǔ dì'er** penultimate

倒数数 **dào shǔshù** countdown

倒塌 **dǎotā** collapse, cave in

倒台 **dǎotái** fall

稻田 **dàotián** paddy field, ricefield

倒下 **dǎoxià** fall down; collapse

导线 **dǎoxiàn** (electrical) wire; cable

倒叙 **dàoxù** flashback

导演 **dǎoyǎn** direct *play, movie* ◊ direction ◊ director

盗用 **dàoyòng** embezzle ◊ embezzlement

导游 **dǎoyóu** courier; guide

导游旅游 **dǎoyóu lǚyóu** guided tour

岛屿 **dǎoyǔ** island

岛屿人 **dǎoyǔ rén** islander

导致 **dǎozhì** result in; set off

倒置 **dàozhì** invert

稻子 **dàozi** paddy

大炮 **dàpào** artillery; cannon

打喷嚏 **dǎ pēntì** sneeze

打屁股 **dǎ pìgǔ** spank

打平局 **dǎ píngjú** draw (*in match*)

大皮箱 **dà píxiāng** trunk

打破 **dǎpò** break; 打破沉默 **dǎpò chénmò** break the ice

打破纪录 **dǎpò jìlù** record-breaking

大气 **dàqì** atmosphere

大气外层 **dàqì wàicéng** upper atmosphere

大气污染 **dàqì wūrǎn** atmospheric pollution

打圈 **dǎquān** circle

大群 **dàqún** swarm; crowd

打扰 **dǎrǎo** disturb; trespass on

打入 **dǎrù** infiltrate; penetrate

打扫 **dǎsǎo** sweep; clean

大扫除 **dà sǎochú** spring-cleaning

打扫干净 **dǎsǎo gānjìng** clean out

大厦 **dàshà** high-rise building

打闪 **dǎshǎn** flash (*of lightning*)

打伤 **dǎshāng** wound

大赦 **dàshè** amnesty

大声 **dàshēng** in a loud voice

大声点 **dàshēng diǎn** speak up

大声呼喊 **dàshēng hūhǎn** give a cry; shout

大声说出 **dàshēng shuōchū** cry out

大声笑 **dàshēng xiào** roar with laughter

大使 **dàshǐ** ambassador

大使馆 **dàshǐguǎn** embassy

大手大脚的人 **dàshǒu dàjiǎo** wasteful; extravagant; 大手大脚 地花钱 **dàshǒu dàjiǎo di huāqián** splash out

打手势 **dǎ shǒushì** gesticulate

打算 **dǎsuàn** intend; plan

大蒜 **dàsuàn** garlic

打碎 **dǎsuì** shatter; break ◊ broken, bust

大体来说 **dàtǐ láishuō** broadly speaking

打听 **dǎtīng** pry; inquire about; make enquiries; 向 X 打听 Y **xiàng X dǎtīng Y** ask X about Y

大厅 **dàtīng** hall

大提琴 **dà tíqín** cello

大体上 **dàtǐshang** in general

打通 **dǎtōng** (*on telephone*) get through

大头针 **dàtóuzhēn** pin

大腿 **dàtuǐ** thigh

打退堂鼓 **dǎ tuìtánggǔ** back off; get cold feet, chicken out

大屠杀 **dà túshā** carnage; massacre

大为 **dàwéi** great achievement ◊ greatly; 使大为吃惊 **shǐ dàwéi chījīng** amaze; 大为惊讶 **dàwéi jīngyà** marvel at

大乌鸦 **dà wūyā** raven

大虾 **dàxiā** shrimp

大象 dàxiàng elephant

大小 dàxiǎo size

打消疑虑 dǎxiāo yílǜ reassure

大写 dàxiě print (in block letters) ◊ capitalization; full form of Chinese numeral

大写字母 dàxiě zìmǔ capital letter(s)

)大型 dàxíng large-scale

猩猩 dàxīngxing gorilla

大型衣柜 dàxíng yīguì walk-in closet

大型游艇 dàxíng yóutǐng cruise liner

大修 dàxiū overhaul

大西洋 Dàxīyáng Atlantic

大学毕业后 dàxué bìyèhòu postgraduate

大削减 dà xuējiǎn slash, cut

大学生 dàxué shēng (college) student; undergraduate

大烟囱 dà yāncōng stack

打哑语 dǎ yǎyǔ mime

大衣 dàyī overcoat

大意 dàyì gist

大意 dàyì careless

打印 dǎyìn print, run off

答应 dāying reply; agree

打印机 dǎyìnjī printer

打印文本 dǎyìn wénběn hard copy

大雨 dàyǔ deluge; 大雨倾盆 dàyǔ qīngpén it's pouring (with rain)

大约 dàyuē approximate ◊ approximately, around, in the region of ◊ thereabouts

大跃进 Dàyuèjìn Great Leap Forward

大运河 Dàyùnhé Grand Canal

大斋节 Dàzhāijié Lent

打颤 dǎzhàn chatter

大帐篷 dàzhàngpéng marquee

打招呼 dǎ zhāohu greet

打折扣 dǎ zhékòu discount

大致 dàzhì more or less

大致说来 dàzhì shuōlái basically

打中 dǎzhòng hit *target*

大众 dàzhòng the masses

大众传媒 dàzhòng chuánméi

mass media

大众化 dàzhònghuà popularize

打字 dǎzì type

大字标题 dàzì biāotí headline

打字机 dǎzì jī typewriter

打字员 dǎzìyuán typist

大宗 dàzōng block

大走财运 dàzǒucáiyùn make a killing

打坐 dǎzuò meditate ◊ meditation

大作 dàzuò great work, masterpiece

的名字 shūde míngzi the title of the book ◊ (*makes adjectives attributive*): 漂亮的姑娘 piàoliangde gūniang a beautiful girl ◊ (*introducing relative clause*): 我喜欢的宾馆 wǒ xǐhuande bīnguǎn the hotel which I prefer

得 de (*before a qualifying word*): 好得多 / 容易得多 hǎo de duō / róngyì de duō a lot better / a lot easier ◊ (*when result of an action is expressed*): 看得见 kàn de jiàn be able to see

地 de (*to form adverbs*): 高兴地 gāoxìngde happily

得 dé get, obtain

德 dé morals; virtue

得不偿失 dé bùchángshī the loss outweighs the gain; 做 X 得不偿失 zuò X dé bùchángshī it doesn't pay to do X

得到 dédào get, obtain; reach *decision*

得到 ... 的风声 dédào ... de fēngshēng get wind of

得到消息 dédào xiāoxi hear from; get news of

得分 défēn score

得分运动员 défēn yùndòngyuán scorer

得感冒 dé gǎnmào catch (a) cold

德国 Déguó Germany ◊ German

得过且过 déguòqiěguò muddle along

得啦 , 得啦 déla, déla now, now!

得了 déle alright, that's enough!; 得了吧！déleba! will you stop that!

得了 … 病 déle … bìng be sickening for

得力助手 délì zhùshǒu righthand man

灯 dēng light; lamp

登 dēng climb

等 děng wait; grade, class; 你 等 着 吧 ! **nǐ děngzhe ba!** just you wait!; 让 X 等 **ràng X děng** keep X waiting; 我们 等 他 准备 好 **wǒmen děng tā zhǔnbèihǎo** we'll wait until he's ready

凳 dèng stool

登场 dēngchǎng appear ◊ appearance (*in movie*)

等待 děngdài wait; wait for ◊ waiting

等等 děngděng and so on, etc ◊ hang on

登高 dēnggāo climb a mountain

登广告 dēng guǎnggào advertise

登广告者 dēng guǎnggào zhě advertiser

等候 děnghòu wait

等候室 děnghòushì waiting room

等候者名单 děnghòuzhě míngdān waiting list

登记 dēngjì check in; register; book ◊ registration

等级 děngjí class; classification; grade; rank

等价 děngjià of equivalent value

登记簿 dēngjì bù register

登机卡 dēngjī kǎ boarding card

登机口 dēngjīkǒu gate (*at airport*)

登记人 dēngjì rén registrar

等级制度 děngjí zhìdù hierarchy

灯笼 dēnglong lantern

灯泡 dēngpào light bulb

登山 dēngshān mountaineering

登山者 dēngshān zhě mountaineer, climber

等式 děngshì equation

灯塔 dēngtǎ lighthouse

等同 děngtóng equal

等退票 děng tuìpiào on standby

等退票旅客 děng tuìpiào lǚkè standby passenger

邓小平 Dèng Xiǎopíng Deng Xiaoping

邓小平理论 Dèng Xiǎopíng lǐlùn Deng Xiaoping theory

灯芯绒 dēngxīnróng corduroy

灯芯绒裤 dēngxīnróng kù cords

等一下 děngyíxià hold on; wait a moment

等于 děngyú equal; correspond to

灯罩 dēngzhào (lamp)shade

凳子 dèngzi stool

得体 déti proper; tactful

得知 dézhī become aware of

得罪 dézuì insult; offend

滴 dī drop; blob ◊ drip; trickle

堤 dī dike

低 dī low; junior

笛 dí bamboo flute

敌 dí enemy

底 dǐ bottom

递 dì pass

帝 dì emperor

弟 dì younger brother

第 dì *used to create ordinal numbers*

递 dì hand over, deliver

地 dì the earth; land; ground

堤岸 dī'àn embankment

点 diǎn dot; (decimal) point; point; drop; spot ◊ dip; dunk ◊ a little, some ◊ o'clock 好 / 容易 点 儿 了 吗 ? **hǎo / róngyì diǎnr le ma?** is that any better / easier?; 几 点 了 ? **jǐdiǎnle?** what's the time?

碘 diǎn iodine

电 diàn electric(al) ◊ electricity

垫 diàn cushion; mat

店 diàn store; shop

电报 diànbào telegram

颠簸 diānbǒ jolt ◊ bumpy

点菜 diǎncài order (*in restaurant*)

电唱机 diànchàngjī record player

电唱盘 diànchàng pán turntable

电车 diànchē streetcar

垫衬 diànchèn pad

电池 diànchí battery

典当 diǎndàng pawn

颠倒 diāndǎo reverse; 把 X 上 下 颠 倒 过 来 **bǎ X shàngxià diāndǎo guòlái** turn X upside down

颠倒黑白 diāndǎo hēibái topsy-turvy

电灯 diàndēng electric light

电灯泡 **diàndēng pào** light bulb

点滴 **diǎndī** drip MED

电动机 **diàndòng jī** dynamo

典范 **diǎnfàn** characterize ◊ example; model

电饭锅 **diànfànguō** rice cooker

淀粉 **diànfěn** starch; cornstarch

颠覆分子 **diānfù fènzǐ** subversive

电工 **diàngōng** electrician

佃户 **diànhù** tenant

电话 **diànhuà** telephone; 打个电话 **dǎ ge diànhuà** make a telephone call

电话簿 **diànhuà bù** phone book

电话磁卡 **diànhuà cíkǎ** phonecard

电话费 **diànhuà fèi** toll TELEC

电话号码 **diànhuà hàomǎ** telephone number

电话机 **diànhuàjī** telephone

电话交换台 **diànhuà jiāohuàntái** switchboard

电话亭 **diànhuà tíng** phone booth

电话线 **diànhuà xiàn** telephone line

点火 **diǎnhuǒ** light *fire*

点击 **diǎnjī** click COMPUT

电级 **diànjí** electrode

电缆 **diànlǎn** electricity cable

电缆塔 **diànlǎntǎ** pylon

典礼 **diǎnlǐ** ceremony ◊ ceremonial

垫料 **diànliào** pad; padding; upholstery

电流 **diànliú** electric current

电炉 **diànlú** hotplate; electric stove

点名 **diǎnmíng** roll call

电脑 **diànnǎo** computer

电脑化 **diànnǎo huà** computerize

电脑空间 **diànnǎo kōngjiān** cyberspace

电脑控制 **diànnǎo kòngzhì** computer-controlled

电脑使用 **diànnǎo shǐyòng** computing

惦念 **diànniàn** worry; worry about

电脑站 **diànnǎo zhàn** computer terminal

垫片 **diànpiàn** gasket; washer

电气 **diànqì** electricity

电器 **diànqì** electrical appliance

点燃 **diǎnrán** ignite

电热水器 **diàn rèshuǐqì** immersion heater

电热毯 **diànrètǎn** electric blanket

电扇 **diànshàn** electric fan

电视 **diànshì** television; 电视上 **diànshì shang** on TV

电视会议 **diànshì huìyì** video conference

电视机 **diànshì jī** television set

电视节目 **diànshì jiémù** television program

电视摄影室 **diànshì shèyǐng shì** television studio

电视游戏 **diànshì yóuxì** video game

电死 **diànsǐ** electrocute

电台 **diàntái** station RAD, TV

电梯 **diàntī** elevator

电筒 **diàntǒng** flashlight

点头 **diǎntóu** nod

玷污 **diànwū** taint; cast a slur on

癫痫 **diānxián** epileptic

点线 **diǎnxiàn** dotted line

电线 **diànxiàn** cable; wire; power line

癫痫发作 **diānxián fāzuò** epileptic fit

电线杆 **diànxiàn gān** telegraph pole

癫痫症 **diānxiánzhèng** epilepsy

点心 **diǎnxīn** dim sum

电信 **diànxìn** telecommunications

典型 **diǎnxíng** characteristic; classic; representative; typical ◊ typically; 典型美国人 **diǎnxíng měiguórén** typically American

电压 **diànyā** voltage

点烟 **diǎnyān** light up *cigarette*

电椅 **diànyǐ** electric chair

电影 **diànyǐng** movie, motion picture

电影剧本 **diànyǐng jùběn** screenplay

电影迷 **diànyǐng mí** movie buff

电影明星 **diànyǐng míngxīng** movie star

电影院 **diànyǐng yuàn** movie theater

电影预告片 diànyǐng yùgào piān trailer

店员 diànyuán sales clerk

电源电缆 diànyuán diànlǎn power cable

点钟 diǎnzhōng o'clock; 五点钟 wǔdiǎnzhōng five o'clock

店主 diànzhǔ landlord; shopkeeper

点缀 diǎnzhuì decorate; jazz up

点子 diǎnzi pointer; 出点子 chū diǎnzi give advice

电子 diànzǐ electron ◊ electronic

垫子 diànzi cushion; padding

电子表 diànzǐbiǎo quartz watch

电子数据处理 diànzǐ shùjù chǔlǐ electronic data processing, EDP

电子信箱 diànzǐ xìnxiāng e-mail address

电子学 diànzǐxué electronics

电子邮件 diànzǐ yóujiàn e-mail; 打电子邮件 dǎ diànzǐ yóujiàn e-mail, send an e-mail

电子遊戏 diànzǐ yóuxì computer game

凋 diāo wither

雕 diāo carve; engrave

刁 diāo wily

调 diào move, transfer

吊 diào hang; suspend

钓 diào fish with hook and line

掉 diào come out (of stain) ◊ (getting rid of): 吃掉 chī diào eat up; 擦掉 cā diào wipe off; 卖掉 mài diào sell off; 掉了 diàole come away (of button etc)

碉堡 diāobǎo fortress

调查 diàochá look into, check out; investigate; poll; survey ◊ investigation

调查方法 diàochá fāngfǎ line of inquiry

吊床 diàochuáng hammock

钓到 diàodào catch fish

吊灯 diàodēng chandelier

调动 diàodòng transfer

钓竿 diàogān fishing rod

调换 diàohuàn exchange

吊架 diàojià trapeze

雕刻 diāokè carve; engrave

雕刻 (塑) diāokè (sù) sculpture

雕刻 (塑) 家 diáokè (sù) jiā sculptor

吊裤带 diàokùdài suspenders

掉落 diàoluò fall out

刁难 diāonàn give a hard time; create difficulties; be obstructive

貂皮 diāopí mink

貂皮大衣 diāopí dàyī mink (coat)

吊桥 diàoqiáo suspension bridge

掉色 diàoshǎi fade

吊死 diàosǐ hang

雕塑 diāosù sculpture

吊索运输车 diàosuǒ yùnshūchē ski lift

调头 diàotóu turn around

吊袜带 diàowàdài garter

凋谢 diāoxiè wither

吊唁 diàoyàn offer condolences

钓鱼 diàoyú go fishing

钓鱼杆 diàoyúgān fishing rod

掉转 diàozhuǎn steer; turn

第八 dì bā eighth

地板 dìbǎn floor; floorboard

第八十 dì bāshí eightieth

底部 dǐbù base; bottom

地产 dìchǎn estate

低潮 dīcháo low tide

底朝上 dǐ cháo shàng upside down

低沉 dīchén low; deep; oppressive

滴答 dīdā tick (of clock)

抵达 dǐdá arrive at

地带 dìdài zone; area

抵挡 dǐdǎng resist; repel

地道 dìdào authentic; idiomatic

低地 dīdì lowlands

弟弟 dìdi younger brother

地点 dìdiǎn place; spot; location

低调 dī diào low key

敌对 díduì hostile

跌 diē fall; stumble

爹 diē dad, pop

叠 dié stack, pile

蝶 dié butterfly

跌倒 diēdǎo fall over

爹爹 diēdie dad, pop

喋喋不休 diédié bùxiū chatter

跌跌撞撞 diēdie zhuàngzhuàng stagger

跌价 **diējià** price drop

跌落 **diēluò** drop

第二 **dì'èr** second; 第二大 **dì'èr dà** second biggest; 第二好 **dì'èr hǎo** second best

第二点 **dì'èrdiǎn** secondly

第二十 **dì'èrshí** twentieth

第二天 **dì'èr tiān** the day after

蝶泳 **diéyǒng** butterfly stroke

碟子 **diézi** dish

提防 **dīfáng** be on one's guard against

地方 **dìfāng** place ◊ local

地方政府 **dìfāng zhèngfǔ** local government

低峰时间 **dīfēng shíjiān** off-peak

滴干 **dīgān** drip-dry

低估 **dīgū** underestimate; undervalue

帝国 **dìguó** empire

帝国主义 **dìguó zhǔyì** imperialism

诋毁 **dǐhuǐ** slur

低级 **dījí** low; crude

地基 **dìjī** foundations

地极 **dìjí** pole ◊ polar

递交 **dìjiāo** hand over; deliver

地窖 **dìjiào** cellar; vaults

缔结 **dìjié** conclude *contract*

第九 **dì jiǔ** ninth

第九十 **dì jiǔshí** ninetieth

低卡路里 **dī kǎlùlǐ** low-calorie

抵抗 **dǐkàng** resist ◊ resistance

地雷 **dìléi** (land) mine

地理 **dìlǐ** geography

低廉 **dīlián** knockdown price

低领口 **dī lǐngkǒu** low-cut

第六 **dìliù** sixth

第六十 **dì liùshí** sixtieth

地理学 **dìlǐxué** geography

低落 **dīluò** subdued

弟妹 **dìmèi** sister-in-law (*younger brother's wife*); younger brothers and sisters

地面 **dìmiàn** ground; bottom

地面控制 **dìmiàn kòngzhì** ground control

低能 **dīnéng** ineffectual; mentally handicapped

低能儿 **dīnéng'ér** imbecile

叮 **dīng** sting; stab

钉 **dīng** nail; staple

丁 **dīng** cube

盯 **dīng** stare

顶 **dǐng** top; crest ◊ replace; cope with; push up ◊ very ◊ *measure word for hats*: 一顶草帽 **yìdǐng cǎomào** a straw hat

锭 **dìng** ingot

定 **dìng** set, fix; 那就定了！ **nà jiù dìng le!** that settles it!

订 **dìng** order; subscribe

钉 **dìng** nail

定菜单 **dìng càidān** order (*in restaurant*)

定餐 **dìngcān** set meal

顶层公寓 **dǐngcéng gōngyù** penthouse

顶层楼座 **dǐngcéng lóuzuò** gallery

订单 **dìngdān** order (*for goods*); order form

叮当声 **dīngdāng shēng** tinkle; clink

顶点 **dǐngdiǎn** summit; culmination

定额 **dìng'é** quota; target

定发胶 **dìng fàjiāo** lacquer

顶峰 **dǐngfēng** high point, peak

顶风 **dǐngfēng** against the wind ◊ headwind

定购 **dìnggòu** order

定冠词 **dìngguàncí** definite article

订户 **dìnghù** customer; subscriber

订婚 **dìnghūn** engaged ◊ get engaged ◊ engagement

订婚戒指 **dìnghūn jièzhǐ** engagement ring

订货 **dìnghuò** order goods

定价 **dìngjià** price *goods*; set a price

订计划 **dìng jìhuà** plan

定金 **dìngjīn** deposit; down payment

订机票 **dìng jīpiào** book a flight

定居 **dìngjū** settle (down)

钉牢 **dìngláo** fix

定量 **dìngliàng** quota

定量供应 **dìngliàng gōngyìng** ration

顶楼 **dǐnglóu** garret

定论 **dìnglùn** verdict

钉帽 **dīngmào** head (*of nail*)

定名 **dìngmíng** entitled *book*

定期 **dìngqī** regular ◊ periodically ◊ set a date

定期航班 **dìngqī hángbān** scheduled flight

盯梢 **dīngshāo** tail, shadow

定时器 **dìngshíqì** timer; time switch

定时炸弹 **dìngshí zhàdàn** time bomb

订书钉 **dìngshūdīng** staple

订书机 **dìngshūjī** stapler

定位 **dìngwèi** location

丁香 **dīngxiāng** lilac

定向发射 **dìngxiàng fāshè** beam

丁香花 **dīngxiāng huā** lilac

定义 **dìngyì** definition

订阅 **dìngyuè** subscribe to *publication*

订阅者 **dìngyuè zhě** subscriber (*to publication*)

盯着 **dīngzhe** stare at; 盯着 X 的眼睛 **dìngzhe X de yǎnjīng** look X straight in the eye

顶针 **dīngzhēn** thimble

顶住 **dǐngzhù** resist

订桌 **dìngzhuō** book a table

钉子 **dīngzi** brush-off; snub; nail; 钉钉子 **dìng dīngzi** hammer in a nail

定罪 **dìngzuì** conviction (*criminal*) ◊ convict

定做 **dìngzuò** made-to-measure; tailor-made

底盘 **dǐpán** chassis

地皮 **dìpí** plot of land to build on

底片 **dǐpiàn** negative (*photographic*)

地平线 **dìpíngxiàn** horizon

第七 **dì qī** seventh

地勤人员 **dìqín rényuán** ground crew, ground staff

第七十 **dì qīshí** seventieth

地球 **dìqiú** earth; world; globe

地球居民 **dìqiú jūmín** terrestrial

地球仪 **dìqiúyí** globe

低气压区 **dī qìyā qū** low (*in weather*)

地区 **dìqū** area; neighborhood; region ◊ regional

的确 **díquè** indeed; undeniably

敌人 **dírén** enemy

第三 **dìsān** third ◊ thirdly

第三方保险 **dìsān fāng bǎoxiǎn** third-party *or* liability insurance

第三个 **dìsān gè** third

第三十 **dìsānshí** thirtieth

第三世界 **Dìsān Shìjiè** Third World

第三者 **dìsānzhě** third party

低声 **dīshēng** softly

低声说 **dīshēng shuō** whisper; mutter

第十 **dìshí** tenth

地势 **dìshì** terrain

第十八 **dì shíbā** eighteenth

第十二 **dì shí'èr** twelfth

第十六 **dì shíliù** sixteenth

第十七 **dì shíqī** seventeenth

第十三 **dì shísān** thirteenth

第十四 **dìshísì** fourteenth

第十五 **dì shíwǔ** fifteenth

第十一 **dì shíyī** eleventh

滴水 **dīshuǐ** drain

第四 **dìsì** fourth

迪斯科 **dísīkē** disco

第四十 **dìsìshí** fortieth

递送 **dìsòng** deliver

地毯 **dìtǎn** carpet

地铁 **dìtiě** subway

迪厅 **dítīng** disco

低头 **dītóu** bow; duck *head*

地图 **dìtú** map

地图册 **dìtúcè** atlas

丢 **diū** lose; throw away

丢掉 **diūdiào** throw away

丢脸 **diūliǎn** lose face ◊ humiliating

丢弃 **diūqì** dump

丢失 **diūshī** lose

丢下 X 不管 **diūxià X bùguǎn** leave X unattended

低微 **dīwēi** humble

地位 **dìwèi** position, standing, status

地位低 **dìwèi dī** junior

地位低下 **dìwèi dīxià** underprivileged

第五 **dìwǔ** fifth

第五十 **dì wǔshí** fiftieth

低下 dīxià menial
地下 dìxià underground
地线 dìxiàn ground ELEC
抵消 dǐxiāo offset
地下室 dìxiàshì basement
地下通道 dìxià tōngdào underpass
地形 dìxíng geography; terrain
抵押 dǐyā mortgage
低压地区 dīyā dìqū low-pressure area
低压区 dīyā qū depression (*meteorological*)
敌意 díyì animosity, antagonism, hostility
第一 dìyī first; leading
第一百 dì yìbǎi hundredth
第一次 dìyīcì the first time
第一个 dìyīgè first
第一流 dìyīliú ace; first-class
低音提琴 dīyīn tíqín double-bass
低音乐器 dīyīn yuèqì bass
第一千个 dì yì qiān gè thousandth
第一手 dìyīshǒu at first hand
低于 dīyú below, beneath
低语 dīyǔ murmur
地狱 dìyù hell
低噪音 dī zàoyīn quiet
地震 dìzhèn earthquake
地震学 dìzhènxué seismology
地支 dìzhī earthly branches (*in Chinese calendar*)
抵制 dǐzhì resist; boycott
地址 dìzhǐ address
地质 dìzhì geology ◊ geological
低脂肪 dīzhīfáng low-fat
地质学 dìzhìxué geology
地质学者 dìzhìxué zhě geologist
地主 dìzhǔ land owner
笛子 dízi flute
底座 dǐzuò base
东 dōng east
鸫 dōng robin
冬 dōng winter
懂 dǒng understand; know
洞 dòng hole; cave
动 dòng move; 别动来动去! *bié dònglái dòngqù!* keep still!
冻 dòng freeze; 我冻坏了 *wǒ dònghuài le* I'm frozen

栋 dòng *measure word for houses*; 一栋房屋 *yídòng fángwū* a house
东北 dōngběi northeast
东部 dōngbù eastern
洞察 dòngchá insight
洞察力 dòngchálì perception
动产 dòngchǎn moveable assets
冻疮 dòngchuāng chilblain
动词 dòngcí verb
动荡不定 dòngdàng búdìng unstable
东道主 dōngdàozhǔ host
东方 dōngfāng east; the East; Orient ◊ eastern; oriental; Oriental
东方人 dōngfāng rén Oriental
冬菇 dōnggū dried winter mushroom
东海 Dōnghǎi East China Sea
懂行 dǒngháng expert
恫吓 dònghè threaten; intimidate
动画片 dònghuà piān animated cartoon
动画片摄制 dònghuà piān shèzhì animation
动机 dòngjī motive
冻僵 dòngjiāng numb with cold, frozen stiff
冻结 dòngjié freeze
冬季运动 dōngjì yùndòng winter sports
东拉西扯 dōnglā xīchě ramble (*in speaking*) ◊ rambling
动力 dònglì driving force; dynamism; momentum; incentive; stimulus; motivation
动乱 dòngluàn turmoil; unrest; upheaval
动脉 dòngmài artery
冬眠 dōngmián hibernation ◊ hibernate
东南 dōngnán southeast, southeastern
东南部 dōngnán bù southeast
东南亚 Dōngnán Yà Southeast Asia ◊ Southeast Asian
鸫鸟 dōngniǎo thrush
冬青 dōngqīng holly
动人 dòngrén moving
冻伤 dòngshāng frostbite ◊ frostbitten

东山再起 **dōngshān zàiqǐ** make a comeback

动身 **dòngshēn** set off

懂事 **dǒngshì** understanding; sensible

董事 **dǒngshì** board member; director

董事会 **dǒngshì huì** board of directors

董事会会议 **dǒngshìhuì huìyì** board meeting

董事长 **dǒngshìzhǎng** chairman of the board

动手 **dòngshǒu** get to work

动手动脚 **dòngshǒu dòngjiǎo** touch up; make a pass; get fresh

动手术 **dòng shǒushù** operate MED

冻死 **dòngsǐ** freeze to death; 我冻死了 **wǒ dòngsǐle** I'm freezing

冬天 **dōngtiān** winter

动物 **dòngwù** animal

动物学 **dòngwù xué** zoology ◊ zoological

动物园 **dòngwù yuán** zoo

东西 **dōngxi** thing

洞穴 **dòngxué** cave

动摇 **dòngyáo** waver

动作 **dòngzuò** movement

都 **dōu** all; both ◊ even

陡 **dǒu** steep ◊ suddenly

抖 **dǒu** tremble; shake

豆 **dòu** bean

斗 **dòu** fight; struggle

逗 **dòu** tease; amuse ◊ funny

豆瓣酱 **dòubànjiàng** black bean sauce

兜捕 **dōubǔ** round up ◊ round-up

斗橱 **dōuchú** bureau; chest of drawers

逗点 **dòudiǎn** comma

抖动 **dǒudòng** shake

兜风 **dōufēng** drive

豆腐 **dòufu** tofu, bean curd

逗号 **dòuhào** comma

豆浆 **dòujiāng** soy milk

逗留 **dòuliú** stay; stop over; linger

抖擞 **dǒusǒu** shake off

逗弄 **dòunòng** tease

斗殴 **dòu ōu** brawl

斗篷 **dǒupeng** cape

豆芽 **dòuyá** beansprouts

窦炎 **dòuyán** sinusitis

豆油 **dòuyóu** soy bean oil

斗争 **dòuzhēng** battle; struggle; fight for

都 **dū** city; capital

督 **dū** supervise

读 **dú** read; 他在读大学 **tā zài dú dàxué** he is at university

毒 **dú** poison; narcotics ◊ poisonous; toxic

独 **dú** only; alone

肚 **dǔ** tripe

堵 **dǔ** block

赌 **dǔ** gamble

肚 **dù** belly; stomach

度 **dù** degree ◊ spend, pass *time*

渡 **dù** cross *water*; ferry

妒 **dù** envy

端 **duān** end; extremity ◊ carry

短 **duǎn** short

段 **duàn** section; paragraph

缎 **duàn** satin

断 **duàn** break

短波 **duǎnbō** short wave

短处 **duǎnchù** shortcoming

断定 **duàndìng** conclude; decide

短棍 **duǎngùn** baton

断绝 **duànjué** break off

断绝关系 **duànjué guānxi** drop; 与 X 断绝关系 **yǔ X duànjué guānxi** finish with X, drop X

端口 **duānkǒu** port COMPUT

短裤 **duǎnkù** shorts

锻炼 **duànliàn** exercise; gymnastics; workout

断裂 **duànliè** snap, break

短路 **duǎnlù** short circuit

断路开关 **duànlù kāiguān** circuit breaker

段落 **duànluò** paragraph

短跑 **duǎnpǎo** sprint

短跑运动员 **duǎnpǎo yùndòng yuán** sprinter

短篇小说 **duǎnpiān xiǎoshuō** short story

短期 **duǎnqī** short term

短缺 **duǎnquē** shortage

断然 **duànrán** point blank

端上 **duānshang** serve

断头 **duàntóu** break

短袜 **duǎnwà** sock

短文 **duǎnwén** essay

端午节 **Duānwǔjié** Dragon Boat Festival

断线 **duànxiàn** cut off *telephone*

短袖 **duǎnxiù** short-sleeved

断言 **duànyán** maintain, argue; affirm

短暂 **duǎnzàn** momentary, fleeting, short-lived

锻造 **duànzào** forge

缎子 **duànzi** satin

赌博 **dǔbó** bet; gamble ◊ gambling

独裁 **dúcái** dictatorial

独裁者 **dúcái zhě** dictator

赌场 **dǔchǎng** casino

独唱曲 **dúchàng qǔ** solo

独唱演员 **dúchàng yǎnyuán** soloist

堵车 **dǔchē** traffic jam

都城 **dūchéng** capital

渡船 **dùchuán** ferry

独创力 **dúchuànglì** originality

督促 **dūcù** urge; press

读错 **dúcuò** misread

嘟嘟声 **dūdū shēng** beep

读给 X 听 **dúgěi X tīng** read to X

度过 **dùguò** pass, spend *time*

毒害 **dúhài** poison

堆 **duī** heap, pile, mound ◊ pile up, stack

兑 **duì** exchange

对 **duì** correct; right ◊ against; toward; facing; opposite; with regard to; for; to ◊ pair ◊ face; 对啊 ! **duì a!** that's right!; 对了 ! **duìle!** that's it!, that's right!; X 对 Y **X duì Y** X against Y; X versus Y

队 **duì** team; line

对半 **duìbàn** fifty-fifty

对比 **duìbǐ** compare

对不起 **duìbùqǐ** sorry; I'm sorry; pardon me

对称 **duìchèn** symmetrical ◊ symmetry

堆成堆 **duīchéngduī** pile up

对待 **duìdài** treat ◊ treatment; 认真对待 X **rènzhēn duìdài X** take X seriously

对等 **duìděng** corresponding

对方 **duìfāng** opposite side

对付 **duìfu** handle; 对付 X **duìfu X** have X to reckon with

对话 **duìhuà** dialog

兑换 **duìhuàn** exchange

兑换率 **duìhuànlǜ** exchange rate

堆积 **duījī** pile up, heap up

对讲机 **duìjiǎngjī** intercom

对接处 **duì jiē chù** dock (*of spaceship*)

对抗 **duìkàng** opposite ◊ defiance

对立 **duìlì** oppose ◊ opposite; contrast ◊ contrary; 与 X 对立 **yǔ X duìlì** be at odds with X

对面 **duìmiàn** opposite; 邮局在银行的对面 **yóujú zài yínháng de duìmiàn** the post office is opposite the bank

对手 **duìshǒu** opponent, adversary

对外贸易 **duìwài màoyì** foreign trade

队伍 **duìwǔ** troops; ranks

兑现 **duìxiàn** cash *check*

对象 **duìxiàng** target; boyfriend; girlfriend

对象市场 **duìxiàng shìchǎng** target market

对象组 **duìxiàng zǔ** target group

队长 **duìzhǎng** captain (*of team*)

对照 **duìzhào** contrast

对折 **duìzhé** double

对质 **duìzhì** confront

对准 **duìzhǔn** point

妒忌 **dùjì** jealous ◊ jealousy; envy; 妒忌 … **dùjì …** be jealous of …

独家 **dújiā** exclusive

度假 **dùjià** spend one's vacation

度假胜地 **dùjià shèngdì** resort

镀金材料 **dùjīn cáiliào** gilt

赌纪人 **dǔjì rén** bookmaker, bookie

独立 **dúlì** independence ◊ independent ◊ independently

度量衡 **dùliánghéng** system of measurement

独立日 **Dúlìrì** Independence Day

独立生活 **dúlì shēnghuó** fend for oneself

独轮车 **dúlún chē** barrow

独木舟 **dúmù zhōu** canoe

蹲 **dūn** squat, crouch

吨 **dūn** ton

钝 **dùn** blunt; dull

炖 **dùn** braise; simmer; stew

盾 **dùn** shield

顿 **dùn** *measure word for meals*; 一顿饭 **yídùn fàn** a meal

敦促 **dūncù** call on, urge; press

独女 **dúnǚ** only daughter

钝吻鳄 **dùnwěn'è** alligator

多 **duō** a lot of; many; much; more ◊ how; however; 比 …多 **bǐ … duō** above, more than; 好得多 **hǎo dé duō** much better; 好／容易多了 **hǎo／róngyì duōle** so much better／easier; 多滑稽／悲哀！**duō huájí／bēiāi!** how funny／sad!; 你／他多大年纪了？**nǐ／tā duōdà niánji le?** how old are you／is he?; 要多长时间？**yào duōcháng shíjiān?** how long does it take?; 多经常？**duō jīngcháng?** how often?

夺 **duó** take by force

朵 **duǒ** *measure word for flowers, clouds*; 一朵花 **yìduǒ huā** a flower

躲 **duǒ** hide; dodge

跥 **duò** chop

舵 **duò** helm; rudder

堕 **duò** fall; sink

跥 **duò** stamp *foot*

多半儿 **duōbànr** in all likelihood ◊ the majority

躲避 **duǒbì** dodge; elude

多变 **duōbiàn** variable

多病 **duōbìng** sickly

踱步 **duóbù** pace up and down

多才多艺 **duōcái duōyì** versatile ◊ versatility

躲藏 **duǒcáng** hide; 躲藏起来 **duǒcáng qǐlái** go into hiding; 躲藏着 **duǒcángzhe** be in hiding

躲藏处 **duǒcángchù** hiding place

多草 **duōcǎo** grassy

多产 **duōchǎn** productive; prolific

多尘土 **duō chéntǔ** dusty

多愁善感 **duōchóu shàngǎn** corny

多刺 **duōcì** prickly

多次 **duōcì** time and again

夺得 **duódé** snatch

多风 **duōfēng** windy

多个 **duōgè** multiple

多功能 **duō gōngnéng** versatile ◊ versatility

多关系户 **duō guānxi hù** be well-connected

多国 **duōguó** multinational

多花 **duōhuā** flowery

夺回 **duóhuí** recapture

跺脚 **duòjiǎo** stamp one's feet

多久 **duōjiǔ** how long; 多久之前？**duōjiǔ zhīqián?** how long ago?

多亏 **duōkuī** fortunately

堕落 **duòluò** degenerate; 使堕落 **shǐ duòluò** corrupt

多毛 **duōmáo** hairy

多么 **duōme** how; what; 多么蓝的天啊！**duōme lán de tiān a!** what a blue sky!

多媒体 **duōméitǐ** multimedia

夺取 **duóqǔ** conquer; overcome

堕入 **duòrù** sink into

多沙 **duōshā** sandy

多山 **duōshān** mountainous

多少 **duōshǎo** much; many ◊ how much; how many; 你需要多少？**nǐ xūyào duōshao?** how many do you need?; 多少钱？**duōshao qián?** how much is it?

多石 **duōshí** stony

多数 **duōshù** majority ◊ most; 占多数 **zhàn duōshù** be in the majority

多水 **duōshuǐ** watery

哆嗦 **duōsuo** quake

堕胎 **duòtāi** abortion ◊ have an abortion

多雾 **duōwù** foggy

多险 **duōxiǎn** perilous

多香料 **duō xiāngliào** spicy

多谢 **duōxiè** thanks very much

多雪 **duōxuě** snowy

多烟 **duōyān** smoky

多样化 **duōyàng huà** diverse ◊ diversity; variety

多岩石 **duō yánshí** rocky

多疑 **duōyí** paranoid

多用途 **duō yòngtú** all-purpose

多于 **duōyú** excess ◊ in excess of, more than

多余 duōyú spare; redundant, superfluous

多雨 duōyǔ rainy

多云 duōyún overcast

多汁 duōzhī juicy

多种经营 duōzhǒng jīngyíng diversification ◊ diversify

多皱纹 duō zhòuwén rugged

毒品 dúpǐn drugs, narcotics

毒品贩子 dúpǐn fànzi pusher

肚脐 dùqí navel

堵塞 dǔsāi block, block up ◊ blockage; congestion ◊ congested

堵塞 dǔsè block; jam ◊ blocked

独身 dúshēn single

都市 dūshì metropolis

读数 dúshù reading

毒死 dúsǐ poison

杜松子酒 dùsōngzǐjiǔ gin

独特 dútè unique

独特性 dútèxìng peculiarity

赌徒 dǔtú gambler

读物 dúwù reading material

妒羡 dùxiàn envy

毒药 dúyào poison

毒液 dúyè venom

镀银 dùyín silver-plated

独一无二 dúyīwú'èr unique

独有 dúyǒu exclusive

独占 dúzhàn monopoly

读者 dúzhě reader

赌咒 dǔzhòu swear; take an oath

赌注 dǔzhù bet; stake

堵住 dǔzhù block in; clog up; 堵住了 **dǔzhùle** stuck fast

杜撰 dùzhuàn make up; invent

独自 dúzì alone; by itself; by myself; single-handed; 她独自 **tā dúzì** by herself

肚子 dùzi stomach; abdomen; belly

独子 dúzǐ only son

肚子疼 dùzi téng stomach-ache

独自一人 dúzì yīrén solitude

独奏曲 dúzòu qǔ solo

独奏演员 dúzòu yǎnyuán soloist

# E

额 é forehead; volume (*of business*)
鹅 é goose
蛾 é moth
恶 è evil
腭 è palate
饿 è hunger ◊ hungry; 我饿了 **wǒ è le** I'm hungry
恶霸 èbà bully; despot
恶臭 èchòu stench
恶毒 èdú malevolent; savage; vicious
恶棍 ègùn gangster; ruffian
恶化 èhuà deteriorate
饿坏了 èhuàile ravenous
恶劣 èluè foul, nasty; vile
俄罗斯 Éluósī Russia ◊ Russian
恶梦 èmèng nightmare
恶魔 èmó devil; demon
恩 ēn favor; kindness
而 ér and; but
儿 ér child; son
耳 ěr ear
二 èr two
耳背 ěrbèi hard of hearing
而不是 ér búshì instead of
二冲程 èrchōngchéng two-stroke
二档 èrdǎng second gear
二等 èrděng second class
耳朵 ěrduǒ ear
儿歌 érgē nursery rhyme
耳垢 ěrgòu (ear)wax
耳光 ěrguāng clip around the ear
而后 érhòu then
耳环 ěrhuán earring
耳机 ěrjī headphones, earphones
二进制 èrjìn zhì binary
二进制位 èrjìn zhì wèi bit
COMPUT

儿科学 érkēxué pediatrics
儿科学家 érkēxuéjiā pediatrician
二流 èrliú second-rate
二年级 èrniánjí sophomore
而且 érqiě moreover; plus
二十 èrshí twenty
三十分之一 èrshífēnzhīyī twentieth
二手 èrshǒu secondhand
儿童 értóng children
耳痛 ěrtòng earache
儿童节 Értóng Jié Children's Day
二头肌 èrtóu jī biceps
儿媳妇 érxífu daughter-in-law
耳语 ěryǔ whisper
二月 èryuè February
儿子 érzi son
扼杀 èshā strangle, throttle
饿死 èsǐ starve to death; 我饿死了 **wǒ èsǐ le** I'm starving
扼死 èsǐ strangle
额外 éwài additional, extra
额外品 éwài pǐn bonus
恶习 èxí vice
恶心 ěxīn nausea ◊ revolting ◊ feel nauseous; 我感到恶心 **wǒ gǎndào ěxīn** I feel nauseous; 使恶心 **shǐ ěxīn** nauseate
恶性 èxìng malignant; virulent
恶意 èyì ill will; malice, spite ◊ malicious, spiteful
俄语 Éyǔ Russian (*language*)
鳄鱼 èyú crocodile
恶运，厄运 èyùn jinx
遏制 èzhì bottle up
蛾子 ézi moth
恶作剧 èzuòjù mischief; practical joke, prank

# F

发 fā send out; give out; issue; emit

阀 fá valve

罚 fá punish

乏 fá lack ◊ exhausted

筏 fá raft

法 fǎ law; method

发 fà hair

发表 fābiǎo publish; issue

发表意见 fābiǎo yìjiàn comment; express an opinion

发财 fācái make a fortune; get rich

发愁 fāchóu worry; be anxious

发出 fāchū send off, dispatch; give off; issue

发错 fācuò mispronounce

发达 fādá developed ◊ develop

发大财 fā dàcái hit the jackpot

发达国家 fādá guójiā developed country

发呆 fādāi be in a daze

发电 fādiàn generate electricity

法典 fǎdiǎn code; statutes

发电机 fādiànjī generator

发电站 fādiànzhàn power station

法定 fǎdìng legal; statutory; 未到法定年龄 wèidào fǎdìng niánlíng below the legal age

发动 fādòng start; launch; mobilize

发动机 fādòngjī motor

发抖 fādǒu shake; shudder; tremble

发奋 fāfèn make an effort

发疯 fāfēng go crazy; 使 X 发疯 shǐ X fāfēng drive X mad

法官 fǎguān judge; 法官判定 … fǎguān pàndìng … the judge ruled that …

发光 fāguāng glow; shine

发光二极管 fāguāng èrjí guǎn LED, light-emitting diode

法规 fǎguī law; act; legislation

法国 Fǎguó France ◊ French

发慌 fāhuāng feel nervous

发挥 fāhuī summon up

发昏 fāhūn dazed

发火 fāhuǒ erupt; get angry

发货 fāhuò send goods

法家 fǎjiā legalism (*philosophy*)

法家 fǎjiā legalist

发夹 fàjiā hairpin

发奖 fājiǎng award prizes

发酵 fājiào ferment ◊ fermentation

罚金 fájīn fine

发掘 fājué find, uncover, unearth

罚款 fákuǎn fine

发狂 fākuáng go crazy

发困 fākùn drowsy

珐琅质 fàlángzhì enamel

法兰绒 fǎlánróng washcloth

发牢骚 fā láosāo grumble, complain, bitch; 爱发牢骚的人 ài fā láosāo de rén grumbler

乏力 fálì weak

发亮 fāliàng shiny

法令 fǎlìng law; statute; court order

法律 fǎlǜ law ◊ legal

法轮功 fǎlúngōng Falungong sect

发麻 fāmá pins and needles ◊ get pins and needles; go numb

发霉 fāméi go moldy

发明 fāmíng invent ◊ invention

发明者 fāmíng zhě inventor

翻 fān overturn; roll over

帆 fān sail

烦 fán annoyed

反 fǎn anti-; counter- ◊ reverse; inside-out; 穿反了 chuānfǎnle back to front

返 fǎn return

饭 fàn (cooked) rice; food; meal

犯 fàn commit *crime, blunder*

帆 fānbǎn sailboard; windsurfer

翻版 fānbǎn reprint

帆板运动 fānbǎn yùndòng

windsurfing

帆板运动员 **fānbǎn yùndòngyuán** windsurfer

反驳 **fǎnbó** contradict; counter; retort

帆布 **fānbù** canvas

帆布篷 **fānbùpéng** tarpaulin; awning

帆布鞋 **fānbùxié** sneakers

饭菜 **fàncài** food

反常 **fǎncháng** unnatural; warped;

反常现象 **fǎncháng xiànxiàng** freak

范畴 **fànchóu** category

翻船 **fānchuán** capsize

帆船 **fānchuán** junk; sailboat

饭店 **fàndiàn** hotel; restaurant

贩毒 **fàndú** drug dealing; drug trafficking ◊ push

反对 **fǎnduì** oppose; be against; take exception to; object; protest ◊ opposition; objection; 我抽烟你不反对吗? **wǒ chōuyān nǐ bù fǎnduì ma?** do you mind if I smoke?

反毒警 **fǎndú jǐng** narcotics agent

贩毒者 **fàndú zhě** drug dealer

犯法 **fànfǎ** break the law

反复 **fǎnfù** repeated

反复无常 **fǎnfù wúcháng** unpredictable; unstable; volatile

方 **fāng** square; to the power of MATH

房 **fáng** house; room

防 **fáng** prevent

妨 **fáng** hinder; obstruct

纺 **fǎng** spin

访 **fǎng** visit

仿 **fǎng** copy; imitate

放 **fàng** place, put, set; put on; release; 放在一边 **fàngzài yìbiān** put aside; 放风筝 **fàng fēngzhēng** fly a kite

犯病 **fànbìng** relapse MED

妨碍 **fáng'ài** hinder; obstruct

反感 **fǎn'gǎn** aversion; antipathy; dislike; revulsion; 使反感 **shǐ fǎngǎn** disgust

方案 **fāng'àn** plan; program

方便 **fāngbiàn** convenience ◊ convenient; 在你方便的时候

*zài nǐ fāngbiàn de shíhòu* at your convenience

方便面 **fāngbiànmiàn** instant noodles

方便食品 **fāngbiàn shípǐn** convenience food

防波堤 **fángbōdī** jetty

放长 **fàngcháng** let down *pants etc*

防虫药 **fángchóngyào** insect repellent

放大 **fàngdà** amplify; enlarge; magnify

放大镜 **fàngdàjìng** magnifying glass

防弹 **fángdàn** bullet-proof

放荡 **fàngdàng** debauchery ◊ debauched, dissolute; loose

放荡女子 **fàngdàng nǚzǐ** slut

放大器 **fàngdàqì** amplifier

房地产 **fángdìchǎn** property; real estate

房地产开发人 **fángdìchǎn kāifārén** property developer

房东 **fángdōng** landlord; landlady

方法 **fāngfǎ** method, means, way

防腐剂 **fángfǔjì** preservative

方格 **fānggé** check (*pattern*); box (*on form*)

放过 **fàngguò** let off; pass up

防护 **fánghù** protect

防滑 **fánghuá** nonskid

防滑链 **fáng huá liàn** snow chains

放回 **fànghuí** put back; return; replace

放回原处 **fànghuí yuánchù** put back

防火 **fánghuǒ** fire prevention

放火 **fànghuǒ** set fire to

放假 **fàngjià** be on leave; have a day off; have a vacation; 放假一星期 **fàngjià yìxīngqī** take a week off

房间 **fángjiān** room

放进去 **fàngjìnqù** put in; get in

放开 **fàngkāi** open up; let go of

房客 **fángkè** lodger; tenant

方块儿 **fāngkuàir** diamond

放慢 **fàngmàn** slacken off

方面 **fāngmiàn** aspect; side; 在这方面 *zài zhè fāngmiàn* in this respect

防抹舌 fángmǒshé tab

放屁 fàngpì fart; break wind

放弃 fàngqì abandon; give up; jettison

防窃警报器 fángqiè jīngbào qì burglar alarm

放晴 fàngqíng clear up (of weather)

防热 fángrè heat-resistant

放任 fàngrèn permissive

防晒膏 fángshàigāo sun block

放哨 fàngshào keep watch

放射 fàngshè radiate

放射尘 fàngshèchén fallout

放射疗法 fàngshè liáofǎ radiotherapy

放声大哭 fàngshēng dàkū burst into tears

放射性 fàngshè xìng radioactive ◊ radioactivity

方式 fāngshì way; manner; mode; approach; pattern

防守 fángshǒu defense

防水 fángshuǐ waterproof

放肆 fàngsì impertinent; audacious; presumptuous

放松 fàngsōng ease; relieve; lighten up; relax, unwind ◊ relaxed, easy ◊ relaxation

方糖 fāngtáng sugar cubes

反光 fǎn'guāng reflect

泛光灯 fàn'guāngdēng floodlight

反光镜 fǎn'guāngjìng mirror

犯规 fàn'guī break the rules; foul SP

翻滚 fān'gǔn roll

翻过来 fān guòlái turn over; overturn

方位 fāng'wèi directions

防卫 fángwèi defend; protect

访问 fǎngwèn pay a visit

放下 fàngxià put down, lay down; lower

芳香 fāngxiāng bouquet; fragrance

方向 fāngxiàng direction

方向盘 fāngxiàng pán steering wheel

方向指示器 fāngxiàng zhǐshìqì indicator

仿效者 fǎngxiào zhě imitator

放心 fàngxīn put one's mind at rest; rest assured

防锈 fángxiù rustproof

方言 fāngyán dialect

放映 fàngyìng screen movie

放映机 fàngyìngjī projector

防雨 fángyǔ showerproof

防御 fángyù defend ◊ defensive ◊ defense

仿造 fǎngzào copy ◊ imitation

放债者 fàngzhài zhě money-lender

仿照 fǎngzhào copy; imitate

方针 fāngzhēn policy; guideline

防止 fángzhǐ guard against; prevent

纺织 fǎngzhī textile

仿制 fǎngzhì fake

纺织品 fǎngzhīpǐn textiles

防撞头盔 fángzhuàng tóukuī crash helmet

房子 fángzi house; building

放纵 fàngzòng indulgence ◊ indulge; pamper

房租 fángzū rent

返回 fǎnhuí return; turn back; 顺原路返回 shùn yuánlù fǎnhuí retrace

反击 fǎnjī counter; hit back ◊ counter-attack

反间谍活动 fǎn jiàndié huódòng counterespionage

烦交 fánjiāo c/o, care of

反诘问 fǎn jiéwèn cross-examine

翻筋斗 fān jīndǒu somersault

反抗 fǎnkàng revolt

饭筐 fànkuāng hamper

反馈信息 fǎnkuì xìnxī feedback

泛滥 fànlàn overflow; flood

烦劳 … fánláo … would you mind …?

翻了三番 fānle sān fān treble

翻领 fānlǐng lapel

贩卖 fànmài traffic in; peddle

繁忙 fánmáng busy

反面 fǎnmiàn reverse (side); opposite

烦恼 fánnǎo annoyance ◊ vexed; 令人烦恼 lìngrén fánnǎo annoying

反叛 fǎnpàn rebellion; mutiny

反叛军队 fǎnpàn jūnduì rebel troops

反叛者 **fǎnpàn zhě** rebel

翻篇儿 **fān piānr** turn over *page*; turn the page

翻起 **fānqǐ** turn up; turn over

蕃茄 **fānqié** tomato

番茄酱 **fānqiéjiàng** tomato ketchup

烦扰 **fánrǎo** bother, plague

烦人 **fánrén** irritating; troublesome ◊ nuisance

繁荣 **fánróng** boom ◊ flourishing, thriving; prosperous ◊ promote; develop

反射 **fǎnshè** reflect, mirror ◊ reflection

翻身 **fānshēn** turn over, roll over; toss and turn

反手击球 **fǎnshǒu jīqiú** backhand SP

繁体字 **fántǐzì** traditional Chinese characters

发怒 **fānù** flare up; be in a rage; get angry

饭碗 **fànwǎn** rice bowl

范围 **fànwéi** range; scope; 在一定范围内 **zài yídìng fànwéi nèi** within specific limits

反问 **fǎnwèn** rhetorical question

翻下 **fānxià** turn down

反响 **fǎnxiǎng** echo; repercussion

反省 **fǎnxǐng** reflect, think ◊ reflection, consideration

翻寻 **fānxún** rummage around

翻译 **fānyì** translate; interpret ◊ translation; interpretation; translator; interpreter; 翻译成英语 **fānyì chéng Yīngyǔ** translate into English

翻一番 **fānyīfān** double

反应 **fǎnyìng** react ◊ reaction

反应堆 **fǎnyìng duī** reactor

反应能力 **fǎnyìng nénglì** reflex

反右运动 **Fǎnyòu Yùndòng** Anti-rightists Campaign

犯有罪恶 **fànyǒu zuì'è** sin, commit a sin

繁育 **fányù** fertility ◊ breed; reproduce

翻阅 **fānyuè** leaf through

烦躁 **fánzào** fret ◊ irritable ◊ irritation

烦躁不安 **fánzào bù'ān** fidget

反证 **fǎnzhèng** disprove

反正 **fǎnzhèng** in any case; anyway

繁殖 **fánzhí** breed; reproduce ◊ reproduction ◊ reproductive

反之亦然 **fǎnzhī yìrán** vice versa

翻转 **fānzhuàn** overturn

犯罪 **fànzuì** commit a crime

犯罪率 **fànzuì lǜ** crime rate

反作用 **fǎnzuòyòng** reaction; counteraction

发牌 **fāpái** deal; deal the cards

发牌者 **fāpái zhě** dealer (*cards*)

发胖 **fāpàng** put on weight

发票 **fāpiào** receipt; invoice

发脾气 **fā píqì** huff; tantrum ◊ be in a huff; be in a temper; lose one's temper, get angry 爱发脾气 **ài fā píqì** short-tempered

发起 **fāqǐ** mount *campaign*; originate; initiate; launch; sponsor

发卡 **fàqiǎ** barrette; hairpin

发起人 **fāqǐ rén** creator; originator; sponsor

发球 **fāqiú** serve SP

罚球 **fáqiú** penalty SP

发球得分 **fāqiú défēn** ace (*in tennis*)

罚球区 **fáqiúqū** penalty area

发球人 **fāqiúrén** server (*in tennis*)

法人 **fǎrén** legal person; legal entity

发热器 **fārèqì** heater

发烧 **fāshāo** have a fever

发射 **fāshè** launch; blast off

发生 **fāshēng** happen, occur; take place

发生冲突 **fāshēng chōngtū** clash

发生的事情 **fāshēng de shìqíng** goings-on

发生关系 **fāshēng guānxì** have a relationship (*sexual*)

发生故障 **fāshēng gùzhàng** malfunction

发射上天 **fāshè shàngtiān** blast off

发射台 **fāshè tái** launch pad

发誓 **fāshì** swear; vow; pledge

发式 **fàshì** hairdo

发条 **fātiáo** clockwork

法庭 **fǎtíng** (law) court

乏味 **fáwèi** tasteless; bland; boring

发微光 **fāwēiguāng** glimmer

发现 **fāxiàn** discover; find; realize; notice ◊ discovery

发泄 **fāxiè** give vent to; release

发薪 **fāxīn** pay wages; pay salary

发信 **fāxìn** send off a letter

发行 **fāxíng** issue; publish; launch; release; distribute; put on sale

发型 **fāxíng** hairstyle

发薪日 **fāxīnrì** payday

法西斯 **fǎxīsī** fascist

法西斯主义 **fǎxīsī zhǔyì** fascism

法西斯主义者 **fǎxīsī zhǔyì zhě** fascist

法学 **fǎxué** law

发芽 **fāyá** sprout; germinate

发言 **fāyán** speak

发炎 **fāyán** inflammation ◊ become inflamed

发痒 **fāyǎng** itch; tickle; 使发痒 **shǐ fāyǎng** tickle

发扬 **fāyáng** develop; make the most of

发炎膏 **fāyánggāo** inflammation

发言人 **fāyán rén** spokesman; spokeswoman; spokesperson

法衣 **fǎyī** robe

发音 **fāyīn** pronounce ◊ pronunciation

发音错误 **fāyīn cuòwù** mispronunciation

发育 **fāyù** grow ◊ growth

法语 **Fǎyǔ** French (*language*)

发源 **fāyuán** spring; rise; originate

法院 **fǎyuàn** court; courthouse

发展 **fāzhǎn** develop, build up; grow ◊ development; growth

发展中国家 **fāzhǎn zhōng guójiā** developing country

发作 **fāzuò** bout; seizure

非本意 **fēiběnyì** involuntary

飞 **fēi** fly

非 **fēi** not

肥 **féi** fat; fatty; fertile ◊ fertilizer

费 **fèi** cost; fee ◊ cost; spend; expend

肺 **fèi** lung

吠 **fèi** bark (*of dog*)

废 **fèi** useless

沸 **fèi** boil

非 ... 非 ... **fēi ... fēi ...** neither ... nor ...

非 ... 即 ... **fēi ... jí ...** either ... or ...

肺癌 **fèi'ái** lung cancer

诽谤 **fěibàng** libel; slander ◊ defamation ◊ defamatory

诽谤活动 **fěibàng huódòng** smear campaign

非暴力 **fēi bàolì** nonviolence ◊ nonviolent

飞奔 **fēibēn** dash; run quickly

非常 **fēicháng** extraordinary ◊ extremely, very; 非常感谢 **fēicháng gǎnxiè** thanks very much

非常规 **fēi chángguī** nonstandard

废除 **fèichú** abolish, do away with; repeal, revoke; undo

肥大 **féidà** bulky

飞到 **fēidào** fly in; fly to

废掉 **fèidiào** scrap

飞碟 **fēidié** flying saucer

非法 **fēifǎ** illegal; 非法麻醉品 **fēifǎ mázuì pǐn** illegal drugs

非凡 **fēifán** remarkable; phenomenal ◊ remarkably

非法侵入 **fēifǎ qīnrù** trespass (on)

非法侵入者 **fēifǎ qīnrù zhě** trespasser

狒狒 **fèifei** baboon

飞过 **fēiguò** whizz by

废话 **fèihuà** nonsense; gibberish

飞回 **fēihuí** fly back

飞机 **fēijī** airplane

飞溅 **fēijiàn** splash

飞机场 **fēijīchǎng** airport

费解 **fèijiě** inexplicable; puzzling

飞机库 **fēijīkù** hangar

费劲 **fèijìn** strenuous

废金属 **fèijīnshǔ** scrap metal

飞机失事 **fēijī shīshì** plane crash

飞快 **fēikuài** lightning fast; quick as a flash

费力 **fèilì** effort; exertion; hard work ◊ laborious; strenuous; exhausting

肥料 **féiliào** fertilizer; manure

废料堆 **fèiliàoduī** scrap heap

菲律宾 **Fēilǜbīn** the Philippines

肥胖 **féipàng** plump; chubby; stout

肥胖症 **féipàngzhèng** obesity

飞跑 **fēipǎo** rush, fly; gallop

废品 **fèipǐn** trash, junk; waste product

废品站 **fèipǐnzhàn** junkyard

废气 **fèiqì** exhaust; fumes

废弃 **fèiqì** abandon ◊ disused; waste

非人造 **fēi rénzào** natural, non-artificial

飞逝 **fēishì** fly past (of time)

费事 **fèishì** painful

飞速 **fēisù** very fast; meteoric

沸腾 **fèiténg** boil

飞脱 **fēituō** fly off (of hat etc)

肥沃 **féiwò** fertile ◊ fertility

废物 **fèiwù** waste

飞行 **fēixíng** flight; flying ◊ fly

飞行甲板 **fēixíng jiǎbǎn** flight deck

飞行记录仪 **fēixíng jìlùyí** flight recorder

飞行路线 **fēixíng lùxiàn** flight path

飞行时间 **fēixíng shíjiān** flight time

飞行员 **fēixíngyuán** pilot

飞行中 **fēixíngzhōng** in-flight

废墟 **fèixū** ruins; wasteland

肺炎 **fèiyán** pneumonia

沸溢 **fèiyì** boil over

费用 **fèiyòng** charge; fee; costs; expenses

鲱鱼 **fēiyú** herring

飞跃 **fēiyuè** leap; become popular; take off

肥皂 **féizào** soap

肥皂剧 **féizào jù** soap opera

非正式 **fēi zhèngshì** informal; unofficial ◊ unofficially

非正义 **fēizhèngyì** injustice ◊ unjust

废纸 **fèizhǐ** wastepaper; scrap paper

废纸篓 **fèizhǐlǒu** wastepaper basket

非洲 **Fēizhōu** Africa ◊ African

痱子 **fèizi** prickly heat

飞走 **fēizǒu** fly away

分 **fēn** divide; split; share ◊ cent; minute fraction ◊ measure word for time, money, length

坟 **fén** grave

焚 **fén** burn

粉 **fěn** powder ◊ pink

份 **fèn** portion; share; part; copy ◊ measure word for newspapers, documents; 一份报纸 **yífèn bàozhǐ** a newspaper; 一份饭 **yífèn fàn** a helping of food

粪 **fèn** excrement; dung

分包合同 **fēnbāo hétong** subcontract

分包人 **fēnbāo rén** subcontractor

分贝 **fēnbèi** decibel

粉笔 **fěnbǐ** chalk

粪便 **fènbiàn** dung

分别 **fēnbié** separate ◊ separately; respectively

分不开 **fēnbùkāi** inseparable

分岔 **fēnchà** branch off

分岔处 **fēnchàchù** fork

分成两半 **fēnchéng liǎngbàn** halve

分成四份 **fēnchéng sìfèn** quarter

粉刺 **fěncì** acne; pimples

分店 **fēndiàn** branch

奋斗 **fèndòu** strive, struggle

份额 **fèn'é** share

分发 **fēnfā** give out; distribute ◊ distribution

分房 **fēnfáng** allocate accommodation

粪肥 **fènféi** manure

封 **fēng** seal; board up ◊ measure word for letters; 三封信 **sānfēng xìn** three letters

锋 **fēng** edge; front (weather)

疯 **fēng** mad

枫 **fēng** maple

风 **fēng** wind; style; tendency

丰 **fēng** abundant

蜂 **fēng** bee

峰 **fēng** summit; peak

缝 **féng** sew; stitch

缝 **fèng** crack; seam; part (in hair)

凤 **fèng** phoenix

风暴 **fēngbào** storm

风暴警报 **fēngbào jǐngbào** storm warning

封闭 **fēngbì** seal; close up

风车 **fēngchē** windmill

奉承 **fèngchéng** flatter; suck up to ◊ flattery

讽刺 **fěngcì** mock, deride, ridicule ◊ ironic(al); satirical ◊ irony; satire

讽刺画 **fěngcì huà** cartoon; caricature

讽刺者 **fěngcì zhě** satirist

分割 **fēn'gē** division; split

分隔 **fēn'gé** isolate

分给 **fēn'gěi** distribute

蜂房 **fēngfáng** hive

丰富 **fēngfù** abundance ◊ abundant ◊ enrich; 丰富多彩的活动 **fēngfù duōcǎi de huódòng** a variety of things to do

风干 **fēnggān** seasoned *wood*

风格 **fēnggé** method; style; format

风寒 **fēnghán** cold

缝合 **fénghé** sew up

风和日丽 **fēnghé rìlì** *a gentle breeze and glorious sunshine*

凤凰 **fènghuáng** phoenix

风景 **fēngjǐng** view; landscape

风景画 **fēngjǐng huà** landscape (*painting*)

疯狂 **fēngkuáng** insane, crazy ◊ insanity ◊ insanely

锋利 **fēnglì** sharp

风凉话 **fēngliánghuà** wisecrack

风流 **fēngliú** romantic; unrestrained; admirable

风流人物 **fēngliú rénwù** influential person; moldbreaker; romantic hero; great man

风流韵事 **fēngliú yùnshì** love affair; romance

丰满 **fēngmǎn** busty; plump; rounded

风帽 **fēngmào** hood

蜂蜜 **fēngmì** honey

封面 **fēngmiàn** (front) cover

蜂鸣器 **fēngmíng qì** buzzer

分公司 **fēn gōngsī** branch (*of company*)

奉陪 **fèngpéi** *fml* accompany; 我有急事，不能奉陪 **wǒ yǒu jíshì, bù néng fèngpéi** I'm sorry, I can't make it due to a prior engagement

风琴 **fēngqín** organ MUS

奉劝 **fèngquàn** *fml* advise

疯人 **fēngrén** madman

缝纫 **féngrèn** sew ◊ sewing

缝纫机 **féngrènjī** sewing machine

缝上 **féngshang** sew on

风扇皮带 **fēngshàn pídài** fan belt

丰盛 **fēngshèng** rich; copious; 丰盛可口 **fēngshèng kěkǒu** magnificent *meal*

风湿 **fēngshī** rheumatism

丰收 **fēngshōu** good harvest

封锁 **fēngsuǒ** blockade ◊ cordon off; seal off

风俗习惯 **fēngsú xíguàn** traditions, customs

风头主义者 **fēngtóu zhǔyì zhě** exhibitionist

蜂王 **fēngwáng** queen bee

风味 **fēngwèi** savor

缝隙 **fèngxì** crack

风险 **fēngxiǎn** risk; 有风险 **yǒu fēngxiǎn** adventurous; risky

蜂箱 **fēngxiāng** beehive

风行一时 **fēngxíng yìshí** all the rage

风信子 **fēngxìnzǐ** hyacinth

风雪大衣 **fēngxuě dàyī** parka

蜂拥 **fēngyōng** swarm

缝针 **féngzhēn** stitches

风筝 **fēngzheng** kite

疯子 **fēngzi** lunatic

风钻 **fēngzuàn** pneumatic drill

分行 **fēnháng** branch (*of bank, company*)

分号 **fēnhào** semicolon

粉红 **fěnhóng** pink

焚化炉 **fénhuàlú** incinerator

分机 **fēnjī** extension

分解 **fēnjiě** break up

分居 **fēnjū** separate; live apart

分开 **fēnkāi** break; part; separate; detach; 把 X 与 Y 分开 **bǎ X yǔ Y fēnkāi** separate X from Y

愤慨 **fènkǎi** indignant ◊ indignation

芬兰 **Fēnlán** Finland ◊ Finnish

分类 **fēnlèi** break down; classify;

group ◊ breakdown; classification; 给 … 分类 **gěi … fēnlèi** grade

分类广告 **fēnlèi guǎnggào** classified advertisement

分离 **fēnlí** separate ◊ separation

分裂 **fēnliè** division; partition; breach; rift; split ◊ divide; splinter

分裂人格 **fēnliè réngé** split personality

分流术 **fēnliú shù** bypass

分泌 **fēnmì** secrete ◊ secretion

分娩 **fēnmiǎn** childbirth; labor; delivery; 在分娩中 **zài fēnmiǎn zhōng** in labor

分泌物 **fēnmìwù** secretion

粉末 **fěnmò** powder

坟墓 **fénmù** grave; tomb

愤怒 **fènnù** anger ◊ angry

分配 **fēnpèi** allot; assign; allocate; distribute ◊ distribution

分批 **fēnpī** in groups; partially

分歧 **fēnqí** difference; gulf

分期付款 **fēnqī fùkuǎn** pay in installments ◊ installment plan

分散 **fēnsàn** scattered

分散注意力 **fēnsàn zhùyì lì** distract

焚烧 **fénshāo** burn

粉饰 **fěnshì** gloss over

愤世嫉俗 **fènshì jísú** cynical ◊ cynicism

愤世嫉俗者 **fènshì jísú zhě** cynic

分手 **fēnshǒu** split up; break up ◊ breakup; separation ◊ separated

分数 **fēnshù** fraction; mark

粉刷 **fěnshuā** paintwork ◊ whitewash

粉刷工 **fěnshuāgōng** painter

粉丝 **fěnsī** Chinese vermicelli, rice noodles

粉碎 **fěnsuì** shatter; pulverize

分析 **fēnxì** analysis ◊ analyze

分享 **fēnxiǎng** share

分心 **fēnxīn** distract; 使 X 分心 **shǐ X fēnxīn** drive X to distraction

分着 **fēnzhe** separately

分钟 **fēnzhōng** minute

分子 **fēnzǐ** numerator MATH; molecule ◊ molecular

分组 **fēnzǔ** divide into groups

佛 **Fó** Buddha

佛教 **Fójiào** Buddhism ◊ Buddhist

佛教徒 **Fójiào tú** Buddhist

否 **fǒu** no; not

否定 **fǒudìng** negative ◊ negate; deny; repudiate; 给予否定的回答 **jǐyǔ fǒudìngde huídá** answer in the negative

否决 **fǒujué** overrule; throw out; veto

否决权 **fǒujué quán** veto

否认 **fǒurèn** denial ◊ deny; disclaim; 否认自己和 X 有关系 **fǒurèn zìjǐ hé X yǒu guānxi** dissociate oneself from X

否则 **fǒuzé** or else; otherwise

佛爷 **Fóye** Buddha

夫 **fū** husband; man

敷 **fū** apply

孵 **fū** hatch; incubate

肤 **fū** skin

扶 **fú** hold up; support

福 **fú** luck; happiness; fortune

辐 **fú** spoke

幅 **fú** measure word for paintings, cloth; 一幅画 **yìfú huà** a picture

浮 **fú** float

服 **fú** take medicine

斧 **fǔ** ax

腐 **fǔ** rotten; stale

抚 **fǔ** stroke

附 **fù** attach; enclose

副 **fù** vice-; deputy; assistant ◊ pack (of cards)

付 **fù** pay

父 **fù** father

富 **fù** rich, wealthy

复 **fù** again ◊ duplicate ◊ reply

腹 **fù** abdomen; stomach

负 **fù** negative; minus ◊ bear

妇 **fù** wife; woman

腐败 **fùbài** corrupt

副本 **fùběn** copy

辅币 **fǔbì** token

浮标 **fúbiāo** buoy

副标题 **fùbiāotí** subheading

服兵役 **fú bīngyì** do military service

敷布 **fūbù** compress

腹部 **fùbù** stomach ◊ abdominal

复查 **fùchá** doublecheck

副产品 fù chǎnpǐn by-product

扶车 fúchē walker

俯冲 fúchōng dive

孵出 fūchū hatch out

付出 fùchū pay out; stump up; put in *time*; donate ◊ donation; 付出的款项 **fùchūde kuǎnxiàng** payment

副词 fùcí adverb

服从 fúcóng obey; comply ◊ obedience ◊ obedient; 服从命令 **fúcóng mìnglìng** obey orders

附带 fùdài incidental; supplementary ◊ incidentally

附带条件 fùdài tiáojiàn proviso

负担 fùdān load; burden

辅导 fǔdǎo counsel; tutor ◊ counseling; tuition

辅导课 fǔdǎokè tutorial

副导演 fù dǎoyǎn assistant director

辅导员 fǔdǎo yuán counselor; tutor

负电 fùdiàn negative ELEC

浮雕 fúdiāo relief (*in sculpture*)

浮动 fúdòng float

复发 fùfā relapse

复方药 fùfāngyào mixture (*medicine made from a combination of compounds*)

夫妇 fūfù (married) couple

覆盖 fùgài cover

讣告 fùgào obituary

副歌 fùgē refrain MUS

浮垢 fúgòu scum

腹股沟 fùgǔgōu groin

敷裹 fūguǒ dress

符号 fúhào symbol

符合 fúhé agreement ◊ accordingly ◊ tally (with); conform (to) ◊ compatible; 符合标准 **fúhé biāozhǔn** be up to standard

复合 fùhé overlap

负荷 fùhè load; 负荷过重 **fùhè guòzhòng** overload

符合性 fúhé xìng compatibility

孵化器 fūhuàqì incubator

付回款 fùhuíkuǎn repayment

复活 fùhuó resurrection

复活节 Fùhuójié Easter

伏击 fújī ambush

附加 fùjiā add ◊ additional

附加费 fùjiāfèi extra charge; supplement; surcharge

附件 fùjiàn accessory; add-on; enclosure; attachment (*to e-mail*) ◊ enclose (*in letter*); attach

复件 fùjiàn duplicate

副教授 fù jiàoshòu associate professor

副驾驶员 fù jiàshǐ yuán co-pilot

附加物 fùjiāwù frill; extra; insert

附近 fùjìn close by ◊ neighboring; 他住在附近 **tā zhù zài fùjìn** he lives around here

副经理 fù jīnglǐ assistant manager

妇科医生 fùkē yīshēng gynecologist

付款 fùkuǎn pay ◊ payment

付款人 fùkuǎn rén payer

付款台 fùkuǎn tái cash desk

腐烂 fǔlàn decay; perish; rot ◊ rotten

富丽 fùlì palatial

敷料 fūliào dressing MED

福利 fúlì welfare

福利工作 fúlì gōngzuò welfare work

福利国家 fúlì guójiā welfare state

福利救济 fúlì jiùjì welfare

俘虏 fúlǔ capture ◊ prisoner; captive; 俘虏 X **fúlǔ X** take X prisoner

附录 fùlù appendix

负面 fùmiàn unfavorable, negative

覆灭 fùmiè demise; downfall

抚摸 fǔmō stroke; caress

抚摩 fǔmó stroke; caress

父母 fùmǔ parents ◊ parental

妇女 fùnǚ woman

夫妻 fūqī married couple

福气 fúqì luck; happiness

肤浅 fúqiǎn superficial; sketchy

付钱 fùqián pay

父亲 fùqīn father

付清 fùqīng pay off *debt*

父亲身分 fùqīn shēnfèn paternity

夫人 fūrén Mrs; wife

富人 fùrén the rich; rich person

附入 fùrù enclose; add

服丧 **fúsāng** mourning; 在服丧 **zài fúsāng** in mourning

肤色 **fūsè** skin color

负伤 **fùshāng** injured

敷设 **fūshè** lay *cable*

辐射 **fúshè** radiate ◊ radiation

服侍 **fúshì** attend to

服饰 **fúshì** clothes and accessories; get-up

腐蚀 **fǔshí** corrode ◊ corrosion

俯视 **fǔshì** overlook

扶手 **fúshǒu** armrest; handrail; banister; balustrade

副手 **fùshǒu** mate

扶手椅 **fúshǒu yǐ** armchair

复数 **fùshù** plural

复述 **fùshù** relate; repeat

负数 **fùshù** negative (number)

附属公司 **fùshǔ gōngsī** subsidiary (company)

复数形式 **fùshù xíngshì** plural

伏特 **fútè** volt

伏特加 **fútèjiā** vodka

伏天 **fútiān** dog days

服贴 **fútiē** obedient; manageable

斧头 **fǔtóu** ax

浮凸 **fútū** emboss

富翁 **fùwēng** rich man

俯卧撑 **fǔ wòchēng** push-up

服务 **fúwù** serve ◊ service

服务费 **fúwùfèi** service charge

服务行业 **fúwù hángyè** service industry; service sector

服务器 **fúwùqì** server COMPUT

服务区 **fúwùqū** service area

服务台 **fúwùtái** reception

服务员 **fúwù yuán** attendant; maid; clerk; waiter; waitress

复习 **fùxí** review; revise

父系 **fùxì** paternal

复写 **fùxiě** copy; duplicate

腹泻 **fùxiè** diarrhea

复习课程 **fùxí kèchéng** refresher course

附信 **fùxìn** covering letter

复兴 **fùxīng** revival ◊ revive

敷衍 **fūyǎn** stall; hold off ◊ perfunctory

抚养 **fǔyǎng** raise

抚养费 **fúyǎngfèi** maintenance (*money*)

扶养权 **fúyǎng quán** custody

副业 **fùyè** sideline

附议 **fùyì** second *motion*

福音 **fúyīn** gospel

辅音 **fūyīn** consonant

复印 **fùyìn** copy; photocopy; duplicate

复映 **fùyìng** rerun

复印机 **fùyìn jī** copier

复印件 **fùyìn jiàn** copy

浮油 **fúyóu** (oil) slick

富有 **fùyǒu** wealthy; rich in; with a lot of ◊ be rich in; have plenty of

富有表情 **fùyǒu biǎoqíng** expressive

富裕 **fùyù** affluent, well-off

赋予权利 **fùyù quánlì** entitled; empowered

复杂 **fùzá** complex, complicated; intricate; involved; mixed *feelings*

负载 **fùzài** load ELEC

负责 **fùzé** answer for; take care of; be in charge of; accept responsibility for ◊ responsible; liable; conscientious

负责人 **fùzé ren** person in charge

负责任 **fù zérèn** be held accountable ◊ responsible

付账 **fùzhàng** pay the bill

复职 **fùzhí** be reinstated

复制 **fùzhì** copy; duplicate; clone; 复制一份档案 **fùzhì yífèn dǎng'an** make a copy of a file

复制品 **fùzhì pǐn** copy; replica; reproduction

复制钥匙 **fùzhì yàoshi** duplicate key

负重 **fùzhòng** burden

符咒 **fúzhòu** magic spell

辅助 **fúzhù** auxiliary

服装 **fúzhuāng** dress; clothing; garment; costume; uniform

副主管 **fù zhǔguǎn** assistant director

副总管 **fù zǒngguǎn** deputy leader

副总统 **fù zǒngtǒng** vice president

富足 **fùzú** plenty

服罪 **fúzuì** plead guilty

副作用 **fùzuòyòng** side effect

# G

嘎嘎声 **gāgā shēng** rattle

该 **gāi** be supposed to; should; be next; 我该做什么？**wǒ gāi zuò shénme?** what should I do?; 该你了 **gāi nǐ le** it's your turn; over to you

改 **gǎi** change; correct

盖 **gài** cover ◊ top; lid; 盖好被子 **gàihǎo bèizi** tuck in

钙 **gài** calcium

改编 **gǎibiān** adapt; arrange; reorganize ◊ adaptation; arrangement

改变 **gǎibiàn** change, alter; transform; vary ◊ shift; transformation; change; 改变话题 **gǎibiàn huàtí** change the subject

改编本 **gǎibiān běn** version; adaptation

改革 **gǎigé** reform

改换 **gǎihuàn** switch; change

改建 **gǎijiàn** convert

改进 **gǎijìn** improve; upgrade ◊ development; improvement

概况 **gàikuàng** survey; overview

概括 **gàikuò** generalization ◊ generalize; sum up; summarize

概括性 **gàikuò xìng** broad; general

盖了帽了 **gàilemàole** terrific, awesome

概念 **gàiniàn** concept

改期 **gǎiqī** be postponed; be rescheduled

改日 **gǎirì** sometime; another day

改善 **gǎishàn** improve

概述 **gàishù** sum up ◊ summary

该死 **gāisǐ** damn

改天 **gǎitiān** another day; another time

改线 **gǎixiàn** diversion ◊ divert

改小 **gǎixiǎo** take in, make narrower

改写 **gǎixiě** rewrite; transliterate; paraphrase

改邪归正 **gǎixiéguīzhèng** rehabilitate; go straight

概要 **gàiyào** outline; overview

改用 **gǎiyòng** adapt

盖章 **gàizhāng** stamp; seal

改正 **gǎizhèng** amend; correct

盖住 **gàizhù** cover up

改装 **gǎizhuāng** do up; make over

盖子 **gàizi** lid; cap

改组 **gǎizǔ** reorganization ◊ reorganize

咖喱 **gālí** curry

干 **gān** dry; dried; empty ◊ dry; empty ◊ in vain

肝 **gān** liver

杆 **gān** pole

竿 **gān** rod

甘 **gān** sweet

敢 **gǎn** dare; 你敢！**nǐgǎn!** how dare you!

赶 **gǎn** drive out; banish; rush; catch up with; hurry; 赶时髦 **gǎn shímáo** keep up with the latest fashions

秆 **gǎn** stalk; straw

擀 **gǎn** roll out

感 **gǎn** feel; sense

干 **gàn** do ◊ stem; trunk; 你今晚干什么？**nǐ jīnwǎn gàn shénme?** what are you doing tonight?; 干吧 **gàn ba** go ahead

干爸 **gānbà** godfather

干杯 **gānbēi** cheers!; 为 ... 干杯 **wèi ... gānbēi** toast; propose a toast to

干部 **gànbu** cadre; official

干草 **gāncǎo** hay

甘草 **gāncǎo** licorice

甘草栗子 **gāncǎo lìzi** water chestnut

赶超 **gǎnchāo** emulate; surpass

赶出 **gǎnchū** drive out; flush out

感到 gǎndào feel; 感到无聊 **gǎndào wúliáo** feel bored

赶掉 gǎndiào chase away

干掉 gàndiào kill, eliminate ◊ murder, elimination

感动 gǎndòng affect; move, touch ◊ moved, touched

干豆腐 gāndòufu dried bean curd

干儿子 gān érzi godson

感恩 gǎn'ēn gratitude

感恩节 Gǎn'ēn Jié Thanksgiving Day

钢 gāng steel

缸 gāng earthenware vessel; vat; jar

刚 gāng just

港 gǎng harbor, port

杠 gàng lever

尴尬 gān'gà embarrassed; awkward ◊ feel awkward ◊ embarrassment; 令人尴尬 **lìngrén gāngà** embarrassing

钢笔 gāngbǐ fountain pen

港币 gǎngbì Hong Kong dollar

刚才 gāngcái just now

杠杆 gànggǎn lever

刚刚 gānggang (only) just; 我刚刚看到她 **wǒ gānggang kàndào tā** I've just seen her

杠杆力量 gànggǎn lìliàng leverage

刚好 gānghǎo just right; exact ◊ exactly

钢筋混凝土 gāngjīn hùnníng tǔ reinforced concrete

港口 gǎngkǒu port, harbor

肛门 gāngmén anus

钢琴 gāngqín piano

钢琴家 gāngqínjiā pianist

岗哨 gǎngshào guard; lookout

港市 gǎngshì port (city)

钢丝绳 gāngsī shéng cable; high wire; tight-rope

钢铁厂 gāngtiěchǎng ironworks

港湾 gǎngwān harbor; bay

岗位 gǎngwèi guard

港务局 gǎngwùjú port authorities

缸子 gāngzi beaker; mug; bowl

干旱 gānhàn drought

干涸 gānhé dry out; dry up

感激 gǎnjī appreciation ◊ appreciate; feel grateful; be thankful ◊ thankfully

赶集 gǎnjí go to market

赶紧 gǎnjǐn hurry

干净 gānjìng clean

柑桔 gānjú tangerine

感觉 gǎnjué feeling; sensation; sense ◊ feel; experience; 我感觉累了 **wǒ gǎnjué lèi le** I feel tired

干枯 gānkū dry up ◊ dried up

甘苦 gānkǔ ups and downs

赶快 gǎnkuài hurry ◊ quickly

橄榄 gǎnlǎn olive

橄榄球 gǎnlǎn qiú rugby; football

橄榄油 gǎnlǎn yóu olive oil

干酪 gānlào cheese

干裂 gānliè dry and cracked; chapped

赶拢 gǎnlǒng round up

干妈 gānmā godmother

感冒 gǎnmào cold; flu ◊ catch a cold; 我感冒了 **wǒ gǎnmàole** I have a cold

甘美 gānměi luscious

擀面杖 gǎnmiànzhàng rolling pin

干女儿 gān nǚ'ér goddaughter

赶跑 gǎnpǎo chase off; see off

感情 gǎnqíng expression; feeling; emotion; 我对他有很多矛盾的感情 **wǒ duì tā yǒu hěn máodùnde gǎnqíng** I have mixed feelings about him

感染 gǎnrǎn contract, pick up; infect; influence; affect; become infected ◊ infected; infectious; septic

干扰 gānrǎo disturbance; interference ◊ interfere with; jam

感人 gǎnrén moving, touching

赶上 gǎnshàng catch; catch up

干涉 gànshè interfere; intervene; meddle ◊ interference

感叹 gǎntàn exclamation

感叹号 gǎntànhào exclamation point

干洗 gānxǐ dryclean ◊ drycleaning

干线 gànxiàn arterial road

干洗店 gānxǐ diàn dry cleaner

感谢 gǎnxiè thanks ◊ thank; say

thanks; be grateful

甘心 gǎnxīn willingly ◊ resign oneself to

感性 gǎnxìng sensory

感兴趣 gǎn xìngqù be interested

甘心情愿 gānxīn qíngyuàn willingly

甘心于 gānxīn yú reconcile oneself to

干洗衣物 gānxǐ yīwù drycleaning

肝炎 gānyán hepatitis

干预 gānyù poke one's nose into

敢于 gǎnyú dare

肝藏 gānzàng liver

干燥 gānzào dry

甘蔗 gānzhe sugar cane

感知 gǎnzhī feel

赶制 gǎnzhì run up *clothes*

感知能力 gǎnzhī nénglì perception

杆子 gānzi post (*wooden*)

赶走 gǎnzǒu chase away; banish ◊ family name

高 gāo big; tall; high ◊ top (*gear*)

比高 **bǐ ... gāo** above; higher/ taller than

膏 gāo ointment; cream

糕 gāo cake

搞 gǎo do; make

高傲 gāo'ào lofty

高保真电器 gāo bǎozhēn diànqì hi-fi

告别 gàobié say goodbye; 向死者告别 **xiàng sǐzhě gàobié** pay one's last respects

告别会 gàobié huì leaving party

高超 gāochāo masterly

高潮 gāocháo climax; high tide

高大 gāodà enormous; massive

高等 gāoděng higher; advanced; elite

高等教育 gāoděng jiàoyù higher education

糕点 gāodiǎn bread; cakes and pastries

高调 gāodiào highbrow

高顶帽 gāodǐngmào top hat

高度 gāodù height; altitude

高尔夫俱乐部 gāo'ěrfū jùlèbù golf club (*organization*)

高尔夫(球) gāo'ěrfū(qiú) golf

高尔夫球场 gāo'ěrfū qiúchǎng golf course

高尔夫球棍 gāo'ěrfū qiúgùn golf club (*stick*)

告发 gàofā inform; inform on; 向警方告发 X **xiàng jǐngfāng gàofā X** report X to the police

告发人 gàofā rén informer

高峰 gāofēng peak; summit

高峰时间 gāofēng shíjiān peak hours; rush hour

高跟 gāogēn high-heeled

高跟鞋 gāogēn xié high heels; high-heeled shoes

高贵 gāoguì noble

搞鬼 gǎoguǐ cheat; play tricks; cause trouble

高呼 gāohū chant

搞坏 gǎohuài mess up, ruin

高级 gāojí high-class; high-level; select; upmarket; senior; top

稿件 gǎojiàn manuscript; article

高脚椅 gāojiǎoyǐ highchair

高架铁路 gāojià tiělù elevated railroad

高阶层 gāo jiēcéng high-level

高级法庭 gāojí fǎtíng Supreme Court

高空跳水 gāokōng tiàoshuǐ high diving

高粱 gāoliáng sorghum

高楼大厦 gāolóu dàshà high-rise buildings

高炉 gāolú blast furnace

搞乱 gǎoluàn confuse; mix up; mess up

告密 gàomì sneak; inform on

高明 gāomíng masterly

高能 gāonéng high-energy; high-power

高能汽车 gāonéng qìchē performance car

高能转向 gāonéng zhuǎnxiàng power steering

高频 gāopín high-frequency

高人一等 gāorén yìděng patronizing; superior; 他觉得自己高人一等 **tā juéde zìjǐ gāorén yìděng** he feels superior to others

高尚 gāoshàng noble

高烧 gāoshāo high fever

高耸于 **gāosǒng yú** dominate

高速 **gāosù** high-speed

告诉 **gàosu** tell; say; 别告诉妈妈 **bié gàosu māma** don't tell Mom

高速公路 **gāosù gōnglù** freeway; expressway

高速缓存 **gāosù huǎncún** cache COMPUT

高速火车 **gāosù huǒchē** high-speed train

睾丸 **gāowán** testicles

高效率 **gāo xiàolǜ** efficient; streamlined

高效益 **gāo xiàoyì** businesslike; highly efficient

高兴 **gāoxìng** happy; pleased, glad, delighted ◊ happily; 见到你真高兴！ **jiàndào nǐ zhēn gāoxìng!** great to see you!

高新技术 **gāoxīn jìshù** high tech

高血压 **gāoxuèyā** hypertension, high blood pressure

高压 **gāoyā** high pressure; high-tension

高雅 **gāoyǎ** elegance ◊ elegant

羔羊 **gāoyáng** lamb

膏药 **gāoyao** plaster MED

高要求 **gāo yāoqiú** demanding ◊ tall order

高音 **gāoyīn** soprano

高音调 **gāoyīndiào** high-pitched

高原 **gāoyuán** plateau

搞运动 **gǎo yùndòng** campaign

搞糟 **gǎozāo** bungle; mess up

高涨 **gāozhǎng** upturn

告知 **gàozhī** inform

告终 **gàozhōng** culminate

稿子 **gǎozi** copy

嘎吱作声 **gāzhī zuòshēng** crunch

搁 **gē** put; add; put aside; deposit; 搁在 ... 上 **gē zài ... shàng** rest on, lean on

割 **gē** cut; mow

哥 **gē** elder brother

歌 **gē** song

鸽 **gē** dove; pigeon

格 **gé** grid; grating; square (*in board game*)

革 **gé** leather

嗝 **gé** hiccups

隔 **gé** cut off; separate

铬 **gè** chrome, chromium

个 **gè** *general purpose measure word*; 两个问题 **liǎnggè wèntí** two questions; 一个人 **yígè rén** a person

各 **gè** each; every; various

隔壁 **gébì** adjoining ◊ next door ◊ next-door neighbor

个别 **gèbié** individual

戈壁滩 **Gēbìtān** Gobi Desert

胳膊 **gēbo** arm

胳膊肘儿 **gēbozhǒur** elbow

割草机 **gécǎo jī** lawn mower

歌唱家 **gēchàng jiā** vocalist

歌唱团 **gēchàng tuán** vocal group

各处 **gèchù** everywhere

歌词 **gēcí** lyrics

疙瘩 **gēda** boil; pimple; lump; knot

格调 **gédiào** style

格斗 **gédòu** struggle

隔断 **géduàn** separate

哥哥 **gēge** elder brother

格格不入 **gégébúrù** go against the grain

咯咯地笑 **gēgē de xiào** giggle; gurgle; chuckle

给 **gěi** give; administer ◊ for; to; for the attention of

给以荣誉 **gěiyǐ róngyù** honor

歌剧 **gējù** opera

隔绝 **géjué** cut off; isolate

歌剧院 **gējù yuàn** opera house

隔开 **gékāi** partition off

蛤蜊 **gélí** clam

隔离 **gélí** isolate; segregate ◊ isolation; segregation; quarantine

隔帘 **gélián** screen

隔离间 **gélíjiān** isolation ward

格林威治标准时间 **Gélínwēizhì Biāozhǔn Shíjiān** Greenwich Mean Time

阁楼 **gélóu** attic; loft

哥们儿 **gēmenr** pal, buddy

革命 **gémìng** revolution ◊ revolutionary

革命家 **gémìng jiā** revolutionary

隔膜 **gémó** diaphragm

根 gēn root

跟 gēn follow ◊ with ◊ and ◊ heel

根本 gēnběn ultimate; underlying ◊ at all; fundamentally ◊ base; foundation; 他们根本不像 tāmen gēnběn búxiàng they're not at all alike

根除 gēnchú eradicate

耕 gēng plow

更 gēng change ◊ watch (*2 hour period*)

梗 gěng stalk

更 gèng more; even more; 更好 *gèng hǎo* better; 我更喜欢她了 *wǒ gèng xǐhuān tā le* I like her better

耕地 gēngdì plow ◊ arable land

更多 gèngduō more

更改 gēnggǎi alter ◊ alteration; 更改线路 *gēnggǎi xiànlù* reroute

更坏 gènghuài worse

更换 gēnghuàn exchange

耕牛 gēngniú (draft) ox

更新 gēngxīn renew; replace; upgrade

更衣室 gēngyī shì cubicle

耕种 gēngzhòng till; cultivate

耕作 gēngzuò cultivate ◊ cultivation

根基 gēnjī roots

根据 gēnjù basis ◊ according to; 根据具体环境来考虑 X *gēnjù jùtǐ huánjìng lái kǎolǜ X* look at X in context

根据地 gēnjùdì stronghold

跟上 gēnshàng keep up

根深蒂固 gēnshēndìgù entrenched

跟随 gēnsuí follow; string along

根源 gēnyuán origin; source ◊ originate

跟着 gēnzhe follow

跟踪 gēnzōng stalk; trace; trail

跟踪会议 gēnzōng huìyì follow-up meeting

跟踪者 gēnzōng zhě stalker

跟踪追捕 gēnzōng zhuībǔ track down

歌曲 gēqǔ song

个儿 gèr height

隔热 gérè insulate ◊ insulation

隔热垫 gérèdiàn mat

个人 gèrén individual ◊ personal ◊ privately

个人电脑 gèrén diànnǎo personal computer

个人卫生 gèrén wèishēng personal hygiene

个人主义者 gèrénzhǔyì zhě individualist

哥儿们 gērmen buddy, pal

各色各样 gèsè gèyàng all kinds; a choice

格式 géshì layout

各式各样 gèshì gèyàng assortment

格式设定 géshì shèdìng format

歌手 gēshǒu singer

个体 gètǐ freelance; self-employed

个体户 gètǐhù privately owned small business; freelancer

个体遗传性征 gètǐ yíchuán xìngzhēng genetic fingerprint

格外 géwài particularly; extra

割腕 gēwàn slash one's wrists

歌舞表演 gēwǔ biǎoyǎn song and dance performance; cabaret

歌舞剧 gēwǔjù musical

革新 géxīn innovation ◊ innovative

个性 gèxìng personality; character; 他很有个性 *tā hěn yǒu gèxìng* he's a real character

革新者 géxīn zhě innovator

隔音 géyīn soundproof

胳肢 gēzhi tickle

革制品 gézhìpǐn leather goods

各种各样 gèzhǒng gèyàng mixed, varied; miscellaneous; 各种各样的人 *gèzhǒng gèyàngde rén* all kinds of people

鸽子 gēzi dove; pigeon

格子 gézi checked ◊ grille

各自 gèzì respective ◊ individually; each; 各自付款 *gèzì fùkuǎn* go Dutch

弓 gōng bow

工 gōng work; worker

攻 gōng attack

功 gōng merit; service

供 gōng supply; provide

恭 gōng respectful

公 gōng public; male
宫 gōng palace
拱 gǒng arch
共 gòng common; joint; mutual ◊ together; altogether
公安局 Gōng'ān jú Public Security Bureau
公布 gōngbù announce; declare; release
共产党 Gòngchǎndǎng Communist Party
共产党员 Gòngchǎndǎng yuán Communist Party member
工厂 gōngchǎng factory
共产主义 gòngchǎn zhǔyì communism ◊ communist
工程 gōngchéng construction; engineering
工程师 gōngchéngshī engineer
共处 gòngchǔ coexist ◊ coexistence
供词 gòngcí confession
共存 gòngcún coexist ◊ coexistence
公道 gōngdào justice
工地 gōngdì building site
宫殿 gōngdiàn palace
拱顶 gǒngdǐng vault
攻读 gōngdú study
公愤 gōngfèn outrage
功夫 gōngfu kung-fu
公告牌 gōnggào pái bulletin board
公共 gōnggòng public
公共汽车 gōnggòng qìchē bus
公共汽车总站 gōnggòng qìchē zǒngzhàn bus station
公关 gōngguān public relations
公害 gōnghài environmental damage
公函 gōnghán official letter
恭贺 gōnghè congratulate
共和国 gònghé guó republic
共和主义 gònghé zhǔyì republicanism ◊ republican
共和主义者 gònghé zhǔyì zhě republican
工会 gōnghuì labor union
工会发言人 gōnghuì fāyánrén shop steward
公鸡 gōngjī rooster

攻击 gōngjí attack, assault; go for ◊ offensive
供给 gōngjǐ supply
弓箭 gōngjiàn bow and arrow
弓箭手 gōngjiàn shǒu archer
共计 gòngjì amount to, add up to
公斤 gōngjīn kilogram
恭敬 gōngjìng respect
工具 gōngjù tool; implement
公爵 gōngjué duke
工具格 gōngjùgé toolbar COMPUT
公开 gōngkāi public; open
功劳 gōngláo merit; service
公里 gōnglǐ kilometer
公路 gōnglù highway; road
公路赛车 gōnglù sàichē rally MOT
公路支线 gōnglù zhīxiàn access road
公猫 gōngmāo tomcat
拱门 gǒngmén archway
公民 gōngmín citizen ◊ civic; civil
公民权 gōngmín quán civil rights
公民投票 gōngmín tóupiào referendum
公墓 gōngmù graveyard, cemetery
功能 gōngnéng function
公鸟 gōngniǎo cock (male bird)
公牛 gōngniú bull
供暖 gōngnuǎn heating
公公 gōnggōng father-in-law (husband's father)
贡品 gòngpǐn tribute
公平 gōngpíng fair, just; balanced ◊ justice
公婆 gōngpó in-laws (husband's parents)
供求 gōngqiú supply and demand
公顷 gōngqǐng hectare
工人 gōngrén worker; workman
供认 gòngrèn confess ◊ confession
工人阶级 gōngrén jiējí working class
工伤 gōngshāng industrial accident
工商管理学硕士 gōngshāng guǎnlǐxué shuòshì MBA, master of business administration
公社 gōngshè commune

公升 gōngshēng liter
公式 gōngshì formula
供水 gōngshuǐ water supply
公司 gōngsī company; business; firm ◊ incorporated
公司车 gōngsī chē company car
公司法 gōngsī fǎ company law
公司形象 gōngsī xíngxiàng corporate image
公诉人 gōngsùrén (public) prosecutor
共同 gòngtóng collective; common; joint; shared; 和 X 有共同之处 hé X yǒu gòngtóng zhīchù have something in common with X
共同体 gòngtóngtǐ community
恭维 gōngwei compliment; flatter
公文 gōngwén document
公文包 gōngwén bāo briefcase
公物 gōngwù public property
公务员 gōngwùyuán civil servant
攻下 gōngxià capture
贡献 gòngxiàn contribute; devote ◊ contribution
恭喜 gōngxǐ congratulations
恭喜发财 gōngxǐ fācái wishing you prosperity (a New Year greeting)
公学 gōngxué public school
公羊 gōngyáng ram (male sheep)
供养 gōngyǎng keep, maintain, provide for
工业 gōngyè industry ◊ industrial
工业废料 gōngyè fèiliào industrial waste
工业化 gōngyèhuà industrialize
工业行动 gōngyè xíngdòng industrial action
工艺 gōngyì craft; technology
工艺美术 gōngyì měishù arts and crafts
供应 gōngyìng supply, provide ◊ provision
供应品 gōngyìngpǐn supplies
供应商 gōngyìngshāng supplier
供应与需求 gōngyìng yǔ xūqiú supply and demand
公用 gōngyòng communal; public
公用电话 gōngyòng diànhuà pay phone

公用实业 gōngyòng shíyè public utilities
共有者 gòngyǒu zhě part owner
公寓 gōngyù apartment
公园 gōngyuán park
公寓大厦 gōngyù dàshà apartment block
公约 gōngyuē pact; convention
公正 gōngzhèng fair, just; impartial ◊ fairly, justly ◊ fairness
公证 gōngzhèng authenticate; witness
公证人 gōngzhèng rén notary
公制 gōngzhì metric system
供职 gòngzhí serve; hold office
公职人员 gōngzhí rényuán official
公众 gōngzhòng public
公众交通运输工具 gōngzhòng jiāotōng yùnshū gōngjù public transportation
公主 gōngzhǔ princess
工资 gōngzī wage; salary
工资袋 gōngzīdài pay envelope
工作 gōngzuò work; job; business; employment ◊ work; 她很会工作 tā hěn huì gōngzuò she's a good worker; 工作的满足感 gōngzuò de mǎnzúgǎn job satisfaction
工作狂 gōngzuòkuáng workaholic
工作量 gōngzuòliàng workload
工作期间 gōngzuò qījiān work hours
工作日 gòngzuòrì work day
工作室 gōngzuòshì studio
工作台 gōngzuò tái workbench
工作许可 gōngzuò xǔkě work permit
工作站 gōngzuòzhàn work station
沟 gōu trench; ditch; channel
钩 gōu hook; jack (playing cards) ◊ crochet
狗 gǒu dog
购 gòu buy
够 gòu sufficient; enough; 够朋友 gòu péngyǒu true friend; 够大 gòudà quite big; big enough; 够

了 **gòule** that's enough; stop that!;
我受够了 **wǒ shòugòu le** I've had enough; 五十美元够了吗? **wǔshí měiyuán gòule ma?** will $50 be enough?

构成 **gòuchéng** comprise, constitute

狗狗 **gǒugǒu** doggie

篝火 **gōuhuǒ** fire

构架 **gòujià** structure ◊ structural

勾结 **gōujié** collaborate

勾结者 **gōujié zhě** collaborator

购买 **gòumǎi** purchase

狗屁 **gǒu pì!** V bullshit!

狗屎不如 **gǒushǐ bùrú** V dirtier than dog shit; lowest of the low

沟通 **gōutōng** communicate ◊ communication

狗窝 **gǒuwō** kennel

购物 **gòuwù** shopping ◊ do one's shopping

购物人 **gòuwùrén** shopper

购物中心 **gòuwù zhōngxīn** (shopping) mall

勾销 **gōuxiāo** write off *debt*

勾引 **gōuyǐn** pick up; seduce

构造 **gòuzào** construction; design

钩针 **gōuzhēn** crochet hook

钩子 **gōuzi** hook

姑 **gū** aunt (*father's sister*); sister-in-law (*husband's sister*)

箍 **gū** hoop

估 **gū** estimate

孤 **gū** orphaned; lonely

鼓 **gǔ** drum

股 **gǔ** share, stock ◊ *measure word for smells, wind*; 一股风 **yīgǔ fēng** a gust of wind; 一股味 **yīgǔ wèi** a smell

古 **gǔ** ancient; antiquated

骨 **gǔ** bone

谷 **gǔ** valley; grain

雇 **gù** take on; employ; 他被雇作 … **tā bèi gù zuò …** he's employed as a

顾 **gù** look around

故 **gù** therefore

固 **gù** solid; firm

瓜 **guā** melon

刮 **guā** scrape; shave

挂 **guà** hang; drape

刮擦 **guācā** scrape

刮掉 **guādiào** shave off; scrape off

挂断 **guàduàn** hang up TELEC

刮风 **guāfēng** blow

寡妇 **guǎfù** widow

挂钩 **guàgōu** hook, peg

呱呱叫 **guāguājiào** great

呱呱叫声 **guāguā jiàoshēng** croak; quack

挂号 **guàhào** register

挂号信 **guàhào xìn** registered letter; 寄挂号信 **jì guàhào xìn** send a letter registered

乖 **guāi** good; well-behaved

拐 **guǎi** turn; 向右拐 **xiàng yòu guǎi** turn to the right

怪 **guài** strange

拐棍 **guǎigùn** crook; walking stick

拐角 **guǎijiǎo** turning

乖戾 **guāilì** surly

乖僻 **guāipì** morose

拐骗 **guǎipiàn** kidnap

怪人 **guàirén** freak, weirdo; crank; nerd

拐弯 **guǎiwān** turn off; turn; corner; twist

拐弯抹角 **guǎiwān mòjiǎo** beat around the bush

怪物 **guàiwu** monster

怪相 **guàixiàng** grimace

怪异 **guàiyì** weird ◊ peculiarity

拐杖 **guǎizhàng** walking stick

呱啦呱啦 **guālā guālā** yap, yak

刮脸 **guāliǎn** shave, have a shave

关 **guān** close, shut; turn off; 他们已经关了 **tāmen yǐjīng guānle** they were shut

官 **guān** official

棺 **guān** casket, coffin

鳏 **guān** widower ◊ widowed

观 **guān** look at; observe

管 **guān** manage; control; concern oneself with; bother ◊ tube; pipe; 不要管 **bùyào guǎn** take no notice of

罐 **guàn** jar; pitcher

冠 **guàn** hat; crown

灌 **guàn** pour into

鹳 **guàn** stork

惯 **guàn** used to; accustomed

关隘 **guān'ài** pass

关闭 **guānbì** close (down), shut (down); wind up ◊ closure ◊ closed

棺材 **guāncai** casket, coffin

观测 **guāncè** observe

观察 **guānchá** keep an eye on; monitor ◊ observation

惯常 **guàncháng** habitual

观察员 **guānchá yuán** observer

罐车 **guànchē** tanker (*truck*)

贯彻 **guànchè** implement; carry out

贯穿 **guànchuān** throughout

冠词 **guàncí** article

管道 **guǎndào** pipeline; tube; pipe

管道装置 **guǎndào zhuāngzhì** plumbing

观点 **guāndiǎn** point of view; view; slant

关掉 **guāndiào** turn off; be off

官方 **guānfāng** formal; official ◊ officially

鳏夫 **guānfū** widower

官服 **guānfú** robe

光 **guāng** light; brightness; glory ◊ finished; gone; bare; naked ◊ only

广 **guǎng** wide; broad; extensive

逛 **guàng** wander; stroll; 逛商店 **guàng shāngdiàn** walk around the stores

灌溉 **guàngài** irrigate ◊ irrigation

灌溉渠 **guàngài qú** irrigation canal

光笔 **guāngbǐ** light pen

光标 **guāngbiāo** cursor

广播 **guǎngbō** broadcast

广播电台 **guǎngbō diàntái** radio station

光彩 **guāngcǎi** brilliance

广场 **guǎngchǎng** square; place

光导纤维 **guāngdǎo xiānwéi** fiber optics

光点 **guāngdiǎn** blip

光碟 **guāngdié** disc

广东 **Guǎngdōng** Canton ◊ Cantonese

广东话 **Guǎngdōnghuà** Cantonese

广度 **guǎngdù** width; breadth

广而言之 **guǎng ér yán zhī** in general

广泛 **guǎngfàn** wide, extensive ◊ widely

广告 **guǎnggào** advertisement

广告公司 **guǎnggào gōngsī** advertising agency

广告牌 **guǎnggào pái** billboard

广告业 **guǎnggào yè** advertising (industry)

光顾 **guānggù** patronize

光滑 **guānghuá** smooth; glossy

光滑面 **guānghuámiàn** glaze

光环 **guānghuán** halo

光辉 **guānghuī** glow

光辉灿烂 **guānghuī cànlàn** splendor

光脚 **guāngjiǎo** be barefoot

光洁 **guāngjié** clear

广阔 **guǎngkuò** wide; great; enormous

光芒四射 **guāngmáng sìshè** radiate

光面 **guāngmiàn** glossy

光明 **guāngmíng** bright; rosy

光年 **guāngnián** light year

光盘 **guāngpán** CD-ROM; CD

光驱 **guāngqū** CD-ROM drive

光圈 **guāngquān** aperture

光荣 **guāngróng** honor; glory ◊ honorable; glorious

光天化日 **guāngtiān huàrì** in broad daylight

光秃秃 **guāng tūtū** bare; bald

观光 **guānguāng** look around; go sightseeing

观光客 **guānguāngkè** sightseer; tourist

观光旅游 **guānguāng lǚyóu** sightseeing tour

光纤 **guāng xiān** fiber optics

光线 **guāngxiàn** light; ray

光学 **guāngxué** optics

光泽 **guāngzé** shine; luster

光着头 **guāngzhe tóu** bareheaded

关怀 **guānhuái** show sympathy for; show concern for

关机 **guānjī** shut down COMPUT

管家 **guǎnjiā** housekeeper; butler ◊ run a household

关键 **guānjiàn** key, crucial, vital ◊ key; crux; bolt (*of door*)

关键钮 **guān jiànniǔ** off switch

关节 **guānjié** joint

关节炎 **guānjié yán** arthritis

关进 **guānjìn** put away

冠军 **guànjūn** champion; championship

观看 **guānkàn** watch

官吏 **guānlì** mandarin

管理 **guǎnlǐ** control; manage; administer; operate; run ◊ administration; management

关联 **guānlián** relevance

官僚 **guānliáo** bureaucrat ◊ bureaucratic

官僚程序 **guānliáo chéngxù** red tape

官僚制度 **guānliáo zhìdù** bureaucracy

官僚主义 **guānliáo zhǔyì** bureaucracy

惯例 **guànlì** custom; habit

管理人员 **guǎnlǐ rényuán** administrator; management team

管理学 **guǎnlǐxué** management studies

管理员 **guǎnlǐyuán** superintendent

关门 **guānmén** close *store etc*; close down; close the door ◊ closed

关门时间 **guānmén shíjiān** closing time

灌木 **guànmù** bush; shrub

灌木丛 **guànmùcóng** shrubbery; undergrowth

官能 **guānnéng** sense

关卡 **guānqiǎ** checkpoint

灌输 **guànshū** indoctrinate

关税 **guānshuì** customs duty, tariff

罐头 **guàntou** can (*for drinks etc*)

观望点 **guānwàng diǎn** vantage point

关系 **guānxi** connection, relation; relationship; 没关系 **méi guānxi** it doesn't matter; 外交关系 **wàijiāo guānxi** diplomatic relations; 与 X 关系好 **yǔ X guānxì hǎo** be on good terms with X

管弦乐 **guǎnxiányuè** orchestral

music

管弦乐队 **guǎnxián yuèduì** orchestra

关小 **guānxiǎo** turn down *volume*

关系到 **guānxì dào** apply to, affect

关心 **guānxīn** concern; care; consideration ◊ be concerned about; care about

冠心病 **guànxīnbìng** coronary disease

惯性 **guànxìng** inertia

盥洗室 **guànxǐshì** washroom

关押 **guānyā** lock up

惯用 **guànyòng** commonly use; 惯用法 **guànyòngfǎ** common usage; habitual; 惯用左手 **guànyòng zuǒshǒu** left-handed

关于 **guānyú** with reference to, regarding; about

官员 **guānyuán** official

管乐器 **guǎnyuèqì** wind instrument

馆长 **guǎnzhǎng** curator

管制措施 **guǎnzhì cuòshī** controls, restrictions

观众 **guānzhòng** audience; crowd; spectators; viewers

罐装 **guànzhuāng** can ◊ canned

冠状动脉 **guànzhuàng dòngmài** coronary artery

冠状动脉血栓 **guànzhuàng dòngmài xuèshuān** coronary thrombosis

管子 **guǎnzi** pipe; tube

馆子 **guǎnzi** restaurant

管嘴 **guǎnzuǐ** jet

刮水器 **guāshuǐqì** windshield wiper

挂锁 **guàsuǒ** padlock

挂毯 **guàtǎn** tapestry; wall hanging

挂衣钩 **guàyīgōu** coat hook

瓜子 **guāzǐ** melon seed

古巴 **Gǔbā** Cuba ◊ Cuban

古板 **gǔbǎn** straitlaced, stuffy

鼓吹 **gǔchuī** advocate

鼓槌 **gǔchuí** drumstick

古代 **gǔdài** antiquity; ancient times; ancient China ◊ ancient

孤单 **gūdān** alone; solitary

古典 gǔdiǎn classic; classical

古典音乐 gǔdiǎn yīnyuè classical music

固定 gùdìng fasten; fix ◊ fixed; 把 X 固定在 Y 上 bǎ X gùdìng zài Y shang fasten X onto Y; 用针固定 yòng zhēn gùdìng pin

固定装置 gùdìng zhuāngzhì fixture

股东 gǔdōng stockholder, shareholder

古董 gǔdǒng antique

股东公司 gǔdōng gōngsī holding company

古董商 gǔdǒng shāng antique dealer

孤独 gūdú lonely; solitary

孤独感 gūdú gǎn loneliness

孤儿 gū'er orphan

孤儿院 gū'er yuàn orphanage

股份 gǔfèn stock, share

股份公司 gǔfèn gōngsī joint-stock company

股份有限公司 gǔfèn yǒuxiàn gōngsī corporation

姑父 gūfu uncle (father's sister's husband)

辜负 gūfù disappoint

毂盖 gǔgài hubcap

故宫 Gùgōng the former imperial palace in Beijing; the Forbidden City

姑姑 gūgu auntie (father's sister)

古怪 gǔguài funny, odd; eccentric; 古怪的人 gǔguài de rén eccentric; weirdo

汩汩地流 gǔgǔ de liú gurgle

鼓鼓囊囊 gǔgu nāngnang bulging

固化 gùhuà solidify

骨灰 gǔhuī ashes (after cremation)

骨灰盒 gǔhuīhé urn (for ashes)

硅 guī silicon

归 guī return; belong to

龟 guī turtle; tortoise

轨 guǐ rail; track

鬼 guǐ ghost

贵 guì expensive; noble

桂 guì cassia; laurel; osmanthus

柜 guì cupboard

跪 guì kneel

鬼把戏 guǐbǎxì gimmick

贵宾 guìbīn guest of honor

归并 guībìng merge; 把 … 归并在一起 bǎ … guībìng zài yìqǐ lump together

轨道 guǐdào track; orbit; 绕轨道运行 rào guǐdào yùnxíng orbit

鬼地方 guǐdìfāng horrible place; dump

规定 guīdìng stipulate ◊ stipulation; regulation; rule; 违约罚款的规定 wéiyuē fákuǎn de guīdìng penalty clause; 规定的任期 guīdìng de rènqī stint; period of office

规范 guīfàn rules; standard

归附者 guīfù zhě convert

规格 guīgé specifications

归根结底 guīgēn jiédǐ boil down to

归功 guīgōng owing to; thanks to

鬼鬼祟祟 guǐguǐ suìsuì shifty-looking; sneaky

规划 guīhuà plan ◊ planning

归还 guīhuán give back; return

归家 guījiā homecoming

诡计多端 guǐjì duōduān scheming

规矩点！guījǔ diǎn! behave (yourself)!

归类 guīlèi classify

规模 guīmó scale

桂皮 guìpí cinnamon

硅片 guīpiàn silicon chip

归属 guīshǔ belong to

柜台 guìtái counter, bar

归途 guītú way back

跪下 guìxià kneel

规则 guīzé rule; regulations

诡诈 guǐzhà underhand

规章 guīzhāng regulation

贵重 guìzhòng valuable

贵重物品 guìzhòng wùpǐn valuables

柜子 guìzi cabinet; cupboard

刽子手 guìzishǒu executioner

贵族 guìzú nobility

估计 gūjì calculate; estimate; assess; put the cost at ◊ estimate; valuation

古迹 gǔjì antiquities; historical

sites

顾及 **gùjí** take into account; consider

估价 **gūjià** appraise; value

骨节嶙峋 **gǔjié línxún** gnarled

故居 **gùjū** former residence

顾客 **gùkè** client, customer; consumer

顾客关系 **gùkè guānxi** customer relations

古老 **gǔlǎo** ancient

谷类 **gǔlèi** cereal

孤立 **gūlì** isolate; separate ◊ isolated

鼓励 **gǔlì** encourage; urge on ◊ encouragement; 鼓励的话 **gǔlìde huà** pep talk

谷粒 **gǔlì** grain

估量 **gūliáng** size up, weigh up; assess; estimate

孤零零 **gū línglíng** solitary; all alone

孤立无援 **gūlì wúyuán** defenseless

顾虑 **gùlù** misgivings, scruples

鼓膜 **gǔmó** eardrum

滚 **gǔn** roll ◊ get lost!

棍 **gùn** rod

滚出去！ **gǔnchūqù!** get out!

滚蛋！ **gǔndàn!** get lost!

滚动 **gǔndòng** roll

姑娘 **gūniang** girl

牯牛 **gǔniú** bull

滚开！ **gǔnkāi!** ∨ fuck off!

咕哝 **gūnong** mumble, mutter

滚烫 **gǔntàng** piping hot

滚珠轴承 **gǔnzhū zhóuchéng** ball bearing

棍子 **gùnzi** stick; rod

锅 **guō** pot, pan; wok

国 **guó** state; country

果 **guǒ** fruit; result

裹 **guǒ** wrap

过 **guò** across; over ◊ pass; cross; spend; 走过 **zǒuguò** walk past ◊ (*past indicator*): 我去过中国 **wǒ qùguo Zhōngguó** I've been to China; 我吃过了 **wǒ chīguò le** I have eaten

锅铲 **guōchǎn** spatula

过程 **guòchéng** process

过错 **guòcuò** error; mistake

过道 **guòdào** corridor

过得快乐 **guòde kuàilè** enjoy oneself

过得去 **guòdequ** tolerable; acceptable ◊ be able to get by; be able to get through

过低评价 **guòdī píngjià** underrate

果冻 **guǒdòng** jelly

过度 **guòdù** excess ◊ excessive; undue; 过度感光 **guòdù gǎnguāng** overexpose

过渡 **guòdù** transition ◊ transitional

果断 **guǒduàn** decisive

过度紧张 **guòdù jǐnzhāng** hypertension

国防部 **Guófáng Bù** Department of Defense

国防部长 **Guófáng Bùzhǎng** Defense Secretary

国防开支 **guófáng kāizhī** defense budget

过分 **guòfèn** excessive; unreasonable ◊ unduly; 他太过分了 **tā tài guòfènle** he's gone too far; he's too much

果脯 **guǒfǔ** candied fruit

过高 **guògāo** exorbitant; extortionate; too high

过高估计 **guògāo gūjì** overestimate ◊ overrated

过高要价 **guògāo yàojià** overcharge

国歌 **guógē** national anthem

国会 **guóhuì** Congress ◊ Congressional

国会议员 **guóhuì yìyuán** Congressman, member of Congress

过火 **guòhuǒ** exaggerated; overdone ◊ exaggerate

国籍 **guójí** citizenship; nationality

国际 **guójì** international ◊ internationally

国家 **guójiā** country; nation; state ◊ national

国家队 **guójiāduì** national team

国家公园 **guójiā gōngyuán** national park

果酱 **guǒjiàng** jam; conserve

国际比赛 **guójì bǐsài** international (match)

过节 **guòjié** celebrate a festival

国际法庭 **Guójì Fǎtíng** International Court of Justice

国际货币基金 **Guójì Huòbì Jījīn** International Monetary Fund

国际劳动节 **Guójì Láodòngjié** International Labor Day

过境 **guòjìng** be in transit (*between countries*)

过境签证 **guòjìng qiānzhèng** transit visa

国际收支差额 **guójì shōuzhī chā'é** (international) balance of payments

过来 **guòlái** step in; come over ◊ across

国立 **guólì** national; state-run

过量 **guòliàng** overdose

锅炉 **guōlú** boiler

过滤 **guòlǜ** filter; strain; 过滤式咖啡壶 **guòlǜshì kāfēihú** percolator

过滤器 **guòlǜ qì** filter; strainer

过路人 **guòlùrén** passer-by

过滤嘴香烟 **guòlǜzuǐ xiāngyān** filter-tipped cigarette

国民 **guómín** national

过敏 **guòmǐn** allergy ◊ hypersensitive

国民党 **Guómíndǎng** Kuomintang, KMT, Nationalist Party

国民生产总值 **guómín shēngchǎn zǒngzhí** GNP, gross national product

国内 **guónèi** domestic; internal; 在国内 **zài guónèi** at home (*in country*)

国内航班 **guónèi hángbān** domestic flight

国内贸易 **guónèi màoyì** internal trade

国内生产总值 **guónèi shēngchǎn zǒngzhí** GDP, gross domestic product

国内外 **guónèiwài** at home and abroad

过年 **guònián** celebrate Chinese New Year

果皮 **guǒpí** peel (*of fruit*)

国旗 **guóqí** national flag

过期 **guòqī** out of date

国庆节 **Guóqìngjié** National Day

过去 **guòqù** past ◊ go by; 那都已经过去了 **nà dōu yǐjīng guòqù le** that's all past now; 在过去 **zài guòqù** in the past

过去分词 **guòqù fēncí** past participle

过去时 **guòqùshí** past tense

果然如此 **guǒrán rúcǐ** sure enough

果肉 **guǒròu** flesh (*of fruit*); pulp

过山车 **guò shān chē** roller coaster

过剩 **guòshèng** surplus

果实 **guǒshí** fruit

过时 **guòshí** out of date; dated; old-fashioned; out of fashion; stale *news*

果树 **guǒshù** fruit tree

过堂风 **guòtáng fēng** draft

国外 **guówài** abroad ◊ foreign

国王 **guówáng** king

国务访问 **guówù fǎngwèn** state visit

国务卿 **Guówùqīng** Secretary of State

国务院 **Guówùyuàn** Department of State, State Department

果馅饼 **guǒxiànbǐng** flan

果馅儿饼 **guǒxiànr bǐng** tart

国宴 **guóyàn** state banquet

过夜 **guòyè** stay the night, spend the night

过一会儿 **guò yíhuìr** by and by, soon

国营 **guóyíng** state-owned; state-run

国有化 **guóyǒu huà** nationalize

过于 **guòyú** excessively; too

果园 **guǒyuán** orchard

过早 **guòzǎo** untimely

国债 **guózhài** national debt

果汁 **guǒzhī** fruit juice

骨盆 **gúpén** pelvis

孤僻 **gūpì** withdrawn; autistic

股票 **gǔpiào** stock, share

股票交易所 **gǔpiào jiāoyìsuǒ**

stock exchange

股票经纪人 gǔpiào jīngjì rén stockbroker

股票市场 gǔpiào shìchǎng stock market; 股票市场暴跌 *gǔpiào shìchǎng bàodiē* stockmarket crash

鼓起 gǔqǐ drum up; rouse

鼓起劲儿来！gǔ qǐ jìnr lái! cheer up!

鼓起勇气 gǔqǐ yǒngqì pluck up courage

故事 gùshi story; tale; narrative; joke

鼓手 gǔshǒu drummer

固守 gùshǒu cling to

骨髓 gǔsuǐ bone marrow

固体 gùtǐ solid

骨头 gǔtou bone

顾问 gùwèn adviser; consultant

鼓舞 gǔwǔ encourage; 令人鼓舞 *lìngrén* gǔwǔ encouraging

股息 gǔxī dividend

故乡 gùxiāng home town; homeland

古雅小巧 gǔyǎ xiǎoqiǎo quaint

故意 gùyì deliberate; willful ◊ deliberately, on purpose

雇佣 gùyōng employ

雇佣兵 gùyōngbīng mercenary

固有 gùyǒu inherent

雇员 gùyuán employee; staff

鼓掌 gǔzhǎng applaud ◊ applause

故障 gùzhàng breakdown; defect; bug COMPUT

骨折 gǔzhé break, fracture ◊ broken

固执 gùzhí persistent, dogged; inflexible; stubborn; willful

孤注一掷 gūzhù yízhì desperate ◊ desperation; 孤注一掷之举 *gūzhù yízhì zhījǔ* an act of desperation

故作姿态 gùzuò zītài put on an act, put on airs

# H

哈 **hā** exhale ◊ ha-ha

嗨，咳 **hāi** (*regret*): 嗨，我怎么给忘了呢? *hāi, wǒ zěnme gěi wàng le?* oh no, how come I forgot it?

还 **hái** still; as well as; yet; quite; even more; also; 还有什么? *háiyǒu shénme?* anything else?; 你还要吗? *nǐ háiyào ma?* do you still want it?

海 **hǎi** sea

害 **hài** harm

海岸 **hǎi'àn** coast

海岸线 **hǎi'àn xiàn** coastline

海拔 **hǎibá** altitude; elevation; height above sea level

海报 **hǎibào** poster, bill

海豹 **hǎibào** seal (*animal*)

海边 **hǎibiān** seaside

海滨 **hǎibīn** seaside

海滨砂石 **hǎibīn shāshí** shingle

海滨胜地 **hǎibīn shèngdì** seaside resort

害虫 **hàichóng** pest; vermin

害处 **hàichu** damage; harm

海带 **hǎidài** kelp, (edible) seaweed

海胆 **hǎidǎn** sea urchin

海港 **hǎigǎng** seaport

海关 **hǎiguān** customs

海关官员 **hǎiguān guānyuán** customs officer

还好 **háihǎo** alright, not bad

海军 **hǎijūn** navy ◊ naval

海军基地 **hǎijūn jīdì** naval base

海军兰 **hǎijūn lán** navy blue

海军强国 **hǎijūn qiángguó** sea power

海军上将 **hǎijūn shàngjiàng** admiral

海里 **hǎilǐ** nautical mile

海陆兵 **hǎilùbīng** marine MIL

海洛因 **hǎiluòyīn** heroin

海绵 **hǎimián** sponge; foam rubber

海南岛 **Hǎinán Dǎo** Hainan Island

害鸟 **hàiniǎo** pest (*bird*)

海鸥 **hǎi'ōu** seagull

害怕 **hàipà** be afraid, be frightened; be afraid of, dread

海平面 **hǎipíngmiàn** sea level

骇人听闻 **hài rén tīngwén** hideous; shocking

海上 **hǎishàng** maritime; seafaring

还是 **háishi** or

海市蜃楼 **hǎishì shènlóu** mirage

害兽 **hàishòu** pest

海难 **hǎinàn** shipwreck; 遇海难 *yù hǎinàn* be shipwrecked

海损 **hǎisǔn** maritime damage

海滩 **hǎitān** beach

海豚 **hǎitún** dolphin

海外 **hǎiwài** overseas

海湾 **hǎiwān** gulf; inlet

海味 **hǎiwèi** seafood

海峡 **hǎixiá** channel; strait

海星 **hǎixīng** starfish

害羞 **hàixiū** shy

海洋 **hǎiyáng** ocean ◊ marine

海员 **hǎiyuán** sailor

海运 **hǎiyùn** ship; shipping

海蜇 **hǎizhé** jellyfish

孩子 **háizi** child

孩子气 **háiziqì** infantile

哈喇 **hāla** rancid

蛤蟆 **háma** toad

寒 **hán** cold

含 **hán** contain; suck

函 **hán** letter

喊 **hǎn** shout

汉 **Hàn** Han

汗 **hàn** sweat

旱 **hàn** dryness

焊 **hàn** weld

汉堡包 **hànbǎobāo** hamburger, beefburger

旱冰鞋 **hànbīng xié** roller skate;

四轮旱冰鞋 **silún hànbīng xié** in-line skate, rollerblade®

汉朝 Hàncháo Han Dynasty

行 háng line; row; trade; profession

航班 hángbān flight

航班号 **hángbān hào** flight number

航标 hángbiāo buoy

航程 hángchéng voyage

行道 hángdào lane (*on freeway*)

航海 hánghǎi voyage ◊ nautical ◊ navigate

航海家 hánghǎi jiā navigator

航海图 hánghǎi tú chart

行话 hánghuà jargon, slang

行家 hángjia expert; connoisseur

航空 hángkōng aviation ◊ aeronautical ◊ by air

航空公司 **hángkōng gōngsī** airline

航空母舰 **hángkōng mǔjiàn** aircraft carrier

航空摄影 hángkōng shèyǐng aerial photography

航空图 hángkōng tú chart

航空信件 hángkōng xìnjiàn air letter, airmail

航空邮件 hángkōng yóujiàn air letter, airmail

行列 hángliè procession

航天 hángtiān space flight

航天飞机 **hángtiān fēijī** space shuttle

航线 hángxiàn airline; flight route

航向 hángxiàng course

航行 hángxíng cruise

航行学 hángxíng xué navigation

行业 hángyè trade; profession

含糊 hánhú ambiguous

含糊不清 hánhú bùqīng unclear; 含糊地说 **hánhude shuō** mumble

含糊其辞 hánhu qící oblique; coy

旱季 hànjì dry season

罕见 hǎnjiàn rare

喊叫 hǎnjiào call; cry; cry out ◊ shouting

喊叫声 **hǎnjiào shēng** yell; scream

焊接 hànjiē weld; solder

焊接工人 hànjiē gōngrén welder

含酒精 hán jiǔjīng alcoholic

寒冷（刺骨） **hánlěng (cìgǔ)** icy cold, bitterly cold

含量 hánliàng content

汗淋淋 hànlínlín sweaty

寒流 hánliú stream of cold air

含氯氟烃 hán lǜfútīng chlorofluorocarbon, CFC

汗沫儿 hànmòr sweat; lather

汗衫 hànshān T-shirt

鼾声 hánshēng snoring

喊声 hǎnshēng shout

函授 hánshòu correspondence course

寒暑表 hánshǔbiǎo thermometer

酣睡 hānshuì sound sleep

汗水 hànshuǐ sweat, perspiration

寒酸 hánsuān shabby

捍卫 hànwèi defend ◊ defense

捍卫者 hànwèi zhě champion

含蓄 hánxù reserve ◊ implicit

汉学 hànxué sinology

汉学家 hànxuéjiā sinologist

含药物 hán yàowù medicated

含义 hányì meaning

汉语 Hànyǔ Chinese

旱灾 hànzāi drought

汉藏 Hànzàng Sino-Tibetan

汉字 Hànzì Chinese character

汉族 Hànzú the Han people

蚝 háo oyster

毫 háo milli- ◊ in the least

好 hǎo good; fine ◊ well; quite; very; 比 ... 好 **bǐ ... hǎo** better than; 太好了！ **tàihǎole!** great!

耗 hào use; consume

号 hào number

好 hào like

好吧 hǎoba very well, ok

毫不犹豫 háobù yóuyù like a shot, without the least hesitation

好吵闹 hào chǎonào rowdy

号称 hàochēng be called

好吃 hǎochī delicious; good to eat

好处 hǎochù advantage, benefit; compensation; 对你有好处 **duì nǐ yǒu hǎochù** it's to your advantage; it's good for you

耗费 hàofèi spend; use

好感 **hǎogǎn** fondness; affection

好管闲事 **hàoguǎn xiánshì** nosy

豪华 **háohuá** luxury ◊ luxurious; de luxe; plush; 豪华的生活方式 **háohuáde shēnghuó fāngshì** high life

嚎叫 **háojiào** howl

浩劫 **hàojié** havoc

好极了 **hǎojíle** excellent, very good

耗尽 **hàojìn** run down; use up; run out

好竞争 **hào jìngzhēng** competitive

好看 **hǎokàn** good-looking

毫克 **háokè** milligram

好客 **hàokè** hospitable; 好客的主人 **hàokè de zhǔrén** a congenial host

好了，好了！ **hǎole, hǎole!** there, there!

号码 **hàomǎ** number; size

毫米 **háomǐ** millimeter

好奇 **hàoqí** curious, inquisitive ◊ curiously

好强 **hàoqiáng** ambitious

好球 **hǎoqiú** strike (*in baseball*)

好奇心 **hàoqí xīn** curiosity; 引起好奇心 **yǐnqǐ hàoqí xīn** intrigue

好听 **hǎotīng** melodious; nice-sounding

好哇 **hǎowa** hurray

毫无 **háowú** not in the least; 毫无用处 **háowú yòngchù** no use at all

毫无顾忌 **háowú gùjì** regardless

好象 **hǎoxiàng** seem; resemble; look like ◊ apparently ◊ as if, as though

好笑 **hǎoxiào** amusing, funny; jovial

好心 **hǎoxīn** kind-hearted, sweet

好学 **hàoxué** academic, studious

好意 **hǎoyì** kindness

耗用 **hàoyòng** consume, use

蚝油 **háoyóu** oyster sauce

号召 **hàozhào** call; call on

豪猪 **háozhū** porcupine

好转 **hǎozhuǎn** get better, improve ◊ improvement, upturn

哈萨克斯坦 **Hāsàkèsītǎn** Kazakhstan ◊ Kazahk

哈腰 **hāyāo** stoop; bow

喝 **hē** drink

和 **hé** and; along with ◊ harmonious; mild ◊ sum; peace; 和 ... 一起 **hé ... yìqǐ** with

盒 **hé** case; box; container

颌 **hé** jaw

何 **hé** who; what; which; why; how

核 **hé** core, center; pip, pit

河 **hé** river

荷 **hé** lotus

合 **hé** join; fit; suit; 合你口味儿 **hé nǐ kǒuwèir** to your liking

褐 **hè** brown

贺 **hè** congratulate

和蔼可亲 **hé'ǎi kěqīn** amiable

河岸 **hé'àn** river bank

荷包蛋 **hébao dàn** fried egg

合抱双臂 **hébào shuāngbì** fold one's arms

河边 **hébiān** riverside

合并 **hébìng** merge, amalgamate ◊ merger

合不来 **hébùlái** not get on; be incompatible

喝采 **hècǎi** applaud; cheer; cheer on

合唱 **héchàng** sing in chorus ◊ choir

合成 **héchéng** synthesis

合成代谢激素 **héchéng dàixiè jīsù** anabolic steroid

河床 **héchuáng** riverbed

喝倒彩 **hè dàocǎi** boo

合得来 **hédélái** get on well; be compatible

合调 **hédiào** in tune

核对 **héduì** check

荷尔蒙 **hé'ěrméng** hormone

合法 **héfǎ** legal; legitimate; lawful

核反应堆 **hé fǎnyìng duī** nuclear reactor

合法性 **héfǎ xìng** legality

核废物 **hé fèiwù** nuclear waste

和服 **héfú** kimono

合格 **hégé** qualified; eligible; competent

合格会计师 **hégé kuàijì shī** certified public accountant

喝光 **hēguāng** drink up

和好 **héhǎo** make it up; be reconciled

和平 **héhu** conform with; 和平语法 **héhu yǔfǎ** grammatical

荷花 **héhuā** lotus (flower)

和缓 **héhuǎn** gentle, mild

合伙 **héhuǒ** team up; form a partnership; 合伙攻击 **héhuǒ gōngjī** gang up on; 合伙经营 **héhuǒ jīngyíng** partnership COM

合伙人 **héhuǒ rén** partner

嘿 **hēi** (appreciation): 嘿，这可不错 **hēi, zhè kě búcuò** hey, this isn't bad at all

黑 **hēi** black; dark

黑暗 **hēi'àn** blackness; dark, darkness

黑白片 **hēibái piàn** black and white movie

黑板 **hēibǎn** blackboard

黑板擦 **hēibǎncā** blackboard eraser

黑板架 **hēibǎnjià** (blackboard) easel

黑客 **hēikè** hacker

黑麦 **hēimài** rye

黑莓 **hēiméi** blackberry

黑名单 **hēi míngdān** blacklist

黑啤酒 **hēi píjiǔ** dark beer

黑钱 **hēiqián** slush fund

黑人 **hēirén** black (person)

黑色 **hēisè** black (color)

黑社会 **hēi shèhuì** underworld

黑市 **hēishì** black market

黑市经济 **hēishì jīngjì** black economy

黑手党 **Hēishǒudǎng** Mafia

黑桃 **hēitáo** spades (in cards)

黑线鳕 **hēixiàn xuě** haddock

黑匣子 **hēi xiázi** black box

黑猩猩 **hēi xīngxing** chimpanzee

黑眼镜 **hēi yǎnjìng** dark glasses

核计 **héjì** calculate

合计 **héjì** add up

和解 **héjiě** make up

合金 **héjīn** alloy

喝酒 **hējiǔ** drink; drinking; 我不喝酒 **wǒ bù hējiǔ** I don't drink

河口 **hékǒu** rivermouth

河口湾 **hékǒu wān** estuary

荷兰 **Hélán** Holland, the

Netherlands ◊ Dutch

合礼 **hélǐ** kosher

合理 **hélǐ** rational, reasonable; sensible, sound ◊ reasonably, rationally

核裂变 **hé lièbiàn** nuclear fission

合理化 **hélǐ huà** rationalize ◊ rationalization

河流 **héliú** river

合理性 **hélǐ xìng** rationality

河马 **hémǎ** hippopotamus

褐煤 **hèméi** brown coal

和睦 **hémù** harmony

痕 **hén** mark; trace; scar

很 **hěn** very; quite

狠 **hěn** hard-hearted

恨 **hèn** hate ◊ hatred

很棒 **hěnbàng** great

狠毒 **hěndú** malicious; venomous

核能 **hénéng** nuclear power, nuclear energy

核能站 **hénéng zhàn** nuclear power station

横 **héng** horizontal

哼唱 **hēngchàng** hum

横冲直撞 **héngchōng zhízhuàng** rampage

横渡 **héngdù** crossing NAUT

横幅 **héngfú** banner, streamer

横杆 **hénggān** crossbar (of high jump)

横贯 **héngguàn** cross

横跨 **héngkuà** span

横跨大西洋 **héngkuà Dàxīyáng** transatlantic

横梁 **héngliáng** beam

衡量 **héngliáng** consider; weigh up

衡量标准 **héngliáng biāozhǔn** yardstick

横木 **héngmù** crossbar (of goal)

横排 **héngpái** landscape print

恒温器 **héngwēn qì** thermostat

恒温育婴箱 **héngwēn yùyīng xiāng** incubator

横向 **héngxiàng** thwart

恒心 **héngxīn** stamina; persistence

痕迹 **hénjì** evidence; trail; traces

狠揍 **hěnzòu** beat up

和平 **hépíng** peace

和平队 **Hépíngduì** Peace Corps

和平主义 **hépíng zhǔyì** pacifism

和平主义者 **hépíng zhǔyì zhě** pacifist

和气 **héqi** polite; friendly; peaceable

呵欠 **hēqiàn** yawn

合群 **héqún** sociable ◊ fit in

和善 **héshàn** friendly

和尚 **héshàng** Buddhist monk

合身 **héshēn** fit

和声 **héshēng** harmony

核实 **héshí** verification ◊ verify

合适 **héshì** suitable, appropriate; right; convenient ◊ fit; 合适的位置 *héshìde wèizhi* niche

合算 **hésuàn** profitable

喝汤 **hētāng** drink soup

核桃 **hétáo** walnut

合同 **hétóng** contract ◊ contractual

合为一体 **hé wéi yītǐ** merge

核武器 **hé wǔqì** nuclear weapons

贺喜 **hèxǐ** congratulate

和谐 **héxié** harmonious

核心 **héxīn** core; kernel

贺信 **hèxìn** letter of congratulation

合意 **héyì** please; appeal to

合意男士 **héyì nánshì** eligible bachelor

合影 **héyǐng** group photo

合用 **héyòng** double up, share

和约 **héyuē** peace treaty

盒子 **hézi** box

合资企业 **hézī qǐyè** joint venture

合组 **hézǔ** consortium

喝醉 **hēzuì** get drunk

喝醉了 **hēzuìle** drunk; drunken

合作 **hézuò** cooperate, collaborate ◊ cooperation, collaboration ◊ cooperative

合作社 **hézuò shè** cooperative

合作者 **hézuò zhě** collaborator

轰 **hōng** chuck out, drive away

红 **hóng** red

虹 **hóng** rainbow

洪 **hóng** big ◊ flood

哄 **hǒng** coax

红宝石 **hóng bǎoshí** ruby

红茶 **hóngchá** black tea

红肠面包 **hóngcháng miànbāo** hot dog

宏大 **hóngdà** great

红灯 **hóngdēng** red light

红灯区 **hóngdēng qū** red light district

轰的一声 **hōngde yīshēng** bang

轰动 **hōngdòng** cause a sensation ◊ sensation ◊ sensational

红光满面 **hóngguāng mǎnmiàn** radiant

轰击 **hōngjī** shoot at; bombard

红军 **Hóngjūn** Red Army

烘烤 **hōngkǎo** toast

洪亮 **hóngliàng** sonorous

红绿灯 **hónglǜdēng** traffic light

轰鸣 **hōngmíng** roar

轰鸣声 **hōngmíng shēng** roar

虹膜 **hóngmó** iris *(of eye)*

哄骗 **hǒngpiàn** deceive; swindle

红润 **hóngrùn** glow ◊ rosy; ruddy

红色 **hóngsè** red

红色中国 **Hóngsè Zhōngguó** Red China

红十字 **Hóngshízì** Red Cross

红薯 **hóngshǔ** sweet potato

洪水 **hóngshuǐ** flood

洪水泛滥 **hóngshuǐ fànlàn** flooding

红桃 **hóngtáo** hearts *(in cards)*

红外线 **hóngwàixiàn** infra-red rays

宏伟 **hóngwěi** grandiose

红卫兵 **Hóngwèibīng** Red Guard

轰炸 **hōngzhà** bomb

轰炸机 **hōngzhà jī** bomber *(plane)*

轰炸警告 **hōngzhà jǐnggào** bomb scare

猴 **hóu** monkey

喉 **hóu** throat

吼 **hǒu** roar

后 **hòu** back; rear; behind

厚 **hòu** thick

候 **hòu** wait

厚板 **hòubǎn** slab

后背 **hòubèi** back

后备 **hòubèi** back up ◊ backup

后部 **hòubù** back

候车场 **hòuchē chǎng** cab rank, cab stand

候车室 **hòuchē shì** waiting room

后代 **hòudài** offspring; posterity

后跟 **hòugēn** heel

后果 **hòuguǒ** consequence; effect

后花园 **hòu huāyuán** backyard

后悔 **hòuhuǐ** regret; repent; be sorry

吼叫 **hǒujiào** bellow

吼叫声 **hǒujiào shēng** bellow

喉结 **hóujié** Adam's apple

候机室 **hòují shì** departure lounge

后来 **hòulái** after; afterward; later, later on; subsequently

喉咙 **hóulóng** throat

后门 **hòumén** backdoor

后面 **hòumian** behind, in back

候鸟 **hòuniǎo** bird of passage

后勤学 **hòuqín xué** logistics

喉舌 **hóushé** mouthpiece, spokesperson

吼声 **hǒushēng** bellow

后视镜 **hòushì jìng** rear-view mirror

后天 **hòutiān** the day after tomorrow

后退 **hòutuì** back away; back off; back up (*in car*); stand back ◊ retrograde

后卫 **hòuwèi** back SP

候选人 **hòuxuǎn rén** candidate

后续 **hòuxù** follow up

喉炎 **hóuyán** laryngitis

厚颜无耻 **hòuyán wúchǐ** outrageous; impertinent

后腰 **hòuyāo** small of the back

后裔 **hòuyì** descendant

后院 **hòuyuàn** backyard

后者 **hòuzhě** latter

猴子 **hóuzi** monkey

呼 **hū** beep

忽 **hū** overlook ◊ suddenly

壶 **hú** jug; kettle; pot

湖 **hú** lake

核 **hú** pit (*in fruit*)

胡 **hú** mustache; beard

糊 **hú** stick

煳 **hú** burnt

虎 **hǔ** tiger

糊 **hú** mush

户 **hù** door; household; bank account

护 **hù** protect

互 **hù** mutual

花 **huā** flower; blossom ◊ spend; cost; 他们花了五百美金 **tāmen huāle wǔbǎi měijīn** it cost them $500

划 **huá** row; paddle; strike *match*

滑 **huá** slide; slip ◊ slippery, icy

华 **huá** glory; China

画 **huà** draw; paint; portray ◊ drawing; painting

话 **huà** talk; words; remark

化 **huà** change; melt; dissolve ◊ (*to make adjectives and nouns into verbs*) -ize; 大众化 **dàzhònghuà** popularize; 简化 **jiǎnhuà** simplify

画 **huà** stroke (*in character*); picture ◊ paint

花瓣 **huābàn** petal

滑板 **huábǎn** skateboard

画报 **huàbào** magazine

画笔 **huàbǐ** paintbrush

花边 **huābiān** lace

哗变 **huábiàn** mutiny

滑冰 **huábīng** skate ◊ skating

化冰 **huàbīng** defrost

滑冰场 **huábīng chǎng** ice rink

滑冰人 **huábīng rén** skater

划船 **huáchuán** row; paddle

花点 **huādiǎn** spotted

划掉 **huádiào** delete; strike out

化冻 **huàdòng** thaw

花朵 **huāduǒ** bloom

华而不实 **huá ér bùshí** ornate

华尔街 **Huá'ěrjiē** Wall Street

华尔兹 **huá'ěrzī** waltz

花费 **huāfèi** spend ◊ expenditure

化肥 **huàféi** artificial fertilizer

花粉 **huāfěn** pollen

划分 **huàfēn** divide; 划分轻重缓急 **huàfēn qīngzhòng huǎnjí** prioritize

花粉计数 **huāfěn jìshù** pollen count

花粉热 **huāfěn rè** hay fever

花岗石 **huāgāng shí** granite

花岗岩 **huāgāng yán** granite

化工 **huàgōng** chemical industry

滑旱冰 **huá hànbīng** skate

化合 **huàhé** combine

划痕 **huáhén** cut; score ◊ scratch

化合物 **huàhé wù** compound CHEM

画画 **huàhua** draw

花花公子 **huāhuā gōngzǐ** playboy

花环 **huāhuán** garland

怀 **huái** bosom ◊ cherish; 怀好意 **huái hǎoyì** mean well

踝 **huái** ankle

坏 **huài** bad

坏处 **huàichu** disadvantage

坏蛋 **huàidàn** gangster; villain

怀旧 **huáijiù** nostalgia ◊ nostalgic ◊ reminisce

怀念 **huáiniàn** long for

坏人 **huàirén** rogue

坏事 **huàishì** evil; evil thing

槐树 **huáishù** scholar tree

怀疑 **huáiyí** doubt; suspect; question ◊ suspicion ◊ skeptical

怀疑论者 **huáiyílùn zhě** skeptic

怀疑态度 **huáiyí tàidù** skepticism

怀有 **huáiyǒu** harbor *grudge etc*; 怀有恶意 **huáiyǒu èyì** spiteful; 怀有希望 **huáiyǒu xīwàng** expectant

怀孕 **huáiyùn** conceive; expect ◊ pregnant ◊ pregnancy; conception

怀着 **huáizhe** carry (*of pregnant woman*)

滑稽 **huájī** comical ◊ funnily; 滑稽的模仿 **huájī de mófǎng** (comic) impression; 滑稽短剧 **huájī duǎnjù** (comedy) sketch

画家 **huàjiā** artist, painter

花椒 **huājiāo** Sichuan pepper

花轿 **huājiào** bridal palanquin

滑稽可笑 **huájī kěxiào** very funny, hysterical

哗啦 **huālā** crash; clatter; crackle

滑来滑去 **huálái huáqù** slither

画廊 **huàláng** art gallery

哗啦声 **huālā shēng** crash; clatter; crackle

花蕾 **huālěi** bud

华丽的词藻 **huálìde cízǎo** rhetoric

滑轮 **huálún** pulley

画面 **huàmiàn** image

化名 **huàmíng** pseudonym

欢 **huān** happy

还 **huán** return, give back; 将X还给Y **jiāng X huángěi Y** give X back to Y

环 **huán** ring; circle

缓 **huǎn** slow; leisurely ◊ postpone, put off

换 **huàn** change; swap; switch; 换衣服 **huàn yīfu** change clothes; 用X换Y **yòng X huàn Y** exchange X for Y

患 **huàn** worry; catch *disease*

唤 **huàn** shout

幻 **huàn** unreal; magic

换班 **huànbān** change shifts

环保 **huánbǎo** environmental protection

患病 **huànbìng** be ill

欢畅 **huānchàng** cheerful

缓冲器 **huǎnchōng qì** buffer COMPUT

换档键 **huàndǎng jiàn** shift key

幻灯 **huàndēng** slide show

幻灯片 **huàndēng piàn** slide; transparency

荒 **huāng** desolate

慌 **huāng** nervous; 别慌 **biéhuāng** don't panic

黄 **huáng** yellow

晃 **huǎng** dazzle

谎 **huǎng** lie

晃 **huàng** swing; wave

蝗虫 **huángchóng** locust

荒诞 **huāngdàn** absurd; grotesque

黄疸 **huángdǎn** jaundice

黄道带 **huángdào dài** zodiac

黄道十二宫图 **huángdào shí'èr gōngtú** signs of the zodiac

荒地 **huāngdì** wasteland; heath

皇帝 **huángdì** emperor ◊ imperial

黄帝 **Huángdì** Yellow Emperor

晃动 **huàngdòng** shake; waggle

黄豆 **huángdòu** soybean

荒废 **huāngfèi** lie fallow

黄蜂 **huángfēng** wasp

皇宫 **huánggōng** imperial palace

黄瓜 **huángguā** cucumber

黄海 **Huánghǎi** Yellow Sea

黄河 **Huánghé** Yellow River

皇后 **huánghòu** empress; queen

恍惚 **huǎnghū** trance

谎话 **huǎnghuà** lie

黄昏 **huánghūn** dusk, twilight

皇家 **huángjiā** royal family ◊ royal

黄金 **huángjīn** gold

黄金时间 **huángjīn shíjiān** prime time

荒凉 **huāngliáng** bleak; deserted; desolate; stark

慌忙 **huāngmáng** hurried

荒谬 **huāngmiù** preposterous, ridiculous ◊ ridiculously

荒漠 **huāngmò** barren

荒僻 **huāngpì** remote, out-of-the-way

黄色 **huángsè** yellow ◊ pornographic

黄色电影 **huángsè diànyǐng** blue movie

黄色杂志 **huángsè zázhì** pornographic magazine

黄色作品 **huángsè zuòpǐn** pornography

荒疏 **huāngshū** lose the knack

荒唐 **huāngtáng** ludicrous, absurd ◊ absurdity

黄铜 **huángtóng** brass

环顾 **huángù** look around

荒无人烟 **huāng wú rényān** uninhabited

荒野 **huāngyě** the bush; the wilds

黄油 **huángyóu** butter

荒原 **huāngyuán** wilderness

慌张 **huāngzhāng** nervous

幌子 **huǎngzi** front

皇族 **huángzú** royalty

缓和 **huǎnhé** lighten; soften; tone down ◊ détente; respite

欢呼 **huānhū** cheer ◊ cheering

还击 **huánjī** hit back

环礁湖 **huánjiāo hú** lagoon

缓解 **huǎnjiě** relax; alleviate; ease off; smooth over

环境 **huánjìng** environment; surroundings; setting

环境保护 **huánjìng bǎohù** environmental protection

环境保护论者 **huánjìng bǎohùlùn zhě** environmentalist

环境卫生部门 **huánjìng wèishēng bùmén** sanitation department

环境污染 **huánjìng wūrǎn** environmental pollution

欢聚 **huānjù** social gathering, get-together

欢快 **huānkuài** bright ◊ brightness

欢乐 **huānlè** happy; cheerful; convivial ◊ merriment

还礼 **huánlǐ** return the salute, salute back

缓慢 **huǎnmàn** slow; leisurely; tardy; 缓慢进行 *huǎnmàn jìnxíng* plod along, plod on

幻灭 **huànmiè** disillusionment

化脓 **huànóng** fester

唤起 **huànqǐ** evoke; arouse; call up

还钱 **huánqián** pay back

换钱 **huànqián** change money

欢庆 **huānqìng** festivities

还清 **huánqīng** pay off

换取 **huànqǔ** exchange; 用来换取 *yònglái huànqǔ* in exchange for

焕然一新 **huànrán yìxīn** renew; take on a new look

环绕 **huánrào** surround, encircle

涣散 **huànsàn** loose; limp

换算 **huànsuàn** convert

换算表 **huànsuàn biǎo** conversion table

欢喜 **huānxǐ** rapturous

幻想 **huànxiǎng** illusion; fantasy

幻象 **huànxiàng** illusion; 使幻想破灭 *shǐ huànxiǎng pòmiè* disillusion

欢笑 **huānxiào** mirth

欢欣 **huānxīn** jubilation

缓刑 **huǎnxíng** reprieve ◊ probation

唤醒 **huànxǐng** wake; rouse

唤醒电话 **huànxǐng diànhuà** wake-up call

缓刑监督官 **huǎnxíng jiāndūguān** probation officer

浣熊 **huànxióng** raccoon

还押 **huányā** be on remand

欢迎 **huānyíng** welcome ◊ reception; 受欢迎 *shòu huānyíng* be popular; go down well

患有 **huànyǒu** be suffering from

花盆 **huāpén** flowerpot

花瓶 **huāpíng** vase

花钱 **huāqián** spend

华侨 **Huáqiáo** overseas Chinese

划清界线 **huàqīng jièxiàn** delimit

花圈 **huāquān** wreath

花色俱全 **huāsè jùquán** assortment

花色牌 **huāsè pái** suit (*in cards*)

花商 **huāshāng** florist

花哨 **huāshao** flashy, gaudy

化身 **huàshēn** embodiment

花生 **huāshēng** peanut

华盛顿 **Huáshèngdùn** Washington

花生酱 **huāshēng jiàng** peanut butter

华氏 **huáshì** Fahrenheit

化石 **huàshí** fossil

划时代 **huàshídài** epoch-making

花时间 **huā shíjiān** time-consuming

花束 **huāshù** bouquet

滑水 **huáshuǐ** waterskiing

划算 **huásuàn** pay off; be worthwhile ◊ cost-effective

花坛 **huātán** flowerbed

滑梯 **huátī** slide

话题 **huàtí** topic of conversation

划艇 **huátǐng** rowboat

话务员 **huàwù yuán** telephonist; switchboard operator

化纤 **huàxiān** synthetic fiber

划线标出 **huàxiàn biāochū** mark out

滑翔 **huáxiáng** glide

滑翔机 **huáxiáng jī** glider

滑翔运动 **huáxiáng yùndòng** gliding

滑翔者 **huáxiáng zhě** glider (*person*)

滑行 **huáxíng** glide; slide; coast; taxi (*of airplane*)

滑行运动 **huáxíng yùndòng** gliding; sliding; coasting; taxiing

滑雪 **huáxuě** ski ◊ skiing

化学 **huàxué** chemistry ◊ chemical

滑雪道 **huáxuě dào** ski run

化学家 **huàxué jiā** chemist

化学疗法 **huàxué liáofǎ** chemotherapy

化学战 **huàxué zhàn** chemical warfare

滑雪杖 **huáxuě zhàng** ski pole

滑雪者 **huáxuě zhě** skier

化学制品 **huàxué zhìpǐn** chemical

花样滑冰 **huāyàng huábīng** figure skating

化验室 **huàyàn shì** laboratory

华裔 **Huáyì** person of Chinese descent

花园 **huāyuán** garden

画展 **huàzhǎn** exhibition of paintings

花招 **huāzhāo** trick

化妆 **huàzhuāng** put on make-up

化妆品 **huàzhuāng pǐn** make-up; cosmetics

化装室 **huàzhuāng shì** dressing room

化妆晚会 **huàzhuāng wǎnhuì** fancy-dress party

划子 **huázi** rowboat

护板 **hùbǎn** shield

湖滨 **húbīn** shore, lakeside

胡茬子 **húcházi** stubble

胡扯 **húchě** rave

呼出 **hūchū** breathe; breathe out

护创膏 **hùchuàng gāo** sticking plaster

蝴蝶 **húdié** butterfly

蝴蝶结 **húdié jié** bow (*knot*)

忽动忽停 **hūdòng hūtíng** jerky

护发剂 **hùfà jì** conditioner

糊饭 **húfàn** burnt rice

胡蜂 **húfēng** wasp

护封 **hùfēng** jacket (*of book*)

呼喊 **hūhǎn** call

呼唤 **hūhuàn** call; bleep

互换 **hùhuàn** exchange

互惠 **hùhuì** bilateral; reciprocal

灰 **huī** ash; dust

挥 **huī** wave

回 **huí** return; go back

悔 **huǐ** regret

毁 **huǐ** damage

会 **huì** be able to; meet ◊ meeting; 你会说法语吗？**nǐ huì shuō Fǎyǔ ma?** can you speak French?; 我说过我会去 **wǒ shuōguò wǒ huì qù** I said that I could go; 会用

电脑 **huìyòng diànnǎo** computer literate

嚎 **huì** beak; snout

汇 **huì** converge

绘 **huì** paint; draw

灰暗 **huī'àn** dark; somber

回报 **huíbào** return *favor, invitation*

汇报 **huìbào** report card

回避 **huíbì** evade; duck

会场 **huìchǎng** meeting place

回车健 **huíchē jiàn** return key COMPUT

灰尘 **huīchén** dust

回程 **huíchéng** return journey

回程飞机 **huíchéng fēijī** return flight

回答 **huídá** answer, reply

回荡 **huídàng** echo

回到 **huídào** return, get back

回电话 **huí diànhuà** call back; 他能给我回电话吗? **tā néng gěi wǒ huí diànhuà ma?** can he call me back?

挥动 **huīdòng** swing; wield; brandish

汇兑 **huìduì** transfer *money*

挥发 **huīfā** evaporate

回放 **huífàng** playback

会费 **huìfèi** membership fee

恢复 **huīfù** recover; restore; return; bring back; resume ◊ recovery; 他恢复得很好 **tā huīfù de hěnhǎo** he has made a good recovery

恢复元气 **huīfù yuánqì** recuperate

恢复知觉 **huīfù zhījué** regain consciousness

回顾 **huígù** look back ◊ retrospective

惠顾 **huìgù** custom, patronage

回归线 **huíguī xiàn** tropic

回国 **huíguó** go home (*to one's own country*)

回合 **huíhé** round (*in boxing*)

汇合 **huìhé** join

会合 **huìhé** meet; convene; link up

悔恨 **huǐhèn** regret

绘画 **huìhuà** paint ◊ painting; picture

毁坏 **huǐhuài** destroy; ruin; wreck; mangle

辉煌 **huīhuáng** brilliant; glorious

挥霍 **huīhuò** wasteful; extravagant; lavish ◊ squander

回家 **huíjiā** go home

会见 **huìjiàn** meeting

灰浆 **huījiāng** mortar

回教 **Huíjiào** Islam

灰烬 **huījìn** ash

扣扣 **huíkòu** bribe, kickback

汇款单 **huìkuǎn dān** money order

回来 **huílái** come back

贿赂 **huìlù** bribe ◊ bribery

汇率 **huìlǜ** exchange rate

会面 **huìmiàn** meet

毁灭 **huǐmiè** wreck; obliterate

灰泥 **huīní** plaster

汇票 **huìpiào** bill of exchange

会签 **huìqiān** countersign

回球 **huíqiú** return (*in tennis*)

回去 **huíqù** go back, return

毁容 **huǐróng** disfigure

灰色 **huīsè** gray

灰色跑犬 **huīsè pǎoquǎn** grayhound

回声 **huíshēng** echo

挥手 **huīshǒu** wave

回收 **huíshōu** recycle ◊ recycling

会谈 **huìtán** have a conversation

回头 **huítóu** turn back

回头生意 **huítóu shēngyì** repeat business

绘图 **huìtú** drawing

绘图人 **huìtú rén** illustrator

绘图仪 **huìtú yí** plotter COMPUT

绘图员 **huìtú yuán** draftsman

挥舞 **huīwǔ** wave

污物 **huìwù** filth

会晤 **huìwù** meet with

回响 **huíxiǎng** reverberate

回想 **huíxiǎng** think back

诙谐 **huīxié** humorous

灰心 **huīxīn** discouraged; frustrated; frustrating ◊ frustratingly

回信 **huíxìn** reply, write back ◊ (letter of) reply

彗星 **huìxīng** comet

回形针 **huíxíngzhēn** paper clip

会演 **huìyǎn** festival

回忆 **huíyì** recollect ◊ recollection; 引起 X 的回忆 **yǐnqǐ X de huíyì** jog X's memory

会议 **huìyì** convention, conference; congress; meeting

回忆录 **huíyìlù** memoirs

会议室 **huìyì shì** board room; meeting room

会议中心 **huìyì zhōngxīn** convention center

徽章 **huīzhāng** button, badge, pin

绘制 **huìzhì** draw

回转 **huízhuǎn** turn around

回嘴 **huízuǐ** answer back

护甲 **hùjiǎ** armor

胡椒 **hújiāo** pepper

胡椒薄荷 **hújiāo bòhé** peppermint

胡椒粉 **hújiāofěn** (ground) pepper

呼叫机 **hūjiào jī** bleeper

呼救 **hūjiù** emergency call

户口 **hùkǒu** household registration

狐狸 **húli** fox

护理 **hùlǐ** nurse ◊ nursing

护林员 **hùlínyuán** forest ranger

护理人员 **hùlǐ rényuán** nursing staff

胡乱 **húluàn** carelessly; 胡乱摆弄 **húluàn bǎinòng** fiddle around with

忽略 **hūlüè** neglect ◊ overlook, ignore

胡萝卜 **húluóbo** carrot

呼噜声 **hūlushēng** grunt; purr

护目镜 **hùmùjìng** goggles

荤 **hūn** meat or fish

昏 **hūn** dark ◊ swoon

婚 **hūn** marriage ◊ marry

混 **hùn** mix

昏暗 **hūn'an** dark; dim; obscure; dingy

胡闹 **húnào** make trouble; fool around

混蛋 **húndàn** bastard; pig

昏倒 **hūndǎo** faint

混合 **hùnhé** mix; combine; mingle; blend

混合物 **hùnhéwù** mix; mixture

昏厥 **hūnjué** fit MED ◊ pass out

婚礼 **hūnlǐ** marriage; wedding

婚礼蛋糕 **hūnlǐ dàngāo** wedding cake

婚礼日 **hūnlǐrì** wedding day

混乱 **hùnluàn** chaos; muddle ◊ chaotic; turbulent; 我的思维一片混乱 **wǒde sīwéi yípiàn hùnluàn** my mind is in a whirl

昏迷 **hūnmí** black out ◊ blackout; coma ◊ unconscious

混凝土 **hùnníngtǔ** concrete

糊弄 **hùnong** mess around

婚前 **hūnqián** premarital

婚纱 **hūnshā** wedding dress

浑身 **húnshēn** the entire body ◊ all over; 我浑身都疼 **wǒ húnshēn dōu téng** it hurts all over

馄饨 **húntun** won ton (type of dumpling)

婚外 **hūnwài** extramarital

混淆 **hùnxiáo** confuse ◊ confusion

混血儿 **hùnxuè'ér** half-caste

婚姻 **hūnyīn** marriage ◊ marital

婚姻顾问 **hūnyīn gùwèn** marriage counselor

婚约 **hūnyuē** engagement

浑浊 **húnzhuó** cloudy; muddy

或 **huò** or

活 **huó** live ◊ alive ◊ work; 你有活儿干了 **nǐ yǒu huór gànle** you'll have a job, it won't be easy

火 **huǒ** fire

货 **huò** stock; goods

祸 **huò** accident

获 **huò** achieve

火把 **huǒbǎ** torch

伙伴 **huǒbàn** buddy

货板 **huòbǎn** pallet

活板门 **huóbǎnmén** trapdoor

货币 **huòbì** currency ◊ monetary

货舱 **huòcāng** hold

火柴 **huǒchái** match

火柴盒 **huǒcháihé** matchbox

货车 **huòchē** truck; freight car

火车 **huǒchē** train;

火车头 **huǒchētóu** locomotive

货车厢 **huòchēxiāng** freight car

火车站 **huǒchē zhàn** train station

货船 **huòchuán** freighter

货到付款 huòdào fùkuǎn collect on delivery

获得 huòdé acquire, get; achieve; capture; 获得成功 *huòdé chénggōng* achieve success; make it

活动 huódòng activity; pastime; pursuit ◊ move ◊ mobile

活动扳手 huódòng bānshǒu monkey wrench

活动边 huódòngbiān flap (of table)

活动过度 huódòng guòdù hyperactive

活动家 huódòngjiā campaigner

活动住房 huódòng zhùfáng mobile home

火锅 huǒguō hot pot

火红 huǒhóng lurid; fiery

火花 huǒhuā spark

火化 huǒhuà cremate ◊ cremation

火化场 huǒhuà chǎng crematorium

火花塞 huǒhuāsāi spark plug

火鸡 huǒjī turkey

货价 huòjià cost (of goods)

火箭 huǒjiàn rocket

获奖 huòjiǎng prizewinning ◊ win a prize

获奖者 huòjiǎng zhě prizewinner

火警 huǒjǐng fire alarm

火炬 huǒjù torch

活力 huólì vigor; vitality; spirit

霍乱 huòluàn cholera

货品 huòpǐn merchandise

活泼 huópo animated; brisk; lively; sprightly; vivacious

活泼有力 huópo yǒulì frisky

获取 huòqǔ extract

活塞 huósāi piston

火山 huǒshān volcano

火山口 huǒshān kǒu crater

获胜 huòshèng win ◊ winning ◊ winner

祸首 huòshǒu instigator; culprit; ringleader

货摊 huòtān booth

火腿 huǒtuǐ ham

货物 huòwù goods; cargo; freight; consignment, shipment

获悉 huòxī discover

火星 huǒxīng spark

活性洗涤剂 huóxìng xǐdí jì biological detergent

或许 huòxǔ perhaps

火焰 huǒyàn flame

活页夹 huóyè jiá binder (for papers)

活跃 huóyuè active; effervescent; vivid

货运列车 huòyùn lièchē freight train

货运站 huòyùnzhàn freight depot

活着 huózhe alive; living ◊ live

或者 huòzhě or; alternatively; 或者 … 或者 *huòzhě … huòzhě* either … or

获知 huòzhī find out

虎皮鹦鹉 hǔpí yīngwǔ budgerigar

糊墙纸 húqiángzhǐ wallpaper

忽然 hūrán suddenly

呼声 hūshēng clamor

忽视 hūshì neglect; disregard

护士 hùshì nurse

胡刷 húshuā shaving brush

胡说 húshuō nonsense

胡说八道 húshuō bādào nonsense

胡同 hútòng alley, lane

户头 hùtóu account

糊涂 hútu confused; 令人糊涂 *lìngrén hútú* confusing

护卫 hùwèi escort

互为补充 hùwéi bǔchōng complementary

呼吸 hūxī breath; breathing ◊ breathe

互相 hùxiāng reciprocal; mutual ◊ mutually; each other; one another

互相传 hùxiāng chuán pass around

弧形 húxíng arched

呼吁 hūyù appeal

护照 hùzhào passport

护照检查处 hùzhào jiǎncháchù passport control

互撞 hùzhuàng collision

胡子 húzi beard; mustache; whiskers; sideburns

胡子楂 húzi chá bristles

# J

击 jī attack; strike; knock ◊ blow

鸡 jī chicken

基 jī base; foundation

机 jī machine; airplane; opportunity

奇 jī odd *number*

即 jí namely; promptly

吉 jí lucky; auspicious

集 jí collect ◊ episode

及 jí and ◊ reach

极 jí extreme ◊ extremely

级 jí level; grade; 我们是同级的 **wǒmen shì tóngjí de** we were in the same year

急 jí impatient; in a hurry; urgent

脊 jí ridge

几 jǐ some; a few; several; how many?; 几百美元 **jǐbǎi měiyuán** a few hundred dollars; 几张票 **jǐzhāng piào** a few tickets

系 jì fasten; tie; buckle

迹 jì mark; trace

计 jì calculate; count

技 jì skill

妓 jì prostitute

寄 jì send; mail

季 jì season

既 jì already ◊ since

记 jì remember; 记笔记 **jì bǐjì** take notes; 记不得 **jìbudé** I don't remember; 记不住 **jìbuzhù** I can't remember

忌 jì envy

纪 jì record

继 jì continue

系 jì button up; tie up

既 ... 又 ... jì ... yòu ... both ... and ...

加 jiā add ◊ plus

夹 jiā clip ◊ squeeze

家 jiā home; family; 在家 **zài jiā** at home

痂 jiā scab

佳 jiā very good; fine; beautiful

颊 jiá cheek

假 jiǎ false, fake; bogus; 假钞票 **jiǎchāopiào** counterfeit bill

甲 jiǎ first; armor; nail; A; *unspecified person or thing in lists etc*

架 jià shelf; rack; frame

价 jià price

假 jià vacation

驾 jià drive

加班 jiābān work overtime

甲板 jiǎbǎn deck

假扮 jiǎbàn impersonate

夹板 jiābǎn jiá splint

加倍 jiābèi double

加标点 jiā biāodiǎn punctuate

加冰 jiābīng iced

夹层 jiácéng compartment

家常闲话 jiācháng xiánhuà chitchat; gossip

甲虫 jiǎchóng beetle

家畜 jiāchù domestic animal

假定 jiǎdìng assume

加法 jiāfǎ addition MATH

假发 jiǎfà wig

价格 jiàgé price; cost

价格战 jiàgézhàn price war

加工 jiāgōng process; embellish

加固 jiāgù fasten; secure

加号 jiāhào plus sign

家伙 jiāhuo guy, fellow

嘉奖 jiājiǎng praise

佳节 jiājié celebration; festival

嫁接 jiàjiē graft BOT

夹紧 jiājǐn clamp

家具 jiājù furniture; 一件家具 **yíjiàn jiājù** a piece of furniture; 一套家具 **yítào jiājù** suite

加剧 jiājù intensify

家具罩 jiājù zhào dust cover

家具装饰材料 jiājù zhuāngshì cáiliào upholstery

茄克 jiākè jacket; coat

架空 jiàkōng overhead

加快 jiākuài accelerate, speed up

加宽 jiākuān widen

假面具 jiǎ miànjù disguise

价目表 jiàmùbiǎo tariff

煎 jiān shallow fry

尖 jiān tip, point ◊ pointed; sharp; acute

肩 jiān shoulder

监 jiān prison ◊ supervise

坚 jiān solid; firm

艰 jiān difficult

奸 jiān traitor; adultery ◊ wicked, evil; cunning

剪 jiān cut; clip; 把头发剪了 **bǎ tóufa jiǎn le** get one's hair cut

减 jiǎn reduce; take away, subtract ◊ minus

简 jiǎn uncomplicated, straightforward, simple

检 jiǎn inspect, check

捡 jiǎn collect, pick up

键 jiàn key

见 jiàn see; meet

溅 jiàn splash; splatter

剑 jiàn sword

腱 jiàn tendon

渐 jiàn gradually

舰 jiàn warship

箭 jiàn arrow

件 jiàn *measure word for items, matters, clothing, furniture*; 三件行李 **sānjiàn xíngli** three pieces of baggage; 一件 yíjiàn an article, an item; 一件短上衣 **yíjiàn duǎnshàngyī** a jacket

建 jiàn build; put up

健 jiàn healthy

加拿大 Jiānádà Canada ◊ Canadian

肩膀 jiānbǎng shoulder

简报 jiǎnbào briefing; clipping

简便机场 jiǎnbiàn jīchǎng landing strip

鉴别 jiànbié identify; differentiate

兼并 jiānbìng take over ◊ takeover

剑柄 jiànbìng hilt

兼并投标 jiānbìng tóubiāo takeover bid

剪裁 jiǎncái cut to size; cut out

剪草钳 jiǎncǎo qián clippers

检查 jiǎnchá check; examine; inspect ◊ examination; inspection;

检查 … 的拼写 jiǎnchá … de pīnxiě do a spellcheck on …

检察 jiǎnchá prosecute

检察官 jiǎncháguān prosecuting attorney

减产 jiǎnchǎn wind down production

检查员 jiǎncháyuán inspector

简称 jiǎnchēng abbreviation

建成 jiànchéng construct; be up; be built

坚持 jiānchí maintain; insist; hold; adhere; stand by, stick to ◊ insistent; 坚持自己的立场 **jiānchí zìjǐ de lìchǎng** stand one's ground; assert oneself

坚持不懈 jiānchí búxiè persistence, perseverance

剪出 jiǎnchū cut out

肩带 jiāndài shoulder strap; sash

煎蛋 jiāndàn fried egg

简单 jiǎndān simple; straightforward; humble ◊ briefly; simply ◊ simplicity

煎蛋卷 jiān dànjuǎn omelet

剪刀 jiǎndāo scissors

剪掉 jiǎndiào cut off

间谍 jiàndié spy

间谍活动 jiàndié huódòng espionage

坚定 jiāndìng firm; determined; confirmed; stalwart, staunch ◊ be firm, put one's foot down

鉴定 jiàndìng survey; assess

鉴定人 jiàndìng rén surveyor

监督 jiāndū supervise; monitor

尖端 jiānduān point (*of knife etc*)

简短 jiǎnduǎn brief

尖端产品 jiānduān chǎnpǐn top-quality product

舰队 jiànduì fleet

简而言之 jiǎn ér yánzhī in short

减肥 jiǎnféi slim, diet; lose weight

减肥食品 jiǎnféi shípǐn diet

姜 jiāng ginger (*spice*)

将 jiāng take; will; 将东西装入 **jiāng dōngxi zhuāngrù** pack; 将头发分开 **jiāng tóufà fēnkāi** part one's hair; 将 … 归档 **jiāng … guīdàng** file away; 他将去旅行 **tā jiāng qù lǚxíng** he's going to travel around

僵 jiāng stiff

缰 jiāng rein

桨 jiāng paddle; oar

讲 jiǎng speak; talk; tell; 讲电话 *jiǎng diànhuà* be on the telephone

奖 jiǎng award; prize

降 jiàng lower; sink

酱 jiàng paste; sauce

奖杯 jiǎngbēi trophy

讲道 jiǎngdào sermon

讲道德 jiǎngdàodé moral

降低 jiàngdī decline; die down; lower; reduce; 使降低 *shǐ jiàngdī* bring down

降低标价 jiàngdī biāojià mark down

降低等级 jiàngdī děngjí downgrade

间隔 jiàngé interval; distance

浆果 jiāngguǒ berry

糨糊 jiànghú paste

讲话 jiǎnghuà speak; deliver a speech

姜黄色 jiānghuángsè red; ginger

讲价 jiǎngjià haggle; bargain

降价 jiàngjià get cheaper, drop in price; drop (its) prices

讲解 jiǎngjiě explain

蒋介石 Jiǎng Jièshí Chiang Kai-shek

将近 jiāngjìn almost

奖金 jiǎngjīn bonus

将就 jiāngjiù make do with

讲究 jiǎngjiu fussy, particular ◊ be particular about

讲究细节 jiǎngjiu xìjié finicky

僵局 jiāngjú deadlock, impasse; stalemate

将军 jiāngjūn general ◊ check (*in chess*)

讲课 jiǎngkè give a lecture

将来 jiānglái in the future; 不远的将来 *bùyuǎnde jiānglái* in the near future

将来时 jiāngláishí future tense

讲理 jiǎnglǐ reason with ◊ reasonable

奖励 jiǎnglì award; reward

降临 jiànglín onset ◊ strike

降落 jiàngluò land

降落伞 jiàngluòsǎn parachute

奖品 jiǎngpǐn prize

奖赏 jiǎngshǎng prize

缰绳 jiāngsheng lead, leash; rein

讲师 jiǎngshī lecturer

讲实际 jiǎng shíjì hardheaded

讲述 jiǎngshù tell

将死 jiàngsǐ checkmate

讲台 jiǎngtái rostrum

坚固 jiāngù strong, solid; resistant; robust

兼顾 jiāngù combine; do both ... and ...; 兼顾 X 和 Y *jiāngù X hé Y* combine X with Y

见怪 jiànguài take badly; mind; take offense

监管人 jiānguǎn rén prison guard

坚果 jiānguǒ nut

坚果钳 jiānguǒ qián nutcrackers

坚果味儿 jiānguǒ wèir nutty *taste*

降温 jiàngwēn drop in temperature

讲习班 jiǎngxíbān workshop, seminar

奖学金 jiǎngxuéjīn scholarship

讲演 jiǎngyǎn lecture

讲演厅 jiǎngyǎn tīng lecture hall

将要 jiāngyào about to

僵硬 jiāngyìng stiff

酱油 jiàngyóu soy sauce

疆域 jiāngyù territory

降雨量 jiàngyǔ liàng rainfall

奖章 jiǎngzhāng medal

奖章获得者 jiǎngzhāng huòdé zhě medalist

降职 jiàngzhí downgrade

讲座 jiǎngzuò course; lecture

减号 jiǎnhào minus sign

简化 jiǎnhuà simplify

减缓 jiǎnhuǎn drop; ease off; slacken off

监护人 jiānhùrén guardian

剪辑 jiǎnjí clip; cutting; editing ◊ edit ◊

减价 jiǎnjià reduce the price; 减价二十美元 *jiǎnjià èrshí měiyuán* knock $20 off

肩胛骨 jiānjiǎgǔ shoulder blade

渐渐 jiànjiàn gradually

尖叫 jiānjiào scream, shriek; yelp

建交 jiànjiāo establish diplomatic

尖叫声 **jiānjiàoshēng** scream, screech

剪接 **jiǎnjiē** edit

简洁 **jiǎnjié** concise; lean

简介 **jiǎnjiè** blurb

间接 **jiànjiē** indirect ◊ indirectly

监禁 **jiānjìn** imprison; confine ◊ imprisonment; confinement

坚决 **jiānjué** determined, resolute; decided; strong; 坚决要求 **jiānjué yāoqiú** insist on

键卡 **jiànkǎ** keycard

健康 **jiànkāng** fit; healthy ◊ fitness; health; well-being, welfare ◊ be well

健康保险 **jiànkāng bǎoxiǎn** health insurance

健康检查 **jiànkāng jiǎnchá** checkup

健康食品 **jiànkāng shípǐn** health food

健康食品店 **jiànkāng shípǐndiàn** health food store

健康证书 **jiànkāng zhèngshū** medical certificate

尖刻 **jiānkè** cutting; bitter; harsh

艰苦 **jiānkǔ** difficult; strenuous

尖利 **jiānlì** sharp; piercing

建立 **jiànlì** establish, set up, found

建立桥梁 **jiànlì qiáoliáng** bridge gap

尖利声 **jiānlìshēng** screech

简陋 **jiǎnlòu** primitive, crude; humble

溅落 **jiànluò** splash down

减慢 **jiǎnmàn** slow down

健美锻炼 **jiànměi duànliàn** bodybuilding

见面 **jiànmiàn** meet

简明 **jiǎnmíng** concise

艰难 **jiānnán** difficult ◊ difficulty; hardship

艰难行走 **jiānnán xíngzǒu** plod

键盘 **jiànpán** keyboard

剪票 **jiǎnpiào** punch a ticket

简朴 **jiǎnpǔ** austere

柬埔寨 **Jiǎnpǔzhài** Cambodia ◊ Cambodian

拣起 **jiǎnqǐ** pick up

坚强 **jiānqiáng** strong; tough; forceful

剪切 **jiǎnqiē** cut

减轻 **jiǎnqīng** alleviate; relieve; lighten; ease; soften; 减轻的情节 **jiǎnqīngde qíngjié** mitigating circumstances

减去 **jiǎnqù** minus ◊ subtract

尖儿 **jiānr** ace (*in cards*)

坚韧 **jiānrèn** tough; tenacious

键入 **jiànrù** key in, enter COMPUT

尖锐 **jiānruì** incisive; penetrating; pointed; sharp; shrill

尖锐刺耳 **jiānruì cì'ěr** strident

尖锐而深刻 **jiānruì ér shēnkè** searching

减弱 **jiǎnruò** die down; subside; moderate; shrink; wane ◊ muted

减色 **jiǎnsè** detract from

减少 **jiǎnshǎo** reduce; cut down; decline; dwindle ◊ reduction; 使减少 **shǐ jiǎnshǎo** diminish; deaden

建设 **jiànshè** build; construct; develop ◊ construction; development

健身 **jiànshēn** keep fit

尖声说出 **jiānshēng shuōchū** shriek

健身俱乐部 **jiànshēn jùlèbù** health club

健身中心 **jiànshēn zhōngxīn** fitness center

建设性 **jiànshè xìng** constructive

坚实 **jiānshí** solid

监视 **jiānshì** oversee; watch

见识 **jiànshi** experience; common sense

监视器 **jiānshìqì** monitor COMPUT

减速 **jiǎnsù** decelerate, slow down

尖酸刻薄 **jiānsuān kèbó** sour

尖塔 **jiāntǎ** spire, steeple

健谈 **jiàntán** talkative, chatty

剪贴板 **jiǎntiē bǎn** clipboard COMPUT

剪贴簿 **jiǎntiēbù** scrapbook

监听 **jiāntīng** listen to; listen in on; tap; bug

坚挺 **jiāntǐng** strong *currency*

简体字 **jiǎntǐzì** simplified characters

箭头 **jiàntóu** arrow; arrowhead

健忘 **jiànwàng** forgetful;

scatterbrained

奸污 jiānwū rape

见习 jiànxí become familiar with one's work; train

间隙 jiànxì gap

尖笑 jiānxiào smirk

尖啸 jiānxiào wail

减小 jiǎnxiǎo taper

见效 jiànxiào effective

尖啸声 jiānxiàoshēng wail

间歇 jiànxiē interval; lull

艰辛 jiānxīn suffering; hardship

减刑 jiǎnxíng commute a sentence

饯行 jiànxíng have a farewell meal

尖牙 jiānyá fang

检验 jiǎnyàn test

简要 jiǎnyào succinct

检疫 jiǎnyì quarantine

建议 jiànyì suggest, propose ◊ suggestion, proposition; 一项建议 *yīxiàng jiànyì* a piece of advice; a proposal

坚硬 jiānyìng rigid; hard

监狱 jiānyù prison, jail; penitentiary

鉴于 jiànyú in view of

检阅 jiǎnyuè review *troops*

建造 jiànzào build, construct ◊ building, construction *(activity)*; 在建造中 *zài jiànzào zhōng* under construction

见证人 jiànzhèng rén witness

减震器 jiǎnzhènqì shock absorber

减震装置 jiǎnzhèn zhuāngzhì suspension

兼职 jiānzhí moonlight

简直 jiǎnzhí simply; utterly; 简直是最好的 *jiǎnzhí shì zuìhǎode* it is simply the best; 简直了 *jiǎnzhí le!* amazing!

剪纸 jiǎnzhǐ paper cut

建筑 jiànzhù building, construction; architecture

健壮 jiànzhuàng robust

建筑工地 jiànzhù gōngdì construction site

建筑工人 jiànzhù gōngrén construction worker

建筑公司 jiànzhù gōngsī construction company

建筑区 jiànzhù qū built-up area

建筑师 jiànzhù shī architect

建筑物 jiànzhùwù structure

建筑学 jiànzhù xué architecture

建筑业 jiànzhù yè construction industry

尖子 jiānzi top

剪子 jiǎnzi scissors

胶 jiāo glue

教 jiāo teach

礁 jiāo reef

浇 jiāo pour; water

交 jiāo hand over; cross; 把X交给Y *bǎ X jiāogěi Y* send X to Y; 交朋友 *jiāo péngyǒu* make friends; 与X交朋友 *yǔ X jiāo péngyǒu* make friends with X

郊 jiāo suburbs

焦 jiāo burnt

嚼 jiáo chew

脚 jiǎo foot; bottom

角 jiǎo corner; horn; jiao *(Chinese money)*

搅 jiǎo stir

叫 jiào call; be called; summon; ask; draw, lead; 叫X帮忙 *jiào X bāngmáng* enlist the help of X; 叫X进去 *jià X jìnqù* send in X

较 jiào relatively

教 jiào teach ◊ religion

轿 jiào palanquin, sedan chair

校 jiào check; proofread

骄傲 jiāo'ào proud

骄傲自大 jiāo'ào zìdà arrogant

搅拌 jiǎobàn stir; whisk

搅拌器 jiǎobànqì mixer

脚背 jiǎobèi instep

脚本 jiǎoběn script

教鞭 jiàobiān pointer

胶布 jiāobù adhesive tape

脚步 jiǎobù footstep

叫菜 jiàocài order *food*

窖藏 jiàocáng hoard

交叉 jiāochā cross, intersect

交叉道 jiāochādào interchange

交叉路口 jiāochā lùkǒu junction

交叉双腿 jiāochā shuāngtuǐ cross one's legs

轿车 jiàochē car

交出 jiāochū give in, hand in, surrender

搅打 jiǎodǎ whip

胶带 jiāodài adhesive tape

搅蛋器 jiǎodànqì egg whisk

教导 jiàodǎo civilize; educate; instruct ◊ instruction

脚灯 jiǎodēng footlights

焦点 jiāodiǎn focus; 在焦点上 zài jiāodiǎn shang be in focus

脚底板 jiǎodǐ bǎn sole

搅动 jiǎodòng stir; move

角度 jiǎodù angle

交锋 jiāofēng cross swords; fight

焦干 jiāogān parched; very dry

娇惯 jiāoguàn spoil (indulge)

叫喊 jiàohǎn shout, yell

搅和 jiǎohe blend in

胶合板 jiāohébǎn plywood

搅和机 jiǎohéjī blender

脚后跟 jiǎohòugēn heel

狡猾 jiǎohuá crafty; cunning; devious; sly

交换 jiāohuàn exchange, swap; barter; trade; 交换意见 jiāohuàn yìjiàn confer

教皇 jiàohuáng pope

教诲 jiàohuì explain; instruct ◊ explanation; instruction

交货 jiāohuò deliver goods

搅和 jiǎohuo mix

交货付款 jiāohuò fùkuǎn collect on delivery

交互式 jiāohùshì interactive

焦急 jiāojí anxious ◊ anxiety; 焦急等待 jiāojí děngdài be anxious for

交际 jiāojì communication; contact

交界 jiāojiè border (on)

铰接车 jiǎojiēchē semi trailer

绞尽脑汁 jiǎojìn nǎozhī rack one's brains

焦距 jiāojù focal length

教具 jiàojù teaching aid

胶卷 jiāojuǎn film (for camera)

教科书 jiàokē shū textbook

交口称赞 jiāokǒu chēngzàn rave review

教练 jiàoliàn coach

较量 jiàoliàng compete; compare

教练员 jiàoliàn yuán trainer

交流 jiāoliú exchange; flow

交流电 jiāoliúdiàn alternating current

交流量 jiāoliú liàng traffic

角楼 jiǎolóu turret

焦虑 jiāolǜ agitation

焦虑不安 jiāolǜ bù'ān agitated

脚轮 jiǎolún caster

角落 jiǎoluò corner

角膜 jiǎomó cornea

酵母 jiàomǔ yeast

胶囊 jiāonáng capsule (of medicine)

娇嫩 jiāonèn tender; sensitive

教派 jiàopài denomination REL

交配 jiāopèi mate

脚蹼 jiǎopǔ flipper

娇气 jiāoqì squeamish; fragile

娇气包 jiāoqìbāo wimp

角球 jiǎoqiú corner (kick)

郊区 jiāoqū suburbs; outskirts ◊ suburban

教区牧师 jiàoqū mùshī vicar

教区牧师住所 jiàoqū mùshī zhùsuǒ vicarage

绞肉机 jiǎoròujī meat grinder

矫揉造作 jiǎoróu zàozuò affected

娇生惯养 jiāoshēng guànyǎng coddle

礁石 jiāoshí reef

教师 jiàoshī teacher

教室 jiàoshì classroom

教师培训 jiàoshī péixùn teacher training

教授 jiàoshòu professor

脚手架 jiǎoshǒujià scaffolding

教授职位 jiàoshòu zhíwèi chair (at university)

教书 jiàoshū teach

浇水筒 jiāoshuǐtǒng watering can

教唆 jiàosuō instigate

脚踏车 jiǎotàchē bicycle

交谈 jiāotán talk, converse

焦炭 jiāotàn coke

教堂 jiàotáng church

教堂集会 jiàotáng jíhuì congregation

脚踏实地 jiǎotà shídì down-to-earth

交替 jiāotì alternate

教条 jiàotiáo doctrine; dogma

教条主义 jiàotiáo zhǔyì dogmatism ◊ dogmatic

交通 **jiāotōng** traffic

绞痛 **jiāotòng** colic

交通标志 **jiāotōng biāozhì** traffic sign

交通部 **Jiāotōng Bù** Department of Transportation

交通岛 **jiāotōng dǎo** traffic island

交通堵塞 **jiāotōng dǔsè** traffic jam; gridlock

交通费用 **jiāotōng fèiyòng** travel expenses

交通工具 **jiāotōng gōngjù** means of transportation

交通警 **jiāotōng jǐng** traffic cop; traffic police

焦头烂额 **jiāotóulàn'é** stressed out

脚腕 **jiǎowàn** ankle

交往 **jiāowǎng** mingle; mix with; contact ◊ dealings; contract; association

交响乐 **jiāoxiǎngyuè** symphony

娇小 **jiāoxiǎo** petite

胶鞋 **jiāoxié** sneakers

矫形 **jiǎoxíng** orthopedic ◊ orthopedics

侥幸 **jiǎoxìng** lucky; 他侥幸得以逃生 **tā jiǎoxìng déyǐ táoshēng** he's lucky to be alive

叫醒 **jiàoxǐng** wake

绞刑架 **jiǎoxíngjià** gallows

矫形外科 **jiǎoxíng wàikē** orthopedics; orthopedic surgery

教学 **jiàoxué** teaching

教训 **jiàoxun** lesson; moral; 教训 X **jiàoxun X** teach X a lesson

教养 **jiàoyǎng** upbringing; manners; breeding ◊ bring up; train

校样 **jiàoyàng** proof (of book)

交易 **jiāoyì** deal; transaction ◊ transact

交易会 **jiāoyìhuì** trade fair

脚印 **jiǎoyìn** footprint

交易所 **jiāoyìsuǒ** exchange

郊游 **jiāoyóu** excursion

教育 **jiàoyù** education ◊ educational ◊ educate

教员 **jiàoyuán** teacher

教员室 **jiàoyuán shì** staffroom

教育学 **jiàoyùxué** (the study of) education

焦躁 **jiāozào** harassed

交战 **jiāozhàn** (military) engagement ◊ fight ◊ belligerent

矫正 **jiāozhèng** correct; adjust

校正 **jiàozhèng** correct ◊ correction

脚指 **jiǎozhǐ** toe

浇铸 **jiāozhù** cast; mold

脚注 **jiǎozhù** footer; footnote

骄子 **jiāozǐ** very talented person; whizzkid

饺子 **jiǎozi** Chinese dumpling

叫做 **jiàozuò** be called

家谱 **jiāpǔ** family tree

假期 **jiàqī** vacation; leave

加强 **jiāqiáng** intensify; reinforce; strengthen

家禽 **jiāqín** poultry (birds)

家禽肉 **jiāqínròu** poultry (meat)

加燃料 **jiā ránliào** refuel

加热 **jiārè** heat up

家人 **jiārén** family members

加热器 **jiārè qì** stove

假日 **jiàrì** (public) holiday

加入 **jiārù** add; join; 加入国籍 **jiārù guójí** become naturalized; 加入交易 **jiārù jiāoyì** come in on a deal

加上 **jiāshàng** add on ◊ plus; 加上一层 **jiāshàng yìcéng** cover, coat

假设 **jiǎshè** suppose ◊ assuming ◊ hypothesis ◊ hypothetical

加深 **jiāshēn** deepen

夹生 **jiāshēng** half-done

假释 **jiǎshì** parole; 获得假释 **huòdé jiǎshì** be on parole

驾驶 **jiàshǐ** drive; steer; fly; sail ◊ driving; driver; 左/右座驾驶 **zuǒ/yòu zuò jiàshǐ** left-/right-hand drive

驾驶船 **jiàshǐchuán** sail a boat

驾驶教练 **jiàshǐ jiàoliàn** driving instructor

驾驶机构 **jiàshǐ jīgòu** steering

驾驶室 **jiàshǐ shì** cab (of truck)

驾驶台 **jiàshǐ tái** bridge

驾驶学校 **jiàshǐ xuéxiào** driving school

驾驶学员 **jiàshǐ xuéyuán** beginner driver

驾驶员 **jiàshǐ yuán** driver

驾驶执照 jiàshǐ zhízhào driver's license

家属 jiāshǔ family members; household

加速 jiāsù accelerate; speed up ◊ acceleration

家庭 jiātíng family ◊ domestic

家庭妇女 jiātíng fùnǚ housewife

家庭录象 jiātíng lùxiàng home movie

家庭医生 jiātíng yīshēng family doctor

家庭主妇 jiātíng zhǔfù housewife

家庭作业 jiātíng zuòyè homework

家兔 jiātù rabbit

家务 jiāwù housework; chores

家务管理 jiāwù guǎnlǐ housekeeping

家务开消 jiāwù kāixiāo housekeeping (money)

家乡 jiāxiāng home; home town

假想 jiǎxiǎng imaginary, make-believe

加楔儿 jiāxiēr shove in

假惺惺 jiǎxīngxīng hypocritical ◊ hypocritically

假牙 jiǎyá dentures, false teeth

家用电脑 jiāyòng diànnǎo home computer

家用器械 jiāyòng qìxiè (household) appliance

加油 jiāyóu fill up; refuel; oil; come on!; go!

加油站 jiāyóuzhàn gas station

家喻户晓 jiāyù hùxiǎo household name

加载 jiāzài upload COMPUT

家长 jiāzhǎng head of household; parent

家长主义 jiāzhǎng zhǔyì paternalism

家长作风 jiāzhǎng zuòfēng paternalistic

假正经 jiǎzhèngjing prude ◊ prudish

假肢 jiǎzhī artificial limb

价值 jiàzhí value; worth; 价值上升/下降 jiàzhí shàngshēng/xiàjiàng rise/fall in value

jiàzhí kǎoshì driving test 驾驶

考试

加重 jiāzhòng become heavier; deepen

假装 jiǎzhuāng pretend; (play)act; make believe; put on ◊ masquerade

甲状腺 jiǎzhuàngxiàn thyroid gland

假珠宝 jiǎ zhūbǎo costume jewelry

夹竹桃 jiāzhútáo oleander

夹子 jiāzi clip; clamp; clasp

架子 jiàzi stand; frame; shelf; airs

家族 jiāzú clan

鸡巴 jībā ∨ prick

击败 jībài beat, defeat; overpower

基本 jīběn basic, fundamental; main; essential ◊ foundation ◊ basically

急奔 jí bēn dash; race

基本利率 jīběn lìlǜ base rate

基本上 jīběnshang basically; essentially

基本原理 jīběn yuánlǐ basic principles

基本知识 jīběn zhīshí basic knowledge

级别 jíbié rank; level

级别条纹 jíbié tiáowén stripe (indicating rank)

疾病 jíbìng disease; illness; sickness

既不 … 也不 … jìbù … yěbù … neither … nor …

机场 jīchǎng airport; airfield

继承 jìchéng inherit; 剥夺继承权 bōduó jìchéng quán disinherit

计程表 jìchéngbiǎo meter; taxi meter

计程车 jìchéngchē taxi

计程车司机 jìchéngchē sījī taxi driver

集成电路 jíchéng diànlù integrated circuit

继承人 jìchéngrén heir

急冲 jíchōng dash

基础 jīchǔ basis; foundation; 以 … 为基础 yǐ … wéi jīchǔ base on; be based on

挤出 jǐchū squeeze out

基础工作 jīchǔ gōngzuò

groundwork

基础结构 **jīchǔ jiégòu** infrastructure

击打 **jīdǎ** beat; hit; punch

即达 **jídá** incoming

极大 **jídà** enormous

鸡蛋 **jīdàn** egg

鸡蛋杯 **jīdànbēi** eggcup

击倒 **jīdǎo** knock out; flatten ◊ knockout

记得 **jìde** remember

基地 **jīdì** base

激动 **jīdòng** excite; inflame ◊ feverish; impassioned

机动 **jīdòng** flexible

机动车 **jīdòngchē** motor vehicle

激动人心 **jīdòng rénxīn** stirring

基督 **Jīdū** Christ ◊ Christian

嫉妒 **jídù** jealousy ◊ be jealous; envy; be envious

极度 **jídù** extreme; utmost ◊ extremely

忌妒 **jìdu** envy ◊ envious

季度 **jìdù** quarter ◊ quarterly

极端 **jíduān** drastic; extreme; unbelievable ◊ exceedingly

极端主义者 **jíduānzhǔyì zhě** extremist

基督教 **Jīdūjiào** Christianity ◊ Christian

基督徒 **Jīdū tú** Christian

饥饿 **jī'è** starvation; hunger ◊ hungry

街 **jiē** street

接 **jiē** contact; join; call for, collect; pick up; fetch; catch

结 **jiē** bear *fruit*

揭 **jiē** take off *lid*

阶 **jiē** steps; stairs

结 **jié** knot

节 **jié** festival; knot; verse ◊ *measure word for sections, lengths*; 一节竹子 **yìjié zhúzi** a length of bamboo

解 **jiě** untie

姐 **jiě** older sister

借 **jiè** borrow; lend ◊ loan; 借个手，行吗？ **jiè gè shǒu, xíng ma?** can you lend me a hand?; 借给 X Y **jiègěi X Y** lend X to Y

戒 **jiè** cut out; give up

界 **jiè** border; limit

结巴 **jiēba** stammer; stutter

接班人 **jiēbān rén** successor

戒备 **jièbèi** vigilance ◊ vigilant

结冰 **jiébīng** freeze; ice up

阶层 **jiēcéng** (social) class

截查 **jiéchá** intercept

结肠 **jiécháng** bowels; colon

劫车 **jiéchē** hijack a car

劫车者 **jiéchē zhě** carjacker

劫持 **jiéchí** hijack; abduct

接触 **jiēchù** contact ◊ touch

杰出 **jiéchū** brilliant, outstanding; eminent

解除 **jiěchú** take away

戒除 **jièchú** remove; get rid off; kick *habit*; 解除武装 **jiěchú wǔzhuāng** disarm ◊ disarmament

揭穿 **jiēchuān** expose ◊ exposure

介词 **jiècí** preposition

结存 **jiécún** balance FIN

解答 **jiědá** solution; answer; reply

接待 **jiēdài** greet; receive

接待处 **jiēdài chù** reception (area)

接待员 **jiēdài yuán** receptionist; desk clerk

街道 **jiēdào** street

街灯 **jiēdēng** streetlight

解冻 **jiědòng** defrost; thaw

戒毒 **jièdú** withdrawal (*from drugs*)

街段 **jiēduàn** block

阶段 **jiēduàn** phase; stage

截短 **jiéduǎn** cut short, curtail

解毒药 **jiědúyào** antidote

揭发 **jiēfā** uncover; discover

解放 **jiěfàng** liberate ◊ emancipated ◊ liberation; emancipation; the 1949 Communist victory in China

借方 **jièfāng** debit ◊ debtor

解放军 **Jiěfàngjūn** People's Liberation Army, PLA; PLA soldier

姐夫 **jiěfu** brother-in-law (*elder sister's husband*)

结构 **jiégòu** structure

解雇 **jiěgù** dismiss, sack; lay off ◊ dismissal

接管 **jiēguǎn** take charge, take over

结果 **jiéguǒ** result, outcome ◊ end

结核病 jiéhé bìng tuberculosis, TB

接合器 jiēhé qì adapter

结婚 jiéhūn marry; get married; 跟 X 结婚 gēn X jiéhūn get married to X

结婚公告 jiéhūn gōnggào banns

结婚戒指 jiéhūn jièzhǐ wedding ring

结婚礼服 jiéhūn lǐfú wedding gown

结婚证书 jiéhūn zhèngshū marriage certificate

结婚周年 jiéhūn zhōunián wedding anniversary

劫机 jiéjī hijack a plane

阶级 jiējí (social) class; 阶级斗争 jiējí dòuzhēng class warfare

截击 jiéjī intercept *missile*

节俭 jiéjiǎn economic ◊ economically

街角 jiējiǎo street corner

结交 jiéjiāo associate with

姐姐 jiějie older sister

结结巴巴 jiējie bābā broken *English etc*

接近 jiējìn near (*access*) ◊ verge on

竭尽 jiéjìn exhaust; use up; 竭尽所能 jiéjìn suǒnéng do one's utmost

洁净 jiéjìng clean; pure

捷径 jiéjìng short cut

解救 jiéjiù extricate

戒酒 jièjiǔ give up alcohol; be on the wagon

劫机者 jiéjī zhě hijacker

结局 jiéjú outcome; ending

借据 jièjù IOU

解决 jiéjué solve; settle *dispute*; sort out *problem* ◊ fix; settlement

解开 jiěkāi undo; loosen; unfasten; untie; 解开纽扣 jiěkāi niǔkòu unbutton

捷克 Jiékè Czech

捷克共和国 Jiékè Gònghéguó Czech Republic

借口 jièkǒu excuse; pretext

结块 jiékuài clot (*of blood*)

解缆 jiělǎn cast off

接连不断 jiēlián búduàn successive; 接连五天 jiēlián wǔ

天 tiān 5 days in a row

接力赛 jiēlì sài relay (race)

节流阀 jiéliú fá throttle (*on motorbike etc*)

揭露 jiēlù expose; reveal

节录 jiélù excerpt

结论 jiélùn conclusion

睫毛 jiémáo eyelash

睫毛膏 jiémáogāo mascara

姐妹 jiěmèi sisters; 同父异母姐妹 tóngfù yìmǔ jiěmèi, 同母异父姐妹 tóngmǔ yìfù jiěmèi stepsister

界面 jièmiàn interface

解密码 jiě mìmǎ decipher

芥末 jièmò mustard

结膜炎 jiémó yán conjunctivitis

揭幕 jiēmù unveil

节目 jiémù program; show; 今晚有什么节目? jīnwǎn yǒu shénme jiémù? what's on tonight?

节目表 jiémù biǎo listings magazine

节目单 jiémùdān program

接纳 jiēnà admit

节能 jiénéng save energy ◊ energy-saving

节拍 jiépāi rhythm; beat

解剖 jiěpōu dissect ◊ dissection; anatomy

揭起 jiēqǐ take up

截球 jiéqiú tackle SP

接球者 jiēqiú zhě receiver SP

接壤 jiērǎng border (on)

截然相反 jiérán xiāngfǎn contrasting; diametrically opposed

节日 jiérì festival; (public) holiday

吉尔吉斯 Jíěrjísī Kyrgyzstan ◊ Kirg(h)iz

介入 jièrù intervene ◊ intervention; 他不想介入 tā bùxiǎng jièrù he won't have anything to do with it

街上 jiēshang in the street

介绍 jièshào introduce ◊ introduction; profile; 我来介绍一下... wǒ lái jièshào yíxià ... may I introduce ...?; 向 X 介绍 Y xiàng X jièshào Y brief X on Y

介绍信 jièshào xìn testimonial

节省 jiéshěng economize on;

save; stint on ◊ economy; saving ◊ economical

节省时间 **jiéshěng shíjiān** timesaving

结实 **jiēshi** sturdy; firm

解释 **jiěshì** explain; account for; interpret; rationalize ◊ explanation

接收 **jiēshōu** receive

接手 **jiēshǒu** take over ◊ catcher SP

接受 **jiēshòu** accept; take; receive; admit ◊ acceptance; 接受手术治疗 **jiēshòu shǒushù zhìliáo** undergo surgery; 我接受你的提议 **wǒ jiēshòu nǐde tíyì** I'll take you up on your offer; 接受 X 的意见 **jiēshòu X de yìjiàn** take X's advice

接收力 **jiēshōu lì** reception (for TV etc)

接收人 **jiēshōu rén** recipient

结束 **jiéshù** end, finish, conclude; put an end to

结算 **jiésuàn** balance the books; settle bill

结算单 **jiésuàn dān** (bank) statement

阶梯 **jiētī** step; stairs

接替 **jiētì** replace; relieve

解体 **jiětǐ** disintegrate

接通 **jiētōng** connect; put through

接通电源 **jiētōng diànyuán** plug in

解脱开 **jiětuō kāi** disentangle

结网 **jiéwǎng** spin web

结尾 **jiéwěi** conclusion, end

接吻 **jiēwěn** kiss

接下来 **jiēxiàlái** succeeding

界限 **jièxiàn** border; parameter

接线生 **jiēxiàn shēng** operator

戒严令 **jièyánlìng** martial law

解压缩 **jiě yāsuō** unzip COMPUT

介意 **jièyì** mind, object; object to; 我抽烟你介意吗？**wǒ chōuyān nǐ jièyì ma?** would you mind if I smoked?

解疑屏幕 **jiěyí píngmù** help screen

借用 **jièyòng** borrow ◊ on loan

节育 **jiéyù** birth control

节约 **jiéyuē** economize; save ◊

thrift ◊ thrifty; cost-conscious

解约 **jiěyuē** cancel a contract

节约行动 **jiéyuē xíngdòng** economy drive

结扎 **jiézā** sterilize

结账 **jiézhàng** checkout ◊ check out; settle an account; pay the bill

结账时间 **jiézhàng shíjiān** checkout time

接着 **jiēzhe** following

节肢 **jiézhī** amputate

节制 **jiézhì** moderation, restraint

戒指 **jièzhǐ** ring (on finger)

接种 **jiēzhòng** vaccinate; inoculate ◊ vaccination; inoculation; 接种 X 疫苗 **jiēzhòng X yìmiáo** be vaccinated against X

接种疫苗 **jiēzhòng yìmiáo** vaccinate

接住 **jiēzhù** catch

疖子 **jiēzi** boil

节奏 **jiézòu** rhythm; beat

杰作 **jiézuò** masterpiece

激发 **jīfā** arouse; work up

记分 **jìfēn** (keep the) score

讥讽 **jīfěng** sarcasm ◊ sarcastic

季风 **jìfēng** monsoon

季风雨季 **jìfēng yǔjì** monsoon season

记分员 **jìfēnyuán** scorer

继父 **jìfù** stepfather

挤干 **jǐgān** squeeze dry

及格 **jígé** pass (in exam)

几个 **jǐge** a few, several; how many?

及格分 **jígéfēn** pass mark

技工 **jìgōng** mechanic; skilled worker

机构 **jīgòu** organization; institution; structure; mechanism

籍贯 **jíguàn** home; birthplace

激光 **jīguāng** laser

激光唱片 **jīguāng chàngpiàn** compact disc

激光打印机 **jīguāng dǎyìn jī** laser printer

激光光束 **jīguāng guāngshù** laser beam

极好 **jí hǎo** fabulous, swell, marvelous

记号 **jìhao** mark, sign

集合 **jíhé** meet; assemble;

combine; pool ◊ set MATH

记恨 jìhèn bear a grudge

几何学 jǐhéxué geometric ◊ geometrical

几乎 jīhū almost

激化 jīhuà intensify; increase

计划 jìhuà plan; project; figure on; structure ◊ planning; program; project

计划表 jìhuàbiǎo schedule

极坏 jíhuài rotten

饥荒 jīhuāng famine

计划生育 jìhuà shēngyù family planning; birth control; one child policy

击毁 jīhuǐ destroy

机会 jīhuì opportunity, chance

集会 jíhuì meeting; assembly; rally; function

积极 jījí active; dynamic; positive; energetic

击剑 jījiàn fencing

即将 jíjiāng about to; on the brink of ◊ soon

即将来临 jíjiāng láilín upcoming

计件工作 jìjiàn gōngzuò piecework

寄件人 jìjiànrén sender

集结 jíjié mass

季节 jìjié season

积极分子 jījí fènzi activist; militant

唧唧叫 jījī jiào chirp

基金 jījīn fund

激进 jījìn radical

挤紧 jǐjǐn squeeze up

挤进 jǐjìn jam, squeeze

机警 jījǐng on the ball; alert

寂静 jìjìng quiet

基金会 jījīnhuì foundation

激进主义 jījìn zhǔyì radicalism

激进主义者 jījìn zhǔyì zhě radical

急救 jíjiù first aid

急救箱 jíjiùxiāng first-aid box, first-aid kit

积极性 jījíxìng initiative; dynamism; activity

积聚 jījù build-up ◊ build up, mount up

急剧 jíjù rapid; abrupt

即刻 jíkè immediate, instantaneous ◊ immediately, instantly; momentarily

疾苦 jíkǔ suffering

系牢 jìláo do up

积累 jīlěi accumulate; pile up

激励 jīlì boost; spur; stimulation; 激励 ... 前进 jīlì ... qiánjìn spur on

吉利 jílì fortunate; favorable; lucky

剂量 jìliàng dose

脊梁骨 jǐliáng gǔ backbone; spine

计量器 jìliángqì gauge

激烈 jīliè intense; fierce; heated

机灵 jīling smart; sharp; nimble

急流 jíliú rapids; torrent

纪录 jìlù record; note ◊ minutes; log; 纪录保持者 jìlù bǎochí zhě record holder

纪律 jìlǜ discipline

击落 jīluò shoot down

纪录片 jìlù piān documentary

记录 X jìlù X keep track of X

挤满 jǐmǎn be full of

急忙 jímáng hurried; in a hurry

机密 jīmì classified; confidential; top secret

机敏 jīmǐn quickwitted

寂寞 jìmò lonely

计谋 jìmóu trick

继母 jìmǔ stepmother

金 jīn gold ◊ golden

津 jīn ford; ferry crossing

巾 jīn cloth

今 jīn now; today; the present

筋 jīn tendon

斤 jīn jin (500 grams)

紧 jǐn tight; tense; taut

锦 jǐn brocade

仅 jǐn only

尽 jǐn furthest; 尽里面 jǐn lǐmiàn back; very back; furthest back

尽 jìn exhaust; try one's best ◊ exhausted; finished ◊ to the limit

近 jìn close, near

进 jìn go in; enter; 请进 !qǐngjìn! come in!

禁 jìn prohibit

劲 jìn strength; energy

浸 jìn soak

缉拿 jīná manhunt

挤奶 jǐnǎi milk

金边儿股票 jīnbiānr gǔpiào gilts

锦标旗 jǐnbiāoqí pennant

锦标赛 jǐnbiāo sài championship; tournament

进步 jìnbù advance; progress ◊ progressive

禁不住 jīnbúzhù can't help; 我禁不住笑了 **wǒ jīnbúzhù xiàole** I couldn't help laughing

进餐时间 jìncān shíjiān mealtime

进程 jìnchéng proceedings; course; process

紧凑 jǐncòu tight *timing*; compact; terse

禁得住 jīndezhù withstand

禁地 jìndì restricted area

筋斗 jīndǒu somersault

金额 jīn'é amount

技能 jìnéng technique; skills; knowhow

金发 jīnfà blond hair

谨防 jǐnfáng be wary of

劲风 jìnfēng high wind

茎 jīng stem

鲸 jīng whale

京 jīng capital city

惊 jīng alarm; surprise

精 jīng essence; spirit; seed; semen ◊ refined; excellent

晶 jīng crystal

经 jīng warp; longitude ◊ experience

井 jǐng well (*for water*)

警 jǐng warn ◊ alarm; police

景 jǐng landscape; scenery

颈 jǐng neck; throat

净 jìng clean; net

境 jìng border

镜 jìng mirror

静 jìng quiet

敬 jìng respect ◊ respectful

径 jìng path; diameter

紧盖器 jǐn'gàiqì fastener

金刚石 jīngāngshí diamond

警报 jǐngbào alarm; alert

胫部 jìngbù shin

精彩 jīngcǎi wonderful

警察 jǐngchá police; police oficer

警察国家 jǐngchá guójiā police state

警察纠捕队 jǐngchá jiūbǔ duì vice squad

警察局 jǐngchájú police station, station house

经常 jīngcháng often ◊ frequent; habitual

惊呆 jīngdāi bowl over, amaze

精打细算 jīngdǎ xìsuàn be on a budget

境地 jìngdì situation; position

静电 jìngdiàn static electricity

经典作品 jīngdiǎn zuòpǐn classic

经度 jīngdù longitude

精读课 jīngdúkè intensive course

惊愕 jīng'è stupefied

警方 jǐngfāng police

警告 jǐnggào warn ◊ warning

胫骨 jìnggǔ shin; shinbone

警官 jǐngguān police officer

警棍 jǐnggùn nightstick

经过 jīngguò pass by; pass ◊ past; by; via; through

精华 jīnghuá essence; goodness

净化 jìnghuà purify

惊慌 jīnghuāng alarmed ◊ get alarmed

惊惶失措 jīnghuáng shīcuò panic-stricken

静火山 jìng huǒshān dormant volcano

经济 jīngjì economy ◊ economic; economical

竞技 jìngjì athletics; sports

精简 jīngjiǎn abridge

惊叫 jīngjiào exclaim

经济舱 jīngjìcāng economy class

警戒 jǐngjiè warn

警戒线 jǐngjiè xiàn cordon

经济紧缩 jīngjì jǐnsuō austerity

井井有条 jǐngjǐng yǒutiáo in good trim; in order

经济气候 jīngjì qìhòu economic climate

经济情况 jīngjì qíngkuàng economics; financial circumstances

纪人 jīngjì rén broker; middleman

经济上 jīngjì shang economically; in financial terms

经济特区 jīngjì tèqū special economic zone, SEZ

经济学 jīngjìxué economics

(subject)

经济学家 jīngjìxuéjiā economist

京剧 Jīngjù Peking Opera

警觉 jīngjué alert

惊恐 jīngkǒng consternation; scare

净空高度 jìngkōng gāodù headroom

镜框 jìngkuàng frame (of picture, glasses)

境况 jìngkuàng circumstances

经理 jīnglǐ manager

经历 jīnglì experience; background ◊ go through

精力 jīnglì energy; drive

敬礼 jìnglǐ salute

精力充沛 jīnglì chōngpèi dynamic; vigorous; inexhaustible ◊ nervous energy

痉挛 jìngluán cramp

静脉 jìngmài vein

静脉内 jìngmàinèi intravenous

静脉曲张 jìngmài qūzhāng varicose vein

精美 jīngměi exquisite, beautiful

精密 jīngmì precise; accurate; sophisticated, complex

精明 jīngmíng clever; ingenious; calculating; shrewd ◊ ingenuity

进攻 jìngōng advance MIL; charge

惊跑 jīngpǎo stampede

敬佩 jìngpèi respect

精辟 jīngpì profound

惊奇 jīngqí amazement, surprise; wonder ◊ be amazed

精确 jīngquè precise; rigorous ◊ precisely ◊ precision

井然 jǐngrán neat; proper

惊人 jīngrén amazing, mind-boggling, breathtaking ◊ phenomenally

竞赛 jìngsài race; racing ◊ run

径赛 jìngsài track event; athletics meeting

景色 jǐngsè scenery

精神 jīngshen vigor; energy ◊ lively; vigorous; smart

精神 jīngshén soul; spirit; mind; essence ◊ mental; 精神好／坏 jīngshén hǎo/huài be in good/poor spirits

精神崩溃 jīngshén bēngkuì nervous breakdown

精神变态者 jīngshén biàntài zhě psychopath

精神病 jīngshénbìng mental illness ◊ psychiatric

精神病学 jīngshénbìngxué psychiatry

精神病院 jīngshénbìngyuàn mental hospital

精神错乱 jīngshén cuòluàn demented

精神分裂 jīngshén fēnliè schizophrenic

精神分裂症 jīngshén fēnlièzhèng schizophrenia

精神分裂症患者 jīngshén fēnlièzhèng huàn zhě schizophrenic

精神分析 jīngshén fēnxī psychoanalysis

精神分析学家 jīngshén fēnxīxuéjiā psychoanalyst

精神恍惚 jīngshén huǎnghū dreamy

精神科医生 jīngshénkē yīshēng psychiatrist

精神虐待 jīngshén nüèdài mental cruelty

精神失常 jīngshén shīcháng madness ◊ mentally disturbed

紧身套衫 jǐnshēn tàoshān sweater

经受 jīngshòu undergo; suffer

景泰蓝 jǐngtàilán cloisonné

惊叹 jīngtàn exclaim; admire; marvel at; 令人惊叹 *lìngrén jīngtàn* amazing; shattering

晶体 jīngtǐ crystal

警惕 jǐngtì alert ◊ watchful ◊ warily

惊跳 jīngtiào jump

晶体管 jīngtǐguǎn transistor

晶体管收音机 jīngtǐguǎn shōuyīnjī transistor radio

精通 jīngtōng be expert at; master ◊ impeccable; proficient ◊ mastery

精通世故 jīngtōng shìgù sophisticated

镜头 jìngtóu shot; scene;

photograph; lens

镜头盖 jìngtóu gài lens cover

尽管 jǐnguǎn although; despite, in spite of

尽管如此 jǐnguǎn rúcǐ all the same, nevertheless

警卫 jǐngwèi guard

紧握 jǐngwò clasp

精细 jīngxì meticulous; refined

惊吓 jīngxià fright ◊ frighten, scare; startle

惊险电影 jīngxiǎn diànyǐng thriller (movie)

惊险小说 jīngxiǎn xiǎoshuō thriller (novel)

经销 jīngxiāo distribute ◊ distribution

经销商 jīngxiāo shāng distributor

精心 jīngxīn carefully; nicely

精心制作 jīngxīn zhìzuò elaborate

精选 jīngxuǎn choice

竞选 jìngxuǎn run (for election)

竞选活动 jìngxuǎn huódòng election campaign

竞选人 jìngxuǎn rén contender

竞选总统 jìngxuǎn zǒngtǒng run for President

惊讶 jīngyà astonishment ◊ be astonished

经验 jīngyàn experience

敬仰 jìngyǎng admire; worship

精液 jīngyè sperm; semen

惊异 jīngyì stunned, amazed

敬意 jìngyì respect; deference; 表示敬意 biǎoshì jìngyì deferential; 令人惊异 lìngrén jīngyì stunning

精英 jīngyīng elite

经营 jīngyíng manage; operate; run ◊ running; trade; operations ◊ managerial

经营顾问 jīngyíng gùwèn management consultant

经由 jīngyóu by way of

鲸鱼 jīngyú whale

竞争 jìngzhēng compete; contend for ◊ competition; contest; rivalry

竞争对手 jìngzhēng duìshǒu competitor

竞争力很强 jìngzhēnglì

很强 hěnqiáng competitive

竞争者 jìngzhēng zhě contender; rival; contestant

精致 jīngzhì delicate; fancy; exquisite ◊ delicacy

径直 jìngzhí straight

晶质玻璃 jīngzhì bōli crystal

警钟 jǐngzhōng alarm

净重 jìngzhòng net weight

精子 jīngzǐ sperm

镜子 jìngzi mirror; glasses, specs

精子库 jīngzǐ kù sperm bank

今后 jīnhòu in future

进化 jìnhuà evolve ◊ evolution

金婚纪念 jīnhūn jìniàn golden wedding anniversary

纪念 jìniàn commemorate, mark ◊ memorial; 作为对 X 的纪念 zuòwéi duì X de jìniàn in memory of X

纪念碑 jìniànbēi memorial; monument

纪念品 jìniàn pǐn souvenir; memento

紧急 jǐnjí urgent; imperative ◊ urgency

晋级 jìnjí promotion

近郊 jìnjiāo environs

紧急出口 jǐnjí chūkǒu emergency exit

紧接着 jǐnjiēzhe in the wake of

仅仅 jǐnjǐn only; merely; barely; solely

紧急情况 jǐnjí qíngkuàng emergency

近几天 jìnjǐtiān the past few days

禁酒 jìnjiǔ dry

紧急着落 jǐnjí zháoluò emergency landing

紧急状态 jǐnjí zhuàngtài state of emergency

尽可能 jìn kěnéng as far as possible; 尽可能最好 ... jìn kěnéng zuìhǎo ... the best possible ...

进口 jìnkǒu import

进口商 jìnkǒushāng importer

金库 Jīnkù National Treasury

尽快 jǐnkuài as soon as possible

近况如何? jìnkuàng rúhé? how are things?

近来 jìnlái recent ◊ recently

尽力 jìnlì endeavor

尽量 jǐnliàng as well as one can

尽量利用 jǐnliàng lìyòng make the most of

尽力而为 jìnlì érwéi do one's best

尽力解决 jìnlì jiějué grapple with

紧邻 jǐnlín the immediate neighborhood

禁令 jìnlìng ban

浸满水 jìnmǎnshuǐ waterlogged

今年 jīnnián this year

金牌 jīnpái gold medal

浸泡 jìnpào soak; immerse ◊ infusion

筋疲力尽 jīnpí lìjìn exhaust; drain ◊ exhausted; shattered

紧迫 jǐnpò extremely urgent

谨启 jǐnqǐ yours sincerely

金枪鱼 jīnqiāng yú tuna

近亲繁殖 jìnqīn fánzhí inbreeding

进去 jìnqu go in

禁区 jìnqū no-go area

进取心 jìnqǔ xīn enterprise, initiative

金融 jīnróng finance ◊ financial

金融家 jīnróng jiā financier

金融市场 jīnróng shìchǎng money market

进入 jìnrù enter; get in ◊ entrance; entry

金色 jīnsè golden

紧身 jǐnshēn tight-fitting; skin-tight

谨慎 jǐnshèn careful, cautious; discreet ◊ caution; tact, delicacy

晋升 jìnshēng promote

紧身套衫 jǐnshēn tàoshān sweater; sweatshirt

紧身胸衣 jǐnshēn xiōngyī bodice

紧身衣 jǐnshēn yī body suit; leotard

近视 jìnshi shortsighted ◊ myopia

浸湿 jìnshī soak

禁食 jìnshí fast (not eating)

近视眼 jìnshìyǎn shortsighted ◊ myopia

金首饰商 jīnshǒushìshāng goldsmith

金属 jīnshǔ metal

金属器具 jīnshǔ qìjù hardware

金属丝 jīnshǔsī wire

金属网 jīnshǔwǎng wire netting

近似 jìnsì almost; roughly ◊ border on

金丝雀 jīnsīquè canary

紧缩开支 jǐnsuō kāizhī economize

今天 jīntiān today; 今天几号？ jīntiān jǐhào? what's the date today?; 今天上午 jīntiān shàngwǔ this morning; 今天晚上 jīntiān wǎnshang this evening; 今天下午 jīntiān xiàwǔ this afternoon; 今天星期几？ jīntiān xīngqī jǐ? what day is it today?; 今天早晨 jīntiān zǎochén this morning

津贴 jīntiē subsidy; allowance

尽头 jìntóu end

劲头 jìntóu enthusiasm

浸透 jìntòu soak (through), saturate

进退两难 jìntuì liǎngnán dilemma

激怒 jīnù incense, infuriate; provoke ◊ enraged

妓女 jìnǚ prostitute

继女 jìnǚ stepdaughter

今晚 jīnwǎn tonight

紧握 jǐnwò clutch; grip

进行 jìnxíng carry out; execute; progress, move on; 在进行中 zài jìnxíngzhōng be under way

进修 jìnxiū continue one's education

紧要 jǐnyào critical

紧要关头 jǐnyào guāntóu tension

襟翼 jīnyì flap

进一步 jìnyíbù a step further; further

金银丝 jīnyín sī tinsel

禁用 jìnyòng heavy-duty; long-lasting; hard-wearing

金鱼 jīnyú goldfish

禁运 jìnyùn embargo

尽早 jǐnzǎo as early as possible

进站 jìn zhàn pull in, arrive

进展 jìnzhǎn proceed, progress

紧张 jǐnzhāng nervous; tense; uptight; stressed ◊ get nervous;

get flustered; tense up ◊
nervousness; tension; 别 紧张 **bié
jǐnzhāng** take it easy!

紧张感 jǐnzhānggǎn suspense

紧张慌乱 jǐnzhāng huāngluàn
be in a flap

禁止 jìnzhǐ ban, forbid, prohibit ◊
ban, prohibition; 禁止 X 做 Y
**jìnzhǐ X zuò Y** forbid X to do Y

禁止入内 jìnzhǐ rùnèi no
admittance; off limits

禁止停车 jìnzhǐ tíngchē no
parking

禁止吸烟 jìnzhǐ xīyān no
smoking

窘况 jiǒngkuàng predicament

窘迫 jiǒngpò poverty-stricken; in
a predicament

麂皮 jǐpí chamois (leather)

鸡皮疙瘩 jīpí gēda gooseflesh; 他
使我浑身起鸡皮疙瘩 **tā
shǐwǒ húnshēn qǐ jīpí gēda** he
gives me the creeps

祭品 jìpǐn sacrifice

击破 jīpò strike down; fell

急迫 jípò urgent

吉普车 jípǔchē jeep

吉普赛人 jípǔsài rén gipsy

激起 jīqǐ prompt; cause; excite;
work up

机器 jīqì machine; machinery

极其 jíqí extremely

记起 jìqǐ recall; remember

机枪 jīqiāng machine gun

技巧 jìqiǎo skill; knack

急切 jíqiè eager

激情 jīqíng machine gun

机器人 jīqìrén robot

击球 jīqiú bat; strike *ball* ◊ batting

击球员 jīqiú yuán batter

寄去 jìqù send in, mail in

极权主义 jíquán zhǔyì
totalitarian

既然 jìrán since

既然这样 jìrán zhèyàng in that
case

急人 jírén frightening; worrying

继任 jìrèn succeed (to office etc)

继任人 jìrènrén successor

鸡肉 jīròu chicken (meat)

肌肉 jīròu muscle

肌肉发达 jīròu fādá muscular

机身 jīshēn fuselage

寄生虫 jìshēngchóng parasite;
sponger, freeloader

及时 jíshí prompt; timely ◊
promptly; in time

即时 jíshí immediately

即使 jíshí even if

疾驶 jíshǐ speed

集市 jíshì market

几时 jǐshí when; what time

集市广场 jíshì guǎngchǎng
market place

计时钟 jìshízhōng time clock (in
factory)

棘手 jíshǒu tricky

奇数 jīshù odd number

技术 jìshù skill; technique;
technology ◊ technological

计数 jìshù count

技术娴熟 jìshù xiánshú
workmanlike

技术性 jìshù xìng technical

技术员 jìshùyuán technician

祭祀 jìsì sacrifice

激素 jīsù steroids

计算 jìsuàn calculate; count;
budget for; allow

计算出 jìsuànchù figure out

计算机 jìsuànjī computer;
calculator

计算结果 jìsuàn jiēguǒ
calculation

计算机科学 jìsuànjī kēxué
computer science

计算机科学家 jìsuànjī kēxué jiā
computer scientist

计算器 jìsuàn qì calculator

寄宿生 jìsù shēng boarder (at
school)

急速行驶 jísù xíngshǐ zoom, race

寄宿学校 jìsù xuéxiào boarding
school

吉他 jítā guitar

祭坛 jìtán altar

集体 jítǐ collective

几天 jǐtiān a few days, a couple of
days

集体精神 jítǐ jīngshén team spirit

集体抛售 jítǐ pāoshòu raid FIN

集体协定 jítǐ xiédìng collective

bargaining

集团 jítuán group; bloc ◊ corporate

鸡腿 jītuǐ drumstick (*chicken leg*)

击退 jītuì repel

阄 jiū: 抓阄儿 **zhuājiūr** draw lots

酒 jiǔ alcoholic drink; liquor

九 jiǔ nine

久 jiǔ a long time

舅 jiù uncle (*mother's brother*); brother-in-law (*wife's brother*)

旧 jiù old; obsolete; former; threadbare

就 jiù right; directly; just; only; regarding; 就我而言 **jiù wǒ ér yán** as far as I'm concerned

救 jiù save; rescue

酒吧 jiǔbā bar

旧病复发 jiùbìng fùfā relapse ◊ have a relapse

韭菜 jiǔcài Chinese chives

纠察 jiūchá picket

纠察队 jiūcháduì picket

纠缠 jiūchán badger, pester

纠察线 jiūcháxiàn picket line

旧城区 jiùchéngqū inner city

白齿 jiùchǐ molar

韭葱 jiǔcōng leek

酒店 jiǔdiàn bar; wineshop; restaurant

酒店伙计 jiǔdiàn huǒjì bartender

纠纷 jiūfēn dispute; quarrel

纠葛 jiūgé dispute; involvement

酒鬼 jiǔguǐ drunk; alcoholic

酒后开车 jiǔhòu kāichē drunk driving

救护车 jiùhùchē ambulance

旧货 jiùhuò second-hand goods

救急 jiùjí urgent

究竟 jiūjìng actually; at the end of the day; 你究竟在干什么？**nǐ jiūjìng zài gàn shénme?** what the hell are you doing?

酒精 jiǔjīng alcohol

酒精饮料 jiǔjīng yǐnliào liquor

舅舅 jiùjiu uncle (*mother's brother*)

救济院 jiùjìyuàn hospice

旧历 jiùlì Chinese lunar calendar

九龙 Jiǔlóng Kowloon

救命 jiùmìng save s.o.'s life ◊ help!

就寝 jiùqǐn go to bed

救球 jiùqiú save SP

救生 jiùshēng life-saving

救生圈 jiùshēng quān life belt

救生艇 jiùshēng tǐng lifeboat

救生衣 jiùshēng yī life jacket

救生员 jiùshēng yuán lifeguard

九十 jiǔshí ninety

就是 jiùshi exactly!

就事论事 jiùshìlùnshì *prov* call a spade a spade

就是说 jiùshìshuō that is to say

救世主 jiùshìzhǔ savior

灸术 jiǔshù moxibustion

九死一生 jiǔsǐyìshēng have a narrow escape

酒窝 jiǔwō dimple

酒席 jiǔxí banquet

就医 jiùyī go to the doctor

久远 jiǔyuǎn remote *ancestor*

九月 jiǔyuè September

纠正 jiūzhèng correct

纠正错误 jiūzhèng cuòwù put things right

就职 jiùzhí inauguration ◊ inaugural

就职仪式 jiùzhí yíshì induction ceremony

酒钻 jiǔzuàn corkscrew

就座 jiùzuò take a seat

就座勿动 jiùzuò wùdòng please remain seated

极为 jíwéi extremely

即位 jíwèi succeed ◊ succession

鸡尾酒 jīwěijiǔ cocktail

极微小 jíwēixiǎo microscopic

极限 jíxiàn limit; frontier

吉祥 jíxiáng lucky

挤向 jǐxiàng crowd

迹象 jīxiàng mark; pointer; sign

集线器 jíxiànqì hub COMPUT

讥笑 jīxiào scoff; laugh at

极小 jíxiǎo tiny; remote *possibility*

机械 jīxiè machinery; mechanism ◊ mechanical ◊ mechanically

机械化 jīxièhuà mechanize

机械装置 jīxiè zhuāngzhì mechanism

畸形 jīxíng freak; monstrosity ◊ misshapen; monstrous

疾行 jíxíng race; run

即兴 jíxìng improvise

急性 jíxìng acute *illness*

记性 jìxing memory

鸡心领 jīxīn lǐng V-neck

继兄弟 jìxiōngdì stepbrother

积蓄 jīxù save up; keep ◊ savings

急需 jíxū be in urgent need of

继续 jìxù continue; go on; keep on; carry on; conduct

积雪 jīxuě snowy

挤压 jǐyā press

鸡眼 jīyǎn corn (on foot)

给养 jǐyǎng provisions

技艺 jìyì skill; art; craft; workmanship

记忆 jìyì remember ◊ memory; recollection

记忆力 jìyìlì memory; 记忆力好 / 坏 jìyìlì hǎo / huài have a good / bad memory

基因 jīyīn gene

集邮 jíyóu stamp collecting

极右主义 jíyòu zhǔyì right-wing extremism

给予 jǐyǔ render; provide; give *answer*

基于 jīyú because of; on the basis of

机遇 jīyù chance; stroke of luck

积怨 jīyuàn rancor

纪元 jìyuán era, epoch

妓院 jìyuàn brothel

给予优先 jǐyǔ yōuxiān prioritize

记载 jìzǎi record

及早 jízǎo early; premature

急躁 jízào on edge

激增 jīzēng sudden increase; surge; explosion (in population)

机长 jīzhǎng captain (of aircraft)

记账 jìzhàng bookkeeping ◊ do the books; charge

记账人 jìzhàng rén bookkeeper

记者 jìzhě reporter; journalist

急诊医生 jízhěn yīshēng emergency doctor

记者招待会 jìzhě zhāodàihuì press conference

机制 jīzhì machine

机智 jīzhì tact; wit ◊ witty; resourceful

机智幽默 jīzhì yōumò wit

集中 jízhōng assemble; collect;

centralize; concentrate ◊ cluster; focus (of attention)

集中精力 jízhōng jīnglì concentrate

脊柱 jǐzhù spine; spinal column ◊ spinal

记住 jìzhù remember; memorize

记住锁门 jìzhù suǒmén remember to lock the door

系住 jìzhù tie up

集装箱 jízhuāng xiāng container

集装箱船 jízhuāng xiāng chuán container ship

急转弯 jízhuǎnwān hairpin curve

脊椎 jǐzhuī vertebra; 有脊椎 yǒu jǐzhuī vertebrate

基准 jīzhǔn benchmark

髻子 jìzi bun (in hair)

继子 jìzǐ stepson

机组 jīzǔ air crew

基座 jīzuò pedestal

拘 jū restrict

驹 jū foal

居 jū live; reside; occupy ◊ house; residence; 居要位 jū yàowèi have priority

局 jú department; office; game; set; situation

举 jǔ raise; hold up; elect ◊ act; deed

剧 jù drama; play; theater

锯 jù saw

聚 jù assemble; get together

巨 jù giant, huge

具 jù tool, utensil

句 jù sentence

据 jù according to; 据我所知 jù wǒ suǒzhī as far as I know, to the best of my knowledge

捐 juān donate; contribute

卷 juǎn roll; reel; coil ◊ curly, frizzy; 把 X 卷成球 bǎ X juǎn chéngqiú roll X into a ball

卷 juàn volume

圈 juàn pen; enclosure

卷尺 juǎnchǐ tape measure

卷发 juǎnfà curly hair

卷发卷 juǎnfà juǎn roller; tongs (for hair)

绢纺 juànfǎng silk spinning

卷角 juǎnjiǎo dog-eared

捐款 juānkuǎn donation;

contribution

捐款人 **juānkuǎn rén** contributor; donor

卷盘 **juǎnpán** spool

卷起来 **juǎn qǐlái** roll up; coil up

卷入 X **juǎnrù** involvement; 卷入 X **juǎnrù X** get involved with X

捐献 **juānxiàn** contribute; donate ◊ contribution; donation

捐献者 **juānxiàn zhě** donor

卷心菜 **juǎnxīn cài** cabbage

捐赠 **juānzèng** donate; contribute

举办 **jǔbàn** organize; hold

具备 **jùbèi** own; have

剧本 **jùběn** (stage) play

聚苯乙烯 **jùběnyǐxī** polystyrene

剧变 **jùbiàn** upheaval

局部 **júbù** partial ◊ partially

剧场 **jùchǎng** theater

局促不安 **júcù bù'ān** feel ill at ease; squirm

举措 **jǔcuò** move

巨大 **jùdà** enormous, immense, vast; astronomical

锯掉 **jùdiào** saw off

蕨 **jué** fern

觉 **jué** sense; feel ◊ feeling

角 **jué** role

决 **jué** decide

掘 **jué** dig

绝 **jué** cut off ◊ absolute

绝版 **juébǎn** out of print

决不 **juébù** on no account, under no circumstances

决策者 **juécè zhě** mastermind; decision maker

觉察 **juéchá** perceive

觉得 **juéde** feel; think; 我觉得很冷 **wǒ juéde hěnlěng** I feel cold; 你觉得怎么样? **nǐ juéde zěnmeyàng?** what do you make of it?

决定 **juédìng** decide, make up one's mind ◊ decision; resolution; 你来决定 **nǐ lái juédìng** you decide, it's up to you

决定性 **juédìng xìng** decisive, conclusive ◊ decidedly

决断力 **juéduànlì** judgment

绝对 **juéduì** absolute; total ◊ definitely, absolutely; 绝对不行! **juéduì bùxíng!** no way!,

certainly not!

倔强 **juéjiàng** disobedient

绝交 **juéjiāo** sever relations; 我与 X 绝交 **wǒ yǔ X juéjiāo** I'm through with X

绝经期 **juéjīngqī** menopause

绝密 **juémì** top secret

绝妙 **juémiào** sensational, tremendous; magic

掘起 **juéqǐ** dig up

诀窍 **juéqiào** knack

决赛 **juésài** decider; final SP; 参加决赛者 **cānjiā juésài zhě** finalist

角色 **juésè** part, role

绝食 **juéshí** hunger strike

爵士音乐 **juéshì yīnyuè** jazz

爵士乐队 **juéshì yuèduì** jazz band

决算 **juésuàn** balance (sheet)

掘土机 **juétǔjī** excavator

绝望 **juéwàng** despair

决心 **juéxīn** determination, resolution

决选 **juéxuǎn** shortlist

决议 **juéyì** decision; resolution

绝缘 **juéyuán** insulation

绝缘材料 **juéyuán cáiliào** insulation

绝缘胶布 **juéyuán jiāobù** friction tape

绝种 **juézhǒng** extinct ◊ extinction

撅嘴 **juēzuǐ** pout

句法 **jùfǎ** syntax

飓风 **jùfēng** hurricane

拒服兵役者 **jù fú bīngyì zhě** conscientious objector

鞠躬 **jūgōng** bow

聚光灯 **jùguāng dēng** spotlight

句号 **jùhào** period, full stop

聚合 **jùhé** meet (of committee)

菊花 **júhuā** chrysanthemum

聚会 **jùhuì** gathering; get-together

聚集 **jùjí** assemble; gather; congregate

聚焦于 **jùjiāo yú** focus on

拘谨 **jūjǐn** stiff; uptight; reserved

拘禁 **jūjìn** lock up

狙击手 **jūjīshǒu** sniper

拒绝 **jùjué** refusal; denial; rejection; refuse; deny; reject; 拒绝参加 **jùjué cānjiā** boycott; refuse to take part in

锯开 jùkāi saw

俱乐部 jùlèbù club

距离 jùlí distance ◊ apart

剧烈 jùliè fierce; energetic; 剧烈的头痛 jùliè de tóutòng splitting headache

拘留 jūliú detain; intern ◊ detention; 被拘留 bèi jūliú in custody

居留 jūliú stay; reside

居留证 jūliúzhèng residence permit

聚氯乙烯 jùlǜyǐxī PVC

局面 júmiàn situation

居民 jūmín inhabitant; resident

锯末 jùmò sawdust

军 jūn army

均 jūn same; equal ◊ all; both

君 jūn king; gentleman ◊ you fml

郡 jùn county; prefecture (in old China)

军备 jūnbèi armament

均等 jūnděng equal ◊ equality

军队 jūnduì army; the military; the services; troops

军阀 jūnfá warlord

军官 jūnguān officer MIL

均衡 jūnhéng balance; equalize (pressure etc)

均衡饮食 jūnhéng yǐnshí balanced diet

军火 jūnhuǒ ammunition

军舰 jūnjiàn warship

军警 jūnjǐng military police

岭 jùnlǐng high mountains

军旗 jūnqí colors MIL

军人 jūnrén serviceman; soldier

军事 jūnshì military

军事法庭 jūnshì fǎtíng court martial

军事学院 jūnshì xuéyuàn military academy

军事装备 jūnshì zhuāngbèi military installation

军衔 jūnxián rank

均匀 jūnyún even, regular ◊ evenly

君主 jūnzhǔ monarch

君子 jūnzǐ gentleman

举起 jǔqǐ lift; put up; 举起手来！jǔqǐshǒulái! hands up!

巨人 jùrén giant

沮丧 jǔsàng dejected; depressed; downcast; frustrated; 令人沮丧 lìngrén jǔsàng dismal

居士 jūshì hermit

居首位 jū shǒuwèi take the lead

拘束 jūshù awkward; constrained; unnatural; 别拘束 bié jūshù make yourself at home

据说 … jùshuō … it is said that …; they say …; be supposed to …; 据说他在香港 jù shuō tā zài Xiānggǎng he is reported to be in Hong Kong; 据说这首诗是 … 所作 jùshuō zhèi shǒu shī shì … suǒzuò the poem has been attributed to …

具体 jùtǐ concrete; specific

具体细致 jùtǐ xìzhì in minute detail

巨头 jùtóu tycoon

据为己有 jùwéi jǐyǒu pocket

据悉 … jùxī … it has emerged that …

局限 júxiàn limit; confine ◊ limitation

举行 jǔxíng stage; organize; hold

句型 jùxíng sentence pattern

举行罢工 jǔxíng bàgōng go on strike

聚乙烯 jùyǐxī polyethylene

具有 jùyǒu own; have; 具有想象力 jùyǒu xiǎngxiànglì imaginative

剧院 jùyuàn theater; opera house

剧增 jùzēng increase suddenly

举止 jǔzhǐ conduct, behavior

举止不当 jǔzhǐbúdàng misbehave

举止粗鲁 jǔzhǐ cūlǔ ill-mannered

聚酯纤维 jùzhǐxiānwéi polyester

举重 jǔzhòng weightlifting

举重运动员 jǔzhòng yùndòngyuán weightlifter

居住 jūzhù live

居住者 jūzhù zhě occupant

橘子 júzi mandarin orange

句子 jùzi sentence GRAM

锯子 jùzi saw

剧作家 jùzuò jiā dramatist, playwright

# K

卡 kǎ card

喀嚓声 kāchāshēng snap, click

卡车 kǎchē truck

卡车司机 kǎchē sījī truck driver, teamster

咖啡 kāfēi coffee

咖啡店 kāfēi diàn coffee shop

咖啡馆 kāfēiguǎn café

咖啡壶 kāfēi hú coffee pot

咖啡机 kāfēi jī coffee maker

咖啡因 kāfēiyīn caffeine

开 kāi open; turn on; start; drive; boil; write *check* ◊ (*away*): 离开 *líkāi* leave; 走开 *zǒukāi* go away; 开户 *kāi hù* open a bank account

揩 kāi wipe

开本 kāiběn format

开采 kāicǎi mine; mine for

开叉 kāichà slit

开车 kāichē drive (a car)

开除 kāichú expel; discharge ◊ expulsion

开创 kāichuàng initiate ◊ initiation

开大 kāidà turn up *volume*

开刀 kāidāo operate; perform surgery

开灯 kāidēng turn the light on

开动 kāidòng work (*of machine*)

开端 kāiduān start, beginning

开发 kāifā develop

开放政策 kāifàng zhèngcè open-door policy

开发区 kāifāqū development area

开关 kāiguān switch

揩汗 kāihàn wipe away perspiration

开花 kāihuā bloom, blossom

开会 kāihuì hold a meeting; 他在开会 *tā zài kāihuì* he's in a meeting

开机 kāijī boot up

开奖 kāijiǎng draw; lottery result

开襟毛衣 kāijīn máoyī cardigan

开扣 kāikòu fly (*on pants*)

开阔 kāikuò extensive

开朗 kāilǎng open; clear; outgoing; cheerful

开门 kāimén open the door

开明 kāimíng enlighten ◊ progressive; enlightened

开幕 kāimù open; inaugurate; raise the curtain

开枪 kāiqiāng fire a gun

开球 kāiqiú kickoff ◊ kick off

开始 kāishǐ begin, start ◊ beginning ◊ initially

开始曲 kāishǐqǔ signature tune

开水 kāishuǐ boiled water

开庭 kāitíng sitting; hearing

开头 kāitóu start

开拓 kāituò pioneering; 开拓殖民地 *kāituò zhímíndì* colonize

开玩笑 kāi wánxiào joke; kid ◊ joking; 别开玩笑了! *bié kāi wánxiào le!* you can't be serious!, you must be joking!

开胃 kāiwèi appetizing

开胃酒 kāiwèi jiǔ aperitif

开胃品 kāiwèi pǐn appetizer

开小差 kāi xiǎochāi desert ◊ desertion

开心 kāixīn have a good time; 玩儿得很开心 *wánr de hěn kāixīn* it was great fun

凯旋 kǎixuán triumph

开演 kāiyǎn be on (*of program*)

开药方 kāi yàofāng prescribe

开业 kāiyè start a business

开账单 kāi zhàngdān bill, invoice

开着 kāizhe open

开支 kāizhī budget; expenditure; expenses

开走 kāizǒu drive

卡拉 OK kǎlā OK karaoke

卡路里 kǎlùlǐ calorie

刊 kān publication

砍 kǎn chop

看 **kàn** look at; see; watch; read; visit ◊ look, glance; 看电视 **kàn diànshì** watch television; 看天气吧 **kàn tiānqì ba** it depends on the weather; 我看是这样 **wǒ kàn shì zhèyàng** I suppose so; 我能看一下吗? **wǒ néng kàn yíxià ma?** can I have a look?

看病 **kànbìng** see a doctor

看不起 **kànbuqǐ** look down on, despise

刊出 **kānchū** publish

看穿 **kànchuān** see through

看待 **kàndài** view

砍刀 **kǎndāo** chopper

砍倒 **kǎndǎo** chop down

看得见 **kàndejiàn** be visible; show

砍掉 **kǎndiào** lop off

砍伐 **kǎnfá** fell *trees*

看法 **kànfǎ** view; belief; idea

康 **kāng** healthy

抗 **kàng** resist; fight

抗病毒程序 **kàng bìngdú chéngxù** antivirus program

康采恩 **kāngcǎi'ēn** group (*of companies*); concern

康复 **kāngfù** get well again; recuperate

抗菌 **kàngjūn** antiseptic

抗菌剂 **kàngjūnjì** antiseptic

抗菌素 **kàngjūnsù** antibiotic

慷慨 **kāngkǎi** generous; liberal; magnanimous

康乃馨 **kāngnǎixīn** carnation

抗热 **kàngrè** heatproof, heat-resistant

抗日战争 **Kàngrì Zhànzhēng** Anti-Japanese War

抗体 **kàngtǐ** antibody

看管 **kānguǎn** guard; look after

看管人 **kānguǎn rén** caretaker

抗议 **kàngyì** protest

看护 **kānhù** look after; nurse

看见 **kànjiàn** see; catch sight of, catch a glimpse of

看来 **kànlái** seemingly, it appears that ...; 在我看来 **zài wǒ kànlái** in my opinion

看门人 **kānmén rén** doorman; janitor

看起来 **kànqǐlái** seem, appear to be

看上去 **kànshàngqu** seemingly

看守 **kānshǒu** guard, lookout

勘探 **kāntàn** prospect for

看望 **kànwàng** visit

刊物 **kānwù** publication; periodical

看作 **kànzuò** regard as, look on as; 把 X 看作 Y **bǎ X kànzuò Y** regard X as Y

烤 **kǎo** barbecue; broil; roast; bake ◊ barbecued; broiled; roast; baked; 烤牛肉 **kǎo niúròu** roast beef; barbecued beef; 烤猪肉 **kǎo zhūròu** roast pork; barbecued pork

考 **kǎo** examine, test *student*; take *exam*; 考驾照 **kǎo jiàzhào** take one's driving test

靠 **kào** lean against; be near; rely on; 靠 ... 生活 **kào ... shēnghuó** live on, subsist on

靠岸 **kào'àn** dock

靠背 **kàobèi** back (*of chair*)

靠不住 **kàobuzhù** unreliable; deceptive; dubious, shady

考察 **kǎochá** inspect; explore

考查 **kǎochá** examine

靠窗座位 **kàochuāng zuòwei** window seat

靠垫 **kàodiàn** cushion

考古学 **kǎogǔ xué** archeology

考古学家 **kǎogǔ xué jiā** archeologist

靠近 **kàojìn** by, near

靠拢 **kàolǒng** move closer; close up

烤炉 **kǎolú** oven

考虑 **kǎolǜ** consider; think over ◊ consideration, thought

考虑不周 **kǎolǜ bùzhōu** inconsiderate

考虑到 **kǎolǜ dào** allow for, take account of; make allowances

考虑周到 **kǎolǜ zhōudào** discreet

烤面包 **kǎo miànbāo** toast

烤肉 **kǎoròu** roast; barbecue

考试 **kǎoshì** exam

考试卷 **kǎoshìjuàn** exam paper

烤土豆 **kǎo tǔdòu** baked potato

烤箱 **kǎoxiāng** oven

考验 **kǎoyàn** test

靠着 **kàozhe** lean on; rely on

卡片 **kǎpiàn** card

卡片目录 **kǎpiàn mùlù** card index

卡片钥匙 **kǎpiàn yàoshí** card key

卡通片 **kǎtōng piàn** cartoon

棵 **kē** *measure word for trees*; 一棵树 **yìkē shù** a tree

颗 **kē** *measure word for small round things*; 三颗米 **sānkē mǐ** three grains of rice

科 **kē** department

咳 **ké** cough

壳 **ké** shell

渴 **kě** thirst ◊ thirsty

可 **kě** can; may ◊ -able; 可变 **kěbiàn** changeable; variable

刻 **kè** carve ◊ quarter of an hour; 五点一刻 **wǔdiǎn yíkè** quarter after 5

课 **kè** class; lesson; subject

克 **kè** gram

客 **kè** guest

可爱 **kě'ài** delightful; lovable; cute

刻板 **kèbǎn** rigid

可悲 **kěbēi** pathetic

课本 **kèběn** textbook

可鄙 **kěbǐ** pitiful

可变 **kěbiàn** changeable; variable

可辨认出 **kě biànrèn chū** discernible

刻薄 **kèbó** scathing; unkind, hurtful

客车 **kèchē** passenger train

课程 **kèchéng** course; curriculum

课程表 **kèchéngbiǎo** schedule

可耻 **kěchǐ** dishonorable

可充气 **kě chōngqì** inflatable

客店 **kèdiàn** guest house; inn

可调换 **kě diàohuàn** transferable

蝌蚪 **kēdǒu** tadpole

刻度 **kèdù** scale

客房 **kèfáng** guest room; spare room

克服 **kèfú** overcome, surmount

可观 **kěguān** substantial

客观 **kèguān** objective

可贵 **kěguì** valuable; praiseworthy

刻痕 **kèhén** nick; cut

科幻 **kēhuàn** science fiction

科技 **kējì** science and technology

敬可敬 **kějìng** worthy; venerable

可靠 **kěkào** reliable; responsible; trustworthy

可靠性 **kěkào xìng** reliability

可卡因 **kěkǎyīn** cocaine

苛刻 **kēkè** demanding; severe

可可 **kěkě** cocoa

可口 **kěkǒu** tasty

可口可乐 **Kěkǒu Kělè** Coca Cola®

刻苦 **kèkǔ** hard-working

克拉 **kèlā** carat

可怜 **kělián** pitiful; pitiable

客满 **kèmǎn** fully booked ◊ no vacancies

科目 **kēmù** subject

啃 **kěn** chew; gnaw; nibble

肯 **kěn** be willing to

肯定 **kěndìng** confirm; be sure about ◊ sure, certain, definite; positive GRAM ◊ certainly, definitely; 你能不能肯定？ **nǐ néngbùnéng kěndìng?** are you definite about that?; 他们现在肯定到了 **tāmen xiànzài kěndìng dàole** they must have arrived by now

可能 **kěnéng** possibility; chance ◊ possible; likely, probable ◊ possibly; maybe; 可能会下雨 **kěnéng huì xiàyǔ** it may rain

可能性 **kěnéng xìng** possibility; liability; likelihood; probability; prospect ◊ must

坑 **kēng** ditch; pit

坑道 **kēngdào** gallery; tunnel

坑害 **kēnghài** set up; frame

坑洼 **kēngwā** pothole

恳切请求 **kěnqiè qǐngqiú** appeal for

恳求 **kěnqiú** implore; plead for ◊ plea

可怕 **kěpà** terrible; terrifying; horrifying; formidable

客气 **kèqi** polite; friendly; 别客气 **biékèqi** you're welcome

苛求 **kèqiú** pushy

可取 **kěqǔ** advisable

客人 **kèrén** visitor; guest

可溶 **kěróng** soluble

可食用 **kě shíyòng** edible

瞌睡 **kēshuì** sleepy ◊ snooze

咳嗽 **késou** cough

可塑 **kěsù** pliable

课堂 **kètáng** classroom; lecture room

课题 **kètí** subject, topic

客厅 **kètīng** living room

磕头 **kētóu** kowtow

渴望 **kěwàng** crave; yearn for, long for ◊ craving; longing ◊ eager; wistful

可恶 **kěwù** horrible, repulsive

可惜 **kěxī** what a shame ◊ unfortunately

可笑 **kěxiào** funny, amusing; ridiculous

可信 **kěxìn** trusted; credible; reliable

可行 **kěxíng** workable; feasible

可行性研究 **kěxíngxìng yánjiū** feasibility study

可信度 **kěxìn dù** credibility

科学 **kēxué** science ◊ scientific

科学家 **kēxuéjiā** scientist

可疑 **kěyí** suspicious

可以 **kěyǐ** can; may ◊ OK ◊ -able ◊ not bad; 可以吗? – 可以 **kěyǐma? – kěyǐ** can I/he? – ok, you/he can; 可以喝 **kěyǐ hē** drinkable; 还可以 **hái kěyǐ** not bad; 我觉得可以 **wǒ juédé kěyǐ** that's OK *or* fine by me

可以忍受 **kěyǐ rěnshòu** tolerable, bearable

可以容忍 **kěyǐ róngrěn** acceptable

可以想象 **kěyǐ xiǎngxiàng** imaginable, conceivable

可再用 **kě zài yòng** reusable, recyclable

可争论 **kě zhēnglùn** debatable ◊ arguably

克制 **kèzhì** control oneself

空 **kōng** empty; bare; vacant ◊ sky; air

恐 **kǒng** be afraid; fear

孔 **kǒng** hole

空 **kòng** spare time; leisure time

控 **kòng** control

空白 **kòngbái** gap; hole; empty space; margin ◊ blank

恐怖 **kǒngbù** terror; horror ◊ scary

恐怖电影 **kǒngbù diànyǐng** horror movie

恐怖分子 **kǒngbù fènzi** terrorist

恐怖机构 **kǒngbù jīgòu** terrorist organization

恐怖症 **kǒngbùzhèng** phobia

恐怖主义 **kǒngbù zhǔyì** terrorism

空挡 **kōngdǎng** neutral

空洞 **kōngdòng** empty; meaningless

空洞无物 **kōngdòng wúwù** wishy-washy

空额 **kòng'é** opening (*at work*)

空腹 **kōngfù** empty stomach

控告 **kònggào** indict; charge; sue ◊ charge; 被控告 ... **bèi kònggào** ... be accused of ...

空隔键 **kònggé jiàn** space-bar

控股权益 **kònggǔ quányì** controlling interest

恐吓 **kǒnghè** terrify; terrorize

恐慌 **kǒnghuāng** panic

空间 **kōngjiān** space; room; void

空姐 **kōngjiě** air hostess

空军 **kōngjūn** air force

空军基地 **kōngjūn jīdì** airbase

空旷 **kōngkuàng** open *countryside*

恐龙 **kǒnglóng** dinosaur

空落落 **kōng luòluo** stark *decor, room*

恐怕 **kǒngpà** I'm afraid (*regret*)

空气 **kōngqì** air

空前 **kōngqián** unprecedented

空气动力 **kōngqì dònglì** aerodynamic

空气污染 **kōngqì wūrǎn** air pollution

孔雀 **kǒngquè** peacock

空缺 **kòngquē** opening

空儿 **kòngr** parking space

空手道 **kōngshǒudào** karate

控诉 **kòngsù** bring charges

空谈 **kōngtán** empty talk; 他只是空谈 **tā zhǐshì kōngtán** he's all talk

空调 **kōngtiáo** air-conditioning

空头支票 **kōngtóu zhīpiào** blank check

空位 **kòngwèi** blank; space

空隙 **kòngxì** opening; gap

空闲 **kòngxián** leisure; leisure time ◊ unoccupied; at a loose end

空想 **kōngxiǎng** daydream; utopian fantasy

空心 **kōngxīn** hollow

空虚 **kōngxū** empty; meaningless ◊ emptiness; void

空域 **kōngyù** airspace

空余 **kòngyú** free *room, table*

空运 **kōngyùn** air transport

空晕病 **kōngyùnbìng** airsickness

空余时间 **kòngyú shíjiān** leisure time

空着 **kōngzhe** empty; unoccupied *room*

控制 **kòngzhì** control; regulate; dominate ◊ control; domination; 我们无法控制的因素 **wǒmén wúfǎ kòngzhì de yīnsù** circumstances beyond our control

控制键 **kòngzhìjiàn** control key

控制盘 **kòngzhì pán** control panel

控制中心 **kòngzhì zhōngxīn** control center

空中交通 **kōngzhōng jiāotōng** air traffic

空中交通控制 **kōngzhōng jiāotōng kòngzhì** air-traffic control

空中交通控制人员 **kōngzhōng jiāotōng kòngzhì rényuán** air-traffic controller

空中小姐 **kōngzhōng xiǎojie** air hostess

空转 **kōngzhuàn** idling; in neutral

孔子 **Kǒngzǐ** Confucius

口 **kǒu** mouth

扣 **kòu** button up

口才 **kǒucái** eloquence

口吃 **kǒuchī** stutter; speech impediment

口齿不清 **kǒuchǐ bùqīng** inarticulate

扣除 **kòuchú** deduct; subtract ◊ deduction

口袋 **kǒudài** pocket

口服避孕药 **kǒufú bìyùnyào** contraceptive pill

口供 **kǒugōng** statement (*to police*)

口号 **kǒuhào** slogan

口红 **kǒuhóng** lipstick

叩击 **kòujī** rap; knock on

口径 **kǒujìng** caliber (*of gun*)

叩击声 **kòujī shēng** rap; knock

口技艺人 **kǒujì yìrén** ventriloquist

渴 **kě** thirsty

扣扣子 **kòu kòuzi** button up

口令 **kǒulìng** password

抠门儿 **kōuménr** stingy; tight-fisted

口腔卫生 **kǒuqiāng** oral hygiene

口琴 **kǒuqín** mouth organ

扣球 **kòuqiú** smash (*in tennis*)

扣人心弦 **kòu rén xīnxián** gripping

口哨声 **kǒushàoshēng** whistle (*sound*)

口授 **kǒushòu** dictate ◊ dictation

口水 **kǒushuǐ** saliva

口试 **kǒutuò** oral exam

口头 **kǒutóu** oral

口吐狂言 **kǒutù kuángyán** rant and rave

口香糖 **kǒuxiāng táng** chewing gum

扣押 **kòuyā** seize; impound ◊ seizure

扣眼儿 **kòuyǎnr** buttonhole

口译 **kǒuyì** interpret ◊ interpretation

口音 **kǒuyīn** accent

口淫 **kǒuyín** oral sex; blow job

口译者 **kǒuyì zhě** interpreter

口语 **kǒuyǔ** colloquial language ◊ colloquial; conversational

口子 **kǒuzi** tear; slit

扣子 **kòuzi** button

哭 **kū** cry

枯 **kū** dried up; parched

苦 **kǔ** bitter ◊ bitterness

酷 **kù** cool, great

库 **kù** storehouse; warehouse

裤 **kù** pants

夸 **kuā** praise; exaggerate

跨 **kuà** step; step across

胯 **kuà** hip

夸大 **kuādà** exaggerate

垮掉 **kuǎdiào** crack up; have a breakdown

酷爱 **kù'ài** go in for; enjoy

块 **kuài** piece; block; dollar; yuan; lump (*of sugar*); pane (*of glass*) ◊ measure word for money, pieces; 五块钱 **wǔkuài qián** five yuan; 一块派／面包 **yíkuài pài／miànbāo** a piece of pie／bread

快 **kuài** quick; rapid; sharp ◊ quickly; soon; 他快五十了 **tā kuài wǔshí le** he's getting on for 50

酷爱 **kù'ài** be in love with *job, hobby*

快餐 **kuàicān** fast food; quick snack

快餐店 **kuàicāndiàn** fast food restaurant

快车 **kuàichē** fast train

快吃 **kuàichī** eat quickly; bolt

快点儿! **kuàidiǎnr!** hurry up!; come on!

快感 **kuàigǎn** pleasurable feeling; thrill

快活 **kuàihuó** cheerful

会计 **kuàijì** accounting ◊ accountant; bookkeeper

快捷键 **kuàijiéjiàn** hot key

快进 **kuàijìn** fast forward

快乐 **kuàilè** joy; pleasure; bliss ◊ happy; 使人快乐 **shǐrén kuàilè** entertain

快门儿 **kuàiménr** shutter PHOT

快速 **kuàisù** fast; rapid; express ◊ velocity; rapidity

快艇 **kuàitǐng** speedboat

筷子 **kuàizi** chopsticks

快走 **kuàizǒu** hurry

夸奖 **kuājiǎng** praise

垮了 **kuǎle** break down; have a breakdown; be exhausted

宽 **kuān** broad; 十米宽 **shímǐkuān** 10m across

款 **kuǎn** sum of money; article (*of law, act*)

宽敞 **kuānchang** spacious

宽大 **kuāndà** spacious; lenient

款待 **kuāndài** treat; 用 Y 款待 X **yòng Y kuǎndài X** treat X to Y

宽度 **kuāndù** width

筐 **kuāng** basket

狂 **kuáng** crazy

框 **kuàng** frame

矿 **kuàng** mine

旷 **kuàng** spacious

狂暴 **kuángbào** turbulent; ferocious ◊ turbulence; ferocity; rage

矿藏 **kuàngcáng** mineral resources

矿层 **kuàngcéng** seam (*of ore*)

旷工 **kuànggōng** skip work ◊ absence (from work) ◊ absent

矿工 **kuànggōng** miner

狂欢 **kuánghuān** live it up

狂欢节 **kuánghuānjié** carnival

框架 **kuàngjià** outline; framework

矿井 **kuàngjǐng** mine shaft

旷课 **kuàngkè** play hookey ◊ absence (from school) ◊ absent

矿坑 **kuàngkēng** mine; pit

况且 **kuàngqiě** furthermore

狂犬病 **kuángquǎn bìng** rabies

矿泉水 **kuàngquánshuǐ** mineral water

狂热 **kuángrè** craze, fad ◊ fanatical; feverish

狂人 **kuángrén** madman, maniac

狂热者 **kuángrè zhě** fanatic

矿山 **kuàngshān** mine

矿石 **kuàngshí** ore

狂妄 **kuángwàng** arrogant; presumptuous

矿物 **kuàngwù** mineral

狂喜 **kuángxǐ** joy; rejoicing ◊ exult; rejoice ◊ overjoyed

狂笑 **kuángxiào** guffaw; howl with laughter ◊ guffaw, howl; hysterics

矿业 **kuàngyè** mining

狂饮 **kuángyǐn** bender (*drinking*)

宽宏大量 **kuānhóng dàliàng** generous

宽厚 **kuānhòu** lenient; soft

宽阔 **kuānkuò** wide *street, field*

宽容 **kuānróng** tolerant; lenient;

forbearing; broad *smile* ◊
tolerance ◊ condone

宽容度 **kuānróng dù** freedom;
latitude

款式 **kuǎnshì** cut (*of clothes, hair*)

宽恕 **kuānshù** forgive

宽松 **kuānsōng** loose; baggy

宽松裤 **kuānsōng kù** slacks

宽慰 **kuānwèi** relief ◊ be relieved

垮台 **kuǎtái** downfall; fall; 使 ... 垮
台 *shǐ ... kuǎtái* bring down

夸脱 **kuātuō** quart

夸耀 **kuāyào** showy; ostentatious

跨越 **kuàyuè** cross; pass; exceed

夸张 **kuāzhāng** exaggerate;
overdo ◊ ostentatious

裤衩 **kùchǎ** underpants; panties

库存 **kùcún** stock

裤兜 **kùdōu** pants pocket

苦干 **kǔgàn** toil

亏 **kuī** lose

盔 **kuī** helmet

窥察 **kuīchá** snoop around

葵花 **kuíhuā** sunflower

窥孔 **kuīkǒng** peephole

傀儡 **kuǐlěi** puppet

傀儡政府 **kuǐlěi zhèngfǔ** puppet
government

亏损 **kuīsǔn** deficit; loss ◊ make a
loss

魁梧 **kuíwú** burly ◊ great hunk

溃疡 **kuìyáng** ulcer

骷髅 **kūlóu** skeleton

捆 **kǔn** bundle

困 **kùn** tired

苦难 **kǔnàn** difficulty; suffering

苦难的经历 **kǔnànde jīnglì**
ordeal

苦恼 **kǔnǎng** distress; mental
suffering

苦恼 **kǔnǎo** vexed; worried ◊

worry; trouble; grief

哭闹纠缠 **kūnào jiūchán** whine

昆虫 **kūnchóng** insect; bug

困乏 **kùnfá** weary; 使人困乏
*shǐrén kùnfá* wearing

困惑 **kùnhuò** confused; perplexed
◊ perplexity; 使 ... 困惑 *shǐ ...
kùnhuò* puzzle, perplex

困境 **kùnjìng** mess, jam; plight

困倦 **kùnjuàn** sleepy

困难 **kùnnan** difficulty; trouble;
complication

困扰 **kùnrǎo** nagging; niggling

捆住 **kǔnzhù** tie down; make fast

扩 **kuò** expand

阔 **kuò** wide; rich

括 **kuò** include

扩充 **kuòchōng** branch out

扩大 **kuòda** expand; enlarge;
extend ◊ expansion; enlargement;
extension

括号 **kuòhào** brackets;
parentheses

扩建 **kuòjiàn** extension (*on house*)

扩军 **kuòjūn** arm; build up the
army

阔气 **kuòqi** wealthy

蛞蝓 **kuòyú** slug (*animal*)

扩张 **kuòzhāng** dilate (*of pupils*)

哭泣 **kūqì** weep

酷热 **kùrè** sweltering, very hot

哭诉 **kūsù** moan

枯萎 **kūwěi** droop; wilt ◊ wilting;
drooping

裤线 **kùxiàn** crease (*in pants*)

苦笑 **kǔxiào** wry smile

苦心 **kǔxīn** pains; 费苦心 *fèi
kǔxīn* take pains

枯燥 **kūzào** boring

枯燥无味 **kūzào wúwèi** bland

裤子 **kùzi** pants

# L

拉 **lā** pull; draw; drag
辣 **là** hot, spicy
蜡 **là** wax
喇叭 **lǎba** trumpet; horn; loudspeaker; 按喇叭 **àn lǎba** hoot; sound one's horn
喇叭状 **lǎbazhuàng** flare (*in dress*)
拉丁美洲 **Lādīng Měizhōu** Latin America
拉丁字母 **Lādīng zìmǔ** Roman alphabet
拉肚子 **lādùzi** diarrhea
拉关系 **lā guānxi** pull strings
拉过来 **lā guòlái** draw up *chair*
拉环 **lāhuán** ring-pull
来 **lái** come ◊ (*toward speaker*): 拿进来 **nájìn lai** bring in; 过来 **guòlai** come over
来迟 **láichí** belated
癞蛤蟆 **làiháma** toad
来回 **láihuí** back and forth; there and back; to and fro
来回票 **láihuí piào** round trip ticket
来历 **láilì** origin
来临 **láilín** approach; come; fall (*of night*)
来世 **láishì** afterlife
来往 **láiwǎng** contact; dealings
来由 **láiyóu** reason; cause
来源 **láiyuán** source
来自 **láizì** come from; originate in, stem from
垃圾 **lājī** garbage, trash; litter
辣椒 **làjiāo** chili pepper
拉紧 **lājǐn** pull tight
拉近 **lājìn** zoom in on
垃圾桶 **lājītǒng** trashcan
垃圾箱 **lājīxiāng** garbage can
垃圾站 **lājī zhàn** garbage dump
拉开 **lākāi** draw back, pull back; pull apart, separate

拉开拉链 **lākāi lāliàn** unzip
啦啦队 **lālā duì** cheerleaders
拉力 **lālì** tension
拉链 **lāliàn** fastener, zipper; 拉拉链 **lā lāliàn** zip up
喇嘛 **lǎma** lama
拉门 **lāmén** sliding door
拉面 **lāmiàn** hand-pulled noodles
栏 **lán** railing; hurdle; column (*of text*)
兰 **lán** orchid
拦 **lán** block; obstruct
蓝 **lán** blue
篮 **lán** basket
懒 **lǎn** lazy
缆 **lǎn** cable; rope
烂 **làn** decayed; rotten
滥 **làn** excessive
蓝宝石 **lánbǎoshí** sapphire
缆车 **lǎnchē** cable car
蓝调 **lándiào** blues
懒惰 **lǎnduò** laziness, indolence ◊ lazy, indolent
狼 **láng** wolf
浪 **làng** wave
栏杆 **lángān** barrier; railings
浪潮 **làngcháo** tide; wave
朗读 **lǎngdú** read aloud
浪费 **làngfèi** waste
浪花 **lànghuā** seaspray; foam
浪漫 **làngmàn** romantic ◊ romance
朗诵 **lǎngsòng** read out
榔头 **lángtou** hammer
浪头 **làngtóu** trend; wave; 赶浪头 **gǎn làngtóu** jump on the bandwagon
狼吞虎咽 **lángtūn hǔyàn** devour, wolf down ◊ voracious
懒鬼 **lǎnguǐ** idle, lazy
懒汉 **lǎnhàn** bum; hobo
拦河坝 **lánhébà** dam
兰花 **lánhuā** orchid

拦截 **lánjié** intercept *ball*

蓝领工人 **lánlǐng gōngrén** blue-collar worker

褴褛 **lánlǚ** ragged

烂泥 **lànní** mud

篮球 **lánqiú** basketball

懒散 **lǎnsǎn** laze around ◊ lethargic

蓝色 **lánsè** blue

蓝图 **lántú** blueprint

阑尾 **lánwěi** appendix

阑尾炎 **lánwěiyán** appendicitis

懒洋洋 **lǎnyángyáng** unenthusiastic; listless

蓝眼睛 **lányǎnjing** blue eyes ◊ blue-eyed

滥用 **lànyòng** misuse; abuse

拦住 **lánzhù** hold back; stop; accost

篮子 **lánzi** basket

牢 **láo** pen; prison ◊ solid; sturdy

劳 **láo** work

老 **lǎo** old ◊ F very, dead; always; 他老迟到 **tā lǎo chídào** he's always late; 老了 **lǎo le** get on, grow old; pass away

老板 **lǎobǎn** owner (of a business); proprietor; boss; landlord

老板娘 **lǎobǎnniáng** landlady; proprietress

老成练达 **lǎochéng liàndá** worldly; sophisticated

唠叨 **láodao** go on; go on at

唠叨不停 **láodao bùtíng** nag

劳动 **láodòng** work; labor

劳动节 **Láodòngjié** Labor Day

劳动力 **láodònglì** manpower; workers; workforce

劳动日 **láodòngrì** working day

劳动者 **láodòng zhě** laborer

牢房 **láofáng** prison cell

牢固 **láogù** solid; sturdy; durable

老虎 **lǎohǔ** tiger

老虎机 **lǎohǔjī** slot machine; gambling machine

老虎钳 **lǎohǔqián** pliers; pincers

劳驾 **láojià** excuse me; would you mind; 劳驾帮帮忙 **láojià bāngbang máng** could you help me?

老家 **lǎojiā** home

姥姥 **lǎolao** grandma

劳累 **láolèi** tire ◊ tired

老练 **lǎoliàn** diplomacy, tact ◊ diplomatic; veteran

老年 **lǎonián** geriatric ◊ old age

老年病学 **lǎonián bìngxué** geriatrics

老气 **lǎoqì** old-fashioned *clothes*

老前辈 **lǎoqiánbèi** senior citizen; senior

老人 **lǎorén** old person; senior citizen

老人院 **lǎorényuàn** old people's home, nursing home

牢骚 **láosao** complaint

老实 **lǎoshi** honest

老师 **lǎoshī** teacher

老式 **lǎoshì** old-fashioned *equipment*

老是 **lǎoshì** always

老鼠 **lǎoshǔ** rat; mouse

劳损 **láosǔn** strain

老外 **lǎowài** foreigner; layman

老挝 **Lǎowō** Laos ◊ Laotian

老兄 **lǎoxiōng** pal, buddy

老早 **lǎozǎo** long ago

老子 **Lǎozǐ** Lao-tzu (*Taoist sage*)

劳资纠纷 **láozī jiūfēn** industrial dispute

拉票 **lāpiào** canvass POL

拉平 **lāpíng** even out; smooth out; 拉平比分 **lāpíng bǐfēn** even the score; 和 … 拉平 **hé … lāpíng** draw level with

拉萨 **Lāsà** Lhasa

拉伤 **lāshāng** pull, strain

拉舌 **lāshé** tab

拉屎 **lāshǐ** shit

拉手 **lāshǒu** doorknob

邋遢 **lāta** messy *person*; scruffy; slovenly

拉下 **lāxià** pull down; lower

蜡烛 **làzhú** candle

了 **le** (*particle indicating completed action*): 雨停了 **yǔtíngle** it has stopped raining ◊ (*particle indicating change of state*): 头发白了 **tóufa báile** his hair is going gray; 我买了 **wǒ mǎi le** I'll take it ◊ (*for emphasis*): 你太好了 **nǐ** *tài hǎo le* that's very kind

勒 **lè** rein in; check

乐 **lè** joy; happiness

乐观 **lèguān** optimistic; hopeful; positive ◊ optimism

乐观者 **lèguān zhě** optimist

雷 **léi** thunder

累 **léi** accumulate

泪 **lèi** tear

累 **lèi** tired

类 **lèi** sort, type, kind

肋 **lèi** side (of body)

肋部 **lèibù** flank; side (of body)

雷达 **léidá** radar

雷锋叔叔 **Léi Fēng shūshu** do-gooder

肋骨 **lèigǔ** rib

累积 **léijī** accumulate

雷鸣 **léimíng** thunder

类似 **lèisì** similar; comparable ◊ likeness

累死了 **lèi sǐ le** dead tired

类型 **lèixíng** type

雷雨 **léiyǔ** thunderstorm

雷阵雨 **léizhènyǔ** thundery shower

累赘 **léizhuì** cumbersome

勒令停职 **lèlìng tíngzhí** suspend

冷 **lěng** cold

棱 **léng** edge

冷冰冰 **lěng bīngbing** cold; icy

冷藏 **lěngcáng** chill; refrigerate ◊ refrigeration

冷淡 **lěngdàn** chilly; indifferent; impassive; frigid

冷冻 **lěngdòng** freeze ◊ frozen

冷冻室 **lěngdòngshì** freezer

冷冻食品 **lěngdòng shípǐn** frozen food

冷静 **lěngjìng** calm, collected

冷酷 **lěngkù** in cold blood ◊ cold-blooded; heartless

冷气 **lěngqì** chill (in air)

冷门 **lěngmén** outsider

冷面 **lěngmiàn** cold noodles

冷漠 **lěngmò** cool; remote, unfriendly; unconcerned; apathetic

冷凝 **lěngníng** condense ◊ condensation

冷盘 **lěngpán** cold cuts

冷却 **lěngquè** cool ◊ cooling

冷杉 **lěngshān** fir

冷烫 **lěngtàng** cold wave (in hairdressing)

冷笑 **lěngxiào** sneer

冷血 **lěngxuè** cold-blooded

冷饮 **lěngyǐn** cold drinks

棱锥体 **léngzhuītǐ** pyramid

乐趣 **lèqù** amusement; enjoyment; fun; pleasure

勒索 **lèsuǒ** extort; blackmail ◊ extortion; blackmail

乐意 **lèyì** with pleasure; willingly

乐于 **lèyú** willing; 乐于助人 **lèyú zhùrén** obliging

乐园 **lèyuán** paradise; amusement park

狸 **lí** beaver

梨 **lí** pear

犁 **lí** plow

离 **lí** leave ◊ from; 离这儿很远 **lí zhèr hěn yuǎn** it's far from here; 离圣诞节还有六星期 **lí Shèngdànjié háiyǒu liù xīngqī** Christmas is still six weeks away

礼 **lǐ** rite; ritual; etiquette

李 **lǐ** plum

里 **lǐ** in; inside ◊ neighborhood; *measure of distance, approx. one third of a mile*

理 **lǐ** reason ◊ pay attention to; put in order, sort

粒 **lì** grain, speck; particle

力 **lì** strength; power

立 **lì** stand

利 **lì** sharp ◊ profit; benefit

例 **lì** example

历 **lì** experience; calendar

俩 **liǎ** both; two; 他们俩儿 **tāmén liǎ** the two of them, both of them

帘 **lián** curtain; blind

联 **lián** join; unite with

连 **lián** link; connect ◊ even; 连 … 也不 **lián … yěbù** not even

莲 **lián** lotus

脸 **liǎn** face

恋 **liàn** love

炼 **liàn** refine

练 **liàn** practise; train

链 **liàn** chain

恋爱 **liàn'ài** love

联邦 **liánbāng** federation; union

联邦调查局 **Liánbāng Diàochájú** FBI, Federal Bureau of Investigation

联邦制 **liánbāngzhì** federal

连播 **liánbō** serialize

脸蛋儿 **liǎndànr** face

镰刀 **liándāo** sickle

凉 **liáng** cool; cold

良 **liáng** good

粮 **liáng** grain

量 **liáng** measure; 量体温 **liáng tǐwēn** take sb's temperature

两 **liǎng** two; 两盘磁带 **liǎngpán cídài** two cassettes

量 **liàng** capacity; quantity; volume

谅 **liàng** forgive

亮 **liàng** bright; light; clear

辆 **liàng** *measure word for vehicles*; 一辆小汽车 **yíliàng xiǎoqìchē** a car

炼钢厂 **liàngāngchǎng** steelworks

两倍 **liǎngbéi** double

两边 **liǎngbiān** bilateral

粮仓 **liángcāng** barn

两重 **liǎngchóng** double; dual

量出 **liángchū** measure out

两次 **liǎngcì** twice

亮度 **liàngdù** lightness; brightness

晾干 **liànggān** air-dry

谅解 **liàngjiě** understand; forgive

两极分化 **liǎngjí fēnhuà** polarize; split

量具 **liángjù** measuring instrument

凉开水 **liáng kāishuǐ** cold boiled water

凉快 **liángkuai** pleasantly cool

两面派 **liǎngmiànpài** two-faced

椋鸟 **liángniǎo** starling

两栖 **liǎngqī** amphibious

踉跄 **liàngqiàng** stagger; sway

俩儿 **liǎngr** two; both

粮食 **liángshi** grain; cereal

良师益友 **liángshī yìyǒu** mentor

凉爽 **liángshuǎng** cool; crisp; fresh ◊ freshness

凉台 **liángtái** balcony

连贯 **liánguàn** coherent; lucid

连贯性 **liánguàn xìng** continuity

两位数 **liǎngwèi shù** double figures

凉鞋 **liángxié** sandal

良心 **liángxīn** conscience

良性 **liángxìng** benign

联合 **liánhé** unite; form an alliance ◊ alliance; union ◊ concerted

联合国 **Liánhéguó** United Nations

联合企业 **liánhé qǐyè** cartel

联合收割机 **liánhé shōugējī** combine harvester

联合王国 **Liánhé Wángguó** United Kingdom

脸红 **liǎnhóng** blush

连环漫画 **liánhuán mànhuà** comic strip

连环碰撞 **liánhuán pèngzhuàng** pile-up, crash

恋家 **liànjiā** homeloving

廉价出售 **liánjià chūshòu** be on sale

离岸价格 **lí'àn jiàgé** FOB, free on board

连接 **liánjiē** join, connect; link

联接 **liánjiē** link; connect

联结 **liánjié** bond

连接处 **liánjiēchù** joint

联结处 **liánjiéchù** join

连接词 **liánjiēcí** conjunction GRAM

连接器 **liánjiē qì** connector COMPUT

连襟儿 **liánjīnr** brother-in-law

连裤袜 **liánkùwà** pantyhose

连累 **liánlěi** get … involved

联络 **liánluò** contact, get in touch with ◊ liaison

联络网 **liánluò wǎng** network

联盟 **liánméng** coalition; league; union; alliance

连绵 **liánmián** continuous; 连绵一百英里 **liánmián yìbǎi yīnglǐ** it stretches for 100 miles

怜悯 **liánmǐn** sympathize with

脸盆 **liǎnpén** washbasin

莲蓬头 **liánpengtóu** shower head

脸皮厚 **liǎnpí hòu** thick-skinned; insensitive; shameless

连日 **liánrì** lasting for days

炼乳 **liànrǔ** condensed milk

联赛 liánsài league sp
脸色 liǎnsè color (in cheeks)
脸色苍白 liǎnsè cāngbái pallor
连锁店 liánsuǒ diàn chain store
连锁反应 liánsuǒ fǎnyìng chain reaction
链条 liàntiáo chain
连体双胞胎 liántǐ shuāngbāotāi Siamese twins
连同 liántóng in conjunction with
联系 liánxì contact; connect ◊ connection; 将 X 与 Y 联系起来 jiāng X yǔ Y liánxì qǐlái relate X to Y; 我们保持联系 wǒmén bǎochí liánxì we keep in touch
练习 liànxí practice; training; exercise
练习本 liànxíběn exercise book
联系电话 liánxì diànhuà contact number
连续 liánxù continuous; uninterrupted; consecutive; 连续两天 liánxù liǎngtiān for two days running
连续不断 liánxù búduàn continuous ◊ persistently
连衣裤 liányīkù dungarees
连衣裙 liányīqún dress
联运 liányùn connection (train etc)
帘子 liánzi curtain
连字号 liánzìhào hyphen
聊 liáo chat
疗 liáo treat ◊ treatment
了 liǎo finish, end ◊ understand; 对 X 了如指掌 duì X liǎo rú zhǐzhǎng have X at one's fingertips ◊ (completed action): 吃了 chī liǎo eat up ◊ (ability): 我去不了 wǒ qù bu liǎo I can't go; 我办得了 wǒ bàn de liǎo I can manage it
料 liào material, fabric
了不起 liǎobùqǐ terrific, fantastic
潦草的字迹 liáocǎode zìjì scrawl, messy; 潦草的字迹 liáocǎode zìjì scrawl, scribble
疗程 liáochéng course of treatment
疗法 liáofǎ cure; remedy; therapy
了结 liǎojié deal with; settle
了解 liǎojiě understand; 据了解

他们在加拿大 jù liáojiě tāmén zài Jiānádà they are understood to be in Canada
料理 liàolǐ take care of
聊天 liáotiān chat
料想 liàoxiǎng suppose
疗养 liáoyǎng convalesce
疗养地 liáoyǎngdì health resort
疗养期 liáoyǎng qī convalescence
疗养院 liáoyǎngyuàn sanatorium
篱笆 líba fence
离别 líbié separation ◊ separate; part from (of people)
利比亚 Lìbǐyà Libya ◊ Libyan
立场 lìchǎng standpoint; point of view
里程 lǐchéng mileage
里程碑 lǐchéngbēi milestone
里程表 lǐchéng biǎo odometer
里道 lǐdào inside lane (of road)
列 liè list ◊ column, row ◊ measure word for trains; 一列火车 yīliè huǒchē a train
裂 liè crack; split
烈 liè intense
劣 liè inferior; poor
猎 liè hunt
列车 lièchē train
列车长 lièchē zhǎng conductor (on train)
裂缝 lièfèng crack; crevice; gap; slit, opening
裂痕 lièhén crack
烈酒 lièjiǔ hard liquor
列举 lièjǔ enumerate
裂开 lièkāi disintegrate; split; damage; gape ◊ gaping hole
裂口 lièkǒu tear (in cloth, paper); burst; chip (in cup); split
列宁 Lièníng Lenin
猎枪 lièqiāng shotgun
猎区 lièqū hunting ground
猎取 lièqǔ hunt; prey on
猎犬 lièquǎn hunting dog; retriever
猎人 lièrén hunter
列入计划 lièrù jìhuà schedule
烈士 lièshì martyr
猎手 lièshǒu hunter
猎物 lièwù prey
烈性 lièxìng strong drink

劣质 **lièzhì** inferior; shoddy; trashy

咧嘴 **liězuǐ** grin

理发 **lǐfà** haircut; hairdressing ◊ style hair

立法 **lìfǎ** legislate ◊ legislation ◊ legislative

立法过程 **lìfǎ guòchéng** legislation

立法机构 **lìfǎ jīgòu** legislature

立方 **lìfāng** cubic

立方米 **lìfāngmǐ** cubic meter

立方形 **lìfāng xíng** cube

理发师 **lǐfàshī** hairdresser

理发厅 **lǐfàtīng** hairdressing salon; barber shop

礼服 **lǐfú** formal wear; tuxedo

利害 **lìhai** severe; tough; formidable

离合器 **líhéqì** clutch

离婚 **líhūn** divorce; get divorced ◊ divorced

里脊 **lǐjǐ** fillet

痢疾 **lìji** dysentery

立即 **lìjí** immediate ◊ immediately

理解 **lǐjiě** understand; view, perceive ◊ comprehension; understanding

离开 **líkāi** leave, depart; go away; quit; 我们明天离开 **wǒmén míngtiān líkāi** we're off tomorrow

立刻 **lìkè** immediately; in no time

力量 **lìliàng** power; strength; force; might

理疗 **lǐliáo** physiotherapy

理疗医生 **lǐliáo yīshēng** physiotherapist

利率 **lìlǜ** interest rate

理论 **lǐlùn** theory ◊ theoretical

利落 **lìluo** clear and concise; snappy

礼貌 **lǐmào** courtesy; politeness ◊ courteously; 有／没有礼貌 **yǒu／méiyǒu lǐmào** have good／bad manners

厘米 **límǐ** centimeter

里面 **lǐmiàn** inside

黎明 **límíng** daybreak

林 **lín** wood; forest

淋 **lín** drip; soak

临 **lín** overlook ◊ be about to

邻 **lín** neighbor; neighborhood

淋巴结 **línbājié** lymph gland

临床 **línchuáng** clinical

铃 **líng** bell

零 **líng** zero; nil; 零下十度 **língxià shídù** 10 degrees below zero; 从零开始 **cóng líng kāishǐ** start from scratch

陵 **líng** mound; tomb

灵 **líng** spirit; soul

领 **líng** neck; collar ◊ claim; withdraw *money*

另 **lìng** other; in addition

令 **lìng** order

领班 **língbān** foreman

灵车 **língchē** hearse

凌晨 **língchén** early morning

领带 **língdài** necktie

领导 **língdǎo** leader; head; boss ◊ lead; 在他的领导下 **zài tāde língdǎo xià** under his leadership

领导技巧 **língdǎo jìqiǎo** leadership skills

领导人 **língdǎo rén** leader; manager

零度 **língdù** zero degrees

领队 **língduì** bandleader

灵感 **línggǎn** inspiration; brainwave

领海 **línghǎi** territorial waters

领会 **línghuì** grasp; comprehend; digest *information*

灵魂 **línghún** soul; spirit; 灵魂转世 **línghún zhuǎnshì** reincarnation

灵活 **línghuó** flexible; agile

零下 **língxià** below zero

灵机 **língjī** inspiration; 灵机一动 **língjīyídòng** have a flash of inspiration

零件 **língjiàn** (spare) part

领结 **língjié** bow tie

领口 **língkǒu** neckline

铃兰 **línglán** lily of the valley

伶俐 **línglì** quick; nimble; apt

领路 **línglù** navigation

凌乱 **língluàn** untidy; messy

灵敏 **língmǐn** sharp; quick *mind*

陵墓 **língmù** mausoleum

零钱 **língqián** loose change, coins

灵巧 **língqiǎo** deft; quick

令人 **lìngrén** (*causing a person to*

*feel something*): 令人恶心 **língrén èxīn** disgusting, revolting; 令人愉快 **língrén yúkuài** enjoyable; 令人失望 **língrén shīwàng** disappointing

零散 **língsǎn** sporadic
零食 **língshí** snacks; nibbles; candy
领事 **língshì** consul
领事馆 **língshì guǎn** consulate
零售 **língshòu** retail
零售价 **língshòu jià** retail price
零售商 **língshòu shāng** retailer
零碎 **língsuì** incomplete; fragmented
领头 **língtóu** lead *race, procession*
领土 **língtǔ** territory; territorial
另外 **língwài** other ◊ in addition; apart from that
另外收费 **língwài shōufèi** be extra
领先 **língxiān** be in the lead; be ahead of ◊ in front; leading ◊ lead (*in race*)
零星 **língxīng** scattered
菱形 **língxíng** diamond; lozenge
另行通知 **língxíng tōngzhī** until further notice
领袖 **língxiù** leader
领养 **língyǎng** adopt ◊ adoption
另一个 **líng yígè** another
另一件事 **líng yíjiàn shì** another matter; a different ball game
零用钱 **língyòng qián** allowance
零用现金 **língyòng xiànjīn** petty cash
领域 **língyù** territory; field; preserve; sphere; 戏剧领域 **xìjù língyù** the world of the theater
领子 **língzi** collar
临海 **línhǎi** coastal
林火 **línhuǒ** forest fire
临街店铺 **línjiē diànpù** storefront
邻近 **línjìn** adjacent
临近 **línjìn** approach ◊ proximity
邻居 **línjū** neighbor
鳞片 **línpiàn** scale (*on fish*)
吝啬 **lìnsè** miserly, tight-fisted
吝啬鬼 **lìnsèguǐ** miser
临时 **línshí** provisional; temporary; casual
临时担任 **línshí dānrèn** act as,

fill in as
临时工 **línshígōng** temp
林荫道 **línyìndào** avenue
淋浴 **línyù** take a shower ◊ shower
淋浴帘 **línyùlián** shower curtain
礼炮 **lǐpào** salute
礼品 **lǐpǐn** gift, present
离奇 **líqí** strange; uncanny
离弃 **líqì** abandon
力气 **lìqi** strength (*physical*)
沥青 **lìqīng** asphalt
里圈跑道 **lǐquān pǎodào** inside lane SP
例如 **lìrú** for instance, e.g.
利润 **lìrùn** profit
利润率 **lìrùnlǜ** profit margin
理事 **lǐshì** director; trustee
砾石 **lìshí** gravel
历史 **lìshǐ** history
历史性 **lìshǐxìng** historic; historical
历史学家 **lìshǐ xuéjiā** historian
理所当然 **lǐsuǒ dāngrán** naturally; of course
礼堂 **lǐtáng** (ceremonial) hall; church
离题 **lítí** beside the point
立体声装置 **lìtǐshēng zhuāngzhì** stereo system
留 **liú** stay; keep; let grow *hair*; 你留着吧 **nǐ liúzhe ba** please keep it, I insist
流 **liú** flow, run
硫 **liú** sulfur
柳 **liǔ** willow
六 **liù** six
遛 **liù** walk; 遛狗 **liùgǒu** walk the dog
遛冰场 **liūbīng chǎng** ice rink
流鼻涕 **liú bítì** runny nose
流鼻血 **liú bíxuè** nosebleed
流产 **liúchǎn** miscarriage
流畅 **liúchàng** smooth; fluent
流程图 **liúchéngtú** flowchart
流传 **liúchuán** spread; circulate
溜出去 **liūchūqù** slip out
流弹 **liúdàn** stray bullet
流荡 **liúdàng** drift
流动 **liúdòng** flow
流动工人 **liúdòng gōngrén** migrant worker

流动基金 liúdòng jījīn cash flow

流放 liúfàng exile

流感 liúgǎn flu

刘海 liúhǎi bangs; fringe

留话 liúhuà leave a message

硫磺 liúhuáng sulfur

流口水 liú kǒushuǐ dribble; slobber

浏览 liúlǎn skim; browse; flick through

流浪汉 liúlànghàn drifter; hobo

浏览器 liúlǎn qì browser COMPUT

流泪 liúlèi shed tears

流利 liúlì fluent ◊ fluency; 他讲一口流利的汉语 **tā jiǎng yìkǒu liúlìde Hànyǔ** he speaks fluent Chinese

流氓 liúmáng hoodlum; hooligan

留念 liúniàn keep as a memento

流沙 liúshā quicksand

留神 liúshén look out; pay attention

流逝 liúshì slip away; elapse; pass

六十 liùshí sixty

柳树 liǔshù willow

流水 liúshuǐ running water

六四 Liùsì Tiananmen Square (incident)

流苏 liúsū tassel

流体 liútǐ fluid

流亡 liúwáng exile

留下 liúxià bequeath; leave

流线型 liúxiànxíng streamlined

留心 liúxīn be alert, be observant; listen to, heed

流星 liúxīng meteor; falling star

流行 liúxíng in fashion, fashionable; popular; pop

流行病 liúxíngbìng epidemic

流行歌曲 liúxíng gēqǔ pop song; hit

流行款式 liúxíng kuǎnshì style, fashion

流行性 liúxíngxìng epidemic

流行性感冒 liúxíngxìng gǎnmào influenza

流行音乐 liúxíng yīnyuè pop music

留学 liúxué study abroad

流血 liúxuè bleed ◊ bleeding; bloodshed

留言 liúyán leave a message

流言蜚语 liúyán fēiyǔ gossip; scandal

流走 liúzǒu drain, flow away

例外 lìwài exception

礼物 lǐwù gift

利息 lìxī interest

离线 líxiàn go off-line

理想 lǐxiǎng ideal

理想化 lǐxiǎnghuà idealistic

理性 lǐxìng reason; sense

利息率 lìxīlǜ interest rate

力学 lìxué mechanics

离异 líyì break up (of couple)

礼仪 lǐyí protocol; etiquette; ceremony

利益 lìyì interest; advantage; benefit

利用 lìyòng use; exploit; take advantage of

理由 lǐyóu reason; cause; grounds

鲤鱼 lǐyú carp

俚语 lǐyǔ slang

例证 lìzhèng illustration; example

理智 lǐzhì reason (faculty)

荔枝 lìzhī lychee

李子 lǐzi plum

里子 lǐzi lining

例子 lìzi example; case; instance

栗子 lìzi chestnut

粒子 lìzǐ particle PHYS

栗子树 lìzi shù chestnut tree

笼 lóng cage

聋 lóng deaf ◊ deafness

龙 lóng dragon

隆冬季节 lóngdōng jìjié in the depths of winter

垄断 lǒngduàn monopolize ◊ monopoly

龙骨 lónggǔ keel

龙卷风 lóngjuǎn fēng tornado; whirlwind

隆隆声 lónglong shēng boom; peal (of thunder)

笼统 lóngtǒng sweeping statement

龙头 lóngtóu faucet

龙虾 lóngxiā lobster

聋哑 lóngyǎ deaf-and-dumb

笼罩 lǒngzhào descend (of mood,

*darkness*)

隆重 **lóngzhòng** festive

笼子 **lóngzi** cage

楼 **lóu** building; story, floor

搂 **lǒu** hug, embrace

漏 **lòu** seep; drip; leak ◊ leaky

楼层 **lóucéng** floor, story

漏出 **lòuchū** escape, leak; seep

漏洞 **lòudòng** leak; loophole

漏斗 **lòudǒu** funnel

楼房 **lóufáng** building

露面 **lòumiàn** turn up; put in an appearance

漏气 **lòuqì** leak out (*of air, gas*)

楼上 **lóushàng** upstairs

楼梯 **lóutī** stairs, staircase

楼厅 **lóutīng** balcony

楼下 **lóuxià** downstairs

炉 **lú** oven

橹 **lǔ** paddle

鹿 **lù** deer

路 **lù** road; way; possibility; 五路有轨电车 **wǔlù yǒuguǐdiànchē** streetcar line 5

露 **lù** dew ◊ reveal

录 **lù** record

驴 **lǘ** donkey

铝 **lǚ** aluminum

缕 **lǚ** strand, lock

氯 **lǜ** chlorine

滤 **lǜ** filter, strain

率 **lǜ** level, amount, rate (*of pay*)

绿 **lǜ** green

卵 **luǎn** (human) egg

乱 **luàn** chaotic, in a mess ◊ chaos

卵巢 **luǎncháo** ovary

乱砍 **luànkǎn** slash

乱伦 **luànlún** incest

乱蓬蓬 **luàn péngpeng** ragged

乱七八糟 **luànqī bāzāo** in a mess, in confusion, topsy-turvy

卵石 **luǎnshí** pebble

乱弹 **luàntán** strum

乱涂 **luàntú** daub

乱写 **luànxiě** scrawl, scribble

绿宝石 **lǜbǎoshí** emerald

路边 **lùbiān** roadside

路标 **lùbiāo** roadsign; signpost; landmark

铝箔 **lǚbó** aluminum foil

绿茶 **lǜchá** green tea

旅程 **lǚchéng** itinerary

露出 **lùchū** expose, reveal

屡次 **lǚcì** over and over again

路堤 **lùdī** embankment

陆地 **lùdì** land, shore, dry land; mainland ◊ terrestrial

旅店 **lǚdiàn** hostel; inn

掠夺 **lüèduó** loot

掠夺者 **lüèduó zhě** looter

掠过 **lüèguò** skim *surface*

略过 **lüèguò** skip, omit

略微 **lüèwēi** hint, trace

滤干 **lǜgān** strain; drain

路过 **lùguò** pass by

绿化 **lǜhuà** put plants / trees in, plant up

鹿角 **lùjiǎo** antlers

路径 **lùjìng** path

旅客 **lǚkè** passenger

履历 **lǚlì** résumé

陆路 **lùlù** track; overland route

鲁莽 **lǔmǎng** rash, impetuous

路面 **lùmiàn** pavement, road surface

轮 **lún** wheel; round (*of drinks*)

论 **lùn** discuss

轮齿 **lúnchǐ** cog

轮船 **lúnchuán** steamer; ship

论点 **lùndiǎn** thesis

伦敦 **Lúndūn** London

轮毂 **lúngǔ** hub (*of wheel*)

轮换 **lúnhuàn** alternate

论据 **lùnjù** argument; reasoning

轮廓 **lúnkuò** contour, outline; silhouette

轮流 **lúnliú** alternate ◊ alternately; 轮流做 **lúnliú zuò** do in rotation, take turns in doing

伦理学 **lúnlǐxué** ethics

轮盘赌 **lúnpán dǔ** roulette

轮胎 **lúntāi** tire

论文 **lùnwén** thesis, dissertation, treatise; paper

轮椅 **lúnyǐ** wheelchair

论语 **Lúnyǔ** Analects of Confucius

轮缘 **lúnyuán** rim (*of wheel*)

轮值表 **lúnzhí biǎo** rota

轮轴 **lúnzhóu** axle

轮子 **lúnzi** wheel

落 **luò** fall; sink; land (*of ball etc*); set (*of sun*)

锣 **luó** gong

骡 **luó** mule

裸 **luǒ** naked, bare

萝卜 **luóbo** turnip; radish

落地窗 **luòdìchuāng** French doors

落地灯 **luòdìdēng** floor lamp

落后 **luòhòu** backward ◊ be behind, trail; lose the lead; 在 X 方面落后 *zài X fāngmiàn luòhòu* be behind with X

落花生 **luòhuāshēng** groundnut

逻辑 **luóji** logic ◊ logical

落空 **luòkōng** fall through, fail

罗马数字 **Luómǎ shùzì** Roman numerals

螺母 **luómǔ** nut (*for bolt*)

罗盘仪 **luópán yí** compass

落泊 **luòpò** comedown

罗圈腿 **luóquān tuǐ** bandy

络腮胡子 **luòsāi húzi** full beard

螺栓 **luóshuān** bolt

落水 **luòshuǐ** fall into the water; 有人落水！*yǒurén luòshuǐ!* man overboard!

螺丝 **luósī** screw

螺丝刀 **luósīdāo** screwdriver

螺丝钉 **luósīdīng** screw

裸体 **luǒtǐ** naked, nude

裸体画 **luǒtǐ huà** nude

裸体主义者 **luǒtǐ zhǔyì zhě** nudist

骆驼 **luòtuo** camel

螺纹 **luówén** thread (*of screw*)

落下 **luòxià** go down, sink

裸胸 **luǒxiōng** topless

螺旋 **luóxuán** spiral

螺旋桨 **luóxuánjiǎng** propeller

录取 **lùqǔ** admit, take in

鹿肉 **lùròu** venison

绿色 **lǜsè** green

律师 **lǜshī** attorney, lawyer

露水 **lùshuǐ** dew

露宿街头 **lùsù jiētóu** sleep rough

芦笋 **lúsǔn** asparagus

露天 **lùtiān** open-air ◊ in the open air

旅途 **lǚtú** ride, drive; travels

芦苇 **lúwěi** reed

路线 **lùxiàn** route; way

录像 **lùxiàng** video; video recording

录像带 **lùxiàng dài** video cassette; videotape

录像机 **lùxiàng jī** video recorder, VCR

履行 **lǚxíng** fulfill ◊ fulfillment

旅行 **lǚxíng** travel; get around ◊ journey, trip; traveling

旅行包 **lǚxíngbāo** travel bag

旅行保险 **lǚxíng bǎoxiǎn** travel insurance

旅行袋 **lǚxíng dài** travel bag

旅行社 **lǚxíng shè** travel agency

旅行推销员 **lǚxíng tuīxiāo yuán** commercial traveler

旅行者 **lǚxíng zhě** traveler

旅行支票 **lǚxíng zhīpiào** traveler's check

陆续 **lùxù** one after the other

录音 **lùyīn** (tape) recording ◊ (tape) record ◊ audio

录音电话 **lùyīn diànhuà** answerphone

露营 **lùyíng** camp ◊ camping

录音机 **lùyīnjī** cassette player; cassette recorder; tape recorder

录音室 **lùyīn shì** recording studio

录音座 **lùyīnzuò** tape deck

旅游 **lǚyóu** tour ◊ tourism; tour

旅游公司 **lǚyóu gōngsī** tour operator

旅游业 **lǚyóu yè** tourism

旅游者 **lǚyóu zhě** tourist

旅游指南 **lǚyóu zhǐnán** guidebook

路障 **lùzhàng** barricade; roadblock

绿洲 **lǜzhōu** oasis

炉子 **lúzi** stove; furnace

# M

妈 **mā** mom, ma

抹 **mā** wipe

麻 **má** hemp

马 **mǎ** horse; 老马识途 **lǎo mǎ shí tú** *prov* the old horse knows the way

码 **mǎ** yard

骂 **mà** curse, swear

吗 **ma** (*question indicator*): 你认识他吗? **nǐ rènshi tā ma?** do you know him?

马表 **mǎbiǎo** stopwatch

抹布 **mābù** cloth; dish cloth

马车 **mǎchē** cart

马达 **mǎdá** motor, engine

马大哈 **mǎdàhā** disaster area *fig* 妈的! **māde!** V shit!

麻烦 **máfán** bother, trouble; 太麻烦你了 **tài máfán nǐle** you needn't have bothered

吗啡 **mǎfēi** morphine

马夫 **mǎfū** groom (*for horse*)

马虎 **mǎhū** careless, sloppy

埋 **mái** bury; 埋头于工作 **máitóu yú gōngzuò** bury oneself in work

买 **mǎi** buy

麦 **mài** wheat

迈 **mài** step

脉 **mài** blood vessel

卖 **mài** sell

迈步 **màibù** stride

买不到 **mǎi bú dào** unobtainable

埋藏 **máicáng** bury

买单 **mǎidān** pay the bill

买东西 **mǎi dōngxi** shop

卖方 **màifāng** seller

埋伏 **máifú** ambush

卖高价票 **mài gāojià piào** scalper

买家 **mǎijiā** buyer

麦克风 **màikèfēng** microphone

买卖 **mǎimài** buying and selling; business; 做 X 的买卖 **zuò X de**

买卖 **mǎimài** trade in X

麦片 **màipiàn** rolled oats

卖俏 **màiqiào** flirt

卖肉的 **màiròu de** butcher

麦乳精 **màirǔjīng** malted milk

卖艺 **màiyì** work as a performer

卖淫 **màiyín** prostitute oneself

埋葬 **máizàng** bury

买主 **mǎizhǔ** purchaser; customer

卖主 **màizhǔ** seller, vendor

麦子 **màizi** wheat

麻将 **májiàng** mah-jong

马厩 **mǎjiù** stable

马克 **mǎkè** mark (*currency*)

马克思 **Mǎkèsī** Marx

马克思主义 **Mǎkèsīzhǔyì** Marxism ◊ Marxist

马克思主义者 **Mǎkèsīzhǔyì zhě** Marxist

马来西亚 **Mǎláixīyà** Malaysia ◊ Malaysian

马来语 **Mǎlái yǔ** Malay (*language*)

马拉松 **mǎlāsōng** marathon

马力 **mǎlì** horsepower

马列主义 **Mǎlièzhǔyì** Marxism-Leninism

马列主义者 **Mǎlièzhǔyì zhě** Marxist-Leninist

马笼头 **mǎ lóngtóu** bridle

马路 **mǎlù** street

妈妈 **māma** mom, ma

马马虎虎 **mǎma hūhū** so-so, average, mediocre

麻木 **mámù** numb

蛮 **mán** quite; very

鳗 **mán** eel

瞒 **mán** conceal; keep secret

满 **mǎn** full

慢 **màn** slow

漫 **màn** overflow

漫步 **mànbù** ramble; saunter; wander ◊ rambling

满不在乎 **mǎn bù zàihu** not care at all

漫步者 **mànbù zhě** rambler

漫长 **màncháng** lengthy

慢动作 **màndòngzuò** slow motion

盲 **máng** blind

忙 **máng** busy ◊ be in a rush; 忙什么? **máng shénme?** what's the big rush?

盲点 **mángdiǎn** blind spot

芒果 **mángguǒ** mango

忙碌 **mánglù** busy; hectic; on the go ◊ bustle around; be busy; rush, scramble

盲目 **mángmù** blind; wild, crazy *scheme*

茫然 **mángrán** blank, vacant *look*

盲人 **mángrén** blind person; the blind

盲文 **mángwén** braille

蛮横 **mánhèng** harden *attitude* ◊ insolent

漫画 **mànhuà** comic

漫画书 **mànhuà shū** comic book

慢跑 **mànpǎo** jog ◊ jogging

满身 **mǎn shēn** the whole body; all over

蔓生植物 **mànshēng zhíwù** climbing plant

漫谈 **màntán** ramble ◊ rambling, incoherent

馒头 **mántou** steamed bun

漫无目的 **màn wú mùdì** aimless

慢性 **mànxìng** chronic

蔓延 **mànyán** spread (*of fire, disease, belief*); sprawl (*of city*); be overrun with ◊ contagious *fear, laughter*; sprawling; 四处蔓延 **sìchù mànyán** run wild

满意 **mǎnyì** satisfied; 令人满意 **lìngrén mǎnyì** fulfilling; satisfactory

漫游 **mànyóu** roam, wander around

满员 **mǎnyuán** full; booked up; packed

满月 **mǎnyuè** full moon

满洲 **Mǎnzhōu** Manchuria

慢走 **mànzǒu** goodbye, so long

满足 **mǎnzú** satisfy *needs, desires* ◊ satisfied, content, contented ◊ contentment; fulfillment; satisfaction

满族 **Mǎnzú** Manchu

猫 **māo** cat

锚 **máo** anchor

毛 **máo** hair; bristles; wool; mao (*Chinese money*)

矛 **máo** spear; javelin

铆 **mǎo** rivet

冒 **mào** emit, give off

毛笔 **máobǐ** writing brush

毛病 **máobìng** fault, defect; 车有点毛病 **chē yǒu diǎn máobìng** there is something wrong with the car

毛虫 **máochóng** caterpillar

冒充 **màochōng** impersonate, pose as

铆钉 **mǎodīng** rivet

矛盾 **máodùn** contradiction ◊ contradictory

冒犯 **màofàn** offend, insult

毛纺厂 **máofǎngchǎng** textile mill

毛骨悚然 **máogǔ sǒngrán** terrifying, hair-raising

冒号 **màohào** colon GRAM

铆接 **mǎojiē** rivet

毛巾 **máojīn** towel; washcloth

毛巾架 **máojīn jià** towel rail

毛孔 **máokǒng** pore

毛毛雨 **máomao yǔ** drizzle

猫咪 **māomī** puss, pussycat

牦牛 **máoniú** yak

毛皮 **máopí** coat, fur

茅舍 **máoshè** hovel

帽舌 **màoshé** visor

茂盛 **màoshèng** rampant; flourishing; luxuriant

冒失 **màoshī** presumptuous

毛毯 **máotǎn** blanket

猫头鹰 **māotóuyīng** owl

毛线 **máoxiàn** knitting wool

冒险 **màoxiǎn** adventure; venture, undertaking ◊ take a risk; venture into ◊ dangerous, risky; bold, audacious

冒险家 **màoxiǎnjiā** adventurer

帽檐 **màoyán** brim (*of hat*)

毛衣 **máoyī** sweater

贸易 **màoyì** trade, commerce

贸易差额 **màoyì chā'é** balance

of trade

贸易关系 **màoyì guānxi** trade relations

毛泽东 **Máo Zédōng** Mao Tse-tung, Mao Zedong

毛泽东思想 **Máo Zédōng sīxiǎng** Mao Zedong thought

毛毡 **máozhān** felt

毛主席 **Máo Zhǔxí** Chairman Mao

毛主席像章 **Máo Zhǔxí xiàngzhāng** Mao badge

毛主席语录 **Máo Zhǔxí Yǔlù** Little Red Book

帽子 **màozi** cap; hat

麻雀 **máquè** sparrow

骂人 **màrén** curse, swear

骂人话 **màrénhuà** swearword

马赛克 **mǎsàikè** mosaic

马上 **mǎshàng** immediately, right now, straight away

马蹄 **mǎtí** hoof

马蹄铁 **mǎtítiě** horseshoe

马桶 **mǎtǒng** lavatory

码头 **mǎtóu** dock; wharf; port

马尾辫 **mǎwěibiàn** pigtail

马尾发 **mǎwěifà** ponytail

马戏团 **mǎxìtuán** circus

蚂蚁 **mǎyǐ** ant

麻油 **máyóu** sesame oil

马掌 **mǎzhǎng** horseshoe

麻疹 **mázhěn** measles

麻醉 **mázuì** anesthetize; drug ◊ anesthesia; anesthetic; drug ◊ high, stoned

麻醉剂 **mázuìjì** anesthetic; narcotic

麻醉品 **mázuìpǐn** narcotic; drug

麻醉师 **mázuì shī** anesthetist

煤 **méi** coal

霉 **méi** mold, mildew

没 **méi** not ◊ have not; 我没钱 **wǒ méi qián** I've got no money; 我没看过这本书 **wǒ méi kànguo zhè běn shū** I haven't read this book; 没多少 **méi duōshǎo** nothing much ◊ (*in questions*): 你去没去? **nǐ qù méi qù?** did you go or not?

梅 **méi** plum

眉 **méi** eyebrow

每 **měi** every; each; per

美 **měi** beautiful, pretty, lovely

妹 **mèi** younger sister

美餐 **měicān** good meal

每次 **měicì** each time

美德 **měidé** morality

没的比 **méidebǐ** there's no comparison

梅毒 **méidú** syphilis

妹夫 **mèifū** brother-in-law (*younger sister's husband*)

没赶上 **méigǎnshàng** miss

每隔 **měigé** alternate

每个 **měigè** each

每个人 **měigè rén** everyone

每隔一天 **měigéyìtiān** every other day

湄公河 **Méigōnghé** Mekong River

没工作 **méi gōngzuò** jobless

美观 **měiguān** esthetic

没关系 **méi guānxi** it doesn't matter, never mind; it's a pleasure, you're welcome

玫瑰 **méigui** rose

美国 **Měiguó** America, USA ◊ American

美国人 **Měiguó rén** American

没骨气 **méi gǔqì** spineless

美好 **měihǎo** wonderful; good

美化 **měihuà** make more attractive; brighten up

没化妆 **méi huàzhuāng** unmade-up, without make-up

媒介 **méijiè** medium; means

没经验 **méi jīngyàn** inexperienced

没开 **méikāi** be off (*of TV, machine, light*)

煤矿 **méikuàng** coal-mine

美丽 **měilì** beautiful, lovely ◊ beauty

魅力 **mèilì** attraction, magnetism; charm; glamor

美利坚合众国 **Měilìjiān Hézhòngguó** United States of America

没礼貌 **méilǐmào** have no manners

眉毛 **méimao** eyebrow

美貌 **měimào** looks

妹妹 **mèimèi** younger sister

没门儿！**méiménr!** no way!

美妙 **měimiào** wonderful

每年 **měinián** yearly ◊ per annum

美女 **měinǚ** pin-up; pretty girl

煤气 **méiqì** coal gas

没前途 **méi qiántú** have no future ◊ hopeless, useless; 没前途的工作 **méi qiántú de gōngzuò** dead-end job

煤气灶 **méiqìzào** gas stove

没人 **méirén** nobody

每日 **měirì** daily

美容 **měiróng** cosmetic

美容家 **měiróng jiā** beautician

美容洗液 **měiróng xǐyè** face lotion

美容院 **měiróng yuàn** beauty parlor

美食 **měishí** delicacy

没事儿 **méi shìr** it's alright; 我没事儿 **wǒ méi shìr** I'm alright

美术片 **měishùpiàn** animation

每天 **měitiān** daily, everyday ◊ every day

媒体渲染 **méitǐ xuànrǎn** media hype

没完 **méiwán** never-ending

每晚 **měiwǎn** every evening

没完没了 **méiwán méiliǎo** on and on, endlessly; 没完没了地要 X 去做 Y **méiwán méiliǎo de yào X qù zuò Y** go on and on at X to do Y

没完全准备好 **méi wánquán zhǔnbèi hǎo** not quite ready

美味 **měiwèi** delicacy

没味儿 **méiwèir** tasteless

没问题 **méi wèntí** certainly, no problem

每小时 **měi xiǎoshí** hourly; 每小时一百五十公里 **měi xiǎoshí yībǎi wǔshí gōnglǐ** at 150 km/h

没兴趣 **méi xìngqu** uninterested; uninteresting

没修面 **méi xiūmiàn** unshaven

美学 **měixué** esthetics

没牙 **méiyá** toothless

没一个 **méi yīgè** none

没用 **méiyòng** useless ◊ it's no use; 试也没用 **shì yě méiyòng** it's useless trying

没用的东西 **méiyòng de dōngxi** bum

没用的人 **méiyòng de rén** good-for-nothing

煤油 **méiyóu** paraffin; kerosene

没有 **méiyǒu** without ◊ no ◊ not ◊ there is / are not; 没有多少 **méiyǒu duōshao** not much; not many; 没有咖啡 / 茶了 **méiyǒu kāfēi / chá le** there's no coffee / tea left; 没有钱 **méiyǒu qián** have no money ◊ (in questions): 你去了没有？**nǐ qùle méiyou?** did you go or not?

没有结果 **méiyǒu jiéguǒ** unproductive

没有察觉到 **méiyǒu juéchádào** be unaware of

没有什么 **méiyǒu shénme** nothing

没有时间 **méiyǒu shíjiān** have no time; be booked up

没有图案 **méiyǒu tú'àn** plain, unadorned

没有问题 **méiyǒu wèntí** no problem; without a hitch

没有希望 **méiyǒu xīwàng** hopeless

没有音乐天赋 **méiyǒu yīnyuè tiānfù** unmusical

美元 **měiyuán** US dollar

每月 **měiyuè** monthly

没粘住 **méi zhānzhù** come unstuck

没治了 **méizhìle** amazing

美洲 **Měizhōu** (continent of) America

美洲鹫 **měizhōu jiù** vulture

美洲山核桃 **měizhōu shānhétáo** pecan

每周一次 **měizhōu yīcì** weekly

闷 **mēn** stuffy, airless

门 **mén** door

闷 **mèn** bored; 闷死了 **mènsǐle** be bored to death

门把手 **mén bǎshǒu** doorknob

门垫 **méndiàn** doormat

蒙 **méng** cover

猛 **měng** fierce

梦 **mèng** dream

蒙蔽 **méngbì** deceive ◊ deception, deceit

蠓虫 **měngchóng** midge, gnat

蒙古 **Měnggǔ** Mongolia ◊ Mongolian

猛击 **měngjī** bang; blow ◊ blaze away

孟加拉 **Mèngjiālā** Bangladesh ◊ Bangladeshi

梦见 **mèngjian** dream about

猛拉 **měnglā** jerk, wrench

猛烈 **měngliè** fierce, violent; passionate ◊ with a vengeance

朦朦胧胧 **méngméng lónglóng** misty *color*

蒙蒙细雨 **méngméng xìyǔ** drizzle

蒙骗 **mēngpiàn** cheat, deceive

猛扑 **měngpū** pounce, swoop

猛抬物价 **měngtái wùjià** bump up *prices*

猛推 **měngtuī** thrust, force

梦想 **mèngxiǎng** dream, fantasize

梦想家 **mèngxiǎng jiā** dreamer

萌芽 **méngyá** shoot, sprout

梦游者 **mèngyóu zhě** sleep walker

猛增 **měngzēng** jump, soar

猛掷 **měngzhì** hurl

蒙住眼睛 **méngzhù yǎnjīng** blindfold

孟子 **Mèngzǐ** Mencius

门阶 **ménjiē** doorstep

门槛 **ménkǎn** threshold

门口 **ménkǒu** gateway

门廊 **ménláng** porch, stoop

门铃 **ménlíng** doorbell

闷闷不乐 **mènmèn bùlè** sullen

门牌号 **ménpáihào** house number

门票 **ménpiào** entrance ticket

闷热 **mēnrè** clammy, sultry

闷人 **mènrén** bore

门闩 **ménshuān** bolt; latch

闷死 **mēnsǐ** suffocate

门厅 **méntīng** lobby

门卫 **ménwèi** porter, doorman

门诊部 **ménzhěnbù** outpatient department

门诊治疗 **ménzhěn zhìliáo** outpatient treatment

闷住 **mēnzhù** smother

门柱 **ménzhù** goalpost

迷 **mí** lost ◊ fan; 足球迷 **zúqiúmí** soccer fan

谜 **mí** mystery; riddle

米 **mǐ** rice; meter

密 **mì** thick; close

秘 **mì** secret

蜜 **mì** honey

棉 **mián** cotton

眠 **mián** sleep

免 **miǎn** avoid; prohibit

面 **miàn** face; side; flour; noodle

面包 **miànbāo** bread

面包店 **miànbāo diàn** bakery

面包渣 **miànbāo zhā** breadcrumbs

棉布 **miánbù** cotton

面部 **miànbù** face; 面部拉皮手术 **miànbù lāpí shǒushù** facelift

免除 **miǎnchú** immune ◊ be exempt from; 免除 X 的 Y **miǎnchú X de Y** excuse X from Y

面的 **miàndī** cab, taxi

缅甸 **Miǎndiàn** Burma ◊ Burmese

面的司机 **miàndī sījī** cab driver

面对 **miànduì** confront, stand up to; face (toward)

面对面 **miàn duì miàn** face to face

面额 **miàn'é** denomination (*of money*)

免费 **miǎnfèi** free, free of charge; 免费入场 **miǎnfèi rùchǎng** admission free

免费样品 **miànfèi yàngpǐn** free sample

面粉 **miànfěn** (wheat) flour

面糊 **miànhú** batter

棉花 **miánhua** cotton

棉花糖 **miánhuā táng** cotton candy; marshmallow

面积 **miànjī** area; proportions

面颊 **miànjiá** cheek

面具 **miànjù** mask

面孔 **miànkǒng** face

勉励 **miǎnlì** encourage

面貌 **miànmào** face; appearance

面前 **miànqián** in front of; 在 X 面前 **zài X miànqián** in the presence of X

勉强 **miǎnqiǎng** manage with difficulty ◊ reluctant, grudging, forced ◊ reluctantly; 勉强及格 *miǎnqiǎng jígé* scrape through; 勉强维持生活 *miǎnqiǎng wéichí shēnghuó* scrape a living

面色 **miànsè** complexion

面纱 **miànshā** veil

面食 **miànshí** pasta; pastry

面试 **miànshì** (job) interview

面熟 **miànshú** seem familiar

免税 **miǎnshuì** tax-free; duty-free

免税商店 **miǎnshuì shāngdiàn** duty-free store

免税物品 **miǎnshuì wùpǐn** duty-free goods

缅腆 **miǎntiǎn** shy; timid; retiring ◊ shyness; timidity

面条 **miàntiáo** noodle

面团 **miàntuán** dough

绵羊 **miányáng** sheep

免疫 **miǎnyì** immune ◊ immunity

免疫性 **miǎnyìxìng** immune ◊ immunity

免疫系统 **miǎnyì xìtǒng** immune system

免职 **miǎnzhí** oust

免租 **miǎnzū** rent-free

免罪 **miǎnzuì** redeem *sinner*

喵 **miāo** miaow

苗 **miáo** young plant

秒 **miǎo** second

庙 **miào** temple; temple market

妙 **miào** wonderful; 妙极了！ *miàojíle!* fantastic!

秒表 **miǎobiǎo** stopwatch

妙不可言 **miàobùkěyán** magical, enchanting

描绘 **miáohuì** portray, represent; describe

庙会 **miàohuì** carnival

苗圃 **miáopǔ** nursery (*for plants*)

描述 **miáoshù** describe; depict, portray ◊ description; portrayal

苗条 **miáotiáo** slim, slight; trim

描写 **miáoxiě** describe ◊ description; portrayal

妙语 **miàoyǔ** punch line

庙宇 **miàoyǔ** temple

妙语 **miàoyǔ** witticism

秒针 **miǎozhēn** second hand

瞄准 **miáozhǔn** aim ◊ be aimed at

弥补 **míbǔ** catch up on; make up for; recoup; rectify ◊ compensation

灭 **miè** extinguish, put out

灭火 **mièhuǒ** put out a fire

灭火器 **mièhuǒqì** fire extinguisher

灭绝 **mièjué** die out; wipe out, eradicate, exterminate

灭亡 **mièwáng** decline, disappearance ◊ go under, be ruined

米粉 **mǐfěn** rice noodles; vermicelli

密封 **mìfēng** airtight ◊ seal

蜜蜂 **mìfēng** bee

迷宫 **mígōng** maze

猕猴桃 **míhóutáo** kiwi fruit

迷惑 **míhuò** mystify; mislead; confuse ◊ disoriented

密集 **mìjí** dense *crowd* ◊ swarm

米酒 **mǐjiǔ** rice wine

秘诀 **mìjué** formula

迷恋 **míliàn** be infatuated with, be nuts about

迷路 **mílù** lose one's way; 我迷路了 *wǒ mílù le* I'm lost

密码 **mìmǎ** code; combination; PIN; 通路密码 *tōnglù mìmǎ* access code

秘密 **mìmì** secret ◊ covert, under-cover

靡靡之音 **mǐmǐ zhī yīn** schmaltzy music; schmaltzy song

密谋 **mìmóu** conspire, plot

民 **mín** people; folk

民兵 **mínbīng** militia

名 **míng** name

鸣 **míng** ring, chime; toll; cry (*of birds, animals*)

明 **míng** bright; light

命 **mìng** life

敏感 **mǐngǎn** sensitive; touchy; acute *sense* ◊ sensitivity; 对冷／热敏感 *duì lěng／rè mǐngǎn* be sensitive to the cold／heat

敏感性 **mǐngǎnxìng** sensitivity

明白 **míngbái** understand ◊ clear

名册 **míngcè** roll, list

明朝 **Míngcháo** Ming Dynasty

明晨 **míngchén** tomorrow morning

名称 **míngchēng** name; designation

名词 **míngcí** noun

名次 **míngcì** place, position

民歌 **míngē** folk song

民歌手 **míngēshǒu** folk singer

明亮 **míngliàng** bright; light, brilliant ◊ brightness

明了 **míngliǎo** lucid

命令 **mìnglìng** command, order

命令式 **mìnglìng shì** dictatorial

鸣锣令 **míngluó lìng** gong; bell

命名 **mìngmíng** name

明年 **míngnián** next year

名牌 **míngpái** well-known brand

名牌服装 **míngpái fúzhuāng** designer clothes

名牌商品 **míngpái shāngpǐn** brand name

名片 **míngpiàn** business card, visiting card

明确 **míngquè** define ◊ definite; pronounced; explicit

明确指出 **míngquè zhǐchū** pinpoint

名人 **míngrén** prominent figure; celebrity

名声 **míngshēng** reputation; 有好/坏名声 **yǒuhǎo/huài míngshēng** have a good/bad reputation

名胜 **míngshèng** scenic spot

明天 **míngtiān** tomorrow; 明天上午 **míngtiān shàngwǔ** tomorrow morning (*between 10am and noon*); 明天早晨 **míngtiān zǎochén** tomorrow morning (*before 10am*)

铭文 **míngwén** inscription

明显 **míngxiǎn** clear, obvious; transparent

明星 **míngxīng** star

明信片 **míngxìnpiàn** postcard

名义上 **míngyì shàng** nominal

名誉 **míngyù** fame; reputation

明智 **míngzhì** wise; sensible

名字 **míngzi** name; given name; 你叫什么名字? **nǐ jiào shénme míngzi?** what's your name?

民航 **mínháng** civil aviation

民间 **mínjiān** civil; folk

民间舞 **mínjiānwǔ** folk dance

敏捷 **mǐnjié** quick, rapid; nimble; sharp, smart

民谣 **mínyáo** ballad

民意测验 **mínyì cèyàn** poll, survey

民意调查 **mínyì diàochá** poll, survey

民营企业 **mínyíng qǐyè** private sector

民乐 **mínyuè** folk music

民众 **mínzhòng** the people; the public

民主 **mínzhǔ** democracy ◊ democratic

民主党 **Mínzhǔ Dǎng** Democratic Party

民主主义者 **mínzhǔ zhǔyì zhě** democrat

民族 **mínzú** people; ethnic group; race; nation; nationality

民族主义 **mínzú zhǔyì** nationalism

密切 **mìqiè** intimate, close

迷人 **mírén** fascinating; charming; enchanting

弥撒 **mísa** mass REL

米色 **mǐsè** cream (*color*)

秘书 **mìshū** secretary ◊ secretarial

迷途知返 **mítú zhīfǎn** straighten out

迷惘 **míwǎng** be mixed up

迷信 **míxìn** superstition ◊ superstitious

密友 **mìyǒu** crony, pal

谜语 **míyǔ** riddle

蜜月 **mìyuè** honeymoon

迷住 **mízhù** enthrall, bewitch; 被X迷住 **bèi X mízhù** be hooked on X

摸 **mō** touch, feel; grope

膜 **mó** membrane

磨 **mó** grind; sharpen

魔 **mó** demon

抹 **mǒ** spread *butter etc*

磨 **mò** grind (down)

末 **mò** end

墨 **mò** ink

没 **mò** sink

殁 mò perish, meet one's end

末班车 mòbānchē last bus; last train

漠不关心 mò bù guānxīn indifference ◊ indifferent; nonchalant

摸不着头脑 mōbùzháo tóunǎo be baffled

摩擦 mócā friction ◊ rub

末代皇帝 Mòdài Huángdì Last Emperor

磨掉 módiào rub off (of paint etc)

抹掉 mǒdiào erase, wipe

魔法 mófǎ magical

模范 mófàn example, model ◊ exemplary

模仿 mófǎng imitate, mimic; forge ◊ imitation, impersonation

磨坊 mòfáng mill

蘑菇 mógū mushroom

磨光 móguāng polish

魔鬼 móguǐ devil; demon

模糊 móhu vague; indistinct; fuzzy, hazy; misty ◊ blur ◊ mist over

墨家 Mòjiā Mohism ◊ Mohist

墨镜 mòjìng sunglasses

魔力 mólì magic

茉莉 mòli jasmine

茉莉花茶 mòlihuāchá jasmine tea

莫名其妙 mò míng qí miào mysterious

模拟 mónǐ analog

摹拟 mónǐ mock, simulated, imitation ◊ simulate

末期 mòqī final stage; 十九／二十世纪末期 shíjiǔ／èrshí shìjì mòqī the late 19th／20th century

默契 mòqì chemistry (between people)

磨砂玻璃 móshā bōli frosted glass

陌生 mòshēng strange, unfamiliar; alien

陌生人 mòshēng rén stranger

模式 móshì model, pattern

没收 mòshōu confiscate

墨守成规者 mòshǒu chéngguī zhě stick-in-the-mud

魔术 móshù conjuring tricks, magic

墨水 mòshuǐ ink

魔术师 móshùshī magician, conjurer

莫斯科 Mòsīkē Moscow

磨碎 mósuì grate

磨损 mósǔn wear; abrasion ◊ wear away, wear out ◊ worn

摸索 mōsuǒ grope

模特儿 mótèr (fashion) model

摩天大楼 mótiān dàlóu skyscraper

摩托 mótuō motor, engine

摩托车 mótuōchē motorcycle

谋 móu scheme

某 mǒu certain; some; 某处 mǒuchù somewhere; 某人 mǒurén a certain person, someone

谋杀 móushā murder

谋生 móushēng living ◊ earn one's living

末尾 mòwěi end

墨西哥 Mòxīgē Mexico ◊ Mexican

模型 móxíng model; prototype; cast, mold

磨牙 móyá molar

墨鱼 mòyú cuttlefish

某种 mǒuzhǒng certain, particular

母 mǔ mother; female (of animal or bird)

幕 mù curtain; act (of play)

木 mù wood

墓 mù grave

目 mù eye

牧 mù tend livestock

母爱 mǔ'ài motherly love

母斑 mǔbān birthmark

母板 mǔbǎn motherboard

木板 mùbǎn plank

墓碑 mùbēi tombstone, gravestone

目标 mùbiāo aim, objective; goal; target

木材 mùcái lumber, wood

牧草 mùcǎo graze

木柴 mùchái firewood

牧场 mùchǎng pasture

牧场主 mùchǎng zhǔ rancher

牡丹 mǔdān peony

目瞪口呆 mùdèng kǒudāi stupefied, astonished

墓地 mùdì graveyard, cemetery

目的 mùdì purpose, aim, end

目的地 mùdìdì destination

木耳 mù'ěr wood-ear mushroom

木筏 mùfá raft

木工 mùgōng carpenter; joiner

木工活 mùgōnghuó woodwork (*activity*)

母狗 mǔgǒu bitch (*dog*)

目光 mùguāng look

木棍 mùgùn stick; club

幕后 mùhòu behind the scenes

幕后策划 mùhòu cèhuà mastermind, organize

母鸡 mǔjī hen

目击 mùjī witness

幕间 mùjiān interlude

木匠 mùjiàng carpenter

幕间休息 mùjiān xiúxī intermission

目击者 mùjīzhě eyewitness

募捐 mùjuān collect donations

募捐者 mùjuān zhě fundraiser

木刻 mùkè wood carving

母鹿 mǔlù doe

目录 mùlù catalog; directory; list; table of contents

暮 mù evening

母马 mǔmǎ mare

牡马 mǔmǎ stallion

牧民 mùmín herdsman

母牛 mǔniú cow

木偶 mù'ǒu puppet

木偶戏 mù'ǒuxì puppet show

木排 mùpái raft

目前 mùqián at present, currently

母亲 mǔqīn mother

母亲节 Mǔqīnjié Mother's Day

暮色降临 mùsè jiànglín get dark

牧师 mùshī priest, minister, clergyman, pastor

穆斯林 Mùsīlín Muslim

木炭 mùtàn charcoal

木纹 mùwén grain

木屋 mùwū log cabin

木屑 mùxiè chip (*of wood*)

母性 mǔxìng maternity ◊ motherly

母羊 mǔyáng ewe

牧羊犬 mùyángquǎn sheepdog

牧羊人 mùyáng rén shepherd

母语 mǔyǔ mother tongue

拇指 mǔzhǐ thumb

木制 mùzhì wooden

木制管乐器 mùzhì guānyuèqì woodwind instrument

墓志铭 mùzhìmíng epitaph

木制品 mùzhìpǐn woodwork (*object*)

目中无人 mùzhōng wúrén snooty

母猪 mǔzhū sow (*pig*)

木柱 mùzhù pin, skittle

模子 múzi mold

# N

拿 **ná** carry (*in hand*); hold; fetch; collect; take, remove

哪 **nǎ** which; 哪一个？*nǎ yīgè?* which one?

那 **nà** that; those ◊ then; 那不行 *nà bùxíng* that's not right, that's not allowed; 那两人 *nà liǎngrén* those two people; 那是什么？*nà shì shénme?* what is that?; 那又怎么样？*nà yòu zěnmeyàng?* so what?

拿不准 **ná bùzhǔn** be doubtful

拿出 **náchū** produce, take out

纳粹 **Nàcuì** Nazi

拿掉 **nádiào** get off, remove

拿动 **nádòng** manage

哪个 **nǎge** which; which one; who; 哪个是你的？*nǎge shì nǐde?* which one is yours?; 哪个都行 *nǎge dōuxíng* either

那个 **nàge** that, that one

奶 **nǎi** milk

耐穿 **nàichuān** sturdy, hardwearing

耐久 **nàijiǔ** durable

奶酪 **nǎilào** cheese

耐力 **nàilì** stamina, endurance

奶奶 **nǎinai** grandma (*paternal*)

奶瓶 **nǎipíng** baby's bottle

耐心 **nàixīn** patience; 耐心点儿！*nàixīn diǎnr!* just be patient!

耐用 **nàiyòng** hardwearing ◊ wear, last

奶油 **nǎiyóu** cream

奶子 **nǎizi** tit, boob

奶嘴 **nǎizuǐ** pacifier; nipple

拿来 **nálái** bring

哪里 **nǎli** where, whereabouts

那里 **nàli** there

那么 **nàme** such a ◊ (so) that ◊ then, therefore; 那么大／贵 *nàme dà／guì* that big／expensive; 那么多？*nàme duō?* as much as that?

南 **nán** south ◊ southern; southerly

难 **nán** difficult, hard

男 **nán** male

难 **nàn** disaster

男扮女装 **nánbàn nǚzhuāng** in drag ◊ transvestite

南边 **nánbiān** south; the south side; 在 X 的南边 *zài X de nánbiān* to the south of X

男傧相 **nán bīnxiàng** best man

南部 **nánbù** south

男厕 **náncè** men's room, washroom

难道 …？ **nándào …?** can it be that …?; 你难道没看见？*nǐ nándào méi kànjiàn?* can't you see?

难度 **nándù** difficulty, hardness

南方 **nánfāng** south

南非 **Nánfēi** South Africa ◊ South African

南风 **nánfēng** southerly wind

男服务员 **nán fúwùyuán** waiter

男高音 **nán gāoyīn** tenor

难怪！**nánguài!** no wonder!

南瓜 **nánguā** squash, pumpkin

难过 **nánguò** upset; sad, unhappy; sorry; 令人难过 *lìngrén nánguò* upsetting

囊肿 **nángzhǒng** cyst

男孩 **nánhái** boy

南海 **Nánhǎi** South China Sea

南韩 **Nánhán** South Korea ◊ South Korean

男护士 **nán hùshì** male nurse

南极 **Nánjí** South Pole ◊ Antarctic

男妓 **nánjì** male prostitute

难解 **nánjiě** obscure, difficult

难接近 **nán jiējìn** inaccessible

难堪 **nánkān** embarrassed; 使 X 难堪 *shǐ X nánkān* embarrass X, put X on the spot

难看 **nánkàn** ugly

难理解 **nán lǐjiě** unintelligible

南美 **Nánměi** South America ◊ South American

难免 **nánmiǎn** inevitable; inescapable

难民 **nànmín** refugee

男模特儿 **nán mótèr** male model

男朋友 **nán péngyou** boyfriend

男仆从 **nán púcóng** valet

男人 **nánrén** man, male

南沙群岛 **Nánshā Qúndǎo** Spratley Islands

男士护肤液 **nánshì hùfū yè** aftershave

难受 **nánshòu** feel ill-at-ease

难忘 **nánwàng** unforgettable

难为情 **nánwéiqíng** ashamed, embarrassed

难闻 **nánwén** foul-smelling

男性 **nánxìng** masculine, male

南亚 **Nányà** South Asia ◊ South Asian

难以 **nányǐ** difficult to

难以表述 **nányǐ biǎoshù** inexpressible

难以察觉 **nányǐ chájué** imperceptible

难以对付 **nányǐ duìfù** awkward, obstreperous

难以估量 **nányǐ gūliàng** inestimable

难以解答 **nányǐ jiědá** baffling

难以接近 **nányǐ jiējìn** unapproachable

难以描述 **nányǐ miáoshù** indefinable

难以扑捉 **nányǐ pūzhuō** elusive

难以确定 **nányǐ quèdìng** be in doubt

难以忍受 **nányǐ rěnshòu** unbearable

难以容忍 **nányǐ róngrěn** trying

难以想象 **nányǐ xiǎngxiàng** unimaginable

难以形容 **nányǐ xíngróng** indescribable

难以预料 **nányǐ yùliào** it is doubtful whether

难以置信 **nányǐ zhìxìn** unbelievable

男用卫生间 **nányòng**

卫生间 **wèishēngjiān** washroom, men's room

难住 **nánzhù** baffle, stump

男子汉气 **nánzǐhànqì** manhood; manliness

男子气 **nánzǐqì** masculine

男子气概 **nánzi qìgài** virility; machismo

脑 **nǎo** brain

闹 **nào** noisy ◊ make a noise; beef, bellyache

闹别扭 **nào bièniu** fall out, argue

闹鬼 **nàoguǐ** haunted

恼火 **nǎohuǒ** mad, sore ◊ be mad, be sore

闹剧 **nàojù** farce

脑门儿 **nǎoménr** forehead, brow

脑膜炎 **nǎomóyán** meningitis

恼怒 **nǎonù** annoyed, pissed

恼人 **nǎorén** annoying

闹事 **nàoshì** make a scene; riot

闹事者 **nàoshì zhě** rioter

脑髓 **nǎosuǐ** brain

脑外科医生 **nǎo wàikē yīshēng** brain surgeon

脑震荡 **nǎozhèndàng** concussion

闹着玩儿 **nào zhe wánr** playful; joking; 不是闹着玩儿的 **búshì nàozhe wánr de** it's no joke

闹钟 **nàozhōng** alarm clock

脑子 **nǎozi** brains, intelligence

拿起 **náqǐ** pick up

哪儿 **nǎr** where; 我哪儿都找不着 **wǒ nǎr dōu zhǎobùzháo** I can't find it anywhere

那儿 **nàr** there; 他在那儿！ **tā zài nàr!** there he is!

拿上去 **ná shàngqù** take up, fetch up

那时 **nàshí** then

那时候 **nàshíhòu** in those days

拿手好菜 **náshǒu hǎocài** specialty

纳税人 **nàshuì rén** taxpayer

那天 **nàtiān** the other day

哪些 **nǎxiē** which; which ones; who

那些 **nàxiē** those

捺着性子 **nàzhe xìngzi** keep one's temper

拿走 **názǒu** take away, remove

呢 ne *(in questions)*:你呢？*nǐ ne?* and you? ◊ *(emphasis)*: 他还没来呢！*ta hái méi lái ne!* he still hasn't come!

哪 něi which

内 nèi inside ◊ inner; internal

那 nèi that; those

内部 nèibù inside, interior ◊ internal; inward; inner ◊ internally

内部人 nèibùrén insider

内部消息 nèibù xiāoxi inside information

内部装修 nèibù zhuāngxiū interior decoration

内存 nèicún RAM, random access memory

内弟 nèidì brother-in-law *(wife's younger brother)*

内地 nèidì interior; inland

内阁 nèigé cabinet POL

内含 nèihán built-in

内涵 nèihán hidden

内疚 nèijiù guilt; guilty conscience ◊ guilty; 我一直感到内疚 *wǒ yizhí gǎndào nèijiù* it has been on my conscience

内科医生 nèikē yīshēng internist

内裤 nèikù underpants, panties

内陆 nèilù interior, inland

内蒙古 Nèiménggǔ Inner Mongolia ◊ Inner Mongolian

内蒙古大草原 Nèiménggǔ Dà Cǎo Yuán Inner Mongolian Grasslands

内幕交易 nèimù jiāoyì insider trading

内燃机 nèiránjī internal combustion engine

内容 nèiróng content; contents

内胎 nèitāi inner tube

内向 nèixiàng reserved; introverted

内斜视 nèi xiéshì cross-eyed

内心 nèixīn privately, inwardly

内兄 nèixiōng brother-in-law *(wife's older brother)*

内衣 nèiyī underwear

内脏 nèizàng guts; giblets

内战 nèizhàn civil war

内政 nèizhèng domestic policy; domestic affairs

内政部 Nèizhèng Bù Department of the Interior

内装 nèizhuāng built-in

嫩 nèn tender

能 néng can, be able to ◊ energy; 你能帮我吗？*nǐ néng bāng wǒ ma?* can you help me?

能干 nénggàn capable

能够 nénggòu be able to

能见度 néngjiàn dù visibility

能力 nénglì ability, capacity; competence; faculty *(hearing, vision etc)*

能量 néngliàng power, energy; 能量爆发 *néngliàng bàofā* in a burst of energy

能量单位 néngliàng dānwèi power unit

能耐梗 néngnàigěng wise guy

能胜任 néngshèngrèn be equal to

能生育 néng shēngyù fertile

能手 néngshǒu expert

能养活 néng yǎnghuó viable *life form*

能源 néngyuán energy *(gas etc)*

嫩鸡 nènjī broiler *(chicken)*

嫩芽 nènyá shoot BOT

嗯 ńg *(questioning)*: 嗯，你说什么？*ńg, ni shuō shénme?* huh?, what did you say?

嗯 ng *(promising)*: 嗯！就这么办吧！*ng! jiù zhème bàn ba* ok, it's a deal!

泥 ní mud

你 nǐ you *sg* ◊ your *sg*

拟 nǐ draft, draw up

溺爱 nì'ài mollycoddle

年 nián ◊ annual

粘 nián sticky ◊ stick

念 niàn think of; read (out loud); study

黏稠度 niánchóu dù consistency, texture

年初 niánchū start of the year

年底 niándǐ end of the year

年度 niándù year ◊ annual

粘附 niánfù adhere to

娘 niáng mother; woman

酿 niàng ferment; brew

娘家姓 niángjiāxìng maiden name

酿酒厂 niàngjiǔchǎng distillery; winery

娘儿们 niángrmen broad, chick

酿造 niàngzào brew

酿造厂 niàngzào chǎng brewery

酿造者 niàngzào zhě brewer

黏糊糊 nián húhu sticky, clammy

年级 niánjí grade, class EDU

年纪 niánjì age

粘结 niánjié bond, stick

年龄 niánlíng age; 年龄为 **niánlíng wéi** at the age of

碾灭 niǎnmiè stub out

粘膜 niánmó mucous membrane

年青 niánqīng young

碾碎 niǎnsuì grind

捻碎 niǎnsuì scrunch up

念头 niàntou thought, idea

粘土 niántǔ clay

粘液 niányè mucus

年长 niánzhǎng senior; elder; eldest

年长者 niánzhǎngzhě elder

粘住 niánzhù stick, glue, adhere

撵走 niǎnzǒu throw out, expel

鸟 niǎo bird

尿 niào urine, piss

尿布 niàobù diaper

鸟类保护区 niǎo lèibǎohù qū bird sanctuary

鸟笼 niǎolóng birdcage

尿片 niàopiàn diaper

鸟嘴 niǎozuǐ bill, beak

尼泊尔 Níbó'ěr Nepal ◊ Nepalese

昵称 nìchēng pet name

你的 nǐde your sg ◊ yours sg; 你的朋友 **nǐde péngyǒu** a friend of yours

拟订 nǐdìng draft, draw up

捏 niē pinch; 一捏 **yīniē** a pinch (of salt etc)

镍 niè nickel

啮合 nièhé engage, become operative

捏造 niēzào invent

镊子 nièzi tweezers

逆风 nìfēng headwind

尼姑 nígū Buddhist nun

你好 nǐ hǎo hello, hi; 你好吗？ **nǐ hǎo ma?** how do you do?; how are you?

霓虹灯 níhóng dēng neon light

霓虹灯管 níhóng dēngguǎn neon strip

泥浆 níjiāng slime

尼龙 nílóng nylon

你们 nǐmen you pl ◊ your pl

你们的 nǐmende your pl ◊ yours pl

你们自己 nǐmén zìjǐ yourselves ◊ by yourselves

匿名 nìmíng anonymous

您 nín you polite ◊ your polite

您的 nínde your polite ◊ yours polite

宁 níng peaceful

拧 níng twist; pinch

凝 níng condense; congeal

拧出 níngchū wring out

拧干 nínggān wring dry

凝固 nínggù freeze; congeal

凝结 níngjié set; coagulate; curdle

宁静 níngjìng peace, tranquility ◊ serene; tranquil, quiet, peaceful

拧开 níngkāi unscrew lid

柠檬 níngméng lemon

柠檬茶 níngméng chá lemon tea

柠檬汽水 níngméng qìshuǐ carbonated lemonade

柠檬水 níngméng shuǐ lemonade

柠檬汁儿 níngméng zhīr lemon juice

凝视 níngshì gaze; peer; gaze at ◊ stare; gaze

宁愿 nìngyuàn would rather

泥泞 nínìng muddy

泥石流 níshí liú landslide

逆时针 nì shízhēn counterclockwise

妞 niū chick, babe

牛 niú cattle; cow; bull; ox

扭 niǔ twist

扭打 niǔdǎ scuffle; fight

扭动 niǔdòng squirm, wriggle, writhe; wiggle

牛犊 niúdú calf

牛奶 niúnǎi (cow's) milk

牛奶场 niúnǎichǎng dairy

牛奶加工 niúnǎi jiāgōng dairy

忸怩 niǔní bashful

牛排 niúpái steak

牛皮纸 niúpí zhǐ brown paper

扭曲 niǔqū screw up, contort ◊ gnarled

牛肉 niúròu beef

牛肉面 niúròumiàn beef noodles

扭伤 niǔshāng sprain, wrench

纽约 Niǔyuē New York

牛仔 niúzǎi cowboy

牛仔布 niúzǎi bù denim

牛仔裤 niúzǎikù jeans

扭转 niǔzhuǎn deflect; turn around

扭转方向 niǔzhuǎn fāngxiàng deflect

泥瓦工 níwǎgōng bricklayer

泥瓦匠 níwǎ jiàng bricklayer; mason

你自己 nǐ zìjǐ yourself

脓 nóng pus

浓 nóng thick; strong *tea etc*

农 nóng agriculture, farming; farmer; peasant ◊ agricultural

弄 nòng do; make; obtain

脓包 nóngbāo pimple

农场 nóngchǎng farm

农场工人 nóngchǎng gōngrén farmworker

弄出 nòngchū get out, extract

农村 nóngcūn village; countryside ◊ rural

弄错 nòngcuò be mistaken

弄掉 nòngdiào shift, get rid of

浓度 nóngdù depth (*of color*); level

弄短 nòngduǎn shorten

弄翻 nòngfān upset, spill

农夫 nóngfū farmer

浓厚 nónghòu dense, thick; strong

农户 nónghù farm

弄坏 nònghuài break; wear out; spoil

弄糊涂 nòng hútu muddle

浓裂 nóngliè strong

弄乱 nòngluàn mess up; be in a mess; ruffle *hair*

浓密 nóngmì bushy

农民 nóngmín farmer; peasant

弄明白 nòng míngbái work out

弄清 nòngqīng make clear

农舍 nóngshè farmhouse

弄湿 nòng shī dampen, moisten

弄死 nòngsǐ kill

弄碎 nòngsuì crumble *stock cube*

浓缩 nóngsuō concentrated

农田 nóngtián field

浓烟 nóngyān smoke

农业 nóngyè agriculture ◊ agricultural

弄脏 nòngzāng dirty, soil; smudge

弄糟 nòngzāo screw up; spoil

弄直 nòngzhí straighten

脓肿 nóngzhǒng abscess

奴 nú slave

怒 nù anger; rage

女 nǚ female; feminine

暖 nuǎn warm

暖房 nuǎnfáng hothouse; greenhouse; conservatory

暖和 nuǎnhuo warm, snug

暖瓶 nuǎnpíng flask

暖气 nuǎnqì heating; central heating; radiator

女厕 nǚcè ladies room

女厕所 nǚcèsuǒ ladies room, powder room

女店主 nǚ diànzhǔ landlady

虐待 nüèdài ill-treat, abuse ◊ ill-treatment, abuse

疟疾 nüèji malaria

女儿 nǚ'ér daughter

女服务员 nǚ fúwùyuán waitress; (chamber)maid

女孩 nǚhái girl

怒号 nùháo howl; roar

怒吼 nùhǒu howl; roar; bellow

女皇 nǚhuáng empress

女继承人 nǚ jìchéng rén heiress

女警察 nǚ jǐngchá policewoman

奴隶 núlì slave

努力 nǔlì effort, attempt; endeavor ◊ laborious ◊ struggle; work hard

努力不懈 nǔlì búxiè plug away, persevere

怒目而视 nùmù ér shì glare at

女牧师 nǚ mùshī woman priest

挪 nuó slide

挪动 nuódòng move, shift; stir (*in sleep*)

懦夫 nuòfū coward ◊ cowardly

糯米 nuòmì glutinous rice

挪威 **Nuówēi** Norway ◊
  Norwegian

诺言 **nuòyán** promise, word

女朋友 **nǚ péngyou** girlfriend (*of boy*)

女仆 **nǚpú** maid

女权 **nǚquán** women's rights

女权主义 **nǚquán zhǔyì** feminism

女权主义者 **nǚquán zhǔyì zhě** feminist

女人 **nǚrén** woman; female

女人气 **nǚrénqì** effeminate

怒容 **nùróng** scowl

女神 **nǚshén** goddess

女生 **nǚshēng** female student

怒视 **nùshì** scowl

女士 **nǚshì** lady ◊ ma'am ◊ Ms; Miss

女同性恋者 **nǚtóng xìngliàn zhě** lesbian

女王 **nǚwáng** queen

女巫 **nǚwū** witch

女性 **nǚxìng** female

女性朋友 **nǚxìng péngyou** girlfriend (*of girl*)

女婿 **nǚxù** son-in-law

女招待 **nǚzhāodài** hostess (*in bar*)

女主人 **nǚzhǔ rén** mistress (*employer, owner*); hostess

# O

噢，喔 ō (*understanding*): 噢，我 明 白 了 ō, **wǒ míngbái le** oh, I see

哦 ó (*doubt*): 哦，你 确 定 吗？ **ó, ni quèdìng ma?** really? are you sure?

鸥 ōu gull

偶 ǒu mate

藕 ǒu lotus root

殴 打 ōudǎ assault, attack

偶 尔 ǒu'ěr every now and then, occasionally ◊ occasional

欧 化 ōuhuà westernize

偶 然 ǒurán chance ◊ by chance; occasionally; 偶 然 发 现 **ǒurán fāxiàn** happen across

偶 然 性 ǒuránxìng haphazard

偶 数 ǒushù even *number*

呕 吐 ǒutù bring up, throw up ◊ vomiting; vomit

偶 像 ǒuxiàng heart throb, idol

欧 元 ōuyuán euro

欧 洲 Ōuzhōu Europe ◊ European

# P

趴 pā lie on one's stomach
爬 pá climb; crawl
耙 pá rake
怕 pà fear
啪嗒声 pādāshēng patter
拍 pāi take *photograph*; shoot *film*; beat, pound; clap; pat
牌 pái plate; board; brand; card
排 pái line, row; tier; cluster; platoon ◊ rank (*in order*); discharge, expel; 排成长龙 **páichéng chánglóng** be backed up (*of traffic*)
派 pài group; pie
排版 páibǎn typeset
陪伴 péibàn companionship
派别 pàibié group; faction; sect
排斥 páichì exclude, bar; push away
排出 páichū discharge
排出的废气 páichūde fèiqì exhaust fumes
排除 páichú eliminate; cut out; exclude; rule out ◊ removal
排除故障 páichú gùzhàng troubleshooting
派出所 pàichūsuǒ police station
排除在外 páichú zàiwài exclude; ignore
拍打 pāidǎ buffet; patter; smack
排队 páiduì stand in line
排房 páifáng row house
排放 páifàng emission
排干 páigān drain *liquid*
排骨 páigǔ chop; spare ribs
排挤 páijǐ displace
迫击炮 pǎijīpào mortar
排练 páiliàn rehearse ◊ rehearsal
排列 páiliè sort COMPUT
拍卖 pāimài auction
拍卖掉 pāimài diào auction off
拍马屁 pāi mǎpì brown-nose
排尿 páiniào urinate, pass water
拍拍 pāipāi pat *dog etc*

派遣 pàiqiǎn send
排气管 páiqìguǎn exhaust (pipe)
排球 páiqiú volleyball
排去 páiqù drain away; drain off
派人去找 pàirén qùzhǎo send for
拍摄 pāishè film, shoot; photograph
派生 pàishēng derivative
拍摄场地 pāishè chǎngdì (film) set
拍手 pāishǒu clap, applaud
排水 páishuǐ drainage
排水工程 páishuǐ gōngchéng sewerage
排水沟 páishuǐgōu gutter
排水管 páishuǐ guǎn drainpipe
派往 pàiwǎng post; transfer
排演 páiyǎn rehearse ◊ rehearsal
拍照 pāizhào photograph
牌照 páizhào vehicle registration
拍子 pāizi bat; racket; club; stick
牌子 páizi sign; nameplate; brand; make
攀 pān climb
盘 pán dish; plate; set (*in tennis*) ◊ *measure word for cassettes, CDs*
判 pàn judge
叛 pàn betray
盼 pàn hope for; expect
攀登 pāndēng climb; scramble
盘点 pándiǎn take stock ◊ stocktaking
判断 pànduàn judge; make a judgment
判断能力 pànduàn nénglì discretion, judgment
旁 páng side
胖 pàng fat
旁边 pángbiān side; 在 X 的旁边 **zài X de pángbiān** next to X, beside X
庞大 pángdà enormous
判给 pàngěi award
旁观 pángguān look on, watch

膀胱 pángguāng bladder

旁观者 pángguān zhě bystander, onlooker

胖乎乎 pànghūhū plump

庞然大物 pángrán dàwù monster

旁听 pángtīng listen in; audit *course*

滂沱 pāngtuó pouring; 大雨滂沱 dàyǔ pāngtuó pouring with rain

叛国罪 pànguó zuì treason

螃蟹 pángxiè crab

胖子 pàngzi fat person, fatso

判决 pànjué pass judgment ◊ judgment, verdict

叛乱 pànluàn mutiny

叛逆 pànnì rebel

蹒跚 pánshān hobble; lurch; totter

叛徒 pàntú traitor

盼望 pànwàng long for

盘问 pánwèn question, quiz

判刑 pànxíng sentence; pass sentence; 判死刑 pàn sǐxíng condemn to death

盘旋 pánxuán twist, wind; circle

攀缘 pānyuán climb

盘子 pánzi plate

抛 pāo throw

跑 pǎo run; run away

泡 pào bubble ◊ soak, steep; brew, infuse (*of tea*)

炮 pào cannon; gun

炮兵 pàobīng artillery

跑步 pǎobù run, jog

泡菜 pàocài pickles

泡茶 pàochá make tea

跑车 pǎochē sports car

刨出 páochū dig out; dig up

炮弹 pàodàn shell MIL

跑道 pǎodào runway; racetrack; lane

跑掉 pǎodiào run off; run away

炮火 pàohuǒ gunfire; shelling

炮击 pàojī shell MIL

跑马 pǎomǎ the races

跑马道 pǎomǎ dào racecourse

抛锚 pāomáo break down; stall (*of vehicle*); anchor (*of ship*)

泡沫 pàomò foam, froth; suds; lather

泡沫橡胶 pàomò xiàngjiāo foam rubber

泡泡糖 pàopao táng bubble gum

抛起 pāoqǐ throw up *ball*

抛弃 pāoqì abandon; leave; discard; ditch ◊ desertion

跑气 pǎoqì flat *beer*

跑腿 pǎotuǐ run errands

咆哮 páoxiào growl; roar

疱疹 pàozhěn herpes; 嘴边疱疹 zuǐbiān pàozhěn cold sore

扒手 páshǒu pickpocket

爬行 páxíng creep; crawl

爬行动物 páxíng dòngwù reptile

耙子 pázi rake

呸 pēi (*scorn*): 呸！谁要你的臭钱！pēi! shéi yào nǐde chòuqián! bah!, who needs your damn money!

陪 péi accompany, go with; escort

赔 péi pay compensation

配 pèi match, go together; 配钥匙 pèi yàoshi copy a key

陪伴 péibàn accompany

赔本 péiběn make a loss

赔偿 péicháng compensate ◊ compensation; damages

佩服 pèifu admire

配合 pèihé cooperate ◊ teamwork

配给 pèijǐ ration; 少量配给 shǎoliàng pèijǐ dole out

配给量 pèijǐ liàng ration

赔礼 péilǐ apologize

配偶 pèi'ǒu spouse

赔钱 péiqián be out of pocket

陪审团 péishěntuán jury

陪审员 péishěnyuán juror

胚胎 pēitāi embryo

陪同 péitóng escort; accompany

陪同者 péitóngzhě escort; companion; accompanist

培训 péixùn train; groom, prepare ◊ training

培训课程 péixùn kèchéng training course

培养 péiyǎng raise; develop; train; cultivate *plants*

配音 pèiyīn dub *movie*

配乐 pèiyuè soundtrack, score

培植 péizhí breeding ◊ cultivate *plants*

盆 pén bowl; plant pot; 一盆花 **yīpén huā** a potted plant

喷出 pēnchū spout, spurt

盆地 péndì basin (*geographical*)

喷发胶 pēnfà jiāo hair spray

砰 pēng thump

烹 pēng cook

棚 péng shed; stall, pen

碰 pèng touch; knock; push; bump into; meet; 别碰！**bié pèng!** hands off!

碰杯 pèngbēi clink glasses

篷车 péngchē trailer

碰钉子 pèng dīngzi get the brushoff

捧腹大笑 pěngfù dàxiào crack up, laugh

抨击 pēngjī hit out at, criticize, attack

碰见 pèngjiàn bump into, meet

蓬乱 péngluàn unkempt, dishevelled; tousled

碰碰车 pèngpèngchē bumper car, dodgem®

捧起 pěngqǐ scoop up

碰巧 pèngqiǎo by chance, coincidentally; 如果 你 碰巧见到 他 **rúguǒ nǐ pèngqiǎo jiàndào tā** if you happen to see him

烹饪书 pēngrèn shū cookbook

碰伤 pèngshāng bruise (*of fruit*)

蓬松 péngsōng fluffy

烹调 pēngtiáo cook ◊ cookery ◊ culinary

碰头 pèngtóu meet

棚屋 péngwū hut

朋友 péngyou friend

膨胀 péngzhàng expand; bulge; inflate *economy* ◊ expansion ◊ swollen; puffy

碰撞 pèngzhuàng collide

棚子 péngzi shack

喷壶 pēnhú watering can

盆景 pénjǐng bonsai

喷沫 pēnmò aerosol

喷墨（打印机）pēnmò (dǎyìnjī) inkjet (printer)

喷漆 pēnqī spray paint

喷枪 pēnqiāng spraygun

喷气发动机 pēnqì fādòngjī jet engine

喷气式 pēnqìshì jet

喷气式飞机 pēnqìshì fēijī jet plane

喷泉 pēnquán fountain

喷射 pēnshè squirt; spurt

喷嚏 pēntì sneeze

喷雾器 pēnwù qì spray

喷嘴 pēnzuǐ nozzle

劈 pī split *logs etc*

批 pī batch

披 pī put on; drape

脾 pí spleen

皮 pí skin; hide; leather; shell

癖 pí addiction; obsession

匹 pǐ *measure word for horses*; 四匹马 **sìpī mǎ** four horses

屁 pì fart; ass, butt

偏 piān leaning to one side; partial; 偏大 / 小 **piāndà / xiǎo** on the big / small side

篇 piān piece of writing ◊ *measure word for paper, books etc*; 一篇文章 **yìpiān wénzhāng** an article

骗 piàn cheat, deceive, con

片 piàn slice (*of bread etc*); stretch (*of land etc*) ◊ *measure word for slices, flat things*; 两片安眠药 **liǎngpiàn ānmiányào** two sleeping pills

偏爱 piān'ài favorite ◊ be partial to; have a soft spot for ◊ preference

偏差 piānchā difference; deviation

偏高 piāngāo sharp MUS

偏激 piānjī extreme *views*

骗计 piànjì swindle

偏见 piānjiàn prejudice; bias

骗局 piànjú deception; fraud; con; racket

片刻 piànkè moment

偏离 piānlí deviate; differ ◊ departure

片面 piànmiàn biased

篇名 piānmíng title (*of novel etc*)

偏僻 piānpì remote

偏偏 piānpiān of all people; just; 他偏偏不做 **tā piānpiān bú zuò** he just won't do it

骗取 piànqǔ defraud

偏袒 piāntǎn bias (*in favor of*) ◊ biased

偏头痛 piāntóutòng migraine

偏向 piānxiàng take sides

偏心 piānxīn prejudiced

便宜 piányi cheap; inexpensive

便宜货 piányí huò buy; bargain

片语 piànyǔ phrase

篇章 piānzhāng chapter

骗子 piànzi cheat; fraud; crook; con man

飘 piāo drift

瓢 piáo ladle

票 piào ticket

漂白剂 piǎobái jì bleach

漂泊 piāobó drift

瓢虫 piáochóng ladybug

飘荡 piāodàng drift; float

飘动 piāodòng flutter (*of flag*)

票贩子 piàofànzi scalper

漂浮 piāofú float; drift ◊ afloat

票价 piàojià fare

漂亮 piàoliang pretty, beautiful, lovely

漂亮的一举 piàoliàng de yījǔ coup, feat

票面价值 piàomiàn jiàzhí face value

瓢泼大雨 piáopō dàyǔ cloudburst

票券 piàoquàn voucher

漂洗 piǎoxǐ rinse

飘扬 piāoyáng flutter; flap; blow; fly (*of flag*)

皮包骨 píbāogǔ skinny

疲惫 píbèi exhausted

皮带 pídài leather belt

皮蛋 pídàn preserved egg

匹敌 pǐdí equal; evenly matched; 与 X 匹敌 yǔ X pǐdí match X

屁兜儿 pìdōur hip pocket

撇号 piěhào apostrophe

瞥见 piējiàn glimpse; catch a glimpse of; peek

撇去 piēqù skim *milk*

批发 pīfā wholesale

疲乏 pífá tired

批发商 pīfāshāng wholesaler

皮肤 pífū skin

批改 pīgǎi mark EDU

皮革 pígé leather

皮革制品 pígé zhìpǐn leather goods

屁股 pìgu bottom, butt

癖好 pǐhào mania, passion

披肩 pījiān shawl

僻静处 pìjìngchù hideaway

否极泰来 pǐjítàilái *prov* good luck comes after a lot of misfortune

啤酒 píjiǔ beer

啤酒厂 píjiǔchǎng brewery

啤酒花 píjiǔhuā hops

疲倦 píjuàn tire ◊ tiredness; fatigue ◊ tired; run-down; 令人疲倦 lìngrén píjuàn exhausting; 使 ... 疲倦 shǐ ... píjuàn wear out

劈开 pīkāi split

疲劳 píláo exhausted; 疲劳不堪 píláo bùkān totally exhausted

劈雳 pīlì crash (*of thunder*)

皮毛 pímáo fur, coat; skin; fleece

拼 pīn put together; spell

频 pín frequency

贫 pín poor

品 pǐn item, article

品尝 pǐncháng savor; taste, sample

拼凑 pīncòu piece together; pad *speech etc*

频道 píndào channel (*TV etc*)

品德 pǐndé virtue

频繁 pínfán frequently

瓶 píng bottle; jar

平 píng even, level; peaceful; safe; 二平 èrpíng two all

评 píng criticize

凭 píng rely on; lean on

平安 píng'ān safe ◊ safely; 平安到达 píng'ān dàodá arrive safe and sound; 平安无恙 píng'ān wúyàng unharmed

平常 píngcháng usually, normally ◊ common; conventional

平淡 píngdàn bland; tame; uneventful; flat *tone of voice*

平等 píngděng equal ◊ equality

平等主义 píngděngzhǔyì egalitarian

平底 píngdǐ flat *shoes*

平底锅 píngdǐguō frying pan; pan

平底雪橇 píngdǐ xuěqiāo toboggan

平凡 píngfán usual; normal

平方 píngfāng square MATH

平方根 píngfāng gēn square root

平放着 píng fàngzhe lie (*of object*)

平分 píngfēn share out

屏风 píngfēng partition, screen

平分球 píngfēnqiú equalizer SP

评估 pínggū evaluate, assess; take stock ◊ evaluation

苹果 píngguǒ apple

苹果酒 píngguǒ jiǔ cider

苹果派 píngguǒ pài apple pie

苹果汁儿 píngguǒ zhīr apple sauce

平衡 pínghéng balance; equilibrium ◊ balance; stabilize ◊ balanced

平衡力 pínghéng lì counterbalance

评价 píngjià assess, evaluate

平静 píngjìng quiet; calm; peaceful

平静下来 píngjìng xiàlái calm down

平局 píngjú draw, tie; deuce (*in tennis*)

凭据 píngjù evidence

平均 píngjūn average; 平均来说 *píngjūn láishuō* on average

平均水准 píngjūn shuǐzhǔn average; 高于／低于平均水准 *gāoyú / dīyú píngjūn shuǐzhǔn* above / below average

凭空 píngkōng unfounded, baseless

凭空想出 píngkōng xiǎngchū dream up

平乱警察 píngluàn jǐngchá riot police

评论 pínglùn review, write-up; commentary ◊ review; remark, comment

评论家 pínglùn jiā critic; commentator; reviewer

平面 píngmiàn plane ◊ level; graphic

平面交叉 píngmiàn jiāochā grade crossing

平面图 píngmiàntú ground plan

平民 píngmín civilian

屏幕 píngmù screen COMPUT

屏幕保护器 píngmù bǎohùqì screen saver

兵乓球 pīngpāngqiú table tennis; ping-pong

瓶塞 píngsāi cork; stopper

平时 píngshí ordinarily; usually

平台 píngtái patio

平坦 píngtǎn flat, level

平头 píngtóu crew cut

评委 píngwěi judge (*in competition*)

平稳 píngwěn smooth; steady

平息 píngxī cool down; die down; subside; appease

平行 píngxíng parallel

平行线 píngxíngxiàn parallel line

平胸 píngxiōng flat-chested

平易近人 píngyì jìnrén approachable

平庸 píngyōng commonplace; mediocre ◊ mediocrity

平庸的人 píngyōngde rén mediocrity

评语 píngyǔ comment; assessment

平原 píngyuán plain, prairie

平直 píngzhí straight; lank

平装书 píngzhuāng shū paperback, pocketbook

瓶装水 píngzhuāng shuǐ bottled water

瓶子 píngzi bottle

贫瘠 pínjí barren

聘金 pìnjīn retainer

贫困 pínkùn poor, deprived; destitute; impoverished ◊ poverty

贫困不堪 pínkùn bùkān poverty-stricken

频率 pínlǜ frequency

拼命 pīnmìng all out, like mad

贫民窟 pínmínkū slum

品牌 pǐnpái kind, variety; brand

拼盘 pīnpán cold platter

贫穷 pínqióng poor

品脱 pǐntuō pint

拼图游戏 pīntú yóuxì jigsaw (puzzle)

品位 pǐnwèi taste

拼写 pīnxiě spell

品行 pǐnxíng conduct, behavior

贫血 pínxuè anemia ◊ anemic

拼音 pīnyīn pinyin

聘用 pìnyòng hire, take on

品种 pǐnzhǒng breed

批评 pīpíng criticize ◊ criticism

脾气 píqi temperament; temper;
脾气好 *píqì hǎo* good-natured;
脾气坏 *píqì huài* bad-tempered,
ill-natured

皮箱 píxiāng suitcase

皮鞋 píxié leather shoes

癖性 pǐxìng idiosyncrasy

屁眼儿 pìyǎnr asshole

皮衣 píyī leather garment; leather
clothing

皮疹 pízhěn rash MED

批准 pīzhǔn approve, pass ◊
approval, sanction

坡 pō slope

泼 pō splash

婆 pó old woman

破 pò break ◊ broken

迫 pò force; press ◊ pressing

破冰船 pòbīngchuán icebreaker

迫不及待 pòbù jídài pressing,
urgent ◊ can't wait

破产 pòchǎn bankrupt ◊ go
bankrupt; go into liquidation; be
in receivership ◊ bankruptcy

坡道 pōdào ramp

坡顶 pōdǐng brow (*of hill*)

泼妇 pōfù bitch; dragon (*woman*)

迫害 pòhài persecute ◊
persecution

破坏 pòhuài ruin; destroy;
sabotage; corrupt COMPUT ◊
destruction; disruption; sabotage

破坏公共财产行为 pòhuài
gōnggòng cáichǎn xíngwéi
vandalism

破坏公共财产者 pòhuài
gōnggòng cáichǎn zhě vandal

破坏性 pòhuài xìng destructive;
disruptive

迫降 pòjiàng forced landing

迫近 pòjìn close in; be imminent ◊
imminent

破旧 pòjiù beat-up; worn-out; run-
down; seedy

破烂 pòlàn ragged, tattered ◊
trash, crap

破牢 pòláo break out, escape

破裂 pòliè rupture; burst ◊
rupture; bust-up ◊ broken; in
ruins; cracked

破门而入 pòmén ér rù break in

破灭 pòmiè dash, shatter *hopes*

婆婆 pópó mother-in-law (*of
woman*)

破破烂烂 pòpo lànlan in tatters

迫切 pòqiè pressing

迫切需要 pòqiè xūyào cry out
for

破伤风 pòshāngfēng tetanus

迫使 pòshǐ force

破碎 pòsuì break, smash ◊ broken

剖 pōu cut open; dissect; analyze

剖腹产 pōufùchǎn cesarean

剖面 pōumiàn profile; section

破晓 pòxiǎo daybreak, dawn

破译 pòyì crack, solve

迫在眉睫 pò zài méijié
impending

破折号 pòzhé hào dash (*in
punctuation*)

铺 pū spread; unfold; pave

谱 pǔ musical notation

普遍 pǔbiàn general, widespread;
universal

普遍存在 pǔbiàn cúnzài
pervasive

瀑布 pùbù waterfall

铺床 pūchuáng make the bed

仆从 púcóng henchman

扑动 pūdòng flutter (*of heart*)

扑粉 pūfěn powder

匍匐植物 púfú zhíwù creeper

曝光 pùguāng expose ◊ exposure

普及 pǔjí generalize; popularize ◊
widespread; universal

扑克 pūkè poker; playing cards

扑克牌 pūkèpái playing cards

铺路石板 pūlù shíbǎn paving
stone

扑灭 pūmiè extinguish

谱曲 pǔqǔ compose

仆人 púrén servant

菩萨 Púsà Bodhisattva; Buddha

铺设 pūshè pave; lay

朴素 pǔsù modest; plain, simple ◊
modesty

葡萄 pútao grape; vine

葡萄干 pútáo gān raisin

葡萄酒 **pútaojiǔ** wine
葡萄糖 **pútaotáng** glucose
葡萄牙 **Pútaoyá** Portugal ◊ Portuguese
葡萄柚 **pútaoyòu** grapefruit
葡萄柚汁 **pútaoyòu zhī** grapefruit juice
葡萄园 **pútáo yuán** vineyard
扑通 **pūtōng** splash (noise)
普通 **pūtōng** ordinary; common, standard; plain features etc

普通股 **pūtōnggǔ** equity
普通话 **Pūtōnghuà** Mandarin, Putonghua
普通邮件 **pūtōng yóujiàn** surface mail
铺位 **pùwèi** berth
普选 **pǔxuǎn** general election
溥仪 **Pǔ Yí** Pu Yi (last Emperor of China)

# Q

漆 **qī** paint
妻 **qī** wife
七 **qī** seven
期 **qī** period; issue, edition
欺 **qī** cheat, deceive
鳍 **qí** fin
旗 **qí** flag
骑 **qí** ride; pedal
齐 **qí** even; neat
其 **qí** his; her; its
启 **qǐ** open; start; enlighten
起 **qǐ** get up; 起风了 **qǐ fēng le** it's getting windy ◊ (*ability*): 买得起 **mǎi de qǐ** be able to afford
器 **qì** device; utensil; meter
汽 **qì** vapor; steam
气 **qì** air; gas; 胃肠中的气 **wèicháng zhōng de qì** wind, flatulence
迄 **qì** until; by
掐 **qiā** nip
卡 **qiǎ** jam; choke
恰当 **qiàdàng** proper, correct; appropriate; applicable
恰到好处 **qiàdào hǎochù** to perfection
恰好 **qiàhǎo** just; in the nick of time
亲爱 **qī'ài** darling
千 **qiān** thousand
铅 **qiān** lead (*metal*)
牵 **qiān** pull; lead
签 **qiān** sign
迁 **qiān** move
前 **qiān** before; in front of; ex-, former; 两天前 **liǎngtiān qián** 2 days ago; 前一个星期 **qián yīgè xīngqī** the week before
潜 **qián** dive; submerge ◊ hidden
钱 **qián** money; 我欠你多少？ **wǒ qiàn nǐ duōshǎo?** how much do I owe you?
浅 **qiǎn** shallow; light
欠 **qiàn** owe ◊ due, owed

钱包 **qiánbāo** wallet, billfold; purse
谦卑 **qiānbēi** humble
前辈 **qiánbèi** senior; elder
铅笔 **qiānbǐ** pencil
前臂 **qiánbì** forearm
浅薄 **qiānbó** shallow, superficial
前部 **qiánbù** foreground; 在 X 的前部 **zài X de qiánbù** at the front of X
潜藏 **qiáncáng** lurk
浅尝 **qiǎncháng** foretaste
虔诚 **qiánchéng** devout; pious; ardent
嵌齿轮 **qiàn chǐlún** cogwheel
前灯 **qiándēng** headlight
签订 **qiāndìng** sign; conclude *contract*
前额 **qián'é** forehead, brow
签发 **qiānfā** issue
前锋 **qiánfēng** forward SP
千分之一 **qiānfēnzhīyī** thousandth
前夫 **qiánfū** ex(-husband)
潜伏 **qiánfú** latent; potential
枪 **qiāng** gun
强 **qiáng** strong
墙 **qiáng** wall
抢 **qiǎng** rob; snatch, nab
强暴 **qiángbào** violent ◊ violently ◊ rape
墙报 **qiángbào** wall news-sheet
枪毙 **qiāngbì** shoot dead
墙壁 **qiángbì** wall
强大 **qiángdà** powerful
强盗 **qiángdào** robber; bandit
强调 **qiángdiào** emphasize, stress; accentuate
强度 **qiángdù** strength, force
抢购 **qiǎnggòu** snap up, buy
强化 **qiánghuà** intensive
强奸 **qiángjiān** rape
强奸犯 **qiángjiān fàn** rapist
抢劫 **qiǎngjié** rob; hold up ◊

robbery; holdup; raid; 我被抢劫了 **wǒ bèi qiǎngjié le** I've been robbed

抢劫犯 **qiǎngjié fàn** robber; raider

强劲 **qiángjìn** strong; virile

抢救 **qiǎngjiù** rescue; recover; save; salvage

跄踉 **qiàngliàng** stumble

强烈 **qiángliè** strong; fierce; keen ◊ intensity

谦恭 **qiāngōng** humility

钳工 **qiángōng** fitter

强迫 **qiǎngpò** coerce; compel; put pressure on

枪伤 **qiāngshāng** gunshot wound

牵挂 **qiānguà** worry about

抢先报道 **qiǎngxiān bàodào** scoop

强硬路线者 **qiángyìng lùxiàn zhě** hardliner

强有力 **qiángyǒulì** powerful

枪支 **qiāngzhī** firearm

墙纸 **qiángzhǐ** wallpaper

强制 **qiángzhì** force ◊ mandatory

强壮 **qiángzhuàng** strong; sound; hardy

前后颠倒 **qiánhòu diāndǎo** back to front

千斤顶 **qiānjīndǐng** jack MOT

前景 **qiánjǐng** view; prospects

迁就 **qiānjiù** accommodate

迁居 **qiānjū** move house ◊ move; migration

千克 **qiānkè** kilogram

潜力 **qiánlì** potential

牵连 **qiānlián** involve; 与 X 有牵连 **yǔ X yǒu qiānlián** be mixed up in X

前门 **qiánmén** front door

千米 **qiānmǐ** kilometer

前面 **qiánmiàn** front; in front; ahead; 在 X 的前面 **zài X de qiánmiàn** in front of X

签名 **qiānmíng** sign ◊ signature

前排 **qiánpái** front row

前妻 **qiánqī** ex(-wife)

牵强 **qiānqiáng** farfetched

欠缺 **qiànquē** go without; lack

前任者 **qiánrèn zhě** predecessor

潜入 **qiánrù** submerge

遣散 **qiǎnsàn** discharge

浅色 **qiǎnsè** light-colored; fair *hair*

牵涉 **qiānshè** entail

歉收 **qiànshōu** crop failure

签署 **qiānshǔ** sign

潜水 **qiánshuǐ** dive ◊ diving

潜水艇 **qiánshuǐtǐng** submarine

潜水员 **qiánshuǐyuán** diver

前所未闻 **qián suǒ wèi wén** unheard-of

潜逃车 **qiántáochē** getaway car

前提 **qiántí** prerequisite; condition

前天 **qiántiān** the day before yesterday

潜艇 **qiántǐng** submarine

前途 **qiántú** future; prospects

欠妥 **qiàntuǒ** inappropriate

前途未卜 **qiántú wèibǔ** journey into the unknown

前夕 **qiánxī** eve

前线 **qiánxiàn** front, frontline

前行 **qiánxíng** proceed

潜行 **qiánxíng** prowl

谦虚 **qiānxū** modest, unassuming

谦逊 **qiānxùn** modest, unassuming ◊ modesty

前言 **qiányán** foreword; preface

迁移 **qiānyí** move; migrate; transfer

潜意识 **qiányìshí** subconscious

签约方 **qiānyuēfāng** signatory

潜在 **qiánzài** potential

谴责 **qiǎnzé** condemn; accuse ◊ condemnation; accusation

欠债 **qiànzhài** be in debt; 欠 X 债 **qiàn X zhài** be indebted to X

千兆字节 **qiānzhào zìjié** gigabyte

前者 **qiánzhě** the former

签证 **qiānzhèng** visa

牵制 **qiānzhì** diversion

钳制 **qiánzhì** clamp down on; 钳制新闻 **qiánzhì xīnwén** muzzle the press

前缀 **qiánzhuì** prefix

签字 **qiānzì** sign *check etc*

钳子 **qiánzi** forceps; pliers; tongs

千字节 **qiānzìjié** kilobyte

前奏 **qiánzòu** overture; prelude

敲 **qiāo** knock

锹 **qiāo** spade

桥 qiáo bridge

瞧 qiáo look

巧 qiǎo skillful; coincidental

鞘 qiào sheath (*for knife*)

瞧不起 qiáobuqǐ look down on

憔悴 qiáocuì gaunt, haggard

敲打 qiāodǎ beat; drum

巧合 qiǎohé coincide ◊ coincidence

侨居 qiáojū live abroad

撬开 qiàokāi lever open

巧克力 qiǎokèlì chocolate

巧克力蛋糕 qiǎokèlì dàngāo chocolate cake

翘棱 qiáoleng warp

巧妙 qiǎomiào clever; neat; subtle

巧妙地安排 qiǎomiàode ānpái engineer, arrange

巧妙的手法 qiǎomiàode shǒufǎ sleight of hand

桥牌 qiáopái bridge (*cards*)

俏皮话 qiàopí huà quip

悄悄 qiāoqiao stealthy

跷跷板 qiāoqiāobǎn seesaw

悄然去逝 qiāorán qùshì slip away

敲响 qiāoxiǎng strike

敲诈 qiāozhà blackmail

敲钟 qiāozhōng ring

敲竹杠 qiāo zhúgàng cheat, rip off

恰恰 qiàqià exactly

恰如其分 qiàrú qífèn apt; applicable; accurate

洽商 qiàshāng negotiate

洽谈 qiàtán discuss; negotiate

卡住 qiǎzhù jam; lodge; be jammed; seize up

起搏器 qǐbóqì pacemaker MED

器材 qìcái equipment

蛴螬 qícáo grub (*of insect*)

起草 qǐcǎo draw up

起草稿 qǐ cǎogǎo draft

起草人 qǐcǎo rén draftsman

汽车 qìchē automobile

汽车道 qìchē dào driveway

汽车旅馆 qìchē lǚguǎn motel

汽车喇叭 qìchē lǎba (car) horn

启程 qǐchéng leave

启程时间 qǐchéng shíjiān departure time

汽车棚 qìchēpéng car port

汽车修理站 qìchē xiūlǐzhàn garage

汽车业 qìchē yè automobile industry

汽车站 qìchē zhàn depot, bus station

气冲冲 qìchōngchōng furious

起初 qǐchū at first

汽船 qìchuán motorboat

气喘 qìchuǎn gasp ◊ asthma; 气喘嘘嘘 qìchuǎn xūxū be out of breath

起床 qǐchuáng get up; get out of bed; 起床走动 qǐchuáng zǒudòng be up and about

其次 qícì secondly

期待 qīdài expect; look forward to

脐带 qídài umbilical cord

期待以久 qīdài yǐjiǔ overdue; long-awaited

祈祷 qídǎo pray; wish for

启迪 qǐdí enlighten

起点 qǐdiǎn starting point

气垫船 qìdiànchuán hovercraft

启动 qǐdòng boot up

起动装置 qǐdòng zhuāngzhì starter motor; trigger; record button

切 qiē cut; carve *meat*

姜 qiè concubine

窃 qiè steal

企鹅 qǐ'é penguin

怯场 qièchǎng stage fright

切成薄片 qiēchéng báopiàn slice

切成丁 qiēchéng dīng dice

切成小条 qiēchéng xiǎotiáo shred

切除 qiēchú remove; cut out

切断 qiēduàn cut off, disconnect; sever

切合实际 qièhé shíjì realistic

切开 qiēkāi incision

切口 qiēkǒu cut

切片面包 qiēpiàn miànbāo sliced bread

窃窃私语 qièqiè sīyǔ whisper

切实可行 qièshí kěxíng viable, feasible

切碎 qiēsuì chop, mince

切碎机 qiēsuìjī (document) shredder

窃听 qiètīng eavesdrop; tap

窃听器 qiètīng qì bug; 装窃听器 **zhuāng qiètīng qì** bug; tap; wire up

茄子 qiézi eggplant

起反作用 qǐ fǎn zuòyòng counterproductive

启发性 qǐfāxìng illuminating

起飞 qǐfēi take off ◊ takeoff

起飞时间 qǐfēi shíjiān flight time

气氛 qìfēn atmosphere, mood; tone

气愤 qìfèn outraged

欺负 qīfu bully, pick on

起伏 qǐfú swell (of sea)

乞丐 qǐgài beggar

汽缸 qìgāng cylinder (of engine)

漆革 qīgé patent leather

气功 qìgōng qigong (Chinese system of breath control)

奇怪 qíguài strange, odd

器官 qìguān organ

妻管严 qīguǎnyán henpecked

气管炎 qìguǎn yán bronchitis

旗鼓相当 qígǔ xiāngdāng meet one's match

启航 qǐháng sail, depart

漆黑 qīhēi pitch black

起哄 qǐhòng jeer

气候 qìhòu climate

汽化 qìhuà vaporize

汽化器 qìhuàqì carburetor

期货 qīhuò futures

期货市场 qīhuò shìchǎng futures market

奇迹 qíjī miracle ◊ miraculous

期间 qíjiān duration; 夏季期间 **xiàjì qíjiān** through the summer; 在 X 期间 **zài X qíjiān** during X

奇迹般 qíjībān miraculous

迄今 qìjīn yet, so far

骑警 qíjǐng mounted police

汽酒 qìjiǔ sparkling wine

器具 qìjù device, gadget

起居室 qǐjū shì lounge

期刊 qīkān periodical; magazine

起来 qǐlai rise, stand up ◊ (start of action): 唱起来 **chàng qǐlai** start singing

起立 qǐlì stand, rise

气轮机 qìlún jī turbine

起落架 qǐluòjià undercarriage

起落装置 qǐluò zhuāngzhì landing gear

骑马 qímǎ ride (a horse) ◊ riding ◊ on horseback

起码 qǐmǎ at least

期满 qīmǎn expire ◊ expiry

起锚 qǐmáo weigh anchor

骑马人 qímǎ rén rider

妻妹 qīmèi sister-in-law (wife's younger sister)

奇妙 qímiào wonderful

器皿 qìmǐn vessel; container

起名 qǐmíng name, call

骑摩托车的人 qí mótuōchē de rén motorcyclist

亲 qīn kiss ◊ intimate ◊ relatives

侵 qīn invade

禽 qín bird; fowl

勤 qín hardworking

亲爱 qīn'ài dear; darling; 亲爱的 王丽 **qīn'àide Wáng Lì** Dear Wang Li

亲爱的 qīn'àide darling, honey

亲笔签名 qīnbǐ qiānmíng autograph

芹菜 qíncài celery

秦朝 Qín Cháo Qin Dynasty

气馁 qìněi demoralized; 令人气馁 **lìngrén qìněi** unnerving; 使 ... 气馁 **shǐ ... qìněi** daunt

侵犯 qīnfàn encroach; breach; intrude ◊ intrusion

侵犯行为 qīnfàn xíngwéi aggression

侵犯者 qīnfàn zhě intruder

勤奋 qínfèn diligent, hard-working, industrious

氢 qīng hydrogen

轻 qīng light ◊ lightness

青 qīng green; blue; black; young

清 qīng clear; pure

倾 qīng incline

情 qíng feeling

晴 qíng sunny; clear

请 qǐng please ◊ ask; invite; 我可以请你吃顿饭吗？**wǒ kěyǐ qǐng nǐ chī dùn fàn ma?** can I invite you for a meal?; 请勿吸

烟！**qǐng wù xīyān!** no smoking, please!; 请勿打搅 **qǐngwù dǎjiǎo** please do not disturb

庆 **qìng** celebrate

清白 **qīngbái** pure; clear; flawless

情报 **qíngbào** intelligence; information; news

情报局 **qíngbàojú** intelligence service

轻便 **qīngbiàn** handy

请便 **qǐngbiàn** please yourself

轻擦 **qīngcā** dab

清仓大拍卖 **qīngcāng dà pāimài** clearance sale

清偿 **qīngcháng** settle; pay off ◊ settlement

清朝 **Qīng Cháo** Qing Dynasty

清澈 **qīngché** clear *water, eyes*

清晨 **qīngchén** early morning

清楚 **qīngchu** clear ◊ understand (clearly); 我没讲清楚 **wǒ méi jiǎng qīngchu** I didn't make myself clear

清除 **qīngchú** clear *road, table*; clean up, purge

轻触 **qīngchù** brush, touch

清除堵塞 **qīngchú dǔsè** unblock

青春 **qīngchūn** youth

青春年代 **qīngchūn niándài** youth

青春期 **qīngchūn qī** adolescent ◊ adolescence; puberty

清单 **qīngdān** checklist

氢弹 **qīngdàn** hydrogen bomb

清淡 **qīngdàn** mild; weak; plain, simple; slack *period*

清淡色 **qīngdànsè** pastel

倾倒 **qīngdào** tip over; overturn

倾倒 **qīngdào** dump

轻而薄 **qīng'érbó** flimsy

轻浮 **qīngfú** flighty

情妇 **qíngfù** mistress (*lover*)

情感 **qínggǎn** emotion; passion ◊ emotional

请假 **qǐngjià** ask for leave

请教 **qǐngjiào** ask for advice

清教徒 **qīngjiàotú** puritan

清教徒式 **qīngjiàotúshì** puritanical

清洁 **qīngjié** cleanse ◊ clean, sanitary

情节 **qíngjié** plot

清洁工 **qīngjié gōng** cleaner

清洁剂 **qīngjié jì** cleanser

清洁女工 **qīngjié nǚgōng** cleaning woman

情景 **qíngjǐng** scene, sight

情景喜剧 **qíngjǐng xǐjù** sitcom

请客 **qǐngkè** invite guests; pay

轻快 **qīngkuài** brisk; springy

情况 **qíngkuàng** circumstances, situation; scenario; 在这种情况下 **zài zhèzhǒng qíngkuàng xià** under the circumstances

晴朗 **qínglǎng** bright, fine, sunny; clear

清理 **qīnglǐ** clear out

清凉 **qīngliáng** refreshing

轻量级 **qīngliàng jí** lightweight

情侣 **qínglǚ** couple

青绿色 **qīnglǜsè** turquoise

青霉素 **qīngméisù** penicillin

轻描淡写 **qīngmiáo dànxiě** downplay

轻蔑 **qīngmiè** contempt ◊ contemptuous; 用轻蔑的口吻谈 X **yòng qīngmiède kǒuwěn tán X** pour scorn on X

清明节 **Qīngmíngjié** Tomb Sweeping Day

青年 **qīngnián** youth

青年旅社 **qīngnián lǚshè** youth hostel

青年人 **qīngnián rén** young people; young person

青年招待所 **qīngnián zhāodài suǒ** youth hostel

轻拍 **qīngpāi** pat

倾盆大雨 **qīngpén dàyǔ** downpour, cloudburst ◊ be pouring

清漆 **qīngqī** varnish

轻敲 **qīngqiāo** tap

轻轻 **qīngqīng** lightly

轻轻移动 **qīngqīng yídòng** prowl

轻轻走 **qīngqīng zǒu** pad

请求 **qǐngqiú** ask; plead

情人 **qíngrén** lover

情人节 **Qíngrénjié** Valentine's Day

清嗓子 **qīng sǎngzi** clear one's throat

青少年 qīngshàonián teenager; youngster; young people ◊ teenage

轻视 qīngshì despise; scorn; put down, belittle

情书 qíngshū love letter

轻率 qīngshuài impetuous; indiscreet ◊ indiscretion

清爽 qīngshuǎng refreshing

轻松 qīngsōng relaxed

倾诉 qīngsù pour out

清算 qīngsuàn liquidation

青苔 qīngtái moss

轻弹 qīngtán flick

晴天霹雳 qíngtiān pīlì like a bolt from the blue

请帖 qǐngtiě invitation (card)

倾听 qīngtīng listen

蜻蜓 qīngtíng dragonfly

青铜 qīngtóng bronze

轻推 qīngtuī nudge

青蛙 qīngwā frog

请问 qǐngwèn excuse me; may I ask?; 请问几点了? qǐngwèn jǐdiǎnle? excuse me, what time is it?; 请问贵姓? qǐngwèn guìxìng? may I ask your name?

清晰 qīngxī vivid

清洗 qīngxǐ rinse; flush

倾向 qīngxiàng tendency; trend; current; disposition; 有 X 的倾向 yǒu X de qīngxiàng be subject to X

倾向于 qīngxiàng yú incline toward; tend toward

轻笑 qīngxiào chuckle

清晰度 qīngxīdù clarity; resolution

倾斜 qīngxié slope; tilt; lurch; dip ◊ slanting

轻信 qīngxìn credulous

清醒 qīngxǐng awake; conscious; sober

轻型小货车 qīngxíng xiǎohuòchē pick-up (truck)

清新悦目 qīngxīn yuèmù refreshing

轻信者 qīngxìn zhě sucker

情绪 qíngxù mood; spirits ◊ sentimental; 情绪低落 qíngxù dīluò be down; 情绪好 / 坏

qíngxù hǎo / huài be in a good / bad mood; 情绪稳定 qíngxù wěndìng well-balanced

轻摇 qīngyáo rock

轻音乐 qīngyīnyuè light music

情愿 qíngyuàn prefer; 我情愿在这儿住 wǒ qíngyuàn zài zhèr zhù I'd prefer to stay here

请愿书 qǐngyuàn shū petition

晴雨表 qíngyǔ biǎo barometer; indicator

青藏高原 Qīngzàng Gāoyuán Tibetan Plateau

请找 … ? qǐngzhǎo …? can I talk to …?

清真寺 qīngzhēnsì mosque

庆祝 qìngzhù celebrate

庆祝会 qìngzhù huì celebration, party

庆祝活动 qìngzhù huódòng celebration, party

亲自动手 qīnzì dòngshǒu hands-on

轻罪 qīngzuì misdemeanor

亲和性 qīnhéxìng friendly

亲近 qīnjìn familiar ◊ affinity; 和 X 亲近 hé X qīnjìn be close to X

寝具 qǐnjù bedding

勤快 qínkuai hardworking

勤劳 qínláo hardworking

侵略 qīnlüè invade ◊ invasion; aggression

亲密 qīnmì close; intimate ◊ intimacy

勤勉 qínmiǎn hard-working

亲昵 qīnnì (sexually) intimate ◊ intimacy

钦佩 qīnpèi admire ◊ admiration; 令人钦佩 lìngrén qīnpèi admirable

亲戚 qīnqi relatives

亲切 qīnqiè kind; familiar; genial

侵入 qīnrù intrude

亲身 qīnshēn bodily; firsthand

亲生父母 qīnshēng fùmǔ biological parents

侵蚀 qīnshí erode ◊ erosion

秦始皇 Qínshǐhuáng First Emperor of China

亲手 qīnshǒu in person; with one's own hands

亲属 qīnshǔ relation

侵吞 qīntūn embezzle; misappropriate

亲吻 qīnwěn kiss

侵袭 qīnxí affect MED; strike

勤杂工 qínzá gōng (hospital) orderly

侵占 qīnzhàn encroach on; overrun

亲自 qīnzì in person; personally

穷 qióng poor

穷困潦倒 qióngkùn liáodǎo down-and-out

穷人 qióngrén the poor; poor person

穷乡僻壤 qióngxiāng pìrǎng hick town ◊ out in the boonies

穷凶极恶 qióngxiōng jí'è enormity

棋盘 qípán board; chessboard

旗袍 qípáo qipao, cheongsam (high-necked Chinese dress with side slits)

起泡 qìpào carbonated

气泡 qìpào bubble

起泡沫 qǐ pàomò frothy

漆皮 qīpí patent leather

欺骗 qīpiàn deceive; delude; doublecross; trick ◊ deceit; deception; fraud; hoax; trickery

欺骗性 qīpiànxìng fraudulent

漆器 qīqì lacquerware

乞求 qǐqiú bum; cadge; 跟 Y 乞求 X gēn Y qǐqiú X cadge X from Y

气球 qìqiú balloon

崎岖 qíqū rugged

齐全 qíquán complete

弃权 qìquán abstain ◊ abstention

骑上 qíshàng mount

祈神赐福 qíshén cìfú blessing

七十 qīshí seventy

骑师 qíshī jockey

祈使 qíshǐ imperative

歧视 qíshì discriminate against ◊ discrimination

启示 qǐshì message

漆刷 qīshuā paintbrush

汽水 qìshuǐ carbonated mineral water; carbonated drink

起水疱 qǐ shuǐpào blister

起诉 qǐsù sue; bring an action

against, prosecute ◊ prosecution

其他 qítā other (of people)

其它 qítā other (of things)

其他的 qítāde the others (people)

其它的 qítāde the others (things)

奇谈 qítán yarn, story

乞讨 qǐtǎo beg

奇特 qítè original; unique; strange; curious

奇特服装 qítè fúzhuāng fancy dress

气体 qìtǐ gas

汽艇 qìtǐng motor boat

企图 qìtú try, attempt

起推进作用 qǐ tuījìn zuòyòng propellant

秋 qiū fall, autumn

球 qiú ball

求 qiú implore, beseech

囚 qiú imprison ◊ prisoner

囚车 qiúchē patrol wagon

球队 qiúduì team (for ball game)

囚犯 qiúfàn prisoner; convict

秋分 qiūfēn autumn equinox

球杆 qiúgān cue (for pool); club (for golf)

球棍 qiúgùn bat

求婚 qiúhūn propose ◊ proposal

球茎 qiújīng bulb

求救 qiújiù call for help

求救信号 qiújiù xìnhào distress signal

丘陵 qiūlíng hill

球拍 qiúpāi bat; racket

秋千 qiūqiān swing

球体 qiútǐ sphere

秋天 qiútiān fall, autumn

蚯蚓 qiūyǐn earthworm

球员 qiúyuán soccer player; player

丘疹 qiūzhěn spot

球座 qiúzuò tee

期望 qīwàng hope for; expect ◊ prospect; expectation

气味 qìwèi smell, odor

气温 qìwēn temperature

栖息 qīxī perch

期限 qīxiàn deadline; time limit

气象 qìxiàng weather

气象学 qìxiàngxué meteorology ◊ meteorological

气象学家 qìxiàngxuéjiā meteorologist

气象预报员 qìxiàng yùbàoyuán weatherman

栖息处 qīxīchù perch

栖息地 qīxīdì habitat

器械 qìxiè apparatus; appliance

气压 qìyā air pressure

气压表 qìyā biǎo barometer

企业 qìyè enterprise

企业家 qìyèjiā entrepreneur

起义 qǐyì uprising

奇异的事物 qíyìde shìwù marvel

汽油 qìyóu gasoline, gas

汽油泵 qìyóubèng gas pump

其余 qíyú the remainder, the rest

起于 qǐyú result from

起源 qǐyuán be derived from; stem from ◊ origin, beginning

七月 qīyuè July

契约 qìyuē contract; deed

气质 qìzhí charisma

其中 qízhōng among; among which; of which

起重机 qǐzhòng jī crane; hoist

妻子 qīzi wife

妻姊 qīzǐ sister-in-law (wife's elder sister)

旗子 qízi flag

棋子 qízǐ man, piece (in chess etc)

骑自行车 qí zìxíngchē cycle, ride ◊ cycling

骑自行车的人 qí zìxíngchē de rén cyclist

区 qū district; zone

蛆 qū maggot

曲 qū curved

取 qǔ take; fetch; get

曲 qǔ tune; song; music

去 qù go; 去 X 的火车 qù X de huǒchē a train for X; 到 X 去有多远？ dào X qù yǒu duōyuǎn? how far is it to X?; 去你的！ qùnǐde! go to hell!

圈 quān ring, circle; lap; circuit; loop

拳 quán fist ◊ punch

泉 quán spring; stream

权 quán right; power; authority

全 quán whole; entire

犬 quǎn dog

劝 quàn persuade

全部 quánbù all; entire

全部付清 quánbù fùqīng pay up; pay in full

全部湿透 quánbù shītòu dripping (wet)

全长 quáncháng full-length

劝导 quàndǎo teach; advise; instruct

鬈发 quánfà curl; curly hair

蜷伏 quánfú snuggle down

劝告 quàngào advise, counsel

颧骨 quángǔ cheekbone

全国人大 Quánguó Réndà National People's Congress, NPC

权衡 quánhéng weigh up

拳击 quánjī box ◊ boxing; fight

全集 quánjí collected

拳击比赛 quánjī bǐsài boxing match

拳击场 quánjī chǎng ring

全景 quánjǐng panorama ◊ panoramic

拳击手 quánjī shǒu boxer, fighter

权力 quánlì power, authority

权利 quánlì right

全面 quánmiàn comprehensive; overall; all-round

全民所有制 quánmín suǒyǒuzhì national property; property of the people

全能者 Quánnéng zhě the Almighty

全球 quánqiú global

全球经济 quánqiú jīngjì global economy

全球气温升高 quánqiú qìwēn shēnggāo global warming

全球市场 quánqiú shìchǎng global market

拳曲 quánqū curl (up) ◊ curly

全权 quánquán power of attorney; full powers

全权代表 quánquán dàibiǎo authorized representative

全人类 quánrénlèi all humankind

全日 quánrì full-time

全日制 quánrìzhì full-time

全盛期 quánshèngqī heyday

全神贯注于 quánshén guànzhù yú engrossed in

全世界 quánshìjiè worldwide

全食宿 quán shísù full board

泉水 quánshuǐ spring water

劝说 quànshuō persuade ◊ persuasion

蜷缩 quánsuō writhe; double up; curl up; cower; 蜷缩在一起 quánsuō zài yìqǐ huddle together

圈套 quāntào trap; snare; noose; 设圈套 shè quāntào trap; set up

全体 quántǐ all; whole ◊ totality; 全体选民 quántǐ xuǎnmín electorate

拳头 quántou fist

权威 quánwēi authority

权威性 quánwēi xìng classic; definitive; authoritative

全心全意 quánxīn quányì whole-hearted

全息图 quánxītú hologram

痊愈 quányù recuperate; convalesce

劝止 quànzhǐ dissuade

圈子 quānzi circle

劝阻 quànzǔ advise against; 劝阻 X不要去做Y quànzǔ X bùyào qù zuò Y dissuade X from doing Y

区别 qūbié distinguish, discriminate between ◊ distinction; 区别好坏 qūbié hǎohuài know right from wrong

驱车离开 qūchē líkāi drive away; drive off

龋齿 qǔchǐ cavity

驱虫剂 qūchóng jì repellent

驱除 qūchú remove; drive out; boot out

取出 qǔchū take out, extract

驱除出境 qūchú chūjìng deport ◊ deportation

驱除舰 qūchú jiàn destroyer

驱除令 qūchú lìng deportation order

取代 qǔdài substitution; 用X取代Y yòng X qǔdài Y substitute X for Y

渠道 qúdào drain

取得 qǔdé gain; achieve; acquire; obtain

曲调 qǔdiào tune

去掉 qùdiào remove; get rid of

驱动 qūdòng drive; 四轮驱动 sìlún qūdòng all-wheel drive

驱动器 qūdòngqì disk drive

缺 quē lack; miss

瘸 qué lame

雀 què sparrow

雀斑 quèbān freckle

缺点 quēdiǎn disadvantage; weakness, shortcoming

确定 quèdìng confirm, make certain; be sure

确定不变 quèdìng búbiàn fixed

缺乏 quēfá absence; deficiency; shortage ◊ lack; be short of

缺口 quēkǒu niche

缺钱 quēqián hard up

确切 quèqiè exact

确认 quèrèn confirm

缺少 quēshǎo lack

确实 quèshí really; actually

缺席 quēxí absent ◊ absence

缺陷 quēxiàn defect; downside

确信 quèxìn be convinced ◊ certainty, conviction; 使 … 确信 shǐ … quèxìn assure

确证 quèzhèng validate

瘸子 quézi cripple

区分 qūfēn differentiate between; tell the difference between; 区分 X和Y qūfēn X hé Y distinguish between X and Y

屈服 qūfú give in; succumb; knuckle under

驱赶 qūgǎn repel; chase away; dispel

躯干 qūgàn trunk

去骨 qùgǔ bone

去国者 qùguó zhě exile

区号 qūhào area code

取回 qǔhuí pick up

曲解 qūjiě misinterpret ◊ misinterpretation

曲径 qūjìng maze

取景器 qǔjǐng qì viewfinder

取决于 qǔjuéyú depend on

取款机 qǔkuǎn jī ATM, cash machine

取乐 qǔlè have fun

群 qún group; crowd; flock; cluster; 一群人 **yìqún rén** a crowd of people

裙 qún skirt

区内电话 qūnèi diànhuà local call

去年 qùnián last year

取暖 qǔnuǎn warm up

取暖器 qǔnuǎn qì radiator

群众 qúnzhòng the masses

裙子 qúnzi skirt

去皮 qùpí skin

曲奇 qǔqí cookie

驱散 qūsàn break up; disperse

趋势 qūshì tendency, trend

去世 qùshì pass away, die ◊ demise

躯体 qūtǐ body

去污剂 qùwū jì stain remover

取下 qǔxià take down; take off

曲线 qūxiàn curve

趋向 qūxiàng trend

取消 qǔxiāo cancel; revoke ◊ cancellation

取笑 qǔxiào deride; mock, send up ◊ derision; banter

区域 qūyù region, area

取悦 qǔyuè ingratiate oneself with

曲折 qūzhé twist

曲折行进 qūzhé xíngjìn zigzag

取之不尽 qǔ zhī bù jìn inexhaustible

曲轴 qūzhóu crankshaft

驱逐 qūzhú expel; deport; kick out ◊ expulsion

屈尊 qūzūn deign to

# R

燃 **rán** burn; ignite

染 **răn** color; dye

然而 **rán'ér** but, however; nonetheless; though

染发 **rănfà** dye one's hair

让 **ràng** let, allow; give way; make, cause; 让他进来 **ràng tā jìnlái** let him come in; 让我走! **ràng wǒ zǒu!** let me go!; 让人听懂 **ràng ren tīng dǒng** get through, make oneself understood; 让 X 等 **ràng X děng** keep X waiting

让步 **ràngbù** give way, capitulate; relent ◊ concession

让路 **rànglù** yield, give way

嚷嚷 **rāngrang** yell

让位 **ràngwèi** step down

然后 **ránhòu** then; next; afterward

燃料 **ránliào** fuel

染料 **rănliào** dye

染色 **rănsè** color; dye; stain; tint

染色剂 **rănsè jì** (wood) stain

染上 **rănshàng** catch

燃烧 **ránshāo** burn ◊ combustion

燃烧弹 **ránshāodàn** incendiary device

绕 **rào** around

绕道 **ràodào** go around; detour

绕道行驶 **ràodào xíngshǐ** detour

绕杆 **ràogān** turnstile

绕过 **ràoguò** bypass

扰乱 **răoluàn** disrupt ◊ disruption

扰频 **răopín** scramble

饶舌者 **ráoshé zhě** chatterbox

绕行 **ràoxíng** round

惹 **rě** start; cause; provoke; 惹麻烦 **rě máfan** cause trouble; play up; 惹人喜爱 **rě rén xǐ'ài** sweet, cute

热 **rè** hot; warm ◊ heat ◊ warm up

热爱 **rè'ài** love passionately

热忱 **rèchén** enthusiastic; hearty

热诚 **rèchéng** fervent

热带 **rèdài** tropics ◊ tropical

热带地区 **rèdài dìqū** tropics

热带雨林 **rèdài yǔlín** tropical rain forest

热点 **rèdiǎn** hot spot

热浪 **rèlàng** heatwave

热恋 **rèliàn** have a crush on ◊ madly in love; passionate

热烈 **rèliè** enthusiastic; heated discussion; wild applause

热门 **rèmén** popular; sought-after; blue chip

人 **rén** person; human being; people; man ◊ used to form nationality words: 法国人 **Făguó rén** Frenchman; Frenchwoman; the French

忍 **rěn** endure

认 **rèn** recognize; 认不出来了 **rèn bū chūlái le** beyond recognition

刃 **rèn** blade

任 **rèn** task; mission; term ◊ take responsibility

惹恼 **rěnǎo** exasperate

热闹 **rènao** exciting; lively ◊ hustle and bustle

忍不住 **rěnbúzhù**: 我忍不住 **wǒ rěnbúzhù** I can't help it

人称代词 **rénchēng dàicí** personal pronoun

认出 **rènchū** recognize, know; pick out

仁慈 **réncí** clemency; humanity; mercy; philanthropy ◊ kind; merciful; philanthropic

韧带 **rèndài** ligament

人道 **réndào** humane ◊ humanity

人道主义者 **réndào zhǔyì zhě** humanitarian

认得 **rènde** recognize

认定 **rèndìng** be sure of; identify

扔 **rēng** throw; throw away; drop; dump

仍 **réng** still, yet

扔掉 rēngdiào get rid of, dispose of; throw away ◊ disposal

人格 réngé personality

人工 réngōng man-made, artificial

人工呼吸器 réngōng hūxī qì respirator

人工流产 réngōng liúchǎn abortion

人工智能 réngōng zhìnéng artificial intelligence

仍然 réngrán still; 她可能仍然会来 tā kěnéng réngrán huìlái she might still come

扔下 rēngxià leave behind; 扔下 X 不管 rēngxià X bùguǎn turn one's back on X

任何 rènhé any; whatever; whichever

任何东西 rènhé dōngxi anything

任何人 rènhé rén anybody

人际罕至 rénjì hǎnzhì secluded

认可 rènkě acknowledgement

人口 rénkǒu population; 人口密集 rénkǒu mìjí densely populated

人类 rénlèi human race, man, mankind ◊ human

人类丧失免疫力病毒 rénlèi sàngshī miǎnyìlì bìngdú HIV

人类资源 rénlèi zīyuán human resources

人力 rénlì labor; manpower

人力车 rénlìchē rickshaw

人们 rénmen people, folk

人民 rénmín the people

人民币 rénmínbì renminbi, RMB

人民大会堂 Rénmín Dàhuìtáng Great Hall of the People

人民代表大会 Rénmín Dàibiǎo Dàhuì People's Congress

任命 rènmìng appointment; nomination ◊ appoint; designate

人民公社 Rénmín Gōngshè People's Commune

人民解放军 Rénmín Jiěfàngjūn People's Liberation Army

人民日报 Rénmín Rìbào People's Daily

忍耐 rěnnài endure

忍耐力 rěnnàilì endurance

任期 rènqī term of office

人权 rénquán human rights

人群 rénqún crowd, throng

参人参 rénshēn ginseng

人生 rénshēng (human) life

认生 rènshēng be afraid of strangers

认识 rènshi know; get to know; recognize; 很高兴认识你 hěn gāoxìng rènshí nǐ pleased to meet you; 她认识汉字 tā rènshí Hànzì she can read Chinese characters

人事部 rénshìbù personnel (department)

人事部主任 rénshìbù zhǔrèn personnel manager

人世间 rénshìjiān the world ◊ earthly

忍受 rěnshòu accept; put up with, bear

人寿保险 rénshòu bǎoxiǎn life insurance

人体模型 réntǐ móxíng mannequin, dummy (for clothes)

认同 rèntóng approve of

惹怒 rěnù irritate

认为 rènwéi consider; believe, think; feel; 我不认为如此 wǒ bú rènwéi rúcǐ I don't think so; 认为有能力做 rènwéi yǒu nénglì zuò feel up to

人物 rénwù figure, personality; character (in book)

任务 rènwù assignment, mission; job, task

任务钮 rènwùniǔ task button

人性 rénxìng human ◊ humanity

任性 rènxìng headstrong

人行道 rénxíngdào sidewalk

人行横道 rénxíng héngdào (pedestrian) crosswalk

人烟稀少 rényān xīshǎo sparsely populated

任意 rènyì arbitrary

任意而为 rènyì ér wéi indiscriminate

任一个 rèn yígè either; any

任意球 rènyì qiú free kick

人员 rényuán personnel, staff

人造 rénzào artificial, man-made, synthetic

人造黄油 rénzào huángyóu margarine

人造卫星 rénzào wèixīng satellite

忍着 rěnzhe stifle, repress

认真 rènzhēn serious; earnest; conscientious ◊ in earnest; religiously

人质 rénzhì hostage; 被扣作人质 bèi kòuzuò rénzhì be taken hostage

人种 rénzhǒng race

认罪书 rènzuì shū confession

热切 rèqiè eager

热起来 rèqǐlái warm up

热情 rèqíng enthusiastic; warm; passionate ◊ warmth; enthusiasm; zest; passion

热气球 rè qìqiú balloon

热水袋 rèshuǐdài hot-water bottle

热水瓶 rèshuǐpíng vacuum flask

热死了 rè sǐle scorching hot

热腾腾 rè téngteng red-hot

热心 rèxīn enthusiastic; warm-hearted ◊ eagerness; zeal

热心肠 rèxīncháng warmhearted

热衷于 rèzhōng yú be wild about; 热衷于做 X rèzhōng yú zuò X be eager to do X

热中者 rèzhōngzhě enthusiast

日 rì sun; day

日报 rìbào daily paper

日本 Rìběn Japan ◊ Japanese

日本人 Rìběn rén Japanese

日常 rìcháng everyday; daily

日出 rìchū sunrise

日光 rìguāng daylight

日光灯 rìguāngdēng fluorescent light

日晷 rìguǐ sundial

日记 rìjì diary; journal

日间服 rìjiānfú day wear

日历 rìlì calendar

日落 rìluò sunset

日期 rìqī date

日晒肤色 rì shài fūsè tan

日蚀 rìshí eclipse

日语 Rìyǔ Japanese (language)

日元 rìyuán yen FIN

日志 rìzhì logbook

绒 róng down (feathers)

容 róng contain; tolerate ◊ face

溶 róng dissolve

荣 róng honor

融 róng melt; meld; merge; 融为一体 róng wéi yìtǐ integrate

冗长 rǒngcháng lengthy

融和 rónghé blend in

熔合 rónghé fusion

融化 rónghuà melt; thaw ◊ molten

熔化 rónghuà smelt

熔毁 rónghuǐ melt down

容积 róngjī volume

溶解 róngjiě dissolve

容积量 róngjī liàng cubic capacity

容量 róngliàng volume; capacity

熔流 róngliú torrent

熔炉 rónglú melting pot

绒毛 róngmáo down (on bird)

容貌 róngmào feature

绒面革 róngmiàngé suede

容纳 róngnà hold, contain

容器 róngqì container

融洽 róngqià peaceable; 与 X 关系融洽 yǔ X guānxi róngqià be friendly with X

容忍 róngrěn tolerate, stand for

荣幸 róngxìng privilege ◊ privileged

容许 róngxǔ permit, allow; tolerate

溶液 róngyè solution

容易 róngyì easy; effortless ◊ ease

容易饱人 róngyì bǎorén filling

容易上口 róngyì shàngkǒu catchy

荣誉 róngyù glory; honor; kudos

柔 róu soft; gentle

揉 róu knead; rub

鞣 róu tan

肉 ròu meat

柔道 róudào judo

肉店 ròudiàn butcher shop

肉冠 ròuguàn crest

肉桂 ròuguì cinnamon

柔和 róuhé soft; mild; subdued; mellow

肉麻 ròumá nauseating

肉末 ròumò ground meat

柔懦情调 róunuò qíngdiào

sentimentality

柔懦情感 **róunuò qínggǎn** sentiment

柔软 **róuruǎn** soft; supple

肉体 **ròutǐ** flesh

肉丸子 **ròuwánzi** meatball

肉馅 **ròuxiàn** mincemeat

肉眼 **ròuyǎn** naked eye

肉欲 **ròuyù** lust; sensuality

肉汁 **ròuzhī** gravy

如 **rú** like; as; if

乳 **rǔ** breast; milk; gel

辱 **rǔ** disgrace

入 **rù** enter

乳癌 **rǔ'ái** breast cancer

软 **ruǎn** soft; tender ◊ tenderness

软磁盘 **ruǎn cípán** diskette

软膏 **ruǎngāo** ointment; balm

软骨 **ruǎngǔ** gristle

软管 **ruǎnguǎn** hose

软件 **ruǎnjiàn** software

软木 **ruǎnmù** cork (*wood*)

软木塞 **ruǎnmùsāi** cork (*stopper*)

软盘 **ruǎnpán** floppy disk

软驱 **ruǎnqū** floppy drive

软弱 **ruǎnruò** weak

软卧 **ruǎnwò** soft sleeper (*on train*); first-class sleeping car

软性饮料 **ruǎnxìng yǐnliào** soft drink

软座 **ruǎnzuò** soft seat

入场费 **rùchǎngfèi** entrance fee

如此 **rúcǐ** thus, in this way; 我希望如此 **wǒ xīwàng rúcǐ** I hope so

入店行窃 **rùdiàn xíngqiè** shoplifter

蠕动 **rúdòng** squirm, writhe

乳房 **rǔfáng** breast

如果 **rúguǒ** if

如画 **rúhuà** picturesque

蚋 **ruì** gnat

锐 **ruì** sharp

锐不可当 **ruì bù kě dāng** inexorable; irresistible

瑞典 **Ruìdiǎn** Sweden ◊ Swedish

锐利 **ruìlì** piercing

瑞士 **Ruìshì** Switzerland ◊ Swiss

儒家 **Rújiā** Confucianism

如今 **rújīn** nowadays; at present, currently

入境 **rùjìng** enter *country*

入境签证 **rùjìng qiānzhèng** entry visa

入口 **rùkǒu** way in, entrance; inlet

辱骂 **rǔmà** abuse

入迷 **rùmí** be fascinated; be spellbound

润 **rùn** moist ◊ profit

润肤膏 **rùnfūgāo** moisturizer

润肤霜 **rùnfūshuāng** moisturizer

润喉糖 **rùnhóu táng** throat lozenges

润滑 **rùnhuá** lubricate ◊ lubrication

润滑剂 **rùnhuá jì** lubricant

润滑油箱 **rùnhuá yóuxiāng** sump

闰年 **rùnnián** leap year

润色 **rùnsè** polish

弱 **ruò** weak

若 **ruò** if ◊ like

弱点 **ruòdiǎn** weakness

若干 **ruògān** some; a number

弱小 **ruòxiǎo** puny

弱者 **ruòzhě** weakling

入神 **rùshén** be engrossed; be entranced

入室抢劫 **rùshì qiǎngjié** housebreaking

乳霜 **rǔshuāng** cream

入睡 **rùshuì** fall asleep

如同 **rútóng** just like; 如同往常 **rútóng wǎngcháng** as usual

乳头 **rǔtóu** nipple; teat

如下 **rúxià** the following ◊ as follows; see below

入乡随俗 **rùxiāngsuísú** *prov* when in Rome …

乳牙 **rǔyá** milk tooth

如意 **rúyì** hunky-dory

如愿 **rúyuàn** as planned; as hoped

乳罩 **rǔzhào** brassière

乳制品 **rǔzhì pǐn** dairy products

乳猪 **rǔzhū** sucking pig

# S

撒 sǎ scatter; sprinkle
洒 sǎ sprinkle; spill
撒旦 Sādàn Satan
撒谎 sāhuǎng fib, lie
塞 sāi cram; jam; plug; squeeze in; stick in; 把 X 塞入 Y 手中 **bǎ X sāirù Y shǒu zhōng** thrust X into Y's hands
腮 sāi cheek
赛 sài competition; race
赛车 sàichē racing car
赛车运动员 sàichē yùndòngyuán racing driver
塞进 sāijìn tuck
赛马 sàimǎ horse race
赛跑 sàipǎo race (on foot)
赛跑者 sàipǎo zhě runner
腮腺炎 sāixiànyán mumps
塞住 sāizhù clog up; 塞住… 的嘴 **sāizhù … de zuǐ** gag
塞子 sāizi plug, stopper
萨克斯管 sàkèsīguǎn saxophone
三 sān three
伞 sǎn umbrella
散 sǎn scattered; loose
散 sàn spread; distribute; disseminate
三八妇女节 Sānbā Fùnǚjié Women's Day
三胞胎 sānbāotāi triplets
三倍 sānbèi treble
伞兵 sǎnbīng paratrooper
散步 sànbù stroll ◊ take a stroll
散布 sànbù spread
三重唱 sān chóng chàng trio
三等仓 sāndǐngcāng third-class cabin
散发 sànfā distribute
丧 sāng mourning; 穿丧服 **chuān sāngfú** wear mourning
桑 sāng mulberry
丧 sàng lose
丧礼 sānglǐ funeral service
丧命 sàngmìng die

桑拿浴 sāngnáyù sauna
丧失 sàngshī loss ◊ forfeit; 使丧失名誉 **shǐ sàngshī míngyù** discredit
丧失志气 sàngshī zhìqì demoralized
桑树 sāngshù mulberry tree
三国 Sānguó Three Kingdoms
嗓音 sǎngyīn voice ◊ vocal
嗓子 sǎngzi throat
撒尿 sāniào pee, piss
三脚架 sānjiǎojià tripod
三角裤 sānjiǎo kù briefs
三角形 sānjiǎo xíng triangle ◊ triangular
伞菌 sǎnjūn toadstool
散开 sànkāi scatter
三轮车 sānlúnchē tricycle; pedicab
三明治 sānmíngzhì sandwich
三色堇 sānsèjǐn pansy
三十 sānshí thirty
散文 sǎnwén prose
三峡 Sānxiá Three Gorges
三心二意 sānxīn èryì half-hearted
三月 sānyuè March
搔 sāo scratch
扫 sǎo sweep; drag
扫除 sǎochú root out
搔动 sāodòng commotion
扫雷艇 sǎoléi tǐng minesweeper
扫拢 sǎolǒng sweep up
骚乱 sāoluàn commotion; turmoil; trouble; disturbances
扫描 sǎomiáo scan
扫描器 sǎomiáoqì scanner MED
扫描仪 sǎomiáoyí scanner COMPUT
扫灭 sǎomiè mow down
骚扰 sāorǎo harass; molest ◊ harassment
扫射 sǎoshè burst (of gunfire)
扫视 sǎoshì glance; glance at; scan

扫兴 **sǎoxìng** be disappointed

搔痒 **sāoyǎng** scratch, have a scratch

扫帚 **sàozhou** broom

嫂子 **sǎozi** sister-in-law (*older brother's wife*)

撒手 **sāshǒu** release one's grip, let go; back out

撒种 **sǎzhǒng** sow *seeds*

涩 **sè** sharp, tart; tight

色 **sè** color

色彩 **sècǎi** color, tone

色彩设计 **sècǎi shèjì** color scheme

色度 **sèdù** shade

色鬼 **sèguǐ** womanizer

色拉 **sèlā** salad

色狼 **sèláng** wolf, womanizer

色盲 **sèmáng** color-blind

森林 **sēnlín** forest

森林学 **sēnlínxué** forestry

色情 **sèqíng** pornographic; erotic

色情作品 **sèqíng zuòpǐn** pornography

刹 **shā** brake

沙 **shā** sand

鲨 **shā** shark

杀 **shā** kill, slay

砂 **shā** sand

纱 **shā** thread, yarn

傻 **shǎ** dumb, dim; brainless; silly

纱布 **shābù** gauze

刹车 **shāchē** brake; skid ◊ brakes

刹车灯 **shāchē dēng** stoplight

刹车踏板 **shāchē tàbǎn** brake pedal

杀虫剂 **shāchóngjì** pesticide; insecticide

沙袋 **shādài** sandbag

沙丁鱼 **shādīngyú** sardine

沙发 **shāfā** sofa

沙发床 **shāfā chuáng** sofa bed

傻瓜 **shǎguā** idiot, moron

杀害 **shāhài** kill; murder

筛 **shāi** sift

晒 **shài** put out in the sun ◊ too sunny

晒斑 **shàibān** sunburn

晒黑 **shài hēi** tan ◊ tanned

晒伤 **shàishāng** burn ◊ sunburnt

晒太阳 **shài tàiyáng** sunbathe; bask

筛子 **shāizi** sieve

色子 **shāizi** dice

砂浆 **shājiāng** mortar

沙坑 **shākēng** sandpit

砂砾 **shālì** grit

沙龙 **shālóng** salon

杀戮 **shālù** slaughter

沙漠 **shāmò** desert

山 **shān** mountain; mount

闪 **shǎn** flash

疝 **shàn** hernia

扇 **shàn** fan ◊ *measure word for doors and windows*; 两扇窗 **liǎngshàn chuāng** two windows; 给自己扇风 **gěi zìjǐ shānfēng** fan oneself

善 **shàn** good; kind-hearted

刹那 **shànà** instant

擅长 **shàncháng** be good at, excel at

删除 **shānchú** delete; erase; take out ◊ deletion

闪电 **shǎndiàn** lightning; flash of lightning

闪电般 **shǎndiànbān** in a flash

山地车 **shāndìchē** mountain bike

山顶 **shāndǐng** peak, summit

煽动 **shāndòng** incite; rouse; stir up; 煽动 X 做 Y **shāndòng X zuò Y** incite X to do Y

闪动 **shǎndòng** flicker

山东半岛 **Shāndōng Bàndǎo** Shandong Peninsula

煽动者 **shàndòng zhě** agitator

山峰 **shānfēng** peak, summit

伤 **shāng** hurt; strain ◊ wound

商 **shāng** business; quotient ◊ commercial

赏 **shǎng** reward

上 **shàng** on; at the top; up ◊ get on, board; 上车 **shàng chē** get on the bus/train; 在屋顶上 **zài wūdǐng shang** up on the roof

删改 **shāngǎi** censor

上岸 **shàng'àn** go ashore

伤疤 **shāngbā** scar

上班 **shàngbān** go to work; be at work; 我坐公车去上班 **wǒ zuò gōngchē qù shàngbān** I go to work by bus

上臂 **shàngbì** upper arm

商标 **shāngbiāo** brand name; trademark

商标概念 **shāngbiāo gàiniàn** brand image

上部 **shàngbù** top part, upper part

上菜 **shàng cài** serve (the food)

上层 **shàngcéng** upper

上层社会 **shàngcéng shèhuì** upper class

商场 **shāngchǎng** department store; bazaar

上场 **shàngchǎng** enter (of actors)

上车 **shàngchē** get on a train/bus/bicycle

上船 **shàngchuán** go aboard (a ship)

上床 **shàngchuáng** go to bed, turn in; 和 … 上床 **hé … shàngchuáng** go to bed with …

上等货 **shàngděnghuò** top-quality goods

上等阶层 **shàngděng jiēcéng** upper classes

上帝 **Shàngdì** God

商店 **shāngdiàn** shop; store

上吊 **shàngdiào** hang oneself

商定 **shāngdìng** agree; arrange

上发条 **shàng fātiáo** wind up

上飞机 **shàng fēijī** board a plane

伤风 **shāngfēng** catch a cold

伤感情 **shānggǎnqíng** hurt (emotionally)

伤害 **shānghài** wound; injury; bruise ◊ injure

上海 **Shànghǎi** Shanghai

伤寒 **shānghán** typhoid (fever)

商会 **shānghuì** chamber of commerce

上火车 **shàng huǒchē** board a train

上机 **shàngjī** log on

上级 **shàngjí** boss; superior

上交 **shàngjiāo** hand over

伤口 **shāngkǒu** wound; injury; cut

上来 **shànglái** board

商量 **shāngliang** discuss

上流 **shàngliú** high-class

上流社会 **shàngliú shèhuì** high society

上面 **shàngmian** top ◊ at the top ◊ up ◊ upper

伤脑筋 **shāng nǎojīn** annoying; frustrating

上年纪 **shàng niánjì** elderly, getting on in years; 他上了年纪 **tā shàngle niánjì** he's getting on

上牌 **shàngpái** register

商品 **shāngpǐn** commodity; goods

商品陈列室 **shāngpǐn chénlièshì** showroom

商品券 **shāngpǐn quàn** token

商品特色 **shāngpǐn tèsè** selling point

上坡 **shàngpō** uphill

上去 **shàngqù** come up; go up ◊ up

商人 **shāngrén** businessman; dealer; merchant; trader

伤人感情 **shāngrén gǎnqíng** cutting

上色 **shàngshǎi** brown (in cooking)

上身 **shàngshēn** upper body

上升 **shàngshēng** rise; climb

赏识 **shǎngshí** have great respect for

上市 **shàngshì** on the market ◊ launch

上述 **shàngshù** above-mentioned

上水 **shàngshuǐ** upstream

上司 **shàngsi** boss, chief

上诉 **shàngsù** appeal

商谈 **shāngtán** discuss, kick around

商讨 **shāngtǎo** discuss

上调 **shàngtiáo** push up

山谷 **shāngǔ** valley

闪光 **shǎnguāng** glisten

闪光灯 **shǎnguāngdēng** flash; flashlight

闪光指示灯 **shǎnguāng zhǐshìdēng** flasher MOT

闪光装置 **shǎnguāng zhuāngzhì** flare

上网 **shàngwǎng** log on; go on-line ◊ on-line

伤亡人士 **shāngwáng rénshì** casualties

上午 **shàngwǔ** morning ◊ in the morning; 上午好 **shàngwǔ hǎo** good morning

商务舱 shāngwù cāng business class

上相 shàngxiàng photogenic

上校 shàngxiào colonel

上下文 shàngxià wén context

伤心 shāngxīn sad; broken-hearted; heartrending ◊ distress;

令人伤心 lìngrén shāngxīn upsetting; depressing; disheartening

伤心事 shāngxīn shì sorrow

上学 shàngxué go to school

上演 shàngyǎn perform, put on

商业 shāngyè business; commerce ◊ commercial

上夜班 shàng yèbān work nights

商业化 shāngyè huà commercialize

商业会议 shāngyè huìyì business meeting

商业秘密 shāngyè mìmì trade secret

商业午餐 shāngyè wǔcān business lunch

商业信用书 shāngyè xìnyòng shū letter of credit

商业学 shāngyè xué business studies

商业学校 shāngyè xuéxiào business school

上衣 shàngyī top (clothing)

上一次 shàng yīcì last ◊ last time

上瘾 shàngyǐn be addicted to

上映 shàngyìng show

上游 shàngyóu upper reaches of a river

伤员 shāngyuán casualty

上闸 shàngzhá put the brakes on

上涨 shàngzhǎng rise; go up

珊瑚 shānhú coral

闪回 shǎnhuí flashback

山脊 shānjí ridge

闪开 shǎnkāi dodge

闪亮 shǎnliàng flash

善良 shànliáng generous; kind

山麓小丘 shānlù xiǎoqiū foothills

山脉 shānmài mountain range

山猫 shānmāo lynx

山毛榉 shānmáo jǔ beech

山坡 shānpō hill; hillside

山穷水尽 shānqióng shuǐjìn be at the end of one's tether

山区 shānqū mountainous area

删去 shānqù delete

山雀 shānquè tit (bird)

闪闪发光 shǎnshǎn fāguāng glitter

闪烁 shǎnshuò flash; glint; blink ◊ gleam

膳宿 shànsù board with

山头 shāntóu mountain top

善行 shànxíng goodness

山羊 shānyáng goat

赡养 shànyǎng support

赡养费 shànyǎng fèi alimony

闪耀 shǎnyào sparkle; twinkle; glare

善意 shànyì goodwill

善于 shànyú be good at

山楂 shānzhā haw (berry)

擅自 shànzì unauthorized

扇子 shànzi fan

擅自占地者 shànzì zhàndì zhě squatter

擅自占用 shànzì zhànyòng squat

烧 shāo burn; fry

稍 shāo slightly; 稍醉 shāo zuì slightly drunk, tipsy

勺 sháo spoon; 两勺糖 liǎng sháo táng two spoonfuls of sugar

少 shǎo few; less ◊ lack, be without; 少吃／说 shǎo chī／shuō eat／talk less

哨 shào whistle

少 shào young

哨兵 shàobīng sentry

少不得 shǎobude essential, indispensable

烧断 shāoduàn blow (of fuse)

烧毁 shāohuǐ burn down

烧焦 shāojiāo burn; singe ◊ charred

烧开 shāokāi boil

少量 shǎoliàng small amount ◊ meager

少男 shàonán teenage boy

少年 shàonián young person (in early teens)

少年犯 shàoniánfàn juvenile

delinquent

少年犯罪 **shàonián fànzuì** juvenile delinquency

少女 **shàonǚ** teenage girl

烧伤 **shāoshāng** burn

少数 **shǎoshù** few ◊ minority

少数几个 **shǎoshù jǐgè** few

少数民族 **shǎoshù mínzú** ethnic minority

稍微 **shāowēi** a little; some ◊ slightly; marginally

少校 **shàoxiào** major MIL

稍许 **shāoxǔ** a little

少许 **shāoxǔ** a little

少有 **shǎoyǒu** infrequent

少于 … **shǎoyú** … fewer than …

烧着 **shāozhe** burn; catch fire

哨子 **shàozi** whistle

杀气腾腾 **shāqì téngténg** murderous

沙丘 **shāqiū** (sand) dune

杀人犯 **shārénfàn** murderer

沙色 **shāsè** sandy color

沙沙声 **shāshāshēng** rustle

杀死 **shāsǐ** kill

沙滩 **shātān** sandy beach

砂糖 **shātáng** granulated sugar

沙特阿拉伯 **Shātè'Ālābó** Saudi (Arabia) ◊ Saudi

纱线 **shāxiàn** yarn, thread

傻笑 **shǎxiào** giggle; titter

沙哑 **shāyǎ** rough; husky *voice*

沙岩 **shāyán** sandstone

鲨鱼 **shāyú** shark

砂纸 **shāzhǐ** sandpaper

砂质土壤 **shāzhì tǔrǎng** sandy soil

傻子 **shǎzi** dope, idiot

蛇 **shé** snake

舌 **shé** tongue

社 **shè** society

设 **shè** set up, establish

射 **shè** shoot

设备 **shèbèi** equipment

设备齐全 **shèbèi qíquán** self-contained

射程 **shèchéng** range

奢侈 **shēchǐ** extravagant; luxurious; magnificent ◊ extravagance

社工 **shègōng** social worker

社会 **shèhuì** society ◊ social

社会工作 **shèhuì gōngzuò** social work

社会习俗 **shèhuì xísú** convention

社会学 **shèhuì xué** sociology

社会渣滓 **shèhuì zhāzǐ** the dregs of society

社会主义 **shèhuì zhǔyì** socialism ◊ socialist

社会主义者 **shèhuì zhǔyì zhě** socialist

谁 **shéi** who; 谁是第一个？ **shéi shì dìyīgè?** who's first please?

谁的 **shéide** whose

射击 **shèjī** fire, shoot ◊ gunshot

涉及 **shèjí** involve; concern ◊ reference

设计 **shèjì** design; plan; create

社交 **shèjiāo** social interaction ◊ socialize

社交礼节 **shèjiāo lǐjié** social niceties

射击声 **shèjīshēng** shot

设计师 **shèjì shī** designer

设计失误 **shèjì shīwù** design fault

设计图 **shèjìtú** plan; design

设计学院 **shèjì xuéyuàn** design school

设计者 **shèjì zhě** creator

设立 **shèlì** set up, establish

社论 **shèlùn** editorial

蛇麻草 **shémácǎo** hop (*plant*)

赦免 **shèmiǎn** pardon; amnesty ◊ absolve

深 **shēn** deep ◊ dearly *love*; 深绿／蓝 **shēn lǜ / lán** dark green / blue

身 **shēn** body

伸 **shēn** stretch; 伸长脖子 **shēncháng bózi** crane one's neck

神 **shén** god; deity ◊ divine; spiritual

肾 **shèn** kidney

渗 **shèn** seep; leak

深奥 **shēn'ào** deep; mysterious; baffling

申辩 **shēnbiàn** defend oneself

身材 **shēncái** build; figure

审查 **shēnchá** check; examine;

review

审查制度 shěnchá zhìdù censorship

深沉 shēnchén deep

申斥 shēnchì reprimand

伸出 shēnchū jut out, stick out; hold out

渗出 shènchū ooze

深度 shēndù depth

身分 shēnfen identity; status

身份的象征 shēnfènde xiàngzhēng status symbol

身分证 shēnfenzhèng identity card

身分证明 shēnfen zhèngmíng identification

生 shēng give birth to; grow; live ◊ raw; unripe; ... 有点儿生了 ... *yǒudiǎnr shēng le* ... is a little rusty

升 shēng rise; hoist ◊ liter

声 shēng sound

绳 shéng cord; rope

省 shěng province ◊ provincial

盛 shèng height ◊ flourishing, prosperous

剩 shèng remain, be left over; 没剩什么 *méishèng shénme* there is nothing left

胜 shèng win ◊ victory

圣 shèng saint; sage

身高 shēngāo height

声辩 shēngbiàn protest

生病 shēngbìng fall ill, be taken ill ◊ sick

声部 shēngbù part

生菜叶 shēngcài yè lettuce

生产 shēngchǎn produce; output ◊ childbirth; production

生产耗资 shēngchǎn chéngběn production costs

生产力 shēngchǎnlì productivity

生产能力 shēngchǎn nénglì production capacity

生产线 shēngchǎn xiàn production line

生产者 shēngchǎn zhě manufacturer

声称 shēngchēng claim; profess

生成 shēngchéng generate

牲畜 shēngchù stock; livestock

生存 shēngcún exist; live ◊ existence; being

声带 shēngdài vocal cords

圣诞节 Shèngdàn Jié Christmas; Christmas Day

圣诞卡 Shèngdàn kǎ Christmas card

圣诞快乐！Shèngdàn kuàilè! Merry Christmas!

圣诞老人 Shèngdàn Lǎorén Santa Claus

圣诞礼物 Shèngdàn lǐwù Christmas present

圣诞树 Shèngdàn shù Christmas tree

圣诞夜 Shèngdàn Yè Christmas Eve

圣地 shèngdì sanctuary

声调 shēngdiào tone of voice; ring

省掉 shěngdiào spare

生动 shēngdòng vivid; graphic; lifelike

升高 shēnggāo raise

胜过 shèngguò outdo; eclipse

生孩子 shēng háizi give birth

省会 shěnghuì provincial capital

生活 shēnghuó live ◊ life

生活水平 shēnghuó shuǐpíng standard of living

生活方式 shēnghuò fāngshì way of life

生活费用 shēnghuó fèiyòng cost of living

生活史 shēnghuó shǐ life history

生活水准 shēnghuó shuǐzhǔn standard of living

升级 shēngjí escalation

生计 shēngjì livelihood; keep

圣经 Shèngjīng the Bible

声卡 shēngkǎ sound card

盛开 shèngkāi in full bloom

牲口 shēngkou livestock

生来 shēnglái genetically ◊ inborn; 他生来如此 *tā shēnglái rúcǐ* it's in his genes

胜利 shènglì victory, win ◊ victorious; 胜利的喜悦 *shènglì de xǐyuè* triumph

圣灵 Shènglíng Holy Spirit

胜利者 shènglì zhě victor

省略 **shěnglüè** leave out, omit

生闷气 **shēng mènqì** sulk; brood ◊ sulky

生面团 **shēngmiàn tuán** dough

声明 **shēngmíng** declare; state ◊ declaration; statement

生命 **shēngmìng** life

声名 **shēngmíng** reputation

声名败坏 **shēngmíng bàihuài** disreputable

声名狼籍 **shēngmíng lángjí** notorious

申明缘由 **shēnmíng yuányóu** justify *text*

盛年 **shèngnián** prime of one's life

生啤酒 **shēng píjiǔ** draft (beer)

举起 **shēngqǐ** hoist

升起 **shēngqǐ** rise; be up (*of sun*)

生气 **shēngqì** annoy; be annoyed; get worked up; 令人生气 *lìngrén shēngqì* infuriating; 使 X 生气 *shǐ X shēngqì* make X angry; 跟 X 生气 *gēn X shēngqì* be angry with X

生气勃勃 **shēngqì bóbó** spirited; energetic

升起来 **shēng qǐlái** come up

省却 **shěngquè** dispense with

圣人 **shèngrén** saint; sage

胜任 **shèngrèn** be equal to, be able to manage; 我觉得自己不能胜任 *wǒ juédé zìjǐ bùnéng shèngrèn* I don't feel up to it

生日 **shēngrì** birthday; 生日快乐! *shēngrì kuàilè!* happy birthday!

升入 **shēngrù** soar (*of rocket*)

生手 **shēngshǒu** greenhorn

生疏 **shēngshū** rusty *subject*

声嘶力竭 **shēngsī lìjié** strident

生态 **shēngtài** ecology ◊ ecological

生态平衡 **shēngtài pínghéng** ecological balance

生态系统 **shēngtài xìtǒng** ecosystem

生态学 **shēngtàixué** ecology

生态学家 **shēngtài xuéjiā** ecologist

圣坛 **shèngtán** altar

生铁 **shēngtiě** cast iron

圣徒 **shèngtú** saint

深谷 **shēngǔ** ravine

声望 **shēngwàng** popularity; reputation; standing

生物 **shēngwù** being; organism ◊ biological

生物工艺学 **shēngwù gōngyì xué** biotechnology

生物学 **shēngwù xué** biology

生息 **shēngxī** yield

剩下 **shèngxia** be left, remain; 有五个剩下 *yǒu wǔgè shèngxià* there were five to spare

盛夏 **shèngxià** height of summer

声响 **shēngxiǎng** sound

圣像 **shèngxiàng** icon

生效 **shēngxiào** take effect; come into force; 使 … 生效 *shǐ … shēngxiào* validate

生肖 **shēngxiào** *the twelve animals of the Chinese horoscope*

盛行 **shèngxíng** prevailing

生锈 **shēngxiù** rust ◊ rusty

生涯 **shēngyá** career

盛宴 **shèngyàn** feast; spread

生意 **shēngyì** business; trade

声音 **shēngyīn** sound; noise; voice

生硬 **shēngyìng** abrupt, brusque; brisk

生意兴隆 **shēngyì xīnglóng** busy

生育 **shēngyù** bear *child*

声誉 **shēngyù** reputation; renown, fame

剩余 **shèngyú** surplus; remainder, rest ◊ be over, be left

声誉不好 **shēngyù bùhǎo** disreputable

剩余收入 **shèngyú shōurù** disposable income

生长 **shēngzhǎng** grow

升值 **shēngzhí** revalue

生殖 **shēngzhí** reproduce

生殖器 **shēngzhíqì** genitals

绳子 **shéngzi** cord

审核 **shěnhé** audit

深红色 **shēnhóng sè** dark red; crimson

深厚 **shēnhòu** deep, profound

神话 **shénhuà** myth

神话故事 **shénhuà gùshì** fairy tale

神话学 **shénhuà xué** mythology

深呼吸 **shēn hūxī** breathe deeply

审计 **shěnjì** audit

伸脚空间 **shēnjiǎo kōngjiān** leg room

肾结石 **shènjiéshí** kidney stone

神经 **shénjīng** nerve ◊ screwed up

神经崩溃 **shénjīng bēngkuì** nervous breakdown

神经病 **shénjīng bìng** mental illness ◊ crazy

神经病学家 **shénjīngbìng xuéjiā** neurologist

神经过敏 **shénjīng guòmǐn** neurotic

神经机能病 **shénjīng jīnéng bìng** neurosis

神经性 **shénjīng xìng** nervous

神经质 **shénjīng zhì** neurotic

审计师 **shěnjì shī** auditor

伸开四肢 **shēnkāi sìzhī** sprawl

神龛 **shénkān** shrine

深刻 **shēnkè** deep; 给人以深刻印象 **gěi rén yǐ shēnkè yìnxiàng** impressive, which makes a deep impression

伸懒腰 **shēn lǎnyāo** stretch

渗漏 **shènlòu** leak; drip; seep out

什么 **shénme** what ◊ anything; 什么事? **shénme shì?** what is it?; 那是什么? **nà shì shénme?** what is that?; 我没听见什么 **wǒ méi tīngjiàn shénme** I didn't hear anything; 什么时候还给我? **shénme shíhou huángěi wǒ?** when can I have it back?; 什么也不缺 **shénme yě bùquē** want for nothing

神秘 **shénmì** mysterious; occult

申明 **shēnmíng** declare, profess; protest

深明真相 **shēnmíng zhēnxiàng** penetrating

审判 **shěnpàn** try ◊ trial

审判室 **shěnpàn shì** courtroom

神奇 **shénqí** supernatural

深切 **shēnqiè** profound

申请 **shēnqǐng** apply for; put in for ◊ application

申请表格 **shēnqǐng biǎogé** application form

申请人 **shēnqǐng rén** applicant; claimant

深入 **shēnrù** deep ◊ in depth

渗入 **shènrù** sink in

深深 **shēnshēn** profoundly; head over heels; 深深地爱上 X **shēnshen de àishàng X** fall madly in love with X

审慎 **shěnshèn** prudent; scrupulous ◊ prudence

神圣 **shénshèng** holy, sacred ◊ sanctity

绅士 **shēnshì** gentleman

审视 **shěnshì** survey

身势语 **shēnshì yǔ** body language

伸手 **shēnshǒu** stretch

深思 **shēnsī** ponder

申诉 **shēnsù** lodge a complaint ◊ complaint

伸缩 **shēnsuō** flexible; stretchy

身体 **shēntǐ** body ◊ physical; 身体不好 **shēntǐ bùhǎo** be in poor health

身体上 **shēntǐ shang** physically

神童 **shéntóng** (infant) prodigy

身为人父 **shēnwéi rénfù** fatherhood

审问 **shěnwèn** question

审问者 **shěnwèn zhě** interrogator

身陷困境 **shēnxiàn kùnjìng** deep trouble

神学 **shénxué** theology

审讯 **shěnxùn** examine; hear ◊ hearing; inquest

深夜 **shēnyè** in the dead of night

呻吟 **shēnyín** groan; moan

深渊 **shēnyuān** abyss

深远 **shēnyuǎn** far-reaching

深造 **shēnzào** continue one's education

伸展 **shēnzhǎn** stretch; extend; spread

伸展四肢 **shēnzhǎn sìzhī** stretch

甚至 **shènzhì** even; to the extent that

神志不清 **shénzhì bùqīng** stupor ◊ in a stupor

神志清醒 **shénzhì qīngxǐng** lucid ◊ lucidity

神职人员 shénzhí rényuán clergy

神志正常 shénzhì zhèngcháng sane ◊ sanity

慎重 shènzhòng careful

舍弃 shěqì abandon

赊欠 shēqiàn credit FIN

社区 shèqū community

设施 shèshī facilities

摄氏 shèshì Celsius; centigrade; 摄氏十度 *shèshì shídù* 10 degrees centigrade

射手 shèshǒu marksman

舌舔 shétiǎn lick

舌头 shétóu tongue

社团 shètuán society, organization

设想 shèxiǎng conceive of; visualize ◊ assumption

摄像机 shèxiàng jī video camera; camcorder

摄影 shèyǐng photography

摄影棚 shèyǐng péng studio

摄影师 shèyǐng shī photographer; cameraman

摄远镜头 shèyuǎn jìngtóu telephoto lens

设置 shèzhì locate

射中 shèzhòng shoot

诗 shī poem; verse; poetry

湿 shī wet; damp

师 shī master

狮 shī lion

失 shī lose

施 shī carry out

尸 shī corpse

十 shí ten

实 shí real; solid

识 shí know; recognize

石 shí stone

时 shí time; hour; 十八岁时 *shíbāsuì shí* at the age of 18; 午夜时 *wǔyèshí* at midnight

食 shí food ◊ eat

屎 shǐ feces, shit

史 shǐ history

使 shǐ cause; make; 使 ... 吃亏 *shǐ ... chīkuī* put at a disadvantage; 使 ... 不高兴 *shǐ ... bù gāoxìng* displease; 使 ... 尴尬 *shǐ ... gāngà* embarrass

始 shǐ begin, start

事 shì matter, affair

是 shì be ◊ yes; 是，我知道 *shì, wǒ zhīdào* yes, I know

室 shì room

市 shì city; market

式 shì type; style

试 shì try; 试做 X *shì zuò X* have a try at X

示 shì show; indicate

视 shì see; watch; 视 ... 而定 *shì ... érdìng* conditional on ...

誓 shì vow

势 shì power

氏 shì family name

十八 shíbā eighteen

失败 shībài fail; lose ◊ failure; defeat

失败者 shībài zhě loser

失败主义 shībài zhǔyì defeatism ◊ defeatist

饰板 shìbǎn plaque

施暴虐 shī bàonüè tyrannize

饰边 shìbiān frill; fringe

事变 shìbiàn incident

识别 shíbié recognize; distinguish

士兵 shìbīng soldier; private; the ranks

时差 shíchā time difference

视察 shìchá inspect ◊ inspection

时差反应 shíchā fǎnyìng jetlag

失常 shīcháng unbalanced; abnormal

时常 shícháng frequently, often

市场 shìchǎng market; marketplace

市场调查 shìchǎng diàochá market survey

市场经济 shìchǎng jīngjì market economy

市场力量 shìchǎng lìliàng market forces

市场占有率 shìchǎng zhànyǒulǜ market share

市场主导 shìchǎng zhǔdǎo market leader

试车 shìchē test drive; trial run

世仇 shìchóu feud

驶出 shìchū pull out (of train, ship)

试穿 shìchuān try on

视窗 shìchuāng window

时代 **shídài** age, era; generation

实弹 **shídàn** live ammunition

适当 **shìdàng** proper, appropriate, suitable ◊ properly; duly

食道 **shídào** gullet

使得 **shǐde** so; so that ◊ make; cause

是的 **shìde** yes; that's right

实得工资 **shídé gōngzī** take-home pay

湿度 **shīdù** humidity

适度 **shìdù** moderate ◊ mildly; moderately; in moderation

十二 **shí'èr** twelve, dozen

视而不见 **shì'ér bújiàn** blind to

十二分之一 **shí'èr fēn zhīyī** twelfth

十二月 **shí'èryuè** December

示范 **shìfàn** demonstrate ◊ demonstration, demo

示范碟 **shìfàn dié** demo disk

释放 **shìfàng** release, free

施肥 **shīféi** fertilize

是否 **shìfǒu** whether or not

师傅 **shīfu** master

石膏 **shígāo** plaster

石膏绷带 **shígāo bēngdài** plaster cast

诗歌 **shīgē** poem; poetry

施工工地 **shīgōng gōngdì** construction site

石工技巧 **shígōng jìqiǎo** masonry (skill)

尸骨 **shīgǔ** skeleton

事故 **shìgù** accident; crash; 在事故中丧生 **zài shìgù zhōng sàngshēng** be killed in an accident

使馆 **shǐguǎn** embassy

试管 **shìguǎn** test tube

试管婴儿 **shìguǎn yīng'ér** test-tube baby

嗜好 **shìhào** hobby; addiction; 有吸毒嗜好 **yǒu xīdú shìhào** be on drugs

适合 **shìhé** suit; fit; be in accordance with; 适合于 X **shìhé yú X** be cut out for X

事后 **shìhòu** subsequent ◊ subsequently, afterward

石灰 **shíhuī** lime

失火 **shīhuǒ** fire ◊ catch fire

实际 **shíjì** real, actual; practical; substantive

世纪 **shìjì** century

时间 **shíjiān** time; while; interlude; 请再给我一些时间？ **qǐng zài gěi wǒ yìxiē shíjiān?** can I have more time?; 时间自会定论 **shíjiān zì huì dìnglùn** time will tell

实践 **shíjiàn** practice

事件 **shìjiàn** event, happening; incident; business

时间安排 **shíjiān ānpái** timing

时间表 **shíjiān biǎo** timetable

时刻表 **shíkè biǎo** schedule

时间段 **shíjiānduàn** sitting

时间范围 **shíjiān fànwéi** timescale

时间间隔 **shíjiān jiàngé** time-lag

时间顺序 **shíjiān shùnxù** chronological

市郊 **shìjiāo** suburbs

施加压力 **shījiā yālì** put pressure on

世界 **shìjiè** world

世界大战 **shìjiè dàzhàn** world war

世界地图 **shìjiè dìtú** map of the world; atlas

世界观 **shìjièguān** world view

世界冠军 **shìjiè guànjūn** world champion

世界记录 **shìjiè jìlù** world record

世界强国 **shìjiè qiángguó** world power

世界性 **shìjiè xìng** cosmopolitan

世界著名 **shìjiè zhùmíng** world-famous

什锦 **shíjǐn** mixed; miscellaneous

试镜 **shìjìng** screen test

实际上 **shíjì shàng** actually, in fact; in practice

十几岁 **shíjǐ suì** be in one's teens

十九 **shíjiǔ** nineteen

诗句 **shījù** verse

视觉 **shìjué** vision ◊ visual; 视觉上来说 **shìjué shàng láishuō** visually

势均力敌 **shìjūn lìdí** evenly matched

时刻 **shíkè** moment ◊ constantly

时刻表 **shíkèbiǎo** schedule

蚀刻术 **shíkèshù** etching

石窟 **shíkū** grotto

实况 **shíkuàng** live

实况转播 **shíkuàng zhuǎnbō** live transmission

湿冷 **shīlěng** cold and damp

失利 **shīlì** lose out

实力 **shílì** strength

势力 **shìlì** strength, power

视力 **shìlì** sight, eyesight, vision

势利 **shìlì** snobbish

失恋 **shīliàn** be jilted

势力范围 **shìlì fànwéi** sphere of influence

失灵 **shīlíng** out of order; dead ◊ malfunction; jam ◊ be down

石榴 **shíliu** pomegranate

十六 **shíliù** sixteen

势利眼 **shìliyǎn** snob

时髦 **shímáo** fashionable

失眠 **shīmián** insomnia

市民 **shìmín** city dweller

失明 **shīmíng** go blind

使命 **shǐmìng** mission; vocation

室内 **shìnèi** indoors; inside

室内设计 **shìnèi shèjì** interior design

室内设计者 **shìnèi shèjì zhě** interior designer

十年 **shínián** decade

施虐狂 **shīnüèkuáng** sadism

失陪 **shīpéi** please excuse me

食品 **shípǐn** food

视频 **shìpín** video COMPUT

食品杂货业 **shípǐn záhuò yè** grocery business

识破 **shípò** see through

食谱 **shípǔ** recipe; cookbook

十七 **shíqī** seventeen

时期 **shíqī** term; period

拾起 **shíqǐ** lift, pick up

士气 **shìqì** morale

史前 **shǐqián** prehistoric

事情 **shìqíng** issue; matter

失去 **shīqù** lose; 失去控制 **shīqù kòngzhì** lose control; 失去知觉 **shīqù zhījué** lose consciousness

时区 **shíqū** time zone

拾取 **shíqǔ** pick up

市区 **shìqū** city area

湿热 **shīrè** humid

诗人 **shīrén** poet; 抒情诗人 **shūqíng shīrén** lyric poet

使人 **shǐrén** *causative:* 使人困乏 **shǐrén kùnfá** wearing, tiring; 使人兴奋 **shǐrén xīngfèn** exciting

食肉动物 **shíròu dòngwù** carnivore; predator

湿软 **shīruǎn** swampy

湿润 **shīrùn** moisture ◊ moist; soggy

失散 **shīsàn** stray

十三 **shísān** thirteen

时尚 **shíshàng** fashion

失身 **shīshēn** lose one's virginity

失声 **shīshēng** let out a cry

失势 **shīshì** fall from power

失事 **shīshì** have an accident

实施 **shíshī** implement; execute ◊ execution

实时 **shíshí** real time

时事 **shíshì** current affairs, current events

史诗 **shǐshī** epic

试试 **shìshi** try; 让我试试 **ràng wǒ shìshi** can I have a try?

事实 **shìshí** fact; truth

适时 **shìshí** well-timed

逝世 **shìshì** pass away

实事求是 **shíshì qiúshì** practical; down-to-earth

事实上 **shìshí shang** indeed, as a matter of fact

时事讨论节目 **shíshì tǎolùn jiémù** current affairs program

尸首分离 **shīshǒu fēnlí** decapitate

十四 **shísì** fourteen

时速 **shísù** speed

世俗 **shìsú** worldly; secular

失算 **shīsuàn** miscalculate

时态 **shítài** tense

食堂 **shítáng** cafeteria; canteen

食糖 **shítáng** sugar

尸体 **shītǐ** corpse, cadaver

失调 **shītiáo** disorder

视听 **shìtīng** audiovisual

湿透 **shītòu** soaked ◊ be wet through

石头 **shítou** stone

试图 **shìtú** attempt

室外 **shìwài** outdoors; outside ◊ outdoor

世外桃源 **shìwài táoyuán** oasis *fig*

失望 **shīwàng** be disappointed ◊ disappointment ◊ disappointed; 令人失望 **lìngrén shīwàng** disappointing ◊ dismay; 使 ... 失望 **shǐ ... shīwàng** disappoint; 让 X 失望 **ràng X shīwàng** let X down

视网膜 **shìwǎngmó** retina

示威 **shìwēi** demonstration, protest ◊ demonstrate

示威游行 **shìwēi yóuxíng** demonstration

示威者 **shìwēi zhě** demonstrator, protester

失误 **shīwù** mistake, error

十五 **shíwǔ** fifteen

食物 **shíwù** food; diet

事务 **shìwù** concern; affair

食物搅拌器 **shíwù jiǎobànqì** food mixer

史无前例 **shǐ wú qiánlì** unprecedented

事物 **shìwù** thing

失物招领处 **shīwù zhāolǐng chù** lost-and-found (office)

食物中毒 **shíwù zhòngdú** food poisoning

实习 **shíxí** work as an intern ◊ internship

世袭 **shìxí** hereditary; inherited

实现 **shíxiàn** fulfill; realize; come true ◊ realization

事先 **shìxiān** beforehand ◊ prior

事先形成 **shìxiān xíngchéng** preconceived

实习护士 **shíxí hùshi** student nurse

实习教师 **shíxí jiàoshī** student teacher

时新 **shíxīn** fashionable, stylish

实行 **shíxíng** implement, carry out

失信 **shīxìn** go back on one's word, break one's promise

实习期 **shíxí qī** trial period

实习生 **shíxí shēng** trainee

失修 **shīxiū** in a state of disrepair; run-down; derelict

世袭遗产 **shìxí yíchǎn** heritage

实验 **shíyàn** experiment

誓言 **shìyán** oath, vow

试演 **shìyǎn** audition

试验 **shìyàn** test; experiment; trial; 试验 X **shìyàn X** have X on trial; test X

试验方案 **shìyàn fāng'àn** pilot scheme

试样 **shìyàng** sample

式样 **shìyàng** style; type

试验期 **shìyàn qī** trial period

试验区 **shìyàn qū** pilot plant

使眼色 **shǐ yǎnsè** wink

实验室 **shíyàn shì** lab, laboratory

实验室技师 **shíyàn shì jìshī** laboratory technician

失业 **shīyè** unemployed, out of work ◊ unemployment

视野 **shìyě** vision; outlook; 使视野开阔 **shǐ shìyě kāikuò** broaden one's mind; 在 X 视野之内 **zài X shìyě zhī nèi** within sight of X

事业 **shìyè** undertaking; career

实业家 **shíyèjiā** industrialist

失业者 **shīyè zhě** unemployed

诗意 **shīyì** poetic

十一 **shíyī** eleven

十亿 **shíyì** billion

适宜 **shìyí** appropriate, suitable

释义 **shìyì** paraphrase

示意 **shìyì** sign, signal; 他示意我前行 **tā shìyì wǒ qiánxíng** he motioned me forward

石英 **shíyīng** quartz

适应 **shìyìng** adapt; acclimate, acclimatize; adjust

侍应生 **shìyìng shēng** busboy

石英钟 **shíyīng zhōng** quartz clock

十一月 **shíyíyuè** November

食用 **shíyòng** consume

实用 **shíyòng** practical; useful

使用 **shǐyòng** apply, use, employ; access

适用 **shìyòng** applicable ◊ apply

试用 **shìyòng** probation ◊ try out

试用期 **shìyòng qī** probation period

使用时间 **shǐyòng shíjiān** access time

使用说明书 shǐyòng shuōmíng shū instruction manual

实用主义 shíyòng zhǔyì pragmatism

石油 shíyóu oil; petroleum

食油 shíyóu cooking oil

石油公司 shíyóu gōngsī oil company

石油化学产品 shíyóu huàxué chǎnpǐn petrochemical

石油输出国组织 Shíyóu Shūchūguó Zǔzhī OPEC, Organization of Petroleum Exporting Countries

食欲 shíyù appetite

十月 shíyuè October

誓约 shìyuē vow

适于 shìyú: 适于居住 *shìyú jūzhù* habitable, inhabitable; 适于青年 *shìyú qīngnián* youthful *fashion, music*; 适于远航 *shìyú yuǎnháng* seagoing

实在 shízài real ◊ really

施展 shīzhǎn unfold, develop; display

市长 shìzhǎng mayor

使者 shìzhě envoy

侍者 shìzhě bellhop

湿疹 shīzhěn eczema

市镇 shìzhèn urban

实证 shízhèng testament

市政 shìzhèng municipal

市政厅 shìzhèng tīng city hall

食指 shízhǐ forefinger, index finger

实质 shízhì essence; substance

实质上 shízhì shang substantially

始终 shǐzhōng from start to finish

始终不渝 shǐzhōng bù yú consistent ◊ consistently

市中心 shì zhōngxīn down-town ◊ city center

施主 shīzhǔ benefactor

时装 shízhuāng fashion

时装表演 shízhuāng biǎoyǎn fashion show

时装商店 shízhuāng shāngdiàn boutique

时装设计师 shízhuāng shèjìshī fashion designer

时装展览 shízhuāng zhǎnlǎn collection

狮子 shīzi lion

虱子 shīzi louse

师资 shīzī teachers

柿子 shìzi persimmon

十字架 shízìjià cross, crucifix

十字路口 shízì lùkǒu crossroads; intersection

狮子舞 shīziwǔ lion dance

失踪 shīzōng missing ◊ disappearance

十足 shízú absolute, complete; downright

氏族 shìzú family, kin; clan

失足跌倒 shīzú diēdǎo lose one's footing

收 shōu receive; accept

熟 shóu ripe; cooked; familiar ◊ ripeness ◊ soundly

手 shǒu hand

守 shǒu keep watch; guard; abide by

首 shǒu head ◊ first

瘦 shòu thin; lean

兽 shòu beast; animal

受 shòu receive; accept; 不受诱惑 *búshòu yòuhuò* resist temptation; 受感染 *shòu gǎnrǎn* go septic

授 shòu give; teach

售 shòu sell

售报亭 shòubào tíng newsstand

手臂 shǒubì arm

手边 shǒubiān within reach

手表 shǒubiǎo wristwatch

守财奴 shǒucái nú miser

收藏 shōucáng tuck away

收藏家 shōucáng jiā collector

收藏品 shōucáng pǐn collection

手册 shǒucè handbook

首倡 shǒuchàng pioneer

收成 shōucheng crop, harvest

首次公演 shǒucì gōngyǎn première

手袋 shǒudài purse

收到 shōudào receive, get

手电筒 shǒudiàntǒng flashlight

首都 shǒudū capital

收短 shōuduǎn take up *dress etc*

手段 shǒuduàn means

守法 shǒufǎ comply with the law

收费 shōufèi charge

收费处 shōufèi chù toll booth

收费公路 shōufèi gōnglù toll road

手风琴 shǒufēng qín accordion

手稿 shǒugǎo manuscript

收割 shōugē reap

手工 shǒugōng manual ◊ handiwork

手工业 shǒugōngyè craft; handicraft

手工业者 shǒugōngyè zhě craftsman

手工艺 shǒugōngyì handicraft

手工艺者 shǒugōngyì zhě craftsman

手工制作 shǒugōng zhìzuò handmade

收购 shōugòu purchase ◊ purchasing

守规矩 shǒu guījǔ behave (oneself)

受过教育 shòuguò jiàoyù educated

受害 shòuhài sustain damage; suffer an injury

受害者 shòuhài zhě victim

首航 shǒuháng maiden voyage

守候 shǒuhòu watch for

售后服务 shòuhòu fúwù after-sales service

守护 shǒuhù look after, watch

受欢迎 shòu huānyíng popular; welcome; well-received

收回 shōuhuí repossess; reclaim; retract

受贿 shòuhuì corruption

收获 shōuhuò harvest

售货亭 shòuhuò tíng kiosk

售货员 shòuhuò yuán sales clerk

收集 shōují collect

售价 shòujià retail price

收件人 shōujiàn rén addressee

手巾 shǒujīn towel

受惊 shòujīng panic

受精 shòujīng be fertilized; 使 ... 受精 shǐ ... shòujīng fertilize

受惊吓 shòujīngxià petrified

守旧 shǒujiù provincial

熟记 shóujì know by heart

收据 shōujù receipt

手绢 shǒujuàn handkerchief

收看 shōukàn view; tune in; tune in to

手铐 shǒukào handcuffs

受苦 shòukǔ suffer

收款人 shōukuǎn rén recipient; payee

收款台 shōukuǎn tái till, cash register

受冷遇 shòu lěngyù get the cold shoulder; be in the doghouse

受连累 shòu liánlèi incriminate oneself

狩猎 shòuliè hunt

首领 shǒulǐng leader

收留 shōuliú take in

手榴弹 shǒuliúdàn grenade

收买 shōumǎi purchase; buy off, bribe

守门人 shǒumén rén doorman; super

守门员 shǒumén yuán goalkeeper

寿命 shòumìng life, lifetime

受虐狂 shòunüèkuáng masochism

受虐狂者 shòunüèkuáng zhě masochist

受骗 shòupiàn be deceived; 易受骗 yì shòupiàn gullible

售票处 shòupiào chù box office, ticket office

售票机 shòupiào jī ticket machine

收票员 shòupiào yuán ticket collector

售票员 shòupiào yuán booking clerk, ticket seller

收瓶处 shōupíng chù bottle bank

手枪 shǒuqiāng handgun; pistol

收起来 shōuqǐlái put away

授权 shòuquán authorize; warrant; delegate ◊ mandate; power of attorney

兽群 shòuqún herd

熟人 shóurén acquaintance; friend

收入 shōurù income; revenue

受伤 shòu shāng wounded; 腿受

伤 **tuǐ shòu shāng** wounded in the leg

受伤害 **shòu shānghài** injured

受伤者 **shòu shāng zhě** the injured

受伤至残 **shòu shāng zhì cán** cripple

受审 **shòushěn** on trial

收拾 **shōushi** clear away; clear up, tidy up; pack up

首饰 **shǒushi** jewelry

守时 **shǒushí** be punctual ◊ punctuality

手势 **shǒushì** gesture

熟食店 **shóushí diàn** delicatessen, deli

收拾干净 **shōushi gānjìng** clean up

手势语言 **shǒushì yǔyán** sign language

手术 **shǒushù** surgery; operation; 做手术 **zuò shǒushù** have an operation

手术刀 **shǒushù dāo** scalpel

手术室 **shǒushù shì** operating room

收缩 **shōusuō** contract, shrink

手套 **shǒutào** glove

手提包 **shǒutí bāo** bag; purse

手提电话 **shǒutí diànhuà** cell phone

收听 **shōutīng** tune in; tune in to

手提式 **shǒutíshì** portable

手提行李 **shǒutí xíngli** hand baggage

手提衣箱 **shǒutí yīxiāng** suitcase

手推车 **shǒutuīchē** wheelbarrow

受托集团 **shòutuō jítuán** trust FIN

手腕 **shǒuwàn** wrist

售完为止 **shòuwán wéizhǐ** subject to availability

守卫 **shǒuwèi** guard

守卫队员 **shǒuwèi duìyuán** defense player

守卫者 **shǒuwèi zhě** guard, watchman

首先 **shǒuxiān** firstly, to begin with, in the first place

首相 **shǒuxiàng** prime minister

受限制 **shòu xiànzhì** restricted

手写 **shǒuxiě** handwritten ◊ write by hand

收信人 **shōuxìn rén** addressee; receiver

首席小提琴演奏者 **shǒuxí xiǎotíqín yǎnzòu zhě** concertmaster

手续 **shǒuxù** formality; procedure

授勋 **shòuxūn** decorate

首演 **shǒuyǎn** début

收养 **shōuyǎng** adopt

手摇风琴 **shǒuyáo fēngqín** barrel organ

收益 **shōuyì** return, yield

兽医 **shòuyī** veterinary surgeon

受益 **shòuyì** benefit

手淫 **shǒuyín** masturbate

手印 **shǒuyìn** fingerprint

收音机 **shōuyīnjī** radio; 收音机里 **shōuyīnjī lǐ** on the radio

手艺人 **shǒuyì rén** craftsman; artisan

授予 **shòuyǔ** grant; present; confer

受约束 **shòu yuēshù** be bound, be committed; 受约束去做 X **shòu yuēshù qùzuò X** be bound to do X

受灾地区 **shòuzāi dìqū** disaster area

守则 **shǒuzé** rules

手轧 **shǒuzhá** parking brake

手掌 **shǒuzhǎng** palm

手杖 **shǒuzhàng** walking stick

手指 **shǒuzhǐ** finger

手指甲 **shǒuzhǐjiǎ** fingernail

收支平衡 **shōuzhī pínghéng** balance ◊ break even

受重伤 **shòu zhòngshāng** seriously injured

手爪子 **shǒuzhuǎzi** paw

手镯 **shǒuzhuó** bracelet

手足之情 **shǒuzú zhī qíng** fraternal love

书 **shū** book

梳 **shū** comb

输 **shū** lose

叔 **shū** uncle

熟 **shú** cooked; ripe; familiar ◊ ripeness ◊ soundly

赎 **shú** redeem

数 **shǔ** count

鼠 shǔ mouse; rat

暑 shǔ summer heat

属 shǔ belong to; 我属龙 **wǒ shǔ lóng** I was born in the year of the dragon

数 shù number

树 shù tree

竖 shù vertical

术 shù skill; art

述 shù tell, narrate

束 shù bundle, bunch, sheaf; 一束玫瑰 **yīshù méiguī** a bunch of roses

刷 shuā clean ◊ brush

刷掉 shuādiào brush off

耍滑头 shuǎ huátóu try to be clever; 跟 X 耍滑头 **gēn X shuǎ huátóu** get smart with X

摔 shuāi fall; drop; throw down

帅 shuài handsome; snazzy

衰败 shuāibài go to seed

摔倒 shuāidǎo fall, fall down

甩干 shuǎigān spin-dry

甩干机 shuǎigān jī (spin-)dryer, (tumble-)dryer

摔跤 shuāijiāo fall; slip; wrestle

摔跤比赛 shuāijiāo bǐsài wrestling match

摔跤运动 shuāijiāo yùndòng wrestling

摔跤运动员 shuāijiāo yùndòng yuán wrestler

衰老 shuāilǎo senile

衰老状态 shuāilǎo zhuàngtài senility

衰落 shuāiluò go downhill, deteriorate

衰弱 shuāiruò weak ◊ waste away

衰退 shuāituì decay; decline

率直 shuàizhí plain; blunt

刷净 shuājìng scour

刷卡 shuākǎ smartcard

闩 shuān bolt ◊ catch (on door)

拴 shuān tie up, tether; 把 X 拴在 Y 上 **bǎ X shuān zài Y shàng** hitch X to Y; chain X to Y

双 shuāng both; even; double; dual; twin ◊ measure word for pairs; 一双袜子 **yīshuāng wàzi** a pair of socks

霜 shuāng frost

双胞胎 shuāng bāo tāi twins

双倍 shuāngbèi double

双边 shuāngbiān bilateral

双层玻璃 shuāngcéng bōli double glazing

双层床 shuāngcéng chuáng bunk beds

双重 shuāngchóng double

双打 shuāngdǎ doubles SP

霜冻 shuāngdòng frost

双方 shuāngfāng both sides

媚妇 shuāngfù widow

双关语 shuāngguānyǔ pun

双击 shuāngjī double click

爽快 shuǎngkuài refreshed; invigorating

双排扣式 shuāngpái kòushì double-breasted

双人床 shuāngrén chuáng double bed

双人房 shuāngrén fáng double (room)

爽身粉 shuǎngshēnfěn talcum powder

双数 shuāngshù even number

双下巴 shuāngxiàbā double chin

双向交通 shuāngxiàng jiāotōng two-way traffic

双性 shuāngxìng bisexual

双语 shuāngyǔ bilingual

栓剂 shuānjì suppository

栓牢 shuānláo attach

栓塞 shuānsè embolism

栓住 shuānzhù bolt; hitch

耍小聪明 shuǎ xiǎo cōngmíng smart, cute

刷牙 shuāyá brush one's teeth

刷子 shuāzi brush

鼠标 shǔbiāo mouse COMPUT

鼠标垫 shǔbiāodiàn mouse mat

数不清 shùbuqīng innumerable; incalculable; countless

蔬菜 shūcài vegetable

蔬菜农场 shūcài nóngchǎng truck farm

蔬菜水果商 shūcài shuǐguǒ shāng greengrocer

输出 shūchū output; export

书呆子 shūdāizi bookworm;

pedant

竖笛 shùdí recorder MUS
书店 shūdiàn bookstore
输掉 shūdiào lose
数额 shù'é amount, sum
书法 shūfǎ calligraphy
书房 shūfáng study, den
竖放 shùfàng stand
舒服 shūfu comfortable ◊ well
束缚 shùfù tie; bind
树干 shùgàn trunk
疏忽 shūhū oversight
谁 shuí who
水 shuǐ water
睡 shuì sleep; 我睡不着 **wǒ shuìbùzháo** I couldn't get to sleep; 睡个懒觉 **shuìgè lǎnjiào** sleep late
税 shuì tax; duty; tariff
水坝 shuǐbà dam
水边 shuǐbiān waterside
水彩 shuǐcǎi watercolor
水彩画 shuǐcǎihuà watercolor (painting)
水池 shuǐchí pond; basin
睡袋 shuìdài sleeping bag
水电站 shuǐdiànzhàn hydroelectric power plant
水痘 shuǐdòu chicken pox
睡房 shuìfáng bedroom
水肺 shuǐfèi air tank, aqualung
水管 shuǐguǎn water pipe
水果 shuǐguǒ fruit
水果色拉 shuǐguǒ sèlā fruit salad
睡过头 shuì guòtóu oversleep
水花 shuǐhuā spray
睡觉 shuìjiào sleep; go to bed; 我需要好好睡一觉 **wǒ xūyào hǎohǎo shuìyìjiào** I need a good sleep; 和 … 睡觉 **hé … shuìjiào** sleep with …
水晶 shuǐjīng crystal
水坑 shuǐkēng puddle
水库 shuǐkù reservoir
睡裤 shuìkù pajama pants
睡懒觉 shuì lǎnjiào sleep late
水冷却 shuǐlěngquè water-cooling
水力发电 shuǐlì fādiàn hydroelectric

水龙头 shuǐlóngtóu faucet
水路 shuǐlù waterway
水面 shuǐmiàn surface (of water)
睡眠 shuìmián sleep
水墨画 shuǐmòhuà ink wash painting
水泥 shuǐní cement
水牛 shuǐniú water buffalo
水暖工 shuǐnuǎngōng plumber
水疱 shuǐpào blister
水平 shuǐpíng standard, level; horizontal
水平面 shuǐpíngmiàn water level; level surface
水栖 shuǐqī aquatic, water-dwelling
水上运动 shuǐshàng yùndòng watersports
水手 shuǐshǒu sailor, seaman
税收 shuìshōu tax revenue
水手领 shuǐshǒu lǐng crew neck
水獭 shuǐtǎ otter
水桶 shuǐtǒng pail, bucket
水位 shuǐwèi water level
税务调查员 shuìwù diàocháyuán tax inspector
税务局 shuìwùjú tax office
水箱 shuǐxiāng cistern
睡醒 shuìxǐng wake up
睡眼惺忪 shuìyǎn xīngsōng bleary-eyed
睡衣 shuìyī nightdress; pajamas; pajama jacket
睡衣裤 shuìyīkù pajamas; pajama pants
水银 shuǐyín mercury, quicksilver
水翼艇 shuǐyìtǐng hydrofoil
水域 shuǐyù waters; area of water
睡着 shuìzháo fall asleep
水准仪 shuǐzhǔn yí spirit level
水准 shuǐzhǔn standard, level
水族馆 shuǐzú guǎn aquarium
书脊 shūjí spine
书籍 shūjí books
书架 shūjià bookcase
暑假 shǔjià summer vacation
树胶 shùjiāo gum
赎金 shújīn ransom
数据 shùjù data
数据保护 shùjù bǎohù data protection

数据储存 shùjù chǔcún data storage

数据处理 shùjù chǔlǐ data processing

数据俘获 shùjù fúhuò data capture

数据库 shùjù kù database

疏浚 shūjùn dredge

数据载体 shùjù zàitǐ data carrier

熟客 shúkè regular visitor

漱口 shùkǒu gargle

漱口剂 shùkǒujì mouthwash

树篱 shùlí hedge

熟练 shúliàn skillful; proficient; practised ◊ proficiency

数量 shùliàng amount

熟练技巧 shúliàn jìqiǎo dexterity

树林 shùlín wood

数落 shǔluò tell off, chew out

书面 shūmiàn written ◊ in writing; 以书面形式 yǐ shūmiàn xíngshì in writing

数目 shùmù number, numeral; sum

吮 shǔn suck

顺便 shùnbiàn in passing

顺便过访 shùnbiàn guòfǎng stop by

顺便看望 shùnbiàn kànwàng look in on

顺便来访 shùnbiàn láifǎng drop in

顺便问一下 shùnbiàn wènyīxià by the way, incidentally

顺从 shùncóng obey; submit ◊ obedient; submissive; docile

顺从的人 shùncóng de rén conformist

顺风 shùnfēng tail wind

枢纽 shūniǔ hub; center

瞬间 shùnjiān moment, instant ◊ momentarily

顺口溜 shùnkǒuliū jingle

顺利 shùnlì smooth ◊ smoothly

顺势疗法 shùnshì liáofǎ homeopathy

顺时针 shùn shízhēn clockwise

吮吸 shǔnxī suck; 吮吸拇指 shǔnxī mǔzhǐ suck one's thumb

顺心 shùnxīn satisfactory

顺序 shùnxù sequence

说 shuō talk; speak; say; 你说呢？ nǐ shuō ne? what do you think?; 你说什么？ nǐ shuō shénme? pardon me? what did you say?; 那就是说 nà jiùshì shuō that is to say; 说吧 shuō ba go ahead; 说正经的 shuō zhèngjing de seriously, joking apart; 我在说正经的 wǒ zài shuō zhèngjing de I'm serious

说唱音乐 shuōchàng yīnyuè rap MUS

说定 shuōdìng agree on; arrange; 说定了 shuōdingle and that's flat; that's settled

说法 shuōfǎ way of saying something; version

说服 shuōfú persuade, convince; 说服X做Y shuōfú X zuò Y persuade X to do Y, talk X into doing Y

说话 shuōhuà speak

说话方式 shuōhuà fāngshì speech, way of speaking

说话能力 shuōhuà nénglì speech, ability to speak

说谎话 shuō huǎnghuà lie

说谎者 shuōhuǎng zhě liar

说教 shuōjiào preach

说明 shuōmíng explain ◊ explanation; caption

说明书 shuōmíng shū instruction manual

硕士 shuòshì master's (degree)

说说而已 shuōshuo ér yǐ all talk and no action

说笑话 shuō xiàohuà joke; crack a joke

说真的 shuōzhēnde honestly; 说真的吗？ shuōzhènde ma? seriously?

说正事 shuō zhèngshì get to the point

竖排 shùpái portrait print

书皮 shūpí dust cover

树皮 shùpí bark

薯片 shǔpiàn (potato) chips

鼠疫 shǔpiàn rat race

述评 shùpíng comment ◊ commentary

竖起 **shùqǐ** erect, put up ◊ erection

书签 **shūqiān** bookmark

竖起耳朵 **shùqǐ ěrduo** prick up one's ears

竖琴 **shùqín** harp

熟人 **shúrén** acquaintance; friend

输入 **shūrù** input; import

输入端口 **shūrù duānkǒu** input port

疏散 **shūsàn** disperse; decentralize

书商 **shūshāng** bookseller

树梢 **shùshāo** tree top

舒适 **shūshì** cozy; comfortable

熟食 **shúshí** cooked meal

竖式(钢琴) **shùshì (gāngqín)** upright (piano)

叔叔 **shūshu** uncle (*father's younger brother*); *also used to address non-related men*

数数 **shǔshù** count

熟睡 **shúshuì** fast asleep

输送 **shūsòng** transport; convey; inject *fuel*

书摊 **shūtān** bookstall

薯条 **shǔtiáo** (French) fries

熟透 **shútòu** well-done, cooked through

鼠尾草 **shǔwěicǎo** sage

梳洗 **shūxǐ** clean up, freshen up

熟悉 **shúxī** know; be familiar with

书写体 **shūxiětǐ** script

书写体系 **shūxiě tǐxì** writing

书信往来 **shūxìn wǎnglái** correspondence

输血 **shūxuè** (blood) transfusion

数学 **shùxué** mathematics ◊ mathematical

数学家 **shùxué jiā** mathematician

输血者 **shūxuè zhě** blood donor

输液 **shūyè** infusion

树液 **shùyè** sap

鼠疫 **shǔyì** plague

属于 **shǔyú** belong; belong to; 我不属于这里 *wǒ bù shǔyú zhèlǐ* I don't belong here

术语 **shùyǔ** terminology; term

疏远 **shūyuǎn** drift apart; alienate; distance oneself ◊ estranged

疏于练习 **shūyú liànxí** be out of practice

输者 **shūzhě** loser

树枝 **shùzhī** branch

树脂 **shùzhī** resin

树桩 **shùzhuāng** stump

梳妆台 **shūzhuāng tái** dressing table, dresser

书桌 **shūzhuō** desk

梳子 **shūzi** hairbrush; comb

数字 **shùzì** number, digit, figure ◊ digital; 四位数字 *sìwèi shùzì* four digit number

数字视频光盘 **shùzì shìpín guāngpán** DVD

嘶 **sī** neigh

撕 **sī** tear (up)

思 **sī** think; consider

私 **sī** private

丝 **sī** silk

死 **sǐ** die ◊ death ◊ dead; 死于癌症 *sǐyú áizhèng* die of cancer

寺 **sì** Buddhist temple

四 **sì** four

似 **sì** resemble, be like; seem

饲 **sì** feed, fodder

四胞胎 **sì bāotāi** quadruplets

私奔 **sībēn** elope

四边形 **sìbiān xíng** quadrangle; rectangle

死不开口 **sǐ bù kāikǒu** clam up

死产 **sǐchǎn** be stillborn

撕成碎片 **sīchéng suìpiàn** shred

四重唱 **sì chōngchàng** quartet

四重奏 **sì chóngzòu** quartet

丝绸 **sīchóu** silk

丝绸之路 **Sīchóu zhī lù** Silk Road

四川 Sichuan, Szechuan

四川盆地 **Sìchuān Péndì** Sichuan Basin

四次 **sìcì** four times

丝带 **sīdài** ribbon

斯大林 **Sīdàlín** Stalin

死定了 **sǐdìngle** doomed

司法 **sīfǎ** justice ◊ judicial

四方形 **sìfāng xíng** square

四方院 **sìfāng yuàn** quadrangle

司法权 **sīfǎquán** jurisdiction

似非而是 **sìfēi'érshì** paradoxical ◊ paradoxically

四分音符 **sì fēn yīnfú** quarternote

四分之三 **sì fēn zhī sān** three-quarters

四分之一 **sì fēn zhī yī** quarter

丝瓜 **sīguā** loofah

丝毫 **sīháo** shred, vestige

似乎 **sìhū** looks like; seems ◊ apparently; 她似乎是 … **tā sìhū shì …** she comes across as …

撕毁 **sīhuǐ** tear up

厮混 **sīhùn** play around, be unfaithful; 与 X 厮混 **yǔ X sīhùn** get mixed up with X

死胡同 **sǐ hútòng** dead end, blind alley

司机 **sījī** driver; motorist; chauffeur

四季豆 **sìjìdòu** green bean

撕开 **sīkāi** slit; rip open

思考 **sīkǎo** contemplate, think about

司库 **sīkù** treasurer

私利 **sīlì** self-interest

饲料 **sìliào** fodder

撕裂 **sīliè** rip

司炉 **sīlú** stoker, boilerman

思路 **sīlù** line of thought

思念 **sīniàn** long for, pine for

死气沉沉 **sǐqì chénchén** dead *place* ◊ dull, boring

私人 **sīrén** private, personal; intimate

死人 **sǐrén** the dead; dead person

四人帮 **Sìrénbāng** Gang of Four

私人财产 **sīrén cáichǎn** private property

私人教师 **sīrén jiàoshī** (private) tutor

私人空间 **sīrén kōngjiān** privacy

私人助理 **sīrén zhùlǐ** personal assistant

丝绒 **sīróng** velvet

私生 **sīshēng** illegitimate

私生活 **sīshēnghuó** private life

私生子 **sīshēngzǐ** illegitimate child, bastard

死尸 **sǐshī** corpse

四十 **sìshí** forty

撕碎 **sīsuì** tear to pieces

私通 **sītōng** adultery ◊ commit adultery

死亡 **sǐwáng** death; fatality

死亡率 **sǐwáng lǜ** mortality, death rate

死亡总数 **sǐwáng zǒngshù** death toll

私下 **sīxià** in private, privately

撕下 **sīxià** tear out; tear off

思想 **sīxiǎng** thought; thinking; idea; ideology

死刑 **sǐxíng** capital punishment, death penalty; execution

私刑处死 **sīxíng chùsǐ** lynch

四星级 **sìxīngjí** four-star

嘶哑 **sīyǎ** hoarse

饲养 **sìyǎng** breed ◊ breeding

饲养员 **sìyǎng yuán** breeder

司仪 **sīyí** marshal; master of ceremonies

肆意破坏 **sìyì pòhuài** vandalize

私语 **sīyǔ** whisper

寺院 **sìyuàn** temple

四月 **sìyuè** April

死者 **sǐzhě** the deceased

丝制 **sīzhì** silk

四肢 **sìzhī** limbs

丝织品 **sīzhīpǐn** silk goods

四周 **sìzhōu** all around

四足动物 **sìzú dòngwù** quadruped

松 **sōng** pine ◊ loose ◊ loosely; 松一口气 **sōng yìkǒu qì** heave a sigh of relief

送 **sòng** deliver; give; accompany, escort; 我送你到门口 **wǒ sòng nǐ dào ménkǒu** I'll see you to the door

送别 **sòngbié** see off

送别宴会 **sòngbié yànhuì** farewell party

宋朝 **Sòng Cháo** Song Dynasty

松弛 **sōngchí** slack; flabby ◊ slacken; 松弛的肌肉 **sōngchíde jīròu** flab

宋词 **Sòngcí** Song Dynasty lyric poetry

松动 **sōngdong** loose ◊ work loose; loosen up

颂歌 **sònggē** carol

送回 **sònghuí** send back

送回国 **sòng huíguó** repatriate

送货 **sònghuò** delivery

送货车 **sònghuò chē** delivery

van

送货单 **sònghuò dān** delivery note

送货日期 **sònghuò rìqī** delivery date

耸肩 **sǒngjiān** shrug; 他耸了耸肩就走了 **tā sǒnglesǒng jiān jiù zǒule** he gave a shrug and left

松紧带 **sōngjǐndài** elastic

松开 **sōngkāi** release

松垮 **sōngkuǎ** lax

耸立 **sǒnglì** tower; rise

送礼 **sònglǐ** offer a present; give a bribe

松木 **sōngmù** pine (*wood*)

耸人听闻 **sǒngrén tīngwén** lurid

松软 **sōngruǎn** floppy; fluffy

松手 **sōngshǒu** let go

松鼠 **sōngshǔ** squirrel

松树 **sōngshù** pine (*tree*)

送送 **sòngsòng** see out, see to the door

松塔 **sōngtǎ** (pine) cone

松香 **sōngxiāng** resin

松懈 **sōngxiè** relax

送行 **sòngxíng** see off

怂恿 **sǒngyǒng** egg on

馊 **sōu** sour

搜捕 **sōubǔ** search

搜查 **sōuchá** search; frisk

搜查证 **sōucházhèng** search warrant

搜集 **sōují** gather; save

搜索 **sōusuǒ** search; scour; scan

搜索队 **sōusuǒduì** search party

搜寻 **sōuxún** search ◊ hunt for; scour; comb; surf (the Net)

酥 **sū** crisp

俗 **sú** vulgar; common

宿 **sù** stay overnight

塑 **sù** mold; sculpt

素 **sù** plain; white ◊ vegetarian food

速 **sù** fast

酸 **suān** acid ◊ acidic; sour; aching; sore

算 **suàn** count, include

蒜 **suàn** garlic

酸橙 **suānchéng** lime

酸辣汤 **suānlàtāng** hot and sour soup

算命 **suànmìng** tell s.o.'s fortune; tell fortunes

算命者 **suànmìng zhě** fortune-teller

酸奶 **suānnǎi** yogurt

算盘 **suànpán** abacus

算术 **suànshù** arithmetic; sum

算算术 **suàn suànshù** add

酸味 **suānwèi** acidity; sourness

酸雨 **suānyǔ** acid rain

算帐 **suànzhàng** settle accounts; settle scores; 跟 X 算旧帐 **gēn X suàn jiùzhàng** have an old score to settle with X

酥饼 **sūbǐng** flaky pastry

俗不可耐 **sú bù kě nài** garish

素菜 **sùcài** vegetarian dish

速成课 **sùchéng kè** crash course

酥脆 **sūcuì** crispy; crunchy

苏打 **sūdá** soda

速冻 **sùdòng** quick-freeze ◊ quick-frozen

速度 **sùdù** speed, pace, rate; tempo; 速度每小时一百五十英里 **sùdù měi xiǎoshí yìbǎi wǔshí yīnglǐ** at a speed of 150 mph

速度极限 **sùdù jíxiàn** speed limit

苏格兰 **Sūgélán** Scotland ◊ Scottish

虽 **suī** although

髓 **suǐ** pith

随 **suí** follow; 随你的便！ **suí nǐde biàn!** suit yourself!

穗 **suì** ear (*of corn*)

碎 **suì** shatter ◊ shattered

岁 **suì** year; years old; 她五岁了 **tā wǔsuì le** she's five years old

随便 **suíbiàn** arbitrary; casual ◊ at random; at will; 随便拿 **suíbiàn ná** take as much as you want; help yourself; 随便你 **suíbiàn nǐ** if you like; suit yourself

随便看看 **suíbiàn kànkan** browse

随从人员 **suícóng rényuán** entourage

穗带 **suìdài** braid

隧道 **suìdào** tunnel

随和 **suíhé** easy-going

随后 **suíhòu** afterward,

subsequently ◊ subsequent

随机 **suíjī** random

随机抽样 **suíjī chōuyàng** random sample

碎块 **suìkuài** fragment

碎裂 **suìliè** break up; crumble

碎片 **suìpiàn** piece; flake; shred; splinter; fragment

虽然 **suīrán** although, while

碎肉 **suìròu** ground meat

随身听 **suíshēntīng** Walkman®, personal stereo

随时 **suíshí** at any time

碎石 **suìshí** gravel

随意 **suíyì** as one likes; 你要吃什么? – 随意 **nǐ yào chī shénme?** – **suíyì** what would you like to eat? – anything will be fine

速记 **sùjì** shorthand ◊ take shorthand

肃静! **sùjìng!** silence!

诉苦 **sùkǔ** complain

苏联 **Sūlián** Soviet Union

塑料 **sùliào** plastic

塑料袋 **sùliào dài** plastic bag

素描簿 **sùmiáo bò** sketchbook

宿命 **sùmìng** predestination

塑膜 **sùmó** shrink-wrapping

塑膜包装 **sùmó bāozhuāng** shrink-wrap ◊ shrink-wrapping

孙 **sūn** grandson

笋 **sǔn** bamboo shoot

损害 **sǔnhài** harm, damage; impair

损耗 **sǔnhào** wear (and tear)

损坏 **sǔnhuài** break; damage

损坏表面 **sǔnhuài biǎomiàn** deface

孙女 **sūnnǚ** granddaughter (*son's daughter*)

损伤 **sǔnshāng** damage; mutilate; 未受损伤 **wèi shòu sǔnshāng** uninjured; unscathed; undamaged

损失 **sǔnshī** damage; loss; toll

损失惨重 **sǔnshī cǎnzhòng** disastrous

孙中山 **Sūn Zhōngshān** Sun Yat-sen

孙子 **sūnzi** grandson (*son's son*)

锁 **suǒ** lock; 锁在里面 **suǒ zài lǐmiàn** lock in; 锁在外面 **suǒ zài wàimiàn** lock out

缩 **suō** shrink, contract; retract

索 **suǒ** rope

所 **suǒ** what, that which; 据我所知 **jù wǒ suǒ zhī** according to what I know ◊ *measure word for institutions*; 一所学校 **yì suǒ xuéxiào** a school

索道 **suǒdào** cable railroad

所得税 **suǒdéshuì** income tax

缩短 **suōduǎn** shorten; 缩短会议 **suōduǎn huìyì** cut a meeting short

缩格书写 **suōgé shūxiě** indent text

锁骨 **suǒgǔ** collarbone

缩回 **suōhuí** draw back

缩减 **suōjiǎn** decrease; cut back

锁匠 **suǒjiàng** locksmith

缩进 **suōjìn** retract

缩进排印 **suōjìn páiyìn** indent (*in text*)

锁孔 **suǒkǒng** keyhole

索赔 **suǒpéi** claim

锁起来 **suǒ qǐlái** lock away

索取 **suǒqǔ** claim

索取单 **suǒqǔ dān** coupon

琐事 **suǒshì** triviality, trifle

所述 **suǒshù** above-mentioned

缩水 **suōshuǐ** shrink

琐碎事 **suǒsuì shì** odds and ends; trivia; minor details

所谈 **suǒtán** in question

所谓 **suǒwèi** alleged; so-called

缩微胶卷 **suōwēi jiāojuǎn** microfilm

缩小 **suōxiǎo** reduce, make smaller

缩写 **suōxiě** abbreviate ◊ abbreviation

所以 **suǒyǐ** therefore; so; consequently

索引 **suǒyǐn** index

索引卡 **suǒyǐn kǎ** index card

所有 **suǒyǒu** own ◊ all; 他把所有的东西都吃了 **tā bǎ suǒyǒude dōngxi dōu chī le** he ate all of it

所有权 **suǒyǒu quán** ownership; title

所有物 **suǒyǒu wù** belongings, possessions, stuff, things

所在地 **suǒzàidì** seat; site

锁住 **suǒzhù** immobilize

俗气 **súqi** tacky

肃清 **sùqīng** mop up MIL

速溶咖啡 **sùróng kāfēi** instant coffee

宿舍 **sùshè** hostel; boarding house; dormitory

素食 **sùshí** vegetarian

素食者 **sùshí zhě** vegetarian

素食主义 **sùshí zhǔyì** vegan

素食主义者 **sùshí zhǔyì zhě** vegan

诉讼 **sùsòng** lawsuit

诉讼细节 **sùsòng xìjié** legal technicality

俗套 **sútào** corny

俗套情节 **sútào qíngjié** hokum

塑像 **sùxiàng** statue

苏醒 **sūxǐng** come around, come to ◊ revival; 使 .. 苏醒 **shǐ ... sūxǐng** revive

俗艳 **súyàn** loud *color*

宿营地 **sùyíngdì** quarters

酥油 **sūyóu** butter; cream

塑造 **sùzào** form, shape

素质 **sùzhì** constitution, make-up; qualities

# T

他 tā he; him ◊ his
她 tā she; her
它 tā it ◊ its
塔 tǎ tower
獭 tǎ otter
踏 tà step, tread
踏板 tàbǎn pedal; treadle
踏板车 tàbǎnchē scooter
塌鼻 tābí snub-nosed
她的 tāde her ◊ hers
他的 tāde his
它的 tāde its
塌方 tāfāng landslide
胎 tāi embryo; fetus
苔 tái moss
台 tái platform; terrace; Taiwan
太 tài too; very 太多饭 tài duō fàn too much rice; 太大 tài dà too big
台北 Táiběi Taipei
台布 táibù tablecloth
台词 táicí speech
态度 tàidù attitude, manner
胎儿 tāi'ér embryo; fetus
太妃糖 tàifēi táng toffee
台风 táifēng typhoon
泰国 Tàiguó Thailand ◊ Thai
太极拳 tàijíquán tai chi
太空 tàikōng (outer) space
太空舱 tàikōng cāng (space) capsule
胎面 tāimiàn tread
太平间 tàipíngjiān mortuary
太平洋 Tàipíngyáng Pacific Ocean
太平洋岸 Tàipíngyáng àn Pacific Rim
太平洋岸国家 Tàipíngyáng àn guójiā Pacific Rim countries
台球 táiqiú snooker; billiards
泰然自若 tàirán zìruò poised
泰山 Tàishān Mount Tai
台式机 táishìjī desk top computer
太太 tàitai Mrs ◊ wife
台湾 Táiwān Taiwan ◊ Taiwanese

台湾海峡 Táiwān Hǎixiá Taiwan Straits
台湾话 Táiwān huà Taiwanese
台湾人 Táiwān rén Taiwanese
太阳 tàiyáng sun
太阳电池板 tàiyáng diànchí bǎn solar panel
太阳镜 tàiyáng jìng sunglasses
太阳能 tàiyáng néng solar energy
太阳穴 tàiyáng xuè temple
踏脚石 tàjiǎo shí stepping stone
塔吉克 Tǎjíkè Tajikistan ◊ Tajiki
他妈的 tāmāde ∨ damn, fuck ◊ fucking; 去他妈的！qù tāmāde! fuck!; fuck him/that!
他们 tāmen they; them ◊ their
她们 tāmen they; them ◊ their (female only)
她们的 tāmende their ◊ theirs (female only)
他们的 tāménde their ◊ theirs
他们自己 tāmen zìjǐ themselves
摊 tān pool
贪 tān covet
瘫 tān paralyzed
坛 tán bed (of flowers)
谈 tán talk; 我会和他谈 wǒ huì hé tā tán I'll talk to him about it
痰 tán spit, spittle
弹 tán play string instrument; 弹钢琴 tán gāngqín play the piano; 弹吉他 tán jítā play the guitar
叹 tàn sigh
碳 tàn carbon
炭 tàn charcoal
坦白 tǎnbái confess ◊ frankly ◊ open; 坦白告诉我 tǎnbái gàosù wǒ give it to me straight
炭笔 tànbǐ charcoal (for drawing)
探测 tàncè probe
探测器 tàncè qì detector
探查 tànchá probe
摊贩 tānfàn street trader

探访者 **tànfǎng zhě** caller, visitor

汤 **tāng** soup; stock; broth

糖 **táng** sugar; candy

躺 **tǎng** lie

淌 **tǎng** run (of nose etc)

烫 **tàng** hot

唐朝 **Táng Cháo** Tang Dynasty

汤匙 **tāngchí** spoon; soup spoon

搪瓷 **tángcí** enamel

糖醋 **tángcù** sweet and sour

堂弟 **tángdì** cousin (younger male on father's side)

探戈舞 **tàngē wǔ** tango

烫发 **tàngfà** have a perm ◊ perm

糖粉 **tángfěn** confectioners' sugar

糖罐 **tángguàn** sugar bowl

糖果 **tángguǒ** candy

糖浆 **tángjiāng** molasses, syrup

烫焦 **tàngjiāo** scorch; singe

堂姐 **tángjiě** cousin (older female on father's side)

糖精 **tángjīng** saccharin

淌流 **tǎngliú** run (of nose)

堂妹 **tángmèi** cousin (younger female on father's side)

汤面 **tāngmiàn** noodle soup

糖尿病 **tángniàobìng** diabetes ◊ diabetic

唐人街 **Tángrénjiē** Chinatown

唐三彩 **tángsāncǎi** Tang ceramics glazed in three colors

搪塞 **tángsè** stonewall, stall

烫伤 **tàngshāng** scald

唐诗 **Tángshī** Tang poetry

糖霜 **tángshuāng** frosting

趟水 **tāngshuǐ** wade; paddle

唐突 草率 **tángtū cǎoshuài** curt

汤碗 **tāngwǎn** soup bowl

躺下 **tǎngxia** lie down

堂兄 **tángxiōng** cousin (older male on father's side)

躺椅 **tǎngyǐ** deck chair; lounger

谈话 **tánhuà** talk

谈话节目 **tánhuà jiémù** talk show

瘫痪 **tānhuàn** paralysis ◊ paralyze; 使 ... 瘫痪 **shǐ ... tānhuàn** immobilize

弹簧 **tánhuáng** spring

坍毁 **tānhuǐ** dilapidated

弹回来 **tán huílái** rebound

摊开 **tānkāi** open; unfold; spread

坦克 **tǎnkè** tank MIL

贪婪 **tānlán** greedy; acquisitive

谈恋爱 **tán liàn'ài** date

摊凉 **tānliáng** cool (down)

谈判 **tánpàn** negotiate ◊ negotiations

谈判员 **tánpàn yuán** negotiator

弹起 **tánqǐ** bounce

叹气 **tànqì** sigh

弹射 **tánshè** eject

贪食 **tānshí** gluttony ◊ gluttonous

贪食者 **tānshí zhě** glutton

坦率 **tǎnshuài** frank, open, candid ◊ candor

碳水化合物 **tànshuǐ huàhéwù** carbohydrate

探索 **tànsuǒ** exploration ◊ seek

探索性 **tànsuǒ xìng** exploratory

探索者 **tànsuǒ zhě** explorer

坍塌 **tāntā** give way

探讨 **tàntǎo** explore

弹跳 **tántiào** bounce

探听 **tàntīng** investigate; nose around

探望时间 **tànwàng shíjiān** visiting hours

贪污 **tānwū** embezzle ◊ embezzlement

叹息 **tànxī** sigh

探险 **tànxiǎn** expedition

贪心 **tānxīn** greed

弹性 **tánxìng** elasticity

探照灯 **tànzhàodēng** searchlight

摊子 **tānzi** stall, stand, booth

毯子 **tǎnzi** blanket, rug

弹奏 **tánzòu** play

逃 **táo** flee; escape

桃 **táo** peach

讨 **tǎo** discuss

套 **tào** set; suit; suite ◊ measure word for rooms, furniture, clothes; 一套家具 **yītào jiājù** a suite of furniture

逃避 **táobì** escape, elude; shirk ◊ evasion

逃兵 **táobīng** deserter

绦虫 **tāochóng** tapeworm

掏出 **tāochū** get out; cough up money

陶瓷 **táocí** ceramics

逃犯 táofàn fugitive

套服 tàofú suit

陶工 táogōng potter

讨好 tǎohǎo flatter ◊ flattering

讨价还价 tǎojià huánjià bargain, haggle

套间 tàojiān suite (of rooms)

掏空 tāokōng empty

讨论 tǎolùn discuss, talk over; debate ◊ discussion

讨论会 tǎolùn huì conference

逃跑 táopǎo run away, flee ◊ flight; getaway

陶器 táoqì ceramics, pottery, earthenware

淘气 táoqì naughty

掏钱 tāoqián cough up, pay

淘气包 táoqìbāo rogue; brat

陶器作坊 táoqì zuōfang pottery (place)

讨人喜欢 tǎorén xǐhuān endearing

淘汰 táotài eliminate; weed out ◊ elimination

淘汰赛 táotàisài knockout competition

滔滔不绝 tāotao bùjué torrent (of words)

逃脱 táotuō escape; 逃脱处分 táotuō chǔfèn get off, escape punishment

逃学 táoxué play hookey

讨厌 tǎoyàn disgusting; tiresome ◊ detest, loathe ◊ what a nuisance!

令人讨厌 lìngrén tǎoyàn rotten trick; unsavory; bitchy

讨厌鬼 tǎoyàngǔi pest, so-and-so; creep

套装 tàozhuāng outfit

桃子 táozi peach

套子 tàozi housing; case

逃走 táozǒu flee, run away

逃罪 táozuì get away with

陶醉 táozuì intoxicated; high

她自己 tā zìjǐ herself

他自己 tā zìjǐ himself

它自己 tā zìjǐ itself

特 tè special

特别 tèbié special, specific, particular, ◊ specially, specifically, particularly

特别工作组 tèbié gōngzuòzǔ task force

特产 tèchǎn specialty

特大 tèdà king-size(d)

特大号 tè dàhào outsize

特等包厢 tèděng bāoxiāng dress circle

特地 tèdì expressly

特点 tèdiǎn characteristic, peculiarity

特工人员 tègōng rényuán secret agent

特护（部）tèhù (bù) intensive care (unit)

特技 tèjì trick; stunt

特快 tèkuài express

特免 tèmiǎn immunity, exemption

疼 téng pain, hurt ◊ sore; 疼不疼？téng bùténg? is it sore?, does it hurt?

腾出 téngchū vacate

藤条 téngtiáo wicker

疼痛 téngtòng hurt, pain ◊ painful

藤椅 téngyǐ wicker chair

特权 tèquán privilege

特色 tèsè feature, characteristic

特殊 tèshū special, particular; exceptional; 特殊情况 tèshū qíngkuàng one-off, exception; special circumstances

特务 tèwu secret agent

特务机关 tèwù jīguān secret service

特写镜头 tèxiě jìngtóu close-up

特性 tèxìng quality, trait

特有 tèyǒu distinctive; peculiar to

特征 tèzhēng attribute, characteristic

特种 tèzhǒng special ◊ special type

特种饮食 tèzhǒng yǐnshí special diet

踢 tī kick; 踢足球 tī zúqiú play soccer

梯 tī ladder; steps

蹄 tí hoof

题 tí subject, theme

提 tí carry; lift; raise; 不提 X 的事 bù tí X de shì keep quiet about X

体 tǐ body

剃 tì shave

替 **tì** replace; substitute ◊ in behalf of; 替我问她好 **tì wǒ wèn tā hǎo** remember me to her

添 **tiān** add

甜 **tián** sweet

填 **tián** fill out, fill in

田 **tián** field

舔 **tiǎn** lick; lap up

天安门广场 **Tiān'ānmén Guǎngchǎng** Tiananmen Square

填表 **tiánbiǎo** fill out a form

天才 **tiāncái** talent; genius ◊ ingenious

甜菜 **tiáncài** sugar beet

填充 **tiánchōng** stuff *turkey etc*

天窗 **tiānchuāng** skylight

田地 **tiándì** field; farmland

天鹅 **tiān'é** swan

天鹅绒 **tiān'éróng** velvet

天份 **tiānfèn** gift, talent; flair

天赋 **tiānfù** gift, talent

天沟 **tiāngōu** gutter

天黑 **tiānhēi** dark; 天黑以后 **tiānhēi yǐhòu** after dark

天花 **tiānhuā** smallpox

天花板 **tiānhuābǎn** ceiling

添加 **tiānjiā** add

添加剂 **tiānjiā jì** additive

田径 **tiánjìng** track and field; athletics

天空 **tiānkōng** sky

填料 **tiánliào** stuffing

填满 **tiánmǎn** fill up; fill in

天哪！ **tiānna!** good heavens!; oh God!

甜品 **tiánpǐn** dessert

天平 **tiānpíng** scales

天气 **tiānqì** weather; 天气很冷 **tiānqì hěnlěng** it's cold; 天气晴朗 **tiānqì qínglǎng** it's sunny

天气预报 **tiānqì yùbào** weather forecast

天然 **tiānrán** natural ◊ naturally

天然气 **tiānrán qì** natural gas

田赛 **tiánsài** field events

天生 **tiānshēng** innate ◊ naturally; 天生的 … **tiānshēngde …** be a natural …

天使 **tiānshǐ** angel

甜食 **tiánshí** confectionery

田鼠 **tiánshǔ** vole

天坛 **Tiāntán** Temple of Heaven

天堂 **tiāntáng** heaven; paradise

天体 **tiāntǐ** heavenly body

天体运行轨道 **tiāntǐ yùnxíng guǐdào** orbit

甜味剂 **tiánwèijì** sweetener

天文 **tiānwén** astronomy

天文台 **tiānwén tái** observatory

天文学 **tiānwén xué** astronomy

天文学家 **tiānwén xuéjiā** astronomer

天线 **tiānxiàn** aerial, antenna

天线塔 **tiānxiàntǎ** (radio) mast

填写 **tiánxiě** fill out, fill in, complete

天性 **tiānxìng** disposition, nature

填鸭式灌输 **tiányā shì guànshū** spoonfeed

天衣无缝 **tiān yī wú fèng** perfect

田园式 **tiányuánshì** idyllic

甜玉米 **tián yùmǐ** sweetcorn

天真 **tiānzhēn** naive; childlike

天真无邪 **tiānzhēn wúxié** childlike; innocent

天主教 **Tiānzhǔjiào** (Roman) Catholic

天主教徒 **Tiānzhǔjiào tú** (Roman) Catholic

天资 **tiānzī** aptitude

挑 **tiāo** choose, pick

条 **tiáo** strip; item ◊ *measure word for long thin things*; 一条裤子 **yìtiáo kùzi** a pair of pants; 一条香烟 **yìtiáo xiāngyān** a carton of cigarettes; 一条新闻 **yìtiáo xīnwén** a bit of news

调 **tiáo** adjust

挑 **tiǎo** push; provoke

跳 **tiào** jump, leap, hop; skip

跳板 **tiàobǎn** springboard; gangway

挑拨 **tiǎobō** provoke

挑出 **tiāochū** single out

挑刺儿 **tiāocìr** be critical ◊ critical

挑动 **tiǎodòng** stir up

跳动 **tiàodòng** beat, throb

挑逗 **tiǎodòu** provoke ◊ provocative; 挑斗 X 去做 Y **tiǎodòu X qù zuò Y** dare X to do Y

挑逗嗯哨 **tiǎodòu hūshào** wolf whistle

跳高 **tiàogāo** high jump

调羹 **tiáogēng** spoon

调合 **tiáohé** set *alarm clock etc*

挑拣 **tiāojiǎn** be selective ◊ selective

条件 **tiáojiàn** condition, term, requirement, stipulation ◊ conditional

条件反射 **tiáojiàn fǎnshè** conditioning

调节 **tiáojié** adjust

调解 **tiáojiě** mediate; reconcile ◊ mediation; reconciliation

调解人 **tiáojiě rén** mediator; troubleshooter

条款 **tiáokuǎn** clause; provision

跳栏 **tiàolán** hurdle; hurdles

跳栏运动员 **tiàolán yùndòng yuán** hurdler

调料 **tiáoliào** spice; herb; condiment; ingredient

调配饮料 **tiáopèi yǐnliào** mixer (*drink*)

调皮 **tiáopí** naughty; rude

调皮鬼 **tiáopíguǐ** little monkey; scamp

跳棋 **tiàoqí** Chinese checkers

调情 **tiáoqíng** flirt; 向 X 调情 **xiàng X tiáoqíng** make a pass at X

调情者 **tiáoqíng zhě** flirt (*person*)

跳棋盘 **tiàoqí pán** checkerboard

跳伞 **tiàosǎn** parachute; bail out

挑三拣四 **tiāosān jiǎnsì** choosey, discriminating

跳伞者 **tiàosǎn zhě** parachutist

调色剂 **tiáosè jì** toner

跳绳 **tiàoshéng** jump rope

跳水 **tiàoshuǐ** dive; diving

跳水板 **tiàoshuǐ bǎn** diving board

跳水者 **tiàoshuǐ zhě** diver

挑剔 **tiāotī** fussy, particular, choosey, picky; 挑剔食物的人 **tiāotī shíwù de rén** fussy eater

挑挑拣拣 **tiāotiāo jiǎnjiǎn** pick and choose ◊ picky, choosey

调停 **tiáotíng** arbitrate, intercede

调味 **tiáowèi** season; 给 X 调味 **gěi X tiáowèi** flavor X

调味品 **tiáowèipǐn** flavoring, seasoning

调味汁儿 **tiáowèi zhīr** dressing

条纹 **tiáowén** streak; stripe

跳舞 **tiàowǔ** dance

调谐 **tiáoxié** tune up

调谐器 **tiáoxié qì** tuner

挑衅 **tiáoxìn** provoke ◊ provocation ◊ provocative

条形码 **tiáoxíng mǎ** bar code

挑选 **tiāoxuǎn** choose, select

调音 **tiáoyīn** tune up

跳远 **tiàoyuǎn** long jump

条约 **tiáoyuē** treaty, pact

跳跃 **tiàoyuè** jump, bound, spring

跳蚤 **tiàozao** flea

跳蚤市场 **tiàozao shìchǎng** flea market

挑战 **tiǎozhàn** challenge; 挑战 X 做 Y **tiǎozhàn X zuò Y** challenge X to Y

挑战者 **tiǎozhàn zhě** challenger

调整 **tiáozhěng** adjust

调制 **tiáozhì** concoct

调制解调器 **tiáozhì jiětiáoqì** modem

调制品 **tiáozhì pǐn** concoction

笤帚 **tiáozhǒu** broom

体操 **tǐcāo** gymnastics

体操家 **tǐcāojiā** gymnast

提倡 **tíchàng** advocate

提出 **tíchū** bring up, broach, raise; advance; 提出辞职通知 **tíchū cízhí tōngzhī** hand in one's notice

提词 **tící** prompt

题词 **tící** dedication ◊ dedicate

替代 **tìdài** replace; deputize for

替代演员 **tìdài yǎnyuán** double (*of actor*)

提到 **tídào** mention, touch on, refer to

剃刀 **tìdāo** shaver

踢踏舞 **tīda wǔ** tap dance

贴 **tiē** stick; 贴壁纸 **tiē bìzhǐ** wallpaper

铁 **tiě** iron

贴边 **tiēbiān** hem; seam; edge

贴标签 **tiē biāoqiān** label

铁饼 **tiěbǐng** discus

铁饭碗 **tiě fànwǎn** iron rice bowl, job for life

铁轨 **tiěguǐ** rail

铁匠 **tiějiàng** blacksmith

铁路 **tiělù** railroad

贴签 **tiēqiān** sticky label

铁锹 **tiěqiāo** shovel, spade

贴身 **tiēshēn** skin-tight ◊ cling

贴邮票 **tiē yóupiào** stamp

体罚 **tǐfá** corporal punishment

提高 **tígāo** raise, elevate; increase; improve ◊ rise

提高 ... 等级 **tígāo ... děngjí** upgrade

提高标价 **tígāo biāojià** mark up

提高价值 **tígāo jiàzhí** appreciate FIN

提高效率 **tígāo xiàolǜ** streamline

体格 **tǐgé** physique; 体格健美 **tǐgé jiànměi** athletic

体格检查 **tǐgé jiǎnchá** physical, medical check-up

提供 **tígōng** supply, provide, furnish; offer; 提供资金 **tígōng zījīn** finance

提供信息 **tígōng xìxī** inform ◊ informative

提供消息人 **tígōng xiāoxī rén** informant

剃光 **tìguāng** shaven

柜橱 **tì guì** chest of drawers

替换 **tìhuàn** substitute, replace; 替换队员 **tìhuàn duìyuán** make a substitution

替换衣服 **tìhuàn yīfu** change one's clothes

剃胡子 **tì húzi** shave

梯级 **tījí** stair; rung

提及 **tíjí** mention

体积 **tǐjī** volume

替件 **tìjiàn** replacement part

提款 **tíkuǎn** withdraw ◊ withdrawal

提炼 **tíliàn** refine

提炼厂 **tíliàn chǎng** refinery

体面 **tǐmiàn** face; dignity ◊ respectable

提名 **tímíng** nominate ◊ nomination

题目 **tímù** topic

体内 **tǐnèi** internally

厅 **tīng** hall; auditorium

听 **tīng** listen; listen to; obey; 我听你之便 **wǒ tīng nǐ zhī biàn** I am at your disposal; 听电话 **tīng**

电话 **diànhuà** answer the telephone

停 **tíng** stop; 停了 **tíngle** come to a stop

亭 **tíng** pavilion

挺 **tǐng** very, quite; 挺好 **tǐng hǎo** very good, terrific

停泊 **tíngbó** moor

停泊区 **tíngbó qū** moorings

听不见 **tīngbújiàn** inaudible

停车 **tíngchē** park ◊ parking

停车标志 **tíngchē biāozhì** stop sign

停车场 **tíngchē chǎng** parking lot; 室内停车场 **shìnèi tíngchē chǎng** parking garage

停车处 **tíngchē chù** parking place

听从 **tīngcóng** obey; respond

听到 **tīngdào** hear; hear about

听得见 **tīngde jiàn** audible

停电 **tíngdiàn** power cut, blackout

停顿 **tíngdùn** pause; disruption ◊ be at a standstill; 使停顿 **shǐ tíngdùn** disrupt

停放 **tíngfàng** park MOT

听话 **tīnghuà** listen; obey ◊ obedient

停火 **tínghuǒ** cease-fire

听见 **tīngjiàn** hear

听距 **tīngjù** within hearing

挺括 **tǐngkuò** crisp

听力 **tīnglì** hearing; comprehension

听起来 **tīngqǐlái** sound; 听起来很有趣 **tīngqǐlái hěn yǒuqù** that sounds interesting

听清楚 **tīng qīngchu** hear, catch

听其自然 **tīngqí zìrán** resign oneself to

听取意见 **tīngqǔ yìjiàn** canvass

挺身而出 **tǐngshēn ér chū** come forward

停尸房 **tíngshīfáng** morgue

听说 ... **tīngshuō ...** people say ..., they say that ...

听天由命 **tīngtiān yóumìng** resigned

听筒 **tīngtǒng** receiver TELEC

停业 **tíngyè** shut down, fold, cease trading

听诊 **tīngzhěn** sound MED

听诊器 **tīngzhěnqì** stethoscope

停职 **tíngzhí** suspension (*from duty*)

停止 **tíngzhǐ** stop, halt; let up

停滞 **tíngzhì** stagnant

挺直 **tǐngzhí** straighten up

停滞不前 **tíngzhì bù qián** come to a halt

停止生产 **tíngzhǐ shēngchǎn** discontinue

听众 **tīngzhòng** audience; listeners

停住 **tíngzhù** stop

亭子 **tíngzi** kiosk; pavilion

提起 **tíqǐ** pull up

提前 **tíqián** early, in advance

提起公诉 **tíqǐ gōngsù** prosecute

提取 **tíqǔ** withdraw; extract

体弱 **tǐruò** infirm; weak ◊ infirmity; 体弱的人 **tǐruò de rén** weakling

提神 **tíshén** freshen up; refresh oneself

提升 **tíshēng** promote

替身演员 **tìshēn yǎnyuán** stuntman

提示 **tíshì** point out; hint ◊ cue

提示符 **tíshìfú** prompt

梯田 **tītián** terraced field, terrace

体贴 **tǐtiē** nice; considerate

剃头匠 **tìtóu jiàng** barber

提问 **tíwèn** ask

体温 **tǐwēn** (body) temperature

体温过低 **tǐwēn guòdī** hypothermia

题献 **tíxiàn** dedicate

体现 **tǐxiàn** embody

提心吊胆 **tíxīn diàodǎn** be on tenterhooks

提醒 **tíxǐng** remind; 提醒X做Y **tíxǐng X zuò Y** remind X to do Y

体臭 **tǐxiù** BO, body odor

剃须刀 **tìxū dāo** razor

剃须刀刀片 **tìxū dāo dāopiàn** razor blade

剃须膏 **tìxūgāo** shaving soap

体验 **tǐyàn** experience

提议 **tíyì** suggest, propose ◊ proposal, motion

体育 **tǐyù** sport

体育版 **tǐyù bǎn** sports page

体育场 **tǐyù chǎng** stadium

体育馆 **tǐyù guǎn** gymnasium

体育记者 **tǐyù jìzhě** sports journalist

体育新闻 **tǐyù xīnwén** sports news

体育运动 **tǐyù yùndòng** sport ◊ sporting

体质 **tǐzhì** physique; constitution

体制 **tǐzhì** system

体重 **tǐzhòng** (body) weight

梯子 **tīzi** ladder

替罪羊 **tìzuìyáng** scapegoat

通 **tōng** through; 通了 **tōngle** you're through TELEC

铜 **tóng** copper

童 **tóng** child

瞳 **tóng** pupil

同 **tóng** same; similar; with; and

桶 **tǒng** barrel, drum; tub; pail

捅 **tǒng** poke, prod

统 **tǒng** unite

痛 **tòng** pain, hurt; ache ◊ sore, aching; 痛不痛? **tòng bútòng?** does it hurt?

同伴 **tóngbàn** partner

铜版画 **tóngbǎnhuà** copperplate

同胞 **tóngbāo** fellow citizen; fellow countryman

同步 **tóngbù** same speed; 使...同步 **shǐ...tóngbù** synchronize

统舱 **tǒngcāng** lower deck

通常 **tōngcháng** usual, normal; usually, normally

通常开支 **tōngcháng kāizhī** overhead FIN

痛打 **tòngdǎ** thrashing, hiding ◊ lay into

同代人 **tóngdài rén** contemporary

通道 **tōngdào** passage; aisle

同等 **tóngděng** equal ◊ equally; 同等价值 **tóngděng jiàzhí** of equal value

同等人 **tóngděngrén** peer

通风 **tōngfēng** air; ventilate ◊ airy; drafty ◊ ventilation

通风报信 **tōngfēng bàoxìn** tip off

通风井 **tōngfēng jǐng** ventilation shaft

通风孔 tōngfēng kǒng vent

通风设备 tōngfēng shèbèi ventilator

同感 tónggǎn sympathy

通告 tōnggào notice

通关 tōngguān customs clearance

铜管乐队 tóngguǎn yuèduì brass band

通过 tōngguò pass, get by ◊ via, through; 通过考试 tōngguò kǎoshì pass an exam; 通过他安排 tōngguò tā ānpái arranged through him

童话 tónghuà fairy tale

通货膨胀 tōnghuò péngzhàng inflation

通货再膨胀 tōnghuò zài péngzhàng reflation

通缉 tōngjí: 被通缉 bèi tōngjí wanted

统计 tǒngjì statistics ◊ statistical

同届 tóngjiè contemporary

统计学 tǒngjì xué statistics; 从统计学角度来说 cóng tǒngjìxué jiǎodù láishuō statistically

统计资料 tǒngjì zīliào statistics

同居 tóngjū cohabit; 和X同居 hé X tóngjū live with X

瞳孔 tóngkǒng pupil

痛哭 tòngkū bawl, wail

恸哭 tòngkū bawl, wail

痛苦 tòngkǔ suffering; misery; distress; discomfort; 令人痛苦 lìngrén tòngkǔ painful; distressing

痛快一番 tòngkuài yīfān go (out) on a spree

恸哭声 tòngkūshēng wail

通力合作 tōnglì hézuò pull together

同卵双胎 tóngluǎn shuāngtāi identical twins

同盟 tóngméng alliance, confederation

同盟者 tóngméng zhě ally

同名人 tóngmíng rén namesake

童年 tóngnián childhood

同年 tóngnián same year ◊ of the same age

铜牌 tóngpái bronze medal

通气 tōngqì ventilate, air

痛切 tòngqiè poignant

通气管 tōngqìguǎn snorkel

同情 tóngqíng pity; sympathize with; empathize with; commiserate ◊ compassion

通情达理 tōngqíng dálǐ understanding

同情心 tóngqíngxīn sympathy

同时 tóngshí at the same time, simultaneously, together; in the meantime ◊ simultaneous

同事 tóngshì colleague, associate

痛惜 tòngxī deplore

通向 tōngxiàng give onto

通宵 tōngxiāo throughout the night

通晓 tōngxiǎo familiarity

通泄药 tōngxiè yào laxative

通信 tōngxìn correspond

通行费 tōngxíng fèi toll

同性恋 tóngxìngliàn homosexual ◊ homosexuality

同性恋者 tóngxìngliàn zhě homosexual; lesbian

通行权 tōngxíng quán right of way

同形异义词 tóngxíng yìyì cí homograph

通行证 tōngxíngzhèng pass

通信联络 tōngxìn liánluò correspondence

通信员 tōngxìn yuán messenger

通信者 tōngxìn zhě correspondent

同学 tóngxué classmate; fellow student

通讯录 tōngxùn lù address book

通讯社 tōngxùn shè news agency

通讯卫星 tōngxùn wèixīng communications satellite

通讯业 tōngxùn yè communications

通讯员 tōngxùn yuán correspondent

同样 tóngyàng same

童谣 tóngyáo nursery rhyme

同意 tóngyì agree, concur; consent; grant ◊ agreement; approval; 我同意这个想法 wǒ tóngyì zhège xiǎngfǎ I am for the idea

统一 **tǒngyī** unite; unify ◊ unified; uniform ◊ uniformly ◊ unity; unification

同义词 **tóngyìcí** synonym

统一收费率 **tǒngyī shōufèilǜ** flat rate

同意资助 **tóngyì zīzhù** underwrite FIN

同狱犯人 **tóngyù fànrén** inmate

通知 **tōngzhī** inform, notify; report ◊ circular; notice

同志 **tóngzhì** comrade

统治 **tǒngzhì** reign; rule

统治者 **tǒngzhì zhě** ruler

童装 **tóngzhuāng** children's clothes

偷 **tōu** take, steal

头 **tóu** head

投 **tóu** hurl, fling, throw; pitch

透 **tòu** pass through

投案 **tóu'àn** give oneself up

头版 **tóubǎn** front page

头版新闻 **tóubǎn xīnwén** front page news

投标 **tóubiāo** tender

偷捕 **tōubǔ** poach

头朝下 **tóu cháoxià** head over heels

投弹手 **tóudàn shǒu** bomber (terrorist)

头等 **tóuděng** first class

头等大事 **tóuděng dàshì** a matter of paramount importance ◊ be paramount

投递 **tóudì** deliver ◊ delivery

头顶 **tóudǐng** top of the head

头顶上 **tóudǐng shàng** overhead

头顶头 **tóudǐngtóu** head-on

偷东西 **tōu dōngxi** steal

头发 **tóufa** hair; 做头发 **zuò tóufa** have one's hair done

头发花白 **tóufa huābái** gray-haired

投稿 **tóugǎo** contribute ◊ contribution

投稿人 **tóugǎo rén** contributor

头昏脑胀 **tóuhūn nǎozhàng** dizzy, giddy

投机活动 **tóujī huódòng** venture

投机买卖 **tóujī mǎimài** speculation

头巾 **tóujīn** (head)scarf

透镜 **tòujìng** lens

投机商 **tóujī shāng** speculator FIN

偷看一眼 **tōukàn yīyǎn** sneak a glance at

头靠 **tóukào** headrest

头盔 **tóukuī** helmet

偷懒 **tōulǎn** laze around; goof off

头栏 **tóulán** header

投篮 **tóulán** shoot (at the basket)

头颅 **tóulú** skull

头路 **tóulù** part (in hair)

透露 **tòulù** leak out; disclose, divulge ◊ disclosure; 未透露 **wèi tòulù** untold

头盖骨 **tóugàigǔ** skull

透露真相 **tòulù zhēnxiàng** revealing

透明 **tòumíng** see-through, transparent

头目 **tóumù** ringleader

偷拿 **tōuná** sneak, steal

头脑 **tóunǎo** mind; chief

头脑简单 **tóunǎo jiǎndān** simple(-minded)

头脑冷静 **tóunǎo lěngjìng** level-headed; 头脑敏锐的人 **tóunǎo mǐnruì de rén** clear thinker

头盘 **tóupán** starter (of meal)

头皮 **tóupí** scalp

投票 **tóupiào** vote ◊ voting; ballot

投票间 **tóupiào jiān** voting booth

投票决定 **tóupiào juédìng** ballot; vote on

投票箱 **tóupiào xiāng** ballot box

投票站 **tóupiàozhàn** polling booth

头皮屑 **tóupíxiè** dandruff

投弃 **tóuqì** jettison

偷窃 **tōuqiè** steal ◊ larceny, theft

投球 **tóuqiú** pitch

投入 **tóurù** put in, insert; plunge into; inject ◊ input; injection

透入 **tòurù** penetrate

头上空间 **tóushang kōngjiān** headroom

投手 **tóushǒu** pitcher

投手场地 **tóushǒu chǎngdì** mound

偷税 **tōushuì** evade taxes

透水汽 **tòu shuǐqì** porous

投诉 **tóusù** complain; make a fuss ◊ complaint

头条新闻 **tóutiáo xīnwén** headline news

偷听 **tōutīng** overhear; eavesdrop

头痛 **tóutòng** headache

偷偷 **tōutōu** furtive; 偷偷溜进房间 **tōutōu liūjìn fángjiān** sneak into the room

头衔 **tóuxián** title

投降 **tóuxiáng** yield, surrender ◊ submission

投影器 **tóuyīng qì** projector

头晕 **tóuyūn** dizzy, giddy ◊ feel dizzy

投掷 **tóuzhì** throw

透支 **tòuzhī** advance

头重脚轻 **tóuzhòng jiǎoqīng** top-heavy

骰子 **tóuzi** dice

投资 **tóuzī** invest ◊ investment

投资者 **tóuzī zhě** investor

偷走 **tōuzǒu** snatch; make off with

突突 **tū** suddenly

秃突 **tū** bald

图突 **tú** picture; diagram

涂突 **tú** apply

屠突 **tú** kill

途突 **tú** path; road; way

徒突 **tú** follower; disciple

土突 **tǔ** earth; land

吐突 **tǔ** spit

吐突 **tù** vomit; 我要吐 **wǒ yào tù** I'm going to throw up

兔突 **tù** rabbit; hare

图案 **tú'àn** pattern; design

团 **tuán** round ◊ gather ◊ group; society; mass; wad; expedition; regiment

团结 **tuánjié** unite ◊ united; 团结在X的周围 **tuánjié zài X de zhōuwéi** rally around X

团结一致 **tuánjié yīzhì** solidarity

团聚 **tuánjù** reunion ◊ reunite

湍流 **tuānliú** turbulence

团体 **tuántǐ** group

团圆 **tuányuán** reunion; get-together

团子 **tuánzi** dumpling

图板 **túbǎn** drawing board

突变 **tūbiàn** sudden change

图标 **túbiāo** icon

图表 **túbiǎo** chart; graph

徒步旅行 **túbù lǚxíng** backpack

徒步旅行者 **túbù lǚxíng zhě** hiker; walker; backpacker

涂层 **túcéng** coat

突出 **tūchū** stick out, project ◊ prominent; imposing; glaring; outstanding, excellent; 突出的椎间盘 **tūchūde zhuījiānpán** slipped disc

吐出 **tǔchū** spit (out); 吐出心里的话 **tǔchū xīnlǐ de huà** get … off one's chest

凸窗 **tūchuāng** bay window

土地 **tǔdì** land; soil

秃顶 **tūdǐng** bald; 他开始秃顶了 **tā kāishǐ tūdǐng le** he's going bald

图钉 **túdǐng** thumbtack

土豆 **tǔdòu** potato

土豆泥 **tǔdòuní** mashed potatoes

土耳其 **Tú'ěrqí** Turkey ◊ Turkish

突发奇想 **tūfā qíxiǎng** whim

土匪 **tǔfěi** bandit

屠夫 **túfū** butcher

涂改液 **túgǎiyè** whiteout (*for text*)

图画 **túhuà** picture; drawing; painting

图画书 **túhuàshū** picture book

推 **tuī** push; jolt

腿 **tuǐ** leg

退 **tuì** move backward; retreat; retire

退步 **tuìbù** go backward; fall behind

推测 **tuīcè** suspect; assume; presume; guess

退场 **tuìchǎng** exit; walk out

退潮 **tuìcháo** ebb tide

推迟 **tuīchí** postpone, put off, defer; delay

推出 **tuīchū** bring out

退出 **tuìchū** withdraw, pull out, stand down, drop out; exit, quit

推辞 **tuīcí** decline

退掉 **tuìdiào** take back; 退掉X **tuìdiào X** take X back to the store

推定 **tuīdìng** presumption

推动 **tuīdòng** push forward; promote; boost; budge

推动力 **tuīdòng lì** impetus

推断 **tuīduàn** conclude ◊ conclusion; 由 Y 推断出 X **yóu Y tuīduàn chū X** conclude X from Y

腿肚子 **tuǐdùzi** calf (of leg)

推翻 **tuīfān** overthrow, topple, overturn

颓废 **tuífèi** decadent

退格 **tuìgé** backspace (key)

推合门 **tuīhémén** swing-door

退化 **tuìhuà** degenerate into

退还 **tuìhuán** return, send back

推挤 **tuījǐ** jostle

推荐 **tuījiàn** recommend ◊ recommendation; reference; 推荐 X 任某个职位 **tuījiàn X rèn mǒugè zhíwèi** recommend X for a post

推荐人 **tuījiàn rén** referee

推进 **tuījìn** propel

推开 **tuīkāi** push away

退款 **tuìkuǎn** refund

推理 **tuīlǐ** deduce

推论 **tuīlùn** deduction

退落 **tuìluò** ebb

蜕皮 **tuìpí** peel; shed its skin

退去 **tuìqù** subside

退让 **tuìràng** retreat

退色 **tuìsè** faded

退烧 **tuìshāo** subside (of fever)

退缩 **tuìsuō** flinch; wince

推土机 **tuītǔ jī** bulldozer

退位 **tuìwèi** abdicate

推诿责任 **tuīwěi zérèn** pass the buck

退伍 **tuìwǔ** discharge

退伍军人 **tuìwǔ jūnrén** veteran

推想 **tuīxiǎng** gather, understand

推销 **tuīxiāo** market, sell; plug ◊ marketing

推销员 **tuīxiāo yuán** salesman

推行 **tuīxíng** implement; pursue

退休 **tuìxiū** retire ◊ retired ◊ retirement

退休金 **tuìxiū jīn** pension

退休老人 **tuìxiū lǎorén** senior citizen

退休年龄 **tuìxiū niánlíng** retirement age

退休者 **tuìxiū zhě** retired person; pensioner

退学学生 **tuìxué xuéshēng** dropout

推移 **tuīyí** pass, go by ◊ passage (of time)

退职金 **tuìzhí jīn** gratuity (on retirement)

推子 **tuīzi** clippers

突击 **tūjī** rush

途经 **tújīng** by way of, via ◊ pass through

途径 **tújìng** way, path; gateway

土块 **tǔkuài** clump

凸块儿 **tūkuàir** bump

徒劳 **túláo** thankless ◊ in vain

图利 **túlì** mercenary

涂料 **túliào** paint; 上涂料 **shàng túliào** paint

吐露 **tùlù** confide

涂满 **túmǎn** be plastered with

涂抹 **túmǒ** smear

图谋 **túmóu** scheme

土木工程师 **tǔmù gōngchéngshī** civil engineer

吞 **tūn** swallow

吞并 **tūnbìng** annex

臀部 **túnbù** buttocks; rump; hip

臀部牛排 **túnbù niúpái** rumpsteak

吞饵 **tūn'ěr** bite (of fish)

囤积 **túnjī** hoard

吞没 **tūnmò** engulf

吞食 **tūnshí** devour

豚鼠 **túnshǔ** guinea pig

吞吞吐吐 **tūntūn tǔtu** cagey

吞下 **tūnxià** down; keep down food

吞咽 **tūnyàn** gulp

脱 **tuō** remove, get off; take down

拖 **tuō** drag; pull

托 **tuō** entrust

妥 **tuǒ** appropriate

拖把 **tuōbǎ** mop

驼背 **tuóbèi** hunchback; hump

拖布 **tuōbù** mop

拖长 **tuōcháng** drag out, spin out

拖车 **tuōchē** trailer; wrecker

拖船 **tuōchuán** tug

拖地 **tuōdì** mop

脱掉 **tuōdiào** slip off

拖动 **tuōdòng** drag

托儿所 **tuō'érsuǒ** day-nursery, crèche

驼峰 **tuófēng** hump

脱光衣服 **tuōguāng yīfu** strip

托架 **tuōjià** bracket (*for shelf*)

脱缰 **tuōjiāng** bolt

脱节 **tuōjié** disjointed

脱臼 **tuōjiù** dislocation

拖拉 **tuōlā** trail

拖拉机 **tuōlājī** tractor

拖缆 **tuōlǎn** towrope

脱离 **tuōlí** break away ◊ out of

脱粒 **tuōlì** thresh

脱离关系 **tuōlí guānxì** disown

脱离危险 **tuōlí wēixiǎn** out of danger

驼鹿 **tuólù** moose, elk

脱落 **tuōluò** come off; fall out; peel; shed

陀螺 **tuóluó** (spinning) top

唾沫 **tuòmo** spittle

鸵鸟 **tuóniǎo** ostrich

拖盘 **tuōpán** tray

拖欠 **tuōqiàn** be in arrears

拖欠款 **tuōqiàn kuǎn** arrears

脱去衣服 **tuōqù yīfu** strip

脱色 **tuōsè** lose its color, fade; 使脱色 **shǐ tuōsè** bleach

脱水 **tuōshuǐ** dehydrated

拖网鱼船 **tuōwǎng yúchuán** trawler

托位 **tuōwèi** dislocate

拖鞋 **tuōxié** slippers; flip-flops; mules

妥协 **tuǒxié** compromise

拖延 **tuōyán** stall

脱氧核糖核酸 **tuōyǎng hétáng hésuān** DNA, deoxyribonucleic acid

托曳 **tuōyè** haul; pull

唾液 **tuòyè** saliva

脱衣服 **tuō yīfu** undress, get undressed

脱颖而出 **tuō yǐng ér chū** come to the fore

椭圆 **tuǒyuán** oval; ellipse

托运 **tuōyùn** ship, send

托运公司 **tuōyùn gōngsī** freight company, freight forwarder

脱脂棉 **tuōzhīmián** absorbent cotton

脱脂乳 **tuōzhīrǔ** skimmed milk

拖走 **tuōzǒu** tow away

涂片 **túpiàn** smear

突破 **tūpò** breakthrough; penetration

土丘 **tǔqiū** mound

突然 **tūrán** suddenly ◊ abrupt, sudden; 突然跌落 **tūrán diēluò** plunge; 突然袭击 **tūrán xíjī** raid; pounce

土壤 **tǔrǎng** soil

土人 **tǔrén** native

屠杀 **túshā** massacre; slaughter

徒手格斗 **túshǒu gédòu** unarmed combat

图书馆 **túshūguǎn** library

图书馆员 **túshūguǎn yuán** librarian

吐痰 **tǔtán** spit

突袭 **tūxí** raid

图形 **túxíng** figure; graphic

徒刑 **túxíng** prison sentence

图形卡 **túxíngkǎ** graphics card

图形控制器 **túxíng kòngzhì qì** graphics controller

图形学 **túxíngxué** graphics

凸印 **tūyìn** emboss

涂油漆 **tú yóuqī** paint

屠宰 **túzǎi** slaughter

屠宰场 **túzǎichǎng** slaughterhouse

突增 **tūzēng** jump

图章 **túzhāng** chop, stamp, seal

途中 **túzhōng** en route

土著 **tǔzhù** native

兔子 **tùzi** rabbit; hare

T字形拐杖 **T zì xíng guǎizhàng** crutch

# UW

U形弯 **U xíngwān** U-turn

挖 **wā** dig

蛙 **wā** frog

瓦 **wǎ** roof tile

袜 **wà** socks; stockings

挖鼻孔 **wā bíkǒng** pick one's nose

挖出 **wāchū** dredge up

歪 **wāi** leaning, slanting; crooked

外 **wài** outside ◊ external; foreign; outward ◊ externally; outwardly

外币 **wàibì** foreign currency

外边 **wàibiān** outside; offside

外表 **wàibiǎo** appearance; exterior; façade; veneer ◊ outward

外部 **wàibù** outside, exterior ◊ outer; external

外出 **wàichū** go out

外出旅程 **wàichū lǚchéng** outward journey

外公 **wàigōng** grandfather (*maternal*)

外观 **wàiguān** exterior; appearance; look

外国 **wàiguó** foreign country ◊ abroad ◊ foreign

外国人 **wàiguó rén** foreigner

外行 **wàiháng** layman; layperson

外号 **wàihào** nickname

外汇 **wàihuì** foreign currency, foreign exchange

外交 **wàijiāo** diplomacy ◊ diplomatic

外交部 **Wàijiāobù** Department of State, Ministry of Foreign Affairs

外交部长 **Wàijiāobù Zhǎng** Secretary of State, Foreign Minister

外交官 **wàijiāo guān** diplomat

外交免疫力 **wàijiāo miǎnyì lì** diplomatic immunity

外交事物 **wàijiāo shìwù** foreign affairs

外交政策 **wàijiāo zhèngcè** foreign policy

外景 **wàijǐng** on location

外科 **wàikē** surgical

外壳 **wàiké** hull; husk

外科医师 **wàikē yīshī** surgeon

外来语 **wàiláiyǔ** foreign word; loan word

外贸 **wàimào** foreign trade

外面 **wàimiàn** outside ◊ external

外婆 **wàipó** grandmother (*maternal*)

歪曲 **wāiqū** distort, misrepresent; 对正义的歪曲 **duì zhèngyì de wāiqū** travesty of justice

外甥 **wàisheng** nephew (*sister's son*)

外甥女 **wàishengnǚ** niece (*sister's daughter*)

外孙女 **wàisūnnǚ** granddaughter (*daughter's daughter*)

外孙子 **wàisūnzi** grandson (*daughter's son*)

外围装置 **wàiwéi zhuāngzhì** peripheral

外星人 **wàixīng rén** alien

外衣 **wàiyī** coat

外语 **wàiyǔ** foreign language

曾外孙 **wàizēngsūn** great-grandson (*daughter's grandson*)

外祖父 **wàizǔfù** grandfather (*maternal*)

外祖父母 **wàizǔfùmǔ** grandparents (*maternal*)

外祖母 **wàizǔmǔ** grandmother (*maternal*)

瓦解 **wǎjiě** disintegrate

挖掘 **wājué** excavate ◊ excavation

挖掘机 **wājuéjī** excavator

挖空 **wākōng** excavate; dig

挖苦 **wākǔ** dry

瓦楞铁 **wǎlèngtiě** corrugated iron

瓦楞纸板 **wǎléng zhǐbǎn** corrugated cardboard

瓦砾 **wǎlì** rubble

湾 **wān** bay

弯 **wān** bend ◊ bent

完 **wán** finish ◊ finished, over; complete; 她还没完呢 **tā hái méiwán ne** she still hasn't finished; 完了 **wánle** be through, be finished; 完了！ **wánle!** that's it!; there you are!

玩 **wán** play

碗 **wǎn** bowl

晚 **wǎn** late ◊ evening; night; 天晚了 **tiānwǎn le** it's getting late

万 **wàn** ten thousand

晚安 **wǎn'ān** good night

晚报 **wǎnbào** evening paper

完毕 **wánbì** finished

晚餐 **wǎncān** dinner

完成 **wánchéng** complete; accomplish ◊ completion

完成式 **wánchéngshì** perfect tense

碗橱 **wǎnchú** cupboard

晚点 **wǎndiǎn** delayed

碗碟柜 **wǎndié guì** dresser

豌豆 **wāndòu** pea

晚饭 **wǎnfàn** supper

王 **wáng** king

网 **wǎng** net; network; web; grid; Internet; 一网鱼 **yìwǎngyú** a haul of fish

往 **wǎng** to; toward ◊ past

忘 **wàng** forget

望 **wàng** look ahead; expect

旺 **wàng** prosperous

网吧 **wǎngbā** Internet café

挽歌 **wǎngē** lament

忘恩负义 **wàng'ēn fùyì** ingratitude

往返 **wǎngfǎn** there and back

王国 **wángguó** kingdom

王后 **wánghòu** queen (*monarch's wife*)

旺火煸炒 **wànghuǒ biānchǎo** stir-fry

忘记 **wàngjì** forget

旺季 **wàngjì** high season

往来 **wǎnglái** contact; dealings; relations

网络 **wǎngluò** network; Internet

网络服务 **wǎngluò fúwù** on-line

service

完工 **wángōng** complete

王牌 **wángpái** trump card

网球 **wǎngqiú** tennis; tennis ball

网球场 **wǎngqiú chǎng** tennis court

网球拍 **wǎngqiú pāi** tennis racket

网球手 **wǎngqiú shǒu** tennis player

网球网 **wǎngqiú wǎng** net (*in tennis*)

忘却 **wàngquè** forget; get over *lover etc*

网上 **wǎngshang** on-line COMPUT

往事 **wǎngshì** the past

顽固 **wángù** obstinate, stubborn; set ◊ obstinacy

汪汪叫 **wāngwang jiào** yap; bark

王位 **wángwèi** throne

往下 **wǎngxià** downward

妄想 **wàngxiǎng** delusion

妄想狂 **wàngxiǎng kuáng** paranoia

网眼 **wǎngyǎn** mesh

望远镜 **wàngyuǎn jìng** telescope; binoculars

网址 **wǎngzhǐ** web site; web page

王子 **wángzǐ** prince

妄自尊大的人 **wàngzì zūndà de rén** squirt

完好无损 **wánhǎo wúsǔn** sound, in good repair

晚会 **wǎnhuì** party; (evening) function

玩忽职守 **wánhū zhíshǒu** misconduct; negligence; malpractice

完结 **wánjié** be over

万金油 **wànjīnyóu** balm

挽救 **wǎnjiù** retrieve

玩具 **wánjù** toy

万里长城 **Wànlǐ Chángchéng** Great Wall of China

晚礼服 **wǎnlǐfú** evening dress

完美 **wánměi** perfect, flawless; beautiful ◊ perfection

完美主义者 **wánměi zhǔyì zhě** perfectionist

万能钥匙 **wànnéng yàoshi** master key, skeleton key

顽皮 **wánpí** mischievous

晚期 wǎnqī terminal ◊ terminally

顽强 wánqiáng stubborn; tenacious

弯曲 wānqū bend ◊ crooked ◊ curve; 使弯曲 shǐ wānqū warp

完全 wánquán complete; total ◊ completely, fully; 完全一样 wánquán yīyàng exactly the same

玩儿 wánr play; party; 玩儿开心点儿 wánr kāixīn diǎnr have a good time

完善 wánshàn perfect

晚上 wǎnshang evening; 晚上十一点 wǎnshàng shíyī diǎn 11 o'clock at night; 晚上好! wǎnshang hǎo! good evening!

弯身 wānshēn bend; double up

玩世不恭 wán shì bù gōng cynically

玩耍 wánshuǎ enjoy oneself

玩童 wántóng urchin

弯弯曲曲 wānwan qūqu twisty

万无一失 wàn wú yì shī unerring

惋惜 wǎnxī pity; 令人惋惜 lìngrén wǎnxī lamentable

玩笑 wánxiào joke

万幸 wànxìng fortunate

蜿蜒 wānyán wind ◊ winding; 蜿蜒行进 wānyán xíngjìn wriggle

晚宴服 wǎnyànfú evening wear

弯腰 wānyāo bend down, stoop

弯腰曲背 wānyāo qūbèi stoop

万一 ... wànyī ... in case ...

玩意儿 wányìr trinket

玩杂耍 wán záshuǎ juggle

玩杂耍的人 wán záshuǎ de rén juggler

完整 wánzhěng complete; thorough ◊ completely

婉转地叫 wǎnzhuǎn de jiào warble

晚走 wǎnzǒu stay behind

蛙人 wārén frogman

瓦特 wǎtè watt

娃娃 wáwa doll

挖心 wāxīn core

蛙泳 wāyǒng breaststroke

袜子 wàzi socks; stockings

煨 wēi poach

微 wēi small; micro-

危 wēi danger

违 wéi break; transgress; violate

围 wéi encircle; surround; besiege; 用栅栏围起 yòng zhàlán wéiqǐ fence in

唯 wéi only

为 wéi be ◊ as ◊ achievement

伪 wéi false

伟 wéi great

尾 wěi tail; end

喂 wèi hello TELEC; hey! ◊ feed animals etc

位 wèi position

为 wèi for; 为 ... 干杯 wèi ... gānbēi toast, propose a toast to; 为 ... 辩护 wèi ... biànhù stick up for

未 wèi not yet; not; 未成文 wèi chéngwén unwritten

味 wèi taste

畏 wèi fear

胃 wèi stomach

卫 wèi guard

尾巴 wěiba tail

违背 wéibèi violate; disobey; go against ◊ violation

卫兵 wèibīng guard

微波 wēibō microwave

微薄 wēibó sparse; scanty ◊ scantily; sparsely; 微薄的工资 wēibóde gōngzī pittance

微波炉 wēibōlú microwave (oven)

微不足道 wēi bù zú dào paltry, derisory

未曾 wèicéng never

围场 wéichǎng pound (for strays)

未成年 wèi chéngnián juvenile; underage

未成年人 wèichéngnián rén minor, juvenile

维持 wéichí maintain; get by; hold out

维持生活 wéichí shēnghuó manage

微处理机 wēichǔlǐjī microprocessor

未出生 wèi chūshēng unborn

为此 wèicǐ for this reason

伟大 wěidà great ◊ greatness

味道 wèidao taste, flavor

尾灯 wěidēng tail light

微电子学 wēidiànzǐ xué

microelectronics

纬度 **wěidù** latitude

纬度线 **wěidùxiàn** parallel

巍峨 **wēi'é** lofty

违法 **wéifǎ** illicit, illegal ◊ illegally

违法者 **wéifǎ zhě** criminal; lawbreaker

违反 **wéifǎn** break, contravene

违犯 **wéifàn** violate, breach ◊ violation

违反合同 **wéifǎn hétóng** breach of contract

违反交通法规 **wéifàn jiāotōng fǎguī** traffic violation

微风 **wēifēng** breeze

未付 **wèifù** nonpayment ◊ outstanding

威佛饼干 **wēifú bǐnggān** wafer

桅杆 **wéigān** mast

微光 **wēiguāng** gleam, glimmer

微观世界 **wēiguān shìjiè** microcosm

危害 **wēihài** damage

威吓 **wēihè** intimidate

维护 **wéihù** defend, stand up for; uphold; preserve ◊ maintenance

未婚 **wèihūn** unmarried

未婚夫 **wèihūnfū** fiancé

未婚妻 **wèihūnqī** fiancée

维护 **wéihù** protect, look after

危机 **wēijī** crisis

危急 **wēijí** critical; desperate ◊ critically

危及 **wēijí** endanger

未解决 **wèi jiějué** unsettled

围巾 **wéijīn** scarf

味精 **wèijīng** monosodium glutamate

未经加工 **wèijīng jiāgōng** raw, unprocessed

微晶片 **wēijīngpiàn** microchip

伪君子 **wěijūnzǐ** hypocrite

违抗 **wéikàng** defy ◊ in defiance of

胃口 **wèikǒu** appetite

围困 **wéikùn** besiege ◊ siege

未来 **wèilái** future

未来式 **wèiláishì** future tense ◊ futuristic

慰劳金 **wèiláojīn** golden handshake

为了 **wèile** for; in order to; because of; 为了我 **wèile wǒ** for my sake

微量 **wēiliàng** trace

帷幕 **wéimù** curtain

喂奶 **wèinǎi** breast-feed

为难 **wéinán** uncomfortable; distressed; 使为难 **shǐ wéinán** disconcert

味浓 **wèinóng** strong

委派 **wěipài** posting

围棋 **Wéiqí** Go

委屈 **wěiqu** injustice

围裙 **wéiqún** apron

围绕 **wéirǎo** surround; revolve around ◊ around

委任 **wěirèn** appoint

微弱 **wēiruò** feeble

伪善 **wěishàn** hypocrisy

未删节 **wèi shānjié** full-length

伪善言词 **wěishàn yáncí** cant

危慑 **wēishè** deter

卫生 **wèishēng** hygienic, sanitary ◊ hygiene

卫生带 **wèishēngdài** sanitary napkin

卫生间 **wèishēngjiān** rest room

卫生间用品 **wèishēngjiān yòngpǐn** toiletries

卫生巾 **wèishēngjīn** sanitary napkin

卫生设备 **wèishēng shèbèi** sanitation

维生素 **wéishēngsù** vitamin

卫生纸 **wèishēngzhǐ** toilet paper

为什么 **wèishénme?** why?; what for?; 为什么不？ **wèishénme bù?** why not?

危慑因素 **wēishè yīnsù** deterrent

威士忌 **wēishìjì** whiskey

卫戍部队 **wèishù bùduì** garrison

畏缩 **wèisuō** recoil; shrink from; shy away

维他命 **wéitāmìng** vitamin

维他命药片 **wéitāmìng yàopiàn** vitamin pill

胃痛 **wèitòng** stomach ache

委托 **wěituō** commission; 把Y委托给X **bǎ Y wěituōgěi X** entrust Y to X

未完待续 **wèiwán dàixù** to be continued

威望 **wēiwàng** prestige

委婉说法 **wěiwǎn shuōfǎ** euphemism

微温 **wēiwēn** lukewarm, tepid

唯物论 **wéiwùlùn** materialistic

唯物主义 **wéiwù zhǔyì** materialism

唯物主义者 **wéiwù zhǔyì zhě** materialist

危险 **wēixiǎn** danger, hazard, peril ◊ dangerous, unsafe; 处于危险境地 **chǔyú wēixiǎn jìngdì** be in jeopardy

危险人物 **wēixiǎn rénwù** security risk

危险者 **wēixiǎn zhě** menace

微小 **wēixiǎo** tiny, minute, minuscule

微笑 **wēixiào** smile; 对 … 微笑 **duì … wēixiào** smile at

威胁 **wēixié** threat; menace; intimidation ◊ threaten, intimidate ◊ menacing

猥亵 **wěixiè** obscene, filthy

微型 **wēixíng** pocket

卫星 **wèixīng** satellite

微型电视 **wēixíng diànshì** portable TV

卫星电视 **wèixīng diànshì** satellite TV

卫星电视盘 **wèixīng diànshì pán** satellite dish

唯心论 **wéixīn lùn** spiritualism

维修 **wéixiū** maintain; service; repair

威严 **wēiyán** majestic

喂养 **wèiyǎng** feed

偎依 **wēiyī** nestle, snuggle; cling

唯一 **wéiyī** sole, only, single ◊ solely

位于 **wèiyú** be situated; lie

委员会 **wěiyuánhuì** commission; committee

未预见到 **wèi yùjiàn dào** unforeseen

伪造 **wěizào** counterfeit, forge; falsify

伪造品 **wěizào pǐn** forgery

伪造人 **wěizào rén** forger

违章停车罚款单 **wéizhāng tíngchē fákuǎndān** parking ticket

位置 **wèizhi** location, position; locality, situation

未知 **wèizhī** unknown

未支付 **wèi zhīfù** unsettled

围住 **wéizhù** enclose

伪装 **wěizhuāng** disguise; camouflage ◊ dress up ◊ phoney; 伪装为 X **wěizhuāng wéi X** masquerade as X

位子 **wèizi** seat, place

围嘴 **wéizuǐ** bib

温 **wēn** warm

闻 **wén** smell, sniff

文 **wén** writing; language; literature; culture

蚊 **wén** mosquito

吻 **wěn** kiss

稳 **wěn** stable; steady

问 **wèn** ask; question, query

闻出 **wénchū** smell

问答比赛 **wèndá bǐsài** quiz

问答卷 **wèndá juàn** questionnaire

稳定 **wěndìng** stable ◊ stability ◊ stabilize

温度 **wēndù** temperature

温度表 **wēndùbiǎo** thermometer

温度计 **wēndùjì** thermometer

稳而有力 **wěn ér yǒulì** firm

翁 **wēng** old man

嗡鸣声 **wēngmíng shēng** drone, droning noise

稳固 **wěngù** rigid

嗡嗡作响 **wēngwēng zuòxiǎng** hum; buzz

问好 **wènhǎo** ask after; send greetings; 向她问好 **xiàng tā wènhǎo** give her my love; send her my best wishes

问号 **wènhào** question mark

温和 **wēnhé** mild; moderate; mellow ◊ mildness

温和派 **wēnhépài** moderate POL

问候 **wènhòu** send one's regards; say hello; ask after; 代我向 X 候 **dài wǒ xiàng X wènhòu** give my regards to X

文化 **wénhuà** culture ◊ cultural

文化冲击 wénhuà chōngjī culture shock

文化大革命 Wénhuà Dàgémìng Cultural Revolution

文件 wénjiàn document; papers; documentation; file

文件管理程序 wénjiàn guǎnlǐ chéngxù file manager

文件夹 wénjiàn jiá folder

文具 wénjù stationery

文具商店 wénjù shāngdiàn stationery store

文科硕士 wénkē shuòshì Master of Arts

文科学位 wénkē xuéwèi arts degree

文盲 wénmáng illiterate

文明 wénmíng civilization; culture

闻名 wénmíng famous

温暖 wēnnuǎn warm

文凭 wénpíng qualification; diploma; certificate

文乞 wénqǐ hack

温柔 wēnróu gentle, soft; tender

纹身 wénshēn tattoo

温室 wēnshì greenhouse, hothouse

温室气体 wēnshì qìtǐ greenhouse gas

温室效应 wēnshì xiàoyìng greenhouse effect

文书工作 wénshū gōngzuò paperwork

温顺 wēnshùn meek

问题 wèntí problem; question, matter; 是钱的问题 shì qián de wèntí it's a question of money

温习 wēnxí brush up; revise

蚊香 wénxiāng mosquito coil

问心有愧 wèn xīn yǒu kuì have a guilty conscience

文学 wénxué literature ◊ literary

问讯处 wènxùn chù information office

问讯台 wènxùn tái information desk

文雅 wényǎ refined; cultivated; elegant

瘟疫 wēnyì epidemic, plague

文艺 wényì art and literature

文章 wénzhāng article

蚊帐 wénzhàng mosquito net

稳重 wěnzhòng sedate; sober

稳住 wěnzhù steady

蚊子 wénzi mosquito

文字 wénzì writing; text

文字处理 wénzì chǔlǐ word processing

文字处理机 wénzì chǔlǐjī word processor

窝 wō nest; socket ◊ measure word for broods, hives of bees etc; 一窝蜜蜂 yìwō mìfēng a hive of bees

我 wǒ I; me ◊ my; 我是 ... wǒ shì ... TELEC it's ... here

卧 wò lie down

握 wò hold; grasp

卧病在床 wò bìng zài chuáng be confined to one's bed

卧车 wòchē sleeping car

卧床不起 wò chuáng bù qǐ bedridden

卧倒 wòdǎo lie flat; drop to the ground

我的 wǒde my; mine

我的天啊！wǒde tiān'a! (oh) dear!, dear me!

握紧 wòjǐn clench

涡轮机 wōlúnjī turbine

我们 wǒmen we; us ◊ our; 我们别吵了 wǒmén bié chǎole let's not argue; 我们走吧 wǒmén zǒu ba let's go

我们的 wǒménde our ◊ ours

我们自己 wǒmen zìjǐ ourselves

蜗牛 wōniú snail

窝棚 wōpeng shed; hovel

卧铺 wòpù place to sleep, bunk (on train)

卧室 wòshì bedroom

握手 wòshǒu handshake ◊ shake hands

我自己 wǒ zìjǐ myself

污 wū dirt

乌 wū black ◊ crow

屋 wū house

无 wú nothing ◊ not; no

五 wǔ five

武 wǔ military

午 **wǔ** midday
舞 **wǔ** dance
雾 **wù** fog; mist
误 **wù** mistake
勿 **wù** do not
物 **wù** thing
五百 **wǔbǎi** five hundred
舞伴 **wǔbàn** (dance) partner
无比 **wúbǐ** incomparable
务必 **wùbì** must; 务必保证做完 X **wùbì bǎozhèng zuòwán X** see to it that X gets done
五彩 **wǔcǎi** colorful; 五彩缤纷 **wǔcǎi bīnfēn** a blaze of color
午餐 **wǔcān** lunch
午餐时间 **wǔcān shíjiān** lunchtime
无常 **wúcháng** erratic
无偿 **wúcháng** unpaid
舞场 **wǔchǎng** dance floor; dance hall
无偿债能力 **wú chángzhài nénglì** insolvent
无产阶级 **wúchǎn jiējí** proletariat
无耻 **wúchǐ** outrageous; shameless
无处 **wúchù** nowhere
无带 **wúdài** strapless
舞蹈 **wǔdǎo** dancing
误导 **wùdǎo** misguided
舞蹈编导 **wǔdǎo biāndǎo** choreographer
舞蹈家 **wǔdǎo jiā** dancer
舞蹈演员 **wǔdǎo yǎnyuán** dancer
无敌 **wúdí** invincible
污点 **wūdiǎn** mark; blot; flaw
屋顶 **wūdǐng** roof
无动于衷 **wú dòng yúzhōng** indifferent; untouched; aloof; unconcerned
无端 **wúduān** unfounded; unprovoked
无法 **wúfǎ** unable to
无法超越 **wúfǎ chāoyuè** insurmountable
无法和解 **wúfǎ héjiě** irreconcilable
无法解释 **wúfǎ jiěshì** unaccountable
无法抗拒 **wúfǎ kàngjù**

irresistible
无法理解 **wúfǎ lǐjiě** be out of one's depth
无法弥补 **wúfǎ míbǔ** irreparable
午饭 **wǔfàn** lunch
无法区别 **wúfǎ qūbié** indistinguishable
无法挽回 **wúfǎ wǎnhuí** irrecoverable
无法慰藉 **wúfǎ wèijiè** inconsolable
无法想象 **wúfǎ xiǎngxiàng** inconceivable
无法形容 **wúfǎ xíngróng** indescribable
无风险 **wúfēngxiǎn** safe
无根据 **wúgēnjù** groundless, baseless, unfounded
污垢 **wūgòu** dirt
无辜 **wúgū** innocent ◊ innocently
无关紧要 **wúguān jǐnyào** immaterial
乌龟 **wūguī** tortoise; turtle
无轨电车 **wúguǐ diànchē** streetcar
无故障 **wú gùzhàng** trouble-free
无害 **wúhài** harmless
无核 **wúhé** nuclear-free
无花果 **wúhuāguǒ** fig
雾化器 **wùhuà qì** atomizer
污秽 **wūhuì** grubby
污秽 **wūhuì** squalor
舞会 **wǔhuì** dance; ball; prom
误会 **wùhuì** misunderstand; misconstrue ◊ misunderstanding
屋脊 **wūjǐ** ridge (of roof)
污迹 **wūjī** smudge; smear; 产生污迹 **chǎnshēng wūjī** stain
无机 **wújī** inorganic
无家 **wújiā** homeless
无价 **wújià** invaluable; priceless
无家的人 **wújiāde rén** the homeless
无家具设备 **wú jiājù shèbèi** unfurnished
物件 **wùjiàn** article, item
误将 X 认作 Y **wùjiāng X rènzuò Y** mistake X for Y
五角大楼 **Wǔjiǎo Dàlóu** the Pentagon
物价上涨 **wùjià shàngzhǎng**

inflationary

无价值 **wú jiàzhí** insignificant; worthless

误解 **wùjiě** misunderstand; misread ◊ misunderstanding, misconception; 使人误解 **shǐrén wùjiě** misleading

无戒心 **wú jièxīn** unsuspecting

无节制 **wú jiézhì** immoderate

无计划性 **wú jìhuà xìng** arbitrary

无精打采 **wújīng dǎcǎi** listless

五金商店 **wǔjīn shāngdiàn** hardware store

无脊椎动物 **wú jízhuī dòngwù** invertebrate

无拘束 **wú jūshù** unrestrained

无咖啡因 **wú kāfēiyīn** decaffeinated

无可奉告 **wúkě fènggào** no comment

无可奈何 **wúkě nàihé** helpless ◊ helplessly ◊ resignation ◊ it can't be helped

无可争辩 **wúkě zhēngbiàn** undisputed ◊ unquestionably

无可指责 **wúkě zhǐzé** beyond reproach, irreproachable

无可指摘 **wúkě zhǐzhāi** irreproachable

无愧 **wúkuì** worthy

无赖 **wúlài** scoundrel; scrounger

无礼 **wúlǐ** rudeness, impertinence ◊ impertinent; saucy

无力 **wúlì** feeble

武力 **wǔlì** force

物理 **wùlǐ** physics

无聊 **wúliáo** boredom; monotony ◊ boring; uninteresting

无力量 **wúlìliàng** powerless

无领长袖衫 **wúlǐng chángxiùshān** sweatshirt

无理性 **wúlǐxìng** irrational

物理学家 **wùlǐ xuéjiā** physicist

无理由 **wúlǐyóu** uncalled-for

乌龙茶 **wūlóngchá** oolong tea

无论哪个 **wúlùn nǎge** whichever

无论哪里 **wúlùn nǎlǐ** wherever

无论如何 **wúlùn rúhé** still, in any case; no matter what

无论什么时候 **wúlùn shénme shíhòu** whenever

无论是谁 **wúlùn shì shéi** whoever

无毛 **wúmáo** hairless

雾蒙蒙 **wùméngméng** hazy

污蔑 **wūmiè** smear; slander; libel

诬蔑 **wūmiè** smear; slander; libel

无名 **wúmíng** obscure; nameless

无名指 **wúmíngzhǐ** ring finger

无内胎 **wú nèitāi** tubeless

无能 **wúnéng** incompetent; incapable; unable ◊ inability

无能为力 … **wú néng wéilì** … be powerless to …

五年计划 **Wǔnián Jìhuà** Five Year Plan

误判 **wùpàn** miscarriage of justice

无偏见 **wú piānjiàn** detached

物品 **wùpǐn** object; item

武器 **wǔqì** arms, armaments; weapon

雾气 **wùqì** mist, haze

无铅 **wúqiān** unleaded

无情 **wúqíng** ruthless; callous ◊ ruthlessly ◊ callously ◊ ruthlessness; 无情的力量 **wúqíngde lìliàng** brute force

无亲戚关系 **wú qīnqī guānxi** unrelated

无穷 **wúqióng** infinity

舞曲 **wǔqǔ** dance music

无权 **wúquán** unauthorized

污染 **wūrǎn** contaminate; pollute; infect ◊ contamination; pollution ◊ tainted

污染物质 **wūrǎn wùzhì** pollutant

无人操纵 **wúrén cāozòng** unmanned

无人承担 **wúrén chéngdān** unoccupied *post*

无人住 **wúrén zhù** unoccupied *building*

侮辱 **wǔrǔ** insult, slight

物色 **wùsè** hunt

物色人才的人 **wùsè réncái de rén** headhunter

无声 **wúshēng** silent; mute ◊ silently

无生命 **wú shēngmìng** inanimate; lifeless

无生气 **wú shēngqì** be in the doldrums

无生殖能力 **wú shēngzhí nénglì** infertility

无神论者 **wú shén lùn zhě** atheist

五十 **wǔshí** fifty

武士 **wǔshì** warrior

务实 **wùshí** pragmatic

无数 **wúshù** countless, innumerable

武术 **wǔshù** martial arts

污水 **wūshuǐ** sewage

午睡 **wǔshuì** afternoon nap

污水管 **wūshuǐ guǎn** sewer

无私 **wúsī** selfless, unselfish

五四运动 **Wǔsì yùndòng** May 4th movement

误算 **wùsuàn** miscalculate ◊ miscalculation

无所谓 **wúsuǒwèi** indifferent ◊ all the same

勿踏草坪 **wùtà cǎopíng** keep off the grass

舞台 **wǔtái** stage, platform

舞台布景 **wǔtái bùjǐng** scenery THEA

无特殊技能 **wú tèshū jìnéng** unskilled

物体 **wùtǐ** object

无条件 **wú tiáojiàn** unconditional

舞厅 **wǔtīng** ballroom; dancehall

无痛 **wútòng** painless

无头脑 **wútóunǎo** mindless

乌托邦 **wūtuōbāng** utopia

勿忘我 **wùwàngwǒ** forget-me-not

无畏 **wúwèi** fearless, intrepid

无味 **wúwèi** tasteless, insipid; dull

无危险 **wúwēixiǎn** safe

污物 **wūwù** sewage

污物处理场 **wūwù chǔlǐ chǎng** sewage plant

无武器 **wú wǔqì** unarmed

无限 **wúxiàn** infinite, unlimited, boundless; untold

无线 **wúxiàn** cordless, wireless

无线电 **wúxiàn diàn** radio, wireless

无线电话 **wúxiàn diànhuà** cordless phone; radio telephone

无线电视 **wúxiàn diànshì** terrestrial TV

无限制 **wúxiànzhì** unlimited, limitless; indefinite ◊ indefinitely

无效 **wúxiào** invalid, null and void; futile; 使无效 **shǐ wúxiào** neutralize; annul

无效率 **wúxiàolǜ** inefficient

无懈可击 **wúxiè kějī** impeccable

无心 **wúxīn** unintentionally

五星红旗 **wǔxīng hóngqí** Chinese national flag

五星级饭店 **wǔxīngjí fàndiàn** five-star hotel

污朽 **wūxiǔ** stale

无袖 **wúxiù** sleeveless

午休 **wǔxiū** lunch break, lunch hour

乌鸦 **wūyā** crow; raven

呜咽 **wūyàn** sob

屋檐 **wūyán** eaves

呜咽 **wūyè** whimper

午夜 **wǔyè** midnight

呜咽声 **wūyèshēng** whimper

午夜时 **wǔyèshí** at midnight

无疑 **wúyí** no doubt, undoubtedly, doubtless; easily

无意 **wúyìde** unintentional ◊ unintentionally

五一节 **Wǔyī Jié** May Day

无意识 **wúyìshí** unconscious ◊ unconsciously

无异议 **wú yìyì** unquestioning

无意义 **wú yìyì** senseless, pointless; meaningless

无用 **wúyòng** useless

无忧虑 **wú yōulǜ** secure *feeling*

无忧无虑 **wúyōu wúlǜ** carefree, happy-go-lucky

无远见 **wú yuǎnjiàn** short-sighted

无缘无故 **wúyuán wúgù** for no reason

五月 **wǔyuè** May

无与伦比 **wú yǔ lúnbǐ** unique

乌云 **wūyún** dark clouds

无增长 **wú zēngzhǎng** zero growth

无债务 **wú zhàiwù** solvent

无障碍 **wú zhàng'ài** open

无政府状态 **wú zhèngfǔ zhuàngtài** anarchy

无知 **wúzhī** ignorance ◊ ignorant

物质 **wùzhì** matter, substance,

material

无止境 **wú zhǐjìng** endless, unending, infinite ◊ endlessly, infinitely

无中止 **wú zhōngzhǐ** without a break

无主 **wúzhǔ** unattended

无助 **wúzhù** helpless

武装 **wǔzhuāng** arms, weapons ◊ arm ◊ armed

武装力量 **wǔzhuāng lìliàng** armed forces

物主代词 **wùzhǔ dàicí** possessive pronoun

无资格 **wú zīgé** ineligible

无子女 **wú zǐnǚ** childless

无罪 **wúzuì** innocent ◊ innocence

无足轻重 **wúzú qīngzhòng** insignificant, of little importance

无组织 **wú zǔzhi** disorganized

# X

X 光照片 **X guāng zhàopiān** X-ray

膝 **xī** knee

吸 **xī** inhale; smoke; suck

稀 **xī** rare; sparse; thin

锡 **xī** tin

西 **xī** west ◊ western

溪 **xī** stream

熄 **xī** extinguish

席 **xí** mat; seat; place; feast

袭 **xí** attack

习 **xí** learn; study; practise

洗 **xǐ** wash, clean; shuffle *cards*; develop *photographs*

喜 **xǐ** pleasure, joy

系 **xì** system; department; faculty ◊ tie

细 **xì** fine; thin

戏 **xì** play

瞎 **xiā** blind

虾 **xiā** shrimp

峡 **xiá** strait

狭 **xiá** narrow

下 **xià** down, downward; below; under; next ◊ get off; come down (*of rain etc*); lay eggs; 下个星期 / 下个月 **xiàgè xīngqī / xiàgè yuè** next week / next month

吓 **xià** scare; 吓了 X 一跳 **xià le X yítiào** give X a scare

夏 **xià** summer

下巴 **xiàba** chin

下班 **xiàbān** finish work; go off duty

下边 **xiàbiān** beneath

下车 **xiàchē** get off; get out

下沉 **xiàchén** sink; settle

下船 **xiàchuán** disembark

下垂 **xiàchuí** droop, sag

瑕疵 **xiácī** flaw, blemish

下次 **xiàcì** next time

吓呆 **xiàdāi** petrify

下等 **xiàděng** third-rate

下等场所 **xiàděng chǎngsuǒ** dive (*bar etc*)

下跌 **xiàdiē** plunge

下定义 **xià dìngyì** define

下毒 **xiàdú** drug

下赌注 **xià dǔzhù** bet on; stake

下飞机 **xià fēijī** disembark (*from plane*)

下岗 **xiàgǎng** unemployed; laid off (*from state enterprise*) ◊ unemployment

下岗工人 **xiàgǎng gōngrén** the unemployed (*from state enterprise*)

峡谷 **xiágǔ** canyon; gorge; glen

吓唬 **xiàhu** browbeat

喜爱 **xǐ'ài** like; love ◊ beloved; fond ◊ favor; fondness

下机 **xiàjī** log off

下级 **xiàjí** subordinate

夏季 **xiàjì** summer

下降 **xiàjiàng** decrease; decline; descend; sink ◊ descent; drop; fall ◊ downward

下降趋势 **xiàjiàng qūshì** downturn

下决心 **xià juéxīn** decide; make up one's mind ◊ determined

下来 **xiàlái** come down, descend ◊ descent

夏令时 **xiàlìngshí** summer time; daylight saving time

下流 **xiàliú** indecent; profane; sleazy; smutty

下流坯 **xiàliúpī** swine (*person*)

下落不明 **xiàluò bùmíng** be missing

下毛毛雨 **xià máomao yǔ** drizzle

下面 **xiàmiàn** underneath; below

先 **xiān** first, beforehand

仙 **xiān** fairy; immortal

鲜 **xiān** fresh

弦 **xián** chord; string

咸 **xián** salty; savory

闲 **xián** idle ◊ leisure

嫌 **xián** dislike ◊ suspicion

显 **xiǎn** show; be obvious

线 **xiàn** line; thread; cord; 一线希望 **yíxiàn xīwàng** glimmer of hope

县 **xiàn** county

馅 **xiàn** filling

腺 **xiàn** gland

现 **xiàn** appear ◊ current, present

献 **xiàn** give; present

陷 **xiàn** trap; pitfall; snare

限 **xiàn** limit

瞎闹 **xiānào** mess around, waste time

现场 **xiànchǎng** on the spot ◊ scene of the crime

现场示范 **xiànchǎng shìfàn** reconstruct *crime*

现场直播 **xiànchǎng zhíbō** live broadcast

现成 **xiànchéng** ready-made; off the peg

县城 **xiànchéng** county town

舷窗 **xiánchuāng** porthole

现存 **xiàncún** existing; in existence; in stock, available

现代 **xiàndài** modern; contemporary ◊ modern times

现代化 **xiàndàihuà** modernize ◊ modernization

显得 **xiǎndé** appear, seem

限定 **xiàndìng** limit

限度 **xiàndù** limit

显而易见 **xiǎn ér yìjiàn** inevitable

宪法 **xiànfǎ** constitution ◊ constitutional

箱 **xiāng** box; crate; case

香 **xiāng** incense; perfume ◊ fragrant, aromatic, nice-smelling; tasty

相 **xiāng** each other

乡 **xiāng** countryside; hometown

详 **xiáng** details

响 **xiǎng** sound ◊ loud

想 **xiǎng** think; want; 好好想想！ **hǎohao xiǎngxiang!** think hard!; 我也是这么想的 **wǒ yě shì zhème xiǎng de** I think so too; 你想去看电影吗？ **nǐ xiǎng qù kàn diànyǐng ma?** would you like to go to the movies?; 想得开 **xiǎng de kāi** try to look on the

bright side of things

享 **xiǎng** enjoy

项 **xiàng** item

相 **xiàng** appearance

向 **xiàng** to; toward; 他向我走过来 **tā xiàng wǒ zǒuguòlái** he came up to me; 向 ... 眨眼 **xiàng ... zhǎyǎn** wink at; 向 X 挥手 **xiàng X huīshǒu** wave to X

象 **xiàng** elephant ◊ look like, resemble

像 **xiàng** look like, resemble

乡巴佬 **xiāngbālǎo** redneck

镶板 **xiāngbǎn** panel; section

向北 **xiàngběi** north ◊ northward

象鼻子 **xiàngbí** (elephant's) trunk

相比 **xiāngbǐ** compare; 与 X 相比 **yǔ X xiāngbǐ** compared with X, next to X

镶边 **xiāngbiān** edge

香槟酒 **xiāngbīn jiǔ** champagne

香草 **xiāngcǎo** vanilla

相册 **xiāngcè** photo album

香肠 **xiāngcháng** sausage

镶齿冠 **xiāng chǐguàn** crown *tooth*

相处 **xiāngchǔ** mix, socialize; 他和人相处不好 **tā hé rén xiāngchù bùhǎo** he doesn't relate to people

想出 **xiǎngchū** think up

相当 **xiāngdāng** quite, considerably ◊ parallel, match; 相当大 **xiāngdāng dà** quite big; sizeable; 相当多 **xiāngdāng duō** quite a few, a lot

相当于 **xiāngdāngyú** equivalent to; be equivalent to; be tantamount to ◊ as much as

想到 **xiǎngdào** think of

向导 **xiàngdǎo** guide

想得开 **xiǎngdekāi** light-hearted

向东 **xiàngdōng** eastward, east

相对 **xiāngduì** relative ◊ relatively

想法 **xiǎngfa** thought, idea

相反 **xiāngfǎn** opposite, reverse; 与 ... 相反 **yǔ ... xiāngfǎn** contrary to ..., as opposed to ...

相反方向 **xiāngfǎn fāngxiàng** opposite direction

相符 **xiāngfú** correspond, match

香港 **Xiānggǎng** Hong Kong

香港回归 **Xiānggǎng huíguī** Hong Kong handover

相关 **xiāngguān** related

向后 **xiànghòu** backward

相互 **xiānghù** mutual

相互对立 **xiānghù duìlì** contradictory

相互关联 **xiānghù guānlián** interrelated

相互依赖 **xiānghù yīlài** interdependent

相互作用 **xiānghù zuòyòng** interaction

想家 **xiǎngjiā** be homesick

香蕉 **xiāngjiāo** banana

橡胶 **xiàngjiāo** rubber

相接 **xiāngjiē** interface

相近 **xiāngjìn** close

香精 **xiāngjīng** scent, perfume

镶框 **xiāngkuàng** frame

项链 **xiàngliàn** necklace

香料 **xiāngliào** spice

相貌 **xiàngmào** features (*facial*)

项目 **xiàngmù** item; project; entry (*in diary etc*)

橡木 **xiàngmù** oak (*wood*)

向南 **xiàng nán** southward

向内 **xiàngnèi** inward

想念 **xiǎngniàn** miss

相配 **xiāngpèi** match, complement

橡皮 **xiàngpí** rubber; eraser

相片 **xiāngpiàn** photo

橡皮筋 **xiàngpíjīn** elastic band

橡皮奶头 **xiàngpí nǎitóu** pacifier

香气 **xiāngqì** smell, fragrance, aroma

想起 **xiǎngqǐ** remember; think of; 使 X 想起 Y **shǐ X xiǎngqǐ Y** remind X of Y

象棋 **xiàngqí** chess

镶嵌 **xiāngqiàn** inlay; paneling ◊ set *jewel*

向前 **xiàngqián** forward, onward

想起来 **xiǎng qǐlái** think of; come up with

详情 **xiángqíng** details

项圈 **xiàngquān** collar

向日葵 **xiàngrìkuí** sunflower

相容 **xiāngróng** compatible

香山 **Xiāngshān** Fragrant Hills

向上 **xiàngshàng** up, upward

响声 **xiǎngshēng** sound

相识 **xiāngshí** know each other

享受 **xiǎngshòu** enjoy

详述 **xiángshù** discuss; expand on

橡树 **xiàngshù** oak tree

香水 **xiāngshuǐ** perfume

乡思 **xiāngsī** homesickness

相似 **xiāngsì** alike, similar ◊ be alike ◊ similarity

相似处 **xiāngsì chù** resemblance

相似之处 **xiāngsì zhī chù** parallel ◊ similarity

相同 **xiāngtóng** equal; equivalent ◊ equally

闲逛 **xiánguàng** wander, stroll

向外 **xiàngwài** outward

向往 **xiàngwǎng** yearning

香味 **xiāngwèi** perfume, scent, aroma

响尾蛇 **xiǎngwěishé** rattlesnake

详细 **xiángxì** detailed, full ◊ in detail, fully; minutely

向西 **xiàngxī** west ◊ westward

乡下 **xiāngxià** country (*as opposed to town*)

向下 **xiàngxià** down ◊ downward; underneath

乡下佬 **xiāngxiàlǎo** *pej* hick

想象 **xiǎngxiàng** imagine; envisage ◊ imagination; 我能想象出来 **wǒ néng xiǎngxiàng chūlái** I can just imagine it

想象力 **xiǎngxiànglì** imagination

乡下人 **xiāngxià rén** *pej* hillbilly

相信 **xiāngxìn** believe; believe in; trust

象牙 **xiàngyá** ivory; tusk

香烟 **xiāngyān** cigarette

象样 **xiàngyàng** respectable

想要 **xiǎngyào** wish

香油 **xiāngyóu** sesame oil

享有 **xiǎngyǒu** enjoy; 享有特权 **xiǎngyǒu tèquán** privileged

相遇 **xiāngyù** meet

香皂 **xiāngzào** toilet soap

象征 **xiàngzhēng** symbol, emblem, token ◊ symbolize

相撞 **xiāngzhuàng** collide; knock together

箱子 **xiāngzi** box; chest; crate;

case; trunk

陷书 xiànshū frame, stitch up

显赫 xiǎnhè influential

鲜红 xiānhóng scarlet

先后顺序 xiānhòu shùnxù order, sequence; 事情发生的先后顺序 *shìqíng fāshēng de xiānhòu shùnxù* the sequence of events

鲜花 xiānhuā fresh flowers

针线活 xiànhuózhēni sewing

献祭 xiànjì sacrifice

先见之明 xiānjiàn zhī míng foresight

线接头 xiàn jiētóu terminal

先进 xiānjìn advance ◊ advanced; progressive

现金 xiànjīn cash

现今 xiànjīn nowadays

现金出纳机 xiànjīn chūnà jī cash register

现金短缺 xiànjīn duǎnquē short of cash

陷阱 xiànjǐng pitfall; trap

现金折扣 xiànjīn zhékòu cash discount

现金支付 xiànjīn zhīfù cash down

先决条件 xiānjué tiáojiàn qualification

现款定金 xiànkuǎn dìngjīn cash in advance

先例 xiānlì precedent

闲聊 xiánliáo chatter; gossip

显露出来 xiǎnlòu be out (*of secret*)

显露 xiǎnlù manifest itself

线路 xiànlù circuit; line; wiring

线路板 xiànlù bǎn circuit board

线路图 xiànlù tú road map

鲜美 xiānměi delicious; succulent

鲜明 xiānmíng stark

羡慕 xiànmù envy; 令 X 羡慕 *lìng X xiànmù* be the envy of X

仙女 xiānnǚ fairy

险情指示灯 xiǎnqíng zhǐshìdēng hazard lights

先驱 xiānqū pioneer, forerunner

线圈 xiànquān coil

显然 xiǎnrán obvious ◊ apparently, evidently

闲人免进！ xiánrén miǎnjìn! keep out!

仙人掌 xiānrénzhǎng cactus

陷入 xiànrù become entangled in; 陷入困境 *xiànrù kùnjìng* be in a fix; 陷入圈套 *xiànrù quāntào* be trapped

先生 xiānsheng mister; sir; teacher; husband

献身于 xiànshēn yú dedicate oneself to

显示 xiǎnshì display, show

现实 xiànshí practical; realistic ◊ reality

现世 xiànshì earthly

显示器 xiǎnshìqì indicator; monitor

现实主义 xiànshí zhǔyì realism

现实主义者 xiànshí zhǔyì zhě realist

咸水 xiánshuǐ salt water

线索 xiànsuǒ clue; thread

献题 xiàntí dedication (*in book*)

先天性 xiāntiān xìng congenital

线条 xiàntiáo line

纤维 xiānwéi fiber

显微镜 xiǎnwēijìng microscope

纤维素 xiānwéisù cellulose

嫌恶 xiánwù distaste

纤细 xiánxì slender

闲暇 xiánxiá leisure, spare time

显现 xiǎnxiàn unfold; show up, reveal

现象 xiànxiàng phenomenon

现行 xiànxíng going, current

献血 xiànxuè donate blood

献血者 xiànxuè zhě blood donor

险崖 xiǎnyá crag

鲜艳 xiānyàn bright; vivid; colorful ◊ brightly

先验 xiānyàn transcendental

显眼 xiǎnyǎn conspicuous ◊ stand out ◊ conspicuously

嫌疑 xiányí suspicion

嫌疑犯 xiányífàn suspect

献殷勤 xiàn yīnqín make advances

现有 xiànyǒu available; in existence

先于 xiānyú precede

陷于 xiànyú get into; 陷于困境 *xiànyú kùnjìng* get into difficulties

弦乐器 **xiányuè qì** stringed instrument

弦乐器演奏者 **xiányuè qì yǎnzòu zhě** string player; strings

现在 **xiànzài** now, at the moment; 现在不行 **xiànzài bùxíng** not now

现在看来 **xiànzài kànlái** in retrospect

现在时 **xiànzàishí** present tense

闲着 **xiánzhe** twiddle one's thumbs

闲置 **xiánzhì** idle *machinery*

限制 **xiànzhì** restriction ◊ restrict; qualify *remark*; 限制 X **xiànzhì X** draw the line at X

线轴 **xiànzhóu** spool

显著 **xiǎnzhù** outstanding; prominent; striking, marked

仙子 **xiānzǐ** fairy; immortal

现做的饭 **xiànzuòde fàn** cooked meal

削 **xiāo** peel, skin; cut, trim; 用刀削净 **yòng dāo xiāojìng** scrape

消 **xiāo** disappear

小 **xiǎo** small, little; young; 她比我小十岁 **tā bǐ wǒ xiǎo shísuì** she is ten years my junior; 从小 **cóng xiǎo** from childhood

晓 **xiǎo** dawn ◊ know

笑 **xiào** laugh

效 **xiào** effect

孝 **xiào** filial

校 **xiào** school

小报 **xiǎobào** tabloid

小便 **xiǎobiàn** urine; pee ◊ urinate; pee

笑柄 **xiàobǐng** butt, target; 变成笑柄 **biànchéng xiàobǐng** become a laughing stock

小病 **xiǎobìng** indisposed

小部分 **xiǎobùfen** fraction

小菜 **xiǎocài** side dish

小菜一碟 **xiǎocài yìdié** small amount

小册子 **xiǎo cèzi** booklet, brochure, pamphlet

消沉 **xiāochén** dismal

小吃 **xiǎochī** snack

小吃店 **xiǎochīdiàn** snack bar

小丑 **xiǎochǒu** clown

消除 **xiāochú** eliminate, get rid of, delete ◊ elimination, deletion

小船 **xiǎochuán** boat; launch; dinghy

哮喘 **xiāochuǎn** asthma

小袋 **xiǎodài** pouch

小刀 **xiǎodāo** pocketknife

小调 **xiǎodiào** minor MUS; D 小调 **D xiǎodiào** in D minor

消毒 **xiāodú** sterilize, disinfect ◊ sterile

小段儿 **xiǎoduànr** bit, length

消毒剂 **xiāodú jì** disinfectant

小儿麻痹症 **xiǎo'ér mábìzhèng** polio

效仿 **xiàofǎng** imitate; 效仿 X **xiàofǎng X** follow in X's footsteps

消防车 **xiāofáng chē** fire truck

消防队 **xiāofáng duì** fire department

消防队员 **xiāofáng duìyuán** fireman, firefighter

消防龙头 **xiāofáng lóngtóu** hydrant, fireplug

消费 **xiāofèi** consume ◊ expense; consumption

小费 **xiǎofèi** tip

消费品 **xiāofèi pǐn** consumer goods

消费者 **xiāofèi zhě** consumer

消费者社会 **xiāofèi zhě shèhuì** consumer society

小公共 **xiǎo gōnggòng** public minibus

小狗 **xiǎogǒu** puppy

小姑 **xiǎogū** sister-in-law (*husband's younger sister*)

效果 **xiàoguǒ** effect; 效果不佳 **xiàoguǒ bùjiā** ineffective

小孩 **xiǎohái** child, kid

消耗 **xiāohào** use; consume ◊ consumption

消耗量 **xiāohào liàng** consumption (*quantity used*)

小河 **xiǎohé** stream, creek

消化 **xiāohuà** digest ◊ digestion; 消化不良 **xiāohuà bùliáng** indigestion

笑话 **xiàohua** joke, crack

小黄瓜 **xiǎohuángguā** gherkin

消化系统 **xiāohuà xìtǒng**

digestive system

销货点 xiāohuò diǎn point of sale

小伙子 xiǎo huǒzi lad, youth

消极 xiāojí negative; destructive

小鸡 xiǎojī chick

削价 xiāojià cut-price

削减 xiāojiǎn cut, ax ◊ cutback

小轿车 xiǎo jiàochē sedan, saloon

小教堂 xiǎo jiàotáng chapel

小姐 xiǎojie Miss ◊ young woman; 王小姐 *Wáng xiǎojiě* Miss Wang

小径 xiǎojìng track, trail

宵禁令 xiāojìn lìng curfew

小孔 xiǎokǒng puncture, hole

小块儿 xiǎokuàir bit

效力 xiàolì effect

小礼服 xiǎo lǐfú dinner jacket

销路 xiāolù sales; circulation

小路 xiǎolù path; back road

效率 xiàolǜ efficiency

小旅馆 xiǎo lǚguǎn inn

小萝卜 xiǎoluóbo radish

小马 xiǎomǎ pony

小麦 xiǎomài wheat

小猫 xiǎomāo kitten

小米 xiǎomǐ millet

消灭 xiāomiè destroy, exterminate, eradicate; 消灭有害动物 *xiāomiè yǒuhài dòngwù* pest control

消磨时间 xiāomó shíjiān pass the time

酵母 xiàomǔ yeast

小牛 xiǎoniú calf

小牛肉 xiǎo niúròu veal

小跑 xiǎopǎo trot

小朋友 xiǎo péngyǒu children

削皮 xiāopí peel, pare

小气 xiǎoqì mean; mean-spirited

消遣 xiāoqiǎn amuse oneself ◊ pastime

削铅笔刀 xiāo qiānbǐ dāo pencil sharpener

小汽车 xiǎo qìchē automobile

小圈子 xiǎo quānzi in-group

小人书 xiǎorén shū picture book

笑容满面 xiàoróng mǎnmiàn beam, smile

削弱 xiāoruò diminish

消散 xiāosàn lift, clear

小山坡 xiǎoshānpō hill

小声 xiǎoshēng quiet

笑声 xiàoshēng laugh ◊ laughter

消失 xiāoshī disappear; go away; pass ◊ disappearance

小时 xiǎoshí hour

小事 xiǎoshì trivial matter

消瘦 xiāoshòu emaciated

销售 xiāoshòu sell, market ◊ sales, marketing

销售点 xiāoshòu diǎn (sales) outlet

销售额 xiāoshòu'é sales figures

销售会议 xiāoshòu huìyì sales meeting

小数 xiǎoshù decimal

小书包 xiǎoshūbāo schoolbag, satchel

小数点 xiǎoshù diǎn decimal point

小睡 xiǎoshuì grab some sleep; snooze

孝顺 xiàoshùn be devoted to

小说 xiāoshuō novel; fiction

小说家 xiǎoshuō jiā novelist

小梳妆盒 xiǎo shūzhuāng hé vanity case

小叔子 xiǎoshūzi brother-in-law (husband's younger brother)

小淘气 xiǎo táoqi bully; rascal

萧条 xiāotiáo depression (economic) ◊ depressed

小题大做 xiǎotí dàzuò make a fuss

小艇 xiǎotǐng motor launch

小提琴 xiǎo tíqín violin, fiddle

小提琴家 xiǎo tíqín jiā violinist

小桶 xiǎotǒng keg

小偷 xiǎotōu thief; burglar

小偷小摸 xiǎotōu xiǎomō pilfering

小团 xiǎotuán pellet

消退 xiāotuì fade

小屋 xiǎowū hut

消息 xiāoxi news

小息 xiǎoxī coffee break

小虾 xiǎoxiā shrimp

小巷 xiǎoxiàng lane; side street

肖像 xiàoxiàng portrait

消息灵通 xiāoxī língtōng be in the know

小心 xiǎoxīn be careful ◊ carefully; 要很小心 **yào hěn xiǎoxīn** it requires great care

笑星 xiàoxīng joker

小型公共汽车 xiǎoxíng gōnggòng qìchē minibus

小型客车 xiǎoxíng kèchē compact MOT

小型摩托车 xiǎoxíng mótuōchē motorscooter

小心谨慎 xiǎoxīn jǐnshèn guarded ◊ gingerly

小心轻放 xiǎoxīn qīngfàng (handle) with care

小学 xiǎoxué elementary school

小学老师 xiǎoxué lǎoshī elementary teacher

小学生 xiǎoxuéshēng schoolchild

小阳春 xiǎoyángchūn Indian summer

逍遥法外 xiāoyáo fǎwài get off scot-free ◊ at large

消音器 xiāoyīn qì silencer

校友 xiàoyǒu schoolmate

校园 xiàoyuán campus

校长 xiàozhǎng principal, head teacher

小折刀 xiǎo zhédāo pocketknife

小玩意zhī xiǎowányìzhī gadget

小字 xiǎozì small print

小卒 xiǎozú pawn

小组 xiǎozú panel

小组委员会 xiǎozú wěiyuánhuì subcommittee

吓跑 xiàpǎo scare away

下坡 xiàpō downhill

下坡滑雪 xiàpō huáxuě downhill skiing

下去 xiàqù go down; continue; 谈下去 **tán xiàqù** talk on, continue talking

吓人 xiàrén frightening; 吓人一跳 **xiàrényítiào** jump, give a jump

下士 xiàshì corporal MIL

下属 xiàshǔ subordinate

下述 xiàshù following

下水 xiàshuǐ launch ◊ downstream

下水道 xiàshuǐ dào drains, drainage

下水系统 xiàshuǐ xìtǒng sanitation

下塌 xiàtà stay

下台 xiàtái step down ◊ downfall

夏天 xiàtiān summer ◊ in the summer

下网 xiàwǎng log off ◊ offline

下午 xiàwǔ afternoon; 下午场 **xiàwǔ chǎng** matinée, afternoon show

下午好 xiàwǔ hǎo good afternoon

下陷 xiàxiàn sink, drop; subside

狭 xiáxiǎo poky

下小雨 xià xiǎoyǔ it's spitting (with rain)

下斜 xiàxié descend (of road)

下雪 xiàxuě snow

侠义 xiáyì chivalrous

狭隘 xiáyì narrow views etc

一步 xià yībù next

下一个 xià yīgè next; 谁是下一个？ **shuí shì xià yīgè?** who's next?

下意识 xiàyìshí subconscious

下雨 xiàyǔ rain; 下雨了 **xiàyǔ le** it's raining

瑕瑜互见 xiáyú hùjiàn patchy

下载 xiàzǎi download

狭窄 xiázhǎi narrow; confined

瞎子 xiāzi blind person

西班牙 Xībānyá Spain ◊ Spanish

细胞 xìbāo cell

西北部 xīběi bù northwest

稀薄 xībó thin

西部 xībù west; western

西部片 xībùpiān western (movie)

西餐 xīcān western cuisine

细察 xìchá scrutinize ◊ scrutiny

细长 xìcháng narrow; slim

洗车处 xǐchē chù car wash

洗车服务 xǐchē fúwù valet service (for cars)

吸尘 xīchén vacuum

吸尘器 xīchén qì vacuum cleaner

洗涤 xǐdí clean, wash; erase tape

洗涤槽 xǐdícáo sink

洗涤剂 xǐdí jì detergent

吸毒成瘾 xīdú chéngyǐn be hooked on drugs

吸毒者 xīdú zhě drug addict

歇 xiē rest

斜 xié slanting, oblique; diagonal

鞋 xié shoe; footwear

携 xié carry; hold

邪 xié evil

写 xiě write

谢 xiè thank

卸 xiè unload

泄 xiè release

蟹 xiè crab

斜槽 xiécáo chute

写出 xiěchū write out

鞋带 xiédài shoelace; strap

携带 xiédài take (along)

懈怠 xièdài slack, lax

携带式电脑 xiédài shì diànnǎo laptop

鞋底 xiédǐ sole

鞋店 xiédiàn shoestore

鞋钉 xiédīng spike (on shoe)

协定 xiédìng agreement

亵渎 xièdú blaspheme

邪恶 xié'è evil, wicked; spiteful

鞋跟 xiégēn heel

邂逅 xièhòu encounter

协会 xiéhuì association, institute

卸货 xièhuò unload

鞋匠 xiéjiang shoemaker, cobbler

邪教 xiéjiào cult, sect

谢绝 xièjué decline, refuse

斜靠 xiékào prop, lean

泄漏 xièlòu break; leak out; give away ◊ leak, disclosure

泄露 xièlòu disclose, reveal ◊ disclosure, revelation

泄密 xièmì reveal a secret

泄密者 xièmì zhě telltale

斜坡 xiépō slope, gradient

胁迫 xiépò blackmail

协商 xiéshāng negotiate ◊ negotiation

写生 xiěshēng sketch

邪视 xiéshì leer

斜视 xiéshì squint; look sideways

鞋刷 xiéshuā shoe brush

歇斯底里 xiēsīdǐlǐ hysteria ◊ hysterical; 歇斯底里的发作 xiēsīdǐlǐde fāzuò hysterics

斜体 xiétǐ italic

谢天谢地！xiètiān xièdì! thank goodness!

协调 xiétiáo harmony;

coordination ◊ coordinate ◊ matching; 和 ... 不协调 hé ... bù xiétiáo clash with

写下 xiěxià write down; put down; enter

卸下 xièxià unload

斜线 xiéxiàn oblique, slash

谢谢 xièxie thank you, thanks

写信 xiěxìn write a letter

泻药 xièyào laxative

斜倚 xiéyǐ recline

协议 xiéyì agreement, understanding; pact

鞋油 xiéyóu shoe cream, shoe polish

斜着 xiézhe sideways

楔子 xiēzi wedge

写字夹板 xiězì jiábǎn clipboard

协奏曲 xiézòu qǔ concerto

写作 xiězuò write (as author) ◊ writing (career)

洗发剂 xǐfà jì shampoo

洗发精 xǐfà jīng shampoo

稀饭 xīfàn rice porridge, congee

西方 xīfāng western; westerly

西方国家 Xīfāng guójiā the West ◊ Western

西方化 Xīfānghuà Westernized

西方人 Xīfāngrén Westerner

细分 xìfēn subdivide

西风 xīfēng westerly

西服 xīfú suit

媳妇 xífú daughter-in-law

膝盖骨 xīgàigǔ kneecap

吸干 xīgān blot

细高跟鞋 xìgāogēnxié stilettos

西瓜 xīguā watermelon

吸管 xīguǎn (drinking) straw

习惯 xíguàn custom; habit ◊ be accustomed to; 不习惯 X bù xíguàn X be unused to X

希罕 xīhan rare ◊ rarity

喜好 xǐhào like; love

西红柿 xīhóngshì tomato

西湖 Xīhú West Lake

喜欢 xǐhuan like, be fond of; enjoy; take to; relish

熄火 xīhuǒ stall (of engine)

袭击 xíjī attack; strike

洗剂 xǐjì lotion

洗劫 xǐjié ransack

细节 xìjié detail

洗洁精 xǐjié jīng dishwashing liquid

喜剧 xǐjù comedy

戏剧 xìjù drama, play ◊ dramatic, theatrical

戏剧家 xìjù jiā dramatist, playwright

细菌 xìjūn germ, bacterium

细菌战争 xìjūn zhànzhēng germ warfare

戏剧性 xìjù xìng dramatic, exciting

喜剧演员 xǐjù yǎnyuán comedian

希腊 Xīlà Greece ◊ Greek

细浪 xìlàng ripple

西兰花 xīlánhuā broccoli

洗礼 xǐlǐ baptize, christen ◊ baptism

细粒 xìlì granule

系列 xìliè series; range

奚落 xīluò ridicule

喜马拉雅山 Xīmǎlāyǎshān Himalayas

西面 xīmiàn west

熄灭 xīmiè put out; quench; go out

心 xīn heart; mind; center

新 xīn new; unused; 我是新来的 wǒ shì xīnlái de I'm new to the job

锌 xīn zinc

辛 xīn bitter; hard

欣 xīn enjoy; appreciate

信 xìn faith; letter ◊ believe, trust; 他信佛 tā xìn Fó he's a Buddhist

西南 xīnán southwest ◊ southwestern

西南部 xīnán bù southwest

洗脑 xǐnǎo brainwash ◊ brainwashing

新兵 xīnbīng recruit

心不在焉 xīnbúzàiyān preoccupied; absent-minded

新潮 xīncháo trendy

新陈代谢 xīnchén dàixiè metabolism

信贷限额 xìndài xiàn'é credit limit

心烦 xīnfán frustrated; annoyed

新方向 xīn fāngxiàng new departure, new direction

心烦意乱 xīnfán yìluàn get ruffled

新发展 xīn fāzhǎn new departure, new development

信封 xìnfēng envelope

信服 xìnfú believe; 令人信服 lìngrén xìnfú compelling, convincing

星 xīng star

兴 xīng rise

行 xíng go ◊ expedition ◊ you're on!, ok!; 星期五行吗？ xīngqī wǔ xíngma? are you ok for Friday?; 行了！ xíngle! enough!, that will do!

形 xíng shape, form

刑 xíng punishment

醒 xǐng awake ◊ rouse

擤 xǐng blow one's nose

杏 xìng apricot

性 xìng nature, character; gender; sex ◊ -ility; 可能性 kě'néngxìng possibility; 灵活性 línghuóxìng flexibility

姓 xìng surname, family name

兴 xìng spirit

幸 xìng lucky, fortunate

性爱 xìng'ài passion

性变态 xìngbiàntài pervert

性别 xìngbié gender, sex

性病 xìngbìng venereal disease

擤鼻涕 xǐng bítì blow one's nose

形成 xíngchéng form; come into existence ◊ formation

行程 xíngchéng trip

性传播疾病 xìng chuánbō jíbìng sexually transmitted disease

幸存 xìngcún survive ◊ survival

幸存者 xìngcún zhě survivor

行动 xíngdòng act ◊ action

幸而 xìng'ér mercifully

刑法 xíngfǎ criminal law, penal law

兴奋 xīngfèn excited ◊ excitement ◊ get excited; 令人兴奋 lìngrén xīngfèn exciting

幸奋 xìngfèn delight; drama, excitement

兴奋剂 xīngfèn jì stimulant

幸福 **xìngfú** happy ◊ happiness

性感 **xìnggǎn** sexy; sultry; sensual

兴高采烈 **xìnggāo cǎiliè** elated, exuberant ◊ elation

性格 **xìnggé** character, nature

星号 **xīnghào** asterisk

型号 **xínghào** model

猩红热 **xīnghóngrè** scarlet fever

性急 **xìngjí** impatient; petulant ◊ impatiently

性交 **xìngjiāo** sexual intercourse ◊ have sex; 与 X 性交 **yǔ X xìngjiāo** have sex with X

行经 **xíngjīng** menstruate

行经期 **xíngjīngqī** menstruation

醒酒 **xǐngjiǔ** sober up

行军 **xíngjūn** march

行军床 **xíngjūn chuáng** cot

幸亏 **xìngkuī** fortunately

醒来 **xǐnglái** wake up

行李 **xínglǐ** luggage, baggage

行李车 **xínglǐ chē** baggage car; baggage cart

行李传送带 **xínglǐ chuánsòngdài** (baggage) carousel

行李存放处 **xínglǐ cúnfàng chù** (baggage) checkroom

行李架 **xíngli jià** luggage rack

行李领取处 **xíngli lǐngqǔ chù** baggage reclaim

行李箱 **xínglǐ xiāng** trunk (*of car*)

兴隆 **xīnglóng** brisk

性能 **xìngnéng** performance; efficiency

星期 **xīngqī** week

行乞 **xíngqǐ** beg, panhandle

星期二 **xīngqī'èr** Tuesday

星期六 **xīngqīliù** Saturday

性情 **xìngqíng** temperament

星期日 **xīngqīrì** Sunday

星期三 **xīngqīsān** Wednesday

星期四 **xīngqīsì** Thursday

星期天 **xīngqītiān** Sunday

星期五 **xīngqīwǔ** Friday

星期一 **xīngqīyī** Monday

兴趣 **xìngqù** interest; 引起 X 的兴趣 **yǐnqǐ X de xìngqù** interest X

行人 **xíngrén** pedestrian

杏仁 **xìngrén** almond

人行道 **rénxíng dào** sidewalk

行人区 **xíngrén qū** pedestrian precinct

形容 **xíngróng** describe; 把 X 形容成 Y **bǎ X xíngróng chéng Y** describe X as Y

形容词 **xíngróngcí** adjective

性骚扰 **xìng sāorǎo** sexual harassment

行善者 **xíngshàn zhě** benefactor

兴盛 **xīngshèng** prosperity

行驶 **xíngshǐ** drive; go; travel; journey

行使 **xíngshǐ** exercise

刑事 **xíngshì** criminal; 有刑事记录 **yǒu xíngshì jìlù** have a criminal record

形势 **xíngshì** situation

形式 **xíngshì** form GRAM; formal; 这只是一种形式 **zhè zhǐshì yìzhǒng xíngshì** it's just a formality

形式上 **xíngshì shàng** formality

形体 **xíngtǐ** figure

星条旗 **Xīngtiáo qí** Stars and Stripes

新贵 **xīnguì** upstart

兴旺 **xīngwàng** flourish ◊ flourishing, prosperous

兴旺的企业 **xīngwàng de qǐyè** going concern

行为 **xíngwéi** behavior; deed; 行为的标准 **xíngwéide biāozhǔn** morals, standards of behavior; 行为规矩 **xíngwéi guījù** well-behaved

醒悟 **xǐngwù** awaken; realize; see things as they are

星象 **xīngxiàng** horoscope

形象 **xíngxiàng** image

形象包装 **xíngxiàng bāozhuāng** packaging, marketing

行销地区 **xíngxiāo dìqū** market

猩猩 **xīngxing** ape

行星 **xíngxīng** planet

行刑人 **xíngxíng rén** executioner

形形色色 **xíngxíng sèsè** varied, diverse

行凶抢劫 **xíngxióng qiǎngjié** mug ◊ mugging

行凶抢劫者 xíngxiōng qiǎngjié zhě mugger

性欲 xìngyù sexual desire, lust

性欲高潮 xìngyù gāocháo orgasm

幸运 xìngyùn fortunate ◊ fortunately ◊ good fortune; lucky break

幸灾乐祸 xìngzāi-lèhuò malicious delight

星占 xīngzhàn horoscope

行政 xíngzhèng administration ◊ administrative

行政机关 xíngzhèng jīguān civil service

行政系统 xíngzhèng xìtǒng bureaucracy

性质 xìngzhì quality; character

形状 xíngzhuàng form, shape

行走 xíngzǒu parade

辛亥革命 Xīnhài Gémìng 1911 Revolution

信号 xìnhào signal

新婚人 xīnhūn rén newlyweds

犀牛 xīniú rhinoceros

心悸 xīnjì palpitations

信笺 xìnjiān writing paper

信件 xìnjiàn letter; correspondence

新教 Xīnjiào Protestant

信教 xìnjiào devout

新教徒 Xīnjiàotú Protestant

新加坡 Xīnjiāpō Singapore ◊ Singaporean

新界 Xīnjiè New Territories

心肌梗塞 xīnjī gěngsè heart attack

薪金 xīnjīn pay

薪金支票 xīnjīn zhīpiào paycheck

心口灼热 xīnkǒu zhuórè heartburn

辛苦 xīnkǔ arduous, strenuous

欣快感 xīnkuàigǎn euphoria

辛辣 xīnlà sharp taste

信赖 xìnlài trust; rely on

新郎 xīnláng bridegroom

心理 xīnlǐ psychological ◊ psychologically, mentally

心理疾病 xīnlǐ jíbìng mental illness ◊ mentally ill

心灵感应 xīnlíng gǎnyìng telepathy ◊ telepathic

心理失调 xīnlǐ shītiáo maladjusted

心力衰竭 xīnlì shuāijié heart failure

心理学 xīnlǐ xué psychology ◊ psychological ◊ psychologically

心理学家 xīnlǐ xuéjiā psychologist

心理状态 xīnlǐ zhuàngtài mentality

心满意足 xīnmǎn yìzú contented, happy

新年 Xīnnián New Year (Western); 新年快乐 Xīnnián kuàilè Happy New Year

信念 xìnniàn conviction, belief

新娘 xīnniáng bride

芯片 xīnpiàn chip COMPUT

新起点 xīn qǐdiǎn new departure

心情 xīnqíng mood, frame of mind; 心情好 xīnqínghǎo good-humored

心儿 xīnr core

欣然 xīnrán readily; 欣然接受 xīnrán jiēshòu lap up, readily accept

新任 xīnrèn incoming, newly appointed

信任 xìnrèn trust ◊ confidence ◊ trusting

欣赏 xīnshǎng appreciate ◊ appreciation

心上人 xīnshàng rén sweetheart

心神不定 xīnshén bùdìng distraught

新生 xīnshēng newborn ◊ freshman

新式 xīnshì up-to-date

信使 xìnshǐ courier

新手 xīnshǒu beginner; rookie

薪水 xīnshuǐ salary

薪水级别 xīnshuǐ jíbié salary scale

薪水名册 xīnshuǐ míngcè payroll (staff)

薪水总额 xīnshuǐ zǒng'é payroll (money)

心算 xīnsuàn mental arithmetic

心碎 xīnsuì broken-hearted; 令人

心碎 **lìngrén xīnsuì** heartbreaking

心跳 xīntiào heartbeat

信条 xìntiáo creed

信徒 xìntú believer

喜怒无常 xǐnù wúcháng moody

新闻 xīnwén news

新闻报导 xīnwén bàodǎo news; news report

新闻播音员 xīnwén bōyīn yuán newsreader

新闻工作者 xīnwén gōngzuò zhě journalist

新闻广播 xīnwén guǎngbō newscast

新闻广播员 xīnwén guǎngbō yuán newscaster; anchor man

新闻界 xīnwénjiè the press

新闻写作 xīnwén xiězuò journalism (*writing*)

新闻业 xīnwényè journalism (*career*)

新闻自由 xīnwén zìyǒu freedom of the press

欣喜 xīnxǐ jubilant

信息 xìnxī information

新鲜 xīnxiān fresh ◊ freshness

信箱 xìnxiāng mailbox

信息技术 xìnxī jìshù information technology, IT

新西兰 Xīnxīlán New Zealand

信心 xìnxīn confidence

心胸宽阔 xīnxiōng kuānkuò broad-minded

心胸狭窄 xīnxiōng xiázǎi narrow-minded

欣喜若狂 xīnxǐ ruò kuáng rapture ◊ ecstatic

信息学 xìnxī xué information science

新芽 xīnyá sprout

信仰 xìnyǎng belief, faith

新颖 xīnyǐng novelty, freshness

新颖事物 xīnyǐng shìwù novelty

信以为真 xìn yǐwéi zhēn fall for

信用 xìnyòng credit FIN

信用卡 xìnyòng kǎ credit card

信誉 xìnyù credibility

新月 xīnyuè new moon

信誉卓著 xìnyù zhuōzhù creditworthy

心脏 xīnzàng heart ◊ cardiac

心脏病 xīnzàng bìng heart disease

心脏停跳 xīnzàng tíngtiào cardiac arrest

心脏移植 xīnzàng yízhí heart transplant

心照不宣 xīnzhào bù xuān knowing; tacit ◊ knowingly

信纸 xìnzhǐ writing paper

胸 xiōng chest; bust

兄 xiōng elder brother

凶 xiōng fierce; terrible; evil

熊 xióng bear

雄 xióng male

雄辩 xióngbiàn eloquent ◊ eloquently

兄弟 xiōngdì brothers

兄弟般 xiōngdì ban fraternal ◊ like brothers

兄弟姐妹 xiōngdì jiěmèi brothers and sisters

熊蜂 xióngfēng bumblebee

雄驹 xióngjū colt

熊猫 xióngmāo panda

凶猛 xiōngměng fierce

胸腔 xiōngqiāng thorax

凶杀 xiōngshā murder

凶手 xiōngshǒu murderer, killer

雄伟 xióngwěi imposing; majestic ◊ majestically

雄心勃勃 xióngxīn bóbo ambitious

雄性 xióngxìng male

熊熊燃烧 xióngxiong ránshāo blaze

匈牙利 Xiōngyálì Hungary ◊ Hungarian

胸罩 xiōngzhào brassière

胸针 xiōngzhēn brooch

锡箔 xīpó tinfoil

锡铅合金 xīqiān héjīn pewter

系起来 xì qǐlái tie up *hair*

喜鹊 xǐque magpie

吸入 xīrù breathe in, inhale

吸入器 xīrù qì inhaler

稀少 xīshǎo rare ◊ rarity

细审 xìshěn sift through

牺牲 xīshēng sacrifice

细绳 xìshéng string

系绳 xìshéng tether

牺牲品 xīshēng pǐn victim

稀释 xīshì dilute, water down

吸收 xīshōu absorb

洗手间 xǐshǒu jiān bathroom

稀疏 xīshū sparse

蟋蟀 xīshuài cricket

嬉水 xīshuǐ splash

习俗 xísú custom

细条纹 xìtiáowén pinstripe

系统 xìtǒng system; set-up ◊ systematic

系统崩溃 xìtǒng bēngkuì system crash

系统分析者 xìtǒng fēnxī zhě systems analyst

羞 xiū shame; embarrass

修 xiū repair; 把车修了 **bǎ chē xiūle** get the car fixed

休 xiū stop; rest; 休病假 **xiū bìngjià** be on sick leave

锈 xiù rust

嗅 xiù smell, sniff

袖 xiù sleeve

秀 xiù beautiful

修补 xiūbǔ mend; darn; reinforce

羞耻 xiūchǐ disgrace, shame

羞答答 xiū dádá coy

修道士 xiūdàoshì monastic

修道院 xiūdàoyuàn convent; monastery

修订 xiūdìng update

修复 xiūfù restore, recondition ◊ restoration

修改 xiūgǎi correct, amend; modify ◊ correction, amendment; modification; 他们要修改法律 **tāmén yào xiūgǎi fǎlǜ** they are going to change the law

休会 xiūhuì adjourn

休假 xiūjià vacation; recess ◊ take a vacation; take leave; 休假一天 **xiūjià yītiān** take a day off

修剪 xiūjiǎn crop; prune

修剪指甲 xiūjiǎn zhǐjiǎ manicure

嗅觉 xiùjué sense of smell

休克 xiūkè shock; 处于休克状态 **chǔyú xiūkè zhuàngtài** be in shock

袖口 xiùkǒu cuff

袖口链扣 xiùkǒu liànkòu cuff

link

羞愧 xiūkuì ashamed

修理 xiūlǐ repair, fix

秀丽 xiùlì beautiful; dainty

修理车间 xiūlǐ chējiān workshop; garage

修理工 xiūlǐ gōng repairman

休眠 xiūmián dormant

修女 xiūnǚ nun

羞怯 xiūqiè shy; sheepish

羞辱 xiūrǔ humiliate ◊ humiliation

修缮 xiūshàn renovate, do up

修饰 xiūshì touch up

袖手旁观 xiùshǒu pángguān stand by

休息 xiūxi rest, take a break ◊ recess; 休息吧！**xiūxìba!** let's call it a day!

休息一下 xiūxi yíxià take a break

休息日 xiūxīrì holiday

休养 xiūyǎng recuperate, recover

休养疗法 xiūyǎng liáofǎ rest cure

休战 xiūzhàn truce

袖珍 xiùzhēn compact; midget

修正 xiūzhèng revise, correct ◊ revision

修正主义 xiūzhèng zhǔyì revisionism ◊ revisionist

袖珍型 xiùzhēn xíng miniature

休止 xiūzhǐ cessation

袖子 xiùzi sleeve

洗碗布 xǐwǎn bù dishcloth

希望 xīwàng hope; wish; 希望如此 **xīwàng rúcǐ** I hope so

洗碗工 xǐwǎn gōng dishwasher (person)

洗碗机 xǐwǎn jī dishwasher (machine)

洗碗水 xǐwǎn shuǐ dishwater

席位 xíwèi seat POL

细微 xìwēi fine distinction

细心 xìxīn careful; considerate

熙熙攘攘 xīxī rǎngrang busy, crowded

信息学家 xìxī xuéjiā information scientist

吸烟 xīyān smoke; have a smoke ◊ smoking; 请勿吸烟 **qǐngwù**

*xīyān* please refrain from smoking

吸烟车厢 **xīyān chēxiāng** smoking compartment

吸烟者 **xīyān zhě** smoker

西药 **xīyào** Western medicine (*drugs etc*)

西医 **xīyī** Western medicine (*science*)

蜥蜴 **xīyì** lizard

洗衣店 **xǐyī diàn** laundry (*place*)

洗衣粉 **xǐyī fěn** soap powder, detergent

洗衣服 **xǐyīfu** get one's laundry done; do the washing

洗衣服务 **xǐyī fúwù** valet service (*for clothes*)

洗衣机 **xǐyī jī** washing machine

吸引 **xīyǐn** attract, draw; fascinate, charm; tempt

吸引力 **xīyǐn lì** attraction; appeal

习以为常 **xí yǐ wéi cháng** usual ◊ used to

洗一洗 **xǐyīxǐ** have a wash, wash up

稀有 **xīyǒu** rare

喜悦 **xǐyuè** happy

西藏 **Xīzàng** Tibet ◊ Tibetan

洗澡 **xǐzǎo** bathe; shower ◊ bathing

洗澡间 **xǐzǎo jiān** bathroom

锡纸 **xīzhǐ** tinfoil

细枝 **xìzhī** twig

西装 **xīzhuāng** suit

戏装 **xìzhuāng** costume (*actor's*)

西装上衣 **xīzhuāng shàngyī** coat (*of a suit*)

席子 **xízi** mat

须 **xū** must ◊ whiskers

需 **xū** need

虚 **xū** empty ◊ void

许 **xǔ** promise; permit

叙 **xù** narrate

序 **xù** order, sequence

续 **xù** continue

宣 **xuān** declare

旋 **xuán** rotate; spin, whirl

悬 **xuán** hang, suspend

选 **xuǎn** choose, pick; elect; highlight COMPUT; 他们选他当总统 **tāmén xuǎn tā dāng zǒngtǒng** they voted him

President

选拔 **xuǎnbá** selection

选拔赛 **xuǎnbásài** qualifier, qualifying game

宣布 **xuānbù** announce, declare, proclaim ◊ declaration

宣布无罪 **xuānbù wúzuì** exonerate

选出 **xuǎnchū** elected

宣传 **xuānchuán** promotion, publicity, propaganda ◊ promote, publicize, plug

宣传家 **xuānchuán jiā** publicist; spin doctor

悬垂 **xuánchuí** dangle

选词 **xuǎncí** word

悬而未决 **xuán ér wèi jué** be pending ◊ undecided

旋风 **xuánfēng** whirlwind

宣告 **xuāngào** announce ◊ announcement

悬挂 **xuánguà** suspend, hang

喧哗 **xuānhuá** din, racket ◊ noisy

喧哗声 **xuānhuá shēng** noise

选举 **xuǎnjǔ** election ◊ elect

选举权 **xuǎnjǔ quán** right to vote; 有选举权 **yǒu xuǎnjǔ quán** have the vote

选举日 **xuǎnjǔ rì** election day

选举投票 **xuǎnjǔ tóupiào** vote, go to the polls

选举制度 **xuǎnjǔ zhìdù** electoral system

旋律 **xuánlù** melody

选民 **xuǎnmín** elector, voter

眩目 **xuànmù** blinding

眩目电闪 **xuànmù diànshǎn** bolt of lightning

喧闹 **xuānnào** racket, tumult ◊ noisy, rowdy; tumultuous ◊ blare out

喧闹声 **xuānnào shēng** din

悬念 **xuánniàn** suspense

宣判 **xuānpàn** pass judgment; 宣判无罪 **xuānpàn wúzuì** acquit; 宣判有罪 **xuānpàn yǒuzuì** convict

选票 **xuǎnpiào** vote

轩然大波 **xuānrán dàbō** fuss, stink

选入 **xuǎnrù** vote in

悬赏 xuánshǎng offer a reward

宣誓 xuānshì swear an oath

选手 xuǎnshǒu competitor

悬殊 xuánshū disparity

旋涡 xuánwō whirlpool

喧器 xuānxiāo uproar, hullabaloo

悬崖 xuányá cliff, bluff

宣言 xuānyán manifest

宣扬 xuānyáng advertising

炫耀 xuànyào show off; parade, flaunt ◊ pretentious

眩晕 xuànyùn giddiness, vertigo

选择 xuǎnzé choice, option ◊ choose, select

选择过程 xuǎnzé guòchéng selection process

宣战 xuānzhàn declare war ◊ declaration of war

旋转 xuánzhuǎn revolve; rotate; spin; whirl ◊ revolution, rotation

旋转门 xuánzhuǎn mén revolving door

旋转木马 xuánzhuǎn mùmǎ carousel

旋转炮塔 xuánzhuǎn pàotǎ turret (of tank)

絮叨 xùdao harp on about

蓄电池 xù diànchí storage battery

许多 xǔduō many; much; a lot of

靴 xuē boot

学 xué study; learn

穴 xué hole; cave

雪 xuě snow

血 xuè blood

雪白 xuěbái snow-white

雪崩 xuěbēng avalanche

雪堆 xuěduī snowdrift

血管 xuèguǎn blood vessel

雪花 xuěhuā snowflake

学会 xuéhuì learn ◊ academy

血迹 xuèjī bloodstain

雪茄 xuějiā cigar

削减 xuējiǎn cut, trim; whittle down

血库 xuèkù blood bank

血块 xuèkuài blood clot

雪犁 xuělí snowplow

雪莲 xuělián snowdrop

雪利酒 xuělì jiǔ sherry

血淋淋 xuè línlin bloody

学年 xuénián academic year

学期 xuéqī semester, term

雪橇 xuěqiāo bobsleigh, bobsled; sled, sleigh

血亲 xuèqīn blood relative

雪球 xuěqiú snowball

血球 xuèqiú corpuscle

雪人 xuěrén snowman

削弱 xuēruò impaired ◊ weaken

学生 xuésheng student

学生时代 xuésheng shídài school days

学术 xuéshù academic

血栓形成 xuěshuān xíngchéng thrombosis

学术成就 xuéshù chéngjiù scholarship (work)

学说 xuéshuō doctrine

血统 xuètǒng breed; pedigree

噱头 xuétóu patter, spiel; publicity stunt

学徒 xuétú apprentice, novice

学位 xuéwèi (university) degree

穴位 xuéwèi acupuncture point

学问 xuéwen knowledge

雪屋 xuěwū igloo

学习 xuéxí study; learn ◊ studying; learning; 学习驾驶 xuéxí jiàshǐ learn to drive; 学习曲线 xuéxí qūxiàn learning curve

学校 xuéxiào school

学校假期 xuéxiào jiàqī school vacation

血型 xuèxíng blood group

血压 xuèyā blood pressure

血液 xuèyè bloodstream

血液循环 xuèyè xúnhuán circulation

血液样本 xuèyè yàngběn blood sample

学员 xuéyuán cadet

学院 xuéyuàn college; academy; school

学者 xuézhě scholar

血肿 xuèzhǒng hematoma

血中毒 xuè zhòngdú blood poisoning

靴子 xuēzi boot

虚构 xūgòu make up ◊ fictitious

虚构情节 xūgòu qíngjié embroider, embellish story

虚话 **xūhuà** myth, fiction

续集 **xùjí** sequel, continuation

虚假 **xūjiǎ** hollow, meaningless ◊ pretense

许久 **xǔjiǔ** a long time

酗酒 **xùjiǔ** drink, booze

酗酒者 **xùjiǔ zhě** alcoholic

许可 **xǔkě** permission, authority ◊ license, permit

许可证 **xǔkě zhèng** permit, warrant

畜牧 **xùmù** raise livestock

序幕 **xùmù** prolog

熏 **xūn** smoke

询 **xún** inquire

寻 **xún** seek

巡 **xún** patrol, cruise

驯 **xún** tame

训 **xùn** instruct, train

迅 **xùn** fast, rapid

巡边员 **xúnbiān yuán** linesman

训斥 **xùnchì** reprimand

殉道者 **xùndào zhě** martyr

驯服 **xùnfú** tame, docile

巡官 **xúnguān** inspector (of police)

驯化 **xùnhuà** domesticate

循环 **xúnhuán** circulate ◊ circulation; cycle

巡回 **xúnhuí** round (of doctor etc)

虚拟现实 **xūnǐ xiànshí** virtual reality

巡警 **xúnjǐng** patrolman

训练 **xùnliàn** train ◊ training

训练班 **xùnliàn bān** training course

训练有素 **xùnliàn yǒusù** skillful; polished

巡逻 **xúnluó** patrol

巡逻车 **xúnluó chē** patrol car

巡逻队 **xúnluó duì** patrol

荨麻 **xúnmá** nettle

训兽者 **xùnshòu zhě** trainer (of dog)

迅速 **xùnsù** swift, speedy; express ◊ speedily, swiftly; 他们沿路迅 速前进 **tāmen yánlù xùnsù qiánjìn** they pelted along the road

迅速上升 **xùnsù shàngshēng** shoot up (of prices)

迅速增长 **xùnsù zēngzhǎng** mushroom, spread

许诺 **xǔnuò** promise

询问 **xúnwèn** inquire; interrogate ◊ inquiry; interrogation

勋章 **xūnzhāng** medal; decoration

寻找 **xúnzhǎo** search for, look for, seek

需求 **xūqiú** demand

序曲 **xùqǔ** overture

虚荣 **xūróng** vanity

虚弱 **xūruò** weak, frail, feeble ◊ frailty, weakness

叙事体 **xùshì tǐ** narrative

叙事者 **xùshì zhě** narrator

叙述 **xùshù** relate, narrate, tell ◊ narration, account, story

虚伪 **xūwěi** hypocrisy; insincerity ◊ hypocritical

虚线 **xūxiàn** perforated line

虚心 **xūxīn** open-minded

嘘嘘声 **xūxu shēng** boo

序言 **xùyán** introduction

需要 **xūyào** need, require; cost; take; entail ◊ requirement, need; 有需要 **yǒu xūyào** in demand

蓄意 **xùyì** systematically

虚张声势 **xūzhāng shēngshì** bravado, bluff

# Y

压 yā press, crush ◊ pressure
鸭 yā duck
鸦 yā crow
押 yā mortgage; pawn
呀 yā (being at loss): 呀，这怎么办呢？ *yā, zhè zěnme bàn ne?* oh god, what am I going to do?
牙 yá tooth
哑 yǎ dumb, mute
亚 yà inferior; second best
牙斑 yábān plaque
牙齿 yáchǐ tooth ◊ dental
牙齿检查 yáchǐ jiǎnchá dental checkup
压低 yādī keep down *voice etc*
牙膏 yágāo toothpaste
雅观 yǎguān graceful; refined
押金 yājīn deposit, security
亚军 yàjūn runner-up
牙科 yákē dentistry ◊ dental
哑口无言 yǎkǒu wúyán speechless
压力 yālì pressure; stress
哑铃 yǎlíng dumbbell
亚麻布 yàmá bù linen
腌 yān salt; pickle; cure
烟 yān smoke
淹 yān drown
言 yán word; words; talking; speech
盐 yán salt
严 yán tight; rigorous
颜 yán face; color
研 yán grind; research
岩 yán cliff; rock
延 yán extend
沿 yán along
演 yǎn perform
眼 yǎn eye
堰 yàn weir
咽 yàn swallow
宴 yàn banquet, feast
燕 yàn swallow (*bird*)
厌 yàn hate; dislike
砚 yàn inkstone

验 yàn test, check
掩蔽 yǎnbì cover, shelter
掩蔽物 yǎnbì wù shelter, screen
演播室 yǎnbō shì (TV) studio
掩藏 yǎncáng hide; disguise *fear etc*
烟草 yāncǎo tobacco
檐槽 yáncáo gutter
延长 yáncháng extend, lengthen; prolong ◊ lengthy, protracted
延迟 yánchí delay
演出 yǎnchū perform ◊ performance
烟囱 yāncōng chimney; ship's funnel
烟蒂 yāndì cigarette butt
烟斗 yāndǒu pipe (*for smoking*)
厌烦 yànfán be fed up
羊 yáng sheep
洋 yáng ocean
阳 yáng yang; sun
杨 yáng poplar
扬 yáng raise
痒 yáng itch
养 yǎng keep, rear *animals*
氧 yǎng oxygen
仰 yǎng look up
样 yàng style; type; sample; model
掩盖 yǎngài cover, cover up; mask
掩盖真相 yǎngài zhēnxiàng coverup
洋白菜 yángbái cài cabbage (*Northern China*)
样本 yàngběn sample, specimen
养病 yǎngbìng convalesce
养蚕业 yǎngcányè silkworm breeding
养成 yǎngchéng pick up *habit*; 养成习惯 *yǎngchéng … xíguàn* take to, make a habit of
洋葱 yángcōng onion
阉割 yāngē neuter; castrate
严格 yángé rigorous, strict ◊ rigor, strictness

扬帆驾驶 yángfān jiàshǐ sailing

养父母 yǎngfùmǔ foster parents

羊倌 yángguān shepherd

阳光 yángguāng sunshine

阳光充足 yángguāng chōngzú sunny

洋鬼子 yáng guǐzi *pej* foreign devil, damn foreigner

氧化物 yǎnghuà wù oxide

养老金 yǎnglǎo jīn pension

养老院 yǎnglǎo yuàn old people's home

羊毛 yángmáo wool

羊毛衣物 yángmáo yīwù woolen clothing

阉公牛 yān gōngniú steer (*animal*)

羊皮 yángpí sheepskin

样品 yàngpǐn specimen, sample

氧气 yǎngqì oxygen

羊绒 yángróng cashmere

羊肉 yángròu mutton

阳伞 yángsǎn sunshade, parasol

养神 yǎngshén relax

扬声器 yángshēng qì loudspeaker

样式 yàngshì pattern

杨树 yángshù poplar tree

阳台 yángtái balcony; patio; terrace

验关 yànguān customs inspection

验光 yànguāng eye test

言过其实 yán guò qí shí exaggeration

仰望 yǎngwàng look up

阳萎 yángwěi impotence ◊ impotent

仰卧 yǎngwò lie on one's back

洋洋大作 yángyang dàzuò blockbuster

仰泳 yǎngyǒng backstroke

养育 yǎngyù bring up

养鱼缸 yǎngyúgāng aquarium

严寒 yánhán frosty

烟盒 yānhé cigarette case

咽喉 yānhóu gullet; larynx

掩护 yǎnhù camouflage

延缓 yánhuǎn postpone, delay

宴会 yànhuì dinner party; banquet

烟灰缸 yānhuī gāng ashtray

烟火 yānhuǒ fireworks

烟火表演 yānhuǒ biǎoyǎn firework display

眼睑 yǎnjiǎn eyelid

演讲 yǎnjiǎng lecture, talk

演讲者 yǎnjiǎng zhě speaker

岩礁 yánjiāo ledge (*on rock face*)

眼睫毛 yǎn jiémáo eyelash

严谨 yánjǐn tight

严禁 yánjìn forbidden

眼睛 yǎnjīng eye

眼镜 yǎnjìng glasses

眼睛疲劳 yǎnjīng píláo eye strain

研究 yánjiū study, research

研究课题 yánjiū kètí research project

研究生 yánjiū shēng postgraduate

研究员 yánjiū yuán researcher

厌倦 yànjuàn be tired of, be sick of

严峻 yánjùn forbidding; somber

眼科医生 yǎnkē yīshēng ophthalmologist

严酷 yánkù stark, grim

眼泪 yǎnlèi teardrop

眼泪汪汪 yǎnlèi wāngwang tearful

严厉 yánlì severe ◊ severely

颜料 yánliào paint

严厉盘问 yánlì pánwèn interrogate, grill

严厉批评 yánlì pīpíng criticize, pan

言论自由 yánlùn zìyóu free speech

燕麦片 yànmài piàn oatmeal; oats

淹没 yānmò flood; submerge; deluge; drown out; 淹没堤岸 yānmò tí'àn flood its banks

赝品 yànpǐn fake

延期 yánqī postpone; extend ◊ postponement; extension

眼球 yǎnqiú eyeball

烟圈儿 yānquānr wisp of smoke

颜色 yánsè color; coloring

延伸 yánshēn stretch, extend

岩石 yánshí rock

掩饰 yǎnshì cover up; 替 X 掩饰 错误缺点 tì X yǎnshì cuòwù quēdiǎn cover up for X

验尸 yànshī autopsy

厌食 **yànshí** be anorexic

验尸官 **yànshī guān** coroner

厌食症 **yànshí zhèng** anorexia

演说家 **yǎnshuō jiā** orator; speaker

淹死 **yānsǐ** drown

严肃 **yánsù** serious; stern; sober; solemn ◊ severity

研讨会 **yántǎo huì** seminar

燕尾服 **yànwěifú** tail coat

烟雾 **yānwù** smog

延误 **yánwù** delay, holdup

厌恶 **yànwù** hate; have an aversion to; 令人厌恶 **lìngrén yànwù** distasteful; sickening; repulsive

演习 **yǎnxí** exercise, drill, maneuver

演戏 **yǎnxì** put on a play; perform

眼下 **yǎnxià** at present

咽峡炎 **yānxiá yán** angina

延续 **yánxù** continue, last

验血 **yànxuè** blood test

眼药水 **yǎnyàoshuǐ** eyedrops

演艺界 **yǎnyìjiè** show business

眼影膏 **yǎnyǐnggāo** eyeshadow

谚语 **yànyǔ** saying, proverb

演员 **yǎnyuán** actor; actress

演员表 **yǎnyuán biǎo** cast

言语矫治师 **yányǔ jiǎozhì shī** speech therapist

言语缺陷 **yányǔ quēxiàn** speech defect

沿着 **yánzhe** follow, go along; stick to *path etc* ◊ down, along; 他们沿着街跑 **tāmen yánzhe jiē pǎo** they ran up the street

验证 **yànzhèng** identification ◊ test; verify

胭脂 **yānzhī** blusher

严重 **yánzhòng** severe, grave; serious; drastic ◊ gravity, seriousness

燕子 **yànzi** swallow (*bird*)

演奏 **yǎnzòu** perform, play *music* ◊ rendition, playing, performance

演奏会 **yǎnzòu huì** recital

演奏者 **yǎnzòu zhě** player, musician

烟嘴 **yānzuǐ** tip (*of cigarette*)

要 **yāo** demand

腰 **yāo** waist

妖 **yāo** monster; ghost

邀 **yāo** invite

幺 **yāo** one (*in phone numbers*)

窑 **yáo** kiln

摇 **yáo** shake

遥 **yáo** far away, distant

咬 **yǎo** bite

舀 **yǎo** scoop

药 **yào** drug, medicine; medication

要 **yào** want; need; must; will ◊ if; 你要什么都行 **nǐ yào shénme dōu xíng** you can have whatever you want; 天也许要下雨 **tiān yěxǔ yào xiàyǔ** it might rain; 我要和你谈话 **wǒ yào hé nǐ táihuà** I need to talk to you

摇摆 **yáobǎi** roll, sway; swing; toss ◊ unsteady

腰包 **yāobāo** fanny pack

腰部 **yāobù** waist

药草 **yàocǎo** herb

药草茶 **yàocǎo chá** herbal tea

舀出 **yǎochū** scoop up

腰带 **yāodài** belt; girdle

要道 **yàodào** main street

要点 **yàodiǎn** key point; core, nub

药店 **yàodiàn** pharmacy, drugstore

摇动 **yáodòng** wave; shake; flap

要饭 **yàofàn** beg

药方 **yàofāng** prescription

药房 **yàofáng** dispensary; pharmacy, drugstore

妖怪 **yāoguài** monster; ghost

摇滚乐 **yáogǔn yuè** rock music, rock and roll

摇滚乐歌星 **yáogǔn yuè gēxīng** rock star

摇晃 **yáohuang** rock; tremble; wobble ◊ shaky

咬紧 **yǎojǐn** clench

要紧 **yàojǐn** important, vital ◊ matter

药剂师 **yàojì shī** druggist, pharmacist

遥控 **yáokòng** remote control

摇篮 **yáolán** cradle

摇橹 **yáolǔ** paddle

幼苗 **yòumiáo** seedling

药片 **yàopiàn** tablet

药品 **yàopǐn** medicine

药签 **yàoqiān** swab

邀请 **yāoqǐng** invite ◊ invitation

要求 **yāoqiú** request, ask for; demand, require ◊ demand; call

要人 **yàorén** VIP

要塞 **yàosài** fort

摇上 **yáoshàng** wind up *window*

钥匙 **yàoshi** key

要是 **yàoshì** if

钥匙圈 **yàoshiquān** keyring

药水 **yàoshuǐ** tonic

腰疼 **yāoténg** lumbago

腰痛 **yāotòng** lumbago

摇头 **yáotóu** shake one's head

摇头丸儿 **yáotóuwánr** ecstasy *(drug)*

药丸 **yàowán** pill

腰围 **yāowéi** waistline

药物 **yàowù** drug

摇下 **yáoxià** wind down *window*

谣言 **yáoyán** rumor

耀眼 **yàoyǎn** dazzle ◊ dazzling

摇摇欲坠 **yáoyao yùzhuì** ramshackle

摇椅 **yáoyǐ** rocking chair

遥远 **yáoyuǎn** far away

腰子 **yāozi** kidney

鸦片 **yāpiàn** opium

鸦片战争 **Yāpiàn Zhànzhēng** Opium War

压迫 **yāpò** oppress

牙签 **yáqiān** toothpick

牙刷 **yáshuā** toothbrush

压缩 **yāsuō** compress; condense, shorten; zip up COMPUT

压缩空气 **yāsuō kōngqì** compressed air

压缩驱动器 **yāsuō qūdòngqì** zip drive

牙套 **yátào** (dental) brace

牙疼 **yáténg** toothache

牙痛 **yátòng** toothache

牙医 **yáyī** dentist

压抑 **yàyì** inhibit; repress; muffle ◊ inhibited; pent-up ◊ inhibition

压印 **yāyìn** imprint *(of credit card)*

牙龈 **yáyín** gum

压韵 **yāyùn** rhyme; 以 ... 压韵 **yǐ ... yāyùn** rhyme with ...

压制 **yāzhì** suppress, clamp down on; silence ◊ repressive

雅致 **yǎzhì** gracious, elegant

亚洲 **Yàzhōu** Asia ◊ Asian

亚洲人 **Yàzhōu rén** Asian

椰 **yē** coconut

爷 **yé** grandpa, grandfather *(paternal)*

也 **yě** too, also, as well; 她也是 **tā yě shì** so is she; 一点也不奇怪 **yìdiǎn yě bù qíguài** not in the least surprised

野 **yě** wild

液 **yè** liquid

夜 **yè** night

页 **yè** page

叶 **yè** leaf

业 **yè** business; industry

夜班 **yèbān** night shift

夜班服务员 **yèbān fúwùyuán** night porter

野餐 **yěcān** picnic

野地 **yědì** wilderness

野鸡 **yějī** unregistered, unlicensed; worthless; mickey-mouse

夜间 **yèjiān** at night; 夜间飞行 **yèjiān fēixíng** night flight; 夜间旅行 **yèjiān lǚxíng** travel by night

液晶体显示器 **yèjīngtǐ xiǎnshìqì** LCD, liquid crystal display

冶炼厂 **yěliàn chǎng** iron and steel works

叶轮机 **yèlún jī** steam turbine

页码 **yèmǎ** page number

野蛮 **yěmán** inhuman

野牛 **yěniú** buffalo

叶片 **yèpiàn** blade *(of grass)*

野人 **yěrén** savage

野生 **yěshēng** wild

野生动物保护区 **yěshēng dòngwù bǎohù qū** animal sanctuary

夜生活 **yè shēnghuó** nightlife

野生鸟兽 **yěshēng niǎoshòu** wildlife

夜市 **yèshì** night market

野兽 **yěshòu** wild beast

耶稣 **Yēsū** Jesus

液体 **yètǐ** liquid

野兔 **yětù** hare

夜晚 **yèwǎn** night

腋窝 **yèwō** armpit

夜校 **yèxiào** evening classes; night

school

野心 yěxīn ambition; greed
野性 yěxìng savage; wild
也许 yěxǔ may, might ◊ perhaps, possibly, maybe; 我也许迟到 wǒ yěxǔ chídào I might be late
液压 yèyā hydraulic
野丫头 yěyātóu tomboy
爷爷 yéye grandpa, grandfather (paternal)
夜莺 yèyīng nightingale
野营车 yěyíng chē camper (vehicle)
野营者 yěyíng zhě camper (person)
业余 yèyú amateur
业余爱好者 yèyú àihào zhě amateur
业余时间 yèyú shíjiān spare time
野猪 yězhū wild boar
业主 yèzhǔ proprietor
液状 yèzhuàng liquid
椰子 yēzi coconut
叶子 yèzi leaf; foliage
椰子奶 yēzi nǎi coconut milk
椰子树 yēzi shù coconut palm
夜总会 yèzǒnghuì nightclub; nightspot
一 yī one
衣 yī clothes; item of clothing
依 yī depend on ◊ according to; 依我看 yī wǒ kàn as far as I can see
医 yī medicine; doctor
姨 yí aunt (mother's sister)
遗 yí lose; leave behind
仪 yí ceremony, rite
移 yí move
疑 yí doubt, suspect
椅 yǐ chair
倚 yǐ lean on; depend on
已 yǐ already
以 yǐ by; according to; 以 X 为目标 yǐ X wéi mùbiāo with a view to X; 以 X 著名 yǐ X zhùmíng be famous for X
意 yì thought, idea; intention; meaning
溢 yì overflow
抑 yì suppress
易 yì easy ◊ change; exchange
义 yì justice

议 yì discuss
亿 yì hundred million
艺 yì art; craft
译 yì translate
异 yì different; strange; foreign
议案 yì'àn POL
一百 yìbǎi one hundred
一百周年 yìbǎi zhōunián centenary, centennial
一般 yìbān ordinary, usual; mediocre ◊ usually, generally
一半 yíbàn half
一帮 yìbāng gang
易饱 yìbǎo stodgy
贻贝 yíbèi mussel
一辈子 yí bèizi one's whole life, a lifetime
一笔 yìbǐ brushstroke
一边 yìbiān aside
易变 yìbiàn unsettled
一边倒 yìbiān dǎo one-sided
易辨认 yìbiànrèn legible
仪表 yíbiǎo dial; dashboard
疑病症患者 yíbìngzhèng huàn zhě hypochondriac
易剥落 yì bōluò flaky
一波三折 yìbō sānzhé stormy relationship
一步 yíbù move (in chess)
一部分 yíbùfen part; portion; fragment
一层 yìcéng blanket (of snow etc)
易察觉 yì chájué visible
遗产 yíchǎn estate; legacy
异常 yìcháng exceptional; unusual ◊ exceptionally; unusually
一尘不染 yìchén bùrǎn spotless
议程 yìchéng agenda
一成不变 yì chéng búbiàn be very set in one's ways
易冲动 yì chōngdòng impulsive
溢出 yìchū overflow, run over; slop
遗传 yíchuán genetic; hereditary ◊ heredity ◊ pass on
遗传工程 yíchuán gōngchéng genetic engineering
遗传学 yíchuán xué genetics
遗传学家 yíchuán xuéjiā geneticist
一触即发 yíchù jífā simmer (with

rage)

易处理 **yì chǔlǐ** manageable

一次 **yīcì** once

依次 **yīcì** in turn

以此 **yǐcǐ** for this reason; consequently; hence; thereby

一次性 **yīcìxìng** disposable ◊ one-off

依从 **yīcóng** obey

意大利 **Yìdàlì** Italy ◊ Italian

一旦 **yídàn** ever; once

一当 **yīdāng** as soon as

一道来 **yīdàolái** come along, come too

胰岛素 **yídǎosù** insulin

一大早 **yīdàzǎo** at daybreak

一点 **yìdiǎn** a bit, a little; 一点水 **yìdiǎn shuǐ** a little water; 一点也不奇怪 **yìdiǎn yě bù qíguài** not in the least surprised; 好一点 **hǎo yìdiǎn** a little better; 一点一点 **yìdiǎn yìdiǎn** little by little, bit by bit

疑点 **yídiǎn** question mark

一点点 **yìdiǎndiǎn** a little bit, not a lot *vague taste*; 我所知道的那一点点 **wǒ suǒ zhīdào de nà yìdiǎndiǎn** the little I know

一点儿 **yìdiǎnr** a bit, a little

一定 **yídìng** definite, certain, sure ◊ definitely, certainly, surely

移动 **yídòng** move; shift; remove ◊ removal; cell phone; 缓慢移动 **huǎnmàn yídòng** edge, move slowly

一动不动 **yídòng búdòng** stand still

移动电话 **yídòng diànhuà** cellular phone

移动性 **yídòng xìng** mobility

易读 **yìdú** readable

一段 **yíduàn** length; passage, extract; period

一段时间 **yíduàn shíjiān** session; spell ◊ for a while

一对 **yíduì** couple; duo

一方 **yīfāng** side, team

已废弃 **yǐ fèiqì** obsolete

一份 **yífèn** helping; share

衣服 **yīfu** clothes, clothing

遗腹 **yífù** posthumous

姨父 **yífù** uncle (*mother's sister's husband*)

衣服架 **yīfújiā** clothes hanger

一个 **yígè** one ◊ single; 一个面包 **yígè miànbāo** a loaf of bread; 一个挨着一个 **yígè āizhe yígè** side by side

一共 **yígòng** altogether; 一共三个 **yígòng sān gè** three in all

义工 **yìgōng** volunteer

衣钩 **yīgōu** coat hook

一贯 **yíguàn** consistent

衣柜 **yīguì** closet

异国 **yìguó** foreign country

一国两制 **yīguó liǎngzhì** one country, two systems

遗憾 **yíhàn** sad ◊ regret; 遗憾…**yíhàn …** it's a pity that …; 令人遗憾 **lìngrén yíhàn** deplorable ◊ sadly

颐和园 **Yíhéyuán** Summer Palace

以后 **yǐhòu** later, afterward; in future; 从那以后 **cóng nà yǐhòu** ever since

易坏 **yìhuài** perishable

议会 **yìhuì** council; assembly; parliament ◊ parliamentary

一会儿 **yíhuìr** a while; 我再等一会儿 **wǒ zài děng yíhuìr** I'll wait a while longer; 一会儿见！**yíhuìr jiàn!** see you later!

已婚 **yǐhūn** married

一伙人 **yìhuǒ rén** crowd, set

异乎寻常 **yì hū xúncháng** uncanny

遗迹 **yíjī** vestige

以及 **yǐjí** and

衣架 **yījià** coathanger

意见 **yìjiàn** opinion; suggestion; complaint; 你有什么意见？**nǐ yǒu shénme yìjiàn?** what's your opinion?

意见分歧 **yìjiàn fēnqí** dissension

意见相左 **yìjiàn xiāngzuǒ** disagree, differ

移交 **yíjiāo** hand over

异教徒 **yìjiàotú** heathen

易激动 **yì jīdòng** temperamental

已经 **yǐjīng** already; 已经晚了**yǐjīng wǎn le** it's getting late

易经 **Yìjīng** I-Ching, Book of

Changes
一经要求 yījīng yāoqiú on request
以旧换新 yǐ jiù huàn xīn trade in
依据 yījù basis; grounds
移居 yíjū immigrate
移居国外 yíjū guówài emigrate ◊ emigration
移开 yíkāi move away
一开始 yīkāishǐ from the start
一开头 yīkāitóu from the outset
依靠 yīkào rely on ◊ reliance; 依靠 X 去做 Y yīkào X qùzuò Y rely on X to do Y; 依靠自己 yīkào zìjǐ self-reliant
倚靠 yǐkào lean against
一刻钟 yīkèzhōng quarter of an hour
一口 yīkǒu bite, mouthful
一口气地说 yìkǒuqìde shuō rattle off poem, list of names
依赖 yīlài depend on ◊ dependent ◊ dependence; dependency
伊拉克 Yīlākè Iraq ◊ Iraqi
一览表 yìlánbiǎo list
伊朗 Yīlǎng Iran ◊ Iranian
依恋 yīliàn be attached to, be fond of
一连串 yìliánchuàn stream, string, succession
医疗 yīliáo medical; therapeutic ◊ (medical) care
医疗保险 yīliáo bǎoxiǎn health insurance
一流 yīliú first-class, first-rate
遗留 yíliú leave behind; bequeath
一楼 yīlóu first floor, ground floor Br
遗漏 yílòu omit ◊ omission
一律 yīlǜ without exception
疑虑重重 yílǜ chóngchong tormented by doubt
一路平安 yílù píng'ān have a good journey
译码 yìmǎ decode
衣帽间 yīmào jiān checkroom (for coats)
疫苗 yìmiáo vaccine
移民 yímín immigrate; emigrate ◊ immigrant; emigrant; immigration; emigration

移民局 Yímínjú Department of Immigration
一模一样 yìmú yíyàng identical
音 yīn sound; tone
因 yīn because ◊ reason
阴 yīn yin; shade; private parts ◊ overcast; 天阴了 tiānyīnle cloud over
银 yín silver
淫 yín lewd
瘾 yǐn addiction; 有 X 的瘾 yǒu X de yǐn be addicted to X
引 yǐn draw, attract
隐 yǐn hide
饮 yǐn drink
印 yìn print ◊ stamp
疑难 yínàn problematic
阴暗 yīn'àn gloomy; dark ◊ gloom
引爆装置 yǐnbào zhuāngzhì detonator, igniter
音标 yīnbiāo phonetics
隐藏 yǐncáng hide, conceal; bury ◊ hidden
阴沉 yīnchén threatening, overcast, dull
印出 yìnchū print out
印戳 yìnchuō stamp
因此 yīncǐ so; therefore; consequently; thus
阴道 yīndào vagina ◊ vaginal
引导 yǐndǎo lead, guide; educate; direct
印第安人 Yìndì'ān rén Indian (Native American)
音调 yīndiào note; pitch; 调准音调 tiáo zhǔn yīndiào tune
音调悦耳 yīndiào yuè'ér tuneful
引渡 yǐndù extradite ◊ extradition
印度 Yìndù India ◊ Indian
引渡公约 yǐndù gōngyuē extradition treaty
印度尼西亚 Yìndùníxīyà Indonesia ◊ Indonesian
印度人 Yìndùrén Indian
印度洋 Yìndùyáng Indian Ocean
印度支那 Yìndùzhīnà Indochina ◊ Indochinese
音符 yīnfú note
鹰 yīng eagle
应 yīng should, ought to
婴 yīng infant, baby

樱 **yīng** cherry

营 **yíng** camp

赢 **yíng** win; beat

迎 **yíng** welcome; meet

影 **yǐng** shadow; image

硬 **yìng** hard

应 **yìng** respond, reply; deal with; adapt to

英镑 **yīngbàng** (pound) sterling

硬邦邦 **yìng bāngbang** solid; stiff

硬币 **yìngbì** coin

迎宾员 **yíngbīn yuán** usher

应承 **yìngchéng** promise

硬扯入 **yìngchě rù** drag in; mention

英尺 **yīngchǐ** foot

英寸 **yīngcùn** inch

应得 **yìngdé** deserve; earn ◊ well-earned

赢得 **yíngdé** gain, earn; win

营地 **yíngdì** campsite

硬度 **yìngdù** hardness

婴儿 **yīng'ér** baby, infant

婴儿车 **yīng'ér chē** baby carriage, buggy

婴儿期 **yīng'ér qī** infancy, babyhood

营房 **yíngfáng** quarters, barracks

应付 **yìngfù** manage, cope; cope with

应该 **yìnggāi** should, ought to

英格兰 **Yīnggélán** England

英国 **Yīngguó** United Kingdom; Britain; England ◊ British; English; Brit

迎合 **yínghé** cater for

樱花树 **yīnghuā shù** cherry tree

营火 **yínghuǒ** bonfire

影集 **yǐngjí** photo album

硬挤 **yìngjǐ** hustle, hurry along

硬件 **yìngjiàn** hardware COMPUT

迎接 **yíngjiē** greet, welcome

应接不暇 **yìngjiē bùxiá** be swamped with

英俊 **yīngjùn** handsome, cute (male)

应考人 **yìngkǎo rén** (exam) candidate

盈亏平衡点 **yíngkuī pínghéng diǎn** break-even point

硬拉 **yìnglā** drag

英里 **yīnglǐ** mile

盈利 **yínglì** profit; surplus

英明 **yīngmíng** brilliant; wise

英亩 **yīngmǔ** acre

因公 **yīngōng** on business

硬盘 **yìngpán** hard disk

硬皮书 **yìngpíshū** hardback

萦绕于心 **yíngrào yú xīn** haunting

应试者 **yìngshì zhě** interviewee

应受指摘 **yìngshòu zhīzhāi** reprehensible

硬刷子 **yìngshuāzi** scrubbing brush

罂粟 **yīngsù** poppy

鹰隼 **yīngsǔn** hawk

樱桃 **yīngtáo** cherry (*fruit*)

硬通货 **yìngtōnghuò** hard currency

硬卧 **yìngwò** hard sleeper (*on train*)

鹦鹉 **yīngwǔ** parrot

影响 **yǐngxiǎng** influence; impact ◊ influence; affect

影响力 **yǐngxiǎnglì** influence; impact

硬行推销 **yìngxíng tuīxiāo** hard sell

英雄 **yīngxióng** hero

营养 **yíngyǎng** nourishment; nutrition

营养不良 **yíngyǎng bùliáng** malnutrition

营养搭配好 **yíngyǎng dāpèihǎo** well-balanced *diet*

营养品 **yíngyǎng pǐn** nutrient

硬要 **yìngyào** impose (oneself)

营业经理 **yíngyè jīnglǐ** sales manager

营业时间 **yíngyè shíjiān** business hours

影印 **yǐngyìn** photocopy

影印本 **yǐngyìn běn** photocopy

影印机 **yǐngyìn jī** photocopier

英勇 **yīngyǒng** heroic

应用 **yìngyòng** use; apply ◊ applied

英勇事迹 **yīngyǒng shìjì** exploit, deed

英语 **Yīngyǔ** English (*language*)

应征 yìngzhēng join the army

应征入伍者 yìngzhēng rùwǔ zhě draftee

硬纸板 yìng zhǐbǎn cardboard

应支付 yìng zhīfù payable, due

影子 yǐngzi shadow

硬座 yìngzuò hard seat (*on train*)

银行 yínháng bank FIN

银行贷款 yínháng dàikuǎn bank loan

银行家 yínháng jiā banker

银行结存 yínháng jiécún bank balance

银行结单 yínháng jiédān bank statement

银行经理 yínháng jīnglǐ bank manager

银行利率 yínháng lìlǜ bank rate

银行信用卡 yínháng xìnyòng kǎ banker's card

银行帐户 yínháng zhànghù bank account

引号 yǐnhào quotation mark

淫秽 yínhuì obscene; bawdy

银婚 yínhūn silver wedding (anniversary)

阴间 yīnjiān underworld (*in mythology*)

音阶 yīnjiē scale MUS

音节 yīnjié syllable

引进 yǐnjìn introduce, bring in ◊ introduction

阴茎 yīnjīng penis

饮酒者 yǐnjiǔ zhě drinker

隐居处 yǐnjū chù retreat

阴凉 yīnliáng shady

音量 yīnliàng volume (*of radio etc*)

阴凉处 yīnliáng chù in the shade

音量调控 yīnliàng tiáokòng volume control

饮料 yǐnliào drink

引路 yǐnlù lead the way

淫乱 yínluàn indecent, obscene

隐瞒 yǐnmán conceal, cover up; disguise

阴毛 yīnmáo pubic hair

隐没 yǐnmò go in

阴谋 yīnmóu conspiracy, plot

阴谋者 yīnmóu zhě plotter

银幕 yínmù screen

银牌 yínpái silver medal

引起 yǐnqǐ cause; produce; inspire; arouse; 引起 X 的注意 yǐnqǐ X de zhùyì catch X's eye

姻亲 yīnqīn in-laws

引擎 yǐnqíng engine

引人反感 yǐn rén fǎngǎn obnoxious

引人入胜 yǐn rén rù shèng compelling

引人注目 yǐn rén zhùmù stand out; attract attention ◊ spectacular; striking

阴森森 yīn sēnsēn spooky

隐士 yǐnshì recluse

印刷 yìnshuā print

印刷厂 yìnshuā chǎng printing works, press

印刷机 yìnshuā jī printing press

印刷品 yìnshuā pǐn printed matter

印刷商 yìnshuā shāng printer

印刷字体 yìnshuā zìtǐ print

饮水 yǐnshuǐ water *animals*

因素 yīnsù ingredient, factor

因特网 yīntèwǎng Internet

阴天 yīntiān cloudy

引退 yǐntuì resign, step down

易怒 yìnù fiery; irritable; snappy

因为 yīnwèi because, since ◊ on account of

淫猥 yínwěi lewd

引文 yǐnwén quotation, quote

阴险 yīnxiǎn devious; insidious ◊ deviously; insidiously

音箱 yīnxiāng speaker (*of sound system*)

音响 yīnxiǎng acoustics; stereo

印象 yìnxiàng impression

印象深刻 yìnxiàng shēnkè impressive

阴性 yīnxìng feminine GRAM; negative *test results*

隐形眼镜 yǐnxíng yǎnjìng contact lens

音译 yīnyì transliterate

引用 yǐnyòng quote

饮用水 yǐnyòng shuǐ drinking water

引诱 yǐnyòu seduce ◊ seduction

音域 yīnyù (vocal) range

音乐 yīnyuè music ◊ musical

音乐会 yīnyuè huì concert

音乐家 yīnyuè jiā musician

音乐片 yīnyuè piān musical (*movie*)

音乐学院 yīnyuè xuéyuàn conservatory, music school

印章 yìnzhāng stamp, seal (*on document*)

引证 yǐnzhèng cite

银制 yínzhì silver

银质 yínzhì silver

印子 yìnzi imprint, impression

一瞥 yīpiē glance, glimpse

一起 yīqǐ together; along; 和 … 一起 hé … yīqǐ with

仪器 yíqì apparatus; instrument

遗弃 yíqì jilt; walk out on

以前 yǐqián before; formerly, previously ◊ former, past; 以前干过吗? yǐqián gàn guò ma? have you done this before?; 他不再和以前一样了 tā búzài hé yǐqián yíyàng le he's not the same any more

一千 yīqiān one thousand

一千年 yīqiānnián millennium

一切 yíqiè everything; all; 一切包括在内 yíqiè bāokuò zàinèi inclusive

一期付款 yīqī fùkuàn installment

意气消沉 yìqì xiāochén despondent

一群 yìqún flock

意趣相投 yìqù xiāngtóu be on the same wavelength

易燃 yìrán combustible, inflammable

易燃烧 yì ránshāo flammable

一日游 yīrìyóu daytrip

以色列 Yǐsèliè Israel ◊ Israeli

医生 yīshēng doctor

一生 yìshēng one's whole life, a lifetime

一声不吭 yīshēng bùkēng stay silent

一时 yìshí a while, a moment

遗失 yíshī lose; mislay

仪式 yíshì ceremony; ritual

意识 yìshí awareness, consciousness; 意识不到 … yìshí búdào … be oblivious of; 意识到 yìshí dào be aware of, realize; 我现在才意识到 … wǒ xiànzài cái yìshí dào … I realize now that …

意识形态 yìshí xíngtài ideology ◊ ideological

艺术 yìshù art ◊ artistic

艺术家 yìshù jiā artist

艺术界 yìshù jiè the arts

艺术品 yìshù pǐn work of art

意思 yìsi meaning, sense; interest; 你什么意思? nǐ shénme yìsi? what are you driving at?

一丝不苟 yìsī bùgǒu scrupulous

一丝不挂 yīsī búguà stark naked

伊斯兰教 Yīsīlánjiào Islam ◊ Islamic

遗俗 yísú relic

易碎 yìsuì fragile; brittle

遗体 yítǐ remains

一天 yìtiān one day

意图 yìtú intention

一团 yìtuán jumble

一团糟 yītuánzāo be a mess ◊ tangle

意外 yìwài accidental; unexpected ◊ by chance; unexpectedly

意外发现 yìwài fāxiàn stumble across

遗忘 yíwàng oblivion ◊ leave behind

意味 yìwèi signify ◊ significance

意味深长 yìwèi shēncháng meaningful

疑问 yíwèn doubt; query; interrogative GRAM

译文 yìwén translation

一文不名 yìwén bùmíng penniless

衣物 yīwù laundry, washing ◊ wardrobe, clothes

遗物 yíwù relic

义务 yìwù obligation, duty ◊ voluntary *work*

义务教育 yìwù jiàoyù compulsory education

一无所有 yìwú suǒyǒu zilch

以下 yǐxià under; following; 十岁以下 shí suì yǐxià under ten years of age; 读以下说明 dú yǐxià shuōmíng read the following instructions

异想天开！ yìxiǎng tiānkāi! it boggles the mind!

一向 yíxiàng always; till now, so far; 一向准时 yíxiàng zhǔnshí have a good record for punctuality

一小袋 yīxiǎodài sachet

一小口 yìxiǎokǒu sip

一小片 yìxiǎopiàn morsel

一下子 yīxiàzi all at once; in one shot

一些 yìxiē some, a few

一系列 yíxìliè succession, series

疑心 yíxīn suspicion; 对 X 有疑心 duì X yǒu yíxīn be suspicious of X

异性爱 yìxìng'ài heterosexual

易兴奋 yìxīngfèn excitable

医学 yīxué medicine ◊ medical

以牙还牙 yǐyá huányá an eye for an eye; tit for tat

一眼 yìyǎn peek

一样 yīyàng just as; just the same; 和 ... 一样高 hé ... yīyàng gāo as high as ...; 看起来一样 kànqǐlái yíyàng look the same

一氧化碳 yīyǎng huàtàn carbon monoxide

一言为定 yī yán wéi dìng it's a deal

一言以蔽之 yìyán yǐ bìzhī in a nutshell

一一 yīyī one by one

意义 yìyì meaning, sense; point, purpose

异议 yìyì objection

一饮而尽 yìyǐn ér jìn gulp down

易于 ... yìyú ... be apt to ...

医院 yīyuàn hospital, infirmary

议员 yìyuán representative; congressman

译员 yìyuán interpreter

意愿 yìyuàn wish; inclination

一月 yíyuè January

依仗 yīzhàng count on

译者 yìzhě translator

一针 yìzhēn stitch

一直 yìzhí all the time, all along

遗嘱 yízhí transplant; graft

遗址 yízhí ruin

一致 yízhì uniform, identical; unanimous ◊ uniformly;

unanimously

意指 yìzhǐ mean

抑制 yìzhì check, restrain; refrain

意志 yìzhì will, willpower

意志力 yìzhìlì willpower

一致同意 yízhì tóngyì unanimous

一致性 yízhì xìng consistency; correspondence

一致意见 yízhì yìjiàn consensus

以至于 yǐzhìyú so that

遗嘱 yízhǔ legacy; will

衣着 yīzhuó clothes; 衣着不整 yīzhuó bùzhěng sloppily dressed; 衣着整洁 yīzhuó zhěngjié well-dressed

椅子 yǐzi chair

易醉 yìzuì heady drink, wine etc

异族通婚 yìzú tōnghūn mixed marriage

拥 yōng embrace; crowd

永 yǒng for ever

涌 yǒng surge

勇 yǒng brave

用 yòng use; apply ◊ with; 用早餐 yòng zǎocān have breakfast; 用电子邮件寄 yòng diànzǐ yóujiàn jì send by e-mail

拥抱 yōngbào cuddle; embrace, hug

用餐 yòngcān dine

涌出 yǒngchū gush, pour

用处 yòngchù usefulness

用错 yòngcuò misuse

用法 yòngfǎ directions; usage

用费 yòngfèi expenses

勇敢 yǒnggǎn brave, courageous, valiant ◊ bravely ◊ bravery

用光 yòngguāng use up, run out of

永恒 yǒnghéng eternal ◊ eternity

拥护 yōnghù welcome

用户 yònghù user; consumer

用坏 yònghuài wear out ◊ wear

用户友好 yònghù yǒuhǎo user-friendly

拥护者 yōnghù zhě supporter, sympathizer

拥挤 yōngjǐ crowd; jostle ◊ crowded, packed

拥挤的人群 yōngjǐ de rénqún crush

涌进 yǒngjìn surge forward

佣金 yòngjīn commission

用尽 yòngjìn exhaust, use up

永久 yǒngjiǔ permanent, everlasting

用具 yòngjù equipment, gear, tackle; utensil

用力 yònglì vigorous ◊ exert oneself; 用力打开 *yònglì dǎkāi* force *door*; 用力举起 *yònglì jǔqǐ* heave

用量 yòngliàng dose, dosage

勇气 yǒngqì courage, nerve; spirit

佣人 yōngrén servant

勇士 yǒngshì tough guy

用途 yòngtú use, purpose

用过 yòngguò used

用完 yòngwán run out; run out of; use up

勇往直前 yǒng wǎng zhí qián carry on undaunted

拥有 yōngyǒu own; keep

拥有者 yōngyǒu zhě owner

永远 yǒngyuǎn for ever, eternally; 他永远不会厌倦 *ta yǒngyuǎn būhuì yànjuàn* he never tires of it

忧 yōu worry ◊ worried

优 yōu excellent, very good

幽 yōu secluded; peaceful

油 yóu oil; fat; grease

铀 yóu uranium

疣 yóu wart

游 yóu travel; float; swim

由 yóu from; 由此发生 … *yóucǐ fāshēng* … it follows from this that …; 由 … 主演 *yóu … zhǔyǎn* feature; 由 … 组成 *yóu … zǔchéng* be comprised of …

邮 yóu mail; 把 X 邮给 Y *bǎ X yóu gěi Y* send X to Y

有 yǒu have, have got; there is; there are ◊ (*forming adjectival constructions*): 有空调 *yǒu kōngtiáo* air-conditioned; 有经验 *yǒu jīngyàn* experienced

友 yǒu friend

右 yǒu right ◊ on the right

幼 yòu child ◊ young

诱 yòu seduce, lure; guide, lead

哟，呦！yōu, yōu! well, well!

又 … 又 … yòu … yòu … both … and …

幽暗 yōu'àn dark

有帮助 yǒu bāngzhù helpful

有把握 yǒu bǎwò safely ◊ self-assured

油泵 yóubèng gas pump

右边 yòubiān right-hand

有别于 yǒubiéyú differ from

幽闭恐怖症 yōubì kǒngbù zhèng claustrophobia

有病 yǒubìng ill

有必要时 yǒu bìyào shí as necessary

油布 yóubù tarpaulin

又不 yòubù nor

油菜 yóucài rape; rapeseed oil, canola

有才华 yǒu cáihuá brilliant

有才能 yǒu cáinéng accomplished

有偿雇佣 yǒucháng gùyōng paid employment

有成效 yǒu chéngxiào productive

幼虫 yòuchóng larva

忧愁 yōuchóu sad; gloomy ◊ sadness

有臭味 yǒu chòuwèi smell ◊ smelly

油船 yóuchuán (oil) tanker

邮戳 yóuchuō postmark

虚弱 yǒu chùtòng tender

由此 yóucǐ from this

有刺铁丝网 yǒucì tiěsī wǎng barbed wire

优待 yōudài favor, special treatment

邮递 yóudì mail delivery

优点 yōudiǎn merit, strength

有点 yǒudiǎn a bit, a little

有颠覆性 yǒu diānfù xìng subversive

有点儿 yǒudiǎnr a bit, a little; 有点儿难过 *yǒudiǎnr nánguò* a bit sad, kind of sad

邮递员 yóudìyuán mailman

有毒 yǒudú poisonous, toxic

有毒瘾者 yǒu dúyǐn zhě junkie

诱饵 yòu'ěr bait; decoy

幼儿 yòu'ér small child, infant

幼儿学校 yòu'ér xuéxiào

kindergarten

幼儿圆 yòu'éryuán kindergarten

幼儿园老师 yòu'éryuán lǎoshī kindergarten teacher

有感染力 yǒu gǎnrǎn lì catching

有根据 yǒu gēnjù valid

有关 yǒuguān concerned, relevant, pertinent ◊ concerning, re

有关系 yǒu guānxì connect

有轨电车 yǒuguǐ diànchē streetcar

有规律 yǒu guīlǜ regular, steady ◊ regularly

有害 yǒuhài harmful; mischievous

有害元素 yǒuhài yuánsù harmful substance

友好 yǒuhǎo friendly, neighborly; kind ◊ goodwill

黝黑 yǒuhēi swarthy

油画 yóuhuà oil painting

油画布 yóuhuà bù canvas

有怀疑 yǒu huáiyí dubious

油灰 yóuhuī putty

邮汇 yóuhuì money order

诱惑 yòuhuò lure, entice ◊ alluring ◊ temptation

有活力 yǒu huólì perky, cheerful

邮寄 yóujì send

有机 yǒujī organic ◊ organically

又及 yòují PS, postscript

邮件 yóujiàn mail

有价证券 yǒujià zhèngquàn bond, security

有价值 yǒu jiàzhí valuable

游击队 yóujíduì guerrilla

有结余 yǒu jiéyú in the black

有技能 yǒu jìnéng skilled

幽静 yōujìng sleepy *town*

油井 yóujǐng oil rig, oil well

有经验 yǒu jīngyàn experienced, seasoned

有竞争力 yǒu jìngzhēng lì competitive

有进取心 yǒu jìnqǔxīn enterprising, go-ahead

有技巧 yǒu jìqiǎo professional

邮寄 yóují mail, send

邮寄人 yóují rén sender

邮局 yóujú post office

游客 yóukè visitor

有可能 yǒu kěnéng possibly;

potentially ◊ be liable to

有空 yǒu kōng have time; be available; 有空吗？*yǒu kōng ma?* can you spare the time?; 有空时 *yǒu kōng shí* at your leisure

有愧 yǒukuì guilt

有困难 yǒu kùnnán in need

由来 yóulái origin

游览 yóulǎn visit; tour; go sightseeing; 游览全中国 *yóulǎn quán Zhōngguó* travel all over China

游廊 yóuláng veranda

有了 yǒule pregnant ◊ be expecting

游乐场 yóulè chǎng amusement park

游乐园 yóulè yuán amusement park

有理 yǒulǐ reasonable; rational; in the right

有利 yǒulì advantageous; favorable

有立法权 yǒu lìfǎ quán legislative

有利可图 yǒulì kětú profitability

有礼貌 yǒu lǐmào respectful, polite, courteous, civil ◊ respectfully

幽灵 yōulíng vision

有利润 yǒu lìrùn be profitable, pay ◊ remunerative

有理由 yǒu lǐyóu justifiable

忧虑 yōulǜ worry, care ◊ worried; distracted

有逻辑 yǒu luójí logical

有毛病 yǒu máobìng faulty

优美 yōuměi lovely; graceful; dainty ◊ grace

有魅力 yǒu mèilì glamorous; attractive; magnetic

有霉味儿 yǒu méiwèir musty

有没有…？ yǒuméiyǒu…? is there …?; are there …?

油门 yóumén accelerator

右面 yòumiàn right-hand side

游民 yóumín hobo

有名生 yǒu míngshēng reputable

幽默 yōumò humor

幽默感 yōumò gǎn sense of

humor

柚木 **yòumù** teak

有耐心 **yǒu nàixīn** patient

有那么点儿 ... **yǒu nàme diǎnr** ... sort of ...

有男性 **yǒu nánxìng** virile

有男子气 **yǒu nánzǐqì** manly

有能力 **yǒu nénglì** able ◊ be capable of

油腻 **yóunì** greasy, oily; rich, heavy

幼年童子军 **yòunián tóngzǐjūn** Brownie

有粘性 **yǒu niánxìng** adhesive

有泥浆 **yǒu níjiāng** slimy

右派 **yòupài** right; right-winger

邮票 **yóupiào** stamp

右撇子 **yòu piě zi** right-handed

有蹼的脚 **yǒu pǔ de jiǎo** webbed feet

尤其 **yóuqí** especially, in particular

有钱 **yǒuqián** rich

有前途 **yǒu qiántú** promising

有气泡 **yǒu qìpào** effervescent

有趣 **yǒuqù** fun, amusing, entertaining; interesting

有权威性 **yǒu quánwēi xìng** authoritative

有缺陷 **yǒu quēxiàn** defective

有人 **yǒurén** someone, somebody ◊ occupied; 有人敲门 **yǒurén qiāomén** there's someone at the door

诱人 **yòurén** seductive, tantalizing

友善 **yǒushàn** amicable

忧伤 **yōushāng** sorrow

有生命危险 **yǒu shēngmìng wēixiǎn** life-threatening

优势 **yōushì** superiority

有事 **yǒu shì** have on; 你今晚有事吗? **nǐ jīnwǎn yǒushì ma?** do you have anything on for tonight?

有时 **yǒushí** sometimes, now and again

优势和劣势 **yōushì hé lièshì** the pros and cons

有施虐狂 **yǒu shīnüèkuáng** sadistic

有失体面 **yǒushī tǐmiàn** disgraceful

有失体统 **yǒu shī tǐtǒng** offensive

有诗意 **yǒu shīyì** poetic

有适应力 **yǒu shìyìng lì** adaptable

有售 **yǒushòu** be on sale

幼兽 **yòushòu** cub

游手好闲 **yóushǒu hàoxián** loaf around

又瘦又高 **yòushòu yòugāo** lanky

有说服力 **yǒu shuōfúlì** forceful, persuasive

有锁柜 **yǒu suǒguì** locker

油台 **yóutái** drilling rig

犹太 **Yóutài** Jewish

犹太人 **Yóutài rén** Jew

有弹性 **yǒu tánxìng** springy, elastic; supple

有特异功能 **yǒu tèyì gōngnéng** psychic

油田 **yóutián** oil field

有天才 **yǒu tiāncái** talented

有天赋 **yǒu tiānfù** gifted

有条不紊 **yǒutiáo bùwěn** methodical ◊ methodically

有条件 **yǒu tiáojiàn** conditional

有条理 **yǒu tiáolǐ** systematic, methodical ◊ systematically

有条纹 **yǒu tiáowén** striped

有挑战性 **yǒu tiǎozhàn xìng** challenging

游艇 **yóutǐng** yacht

游艇驾驶员 **yóutǐng jiàshǐ yuán** yachtsman

游艇停泊港 **yóutǐng tíngbó gǎng** marina

邮筒 **yóutǒng** mailbox

有同情心 **yǒu tóngqíng xīn** compassionate

有投票权者 **yǒu tóupiào quán zhě** voter

有图案 **yǒu tú'àn** patterned

有威望 **yǒu wēiwàng** prestigious

有威胁性 **yǒu wēixié xìng** threatening

有文化 **yǒu wénhuà** be literate

游戏 **yóuxì** play; game

优先 **yōuxiān** preferential, priority ◊ take precedence, take priority

悠闲 **yōuxián** laidback

有限 **yǒuxiàn** limited

右舷 **yòuxián** starboard

有线电视 **yǒuxiàn diànshì** cable

TV

有限度 yǒu xiàndù qualified

邮箱 yóuxiāng mailbox

有香味 yǒu xiāngwèi fragrant

有想像力 yǒu xiǎngxiàng lì imaginative

有象征性 yǒu xiàngzhēng xìng symbolic

优先权 yōuxiān quán priority; 有优先权 *yǒu yōuxiān quán* have priority

优先行驶权 yōuxiān xíngshǐ quán right of way

有嫌疑 yǒu xiányí alleged

有效 yǒuxiào valid; effective

幼小动物 yòuxiǎo dòngwù pup

有效率 yǒu xiàolǜ efficient ◊ efficiently

游戏场 yóuxì chǎng playground

有些 yǒuxiē some; 有些人说 ... *yǒuxiē rén shuō ...* some people say that ...

忧心忡忡 yōuxīn chóngchóng careworn, sad

游行 yóuxíng march, parade

有兴趣 yǒu xìngqù interested

有兴致 yǒu xìngzhì be in the mood for

有信心 yǒu xìnxīn assured

有吸收能力 yǒu xīshōu nénglì absorbent

优秀 yōuxiù excellent ◊ excellence

有修养 yǒu xiūyǎng cultivated, cultured; cultural

有希望 yǒu xīwàng hopeful

有吸引力 yǒu xīyǐn lì attractive; charming; seductive

优雅 yōuyǎ graceful ◊ lightness ◊ beautifully

油烟 yóuyān soot

有眼力 yǒu yǎnlì discerning, discriminating

有烟嘴 yǒu yānzuǐ tipped *cigarettes*

有药性 yǒu yàoxìng medicinal

有益 yǒuyì beneficial; useful; advantageous; expedient

友谊 yǒuyì friendship

有意 yǒuyì intend ◊ intentional, conscious ◊ intentionally, deliberately; 我有意移民 *wǒ*

yǒuyì yímín I'm thinking about emigrating; 有意为 X 准备 *yǒuyì wèi X zhǔnbèi* be meant for X

右翼 yòuyì right wing

又一次 yòu yīcì once again, once more

又一个 yòu yígè another

有益健康 yǒuyì jiànkāng healthy

有影响 yǒu yǐngxiǎng influential

有营养 yǒu yíngyǎng nourishing, nutritious

友谊商店 Yǒuyì Shāngdiàn Friendship Store

友谊市 yǒuyì shì twin town

有艺术性 yǒu yìshù xìng artistic

有意思 yǒu yìsi interesting, intriguing; significant

有一天 yǒu yītiān one day

有意误导 X yǒuyì wùdǎo X string X along

有疑心 yǒu yíxīn suspicious

有意义 yǒu yìyì meaningful

游泳 yóuyǒng swim ◊ swimming

游泳池 yóuyǒng chí swimming pool; 室外游泳池 *shìwài yóuyǒng chí* open-air swimming pool

游泳裤 yóuyǒng kù swimsuit

游泳衣 yóuyǒng yī swimsuit

游泳者 yóuyǒng zhě swimmer

忧郁 yōuyù gloom ◊ glum; melancholy, depressed

鱿鱼 yóuyú squid

由于 yóuyú with; through ◊ because of, due to

犹豫 yóuyù hesitate ◊ hesitation ◊ tentative; 犹豫不决 *yóuyù bù jué* be indecisive; 犹豫不定 *yóuyù búdìng* be indecisive; 对 X 犹豫不定 *duì X yóuyù búdìng* be undecided about X

优越 yōuyuè superior

有余额 yǒu yú'é be in credit

忧郁症 yōuyù zhèng depression

油炸 yóuzhá (deep-)fry

有战斗性 yǒu zhàndòu xìng militant

有朝一日 yǒuzhāo yīrì someday

悠着点儿！ yōu zhe diǎnr! steady on!

有哲理 yǒu zhélǐ philosophical

邮政 **yóuzhèng** mail

邮政编码 **yóuzhèng biānmǎ** zip code

邮政信箱 **yóuzhèng xìnxiāng** P.O. Box

有争议 **yǒu zhēngyì** controversial

优质 **yōuzhì** high-grade

幼稚 **yòuzhì** childish, juvenile; naive ◊ childishness; child

油脂 **yóuzhī** oil; grease; fat

有志向 **yǒu zhìxiàng** ambitious

有秩序 **yǒu zhìxù** orderly

邮资 **yóuzī** postage

柚子 **yòuzi** pomelo

有资格 **yǒuzīgé** entitled

有罪 **yǒuzuì** guilt ◊ guilty

油嘴滑舌 **yóuzuǐ huáshé** glib

有尊严 **yǒu zūnyán** dignified

右座方向盘 **yòuzuò fāngxiàngpán** right-hand drive

鱼 **yú** fish

于 **yú** to; at; in; from

愚 **yú** stupid

渔 **yú** fishing

与 **yǔ** and; with; 与 ... 有关系 **yǔ ... yǒuguānxì** in connection with ...; 与 X 不同 **yǔ X bùtóng** different from X; 与 X 断绝关系 **yǔ X duànjué guānxi** finish with X

雨 **yǔ** rain; 下着雨呢 **xià zhe yǔ ne** it's raining

语 **yǔ** language ◊ used to form language names; 西藏语 **Xīzàngyǔ** Tibetan

羽 **yǔ** feather

玉 **yù** jade

郁 **yù** luxuriant

遇 **yù** meet, encounter

浴 **yù** bath

欲 **yù** desire

愈 **yù** over, more than; 愈快愈好 **yù kuài yù hǎo** the faster the better

预 **yù** beforehand

圆 **yuán** round ◊ circle

元 **yuán** yuan (*Chinese money*)

园 **yuán** garden

原 **yuán** original

远 **yuán** far; distant; 三英里远 **sān yīnglǐ yuǎn** it's three miles off

愿 **yuàn** wish

院 **yuàn** institute

渊博 **yuānbó** vast; high-powered

原材料 **yuán cáiliào** raw materials

元朝 **Yuán Cháo** Yuan Dynasty

远程 **yuǎnchéng** long-range

远处 **yuǎnchù** distant place; 在远处 **zài yuǎnchù** in the distance

元旦 **Yuándàn** New Year's Day

园丁 **yuándīng** gardener

圆顶 **yuándǐng** dome

原定 **yuándìng** default COMPUT

远东 **Yuǎndōng** Far East

缘分 **yuánfèn** destiny

原告 **yuángào** claimant, plaintiff

原告方 **yuángàofāng** prosecution

怨恨 **yuànhèn** grudge

圆滑 **yuánhuá** slick, smooth

元件 **yuánjiàn** unit

远见 **yuǎnjiàn** vision, far-sightedness 援救 **yuánjiù** rescue

援救队 **yuánjiù duì** rescue party

远距离 **yuǎn jùlí** long-distance

援军 **yuánjūn** reinforcements

原来 **yuánlái** original ◊ originally; actually; 原来你在这儿 **yuánlái nǐ zài zhèr** there you are (*finding somebody*)

原谅 **yuánliàng** forgive, excuse, pardon ◊ forgiveness; 请原谅 **qǐng yuánliàng** I beg your pardon

原料 **yuánliào** raw material; ingredient

圆领衫 **yuánlǐng shān** T-shirt

园林师 **yuánlínshī** gardener

圆明园 **Yuánmíngyuán** Old Summer Palace

圆木 **yuánmù** log

圆盘 **yuánpán** disk

圆圈 **yuánquān** circle, ring

原始 **yuánshǐ** primitive

远视 **yuǎnshì** long-sighted, far-sighted

元素 **yuánsù** element CHEM

源头 **yuántóu** source

愿望 **yuànwàng** wish, desire

鸢尾属植物 **yuānwěishǔ zhíwù** iris (*flower*)

原文 **yuánwén** original text

原先 **yuánxiān** originally

元宵节 **Yuánxiāojié** Lantern

Festival

圆形 yuánxíng circular, round

园艺 yuányì gardening; horticulture

愿意 yuànyì willing, ready ◊ willingness, readiness ◊ want

原因 yuányīn cause, reason

元音 yuányīn vowel

原油 yuányóu crude oil

远于 yuǎnyú beyond

远远 yuǎnyuǎn much, way; 远远不如 yuǎnyuǎn bùrú not be a patch on

源源不断 yuányuán búduàn inexhaustible ◊ stream

原则 yuánzé principle; 原则上 yuánzé shang in principle

院长 yuànzhǎng dean

圆周 yuánzhōu circumference

援助 yuánzhù aid

圆柱 yuánzhù column

援助 yuánzhù support, help

圆珠笔 yuánzhūbǐ ballpoint pen

圆锥体 yuánzhuī tǐ cone

圆柱体 yuánzhù tǐ cylinder

原子 yuánzǐ atom ◊ atomic, nuclear

院子 yuànzi yard; courtyard

原子弹 yuánzǐ dàn atom bomb

原子废物 yuánzǐ fèiwù atomic waste

原子核 yuánzǐ hé nuclear

原子核物理 yuánzǐ hé wùlǐ nuclear physics

原子能 yuánzǐ néng atomic energy

远足 yuǎnzú excursion; hike

原作 yuánzuò original

原作品 yuán zuòpǐn original

欲罢不能 yùbà bùnéng compulsive

预报 yùbào forecast

预备 yùbèi prepare

预备队员 yùbèi duìyuán reserve SP

预备性 yùbèi xìng preliminary

预测 yùcè forecast, projection

鱼叉 yúchā harpoon

鱼船 yúchuán fishing boat

愚蠢 yúchǔn stupid, foolish, idiotic ◊ stupidity, folly

鱼刺 yúcì fishbone

遇到 yùdào encounter, meet, run into

雨点儿 yǔdiǎnr raindrop

预定 yùdìng book, reserve ◊ booking, reservation; 预定房间 yùdìng fángjiān book a room

约 yuē arrange

月 yuè month

约 yuè read

越 yuè surpass, exceed; 越 … 越 … yuè … yuè … the more … the more …; 越快越好 yuèkuài yuèhǎo the sooner the better

乐 yuè music

阅兵 yuèbīng parade

月饼 yuèbǐng mooncake

约定 yuēdìng agree; arrange to meet

阅读 yuèdú read ◊ reading; 阅读学习 yuèdú xuéxí read up on

阅读材料 yuèdú cáiliào reading matter

乐队 yuèduì band; orchestra

悦耳 yuè'ěr pleasant-sounding; musical, melodious

越发(多) yuèfā(duō) more and more

岳父 yuèfù father-in-law (wife's father)

月光 yuèguāng moonlight

月桂 yuèguì laurel

越过 yuèguò exceed, pass; get over

约会 yuēhuì appointment; engagement; date, rendez-vous ◊ ask out

约会对象 yuēhuì duìxiàng date (person)

月经 yuèjīng period; menstruation

月经带 yuèjīng dài sanitary napkin

月经栓 yuèjīng shuān tampon

月刊 yuèkān monthly (publication)

越来越 yuè lái yuè increasingly; 越来越多的学生 yuè lái yuè duō de xuéshēng more and more students; 越来越快 yuè lái yuè kuài faster and faster

阅览室 yuèlǎnshì reading room

阅历 yuèlì experience; 她阅历挺

深 **tā yuèlì tǐngshēn** she has been around

月亮 **yuèliàng** moon ◊ lunar

岳母 **yuèmǔ** mother-in-law (*of man*)

越南 **Yuènán** Vietnam ◊ Vietnamese

月票 **yuèpiào** monthly ticket

乐谱 **yuèpǔ** music, score

乐器 **yuèqì** musical instrument

月蚀 **yuèshí** lunar eclipse

约束 **yuēshù** restrain; curb; bind; restrict ◊ restriction

约束力 **yuēshù lì** binding force

越位 **yuèwèi** offside; 未越位 **wèi yuèwèi** onside

月牙形 **yuèyá xíng** crescent

越野 **yuèyě** cross-country; 越野赛 **yuèyě sài** cross-country race

乐音 **yuèyīn** tone

乐章 **yuèzhāng** movement MUS

语法 **yǔfǎ** grammar

鱼贩 **yúfàn** fishmonger

预防 **yùfáng** prevent ◊ prevention ◊ precautionary

预防措施 **yùfáng cuòshī** precaution, preventive measure

预防性 **yùfáng xìng** preventive

渔夫 **yúfū** fisherman

预付 **yùfù** advance (payment) ◊ pay in advance

鱼竿 **yúgān** fishing pole

预感 **yùgǎn** hunch; premonition

浴缸 **yùgāng** bathtub, tub

鱼肝油 **yúgān yóu** cod-liver oil

预告 **yùgào** forecast, predict

鱼钩 **yúgōu** fishhook

宇航 **yǔháng** space travel

宇航服 **yǔháng fú** spacesuit

宇航工业 **yǔháng gōngyè** aerospace industry

宇航员 **yǔháng yuán** astronaut

愈合 **yùhé** heal

迂回 **yūhuí** detour

迂回行进 **yūhuí xíngjìn** weave

与会者 **yùhuì zhě** conventioneer

欲火中烧 **yùhuǒ zhōngshāo** smolder

淤积 **yūjī** deposit

雨季 **yǔjì** rainy season, the rains

郁积 **yùjī** smolder

预计 **yùjì** estimate; plan; 预计到达时间 **yùjì dàodá shíjiān** estimated time of arrival

预见 **yùjiàn** foresee

遇见 **yùjiàn** meet

雨夹雪 **yǔjiáxuě** sleet

余烬 **yújìn** embers

浴巾 **yùjīn** bath towel

郁金香 **yùjīnxiāng** tulip

愉快 **yúkuài** happy, joyful; 令人愉快 **lìngrén yúkuài** nice; enjoyable, pleasant

娱乐 **yúlè** entertainment; amusement; pleasure; recreation

娱乐活动 **yúlè huódòng** amusements

娱乐园 **yúlè yuán** amusement park

娱乐中心 **yúlè zhōngxīn** leisure center; arcade

预料 **yùliào** anticipate, expect; foretell ◊ anticipation

雨林 **yǔlín** rain forest

羽毛 **yǔmáo** feather; plume

浴帽 **yùmào** shower cap

羽毛球 **yǔmáo qiú** badminton; shuttlecock

玉米 **yùmǐ** corn

玉米花 **yùmǐhuā** popcorn

渔民 **yúmín** fisherman

预谋 **yùmóu** premeditated

榆木 **yúmù** elm

云 **yún** cloud

允 **yǔn** permit

熨 **yùn** iron ◊ ironing; 熨衣服 **yùn yīfu** do the ironing

韵 **yùn** rhyme

晕 **yùn** dizzy, giddy

运 **yùn** transport

孕 **yùn** pregnant

遇难 **yùnàn** be killed (in an accident); 遇难船只 **yùnàn chuánzhī** the doomed ship

匀称 **yúnchèn** regular; shapely

匀出 **yúnchū** spare

晕船 **yùnchuán** seasick ◊ get seasick

运动 **yùndòng** move; movement; campaign; sport; exercise; 作运动 **zuò yùndòng** take exercise

运动场 **yùndòng chǎng** playing field

运动会 yùndòng huì meet SP

运动上衣 yùndòng shàngyī sportscoat

运动室 yùndòng shì gym, gymnasium

运动鞋 yùndòng xié sports shoes

运动衣 yùndòng yī jogging suit

运动员 yùndòng yuán sportsman; sportswoman; athlete; player

熨斗 yùndǒu iron

云耳 yún'ěr cloud ear (mushroom)

运费 yùnfèi freight

孕妇 yùnfù pregnant woman

孕妇服装 yùnfù fúzhuāng maternity dress

运河 yùnhé canal

与你无关！ yǔ nǐ wúguān! that's none of your business!, mind your own business!

晕机 yùnjī airsick ◊ airsickness

酝酿 yùnniàng brew

愚弄 yúnòng tease

孕期 yùnqī pregnancy

运气 yùnqì fortune; luck

云雀 yúnquè lark

运输 yùnshū transport; transportation

运输公司 yùnshū gōngsī shipping company; carrier

运输机 yùnshūjī freighter (plane)

运输终点站 yùnshū zhōngdiǎn-zhàn terminal (for containers)

运送 yùnsòng ship; shipping

陨星 yǔnxīng meteorite

运行 yùnxíng move

允许 yǔnxǔ allow, permit

晕眩 yūnxuàn light-headed

熨衣板 yùnyībǎn ironing board

运用 yùnyòng use; apply

运转 yùnzhuàn operate; run; function; revolve; 这东西怎么运转？ zhèi dōngxi zénme yùnzhuǎn? how does this thing work?

浴盆 yùpén bathtub

语气 yǔqì tone

预期寿命 yùqī shòumìng life expectancy

羽绒 yǔróng eiderdown

雨伞 yǔsǎn umbrella

瘀伤 yúshāng bruise

于是 yúshì then; consequently

预示 yùshì usher in

浴室 yùshì bathroom

遇事不慌 yùshì bùhuāng presence of mind

与世隔绝 yǔshì géjué seclusion

余数 yúshù remainder

雨水道 yǔshuǐ dào storm drain

预算 yùsuàn calculate ◊ budget

鱼网 yúwǎng fishing net

欲望 yùwàng appetite; desire; longing

余味儿 yúwèir aftertaste

余下 yúxià the rest, remainder

预先 yùxiān in advance; 预先计划 / 考虑 yùxiān jìhuà / kǎolù plan / think ahead; 四个星期的预先通知 sìgè xīngqī de yùxiān tōngzhī four weeks' notice

雨靴 yǔxuē rain boot

语言 yǔyán language ◊ linguistic

预言 yùyán prophecy; prediction ◊ predict

语言学 yǔyán xué linguistics

语言学家 yǔyán xuéjiā linguist

语言障碍 yǔyán zhàng'ài language barrier

渔业 yúyè fishing industry

雨衣 yǔyī raincoat

羽衣 yǔyī plumage

浴衣 yùyī bathrobe

寓意 yùyì moral

郁郁不乐 yùyù búlè mope

预约 yùyuē arrange; reserve ◊ advance reservation

预展 yùzhǎn preview

预兆 yùzhào omen, sign ◊ ominous

预支 yùzhī get money in advance

预制 yùzhì prefabricated

雨中 yǔzhōng in the rain

与众不同 yǔzhòng bùtóng odd one out ◊ differently ◊ distinguished, dignified

宇宙 yǔzhòu universe

宇宙飞船 yǔzhòu fēichuán spaceship, spacecraft

宇宙空间站 yǔzhòu kōngjiān zhàn space station

鱼子酱 yúzǐ jiàng caviar

# Z

砸 zá crack *nut*

杂 zá mixed, assorted; miscellaneous

杂草 zácǎo weed

杂费 záfèi incidental expenses

杂货 záhuò groceries

杂货店 záhuò diàn grocery store

杂货商 záhuò shāng grocer

灾 zāi disaster

栽 zāi plant; fall; 他栽倒在床上 **tā zāidǎo zài chuáng shàng** he sank onto the bed

再 zài again; further; 再来点儿茶吗？**zài láidiǎn chá ma?** some more tea?; 再走两英里 **zài zǒu liǎng yīnglǐ** two miles further (on)

在 zài at; in; on; 在盒子里 **zài hézi lǐ** in the box; 在华盛顿／中国 **zài Huáshèngdùn／Zhōngguó** in Washington／China ◊ (*continuous tense*): 在服丧 **zài fúsāng** be mourning ◊ (*with sense of be*): be at; be in; be on; 我在火车上 **wǒ zài huǒchē shang** I'm on the train

在 ... 背后 zài ... bèihòu behind

在 ... 的对面 zài ... de duìmiàn opposite

在 ... 的中心 zài ... de zhōngxīn in the center of

在 ... 底下 zài ... dǐxià underneath

在 ... 附近 zài ... fùjìn in the vicinity of

在 ... 后面 zài ... hòumiàn behind

在 ... 里 zài ... lǐ inside

在 ... 里面 zài ... lǐmiàn within

在 ... 旁 zài ... páng beside

在 ... 旁边 zài ... pángbiān beside

在 ... 期间 zài ... qījiān during

在 ... 上 zài ... shàng on, aboard

在 ... 上方 zài ... shàngfāng over

在 ... 上面 zài ... shàngmian on; above

在 ... 时期 zài ... shíqī while

在 ... 条件下 zài ... tiáojiàn xià on the understanding that

在 ... 同时 zài ... tóngshí during

在 ... 下面 zài ... xiàmiàn beneath, under

在 ... 以前 zài ... yǐqián prior to

在 ... 以外 zài ... yǐwài outside

在 ... 之列 zài ... zhī liè rank among

在 ... 之间 zài ... zhījiān between

在 ... 之内 zài ... zhīnèi within

在 ... 之前 zài ... zhīqián before

在 ... 之上 zài ... zhīshàng on top of

在 ... 之中 zài ... zhīzhōng among(st)

在 ... 中 zài ... zhōng in the middle of

在 ... 最上 zài ... zuìshàng at the top of

在岸上 zài ànshàng ashore

再版 zàibǎn reprint

在保 zàibǎo on bail

在场 zàichǎng presence ◊ be present

再次 zàicì again

在此日期前使用 zàicǐ rìqī qián shǐyòng best before date

再发 zàifā recurrent

灾害 zāihài disaster

在行 zàiháng knowledgeable

在乎 zàihu mind, care; 我不在乎咱们做什么 **wǒ bú zàihu zánmen zuò shénme** I don't mind what we do

再婚 zàihūn remarry

灾祸 zāihuò catastrophe, disaster

再见 zàijiàn goodbye, see you

再来 zàilái call back, come back again

再来一个 zàilái yígè encore

灾难 zāinàn disaster, catastrophe

栽培 zāipéi cultivation

再说 **zàishuō** besides

在逃 **zàitáo** be at large; 在逃罪犯 *zàitáo zuìfàn* criminal on the run

再体验 **zài tǐyàn** relive

再现 **zàixiàn** reproduce

灾星 **zāixīng** jinx

再一次 **zàiyícì** once more

再一个 **zài yígè** another

再用 **zàiyòng** reuse

载有 **zàiyǒu** carry

在于 **zàiyú** rest with

再装满 **zài zhuāngmǎn** refill

杂技 **zájì** acrobatics

杂交 **zájiāo** hybrid

杂技演员 **zájì yǎnyuán** acrobat

砸烂 **zálàn** total, write off

杂乱 **záluàn** disorder ◊ disorderly ◊ be a mess

杂乱无章 **záluàn wú zhāng** disorder; mess ◊ messy; chaotic

砸门 **zámén** hammer at the door

暂 **zàn** temporary

赞 **zàn** praise

赞成 **zànchéng** approve, agree with ◊ favorable, agreeable ◊ approval

脏 **zāng** dirty

葬 **zàng** bury

葬礼 **zànglǐ** funeral; burial

脏乱 **zāngluàn** mess

赃物 **zāngwù** loot

脏物 **zāngwù** dirt

暂缓 **zànhuǎn** wait

赞美 **zànměi** praise; compliment ◊ complimentary

赞美诗 **zànměishī** hymn

咱们 **zánmen** we; us; 咱们快走吧 *zánmen kuài zǒu ba* let's get out of here

攒钱 **zǎnqián** save money; 为 … 攒钱 *wèi … zǎnqián* save up for

赞赏 **zànshǎng** appreciate

暂时 **zànshí** temporary ◊ temporarily

暂停 **zàntíng** pause ◊ time out

赞同 **zàntóng** agree with; approve

暂行 **zànxíng** provisional, temporary ◊ temporarily

赞许 **zànxǔ** applaud ◊ consent

赞扬 **zànyáng** credit; praise; applause

赞誉 **zànyù** praise

赞助 **zànzhù** support; patronage; sponsorship

赞助人 **zànzhùrén** patron; backer

糟 **zāo** bad, terrible ◊ damn!

遭 **zāo** meet, encounter

凿 **záo** chisel

枣 **zǎo** Chinese date

早 **zǎo** morning ◊ early; beforehand; 早在一九三五年 *zǎo zài yījiǔ sānwǔ nián* back in 1935

灶 **zào** stove; hearth

噪 **zào** noise

早餐 **zǎocān** breakfast

早产 **zǎochǎn** premature birth

早晨 **zǎochén** morning ◊ in the morning; 早晨好 *zǎochén hǎo* good morning

造成 **zàochéng** form; create; 造成困难 *zàochéng kùnnán* pose a problem

造船厂 **zàochuán chǎng** shipyard

遭到 **zāodào** meet with; 遭到炮火袭击 *zāodào pàohuǒ xíjī* come under shellfire

造反 **zàofǎn** revolt

糟糕 **zāogāo** bad, terrible, awful, horrible ◊ badly, terribly ◊ damn!

早就 **zǎojiù** for a long time; a long time ago

澡盆 **zǎopén** bath

早期 **zǎoqī** early (*farther back in time*)

早日康复！ **zǎorì kāngfù!** get well soon!

早上 **zǎoshang** in the morning; 早上好 *zǎoshang hǎo* good morning

早市 **zǎo shì** early-morning market

遭受 **zāoshòu** suffer

早熟 **zǎoshú** precocious

糟蹋 **zāotà** murder

糟透 **zāotòu** abysmal, atrocious; 糟透了！ *zāotòule!* it stinks!, it's awful!

灶头 **zàotóu** burner

造物主 **Zàowù zhǔ** the Creator

噪音 **zàoyīn** noise

凿子 **záozi** chisel

枣子 **zǎozi** Chinese date

杂耍 **záshuǎ** vaudeville

杂项 **záxiàng** sundries

杂志 **zázhì** magazine, journal

杂种狗 **zázhǒng gǒu** mongrel

责 **zé** duty, responsibility

责备 **zébèi** blame; reproach; reprimand

责怪 **zéguài** blame ◊ accusation

责骂 **zémà** scold

怎 **zěn** how; why

憎 **zēng** hate

增 **zēng** add; increase

赠 **zèng** give; present

增大 **zēngdà** increase; heighten

增多 **zēngduō** increase; multiply

憎恨 **zēnghèn** hate ◊ hatred

增加 **zēngjiā** increase, boost ◊ raise; 增加体重 **zēngjiā tǐzhòng** put on weight

增进 **zēngjìn** promote

增刊 **zēngkān** supplement

增强 **zēngqiáng** strengthen, reinforce

赠券 **zèngquàn** coupon

增湿器 **zēngshī qì** humidifier

赠送 **zèngsòng** give; present ◊ complimentary; 把Y赠送给X **bǎ Y zèngsònggěi X** present Y to X

曾孙 **zēngsūn** great-grandson (*son's grandson*)

曾外祖父 **zēngwài zǔfù** great-grandfather (*maternal*)

曾外祖母 **zēngwài zǔmǔ** great-grandmother (*maternal*)

增长 **zēngzhǎng** grow, expand; increase ◊ growth, expansion

增值 **zēngzhí** increase in value

曾祖父 **zēngzǔfù** great-grandfather (*paternal*)

曾祖母 **zēngzǔmǔ** great-grandmother (*paternal*)

怎么 **zěnme** how; how come; 我不知该怎么办 **wǒ bùzhī gāi zěnmebàn** I don't know what to do; 怎么了? **zěnmele?** what's wrong?, what's the matter?

怎样 **zěnyàng** how

责任 **zérèn** responsibility, duty; blame

诘问 **zéwèn** heckle

闸 **zhá** lock; sluice

眨 **zhǎ** wink; blink

炸 **zhà** blow up, explode

榨 **zhà** squeeze

榨出 **zhàchū** extract; squeeze out ◊ extraction

炸弹 **zhàdàn** bomb

炸弹攻击 **zhàdàn gōngjī** bomb attack

轧辊 **zhágǔn** roller

诈呼 **zhàhu** bluff

摘 **zhāi** pick, pluck

窄 **zhǎi** narrow

债 **zhài** debt

摘除 **zhāichú** pluck

宅第 **zháidì** mansion

债券 **zhàijuàn** bond

摘录 **zhāilù** extract, excerpt

债券 **zhàiquàn** promissory note; bond

债权人 **zhàiquán rén** creditor

债务 **zhàiwù** debt

窄小 **zhǎixiǎo** cramped

摘要 **zhāiyào** précis

债主 **zhàizhǔ** creditor

栅栏 **zhàlán** fence; railings; bars

蚱蜢 **zhàměng** grasshopper

沾 **zhān** dip

粘 **zhān** stick, glue

毡 **zhān** felt

展 **zhǎn** develop; open up

占 **zhàn** occupy; take; constitute, make up

站 **zhàn** stand ◊ stop; station; 站直了! **zhànzhíle!** stand up straight!

战 **zhàn** fight ◊ battle; war

站不住脚 **zhàn búzhù jiǎo** lame excuse

战场 **zhànchǎng** battlefield, battleground

展出 **zhǎnchū** exhibit, display

站点 **zhàndiǎn** web site

战斗 **zhàndòu** combat; fight

战斗机 **zhàndòu jī** warplane, fighter

战俘 **zhànfú** prisoner of war

章 **zhāng** chapter

张 **zhāng** sheet ◊ *measure word for*

*flat things*; 一张 纸 **yìzhāng zhǐ** piece of paper

掌 **zhǎng** palm

涨 **zhǎng** rise

长 **zhǎng** grow ◊ head; 家长 **jiāzhǎng** head of a family

胀 **zhàng** bloated

帐 **zhàng** account

障碍 **zhàng'ài** obstacle, hurdle, stumbling block; barrier

障碍物 **zhàng'ài wù** obstacle; obstruction, barrier, cordon

涨潮 **zhǎngcháo** incoming tide ◊ come in (*of tide*)

章程 **zhāngchéng** rules; statutes

长大 **zhǎngdà** grow up; develop

账单 **zhàngdān** check, bill; invoice

丈夫 **zhàngfu** husband

长高 **zhǎnggāo** shoot up (*of children*)

掌管 **zhǎngguǎn** preside over

掌击 **zhǎngjī** smack; slap; cuff

撞击 **zhuàngjī** smash

涨价 **zhǎngjià** price rise

张开 **zhāngkāi** open, unfold

张口 **zhāngkǒu** gape

蟑螂 **zhāngláng** cockroach

长满青苔 **zhǎngmǎn qīngtái** mossy

长满树木 **zhǎngmǎn shùmù** wooded

帐目 **zhàngmù** accounts; books; account

樟脑 **zhāngnǎo** camphor

长女 **zhǎngnǚ** firstborn (*daughter*)

长胖 **zhǎngpàng** fill out, get fatter

帐篷 **zhàngpeng** tent

掌声 **zhǎngshēng** applause

张贴 **zhāngtiē** put up, post; pin up

战国时期 **Zhànguó Shíqī** Warring States (Period)

掌握 **zhǎngwò** grasp; master; control

章鱼 **zhāngyú** octopus

长子 **zhǎngzǐ** firstborn (son)

粘合剂 **zhānhéjì** adhesive

战后 **zhànhòu** postwar

粘糊糊 **zhānhúhú** sticky

展开 **zhǎnkāi** unfold, unwind; unroll; lay out

粘扣 **Zhānkòu** Velcro®

展览 **zhǎnlǎn** display, exhibit

展览橱窗 **zhǎnlǎn chúchuāng** display cabinet

展览会 **zhǎnlǎnhuì** exhibition

站立 **zhànlì** stand

沾料 **zhānliào** dip (*food*)

站立空间 **zhànlì kōngjiān** standing room

占领 **zhànlǐng** capture; occupy ◊ occupation

战略 **zhànlüè** strategy ◊ strategic

展品 **zhǎnpǐn** exhibit

展期 **zhǎnqī** renew, extend ◊ renewal, extension

战前 **zhànqián** prewar

站起来 **zhàn qǐlái** stand up, get up; jump to one's feet; 他腾地站起来 **tā téngde zhàn qǐlái** he scrambled to his feet

占去 **zhànqù** take up *space, time*

占少数 **zhàn shǎoshù** be in the minority

战胜 **zhànshèng** conquer ◊ victorious; 战胜 X **zhànshèng X** win a victory over X

展示 **zhǎnshì** show; show off; model

战时 **zhànshí** wartime

战士 **zhànshì** soldier; warrior; fighter

战术 **zhànshù** tactics ◊ tactical

站台 **zhàntái** platform; 第十站台 **dì shí zhàntái** track 10

粘贴 **zhāntiē** paste, stick; adhere

毡头油笔 **zhāntóubǐ** felt-tip (pen)

展望 **zhǎnwàng** outlook

谵妄 **zhānwàng** delirious

站位 **zhànwèi** standing room

沾污 **zhānwū** stain

占线 **zhànxiàn** busy ◊ the line is busy

战线 **zhànxiàn** front; battle line

占线声 **zhànxiàn shēng** busy signal

崭新 **zhǎnxīn** brand-new

占星术 **zhànxīng shù** astrology

占星者 **zhànxīng zhě** astrologer

暂休 **zhànxiū** adjourn

战役 **zhànyì** battle

占用 zhànyòng occupy; encroach on

占有 zhànyǒu own, have; take

占优势 zhàn yōushì dominant; predominant ◊ predominate

占有者 zhànyǒu zhě owner

沾沾自喜 zhānzhān zìxǐ gloat

粘着 zhānzhe cling to

站着 zhànzhe stand

战争 zhànzhēng war; warfare; conflict; hostilities

站住 zhànzhù stop

辗转 zhǎnzhuǎn toss and turn

辗转反侧 zhǎnzhuǎn fǎncè toss and turn

招 zhāo beckon

朝 zhāo morning

着 zháo ignite

找 zhǎo look for; ask for

罩 zhào cover

召 zhào convene; summon

照 zhào photograph; license ◊ shine; light up ◊ according to; 照 X 光 zhào X guāng take an X-ray; 照我看来 zhào wǒ kànlái in my estimation

找出 zhǎochū locate, dig out; work out *solution*

找拇 zhǎocuò find fault with

招待 zhāodài entertain; serve *customer*; 热情招待 rèqíng zhāodài hospitality

招待会 zhāodài huì reception

招待所 zhāodàisuǒ guesthouse

找到 zhǎodào find

找工作 zhǎo gōngzuò be job hunting

照顾 zhàogù look after; tend ◊ care

照管 zhàoguǎn look after

照顾不周 zhàogù bùzhōu neglect

召唤 zhāohuàn call out; beckon

召回 zhàohuí recall

找回 zhǎohuí recover, get back ◊ recovery

招魂术者 zhāohúnshù zhě spiritualist

着火 zháohuǒ be on fire; alight, ablaze

着急 zháojí worry; be anxious

召集 zhàojí call, convene; summon

召开 zhàokāi convene; hold

照看 zhàokàn mind, watch, keep an eye on

照亮 zhàoliàng light up

照料 zhàoliào look after; coddle

着陆 zháolù touch down (*of plane*) ◊ touchdown

着迷 zháomí captivate, entrance ◊ obsession ◊ entranced; 使着迷 shǐ zháomí fascinate; 对 X 着迷 duì X zháomí be mad about X

照明 zhàomíng illuminate, light ◊ lighting

召募 zhàomù enlist

招牌 zhāopai sign

照片 zhàopiàn photograph

招聘 zhāopìn recruit ◊ recruitment

找钱 zhǎoqián change ◊ 等一下，我给你找钱 děng yíxià, wǒ gěi nǐ zhǎoqián just a minute, I'll give you the change

朝气蓬勃 zhāoqì péngbó youthful

招认 zhāorèn confess

着色 zháosè tinted

招收 zhāoshōu intake (*of college etc*)

招手 zhāoshǒu wave; beckon

朝霞 zhāoxiá dawn

照相 zhàoxiàng take a photo

照像机 zhàoxiàng jī camera

照耀 zhàoyào shine

罩衣 zhàoyī coveralls

照一照 zhàoyīzhào shine

沼泽 zhǎozé swamp, marsh, bog

招致 zhāozhì incur; 招致麻烦 zhāozhì máfán get into trouble

兆字节 zhàozìjié megabyte

榨取 zhàqǔ bleed; drain; overburden

炸薯片 zhá shǔpiàn potato chip

炸薯条 zhá shǔtiáo fried potatoes

扎眼 zhāyǎn pierce

眨眼 zhǎyǎn blink; wink

炸药 zhàyào dynamite; gunpowder; explosive

complacent

渣子 zhāzi crumb; dregs; scum (*people*)

蜇 zhē sting

遮 zhē cover

折 zhé break; fold

褶 zhě fold; pleat; tuck

这 zhè this; these; the; 这是谁的? **zhè shì shéide?** whose is this?

着 zhe (*continuing action*): 他抱着孩子 **tā bàozhe háizi** he's holding a baby ◊ (*imperative*): 听着！**tīngzhe!** listen!

遮蔽 zhēbì shade; screen; blot out

蜇刺 zhēcì sting

这次 zhècì this time

折叠 zhédié fold ◊ folding *chair etc*, collapsible

折叠椅 zhédiéyǐ folding chair

折断 zhéduàn break; break off; fracture

这个 zhège this ◊ this one

折合 zhéhé convert *unit of measurement*

这 zhèi this; these

折扣 zhékòu discount; rebate

这里 zhèlǐ here

这么 zhème such; so; this; 这么大 **zhème dà** this big; 这么快 **zhème kuài** so quick

折磨 zhémo torment, torture

榛 zhēn hazel

针 zhēn needle; hand (*of clock*)

真 zhēn real, true

侦 zhēn detect

珍 zhēn valuable ◊ value

疹 zhěn rash; blotch

枕 zhěn pillow

镇 zhèn town

震 zhèn tremble, shake; quake; shock

阵 zhèn *measure word for smoke or dust*; 一阵烟/尘土 **yízhèn yān / chéntǔ** a cloud of smoke / dust

珍爱 zhēn'ài fond *memory*

珍宝 zhēnbǎo treasure; gem

针鼻儿 zhēnbír eye of a needle

侦察 zhēnchá reconnoiter ◊ reconnaissance

震颤 zhènchàn throb; tremble; twitch

真诚 zhēnchéng sincere ◊ sincerely ◊ sincerity

针刺 zhēncì acupuncture

震荡 zhèndàng concussion

真的 zhēnde really, actually; 真的吗? **zhēnde ma?** really?

真地 zhēnde truly

阵地 zhèndì position MIL

镇定 zhèndìng calm, composed

镇定自若 zhèndìng zìruò unflappable

震动 zhèndòng shudder; vibrate ◊ vibration; tremor

振动 zhèndòng vibrate ◊ vibration

针对 zhēnduì be aimed at

振奋 zhènfèn feel inspired; 令人振奋 **lìngrén zhènfèn** rousing

阵风 zhènfēng gust of wind

振奋人心 zhènfèn rénxīn stimulating

蒸 zhēng steam

征 zhēng journey ◊ summon; levy *taxes*

争 zhēng struggle; contend

整 zhěng complete, total; all; 三点整 **sāndiǎn zhěng** at 3 o'clock sharp

挣 zhèng earn; struggle

正 zhèng positive; plus; upright; just

证 zhèng evidence

政 zhèng politics ◊ political

争辩 zhēngbiàn dispute; 与X争辩 **yǔ X zhēngbiàn** take issue with X

政变 zhèngbiàn coup

征兵 zhēngbīng draft MIL

政策 zhèngcè policy

政策准则 zhèngcè zhǔnzé component, aspect (*of policy*)

正常 zhèngcháng normal; regular ◊ normally ◊ normality; 一切正常 **yíqiè zhèngcháng** the situation is under control

正常化 zhèngcháng huà normalize

争吵 zhēngchǎo squabble, quarrel

证词 zhèngcí testimony

正当 zhèngdāng proper; legitimate; right

正当理由 zhèngdāng lǐyóu justification

挣得 zhèngde earn

正点 zhèngdiǎn on schedule

争斗 zhēngdòu fight, struggle

整顿 zhěngdùn regulation; arrangement

争夺 zhēngduó dispute; compete for / against ◊ contest

争夺者 zhēngduó zhě contender

蒸发 zhēngfā evaporate; steam

正方形 zhèngfāng xíng square

征服 zhēngfu conquer, overcome ◊ conquest

政府 zhèngfǔ government

政府机构 zhèngfǔ jīgòu public sector

征服者 zhēngfú zhě conqueror

整 zhěng complete; whole; 两点整 liǎngdiǎn zhěng at two o'clock prompt

整个 zhěnggè whole, entire

正规来说 zhèngguī láishuō officially, strictly (speaking)

蒸锅 zhēngguō steamer (for cooking)

正好 zhènghǎo just right

正极 zhèngjí positive ELEC

证件 zhèngjiàn papers, ID

整洁 zhěngjié neat, tidy

整洁漂亮 zhěngjié piàoliàng smart, neat, spruce

拯救 zhěngjiù save ◊ salvation; redemption

证据 zhèngjù evidence; proof

整理 zhěnglǐ order, arrange; sort out; clear up

整理行装 zhěnglǐ xíngzhuāng pack, do one's packing

争论 zhēnglùn argue, contend; dispute ◊ argument; controversy

正门 zhèngmén front entrance

正面 zhèngmiàn front; façade; 正面还是反面? **zhèngmiàn háishì fǎnmiàn?** heads or tails?

正面看台 zhèngmiàn kàntái grandstand

证明 zhèngmíng certify; prove, verify ◊ certificate; confirmation; verification

征募 zhēngmù recruit

正派 zhèngpài decent; law-abiding; straight ◊ decency

整批 zhěngpī in bulk

正片 zhèngpiàn feature movie

蒸汽 zhēngqì steam

整齐 zhěngqí neat, tidy; shipshape

挣钱 zhèngqián earn money

蒸汽电熨斗 zhēngqì diàn yùndǒu steam iron

蒸汽机车 zhēngqì jīchē steam locomotive

蒸汽浴 zhēngqì yù steam bath

争取 zhēngqǔ fight for

政权 zhèngquán regime

证券 zhèngquàn securities

证券市场 zhèngquàn shìchǎng stock market; securities market

正确 zhèngquè correct, right ◊ correctly; properly; 大致正确 **dàzhì zhèngquè** approximately right

正确性 zhèngquè xìng validity

证人 zhèngrén witness

证人席 zhèngrén xí witness stand

整容外科 zhěngróng wàikē cosmetic surgery

整容外科医生 zhěngróng wàikē yīshēng plastic surgeon

正如我言 zhèngrú wǒ yán like I said

证实 zhèngshí confirm; corroborate; back up ◊ confirmation

证实 zhèngshí confirm

正式 zhèngshì formal; official ◊ formally; officially

征收 zhēngshōu impose, levy, collect

整数 zhěngshù in round figures

证书 zhèngshū certificate; qualification

征税 zhēngshuì taxation

整肃 zhěngsù purge

整体 zhěngtǐ whole; 我们必须作为一个整体一起工作 **wǒmen bìxū zuòwéi yígè zhěngtǐ yìqǐ gōngzuò** we must work together as a unit

政务会委员 zhèngwùhuì wěiyuán councilor

正相反 zhèng xiāngfǎn on the contrary

整形外科 zhěngxíng wàikē plastic surgery

整形外科医生 zhěngxíng wàikē yīshēng plastic surgeon

整修 zhěngxiū renovate ◊ renovation

正要 … zhèngyào … be on the point of; 我正要离开，这时 … wǒ zhèngyào líkāi, zhèshí … I was just about to leave when …

争议 zhēngyì conflict

正义 zhèngyì just ◊ justice

正在 zhèngzài currently in the process of

正在流行 zhèngzài liúxíng in vogue

证章 zhèngzhāng badge

征兆 zhēngzhào symptom

争执 zhēngzhí disagreement, dispute

正直 zhèngzhí be right ◊ upright, decent

政治 zhèngzhì politics ◊ political; 政治信仰 zhèngzhì xìnyǎng political beliefs

政治犯 zhèngzhì fàn political detainee

政治家 zhèngzhì jiā politician; statesman

政治局 Zhèngzhìjú Politbureau

郑重 zhèngzhòng solemn, binding

正中要害 zhèngzhòng yàohài hit the bull's eye

症状 zhèngzhuàng symptom MED; 戒毒时的症状 jièdú shí de zhèngzhuàng withdrawal symptoms

正准备 … zhèng zhǔnbèi … be about to …

正字法 zhèngzìfǎ orthography

震撼 zhènhàn shake

赈济 zhènjì charity

针脚 zhēnjiǎo stitch

贞洁 zhēnjié chaste ◊ virginity

震惊 zhènjīng shock; 令人震惊 lìngrén zhènjīng shocking; appalling

镇静 zhènjìng calm, collected, composed ◊ composure

镇静剂 zhènjìng jì tranquilizer

镇静药 zhènjìng yào sedative

针灸 zhēnjiǔ acupuncture

真空 zhēnkōng vacuum

真空包装 zhēnkōng bāozhuāng vacuum-packed

真空吸尘器 zhēnkōng xīchén qì vacuum cleaner

真理 zhēnlǐ truth

珍品 zhēnpǐn gem

真品 zhēnpǐn genuine

侦破 zhēnpò solve, crack

真实性 zhēnshí real; true ◊ really, actually

珍视 zhēnshì prize, value; 不够珍视 X bú gòu zhēnshì X take X for granted, not appreciate X

真是的！ zhēnshide! really! (expressing exasperation etc)

真实性 zhēnshí xìng authenticity

诊所 zhěnsuǒ clinic

侦探 zhēntàn detective

侦探片 zhēntàn piān crime movie

侦探小说 zhēntàn xiǎoshuō detective novel

枕套 zhěntào pillowcase, pillowslip

镇痛 zhèntòng pain-killing, analgesic

针头 zhēntóu needle (for injection)

枕头 zhěntóu pillow

珍惜 zhēnxī cherish, treasure

针线 zhēnxiàn needlework; needle and thread; notions

真相 zhēnxiàng fact; truth

针线活儿 zhēnxiàn huór needlework

镇压 zhènyā repress, suppress ◊ repression, suppression

针叶树 zhēnyè shù conifer

阵雨 zhènyǔ shower (of rain)

真正 zhēnzhèng authentic, real ◊ really

镇政府 zhèn zhèngfǔ town council

针织品 zhēnzhī pǐn knitwear

针织衣服 zhēnzhī yīfú knitwear

震中 zhènzhōng epicenter

珍珠 zhēnzhū pearl

珍珠母 zhēnzhūmǔ mother-of-pearl

榛子 zhēnzi hazelnut

折蓬车 zhépéng chē convertible

折起来 zhé qǐlái fold up *chair etc*

这儿 zhèr here

折算 zhésuàn conversion

折梯 zhétī step ladder

这些 zhèxiē these

哲学 zhéxué philosophy

哲学家 zhéxué jiā philosopher

遮掩 zhēyǎn hush up

这样 zhèyàng like this, this way; so; such; 我认为是这样 **wǒ rènwéi shì zhèyàng** I think so

遮阳帽 zhēyángmào baseball cap

折页 zhéyè hinge

遮阴 zhēyīn shade ◊ shady

之 zhī *fml* (*possessive indicator*): 东方之珠 **dōngfāng zhī zhū** the pearl of the east

只 zhī *measure word for birds, animals, boats*; 两只老虎 **liángzhī lǎohú** two tigers

汁 zhī juice

支 zhī *measure word for pens, pencils, cigarettes and long cylindrical things*

织 zhī weave; knit

知 zhī know

脂 zhī fat; grease

直 zhí straight

职 zhí employment; job

植 zhí plant

值 zhí value ◊ be worth

执 zhí hold

只 zhǐ only

纸 zhǐ paper

指 zhǐ finger ◊ point to

止 zhǐ stop

痣 zhì mole (*on skin*)

掷 zhì toss, throw; 掷色子 **zhì shǎizi** throw dice

治 zhì control

志 zhì will, willpower

至 zhì to; up to ◊ reach; 十至十五人 **shí zhì shíwǔ rén** from 10 to 15 people; 星期一至五 **xīngqī yī zhì wǔ** Monday through Friday

致 zhì send; cause

制 zhì make, manufacture

智 zhì wisdom

质 zhì substance

致癌 zhì'ái carcinogenic

致癌物 zhì'ái wù carcinogen

值班 zhíbān be on duty

纸板 zhǐbǎn cardboard

纸板盒 zhǐbǎn hé cardboard box

纸板火柴 zhǐbǎn huǒchái book of matches

纸杯子 zhǐ bēizi paper cup

直奔 zhíbēn make a beeline for

纸币 zhǐbì (bank)bill

掷币 zhìbì toss a coin

支部 zhībù branch, chapter

只不过 zhǐbúguò mere ◊ merely

织布机 zhībùjī loom

制裁 zhìcái crack down on ◊ crackdown; sanction, penalty

致残 zhìcán maim

支撑 zhīcheng support, hold up; sustain

支撑起 zhīchēngqǐ prop up

支撑住 zhīchēngzhù hold out, manage

支持 zhīchí hold, keep in place; support; back up, endorse ◊ backing; endorsement ◊ supportive; 我支持你 **wǒ zhīchí nǐ** I'm on your side

支持者 zhīchí zhě follower, supporter

支出 zhīchū pay ◊ expenditure

指出 zhǐchū point out

痔疮 zhìchuāng piles MED

直达 zhídá direct, nonstop *flight etc*

纸袋 zhǐdài paper bag

值当 zhídàng be good value

知道 zhīdào know

直到 zhídào until ◊ pending; 直到七月才能完成 **zhídào qǐyuè cái néng wánchéng** it won't be finished until July

指导 zhǐdǎo guide; instruct; coach ◊ directions, instructions; guidance; directory

指导员 zhǐdǎo yuán instructor

指导者 zhǐdǎo zhě supervisor

值得 zhíde deserve, merit; be

worthwhile ◊ desirable; recommended; 值得信任 **zhíde xìnrèn** trustworthy

质地 zhìdì texture

支点 zhīdiǎn pivot

指定 zhǐdìng specify; designate; be meant for, be aimed at; 指定教材 **zhǐdìng jiàocái** set book

制定 zhìdìng enact, institute

指定集合点 zhǐdìng jíhé diǎn rendez-vous; assembly point

制动 zhìdòng brake

制动信号灯 zhìdòng xìnhào dēng brake light

制度 zhìdù system

只读存储器 zhǐdú cúnchǔ qì ROM, read-only memory

只读档案 zhǐdú dǎng'àn read-only file

至多 zhìduō at (the) most

脂肪 zhīfáng fat; 含脂肪多 **hán zhīfáng duo** fatty

支付 zhīfù pay; 支付手段 **zhīfù shǒuduàn** means of payment

制服 zhìfú uniform

至高点 zhìgāodiǎn summit, peak (of powers etc)

趾高气扬 zhǐgāo qìyáng swagger

至高无上 zhìgāo wúshàng supreme

吱嘎声 zhīgā shēng squeak; creak

制革 zhìgé tan leather

职工 zhígōng workforce, staff

直观 zhíguān visual

直观教具 zhíguān jiàojù visual aid

直观显示部件 zhíguān xiǎnshì bùjiàn VDU, visual display unit

至关重要 zhìguān zhòngyào of prime importance

直航飞机 zhíháng fēijī through flight

治好 zhìhǎo cure

纸盒 zhǐhé carton

之后 zhīhòu after

指挥 zhǐhuī conduct ◊ bandmaster

智慧 zhìhuì wisdom; intelligence

指挥调度台 zhǐhuī diàodù tái control tower

指挥官 zhǐhuī guān commander

指挥家 zhǐhuī jiā conductor

指挥台 zhǐhuī tái podium

支架 zhījià upright; support, prop

指甲 zhǐjia fingernail

指甲锉 zhǐjia cuò nail file

指甲刀 zhǐjia dāo nail clippers

指甲剪 zhǐjia jiǎn nail scissors

指尖 zhǐjiān fingertip

纸浆 zhǐjiāng paper pulp

直角 zhíjiǎo right-angle; 成直角 **chéng zhíjiǎo** at right-angles to

指甲油 zhǐjia yóu nail polish

指甲油去除剂 zhǐjia yóu qùchú jì nail polish remover

枝节 zhījié detail

直接 zhíjiē direct ◊ directly, straight

直截了当 zhíjié liǎodàng straightforward, direct ◊ straight out, bluntly

掷界外球 zhì jiè wài qiú throw-in (in soccer)

织锦 zhījǐn tapestry

纸巾 zhǐjīn tissue

至今 zhìjīn until now, up to now

直径 zhíjìng diameter

致敬 zhìjìng salute

纸卷 zhǐjuǎn scroll

知觉 zhījué consciousness; feeling MED; 失去 / 恢复知觉 **shīqù / huīfù zhījué** lose / regain consciousness

直觉 zhíjué intuition

止渴 zhǐkě quench one's thirst

止咳糖 zhǐké táng lozenge

止咳糖浆 zhǐké tángjiāng cough medicine, cough syrup

指控 zhǐkòng accuse; charge ◊ allegation

直立 zhílì erect, upright

治理 zhìlǐ administration ◊ administer, govern

致力 zhìlì dedication

智力 zhìlì intellect; intelligence ◊ intellectual

质量 zhìliàng quality

质量管理 zhìliàng guǎnlǐ quality control

质量控制 zhìliàng kòngzhì quality control

治疗 zhìliáo treatment, therapy ◊

treat

治疗学家 zhìliáo xuéjiā therapist

智力迟钝 zhìlì chídùn retarded

支离破碎 zhīlí pòsuì fragmentary

支流 zhīliú tributary

直流电 zhíliúdiàn direct current

智力游戏 zhìlì yóuxì puzzle

支路 zhīlù side road

指路 zhǐlù navigate (in car)

指路人 zhǐlùrén navigator (in car)

芝麻 zhīma sesame

芝麻油 zhīma yóu sesame oil

殖民地 zhímíndì colony ◊ colonial

知名 zhīmíng famous; prominent

指明 zhǐmíng point out

致命 zhìmìng lethal, fatal ◊ fatally

殖民者 zhímín zhě settler

指南 zhǐnán guidebook; manual

指南针 zhǐnán zhēn compass

执拗 zhíniù stubborn

侄女 zhínǚ niece (brother's daughter)

纸牌 zhǐpái playing card

制片人 zhìpiān rén film-maker; producer

支票 zhīpiào check FIN

支票本 zhīpiào běn checkbook

支票帐户 zhīpiào zhànghù checking account

质朴 zhìpǔ unsophisticated

志气 zhìqì ambition

之前 zhīqián before

支气管炎 zhīqìguǎn yán bronchitis

智穷计尽 zhìqióng jìjìn be at one's wits' end

支取 zhīqǔ withdraw

智商 zhìshāng IQ

至少 zhìshǎo at least

智胜 zhìshèng outwit

直升飞机 zhíshēng fēijī helicopter

知识 zhīshi knowledge; learning

指示 zhǐshì indicate, signal; instruct ◊ indication; directions; **指示 X 做 Y zhǐshì X zuò Y** instruct X to do Y

只是 zhǐshì just, only; except that

知识分子 zhīshì fènzǐ intellectual

指示牌 zhǐshì pái road sign

直率 zhíshuài blunt, direct ◊ bluntly

直爽 zhíshuǎng direct

直说 zhíshuō speak one's mind

制陶术 zhìtáoshù pottery

直通火车 zhítōng huǒchē through train

止痛片 zhítòng piàn painkiller

制图 zhìtú draw charts; make maps

指望 zhǐwàng bank on ◊ expectations

职位 zhíwèi office, position, post

质问 zhìwèn question, challenge

植物 zhíwù plant ◊ botanical

职务 zhíwù duties; job

植物学 zhíwù xué botany

知悉 zhīxī knowingly

窒息 zhìxī suffocate ◊ suffocation; **令人窒息 lìngrén zhìxī** stifling

支线 zhīxiàn branch line

直线 zhíxiàn straight line

纸箱 zhǐxiāng carton, box, pack

指向 zhǐxiàng direct; point at

志向 zhìxiàng ambition

致谢 zhìxiè give one's thanks

窒息而死 zhìxī ér sǐ suffocate

执行 zhíxíng carry out, execute

直系亲属 zhíxì qīnshǔ the immediate family

秩序 zhìxù order, orderliness

止血 zhǐxuè stop bleeding ◊ styptic

智牙 zhìyá wisdom tooth

直言不讳 zhíyán búhuì outspoken; blunt

只要 zhǐyào provided that; so long as

制药 zhìyào pharmaceutical

制药公司 zhìyào gōngsī pharmaceutical company

职业 zhíyè business; profession; occupation ◊ vocational; occupational; professional

职业介绍所 zhíyè jièshàosuǒ employment agency

职业人员 zhíyè rényuán professional

职业杀手 zhíyè shāshǒu hitman

质疑 zhìyí challenge; **对 X 有质疑 duì X yǒu zhìyí** feel

uncomfortable about X; question the validity of X

直译 zhíyì literal translation

致意 zhìyì greeting

指引 zhǐyǐn guide, show, direct

执意做 zhíyì zuò persist in

只有 zhǐyǒu only if; nothing but; 只有几个 zhǐyǒu jǐge just a couple; 只有最好的 zhǐyǒu zuìhǎo de nothing but the best

至于 zhìyú as for

治愈 zhìyù heal, cure

职员 zhíyuán employee; personnel

志愿 zhìyuàn voluntary ◊ volunteer

志愿者 zhìyuàn zhě volunteer

置于两侧 zhìyú liǎngcè flank

制造 zhìzào manufacture, produce ◊ manufacturing

制造厂家 zhìzào chǎngjiā producer

制造商 zhìzào shāng manufacturer

制造者 zhìzào zhě maker

指责 zhǐzé rebuke, reproach ◊ disapproval ◊ reproachful

执照 zhízhào license

执照号码 zhízhào hàomǎ license number

指针 zhǐzhēn needle (on dial); hand (on clock)

执政 zhízhèng in power

直着走 zhízhe zǒu straight ahead ◊ carry straight on

纸制 zhǐzhì paper

制止 zhìzhǐ prevent; deter; stem, block

吱吱声 zhīzhī shēng squeak (of mouse); twitter (of birds)

蜘蛛 zhīzhū spider

支柱 zhīzhù support

止住 zhǐzhù halt

蜘蛛网 zhīzhūwǎng spider's web, cobweb

侄子 zhízi nephew (brother's son)

知足 zhīzú undemanding, modest

制作 zhìzuò make, produce ◊ production

钟 zhōng clock; bell; o'clock

中 zhōng middle; medium; China ◊

be in the process of

忠 zhōng loyal; faithful

终 zhōng end

种 zhǒng species; race; sort, kind; 两种 liǎngzhǒng two kinds of

肿 zhǒng swell ◊ swollen

重 zhòng heavy

种 zhòng plant

中 zhòng hit

众 zhòng crowd

钟表匠 zhōngbiǎo jiàng watchmaker

中波 zhōngbō medium wave

中部 zhōngbù central ◊ central part

仲裁 zhòngcái arbitrate ◊ arbitration

中餐 zhōngcān Chinese food

中产阶级 zhōngchǎn jiējí middle-class ◊ the middle classes

忠诚 zhōngchéng faithful

重大 zhòngdà serious, weighty

中等 zhōngděng medium; average, middling

中等教育 zhōngděng jiàoyù secondary education

终点 zhōngdiǎn finish, end

重点 zhòngdiǎn stress; key point; emphasis; 把重点转移到 bǎ zhòngdiǎn zhuǎnyídào shift the emphasis onto

终点线 zhōngdiǎnxiàn finishing line

终点站 zhōngdiǎn zhàn terminus

中东 Zhōngdōng Middle East

仲冬 zhòngdōng midwinter

重读 zhòngdú stress, emphasize

中毒 zhòngdú poisoning

中断 zhōngduàn interrupt; break off ◊ interruption

终端产品 zhōngduān chǎnpǐn end product

终端用户 zhōngduān yònghù end-user

众多 zhòngduō mass, large amount

中耳炎 zhōng'ěr yán middle ear infection

中饭 zhōngfàn lunch

中风 zhòngfēng stroke MED

重负 zhòngfù strain, stress

忠告 **zhōnggào** advise, recommend

中共 **Zhōnggòng** Chinese Communist Party

重工业 **zhònggōngyè** heavy industry

中共中央委员会 **Zhōnggòng Zhōngyāng Wěiyuánhuì** Central Committee of the Chinese Communist Party

中国 **Zhōngguó** China ◊ Chinese

中国大陆 **Zhōngguó Dàlù** Mainland China

中国国际旅行社 **Zhōngguó Guójì Lǚxíngshè** China International Travel Service, CITS

中国话 **Zhōngguó huà** Chinese (*language*)

中国旅行社 **Zhōngguó Lǚxíngshè** China Travel Service, CTS

中国民航 **Zhōngguó Mínháng** Civil Aviation Administration of China, CAAC

中国人 **Zhōngguó rén** Chinese

中国日报 **Zhōngguó Rìbào** China Daily

中国象棋 **Zhōngguó xiàngqí** Chinese chess

中国银行 **Zhōngguó Yínháng** Bank of China

中国制造 **Zhōngguó zhìzào** made in China

中号 **zhōnghào** medium ◊ medium-sized

中和 **zhōnghé** counteract; neutralize

中华民国 **Zhōnghuá Mínguó** Republic of China, ROC

中华人民共和国 **Zhōnghuá Rénmín Gònghéguó** People's Republic of China, PRC

中级 **zhōngjí** intermediate

重击 **zhòngjī** thump, whack; hammer on

中间 **zhōngjiān** middle ◊ halfway

中间对齐 **zhōngjiān duìqí** center *text*

中坚分子 **zhōngjiān fènzi** hard core POL

中间楼层 **zhōngjiān lóucéng** mezzanine

中间名 **zhōngjiān míng** middle name

中间派 **zhōngjiān pài** center POL

中间人 **zhōngjiān rén** go-between

终究 **zhōngjiū** finally

中肯 **zhòngkěn** apt ◊ aptly

中空 **zhōngkōng** hollow

肿块 **zhǒngkuài** lump, swelling

种类 **zhǒnglèi** kind, type, variety; species

中立 **zhōnglì** disinterested; neutral

重力 **zhònglì** gravity PHYS

重量 **zhòngliàng** weight

中量级 **zhōngliàng jí** middleweight SP

重量极 **zhòngliàng jí** heavyweight SP

中立地位 **zhōnglì dìwèi** neutrality

肿瘤 **zhǒngliú** tumor

钟楼 **zhōnglóu** belfry

钟面 **zhōngmiàn** dial, face (*of clock*)

中年 **zhōngnián** middle age ◊ middle-aged

中篇小说 **zhōngpiān xiǎoshuō** novella

钟情 **zhōngqíng** loving

中秋节 **Zhōngqiūjié** Mid-Autumn Festival, Moon Festival

中人 **zhōngrén** intermediary

中日战争 **Zhōngrì Zhànzhēng** Sino-Japanese war

中山服 **zhōngshānfú** Mao jacket

终身 **zhōngshēn** lifelong; for life

终身伴侣 **zhōngshēn bànlǚ** life partner

钟声 **zhōngshēng** ring (*of bell*)

忠实 **zhōngshí** devoted

中式 **zhōngshì** Chinese-style

中士 **zhōngshì** sergeant

重视 **zhòngshì** value, attach importance to

中世纪 **Zhōngshìjì** Middle Ages ◊ medieval

重事轻说 **zhòngshì qīngshuō** understatement

忠实于 zhōngshí yú be devoted to

中暑 zhòngshǔ heatstroke; 他中暑了 **tā zhòngshǔ le** he has had too much sun

众所周知 zhòng suǒ zhōu zhī well-known

重听 zhòngtīng hard of hearing

中途 zhōngtú midway

中途停留 zhōngtú tíngliú stop over ◊ stopover

中途退出 zhōngtú tuìchū abort COMPUT

中途退学 zhōngtú tuìxué drop out (*of school*)

中尉 zhōngwèi lieutenant

中文 Zhōngwén Chinese (*language*)

中午 zhōngwǔ midday

仲夏 zhòngxià midsummer

中小学教师 zhōngxiǎoxué jiàoshī schoolteacher

中小学女教师 zhōngxiǎoxué nǚ jiàoshī schoolmistress

中小学女生 zhōngxiǎoxué nǚ shēng schoolgirl

中小学男教师 zhōngxiǎoxué nán jiàoshī schoolmaster

中小学男生 zhōngxiǎoxué nánshēng schoolboy

中小学生 zhōngxiǎoxué xuéshēng schoolchild

中心 zhōngxīn center; heart

忠心 zhōngxīn loyal ◊ loyalty

衷心 zhōngxīn sincere; warm

中学 zhōngxué middle school; junior high school

中学生 zhōngxuéshēng middle school student; junior high school student

中央 zhōngyāng central ◊ middle

中央处理机 zhōngyāng chǔlǐ jī CPU, central processing unit

中央电视台 Zhōngyāng Diànshìtái China Central Television, CCTV

中央情报局 Zhōngyāng Qíngbào Jú CIA, Central Intelligence Agency

中药 zhōngyào Chinese medicine

重要 zhòngyào important, significant

重要性 zhòngyào xìng importance, significance

中医 zhōngyī Chinese medicine; Chinese doctor

重音 zhòngyīn accent, emphasis

众议员 zhòngyì yuán representative

众议院 Zhòngyì yuàn House of Representatives

终于 zhōngyú finally, eventually, in the end

忠于 zhōngyú stand by, be loyal to

肿胀 zhǒngzhàng swell up ◊ swollen ◊ swelling

忠贞 zhōngzhēn fidelity

终止 zhōngzhǐ terminate ◊ termination

中止 zhōngzhǐ cease, discontinue

中指 zhōngzhǐ middle finger

终止 zhōngzhǐ end, finish

种植 zhòngzhí grow, cultivate; plant

终止日期 zhōngzhǐ rìqī expiry date

种植园 zhòngzhí yuán plantation

种子 zhǒngzi seed, pip

种子选手 zhǒngzi xuǎnshǒu seed (*in tennis*)

种族 zhǒngzú race, people ◊ ethnic, racial

种族隔离 zhǒngzú gélí racial segregation

重罪 zhòngzuì felony

种族平等 zhǒngzú píngděng racial equality

种族歧视 zhǒngzú qíshì racism ◊ racist

种族歧视者 zhǒngzú qíshì zhě racist

种族社区 zhǒngzú shèqū ethnic group

粥 zhōu rice porridge, congee

洲 zhōu continent

州 zhōu prefecture; state

周 zhōu week; circle

轴 zhóu shaft; axle

肘 zhǒu elbow

皱 zhòu crease, wrinkle

轴承 zhóuchéng bearing TECH

周到 zhōudao considerate; tactful

周恩来 Zhōu Ēnlái Zhou Enlai, Chou En-lai

周刊 zhōukān weekly magazine

咒骂 zhòumà curse, swear; 咒骂 X zhòumà X swear at X

皱眉 zhòuméi frown

周末 zhōumò weekend ◊ on the weekend

周年 zhōunián anniversary

周年大会 zhōunián dàhuì annual general meeting

周期 zhōuqī cycle; period

周期性 zhōuqī xìng periodic; cyclical

骤然下跌 zhòurán xiàdiē decline, slump

周围 zhōuwéi around ◊ surrounding ◊ surroundings

皱纹 zhòuwén crease, wrinkle

绉纹纸 zhòuwén zhǐ crepe paper

骤增 zhòuzēng bulge, sudden increase

州长 zhōuzhǎng governor

猪 zhū hog, pig

珠 zhū pearl; bead

逐 zhú follow

竹 zhú bamboo

煮 zhǔ boil

主 zhǔ main ◊ master, lord

住 zhù live, reside; stop ◊ (showing result): 记住 jì zhù remember; 抓住 zhuā zhù catch

柱 zhù pillar

祝 zhù wish; 祝 X 走运 zhù X zǒuyùn wish X well; 祝你走运! zhù nǐ zǒuyùn! good luck!; 祝你健康! zhù nǐ jiànkāng! your health!

助 zhù help

抓 zhuā grasp; scratch

爪 zhuǎ claw

拽 zhuài pull, tow

抓阄儿 zhuājiūr draw lots

抓牢 zhuā láo tighten one's grip on

专 zhuān special

砖 zhuān brick; tile

转 zhuǎn turn; move, transfer ◊ turning

转 zhuàn turn; revolve

传 zhuàn biography

转变 zhuǎnbiàn shift, change direction ◊ swing; changeover

转播 zhuǎnbō relay signal

专长 zhuāncháng prowess; specialty

转车 zhuǎnchē change (trains / buses)

转达 zhuǎndá communicate, pass on

转达问候 zhuǎndá wènhòu send one's regards

赚的钱 zhuànde qián earnings

转递 zhuǎndì forward letter

转动 zhuǎndòng turn

转动 zhuàndòng turn; revolve; swing

桩 zhuāng stake, peg

装 zhuāng pack; install ◊ clothing; camera

装胶卷 zhuāng jiāojuǎn load camera

庄 zhuāng village

撞 zhuàng hit; bang, bump, strike

壮 zhuàng strong

幢 zhuàng measure word for buildings; 一幢楼房 yīzhuàng lóufáng an apartment block

转告 zhuǎngào relay message

撰稿人 zhuàngǎorén scriptwriter

装扮 zhuāngbàn disguise oneself, dress up; 装扮成 zhuāngbàn chéng disguise oneself as, dress up as

装备 zhuāngbèi equipment ◊ equip; furnish

装玻璃工人 zhuāng bōli de gōngren glazier

装车 zhuāng chē load vehicle

壮大 zhuàngdà healthy

装弹药 zhuāng dànyào load gun

撞倒 zhuàngdǎo run over, knock down; 司机把车撞到 sījī bǎ chē zhuàngdào ... the driver smashed into ...

装钉 zhuāngdīng binding

撞翻 zhuàngfān knock over

壮观 zhuàngguān grand; spectacular ◊ splendor; spectacle

装璜 zhuānghuáng décor; decoration

装潢工人 zhuānghuáng

gōngrén decorator

撞毁 zhuànghuǐ crash *car*

撞击 zhuàngjī knock, hit ◊ blow; impact

庄稼 zhuāngjia crops

装甲车 zhuāngjiǎ chē armored vehicle

撞见 zhuàngjiàn bump into; happen to see; 撞见 X 做 Y *zhuàngjiàn X zuò Y* catch X doing Y

状况 zhuàngkuàng state, condition

壮丽 zhuànglì magnificence

装满 zhuāngmǎn fill up; top up ◊ full

装配 zhuāngpèi set up

装配厂 zhuāngpèi chǎng assembly plant

装配工 zhuāngpèi gōng fitter

装配线 zhuāngpèi xiàn assembly line

装腔作势 zhuāngqiāng zuòshì pose, pretense

装软件 zhuāng ruǎnjiàn load COMPUT

装入口袋 zhuāngrù kǒudài pack, bag up

装饰 zhuāngshì decorate, adorn ◊ decoration, embellishment ◊ decorative, ornamental

装饰物 zhuāngshì wù ornament

装饰性 zhuāngshì xìng cosmetic, superficial

撞碎 zhuàngsuì smash, crash

状态 zhuàngtài condition, state; 处于交战状态 *chǔyú jiāozhàn zhuàngtài* be at war; 处于戒备状态 *chǔyú jièbèi zhuàngtài* be on the alert

装卸工 zhuāngxiè gōng stevedore

装修 zhuāngxiū decorate *room etc*

庄严 zhuāngyán dignified

装有 zhuāngyǒu be supplied with

装载 zhuāngzài load

装置 zhuāngzhì fittings

庄重 zhuāngzhòng grave, solemn

装作 zhuāngzuò pretend; pose as

转航 zhuǎnháng tack (*of yacht*)

专横 zhuānhèng high-handed

转化 zhuǎnhuà convert

转换 zhuǎnhuàn change

转机 zhuǎnjī transfer (*of passengers*)

传记 zhuànjì biography

专家 zhuānjiā expert, specialist

专家建议 zhuānjiā jiànyì expert advice

转机厅 zhuǎnjī tīng transit lounge

专科医生 zhuānkē yīshēng specialist (doctor)

专栏 zhuānlán column

专栏作家 zhuānlán zuòjiā columnist

专利 zhuānlì patent

转脸 zhuǎnliǎn turn away, look away

专门 zhuānmén special; 专门从事 *zhuānmén cóngshì* specialize; specialize in

专门知识 zhuānmén zhīshi expertise

转晴 zhuǎnqíng brighten up, clear up

转让 zhuǎnràng entrust; transfer; 把 X 转让给 Y *bǎ X zhuǎnràng gěi Y* make X over to Y

转让契据 zhuǎnràng qìjù bill of sale

专人 zhuānrén by hand

转入地下 zhuǎnrù dìxià go underground POL

转身 zhuǎnshēn turn around, spin around

砖石结构 zhuānshí jiégòu masonry

转手 zhuǎnshǒu change hands

专题 zhuāntí article, feature

砖头 zhuāntóu brick

转弯 zhuǎnwān turn the corner

转弯处 zhuǎnwān chù curve; corner, bend

转向 zhuǎnxiàng change direction; turn around; move on ◊ change of direction; U-turn

专心 zhuānxīn concentrate ◊ concentration; devotion

专心致志 zhuānxīn zhìzhì single-minded

专业 zhuānyè professional ◊

subject, field; area of expertise

专业知识 zhuānyè zhīshi specialized knowledge

专业人士 zhuānyè rénshì professional (*lawyer etc*)

转移 zhuǎnyí transfer, move; avert

转运商 zhuǎnyùn shāng forwarding agent

转折点 zhuǎnzhé diǎn turning point

专政 zhuānzhèng dictatorship

转租 zhuǎnzū sublet

抓取 zhuāqǔ snatch

抓住 zhuāzhù grab, grasp; grip; scratch

爪子 zhuǎzi claw; paw

主板 zhǔbǎn mainboard COMPUT

珠宝 zhūbǎo jewel; jewelry

珠宝商 zhūbǎo shāng jeweler

逐步 zhúbù progressively, steadily; step by step; 逐步引进 zhúbù yǐnjìn phase in; 逐步中止 zhúbù zhōngzhǐ phase out

逐步发展 zhúbù fāzhǎn progressive

逐步升级 zhúbù shēngjí escalate

贮藏 zhùcáng storage

注册 zhùcè enroll ◊ enrolment

助产士 zhùchǎnshì midwife

主持 zhǔchí present; host; front; chair; preside; 主持会议 zhǔchí huìyì chair a meeting; 主持婚礼 zhǔchí hūnlǐ conduct a wedding

主持人 zhǔchí rén host (*of TV program*)

逐出 zhúchū eject, evict

住处 zhùchù place (where one lives)

贮存 zhùcún store

贮存空间 zhùcún kōngjiān storage space

主导 zhǔdǎo dominant

主祷文 Zhǔdǎo Wén Lord's Prayer

驻地 zhùdì resident; garrison

筑堤坝 zhùdībà dam

注定 zhùdìng condemn, doom; 注定失败 zhùdìng shībài doomed to failure

主动 zhǔdòng initiative ◊ active

GRAM; 主动做 X zhǔdòng zuò X do X on one's own initiative

主动表示 zhǔdòng biǎoshì make overtures to

住房 zhùfáng housing

住房条件 zhùfáng tiáojiàn housing conditions

祝福 zhùfú bless ◊ blessing

逐个 zhúgè one by one

主观 zhǔguān subjective

主管 zhǔguǎn supervisor, boss ◊ be in charge of, oversee

主管人员 zhǔguǎn rényuán executive; management

主观愿望 zhǔguān yuànwàng wishful thinking

煮过火儿 zhǔ guòhuǒr overcook

主好 zhùhǎo best wishes, congratulations ◊ congratulate

祝贺 zhùhè congratulate; 祝贺 zhùhè ... congratulations on ...

追 zhuī chase, pursue

追赶 zhuīgǎn chase, pursue

追赶者 zhuīgǎn zhě pursuer

坠毁 zhuìhuǐ crash

追究 zhuījiū get down to

追求 zhuīqiú seek, pursue

追溯 zhuīsù date back to; backdate ◊ retroactive

追随者 zhuīsuí zhě follower, supporter

追逐 zhuīzhú pursue ◊ pursuit

逐渐 zhújiàn gradual ◊ gradually; 逐渐减少 zhújiàn jiǎnshǎo taper off, decline; 逐渐习惯 zhújiàn xíguàn get accustomed to; 逐渐形成 zhújiàn xíngchéng evolve

珠江 Zhūjiāng Pearl River

珠江三角洲 Zhūjiāng Sānjiǎozhōu Pearl River Delta

主教 zhǔjiào bishop

助教 zhùjiào teaching assistant

主机体 zhǔjītǐ mainframe

猪圈 zhūjuàn pigpen

主角 zhǔjué leading role

主考人 zhǔkǎo rén examiner

助理研究员 zhùlǐ yánjiū yuán research assistant

注满 zhùmǎn fill

著名 zhùmíng famous, distinguished; 以 X 著名 yǐ X

**zhùmíng** be famous for X

注明日期 **zhùmíng rìqī** date *letter etc*

珠穆朗玛峰 **Zhūmùlǎngmǎfēng** Mount Everest

准 **zhǔn** allow ◊ accurate

准备 **zhǔnbèi** plan; prepare; fix ◊ preparation; 把 X 准备好 **bǎ X zhǔnbèi hǎo** get X ready

准备工作 **zhǔnbèi gōngzuò** preparations

准备就绪 **zhǔnbèi jiùxù** readiness

准备练习 **zhǔnbèi liànxí** warm up

准确 **zhǔnquè** accurate; precise

准确性 **zhǔnquè xìng** accuracy

准时 **zhǔnshí** punctual ◊ punctually

准许 **zhǔnxǔ** approve; 准许 X 做 Y **zhǔnxǔ X zuò Y** permit X to do Y

准予 **zhǔnyǔ** grant

准予进入 **zhǔnyǔ jìnrù** entrance, admission

准则 **zhǔnzé** principle; norm; standard

捉 **zhuō** hold; catch

桌 **zhuō** table

啄 **zhuó** peck

着 **zhuó** put on *clothes*

桌布 **zhuōbù** tablecloth

捉到 **zhuōdào** capture

拙劣 **zhuōliè** badly

着陆 **zhuólù** land (*of aircraft*) ◊ landing

桌面排版 **zhuōmiàn páibǎn** desktop publishing, DTP

捉迷藏 **zhuōmícáng** hide-and-seek

啄木鸟 **zhuómù niǎo** woodpecker

捉弄 **zhuōnòng** take in, take for a ride

酌情 **zhuóqíng** use one's discretion; 由你酌情处理 **yóu nǐ zhuóqíng chǔlǐ** deal with it at your discretion

啄食 **zhuóshí** peck at one's food

着手 **zhuóshǒu** initiate; start work

着想 **zhuóxiǎng** consider, show consideration for

卓有成效 **zhuó yǒu chéngxiào** effective; successful

卓越 **zhuóyuè** outstanding; remarkable; notable ◊ remarkably

捉住 **zhuōzhù** catch, capture

茁壮生长 **zhuózhuàng shēngzhǎng** thrive

桌子 **zhuōzi** table

猪皮 **zhūpí** pigskin

主权 **zhǔquán** sovereign, independent ◊ sovereignty, independence

主人 **zhǔrén** host; master, owner

猪肉 **zhūròu** pork

侏儒 **zhūrú** dwarf

注射 **zhùshè** inject ◊ injection, shot

注射器 **zhùshè qì** syringe

主食 **zhǔshí** staple; staple diet

注视 **zhùshì** gaze ◊ gaze at

注释 **zhùshì** note; gloss

助手 **zhùshǒu** assistant, helper

主诉 **zhǔsù** complain of MED

竹笋 **zhúsǔn** bamboo shoots

住所 **zhùsuǒ** residence; accommodations

烛台 **zhútái** candlestick

主题 **zhǔtí** subject, topic, theme ◊ topical

铸铁 **zhùtiě** cast iron

主题歌 **zhǔtí gē** theme song

助听器 **zhùtīng qì** hearing aid

主卧室 **zhǔwòshì** master bedroom

主席 **zhǔxí** chair; chairman; chairwoman; chairperson

主修 **zhǔxiū** major in, specialize in

助学金 **zhùxuéjīn** grant (*for studies*)

主演 **zhǔyǎn** star

主要 **zhǔyào** main, major; chief ◊ mainly, primarily; mostly

主页 **zhǔyè** homepage

主意 **zhǔyì** idea; 好主意 **hǎo zhǔyì** good idea; inspiration

注意 **zhùyì** notice; pay attention to; 注意到 X **zhùyì dào X** take note of X; 引起 X 的注意 **yǐnqǐ X de zhùyì** catch X's eye

注意力 **zhùyìlì** attention

注意形象 **zhùyì xíngxiàng**

image-conscious

猪油 zhūyóu lard

主语 zhǔyǔ subject GRAM

住院 zhùyuàn go into the hospital

住院病人 zhùyuàn bìngrén in-patient

铸造 zhùzào cast

铸造厂 zhùzào chǎng foundry

驻扎 zhùzhā place, station *guard etc*; 驻扎在 *zhùzhā zài* be stationed at

住宅区 zhùzhái qū residential area

主张 zhǔzhāng cause; position ◊ advocate, stand up for; represent

注重 zhùzhòng attach importance to

珠子 zhūzi bead; pearl

竹子 zhúzi bamboo

柱子 zhùzi pillar

住嘴! zhùzuǐ! shut up!

资 zī money, funds

紫 zǐ purple

子 zǐ son; child; seed

字 zì word; character; handwriting

自 zì self ◊ from

自卑感 zìbēi gǎn inferiority complex

资本 zīběn capital

资本家 zīběn jiā capitalist (*businessman*)

资本支出 zīběn zhīchū capital expenditure

资本主义 zīběn zhǔyì capitalism ◊ capitalist

资本主义者 zīběn zhǔyì zhě capitalist

滋补 zībǔ nutritious

资产 zīchǎn asset FIN

资产阶级 zīchǎn jiējí bourgeoisie

自从 zìcóng since; 自从你走以后 *zìcóng nǐ zǒu yǐhòu* since you left

自大 zìdà big-headed

子弹 zǐdàn bullet; cartridge; pellet

子弟 zǐdì disciple

字典 zìdiǎn dictionary

自动 zìdòng automatic ◊ automatically; by itself

自动点唱机 zìdòng diǎnchàngjī jukebox

自动扶梯 zìdòng fútī escalator

自动化 zìdòng huà automation

自动驾驶仪 zìdòng jiàshǐ yí autopilot

自动售货机 zìdòng shòuhuò jī vending machine

自发 zìfā spontaneous

自负 zìfù pompous; arrogant; vain, conceited ◊ conceit

兹附上 zīfùshàng please find enclosed

自高自大 zìgāo zìdà conceited; ostentatious

资格 zīgé qualification; 取得资格 *qǔdé zīgé* qualify; 取消资格 *qǔxiāo zīgé* disqualify; 我不够资格来决定 *wǒ bùgòu zīgé lái juédìng* I am not qualified to judge

子宫 zǐgōng uterus, womb

子宫切除术 zǐgōng qiēchúshù hysterectomy

子宫托 zǐgōng tuō diaphragm

自豪 zìháo pride ◊ proud ◊ proudly; 以 ... 为自豪 *yǐ ... wéi zìháo* be proud of

自己 zìjǐ self; oneself ◊ own ◊ by oneself; 自己做 X *zìjǐ zuò X* do X by oneself; 我自己的公寓/车 *wǒ zìjǐde gōngyù/chē* a car/an apartment of my own

字迹 zìjì writing

字节 zìjié byte

资金 zījīn capital, money

紫禁城 Zǐjìnchéng Forbidden City

自己一个人 zìjǐ yīgè rén alone

自觉 zìjué conscious

自控 zìkòng control oneself

自来水 zìláishuǐ running water

自来水笔 zìláishuǐ bǐ fountain pen

资料保密 zīliào bǎomì data protection

紫罗兰 zǐ luólán violet (*plant*)

紫罗兰色 zǐ luólán sè violet (*color*)

自满 zìmǎn complacent, smug ◊ complacency, smugness

字面 zìmiàn literal ◊ literally

自鸣得意 zìmíng déyì self-satisfied

字母 zìmǔ letter (of alphabet); 依
字母顺序 yī zìmǔ shùnxù
alphabetical order

字幕 zìmù subtitle

字母表 zìmǔbiǎo alphabet

自欺 zìqī delude oneself

子儿 zǐr piece (in chess etc)

自然 zìrán nature ◊ natural ◊
naturally, of course

自然保护区 zìrán bǎohùqū
nature reserve

自然环境 zìrán huánjìng the
environment

自然界 zìrán jiè natural

自然科学 zìrán kēxué natural
science

自然科学家 zìrán kēxué jiā
natural scientist

自然灾害 zìrán zāihài natural
disaster

紫色 zǐsè purple

自杀 zìshā suicide ◊ commit
suicide

滋生地 zīshēng dì breeding
ground

姿势 zīshì position; posture; 摆姿
势 bǎi zīshì pose

字首 zìshǒu monogram ◊
monogrammed

自首 zìshǒu turn in (to police)

自私 zìsī selfish

自私自利 zìsī-zìlì selfish

字体 zìtǐ font; typeface

紫外 zǐwài ultraviolet

滋味 zīwèi flavor, taste

自卫 zìwèi self-defense

自我 zìwǒ self; ego; 以自我为中
心 yǐ zìwǒ wéi zhōngxīn
egocentric

自我表达 zìwǒ biǎodá self-
expression ◊ express oneself

自我控制 zìwǒ kòngzhì self-
control

自我批评 zìwǒ pīpíng self-
criticism

自我约束 zìwǒ yuēshù self-
discipline

仔细 zǐxì careful, thorough ◊
closely; 仔细察看 zǐxì chákàn
study, examine; investigate; 仔细

检查 zǐxì jiǎnchá check, go over;

仔细彻底 zǐxì chèdǐ scrupulous;

仔细考虑 zǐxì kǎolǜ deliberate;
mull over

自相矛盾 zìxiāng máodùn
paradox

自信 zìxìn confident; self-
confident; assertive ◊ self-
confidence

自行车 zìxíngchē bicycle

自行车架 zìxíngchē jià parking
rack (for bicycle)

自信心 zìxìnxīn self-confidence

自选 zìxuǎn self-service ◊ optional

自学 zìxué self-study

咨询 zīxún advice; consultancy

咨询公司 zīxún gōngsī
consultancy

恣意 zìyì wanton

自以为是 zì yǐwéi shì self-
righteous

自由 zìyóu freedom, liberty ◊ free;
liberal POL; 自由放荡 zìyóu
fàngdàng run wild

自由女神像 Zìyóu Nǚshén
Xiàng Statue of Liberty

自由市场经济 zìyóu shìchǎng
jīngjì free market economy

自由泳 zìyóuyǒng crawl,
freestyle

资源 zīyuán resource

自愿 zìyuàn of one's own accord;
voluntary ◊ voluntarily

自治 zìzhì autonomy

自制 zìzhì homemade ◊ self-
possession

自制力 zìzhì lì self control

自治区 zìzhì qū autonomous
region

资助 zīzhù subsidize; back; stake

自传 zìzhuàn autobiography

自助餐 zìzhù cān buffet, self-
service meal

自助餐馆 zìzhù cānguǎn self-
service restaurant

自助式 zìzhù shì self-service

孜孜不倦 zīzī bùjuàn tireless

自尊 zìzūn self-esteem; pride, self-
respect ◊ proud

自尊心 zìzūn xīn self-respect

鬃 zōng mane

踪 **zōng** footprint

总 **zōng** total; general; main; gross FIN ◊ always

纵 **zòng** vertical

总部 **zǒngbù** head office

总裁 **zǒngcái** president

总的 **zǒngde** general, overall; 总的看来 **zǒngde kànlái** on the whole

总额 **zǒng'é** lump sum

总共 **zǒnggòng** altogether; 总共七十美元 **zǒnggòng qīshí měiyuán** that comes to $70 altogether

总公司 **zǒnggōngsī** parent company

综合 **zōnghé** comprehensive; 综合报道 **zōnghé bàodào** news round-up

纵横交错 **zònghéng jiāocuò** checkered

棕褐色 **zōnghè sè** tan (color)

综合性 **zōnghé xìng** full, comprehensive

纵火 **zònghuǒ** arson

踪迹 **zōngjī** track, trace

总机 **zǒngjī** telephone exchange

宗教 **zōngjiào** religion ◊ religious

总计 **zǒngjì** total

总结 **zǒngjié** summary

总经理 **zǒng jīnglǐ** CEO, chief executive officer, managing director

总计为 **zǒngjìwéi** add up to

总理 **zǒnglǐ** premier, prime minister

棕榈树 **zōnglǘshù** palm tree

棕色 **zōngsè** brown

纵深 **zòngshēn** deep

总是 **zǒngshì** always

棕树 **zōngshù** palm tree

总数 **zǒngshù** total; sum

总司令 **zǒngsīlìng** commander-in-chief

总体 **zǒngtǐ** overall

总统 **zǒngtǒng** president ◊ presidential

总统竞选 **zǒngtǒng jìngxuǎn** presidential campaign

总统职位 **zǒngtǒng zhíwèi** presidency

总帐 **zǒngzhàng** ledger

总之 **zǒngzhī** anyhow, in any case; to sum up, briefly

总指挥部 **zǒng zhǐhuībù** headquarters

走 **zǒu** walk; go; move; leave; run; navigate COMPUT; 走吧 **zǒuba** let's go; 走了 **zǒule** walk away; walk out; go ◊ gone 我得走了 **wǒ děi zǒule** I must be going

揍 **zòu** beat up; punch, sock

奏 **zòu** play musical instrument

走调 **zǒudiào** out of tune

走动 **zǒudòng** get around; move around

走狗 **zǒugǒu** pej running dog; yesman

走过 **zǒuguò** tread; walk past

走过来 **zǒu guòlái** approach

走后门儿 **zǒu hòuménr** go through the back door

走火 **zǒuhuǒ** go off (of gun)

走近 **zǒujìn** draw near

走进 **zǒujìn** enter

走开 **zǒukāi** buzz off; walk away

走廊 **zǒuláng** corridor; passageway; hall

走路 **zǒulù** walk, go on foot ◊ walking

走慢 **zǒumàn** lose time (of watch)

走散 **zǒusàn** wander off

走神 **zǒushén** wander (of attention)

走失 **zǒushī** stray

走私 **zǒusī** smuggle ◊ smuggling

走私者 **zǒusī zhě** smuggler

走投无路 **zǒutóu wúlù** desperate

走味儿 **zǒuwèir** stale

奏效 **zòuxiào** work, succeed

走走 **zǒuzou** walk, walk around

走嘴 **zǒuzuǐ** slip of the tongue

租 **zū** rent; hire; lease

卒 **zú** pawn (in chess)

足 **zú** foot ◊ enough

组 **zǔ** group; team, crew

祖 **zǔ** ancestor ◊ ancestral

阻 **zǔ** block; stop

阻碍 **zǔ'ài** hinder, impede, frustrate ◊ setback

钻 **zuàn** drill

钻孔 **zuānkǒng** bore a hole

钻石 zuànshí diamond

钻头 zuàntóu drill

组成 zǔchéng make up, comprise

组成成分 zǔchéng chéngfèn composition, make-up

租出 zūchū lease out

阻挡 zǔdǎng obstruct; keep, detain ◊ tackle SP

阻冻剂 zǔdòngjì antifreeze

组分 zǔfèn constituent, component

阻风门 zǔfēngmén choke MOT

祖父 zǔfù grandfather (paternal)

祖父母 zǔfùmǔ grandparents (paternal)

足够 zúgòu enough, sufficient, ample ◊ amply; 足够多了 zúgòu duō le that's plenty

祖国 zǔguó native country, homeland

组合 zǔhé combination ◊ group

组合成一体 zǔhéchéng yītǐ put together, assemble

组合装置 zǔhé zhuāngzhì system COMPUT

嘴 zuǐ mouth; spout

醉 zuì drunk

最 zuì most; 最漂亮 zuì piàoliàng the most beautiful; 最大 zuìdà the biggest; the eldest

罪 zuì crime

最初 zuìchū first; original; initial

嘴唇 zuǐchún lip

最底 zuìdǐ bottom ◊ minimum; lowest

最低工资 zuìdǐ gōngzī minimum wage

最顶 zuìdǐng top, uppermost

最多 zuìduō maximum; most ◊ at most

罪恶 zuì'è sin

罪犯 zuìfàn criminal; culprit; offender

最高 zuìgāo highest; topmost; tallest

最高档 zuì gāodàng top gear

最高级会议 zuì gāojí huìyì summit meeting

最高权威 zuìgāo quánwēi supremacy

最高限度 zuìgāo xiàndù ceiling, limit

最高一层 zuìgāo yīcéng top floor

最高音部 zuì gāoyīn bù treble MUS

醉鬼 zuìguǐ drunk

最好 zuìhǎo best; 你最好征得同意 nǐ zuìhào zhēngdé tóngyì you'd best ask permission

最后 zuìhòu last, final; ultimate ◊ finally, lastly; in the end; 最后关头 zuìhòu guāntóu at the eleventh hour; 作为最后一招 zuòwéi zuìhòu yīzhāo as a last resort

最后较量 zuìhòu jiàoliàng showdown

最后结果 zuìhòu jiéguǒ upshot

最后面 zuìhòumiàn the very back; bottom (of garden etc)

最后期限 zuìhòu qīxiàn deadline

最后通牒 zuìhòu tōngdié ultimatum

最坏 zuìhuài worst ◊ the worst

最佳 zuìjiā best, optimum

最近 zuìjìn recent; closest ◊ recently; the other day; in the near future; soon; 最近的公共汽车站 zuìjìnde gōnggòng qìchē zhàn the nearest bus stop; 最近在忙些什么? zuìjìn zài mángxiē shénme? what are you up to these days?

最酒会 zuìjiǔhuì cocktail party

最快速度 zuìkuài sùdù top speed

最轻微 zuì qīngwēi least, slightest

罪人 zuìrén sinner; offender

最少 zuìshǎo least; minimum

最深 zuìshēn innermost; deepest

最适宜 zuì shìyí optimum, most suitable

最小 zuìxiǎo least, smallest

最喜欢 zuì xǐhuan favorite; pet

最新 zuìxīn latest; newest; 最新版本 zuìxīn běnběn latest edition

罪行 zuìxíng crime; offense

最优良 zuì yōuliáng state-of-the-art

最优秀 **zuì yōuxiù** top (of class etc)

罪有应得 **zuì yǒu yīngdé** it serves you/him right

最远 **zuìyuǎn** furthest, farthest

最糟 **zuìzāo** worst

最终 **zuìzhōng** eventual; final, ultimate ◊ eventually; in due course; ultimately, finally

最终结果 **zuìzhōng jiéguǒ** end result

最重要 **zuì zhòngyào** most important, central, paramount ◊ above all

租金 **zūjīn** rent, rental

阻力 **zǔlì** resistance

祖母 **zǔmǔ** grandmother (paternal)

祖母绿 **zǔmǔlǜ** emerald green

尊 **zūn** respect

遵 **zūn** follow, abide by

遵从 **zūncóng** follow, comply with ◊ compliance

尊敬 **zūnjìng** respect ◊ honored, esteemed; 尊敬的先生 **zūnjìngde xiānshēng** Dear Sir

遵守 **zūnshǒu** abide by, comply with ◊ observance; 遵守规章 **zūnshǒu guīzhāng** conform, obey the rules

遵循 **zūnxún** follow, keep to

尊严 **zūnyán** dignity

鳟鱼 **zūnyú** trout

尊重 **zūnzhòng** respect; honor

昨 **zuó** yesterday

左 **zuǒ** left

坐 **zuò** sit; sit down; catch, get bus etc; go by car etc

作 **zuò** make, do; be

做 **zuò** do; make; perform, carry out; have operation; 为 X 做好事 **wèi X zuò hǎoshì** do X a good turn; 做吧！ **zuò ba!** go on, do it!

座 **zuò** seat ◊ stand, support ◊ measure word for mountains and buildings; 一座山 **yī zuò shān** a mountain

作伴 **zuòbàn** keep ... company

坐班房 **zuò bānfáng** be behind bars

作弊 **zuòbì** cheat; fix, rig

左边 **zuǒbian** left, left-hand side ◊ left-hand

左边驾驶车 **zuǒbian jiàshǐ chē** left-hand drive

座舱 **zuòcāng** cabin, cockpit

左侧 **zuǒcè** left ◊ to the left

坐车 **zuòchē** go by car; go by train

做出 **zuòchū** arrive at decision etc

坐船 **zuòchuán** go by boat

做出反应 **zuòchū fǎnyìng** respond, react

作出牺牲 **zuòchū xīshēng** make sacrifices

作饭 **zuòfàn** cook

作坊 **zuōfang** workshop

作翻译 **zuò fānyì** interpret; translate

作废 **zuòfèi** expire, become invalid

坐飞机 **zuò fēijī** travel by plane, fly

做工好 **zuògōnghǎo** well-made

作广告 **zuò guǎnggào** publicize; advertize

坐骨神经痛 **zuògǔ shénjīng tòng** sciatica

坐火车 **zuò huǒchē** go by train

作家 **zuòjiā** author, writer

作料 **zuóliào** seasoning

左轮手枪 **zuǒlún shǒuqiāng** revolver

坐落 **zuòluò** be situated

做梦 **zuòmèng** dream; 做梦也想不到 **zuòmèng yě xiǎng bú dào** undreamt-of

琢磨 **zuómó** ponder

作呕 **zuǒ'ǒu** feel nauseous; 令人作呕 **lìngrén zuò'ǒu** nauseating, disgusting

左派 **zuǒpài** the left POL

作品 **zuòpǐn** work (book, painting etc); production (play etc); composition MUS

作评委 **zuò píngwěi** judge competition

坐骑 **zuòqí** mount

坐起来 **zuòqǐlái** sit up (in bed)

作曲家 **zuòqǔ jiā** composer

左手 **zuǒshǒu** left-hand

做手势 **zuò shǒushì** gesticulate

昨天 **zuótiān** yesterday

昨天晚上 zuótiān wǎnshang last night

昨晚 zuówǎn last night

做完 zuòwán finish doing

作为 zuòwéi as; by way of; 作为常规 *zuòwéi chángguī* as a matter of course; 作为秘密 *zuòwéi mìmì* in confidence

座位 zuòwèi place, seat

作伪证 zuò wěizhèng perjury ◊ perjure oneself

作文 zuòwén composition, essay

坐卧两用床 zuòwò liǎngyòng chuáng couchette

坐下 zuòxia sit down

左舷 zuǒxián port(side) NAUT

作业 zuòyè job, task; homework, assignment

左翼 zuǒyì left-wing

作用 zuòyòng function

作用力 zuòyòng lì strain

座右铭 zuòyòumíng motto

作者 zuòzhě author, writer

作证 zuòzhèng testify, give evidence

坐直 zuòzhí sit up straight

做作 zuòzuo theatrical, exaggerated; artificial, insincere ◊ exaggerate

租契 zūqì lease

足球 zúqiú soccer

组曲 zǔqǔ suite MUS

阻塞 zǔsāi obstruct, block ◊ traffic jam

祖先 zǔxiān ancestor; ancestry

足音 zúyīn sound of footsteps

租用 zūyòng lease

租用车 zūyòng chē rental car

租约 zūyuē rental agreement

族长 zúzhǎng (tribal) chief

组织 zǔzhī organization ◊ organize, put together ◊ tissue ANAT

阻止 zǔzhǐ stop, prevent, block; 阻止 X 做 Y *zǔzhǐ X zuò Y* prevent X from doing Y

足智多谋 zúzhì duōmóu resourceful

组织者 zǔzhī zhě organizer

诅咒 zǔzhòu curse

组装 zǔzhuāng assemble, put together ◊ assembly

组装件 zǔzhuāngjiàn (assembly) kit

a, an ◊ (no translation): *a bus* gōnggòng qìchē 公共汽车; *I'm a student* wǒ shì xuésheng 我是学生 ◊ (with a measure word) yī ~; *can I have a cup of coffee?* qǐng gěi wǒ yìbēi kāfēi? 请给我一杯咖啡?; *five men and a woman* wǔge nánde yíge nǚde 五个男的一个女的 ◊ (per): *$50 a time* yícì wǔshí měiyuán 一次五十美元

abandon *object, person* pāoqì 抛弃; *car* líqì 离弃; *plan* fàngqì 放弃

abbreviate suōxiě 缩写

abbreviation suōxiě 缩写

abdicate v/i tuìwèi 退位

abdomen dùzi 肚子

abdominal fùbù 腹部

abduct jiéchí 劫持

◆abide by zūnshǒu 遵守

ability nénglì 能力

ablaze zháohuǒ 着火

able (skillful) yǒu nénglì 有能力; *be ~ to* nénggòu 能够; *I wasn't ~ to see / hear* wǒ dāngshí bùnéng kàn / tīng 我当时不能看 / 听

abnormal bú zhèngcháng 不正常

aboard 1 prep zài … shàng 在 … 上 2 adv: *be ~* (on ship) zài chuán shàng 在船上; (on plane) zài fēijī shàng 在飞机上; *go ~* (on ship) shàng chuán 上船; (on plane) shàng fēijī 上飞机

abolish fèichú 废除

abort v/t mission, rocket launch shǐ zhōngtú shībài 使中途失败; COMPUT program zhōngtú tuìchū 中途退出

abortion réngōng liúchǎn 人工流产; *have an ~* zuò rénliú 做人流

about 1 prep (concerning) … guānyú … 关于 …; *what's it ~?* (book, film) jiǎng shénmede? 讲什么的?; (complaint) shénme shì? 什么事? 2 adv (roughly) dàyuē 大约; ~ *50* dàyuē wǔshí 大约五十; *be ~ to …* zhèng zhǔnbèi … 正准备 …

above 1 prep (higher than) bǐ … gāo 比 … 高; (more than) bǐ … duō 比 … 多; ~ *all* zuì zhòngyào 最重要 2 adv zài shàngtóu 在上头; *on the floor ~* lóushàng 楼上

above-mentioned suǒshù 所述

abrasion mósǔn 磨损

abrasive personality cūbào 粗暴

abridge jīngjiǎn 精简

abroad live guówài 国外; *go ~* chūguó 出国

abrupt departure tūrán 突然; manner shēngyìng 生硬

abscess nóngzhǒng 脓肿

absence (of person) quēxí 缺席; (from school) kuàngkè 旷课; (from work) kuànggōng 旷工; (lack) quēfá 缺乏

absent adj quēxí 缺席; (from school) kuàngkè 旷课; (from work) kuànggōng 旷工

absent-minded xīnbù zàiyān 心不在焉

absolute power juéduì 绝对; idiot shízú 十足

absolutely (completely) wánquán 完全; ~ *not!* bù kěnéng! 不可能!; *do you agree?* – ~ nǐ tóngyì ma? – tóngyì 你同意吗?– 同意

absolve shèmiǎn 赦免

absorb xīshōu 吸收; ~*ed in …* quánshén guànzhùyú … 全神贯注于 …

absorbent yǒu xīshōu nénglì 有吸收能力

absorbent cotton tuōzhīmián 脱脂棉

abstain (from voting) qìquán 弃权

abstention (in voting) qìquán 弃权

abstract adj chōuxiàng 抽象

absurd huāngtáng 荒唐

**absurdity** huāngtáng 荒唐
**abundance** fēngfù 丰富
**abundant** fēngfù 丰富
**abuse**[1] *n* (*insults*) rǔmà 辱骂; (*of child*) nüèdài 虐待; (*of thing*) lànyòng 滥用
**abuse**[2] *v/t* (*physically*) nüèdài 虐待; (*verbally*) rǔmà 辱骂
**abusive**: *language* yǒu nüèdài xìng 有虐待性; *become* ~ kāishǐ chòumà 开始臭骂
**abysmal** (*very bad*) zāotòu 糟透
**abyss** shēnyuān 深渊
**academic 1** *n* xuézhě 学者 **2** *adj* xuéshù 学术; *person* hàoxué 好学; ~ *year* xuénián 学年
**academy** xuéyuàn 学院
**accelerate 1** *v/i* jiāsù 加速 **2** *v/t production* jiākuài 加快
**acceleration** (*of car*) jiāsù 加速
**accelerator** yóumén 油门
**accent** (*when speaking*) kǒuyīn 口音; (*emphasis*) zhòngyīn 重音
**accentuate** qiángdiào 强调
**accept 1** *v/t offer, suggestion, present* jiēshòu 接受; *behavior, conditions* rěnshòu 忍受 **2** *v/i* jiēshòu 接受
**acceptable** kěyǐ róngrěn 可以容忍
**acceptance** jiēshòu 接受
**access 1** *n* (*to a building*) rùkǒu 入口; (*to secrets*) jiējìn 接近; (*to one's children*) jiējìn de quánlì 接近的权利; *have* ~ *to computer* shǐyòng quán 使用权; *child* yǒu jiēchù quán 有接触权 **2** *v/t also* COMPUT shǐyòng 使用
**access code** COMPUT tōnglù mìmǎ 通路密码
**accessible** nénggòu jiējìn 能够接近
**accessory** (*for wearing*) yīshì fùjiàn 衣饰附件; COMPUT fùjiàn 附件; LAW bāngxiōng 帮凶
**access road** gōnglù zhīxiàn 公路支线
**access time** COMPUT shǐyòng shíjiān 使用时间
**accident** (*involving injury or death*) shìgù 事故; (*something not done on purpose*) bùxiǎoxīn 不小心; *by*

~ bùxiǎoxīn 不小心
**accidental** yìwài 意外
**acclimate, acclimatize** *v/t* shìyìng 适应
**accommodate** gěi ... tígòng zhùsuǒ 给 ... 提供住所; *special requirements* qiānjiù 迁就
**accommodations** zhùsuǒ 住所
**accompaniment** MUS bànzòu 伴奏
**accompany** péitóng 陪同; MUS bànzòu 伴奏
**accomplice** bāngxiōng 帮凶
**accomplish** *task* wánchéng 完成; *goal* dádào 达到
**accomplished** yǒu cáinéng 有才能
**accord**: *of one's own* ~ zìyuàn 自愿
**accordance**: *in* ~ *with* gēnjù 根据
**according**: ~ *to* gēnjù 根据
**accordingly** (*consequently*) yīncǐ 因此; (*appropriately*) fúhé 符合
**account** *n* (*financial*) zhàngmù 帐目; (*report, description*) xùshù 叙述; *give an* ~ *of* xùshù 叙述; *on no* ~ juébù 决不; *on* ~ *of* yīnwèi 因为; *take ... into* ~, *take* ... *of* ... kǎolǜ dào ... 考虑到 ...
♦ **account for** (*explain*) jiěshì 解释; (*make up, constitute*) gòngjì dá 共计达
**accountability** zérèn 责任
**accountable**: *be held* ~ fù zérèn 负责任
**accountant** kuàijì 会计
**accounting software** cáiwù ruǎnjiàn 财务软件
**accounts** zhàngmù 帐目
**accumulate** *v/t & v/i* lěijī 累积
**accuracy** zhǔnquè xìng 准确性
**accurate** zhǔnquè 准确
**accusation** zéguài 责怪; (*public*) qiānzé 谴责
**accuse** zhǐkòng 指控; (*publicly*) qiānzé 谴责; *he* ~*d me of lying* tā zhǐkòng wǒ sāhuǎng 他指控我撒谎; *be* ~*d of* ... LAW bèi kònggào ... 被控告 ...
**accused**: *the* ~ LAW bèigào 被告
**accustom**: *get* ~*ed to* zhújiàn

xíguàn 逐渐习惯; **be ~ed to** xíguàn 习惯

**ace** (*in cards*) ⇩ jiānr 尖儿; (*in tennis: shot*) fāqiú défēn 发球得分; (*pilot, designer etc*) dìyīliú 第一流

**ache** n & v/i tòng 痛

**achieve** huòdé chéngjiù 获得成就

**achievement** (*of ambition*) huòdé 获得; (*thing achieved*) chéngjiù 成就

**acid** n suān 酸

**acid rain** suānyǔ 酸雨

**acid test** fig guānjiàn de kǎoyàn 关键的考验

**acknowledge** chéngrèn 承认

**acknowledg(e)ment** rènkě 认可

**acoustics** yīnxiǎng 音响

**acquaint**: **be ~ed with** rènshi 认识

**acquaintance** (*person*) shúrén 熟人

**acquire** *skill, knowledge* huòdé 获得; *property* qǔdé 取得

**acquisitive** tānlán 贪婪

**acquit** LAW xuānpàn wúzuì 宣判无罪

**acre** yīngmǔ 英亩

**acrobat** zájì yǎnyuán 杂技演员

**acrobatics** zájì 杂技

**across 1** prep (*on other side of: of Atlantic etc*) zài … de lìngyībiān 在 … 的另一边; (*of the street, table etc*) zài … de duìmiàn 在 … 的对面; **the post office is ~ the road from the bank** yóujú zài yínháng de duìmiàn 邮局在银行的对面 ◊ (*to other side of: of Atlantic etc*) héngguò 横过; (*of street etc*) guò 过; **he walked ~ America** tā héngguò Měiguó 他横过美国 **2** adv (*to other side*) guòlái 过来; **10 yards ~** shí mǎ kuān 十码宽

**act 1** v/i THEA biǎoyǎn 表演; (*pretend*) jiǎzhuāng 假装; **~ as** línshí dānrèn 临时担任 **2** n (*deed*) xíngdòng 行动; (*of play*) mù 幕; (*in vaudeville*) jiémù 节目; (*pretense*) jiǎzhuāng 假装; (*law*) fǎguī 法规

**acting 1** n (*profession*) biǎoyǎn yè 表演业; (*performance*) biǎoyǎn 表演 **2** adj (*temporary*) dàilǐ 代理

**action** xíngdòng 行动; **out of ~** (*not functioning*) shīlíng 失灵; **take ~** cǎiqǔ xíngdòng 采取行动; **bring an ~ against** LAW qǐsù 起诉

**action replay** TV chóngfù 重复

**active** huóyuè 活跃; *party member* jījí 积极; GRAM zhǔdòng 主动

**activist** POL jījí fènzi 积极分子

**activity** huódòng 活动

**actor** yǎnyuán 演员

**actress** nǚyǎnyuán 女演员

**actual** shíjì 实际

**actually** (*in fact, to tell the truth*) shíjì shàng 实际上; (*surprise*) zhēnde 真的; **~ I do know him** (*stressing converse*) shíjìshàng wǒ rènshì tā de 实际上我认识他的

**acupuncture** zhēnjiǔ 针灸

**acute** *pain* jùliè 剧烈; *sense* mǐngǎn 敏感

**ad** guǎnggào 广告

**adapt 1** v/t (*for TV, movies*) gǎibiān 改编; *machine* gǎiyòng 改用 **2** v/i (*of person*) shìyìng 适应

**adaptable** *person, plant* yǒu shìyìng lì 有适应力; *vehicle etc* kě gǎiyòng 可改用

**adaptation** (*of play etc*) gǎibiān 改编

**adapter** (*electric*) jiēhé qì 接合器

**add 1** v/t MATH, *sugar, salt etc* jiā 加; (*say, comment*) shuō 说 **2** v/i (*of person*) suàn suànshù 算算术

◆**add on** 15% etc jiāshàng 加上

◆**add up 1** v/t jiāqǐlái 加起来 **2** v/i fig hélǐ 合理

**addict** n chéngyǐn zhě 成瘾者

**addicted**: **be ~ to X** yǒu X de yǐn 有X的瘾

**addiction** (*to drugs*) yǐn 瘾; (*to TV, chocolate etc*) chénnì 沉溺

**addictive**: **be ~** (*of drugs, TV, chocolate etc*) chéngyǐn 成瘾

**addition** MATH jiāfǎ 加法; (*to list, company etc*) bǔchōng 补充; **in ~** lìngwài 另外; **in ~ to X** chúle X zhīwài 除了X之外

additional fùjiā 附加

additive tiānjiā jì 添加剂

add-on fùjiàn 附件

address 1 n dìzhǐ 地址; **form of ~** chēnghu 称呼 2 v/t letter xiě dìzhǐ 写地址; audience jiǎnghuà 讲话; person chēnghu 称呼

address book tōngxùn lù 通讯录

addressee shōuxìn rén 收信人

adequate chōngfèn 充分; (satisfactory) jǐn gòu mǎnyì 仅够满意

adhere jiānchí 坚持

♦ adhere to surface niánfù 粘附; rules zūnshǒu 遵守

adhesive yǒu niánxìng 有粘性

adhesive plaster ⬇ chuàngkětiē 创可贴

adhesive tape jiāobù 胶布

adjacent línjìn 邻近

adjective xíngróngcí 形容词

adjoining gébì 隔壁

adjourn v/i (of court) zànxiū 暂休; (of meeting) xiūhuì 休会

adjust v/t tiáozhěng 调整

adjustable kě tiáozhěng 可调整

administer medicine gěi 给; company guǎnlǐ 管理; country zhìlǐ 治理

administration xíngzhèng 行政; (of company) guǎnlǐ 管理; (of country) zhìlǐ 治理; (government) zhèngfǔ 政府

administrative xíngzhèng 行政

administrator guǎnlǐ rényuán 管理人员

admirable lìngrén qīnpèi 令人钦佩

admiral hǎijūn shàngjiàng 海军上将

admiration qīnpèi 钦佩

admire qīnpèi 钦佩

admirer chóngbài zhě 崇拜者

admissible kě yǔnxǔ 可允许

admission (confession) chéngrèn 承认; **~ free** miǎnfèi rùchǎng 免费入场

admit (to a hospital, organization, school) jiēnà 接纳; (confess) chéngrèn 承认; (accept) jiēshòu 接受

admittance: **no ~** jìnzhǐ rùnèi 禁止入内

adolescence qīngchūn qī 青春期

adolescent 1 n qīngshàonián 青少年 2 adj qīngchūn qī 青春期

adopt child lǐngyǎng 领养; plan cǎinà 采纳

adoption (of child) lǐngyǎng 领养; (of plan) cǎinà 采纳

adorable kě'ài 可爱

adore hěn xǐhuān 很喜欢

adult 1 n chéngrén 成人 2 adj chéngrén 成人; **~ film** chéngrén piàn 成人片

adultery sītōng 私通

advance 1 n (money) tòuzhī 透支; (in science etc) xiānjìn 先进; MIL jìngōng 进攻; **in ~** yùfù 预付; (of time) tíqián 提前; (get money) yùzhī 预支; **make ~s** (progress) jìnbù 进步; (sexually) xiàn yīnqín 献殷勤 2 v/i MIL jìngōng 进攻; (make progress) jìnbù 进步 3 v/t theory tíchū 提出; sum of money yùfù 预付; human knowledge, a cause cùjìn 促进

advance booking yùyuē 预约

advanced country xiānjìn 先进; level gāoděng 高等; learner gāojí 高级

advance payment yùfù 预付

advantage hǎochù 好处; **it's to your ~** duì nǐ yǒu hǎochù 对你有好处; **take ~ of** opportunity lìyòng 利用

advantageous yǒulì 有利

adventure màoxiǎn 冒险

adventurous person xǐhuān màoxiǎn 喜欢冒险; investment, policy yǒu fēngxiǎn 有风险

adverb fùcí 副词

adversary duìshǒu 对手

advertise v/t & v/i dēng guǎnggào 登广告

advertisement guǎnggào 广告

advertiser dēng guǎnggào zhě 登广告者

advertising xuānyáng 宣扬; (industry) guǎnggào yè 广告业

advertising agency guǎnggào gōngsī 广告公司

**advice** zīxún 咨询; *take X's* ~ jiēshòu X de yìjiàn 接受X的意见

**advisable** kěqǔ 可取

**advise** *person* quàngào 劝告; *caution etc* zhōnggào 忠告; ~ *X to* ... jiànyì X zuò ... 建议X做 ...

**adviser** gùwèn 顾问

**aerial** tiānxiàn 天线

**aerial photography** hángkōngshèyǐng 航空摄影

**aerobics** ⇩zēng yǎng jiànshēn fǎ 增氧健身法

**aerodynamic** kōngqì dònglì 空气动力

**aeronautical** hángkōng 航空

**aerosol** pēnmò 喷沫

**aerospace industry** yǔháng gōngyè 宇航工业

**affair** *(matter)* shì 事; *(business)* shìwù 事务; *(love)* liàn'ài 恋爱; *foreign ~s* wàijiāo shìwù 外交事务; *have an ~ with* yǔ ... tōngjiān 与 ... 通奸

**affect** *(influence, concern)* yǐngxiǎng 影响; MED qīnxí 侵袭

**affection** àimù 爱慕

**affectionate** yǒu àimù xīn 有爱慕心

**affinity** qīnjìn 亲近

**affirmative**: *answer in the* ~ rènkě de huídá 认可的回答

**affluent** fùyù 富裕; ~ *society* fánróng de shèhuì 繁荣的社会

**afford** *(financially)* fùdān de qǐ 负担得起

**Afghan 1** *adj* Āfùhàn 阿富汗 **2** *n (person)* Āfùhàn rén 阿富汗人

**Afghanistan** Āfùhàn 阿富汗

**afloat** *boat* piāofú 漂浮

**afraid**: *be* ~ hàipà 害怕; *be* ~ *of* hàipà 害怕; *of upsetting s.o. etc* dānxīn 担心; *I'm* ~ *(expressing regret)* kǒngpà 恐怕; *I'm* ~ *so* fēicháng bàoqiàn, zhēnshì zhēnde 非常抱歉，这是真的; *I'm* ~ *not* fēicháng bàoqiàn, bùshì zhèyàng 非常抱歉，不是这样

**Africa** Fēizhōu 非洲

**African 1** *adj* Fēizhōu 非洲 **2** *n* Fēizhōu rén 非洲人

**after 1** *prep (in order, position, time)* zhīhòu 之后; ~ *all* bìjìng 毕竟; ~ *that* zài nà zhīhòu 在那之后; *it's ten* ~ *two* liǎngdiǎn shífēn 两点十分 **2** *adv (afterward)* hòulái 后来; *the day* ~ dì'èrtiān 第二天

**afternoon** xiàwǔ 下午; *in the* ~ zài xiàwǔ 在下午; *this* ~ jīntiān xiàwǔ 今天下午; *good* ~ ⇩xiàwǔ hǎo 下午好

**after sales service** shòuhòu fúwù 售后服务

**aftershave** nánshì hùfū yè 男士护肤液

**aftertaste** yúwèir 余味儿

**afterward** hòulái 后来

**again** zài 再

**against** *lean* kào kào 靠; *X* – *Y* SP X duì Y X对Y; *I'm* – *the idea* zhège zhǔyì wǒ fǎn duì 这个主意我反对; *what do you have* – *her?* nǐ duì tā yǒu shénme yìjiàn? 你对她有什么意见？; ~ *the law* wéifǎ 违法

**age 1** *n (of person, object)* niánjì 年纪; *(era)* shídài 时代; *at the* ~ *of* niánlíng wéi 年龄为; *under* ~ wèidào fǎdìng niánlíng 未到法定年龄; *she's five years of* ~ tā wǔsuì le 她五岁了 **2** *v/i* biànlǎo 变老

**agency** dàilǐ chù 代理处

**agenda** yìchéng 议程; *on the* ~ zài yìchéng shàng 在议程上

**agent** dàilǐ rén 代理人

**aggravate** *(worsen)* shǐ èhuà 使恶化

**aggression** qīnfàn xíngwéi 侵犯行为

**aggressive** hào xúnxìn 好寻衅; *(dynamic)* jījí 积极

**agile** línghuó 灵活

**agitated** jiāolù bù'ān 焦虑不安

**agitation** jiāolù 焦虑

**agitator** shàndòng zhě 煽动者

**ago**: *2 days* ~ liǎngtiān qián 两天前; *long* ~ hěnjiǔ yǐqián 很久以前; *how long* ~? duōjiǔ zhīqián? 多久之前？

**agonizing** nánshòu 难受

**agony** jídù tòngkǔ 极度痛苦

**agree 1** *v/i (of people, figures, accounts)* tóngyì 同意; *I* ~ wǒ tóngyì 我同意; **I don't ~** wǒ bù tóngyì 我不同意; **it doesn't ~ with me** (of food) bú shìhé wǒ 不适合我 2 v/t price shāngdìng 商定; **~ that something should be done** zànchéng yīnggāi cǎiqǔ xíngdòng 赞成应该采取行动

**agreeable** (pleasant) lìngrén yúkuài 令人愉快; (in agreement) zànchéng 赞成

**agreement** (consent) tóngyì 同意; (contract) xiéyì 协议; **reach ~ on** dáchéng xiéyì 达成协议

**agricultural** nóngyè 农业

**agriculture** nóngyè 农业

**ahead: be ~ of** lǐngxiān 领先; **plan / think ~** yùxiān jìhuà / kǎolǜ 预先计划 / 考虑

**aid** n & v/t yuánzhù 援助

**Aids** àizībìng 艾滋病

**ailing** economy xiāotiáo 萧条

**aim** 1 n (in shooting) miáozhǔn 瞄准; (objective) mùbiāo 目标 2 v/i (in shooting) miáozhǔn 瞄准; **~ at doing X, ~ to do X** zhìlìyú zuò X 致力于做 X 3 v/t: **be ~ed at** (of remark etc) zhēnduì 针对; (of guns) miáozhǔn 瞄准

**air** 1 n kōngqì 空气; **by ~ travel** zuò fēijī 坐飞机; send mail hángkōng 航空; **in the open** ~ zài shìwài 在室外; **on the ~** RAD, TV bōsòng 播送 2 v/t room shǐ tōngfēng 使通风; fig: views fābiǎo 发表

**airbase** kōngjūn jīdì 空军基地; **air-conditioned** yǒu kōngtiáo 有空调; **air-conditioning** ⇩ kōngtiáo 空调; **aircraft** fēijī 飞机; **aircraft carrier** hángkōng mǔjiàn 航空母舰; **air cylinder** shuǐfèi 水肺; **airfield** jīchǎng 机场; **air force** kōngjūn 空军; **air hostess** kōngjiě 空姐; **air letter** hángkōng xìnjiàn 航空信件; **airline** hángkōng gōngsī 航空公司; **airmail: by ~** jì hángkōng 寄航空; **airplane** fēijī 飞机; **air pollution** kōngqì wūrǎn 空气污染; **airport** jīchǎng 机场; **airsick: get ~** yǒu kōngyùnbìng 有空晕病; **airspace** kōngyù 空域; **air**

**terminal** jīchǎng zhōngduān 机场终端; airtight container mìfēng 密封; **air traffic** kōngzhōng jiāotōng 空中交通; **air-traffic control** kōngzhōng jiāotōng kòngzhì 空中交通控制; **air-traffic controller** kōngzhōng jiāotōng kòngzhì rényuán 空中交通控制人员

**airy** room tōngfēng 通风; attitude kōngxiǎng 空想

**aisle** tōngdào 通道

**aisle seat** kào tōngdào zuòwèi 靠通道座位

**alarm** 1 n jīngzhōng 警钟; **raise the ~** bàojǐng 报警 2 v/t shǐ kǒnghuāng 使恐慌

**alarm clock** nàozhōng 闹钟

**Albania** Ā'ěrbāníyà 阿尔巴尼亚

**Albanian** 1 adj Ā'ěrbāníyà 阿尔巴尼亚 2 n (person) Ā'ěrbāníyà rén 阿尔巴尼亚人; (language) Ā'ěrbāníyà yǔ 阿尔巴尼亚语

**album** (for photographs) yǐngjí 影集; (record) chàngpiān 唱片

**alcohol** jiǔ 酒

**alcoholic** 1 n xùjiǔ zhě 酗酒者 2 adj hán jiǔjīng 含酒精

**alert** 1 n (signal) jǐngbào 警报; **be on the ~** chùyú jièbèi zhuàngtài 处于戒备状态 2 v/t shǐ jǐngjué 使警觉 3 adj liúxīn 留心

**alibi** n búzài fànzuì xiànchǎng de shēnbiàn 不在犯罪现场的申辩

**alien** 1 n (foreigner) wàiguó rén 外国人; (from space) wàixīng rén 外星人 2 adj mòshēng 陌生; **be ~ to X** (not in keeping with a person's character) yǔ X běnxìng bùfú 与 X 本性不符

**alienate** shūyuǎn 疏远

**alight** adj zháohuǒ 着火

**alike** 1 adj: **be ~** xiāngsì 相似 2 adv xiāngsì 相似; **old and young ~** lǎoshào yīyàng 老少一样

**alimony** shànyǎng fèi 赡养费

**alive: be ~** huózhe 活着

**all** 1 adj dōu 都: **we ~ agree** wǒmen dōu tóngyì 我们都同意; **~ Chinese cities** Zhōngguó suǒyǒude chéngshì 中国所有的城市 2 pron: ~ of us/them wǒ/tāmen dōu 我/他们都; he ate ~ of it tā dōu chī le 他都吃了; that's ~, thanks jiù zhèixiē, xièxie 就这 些, 谢谢; for ~ I care wǒ cái bùguǎn ne 我才不管呢; for ~ I know jù wǒ suǒzhī jùzhè wǒ suǒzhī 据我所知; ~ at once yíxiàzi 一下子; ~ but (nearly) jīhū 几乎; ~ the better gènghǎole 更好了; ~ the time yìzhí 一直; they're not at ~ alike tāmen gēnběn búxiàng 他们根本 不像; not at ~! yìdiǎnr yě bù! 一 点儿也不! two ~ (in score) èrpíng 二平

allegation zhǐkòng 指控
alleged culprit yǒu xiányí 有嫌疑; reason suǒwèi 所谓
allergic: be ~ to ... duì ... guòmǐn 对 ... 过敏
allergy guòmǐn 过敏
alleviate jiǎnqīng 减轻
alley hútòng 胡同
alliance tóngméng 同盟
alligator dùnwěnè 钝吻鳄
allocate ānpái 安排
allot fēnpèi 分配
allow (permit) yǔnxǔ 允许; (calculate for) jìsuàn 计算; it's not ~ed bùxíng 不行; ~ X to ... yǔnxǔ X ... 允许 X ...
◆ allow for kǎolǜ dào 考虑到
allowance (money) jīntiē 津贴; (pocket money) língyòng qián 零 用钱; make ~s (for thing, weather etc) kǎolǜ dào 考虑到; (for person) yuánliàng 原谅
alloy héjīn 合金
all-purpose duō yòngtú 多用途; all-round quánmiàn 全面; all-time: be at an ~ low kōngqián wèiyǒu de dī 空前未有的低
◆ allude to yǐngshè 影射
alluring yòuhuò 诱惑
all-wheel drive sìlún qūdòng 四轮 驱动
ally n tóngméng zhě 同盟者
almond xìngrén 杏仁
almost jīhū 几乎
alone dāndú 单独

along 1 prep: walk ~ this path yánzhe zhètiáo xiǎolù zǒu 沿着 这条小路走 2 adv yìqǐ 一起; ~ with hé 和; all ~ (all the time) yìzhí 一直
aloud chūshēngdi 出声地
alphabet zìmǔ biǎo 字母表
alphabetical order yī zìmǔ shùnxù 依字母顺序
already yǐjīng 已经
alright: that's ~ (doesn't matter) méi guānxi 没关系; (when somebody says thank you) búxiè 不谢; (is quite good) búcuò 不错; I'm ~ (not hurt) wǒ méi shìr 我没事儿; (have got enough) gòule 够了; ~, that's enough! déle 得了; can I? – ~ kěyǐ ma? – kěyǐ 可以吗? – 可以
also yě 也
altar shèngtán 圣坛
alter v/t gǎibiàn 改变
alteration gēnggǎi 更改
alternate 1 v/i jiāotì 交替 2 adj měigé 每隔
alternating current jiāoliúdiàn 交 流电
alternative 1 n xuǎnzé 选择 2 adj lìngyī kě xuǎnzé 另一可选择; lifestyle, music etc bùtóng zhǒng 不 同种
alternatively huòzhě 或者
although jǐnguǎn 尽管
altitude (of plane) gāodù 高度; (of mountain, city) hǎibá 海拔
alt key COMPUT Alt jiàn Alt 键
altogether (completely) wánquán 完全; (in all) yīgòng 一共
altruistic lìrén 利人
aluminum lǚ 铝
always zǒngshì 总是; it's ~ raining here zhèr zǒngshì xià yǔ 这儿总 是下雨
a.m. (in the morning) zǎochén 早晨
amalgamate v/i (of companies) hébìng 合并
amateur n (unskilled) yèyú àihào zhě 业余爱好者; SP yèyú 业余
amaze shǐ dàwéi chījīng 使大为 吃惊
amazement jīngqí 惊奇

**amazing** (*surprising*) jīngrén 惊人; (*very good*) měizhìle 没治了

**ambassador** dàshǐ 大使

**amber: at ~** huáng 黄

**ambiguous** hánhú 含糊

**ambition** zhìxiàng 志向; *pej* yěxīn 野心

**ambitious** yǒu zhìxiàng 有志向; *plan* xióngxīn bóbó dàncái 勃勃

**ambulance** jiùhùchē 救护车

**ambush 1** *n* fújí 伏击 **2** *v/t* máifú 埋伏

**amend** gǎizhèng 改正

**amendment** xiūgǎi 修改

**amends: make ~** bǔguò 补过

**amenities** biànlì shèshī 便利设施

**America** Měiguó 美国

**American 1** *adj* Měiguó 美国 **2** *n* Měiguó rén 美国人

**amiable** hé'ǎi kěqīn 和蔼可亲

**amicable** yǒushàn 友善

**ammunition** jūnhuǒ 军火; *fig* jìngzhēng shǒuduàn 进攻手段

**amnesty** *n* shèmiǎn 赦免

**among(st)** zài … zhīzhōng 在 … 之中

**amount** shùliàng 数量; (*sum of money*) jīn'é 金额

**♦ amount to** děngyú 等于

**ample** chōngzú 充足

**amplifier** fàngdàqì 放大器

**amplify** *sound* fàngdà 放大

**amputate** jiézhī 节肢

**amuse** (*make laugh etc*) dòuxiào 逗笑; (*entertain*) gěi … tígōng yúlè 给 … 提供娱乐

**amusement** (*merriment*) lèqù 乐趣; (*entertainment*) yúlè 娱乐; **~s** (*games*) yúlè huódòng 娱乐活动; *to our great* ~ lìng wǒmen hěn gāoxìng 令我们很高兴

**amusement arcade** yúlè zhōngxīn 娱乐中心

**amusement park** yúlè yuán 娱乐园

**amusing** yǒuqù 有趣

**anabolic steroid** héchéng dàixiè jīsù 合成代谢激素

**Analects of Confucius** Lúnyǔ 论语

**analog** COMPUT móní 模拟

**analogy** bǐyù 比喻

**analysis** fēnxī 分析; (*psychoanalysis*) jīngshén fēnxī 精神分析

**analyze** fēnxī 分析

**anarchy** wúzhèngfǔ zhuàngtài 无政府状态

**anatomy** jiěpōu 解剖

**ancestor** zǔxiān 祖先

**anchor** NAUT **1** *n* máo 锚 **2** *v/i* pāomáo 抛锚

**anchor man** TV xīnwén guǎngbō yuán 新闻广播员

**ancient** *adj* gǔlǎo 古老

**and** ◊ (*joining nouns*) hé 和; *you ~ me* nǐ hé wǒ hé wǒ 你和我 ◊ (*joining adjectives*) yòu … yòu … 又 … 又 …; *tall ~ thin* yòu gāo yòu shòu 又高又瘦 ◊ (*then*) ránhòu 然后; *he checked in ~ went to his room* tā dēngle jì ránhòu qùle tāde fángjiān 他登了记然后去了他的房间 ◊ (*two actions at the same time*) biān … biān … 边 … 边 …; *she was laughing ~ crying* tā yībiān xiào yībiān kū 她一边笑一边哭; *they were eating ~ drinking* tāmen biān chī biān hē 他们边吃边喝 ◊ (*when listing things, not translated*): *two beers ~ a coffee* liǎngge píjiǔ yíge kāfēi 两个啤酒一个咖啡 ◊: *faster ~ faster* yuèláiyuè kuài 越来越快

**anemia** pínxuè 贫血

**anemic: be ~** pínxuè 贫血

**anesthetic** *n* mázuì 麻醉

**anesthetist** mázuì shī 麻醉师

**anger 1** *n* fènnù 愤怒 **2** *v/t* shǐ fènnù 使愤怒

**angina** yānxiá yán 咽峡炎

**angle** *n* jiǎodù 角度

**angry** fènnù 愤怒; *be ~ with X* duì X shēngqì 对X生气

**anguish** jídù tòngkǔ 极度痛苦

**animal** dòngwù 动物

**animated** huópo 活泼

**animated cartoon** dònghuà piān 动画片

**animation** (*liveliness*) huópo 活泼; (*cinematic*) dònghuà piān shèzhì 动画片摄制

animosity díyì 敌意

ankle ⇩jiǎowàn 脚腕

annex 1 n (building) kuòjiàn bùfèn 扩建部分 2 v/t state tūnbìng 吞并

anniversary (wedding ~) zhōunián 周年

announce xuānbù 宣布

announcement xuāngào 宣告

announcer TV, RAD bōyīn yuán 播音员

annoy shǐ fánnǎo 使烦恼; be ~ed shēngqì 生气

annoyance (anger) fán fán 烦; (sth annoying) fánnǎo 烦恼

annoying nǎorén 恼人

annual adj (once a year) nián 年; (of a year) niándù 年度

annul marriage shǐ wúxiào 使无效

anonymous nìmíng 匿名

anorexia yànshí zhèng 厌食症

anorexic: be ~ yànshí 厌食

another adj & pron (different) lìng yígè 另一个; (additional) yòu yígè 又一个; (referring to something that hasn't yet happened) zài yígè 再一个; can I have ~ … ? wǒ kěyǐ zài lái yígè … ma? 我可以再来一个 … 吗?; one ~ hùxiāng 互相

answer 1 n (to letter, person) dáfù 答复; (to problem, question) dá'àn 答案 2 v/t letter, person dáfù 答复; question huídá 回答; ~ the door kāimén 开门; ~ the telephone tīng diànhuà 听电话

♦ answer back 1 v/t person huízuǐ 回嘴 2 v/i huízuǐ 回嘴

♦ answer for fùzé 负责

answerphone ⇩lùyīn diànhuà 录音电话

ant mǎyǐ 蚂蚁

antagonism díyì 敌意

Antarctic Nánjí 南极

antenatal chǎnqián 产前

antenna (of insect) chùjiǎo 触角; (for TV) tiānxiàn 天线

antibiotic n kàngjūnsù 抗菌素

antibody kàngtǐ 抗体

anticipate yùliào 预料

anticipation yùliào 预料

antidote jiědúyào 解毒药

antifreeze zǔdòngjì 阻冻剂

Anti-Japanese War Kàng Rì Zhànzhēng 抗日战争

antipathy fǎngǎn 反感

antiquated chénjiù 陈旧

antique n gǔdǒng 古董

antique dealer gǔdǒng shāng 古董商

Anti-rightists Campaign Fǎnyòu Yùndòng 反右运动

antiseptic 1 adj kàngjūn 抗菌 2 n kàngjūnjì 抗菌剂

antisocial bù héqún 不和群

antivirus program COMPUT kàng bìngdú chéngxù 抗病毒程序

anxiety jiāojí 焦急

anxious jiāojí 焦急; (eager) rèxīn 热心; be ~ for … (for news etc) jiāojí děngdài … 焦急等待 …

any 1 adj: are there ~ diskettes / glasses? yǒuméiyǒu cípán / bēizi? 有没有磁盘 / 杯子?; is there ~ bread / improvement? yǒuméiyǒu miànbāo / jìnbù? 有没有面包 / 进步?; there aren't ~ diskettes / glasses méiyǒu cípán / bēizi méiyǒu 杯子没有磁盘 / 杯子; there isn't ~ bread / improvement méiyǒu miànbāo / jìnbù 没有面包 / 进步; have you ~ idea at all? nǐ dàodǐ míng bù míngbái? 你到底明不明白? 你到底; take ~ one you like suí nǐ ná nǎyígè 随你拿哪一个 2 pron: do you have ~? nǐ yǒu méiyǒu? 你有没有?; there isn't / aren't ~ left méi shèng de le 没剩的了; ~ of them could be guilty tāmen zhīzhōng rèn yīgè dōu kěnéng yǒuzuì 他们之中任一个都可能有罪 3 adv: is that ~ better / easier? hǎo / róngyì diǎnr le ma? 好 / 容易点儿了吗?; I don't like it ~ more wǒ bù xǐhuānle 我不喜欢了

anybody (emphatic) rènhé rén 任何人; ~ can do that rènhé rén dōu kěyǐ zuò 任何人都可以做 ◊ (with negatives): there wasn't ~ there méirén zài nàr 没人在那儿 ◊ (in questions, conditionals) shéi; *if ~ can help* rúguǒ shéi néng bāngmáng 如果谁能帮忙

**anyhow** (*summarizing*) zǒngzhī 总之; (*in any way*) wúlùn yòng hézhǒng fāngfǎ 无论用何种方法; (*at least*) zhìshǎo 至少

**anyone** → **anybody**

**anything** shénme 什么; *I didn't hear* ~ wǒ méi tīngjiàn shénme 我没听见什么; ~ *but* yìdiǎnr yě bù 一点儿也不; ~ *else?* háiyǒu shénme? 还有什么？

**anyway** → **anyhow**

**anywhere** wúlùn nǎli 无论哪里; *I can't find it* ~ wǒ nǎr dōu zhǎobùzháo 我哪儿都找不着

**apart** (*in distance*) jùlí 距离; ~ *live* ~ (*of people*) fēnjū 分居; ~ *from* (*excepting*) chúle 除了; (*in addition to*) cǐwài 此外

**apartment** gōngyù 公寓

**apartment block** gōngyù dàshà 公寓大厦

**apathetic** lěngmò 冷漠

**ape** n xīngxing 猩猩

**aperture** PHOT guāngquān 光圈

**apologize** dàoqiàn 道歉

**apology** dàoqiàn 道歉

**apostrophe** GRAM piěhào 撇号

**appall** 1 v/t shǐ zhènjīng 使震惊

**appalling** lìngrén zhènjīng 令人震惊; *language* cūlǔ 粗鲁

**apparatus** qìxiè 器械

**apparent** míngxiǎn 明显; *become* ~ *that ...* kāishǐ biànde míngxiǎn ... 开始变得明显

**apparently** hǎoxiàng 好象

**appeal** 1 n (*charm*) xīyǐn lì 吸引力; (*for funds etc*) hūyù 呼吁; LAW shàngsù 上诉 2 v/i LAW shàngsù 上诉

♦**appeal for** kěnqiè qǐngqiú 恳切请求

♦**appeal to** (*be attractive to*) duì ... yǒu xīyǐnlì 对 ... 有吸引力

**appear** chūxiàn 出现; (*in film etc*) dēngchǎng 登场; (*of new product*) chūxiàn 出现; (*look, seem*) xiǎnde 显得; *it* ~*s that ...* kànlái ... 看来 ...

**appearance** (*arrival*) dàolái 到来; (*in film etc*) dēngchǎng 登场; (*in court*) chūtíng 出庭; (*look*) wàibiǎo 外表; *put in an* ~ lòumiàn 露面

**appendicitis** lánwěiyán 阑尾炎

**appendix** MED lánwěi 阑尾; (*of book etc*) fùlù 附录

**appetite** wèikǒu 胃口; *fig* yùwàng 欲望

**appetizer** (*food*) kāiwèi pǐn 开胃品; (*drink*) kāiwèi jiǔ 开胃酒

**appetizing** kāiwèi 开胃

**applaud** 1 v/i gǔzhǎng 鼓掌 2 v/t hècǎi 喝采; *fig* zànxǔ 赞许

**applause** gǔzhǎng 鼓掌; (*praise*) zànyáng 赞扬

**apple** píngguǒ 苹果

**apple pie** píngguǒ pài 苹果派

**apple sauce** píngguǒ zhīr 苹果汁儿

**appliance** qìxiè 器械; (*household*) jiāyòng qìxiè 家用器械

**applicable** *ruling* shìyòng 适用

**applicant** shēnqǐng zhě 申请者

**application** (*for job, passport, visa, university etc*) shēnqǐng 申请

**application form** (*for passport, visa, university*) shēnqǐng biǎogé 申请表格

**apply** 1 v/t shǐyòng 使用; *ointment* cāyòng 搽用 2 v/i (*of rule, law*) shìyòng 适用

♦**apply for** *job, passport, university* shēnqǐng 申请

♦**apply to** (*contact*) xiàng ... shēnqǐng 向 ... 申请; (*affect*) guānxì dào 关系到

**appoint** (*to position*) rènmìng 任命

**appointment** (*to position*) rènmìng 任命; (*meeting*) yuēhuì 约会

**appointments diary** yuēhuì rìjìběn 约会日记本

**appreciate** 1 v/t (*value*) xīnshǎng 欣赏; (*be grateful for*) gǎnjī 感激; (*acknowledge*) yìshí dào 意识到; *thanks, I* ~ *it* fēicháng gǎnxiè 非常感谢 2 v/i FIN tígāo jiàzhí 提高价值

**appreciation** (*of kindness etc*) gǎnjī 感激; (*of music etc*) xīnshǎng 欣赏

apprehensive dānxīn 担心

apprentice xuétú 学徒

approach **1** n línjìn 临近; (offer, proposal) tíyì 提议; (to problem) fāngshì 方式 **2** v/t (get near to) línjìn 临近; (contact) liánxì 联系; problem chǔlǐ 处理

approachable person píngyì jìnrén 平易近人

appropriate adj qiàdàng 恰当

approval tóngyì 同意

approve **1** v/i zànchéng 赞成 **2** v/t pīzhǔn 批准
♦approve of rèntóng 认同

approximate adj dàyuē 大约

approximately dàyuē 大约

APR (= annual percentage rate) niánlǜ 年率

apricot xìng 杏

April sìyuè 四月

apt pupil línglì 伶俐; remark qiàrú qífēn 恰如其分; be ~ to ... yìyù ... 易于 ...

aptitude tiānzī 天资

aquarium (large) shuǐzú guǎn 水族馆; (small, at home) yǎngyúgāng 养鱼缸

aquatic (water-dwelling) shuǐqī 水栖; sports (in water) shuǐzhōng 水中; (on water) shuǐshàng 水上; (under water) shuǐxià 水下

Arab **1** adj Ālābó 阿拉伯 **2** n Ālābó rén 阿拉伯人

Arabic **1** adj Ālābó 阿拉伯 **2** n Ālābó yǔ 阿拉伯语

arable gēngzhòng 耕种

arbitrary rènyì 任意; remark suíbiàn 随便; attack wú jìhuà xìng 无计划性

arbitrate v/i (in public affair) zhòngcái 仲裁; (in private) tiáotíng 调停

arbitration (in public affair) zhòngcái 仲裁; (in private) tiáotíng 调停

arch n gǒng 拱

archeologist kǎogǔ xué jiā 考古学家

archeology kǎogǔ xué 考古学

archer gōngjiàn shǒu 弓箭手

architect jiànzhù shī 建筑师

architecture jiànzhù xué 建筑学

archives dǎng'àn 档案

archway gǒngmén 拱门

Arctic Běijí 北极

ardent qiánchéng 虔诚

area (region) dìqū 地区; (of activity, job, study etc) fànwéi 范围; (square metres etc) miànjī 面积

area code TELEC qūhào 区号

arena SP bǐsài chǎng 比赛场

Argentina Āgēntíng 阿根廷

Argentinian **1** adj Āgēntíng 阿根廷 **2** n Āgēntíng rén 阿根廷人

arguably kě zhēnglùn 可争论

argue **1** v/i (quarrel) chǎojià 吵架; (reason) zhēnglùn 争论 **2** v/t: ~ that jiānchí 坚持

argument (quarrel) chǎojià 吵架; (reasoning) zhēnglùn 争论

argumentative ài chǎojià 爱吵架

arid land píngjí 贫瘠

arise (of situation, problem) chéngxiàn 呈现

arithmetic suànshù 算术

arm[1] n (of person) shǒubì 手臂; (of chair) fúshǒu 扶手

arm[2] v/t wǔzhuāng 武装

armaments wǔqì 武器

armchair fúshǒu yǐ 扶手椅

armed wǔzhuāng 武装

armed forces wǔzhuāng lìliàng 武装力量

armed robbery chíxiè qiǎngjié 持械抢劫

armor hùjiǎ 护甲

armored vehicle zhuāngjiǎ chē 装甲车

armpit yèwō 腋窝

arms (weapons) wǔqì 武器

army jūnduì 军队

aroma xiāngwèir 香味儿

around **1** prep (in circle) wéirǎo 围绕; (approximately) dàyuē 大约; it's ~ the corner zài guǎijiǎo nàr 在拐角那儿; we walked ~ the garden wǒmen zài huāyuán lǐ sànbù le 我们在花园里散步了; they all stood ~ him tāmen dōu zhàn zài tāde zhōuwéi 他们都站在他的周围 **2** adv (in the area) zài zhèr 在这儿; (encircling) zhōuwéi 周围; *he lives ~ here* tā zhùzài fùjìn 他住在附近; *walk ~* zǒuzou 走走; *be ~ (somewhere near)* zài fùjìn 在附近; *there are a lot of people ~* yǒu hěnduō rén 有很多人; *she has been ~ (has traveled, is experienced)* tā yuèlì tīngshēn 她阅历挺深

**arouse** *interest, suspicion* yǐnqǐ 引起; *strong feelings* huànxǐng 唤醒; *(sexually)* jīfā 激发

**arrange** *(put in order)* zhěnglǐ 整理; *furniture* bùzhì 布置; *flowers* chā 插; *music* gǎibiān 改编; *meeting, party, time, place etc* ānpái 安排; *I've ~d to meet her* wǒ ānpái hé tā jiànmiàn le 我安排和她见面了

♦**arrange for** ānpái 安排

**arrangement** *(plan)* ānpái 安排; *(agreement)* xiéyì 协议; *(layout: of furniture etc)* bùzhì 布置; *(of flowers)* chāhuā 插花; *(of music)* gǎibiān 改编

**arrears** tuōqiàn kuǎn 拖欠款; *be in ~ (of person)* tuōqiàn 拖欠

**arrest 1** *n* dàibǔ 逮捕; *be under ~* bèibǔ 被捕 **2** *v/t* dàibǔ 逮捕

**arrival** dàodá 到达; *~s (at airport)* dàodá tīng 到达厅

**arrive** dàodá 到达

♦**arrive at** *place* dídá 抵达; *decision etc* zuòchū 做出

**arrogance** àomàn 傲慢

**arrogant** jiāo'ào zìdà 骄傲自大

**arrow** jiàntóu 箭头

**arson** zònghuǒ 纵火

**art** yìshù 艺术; *the ~s* yìshù jiè 艺术界; *~s degree* wénkē xuéwèi 文科学位

**art gallery** huàláng 画廊

**arterial road** gànxiàn 干线

**artery** MED dòngmài 动脉

**arthritis** guānjié yán 关节炎

**article** *(item)* wùjiàn 物件; *(in newspaper)* wénzhāng 文章; *(section of law etc)* kuǎn 款; GRAM guàncí 冠词

**articulate** *adj person* biǎodá nénglì qiáng 表达能力强; *essay* biǎodá de qīngchǔ yǒulì 表达得清楚有力

lì 力

**artificial** rénzào 人造; *(not sincere)* zuòzuò 做作

**artificial intelligence** réngōng zhìnéng 人工智能

**artillery** dàpào 大炮

**artisan** shǒuyì rén 手艺人

**artist** *(painter)* huàjiā 画家; *(artistic person)* yìshù jiā 艺术家

**artistic** *person* yǒu yìshù xìng 有艺术性; *skills* yìshù 艺术

**as 1** *conj* ◊ *(while, when)* dāng ... de shíhou 当...的时候; *~ I was about to leave, the phone rang again* dāng wǒ yào zǒu de shíhou, diànhuà yòu xiǎng le 当我要走的时候, 电话又响了; *I saw him ~ I was cycling along* wǒ qí chēzi de shíhou kànjiàn le tā 我骑车子的时候看见了他 ◊ *(because)* yīnwéi 因为; *I didn't go ~ I wasn't feeling well* wǒ méi qù yīnwéi wǒ bú tài shūfu 因为我不太舒服 ◊ *(like)* xiàng 像; *~ I said* xiàng wǒ shuōde 像我说的; *~ if* hǎoxiàng 好像; *~ usual* rútóng wǎngcháng 如同往常; *~ necessary* yǒu bìyào shí 有必要时 **2** *adv*: *~ high / pretty ~ ...* hé ... yíyàng gāo / piàoliang hé ... 一样高 / 漂亮; *~ much ~ that?* nàme duō? 那么多？ **3** *prep* zuòwéi 作为; *~ a child / schoolgirl* zuòwéi háizi / nǚ xuéshēng 作为孩子 / 女学生; *work ~ a teacher / translator* dāng lǎoshī / fānyì 当老师 / 翻译; *~ for* zhìyú 至于; *~ Hamlet* bànyǎn Hāmǔláitè 扮演哈姆莱特

**asap** (= *as soon as possible*) jìnkuài 尽快

**ash** huī 灰; *~es* huī 灰; *(after cremation)* gǔhuī 骨灰

**ashamed** xiūkuì 羞愧; *be ~ of* wèi ... diūliǎn wéi ... 丢脸; *you should be ~ of yourself* nǐ bū hàisāo 你不害臊

**ash can** lājī xiāng 垃圾箱

**ashore** zài ànshàng 在岸上; *go ~* shàng'àn 上岸

**ashtray** yānhuī gāng 烟灰缸

Asia Yàzhōu 亚洲

Asian 1 adj Yàzhōu 亚洲 2 n Yàzhōu rén 亚洲人

aside yībiān 一边；~ from chúle 除了

ask 1 v/t person wèn 问；(invite) jiào 叫；question tíwèn 提问；favor qǐngqiú 请求；can I ~ you something? kěyǐ wèn nǐ xiē shì ma? 可以问你些事吗？；~ X for ... gēn X yào ... 跟 X 要...；~ X to ... yào X ... 要 X ...；~ X about Y xiàng X dǎting Y 向 X 打听 Y 2 v/i wèn 问

♦ ask after person wènhòu 问候

♦ ask for yāoqiú 要求；person zhǎo 找

♦ ask out (for a drink, night out) yuēhuì 约会

asking price yàojià 要价

asleep: be (fast) ~ shúshuì 熟睡；fall ~ shuìzháo le 睡着了

asparagus lúsǔn 芦笋

aspect fāngmiàn 方面

aspirin āsīpǐlín 阿司匹林

ass¹ (idiot) bèndàn 笨蛋

ass² ∨ (buttocks) pìgu 屁股；(sex) xìng 性

assassin ànshā zhě 暗杀者

assassinate ànshā 暗杀

assassination ànshā 暗杀

assault 1 n gōngjī 攻击；(physical) ōudǎ 殴打；(verbal) wēixié 威胁 2 v/t (physically) ōudǎ 殴打；(verbally) wēixié 威胁

assemble 1 v/t parts zǔzhuāng 组装 2 v/i (of people) jízhōng 集中

assembly (of parts) zǔzhuāng 组装；POL yìhuì 议会

assembly line zhuāngpèi xiàn 装配线

assembly plant zhuāngpèi chǎng 装配厂

assent v/i tóngyì 同意

assert: ~ oneself jiānchí zìjǐde lìchǎng 坚持自己的立场

assertive person zìxìn 自信

assess situation pínggū 评估；value gūjià 估价

asset FIN zīchǎn 资产；fig bǎobèi 宝贝

asshole ∨ pìyǎnr 屁眼儿；(idiot) bèndàn 笨蛋

assign person, thing fēnpèi 分配

assignment (task, study) rènwù 任务

assimilate v/t information xīshōu 吸收；person into group jiēshòu 接受

assist bāngzhù 帮助

assistance bāngzhù 帮助

assistant zhùshǒu 助手

assistant director fù zhǔguǎn 副主管；(of movie) fù dǎoyǎn 副导演

assistant manager fù jīnglǐ 副经理

associate 1 v/t: ~ X with Y X hé Y liánxiǎng zài yìqǐ X 和 Y 联想在一起 2 v/i: ~ with jiéjiāo 结交 3 n tóngshì 同事

associate professor fù jiàoshòu 副教授

association xiéhuì 协会；in ~ with yǔ ... hézuò 与 ... 合作

assortment (of food) huāsè jùquán 花色俱全；(of people) gèshì gèyàng 各式各样

assume (suppose) xiǎngxiàng 想象；(for the sake of argument) jiǎdìng 假定

assumption shèxiǎng 设想

assurance bǎozhèng 保证；(confidence) xìnxīn 信心

assure (reassure) shǐ quèxìn 使确信

assured (confident) yǒu xìnxīn 有信心

asterisk xīnghào 星号

asthma xiàochuǎn 哮喘

astonish shǐ jīngyà 使惊讶；be ~ed jīngyà 惊讶

astonishing lìngrén jīngyà 令人惊讶

astonishment jīngyà 惊讶

astrologer zhānxīng zhě 占星者

astrology zhànxīng shù 占星术

astronaut yǔháng yuán 宇航员

astronomer tiānwén xuéjiā 天文学家

astronomical price etc jùdà 巨大

astronomy tiānwén xué 天文学

asylum (*mental*) jīngshén bìngyuàn 精神病院; (*political*) bìhù bǐhù 庇护

at (*with places*) zài 在; ~ *the cleaner's* zài gānxǐdiàn lǐ 在干洗店里; ~ *Joe's* zài Qiáo jiālǐ 在乔家里; ~ *the door* zài ménkǒu 在门口; ~ *10 dollars* biāojià shí měiyuán 标价十美元; ~ *the age of 18* shíbāsuì shí 十八岁时; ~ *5 o'clock* wǔ diǎnzhōng 五点钟; *be good/bad* ~ *X* shàncháng/bū shàncháng yú X 擅长/不擅长于 X

atheist wú shén lùn zhě 无神论者

athlete yùndòng yuán 运动员

athletic tǐgé jiànměi 体格健美

athletics tiánjìng yùndòng 田径运动

Atlantic Dàxīyáng 大西洋

atlas dìtú jí 地图集

ATM (= *automated teller machine*) qǔkuǎn jī 取款机

atmosphere (*of earth*) dàqì 大气; (*ambiance*) qìfēn 气氛

atmospheric pollution dàqì wūrǎn 大气污染

atom yuánzǐ 原子

atom bomb yuánzǐ dàn 原子弹

atomic yuánzǐ 原子

atomic energy yuánzǐ néng 原子能

atomic waste yuánzǐ fèiwù 原子废物

atomizer wùhuà qì 雾化器

atrocious zāotòu 糟透

atrocity bàoxíng 暴行

attach shuānláo 栓牢; ~ *importance to* zhùzhòng 注重; *be ~ed to* (*fond of: thing*) yīliàn 依恋; (*person*) àimù 爱慕

attachment (*to e-mail*) fùjiàn 附件

attack 1 n (*physical*) ōudǎ 殴打; MIL xíjī 袭击; (*verbal*) pēngjī 抨击 2 v/t (*physically*) ōudǎ 殴打; MIL xíjī 袭击; (*verbally*) pēngjī 抨击

attempt 1 n chángshì 尝试 2 v/t shìtú 试图

attend cānjiā 参加

♦attend to chǔlǐ 处理; *customer* fúshì 服侍

attendance chūqín 出勤

attendant (*in museum*) fúwù yuán 服务员

attention zhùyìlì 注意力; *bring to the* ~ *of* ... shǐ ... zhùyì 使 ... 注意; *your* ~ *please* qǐng zhùyì 请注意; *pay* ~ zhùyì 注意

attentive *listener* rèxīn 热心

attic gélóu 阁楼

attitude tàidù 态度

attn (= *for the attention of*) gěi 给

attorney lǜshī 律师; *power of* ~ shòuquán 授权

attract *person, attention* xīyǐn 吸引; *be ~ed to X* (*person*) àimù X 爱慕 X

attraction xīyǐn lì 吸引力; (*romantic*) mèilì 魅力

attractive yǒu xīyǐn lì 有吸引力

attribute¹ v/t: ~ *X to* ... bǎ X guīyīn yú ... 把 X 归因于 ...; *the poem has been ~d to* ... jùshuō zhèi shǒu shī wéi ... suǒzuò 据说这首诗是 ... 所作

attribute² n tèzhēng 特征

auction n & v/t pāimài 拍卖

♦auction off pāimài diào 拍卖掉

audacious *plan* màoxiǎn 冒险

audacity fàngsì 放肆

audible tīngdejiàn 听得见

audience (*of concert etc*) tīngzhòng 听众; (*in theater, at show, TV*) guānzhòng 观众

audio adj lùyīn 录音

audiovisual shìtīng 视听

audit 1 n shěnjì 审计 2 v/t shěnhé 审核; *course* pángtīng 旁听

audition n & v/i shìyǎn 试演

auditor shěnjì shī 审计师

auditorium (*of theater etc*) tīng 厅

August bāyuè 八月

aunt (*own, maternal*) gū gū 姑姑; (*own, maternal*) yí mā 姨妈; (*somebody else's*) āyí 阿姨

austere jiǎnpǔ 简朴

austerity (*economic*) jīngjì jǐnsuō 经济紧缩

Australasia Àodàlāxīyà 澳大利西亚

Australia Áodàlìyà 澳大利亚

Australian 1 adj Áodàlìyà 澳大利亚 2 n Áodàlìyà rén 澳大利亚人

Austria Áodìlì 奥地利

Austrian 1 adj Áodìlì 奥地利 2 n Áodìlì rén 奥地利人

authentic antique zhēnzhèng 真正; accent dìdào 地道

authenticity zhēnshí xìng 真实性

author zuòzhě 作者

authoritative person, manner ài xià mìnglìng 爱下命令; source of information yǒu quánwēi xìng 有权威性

authority quánwēi 权威; (permission) xǔkě 许可; be an ~ on … shì … de quánwēi 是 … 的权威; the authorities dāngquán zhě 当权者

authorize shòuquán 授权; be ~d to … shòuquán … 授权 …

autistic gūpì 孤僻

auto n qìchē 汽车

autobiography zìzhuàn 自传

autograph qīnbǐ qiānmíng 亲笔签名

automate shǐ zìdònghuà 使自动化

automatic 1 adj zìdòng 自动 2 n (car, gun etc) zìdòng 自动

automatically zìdòng 自动

automation zìdòng huà 自动化

automobile xiǎo qìchē 小汽车

automobile industry qìchē yè 汽车业

autonomous region zìzhìqū 自治区

autonomy zìzhì 自治

autopilot zìdòng jiàshǐ yí 自动驾驶仪

autopsy yànshī 验尸

auxiliary adj fǔzhù 辅助

available facility, service, book, information kě dédào 可得到; person yǒukòng 有空

avalanche xuěbēng 雪崩

avenue dàdào 大道; fig lù 路

average 1 adj píngjūn 平均; (ordinary) pǔtōng 普通; (of mediocre quality) mǎmahūhū 马马虎虎 2 n píngjūn shuǐzhǔn 平均水准; above / below ~ gāoyú /

dīyú píngjūn shuǐzhǔn 高于 / 低于平均水准; on ~ píngjūn láishuō 平均来说 3 v/t píngjūn 平均

♦average out v/t suàn píngjūn shù 算平均数

♦average out at píngjūn shì 平均是

aversion: have an ~ to yànwù 厌恶

avert one's eyes zhuǎnyí 转移; crisis bìmiǎn 避免

aviary niǎoshè 鸟舍

aviation hángkōng 航空

avid rèxīn 热心

avoid bìmiǎn 避免

awake adj xǐng 醒; it's keeping me ~ ràng wǒ shuìbùzháo 让我睡不着

award 1 n (prize) jiǎnglì 奖励 2 v/t jiǎnglì 奖励; damages pàngěi 判给

aware: be ~ of X zhīdào X 知道 X; become ~ of X dézhī X 得知 X

awareness yìshí 意识

away: be ~ (traveling, sick etc) bùzài 不在; walk / run ~ zǒu / pǎo kāi 走 / 跑开; look ~ búkàn 不看; it's 2 miles ~ liǎng yīnglǐ yuǎn 两英里远; Christmas is still six weeks ~ lí shèngdànjié háiyǒu liù xīngqī 离圣诞节还有六星期; take X ~ from Y (something from somebody) cóng Y nàlǐ názǒu X 从Y那里拿走 X; put X ~ bǎ X fànghǎo 把 X 放好

away game SP kèfāng bǐsài 客方比赛

awesome F (terrific) ⇩ gàilemàole 盖了帽了

awful zāogāo 糟糕

awkward (clumsy) bènzhuō 笨拙; (difficult) nányǐ duìfù 难以对付; (embarrassing) gāngà 尴尬; feel ~ gāngà gāngà 尴尬

awning chuánpéng 船篷

ax 1 n fǔ 斧 2 v/t project, budget, jobs etc xiāojiǎn 削减

axle lúnzhóu 轮轴

# B

BA (= *Bachelor of Arts*) wén xuéshì 文学士
baby *n* yīng'ér 婴儿
baby carriage yīng'ér chē 婴儿车; baby-sit kānháizi 看孩子; baby-sitter línshí bǎomǔ 临时保姆
bachelor dānshēn hàn 单身汉
back 1 *n* (*of person*) hòubèi 后背; (*of car, bus*) hòubù 后部; (*of paper, jacket, house, book*) bèimiàn 背面; (*of drawer*) jǐn lǐmiàn 尽里面; (*of chair*) kàobèi 靠背; SP hòuwèi 后卫; *in* ~ zài hòumian 在后面; *in the* ~ *of the car* zài qìchē hòuzuò 在汽车后座; *at the* ~ *of the bus* zài gōnggòng qìchē hòuzuò 在公共汽车后座; ~ *to front* qiánhòu diāndǎo 前后颠倒; *at the* ~ *of beyond* zài huāngwú rényān de dìfang 在荒无人烟的地方 2 *adj* hòu 后; ~ *road* xiǎolù 小路 3 *adv*: *please move / stand* ~ qǐng hòutuì 请后退 2 *meters* ~ *from the edge* lí biānyuán liǎngmǐ 离边缘两米; ~ *in 1935* zǎozài yījiǔsānwǔ nián 早在一九三五年; *give X* ~ *to Y* jiāng X huángěi Y 将 X 还给 Y; *she'll be* ~ *tomorrow* tā míngtiān huílái 她明天回来; *when are you coming* ~? nǐ shénme shíhou huílái? 你什么时候回来?; *take X* ~ *to the store* (*because unsatisfactory*) tuìdiào X 退掉 X; *they wrote / phoned* ~ tāmen huíxìn / dǎhuí diànhuà le 他们回信 / 打回电话了; *he hit me* ~ tā huíshǒu dǎwǒ 他回手打我 4 *v/t* (*support*) zhīchí zhīchí 支持; *car* dǎochē 倒车; *horse* xià dǔzhù 下赌注 5 *v/i* (*of driver*) dǎochē 倒车
♦ back away hòutuì 后退
♦ back down fàngqì 放弃
♦ back off hòutuì 后退; (*from danger*) dǎ tuìtánggǔ 打退堂鼓
♦ back onto bèixiàng 背向
♦ back out (*of commitment*) sāshǒu 撒手
♦ back up 1 *v/t* (*support*) zhīchí 支持; *claim, argument* zhèngshí 证实; *file* hòubèi 后备; *be backed up* (*of traffic*) páichéng chánglóng 排成长龙 2 *v/i* (*in car*) hòutuì 后退
back burner: *put ... on the* ~ bǎ ... fàngzài yībiān 把 ... 放在一边
backdate zhuīsù 追溯
backdoor hòumén 后门
backer zànzhù rén 赞助人
backfire *v/i* *fig* chǎnshēng shì yǔ yuàn wéi de jiéguǒ 产生事与愿违的结果; background bèijǐng 背景; (*of person*) jīnglì jīnglì 经历; (*of situation*) bèijǐng zīliào 背景资料; backhand *n* (*in tennis*) fǎnshǒu jiēqiú 反手击球
backing (*support*) zhīchí 支持; (*musicians*) bànzòu bàn zòu 伴奏; (*singers*) bànchàng 伴唱
backing group bànzòu zǔ 伴奏组; (*singers*) bànchàng zǔ 伴唱组
backlash qiángliè fǎnyìng 强烈反应; backlog jīyā gōngzuò 积压工作; backpack 1 *n* bèibāo 背包 2 *v/i* túbù lǚxíng 徒步旅行; backpacker túbù lǚxíng zhě 徒步旅行者; backpedal *fig* chū'ěr fǎn'ěr 出尔反尔; backspace (key) tuìgé jiàn 退格键; backstairs hòu lóutī 后楼梯; backstroke SP yǎngyǒng 仰泳
backup *also* COMPUT hòubèi 后备; *take a* ~ COMPUT zuò bèiyòng cípán 做备用磁盘
backup disk COMPUT bèiyòng cípán 备用磁盘
backward 1 *adj* *child* chídùn 迟钝;

*society* luòhòu 落后; *glance* xiànghòu 向后 **2** *adv* xiànghòu 向后

**backyard** hòu huāyuán 后花园; *fig* hòuyuàn 后院

**bacon** xūn xiánròu 熏咸肉

**bacteria** xìjūn 细菌

**bad** bùhǎo 不好; *weather, conditions* èliè 恶劣; *cold, headache etc* jùliè 剧烈; *mistake, accident* yánzhòng 严重; *(rotten)* huài 坏; *it's not* ~ hái kěyǐ 还可以; *that's really too* ~ *(shame)* tài yíhàn le 太遗憾了; *feel* ~ *about (guilty)* gǎndào qiànjiù 感到歉疚; *be* ~ *at* bù zhuāngcháng yú 不专长于; *Friday's* ~, *how about Thursday?* xīngqīwǔ bù héshì, xīngqīsì zěnme yàng? 星期五不合适, 星期四怎么样？

**bad debt** wúfǎ shōuhuí de huàizhàng 无法收回的坏账

**bad language** cūhuà 粗话

**badge** zhèngzhāng 证章

**badger** *v/t* jiūchán 纠缠

**badly** *behave* bùhǎo 不好; *injured, damaged* yánzhòng 严重; *perform* chà 差; *he* ~ *needs a haircut / rest* tā jíxū jiǎn tóufa / xiūxi 他急需剪头发 / 休息; *he is* ~ *off (poor)* tā hěn qióng 他很穷

**badminton** yǔmáo qiú 羽毛球

**baffle** shǐ kùnhuò 使困惑; *be* ~d móbùzháo tóunǎo 摸不着头脑

**baffling** *mystery* nányí jiědá 难以解答; *software etc* shēn'ào 深奥

**bag** *(plastic, paper)* dàizi 袋子; *(for school, traveling)* bāo 包; *(purse)* shǒutí bāo 手提包

**baggage** xíngli 行李

**baggage car** RAIL xíngli chē 行李车; **baggage cart** xíngli chē 行李车; **baggage check** cúnfàng xíngli chù 存放行李处; **baggage reclaim** xíngli lǐngqǔ chù 行李领取处

**baggy** kuānsōng 宽松

**bail** *n* LAW bǎoshì 保释; *(money)* bǎoshì jīn 保释金; *on* ~ zàibǎo 在保

♦**bail out 1** *v/t* LAW bǎoshì 保释;

*fig* bāngzhù dùguò nánguān 帮助渡过难关 **2** *v/i (of airplane)* tiàosǎn 跳伞

**bait** *n* yòu'ěr 诱饵

**bake** *v/t* kǎo 烤

**baked potato** kǎo tǔdòu 烤土豆

**baker** miànbāo shīfu 面包师傅

**bakery** miànbāo diàn 面包店

**balance 1** *n* pínghéng 平衡; *(remainder)* chā'é 差额; *(of bank account)* jiécún 结存 **2** *v/t* pínghéng 平衡; ~ *the books* jiésuàn 结算 **3** *v/i* pínghéng 平衡; *(of accounts)* shōuzhī pínghéng 收支平衡

**balanced** *(fair)* gōngpíng 公平; *personality* pínghéng 平衡; ~ *diet* jūnhéng yǐnshí 均衡饮食

**balance of payments** guójì shōuzhī chā'é 国际收支差额

**balance of trade** màoyì chā'é 贸易差额

**balance sheet** juésuàn biǎo 决算表

**balcony** *(of house)* yángtái 阳台; *(in theater)* lóutīng 楼厅

**bald** *man* tūdǐng 秃顶; *he's going* ~ tā kāishǐ tūdǐng le 他开始秃顶了

**ball** qiú 球; *on the* ~ jīngmíng 机警; *play* ~ *fig* hézuò 合作; *the* ~*'s in his court* lúndào tā zuòchū fǎnyìng 轮到他作出反应

**ball bearing** gǔnzhū zhóuchéng 滚珠轴承

**ballerina** bālěiwǔ nǚ yǎnyuán 芭蕾舞女演员

**ballet** bālěiwǔ 芭蕾舞

**ballet dancer** bālěiwǔ yǎnyuán 芭蕾舞演员

**ball game** *(baseball game)* qiúsài 球赛; *that's a different* ~ nà shì lìng yíjiàn shì 那是另一件事

**ballistic missile** dàndào dǎodàn 弹道导弹

**balloon** *(child's)* qìqiú 气球; *(for flight)* rè qìqiú 热气球

**ballot 1** *n* tóupiào 投票 **2** *v/t members* tóupiào juédìng 投票决定

**ballot box** tóupiào xiāng 投票箱

ballpark (*baseball*) bàngqiú chǎng 棒球场; *be in the right ~ fig* dàzhì zhèngquè 大致正确

ballpark figure dàzhì zhèngquè de shùmù 大致正确的数目

ballpoint (pen) ⇩ yuánzhū bǐ 圆珠笔

balls ∨ dàn 蛋; (*courage*) yǒngqì 勇气

bamboo zhúzi 竹子

bamboo shoots zhúsǔn 竹笋

ban 1 *n* jìnlìng 禁令 2 *v/t* jìnzhǐ 禁止

banana xiāngjiāo 香蕉

band (*musical group*) yuèduì 乐队

bandage 1 *n* bēngdài 绷带 2 *v/t* bǎng bēngdài 绑绷带

Band-Aid® ⇩ chuàngkětiē 创可贴

bandit tǔfěi 土匪

bandwagon: *jump on the ~* gǎn làngtóu 赶浪头

bandy *legs* luóquān tuǐ 罗圈腿

bang 1 *n* (*noise*) hōngde yīshēng 轰的一声; (*blow*) měngjī 猛击 2 *v/t door* shuāi 摔; (*hit*) zhuàng 撞 3 *v/i* fāchū pēngde yīxiǎng 发出砰的一响

Bangladesh Mèngjiālā 孟加拉

Bangladeshi 1 *adj* Mèngjiālā 孟加拉 2 *n* (*person*) Mèngjiālā rén 孟加拉人

banjo bānzhuó qín 班卓琴

bank¹ (*of river*) hé'àn 河岸

bank² 1 *n* FIN yínháng 银行 2 *v/i: ~ with* yòng ... yínháng 用 ... 银行 3 *v/t money* chǔcún 储存

♦ bank on zhǐwàng 指望; *don't ~ it* bié nàme kěndìng 别那么肯定

bank account yínháng zhànghù 银行帐户; bank balance yínháng jiécún 银行结存; bank bill chāopiào 钞票

banker yínháng jiā 银行家

banker's card yínháng xìnyòng kǎ 银行信用卡

banker's order chángqī wěituō shū 长期委托书

bank loan yínháng dàikuǎn 银行贷款; bank manager yínháng jīnglǐ 银行经理; Bank of China Zhōngguó Yínháng 中国银行;

bank rate yínháng lìlǜ 银行利率; bankroll *v/t* tígōng zījīn 提供资金

bankrupt 1 *adj* pòchǎn 破产; *go ~* pòchǎn 破产 2 *v/t* pòchǎn 破产

bankruptcy pòchǎn 破产

bank statement yínháng jiédān 银行结单

banner héngfú 横幅

banns jiéhūn gōnggào 结婚公告

banquet yànhuì 宴会

banter *n* qǔxiào qǔxiào 取笑

baptism xǐlǐ 洗礼

baptize xǐlǐ 洗礼

bar¹ (*iron, chocolate*) tiáo 条; (*for drinks*) jiǔbā 酒吧; (*counter*) guìtái 柜台; *a ~ of soap* yīkuài féizào 一块肥皂; *be behind ~s* (*in prison*) zuò bānfáng 坐班房

bar² *v/t* jìnzhǐ 禁止

bar³ *prep* (*except*) chúle 除了

barbecue ⇩ 1 *n* shāokǎo huì 烧烤会; (*equipment*) kǎojià 烤架 2 *v/t* kǎo kǎo 烤烤

barbed wire yǒucì tiěsī 有刺铁丝

barber tìtóu jiàng 剃头匠

bar code ⇩ tiáoxíng mǎ 条形码

bare *adj* (*naked*) guāng 光; (*empty: room*) kōng 空; *mountainside, floor* guāng tūtu 光秃秃

barefoot: *be ~* guāngjiǎo 光脚

barefoot doctor chìjiǎo yīshēng 赤脚医生

bare-headed guāngzhe tóu 光着头

barely jǐnjǐn 仅仅

bargain 1 *n* (*deal*) jiāoyì 交易; (*good buy*) piányí huò 便宜货; *it's a ~!* (*deal*) zhēn piányí! 真便宜! 2 *v/i* tǎojià huánjià 讨价还价

♦ bargain for (*expect*) yùliào 预料

barge *n* NAUT bóchuán 驳船

bark¹ 1 *n* (*of dog*) fèi fèi 吠 *v/i* fèi fèi 吠

bark² (*of tree*) shùpí 树皮

barley dàmài 大麦

barn liángcāng 粮仓

barometer qìyā biǎo 气压表; *fig* qíngyù biǎo 晴雨表

barracks MIL yíngfáng 营房

barrel (*container*) tǒng 桶

barren *land* huāngmò 荒漠

barricade *n* lùzhàng 路障

barrier lángān 栏杆; (*cultural*) zhàng'ài 障碍; *language* ~ yǔyán zhàng'ài 语言障碍

bar tender jiǔdiàn huǒjì 酒店伙计

barter 1 *n* yìhuò màoyì 易货贸易 2 *v/t* jiāohuàn 交换

base 1 *n* (*bottom end*) dǐbù 底部; (*underneath*) dǐzuò 底座; (*center*, MIL) jīdì 基地 2 *v/t* yǐ ... wéi jīchǔ 以 ... 为基础; ~ *X on Y* yǐ Y wéi X de jīchǔ 以 Y 为 X 的基础; *be ~d in* (*in city, country*) yǐ ... wéi jīdì 以 ... 为基地

baseball (*ball*) bàngqiú 棒球; (*game*) bàngqiú yùndòng 棒球运动

baseball bat bàngqiú gùn 棒球棍; baseball cap bàngqiú mào 棒球帽; baseball player bàngqiú yùndòngyuán 棒球运动员

basement (*of house*) dìxiàshì 地下室; (*of store*) dǐcéng 底层

base rate FIN jīběn lìlǜ 基本利率

basic (*rudimentary*) jīběn 基本; (*fundamental*) zhǔyào 主要

basically dàzhì shuōlái 大致说来

basics: *the* ~ jīběn yuánlǐ 基本原理; *get down to* ~ chǎngkāi tiānchuāng shuō liànghuà 敞开天窗说亮话

basin (*for washing*) shuǐchí 水池; (*geographical*) péndì 盆地

basis jīchǔ 基础; (*of argument*) gēnjù 根据

bask shài tàiyáng 晒太阳

basket lánzi 篮子; (*in basketball*) wǎng 网

basketball lánqiú 篮球

bass 1 *n* (*part*) nán dīyīn 男低音; (*singer*) nán dīyīn gēshǒu 男低音歌手; (*instrument*) dīyīn yuèqì 低音乐器 2 *adj* nán dīyīn 男低音

bastard sīshēngzǐ 私生子; F húndàn 混蛋; *poor* ~ / *stupid* ~ F kělián chóng / chǔndàn 可怜虫 / 蠢蛋

bat¹ 1 *n* (*for baseball*) qiúgùn 球棍;

(*for table tennis*) qiúpāi 球拍 2 *v/i* (*in baseball*) jīqiú 击球

bat²: *he didn't ~ an eyelid* tā wúdòng yúzhōng 他无动于衷

bat³ (*animal*) biānfú 蝙蝠

batch *n* pī 批

bath zǎopén 澡盆; *have a* ~, *take a* ~ xǐzǎo 洗澡

bathe *v/i* (*have a bath*) xǐzǎo 洗澡

bath mat dìjīn 地巾; bathrobe yùyī 浴衣; bathroom (*for bath*) xǐzǎo jiān 洗澡间; (*for washing hands*) xǐshǒu jiān 洗手间; (*toilet*) cèsuǒ / xǐshǒu jiān 厕所 / 洗手间; bath towel yùjīn 浴巾; bathtub yùgāng 浴缸

batter *n* miànhú 面糊; (*in baseball*) jīqiú yuán 击球员

battery diànchí 电池; MOT xù diànchí 蓄电池

battle 1 *n* zhànyì 战役; fig dòuzhēng 斗争 2 *v/i* (*against illness etc*) bódòu 搏斗

battlefield, battleground zhànchǎng 战场

bawdy yínhuì 淫秽

bawl (*shout*) dàjiào 大叫; (*weep*) tòngkū 痛哭

◆bawl out *v/t* F chòumà yīdùn 臭骂一顿

bay (*inlet*) wān 湾

bay window tūchuāng 凸窗

be ◊ shì 是; *it's me* shì wǒ 是我; *how much is / are ... ?* ... duōshǎo qián? ... 多少钱 ?; *there is, there are* yǒu 有; ~ *careful* xiǎoxīn 小心; *don't* ~ *sad* bié shāngxīn 别伤心 ◊ (*not translated*): *was she there?* tā zài nàr ma? 她在那儿吗 ?; *I'm happy* wǒ gāoxìng 我高兴; *this book is interereting* zhè běn shū hěn yǒuqù 这本书很有趣 ◊: *has the mailman been?* yóudìyuán láiguò le ma? 邮递员来过了吗 ?; *I've never been to Beijing* wǒ cóngméi qùguò Běijīng 我从没去过北京; *I've been here for hours* wǒ láile hěnjiǔ le 我来了很久了 ◊ (*tags*): *that's right, isn't it?* shìde, duìbuduì? 是的, 对不

对？; *she's Chinese, isn't she?*
tā shì Zhōngguó rén, shìba? 她是
中国人，是吧？◊ *(auxiliary)*: *I
am thinking* wǒ zài xiǎng 我在
想; *he was running* tā zài pǎobù
他在跑步; *you're ~ing silly* nǐ
fànshǎ ne 你犯傻呢 ◊ *(obligation)*: *you are to do what I tell you*
nǐ yào zhào wǒ shuōde qùzuò 你
要照我说的去做; *I was to tell
you this* wǒ běnlái gāi gàosu nǐ 我
本来该告诉你; *you were not to
tell anyone* nǐ bù yīnggāi gàosu
rènhé rén 你不应该告诉任何
人 ◊ *(passive)*: *he was killed* tā bèi
shā sǐ le 他被杀死了; *they have
been sold* tāmen yǐjīng bèi
màidiào le 他们已经被卖掉了

♦ **be in for** *surprise, trouble etc* huì
dédào 会得到

**beach** hǎitān 海滩

**beachwear** hǎibīn fúzhuāng 海滨
服装

**beads** zhūzi 珠子

**beak** huì 喙

**beaker** wúbǐng jiǔbēi 无柄酒杯

**be-all**: *the ~ and end-all* liǎobuqǐ
了不起

**beam 1** *n (in ceiling etc)* héngliáng
横梁 **2** *v/i (smile)* xiàoróng
mǎnmiàn 笑容满面 **3** *v/t
(transmit)* dìngxiàng fāshè 定向发
射

**bean curd** dòufu 豆腐

**beans** dòu 豆; *be full of ~* jīnglì
chōngpèi 精力充沛

**beansprouts** dòuyá 豆芽

**bear**[1] *(animal)* xióng 熊

**bear**[2] **1** *v/t weight* chéngshòu 承受;
*costs* chéngdān 承担; *(tolerate)*
rěnshòu 忍受; *child* shēngyù 生
育 **2** *v/i: bring pressure to ~ on*
shījiā yālì 施加压力

♦ **bear out** *(confirm)* zhèngshí 证实

**bearable** kě róngrěn 可容忍

**beard** húzi 胡子

**bearing** *(in machine)* zhóuchéng 轴
承; *that has no ~ on the case* nà
hé zhège ànjiàn méi shénme
guānxi 那和这个案件没什么
关系

**bear market** FIN dànshì 淡市

**beast** chùsheng 畜生

**beat 1** *n (of heart)* tiàodòng 跳动;
*(of music)* jiézòu 节奏 **2** *v/i (of
heart)* tiàodòng 跳动; *(of rain)*
qiāodǎ 敲打; ~ *about the bush*
guǎiwān mòjiǎo 拐弯抹角 **3** *v/t
(in competition)* jībài 击败; *(hit)* dǎ
打; *(pound)* pāi pāi 拍; ~ *it!* F gǔnkāi!
滚开! ; *it ~s me* F wǒ bū míngbái
我不明白

♦ **beat up** hěnzòu 狠揍

**beaten**: *off the ~ track* xiǎn
yǒurén shèzú 鲜有人涉足

**beating** *(physical)* dǎ dǎ 打

**beat-up** F pòjiù 破旧

**beautician** měiróng jiā 美容家

**beautiful** *woman, house, day* měilì
美丽; *meal* fēngshèng kěkǒu 丰
盛可口; *vacation* wánměi 完美;
*story, movie* dòngrén 动人;
*thanks, that's just ~!* xièxie, wǒ
gòule! 谢谢，我够了！

**beautifully** *cooked, done* gānghǎo
刚好; *simple* yōuyǎ 优雅

**beauty** *(of woman, sunset)* měilì 美
丽

**beauty parlor** měiróng yuàn 美容
院

♦ **beaver away** nǔlì gōngzuò 努力
工作

**because** yīnwèi 因为; ~ *it was too
expensive* yīnwèi tàiguì 因为太
贵; ~ *of* yóuyú 由于

**beckon** *v/i* zhàohuàn 召唤

**become** biànchéng 变成; *what's
~ of her?* tā jiùjìng zěnmeyàng?
她究竟怎么样？

**bed** chuáng 床; *(of flowers)* tán
tǎn 坛; *(of sea, river)* chuáng 床;
*go to ~* shuìjiào 睡觉; *he's still in ~* tā
háiméi qǐchuáng ne 他还没起床
呢; *go to ~ with* hé ... shàng
chuáng hé ... 上床

**bedclothes** chuángshàng yòngpǐn
床上用品

**bedding** qǐnjù 寝具

**bedridden** wòchuáng bùqǐ 卧床不
起; **bedroom** shuìfáng 睡房;
**bedspread** chuángzhào 床罩;
**bedtime** jiùqǐn shíjiān 就寝时间

**bend**

bee mìfēng 蜜蜂

beech shānmáo jǔ 山毛榉

beef 1 n niúròu 牛肉; F (complaint) láosāo 牢骚 2 v/i F (complain) nào 闹

◆beef up chōngshí 充实

beefburger hànbǎo bāo 汉堡包

beef noodles niúròumiàn 牛肉面

beehive fēngxiāng 蜂箱

beeline: make a ~ for zhíbèn 直奔

beep 1 n dūdu shēng 嘟嘟声 2 v/i fāchū dūdu shēng 发出嘟嘟声 3 v/t (call on pager) hū hū 呼呼

beeper kuòjī 扩机

beer píjiǔ 啤酒

beetle jiǎchóng 甲虫

before 1 prep (time, space, order) zhīqián 之前 2 adv yǐqián 以前; the week/day ~ qián yīgè xīngqī/tiān 前一个星期/天 3 conj zhīqián 之前

beforehand shìxiān 事先

beg 1 v/i yàofàn 要饭 2 v/t: ~ X to ... kěnqiú X qùzuò ... 恳求 X 去做 ...

beggar qǐgài 乞丐

begin 1 v/i kāishǐ 开始; to ~ with (at first) běnlái 本来; (in the first place) shǒuxiān 首先 2 v/t kāishǐ 开始

beginner chūxué zhě 初学者

beginner driver jiàshǐ xuéyuán 驾驶学员

beginning kāishǐ 开始; (origin) qǐyuán 起源

behalf: on or in ~ of dàibiǎo 代表; on my/his ~ dàibiǎo wǒ/tā 代表我/他

behave v/i biǎoxiàn 表现; ~ (oneself) shǒu guījǔ 守规矩; ~ (yourself)! guījǔ diǎn! 规矩点!

behavior xíngwéi 行为

behind 1 prep (in position) zài ... hòumian 在 ... 后面; (in progress, in order) luòhòu 落后; be ~ ... (responsible for) zài ... bèihòu zài ... 背后; (support) zhīchí 支持 2 adv (at the back) zài hòumian 在后面; leave, stay liúxià 留下; be ~ with X zài X fāngmiàn luòhòu 在 X 方面落后

Beijing Běijīng 北京

being (existence) shēngcún 生存; (creature) shēngwù 生物

belated láichí 来迟

belch n & v/i dǎgé 打嗝

Belgian 1 adj Bǐlìshí 比利时 2 n Bǐlìshí rén 比利时人

Belgium Bǐlìshí 比利时

belief (trust) xìnrèn 信任; (religion) xìnyǎng 信仰; (opinion) kànfǎ 看法

believe xiāngxìn 相信

◆believe in xiāngxìn 相信; ghosts xìn 信; a person xìnrèn 信任

believer (also fig) xìntú 信徒

bell (on bike, door) líng 铃; (in church, school) zhōng 钟

bellhop shìzhě 侍者

belligerent adj jiāozhàn zhōng 交战中

bellow 1 n hǒushēng 吼声; (of bull) hǒujiào shēng 吼叫声 2 v/i nùhǒu 怒吼; (of bull) hǒujiào 吼叫

belly (of person, animal) dùzi 肚子; (fat stomach) pàng dùzi 胖肚子

bellyache v/i F bàoyuàn 抱怨

belong v/i shǔyú 属于; where does this ~? zhè yīnggāi fàngzài nǎli? 这应该放在哪里?; I don't ~ here wǒ bù shǔyú zhèlǐ 我不属于这里

◆belong to shǔyú 属于; club, organization shì ... chéngyuán 是 ... 成员

belongings suǒyǒu wù 所有物

beloved adj xǐ'ài 喜爱

below 1 prep zài ... de xiàmian 在 ... 的下面; (in amount, rate, level) dīyú 低于 ... 之下; (in text) zài xiàmian 在下面; (in text) zài xiàwén zhōng 在下文中; see ~ rúxià 如下; 10 degrees ~ língxià shídù 零下十度

belt yāodài 腰带; tighten one's ~ fig jiéyuē 节约

bench (seat) chángyǐ 长椅; (work~) gōngzuò tái 工作台

benchmark jīzhǔn 基准

bend 1 n wānqū 弯曲 2 v/t wān wān 弯 3 v/i wān 弯; (of person) wānshēn 弯身

♦**bend down** wānyāo 弯腰

**bender** F kuángyǐn 狂饮

**beneath 1** *prep* zài … xiàmiàn 在 … 下面; (*in status, value*) dīyú 低于 **2** *adv* xiàbian 下边

**benefactor** shīzhǔ 施主

**beneficial** yǒuyì 有益

**benefit 1** *n* hǎochù 好处 **2** *v/t* yǒuyì yú 有益于 **3** *v/i* shòuyì 受益

**benevolent** císhàn 慈善

**benign** cíxiáng 慈祥; MED liángxìng 良性

**bequeath** yíliú 遗留; *fig* liúxià 留下

**bereaved 1** *adj* sàngshī qīnrén 丧失亲人 **2** *n*: **the ~** sàngshī qīnrén de rénmen 丧失亲人的人们

**berry** jiāngguǒ 浆果

**berserk**: *go ~* fāfēng 发疯

**berth** (*for sleeping*) pùwèi 铺位; (*for ship*) chuántái 船台; *give X a wide ~* bìkāi X 避开 X

**beside** zài … pángbiān 在 … 旁边; *be ~ oneself with rage / grief* kuángnù / jí bēishāng 狂怒 / 极悲伤; *that's ~ the point* nàshì wúguān de 那是无关的

**besides 1** *adv* zàishuō 再说 **2** *prep* (*apart from*) chúle 除了

**best 1** *adj* zuìhǎo 最好 **2** *adv* zuìhǎo 最好; *it would be ~ if …* zuìhǎo … 最好 …; *I like her ~* wǒ zuì xǐhuān tā 我最喜欢她 **3** *n*: *do one's ~* jìnlì érwéi 尽力而为; *the ~* (*thing*) zuìhǎo 最好; (*person*) zuìjiā 最佳; *make the ~ of* còuhe 凑和; *all the ~!* zhù yīqiè shùnlì! 祝一切顺利！

**best before date** zài cǐ rìqí qián shǐyòng 在此日期前使用; **best man** (*at wedding*) nán bīnxiàng 男傧相; **best-seller** chàngxiāo shū 畅销书

**bet 1** *n* dǔzhù 赌注 **2** *v/i* dǔbó 赌博; (*reckon*) dǎdǔ 打赌; *you ~!* dāngrán le! 当然了！

**betray** bèipàn 背叛

**betrayal** bèipàn 背叛

**better 1** *adj* gènghǎo 更好; *get ~* gǎijìn 改进; (*in health*) hǎozhuǎn 好转; *he's ~* (*in health*) tā hǎodiǎnr le 他好点儿了 **2** *adv* gènghǎo 更好; *you'd ~ ask permission* nǐ zuìhǎo zhēngdé tóngyì 你最好征得同意; *I'd really ~ not* wǒ háishi bùyào le 我还是不要了; *all the ~ for us* duì wǒmén yǒu hǎochù 对我们有好处; *I like her ~* wǒ gèng xǐhuān tā le 我更喜欢她了

**better off** *adj* fùyù 富裕

**between** *prep* zài … zhījiān 在 … 之间; *~ you and me* nǐwǒ sīxià shuōshuo 你我私下说说

**beverage** *fml* yǐnliào 饮料

**beware**: *~ of* xiǎoxīn 小心

**bewilder** shǐ hútu 使糊涂

**beyond 1** *prep* (*in space*) yuǎnyú 远于; (*in degree, extent*) chāochū 超出; *~ recognition* rèn bù chūlái le 认不出来了; *it's ~ me* (*don't understand*) wǒ bù míngbái 我不明白; (*can't do it*) chāochū wǒde nénglì fànwéi 超出我的能力范围 **2** *adv* gèngyuǎn 更远

**Bhutan** Bùdān 不丹

**Bhutanese 1** *adj* Bùdān 不丹 **2** *n* (*person*) Bùdān rén 不丹人

**bias** *n* (*against*) piānjiàn 偏见; (*in favor of*) piāntǎn 偏袒

**bias(s)ed** (*against*) piānjiàn 偏见; (*in favor of*) piāntǎn 偏袒

**bib** (*for baby*) wéizuǐ 围嘴

**Bible** shèngjīng 圣经

**bibliography** cānkǎo shūmù 参考书目

**biceps** èrtóu jī 二头肌

**bicker** zhēngchǎo 争吵

**bicycle** *n* ⇩ zìxíng chē 自行车

**bid 1** *n* (*at auction*) chūjià 出价; (*attempt*) qǐtú 企图 **2** *v/i* (*at auction*) chūjià 出价

**biennial** *adj* liǎngnián yīcì 两年一次

**big 1** *adj* dà 大; (*tall*) gāo 高; *my brother / sister* wǒ gēge / jiějie 我哥哥 / 姐姐; *~ name* chūmíng 出名 **2** *adv*: *talk ~* chuīniú 吹牛

**bigamy** chónghūn 重婚

**big-headed** zìdà 自大

**bike 1** *n* zìxíng chē 自行车 **2** *v/i* qí

zìxíng chē 骑自行车
bikini bǐjīní 比基尼
bilingual shuāngyǔ 双语
bill 1 n zhàngdān 账单; (*money*) chāopiào 钞票; POL yì'àn 议案; (*poster*) hǎibào 海报 2 v/t (*invoice*) kāi zhàngdān 开账单
billboard guǎnggào pái 广告牌
billfold qiánbāo 钱包
billiards táiqiú 台球
billion shíyì 十亿
bill of exchange huìpiào 汇票
bill of sale zhuǎnràng qìjù 转让契据
bin (*for storage*) xiāngzi 箱子
binary èrjìn zhì 二进制
bind v/t (*connect*) liánjiē 连接; (*tie*) bǎng 绑; (*oblige*) yuēshù 约束
binder (*for papers*) huóyè jiá 活页夹
binding 1 adj agreement, promise yǒu yuēshù lì 有约束力 2 n (*of book*) zhuāngdìng 装钉
binoculars wàngyuǎn jìng 望远镜
biodegradable néng jìnxíng shēngwù jiàngjiě 能进行生物降解
biography zhuànjì 传记
biological shēngwù 生物; ~ **parents** qīnshēng fùmǔ 亲生父母; ~ **detergent** huóxìng xǐdí jì 活性洗涤剂
biology shēngwù xué 生物学
biotechnology shēngwù gōngyì xué 生物工艺学
bird niǎo 鸟
bird of prey měngqín 猛禽
bird sanctuary niǎolèi bǎohù qū 鸟类保护区
birth (*of child*) chūshēng 出生; (*labor*) fēnmiǎn 分娩; *fig of country*) dànshēng 诞生; **give ~ to** child shēng háizi 生孩子; **date of** ~ chūshēng rìqí 出生日期
birth certificate chūshēng zhèng 出生证; **birth control** bìyùn 避孕; **birthday** shēngrì 生日; **happy** ~! shēngrì kuàilè! 生日快乐!; **birthplace** chūshēng dì 出生地; **birthrate** chūshēng lǜ 出生率
biscuit bǐnggān 饼干

bisexual 1 adj shuāngxìng 双性 2 n shuāngxìng rén 双性人
bishop zhǔjiào 主教
bit n (*piece*) xiǎokuàir 小块儿; (*length*) xiǎoduànr 小段儿; (*part*) bùfen 部分; COMPUT èrjìn zhì wèi 二进制位; **a** ~ (*a little*) yǒudiǎnr 有点儿; (*of time*) yīhuìr 一会儿; **a ~ of** (*a little*) yīdiǎn 一点; **a ~ of** **news / advice** yītiáo xīnwén / yīgè gàojiè 一条新闻 / 一个告诫; ~ **by** ~ yīdiǎn yīdiǎn 一点一点; **I'll** **be there in a** ~ (*in a little while*) wǒ yīhuìr huìdào 我一会儿会到
bitch 1 n (*dog*) mǔgǒu 母狗; F (*woman*) pōfù 泼妇 2 v/t F (*complain*) fā láosāo 发牢骚
bitchy F person, remark lìngrén tǎoyàn 令人讨厌
bite 1 n (*of dog, snake*) yǎo 咬; (*of mosquito, flea, spider*) dīng 叮; (*of food*) yīkǒu 一口; **get a** ~ (*of angler*) yú tūněr 鱼吞饵; **let's** **have a** ~ (*to eat*) wǒmen chī diǎnr dōngxi ba 我们吃点儿东西吧 2 v/t (*of dog, snake*) yǎo 咬; (*of mosquito, flea, spider*) dīng 叮 3 v/i yǎo 咬; (*of mosquito, flea*) dīng 叮; (*of fish*) tūněr 吞饵
bitter *taste* kǔ 苦; *person* chōngmǎn yuànhèn 充满怨恨; *weather* hánlěng 寒冷; *argument* jīliè 激烈
bitterly: ~ **cold** hánlěng 寒冷
black 1 adj hēi 黑; *coffee etc* wúnǎi 无奶; *fig* àndàn 暗淡 2 n (*color*) hēisè 黑色; (*person*) hēirén 黑人; **in the** ~ FIN yǒu jiéyú 有结余
♦ **black out** v/i hūnmí 昏迷
black bean sauce dòubànjiàng 豆瓣酱; **blackberry** hēiméi 黑莓; **blackbird** shānniǎo 山鸟; **blackboard** hēibǎn 黑板; **black box** hēi xiázi 黑匣子; **black economy** hēishì jīngjì 黑市经济
blacken person's name fěibàng 诽谤
black eye qīngzhǒng yǎnkuàng 青肿眼眶; **black ice** hēibīng 黑冰; **blacklist 1** n hēi míngdān 黑名单 2 v/t shàng hēi míngdān 上黑名单; **blackmail 1** n xiépò 胁迫;

**emotional ~** gǎnqíng qiāozhà 感情敲诈 2 v/t xiépò 胁迫;
**blackmailer** lèsuǒ zhě 勒索者;
**black market** hēishì 黑市
**blackness** hēi'àn 黑暗
**blackout** ELEC tíngdiàn 停电; MED hūnmí 昏迷; **blacksmith** tiějiàng 铁匠; **black tea** hóngchá 红茶
**bladder** pángguāng 膀胱
**blade** (of knife, sword) rèn 刃; (of helicopter) jiāngyè 浆叶; (of grass) yèpiàn 叶片
**blame 1** n zébèi 责备; (responsibility) zérèn 责任 2 v/t zéguài 责怪; **~ X for Y** yīnwèi Y zébèi X 因为 Y 责备 X
**bland** smile píngdàn 平淡; answer kūzào wúwèi 枯噪无味; food dàn 淡
**blank 1** adj page, tape kòngbái 空白; look mángrán 茫然 2 n (empty space) kòngwèi 空位; **my mind's a ~** wǒ tóunǎo yīpiàn kòngbái 我头脑一片空白
**blank check** kōngtóu zhīpiào 空头支票
**blanket** n tǎnzi 毯子; **a ~ of** fig yīcéng 一层
**blare** v/i xuānnào 喧闹
♦**blare out 1** v/i xuānnào 喧闹 2 v/t dàshēng fāchū 大声发出
**blaspheme** v/i xièdú 亵渎
**blast 1** n (explosion) bàozhà 爆炸; (gust) yīgǔ 一股 2 v/t yòng zhàyào zhà 用炸药炸; **~!** gāisǐ! 该死！
♦**blast off** (of rocket) fāshè shàngtiān 发射上天
**blast furnace** gāolú 高炉
**blast-off** fāshè 发射
**blatant** míngxiǎn 明显
**blaze 1** n (fire) huǒyàn 火焰; **a ~ of color** wǔcǎi bīnfēn 五彩缤纷 2 v/i (of fire) xióngxióng ránshāo 熊熊燃烧
♦**blaze away** (with gun) měngjī 猛击
**blazer** nánshì biàn shàngzhuāng 男式便上装
**bleach 1** n piǎobái jì 漂白剂 2 v/t hair shǐ tuōsè 使脱色
**bleak** countryside huāngliáng 荒凉;

**weather** hánlěng cìgǔ 寒冷刺骨;
**future** àndàn 暗淡
**bleary-eyed** shuìyǎn xīngsōng 睡眼惺忪
**bleat** v/i (of sheep) miēmie jiào 咩咩叫
**bleed 1** v/i liúxuè 流血 2 v/t fig zhàqǔ 榨取
**bleeding** n liúxuè 流血
**bleep 1** n BB shēng BB 声 2 v/i fāchū BB shēng 发出 BB 声 3 v/t (call on pager) hūhuàn 呼唤
**bleeper** hūjiào jī 呼叫机
**blemish 1** n xiácī 瑕疵 2 v/t reputation pòhuài 破坏
**blend** n & v/i hùnhé 混合
♦**blend in 1** v/i rónghé 融和 2 (in cooking) jiǎohé 搅和
**blender** (machine) jiǎohéjī 搅和机
**bless** zhùfú 祝福; **~ you** (in response to sneeze) no equivalent; **be ~ed with** yǒuxìng dédào 有幸得到
**blessing** REL qíshén cìfú 祈神赐福; fig (approval) zànchéng 赞成
**blind 1** adj máng 盲; corner kànbùjiàn lìngyītóu de guǎijiǎo 看不见另一头的拐角; **~ to** shì'ér bùjiàn 视而不见 2 n: **the ~** mángrén 盲人 3 v/t shǐshīmíng 使失明; fig shǐ shīqù pànduàn lì 使失去判断力
**blind alley** sǐ hútòng 死胡同
**blindfold** v/t, n & adv méngzhù yǎnjīng 蒙住眼睛
**blinding** xuànmù 眩目
**blind spot** (in road) mángdiǎn 盲点; fig wúzhī 无知
**blink** v/i (of person) zhǎyǎn 眨眼; (of light) shǎnshuò 闪烁
**blip** (on radar screen) guāngdiǎn 光点; fig zànshí quēxiàn 暂时缺陷
**bliss** kuàilè 快乐
**blister 1** n shuǐpào 水疱 2 v/i qǐ shuǐpào 起水疱; (of paint) qǐ qìpào 起气泡
**blizzard** bàofēngxuě 暴风雪
**bloated** zhàng pàng 胀胖
**blob** (of liquid) dī 滴
**bloc** POL jítuán 集团
**block 1** n kuài 块; (in town) jiēduàn

街段; (of shares) dàzōng 大宗; (blockage) zhàng'ài wù 障碍物 2 v/t dǔsè 堵塞

◆block in (with vehicle) dǔzhù 堵住

◆block out light dǎngzhù 挡住

◆block up v/t sink etc dǔsè 堵塞

blockade n & v/t fēngsuǒ 封锁

blockage dǔsè 堵塞

blockbuster yángyang dàzuò 洋洋大作

block letters dàxiě zìmǔ 大写字母

blond adj jīnfà 金发

blonde n (woman) jīnfà nǚláng 金发女郎

blood xuèyè 血液; in cold ~ cánrěn 残忍

blood bank xuèkù 血库; blood donor ⇩ xiànxuè zhě 献血者;

blood group xuèxíng 血型

bloodless coup wú liúxuè 无流血

blood poisoning xuè zhòngdú 血中毒; blood pressure xuèyā 血压; blood relation, blood relative xuèqīn 血亲; blood sample xuèyè yàngběn 血液样本; bloodshed liúxuè 流血; blood-shot bùmǎn xuèsī 布满血丝; bloodstain xuèjì 血迹; bloodstream xuèliú 血流; blood test yànxuè 验血; blood transfusion shūxuè 输血; blood vessel xuèguǎn 血管

bloody hands etc dàixuè 带血; battle xuè línlín 血淋淋

bloody mary hóng mǎlì hùnhé jiǔ 红玛丽混合酒

bloom 1 n huāduǒ 花朵; in full ~ shèngkāi 盛开 2 v/i kāihuā 开花; fig xīngwàng 兴旺

blossom 1 n huā 花 2 v/i kāihuā 开花; fig fāzhǎn 发展

blot 1 n mòshuǐ zì 墨水渍; fig wūdiǎn 污点 2 v/t paper xīgān 吸干; (wipe dry) cāgān 擦干

◆blot out (hide from view) zhēbì 遮蔽; memory mǒmiè 抹灭

blotch zhěn 疹

blouse chènshān 衬衫

blow¹ n jī 击; (setback) zǔ'ài 阻碍

blow² 1 v/t (of wind) chuī 吹; whistle chuīshào 吹哨; (spend) làngfèi 浪费; opportunity shīqù 失去; ~ one's nose xǐng bítì 擤鼻涕 2 v/i (of wind) guāfēng 刮风; (of whistle) chuīshào 吹哨; (of person) chuīqì 吹气; (of fuse) shāoduàn 烧断; (of tire) bàozhà 爆炸

◆blow off v/t chuīdiào 吹掉

◆blow out v/t & v/i (of candle) chuīmiè 吹灭

◆blow over v/t chuīdǎo 吹倒 2 v/i chuīdǎo 吹倒; (calm down) píngxī 平息; (of argument) bèi dànwàng 被淡忘

◆blow up 1 v/t (with explosives) zhà zhà 炸; balloon chōngqì 充气; photograph fàngdà 放大 2 v/i zhà 炸; (become angry) dàfā píqì 大发脾气

blow-dry v/t chuīgān 吹干; blow job ∨ kǒuyín 口淫; blow-out (of tire) chētāi bàozhà 车胎爆炸; (big meal) měicān 美餐; blow-up (of photo) fàngdà xiàngpiān 放大相片

blue 1 adj lánsè 蓝色; ~ movie huángsè diànyǐng 黄色电影 2 n lánsè 蓝色

blueberry lán jiāngguǒ 蓝浆果; blue chip rèmén 热门; blue-collar worker lánlǐng gōngrén 蓝领工人; blueprint (also fig) lántú 蓝图

blues MUS bólǔsī yīnyuè 勃鲁斯音乐; have the ~ jǔsàng 沮丧

blues singer bólǔsī gēshǒu 勃鲁斯歌手

bluff 1 n (deception) xūzhāng shēngshì 虚张声势 2 v/i zhàhu 诈呼

blunder 1 n dàcuò 大错 2 v/i fàn dà cuòwù 犯大错误

blunt adj dùn chún 钝钝; person zhíshuài 直率

bluntly speak tǎnbái 坦白

blur n & v/t móhu 模糊

blurb (on book) jiǎnjiè 简介

◆blurt out búshèn shuōchū 不慎说出

blush 1 n hóngsè 红色 2 v/i

liǎnhóng 脸红

**blusher** (*cosmetic*) yānzhī 胭脂

**BO** (*body odor*) tǐxiù 体臭

**board 1** *n* bǎn 板; (*for game*) qípán 棋盘; (*for notices*) pái pái 牌; **~** (*of directors*) dǒngshì huì 董事会; **on ~** (*plane*) zài fēijī shàng 在飞机上; (*train*) zài huǒchē shàng 在火车上; (*boat*) zài chuán shàng 在船上; **take on ~** *comments etc* kǎolǜ 考虑; (*fully realize truth of*) yìshídào zhēnxiàng 意识到真相; **across the ~** quánmiàn 全面 **2** *v/t airplane etc* shàng 上 **3** *v/i* (*of passengers*) shànglái 上来

♦**board up** fēng 封

♦**board with** shànsù 膳宿

**board and lodging** chīzhù 吃住

**boarder** jì shànsù zhě 寄膳宿者; EDU jìsù shēng 寄宿生

**board game** qípán yóuxì 棋盘游戏

**boarding card** dēngjī kǎ 登机卡; **boarding house** sùshè 宿舍; **boarding pass** dēngjī kǎ 登机卡; **boarding school** jìsù xuéxiào 寄宿学校

**board meeting** dǒngshìhuì huìyì 董事会会议; **board room** huìyì shì 会议室; **boardwalk** hǎibīn rénxíngdào 海滨人行道

**boast** *n* & *v/i* chuīniú 吹牛

**boat** chuán 船; (*small, for leisure*) xiǎochuán 小船; **go by ~** zuòchuán 坐船

**bob**[1] (*haircut*) duǎnfà 短发

**bob**[2] *v/i* (*of boat etc*) piāolái piāoqù 漂来漂去

♦**bob up** tūrán chūxiàn 突然出现

**bobsleigh, bobsled** xuěqiāo 雪橇

**bodice** jǐnshēn xiōngyī 紧身胸衣

**bodily 1** *adj* shēntǐ 身体 **2** *adv eject* qīnshēn 亲身

**body** shēntǐ 身体; (*dead*) shītǐ 尸体; **~ of water** shuǐtǐ 水体; **~** (*suit*) (*undergarment*) jǐnshēn yī 紧身衣

**bodyguard** bǎobiāo 保镖; **body language** shēnshì yǔ 身势语; **body odor** tǐxiù 体臭; **body shop** MOT chēshēn xiūlǐ chǎng 车

身修理厂; **bodywork** MOT chēshēn 车身

**boggle: it ~s the mind!** yìxiǎng tiānkāi! 异想天开！

**bogus** jiǎ 假

**Bohai Gulf** Bóhǎi Wān 渤海湾

**boil**[1] (*swelling*) jiēzi 疖子

**boil**[2] **1** *v/t liquid, egg, vegetables* zhǔ 煮 **2** *v/i* kāi 开

♦**boil down to** guīgēn jiédǐ 归根结底

♦**boil over** (*of milk etc*) fèiyì 沸溢

**boiled rice** báifàn 白饭

**boiled water** kāishuǐ 开水

**boiler** guōlú 锅炉

**boisterous** xuānnào 喧闹

**bold 1** *adj* dàdǎn 大胆 **2** *n* (*print*) cūtǐ 粗体; **in ~** yòng cūtǐ 用粗体

**bolster** *v/t confidence* zēngqiáng 增强

**bolt 1** *n* luóshuān 螺栓; (*on door*) chāxiāo 插销; (*of lightning*) xuánmù diànshǎn 眩目电闪; **like a ~ from the blue** qíngtiān pīlì 晴天霹雳 **2** *adv*: **~ upright** bǐzhí 笔直 **3** *v/t* (*fix with bolts*) shuānzhù 栓住; (*close*) shuān 闩 **4** *v/i* (*run off*) tuōjiāng 脱缰; (*prisoner*) táopǎo 逃跑

**bomb 1** *n* zhàdàn 炸弹 **2** *v/t* hōngzhà 轰炸

**bombard: ~ with questions** liánzhūpào sìdì tíchū wèntí 连珠炮似地提出问题

**bomb attack** zhàdàn gōngjī 炸弹攻击

**bomber** (*airplane*) hōngzhà jī 轰炸机; (*terrorist*) tóudàn shǒu 投弹手

**bomber jacket** duǎn jiákè 短夹克

**bomb scare** hōngzhà jǐnggào 轰炸警告

**bond 1** *n* (*tie*) liánjié 联结; FIN zhàijuàn 债券 **2** *v/i* (*of glue*) niánjié 粘结

**bone 1** *n* gǔtou 骨头 **2** *v/t meat, fish* qùgǔ 去骨

**bonfire** yínghuǒ 营火

**bonsai** pénjǐng 盆景

**bonus** (*money*) jiǎngjīn 奖金; (*something extra*) éwài pǐn 额外品

boo **1** *n* xūxu shēng 嘘嘘声 **2** *v/t actor, speaker* hè dàocǎi 喝倒彩 **3** *v/i* fāchū xūxu shēng 发出嘘嘘声

book **1** *n* shū 书; **~ of matches** zhǐbǎn huǒchái 纸板火柴 **2** *v/t* (*reserve*) yùdìng 预定; (*of policeman*) dēngjì 登记 **3** *v/i* (*reserve*) yùdìng 预定

bookcase shūjià 书架

booked up kèmǎn 客满; *person* méiyǒu shíjiān 没有时间

bookie F dǔjì rén 赌纪人

booking (*reservation*) yùdìng 预定

booking clerk shòupiào yuán 售票员

bookkeeper jìzhàng rén 记账人

bookkeeping jìzhàng 记账

booklet xiǎo cèzi 小册子

bookmaker dǔjì rén 赌纪人

Book of Changes Yìjīng 易经

books (*accounts*) zhàngmù 帐目; **do the ~** jìzhàng 记账

bookseller shūshāng 书商; **bookstall** shūtān 书摊; **bookstore** shūdiàn 书店

boom[1] *n & v/i* (*in business*) fánróng 繁荣

boom[2] *n* (*noise*) lónglong shēng 隆隆声

boonies F: **out in the ~** qióngxiāng pìràng 穷乡僻壤

boost **1** *n* (*to sales, confidence*) jīlì 激励; (*to economy*) cùjìn 促进 **2** *v/t production, sales* zēngjiā 增加; *prices* tígāo 提高; *confidence, morale* zēngqiáng 增强

boot *n* xuēzi 靴子
♦boot out F qūchú 驱除
♦boot up COMPUT qǐdòng 启动

booth (*at market, fair*) huòtān 货摊; (*at exhibition*) tānzi 摊子; (*in restaurant*) cānzuò 餐座

booze *n* F jiǔ 酒

booze-up Br F kuánghē 狂喝

border *n* (*between countries*) biānjiè 边界; (*edge*) biānyuán 边缘 **2** *v/t country, river* jiāojiè 交界
♦border on *country* jiāojiè 交界; (*be almost*) jìnsì 近似

borderline: **a ~ case of ...** liǎngkě

xìngxíng ... 两可性形 ...

bore[1] *v/t hole* zuānkǒng 钻孔

bore[2] **1** *n* (*person*) mènrén 闷人; **it's such a ~** tài méijìnr le 太没劲 儿了 **2** *v/t shǐ* yànfán 使厌烦

bored: **be ~** mèn 闷; **I'm ~** wǒ hěn mèn 我很闷

boredom wúliáo 无聊

boring fàwèir 乏味儿

born: **be ~** chūshēng 出生; **where were you ~?** nǐ zài nǎr chūshēng? 你在哪儿出生？; **be a ~ ...** tiānshēngde ... 天生的 ...

borrow jiè 借

boss shàngjí 上级
♦boss around chāilái qiǎnqù 拆来遣去

bossy ài guǎnshì 爱管事

botanical zhíwù 植物

botany zhíwù xué 植物学

botch *v/t* gǎode yītuán zāo 搞得一团糟

both **1** *adj & pron* liǎngge 两个; **I know ~** (*of the*) **brothers** liǎng xiōngdì wǒ dōu rènshi 两兄弟我都认识; **~** (*of the*) **brothers there** liǎng xiōngdì dōu zài nàr 两兄弟都在那儿; **~ of them** (*things*) nà liǎngge 那两个; (*people*) nà liǎngrén 那两人 **3** *adv*: **~ ... and ...** yòu ... yòu ... 又 ... 又 ...; **is it business or pleasure? - ~** gōngzuò háishì yúlè? - liǎngyàng dōuyǒu 工作还是娱乐？- 两样都有

bother **1** *n* máfan 麻烦; **it's no ~** méi wèntí 没问题 **2** *v/t* (*disturb*) máfan 麻烦; *person working* dǎjiǎo 打搅; (*worry*) shǐdānxīn 使担心 **3** *v/i* guǎn 管; **don't ~** (*you needn't do it*) búyòngle 不用了; **you needn't have ~ed** tài máfan nǐle 太麻烦你了

bottle **1** *n* píngzi 瓶子; (*for baby*) nǎipíng 奶瓶 **2** *v/t* zhuāngpíng 装瓶
♦bottle up *feelings* èzhì 遏制

bottle bank shōupíng chù 收瓶处

bottled water píngzhuāng shuǐ 瓶装水

bottleneck *n* (*in road, production*)

zǔsāi diǎn 阻塞点
bottle-opener kāipíng qì 开瓶器
bottom 1 adj zuìdī 最低 2 n (on the
inside) dǐbù 底部; (of hill) jiǎo 脚;
(of pile) zuìdī 最底; (underside)
dǐmiàn 底面; (of street) zuìdī chù
最底处; (of garden) zuì hòumiàn
最后面; (buttocks) pìgu 屁股; at
the ~ of the screen zài píngmù
zuìdī chù 在屏幕最底处
♦bottom out dá zuìdī diǎn 达最
低点
bottom line fig (financial outcome)
lìrùn 利润; (the real issue)
zhēnzhèng wèntí 真正问题
boulder dà shítou 大石头
bounce 1 v/t ball tánqǐ 弹起 2 v/i
(of ball) tánqǐ 弹起; (on sofa etc)
tàntiào 弹跳; (of rain etc) sìxià
fēijiàn 四下飞溅; (of check) bèi
jù fù tuìhuí 被拒付退回
bouncer bǎmén rén 把门人
bound¹: be ~ to do X (sure to)
kěndìng zuò X 肯定做X; (obliged
to) shòu yuēshù qùzuò X 受约束
去做X
bound²: be ~ for (of ship) shǐwǎng
驶往
bound³ n & v/i (jump) tiàoyuè 跳跃
boundary biānjiè 边界
boundless wúxiàn 无限
bouquet (flowers) huāshù 花束;
(of wine) fāngxiāng 芳香
bourbon bōpáng wēishìjì jiǔ 波旁
威士忌酒
bout MED fāzuò 发作; (in boxing)
jiàoliàng 较量
boutique shízhuāng shāngdiàn 时
装商店
bow¹ 1 n (as greeting) jūgōng 鞠躬
2 v/i jūgōng 鞠躬 3 v/t head dītóu
低头
bow² (knot) húdié jié 蝴蝶结; MUS
gōng 弓
bow³ (of ship) chuántóu 船头
bowels jiécháng 结肠
bowl¹ (large container) pén 盆;
(small container for rice) wǎn 碗
bowl² 1 n (ball) bǎolíng qiú 保龄
球 2 v/i (in bowling) dǎ bǎolíng qiú
打保龄球

♦bowl over fig jīngdāi 惊呆
bowling bǎolíng qiú 保龄球
bowling alley bǎolíng qiú dào 保
龄球道
bow tie língjié 领结
box¹ n (container) hézi 盒子; (on
form) fānggé 方格
box² v/i quánjí 拳击
boxer quánjí shǒu 拳击手
boxing quánjí 拳击
boxing match quánjí bǐsài 拳击
比赛
box office shòupiào chù 售票处
boy nánháir 男孩儿; (son) érzi 儿
子
boycott dǐzhì 抵制
boyfriend nán péngyou 男朋友
boyish xiàng nánhái yīyàng 象男
孩一样
boyscout tóngzǐ jūnduì yuán 童子
军队员
brace (on teeth) yátào 牙套
bracelet shǒuzhuó 手镯
bracket (for shelf) tuōjià 托架; (in
text) kuòhào 括号
brag v/i chuīniú 吹牛
braid n (in hair) biànzi 辫子;
(trimming) suìdài 穗带
braille mángwén 盲文
brain nǎo 脑
brainless F shǎ 傻
brains (intelligence) nǎozi 脑子
brainstorm (brilliant idea) línggǎn
灵感; brainstorming jítǐ zìyóu
tǎolùn 集体自由讨论; brain
surgeon nǎo wàikē yīshēng 脑外
科医生; brainwash xǐnǎo 洗脑;
brainwashing xǐnǎo 洗脑;
brainwave (brilliant idea) línggǎn
灵感
brainy F cōngmíng 聪明
braise dùn 炖
brake n & v/i shāchē 刹车
brake light zhìdòng xìnhào dēng
制动信号灯
brake pedal shāchē tàbǎn 刹车踏
板
branch n (of tree) shùzhī 树枝; (of
bank) fēnháng 分行; (of company)
fēn gōngsī 分公司; (of chain
store) fēndiàn 分店

♦ branch off (of road) fēnchà 分岔

♦ branch out kuòchōng 扩充

brand 1 n páizi 牌子 2 v/t: **be ~ed a liar** bèi qiǎnzé wéi piànzi 被谴责为骗子

brand image shāngbiāo gàiniàn 商标概念

brandish huīdòng 挥动

brand leader míngpái 名牌儿; brand loyalty míngpái zhōngyú gǎn 名牌忠于感; brand name (famous) míngpái shāngpǐn 名牌商品; (name of a brand) shāngbiāo 商标

brand-new zhǎnxīn 崭新

brandy báilándì 白兰地

brass huángtóng 黄铜

brass band tóngguǎn yuèduì 铜管乐队

brassière xiōngzhào 胸罩

brat pej táoqìbāo 淘气包

bravado xūzhāng shēngshì 虚张声势

brave adj yǒnggǎn 勇敢

bravery yǒnggǎn 勇敢

brawl n & v/i dòu ōu 斗殴

brawny qiángzhuàng 强壮

Brazil Bāxī 巴西

Brazilian 1 adj Bāxī 巴西 2 n Bāxī rén 巴西人

breach (violation) wéifàn 违犯; (in party) fēnliè 分裂

breach of contract LAW wéifàn hétong 违反合同

bread n miànbāo 面包

breadcrumbs miànbāo zhā 面包渣

breadth kuāndù 宽度; (of knowledge) guǎngdù 广度

breadwinner yǎngjiā huókǒu de rén 养家活口的人

break 1 n (in bone) gǔzhé 骨折; (in wire etc) duàntóu 断头; (rest) xiūxi 休息; (in relationship) fēnkāi 分开; **give X a ~** (opportunity) gěi X jīhuì 给 X 机会; **take a ~** xiūxi yíxià 休息一下; **without a ~** work, travel wú zhōngzhǐ 无中止 2 v/t machine, device, toy sǔnhuài 损坏; stick, arm, leg zhéduàn 折断; china, glass, egg shǐ pòsuì 使破

碎; rules, law, promise wéifàn 违反; news bàogào 报告; record dǎpò 打破 3 v/i (of machine, device, toy) sǔnhuài 损坏; (of china, glass, egg) pòsuì破碎; (of stick) zhéduàn 折断; (of news) xièlòu 泄漏; (of storm) tūrán dàzuò 突然大作; (of boy's voice) biànshēng 变声

♦ break away v/i (escape) táopǎo 逃跑; (from family) líkāi 离开; (from organization) bèipàn 背叛; (from tradition) tuōlí 脱离

♦ break down 1 v/i (of vehicle, machine) chū máobìng 出毛病; (of talks) pòliè 破裂; (in tears) kòngzhì bùzhù 控制不住; (mentally) kuǎle 垮了 2 v/t door dǎlàn dǎ lèi 打烂; figures fēnlèi 分类

♦ break even COM shōuzhī pínghéng 收支平衡

♦ break in (interrupt) chāzuǐ 插嘴; (of burglar) pòmén ér rù 破门而入

♦ break off 1 v/t bāixià 掰下; branch zhéduàn 折断; relationship duànjué 断绝; **they've broken it off** tāmen fēnshǒu le 他们分手了 2 v/i (stop talking) zhōngduàn 中断

♦ break out (start up, of disease) bàofā 爆发; (of prisoners) pòláo 破牢; **he broke out in a rash** tā fā hóngzhěn 他发红疹

♦ break up 1 v/t (into component parts) fēnjiě 分解; fight qūsàn 驱散 2 v/i (of ice) suìliè 碎裂; (of couple) líyì 离异; (of band, meeting) fēnshǒu 分手

breakable kě dǎpò 可打破

breakage pòsǔn wù 破损物

breakdown (of vehicle, machine) gùzhàng 故障; (of talks) pòliè 破裂; (nervous ~) bēngkuì 崩溃; (of figures) fēnlèi 分类

break-even point yíngkuī pínghéng diǎn 盈亏平衡点

breakfast n zǎocān 早餐; **have ~** chī zǎocān 吃早餐

break-in dàoqiè 盗窃

breakthrough tūpò 突破

**breakup** (of marriage, partnership) fēnshǒu 分手

**breast** (of woman) rǔfáng 乳房

**breastfeed** v/t bǔrǔ 哺乳

**breaststroke** wāyǒng 蛙泳

**breath** hūxī 呼吸; **be out of ~** chuǎn bū guò qì lái 喘不过气来; **take a deep ~** shēn hūxī 深呼吸

**Breathalyzer®, breath analyzer** hūqì yànzuì qì 呼气验醉器

**breathe** 1 v/i hūxī 呼吸 2 v/t (inhale) xīqì 吸气; (exhale) hūchū 呼出

♦ **breathe in** v/t & v/i xīrù 吸入

♦ **breathe out** v/t & v/i hūchū 呼出

**breathing** hūxī 呼吸

**breathless** chuǎn bū guò qì lái 喘不过气来

**breathlessness** chuǎn bū guò qì 喘不过气

**breathtaking** jīngrén 惊人

**breed** 1 n pǐnzhǒng 品种 2 v/t fánzhí 繁殖; fig yùnniàng 酝酿 3 v/i (of animals) fánzhí 繁殖

**breeder** (of animals) sìyǎng yuán 饲养员

**breeding** (of animals) sìyǎng 饲养

**breeding ground** fig zīshēng dì 滋生地

**breeze** wēifēng 微风

**brew** 1 v/t beer niàngzào 酿造; tea pào 泡 2 v/i (of storm, trouble) yùnniàng 酝酿

**brewer** niàngzào zhě 酿造者

**brewery** niàngzào chǎng 酿造厂

**bribe** n & v/t huìlù 贿赂

**bribery** huìlù 贿赂

**brick** zhuāntóu 砖头

**bricklayer** níwǎ jiàng 泥瓦匠

**bride** xīnniáng 新娘

**bridegroom** xīnláng 新郎

**bridesmaid** bànniáng 伴娘

**bridge**[1] 1 n qiáoliáng 桥; (of nose) bíliáng 鼻梁; (of ship) jiàshǐ tái 驾驶台 2 v/t gap jiànlì qiáoliáng 建立桥梁

**bridge**[2] (card game) qiáopái 桥牌

**brief** adj jiǎnduǎn 简短

**brief**[2] 1 n (mission) rènwù 任务 2 v/t: **~ X on Y** xiàng X jièshào Y 向 X 介绍 Y

**briefcase** gōngwén bāo 公文包

**briefing** jiǎnbào 简报

**briefly** (for a short period of time) yīhuìr 一会儿; (in a few words) jiǎndān 简单; (to sum up) zǒngzhī 总之

**briefs** (for women) duǎn nèikù 短内裤; (for men) sānjiǎo kù 三角裤

**bright** color xiānyàn 鲜艳; light qiángliè 强烈; future guāngmíng 光明; smile huānkuài 欢快; (sunny) qínglǎng 晴朗; room míngliàng 明亮; (intelligent) cōngmíng 聪明

♦ **brighten up** 1 v/t shǐ míngliàng 使明亮; (make more lively) shǐ huóyuè 使活跃 2 v/i (of weather) zhuǎnqíng 转晴; (of face, person) gāoxīng qǐlái 高兴起来

**brightly** smile huānkuài 欢快; shine míngliàng 明亮; colored xiānyàn 鲜艳

**brightness** (of weather) míngliàng 明亮; (of smile) huānkuài 欢快; (intelligence) cōngmíng 聪明

**brilliance** (of person) cáihuá 才华; (of color) guāngcǎi 光彩

**brilliant** sunshine etc míngliàng 明亮; (very good) jiéchū 杰出; (very intelligent) yǒu cáihuá 有才华; idea yīngmíng 英明

**brim** (of container) biānyuán 边缘; (of hat) màoyán 帽檐

**brimful** mǎn 满

**bring** object (not immediate) dàilái 带来; object (more immediate) nálái 拿来; person dài 带; peace, happiness, misery dàilái 带来; **~ it here, will you?** nádào zhèrlái, xíngma? 拿到这儿来，行吗?; **can I ~ a friend?** wǒ néng dàigè péngyǒu láima? 我能带个朋友来吗?

♦ **bring about** dàilái 带来

♦ **bring around** (from a faint) huīfù zhījué 恢复知觉; (persuade) shuōfú 说服

♦ **bring back** (return) huán 还; (reintroduce) huīfù 恢复; memories shǐ huíyì qǐ 使回忆起; (cause to *come back*) lìng ... huílái 令 ... 回来

♦ **bring down** *fence, tree* shǐ dǎoxià 使倒下; *government* shǐ kuǎtái 使垮台; *bird, airplane* shèluò 射落; *rates, inflation, price* shǐ jiàngdī 使降低

♦ **bring in** *interest, income* zhèng 挣; *legislation* yǐnjìn 引进; *verdict* xuānbù 宣布; (*involve*) shǐ jièrù 使介入

♦ **bring out** (*produce: book*) chūbǎn 出版; *video, CD, new product* tuīchū 推出

♦ **bring to** (*from a faint*) huífù zhījué 恢复知觉

♦ **bring up** *child* yǎngyù 养育; *subject* tíchū 提出; (*vomit*) ǒutù 呕吐

**brink** qiàobì biānyuán 峭壁边缘; **on the ~** *fig* jíjiāng 即将

**brisk** *person* huópo 活泼; *voice* shēngyìng 生硬; *walk* qīngkuài 轻快; *trade* xīnglóng 兴隆

**bristles** (*on chin*) húzi chá 胡子楂; (*of brush*) máo 毛

**bristling: be ~ with** (*of person*) húnshēn dùshì 浑身都是; (*of street*) bùmǎn 布满

**Britain** Yīngguó 英国; (*formal use*) Dà Bùlièdiān 大不列颠

**British 1** *adj* Yīngguó 英国; (*formal use*) Dà Bùlièdiān 大不列颠 **2** *n: the ~* Yīngguó rén 英国人; (*formal use*) Dà Bùlièdiān rén 大不列颠人

**Briton** Yīngguó rén 英国人; (*formal use*) Dà Bùlièdiān rén 大不列颠人

**brittle** yìsuì 易碎

**broach** *subject* tíchū 提出

**broad 1** *adj street, shoulders, hips* kuān 宽; *smile* kuānróng 宽容; (*general*) gàikuò xìng 概括性; **in ~ daylight** guāngtiān huàrì 光天化日 **2** n F (*woman*) niángmen 娘儿们

**broadcast** *n & v/t* guǎngbō 广播

**broadcaster** bōyīn yuán 播音员

**broadcasting** bōyīn 播音

**broaden 1** *v/i* biànkuān 变宽 **2** *v/t*

shǐ kuòdà 使扩大; **~ the mind** shǐ shìyě kāikuò 使视野开阔

**broad jump** tiàoyuǎn 跳远

**broadly: ~ speaking** dàtǐ láishuō 大体来说

**broadminded** xīnxiōng kuānkuò 心胸宽阔

**broccoli** xīlánhuā 西兰花

**brochure** xiǎo cèzi 小册子

**broil** *v/t* kǎo 烤

**broiler** *n* (*on stove*) kǎopán 烤盘; (*chicken*) nènjī 嫩鸡

**broke** F (*temporarily*) méiyǒu yīgè zǐr 没有一个子儿; (*long term*) bùmíng yīwén 不明一文; **go ~** (*go bankrupt*) pòchǎn 破产

**broken** *adj* chū máobìng 出毛病; *glass, window* pòsuì 破碎; *neck, arm* gǔzhé 骨折; *home, marriage* pòliè 破裂; *English* jiéjie bābā 结结巴巴

**broken-hearted** xīnsuì 心碎

**broker** yǐngjì rén 经纪人

**bronchitis** qìguǎn yán 气管炎

**bronze** *n* (*metal*) qīngtóng 青铜; (*~ medal*) tóngpái 铜牌

**brooch** xiōngzhēn 胸针

**brood** *v/i* (*of person*) shēng mènqì 生闷气

**broom** tiáozhǒu 笤帚

**broth** (*soup*) tāng 汤; (*stock*) liàotāng 料汤

**brothel** jìyuàn 妓院

**brother** (*own, elder*) gēge 哥哥; (*own, younger*) dìdi 弟弟; (*somebody else's, elder or younger*) xiōngdì 兄弟; **they're ~s** tāmen shì xiōngdì 他们是兄弟; **~s and sisters** xiōngdì jiěmèi 兄弟姐妹

**brother-in-law** (*elder sister's husband*) jiěfū 姐夫; (*younger sister's husband*) mèifū 妹夫; (*husband's younger brother*) xiǎoshūzi 小叔子; (*husband's older brother*) dàbózi 大伯子; (*wife's older brother*) nèixiōng 内兄; (*wife's younger brother*) nèidì 内弟; **they're brothers-in-law** tāmen shì liánjīn 他们是连襟

**brotherly** xiōngdì bān 兄弟般

**brow** (*forehead*) nǎoménr 脑门儿;

(of hill) pōdǐng 坡顶

**browbeat** xiàhu 吓唬

**brown 1** n zōngsè 棕色 **2** adj zōngsè 棕色; (tanned) shàiheīle 晒黑了 **3** v/t & v/i (in cooking) shàngshǎi 上色

**brownbag**: ~ it zìdài wǔfàn shàngbān 自带午饭上班

**Brownie** yòunián tóngzǐjūn 幼年童子军

**brownie** (cake) xiǎo qiǎokèlì dàngāo 小巧克力蛋糕

**brown-nose** v/t F pāi mǎpì 拍马屁

**browse** (in store) suíbiàn kànkan 随便看看; ~ through a book suíbiàn fānyuè běnshū 随便翻阅本书

**browser** COMPUT liúlǎn qì 浏览器

**bruise 1** n cuòshāng 挫伤 **2** v/t person dǎqīng 打青; fruit pèngshāng 碰伤; (emotionally) shānghài 伤害 **3** v/i (of person) yúshāng 瘀伤; (of fruit) pèngshāng 碰伤

**bruising** adj fig yǒu shānghài xìng 有伤害性

**brunch** zǎowǔcān 早午餐

**brunette** zōngfà nǚzǐ 棕发女子

**brunt**: bear the ~ of ... shǒudāng qíchōng ... 首当其冲

**brush 1** n shuā 刷; (conflict) xiǎo chōngtū 小冲突 **2** v/t shuā 刷; (touch lightly) qīngchù 轻触; (move away) chúqù 除去

♦**brush against** cājí 擦及

♦**brush aside** bùtǐng 不听

♦**brush off** shuādiào 刷掉; criticism bùtīng 不听

♦**brush up** chóngwēn 重温

**brushoff** F dīngzǐ 钉子; get the ~ pèng dīngzǐ 碰钉子

**brusque** shēngyìng 生硬

**Brussels sprouts** qiúyá gānlán 球芽甘蓝

**brutal** cánrěn 残忍

**brutality** bàoxíng 暴行

**brutally** cánrěn 残忍; be ~ frank chèdǐdì tǎnbái 彻底地坦白

**brute** chùshēng 畜生

**brute force** wúqíngde lìliàng 无情的力量

**bubble** n qìpào 气泡

**bubble gum** pàopào táng 泡泡糖

**buck**[1] F (dollar) kuài kuài 块

**buck**[2] v/i (of horse) měngrán gōngbèi yuèqǐ 猛然弓背跃起

**buck**[3]: pass the ~ tuīwěi zérèn 推诿责任

**bucket** shuǐtǒng 水桶

**buckle**[1] **1** n dāgōu 搭钩 **2** v/t belt jì 系

**buckle**[2] v/i (of wood, metal) biànxíng 变形

**bud** n BOT huālěi 花蕾

**Buddha** Fó 佛

**Buddhism** Fójiào 佛教

**Buddhist 1** n Fójiào tú 佛教徒; he's a ~ tā xìn Fó 他信佛 **2** adj Fójiào 佛教

**Buddhist temple** sì 寺

**buddy** F huǒbàn 伙伴; (form of address) gērmen 哥儿们

**budge 1** v/t tuīdòng 推动; (make reconsider) shǐ gǎibiàn zhǔyì 使改变主意 **2** v/i yídòng 移动; (change one's mind) gǎibiàn zhǔyì 改变主意

**budgerigar** hǔpí yīngwǔ 虎皮鹦鹉

**budget 1** n yùsuàn 预算; (of family) kāizhī 开支; be on a ~ jīngdǎ xìsuàn 精打细算 **2** v/i zuò yùsuàn 作预算

♦**budget for** jìsuàn 计算

**buff**[1] adj color tǔhuángsè 土黄色

**buff**[2]: a movie / jazz ~ yīge diànyǐng / juéshì yuè mí 一个电影 / 爵士乐迷

**buffalo** yěniú 野牛; water ~ shuǐniú 水牛

**buffer** RAIL fángzhuàng shān 防撞栅; COMPUT huǎnchōng qì 缓冲器; fig huǎnhé zuòyòng 缓和作用

**buffet**[1] (meal) zìzhù cān 自助餐

**buffet**[2] v/t (of wind) pāidǎ 拍打

**bug 1** n (insect) kūnchóng 昆虫; (virus) bìngdú 病毒; (spying device) qiètīng qì 窃听器; COMPUT gùzhàng 故障 **2** v/t telephones, room zhuāng qiètīng qì 装窃听

器; F (*annoy*) shǐ nǎonù 使恼怒

**buggy** (*for baby*) yīng'ér chē 婴儿车

**build 1** *n* (*of person*) shēncái 身材 **2** *v/t* jiànzào 建造

♦**build up 1** *v/t strength* zēngqiáng 增强; *relationship* fāzhǎn 发展; *collection* zhújiàn zàochéng 逐渐造成 **2** *v/i* zhújiàn jījù 逐渐积聚

**builder** (*person*) jiànzhù gōngrén 建筑工人; (*company*) jiànzhù gōngsī 建筑公司

**building** jiànzhù 建筑; (*activity*) jiànzào 建造

**building site** jiànzhù gōngdì 建筑工地

**building trade** jiànzhù yè 建筑业

**build-up** (*accumulation*) jījù 积聚; (*publicity*) yúlùn zhǔnbèi 舆论准备

**built-in** nèizhuāng 内装; *flash* nèihán 内含

**built-up area** jiànzhù qū 建筑区

**bulb** BOT qiújīng 球茎; (*light ~*) diàndēng pào 电灯泡

**bulge 1** *n* (*sudden increase*) zhòuzēng 骤增 **2** *v/i* (*of pocket*) gǔgu nāngnang 鼓鼓囊囊; (*of wall, eyes*) péngzhàng 膨胀

**bulk** dà duōshù 大多数; *in ~* zhěngpī 整批

**bulky** *parcel* tǐjī dà 体积大; *sweater* féidà 肥大

**bull** (*animal*) gōngniú 公牛

**bulldoze** (*demolish*) chǎnpíng 铲平; *~ X into Y fig* xiépò X zuò Y 胁迫 X 作 Y

**bulldozer** tuītǔ jī 推土机

**bullet** zǐdàn 子弹

**bulletin** bùgào 布告

**bulletin board** (*on wall*) bǔgào bǎn 布告板; COMPUT gōnggào pái 公告牌

**bullet point** (*in printing*) biāotídiǎn 标题点

**bullet-proof** fángdàn 防弹

**bull market** FIN shàngzhǎng hángqíng 上涨行情

**bull's-eye** bǎxīn 靶心; *hit the ~* zhèngzhòng yàohài 正中要害

**bullshit** *n* & *v/i* V húshuō bādào 胡

**bully 1** *n* èbà 恶霸; (*child*) xiǎo táoqì 小淘气 **2** *v/t* qīfu 欺负

**bum** F **1** *n* (*tramp*) lǎnhàn 懒汉; (*worthless person*) méiyòng de dōngxi 没用的东西 **2** *adj* (*useless*) sōu 傻 **3** *v/t cigarette etc* qǐqiú 乞求

♦**bum around** F (*travel*) piāobó liúlàng 漂泊流浪; (*be lazy*) fànfan lǎn 犯犯懒

**bumblebee** xióngfēng 熊蜂

**bump 1** *n* (*swelling*) zhǒngkuàir 肿块儿; (*in road*) tūkuàir 凸块儿; *get a ~ on the head* tóushàng zhǒngle yīkuàir 头上肿了一块儿 **2** *v/t* zhuàng 撞

♦**bump into** *table* zhuàng 撞; (*meet*) pèngjiàn 碰见

♦**bump off** F (*murder*) gǎodiào 搞掉

♦**bump up** F *prices* měngtái wùjià 猛抬物价

**bumper 1** *n* MOT bǎoxiǎn gàng 保险杠 **2** *adj harvest* fēngshèng 丰盛; (*extremely good*) jíhǎo 极好

**bumpy** diānbǒ 颠簸

**bun** (*hairstyle*) jìzi 髻子; (*for eating*) xiǎoyuán miànbāo 小圆面包

**bunch** (*of people*) huǒ huǒ 伙伙; (*of keys*) chuàn 串; *a ~ of flowers* yīshù huā 一束花; *a ~ of grapes* yīchuàn pútáo 一串葡萄; *thanks a ~* (*ironic*) duō xièle! 多谢了！

**bundle** (*of clothes*) bāo 包; (*of wood*) kǔn 捆

♦**bundle up** *v/t* bǎ … bāo qǐlái 把 … 包起来; (*dress warmly*) chuānde nuǎnhuó 穿得暖和

**bungle** *v/t* gǎozāo 搞糟

**bunk** *n* chuángpù 床铺

**bunk beds** shuāngcéng chuáng 双层床

**buoy** *n* hángbiāo 航标

**buoyant** *fig* yúkuài 愉快; *economy* fánróng 繁荣

**burden** *n* fùzhòng 负重; *fig* fùdān 负担 **2** *v/t: ~ X with Y* yòng Y lái fánnǎo X 用 Y 来烦恼 X

**bureau** (*chest of drawers*) dǒuchú 斗橱; (*office*) bànshì chù 办事处

**bureaucracy** (*red tape*) guānliáo zhǔyì 官僚主义; (*system*) xíngzhèng xìtǒng 行政系统
**bureaucrat** guānliáo 官僚
**bureaucratic** guānliáo 官僚
**burger** hànbǎobāo 汉堡包
**burglar** xiǎotōu 小偷
**burglar alarm** ⇩ fángqiè jǐngbào qì 防窃警报器
**burglarize** dàoqiè 盗窃
**burglary** dàoqiè 盗窃
**burial** zànglǐ 葬礼
**burly** kuíwú 魁梧
**Burma** Miǎndiàn 缅甸
**Burmese 1** *adj* Miǎndiàn 缅甸 **2** *n* (*person*) Miǎndiàn rén 缅甸人; (*language*) Miǎndiàn yǔ 缅甸语
**burn 1** *n* shāoshāng 烧伤 **2** *v/t* shāo 烧; *toast, meat* shāojiāo 烧焦; (*of sun*) shàishāng 晒伤; (*consume*) shāo 烧 **3** *v/i* shāozháo 烧着; (*of house*) shāohuǐ 烧毁; (*of toast*) shāojiāo 烧焦; (*get sunburnt*) shàishāng 晒伤
♦ **burn down** *v/t* & *v/i* shāohuǐ 烧毁
♦ **burn out**: *burn oneself out* shǐ zìjǐ jīngpí lìjìn 使自己筋疲力尽; *a burned-out car* shāohuǐ de chē 烧毁的车
**burner** (*on cooker*) zàotóu 灶头
**burp** *n, v/i* & *v/t* dǎgé 打嗝
**burst 1** *n* (*in water pipe*) lièkǒu 裂口; (*of gunfire*) sǎoshè 扫射; *a ~ of energy* néngliàng bàofā 能量爆发 **2** *adj* tire bàoliè 爆裂 **3** *v/t* balloon bàoliè 爆裂 **4** *v/i* (*of balloon, tire*) bàoliè 爆裂; *~ into a room* chuǎngrù 闯入; *~ into tears* tūrán dàkū 突然大哭; *~ out laughing* tūrán dàxiào 突然大笑
**bury** máizàng 埋葬; (*conceal*) yǐncáng 隐藏; *be buried under ...* (*covered by*) máizài ... zhīxià 埋在 ... 之下; *~ oneself in work* máitóu yú gōngzuò 埋头于工作
**bus 1** *n* gōnggòng qìchē 公共汽车; (*long distance*) chángtú qìchē 长途汽车 **2** *v/t* yòng gōnggòng qìchē zǎisòng 用公共汽车载送
**busboy** shìyìng shēng 侍应生

**bush** (*plant*) guànmù 灌木; (*land*) huāngyě 荒野
**bushed** F (*tired*) píláo bùkān 疲劳不堪
**bushy** beard nóngmì 浓密
**business** (*trade*) shēngyì 生意; (*company*) gōngsī 公司; (*work*) gōngzuò 工作; (*sector*) zhíyè 职业; (*affair, matter*) shìjiàn 事件; (*as subject of study*) shāngyè 商业; *on ~* yīngōng 因公; *that's none of your ~!, mind your own ~!* yǔ nǐ wúguān! nǐ cāi wúsǐ! 与你无关! 你猜无关!
**business card** míngpiàn 名片; **business class** shāngwù cāng 商务舱; **business hours** yíngyè shíjiān 营业时间; **businesslike** gāo xiàoyì 高效益; **business lunch** shāngyè wǔcān 商业午餐; **businessman** shāngrén 商人; **business meeting** shāngyè huìyì 商业会议; **business school** shāngyè xuéxiào 商业学校; **business studies** shāngyè xué 商业学; **business trip** chūchāi 出差; **businesswoman** nǚshāngrén 女商人
**bus station** gōnggòng qìchē zǒngzhàn 公共汽车总站
**bus stop** chēzhàn 车站
**bust¹** *n* (*of woman*) xiōng 胸
**bust²** F **1** *adj* (*broken*) dǎsuì 打碎; *go ~* pòchǎn 破产 **2** *v/t* dǎsuì 打碎
♦ **bustle around** mánglù 忙碌
♦ **bust-up** F pòliè 破裂
**busty** fēngmǎn 丰满
**busy 1** *adj* máng 忙; *street* yǒu shēngqì 有生气; *store, restaurant*: (*making money*) shēngyì xīnglóng 生意兴隆; (*full of people*) xīxī rǎngrang 熙熙攘攘; TELEC zhànxiàn 占线; *be ~ doing X* mángzhe zuò X 忙着作 X **2** *v/t*: *~ oneself with X* zìjǐ mángyú zìjǐ 自己忙于自己
**busybody** ài guǎn xiánshì de rén 爱管闲事的人
**busy signal** zhànxiàn shēng 占线声
**but 1** *conj* dànshì 但是; *~ that's*

***not fair!*** shízài tàibù gōngpíng le! 实在太不公平了！；***it's not me ~ my father you want*** nǐ yào zhǎode shì wǒ bàba ér búshì wǒ 你要找的是我爸爸而不是我；**then (again)** dàn lìngyī fāngmiàn 但另一方面 **2** *prep*: **all ~ him** chúle tā zhīwài suǒyǒu rén 除了他之外所有人；***the last ~ one*** dàoshǔ dìèr gè 倒数第二个；***the next ~ one*** jiēzhe dìèr 接着第二；***for you*** méiyǒu nǐ 没有你；**nothing ~ the best** zhǐyǒu zuìhǎo de 只有最好的

**butcher** màiròu de 卖肉的；*(murderer)* túfū 屠夫

**butt 1** *n (of cigarette)* yāndì 烟蒂；*(of joke)* xiàobǐng 笑柄；F *(buttocks)* pìgu 屁股 **2** *v/t* yòng tóu zhuàng 用头撞；*(of goat, bull)* yòng tóu dǐng 用头顶

♦**butt in** chāzuǐ 插嘴

**butter 1** *n* huángyóu 黄油 **2** *v/t* mǒ huángyóu 抹黄油

♦**butter up** F fèngchéng 奉承

**butterfly** *(insect)* húdié 蝴蝶

**buttocks** túnbù 臀部

**button 1** *n* kòuzi 扣子；*(on machine)* ànniǔ 按钮；*(badge)* huīzhāng 徽章 **2** *v/t* kòu kòuzi 扣扣子

**buttonhole 1** *n (in suit)* kòuyǎnr 扣眼儿 **2** *v/t* qiángliú jiāotán 强留交谈

**buxom** fēngmǎn 丰满

**buy 1** *n* piányí huò 便宜货 **2** *v/t* mǎi 买；**can I ~ you a drink?** wǒ néng gěinǐ mǎi bēi yǐnliào ma? 我能给你买杯饮料吗？；**$50 doesn't ~ much** wǔshí měiyuán mǎibùliǎo shénme 五十美元买不了什么

♦**buy off** *(bribe)* shōumǎi 收买

♦**buy out** COM mǎixià quánbù gǔfèn 买下全部股份

♦**buy up** dàliàng mǎijìn 大量买进

**buyer** mǎijiā 买家；*(for department store etc)* cǎigòu yuán 采购员

**buzz 1** *n* zàoyīn 噪音；F *(thrill)* xìngfèn gǎn 兴奋感 **2** *v/i (of insect)* fāchū wēngwēng shēng 发出嗡嗡声；*(with buzzer)* àn fēngmíng qì 按蜂鸣器 **3** *v/t (with buzzer)* àn fēngmíng qì jiào 按蜂鸣器叫

♦**buzz off** F zǒukāi 走开

**buzzer** fēngmíng qì 蜂鸣器

**by 1** *prep (agency)* bèi 被；*(near, next to)* kàojìn 靠近；*(no later than)* bù chíyú 不迟于；*(past)* jīngguò 经过；*(mode of transport)* chéng 乘；**side ~ side** yīgè āizhe yīgè 一个挨着一个；**~ day / night** zài báitiān / wǎnshàng 在白天 / 晚上；**~ bus / train** chéng gōnggòng qìchē / huǒchē 乘公共汽车 / 火车；**~ the hour / ton** yǐ xiǎoshí / dūn jìsuàn 以小时 / 吨计算；**~ my watch** ànzhào 按照；**a play ~ ...** yóu ... xiěde jùzuò 由 ... 写的剧作；**~ oneself** zìjǐ 自己；**~ a couple of minutes** yǐ jǐ fēnzhōng zhīchā 以几分钟之差；**2 ~ 4** *(measurement)* èr chéng sì 二乘四；**~ this time tomorrow** míngtiān zhège shíhòu 明天这个时候 **2** *adv*: **~ and ~** *(soon)* guò yīhuìr 过一会儿

**bye(-bye)** zàijiàn 再见

**bygone**: **let ~s be ~s** guòqùde shì ràngtā guòqù ba 过去的事让它过去吧

**bypass 1** *n (road)* pánglù 旁路；MED fēnliú shù 分流术 **2** *v/t* ràoguò 绕过

**by-product** fù chǎnpǐn 副产品

**bystander** pángguān zhě 旁观者

**byte** zìjié 字节

**byword**: **be a ~ for ...** chéngwéi ... de dàihào 成为 ... 的代号

# C

CAAC (= *Civil Aviation Administration of China*) Zhōngguó Mínháng 中国民航

cab (*taxi*) chūzū qìchē 出租汽车; (*van-type ~*) miàndī 面的; (*in Taiwan*) jìchéngchē 计程车; (*of truck*) jiàshǐ shì 驾驶室

cab driver chūzū qìchē sījī 出租汽车司机; (*of van-type cab*) miàndī sījī 面的司机; (*in Taiwan*) jìchéngchē sījī 计程车司机

cabaret gēwǔ biǎoyǎn 歌舞表演

cabbage (*in northern China*) yángbái cài 洋白菜; (*in southern China*) juǎnxīn cài 卷心菜

cabin (*of plane*) zuòcāng 座舱; (*of ship*) chuáncāng 船舱

cabin crew jīzǔ rényuán 机组人员

cabinet (*cupboard*) guìzi 柜子; (*display ~*) chénlièguì 陈列柜; POL nèigé 内阁

cable (*of electrical appliance, telephone*) diànxiàn 电线; (*for securing*) gāngsī shéng 钢丝绳; ~ (*TV*) yǒuxiàn diànshì 有线电视

cable car lǎnchē 缆车

cab stand chūzūchē zhàn 出租车站

cache COMPUT gāosù huǎncún 高速缓存

cactus xiānrénzhǎng 仙人掌

cadaver shītǐ 尸体

CAD-CAM jìsuànjī fǔzhù shèjì hé zhìzào 计算机辅助设计和制造

caddie 1 n (*in golf*) qiútóng 球童 2 v/i: ~ for ... dāng ... de qiútóng 当 ... 的球童

cadet xuéyuán 学员

cadge: ~ X from Y gēn Y qǐqiú X 跟Y乞求X

cadre gànbu 干部

café xiǎo fànguǎn 小饭馆

cafeteria shítáng 食堂

caffeine kāfēiyīn 咖啡因

cage lóng 笼

cagey tūntun tǔtu 吞吞吐吐

cahoots: be in ~ with ... gēn ... tónghuǒ 跟 ... 同伙

cake 1 n dàngāo 蛋糕; be a piece of ~ fig hěn róngyì 很容易 2 v/i (*of mud, blood*) jiékuàir 结块儿

calcium gài 钙

calculate (*work out*) gūjì 估计; (*in arithmetic*) jìsuàn 计算

calculating jīngmíng 精明

calculation jìsuàn jiéguǒ 计算结果

calculator jìsuàn qì 计算器

calendar rìlì 日历

calf¹ (*young cow*) xiǎoniú 小牛

calf² (*of leg*) tuǐdùzi 腿肚子

caliber (*of gun*) kǒujìng 口径; a man of his ~ xiàng tā nàyàng qǐ nénglì de rén 像他那样有能力的人

call 1 n (*phone ~*) diànhuà 电话; (*shout*) hǎnjiào 喊叫; (*demand*) yāoqiú 要求; there's a ~ for you yǒu nǐde diànhuà 有你的电话; give X a call gěi X dǎ diànhuà 给X打电话 2 v/t (*on phone*) dǎ diànhuà gěi 打电话给; (*summon*) jiào 叫; (*meeting*) zhàojí 召集; (*by court*) chuán 传; (*describe as*) shuōchéng shì 说成是; (*shout*) dàhǎn 大喊; what have they ~ed the baby? tāmen gěi háizi qǐ shénme míngzi? 他们给孩子起什么名字？; ~ the manager zhǎo jīnglǐ lái zhǎo jīnglǐ 找经理来; but we ~ him Old Li dàn wǒmen jiào tā Lǎo Lǐ 但我们叫他老李; ~ X names mà X 骂X 3 v/i (*on phone*) dǎ diànhuà 打电话; (*shout*) hūhǎn 呼喊; (*visit*) lái lái 来

♦ call at (*stop at*) qù 去; (*of train*) zài ... tíngchē 在 ... 停车

◆ **call back 1** *v/t* (*on phone*) huí diànhuà 回电话; **call X back** (*summon*) jiào X huíqù 叫 X 回去 **2** *v/i* (*on phone*) zài dǎ diànhuà 再打电话; (*make another visit*) zàilái 再来

◆ **call for** *person* jiē jiē 接; *goods* qùná 去拿; (*demand*) yāoqiú 要求; (*require*) bìxū yǒu 必须要

◆ **call in 1** *v/t* expert qǐng qǐng 请; **call X in** (*summon by person in authority*) jiào X jìnqù 叫 X 进去 **2** *v/i* (*phone*) dǎ diànhuà lái 打电话来; ~ **sick** dǎ diànhuà qǐng bìngjià 打电话请病假

◆ **call off** (*cancel*) qǔxiāo 取消

◆ **call on** (*urge*) dūncù 敦促; (*visit*) bàifǎng 拜访

◆ **call out** (*shout*) dàhǎn 大喊; (*summon*) zhāohuàn 召唤

◆ **call up** *v/t* (*on phone*) dǎ diànhuà gěi 打电话给; COMPUT dǎkāi 打开

**caller** (*on phone*) dǎ diànhuà zhě 打电话者; (*visitor*) tànfǎng zhě 探访者

**call girl** jìnǚ 妓女

**calligraphy** shūfǎ 书法

**callous** wúqíng 无情

**calm 1** *adj* sea, weather píngjìng 平静; person lěngjìng 冷静 **2** *n* (*of countryside*) ānjìng 安静; (*of person*) lěngjìng 冷静

◆ **calm down 1** *v/t*: **calm X down** shǐ X lěngjìng xiàlái 使 X 冷静下来 **2** *v/i* (*of sea, weather, person*) píngjìng xiàlái 平静下来

**calorie** kǎlùlǐ 卡路里

**Cambodia** Jiǎnpǔzhài 柬埔寨

**Cambodian 1** *adj* Jiǎnpǔzhài 柬埔寨 **2** *n* (*person*) Jiǎnpǔzhài rén 柬埔寨人

**camcorder** shèxiàn jī 摄像机

**camera** zhàoxiàng jī 照像机

**cameraman** shèyǐng shī 摄影师

**camouflage 1** *n* wěizhuāng 伪装 **2** *v/t* yǎnhù 掩护

**camp 1** *n* yíng yíng 营 **2** *v/i* lùyíng 露营

**campaign 1** *n* yùndòng 运动; **presidential** ~ zǒngtǒng jìngxuǎn 总统竞选 **2** *v/i* gǎo yùndòng 搞运动

**campaigner** huódòngjiā 活动家

**camper** (*person*) yěyíng zhě 野营者; (*vehicle*) yěyíng chē 野营车

**camping** lùyíng lùyíng 露营

**campsite** yíngdì 营地

**campus** xiàoyuán 校园

**can¹** ◊ (*ability*) néng néng 能; **I ~'t** wǒ bùnéng 我不能; **I ~'t see** wǒ kànbújiàn 我看不见; ~ **you hear me?** nǐ tīngde jiàn wǒ ma? 你听得见我吗 ; ~ **he call me back?** tā néng gěi wǒ huí diànhuà ma? 他能给我回电话吗? ; **as fast as you ~** yuèkuài yuèhǎo 越快越好; **as well as you ~** jìnliàng ba 尽量吧; **you ~'t be serious!** wánxiào le! 别开玩笑了! ; ~ **I help you?** wǒ néng bāng nǐ máng ma? 我能帮你忙吗? ; ~ **you help me?** nǐ néng bāng wǒ ma? 你能帮我吗? ; ~ **I have a beer/ coffee?** qǐng lái bēi píjiǔ/kāfēi? 请来杯啤酒/咖啡? ; **that ~'t be right** bù kěnéng 不可能 ◊ (*with skills*) huì 会; ~ **you speak French?** nǐ huì shuō Fǎyǔ ma? 你会说法语吗? ◊ (*permission*) kěyǐ 可以; ~ **I take this one?** wǒ kěyǐ ná zhège ma? 我可以拿这个吗?

**can²** **1** *n* (*for drinks etc*) guàntóu 罐头 **2** *v/t* (*put in* ~) guànzhuāng 罐装

**Canada** Jiānádà 加拿大

**Canadian 1** *adj* Jiānádà 加拿大 **2** *n* Jiānádà rén 加拿大人

**canal** (*waterway*) yùnhé 运河

**canary** (*bird*) jīnsīquè 金丝雀

**cancel** qǔxiāo 取消

**cancellation** qǔxiāo 取消

**cancer** áizhèng 癌症

**c & f** (*= cost and freight*) chéngběn jiā yùnfèi 成本加运费

**c & i** (*= cost and insurance*) chéngběn jiā bǎoxiǎn fèi 成本加保险费

**candid** tǎnshuài 坦率

**candidacy** hòuxuǎn 候选

candidate (*for position*) hòuxuǎn rén 候选人; (*in exam*) yìngkǎo rén 应考人

candle làzhú 蜡烛

candlestick zhútái 烛台

candor tǎnshuài 坦率

candy táng 糖

cannabis dàmá 大麻

canned *fruit, tomatoes* guànzhuāng 罐装; ~ *laughter* (*recorded*) yùlù xiàoshēng 预录笑声

cannibalize *old car etc* chāijiàn 拆件

cannot → **can**[1]

canoe dúmù zhōu 独木舟

can opener kāiguàn qì 开罐器

cant wěishàn yáncí 伪善言词

can't → **can**[1]

canteen (*in factory*) shítáng 食堂

Canton Guǎngdōng 广东

Cantonese 1 *adj* Guǎngdōng 广东 2 *n* Guǎngdōng rén 广东人; (*language*) Guǎngdōnghuà 广东话

canvas (*for painting*) yóuhuà bù 油画布; (*material*) fānbù 帆布

canvass 1 *v/t* (*seek opinion of*) tīngqǔ yìjiàn 听取意见 2 *v/i* POL lāpiào 拉票

canyon xiágǔ 峡谷

cap (*hat*) màozi 帽子; (*of bottle, lens*) gàizi 盖子; (*of pen*) bǐmào 笔帽

capability (*of person*) nénglì 能力; (*of military*) lìliàng 力量

capable nénggàn 能干; *be ~ of* yǒu nénglì 有能力

capacity (*of container, building*) róngliàng 容量; (*of elevator*) fùhè liàng 负荷量; (*of car engine*) róngliàng 容量; (*of factory*) chǎnliàng 产量; (*ability*) nénglì 能力; *in my ~ as ...* yǐwǒ ... de shēnfèn 以我 ... 的身份

capital *n* (*of country*) shǒudū 首都; (*capital letter*) dàxiě zìmǔ 大写字母; (*money*) zījīn 资金

capital expenditure zīběn zhīchū 资本支出; capital gains tax zīběn shōuyì shuì 资本收益税; capital growth zīběn

chéngzhǎng 资本成长

capitalism zīběn zhǔyì 资本主义

capitalist 1 *adj* zīběn zhǔyì 资本主义 2 *n* (*believer*) zīběn zhǔyì zhě 资本主义者; (*businessman*) zīběn jiā 资本家

capital letter dàxiě zìmǔ 大写字母

capital punishment sǐxíng 死刑

capitulate ràngbù 让步

capsize 1 *v/i* fānchuán 翻船 2 *v/t* shǐ fānchuán 使翻船

capsule (*of medicine*) jiāonáng 胶囊; (*space ~*) tàikōng cāng 太空舱

captain *n* (*of ship*) chuánzhǎng 船长; (*of aircraft*) jīzhǎng 机长; (*of team*) duìzhǎng 队长

caption *n* (*to photo*) shuōmíng 说明

captivate zháomí 着迷

captive fúlǔ 俘虏

captivity bèi guān qǐlái 被关起来

capture 1 *n* (*of city*) zhànlǐng 占领; (*of criminal*) zhuōdào 捉到; (*of animal*) bǔhuò 捕获 2 *v/t person, zhuōdào* 捉到; *animal* bǔhuò 捕获; *city, building* gōngxià 攻下; (*win: market share*) huòdé 获得; (*portray: mood*) miáohuì 描绘; ~ *the moment* zhuāzhù nàyí chànà 抓住那一刹那

car chē 车; (*of train*) chēxiāng 车厢; *by ~* zuòchē 坐车

carafe píng píng 瓶

carat kèlā 克拉

carbohydrate tànshuǐ huàhéwù 碳水化合物

carbonated *drink* qǐpào 起泡

carbon monoxide yīyǎng huàtàn 一氧化碳

carburetor zīhuàqì 汽化器

carcinogen zhì'ái wù 致癌物

carcinogenic zhì'ái 致癌

card (*to mark special occasion*) kǎpiàn 卡片; (*post~*) míngxìnpiànr 明信片儿; (*business ~*) míngpiànr 名片儿; (*playing ~*) zhǐpái 纸牌

cardboard yìng zhǐbǎn 硬纸板

cardiac xīnzàng 心脏

**cardiac arrest** xīnzàng tíngtiào 心脏停跳

**cardigan** kāijīn máoyī 开襟毛衣

**card index** kǎpiàn mùlù 卡片目录

**card key** kǎpiàn yàoshí 卡片钥匙

**care 1** n (of baby, pet, elderly, sick) zhàogù 照顾; (medical ~) yīliáo 医疗; (worry) yōulǜ 忧虑; ~ of (on envelope) fánjiāo 烦交; **take ~** (be cautious) xiǎoxīn 小心; **take ~** (of yourself)! (goodbye) bǎozhòng! 保重！; **take ~** of baby, dog zhàogù 照顾; tool, house, garden àihù 爱护; (deal with) chǔlǐ 处理; project fùzé 负责; **take ~ of the check** fùzhàng 付账; (handle) with ~ (on label) xiǎoxīn qīngfàng 小心轻放 **2** v/i guānxīn 关心; **if you really ~d** (were concerned) yàoshì nǐ zhēnde guānxīn dehuà 要是你真的关心的话; **I don't ~** wǒbú zàihu! 我不在乎！; **I couldn't ~ less** wǒ yīdiǎn yě bú zàihū 我一点也不在乎

◆**care about** guānxīn 关心

◆**care for** (look after) zhàogù 照顾; (like, be fond of) xǐhuān 喜欢; **would you ~ ... ?** nǐ yào ... ma? 你要…吗？

**career** (profession) shìyè 事业; (path through life) jīnglì 经历

**carefree** wúyōu wúlǜ 无忧无虑

**careful** (cautious) jǐnshèn 谨慎; (thorough) zǐxì 仔细; person xìxīn 细心; (be) ~! xiǎoxīn! 小心！

**carefully** (with caution) xiǎoxīn 小心; worded etc jīngxīn 精心

**careless** cūxīn 粗心; work cǎoshuài 草率; **you are so ~!** nǐ tài dàyì le! 你太大意了！

**caress** n & v/t àifǔ 爱抚

**caretaker** kānguǎn rén 看管人

**careworn** yōuxīn chōngchong 忧心忡忡

**cargo** huòwù 货物

**caricature** n (picture) fēngcì huà 讽刺画; (in writing) fēngcì wénzhāng 讽刺文章

**caring** adj yǒu àixīn 有爱心

**carnage** dà túshā 大屠杀

**carnation** kāngnǎixīn 康乃馨

**carnival** miàohuì 庙会

**carol** n sònggē 颂歌

**carousel** (at airport) xínglǐ chuánsòngdài 行李传送带; (at fairground) xuánzhuǎn mùmǎ 旋转木马

**carp** (fish) lǐyú 鲤鱼

**carpenter** mùjiàng 木匠

**carpet** dìtǎn 地毯

**carpool** n héhuǒ yòngchē 合伙用车; **car port** qìchēpéng 汽车棚; **car rental** chūzū qìchē gōngsī 出租汽车公司

**carrier** (company) yùnshū gōngsī 运输公司; (of disease) dàijùn zhě 带菌者

**carrot** húluóbo 胡萝卜

**carry 1** v/t (in hand) ná 拿; (on back) bēi 背; (hold in front) bàozhe 抱; (move: goods) bānyùn 搬运; (have on one's person) dàizhe 带着; (of pregnant woman) huáizhe 怀着; disease dài ... dejùn 带着 ... 的菌; (of ship, plane, bus etc) zàiyǒu ròng 载有; proposal tōngguò 通过; **get carried away** chōnghūn le tóu 冲昏了头 **2** v/i (of sound) chuánsòng 传送

◆**carry on 1** v/i (continue) jiēzhe zuò 接着做; (talking) diédiebùxiū 喋喋不休; (make a fuss) chǎonào 吵闹 **2** v/t jìxù 继续

◆**carry on with** (have an affair with) hé ... yǒu àimèi guānxì 和 ... 有暧昧关系

◆**carry out** survey etc jìnxíng 进行; orders etc zhíxíng 执行

**car seat** (for child) háitóng qìchē zuòyǐ 孩童汽车座椅

**cart** (horsedrawn) mǎchē 马车; (for baggage) xínglǐ chē 行李车

**cartel** liánhé qǐyè 联合企业

**carton** (for storage, transport) zhǐxiāng 纸箱; (for milk, eggs etc) zhǐhé 纸盒; **a ~ of cigarettes** yītiáo xiāngyān 一条香烟

**cartoon** (in newspaper, magazine) fēngcì huà 讽刺画; (on TV, film) kǎtōng piàn 卡通片

**cartridge** (for gun) zǐdàn 子弹

carve *meat* qiē 切; *wood* kè 刻

carving (*figure*) diāokè pǐn 雕刻品

car wash xǐchēchù 洗车处

case[1] (*container*) hé 盒; (*of Scotch, wine*) xiāng 箱; (*suitcase*) píxiāng 皮箱

case[2] n (*instance*) lìzi 例子; (*argument*) gēnjù 根据; (*for police, attorney*) ànjiàn 案件; MED bìnglì 病例; *in ~ ...* wànyī ... 万一 ...; *in any ~* zǒngzhī 总之; *in that ~* jìrán zhèyàng 既然这样

case history MED bìngshǐ 病史

cash 1 n xiànjīn 现金; *short of ~* xiànjīn duǎnquē 现金短缺; *~ down* xiànjīn zhīfù 现金支付; *pay (in) ~* fù xiànjīn 付现金; *~ in advance* xiànkuǎn dìngjīn 现款定金; *~ on delivery* jiāohuò fùkuǎn 交货付款 2 v/t *check* duìxiàn 兑现

♦cash in on cóngzhōng huòlì 从中获利

cash cow jīnkù 金库; cash desk fùkuǎn tái 付款台; cash discount xiànjīn zhékòu 现金折扣; cash flow liúdòng jījīn 流动基金

cashier n (*in store etc*) chūnà yuán 出纳员

cash machine qǔkuǎn jī 取款机

cashmere adj yángróng 羊绒

cash register xiànjīn chūnà jī 现金出纳机

casino dǔchǎng 赌场

casket (*coffin*) guāncai 棺材

cassette cídài 磁带

cassette player lùyīnjī 录音机

cassette recorder lùyīnjī 录音机

cast 1 n (*of play*) yǎnyuán biǎo 演员表; (*mold*) móxíng 模型 2 v/t *metal* jiāozhù 浇铸; *play* fēnpèi juésè 分配角色; *~ X as ... actor* fēnpèi X bànyǎn ... 分配 X 扮演 ...; *~ doubt on* lìngrén huáiyí 令人怀疑

♦cast off v/i (*of ship*) jiělǎn 解缆

caste zhǒngxìng 种姓

caster (*on chair etc*) jiǎolún 脚轮

cast iron n shēngtiě 生铁

cast-iron adj shēngtiě 生铁

castle chéngbǎo 城堡

castrate yāngē 阉割

casual (*chance, offhand, not formal*) suíbiàn 随便; (*not permanent*) línshí 临时

casualty shāngwáng rénshì 伤亡人士

casual wear biànfú 便服

catalog n mùlù 目录

catalyst *fig* dǎohuǒ xiàn 导火线

catalytic converter cuīhuà zhuǎnhuà qì 催化转化器

catastrophe zāinàn 灾难

catch 1 n jiē 接; (*of fish*) bǔhuò wù 捕获物; (*locking device*) shuān 门; (*problem*) wèntí 问题 2 v/t *ball* jiēzhù 接住; *escaped prisoner* zhuōzhù 捉住; (*get on: bus, train*) zuò 坐; (*not miss: bus, train*) gǎnshàng 赶上; *fish with rod* diàodào 钓到; *fish with net* bǔdào 捕到; (*in order to speak to*) zhǎodào 找到; (*hear*) tīng qīngchǔ 听清楚; *illness* rǎnshàng 染上; *~ (a) cold* dé gǎnmào 得感冒; *~ X's eye* (*of person, object*) yǐnqǐ X de zhùyì 引起 X 的注意; *~ sight of, ~ a glimpse of* kànjiàn 看见; *~ X doing Y* zhuàngjiàn X zuò Y 撞见 X 做 Y

♦catch on (*become popular*) shòu huānyíng 受欢迎; (*understand*) lǐjiě 理解

♦catch up v/i gǎnshàng 赶上

♦catch up on míbǔ 弥补

♦catch-22: *it's a ~ situation* jìntuì liǎngnán 进退两难

catcher (*in baseball*) jiēshǒu 接手

catching *disease* chuánrǎn xìng 传染性; *fear, panic* yǒu gǎnrǎn lì 有感染力

catchy *tune* róngyì shàngkǒu 容易上口

category fànchóu 范畴

♦cater for (*meet the needs of*) yínghé 迎合; (*provide food for*) bāobàn 包办

caterer jiǔxí chéngbàn rén 酒席承办人

caterpillar máochóng 毛虫

cathedral dà jiàotáng 大教堂

Catholic 1 adj Tiānzhǔjiào 天主教 2 n Tiānzhǔ jiàotú 天主教徒

catsup fānqié jiàng 蕃茄酱

cattle niú 牛

catty èdú 恶毒

cauliflower càihuā 菜花

cause 1 n yuányīn 原因; (grounds) lǐyóu 理由; (aim of movement, charity etc) zhǔzhāng 主张 2 v/t yǐnqǐ 引起

caution 1 n (carefulness) jǐnshèn 谨慎; ~ is advised jǐnshèn yīxiē 谨慎一些 2 v/t (warn) jǐnggào 警告

cautious jǐnshèn 谨慎

cave dòng 洞

♦ cave in (of roof) dǎotā 倒塌

caviar yúzǐ jiàng 鱼子酱

cavity (in tooth) qǔchǐ 龋齿

cc (= carbon copy) 1 n fùběn 副本 2 v/t fùběn gěi 副本给

CCTV (= China Central Television) Zhōngyāng Diànshìtái 中央电视台

CD (compact disc) guāngpán 光盘

CD-ROM guāngpán 光盘

CD-ROM drive guāngqū 光驱

cease v/t & v/i zhōngzhǐ 中止

cease-fire tínghuǒ 停火

ceiling (of room) tiānhuābǎn 天花板; (limit) zuìgāo xiàngdù 最高限度

celebrate 1 v/i qìngzhù 庆祝 2 v/t qìngzhù 庆祝; (observe) guò 过

celebrated zhùmíng 著名

celebration qìngzhù huì 庆祝会

celebrity míngrén 名人

celery qíncài 芹菜

cell (for prisoner) láofáng 牢房; BIO xìbāo 细胞; COMPUT dānyuán 单元

cellar dìjiào 地窖

cello dà tíqín 大提琴

cellophane bōli zhǐ 玻璃纸

cell(ular) phone ⇩ shǒutí diànhuà 手提电话

Celsius shèshì 摄氏

cement 1 n shuǐní 水泥 2 v/t yòng shuǐní hú 用水泥糊; friendship jiāqiáng 加强

cemetery mùdì 墓地

censor v/t shān'gǎi 删改

censorship shěnchá zhìdù 审查制度

cent fēn 分

centenary, centennial yìbǎi zhōunián 一百周年

center 1 n zhōngxīn 中心; POL zhōngjiān pài 中间派; in the ~ of ... zài ... de zhōngxīn 在 ... 的中心 2 v/t fàngzài zhōngyāng 放在中央; text zhōngjiān duìqí 中间对齐

♦ center on jízhōng yú 集中于

centigrade shèshì 摄氏; 10 degrees ~ shèshì shídù 摄氏十度

centimeter límǐ 厘米

central zhōngbù 中部; location, apartment zhōngyāng 中央; (main) zhǔyào 主要; be ~ to X shì X de zhōngxīn yàodiǎn 是X的中心要点

Central Committee of the Chinese Communist Party Zhōnggòng Zhōngyāng Wěiyuánhuì 中共中央委员会

central heating nuǎnqì 暖气

centralize decision making jízhōng 集中

central processing unit zhōngyāng chǔlǐ jī 中央处理机

central locking MOT zhōngyāng suǒchē 中央锁车

century shìjì 世纪

CEO (= Chief Executive Officer) zǒng jīnglǐ 总经理

ceramic cí 瓷

ceramics (objects) táocí 陶瓷

cereal (grain) gǔlèi 谷类

ceremonial 1 adj diǎnlǐ 典礼 2 n diǎnlǐ 典礼

ceremony (event) diǎnlǐ 典礼; (ritual) yíshì 仪式

certain (sure) kěndìng 肯定; (particular) mǒuzhǒng 某种; it's ~ that ... kěndìng ... 肯定 ...; a ~ Mr S. yígè jiào S xiānshēng de rén 一个叫S先生的人; make ~ quèdìng 确定; know/say for ~ kěyǐ kěndìng 可以肯定

certainly (definitely) yídìng 一定;

(*of course*) méi wèntí 没问题; **~ not!** jué duì bùxíng! 绝对不行！

certainty (*confidence*) quèxìn 确信; (*inevitability*) bìrán xìng 必然性; **it's a ~** kěndìng 肯定

certificate (*qualification*) zhèngshū 证书; (*official paper*) zhèngmíng 证明

certified public accountant hégé kuàijì shī 合格会计师

certify zhèngmíng 证明

Cesarean *n* pōufù 剖腹

cessation xiūzhǐ 休止

c / f (= *cost and freight*) chéngběn jiā yùnfèi 成本加运费

CFC (= *chlorofluorocarbon*) hánlǜ fútīng 含氯氟烃

chain 1 *n* liàntiáo 链条; (*of stores, hotels*) liánsuǒ diàn 连锁店 2 *v/t:* **~ X to Y** bǎ X shuānzài Y shàng 把X拴在Y上

chain reaction liánsuǒ fǎnyìng 连锁反应; chain smoke yìzhī jiē yìzhī de chōuyān 一支接一支地抽烟; chain smoker yānbù líkǒu de rén 烟不离口的人; chain store liánsuǒdiàn 连锁店

chair 1 *n* yǐzi 椅子; (*arm ~*) fúshǒu yǐ 扶手椅; (*at university*) jiàoshòu zhíwèi 教授职位; **the ~** (*electric ~*) diànyǐ 电椅; (*at meeting*) zhǔxí 主席; **go to the ~** zuò diànyǐ 坐电椅; **take the ~** zhǔchí huìyì 主持会议 2 *v/t* meeting zhǔchí 主持

chair lift shēngjiàng yǐ 升降椅

chairman zhǔxí 主席

Chairman Mao Máo Zhǔxí 毛主席

chairperson, chairwoman zhǔxí 主席

chalk (*for writing*) fěnbǐ 粉笔; (*in soil*) báihuī 白灰

challenge 1 *n* (*difficulty, in race, competition*) tiǎozhàn 挑战 2 *v/t* (*defy*) fǎnduì 反对; (*call into question*) zhìyí 质疑; **~ X to Y** tiǎozhàn X zuò Y 挑战X做Y

challenger tiǎozhàn zhě 挑战者

challenging job, undertaking yǒu tiǎozhàn xìng 有挑战性

chambermaid nǚ fúwùyuán 女服务员

Chamber of Commerce shānghuì 商会

chamois (*leather*) jīpí 麂皮

champagne xiāngbīn jiǔ 香槟酒

champion 1 *n* SP guànjūn 冠军; (*of cause*) hànwèi zhě 捍卫者 2 *v/t* (*cause*) zhīchí 支持

championship (*event*) jǐnbiāosài 锦标赛; (*title*) guànjūn 冠军

chance (*possibility*) kěnéng 可能; (*opportunity*) jīhuì 机会; (*risk*) fēngxiǎn 风险; (*luck*) jīyù 机遇; **by ~** yìwài 意外; **take a ~** màoxiǎn 冒险; **I'm not taking any ~s** wǒ bùcún jiǎoxìng zhīxīn 我不存侥幸之心

Chancellor (*in Germany*) Zǒnglǐ 总理; (**of the Exchequer** in *Britain*) Cáizhèngdàchén 财政大臣

chandelier diàodēng 吊灯

Changbai Mountain Chángbáishān 长白山

change 1 *n* (*alteration: to plan, idea, script*) gǎibiàn 改变; (*in society, climate, condition*) biànhuà 变化; (*small coins*) língqián 零钱; (*from purchase*) zhǎoqián 找钱; (*different situation etc*) gēnghuàn 更换; **for a ~** huàn kǒuwèi 换口味; **a ~ of clothes** tìhuàn yīfu 替换衣服 2 *v/t* (*alter*) gǎibiàn 改变; bankbill, trains, planes, one's clothes, (*replace*) huàn 换 3 *v/i* biàn 变; (*put on different clothes*) huàn yīfu 换衣服; (*take different train / bus*) huàn 换

channel (*on TV, radio*) píndào 频道; (*waterway*) hǎixiá 海峡

chant 1 *n* hǎnjiào 喊叫 2 *v/i* gāohū 高呼

chaos hùnluàn 混乱

chaotic hùnluàn 混乱

chapel xiǎo jiàotáng 小教堂

chapped gānliè 干裂

chapter (*of book*) zhāng 章; (*of organization*) zhībù 支部

character (*nature*) běnxìng 本性; (*person*) rén 人; (*in book, play*) rénwù 人物; (*personality*) xìnggé

性格; (*for writing Chinese etc*) zì 字; **he's a real ~** tā hěn yǒu gèxìng 他很有个性

**characteristic 1** *n* tèdiǎn 特点 **2** *adj* diǎnxíng 典型

**characterize** (*be typical of*) diǎnfàn 典范; (*describe*) miáoshù 描述

**charbroiled** kǎo kǎo 烤

**charcoal** (*for barbecue*) mùtàn 木 炭; (*for drawing*) tànbǐ 炭笔

**charge 1** *n* (*fee*) fèiyòng 费用; LAW kònggào 控告; **free of ~** miǎnfèi 免费; **will that be cash or ~?** xiànjīn háishí jìzhàng? 现金还是 记账？; **be in ~** fùzé 负责; **take ~** jiēguǎn 接管 **2** *v/t* (*sum of money*) shōufèi 收费; (*put on account*) jìzhàng 记账; LAW zhǐkòng 指控; battery chōngdiàn 充电 **3** *v/i* (*of troops*) chōngfēng 冲锋; (*of animal*) jìngōng 进攻

**charge account** shēzhàng hùkǒu 赊账户口

**charge card** jìzhàng kǎ 记账卡

**charisma** mèilì 魅力

**charitable** *institution, donation, person* císhàn 慈善

**charity** (*assistance*) zhènjì 赈济; (*organization*) císhàn jīgòu 慈善 机构

**charm 1** *n* (*appealing quality*) mèilì 魅力; (*on bracelet etc*) xiǎo zhuāngshì pǐn 小装饰品 **2** *v/t* (*delight*) xīyǐn 吸引

**charming** mírén 迷人; *idea* yǒu xīyǐn lì 有吸引力

**charred** shāojiāo 烧焦

**chart** (*diagram*) túbiǎo 图表; (*map: for sea*) hánghǎi tú 航海图; (*for airplane*) hángkōng tú 航空图; **the ~s** MUS liúxíng chàngpiān xuǎnmù 流行唱片选目

**charter** *v/t* bāozū 包租

**charter flight** bāojī 包机

**chase 1** *n* zhuīzhú 追逐 **2** *v/t* zhuī 追

♦**chase away** gǎnzǒu 赶走

**chaser** (*drink*) suí lièjiǔ yǐhòu hēde dīdùjiǔ 随烈酒以后喝的低度 酒

**chassis** (*of car*) dǐpán 底盘

**chat 1** *n* liáotiān 聊天 **2** *v/i* liáo 聊

**chatter 1** *n* diédiè xiūxiū 喋喋不 休 **2** *v/i* (*talk*) xiánliáo 闲聊; (*of teeth*) dǎzhàn 打颤

**chatterbox** ráoshé zhě 饶舌者

**chatty** *person* jiàntán 健谈; *letter* jiācháng xiánhuà 家常闲话

**chauffeur** *n* sījī 司机

**chauvinist** (*male ~*) dà nánrén zhǔyì zhě 大男人主义者

**cheap** *adj* (*inexpensive*) piányi 便 宜; (*nasty*) dījí dīcéng 低级; (*mean*) xiǎoqì 小气

**cheat 1** *n* (*person*) piànzi 骗子 **2** *v/t* piàn 骗; **~ X out of Y** cóng Y nàli piànchū X 从Y那里骗出X **3** *v/i* (*in exam*) zuòbì 作弊; (*in cards etc*) gǎoguǐ 搞鬼; **~ on one's husband** gěi zhàngfu dài lù màozi 给丈夫戴绿帽子

**check** *n & adj* (*in pattern*) fānggé 方格

**check**[2] FIN zhīpiào 支票; (*in restaurant etc*) zhàngdān 账单; **the ~ please** zhàngdān 账单

**check**[3] **1** *n* (*to verify sth*) jiǎnchá 检 查; **keep in ~, hold in ~** kòngzhì 控制; **keep a ~ on** héduì 核对 **2** *v/t* (*verify*) cháchá 查查; (*machinery*) jiǎnchá 检查; (*restrain*) yìzhì 抑制; (*stop*) kòngzhì zhù 控制住; (*with a ~mark*) dǎgōu 打勾; (*coat, package etc*) cúnfàng 存放 **3** *v/i* cháchá 查 查; **~ for** jiǎnchá 检查

♦**check in** (*at airport*) lǐng dēngjī kǎ 领登机卡; (*at hotel*) dēngjì 登 记

♦**check off** héduì 核对

♦**check on** chákàn 察看

♦**check out 1** *v/i* (*of hotel*) ⇩ jiézhàng 结账 **2** *v/t* (*look into*) diàochá 调查; *club, restaurant etc* shìshì 试试

♦**check up on** diàochá 调查

♦**check with** (*of person*) wèn 问; (*tally: of information, facts*) fúhé 符 合

**checkbook** zhīpiào běn 支票本

**checked** *material* gézi 格子

**checkerboard** tiàoqí pán 跳棋盘

checkered *pattern* zònghéng-jiāocuò 纵横交错；*career* bǎojīng cāngsāng 饱经沧桑

checkers tiàoqí 跳棋

check-in (counter) lǐng dēngjī kǎ guìtái 领登机卡柜台

checking account zhīpiào zhànghù 支票帐户

check-in time lǐng dēngjī kǎ shíjiān 领登机卡时间

checklist qīngdān 清单；check mark gōuhào 勾号；checkmate *n* jiāngsǐ 将死；checkout (*in supermarket*) guìtái 柜台；checkout time (*from hotel*) ⇩ jiézhàng shíjiān 结账时间；checkpoint (*military, police*) guānqiǎ 关卡；checkroom (*for coats*) yīmào jiān 衣帽间；(*for baggage*) xínglǐ cúnfàng chù 行李存放处；checkup *medical* jiànkāng jiǎnchá 健康检查；*dental* yáchǐ jiǎnchá 牙齿检查

cheek miànjiá 面颊

cheekbone quángǔ 颧骨

cheer 1 *n* huānhū 欢呼；~*s!* (*toast*) gānbēi! 干杯！*v/t* shòu huānyíng 受欢迎 3 *v/i* hècǎi 喝采

♦ cheer on hècǎi 喝采

♦ cheer up 1 *v/i* gāoxìng qǐlái 高兴起来；~! gǔ qǐ jìnr lái! 鼓起劲儿来！2 *v/t*: *cheer X up* ràng X gāoxìng 让 X 高兴

cheerful kuàihuó 快活

cheering huānhū 欢呼

cheerleader lālāduì yuán 啦啦队员

cheese ⇩ nǎilào 奶酪

cheeseburger nǎilào hànbǎobāo 奶酪汉堡包

cheesecake ⇩ nǎilào dàngāo 奶酪蛋糕

chef chúshī 厨师

chemical 1 *adj* huàxué 化学 2 *n* huàxué zhìpǐn 化学制品

chemical warfare huàxué zhàn 化学战

chemist huàxué jiā 化学家

chemistry huàxué 化学；*fig* mòqì 默契

chemotherapy huàxué liáofǎ 化学疗法

cherish *memory, hope* zhēnxī 珍惜

cherry (*fruit*) yīngtáo 樱桃；(*tree*) yīnghuā shù 樱花树

chess xiàngqí 象棋

chessboard qípán 棋盘

chest (*of person*) xiōng 胸；(*box*) xiāngzi 箱子

chestnut lìzi 栗子；(*tree*) lìzi shù 栗子树

chest of drawers tì guì 屉柜

chew *v/t* jiáo 嚼；(*of dog, rats*) kěn 啃

♦ chew out F shǔluò 数落

chewing gum kǒuxiāng táng 口香糖

Chiang Kai-shek Jiǎng Jièshí 蒋介石

chick xiǎojī 小鸡；F (*girl*) niū niū 妞妞

chicken 1 *n* jī 鸡；(*food*) jīròu 鸡肉；F dǎnxiǎo guǐ 胆小鬼 2 *adj* F (*cowardly*) dǎnxiǎo 胆小

♦ chicken out dǎ tuìtánggǔ 打退堂鼓

chickenfeed F méi yóushui 没油水

chicken pox shuǐdòu 水痘

chief 1 *n* (*head*) tóunǎo 头脑；(*of tribe*) zúzhǎng 族长 2 *adj* zhǔyào 主要

chiefly zhǔyào 主要

chilblain dòngchuāng 冻疮

child háizi 孩子；*pej* yòuzhì 幼稚

childbirth shēngchǎn 生产

childhood tóngnián 童年

childish *pej* yòuzhì 幼稚

childless wú zǐnǚ 无子女

childlike tiānzhēn wúxié 天真无邪

Children's Day Értóngjié 儿童节

chill 1 *n* (*in air*) lěngqì 冷气；(*illness*) gǎnmào 感冒 2 *v/t* *wine* lěngcáng 冷藏

chilli (*pepper*) làjiāo 辣椒

chilly *weather* hánlěng 寒冷；*welcome* lěngdàn 冷淡；*I'm~* wǒ yǒudiǎn lěng 我有点冷

chime *v/i* míng 鸣

chimney yāncōng 烟囱

chimpanzee hēi xīngxing 黑猩猩

chin xiàbā 下巴

china cíqì 磁器; (material) cí 磁

China Zhōngguó 中国

China Central Television Zhōngyāng Diànshìtái 中央电视台; China Daily Zhōngguó Rìbào 中国日报; China International Travel Service Zhōngguó Guójì Lǚxíngshè 中国国际旅行社; China Travel Service Zhōngguó Lǚxíngshè 中国旅行社; Chinatown (in other countries) Tángrénjiē 唐人街

Chinese 1 adj Zhōngguó 中国; (in Chinese) Zhōngwén 中文 2 n (written language) Zhōngwén 中文; (spoken language) Zhōngguó huà 中国话; (person) Zhōngguó rén 中国人

Chinese character hànzì 汉字; Chinese checkers tiàoqí 跳棋; Chinese chess xiàngqí 象棋; Chinese doctor zhōngyī 中医; Chinese dumpling jiǎozi 饺子; Chinese foot (measurement) chǐ 尺; Chinese inch (measurement) cùn 寸; Chinese leaf / cabbage báicài 白菜; Chinese leek jiǔcài 韭菜; Chinese medicine zhōngyī 中医; (herbs, drugs) zhōngyào 中药; Chinese New Year Chūnjié 春节; Chinese New Year's Day Chūyī 初一; Chinese New Year's Eve Chúxī 除夕; Chinese onion cōng 葱; Chinese-style Zhōngshì 中式

chink (gap) fèng 缝; (sound) dīngdāng shēng 叮当声

chip 1 n (fragment) suìxiè 碎屑; (damage) liè kǒu 裂口; (in gambling) chóumǎ 筹码; COMPUT xīnpiàn 芯片; potato ~s ⇩ shǔpiàn 薯片 2 v/t (damage) nòng pò yīdiǎn 弄破一点

♦ chip in (interrupt) chāzuǐ 插嘴; (with money) chūqián 出钱

chiropractor ànmójìshī 按摩技师

chirp v/i jījí jiào 唧唧叫

chisel n záozi 凿子

chivalrous xiáyì 侠义

chives jiǔcài 韭菜

chlorine lǜ 氯

chockfull yōngjǐ 拥挤

chocolate qiǎokèlì 巧克力; hot ~ rè qiǎokèlì 热巧克力

chocolate cake qiǎokèlì dàngāo 巧克力蛋糕

choice 1 n xuǎnzé 选择; (selection) gèsè gèyàng 各色各样; (preference) xuǎnzé 选择; I had no ~ wǒ méiyǒu xuǎnzé yúdì 我没有选择余地 2 adj (top quality) jīngxuǎn 精选

choir héchàngtuán 合唱团

choke 1 n MOT zǔfēngmén 阻风门 2 v/i qiǎ ~ kǎ; he ~d on a bone tā qiǎle gǔtóu 他卡了骨头 3 v/t qiā bózi 掐脖子

cholesterol dǎngùchún 胆固醇

choose xuǎnzé 选择 2 v/i tiāoxuǎn 挑选

choosey F tiāotì 挑剔

chop 1 n kǎn 砍; (meat) páigǔ 排骨; (seal) túzhāng 图章 2 v/t wood kǎn 砍; meat, vegetables duò 跺

♦ chop down (tree) kǎndǎo 砍倒

chopper (tool) kǎndǎo 砍刀; F (helicopter) zhíshēng fēijī 直升飞机

chopsticks kuàizi 筷子

chord MUS xián 弦

chore (household task) jiāwù 家务

choreographer wǔdǎo biāndǎo 舞蹈编导

choreography biān wǔ shù 编舞术

chorus (singers) héchàng tuán 合唱团; (of song) héchàng 合唱

Chou En-lai Zhōu Ēnlái 周恩来

Christ Jīdū 基督; ~! wǒde tiān ya! 我的天呀!

christen xǐlǐ 洗礼

Christian 1 n Jīdū tú 基督徒 2 adj Jīdū jiào 基督教; attitude Jīdū jiào 基督教

Christianity Jīdūjiào 基督教

Christian name míng 名

Christmas Shèngdànjié 圣诞节; at ~ Shèngdànjié qījiān 圣诞节期间; Merry ~! Shèngdàn kuàilè! 圣诞快乐!

Christmas card Shèngdàn kǎ 圣

诞卡; Christmas Day
Shèngdànjié 圣诞节; Christmas
Eve Shèngdàn yè 圣诞夜;
Christmas present Shèngdàn
lǐwù 圣诞礼物; Christmas tree
Shèngdàn shù 圣诞树
chrome, chromium gè 铬
chronic mànxìng 慢性
chronological shíjiān shùnxù 时
间顺序; in ~ order àn shíjiān
shùnxù 按时间顺序
chrysanthemum júhuā 菊花
chubby féipàng 肥胖
chuck v/t F rēng 扔
♦chuck out object rēngdiào 扔掉;
person hōng 轰
chuckle 1 n qīngxiào 轻笑 2 v/i
gēgē de xiào 咯咯地笑
chunk dàkuài 大块
church jiàotáng 教堂
chute xiécáo 斜槽; (for garbage)
lājī dào 垃圾道
CIA (= Central Intelligence
Agency) Zhōngyāng Qíngbào Jú
中央情报局
cider píngguǒ jiǔ 苹果酒
CIF (= cost insurance freight)
chéngběn jiā bǎoxiǎn fèi 成本加
保险费
cigar xuějiā 雪茄
cigarette xiāngyān 香烟
cinema (Br: building) diànyǐng
yuàn 电影院; (as institution)
diànyǐng 电影
cinnamon ròuguì 肉桂
circle 1 n yuánquān 圆圈; (group)
quānzi 圈子 2 v/t (draw circle
around) dǎquān 打圈 3 v/i (of
plane, bird) pánxuán 盘旋
circuit Elec xiànlù 线路; (lap) quān
圈
circuit board xiànlù bǎn 线路板
circuit breaker duànlù kāiguān 断
路开关
circular 1 n (giving information)
tōngzhī 通知 2 adj yuánxíng 圆形
circulate 1 v/i xúnhuán 循环 2 v/t
(memo) chuányuè 传阅
circulation BIO xúnhuán 循环; (of
newspaper, magazine) xiāolù 销路
circumference yuánzhōu 圆周

circumstances qíngkuàng 情况;
(financial) jīngjì qíngkuàng 经济
情况; under no ~ juébùnéng 决
不能; under the ~ zài zhèzhǒng
qíng kuàng xià 在这种情况下
circus mǎxìtuán 马戏团
cistern shuǐxiāng 水箱
citizen gōngmín 公民
citizenship guójí 国籍
CITS (= China International Travel
Service) Zhōngguó Guójì
Lǚxíngshè 中国国际旅行社
city chéngshì 城市; ~ center shì
zhōngxīn 市中心; ~ hall shìzhèng
tīng 市政厅
civic adj chéngshì 城市; pride,
responsibilities gōngmín 公民
civil (as opposed to military) mínjiān
民间; disobedience etc gōngmín 公
民; (polite) yǒu lǐmào 有礼貌
civil engineer tǔmù gōngchéngshī
土木工程师
civilian 1 n píngmín 平民 2 adj
clothes biànzhuāng 便装
civilization wénmíng 文明
civilize person jiàodǎo 教导
civil rights gōngmín quán 公民
权; civil servant gōngwùyuán 公
务员; civil service xíngzhèng
jīguān 行政机关; civil war
nèizhàn 内战
claim 1 n (request) suǒpéi 索赔;
(right) quánlì 权利; (assertion)
zhǔzhāng 主张 2 v/t (ask for as a
right) suǒqǔ 索取; (assert)
shēngchēng 声称; lost property
lǐng 领; they have ~ed responsibility for the attack tāmén duì
zhècì gōngjī biǎoshì fùzérèn 他们
对这次攻击表示负责任
claimant shēnqǐng rén 申请人;
LAW yuángào 原告
clam gélí 蛤蜊
♦clam up F sìbù kāikǒu 死不开
口
clammy hands niánhūhu 黏糊糊;
weather mēnrè 闷热
clamor (noise) xuānhuáshēng 喧哗
声; (outcry) hūshēng 呼声
♦clamor for chǎozheyào 吵着要
clamp 1 n (fastener) jiāzi 夹子 2 v/t

*(fasten)* jiājǐn 夹紧
♦ clamp down yāzhì 压制
♦ clamp down on duì … jiāyǐ kòngzhì 对 … 加以控制
clan jiāzú 家族
clandestine mìmì 秘密
clang 1 n kēngqiāngshēng 铿锵声 2 v/i kēngde yīshēng 铿地一声
clap 1 v/i *(applaud)* pāishǒu 拍手 2 v/t pāi 拍
clarify chéngqīng 澄清
clarinet dānhuángguǎn 单簧管
clarity qīngxīdù 清晰度
clash 1 n chōngtū 冲突; *(of personalities)* bù xiétiáo 不协调 2 v/i fāshēng chōngtū 发生冲突; *(of opinions)* bùyīzhì 不一致; ~ **with ...** *(of events)* hé … fāshēng chōngtū 和 … 发生冲突; *(of colors)* hé … bù xiétiáo 和 … 不协调
clasp 1 n jiāzi 夹子 2 v/t *(in hand)* jǐnwò 紧握
class 1 n *(lesson)* kè 课; *(group of people)* bān 班; *(category)* děngjí 等级; *(social ~)* jiēcéng 阶层 2 v/t guīlèi 归类
classic 1 adj *(typical)* diǎnxíng 典型; *(definitive)* quánwēi xìng 权威性 2 n jīngdiǎn zuòpǐn 经典作品
classical *music* gǔdiǎn 古典
classification *(act)* děngjí 等级; *(category)* fēnlèi 分类
classified *information* jīmì 机密
classified ad(vertisement) fēnlèi guǎnggào 分类广告
classify *(categorize)* fēnlèi 分类
classmate tóngxué 同学; classroom jiàoshì 教室; class warfare jiējí dòuzhēng 阶级斗争
classy F gāojí 高级
clatter 1 n huālā 哗啦 2 v/i kuāngdāng kuāngdāng xiǎng 哐当哐当响
clause *(in agreement)* tiáokuǎn 条款; GRAM cóngjù 从句
claustrophobia yōubì kǒngbù zhèng 幽闭恐怖症
claw 1 n *(of lobster, crab)* qiánzi 钳子; *(of cat, woman)* zhuǎzi 爪子 2 v/t *(scratch)* zhuā 抓

clay niántǔ 粘土
clean 1 adj gānjìng 干净 2 adv F *(completely)* wánquán 完全 3 v/t *teeth, shoes* shuā 刷; *house, room* dǎsǎo 打扫; *car, hands, face, clothes* xǐ 洗; **have ... ~ed** bǎ … náqù xǐ 把 … 拿去洗
♦ clean out *room, cupboard* dǎsǎo gānjìng 打扫干净; *fig* bǎ X shū guāng le 把 X 输光了
♦ clean up 1 v/t shōushí gānjìng 收拾干净 2 v/i dǎsǎo dǎ sǎo 打扫; *(wash)* shūxǐ 梳洗; *(on stock market etc)* fācái 发财
cleaner *(person)* qīngjié gōng 清洁工; *dry ~* gānxǐ diàn 干洗店
cleaning woman qīngjié nǚgōng 清洁女工
cleanse *(skin)* qīngjié 清洁
cleanser *(for skin)* qīngjié jì 清洁剂
clear 1 adj *explanation, photograph, voice* qīngchu 清楚; *(obvious)* míngxiǎn 明显; *weather, sky* qínglǎng 晴朗; *water, eyes* qīngchè 清澈; *skin* qīngbái 清白; **a ~ thinker** tóunǎo mǐnruì de rén 头脑敏锐的人; **I'm not ~ about it** wǒ bù dà míngbái 我不大明白; **I didn't make myself ~** wǒ méi jiǎng qīngchu 我没讲清楚 2 adv: **stand ~ of** bùyào kàojìn 不要靠近; **steer ~ of** bǎochí jùlí 保持距离 3 v/t *roads etc* qīngchú 清除; *(acquit)* chéngqīng 澄清; *(authorize)* yǔnxǔ 允许; *(earn)* zhèng 挣; **~ one's throat** qīng sǎngzi 清嗓子 4 v/i *(of sky, mist)* qíngle 晴了; *(of face)* kāilǎng 开朗
♦ clear away v/t shōushí 收拾
♦ clear off v/i táopǎo 逃跑; **~!** gǔnkāi! 滚开!
♦ clear out 1 v/t *(cupboard)* qīnglǐ 清理 2 v/i táopǎo 逃跑
♦ clear up 1 v/i *(tidy up)* shōushí 收拾; *(of weather)* zhuǎnqíng 转晴; *(of illness, rash)* xiāoshī 消失 2 v/t *(tidy)* shōushí 收拾; *mystery, problem* jiějué 解决

clearance (*space*) kōngjiān 空间; (*authorization*) xǔkě 许可

clearance sale qīngcāng dà pāimài 清仓大拍卖

clearly (*with clarity*) qīngchu 清楚; (*evidently*) míngxiǎn 明显

clemency réncí 仁慈

clench *teeth* yǎojǐn 咬紧; *fist* wòjǐn 握紧

clergy shénzhí rényuán 神职人员

clergyman mùshī 牧师

clerk (*administrative*) zhíyuán 职员; (*in store*) fúwùyuán 服務员

clever *person, animal, idea* cōngmíng 聪明; *gadget, device* qiǎomiào 巧妙

click 1 *n* COMPUT diǎnjī 点击 2 *v/i* kādāshēngxiǎng 咔嗒声响

♦ click on COMPUT àn 按

client gùkè 顾客

cliff xuányá 悬崖

climate qìhòu 气候; *economic* ~ jīngjì qìhòu 经济气候

climax *n* gāocháo 高潮

climb 1 *n* (*up mountain*) pāndēng 攀登 2 *v/t* pá 爬 3 *v/i* (*in mountains etc*) pá 爬; *fig* (*inflation etc*) shàngshēng 上升

♦ climb down pá xiàlái 爬下来; *fig* ràngbù 让步

climber (*person*) dēngshān zhě 登山者

clinch: ~ *a deal* dáchéng jiāoyì 达成交易

cling (*of clothes*) tiēshēn 贴身

♦ cling to (*of child*) zhānzhe 粘着; *ideas, tradition* gùshǒu 固守

clingfilm bǎoxiān zhǐ 保鲜纸

clingy *child, boyfriend* chánrén 缠人

clinic zhěnsuǒ 诊所

clinical línchuáng 临床

clink 1 *n* (*noise*) dīngdāngshēng 叮当声 2 *v/i* dīngdāng zuòxiǎng 叮当作响

clip¹ 1 *n* (*fastener*) jiāzi 夹子 2 *v/t* jiā 夹; ~ *X to Y* bǎ X jiādào Y shàng 把 X 夹到 Y 上

clip² 1 *n* (*extract*) jiǎnjí 剪辑 2 *v/t* *hair, hedge, grass* jiǎn 剪

clipboard xiězì jiábǎn 写字夹板;

COMPUT jiǎntiē bǎn 剪贴板

clippers (*for hair*) tuīzi 推子; (*for nails*) zhǐjiǎdāo 指甲刀; (*for gardening*) jiǎncǎo qián 剪草钳

clipping (*from newspaper*) jiǎnbào 剪报

cloak *n* dǒupeng 斗篷

clock zhōng 钟; (*speedometer*) jìchéng qì 记程器

clock radio shōuyīnjī nàozhōng 收音机闹钟

clockwise shùn shízhēn 顺时针

clockwork fātiáo 发条; *it went like* ~ yíqiè shùnlì 一切顺利

♦ clog up 1 *v/i* dǔzhù 堵住 2 *v/t* sāizhù 塞住

close¹ 1 *adj family, friend* qīnmì 亲密; *resemblance* xiāngjìn 相近 2 *adv* jìn 近; ~ *at hand* zài shēnbiān 在身边; ~ *by* fùjìn 附近; *it's* ~ *to the stores* lí shāngdiàn jìn, hěn fāngbiàn 离商店近,很方便; *be* ~ *to X* (*as a friend etc*) hé X qīnjìn 和 X 亲近

close² 1 *v/t* guān 关; (*permanently: business*) guānbì 关闭 2 *v/i* (*of door, store*) guānmén 关门; (*of window*) guān 关; (*of eyes*) bìshàng 闭上; (*of store: permanently*) guānbì 关闭

♦ close down *v/t* & *v/i* guānbì 关闭

♦ close in *v/i* pòjìn 迫近

♦ close up 1 *v/t building* fēngbì 封闭 2 *v/i* (*move closer*) kàolǒng 靠拢

closed *store* guānmén 关门; *eyes* bìshàng 闭上

closed-circuit television bìlù diànshì 闭路电视

closely *listen, watch* zǐxì 仔细; *cooperate* mìqiè 密切

closet yīguì 衣柜

close-up tèxiě jìngtóu 特写镜头

closing time guānmén shíjiān 关门时间

closure guānbì 关闭

clot 1 *n* (*of blood*) xuèkuài 血块 2 *v/i* (*of blood*) jiékuài 结块

cloth (*fabric*) bùliào 布料; (*for kitchen, cleaning*) mābù 抹布

clothes yīfu 衣服

clothes brush shuāzi 刷子

clothes hanger yījià 衣架

clothing yīfu 衣服

cloud n yún 云; a ~ of smoke / dust yízhèn yān / chéntǔ 一阵烟／尘土

♦cloud over (of sky) tiānyīnle 天阴了

cloudburst qīngpéndàyǔ 倾盆大雨

cloudy yīntiān 阴天

clout fig (influence) yǐngxiǎng 影响

clown (in circus) xiǎochǒu 小丑; (joker) chǒujiǎo 丑角; pej chǔncái 蠢材

club n (weapon) mùgùn 木棍; (golf iron) qiúgān 球杆; (organization) jùlèbù 俱乐部

clue xiànsuǒ 线索; I haven't a ~ wǒ wánquán bù zhīdào 我完全不知道

clued-up zàiháng 在行

clump n (of earth) tǔkuài 土块; (group) cuō 撮

clumsiness bènzhuō 笨拙

clumsy person bènshǒu bènjiǎo 笨手笨脚

cluster 1 n (of people) qún 群; (of houses) pái 排 2 v/i (of people) jùjí 聚集; (of houses) jízhōng 集中

clutch 1 n MOT líhéqì 离合器 2 v/t jǐnwò 紧握

♦clutch at shìtú zhuāzhù 试图抓住

Co. (= Company) gōngsī 公司

c/o (= care of) fánjiāo 烦交

coach 1 n (trainer) jiàoliàn 教练 2 v/t zhǐdǎo 指导

coagulate (of blood) níngjié 凝结

coal méi 煤

coalition liánméng 联盟

coal-mine méikuàng 煤矿

coarse fabric cūcāo 粗糙; hair cūyìng 粗硬; (vulgar) cūsú 粗俗

coast n hǎibīn 海边; at the ~ zài hǎibiān 在海边

coastal línhǎi 临海

coastguard hǎi'àn jǐngwèi duì 海岸警卫队; (person) hǎi'àn jǐngwèi 海岸警卫

coastline hǎi'àn xiàn 海岸线

coat 1 n wàiyī 外衣; (over~) dàyī 大衣; (of animal) máopí 毛皮; (of paint etc) céng 层 2 v/t (cover) jiāshàng yīcéng 加上一层

coathanger yījià 衣架

coating céng 层

coax hǒng 哄

cobweb zhīzhūwǎng 蜘蛛网

cocaine kěkǎyīn 可卡因

cock n (chicken) gōngjī 公鸡; (any male bird) gōngniǎo 公鸟

cockeyed idea etc huāngmiù 荒谬

cockpit (of plane) zuòcāng 座舱

cockroach zhāngláng 蟑螂

cocktail jīwěijiǔ 鸡尾酒

cocoa (plant) kěkě shù 可可树; (drink) kěkě 可可

coconut (to eat) yēzi 椰子

coconut milk yēzi nǎi 椰子奶

coconut palm yēzi shù 椰子树

COD (= collect on delivery) huòdào fùkuǎn 货到付款

coddle sick person zhàoliào 照料; child jiāoshēng guànyǎng 娇生惯养

code n mìmǎ 密码

co-educational nánnǚ héxiào 男女合校

coerce qiǎngpò 强迫

coexist gòngcún 共存

coexistence gòngchǔ 共处

coffee kāfēi 咖啡

coffee break xiǎoxī 小息; coffee maker kāfēi jī 咖啡机; coffee pot kāfēi hú 咖啡壶; coffee shop kāfēi diàn 咖啡店; coffee table chájī 茶几

coffin guāncai 棺材

cog lúnchǐ 轮齿

cognac báilándì 白兰地

cogwheel qiàn chǐlún 嵌齿轮

cohabit tóngjū 同居

coherent liánguàn 连贯

coil 1 n (of rope) juǎn 卷 2 v/t juǎn 卷; ~ (up) juǎn qǐlái 卷起来

coin n yìngbì 硬币

coincide qiǎohé 巧合

coincidence qiǎohé 巧合

coke F (cocaine) kěkǎyīn 可卡因

Coke® kěkǒu kělè 可口可乐

cold 1 adj lěng 冷; I'm (feeling) ~

wǒ juéde hěnlěng 我觉得很冷;
*it's ~* tiānqì hěnlěng 天气很冷;
*in ~ blood* lěngkù 冷酷; *get ~
feet* dǎ tuìtánggǔ 打退堂鼓 2 *n*
hánlěng 寒冷; *I have a ~* wǒ
gǎnmàole 我感冒了

cold boiled water liáng kāishuǐ
凉开水; cold-blooded lěngxuè 冷
血; *fig* lěngkù 冷酷; cold cuts
lěngpán 冷盘; cold noodles
lěngmiàn 冷面; cold sore
zuǐbiān pàozhěn 嘴边疱疹

coleslaw (*northern China*) liángbàn
yángbáicài 凉拌洋白菜;
(*southern China*) liángbàn
juǎnxīncài 凉拌卷心菜

colic jiǎotòng 绞痛

collaborate (*in research, etc*) hézuò
合作; (*with enemy*) gōujié 勾结

collaboration hézuò 合作; (*with
enemy*) gōujié 勾结

collaborator hézuò zhě 合作者;
(*with enemy*) gōujié zhě 勾结者

collapse dǎotā 倒塌; (*of person*)
bēngkuì 崩溃

collapsible zhédié 折迭

collar lǐngzi 领子; (*for dog, cat*)
xiàngquān 项圈

collarbone suǒgǔ 锁骨

colleague tóngshì 同事

collect 1 *v/t person* jiē接; *tickets,
cleaning etc* ná 拿; (*gather, as
hobby*) shōují 收集 2 *v/i* (*gather
together*) jízhōng 集中 3 *adv: call
~* shòuhuàrén fùfèi 受话人付费

collect call shòuhuàrén fùfèi 受话
人付费

collected *works, poems etc* quánjí
全集; *person* zhènjìng 镇静

collection (*of art*) shōucángpǐn 收
藏品; (*fashions*) shízhuāng
zhǎnlǎn 时装展览; (*in church*)
mùjuān 募捐

collective 1 *adj* gòngtóng 共同;
POL jítǐ 集体 2 *n* POL jítǐ 集体

collective bargaining jítǐ xiédìng
集体协定

collector shōucáng jiā 收藏家

college xuéyuàn 学院

college exam ⇩ gāokǎo 高考

collide pèngzhuàng 碰撞

collision xiāngzhuàng 相撞

colloquial kǒuyǔ 口语

colon (*punctuation*) màohào 冒号;
ANAT jiécháng 结肠

colonel shàngxiào 上校

colonial *adj* zhímíndì 殖民地

colonize *country* kāituò zhímíndì
开拓殖民地

colony zhímíndì 殖民地

color 1 *n* yánsè 颜色; (*in cheeks*)
liǎnsè 脸色; *in ~* (*movie etc*) cǎisè
彩色; *~s* MIL jūnqí 军旗 2 *v/t
one's hair* rǎnsè 染色 3 *v/i* (*blush*)
liǎnhóng 脸红

color-blind sèmáng 色盲

colored *adj person* hēi 黑

color fast bú tuìsè 不褪色

colorful xiānyàn 鲜艳; *account*
jīngcǎi 精彩

coloring yánsè 颜色; (*of the skin*)
fūsè 肤色

color photograph cǎicè zhàopiān
彩色照片; color scheme sècǎi
shèjì 色彩设计; color TV cǎisè
diànshì 彩色电视

colt xióngjū 雄驹

column liè 列; (*architectural*)
yuánzhù 圆柱; (*of text*) lán lán 栏;
(*newspaper feature*) zhuānlán 专栏

columnist zhuānlán zuòjiā 专栏
作家

coma hūnmí 昏迷

comb 1 *n* shūzi 梳子 2 *v/t* shū 梳;
*area* sōuxún 搜寻

combat 1 *n* zhàndòu 战斗 2 *v/t* yǔ
... zuò dòuzhēng 与 ... 做斗争

combination zǔhé 组合; (*of safe*)
mìmǎ 密码

combine 1 *v/t ingredients* hùnhé 混
合; *~ X with Y* jiāngù X hé Y 兼
顾 X hé Y 2 *v/i* (*of chemical
elements*) huàhé 化合

combine harvester liánhé
shōugējī 联合收割机

combustible yìrán 易燃

combustion ránshāo 燃烧

come (*toward speaker*) lái 来;
(*toward listener*) (*of train,
bus*) láile 来了; *don't ~ too close*
bié tài kàojìn 别太靠近; *in the
years to ~* zài jīnhòu jǐnián 在今

后几年; *how ~?* F zěnme? 怎
么？

♦ **come about** (*happen*) fāshēng 发
生

♦ **come across 1** *v/t items* wúyì
zhōng fāxiàn 无意中发现;
*person* wúyì zhōng yùdào 无意中
遇到 **2** *v/i: it didn't ~* (*of idea,
humor*) méi rén míngbái 没人明
白; *she comes across as …* tā
sìhū shì … 她似乎是 …

♦ **come along** (*come too*) yīdàolái
一道来; (*turn up*) láidào 来到;
(*progress*) jìnzhǎn 进展

♦ **come apart** kě chāizhuāng 可拆
装; (*break*) suìle 碎了

♦ **come around** (*to s.o.'s home*) lái
来; (*regain consciousness*) sūxǐng
苏醒

♦ **come away** (*leave*) líkāi 离开;
(*of button etc*) diàole 掉了

♦ **come back** huílái 回来; *it came
back to me* wǒ xiǎng qǐláile 我想
起来了

♦ **come by 1** *v/i* bàifǎng 拜访 **2** *v/t*
(*acquire*) dédào 得到

♦ **come down** xià lái 下来; (*in
price, amount etc*) xiàjiàng 下降;
(*of rain, snow*) xià 下; *he came
down the stairs* tā zǒuxià lóutī 他
走下楼梯

♦ **come for** (*attack*) gōngjí 攻击;
(*collect: thing*) láiqǔ 来取; (*collect:
person*) láijiē 来接

♦ **come forward** (*present oneself*)
tǐngshēn érchū 挺身而出

♦ **come from** láizì 来自

♦ **come in** zǒu jìnlái 走进来; (*of
train*) dàodá 到达; (*of tide*) zhǎngcháo 涨潮; *~!* qǐngjìn! 请进！;
*the horse came in fourth* nà mǎ
pǎole dìsì 那马跑了第四

♦ **come in for**: *~ criticism* shòudào
pīpíng 受到批评

♦ **come in on**: *~ a deal* jiārù jiāoyì
加入交易

♦ **come off** (*of handle etc*) tuōluò 脱
落

♦ **come on** (*progress*) jìnzhǎn 进
展; *~!* kuàidiǎnr! 快点儿！; (*in
disbelief*) bùkěnéng 不可能

♦ **come out** (*of person*) chū 出; (*of
sun, results, product*) chūlái 出来;
(*of stain*) xiāoshī 消失; (*of book,
record*) fāxíng 发行

♦ **come to 1** *v/t place* dàodá 到达;
(*of hair, dress, water*) dádào 达到;
*that comes to $70* zǒnggòng qīshí
měiyuán 总共七十美元 **2** *v/i*
(*regain consciousness*) sūxǐng 苏醒

♦ **come up** shàngqù 上去; (*of sun*)
shēng qǐlái 升起来; *something
has ~* yǒushì fāshēng 有事发生

♦ **come up with** *new idea etc* xiǎng
qǐlái 想起来

**comeback**: *make a ~* dōngshān
zàiqǐ 东山再起

**comedian** xǐjù yǎnyuán 喜剧演
员; *pej* chǒujiǎo 丑角

**comedown** luòpò 落泊

**comedy** xǐjù 喜剧

**comet** huìxīng 彗星

**comeuppance**: *he'll get his ~* tā
huì dédào bàoyìng 他会得到报
应

**comfort 1** *n* xiǎngshòu 享受;
(*consolation*) ānwèi 安慰 **2** *v/t*
ānwèi 安慰

**comfortable** *chair, house, room*
shūfu 舒服; *be ~* (*of person*) shūfu
舒服; (*financially*) fùyù 富裕

**comic 1** *n* (*to read*) mànhuà 漫画
**2** *adj* yǒuqù 有趣

**comical** huájī 滑稽

**comic book** mànhuà shū 漫画书

**comics** liánhuán mànhuà 连环漫
画

**comma** dòuhào 逗号

**command 1** *n* mìnglìng 命令 **2** *v/t*
mìnglìng 命令

**commander** zhǐhuīguān 指挥官

**commander-in-chief** zǒngsīlìng
总司令

**commemorate** jìniàn 纪念

**commemoration**: *in ~ of …* jìniàn
… 纪念 …

**commence** *v/t & v/i* kāishǐ 开始

**comment 1** *n* yìjiàn 意见; *no ~*
wúkě fènggào 无可奉告 **2** *v/i*
fābiǎo yìjiàn 发表意见

**commentary** pínglùn 评论

**commentator** pínglùn jiā 评论家

commerce shāngyè 商业

commercial 1 *adj* shāngyè 商业 2 *n* (*ad*) guǎnggào 广告

commercial break guǎnggào 广告

commercialize *v/t* shāngyè huà 商业化

commercial traveler lǚxíng tuīxiāo yuán 旅行推销员

commiserate tóngqíng 同情

commission 1 *n* (*payment*) yòngjīn 佣金; (*job*) chéngbāo 承包; (*committee*) wěiyuánhuì 委员会 2 *v/t* (*for a job*) wěituō 委托

commit *money* chéngnuò 承诺; ~ *a crime* fànzuì 犯罪; ~ *oneself* tóurù 投入

commitment zérèn 责任

committee wěiyuánhuì 委员会

commodity shāngpǐn 商品

common (*not rare*) píngcháng 平常; (*shared*) gòngtóng 共同; *in* ~ gòngtóng zhīchù 共同之处; *have something in* ~ *with X* hé X yǒu gòngtóng zhīchù 和 X 有共同之处

common law wife tóngjū qīzi 同居妻子; commonplace *adj* píngyōng 平庸; common sense chángshì 常识

commotion sāodòng 搔动

communal gōngyòng 公用

commune gōngshè 公社

communicate 1 *v/i* (*have contact, make self understood*) gōutōng 沟通 2 *v/t* zhuǎndá 转达

communication gōutōng 沟通

communications tōngxùn yè 通讯业

communications satellite tōngxùn wèixīng 通讯卫星

communicative *person* ài shuōhuà 爱说话

Communism Gòngchǎnzhǔyì 共产主义

Communist 1 *adj* Gòngchǎnzhǔyì 共产主义 2 *n* Gòngchǎndǎngyuán 共产党员

Communist China Zhōnggòng 中共

Communist Party Gòngchǎndǎng 共产党

community shèqū 社区

commute 1 *v/i* (*to work*) chéngchē shàngbān 乘车上班; *he* ~*s to work in Tianjin* tā chéngchē qù Tiānjīn shàngbān 他乘车去天津上班 2 *v/t* LAW jiǎnxíng 减刑

commuter chéngchē shàngbān zhě 乘车上班者; *the trains are packed with* ~*s* huǒchē jǐmǎnle chéngchē shàngbān zhě 火车挤满了乘车上班者

commuter traffic shàngxiàbān jiāotōng 上下班交通

commuter train shàngxià bān huǒchē 上下班火车

compact 1 *adj* xiùzhēn 袖珍 2 *n* MOT xiǎoxíng kèchē 小型客车

compact disc MUS jīguāng chàngpiān 激光唱片; COMPUT guāngpán 光盘

companion bànlǚ 伴侣

companionship péibàn 陪伴

company COM gōngsī 公司; (*companionship*) péibàn 陪伴; (*guests*) kèrén 客人

company car gōngsī chē 公司车

company law gōngsī fǎ 公司法

comparable (*which can be compared*) kě bǐjiào 可比较; (*similar*) lèisì 类似

comparative 1 *adj* (*relative*) xiāngduì 相对; *study* bǐjiào 比较; ~ *form* GRAM bǐjiào jí 比较级 2 *n* GRAM bǐjiào jí 比较级

comparatively xiāngduì éryán 相对而言

compare 1 *v/t* bǐjiào 比较; ~ *X with Y* jiāng X yǔ Y xiāng bǐjiào 将 X 与 Y 相比较; ~*d with X* yǔ X xiāngbǐ 与 X 相比 2 *v/i* bǐjiào 比较

comparison bǐjiào 比较; *there's no* ~ méidebǐ 没的比

compartment (*cupboard*) chúguì 橱柜; (*for credit cards etc*) jiácéng 夹层

compass luópán yí 罗盘仪; (*pair of*) ~*es* yuánguī 园规

compassion tóngqíng 同情

compassionate yǒu tóngqíng xīn

有同情心

**compatibility** fúhé xìng 符合性

**compatible** *people* hédelái 合得来; *blood types, life styles* fúhé 符合; COMPUT xiāngróng 相容; **we're not ~** wǒmen hébùlái 我们合不来

**compel** *(force)* qiǎngpò 强迫; **I felt ~led to …** wǒ bùdebù … wǒ bùdé bù …

**compelling** *argument* lìngrén xìnfú 令人信服; *movie, book* yǐnrén rùshèng 引人入胜

**compensate 1** *v/t (with money)* péicháng 赔偿 **2** *v/i: ~ for* bǔcháng 补偿

**compensation** *(money)* péicháng 赔偿; *(reward)* hǎochù 好处; *(comfort)* ānwèi 安慰

**compete** jìngzhēng 竞争; *(take part)* cānjiā 参加; *~ for* zhēngduó 争夺

**competence, competency** nénglì 能力

**competent** *person* chèngzhí 称职; *work* hégé 合格; **I'm not ~ to judge** wǒ bùgòu zīgé qù pànduàn 我不够资格去判断

**competition** *(contest, competing)* jìngzhēng 竞争; SP bǐsài 比赛; *(competitors)* duìshǒu 对手; **the government wants to encourage ~** zhèngfǔ yào gǔlì jìngzhēng 政府要鼓励竞争

**competitive** *(able to compete: price, offer)* yǒu jìngzhēng lì 有竞争力; *(liking to compete)* hào jìngzhēng 好竞争; *profession, sport* jìngzhēnglì hěnqiáng 竞争力很强

**competitor** *(in contest)* bǐsài zhě 比赛者; COM jìngzhēng duìshǒu 竞争对手

**compile** biānzhì 编制

**complacency** zìmǎn 自满

**complacent** zhānzhan zìxǐ 沾沾自喜

**complain** *v/i* bàoyuàn 抱怨; *(to store, manager)* tóusù 投诉; *~ of* MED zhǔsù 主诉; *~ about X* bàoyuàn X 抱怨 X

**complaint** tóusù 投诉; MED jíbìng

疾病

**complement** *v/t* xiāngpèi 相配; **they ~ each other** tāmén hěn xiāngchèn 他们很相衬

**complementary** hùwéi bǔchōng 互为补充

**complete 1** *adj (total)* shízú 十足; *(full)* wánzhěng 完整; *(finished)* wángōng 完工 **2** *v/t building, course, task etc* wánchéng 完成; *form* tiánxiě 填写

**completely** wánquán 完全

**completion** wánchéng 完成

**complex 1** *adj* fùzá 复杂 **2** *n* PSYCH bìngtài kǒngjù 病态恐惧; *(of buildings)* zhōngxīn 中心

**complexion** *(facial)* miànsè 面色

**compliance** zūncóng 遵从

**complicate** shǐ fùzá huà 使复杂化

**complicated** fùzá 复杂

**complication** kùnnan 困难; *~s* MED bìngfā zhèng 并发症

**compliment 1** *n* zànměi 赞美 **2** *v/t* zànměi 赞美

**complimentary** *speech* zànměi 赞美; *(free)* miǎnfèi 免费; *(in restaurant, hotel)* zèngsòng 赠送; **be very ~ about** jíkǒu chēngzàn 极口称赞

**compliments slip** biàntiáo 便条

**comply** fúcóng 服从; *~ with …* zūnshǒu … 遵守 …

**component** bùfèn 部分

**compose** *v/t* zǔchéng 组成; MUS chuàngzuò 创作; **be ~d of X** yóu X zǔchéng chū X 组成; *~ oneself* shǐ zìjǐ píngjìng xiàlái 使自己平静下来

**composed** *(calm)* píngjìng 平静

**composer** MUS zuòqǔ jiā 作曲家

**composition** *(make-up)* zǔchéng chéngfèn 组成成分; MUS zuòpǐn 作品; *(essay)* zuòwén 作文

**composure** zhènjìng 镇静

**compound** *n* CHEM huàhé wù 化合物

**compound interest** fùlì 复利

**comprehend** *(understand)* lǐjiě 理解

**comprehension** lǐjiě 理解

comprehensive zōnghé xìng 综合性

comprehensive insurance zǒngkuò bǎoxiǎn 总括保险

compress 1 n MED fūbù 敷布 2 v/t air, gas, information yāsuō 压缩

comprise (consist of) bāohán 包含; (make up) gòuchéng 构成; be ~d of ... yóu ... zǔchéng 由 ... 组成

compromise 1 n tuǒxié 妥协 2 v/i tuǒxié 妥协 3 v/t principles fàngqì 放弃; reputation etc sǔnhài 损害; ~ oneself liánlèi zìjǐ 连累自己

compulsion PSYCH qiángpò xìng shénjīng zhì 强迫性神经质

compulsive behavior bùyóu zìzhǔ 不由自主; reading yùbà bùnéng 欲罢不能

compulsory yìwù 义务; class bìxiū 必修; ~ education yìwù jiàoyù 义务教育

computer diànnǎo 电脑; it's on ~ zài diànnǎo shang 在电脑上

computer-controlled diànnǎo kòngzhì 电脑控制

computer game diànzǐ yóuxì 电子游戏

computerize diànnǎo huà 电脑化

computer literate huìyòng diànnǎo 会用电脑; computer science jìsuànjī kēxué 计算机科学; computer scientist jìsuànjī kēxué jiā 计算机科学家

computing diànnǎo shǐyòng 电脑使用

comrade (friend) péngyou 朋友; POL tóngzhì 同志

comradeship yǒuyì 友谊

con F 1 n piànjú 骗局 2 v/t piàn 骗

conceal fact, truth etc yǐnmán 隐瞒; object yǐncáng 隐藏

concede v/t (admit) chéngrèn 承认

conceit zìfù 自负

conceited zìgāo zìdà 自高自大

conceivable kě xiǎngxiàng 可想象

conceive v/i (of woman) huáiyùn 怀孕; ~ of (imagine) shèxiǎng 设想

concentrate 1 v/i (on task) jízhōng jīnglì 集中精力 2 v/t one's attention, energies jízhōng 集中

concentrated juice etc nóngsuō 浓缩

concentration zhuānxīn 专心

concept gàiniàn 概念

conception (of child) huáiyùn 怀孕

concern 1 n (anxiety) dānyōu 担忧; (care) guānxīn 关心; (business) shìwù 事务; (company) gōngsī 公司 2 v/t (involve) shèjí 涉及; (worry) dānyōu 担忧; ~ oneself with guǎn 管

concerned (anxious) gǎndào bù ān 感到不安; (caring) guānxīn 关心; (involved) yǒuguān 有关; as far as I'm ~ jiù wǒ ér yán 就我而言

concerning prep yǒuguān 有关

concert yīnyuè huì 音乐会

concerted (joint) liánhé 联合

concertmaster shǒuxí xiǎo tíqín yǎnzòu zhě 首席小提琴演奏者

concerto xiézòu qǔ 协奏曲

concession (giving in) ràngbù 让步

conciliatory ānfǔ 安抚

concise jiǎnmíng 简明

conclude 1 v/t (deduce) tuīduàn chū 推断出; (end) jiéshù 结束; ~ X from Y yóu Y tuīduàn chū X 由 Y 推断出 X 2 v/i jiéshù 结束

conclusion (deduction) jiélùn 结论; (end) jiéwěi 结尾; in ~ zuìhòu 最后

conclusive juédìng xìng 决定性

concoct meal, drink tiáozhì 调制; excuse, story biānzào 编造

concoction (food, drink) tiáozhì pǐn 调制品

concrete¹ adj (not abstract) jùtǐ 具体

concrete² n hùnníngtǔ 混凝土

concubine qiè 妾

concur v/i tóngyì 同意

concussion zhèndàng 震荡

condemn action qiǎnzé 谴责; building xuāngào ... bù shìyú 宣告 ... 不适于

jūzhù 宣告 ... 不适于居住;
(*doom*) zhùdìng 注定; ~ **to death**
pàn sǐxíng 判死刑
condemnation (*of action*) qiǎnzé
谴责
condensation (*on walls, windows*)
lěngníng wù 冷凝物
condense 1 *v/t* (*make shorter*)
yāsuō 压缩 2 *v/i* (*of steam*) shǐ
lěngníng 使冷凝
condensed milk liànrǔ 炼乳
condescend: **he ~ed to speak to
me** tā fàngxià jiàzi hé wǒ jiǎnghuà
他放下架子和我讲话
condescending (*patronizing*) bào
cǐ'ēn tàidù 抱赐恩态度
condition 1 *n* (*state, of health*)
zhuàngtài 状态; MED bìng bìng 病;
(*requirement, term*) tiáojiàn 条件;
**~s** (*circumstances*) tiáojiàn 条件;
**on ~ that** ... zhǐyào ... 只要 ...
2 *v/t* PSYCH shǐ xíngchéng tiáojiàn
fǎnshè 使形成条件反射
conditional 1 *adj* acceptance yǒu
tiáojiàn 有条件的; ~ **on** ... shì ...
érdìng 视 ... 而定 2 *n* GRAM
tiáojiàn tiáojiàn 条件
conditioner (*for hair*) hùfà jì 护发
剂; (*for fabric*) qiānwēi bǎohù jì
纤维保护剂
conditioning PSYCH tiáojiàn fǎnshè
条件反射
condo → **condominium**
condolences diàoyàn 吊唁
condom ⇩ bìyùn tào 避孕套
condominium = gòngxiáng
gònggòng shèshī de gōngyù 共享
公共设施的公寓
condone actions kuānróng 宽容
conducive: ~ **to** yǒu zhùyú 有助
于
conduct 1 *n* (*behavior*) jǔzhǐ 举止
2 *v/t* (*carry out*) shíshī 实施; ELEC
chuándǎo 传导; MUS zhǐhuī 指挥;
~ **oneself** biǎoxiàn 表现
conducted tour dǎoyóu lǚyóu 导
游旅游
conductor MUS zhǐhuī jiā 指挥家;
(*on train*) lièchē zhǎng 列车长
cone (*in geometry*) yuánzhuī tǐ 圆
锥体; (*of pine tree*) sōngtǎ 松塔;

(*on highway*) zhuīxíng lùbiāo 锥性
路标; **an ice-cream** ~ dànjuǎn
bīngqílín 蛋卷冰淇淋
confectioner tiánpǐn shāng 甜品
商
confectioners' sugar tángfěn 糖
粉
confectionery (*candy*) tiánshí 甜
食
confederation tóngméng 同盟
confer 1 *v/t* (*bestow*) shòuyǔ 授予
2 *v/i* (*discuss*) jiāohuàn yìjiàn 交换
意见
conference tǎolùn huì 讨论会
conference room huìyì tīng 会议
厅
confess 1 *v/t* sin, guilt chéngrèn 承
认; crime tǎnbái 坦白; REL chàn
huǐ 忏悔; **I ~ I don't know** wǒ
chéngrèn wǒ bù zhīdào 我承认
我不知道 2 *v/i* chéngrèn 承认;
(*to priest*) chànhuǐ 忏悔; (*to police*)
tǎnbái 坦白; **to a weakness for
X** chéngrèn xǐ'ài X 承认喜爱X
confession gòngrèn 供认; (*to
police*) rènzuì shū 认罪书; REL
chànhuǐ 忏悔
confessional REL gàojiě shì 告解
室
confessor REL gàojiě shénfù 告解
神父
confide 1 *v/t* tùlù 吐露 2 *v/i*: ~ **in**
... (*trust*) xìnrèn ... 信任 ...
confidence (*assurance*) xìnxīn 信
心; (*trust, secret*) xìnrèn 信任; **in** ~
zuòwéi mìmì 作为秘密
confident (*self-assured*) zìxìn 自信;
(*convinced*) kěndìng 肯定
confidential jīmì 机密
confine (*imprison*) jiānjìn 监禁;
(*restrict*) júxiàn yú 局限于; **be ~d
to one's bed** wòbìng zàichuáng 卧
病在床
confined space xiázhǎi 狭窄
confinement (*imprisonment*)
jiānjìn 监禁; MED fēnmiǎn 分娩
confirm *v/t* quèdìng 确定; theory,
statement, fears zhèngshí 证实
confirmation zhèngmíng 证明; (*of
theory statement, fears*) zhèngshí 证
实

**confirmed** (*inveterate*) jiāndìng 坚定

**confiscate** mòshōu 没收

**conflict 1** *n* (*disagreement*) zhēngyì 争议; (*clash*) chōngtū 冲突; (*war*) zhànzhēng 战争 **2** *v/i* (*clash*) chōngtū 冲突

**conform** zūnshǒu guīzhāng 遵守规章; (*of product*) fúhé 符合; **~ to government standards** fúhé zhèngfǔ biāozhǔn 符合政府标准

**conformist** *n* shùncóng de rén 顺从的人

**confront** (*face*) miànduì 面对; (*tackle*) shǐ duìzhì 使对质

**confrontation** chōngtū 冲突

**Confucianism** Rújiā 儒家

**Confucius** Kǒngzǐ 孔子

**confuse** hùnxiáo 混淆; **~ X with Y** bǎ X dāngchéng Y 把 X 当成 Y

**confused** kùnhuò 困惑

**confusing** lìngrén hútú 令人糊涂

**confusion** (*muddle, chaos*) hùnxiáo 混淆

**congeal** (*of blood, fat*) nínggù 凝固

**congenial** (*pleasant*) lìngrén yúkuài 令人愉快; **a ~ host** hàokè de zhǔrén 好客的主人

**congenital** MED xiāntiān xìng 先天性

**congested** *roads* dǔsè 堵塞

**congestion** (*on roads*) dǔsè 堵塞; (*in chest*) chōngxuè 充血; **traffic ~** jiāotōng dǔsè 交通堵塞

**congratulate** zhùhè 祝贺

**congratulations** zhùhè 祝贺; **~ on ...** zhùhè ... 祝贺 ...

**congregate** (*gather*) jùjí 聚集

**congregation** REL jiàotáng jíhuì 教堂集会

**congress** (*conference*) dàibiǎo dàhuì 代表大会; **Congress** (*of US*) Guóhuì 国会

**Congressional** Guóhuì 国会

**Congressman** Guóhuì yìyuán 国会议员

**conifer** zhēnyè shù 针叶树

**conjecture** *n* (*speculation*) cāicè 猜测

**conjugate** *v/t* GRAM lièjǔ cíxíng biànhuà 列举词形变化

**conjunction** GRAM liánjiē cí 连词; **in ~ with** liántóng 连同

**conjunctivitis** jiémó yán 结膜炎

**♦conjure up** (*produce*) biàn móshù bān biànchū 变魔术般变出; (*evoke*) lìngrén xiǎngqǐ 令人想起

**conjurer, conjuror** (*magician*) móshù shī 魔术师

**conjuring tricks** móshù 魔术

**con man** piànzi 骗子

**connect** (*join*) liánjiē 连接; TELEC jiētōng 接通; (*link*) yǒu guānxì 有关系; (*to power supply*) jiētōng diànlù 接通电路

**connected: be well-~** duō guànxì hù 多关系户; **be ~ with ...** yǔ ... yǒu guānxì 与 ... 有关系

**connecting flight** ⇩ liányùn fēijī 联运飞机

**connection** (*in wiring*) liánjiē 连接; (*link, personal contact*) guānxi 关系; (*when traveling*) liányùn 联运; **in ~ with ...** yǔ ... yǒuguānxi 与 ... 有关系

**connector** COMPUT liánjiē qì 连接器

**connoisseur** hángjia 行家

**conquer** zhēngfú 征服; *fig* (*fear etc*) zhànshèng 战胜

**conqueror** zhēngfú zhě 征服者

**conquest** (*of territory*) zhēngfú 征服

**conscience** liángxīn 良心; **a guilty ~** nèijiù 内疚; **it has been on my ~** wǒ yīzhí gǎndào nèijiù 我一直感到内疚

**conscientious** rènzhēn 认真

**conscientious objector** jù fú bīngyì zhě 拒服兵役者

**conscious** *adj* (*aware*) zìjué 自觉; (*deliberate*) yǒuyì 有意; MED qīngxǐng 清醒; **be ~ of ...** yìshí dào ... 意识到 ...

**consciousness** (*awareness*) yìshí 意识; MED zhījué 知觉; **lose / regain ~** shīqù / huīfù zhījué 失去 / 恢复知觉

**consecutive** liánxù 连续

**consensus** yīzhì yìjiàn 一致意见

**consent 1** n zànxǔ 赞许 **2** v/i tóngyì 同意

**consequence** (*result*) hòuguǒ 后果

**consequently** (*therefore*) suǒyǐ 所以

**conservation** (*preservation*) bǎohù 保护

**conservationist** n tíchàng fánghù zhě 提倡防护者

**conservative** adj (*conventional*), *estimate* bǎoshǒu 保守; *clothes* lǎoqì 老气

**conservatory** (*for plants*) nuǎnfáng 暖房; MUS yīnyuè xuéyuàn 音乐学院

**conserve 1** n (*jelly*) guǒjiàng 果酱 **2** v/t energy, strength bǎocún 保存

**consider** (*regard*) rènwéi 认为; (*show regard for, think about*) kǎolǜ 考虑; *it is ~ed to be ...* zhòngsuǒ zhōuzhī ... 众所周知 ...

**considerable** xiāngdāng dà 相当大

**considerably** zài hěndà chéngdù shàng 在很大程度上

**considerate** tǐtiē 体贴

**consideration** (*thought*) kǎolǜ 考虑; (*thoughtfulness, concern*) guānxīn 关心; (*factor*) yào kǎolǜ de shì 要考虑的事; *take X into ~* kǎolǜ X 考虑 X

**consignment** COM huòwù 货物

♦ **consist of** bāokuò 包括

**consistency** (*texture*) niánchóu dù 黏稠度; (*unchangingness*) yīzhì xìng 一致性

**consistent** (*unchanging*) yīguàn 一贯

**consolation** ānwèi 安慰

**console** v/t ānwèi 安慰

**consonant** n GRAM fǔyīn 辅音

**conspicuous** xiǎnyǎn 显眼

**conspiracy** yīnmóu 阴谋

**conspire** mìmóu 密谋

**constant** (*continuous*) bùduàn 不断

**consternation** jīngkǒng 惊恐

**constipated** biànmì 便秘

**constipation** biànmì 便秘

**constituent** n (*component*) zǔfèn 组分

**constitute** (*account for*) zhàn 占; (*represent*) gòuchéng 构成

**constitution** POL xiànfǎ 宪法; (*of person*) tǐzhì 体质

**constitutional** adj POL xiànfǎ 宪法

**constraint** (*restriction*) xiànzhì 限制

**construct** v/t building etc jiànzào 建造

**construction** (*of building etc*) jiànzào 建造; (*building, trade etc*) jiànzhù 建筑; *under ~* zài jiànzào zhōng 在建造中

**construction industry** jiànzhù yè 建筑业; **construction site** shīgōng gōngdì 施工工地; **construction worker** jiànzhù gōngrén 建筑工人

**constructive** yǒu jiànshè xìng 有建设性

**consul** lǐngshì 领事

**consulate** lǐngshì guǎn 领事馆

**consult** (*seek the advice of*) hé ... shāngliàng hé ... 商量

**consultancy** (*company*) zīxún gōngsī 咨询公司; (*advice*) zīxún 咨询

**consultant** (*adviser*) gùwèn 顾问

**consultation** cuōshāng 磋商

**consume** (*eat, drink*) shíyòng 食用; (*use*) hàoyòng 耗用

**consumer** (*purchaser*) gùkè 顾客

**consumer confidence** gùkè xìnxīn 顾客信心; **consumer goods** xiāofèi pǐn 消费品; **consumer society** xiāofèi zhě shèhuì 消费者社会

**consumption** (*of energy*) xiāohào 消耗; (*quantity used*) xiāohào liàng 消耗量

**contact 1** n (*person*) shóurén 熟人; (*communication, physical*) jiēchù 接触; *keep in ~ with X* yǔ X bǎochí liánluò 与X保持联络 **2** v/t liánluò 联络

**contact lens** yǐnxíng yǎnjìng 隐形眼镜

**contact number** liánxì diànhuà 联

系电话

contagious chuánrǎn 传染; *fig* mànyán 蔓延

contain *tears, laughter* kòngzhì 控制; *it ~ed my camera* wǒde zhàoxiàngjī zài lǐmiàn 我的照像机在里面; *~ oneself* kòngzhì zìjǐ 控制自己

container (*recipient*) róngqì 容器; COM ⇩ jízhuāng xiāng 集装箱

container ship ⇩ jízhuāng xiāng chuán 集装箱船

contaminate wūrǎn 污染

contamination wūrǎn 污染

contemplate *v/t* (*look at*) zhùshì 注视; (*think about*) sīkǎo 思考

contemporary 1 *adj* dāngdài 当代 2 *n* tóngdài rén 同代人; (*at school*) tóngjiè 同届

contempt qīngmiè 轻蔑; *be beneath ~* bùzhí yīgù 不值一顾

contemptible běiliè 卑劣

contemptuous biǎoshì qīngmiè 表示轻蔑

contend: *~ for ...* jìngzhēng ... 竞争 ...; *~ with ...* yìngfù ... 应付 ...

contender (*in sport, competition*) jìngzhēng zhě 竞争者; (*against champion*) zhēngduó zhě 争夺者; POL jìngxuǎn rén 竞选人

content² *n* nèiróng 内容

content² 1 *adj* mǎnzú 满足 2 *v/t*: *~ oneself with ...* mǎnzú yú ... 满足于 ...

contented mǎnzú 满足

contention (*assertion*) lùndiǎn 论点; *be in ~ for ...* zhēngduó ... 争夺 ...

contentment mǎnzú 满足

contents (*of house, letter, bag etc*) nèiróng 内容

contest¹ (*competition*) bǐsài 比赛; (*struggle, for power*) zhēngduó 争夺

contest² *v/t leadership etc* jìngzhēng 竞争; (*oppose*) duì ... tíchū zhìyí 对 ... 提出质疑

contestant cānsài zhě 参赛者

context shàngxià wén 上下文; *look at X in ~* gēnjù jùtǐ huánjìng lái kǎolǜ X 根据具体环境来考

虑 X; *look at X out of ~* tuōlí jùtǐ huánjìng lái kǎolǜ X 脱离具体环境来考虑 X

continent *n* dàlù 大陆

contingency búcè shìjiàn 不测事件

continual búduàn 不断

continuation xùjí 续集

continue 1 *v/t* jìxù 继续; *to be ~d* wèiwán dàixù 未完待续 2 *v/i* jìxù 继续

continuity liánguàn xìng 连贯性

continuous bùtíng 不停

contort *face, body* niǔqū 扭曲

contour lúnkuò 轮廓

contraception bìyùn 避孕

contraceptive *n* (*device*) bìyùn qì 避孕器; (*pill*) bìyùn yào 避孕药

contract¹ *n* hétóng 合同

contract² 1 *v/i* (*shrink*) shōusuō 收缩 2 *v/t illness* gǎnrǎn 感染

contractor chéngbāo rén 承包人

contractual hétóng 合同

contradict *statement* yǔ ... yǒu máodùn 与 ... 有矛盾; *person* fánbó 反驳

contradiction máodùn 矛盾

contradictory *account* xiānghù duìlì 相互对立

contraption F qíyì jīqì 奇异机器

contrary¹ 1 *adj* duìlì 对立; *~ to ...* yǔ ... xiāngfǎn 与 ... 相反 2 *n*: *on the ~* zhèng xiāngfǎn 正相反

contrary² (*perverse*) hào yǔ rén zuòduì 好与人作对

contrast 1 *n* duìzhào 对照 2 *v/t* duìzhào 对照 3 *v/i* xíngchéng duìbǐ 形成对比

contrasting jiérán xiāngfǎn 截然相反

contravene wéifǎn 违反

contribute 1 *v/i* (*with money, material*) juānxiàn 贡献; (*with time*) gòngxiàn 贡献; (*to magazine, paper*) tóugǎo 投稿; (*to discussion*) fābiǎo yìjiàn 发表意见; *~ to* (*help to cause*) cùchéng 促成 2 *v/t money* juānxiàn 捐献; *time, suggestion* gòngxiàn 贡献

contribution (*money*) juānxiàn 捐献; (*to political party, debate, of time, effort*) gòngxiàn 贡献; (*to magazine*) tóugǎo 投稿

**contributor** (*of money*) juānkuǎn rén 捐款人; (*to magazine*) tóugǎo rén 投稿人

**contrive** cémóu 策谋

**control 1** *n* (*of country, emotion etc*) kòngzhì 控制; *be in ~ of …* kòngzhì zhe … 控制着 …; *bring X under ~* déyǐ kòngzhì X 得以控制 X; *get out of ~* shīqù kòngzhì 失去控制; *lose ~ of X* shīqù kòngzhì X 失去控制 X; *lose ~ of oneself* shīqù zìkòng 失去自控; *the situation is under ~* yīqiè zhèngcháng 一切正常; *circumstances beyond our ~* wǒmen wúfǎ kòngzhì de yīnsù 我们无法控制的因素; *~s* (*of aircraft, vehicle*) cāozòng zhuāngzhì 操纵装置; (*restrictions*) guǎnzhì cuòshī 管制措施 **2** *v/t* (*govern*) kòngzhì 控制; (*restrict*) xiànzhì 限制; (*regulate*) guǎnlǐ 管理; *~ oneself* (*not get angry, emotional*) zìkòng 自控; (*not overeat etc*) kèzhì zìjǐ 克制自己

**control center** kòngzhì zhōngxīn 控制中心; **control freak** F kòngzhì kuáng 控制狂; **control key** COMPUT kòngzhìjiàn 控制键

**controlled substance** shòu guǎnzhì yàowù 受管制药物

**controlling interest** FIN kònggǔ quányì 控股权益

**control panel** kòngzhì pán 控制盘

**control tower** zhǐhuī diàodù tái 指挥调度台

**controversial** yǒu zhēngyì 有争议

**controversy** zhēnglùn 争论

**convalesce** yǎngbìng 养病

**convalescence** liáoyǎng qī 疗养期

**convene** *v/t* zhàojí 召集

**convenience** (*of having sth, location*) fāngbiàn 方便; (*of arrangement, time*) shìyí 适宜; *at your/my* ~ zài nǐ/wǒ fāngbiàn de

shíhòu 在你/我方便的时候; *all* (*modern*) ~**s** suǒyǒu xiàndàihuà shèbèi 所有现代化设备

**convenience food** fāngbiàn shípǐn 方便食品

**convenience store** fāngbiàn xiǎo shāngdiàn 方便小商店

**convenient** *location, device* fāngbiàn 方便; *time, arrangement* héshì 合适

**convent** nǚ xiūdào yuàn 女修道院

**convention** (*tradition*) shèhuì xísú 社会习俗; (*conference*) dàhuì 大会

**conventional** *person, ideas, method* píngcháng 平常

**convention center** huìyì zhōngxīn 会议中心

**conventioneer** yǔhuì zhě 与会者

**conversant**: *be ~ with …* shúxī … 熟悉 …

**conversation** jiāotán 交谈

**conversational** kǒuyǔ 口语

**converse** *n* (*opposite*) xiāngfǎn 相反

**conversely** lìngyī fāngmiàn 另一方面

**conversion** (*of figures, money*) zhésuàn 折算

**conversion table** huànsuàn biǎo 换算表

**convert 1** *n* guīfù zhě 归附者 **2** *v/t house, room etc* gǎijiàn 改建; *unit of measurement* zhéhé 折合; *energy* zhuǎnhuà 转化; *person* gǎibiàn xìnyǎng 改变信仰

**convertible** *n* (*car*) zhépéng chē 折蓬车

**convey** (*transmit*) chuándì 传递; (*give*) biǎoshì 表示; (*express*) biǎodá 表达; (*carry*) shūsòng 输送

**conveyor belt** chuánsòng dài 传送带

**convict 1** *n* qiúfàn 囚犯 **2** *v/t* LAW xuānpàn yǒuzuì 宣判有罪; *~ X of Y* yǐ Y zuìxíng xuānpàn X 以 Y 罪行宣判 X

**conviction** LAW dìngzuì 定罪;

*(belief)* quèxìn 确信

**convince** *(persuade)* shuōfú 说服;
*I'm ~d that ...* wǒ kěndìng ... 我肯
定 ...

**convincing** lìngrén xìnfú 令人信
服

**convivial** *(friendly)* huānlè 欢乐

**convoy** *(of ships)* chuánduì 船队;
*(of vehicles)* chēduì 车队

**convulsion** MED chōuchù 抽搐

**cook 1** *n* chúshī 厨师 **2** *v/t* zuò 做;
*(roast, bake)* kǎo 烤; *(steam)* zhēng
蒸; *(stir fry)* chǎo 炒 *a ~ed meal*
xiànzuòde fàn 现做的饭 **3** *v/i* *(of
person)* zuòfàn 做饭; *(roast, bake)*
kǎo 烤; *(steam)* zhēng 蒸; *(stir fry)*
chǎo 炒

**cookbook** pēngrèn shū 烹饪书

**cookery** pēngtiáo 烹调

**cookie** qǔqí 曲奇

**cooking** *(food)* fàncài 饭菜

**cool 1** *n*: *keep one's ~* F bǎochí
lěngjìng 保持冷静; *lose one's ~*
F shīqù kòngzhì 失去控制 **2** *adj*
*weather, breeze* liángshuǎng 凉爽;
*drink* liáng *(calm)* lěngjìng 冷
静; *(unfriendly)* lěngmò 冷漠; F
*(great)* kù 酷 **3** *v/i* *(of food)*
tānliáng 摊凉; *(of tempers)* píngxī
平息; *(of interest)* shīqù rèqíng 失
去热情 **4** *v/t*: *~ it* F lěngjìng xiàlái
冷静下来

♦**cool down 1** *v/i* *(of food, stove)*
tānliáng 摊凉; *(of weather)*
liángkuài qǐlái 凉快起来; *(of
person)* liángkuài 凉快; *fig (of
tempers)* píngxī 平息 **2** *v/t* *food* shǐ
biànliáng 使变凉; *fig* shǐ píngxī
使平息

**cooperate** hézuò 合作

**cooperation** hézuò 合作

**cooperative 1** *n* COM hézuò shè 合
作社 **2** *adj* COM hézuò 合作;
*(helpful)* lèyì pèihé 乐意配合

**coordinate** *activities* xiétiáo 协调

**coordination** *(of activities, body)*
xiétiáo 协调

**cop** F tiáozi 条子

**cope** yìngfu 应付; *~ with ...* yìngfu
... 应付 ...

**copier** *(machine)* fùyìn jī 复印机

**copilot** fù jiàshǐ yuán 副驾驶员

**copious** *notes* hěnduō 很多;
*amount of food* fēngshèng 丰盛

**copper** *n* *(metal)* tóng 铜

**copy 1** *n* *(imitation)* fùzhì pǐn 复制
品; *(duplicate)* fùběn 副本;
*(photocopy)* fùyìn jiàn 复印件;
*(of book)* běn 本; *(of record, CD)*
pán dǐng *(written material)* gǎozi 稿
子; *make a ~ of a file* COMPUT
fùzhì yífèn dǎng'àn 复制一份档
案 **2** *v/t* *(imitate)* fǎngzào 仿造;
*(duplicate)* fùxiě 复写;
*(photocopy)* fùyìn 复印; COMPUT:
*file* fùzhì 复制; *(in writing)*
chāoxiě 抄写; *(in order to cheat)*
chāoxí 抄袭; *~ a key* pèi yàoshi
配钥匙

**copy cat** F fǎngxiào zhě 仿效者;
**copycat crime** fǎngxiào fànzuì 仿
制犯罪; **copyright** *n* bǎnquán 版
权; **copy-writer** *(in advertising)*
guǎngào wénzì zhuàngǎo rén 广
告文字撰稿人

**coral** shānhú 珊瑚

**cord** *(string)* shéng 绳; *(cable)* xiàn
线

**cordial** *adj* rèqíng 热情

**cordless phone** wúxiàn diànhuà
无线电话

**cordon** jǐngjiè xiàn 警戒线

♦**cordon off** fēngsuǒ 封锁

**cords** *(pants)* dēngxīnróng kù 灯
芯绒裤

**corduroy** dēngxīnróng 灯芯绒

**core 1** *n* *(of fruit)* xīnr 心儿; *(of
problem)* yàodiǎn 要点; *(of
organization, party)* héxīn 核心
**2** *v/t* *fruit* wāxīn 挖心 **3** *adj* *issue,
meaning* zuì zhòngyào 最重要

**cork** *(in bottle)* píngsāi 瓶塞;
*(material)* ruǎnmù 软木

**corkscrew** ⇩ luósī qǐzi 螺丝起
子

**corn** yùmǐ 玉米

**corner 1** *n* *(of page)* jiǎo 角; *(of
room)* jiǎoluò 角落; *(of table)*
zhuōjiǎo 桌角; *(of street)* jiējiǎo
街角; *(bend: on road)* zhuǎnwān
转弯; *(in soccer)* jiǎoqiú 角球; *in
the ~* zài jiǎoluò lǐ 在角落里; *on*

***the ~*** (*of street*) zài jiējiǎo 在街角 **2** *v/t person* shǐ zǒutóu wúlù 使走投无路; ~ ***the market*** lǒngduàn shìchǎng 垄断市场 **3** *v/i* (*of driver, car*) guǎiwānr 拐弯儿

**corner kick** (*in soccer*) jiǎoqiú 角球

**cornstarch** diànfěn 淀粉

**corny** F *joke* sútào 俗套; F *gesture* duōchóu shàngǎn 多愁善感

**coronary 1** *adj* guànzhuàng dòngmài 冠状动脉 **2** *n* (*coronary thrombosis*) guànzhuàng dòngmài xuèshuān 冠状动脉血栓; (*heart attack*) guànxīnbìng 冠心病

**coroner** yànshī guān 验尸官

**corporal** *n* xiàshì 下士

**corporal punishment** tǐfá 体罚

**corporate** COM jítuán 集团; ~ ***image*** gōngsī xíngxiàng 公司形象; ***sense of ~ loyalty*** gōngsī guāngróng gǎn 公司光荣感

**corporation** (*business*) gǔfèn yǒuxiàn gōngsī 股份有限公司

**corps** bùduì 部队

**corpse** sǐshī 死尸

**corpulent** féipàng 肥胖

**corpuscle** xuèqiú 血球

**corral** *n* chùlán 畜栏

**correct 1** *adj* zhèngquè 正确 **2** *v/t* jiūzhèng 纠正; *proofs, homework* xiūgǎi 修改

**correction** xiūgǎi 修改

**correspond** (*match*) xiāngfú 相符; (*write letters*) tōngxìn 通信; ~ ***to ...*** děngyú ... 等于 ...; ~ ***with ...*** (*match*) fúhé ... 符合 ...

**correspondence** (*matching*) yī zhìxìng 一致性; (*letters*) xìnjiàn 信件; (*exchange of letters*) tōngxìn liánluò 通信联络

**correspondent** (*letter writer*) tōngxìn zhě 通信者; (*reporter*) tōngxùn yuán 通讯员

**corresponding** (*equivalent*) duìděng 对等

**corridor** (*in building*) zǒuláng 走廊

**corroborate** zhèngshí 证实

**corrode** *v/t* & *v/i* fǔshí 腐蚀

**corrosion** fǔshí 腐蚀

**corrugated cardboard** wǎlèng

zhǐbǎn 瓦楞纸板

**corrugated iron** wǎlèng tiě 瓦楞铁

**corrupt 1** *adj* fǔbài 腐败; COMPUT pòhuài 破坏 **2** *v/t* shǐ duòluò 使堕落; (*bribe*) huìlù 贿赂

**corruption** shòuhuì 受贿

**cosmetic** *adj* měiróng 美容; *fig* zhuāngshì xìng 装饰性

**cosmetics** huàzhuāng pǐn 化妆品

**cosmetic surgeon** zhěngróng wàikē yīshēng 整容外科医生

**cosmetic surgery** zhěngróng wàikē 整容外科

**cosmonaut** yǔháng yuán 宇航员

**cosmopolitan** *city* shìjiè xìng 世界性

**cost 1** *n* (*price*) jiàgé 价格; (*in finance*) chéngběn 成本; *fig* dàijià 代价; ~**s** COM fèiyòng 费用 **2** *v/t* *$50 etc* xūyào 需要; *time* shǐ sàngshī 使丧失; FIN: *project* gūjià 估价; ***how much does it ~?*** duōshao qián? 多少钱？; *it ~ **them $500*** tāmen huāle wǔbǎi měijīn 他们花了五百美金; *it ~ **me my health*** wǒde jiànkāng yīncǐ ér shòusǔn 我的健康因此而受损

**cost and freight** COM huòjià jiā yùnjià 货价加运价; **cost-conscious** jiéyuē 节约; **cost-effective** huásuàn 划算; **cost, insurance and freight** COM huòjià, bǎoxiǎn jiā yùnjià 货价, 保险加运价

**costly** *mistake* dàijià cǎnzhòng 代价惨重

**cost of living** shēnghuó fèiyòng 生活费用

**cost price** chéngběn jiàgé 成本价格

**costume** (*for actor*) xìzhuāng 戏装

**costume jewelry** jiǎ zhūbǎo 假珠宝

**cot** (*camp-bed*) xíngjūn chuáng 行军床

**cottage** cūnshè 村舍

**cottage cheese** nóngjiā xiān gānlào 农家鲜干酪

**cotton 1** *n* miánhua 棉花 **2** *adj*

miánbù 棉布
♦**cotton on** F míngbái 明白
♦**cotton on to** F duì ... chǎnshēng hǎogǎn 对 ... 产生好感
♦**cotton to** F xǐhuān 喜欢
**cotton candy** miánhuā táng 棉花糖
**couch** n cháng shāfā 长沙发
**couch potato** pào diànshì de rén 泡电视的人
**couchette** zuòwò liǎngyòng chuáng 坐卧两用床
**cough** n & vi késou 咳嗽
♦**cough up 1** v/t blood etc ké ké 咳; F money tāochū 掏出 **2** v/i F (pay) tāoqián 掏钱
**cough medicine, cough syrup** zhǐké tángjiāng 止咳糖浆
**could**: ~ I have my key? kěyǐ gěiwǒ yàoshi ma? 可以给我钥匙吗？; ~ you help me? láojià bāngbang máng 劳驾帮帮忙; this ~ be the our bus yěxǔ shì wǒmén de gōnggòng qìchē 也许是我们的公共汽车; you ~ be right méizhǔnr níshì duìde 没准儿你是对的; I ~n't say for sure wǒ bùnéng kěndìng 我不能肯定; he ~ have got lost tā kěnéng mílù le tā 他可能迷路了; you ~ have warned me! zǎo bù shuō! 早不说！
**council** (assembly) yìhuì 议会; (authority) zhèngfǔ 政府
**councilman** zhèngwùhuì wěiyuán 政务会委员
**councilor** zhèngwùhuì wěiyuán 政务会委员
**counsel 1** n (advice) quàngào 劝告; (lawyer) lǜshī 律师 **2** v/t course of action tíyì 提议; person fǔdǎo 辅导
**counseling** fǔdǎo 辅导
**counselor** (adviser) fǔdǎo yuán 辅导员; LAW lǜshī 律师
**count 1** n (number arrived at) zǒngshù 总数; (action of ~ing) shǔshù 数数; (in baseball, boxing) huíjī cìshù 挥击次数; keep ~ of ... shǔ ... de quèqiè shùmù 数 ... 的确切数目; lose ~ of ...

shǔbùqīng ... 数不清 ...; at the last ~ zuìhòu yīcì shǔde shíhou 最后一次数的时候 **2** v/i (to ten etc) shǔ 数; (calculate) jìsuàn 计算; (be important) yǒu zhòngyào yìyì 有重要意义; (qualify) suàn 算 **3** v/t (~ up) shǔ 数; (calculate) jìsuàn 计算; (include) bāokuò 包括
♦**count on** yīkào 依靠
**countdown** dào shǔshù 倒数数
**countenance** v/t zàncháng 赞成
**counter¹** (in store, café) guìtái 柜台; (in game) chóumǎ 筹码
**counter²** 1 v/t fǎnjī 反击 **2** v/i (retaliate) fǎnbó 反驳
**counter³**: run ~ to ... yǔ ... bùxiāng fúhé 与 ... 不相符合
**counteract** zhōnghé 中和
**counter-attack 1** n fǎnjī 反击 **2** v/i jìnxíng fǎnjī 进行反击
**counterbalance** pínghéng lì 平衡力; counterclockwise nì shízhēn 逆时针; counterespionage fǎn jiàndié huódòng 反间谍活动
**counterfeit** v/t & adj wěizào 伪造
**counterpart** (person) duìfāng 对方
**counterproductive** qǐ fǎn zuòyòng 起反作用
**countersign** v/t huìqiān 会签
**countless** shǔbù jìn 数不尽
**country** (nation) guójiā 国家; (as opposed to town) xiāngxià 乡下; in the ~ zài xiāngxià 在乡下
**country and western** MUS xiāngcūn yǔ xībù yīnyuè 乡村与西部音乐; countryman (fellow ~) tóngbāo 同胞; countryside nóngcūn 农村
**county** (in US & China) xiàn 县
**coup** POL zhèngbiàn 政变; fig piàoliàng de yìjǔ 漂亮的一举
**couple** (married) fūqī 夫妻; (man & woman) qínglǚ 情侣; (two people) yīduì 一对; just a ~ zhǐyǒu jǐge 只有几个; a ~ of (people) jǐge 几个; a ~ of days jǐtiān 几天; a ~ of matters shì jǐjiàn shì 几件事; a ~ of tickets jǐzhāng piào 几张票
**coupon** (form) suǒqǔ dān 索取

单; (*voucher*) zèngquàn 赠券

courage yǒngqì 勇气

courageous yǒnggǎn 勇敢

courier (*messenger*) xìnshǐ 信使; (*with tourist party*) dǎoyóu 导游

course (*series of lessons*) kèchéng 课程; (*part of meal*) dàocài 道菜; (*of ship, plane*) hángxiàng 航向; (*for horse race, golf*) chǎng xìng; (*for cross-country running, skiing*) dào dào; of ~ (*certainly*) dāngrán 当然; (*naturally*) zìrán 自然; of ~ not dāngrán bù 当然不; ~ of action cǎiqǔ de xíngdòng 采取的行动; ~ of treatment liáochéng 疗程; in the ~ of … zài … qījiān 在 … 期间

court n LAW fǎtíng 法庭; (*courthouse*) fǎyuàn 法院; SP chǎng xìng; take X to ~ hé X dǎ guānsī 和 X 打官司

court case fǎtíng ànjiàn 法庭案件

courteous yǒu lǐmào 有礼貌

courtesy lǐmào 礼貌

courthouse fǎyuàn 法院; court martial 1 n jūnshì fǎtíng 军事法庭 2 v/t yǐ jūnfǎ shěnpàn 以军法审判; court order fǎlìng 法令; courtroom shěnpàn shì 审判室; courtyard yuànzi 院子

cousin (*older male on father's side*) tángxiōng 堂兄; (*younger male on father's side*) tángdì 堂弟; (*older female on father's side*) tángjiě 堂姐; (*younger female on father's side*) tángmèi 堂妹; (*older male on mother's side*) biǎoxiōng 表兄; (*younger male on mother's side*) biǎodì 表弟; (*older female on mother's side*) biǎojiě 表姐; (*younger female on mother's side*) biǎomèi 表妹

cove (*small bay*) xiǎo hǎiwān 小海湾

cover 1 n (*protective*) zhào zhào; (*of book, magazine*) fēngmiàn 封面; (*for bed*) bèizi 被子; (*shelter*) yǎnbì 掩蔽; (*insurance*) bǎoxiǎn 保险; take ~ from the rain bìyǔ 蔽雨 2 v/t fùgài 覆盖; (*hide*)

yǎngài 掩盖; (*of insurance policy*) bǎoxiǎn 保险; (*distance*) xíngshǐ 行驶; (*of journalist*) bàodào 报道; with his hands ~ed in … mǎnshǒu dōushì … 满手都是 …

♦ cover up 1 v/t gàizhù 盖住; fig yǎngài 掩盖 2 v/i fig yǐnmán 隐瞒; ~ for X tì X yǎnshì cuòwù 替 X 掩饰错误缺点

coverage (*by media*) bàodào 报道

covering letter fùxìn 附信

covert mìmì 秘密

coverup (*concealment*) yǎnshì 掩饰

cow n mǔniú 母牛

coward dǎnxiǎo guǐ 胆小鬼

cowardice dǎnxiǎo 胆小

cowardly dǎnxiǎo 胆小

cowboy niúzǎi 牛仔

cower quánsuō 蜷缩

coy (*evasive*) hánhu qící 含糊其辞; (*flirtatiously*) xiū dádá 羞答答

cozy shūshì 舒适

CPU (= central processing unit) zhōngyāng chǔlǐ jī 中央处理机

crab n pángxiè 螃蟹

crack 1 n lièfèng 裂缝; (*joke*) xiàohua 笑话 2 v/t cup, glass shǐ chǎnshēng lièfèng 使产生裂缝; nut zá 砸; code pòyì 破译; F (*solve*) zhēnpò 侦破; ~ a joke shuō xiàohuà 说笑话 3 v/i liè 裂; get ~ing kāishǐ gàn 开始干

♦ crack down on zhìcái 制裁

♦ crack up (*have breakdown*) kuǎdiào 垮掉; F (*laugh*) pěngfù dàxiào 捧腹大笑

crackbrained yúchūn 愚蠢

crackdown zhìcái 制裁

cracked cup, glass pòliè 破裂; F (*crazy*) fēngkuáng 疯狂

cracker (*to eat*) bócuì bǐnggān 薄脆饼干

crackle v/i (*of fire*) huālā 哗啦

cradle n (*for baby*) yáolán 摇篮

craft¹ NAUT chuán 船

craft² (*skill*) gōngyì 工艺; (*trade*) zhíyè 职业

craftsman shǒuyì rén 手艺人

crafty jiǎohuá 狡猾

crag (*rocky*) xiányá 险崖

cram v/t sāi 塞

cramped *room, apartment* zhǎixiǎo 窄小

cramps chōujīn 抽筋

cranberry yuèjú 越橘

crane 1 *n (machine)* qǐzhòng jī 起重机 2 *v/t:* ~ *one's neck* shēncháng bózi 伸长脖子

crank *n (strange person)* guàirén 怪人

crankshaft qǔzhóu 曲轴

cranky *(bad-tempered)* bàozào 暴躁

crap F shǐ 屎; *(bad quality goods)* pòlàn 破烂; *(nonsense)* húshuō 胡说

crash 1 *n (noise)* huālā shēng 哗啦声; *(of thunder)* pīlì 劈雳; *(accident),* COMPUT shìgù 事故; *(plane ~)* fēijī shīshì 飞机失事; COM dǎobì 倒闭 2 *v/i (of wave)* huālā yīshēng jī 哗啦一声击; *(of vase)* pādī yīshēng diào pāi de yīshēng 啪地一声掉; *(of thunder)* tūrán fāchū 突然发出巨响; *(of car)* zhuàng 撞; *(of airplane)* zhuìhuǐ 坠毁; (COM: *of market)* bàodiē 暴跌; COMPUT chū shìgù 出事故; F *(sleep)* guòyè 过夜 3 *v/t car* zhuànghuǐ 撞毁

♦crash out F *(fall asleep)* shuìzháo 睡着

crash course sùchéng kè 速成课; crash diet kuàisù jiǎnféi 快速减肥; crash helmet fángzhuàng tóukuī 防撞头盔; crash landing shuāijī zháolù 摔机着陆

crate *(packing case)* xiāngzi 箱子

crater *(of volcano)* huǒshān kǒu 火山口

crave kěwàng 渴望

craving kěwàng 渴望; *a* ~ *for ...* fēicháng xiǎngyào ... 非常想要 ...

crawl 1 *n (in swimming)* zìyóuyǒng 自由泳; *at a* ~ *(very slowly)* fēicháng huǎnmàn 非常缓慢 2 *v/i (on floor)* pá 爬; *(move slowly)* huǎnmàn xíngjìn 缓慢行进

♦crawl with jǐmǎn 挤满

crayon làbǐ 蜡笔

craze kuángrè 狂热; *the latest* ~

zuì shímáo de kuángrè 最时髦的狂热

crazy *adj* fāfēng 发疯; *be* ~ *about ...* duì ... zháomí 对 ... 着迷

creak 1 *n* zhīgā zhīgā shēng 吱嘎吱嘎声 2 *v/i* zhīgā zhīgā zuòxiǎng 吱嘎吱嘎作响

cream 1 *n (for skin, coffee, cake)* rǔshuāng 乳霜; *(color)* mǐsè 米色 2 *adj (color)* mǐsè 米色

cream cheese nǎiyóu gānlào 奶油干酪

creamer *(jug)* nǎizhōng 奶盅; *(for coffee)* nǎifěn 奶粉

creamy *(with lots of cream)* duō nǎiyóu 多奶油

crease 1 *n (accidental)* zhòuwén 皱纹; *(deliberate)* kùxiàn 裤线 2 *v/t (accidentally)* nòngzhòu 弄皱

create 1 *v/t (make)* chuàngzào 创造; *(lead to)* yǐnqǐ 引起 2 *v/i (be creative)* chuàngxīn 创新

creation chuàngzào 创造; REL chuàngzào tiāndì 创造天地; *(something created)* chuàngzàode zuòpǐn 创造的作品

creative yǒu chuàngzào nénglì 有创造能力

creator chuàngzào zhě 创造者; *(author)* zuòzhě 作者; *(founder)* fāqǐ rén 发起人; *the Creator* REL Zàowù zhǔ 造物主

creature *(animal)* dòngwù 动物; *(person)* rén 人

credibility *(of person)* xìnyù 信誉; *(of story)* kěxìn xìng 可信性

credible *(believable)* kě xiāngxìn 可相信; *candidate etc* kě xìnrèn 可信任

credit 1 *n* FIN shēqiàn 赊欠; *(use of* ~ *cards)* xìnyòng 信用; *(honor)* zànyáng 赞扬; *(payment received)* dàifāng 贷方; *be in* ~ yǒu yú'é 有余额; *get the* ~ *for X* yǒuyú X dédào zànyáng 由于 X 得到赞扬 2 *v/t (believe)* xiāngxìn 相信; ~ *an amount to an account* cúnrù zhànghù 存入帐户

creditable zhíde zànyáng 值得赞扬

credit card xìnyòng kǎ 信用卡

**credit limit** (*of credit card*) xìndài xiàn'é 信贷限额

**creditor** zhàizhǔ 债主

**creditworthy** xìnyù zhuózhù 信誉卓著

**credulous** qīngxìn 轻信

**creed** (*beliefs*) xìntiáo 信条

**creek** (*stream*) xiǎohé 小河

**creep 1** *n pej* tǎoyàn guǐ 讨厌鬼 **2** *v/i* nièshǒu nièjiǎo de zǒu 蹑手蹑脚地走

**creeper** BOT púfú zhíwù 匍匐植物

**creeps: the house/he gives me the** ~ zhè fángzi/tā shǐwǒ húnshēn qǐ jīpí gēda 这房子/他使我浑身起鸡皮疙瘩

**creepy** lìngrén máogǔ sǒngrán 令人毛骨悚然

**cremate** huǒhuà 火化

**cremation** huǒhuà 火化

**crematorium** huǒhuà chǎng 火化场

**crescent** *n* (*shape*) yuèyá xíng 月牙形

**crest** *n* (*of hill*) dǐng 顶; (*of bird*) ròuguàn 肉冠

**crestfallen** jǔsàng 沮丧

**crevice** lièfèng 裂缝

**crew** *n* (*of ship, airplane*) quántǐ gōngzuò rényuán 全体工作人员; (*of repairmen etc*) zǔ组; (*crowd, group*) yīhuǒ rén 一伙人

**crew cut** píngtóu 平头

**crew neck** shuǐshǒu lǐng 水手领

**crib** *n* (*for baby*) xiǎohái chuáng 小孩床

**crick: ~ in the neck** jǐngbù tòngxìng jìngluán 颈部痛性痉挛

**cricket** (*insect*) xīshuài 蟋蟀

**crime** (*offence*) zuìxíng 罪行; (*shameful act*) lìngrén yíhàn de shì 令人遗憾的事; **the ~ rate** fànzuì lǜ 犯罪率

**criminal 1** *n* zuìfàn 罪犯 **2** *adj* xíngshì 刑事; (*shameful*) lìngrén yíhàn 令人遗憾

**crimson** *adj* shēnhóng sè 深红色

**cringe** xiàde wànghòu suō 吓得往后缩

**cripple 1** *n* (*disabled person*) cánjí rénshì 残疾人士 **2** *v/t person* shòushāng zhì cán 受伤至残; *fig* shǐ xiànyú tānhuàn 使陷于瘫痪

**crisis** wēijī 危机

**crisp** *adj weather, air* liángshuǎng 凉爽; *lettuce, apple* xīnxiān ér cuìshēng 新鲜而脆生; *bacon, toast* cuì 脆; *new shirt, bills* tǐngkuò 挺括

**criterion** (*standard*) biāozhǔn 标准

**critic** pínglùn jiā 评论家

**critical** (*making criticisms*) tiāocìr 挑刺儿; (*serious*) wēijí 危急; *moment etc* jǐnyào 紧要; MED yánzhòng 严重

**critically** *speak etc* yǒu pīpíng xìng 有批评性; ~ *ill* bìngde hěn yánzhòng 病得很严重

**criticism** pīpíng 批评

**criticize** *v/t* pīpíng 批评

**croak 1** *n* (*of frog*) guāgua jiàoshēng 呱呱叫声; (*of person*) dīyǎ de shuōhuà shēng 低哑的说话声 **2** *v/i* (*of frog*) guāgua jiào 呱呱叫; (*of person*) dīyǎ di shuōhuà 低哑地说话

**crockery** táoqì 陶器

**crocodile** èyú 鳄鱼

**crony** F mìyǒu 密友

**crook** *n* (*dishonest*) piànzi 骗子

**crooked** (*not straight*) wānqū 弯曲; (*dishonest*) bù lǎoshí 不老实

**crop 1** *n* shōucheng 收成; *fig* pī 批; **~s** zhuāngjia 庄稼 **2** *v/t hair, photo* xiūjiǎn 修剪

♦ **crop up** (*be mentioned*) tídào 提到; (*happen unexpectedly*) yìwài de fāshēng 意外地发生

**cross 1** *adj* (*angry*) shēngqì 生气 **2** *n* (*X*) chāzi 叉子; (*Christian symbol*) shízìjià 十字架 **3** *v/t* (*go across*) chuānguò 穿过; ~ *oneself* REL yòng shǒu huà shízì huà 用手画十字; ~ *one's legs* jiāochā shuāngtuǐ 交叉双腿; *keep one's fingers* ~*ed* qídǎo zǒuyùn 祈求走运; *it never* ~*ed my mind* wǒ gēnběn jiù méiyǒu xiǎng 我根本就没有想 **4** *v/i* (*go across the road*) guò mǎlù 过马路; (*of lines*)

jiāochā 交叉
♦**cross off**, **cross out** qǔxiāo 取消

**crossbar** (of goal) héngmù 横木; (of bicycle) chējià héngliáng 车架横梁; (in high jump) hénggǎn 横杆

**cross-country** (skiing) yuèyě (huáxuě) 越野（滑雪）

**crossed check** huàxiàn zhīpiào 划线支票

**cross-examine** LAW fǎn jiéwèn 反诘问

**cross-eyed** nèi xiéshì 内斜视

**crossing** NAUT héngdù 横渡

**crossroads** shízì lùkǒu 十字路口; **cross-section** (of people) jùyǒu dàibiǎo xìng de gèsè rénwù 具有代表性的各色人物; **crosswalk** ⇩ rénxíng héngdào 人行横道; **crossword** (puzzle) zònghéng tiánzì mí 纵横填字迷

**crouch** v/i dūn dūn 蹲

**crow** n (bird) wūyā 乌鸦; **as the ~ flies** yán zhíxiàn 沿直线

**crowd** n rénqún 人群; (at sports event) guānzhòng 观众

**crowded** yōngjǐ 拥挤

**crown** 1 n (on tooth) chǐguàn 齿冠 2 v/t tooth xiāng chǐguàn 镶齿冠

**crucial** guānjiàn 关键

**crude** 1 adj (vulgar) cūlǔ 粗鲁; (unsophisticated) jiǎnlòu 简陋 2 n: **~** (oil) yuányóu 原油

**cruel** cánrěn 残忍

**cruelty** cánrěn 残忍

**cruise** 1 n hángxíng 航行 2 v/i (in ship) hángxíng 航行; (of car) huǎnmàn xúnxíng 缓慢巡行; (of plane) yǐ jīngjì xúnxíng sùdù fēixíng 以经济巡行速度飞行

**cruise liner** dàxíng yóutǐng 大型游艇

**cruising speed** jūnsù 均速

**crumb** zhāzi 渣子

**crumble** 1 v/t nòngsuì 弄碎 2 v/i (of bread, stonework) suìliè 碎裂; fig (of opposition etc) bēngkuì 崩溃

**crumple** 1 v/t (crease) nòngzhòu 弄皱 2 v/i (collapse) dǎoxià 倒下

**crunch** 1 n: **when it comes to the ~** F dāng guānjiàn shíkè dàolái shí 当关键时刻到来时 2 v/i (of snow, gravel) gāzhī zuòshēng 嘎吱作声

**crusade** n fig yùndòng 运动

**crush** 1 n (crowd) yōngjǐ de rénqún 拥挤的人群; **have a ~ on** rèliàn 热恋 2 v/t yā yā 压; (crease) nòngzhòu 弄皱; **they were ~ed to death** tāmén bèi yā sǐle 他们被压死了 3 v/i (crease) zhòu zhòu 皱

**crust** (on bread) miànbāo pí 面包皮

**crutch** (for injured person) T zì xíng guǎizhàng T字形拐杖

**cry** 1 n (call) hǎnjiào 喊叫; **have a ~** kū yīchǎng 哭一场 2 v/t (call) hǎnjiào 喊叫 3 v/i (weep) kū 哭
♦**cry out** v/t dàshēng shuōchū 大声说出 v/i hǎnjiào 喊叫
♦**cry out for** (need) pòqiè xūyào 迫切需要

**crystal** (mineral) shuǐjīng 水晶; (glass) jīngzhì bōli 晶质玻璃

**crystallize** 1 v/t jiéjīng 结晶 2 v/i (of thoughts etc) jiéjīng 结晶

**CTS** (= **China Travel Service**) Zhōngguó Lǚxíngshè 中国旅行社

**cub** yòushòu 幼兽

**Cuba** Gǔbā 古巴

**Cuban** 1 adj Gǔbā 古巴 2 n Gǔbā rén 古巴人

**cube** (shape) lìfāng xíng 立方形

**cubic** lìfāng 立方

**cubic capacity** TECH róngjī liàng 容积量

**cubicle** (changing room) gēngyī shì 更衣室

**cucumber** huángguā 黄瓜

**cuddle** n & v/t yōngbào 拥抱

**cuddly** kitten etc dòuren lián'ài 逗人怜爱; (liking cuddles) xǐhuan lǒulou bàobao 喜欢搂搂抱抱

**cue** n (for actor etc) tíshì 提示; (for pool) qiúgān 球杆

**cuff** 1 n (of shirt) xiùkǒu 袖口; (of pants) kùjiǎo fānbiān 裤角翻边; (blow) zhǎngjī 掌击; **off the ~** wèijīng zhǔnbèi 未经准备 2 v/t (*hit*) zhǎngjī 掌击

cuff link xiùkǒu liànkòu 袖口链扣

culinary pēngtiáo 烹调

culminate: ~ *in* ... yǐ ... gàozhōng 以 ... 告终

culmination dǐngdiǎn 顶点

culprit zuìfàn 罪犯

cult (*sect*) zōngpài 宗派

cultivate *land* gēngzuò 耕作; *person* péiyǎng 培养

cultivated *person* yǒu xiūyǎng 有修养

cultivation (*of land*) gēngzuò 耕作

cultural (*relating to the arts*) yǒu xiūyǎng 有修养; (*relating a country's identity*) wénhuà 文化

Cultural Revolution Wénhuà Dàgémìng 文化大革命

culture (*artistic*) wénmíng 文明; (*of a country*) wénhuà 文化

cultured (*cultivated*) yǒu xiūyǎng 有修养

culture shock wénhuà chōngjī 文化冲击

cumbersome léizhuì 累赘

cunning *n & adj* jiǎohuá 狡猾

cup *n* bēi 杯; (*trophy*) bēi 杯; *a ~ of tea* yībēi chá 一杯茶

cupboard guìzi 柜子

curable kěyī 可医

curator guǎnzhǎng 馆长

curb 1 *n* (*of street*) lùyuán 路缘; (*on powers etc*) yuēshù 约束 2 *v/t* kòngzhì 控制

curdle *v/i* (*of milk*) níngjié 凝结

cure 1 *n* MED liáofǎ 疗法 2 *v/t* MED zhìhǎo 治好; *meat, fish* yān 腌

curfew xiāojìn lìng 宵禁令

curiosity (*inquisitiveness*) hàoqí xīn 好奇心

curious (*inquisitive*) hàoqí 好奇; (*strange*) qítè 奇特

curiously (*inquisitively*) hàoqí 好奇; (*strangely*) qíguài 奇怪; *~ enough* qíguàide shì qíguài de shì 奇怪的是

curl 1 *n* (*in hair*) quánfà 鬈发; *~ of smoke* yānquānr 烟圈儿 2 *v/t hair* juǎn 卷; (*wind*) chánrào 缠绕 3 *v/i* (*of hair*) juǎn 卷; (*of leaf, paper etc*) quánqū 蜷曲

♦curl up quánqū 蜷曲

curly *tail* quánqū 蜷曲; *~ hair* quánfà 鬈发

currant (*dried fruit*) xiǎo pútáo gān 小葡萄干

currency (*money*) huòbì 货币; *foreign ~* wàihuì 外汇

current 1 *n* (*in sea*) jīliú 激流; ELEC diànliú 电流; (*of opinions etc*) qīngxiàng 倾向 2 *adj* (*present*) mùqián 目前

current affairs, current events shìshì 时事

current affairs program shìshì tǎolùn jiémù 时事讨论节目

currently mùqián 目前

curriculum kèchéng 课程

curse 1 *n* (*spell*) zǔzhòu 诅咒; (*swearword*) zhòumà 咒骂 2 *v/t* zǔzhòu 诅咒; (*swear at*) zhòumà 咒骂 3 *v/i* (*swear*) màrén 骂人

cursor COMPUT ⇩ guāngbiāo 光标

cursory cūlüè 粗略

curt tángtū cǎoshuài 唐突草率

curtail jiéduǎn 截短

curtain chuānglián 窗帘; THEA wéimù 帷幕

curve 1 *n* qūxiàn 曲线 2 *v/i* (*bend*) wānqū 弯曲

cushion 1 *n* (*for couch etc*) kàodiàn 靠垫 2 *v/t blow, fall* huǎnhé ... de chōngjī 缓和 ... 的冲击

custard dànnǎi hú 蛋奶糊

custody (*of children*) fúyǎng quán 扶养权; *in ~* LAW bèi jūliú 被拘留

custom (*tradition*) xíguàn 习惯; COM huìgù 惠顾; *as was his ~* àn tā píngcháng xíguàn 按他平常习惯

customary chángguī 常规; *it is ~ to ...* chángguī shàng ... 常规上 ...

customer gùkè 顾客

customer relations gùkè guānxi 顾客关系

customs hǎiguān 海关

customs clearance tōngguān 通关; customs inspection yànguān 验关; customs officer hǎiguān guānyuán 海关官员

**cut 1** *n* (*with knife, scissors*) qiēkǒu 切口; (*injury*) shāngkǒu 伤口; (*of garment, hair*) kuǎnshì 款式; (*reduction*) xiāojiǎn 削减; *my hair needs a ~* wǒ gāi jiǎn tóufà le 我该剪头发了 **2** *v/t* qiē 切; (*reduce*) xiāojiǎn 削减; COMPUT: *text* jiǎnqiē 剪切; *get one's hair ~* jiǎn tóufà 剪头发
♦ **cut back 1** *v/i* (*in costs*) suōjiǎn 缩减 **2** *v/t employees* cáiyuán 裁员
♦ **cut down 1** *v/t tree* kǎndǎo 砍倒 **2** *v/i* (*in smoking etc*) jiǎnshǎo 减少
♦ **cut down on:** *~ smoking / drinking* shǎo chōuyān / hējiǔ 少抽烟/喝酒
♦ **cut off** (*with knife, scissors etc*) jiǎndiào 剪掉; (*isolate*) géjué 隔绝; TELEC duànxiàn 断线; *we were cut off* diànhuà duànxiàn le 电话断线了
♦ **cut out** (*with scissors*) jiǎnchū 剪出; *alcohol, smoking* jiè 戒; (*eliminate*) páichú 排除; *cut that out!* F gòule! 够了！; *be ~ for X* shìhé yú X 适合于X
♦ **cut up** *v/t meat etc* qiēsuì 切碎
**cutback** xiāojiǎn 削减
**cute** (*pretty*) kě'ài 可爱; (*sexually attractive, male*) yīngjùn 英俊; (*sexually attractive, female*) piàoliàng 漂亮; (*smart, clever*) shuǎ xiǎo cōngmíng 耍小聪明
**cuticle** biǎopí 表皮
**cut-price** xiāojià 削价
**cut-throat** *competition* cánkù 残酷
**cutting 1** *n* (*from newspaper etc*) jiǎnjí 剪辑 **2** *adj remark* shāngrén gǎnqíng 伤人感情
**cyberspace** diànnǎo kōngjiān 电脑空间
**cycle 1** *n* (*bicycle*) zìxíngchē 自行车; (*series of events*) xúnhuán 循环 **2** *v/i* qí zìxíngchē 骑自行车
**cycling** qí zìxíngchē 骑自行车
**cyclist** qí zìxíngchē de rén 骑自行车的人
**cylinder** (*container*) yuántǒng róngqì 圆筒容器; (*in engine*) qìgāng 汽缸
**cylindrical** yuánzhù xíng 圆柱形
**cynic** fènshì jísú zhě 愤世嫉俗者
**cynical** fènshì jísú 愤世嫉俗
**cynicism** fènshì jísú 愤世嫉俗
**cyst** nángzhǒng 囊肿
**Czech 1** *adj* Jiékè 捷克; *the ~ Republic* Jiékè Gònghéguó 捷克共和国 **2** *n* (*person*) Jiékè rén 捷克人; (*language*) Jiékè yǔ 捷克语

DA (= *district attorney*) dìfāng
jiǎnchá guān 地方检查官

dab 1 *n (small amount)* shǎoliàng 少
量 2 *v/t (remove)* qīngcā 轻擦;
*(apply)* cā 搽

◆dabble in suíbiàn gǎogao 随便
搞搞

dad bà ba 爸爸

dagger bǐshǒu 匕首

daily 1 *n (paper)* rìbào 日报 2 *adj*
měirì 每日

dainty yōuměi 优美

dairy products rǔzhì pǐn 乳制品

dais tái 台

dam 1 *n (for water)* shuǐbà 水坝
2 *v/t river* zhùdībà 筑堤坝

damage 1 *n* sǔnshī 损失; *fig (to
reputation etc)* sǔnhài 损害 2 *v/t*
sǔnhuài 损坏; *fig (reputation etc)*
sǔnshāng 损伤

damages LAW péicháng 赔偿

damaging yǒu pòhuài xìng 有破
坏性

dame F *(woman)* nǚrén 女人

damn 1 *interj* gāisǐ 该死 2 *n: I
don't give a ~!* wǒ cái bùguǎn ne!
我才不管呢！ 3 *adj* gāisǐ 该死
4 *adv* zhēn 真 5 *v/t (condemn)*
qiǎnzé 谴责; ~ *it!* zhēn qìsǐ rén!
真气死人！; *I'm ~ed if ...* wǒ
cái bù ... 我才不 ...

damned → *damn*

damp *building, cloth* shī 湿

dampen nòng shī 弄湿

dance 1 *n* tiàowǔ 跳舞; *(social
event)* wǔhuì 舞会 2 *v/t* tiàowǔ 跳
舞; *would you like to ~?* kěyǐ
qǐngnǐ tiàowǔ ma? 可以请你跳
舞吗？

dancer wǔdǎo jiā 舞蹈家;
*(performer)* wǔdǎo yǎnyuán 舞蹈
演员

dancing wǔdǎo 舞蹈

dandruff tóupíxiè 头皮屑

Dane Dānmài rén 丹麦人

danger wēixiǎn 危险; *out of ~ (of
patient)* tuōlí wēixiǎn 脱离危险

dangerous wēixiǎn 危险;
*assumption* màoxiǎn 冒险

dangle 1 *v/t* yáohuang 摇晃 2 *v/i*
xuánchuí 悬垂

Danish 1 *adj* Dānmài 丹麦 2 *n
(language)* Dānmài yǔ 丹麦语

Danish (pastry) Dānmài dàngāo
丹麦蛋糕

dare 1 *v/i* gǎn 敢; *how ~ you!*
nǐgǎn! 你敢！ 2 *v/t: ~ X to do Y*
tiǎodòu X qù zuò Y 挑斗X去做
Y

daring *adj* dàdǎn 大胆

dark 1 *n* hēi'àn 黑暗; *after ~*
tiānhēi yǐhòu 天黑以后; *keep X
in the ~ fig* bú gàosù X 不告诉X
2 *adj room, night* hēi 黑; *hair, eyes*
shēn yánsè 深颜色; ~
*green / blue* shēn lǜ / lán 深绿／
蓝

darken *(of sky)* biàn hēi 变黑

dark glasses hēi yǎnjìng 黑眼镜

darkness hēi'àn 黑暗

darling 1 *n* qīn'ài de 亲爱的 2 *adj*
qí'ài 亲爱

darn[1] 1 *n (mend)* bǔdīng 补丁 2 *v/t
(mend)* bǔ 补

darn[2], darned → *damn*

dart 1 *n (for throwing)* fēibiāo 飞标
2 *v/i* měngchōng 猛冲

dash 1 *n (punctuation)* pòzhé hào 破
折号; *(small amount)* shǎoliàng
少量; (MOT: *dashboard*) yíbiǎo
bǎn 仪表板; *a ~ of brandy*
shǎoliàng báilándì 少量白兰地;
*make a ~ for* jíchōng 急冲 2 *v/i*
jíchōng 急冲 3 *v/t hopes* pòmiè 破
灭

◆dash off 1 *v/i* gǎnkuài líkāi 赶快
离开 2 *v/t (write quickly)*
cōngmáng xiě 匆忙写

dashboard yíbiǎo bǎn 仪表板

**data** shùjù 数据

**database** shùjù kù 数据库；**data capture** shùjù fúhuò 数据俘获；**data processing** shùjù chǔlǐ 数据处理；**data protection** zīliào bǎomì 资料保密；**data storage** shùjù chǔcún 数据储存

**date²** (*fruit*) zǎo 枣

**date²** 1 *n* rìqī 日期；(*meeting*) yuēhuì 约会；(*person*) yuēhuì duìxiàng 约会对象；**what's the ~ today?** jīntiān jǐhào? 今天几号？；**out of ~** *clothes* guòshí 过时；*passport* guòqī 过期；**up to ~** zuìxīn 最新 2 *v/t letter, cheque* zhùmíng rìqī 注明日期；(*go out with*) tán liàn'ài 谈恋爱；**that ~s you** (*shows your age*) xiǎnshì nǐde niánlíng 显示你的年龄

**dated** guòshí 过时

**daub** *v/t* luàntú 乱涂

**daughter** nǚ'ér 女儿

**daughter-in-law** érxífu 儿媳妇

**daunt** *v/t* shǐ qìněi 使气馁

**dawdle** màntūntún de zuò 慢吞吞地做

**dawn** 1 *n* pòxiǎo 破晓；*fig* (*of new age*) kāiduān 开端 2 *v/i*: **it ~ed on me that ...** wǒ yìshí dào ... 我意识到 ...

**day** tiān 天；**what ~ is it today?** jīntiān xīngqī jǐ? 今天星期几？；**~ off** fàngjià 放假；**by ~** báitiān 白天；**~ by ~** yī tiāntiān di 一天天地；**the ~ after** dì'èr tiān 第二天；**the ~ after tomorrow** hòutiān 后天；**the ~ before** qián yī tiān 前一天；**the ~ before yesterday** qiántiān 前天；**~ in ~ out** měitiān 每天；**in those ~s** nà shíhòu 那时候；**one ~** yǒu yītiān 有一天；**the other ~** (*recently*) zuìjìn 最近；**let's call it a ~!** xiūxība! 休息吧！

**daybreak** pòxiǎo 破晓；**day-dream** 1 *n* báirì mèng 白日梦 2 *v/i* báirì zuòmèng 白日做梦；**daylight** rìguāng 日光；**daytime**: **in the ~** báitiān 白天；**daytrip** yīrìyóu 一日游

**daze**: **in a ~** bùzhī suǒcuò 不知

**所措**

**dazed** (*by good/ bad news*) bùzhī suǒcuò 不知所措；(*by a blow*) fāhūn 发昏

**dazzle** *v/t* (*of light*) huǎng huàng 晃晃；*fig* mízhù 迷住

**dead** 1 *adj person, plant* sǐ 死；*battery, phone, bulb* shīlíng 失灵；F (*place*) sìqì chénchen 死气沉沉 2 *adv* F (*very*) hěn 很；**~ beat, ~ tired** jīnpí lìjìn 筋疲力尽；**that's ~ right** hěn zhèngquè 很正确 3 *n*: **the ~** (*dead people*) sǐrén 死人；**in the ~ of night** shēnyè 深夜

**deaden** *pain, sound* shǐ jiǎnshǎo 使减少

**dead end** (*street*) sǐ hútong 死胡同；**dead-end job** méi qiántú de gōngzuò 没前途的工作；**dead heat** tóngshí dàodá zhōngdiǎn 同时到达终点；**deadline** qīxiàn 期限；(*for newspaper, magazine*) zuìhòu qīxiàn 最后期限；**dead-lock** *n* (*in talks*) jiāngjú 僵局

**deadly** *adj* (*fatal*) zhìmìng 致命；F (*boring*) sǐqì chénchen 死气沉沉

**deaf** lóng 聋

**deaf-and-dumb** lóngyǎ 聋哑

**deafen** shǐ tīng bù jiàn 使听不见

**deafening** jí dàshēng 极大声

**deafness** lóng 聋

**deal** 1 *n* jiāoyì 交易；**it's a ~** (*we have reached an agreement*) chéngjiāo 成交；(*it's a promise*) méi wèntí 没问题；**a good ~** (*bargain*) hǎo jiàqián 好价钱；**a great ~** (*a lot*) hěnduō 很多；**a great ~ of** (*lots*) hěnduō 很多 2 *v/t cards* fāpái 发牌；**a blow to** dǎjī 打击

♦ **deal in**: **~ X** (*trade in*) zuò X mǎimài 做 X 买卖

♦ **deal out** *cards* fāpái 发牌

♦ **deal with** (*handle*) chǔlǐ 处理；(*do business with*) dǎ jiāodào 打交道

**dealer** (*merchant*) shāngrén 商人；(*drug ~*) fàndú zhě 贩毒者；(*in card game*) fāpái zhě 发牌者

**dealing** (*drug ~*) fàndú 贩毒

**dealings** (*business*) jiāowǎng 交往

**dean** (*of college*) yuànzhǎng 院长

**dear** *adj* qīn'ài 亲爱; (*expensive*) guì 贵; **Dear Sir** zūnjìngde xiānshēng 尊敬的先生; **Dear Wang Li** qīn'àide Wáng Lì 亲爱的王丽; (*oh*) ~!, ~ **me!** wǒde tiān'a! 我的天啊!

**dearly** *love* shēn 深

**death** sǐwáng 死亡

**death penalty** sǐxíng 死刑

**death toll** sǐwáng zǒngshù 死亡总数

**debatable** kě zhēnglùn 可争论

**debate 1** *n* (*between opposing sides*) biànlùn 辩论; (*discussion*) tǎolùn 讨论 **2** *v/i* (*discuss*) tǎolùn 讨论; (*between opposing sides*) biànlùn 辩论 **3** *v/t* biànlùn 辩论

**debauchery** fàngdàng 放荡

**debit 1** *n* jièfāng 借方 **2** *v/t* account jièfāng 借方; ~ **his account with $30** zài tāde jièfāng zhàngshang jì sānshí měiyuán 在他的借方帐上记三十美元

**debris** cánjì 残迹

**debt** zhàiwù 债务; **be in** ~ (*financially*) qiànzhài 欠债

**debtor** jièfāng 借方

**debug** *room* chāichú qiètīngqì 拆除窃听器; COMPUT chúcuò 除错

**début** *n* shǒuyǎn 首演

**decade** shínián 十年

**decadent** tuífèi 颓废

**decaffeinated** wú kāfēiyīn 无咖啡因

**decanter** xì jǐng píng 细颈瓶

**decapitate** shīshǒu fēnlí 尸首分离

**decay 1** *n* (*process, matter*) fǔlàn 腐烂; (*of civilization*) shuāituì 衰退; (*in teeth*) làn làn 烂 **2** *v/i* fǔlàn 腐烂; (*of civilization*) shuāituì 衰退; (*of teeth*) làn làn 烂

**deceased: the** ~ sǐzhě 死者

**deceit** qīpiàn 欺骗

**deceitful** bù lǎoshi 不老实

**deceive** qīpiàn 欺骗

**December** shí'èryuè 十二月

**decency** zhèngpài 正派; **he had the** ~ **to ...** tā qǐmǎ zhīdào qù ... 他起码知道去 ...

**decent** *person* zhèngpài 正派; *salary, price* kě jiēshòu 可接受; *size* gòudà 够大; *meal, sleep* zúgòu 足够; **I'm not** ~ **yet!** (*adequately dressed*) wǒ hái méi chuānhǎo yīfu ne! 我还没穿好衣服呢!

**decentralize** *administration* shūsàn 疏散

**deception** qīpiàn 欺骗

**deceptive** kàobuzhù 靠不住

**deceptively: it looks** ~ **simple** kànqǐlái jiǎndān 看起来简单

**decibel** fēnbèi 分贝

**decide 1** *v/t* (*make up one's mind*) juédìng 决定; (*conclude*) xià juéxīn 下决心; (*settle*) pànjué 判决 **2** *v/i* juédìng 决定; **you** ~ nǐ lái juédìng 你来决定

**decided** (*definite*) jiānjué 坚决; (*obvious*) míngxiǎn 明显

**decider** (*match etc*) juédìng sài 决定赛

**decimal** *n* xiǎoshù 小数

**decimal point** xiǎoshù diǎn 小数点

**decimate** èshā dà bùfèn 扼杀大部分

**decipher** jiě mìmǎ 解密码

**decision** juédìng 决定; **come to a** ~ xià juéxīn 下决心

**decision-maker** dāngquán zhě 当权者

**decisive** guǒduàn 果断; (*crucial*) juédìng xìng 决定性

**deck** (*of ship*) jiǎbǎn 甲板; (*of cards*) yìfù zhǐpái 一副纸牌

**deckchair** jiǎbǎn yòng yǐ 甲板用椅

**declaration** (*statement*) shēngmíng 声明; (*of independence*) xuānbù 宣布; ~ **of war** xuānzhàn 宣战

**declare** (*state*) shēngmíng 声明; *independence* xuānbù 宣布; (*at customs*) chéngbào 呈报; ~ **war** xuānzhàn 宣战

**decline 1** *n* (*fall*) xiàjiàng 下降; (*in standards*) jiàngdī 降低; (*in health*) shuāituì 衰退 **2** *v/t invitation* xièjué 谢绝; ~ **to comment / accept** xièjué fābiǎo yìjiàn / jiēshòu 谢绝发表意见/接

受 3 v/i (*refuse*) xièjué 谢绝；(*decrease*) jiǎnshǎo 减少；(*of health*) shuāituì 衰退

**declutch** qǔxià líhéqì 取下离合器

**decode** yìmǎ 译码

**decompose** fǔlàn 腐烂

**décor** zhuānghuáng 装潢

**decorate** (*with paint, paper*) zhuāngxiū 装修；(*adorn*) zhuāngshì 装饰；*soldier* shòuxūn 授勋

**decoration** (*paint, paper*) zhuānghuáng 装潢；(*ornament*) zhuāngshì 装饰

**decorative** zhuāngshì 装饰

**decorator** (*interior ~*) zhuānghuáng gōngrén 装潢工人

**decoy** n yòu'ěr 诱饵

**decrease** 1 n xiàjiàng 下降 2 v/t suōjiǎn 缩减 3 v/i xiàjiàng 下降

**dedicate** *book etc* tíxiàn 题献；*~ oneself to …* xiànshēn yú … 献身于 …

**dedication** (*in book*) xiàntí 献题；(*to cause, work*) zhìlì 致力

**deduce** tuīlǐ 推理

**deduct**: *~ X from Y* cóng Y zhōng jiǎnqù X 从 Y 中减去 X

**deduction** (*from salary*) kòuchú 扣除；(*conclusion*) tuīlùn 推论

**deed** n (*act*) xíngwéi 行为；LAW qìyuē 契约

**deep** *hole, water, color* shēn 深；*shelf* zòngshēn 纵深；*voice* shēnchén 深沉；*thinker* shēnrù 深入；*~ trouble* shēnxiàn kùnjìng 身陷困境

**deepen** 1 v/t bǎ … jiāshēn 把 … 加深 2 v/i biànshēn 变深；(*of crisis, mystery*) jiāzhòng 加重

**deep freeze** n bīngxiāng 冰箱；**deep-frozen food** lěngdòng shípǐn 冷冻食品；**deep-fry** yóuzhá 油炸

**deer** lù 鹿

**deface** sǔnhuài biǎomiàn 损坏表面

**defamation** fěibàng 诽谤

**defamatory** fěibàng 诽谤

**default** adj COMPUT yuándìng 原定

**defeat** 1 n (*conquering*) jībài 击败；

(*losing*) shībài 失败 2 v/t jībài 击败；(*of task, problem*) cuòbài 挫败

**defeatist** adj *attitude* shībài zhǔyì 失败主义

**defect** n quēxiàn 缺陷

**defective** yǒu quēxiàn 有缺陷

**defend** bǎowèi 保卫；*cause* hànwèi 捍卫；(*stand by*) wéihù 维护；(*justify*) biànhù 辩护；*~ X* LAW wèi X biànhù 为 X 辩护

**defendant** bèigào 被告

**defense** n bǎowèi 保卫；SP fángshǒu 防守；LAW bèigào 被告；(*justification*) biànhù 辩护；(*of cause*) hànwèi 捍卫；*come to X's ~* bāngzhù X 帮助 X

**defense budget** POL guófáng kāizhī 国防开支

**defense lawyer** biànhù lǜshī 辩护律师

**defenseless** gūlì wúyuán 孤立无援

**defense player** SP shǒuwèi duìyuán 守卫队员；**Defense Secretary** POL guófáng bùzhǎng 国防部长；**defense witness** LAW biànhù zhèngrén 辩护证人

**defensive** 1 n: *on the ~* cǎiqǔ shǒushì 采取守势；*go on the ~* cǎiqǔ shǒushì 采取守势 2 adj *weaponry* fángyù 防御；*person* zìwǒ biànhù 自我辩护

**defer** v/t tuīchí 推迟

**deference** jìngyì 敬意

**deferential** biǎoshì jìngyì 表示敬意

**defiance** duìkàng 对抗；*in ~ of* wéikàng 违抗

**defiant** tiǎozhàn 挑战

**deficiency** (*lack*) quēfá 缺乏

**deficient**: *be ~ in* quēfá 缺乏

**deficit** kuīsǔn 亏损

**define** *word* xià dìngyì 下定义；*objective* míngquè 明确

**definite** *date, answer, improvement* míngquè 明确；(*certain*) kěndìng 肯定；*are you ~ about that?* nǐ néngbùnéng kěndìng 你能不能肯定？；*nothing ~ has been arranged* zuìhòu ānpái hái méiyǒu quèdìng 最后安排还没有

确定

**definite article** dìngguàncí 定冠词

**definitely** kěndìng 肯定

**definition** (*of word*) dìngyì 定义; (*of objective*) chǎnshù 阐述

**definitive** quánwēi xìng 权威性

**deflect** *ball, blow* shǐ zhuǎnxiàng 使转向; *criticism* niǔzhuǎn 扭转; (*from course of action*) niǔzhuǎn fāngxiàng 扭转方向; *be ~ed from* shǐ cóng ... zhuǎnbiàn fāngxiàng 使从 ... 转变方向

**deform** shǐ chéng jīxíng 使成畸形

**deformity** jīxíng 畸形

**defraud** piànqǔ 骗取

**defrost** *v/t food* jiědòng 解冻; *fridge* huàbīng 化冰

**deft** língqiǎo 灵巧

**defuse** *bomb* chāichú yǐnxìn 拆除引信; *situation* tiáojiě 调解

**defy** wéikàng 违抗

**degenerate** *v/i* duòluò 堕落; *~ into* tuìhuà 退化

**degrade** shǐ diūliǎn 使丢脸

**degrading** *position, work* dǐjí dīsú 低级低俗

**degree** (*from university*) xuéwèi 学位; (*of temperature, angle, latitude*) dù 度; (*amount*) chéngdù 程度; *by ~s* zhújiàn 逐渐; *get one's ~* huòdé xuéwèi 获得学位

**dehydrated** tuōshuǐ 脱水

**de-ice** chúbīng 除冰

**de-icer** (*spray*) chúbīng qì 除冰器

**deign**: *~ to ...* qūzūn ... 屈尊 ...

**deity** shén 神

**dejected** jǔsàng 沮丧

**delay 1** *n* yánchí 延迟 **2** *v/t* tuīchí 推迟; *be ~ed* bèi dāngē 被耽搁 **3** *v/i* tuīchí 推迟

**delegate 1** *n* dàibiǎo 代表 **2** *v/t task, person* shòuquán 授权

**delegation** (*of task, people*) shòuquán 授权

**delete** shānqù 删去; COMPUT shānchú 删除; (*cross out*) huàdiào 划掉

**deletion** (*act*) xiāochú 消除; (*that deleted*) shānchú 删除

**deli** shóushí diàn 熟食店

**deliberate 1** *adj* gùyì 故意 **2** *v/i*

zǐxì kǎolù 仔细考虑

**deliberately** gùyì 故意

**delicacy** (*of fabric*) jīngzhì 精致; (*of problem*) mǐngǎn 敏感; (*of health*) xūruò 虚弱; (*tact*) jǐnshèn 谨慎; (*food*) měishí 美食

**delicate** *fabric* jīngzhì 精致; *problem* mǐngǎn 敏感; *health* xūruò 虚弱

**delicatessen** shóushí diàn 熟食店

**delicious** hǎochī 好吃; *that was ~* zhēn hǎochī 真好吃

**delight** *n* xīngfèn 兴奋

**delighted** gāoxìng 高兴

**delightful** *evening* yúkuài 愉快; *person* kě'ài 可爱

**delimit** huàqīng jièxiàn 划清界线

**delirious** MED zhānwàng 谵妄; (*ecstatic*) jídù xīngfèn 极度兴奋

**deliver** sòng 送; *message* dìjiāo 递交; *baby* shēng 生; *~ a speech* jiǎnghuà 讲话

**delivery** (*of goods, mail*) sònghuò 送货; (*of baby*) fénmiǎn 分娩

**delivery date** sònghuò rìqī 送货日期; **delivery note** sònghuò dān 送货单; **delivery van** sònghuò chē 送货车

**delude** qīpiàn 欺骗; *~ oneself* zìqī 自欺

**deluge 1** *n* dàyǔ 大雨; *fig* fēngyōng érzhì 蜂拥而至 **2** *v/t fig* yānmò 淹没

**delusion** wàngxiǎng 妄想

**de luxe** *adj* háohuá 豪华

**demand 1** *n* yāoqiú 要求; COM xūqiú 需求; *in ~* yǒu xūyào 有需要 **2** *v/t* yāoqiú 要求

**demanding** *job* gāo yāoqiú 高要求; *person* kēkè 苛刻

**demented** jīngshén cuòluàn 精神错乱

**demise** qùshì 去世; *fig* mièwáng 灭亡

**demitasse** xiǎobēi 小杯

**demo** (*protest*) shìwēi 示威; (*of video etc*) shìfàn 示范

**democracy** mínzhǔ 民主

**democrat** mínzhǔ zhǔyì zhě 民主主义者; **Democrat** POL Mínzhǔ dǎngrén 民主党人

democratic mínzhǔ 民主

demo disk shìfàn dié 示范碟

demolish *building* chāihuǐ 拆毁; *argument* cuīhuǐ 摧毁

demolition (*of building*) chāihuǐ 拆毁; (*of argument*) cuīhuǐ 摧毁

demon móguǐ 魔鬼

demonstrate 1 *v/t* (*prove*) zhèngmíng 证明; *machine* shìfàn 示范 2 *v/i* (*politically*) shìwēi 示威

demonstration (*show*) xiǎnshì 显示; (*protest*) shìwēi 示威; (*of machine*) shìfàn 示范

demonstrative: *be ~* gǎnqíng wàilù 感情外露

demonstrator (*protester*) shìwēi zhě 示威者

demoralized qìněi 气馁

demoralizing lìngrén xièqì 令人泄气

den (*study*) shūfáng 书房

Deng Xiaoping Dèng Xiǎopíng 邓小平

Deng Xiaoping theory Dèng Xiǎopíng lǐlùn 邓小平理论

denial (*of rumour, accusation*) fǒurèn 否认; (*of request*) jùjué 拒绝

denim niúzǎi bù 牛仔布

denims (*jeans*) niúzǎikù 牛仔裤

Denmark Dānmài 丹麦

denomination (*of money*) miàn'é 面额; (*religious*) jiàopài 教派

dense (*thick*) nónghòu 浓厚; *foliage* chóumì 稠密; *crowd* mìjí 密集; (*stupid*) chídùn 迟钝

densely: *~ populated* rénkǒu mìjí 人口密集

density (*of population*) chóumì dù 稠密度

dent 1 *n* āochù 凹处 2 *v/t* shǐ āoxià 使凹下

dental *treatment* yáchǐ 牙齿; *hospital* yákē 牙科

dentist yáyī 牙医

dentures jiǎyá 假牙

deny *charge, rumour* fǒurèn 否认; *right, request* jùjué 拒绝

deodorant ⇩ chúxiù jì 除臭剂

depart líkāi 离开; *~ from* (*deviate from*) wéibèi 违背

department (*of company, store*) bùmén 部门; (*of university*) xì 系; (*of government*) bù 部; *Department of Defense* Guófáng bù 国防部; *Department of the Interior* Nèizhèng bù 内政部; *Department of State* Guówùyuàn 国务院

department store bǎihuò shāngchǎng 百货商场

departure (*leaving*) dòngshēn 动身; (*of train, bus*) chūfā 出发; (*of person from job*) líkāi 离开; (*deviation*) piānlí 偏离; *a new ~* (*for government, organization*) xīn qǐdiǎn 新起点; (*for company*) xīn fāzhǎn 新发展; (*for actor, artist, writer*) xīn fāngxiàng 新方向

departure lounge hòujī shì 候机室

departure time qǐchéng shíjiān 启程时间

depend: *that ~s* shì qíngxíng ér dìng 视情形而定; *it ~s on the weather* kàn tiānqì ba 看天气吧; *I ~ on you* wǒ kǎozhe nǐle 我靠着你了

dependable kěkào 可靠

dependence, dependency yīlài 依赖

dependent 1 *n* yīkào zhě 依靠者 2 *adj* yīkào 依靠

depict (*in painting, writing*) miáoshù 描述

deplorable lìngrén yíhàn 令人遗憾

deplore tòngxī 痛惜

deport qūchú chūjìng 驱除出境

deportation qūchú chūjìng 驱除出境

deportation order qūchú lìng 驱除令

deposit 1 *n* (*in bank*) cúnchǔ 存储; (*of mineral*) chénjī 沉积; (*on purchase*) dìngjīn 定金 2 *v/t money* cúnchǔ 存储; (*put down*) gē 搁; *silt, mud* yūjī 淤积

deposition LAW xuānshì zhèng 宣誓证

depot (*train station*) huǒchē zhàn

火车站; (*bus station*) qìchē zhàn 汽车站; (*for storage*) cāngkù 仓库

**depreciate** v/i FIN biǎnzhí 贬值

**depreciation** FIN biǎnzhí 贬值

**depress** *person* shǐ yōuyù 使忧郁

**depressed** *person* yōuyù 忧郁

**depressing** lìngrén shāngxīn 令人伤心

**depression** MED yōuyù zhèng 忧郁症; (*economic*) xiāotiáo 萧条; (*meteorological*) dīyā qū dī压区

**deprive**: ~ *X* of *Y* cóng X nàlǐ názǒu Y 从 X 那里拿走 Y

**deprived** pínkùn 贫困

**depth** (*of water, shelf, thought*) shēndù 深度; (*of voice*) dīchén dù 低沉度; (*of color*) nóngdù 浓度; **in ~** (*thoroughly*) shēnrù 深入; **in the ~s of winter** lóngdōng jìjié 隆冬季节; **be out of one's ~** (*in water*) zài shuǐ shēnde mòdǐng chù 在水深得没顶处; *fig* (*in discussion etc*) wúfǎ lǐjiě 无法理解

**deputation** shòuquán 授权

◆**deputize for** tìdài 替代

**deputy** dàilǐ 代理

**deputy leader** fù zǒngguǎn 副总管

**derail**: **be ~ed** (*of train*) tuōguǐ 脱轨

**deranged** fākuáng 发狂

**derelict** adj shīxiū 失修

**deride** qǔxiào 取笑

**derision** qǔxiào 取笑

**derisive** *remarks, laughter* cháonòng 嘲弄

**derisory** *amount, salary* wēibù zúdào 微不足道

**derivative** (*not original*) pàishēng 派生

**derive** v/t dédào 得到; **be ~d from** (*of word*) qǐyuán yú 起源于

**derogatory** biǎnyì 贬义

**descend 1** v/t xiàlái 下来; **be ~ed from** shì ... de hòuyì 是 ... 的后裔

**descend 2** v/i (*of airplane*) xiàjiàng 下降; (*of road*) xiàxié 下斜; (*of mood, darkness*) lǒngzhào 笼罩

**descendant** hòuyì 后裔

**descent** (*from mountain*) xiàlái 下来; (*of airplane*) xiàjiàng 下降; (*ancestry*) zǔxiān 祖先; **of Chinese ~** huáyí 华裔

**describe** miáoshù 描述; **~ X as Y** bǎ X xíngróng chéng Y 把 X 形容成 Y

**description** miáoxiě 描写; (*of criminal*) miáoshù 描述

**desegregate** qǔxiāo zhǒngzú gélí 取消种族隔离

**desert**[1] n also fig shāmò 沙漠

**desert**[2] **1** v/t (*abandon*) pāoqì 抛弃 **2** v/i (*of soldier*) kāi xiǎochāi 开小差

**deserted** huāngliáng 荒凉

**deserter** MIL táobīng 逃兵

**desertion** (*abandon*) pāoqì 抛弃; MIL kāi xiǎochāi 开小差

**deserve** yīngdé 应得

**design 1** n (*subject, of an object*) shèjì 设计; (*drawing*) shèjì túdìng 设计图; (*pattern*) tú'àn 图案 **2** v/t *building, car, machine* shèjì 设计; **not ~ed for heavy use** zhǐ xiàn qīngyòng zhǐ 只限轻用

**designate** v/t *person* rènmìng 任命; *area* zhǐdìng 指定

**designer** (*of building, car, ship, audio*) shèjì shī 设计师

**designer clothes** míngpái fúzhuāng 名牌服装

**design fault** shèjì shīwù 设计失误

**design school** shèjì xuéyuàn 设计学院

**desirable** *residence* chèngxīn rúyì 称心如意; (*to be recommended*) zhíde 值得

**desire** n (*wish*) yuànwàng 愿望; (*sexual*) xìngyù 性欲

**desk** shūzhuō 书桌; (*in hotel*) wènxùn tái 问讯台

**desk clerk** jiēdàiyuán 接待员; **desktop computer** COMPUT ⇩ táishìjī 台式机; **desktop publishing** zhuōmiàn páibǎn 桌面排版

**desolate** adj *place* huāngliáng 荒凉

**despair 1** n juéwàng 绝望; **in ~**

juéwàng 绝望 2 *v/i* juéwàng 绝望; **~ of** duì … búbào xīwàng 对 … 不抱希望

**desperate** *person* zǒutóu wúlù 走投无路; *action* gūzhù yìzhì 孤注一掷; *situation* wēijí 危急; **be ~ for a drink/cigarette** pòqiè xūyào yínliào/xiāngyān 迫切需要饮料/香烟

**desperation** gūzhù yìzhì 孤注一掷; **an act of ~** gūzhù yìzhì zhījǔ 孤注一掷之举

**despise** kànbùqǐ 看不起

**despite** jǐnguǎn 尽管

**despondent** yìqì xiāochén 意气消沉

**despot** bàojūn 暴君

**dessert** tiánpǐn 甜品

**destination** mùdìdì 目的地

**destiny** yuánfèn 缘分

**destitute** pínkùn 贫困

**destroy** cuīhuǐ 摧毁

**destroyer** (*boat*) qūchú jiàn 驱除舰

**destruction** pòhuài 破坏

**destructive** *power* pòhuài xìng 破坏性; *criticism* xiāojí 消极; *child* táoqì 淘气

**detach** fēnkāi 分开

**detachable** kě fēnkāi 可分开

**detached** (*objective*) wú piānjiàn 无偏见

**detachment** (*objectivity*) bùpiān bǔyǐ 不偏不倚

**detail** *n* (*small point*) zhījié 枝节; (*piece of information*) xìjié 细节; (*irrelevancy*) suǒsuì xiǎoshì 琐碎小事; **in ~** xiángxì 详细

**detailed** xiángxì 详细

**detain** (*hold back*) dāngé 耽搁; (*as prisoner*) jūliú 拘留

**detainee: political ~** zhèngzhì fàn 政治犯

**detect** chájué 察觉; (*of device*) jiǎncè 检测

**detection** (*of criminal, crime*) zhēnchá 侦察; (*of smoke etc*) jiǎncè 检测

**detective** (*policeman*) zhēntàn 侦探

**detective novel** zhēntàn xiǎoshuō

侦探小说

**detector** tàncè qì 探测器

**détente** POL huǎnhé 缓和

**detention** (*imprisonment*) jūliú 拘留

**deter** (*frighten*) wēishè 危慑; (*stop*) zhìzhǐ 制止; **~ X from doing Y** zǔzhǐ X zuò Y 阻止 X 做 Y

**detergent** xǐdí jì 洗涤剂

**deteriorate** èhuà 恶化

**determination** (*resolution*) juéxīn 决心

**determine** (*establish*) chámíng 查明

**determined** xià juéxīn 下决心; *effort* jiānjué 坚决

**deterrent** *n* wēishè yīnsù 危慑因素

**detest** tǎoyàn 讨厌

**detonate 1** *v/t* shǐ bàozhà 使爆炸 **2** *v/i* bàozhà 爆炸

**detour** *n* yūhuí 迂回; (*diversion*) ràodào xíngshí 绕道行驶

♦ **detract from** *achievement, enjoyment* yǒusǔn yú 有损于; *appearance of sth* shǐ jiǎnsè 使减色

**detriment: to the ~ of** duì … búlì 对 … 不利

**detrimental** búlì 不利

**deuce** (*in tennis*) píngjú 平局

**devaluation** (*of currency*) biǎnzhí 贬值

**devalue** *currency* biǎnzhí 贬值

**devastate** *also fig* cuīhuǐ 摧毁

**devastating** cuīhuǐ xìng 摧毁性

**develop 1** *v/t film* chōngxǐ 冲洗; *land, site* jiànshè 建设; *activity, business* kuòdà 扩大; (*originate*) fāmíng 发明; (*improve on*) gǎijìn 改进; *illness, cold* kāishǐ 开始 **2** *v/i* (*grow*) fāzhǎn 发展; (*of person*) zhǎngdà 长大

**developer** (*of property*) búdǒngchǎn shāng 不动产商

**developing country** fāzhǎn zhōng guójiā 发展中国家

**development** (*of film*) chōngxǐ 冲洗; (*of land, site*) jiànshè 建设; (*of business, country*) fāzhǎn 发展; (*event*) shìjiàn 事件; (*origination*) fāmíng 发明; (*improving*) gǎijìn 改进; **~ area** kāifāqū 开发区

device (*tool*) qìjù 器具

devil móguǐ 魔鬼

devious (*sly*) jiǎohuá 狡猾

devise fāmíng 发明

devoid: **~ of** wánquán méiyǒu 完全没有

devote *time, effort* gòngxiàn 贡献

devoted *son etc* zhōngshí 忠实; **be ~ to X** (*to parents, grandparents*) xiàoshùn X 孝顺 X; (*to any other person*) zhōngshí yú X 忠实于 X

devotion zhuānxīn 专心

devour *food* lángtūn hǔyàn 狼吞虎咽; *book* zháomí 着迷

devout qiánchéng 虔诚

dew lùshuǐ 露水

dexterity shúliàn jìqiǎo 熟练技巧

diabetes tángniàobìng 糖尿病

diabetic **1** *n* tángniàobìng huànzhě 糖尿病患者 **2** *adj* tángniàobìng 糖尿病

diagonal *adj* xié 斜

diagram tú 图

dial **1** *n* (*of clock*) zhōngmiàn 钟面; (*of meter*) yíbiǎo 仪表; TELEC bōhào pán 拨号盘 **2** *v/i* TELEC bōhào 拨号 **3** *v/t* TELEC: *number* bō 拨

dialect fāngyán 方言

dialog duìhuà 对话

dial tone bōhàoyīn 拨号音

diameter zhíjìng 直径

diametrically: **~ opposed** jiérán xiāngfǎn 截然相反

diamond (*jewel*) zuànshí 钻石; (*in cards*) fāngkuàir 方块儿; (*shape*) língxíng 菱形

diaper niàobù 尿布

diaphragm ANAT gémó 隔膜; (*contraceptive*) zǐgōng tuō 子宫托

diarrhea fùxiè 腹泻, lādùzi 拉肚子 F

diary rìjì 日记

dice **1** *n* tóuzi 骰子 **2** *v/t* (*cut*) qiē chéng dīng 切成丁

dichotomy liǎng duìlì 两对立

dictate *v/t letter, novel* kǒushòu 口授

dictation kǒushòu 口授

dictator POL dúcái zhě 独裁者

dictatorial *tone of voice* mìnglìng shì 命令式; *person, power* dúcái 独裁

dictatorship zhuānzhèng 专政

dictionary zìdiǎn 字典

die sǐ 死; **~ of cancer / AIDS** sǐyú áizhèng / àizībìng 死于癌症／艾滋病; **I'm dying to know / leave** wǒ jí xiǎng zhīdào / líkāi 我极想知道／离开

♦ **die away** (*of noise*) zhújiàn xiāoshī 逐渐消失

♦ **die down** (*of noise*) jiàngdī 降低; (*of storm*) jiǎnruò 减弱; (*of fire*) biànruò 变弱; (*of excitement*) píngxī 平息

♦ **die out** (*of custom, species*) mièjué 灭绝

diesel (*fuel*) cháiyóu 柴油

diet **1** *n* (*regular food*) shíwù 食物; (*for losing weight*) jiǎnféi shípǐn 减肥食品; (*for health reasons*) tèzhǒng yǐnshí 特种饮食 **2** *v/i* (*to lose weight*) jiǎnféi 减肥

differ (*be different*) bùtóng 不同; (*disagree*) yìjiàn xiāngzuǒ 意见相左

difference chābié 差别; (*disagreement*) fēnqí 分歧; **it doesn't make any ~** (*doesn't change anything*) méi shénme chābié 没什么差别; (*doesn't matter*) méi shénme guānxi 没什么关系

different bùtóng 不同

differentiate: **~ between** qūfēn 区分

differently yǔzhòng bùtóng 与众不同

difficult bù róngyì 不容易

difficulty kùnnan 困难; **with ~** chīlì 吃力

dig **1** *v/t* wā 挖 **2** *v/i*: **it was ~ging into me** juérù wǒ 掘入我

♦ **dig out** (*find*) zhǎochū 找出

♦ **dig up** juéqǐ 掘起; *information* cháchū 查出

digest *v/t* xiāohuà 消化; *information* lǐnghuì 领会

digestible *food* kě xiāohuà 可消化

digestion xiāohuà 消化

digit (number) shùzì 数字; *a four-number* sìwèi shùzì 四位数字

digital shùzì 数字

dignified yǒu zūnyán 有尊严

dignitary dáguān guìrén 达官贵人

dignity zūnyán 尊严

digress zànshí lítí 暂时离题

digression zànshí lítí 暂时离题

dike (wall) dī 堤

dilapidated tānhuǐ 坍毁

dilate (of pupils) kuòzhāng 扩张

dilemma jìntuì liǎngnán 进退两难; *be in a ~* chùyú jìntuì liǎngnán de jìngdì 处于进退两难的境地

diligent qínfèn 勤奋

dilute v/t xīshì 稀释

dim 1 adj room, light hūn'àn 昏暗; outline bù xiǎnzhù 不显著; (stupid) shǎ 傻; prospects bēiguān 悲观 2 v/t: ~ *the headlights* diǎn chē qiándēng àndàn 使车前灯暗淡 3 v/i (of lights) biàn àndàn 变暗淡

dimension (measurement) chǐcun 尺寸

diminish 1 v/t value shǐ jiǎnshǎo 使减少; authority xiāoruò 削弱 2 v/i biànshǎo 变少

diminutive 1 n àichēng 爱称 2 adj xiǎo 小

dimple jiǔwō 酒窝

dim sum diǎnxin 点心

din n xuānnào shēng 喧闹声

dine yòngcān 用餐

diner (person) yòngcān zhě 用餐者; (restaurant) xiǎo cānguǎn 小餐馆

dinghy xiǎochuán 小船

dingy atmosphere hūn'àn 昏暗; (dirty) zāng zhè 脏

dining car cānchē 餐车; dining room cānshì 餐室; dining table cānzhuō 餐桌

dinner (in the evening) wǎncān 晚餐; (at midday) wǔcān 午餐; (gathering) yànhuì 宴会

dinner guest yànhuì kèrén 宴会客人; dinner jacket xiǎo lǐfú 小

礼服; dinner party yànhuì 宴会

dinosaur kǒnglóng 恐龙

dip 1 n (swim) yóuyǒng 游泳; (for food) zhānliào 沾料; (in road) āoxiàn 凹陷 2 v/t zhān 沾; ~ *the headlights* diǎn chē qiándēng àndàn 使车前灯暗淡 3 v/i (of road) qīngxié 倾斜

diploma wénpíng 文凭

diplomacy wàijiāo 外交; (tact) lǎoliàn 老练

diplomat wàijiāo guān 外交官

diplomatic wàijiāo 外交; (tactful) lǎoliàn 老练

dire (urgent) pòbù jídài 迫不及待

direct 1 adj zhíjiē 直接; flight, train zhídá 直达; person zhíshuǎng zào 直爽 2 v/t (to a place) zhǐyǐn 指引; play, movie dǎoyǎn 导演; attention zhǐxiàng 指向

direct current ELEC zhíliú 直流

direction fāngxiàng 方向; (of movie, play) dǎoyǎn 导演; ~s (instructions) zhǐshì 指示; (to a place) fāngwèi 方位; (for use) zhǐdǎo 指导; (for medicine) yòngfǎ 用法

direction indicator MOT fāngwèi zhǐshì 方位指示

directly 1 adv (straight) zhíjiē 直接; (soon) hěnkuài 很快; (immediately) lìjí 立即 2 conj yīdāng 一当

director (of company) zhǔguǎn 主管; (of play, movie) dǎoyǎn 导演

directory zhǐdǎo 指导; TELEC diànhuà bù 电话簿

dirt (grime) zāng dōngxi 脏东西

dirt cheap hěn piányi 很便宜

dirty 1 adj zāng 脏; (pornographic) huángsè 黄色 2 v/t nòngzāng 弄脏

dirty trick bēibǐ xíngwéi 卑鄙行为

disability cánjí 残疾

disabled 1 n cánjí rénshì 残疾人士 2 adj cánjí 残疾

disadvantage (drawback) bùlì zhīchù 不利之处; *be at a ~* chīkuī 吃亏

disadvantaged shèhuì dìwèi dīxià

社会地位低下

**disadvantageous** búlì 不利

**disagree** (*of person*) bù tóngyì 不同意

♦**disagree with**: **~ X** (*of person*) yǔ X yìjiàn bù yīzhì 与X意见不一致; (*of food*) yǔ X bù xiāngyí 与X不相宜

**disagreeable** lìngrén bù yúkuài 令人不愉快

**disagreement** bùtóng yìjiàn 不同意见; (*argument*) zhēngzhí 争执

**disappear** xiāoshī 消失; (*run away*) pǎodiào 跑掉

**disappearance** (*of item*) xiāoshī 消失; (*of person*) shīzōng 失踪

**disappoint** shǐ shīwàng 使失望

**disappointed** shīwàng 失望

**disappointing** lìngrén shīwàng 令人失望

**disappointment** shīwàng 失望

**disapproval** zhǐzé 指责

**disapprove** bū zànchéng 不赞成; **~ of** bū zànchéng 不赞成

**disarm 1** v/t robber jiěchú wǔqì 解除武器; militia shǐ sàngshī shānghài nénglì 使丧失伤害能力 **2** v/i cáijūn 裁军

**disarmament** (*of militia*) jiěchú wǔzhuāng 解除武装; (*of country*) cáijūn 裁军

**disarming** shǐrén xiāochú huáiyí 使人消除怀疑

**disaster** zāinàn 灾难

**disaster area** shòuzāi dìqū 受灾地区; fig (*person*) mǎdàhā 马大哈

**disastrous** sǔnshī cǎnzhòng 损失惨重

**disbelief**: **in ~** bùkě xiāngxìn 不可相信

**disc** (*CD*) guāngdié 光碟

**discard** old clothes etc rēngdiào 扔掉; boyfriend, theory pāoqì 抛弃

**discern** improvement chájué 察觉; (*make out*) biànchū 辨出

**discernible** kě biànrén chū 可辨认出

**discerning** yǒu yǎnlì 有眼力

**discharge 1** n (*from hospital*) chūyuàn 出院; (*from army*) tuìwǔ

退伍; (*of waste*) páichū 排出 **2** v/t (*from hospital*) yǔnxǔ chūyuàn 允许出院; (*from army*) qiǎnsàn 遣散; (*from job*) kāichú 开除; waste páichū 排出

**disciple** (*religious*) zǐdì 子弟

**disciplinary** chéngjiè xìng 惩戒性

**discipline 1** n jìlù 纪律 **2** v/t child, dog, employee chéngfá 惩罚

**disc jockey** DJ DJ

**disclaim** fǒurèn 否认

**disclose** tòulù 透露

**disclosure** (*of information, name*) tòulù 透露; (*about scandal etc*) xièlòu 泄露

**disco** dísīkē 迪斯科; (*place*) ⇩ dítīng 迪厅

**discolor** shǐ biànsè 使变色

**discomfort** n (*pain*) tòngkǔ 痛苦; (*embarrassment*) bú zìzài 不自在

**disconcert** shǐ wéinán 使为难

**disconcerted** jiǒngpò 窘迫

**disconnect** (*detach: hose, electrical / gas appliance*) shǐ bù jiētōng 使不接通; supply, telephones qiēduàn 切断; **I was ~ed** TELEC wǒ bèi qiēduàn le 我被切断了

**disconsolate** jǔsàng 沮丧

**discontent** bùmǎn 不满

**discontented** bù mǎnyì 不满意

**discontinue** product tíngzhǐ shēngchǎn 停止生产; bus, train service, magazine zhōngzhǐ 中止

**discord** MUS bù xiétiáo 不协调; (*in relations*) bù héxié 不和谐

**discotheque** dísīkē 迪斯科; (*place*) ⇩ dítīng 迪厅

**discount 1** n zhékòu 折扣 **2** v/t goods dǎ zhékòu 打折扣; theory bù kǎolǜ 不考虑

**discourage** (*dissuade*) quànzǔ 劝阻; (*dishearten*) shǐ jǔsàng 使沮丧

**discover** fāxiàn 发现

**discoverer** fāxiàn zhě 发现明者

**discovery** fāxiàn 发现

**discredit** v/t person shǐ sàngshī míngyù 使丧失名誉; theory shǐrén bù xiāngxìn 使人不相信

**discreet** person jǐnshèn 谨慎; restaurant kǎolǜ zhōudào 考虑周到

discrepancy chācuò 差错

discretion pànduàn nénglì 判断能力; *at your* ~ yóu nǐ zhuóqíng chǔlǐ 由你酌情处理

discriminate: ~ *against* qíshì 歧视; ~ *between* (*distinguish*) qūbié 区别

discriminating yǒu yǎnlì 有眼力

discrimination (*sexual, racial etc*) qíshì 歧视

discus SP tiěbǐng 铁饼

discuss tǎolùn 讨论; (*of article*) xiángshù 详述

discussion tǎolùn 讨论

disease jíbìng 疾病

disembark v/i (*from plane*) xià fēijī 下飞机; (*from ship*) xià chuán 下船

disenchanted: ~ *with* duì ... shīqù xìngqù 对 ... 失去兴趣

disengage fàngkāi 放开

disentangle jiětuō kāi 解脱开

disfigure shǐ huíróng shǐ 使毁容

disgrace 1 n xiūchǐ 羞耻; *a* ~ (*person*) bù guāngcǎi de rén 不光彩的人; *it's a* ~ bùzhī hàisào 不知害臊; *in* ~ diūliǎn 丢脸 2 v/t shǐ diūliǎn 使丢脸

disgraceful *behaviour, situation* yǒushī tǐmiàn 有失体面

disgruntled bùmǎn 不满

disguise 1 n wěizhuāng 伪装; (*costume, make-up*) jiǎ miànjù 假面具 2 v/t yǐnmán 隐瞒; *fear, anxiety* yǎncáng 掩藏; ~ *oneself as* zhuāngbàn chéng 装扮成; *he was* ~*d as* tā jiǎzhuāng shì 他假装是

disgust 1 n jíwéi fǎngǎn 极为反感 2 v/t shǐ fǎngǎn 使反感

disgusting *habit, smell, food* lìngrén zuò'ǒu 令人作呕

dish (*part of meal*) cài 菜; (*container*) diézi 碟子

dishcloth xǐwǎn bù 洗碗布

disheartened jǔsàng 沮丧

disheartening lìngrén shāngxīn 令人伤心

disheveled bù zhěngqí 不整齐

dishonest bù chéngshí 不诚实

dishonesty bù chéngshí 不诚实

dishonor n chǐrǔ 耻辱; *bring* ~ *on* dàilái chǐrǔ 带来耻辱

dishonorable kěchǐ 可耻

dishwasher (*machine*) xǐwǎn jī 洗碗机; (*person*) xǐwǎn gōng 洗碗工

dishwashing liquid xǐjiéjīng 洗洁精

dishwater xǐwǎn shuǐ 洗碗水

disillusion v/t shǐ huànxiǎng pòmiè 使幻想破灭

disillusionment huànmiè 幻灭

disinclined bú yuànyì 不愿意

disinfect xiāodú 消毒

disinfectant xiāodú jì 消毒剂

disinherit bōduó jìchéng quán 剥夺继承权

disintegrate lièkāi 裂开; (*of marriage, building*) wǎjiě 瓦解

disinterested (*unbiassed*) zhōnglì 中立

disjointed tuōjié 脱节

disk (*shape*) yuánpán 圆盘; COMPUT ⇩ cípán 磁盘; *on* ~ chǔcún zài cípán shàng 储存在磁盘上

disk drive COMPUT ⇩ cípán dàijī 磁盘带机

diskette ⇩ ruǎn cípán 软磁盘

dislike 1 n fǎngǎn 反感 2 v/t bù xǐhuān 不喜欢

dislocate *shoulder* tuōwèi 脱位

dislodge shǐ yídòng 使移动

disloyal bù zhōngchéng 不忠诚

disloyalty bùzhōng 不忠

dismal *weather* zāogāo 糟糕; *news, prospect* lìngrén jǔsàng 令人沮丧; *person* (*sad*) yōuxīn 忧心; *person* (*negative*) xiāochén 消沉; *failure* bēicǎn 悲惨

dismantle *object* chāi 拆; *organization* shǐ jiětǐ 使解体

dismay 1 n (*alarm*) jīng'è 惊愕; (*disappointment*) shīwàng 失望 2 v/t shǐ huīxīn 使灰心

dismiss *employee* jiěgù 解雇; *suggestion, idea* bù kǎolǜ 不考虑; *possibility* bú fàngzài xīnshàng 不放在心上

dismissal (*of employee*) jiěgù 解雇

**disobedience** bù fúcóng 不服从
**disobedient** juéjiàng 倔强
**disobey** wéibèi 违背
**disorder** (*untidiness*) záluàn 杂乱; (*unrest*) bàoluàn 暴乱; MED shītiáo 失调
**disorderly** *room, desk* záluàn 杂乱; *mob* bù shǒu zhìxù 不守秩序
**disorganized** wú zǔzhī 无组织
**disoriented** míhuo 迷惑
**disown** tuōlí guānxì 脱离关系
**disparaging** biǎnyì 贬抑
**disparity** xuánshū 悬殊
**dispassionate** (*objective*) bù piānxīn 不偏心
**dispatch** *v/t* (*send*) fāchū 发出
**dispensary** (*in pharmacy*) yàofáng 药房
**dispense**: ~ **with** shěngquè 省却
**disperse 1** *v/t* qūsàn 驱散 **2** *v/i* (*of crowd*) shūsàn 疏散; (*of mist*) qūsàn 驱散
**displace** (*supplant*) páijǐ 排挤
**display 1** *n* zhǎnlǎn 展览; (*of emotion*) biǎoshì 表示; (*in store window*) chénliè 陈列; COMPUT xiǎnshì 显示; **be on** ~ (*at exhibition*) zhǎnlǎn 展览; (*be for sale*) chénliè 陈列 **2** *v/t emotion* xiǎnshì 显示; (*at exhibition*) zhǎnlǎn 展览; (*for sale*) chénliè 陈列; COMPUT xiǎnshì 显示
**display cabinet** (*in museum, store*) zhǎnlǎn chúchuāng 展览橱窗
**displease** shǐ bù gāoxìng 使不高兴
**displeasure** bùmǎn 不满
**disposable** *diapers, contact lenses* yīcìxìng 一次性; ~ **income** shèngyú shōurù 剩余收入
**disposal** rēngdiào 扔掉; (*of pollutants, nuclear waste*) chǔlǐ 处理; **I am at your** ~ wǒ tīng nǐ zhībiàn 我听你之便; **put X at Y's** ~ ràng Y zìyóu zhīpèi X 让Y自由支配X
**dispose**: ~ **of** rēngdiào 扔掉
**disposed**: **be ~ to do X** (*willing*) yuànyì zuò X 愿意做X; **be well ~ toward X** duì X yǒu hǎogǎn 对X有好感

**disposition** (*nature*) qīngxiàng 倾向
**disproportionate** bùchéng bǐlì 不成比例
**disprove** fǎnzhèng 反证
**dispute 1** *n* zhēnglùn 争论; (*between the two countries*) zhēngbiàn 争辩; (*industrial*) zhēngzhí 争执 **2** *v/t* zhēnglùn 争论; (*fight over*) zhēngduó 争夺
**disqualify** qǔxiāo zīgé 取消资格
**disregard** *n* & *v/t* hūshì 忽视
**disrepair**: **in a state of** ~ shīxiū 失修
**disreputable** shēngmíng bàihuài 声名败坏; *area* shēngyù bùhǎo 声誉不好
**disrespect** bù zūnzhòng 不尊重
**disrespectful** bù lǐmào 不礼貌
**disrupt** *train service* shǐ tíngdùn 使停顿; *meeting, class* pòhuài 破坏; (*intentionally*) rǎoluàn 扰乱
**disruption** (*of train service*) tíngdùn 停顿; (*of meeting, class*) pòhuài 破坏; (*intentional*) rǎoluàn 扰乱
**disruptive** pòhuài xìng 破坏性
**dissatisfaction** bùmǎn 不满
**dissatisfied** bù mǎnyì 不满意
**dissension** yìjiàn fēnqí 意见分歧
**dissent 1** *n* chí yìyì 持异议 **2** *v/i*: ~ **from** chàng fǎndiào 唱反调
**dissident** *n* chí bùtóng zhèngjiàn zhě 持不同政见者
**dissimilar** bùtóng 不同
**dissociate**: ~ **oneself from X** fǒurèn zìjǐ hé X yǒu guānxi 否认自己和X有关系
**dissolute** fàngdàng 放荡
**dissolve** *v/t* & *v/i* róngjiě 溶解
**dissuade** quànzhǐ 劝止; ~ **X from Y** quànzǔ X bùyào qù zuò Y 劝阻X不要去做Y
**distance 1** *n* jùlí 距离; **in the** ~ zài yuǎnchù 在远处 **2** *v/t*: ~ **oneself from X** shǐ zìjǐ yǔ X bǎochí jùlí 使自己和X保持距离
**distant** *place, time, relative* yuǎn 远; *fig* (*aloof*) bǎochí yídìngde jùlí 保持一定的距离
**distaste** xiánwù 嫌恶
**distasteful** lìngrén yànwù 令人厌恶

**distinct** (*clear*) míngxiǎn 明显;
(*different*) bùtóng 不同; *as ~ from
X* yǔ X bùtóng 与X不同

**distinction** (*differentiation*) qūbié
区别; *hotel / product of ~* gāo
zhìliàng lǚguǎn / chǎnpǐn 高质量
旅馆 / 产品

**distinctive** tèyǒu 特有

**distinctly** qīngchǔ 清楚;
(*decidedly*) míngxiǎn 明显

**distinguish** (*see*) biànbié 辨别; *~
between X and Y* qūfēn X hé Y
区分X和Y

**distinguished** (*famous*) zhùmíng
著名; (*dignified*) yǔzhòng bùtóng
与众不同

**distort** wāiqū 歪曲

**distract** *person* shǐ fēnxīn 使分心;
*attention* fēnsàn zhùyì lì 分散注
意力

**distracted** (*worried*) yōulù 忧虑

**distraction** (*of attention*) fēnshén
wù 分神物; (*amusement*) yúlè yú娱
乐; *drive X to ~* shǐ X fēnxīn 使X
分心

**distraught** xīnshén bùdìng 心神
不定

**distress 1** *n* (*mental suffering*)
kǔnǎo 苦恼; (*physical pain*)
tòngkǔ 痛苦; *in ~* (*ship, aircraft*)
wēinàn zhōng 危难中 **2** *v/t*
(*upset*) shāngxīn 伤心

**distress signal** qiújiù xìnhào 求救
信号

**distribute** fēngěi 分给; *leaflets*
sànfā 散发; *wealth* fēnpèi 分配;
COM jīngxiāo 经销

**distribution** (*handing out*) fēnfā 分
发; (*of wealth*) fēnpèi 分配; COM
jīngxiāo 经销

**distribution arrangement** COM
jīngxiāo hétóng 经销合同

**distributor** COM jīngxiāo shāng 经
销商

**district** qū 区

**district attorney** dìfāng jiǎnchá
guān 地方检察官

**distrust** *n & v/t* huáiyí 怀疑

**disturb** (*interrupt*) dǎjiǎo 打搅;
(*upset*) dānyōu 担忧; *do not ~*
qǐngwù dǎjiǎo 请勿打搅

**disturbance** (*interruption*) gānrǎo
干扰; *~s* sāoluàn 骚乱

**disturbed** (*concerned, worried*)
dānxīn 担心; *mentally ~* jīngshén
shīcháng 精神失常

**disturbing** lìngrén shāngxīn 令人
伤心

**disused** fèiqì 废弃

**ditch 1** *n* kēng kǎn 坑坎 **2** *v/t* F (*get rid of*)
pāoqì 抛弃

**dive 1** *n* tiàoshuǐ 跳水;
(*underwater*) qiánshuǐ 潜水; (*of
plane*) fǔchōng 俯冲; F (*bar etc*)
xiàděng chǎngsuǒ 下等场所;
*take a ~* (*of dollar etc*) tūrán
xiàjiàng 突然下降 **2** *v/i* tiàoshuǐ
跳水; (*underwater*) qiánshuǐ 潜
水; (*of plane*) fǔchōng 俯冲

**diver** (*off board*) tiàoshuǐ zhě 跳水
者; (*underwater*) qiánshuǐ zhě 潜
水者

**diverge** chàkāi 岔开

**diverse** duōyàng huà 多样化

**diversification** COM duōzhǒng
jīngyíng 多种经营

**diversify** *v/i* COM duōzhǒng
jīngyíng 多种经营

**diversion** (*for traffic*) gǎixiàn 改
线; (*to distract attention*) qiānzhì 牵
制

**diversity** duōyàng huà 多样化

**divert** *traffic* gǎixiàn 改线; *~ attention* fēnsàn zhùyì lì 分散注
意力

**divest** *~ X of Y* gěi X bōduó Y 给X
剥夺Y

**divide** *fig: country, family*
fēnliè 分裂

**dividend** FIN gǔxī 股息; *pay ~s* fig
lìng shòuyì 令受益

**divine** REL shén 神; F *gài le mào le*
盖了帽了

**diving** (*from board*) tiàoshuǐ 跳水;
(*scuba*) qiánshuǐ 潜水

**diving board** tiàoshuǐ bǎn 跳水板

**divisible** kě chú jìn 可除尽

**division** MATH chúfǎ 除法; (*split: in
party etc*) fēnliè 分裂; (*splitting
into parts*) fēngē 分割; (*of
company*) bùmén 部门

**divorce 1** *n* líhūn 离婚; *get a ~*

líhūn 离婚 **2** *v/t & v/i* líhūn 离婚

divorced líhūn 离婚; *get ~d* líhūn 离婚

divorcee líhūn zhě 离婚者

divulge tòulù 透露

DIY (= *do-it-yourself*) zìjǐ dòngshǒu 自己动手

DIY store zìjǐ dòngshǒu shāngdiàn 自己动手商店

dizzy: *feel ~* tóuyūn 头晕

DNA (= *deoxyribonucleic acid*) tuōyǎng hétáng hésuān 脱氧核糖核酸

do **1** *v/t* zuò 做; *one's hair* shū 梳; *the beds* pū 铺; *French, chemistry etc* xuéxí 学习; *100mph etc* xíngshǐ 行驶; *what are you ~ing tonight?* nǐ jīnwǎn gànshénme? 你今晚干什么?; *I don't know what to ~* wǒ bùzhī gāi zěnme bàn 我不知该怎么办; *no, I'll ~ it* bùyòng, wǒ lái ba 不用,我来吧; *~ it right now!* mǎshàng jiù gàn! 马上就干!; *have you done this before?* yǐqián gàn guò ma? 以前干过吗?; *have one's hair done* zuò tóufa 做头发 **2** *v/i (be suitable, enough)* yě kěyǐ 也可以; *that will ~!* xíng le! 行了!; *~ well (of person)* chénggōng 成功; *(of business)* chāngshèng 昌盛; *well done! (congratulations!)* gōngxǐ! 恭喜!; *how ~ you ~ ?* nǐ hǎoma? 你好吗? **3** *auxiliary:* ~ *you know him?* nǐ rènshi tā ma? 你认识他吗?; *I don't know* wǒ bù zhīdào 我不知道; ~ *you like ... ?* – *yes I* ~ nǐ xǐhuan ... ma? – wǒ xǐhuan 你喜欢...吗? –我喜欢; *he works hard, doesn't he?* tā gōngzuò hái nǔlì, shìba? 他工作还努力,是吧?; *don't you believe me?* nǐ nándào bù xiāngxìn wǒ? 你难道不相信我?; *you* – *believe me, don't you?* nǐ quèshí xiāngxìn wǒ, shìba? 你确实相信我,是吧?; *you don't know the answer, ~ you?* – *no I don't* nǐ bù zhīdào dá'àn, shìba? 你不知道答案,是吧? –我不知道

♦ *do away with* fèichú 废除

♦ *do in: I'm done in* F wǒ lèisǐ le 我累死了

♦ *do out of: do X out of Y* piànXY 骗XY

♦ *do up (renovate)* gǎizhuāng 改装; *(fasten)* jìláo 系牢; *buttons* kòuhǎo 扣好; *laces* bǎng xiédài 绑鞋带

♦ *do with: I could ~ ...* wǒ xiǎngyào ... 我想要...; *he won't have anything to ~ it (won't get involved)* tā bùxiǎng jièrù 他不想介入

♦ *do without* **1** *v/i* méiyǒu yěxíng 没有也行 **2** *v/t* bù xūyào 不需要

docile *person* shùncóng 顺从; *animal* xùnfú 驯服

dock¹ **1** *n* NAUT chuánwù 船坞 **2** *v/i (of ship)* kào mǎtóu 靠码头; *(of spaceship)* duì jiē chù 对接处

dock² LAW bèigào xí 被告席

dockyard chuánchǎng 船厂

doctor *n* MED yīshēng 医生; *(form of address)* yīshēng 医生

doctorate bóshì 博士

doctrine jiàotiáo 教条

docudrama jìshí diànshì jù 记实电视剧

document *n* wénjiàn 文件

documentary *(program)* jìlù piān 纪录片

documentation wénjiàn 文件

dodge *v/t blow* shǎnkāi 闪开; *person, issue* duǒbì 躲避; *question* bìkāi 避开

doe *(deer)* mǔlù 母鹿

dog **1** *n* gǒu 狗 **2** *v/t (of bad luck)* bànsuí 伴随

dog catcher zhuā gǒu rén 抓狗人

dog-eared *book* juǎnjiǎo 卷角

dogged gùzhí 固执

doggie *(in children's language)* gǒugǒu 狗狗

doggy bag gǒu shí dài 狗食袋

doghouse: *be in the ~* shòu lěngyù 受冷遇

dogma jiàotiáo 教条

dogmatic jiàotiáo zhǔyì 教条主义

do-gooder Léi Fēng shūshu 雷锋
叔叔

dog tag MIL shēnfèn shíbié pái 身
份识别牌

dog-tired lèi sǐ le 累死了

do-it-yourself zìjǐ dòngshǒu 自己
动手

doldrums: *be in the ~* (*of economy*)
wú shēngqì 无生气

◆dole out shǎoliàng pèijǐ 少量配
给

doll (*toy*) wáwa 娃娃; F (*woman*)
měimào shàonǚ 美貌少女

◆doll up: *get dolled up* dǎbàn 打
扮

dollar měiyuán 美元

dollop n yídìng liàng 一定量

dolphin hǎitún 海豚

dome (*of building*) yuándǐng 圆顶

domestic adj chores jiātíng 家庭;
news, policy guónèi 国内; (*for
agriculture*) jiāchù 家畜

domesticate animal xùnhuà 驯化;
*be ~d* (*of person*) zuò jiāwù 做家
务

domestic flight guónèi hángbān
国内航班

dominant zhǔyào 主要; *member*
zhǔdǎo 主导; BIO zhàn yōushì 占
优势

dominate kòngzhì 控制; *landscape*
gāosǒng yú 高耸于

domination kòngzhì 控制

domineering bàdào 霸道

donate money juān 捐; toys, books,
MED juānxiàn 捐献; time, energy
fùchū 付出

donation (*of money, toys, books,*
MED juānxiàn 捐献; (*of time,
energy*) fùchū 付出

donkey lǘ 驴

donor (*of money*), MED juānxiàn
zhě 捐献者

donut ⇩ zhá miànbǐngquān 炸面
饼圈

doom n (*fate*) mìngyùn 命运;
(*ruin*) zāinàn 灾难

doomed project zhùdìng shībài 注
定失败; *we are ~* (*bound to fail*)
wǒmen sǐdìng le 我们死定了;
*the ~ ship / plane* yùnàn

chuánzhī / fēijī yùnàn chuánzhī / fēijī 遇难船只 / 飞机

door mén 门; (*entrance*) dàmén 大
门; *there's someone at the ~*
yǒurén qiāomén 有人敲门

doorbell ménlíng 门铃; doorknob mén bǎshǒu 门把手;
doorman shǒumén rén 守门人;
doormat méndiàn 门垫; door-
step ménjiē 门阶; doorway
rùkǒu 入口

dope 1 n (*drugs*) dúpín 毒品;
(*idiot*) shǎzi 傻子; (*information*)
qíngbào 情报 2 v/t shǐ mázuì 使
麻醉

dormant plant xiūmián 休眠; ~
volcano jìng huǒshān 静火山

dormitory sùshè 宿舍

dosage yòngliàng 用量

dose n yòngliàng 用量

dot n (*also in e-mail*) diǎn 点; *on
the ~* (*exactly*) zhǔnshí 准时

◆dote on chǒng'ài 宠爱

dotted line xūxiàn 点线

double 1 n (*amount*) shuāngbèi 双
倍; (*person*) chóngyǐng 重影; (*of
movie star*) tìdài yǎnyuán 替代演
员; (*room*) shuāngrén fáng 双人
房 2 adj (*twice as much*) liǎngbèi
两倍; whisky jiābèi 加倍; sink,
oven shuāng 双; doors liǎngchóng
两重; layer liǎngcéng 两层; *in ~
figures* liǎngwèi shù 两位数
3 adv liǎngbèi 两倍; 4 v/t jiābèi
加倍; (*fold*) duìzhé 对折 5 v/i
fānyīfān 翻一番

◆double back v/i (*go back*) fǎnhuí
返回

◆double up v/i (*in pain*) wānshēn 弯
身; (*share*) héyòng 合用

double-bass dīyīn tíqín 低音提
琴; double bed shuāngrén
chuáng 双人床; double-
breasted shuāngpái kòushì 双排
扣式; doublecheck v/t & v/i
fùchá 复查; double chin
shuāngxiàba 双下巴; double
click COMPUT shuāngjī 双击;
doublecross v/t qīpiàn 欺骗;
double glazing shuāngcéng bōli
双层玻璃; double-quick: *in ~
time* jíkuài 极快; double room

shuāngrén fáng 双人房

**doubles** (in tennis) shuāngdǎ 双打

**doubt 1** n yíwèn 疑问; (uncertainty) yóuyù 犹豫; **be in ~** nányǐ quèdìng 难以确定; **no ~** (probably) wúyí 无疑 **2** v/t huáiyí 怀疑

**doubtful** remark, look zhídé huáiyí 值得怀疑; **be ~** (of person) ná bùzhǔn 拿不准; **it is ~ whether** nányǐ yùliào 难以预料

**doubtfully** huáiyí 怀疑

**doubtless** wúyí 无疑

**dough** shēngmiàn tuán 生面团; F (money) qián 钱

**dove** gēzi 鸽子; fig zhǔhé pài rénwù 主和派人物

**dowdy** bù xiāosǎ 不潇洒

**Dow Jones Average** Dào Qióng píngjūn zhí 道琼平均值

**down**[1] n (feathers) róng róng 绒绒

**down**[2] **1** adv (downward, onto the ground) xià 下; **~ there** zài xiàbiān 在下边; **fall ~** shuāidǎo 摔倒; **$200 ~** (as deposit) xiànfù èrbǎi měiyuán 现付二百美元; **~ south** zài nánfāng 在南方; **be ~** (of price, rate) xiàjiàng 下降; (of numbers, amount) jiǎnshǎo 减少; (not working) shīlíng 失灵; F (depressed) qíngxù dīluò 情绪低落 **2** prep xiàngxià 向下; (along) yánzhe 沿着; **it fell ~ the hole** diào kūlonglǐ le 掉窟窿里了; **go ~ this street** yánzhe zhèitiáo jiē zǒu 沿着这条街走; **there are stores all ~ the street** mǎnjiē dōushì shāngdiàn 满街都是商店; **he walked ~ the hill** tā xià shān le 他下山了 **3** v/t (destroy) jībài 击败

**down-and-out** n qióngkùn liáodǎo 穷困潦倒; **downcast** (dejected) jǔsàng 沮丧; **downfall** n kuàtái 垮台; (reason for ~) kuàtái de yuányīn 垮台的原因; (of politician) xiàtái 下台; **downgrade** v/t jiàngdī děngjí jiàngdī 降低等级; employee jiàngzhí 降职; **downhearted** jǔsàng 沮丧; **downhill** adv xiàpō 下坡; **go ~** fig

zǒu xiàpō lù 走下坡路; **~ skiing** xiàpō huáxuě 下坡滑雪; **download** COMPUT xiàzài 下载; **downmarket** adj dījí 低级; **down payment** dìngjīn 定金; **downplay** v/t qīngmiáo dànxiě 轻描淡写; **downpour** qīngpén dàyǔ 倾盆大雨; **downright 1** adj lie, idiot shízú 十足 **2** adv dangerous, stupid etc shízài shì 实在是; **downside** (disadvantage) quēxiàn 缺陷; **downsize 1** v/t car shēngchǎn xiǎoxíng chē 生产小型车; company cáiyuán cáiyuán 裁员 **2** v/i (of company) cáiyuán 裁员; **downstairs** adj & adv lóuxià 楼下; **down-to-earth** approach jiǎotà shídì 脚踏实地; person shíshí qiúshì 实事求是; **down-town** adj & adv shì zhōngxīn 市中心; **downturn** (in economy) xiàjiàng qūshì 下降趋势

**downward 1** adj glance xiàngxià 向下; trend xiàjiàng 下降 **2** adv wǎngxià 往下

**doze** n & v/i dǎdǔnr 打盹儿

♦ **doze off** dǎ kēshuì 打瞌睡

**dozen** shí'èr 十二, dǎ 打; **~s of X** F jǐshíge X 几十个 X

**drab** dāndiào 单调

**draft 1** n (of air) guòtáng fēng 过堂风; (of document) cǎogǎo 草稿; MIL zhēngbīng 征兵; **~ (beer)**, **beer on ~** zhāng píjiǔ 生啤酒 **2** v/t document qǐ cǎogǎo 起草稿; MIL zhēngbīng 征兵

**draft dodger** táobì bīngyì zhě 逃避兵役者

**draftee** yìngzhēng rùwǔ zhě 应征入伍者

**draftsman** huìtú yuán 绘图员; (of plan) qǐcǎo rén 起草人

**drafty** tōngfēng 通风

**drag 1** n: **it's a ~ having to ...** yào zuò ... shízài shì tài méijìnr le 要做 ... 实在是太没劲了; **he's a ~** tā méi shénme jìn 他没什么劲; **the main ~** jiēdào dàjiē 街道大街; **in ~** nánbàn nǚzhuāng 男扮女装 **2** v/t (pull) lā 拉; person, oneself yìnglā 硬拉; (search) sǎo 扫;

COMPUT tuōdòng 拖动 **3** *v/i (of time)* tuō 拖; *(of show, movie)* méijìnr 没劲儿; ~ **X into Y** *(involve)* yìng bǎ X lāchē jìn Y 硬把 X 拉扯进 Y; ~ **X out of Y** *(get information from)* cóng Y nàlǐ nádào X 从 Y 那里拿到 X

♦ **drag away:** *drag oneself away from the TV* qiángpò zìjǐ bùkàn diànshì 强迫自己不看电视

♦ **drag in** *(into conversation)* yìngchě rù 硬扯入

♦ **drag on** *(last long time)* tuō 拖长

♦ **drag out** *(prolong)* tuōcháng 拖长

♦ **drag up** *(mention)* lǎotí 老提

**dragon** lóng 龙; *fig* pōfù 泼妇

**Dragon Boat Festival** Duānwǔjié 端午节

**dragonfly** qīngtíng 蜻蜓

**drain 1** *n (pipe)* xiàshuǐ guǎndào 下水管道; *(under street)* xiàshuǐ dào 下水道; *a ~ on resources* hàofèi cáifù zhīwù 耗费财富之物 **2** *v/t water* lǜ 滤; *oil* páigān 排干; *vegetables* páigān shuǐfèn 排干水分; *land* shǐ gānhé 使干涸; *glass, tank* dàoguāng 倒光; *(exhaust: person)* jīnpí lìjìn 筋疲力尽 **3** *v/i (of dishes)* dīshuǐ 滴水

♦ **drain away** *(of liquid)* páiqù 排去

♦ **drain off** *water* páiqù 排去

**drainage** *(drains)* xiàshuǐ dào 下水道; *(of water from soil)* páishuǐ 排水

**drainpipe** páishuǐ guǎn 排水管

**drama** *(art form, play in theater)* xìjù 戏剧; *(play on TV)* jiémù 节目; *(dramatic event)* xìjùxìng shìjiàn 戏剧性事件; *(excitement)* xīngfèn 兴奋

**dramatic** xìjù 戏剧; *(exciting)* xìjù xìng 戏剧性; *gesture* zuòzuò 做作

**dramatist** jùzuò jiā 剧作家

**dramatization** *(play)* gǎibiān chéng xìjù 改编成戏剧

**dramatize** *story* gǎibiān chéng xìjù 改编成戏剧; *fig* zuòzuò 做作

**drape** *v/t cloth, coat* guà 挂; ~**d in** *(covered with)* fùgài 覆盖

**drapery** bùshì 布饰

**drapes** chuānglián 窗帘

**drastic** *(extreme)* yánzhòng 严重; *measures* jíduān 极端; *change* jídà 极大

**draw 1** *n (in match, competition)* píngjú 平局; *(in lottery)* kāijiǎng 开奖; *(attraction)* xīyǐn 吸引 **2** *v/t picture, map* huà 画; *cart, curtain* lā 拉; *lottery ticket* chōu 抽; *gun, knife* chōuchū 抽出; *(attract)* xīyǐn 吸引; *(lead)* jiào 叫; *(from bank account)* tíkuǎn 提款 **3** *v/i huàhuà* 画画; *(in match, competition)* dǎ píngjú 打平局; ~ *near (of person)* zǒujìn 走近; *(of date)* línjìn 临近

♦ **draw back 1** *v/i (recoil)* suōhuí 缩回 **2** *v/t (pull back)* lākāi 拉开

♦ **draw on 1** *v/i (advance)* línjìn 临近 **2** *v/t (make use of)* lìyòng 利用

♦ **draw out** *billfold, money* qǔchū 取出

♦ **draw up** *v/t document* qǐcǎo 起草; *chair* lā guòlái 拉过来 **2** *v/i (of vehicle)* tíng 停

**drawback** bìduān 弊端

**drawer**[1] *(of desk etc)* chōutì 抽屉

**drawer**[2]: *she is a good ~* tā hěnhuì huàhuàr 她很会画画儿

**drawing** *(picture)* huà 画; *(skill)* huìtú 绘画

**drawing board** túbǎn 图板; *go back to the ~* chóngxīn kāishǐ 重新开始

**drawl** *n* màn tūntun de jiǎnghuà 慢吞吞地讲话

**dread** *v/t* hàipà 害怕

**dreadful** *(extreme)* zāogāo 糟糕

**dreadfully** *(extremely)* jíduān 极端; *behave* zāogāo 糟糕

**dream 1** *n* mèng 梦 **2** *adj house etc* mèngzhōng 梦中 **3** *v/t & v/i* zuòmèng 做梦; *(day~)* mèngxiǎng 梦想

♦ **dream up** píngkōng xiǎngchū 凭空想出

**dreamer** *(day~)* mèngxiǎng jiā 梦想家

**dreamy** *voice, look* jīngshén huǎnghū 精神恍惚

**dreary** chénmèn 沉闷

dredge *harbour, canal* shūjùn 疏浚

♦ dredge up *fig* wāchū 挖出

dregs *(of coffee)* zhāzi 渣子; *the ~ of society* shèhuì zhāzǐ 社会渣滓

drench *v/t shǐ shītòu* 使湿透; *get ~ed* bèi yǔlín 被雨淋

dress 1 *n (for woman)* ⇩ liányīqún 连衣裙; *(clothing)* fúzhuāng 服装 2 *v/t wound* fūguǒ 敷裹; *~ X person* gěi X chuān yīfu 给 X 穿衣服; *get ~ed* chuān yīfu 穿衣服 3 *v/i (get ~ed)* chuān yīfu 穿衣服; *(well, in black etc)* chuānzhe 穿著

♦ dress up *v/i* dǎbàn 打扮; *(wear a disguise)* wěizhuāng 伪装; *~ as* zhuāngbàn chéng 装扮成

dress circle tèděng bāoxiāng 特等包厢

dresser *(dressing table)* shūzhuāng tái shūzhuāng tái 梳妆台; *(in kitchen)* wǎndié guì 碗碟柜

dressing *(for salad)* tiáowèi zhīr 调味汁儿; *(for wound)* fūliào 敷料

dressing room *(in theater)* huàzhuāng shì 化装室

dressing table shūzhuāng tái 梳妆台

dressmaker cáifeng 裁缝

dress rehearsal cǎipái 彩排

dressy jiǎngjiu 讲究

dribble *v/i (of person, baby)* liú kǒushuǐ 流口水; *(of water)* dī dī 滴; SP dàiqiú 带球

dried *fruit etc* gān 干; *~ bean curd* gāndòufu 干豆腐

drier *(machine)* shuǎigān jī 甩干机

drift 1 *n (of snow)* xuěduī 雪堆 2 *v/i (of snow)* xuě chéngduī 雪成堆; *(of ship)* piāofú 漂浮; *(go off course)* piāobó 漂泊; *(of person)* liúdàng 流荡

♦ drift apart *(of couple)* shūyuǎn 疏远

drifter liúlàng zhě 流浪者

drill 1 *n (tool)* zuàn 钻; *(exercise)* yǎnxí 演习; MIL cāoliàn 操练 2 *v/t hole* zuàn 钻 3 *v/i (for oil)* zuàn 钻; MIL cāoliàn 操练

drilling rig *(platform)* yóutái 油台

drily *remark* lěng bīngbīng 冷冰冰

drink 1 *n* yǐnliào 饮料; *a ~ of water* yìdiǎn shuǐ 一点水; *go for a ~* qù hē diǎn dōngxi 去喝点东西 2 *v/t* hē 喝 3 *v/i* hē 喝; *(consume alcohol)* hējiǔ 喝酒; *I don't ~* wǒ bù hējiǔ 我不喝酒

♦ drink up *v/t & v/i* hēguāng 喝光

drinkable kěyǐ hē 可以喝

drinker yǐnjiǔ zhě 饮酒者

drinking *(of alcohol)* hējiǔ 喝酒

drinking water yǐnyòng shuǐ 饮用水

drip 1 *n (liquid)* dī dī 点滴; MED diǎndī 点滴 2 *v/i* dī dī 滴

dripdry dīgān 滴干

dripping: *~ (wet)* quánbù shītòu 全部湿透

drive 1 *n* lǔtú 旅途; *(outing)* dōufēng 兜风; *(energy)* jīnglì 精力; COMPUT cípán dàijī 磁盘带机; *(campaign)* yùndòng 运动; *left-/right-hand ~* MOT zuǒ / yòu zuò jiàshǐ 左 / 右座驾驶 2 *v/t vehicle* jiàshǐ 驾驶; *(own)* yōngyǒu 拥有; *(take in car)* yòng chē sòng 用车送; TECH qūdòng 驱动; *that noise / he is driving me mad* nàge zàoyīn / tā lìngwǒ fāfēng 那个噪音 / 他令我发疯 3 *v/i* jiàshǐ 驾驶

♦ drive at: *what are you driving at?* nǐ shénme yìsi? 你什么意思？

♦ drive away *v/t* qūchē líkāi 驱车离开; *(chase off)* hōng hōng 哄哄 2 *v/i* qūchē líkāi 驱车离开

♦ drive in *v/t nail* qiāojìn 敲进

♦ drive off *v/i* qūchē líkāi 驱车离开

driver sījī 司机

driver's license jiàshǐ zhízhào 驾驶执照

driveway qìchē dào 汽车道

driving 1 *n* jiàshǐ 驾驶 2 *adj rain* měngliè 猛烈

driving force dònglì 动力; driving instructor jiàshǐ jiàoliàn 驾驶教练; driving lesson xuéchē kèchéng 学车课程; driving school ⇩ jiàshǐ xuéxiào 驾驶学校; driving test jiàzhǐ kǎoshì 驾驶考试

**drizzle 1** n máomao yǔ 毛毛雨
**2** v/i xià máomao yǔ 下毛毛雨

**drone** n (noise) wēngmíng shēng 嗡
鸣声

**droop** v/i xiàchuí 下垂; (of plant)
kūwěi 枯萎

**drop 1** n (of rain) dī 滴; (small
amount) yīdiǎn 一点; (in price,
temperature) xiàjiàng 下降 **2** v/t rēng rēng 扔; (and
lose) diūshī 丢失; person from car
ràng ... xiàchē 让 ... 下车; person
from team chúqù 除去; (stop
seeing) duànjué guānxi 断绝关
系; charges, demand etc qǔxiāo 取
消; (give up) fàngqì 放弃; **~ a line
to** jì fēng duǎn xìn 寄封短信
**3** v/i diēluò 跌落; (decline) xiàjiàng
下降; (of wind) jiǎnhuǎn 减缓

♦ **drop in** (visit) shùnbiàn láifǎng 顺
便来访

♦ **drop off 1** v/t person ràng ...
xiàchē 让 ... 下车; (deliver)
shùnbiàn sòng 顺便送 **2** v/i (fall
asleep) shuìzháo 睡着; (decline)
zhújiàn xiàjiàng 逐渐下降

♦ **drop out** (withdraw) tuìchū 退出;
(of school) zhōngtú tuìxué 中途
退学

**dropout** (from school) tuìxué
xuéshēng 退学学生; (from
society) tuìchū shìsú zhě 退出世
俗者

**drops** (for eyes) yǎn yàoshuǐ 眼药
水

**drought** gānhàn 干旱

**drown 1** v/i yānsǐ 淹死 **2** v/t person
yānsǐ 淹死; sound yānmò 淹没;
**be ~ed** yānsǐ 淹死

**drowsy** fākùn 发困

**drudgery** dāndiào 单调

**drug 1** n MED yào 药; (illegal) dúpǐn
毒品; **be on ~s** yǒu xīdú shìhào
有吸毒嗜好 **2** v/t xiàdú 下毒

**drug addict** xīdú chéngyǐn zhě 吸
毒成瘾者; **drug dealer** fàndú
zhě 贩毒者; **drug trafficking**
fàndú fànmài

**druggist** yàojì shī 药剂师

**drugstore** yàofáng 药房

**drum 1** n MUS gǔ 鼓; (container)

tǒng 桶

♦ **drum into: drum X into Y** xiàng
Y qiángdiào X 向 Y 强调 X

♦ **drum up: ~ support** zhāolǎn
zhīchí 招揽支持

**drummer** gǔshǒu 鼓手

**drumstick** MUS gǔchuí 鼓槌; (of
poultry) jītuǐ 鸡腿

**drunk 1** n zuìguǐ 醉鬼 **2** adj
hēzuìle 喝醉了; **get ~** hēzuì 喝醉

**drunken** voices, laughter hēzuì 喝
醉; **~ party** zuìhuì 醉会; **drunk
driving** jiǔhòu kāichē 酒后
开车

**dry 1** adj skin, clothes, weather, wine
gān 干; (ironic) wākǔ 挖苦;
(alcohol banned) jìnjiǔ 禁酒 **2** v/t
dishes cāgān 擦干 **3** v/i liànggān
晾干

♦ **dry out** (of alcoholic) jièjiǔ 戒酒

♦ **dry up** (of river) gānkū 干枯; (be
quiet) bìzuǐ 闭嘴

**dry-clean** v/t gānxǐ 干洗

**dry cleaner** gānxǐ diàn 干洗店

**dry cleaning** (clothes) gānxǐ yīwù
干洗衣物

**dryer** (machine) shuǎigān jī 甩干
机

**DTP** (= desktop publishing)
zhuōmiàn páibǎn 桌面排版

**dual** shuāng 双

**dub** movie pèiyīn 配音

**dubious** kào bùzhù kàn 靠不住;
(having doubts) yǒu huáiyí 有怀疑

**duck 1** n yā 鸭 **2** v/i duǒcáng 躲藏
**3** v/t one's head dītóu 低头;
question huíbì 回避

**dud** n (false bill) jiǎ chāopiào 假钞
票

**due** (owed) qiàn 欠; (proper)
shìdàng 适当; **is there a train ~?**
huǒchē shìbùshì gāiláile? 火车是
不是该来了？; **when is the
baby ~?** háizi shénme shíhòu
chūshēng? 孩子什么时候出
生?; **~ to** (because of) yóuyú 由于;
**be ~ to X** (be caused by) yīn X ér
chǎnshēng 因 X 而产生; **in ~
course** zuìzhōng 最终

**dull** weather yīn chénchén 阴沉沉;
sound bù qīngcuì 不清脆; pain

dùn 钝；(*boring*) dāndiào 单调

duly (*as expected*) zhǔnshí 准时；
(*properly*) shìdàng 适当

dumb (*mute*) yǎ 哑；(*stupid*) shǎ 傻

dump 1 *n* (*for garbage*) lājī zhàn 垃
圾站；(*unpleasant place*) guǐdìfāng
鬼地方 2 *v/t* (*deposit*) qīngdào 倾
倒；(*dispose of*) rēng 扔；*toxic
waste, nuclear waste* diūqì 丢弃

dumpling tuánzi 团子

dune shāqiū 沙丘

dung fènbiàn 粪便

dungarees lián yīkù 连衣裤

dunk *biscuit* diǎn 点

duo MUS yīduì 一对

duplex (*apartment*) ⇩ èrliánshì
gōngyù 二连式公寓

duplicate 1 *n* fùjiàn 复件；*in* ~
liǎngfèn 两份 2 *v/t* (*copy*) fùzhì 复
制；(*repeat*) chóngfù 重复

duplicate key fùzhì yàoshi 复制
钥匙

durable *material* láo 牢；*relationship*
chíjiǔ 持久

duration qījiān 期间

duress: *under* ~ zài xiépò xià 在胁
迫下

during: ~ *X* zài X qījiān 在 X 期间

dusk huánghūn 黄昏

dust 1 *n* chéntǔ 尘土 2 *v/t*: ~ *X
with Y* (*sprinkle*) bǎ Y sǎzài X
shàng 把 Y 洒在 X 上

dust cover (*for furniture*) jiājù
zhào 家具罩；(*for book*) shūpí 书
皮

duster (*cloth*) mābù 抹布

dust jacket (*of book*) shūjí hùfēng
书籍护封

dustpan bòji 簸箕

dusty duō chéntǔ 多尘土

Dutch 1 *adj* Hélán 荷兰；*go* ~ gèzì
fùkuǎn 各自付款 2 *n* (*language*)
Hélán yǔ 荷兰语；*the* ~ Hélán
rénmín 荷兰人民

duty zérèn 责任；(*task*) rènwù 任
务；(*on goods*) shuì 税；*be on* ~
zhíbān 值班；*be off* ~ xiàbān 下
班

duty-free 1 *adj* miǎnshuì 免税 2 *n*
miǎnshuì wùpǐn 免税物品

duty-free store miǎnshuì
shāngdiàn 免税商店

DVD COMPUT ⇩ shùzì shìpín
guāngpán 数字视频光盘

dwarf 1 *n* zhūrú 侏儒 2 *v/t* shǐ
xiǎnde ǎixiǎo 使显得矮小

◆dwell on lǎoshì xiǎngzhe 老是想
着

dwindle jiǎnshǎo 减少

dye 1 *n* rǎnliào 染料 2 *v/t* rǎnsè 染
色

dying *person* chuísǐ 垂死；*industry,
tradition etc* jíjiāng mièjué 即将灭
绝

dynamic *person* jīnglì chōngpèi 精
力充沛

dynamism (*energy*) dònglì 动力

dynamite *n* zhàyào 炸药

dynamo TECH diàndòng jī 电动机

dynasty cháodài 朝代；*Ming
Dynasty* Míngcháo 明朝

dyslexia sòngdú kùnnán 诵读困
难

dyslexic 1 *adj* sòngdú kùnnán 诵
读困难 2 *n* sòngdú kùnnán bìng
huànzhě 诵读困难病患者

# E

each 1 *adj* měigè 每个 2 *adv* fēnbié 分别; **they're $1.50 ~** měigè yī měiyuán wǔshí měifēn 每个一美元五十美分 3 *pron* měigè 每个; **~ other** bǐcǐ 彼此

eager *adj* kěwàng 渴望; **be ~ to do X** rèzhōngyú zuò X 热衷于做X

eager beaver rèxīnchángde rén 热心肠的人

eagerly rèqiè 热切

eagerness rèxīn 热心

eagle yīng 鹰

ear (*of person, animal*) ěrduǒ 耳朵; (*of corn*) suì 穗

earache ěrtòng 耳痛

eardrum gǔmó 鼓膜

early 1 *adj* (*not late*) zǎo 早; (*ahead of time*) tíqián 提前; (*farther back in time*) zǎoqī 早期; (*in the near future*) xùnsù 迅速 2 *adv* (*not late*) zǎo 早; (*ahead of time*) tíqián 提前

early bird (*in morning*) zǎochén 早晨; (*who arrives early*) xiānxíng zhě 先行者

earmark *money* bōchū 拨出; **~ X for Y** wèi Y ānpái X 为Y安排X

earn zhèng zhēng 挣; *holiday, drink etc* yīngdé 应得; *respect* yíngdé 赢得

earnest rènzhēn 认真; **in ~** rènzhēn 认真

earnings zhuànde qián 赚的钱

earphones ěrjī 耳机; **ear-piercing** *adj* cì'ěr 刺耳; **earring** ěrhuán 耳环; **earshot: within ~** zài tīnglì fànwéi zhīnèi 在听力范围之内; **out of ~** bú zài tīnglì fànwéi zhīnèi 不在听力范围之内

earth (*soil*) tǔ 土; (*world, planet*) dìqiú 地球; **where on ~ ... ?** dàodǐ zài nǎr ... ? 到底在哪儿 ... ?

earthenware *n* táoqì 陶器

earthly xiànshì 现世; **it's no ~ use ...** ... wánquán wúyòng ... 完全无用 ...

earthquake dìzhèn 地震

earth-shattering lìngrénzhènjīng 令人震惊

ease 1 *n* róngyì 容易; **be at (one's) ~, feel at ~** gǎndào shūfu 感到舒服; **be or feel ill at ~** gǎndào bù shūfu 感到不舒服 2 *v/t* (*relieve*) fàngsōng 放松 3 *v/i* (*of pain*) jiǎnqīng 减轻

♦ease off 1 *v/t* (*remove*) xiǎoxīn yídiào 小心移掉 2 *v/i* (*of pain, rain*) jiǎnhuǎn 减缓

easel (*for blackboard*) hēibǎnjià 黑板架; (*for artist*) huàjià 画架

easily (*with ease*) róngyì 容易; (*by far*) wúyí 无疑

east 1 *n* dōngfāng 东方 2 *adj* dōng 东 3 *adv travel* xiàng dōngfāng 向东方

East China Sea Dōnghǎi 东海

Easter Fùhuójié 复活节

Easter egg Fùhuójié cǎidàn 复活节彩蛋

easterly cóng dōng láide 从东来的

eastern dōngbù 东部; (*Oriental*) Dōngfāng 东方

easterner (*from the east coast*) dōnghǎi'àn de rén 东海岸的人

eastward(s) xiàngdōng 向东

easy (*not difficult*) róngyì 容易; (*relaxed*) fàngsōng 放松; **take things ~** (*slow down*) bùjǐnzhāng 不紧张; **take it ~!** (*calm down*) biéjǐnzhāng! 别紧张！

easy chair ānlèyǐ 安乐椅

easy-going suíhé 随和

eat *v/t & v/i* chī 吃

♦eat out chūqù chī 出去吃

♦eat up *food* chīguāng 吃光; *fig* hàojìn 耗尽

eatable kěchī 可吃

eaves wūyán 屋檐

eavesdrop tōutīng 偷听

ebb v/i (of tide) tuìluò 退落

♦ ebb away fig (of courage, strength) jiǎnshǎo 减少

ebb tide tuìcháo 退潮

eccentric 1 adj gǔguài 古怪 2 n gǔguài de rén 古怪的人

echo 1 n huíshēng 回声 2 v/i huídàng 回荡 3 v/t words chóngfù chóngfù 重复; views chóngshēn 重申

eclipse 1 n (of sun) rìshí 日蚀; (of moon) yuèshí 月蚀 2 v/t fig shèngguò 胜过

ecological shēngtài 生态

ecological balance shēngtài pínghéng 生态平衡

ecologically friendly lǜsè 绿色

ecologist shēngtàixuéjiā 生态学家

ecology shēngtàixué 生态学

economic jīngjì 经济

economical (cheap) jīngjì 经济; (thrifty) jiéshěng 节省

economically (in terms of economics) jīngjì shang 经济上; (thriftily) jiéjiǎn 节俭

economics (science) jīngjìxué 经济学; (financial aspects) jīngjì qíngkuàng 经济情况

economist jīngjìxuéjiā 经济学家

economize jǐnsuō kāizhī 紧缩开支

♦ economize on jiéshěng 节省

economy (of a country) jīngjì 经济; (saving) jiéshěng 节省

economy class jīngjìcāng 经济舱; economy drive jiéyuē xíngdòng 节约行动; economy size jīngjìzhuāng 经济装

ecosystem shēngtài xìtǒng 生态系统

ecstasy kuánghxǐ 狂喜; (drug) yáotóuwánr 摇头丸儿

ecstatic xīnxǐ ruò kuáng 欣喜若狂

eczema shīzhěn 湿疹

edge 1 n (of knife) fēng fēng 锋; (of table, road etc) biānyuán 边缘; (in voice) cì'ěr 刺耳; on ~ jízào 急躁 2 v/t xiāngbiān 镶边 3 v/i (move slowly) huǎnmàn yídòng 缓慢移动

edgewise: I couldn't get a word in ~ wǒ chābúshàng huà 我插不上话

edgy jízào 急躁

edible kě shíyòng 可食用

edit text, file, book, newspaper biānjí 编辑; TV program jiǎnjí 剪辑; movie jiǎnjiē 剪接

edition bǎnběn 版本

editor of text, book, newspaper, TV program, movie biānjí 编辑; sports / political ~ tǐyù / zhèngzhì lán biānjí 体育 / 政治栏编辑

editorial 1 adj biānjí 编辑 2 n shèlùn 社论

EDP (= electronic data processing) diànzǐ shùjù chǔlǐ 电子数据处理

educate child jiàoyù 教育; consumers yǐndǎo 引导

educated person shòuguò jiàoyù 受过教育

education jiàoyù 教育

educational jiàoyù 教育; informative yǒu jiàoyù yìyì 有教育意义

eel mán 鳗

eerie guàiyì 怪异

effect n xiàoguǒ 效果; negative hòuguǒ 后果; take ~ (of medicine, drug) shēngxiào 生效; come into ~ (of law) shíshí 实施

effective (efficient) yǒuxiào 有效; (striking) chǎnshēng shēnkè yìnxiàng 产生深刻印象; ~ May 1 cóng wǔyuè yīrì qǐ shēngxiào 从五月一日起生效

effeminate nǚrénqì 女人气

effervescent yǒu qìpào 有气泡; personality huóyuè 活跃

efficiency xiàolǜ 效率

efficient yǒu xiàolǜ 有效率

efficiently yǒu xiàolǜ 有效率

effort (struggle) fèilì 费力; (attempt) nǔlì 努力; make an ~ to do X nǔlì zuò X 努力做X

effortless róngyì 容易

effrontery wúchǐ 无耻

effusive guòyú jīdòng 过于激动

e.g. lìrú 例如

egalitarian *adj* píngděngzhǔyì 平等主义

egg (*of hen*) jīdàn 鸡蛋; (*of bird*) dàn 蛋

♦egg on sǒngyǒng 怂恿

eggcup jīdànbēi 鸡蛋杯; **egg fried rice** dànchǎofàn 蛋炒饭; **egghead** wénrén 文人; **eggplant** qiézi 茄子; **eggshell** dànké 蛋壳

ego PSYCH zìwǒ 自我; (*self-esteem*) zìzūn 自尊

egocentric yǐ zìwǒ wéi zhōngxīn 以自我为中心

Egypt Āijí 埃及

Egyptian 1 *adj* Āijí 埃及 2 *n* Āijírén 埃及人

eiderdown (*quilt*) yǔróng 羽绒

eight bā 八

eighteen shíbā 十八

eighteenth dì shíbā 第十八

eighth dì bā 第八

eightieth dì bāshí 第八十

eighty bāshí 八十

either 1 *adj* rèn yīgè 任一个; (*both*) liǎng 两 2 *pron* nǎgè dōuxíng 哪个都行 3 *adv*: **I won't go ~** wǒ yě bú qù 我也不去 4 *conj*: **~ ... or** huòzhě ... huòzhě 或者 ... 或者

eject 1 *v/t* zhúchū 逐出 2 *v/i* (*from plane*) tánshè 弹射

eke out yányòng 延用

el (*elevated railroad*) gāojià tiělù 高架铁路

elaborate 1 *adj* jīngxīn zhìzuò 精心制作 2 *v/i* xiángjìn jiěshì 详尽解释

elapse liúshì 流逝

elastic 1 *adj* yǒu tánxìng 有弹性 2 *n* sōngjǐndài 松紧带

elastic band xiàngpíjīn 橡皮筋

elasticity tánxìng 弹性

elasticized dài sōngjǐn 带松紧

elated xìnggāocǎiliè 兴高采烈

elation xìnggāocǎiliè 兴高采烈

elbow 1 *n* zhǒu 肘 2 *v/t*: **~ out of the way** yòng zhǒu jíchū yìtiáo lù 用肘挤出一条路

elder 1 *adj* niánzhǎng 年长 2 *n*

niánzhǎngzhě 年长者

elderly shàng niánjì 上年纪

eldest 1 *adj*: **the ~ brother** dàgē 大哥; **the ~ sister** dàjiě 大姐 2 *n*: **the ~** zuìdà 最大

elect *v/t* xuǎn 选; **~ to do X** xuǎnzé zuò X 选择做 X

elected xuǎnchū 选出

election xuǎnjǔ 选举

election campaign jìngxuǎn huódòng 竞选活动

election day xuǎnjǔrì 选举日

elective kěxuǎn 可选

elector xuǎnmín 选民

electoral system xuǎnjǔ zhìdù 选举制度

electorate quántǐ xuǎnmín 全体选民

electric diàn 电; *fig* shǐrén tūrán xīngfèn 使人突然兴奋

electrical diàn 电

electric blanket diànrètǎn 电热毯

electric chair diànyǐ 电椅

electrician diàngōng 电工

electricity diàn 电

electrify shǐ diànqìhuà 使电气化; *fig* cìjī 刺激

electrocute diànsǐ 电死

electrode diànjí 电极

electron diànzǐ 电子

electronic diànzǐ 电子

electronic data processing diànzǐ shùjù chǔlǐ 电子数据处理

electronic mail diànzǐ yóujiàn 电子邮件

electronics diànzǐxué 电子学

elegance gāoyǎ 高雅

elegant gāoyǎ 高雅

element CHEM yuánsù 元素

elementary (*rudimentary*) chūjí 初级

elementary school xiǎoxué 小学

elementary teacher xiǎoxué lǎoshī 小学老师

elephant dàxiàng 大象

elevate tígāo 提高

elevated railroad gāojià tiělù 高架铁路

elevation (*altitude*) hǎibá 海拔

elevator diàntī 电梯

eleven shíyī 十一

eleventh dì shíyī 第十一; *at the hour* zuìhòu guāntóu 最后关头

eligible hégé 合格

eligible bachelor héyì nánshì 合意男士

eliminate (*get rid of*) chúdiào 除掉; (*rule out*) páichú 排除; (*kill*) gàndiào 干掉; *be ~d* (*from competition*) bèi táotài 被淘汰

elimination (*from competition*) táotài 淘汰; (*of poverty*) xiāochú 消除; (*murder*) gàndiào 干掉

elite **1** n jīngyīng 精英 **2** adj gāoděng 高等

elk tuólù 驼鹿

ellipse tuǒyuán 椭圆

elm yúmù 榆木

elope sībēn 私奔

eloquence kǒucái 口才

eloquent xióngbiàn 雄辩

eloquently xióngbiàn 雄辩

else: *anything ~?* hái yào biéde ma? 还要别的吗？; *if you've got nothing ~ to do* rúguǒ nǐ méiyǒu biéde shì yào zuò 如果你没有别的事要做; *no one ~* méiyǒu biérén 没有别人; *everyone ~ is going* biérén dōu qù 别人都去; *who ~ was there?* hái yǒu shéi zài nàr? 还有谁在那儿？; *someone ~* biérén 别人; *something ~* biéde dōngxi 别的东西; *let's go somewhere ~* zánmen qù biéde dìfang ba 咱们去别的地方吧; *or ~* (*otherwise*) fǒuzé 否则

elsewhere biéchù 别处

elude *escape from* táobì 逃避; *avoid* duǒbì 躲避

elusive nányǐ pǔzhuō 难以扑捉

emaciated xiāoshòu 消瘦

e-mail **1** n diànzǐ yóujiàn 电子邮件 **2** v/t person dǎ diànzǐ yóujiàn 打电子邮件; *text* yòng diànzǐ yóujiàn jì 用电子邮件寄

e-mail address diànzǐ xìnxiāng 电子信箱

emancipated *woman* jiěfàng 解放

emancipation jiěfàng 解放

embalm bǎocún 保存

embankment *of river* dī'àn 堤岸; RAIL lùdī 路堤

embargo n jìnyùn 禁运

embark v/i shàngchuán 上船

◆ embark on kāishǐ 开始

embarrass shǐ gāngà 使…尴尬

embarrassed gāngà 尴尬

embarrassing lìngrén gāngà 令人尴尬

embarrassment gāngà 尴尬

embassy dàshǐguǎn 大使馆

embellish zhuāngshì 装饰; *story* jiāgōng 加工

embers yújìn 余烬

embezzle dàoyòng 盗用

embezzlement dàoyòng 盗用

embitter shǐkǔnǎo 使苦恼

emblem xiàngzhēng 象征

embodiment huàshēn 化身

embody tǐxiàn 体现

embolism shuānsè 栓塞

emboss *metal* fútū 浮凸; *paper, fabric* tūyìn 凸印

embrace **1** n yōngbào 拥抱 **2** v/t (*hug*) yōngbào 拥抱; (*take in*) bāokuò 包括 **3** v/i (*of two people*) yōngbào 拥抱

embroider cìxiù 刺绣; *fig* xūgòu qíngjié 虚构情节

embroidery cìxiù 刺绣

embryo pēitāi 胚胎

emerald (*precious stone*) lǜbǎoshí 绿宝石; (*color*) zǔmǔlǜ 祖母绿

emerge (*appear*) chūxiàn 出现; *it has ~d that ...* jùxī ... 据悉…

emergency jǐnjí qíngkuàng 紧急情况; *in an ~* yùdào jǐnjí qíngkuàng 遇到紧急情况

emergency exit jǐnjí chūkǒu 紧急出口

emergency landing jǐnjí zháoluò 紧急着落

emigrant n yīmín 移民

emigrate yíjū guówài 移居国外

emigration yíjū guówài 移居国外

eminent jiéchū 杰出

eminently fēicháng 非常

emission (*of gases*) páifàng 排放

emotion qínggǎn 情感

emotional *problems, development*

qínggǎn 情感; (full of emotion)
fùyú qínggǎn 富于情感

**empathize:** **~ with** tóngqíng 同情

**emperor** huángdì 皇帝

**emphasis** zhòngdiào 重调

**emphasize** qiángdiào 强调

**emphatic** kěndìng 肯定

**empire** dìguó 帝国

**employ** gùyōng 雇佣; (use)
shǐyòng 使用; **he's ~ed as a ...** tā
bèi gù zuò ... 他被雇作 ...

**employee** gùyuán 雇员

**employer** gùzhǔ 雇主

**employment** zhíyè 职业; (work)
gōngzuò 工作; **be seeking ~** zài
qiúzhí 在求职

**employment agency** zhíyè
jièshàosuǒ 职业介绍所

**empress** huánghòu 皇后

**emptiness** kōngxū 空虚

**empty 1** adj kōng 空; promises
kōngdòng 空洞 **2** v/t pockets
tāokōng 掏空; drawer dàokōng 倒
空; glass, bottle dào 倒 **3** v/i (of
room, street) biànkōng 变空

**emulate** gǎnchāo 赶超

**enable** shǐde néngzuò 使得能做

**enact** law zhìdìng 制定; THEA
yǎnchū 演出

**enamel** n tángcí 搪瓷; (on tooth)
fàlángzhì 珐琅质; (paint) cíqī 瓷
漆

**enchanting** smile, village, person
mírén 迷人

**encircle** bāowéi 包围

**enclose** (in letter) fùjiàn 附件; area
wéizhù 围住; **please find ~d ...**
zīfùshàng ... 兹附上 ...

**enclosure** (with letter) fùjiàn 附件

**encore** n zàilái yīgè 再来一个

**encounter 1** n xièhòu 邂逅 **2** v/t
person jiēchù 接触; problem,
resistance yùdào 遇到

**encourage** gǔlì 鼓励

**encouragement** gǔlì 鼓励

**encouraging** lìngrén gǔwǔ 令人
鼓舞

♦**encroach on** land qīnzhàn 侵占;
rights qīnfàn 侵犯; time zhànyòng
占用

**encyclopedia** bǎikēquánshū 百科
全书

**end 1** n (extremity) jìntóu 尽头;
(conclusion) jiéwěi 结尾; (purpose)
mùdì 目的; **in the ~** zuìhòu 最后;
**for hours on ~** chíxùbúduàn 持续
不断; **stand X on ~** zhílì X 直立
X; **at the ~ of July** qīyuèmò 七月
末; **put an ~ to** jiéshù 结束 **2** v/t &
v/i jiéshù 结束

♦**end up** jiéguǒ 结果

**endanger** wēijí 危及

**endangered species** bīnlín
mièjuéde wùzhǒng 濒临灭绝的
物种

**endearing** tǎorén xǐhuan 讨人喜
欢

**endeavor 1** n nǔlì 努力 **2** v/t jìnlì
尽力

**ending** jiéjú 结局; GRAM cíwěi 词
尾

**endless** wúzhǐjìng 无止境

**endorse** check bèishū 背书;
candidacy zhīchí 支持; product
cùxiāo 促销

**endorsement** (of check) bèiqiān 背
签; (of candidacy) zhīchí 支持; (of
product) cùxiāo 促销

**end product** zhōngduān chǎnpǐn
终端产品

**end result** zuìzhōng jiéguǒ 最终
结果

**endurance** rěnnàilì 忍耐力

**endure 1** v/t rěnnài 忍耐 **2** v/i (last)
chíxù 持续

**enduring** chíjiǔ 持久

**end-user** zhōngduān yònghù 终端
用户

**enemy** dírén 敌人

**energetic** jùliè 剧烈; person yǒu
jīngshen 有精神; fig: measures jījí
积极

**energy** (gas, electricity etc)
néngyuán 能源; (of person) jīnglì
精力

**energy-saving** device jiénéng 节能

**enforce** shíshī 实施

**engage 1** v/t (hire) pìnyòng 聘用
**2** v/i TECH niēhé 啮合

♦**engage in** cóngshì 从事

**engaged** (to be married) dìnghūn
订婚; **get ~** dìnghūn 订婚

**engagement** (*appointment*) yuēhuì 约会; (*to be married*) dìnghūn 订婚; MIL jiāozhàn 交战

**engagement ring** dìnghūn jièzhǐ 订婚戒指

**engaging** *smile, person* xīyǐnrén 吸引人

**engine** yǐnqíng 引擎

**engineer** 1 *n* gōngchéngshī 工程师; NAUT lúnjīzhǎng 轮机长; RAIL gōngchéngshī 工程师 2 *v/t fig* (*meeting etc*) qiǎomiàode ānpái 巧妙地安排

**engineering** gōngchéng 工程

**England** Yīnggélán 英格兰

**English** 1 *adj* Yīngguó 英国 2 *n* (*language*) Yīngyǔ 英语; *the ~* Yīnggélán rén 英格兰人

**Englishman** Yīnggélán nánzǐ 英格兰男子

**Englishwoman** Yīnggélán nǚzǐ 英格兰女子

**engrave** diāokè 雕刻

**engraving** (*drawing*) bǎnhuà 版画; (*design*) diāokè 雕刻

**engrossed:** *~ in* quánshén guànzhùyú 全神贯注于

**engulf** tūnmò 吞没

**enhance** zēngqiáng 增强

**enigma** mí 谜

**enigmatic** shénmì 神秘

**enjoy** xǐhuan 喜欢; *~ oneself* guòde kuàilè 过得快乐; *~!* (*said to somebody eating*) chīhǎo! 吃好！

**enjoyable** lìngrén yúkuài 令人愉快

**enjoyment** lèqù 乐趣

**enlarge** kuòdà 扩大

**enlargement** kuòdà 扩大

**enlighten** qǐdí 启迪

**enlist** 1 *v/i* MIL bàomíng cānjūn 报名参军 2 *v/t* zhāomù 召募; *~ the help of X* jiào X bāngmáng 叫 X 帮忙

**enliven** shǐhuóyuè 使活跃

**enormity** (*size*) pángdà 庞大; (*wickedness*) qióngxiōngjí'è 穷凶极恶

**enormous** jùdà 巨大; *satisfaction, patience* jídà 极大

**enormously** fēicháng 非常

**enough** 1 *adj* zúgòu 足够 2 *pron* zúgòu 足够; *will $50 be ~?* wǔshí měiyuán gòu le ma? 五十美元够了吗？; *I've had ~!* wǒ shòugòu le wǒ 我受够了！; *that's ~, calm down!* xíngle, lěngjìngdiǎnr 行了, 冷静点儿！ 3 *adv* zúgòu 足够; *strangely ~* qíguài 奇怪的是

**enquire, enquiry** → *inquire, inquiry*

**enraged** jīnù 激怒

**enrich** *vocabulary* kuòdà 扩大; *somebody's life* fēngfù 丰富

**enroll** *v/i* zhùcè 注册

**enrolment** zhùcè 注册

**ensure** bǎozhèng 保证

**entail** qiánshè 牵涉

**entangle:** *become ~d in* (*in rope*) chánràozài 缠绕在; (*in love affair*) xiànrù 陷入

**enter** 1 *v/t room, house* jìnrù 进入; *competition* cānjiā 参加; *person, horse in race* bàomíng 报名; *write down* xiěxià 写下; COMPUT jiànrù 键入 2 *v/i* jìnrù 进入; THEA shàngchǎng 上场; (*in competition*) bàomíng 报名 3 *n* COMPUT huíchējiàn 回车键

**enterprise** (*initiative*) jìnqǔxīn 进取心; (*venture*) qǐyè 企业

**enterprising** yǒu jìnqǔxīn 有进取心

**entertain** 1 *v/t* (*amuse*) shǐrén kuàilè 使人快乐; (*consider: idea*) yuànyì kǎolù 愿意考虑 2 *v/i* (*have guests*) zhāodài 招待

**entertainer** biǎoyǎnzhě 表演者

**entertaining** *adj* yǒuqù 有趣

**entertainment** yúlè 娱乐

**enthrall** mízhù 迷住

**enthusiasm** rèqíng 热情

**enthusiast** rèzhōngzhě 热中者

**enthusiastic** rèxīn 热心

**entice** yòuhuò 诱惑

**entire** zhěnggè 整个

**entirely** wánquán 完全

**entitle** fùyǔ quánlì 赋予权利

**entitled** *book* dìngmíng 定名

**entrance** *n* (*doorway*) rùkǒu 入口;

*(fact of entering)* jìnrù 进入; THEA chūchǎng 出场; *(admission)* zhǔnyǔ jìnrù 准予进入

**entranced** zháomí 着迷

**entrance fee** rùchǎngfèi 入场费

**entrant** cānjiā zhě 参加者

**entrenched** *attitudes* gēnshēndìgù 根深蒂固

**entrepreneur** qǐyèjiā 企业家

**entrepreneurial** yǒu chuàngyè cáinéng 有创业才能

**entrust** ~ *X with Y*, ~ *Y to X* bǎ Y wěituōgěi X 把 Y 委托给 X

**entry** *(way in)* rùkǒu 入口; *(admission)* jìnrù 进入; *(for competition)* cānjiāzhě 参加者; *(in diary, accounts)* xiàngmù 项目

**entry form** cānsàibiǎo 参赛表

**entry visa** rùjìng qiānzhèng 入境签证

**envelop** bāozhù 包住

**envelope** xìnfēng 信封

**enviable** zhídé xiànmù 值得羡慕

**envious** mǎnhuái jídù 满怀嫉妒; *be ~ of X* xiànmù X 羡慕 X

**environment** *(nature)* zìrán huánjìng 自然环境; *(surroundings)* huánjìng 环境

**environmental** yǒuguān huánjìng 有关环境

**environmentalist** huánjìng bǎohùlùn zhě 环境保护论者

**environmentally friendly** lùsè 绿色

**environmental pollution** huánjìng wūrǎn 环境污染

**environmental protection** huánjìng bǎohù 环境保护

**environs** jìnjiāo 近郊

**envisage** xiǎngxiàng 想象

**envoy** shǐzhě 使者

**envy** 1 *n* jídù 嫉妒; *be the ~ of X* lìng X jídù 令 X 羡慕 2 *v/t*: dùxiàn lù měi; ~ *X Y* xiànmù X de Y 羡慕 X 的 Y

**epic** 1 *n* shǐshī 史诗 2 *adj journey* shǐshībān 史诗般; *a task of ~ proportions* zhòngdà rènwù 重大任务

**epicenter** ⇩ zhènzhōng 震中

**epidemic** liúxíngxìng 流行性

**epilepsy** diānxiánzhèng 癫痫症

**epileptic** *n* diānxián 癫痫

**epileptic fit** diānxián fāzuò 癫痫发作

**epilog** jiéwěi bùfen 结尾部分

**episode** *(of story, soap opera)* yījí 一集; *(happening)* shìjiàn 事件

**epitaph** mùzhìmíng 墓志铭

**epoch** jìyuán 纪元

**epoch-making** huàshídài 划时代

**equal** 1 *adj* xiāngtóng 相同; *be ~ to* *(a task)* néngshèngrèn 能胜任 2 *n* děngtóng 等同 3 *v/t* *(with numbers)* děngyú 等于; *(be as good as)* búxùnsè 不逊色

**equality** píngděng 平等

**equalize** 1 *v/t* jūnhéng 均衡 2 *v/i* SP bānpíng bǐfēn 扳平比分

**equalizer** SP píngfēnqiú 平分球

**equally** tóngděng 同等; ~, ... cǐwài, ... 此外 ...

**equate** ~ *X with Y* děngtóng X hé Y 等同 X 和 Y

**equation** MATH děngshì 等式

**equator** chìdào 赤道

**equilibrium** pínghéng 平衡

**equinox**: *Spring* ~ Chūnfēn 春分; *Autumn* ~ Qiūfēn 秋分

**equip**: ~ *X* zhuāngbèi X 装备 X; *he's not ~ped to handle it* *fig* tā wúlì chǔlǐ cǐshì 他无力处理此事

**equipment** zhuāngbèi 装备

**equity** COM pǔtōnggǔ 普通股

**equivalent** 1 *adj* xiāngtóng 相同; *be ~ to* xiāngdāngyú 相当于 2 *n*: *X is the ~ of Y* X xiāngdāngyú Y X 相当于 Y

**era** jìyuán 纪元

**eradicate** gēnchú 根除

**erase** *(with eraser)* cādiào 擦掉; *tape* xǐdiào 洗掉; COMPUT shānchú 删除

**eraser** *(for blackboard)* hēibǎncā 黑板擦; *(for pencil)* xiàngpí 橡皮

**erect** 1 *adj* zhílì 直立 2 *v/t* shùqǐ 竖起

**erection** *(of building etc)* shùqǐ 竖起; *(of penis)* bóqǐ 勃起

**erode** qīnshí 侵蚀; *fig: rights, power* qīnfàn 侵犯

**erosion** qīnshí 侵蚀; *fig* qīnfàn 侵犯

**erotic** sèqíng 色情

**eroticism** xìngyù 性欲

**errand** chāishǐ 差使; *run ~s* pǎotuǐ 跑腿

**erratic** wúcháng 无常

**error** cuòwù 错误

**error message** COMPUT cuòwù xìnxī 错误信息

**erupt** (*of volcano*) bàofā 爆发; (*of violence*) tūrán fāshēng 突然发生; (*of person*) fāhuǒ 发火

**eruption** (*of volcano*) bàofā 爆发; (*of violence*) tūrán fāshēng 突然发生

**escalate** zhúbù shēngjí 逐步升级

**escalation** shēngjí 升级

**escalator** zìdòngfútī 自动扶梯

**escape 1** *n* (*of prisoner, animal*) táotuō 逃脱; (*of gas*) lòuchū 漏出; *have a narrow ~* jiǔsǐyìshēng 九死一生 **2** *v/i* (*of prisoner, animal*) táotuō 逃脱; (*of gas*) lòuchū 漏出 **3** *v/t: the word ~s me* wǒ xiǎngbùqǐlái zhège cí le 我想不起来这个词了

**escape chute** tuōxiǎn huátī 脱险滑梯

**escort 1** *n* péitóng 陪同; (*guard*) hùwèi 护卫 **2** *v/t* (*socially*) péi péi 陪; (*act as guard to*) hùwèi 护卫

**especially** yóuqí 尤其

**espionage** jiàndié huódòng 间谍活动

**essay** *n* duǎnwén 短文

**essential** *adj* bìyào 必要

**essentially** jīběnshàng 基本上

**establish** *company* chénglì 成立; (*create*) chuàngzào 创造; (*determine*) quèdìng 确定; *~ oneself as* wèi zìjǐ yíngdé 为自己赢得

**establishment** (*firm, store etc*) jīgòu 机构; *the Establishment* dāngquánpài 当权派

**estate** (*area of land*) dìchǎn 地产; (*possessions of dead person*) yíchǎn 遗产

**esthetic** měiguān 美观

**estimate** *n & v/t* gūjì 估计

**estimation**: *he has gone up / down in my ~* zēngjiā / jiàngdī duì tā de zūnjìng 增加 / 降低对他的尊敬; *in my ~* (*opinion*) zhào wǒ kànlái 照我看来

**estranged** *wife, husband* shūyuǎn 疏远

**estuary** hékǒuwān 河口湾

**ETA** (= *estimated time of arrival*) yùjì dàodá shíjiān 预计到达时间

**etching** shíkèshù 蚀刻术

**eternal** yǒnghéng 永恒

**eternity** yǒnghéng 永恒

**ethical** dàodé 道德

**ethics** lúnlǐxué 伦理学

**ethnic** zhǒngzú 种族

**ethnic group** zhǒngzú shèqū 种族社区

**ethnic minority** shǎoshù mínzú 少数民族

**euphemism** wěiwǎn shuōfǎ 委婉说法

**euphoria** xīnkuàigǎn 欣快感

**Europe** Ōuzhōu 欧洲

**European 1** *adj* Ōuzhōu 欧洲 **2** *n* Ōuzhōu rén 欧洲人

**euthanasia** ānlèsǐ 安乐死

**evacuate** (*clear people from*) chèkōng 撤空; (*leave*) chèlí 撤离

**evade** bìkāi 避开

**evaluate** pínggū 评估

**evaluation** pínggū 评估

**evangelist** fúyīn chuándào zhě 福音传道者

**evaporate** (*of water*) zhēngfā 蒸发; (*of confidence*) xiāoshī 消失

**evasion** táobì 逃避

**evasive** bùtǎnshuài 不坦率

**eve** qiánxī 前夕

**even 1** *adj* (*regular*) jūnyún 均匀; (*level*) píng 平; (*number*) ǒushù 偶数; *get ~ with X* bàofù 报复 X **2** *adv* shènzhì 甚至; *~ bigger / better* gèngdà / hǎo 更大 / 好; *not ~ lián . . . yěbù* 连 . . . 也不; *~ so* jìnguǎn rúcǐ 尽管如此; *~ if* jíshǐ 即使 **3** *v/t: ~ the score* lāpíng bǐfēn 拉平比分

**evening** wǎnshang 晚上; *in the ~* wǎnshang 晚上; *this ~* jīntiān wǎnshang 今天晚上; **good ~** wǎnshang hǎo 晚上好

**evening class** yèxiào 夜校; **evening dress** (for man, woman) wǎnlǐfú 晚礼服; **evening paper** wǎnbào 晚报

**evenly** (regularly) jūnyún 均匀

**event** shìjiàn 事件; SP bǐsài 项比赛; **at all ~s** wúlùn rúhé 无论如何

**eventful** yǒu xǔduō dàshì 有许多大事

**eventual** zuìzhōng 最终

**eventually** zhōngyú 终于

**ever** adv (with past or perfect tense questions) céngjīng 曾经; (with past or perfect tense negative) cónglái 从来; (with conditionals) yídàn 一旦; (for emphasis) dàodǐ 到底; **did you ~ go abroad before you were 15?** shíwǔ suì yǐqián nǐ céngjīng chūguó guó ma? 十五岁以前你曾经出过国吗?; **have you ~ been to … ?** nǐ céng dàoguò … ma? 你曾到过 … 吗?; **he hasn't ~ been there** tā cónglái méi qùguò nàr 他从来没去过那儿; **if you ~ come to China, give me a call** nǐ yàoshi yídàn lái Zhōngguó, gěi wǒ dǎge diànhuà 你要是一旦来中国, 给我打个电话; **for ~** yǒngyuǎn 永远; **~ since** cóng nà yǐhòu 从那以后; **~ since he came to China …** cóng tā lái Zhōngguó yǐhòu … 从他来中国以后 …

**Everest: Mount ~** ⇩ Zhūmùlǎngmǎfēng 珠穆朗玛峰

**evergreen** n chángqīng 常青

**everlasting** yǒngjiǔ 永久

**every** měiyī 每一; **~ other day** měigéyìtiān 每隔一天; **~ now and then** ǒu'ěr 偶尔

**everybody** měigèrén 每个人

**everyday** měitiān 每天

**everyone** měigèrén 每个人

**everything** yíqiè 一切

**everywhere** gèchù 各处; (wherever) dàochù 到处

**evict** zhúchū 逐出

**evidence** hénjì 痕迹; LAW zhèngjù 证据; **give ~** zuòzhèng 出证

**evident** míngxiǎn 明显

**evidently** (clearly) míngxiǎn 明显; (apparently) xiǎnrán 显然

**evil 1** adj xié'è 邪恶 **2** n è 恶

**evoke** image huànqǐ 唤起

**evolution** jìnhuà 进化

**evolve** v/i (of animals) jìnhuà 进化; (develop) zhújiàn xíngchéng 逐渐形成

**ewe** mǔyáng 母羊

**ex-** qián qián

**ex** n F (former wife) qiánqī 前妻; (former husband) qiánfū 前夫

**exact** adj quèjiè 确切

**exactly** qiàqià 恰恰; **~!** jiùshì! 就是!; **not ~** bù quánshì 不全是

**exaggerate 1** v/t kuādà 夸大 **2** v/i kuāzhāng 夸张

**exaggeration** yán guò qí shí 言过其实

**exam** kǎoshì 考试; **take an ~** cānjiā kǎoshì 参加考试; **pass / fail an ~** tōngguò / bùtōngguò kǎoshì 通过 / 不通过考试

**examination** (of facts etc) diàochá 调查; (of patient) jiǎnchá 检查; EDU kǎoshì 考试

**examine** study diàochá 调查; patient jiǎnchá 检查; EDU kǎo 考

**examiner** EDU zhǔkǎorén 主考人

**example** lìzi 例子; **for ~** bǐrú 比如; **set a good / bad ~** shùlì hǎo / bùhǎo bǎngyàng 树立好 / 不好榜样

**exasperate** rěnǎo 惹恼

**excavate** v/t (dig) wājué 挖掘; (of archeologist) fājué 发掘

**excavation** wājué 挖掘

**excavator** wājuéjī 挖掘机

**exceed** (be more than) chāoguò 超过; (go beyond) chāochū 超出

**exceedingly** jíduān 极端

**excel 1** v/i shàncháng 擅长; **~ at X** shàncháng X 擅长 X **2** v/t: **~ oneself** shèngguò guòqù 胜过过去

**excellence** yōuxiù 优秀

**excellent** hěn hǎo 很好

**except** chúle 除了; **~ for** chúle X yǐwài 除了 X 以外; **~ that …**

zhǐshì … 只是 …

**exception** lìwài 例外; **with the ~ of** chúle 除了; **take ~ to** fǎnduì 反对

**exceptional** (*very good*) jiéchū 杰出; (*special*) tèshū 特殊

**exceptionally** (*extremely*) yìcháng 异常

**excerpt** jiélù 节录

**excess 1** *n* guòdù 过度; *eat / drink* **to ~** chī/hē wúdù 吃／喝无度; **in ~ of** duōyú 多于 **2** *adj* duōyú 多余

**excess baggage** chāozhòngde xíngli 超重的行李

**excess fare** bǔpiàofèi 补票费

**excessive** guòfèn 过分

**exchange 1** *n* (*of views, information*) jiāohuàn 交换; (*between schools*) jiāoliú 交流; **in ~** zuòwéi jiāohuàn 作为交换; **in ~ for** yònglái huànqǔ 用来换取 **2** *v/t* (*in store*) gēnghuàn 更换; *addresses* hùhuàn 互换; *currency* duìhuàn 兑换; **~ X for Y** yòng X huàn Y 用 X 换 Y

**exchange rate** FIN duìhuànlǜ 兑换率

**excitable** yìxīngfèn 易兴奋

**excite** (*make enthusiastic*) jīdòng 激动

**excited** xīngfèn 兴奋; **get ~** xīngfèn 兴奋; **get ~ about X** wèi X gǎndào xīngfèn 为 X 感到兴奋

**excitement** xīngfèn 兴奋

**exciting** lìngrén xīngfèn 令人兴奋

**exclaim** jīngjiào 惊叫

**exclamation** gǎntàn 感叹

**exclamation point** gǎntànhào 感叹号

**exclude** (*not include*) páichú zàiwài 排除在外; *possibility* páichú 排除; (*bar: from club etc*) páichì 排斥

**excluding** chúle 除了

**exclusive** *hotel, restaurant* dútè 独特; *rights* dúyǒu 独有; *interview* dújiā 独家

**excruciating** *pain* jùliè 剧烈

**excursion** yuǎnzú 远足

**excuse 1** *n* jièkǒu 借口 **2** *v/t*

(*forgive*) yuánliàng 原谅; **please ~ me** (*allow to leave*) shípéi 失陪; **~ X from Y** miǎnchú X zuò Y 免除 X 做 Y; **~ me** (*to get attention*) qǐngwèn 请问; (*to get past*) láojià 劳驾; (*interrupting somebody*) hěn bàoqiàn 很抱歉

**execute** *criminal* chǔjué 处决; *plan* shíshī 实施

**execution** (*of criminal*) sǐxíng 死刑; (*of plan*) shíshī 实施

**executioner** xíngxíngrén 行刑人

**executive** *n* zhǔguǎn rényuán 主管人员

**executive briefcase** zhǔguǎn rényuán gōngshìbāo 主管人员公事包

**executive washroom** zhǔguǎn guànxǐshì 主管盥洗室

**exemplary** mófàn 模范

**exempt: be ~ from** miǎnchú 免除

**exercise 1** *n* (*physical*) duànliàn 锻炼; EDU liànxí 练习; MIL yǎnxí 演习; **take ~** zuò yùndòng 作运动 **2** *v/t muscle* duànliàn 锻炼; *dog* liù 遛; *caution, restraint* yìngyòng 应用 **3** *v/i* duànliàn 锻炼

**exercise book** EDU liànxíběn 练习本

**exert** *authority* xíngshǐ 行使; **~ oneself** yònglì 用力

**exertion** fèilì 费力

**exhale** hūchū 呼出

**exhaust 1** *n* (*fumes*) fèiqì 废气; (*pipe*) páiqìguǎn 排气管 **2** *v/t* (*tire*) shǐpíjuàn 使疲倦; (*use up*) yòngjìn 用尽

**exhaust fumes** páichūde fèiqì 排出的废气

**exhausted** (*tired*) jīnpílìjìn 筋疲力尽

**exhausting** lìngrénpíjuàn 令人疲倦

**exhaustion** láolèi guòdù 劳累过度

**exhaustive** chèdǐ 彻底

**exhaust pipe** páiqìguǎn 排气管

**exhibit 1** *n* (*in exhibition*) zhǎnpǐn 展品 **2** *v/t* (*of gallery*) zhǎnlǎn 展览; (*of artist*) zhǎnchū 展出; (*give evidence of*) xiǎnchū 显出

**exhibition** zhǎnlǎnhuì 展览会; (*of bad behavior*) chūchǒu 出丑; (*of skill*) biǎoyǎn 表演

**exhibitionist** fēngtóu zhǔyì zhě 风头主义者

**exhilarating** lìngrén yúkuài 令人愉快

**exile** 1 *n* liúwáng 流亡; (*person*) qùguó zhě 去国者 2 *v/t* liúfàng 流放

**exist** cúnzài 存在; **~ on X** kào X shēngcún 靠 X 生存

**existence** cúnzài 存在; (*life*) shēngcún 生存; **in ~** xiàncún 现存; **come into ~** xíngchéng 形成

**existing** xiàncún 现存

**exit** 1 *n* (*way out*) chūkǒu 出口; (*from highway*) chūlù 出路; THEA tuìchǎng 退场 2 *v/i* COMPUT tuìchū 退出

**exonerate** xuānbù wúzuì 宣布无罪

**exorbitant** guògāo 过高

**exotic** fùyǒu yìguó qíngdiào 富有异国情调

**expand** 1 *v/t* kuòdà 扩大 2 *v/i* zēngzhǎng 增长; (*of metal*) péngzhàng 膨胀

♦**expand on** xiángshù 详述

**expanse** guǎngkuò 广阔

**expansion** zēngzhǎng 增长; (*of metal*) péngzhàng 膨胀

**expect** 1 *v/t* qīdài 期待; *baby* huáiyùn 怀孕; (*suppose*) rènwéi 认为; (*demand*) yāoqiú 要求 2 *v/i*: **be ~ing** yǒule 有了; **I ~ so** wǒ xiǎng huì de 我想会的

**expectant** huáiyǒu xīwàng 怀有希望

**expectant mother** zhǔn mǔqīn 准母亲

**expectation** qīwàng 期望; **~s** (*demands*) zhǐwàng 指望

**expedient** *n* yǒuyì 有益

**expedition** tànxiǎn 探险; (*group*) tuán 团; (*to do shopping, sightseeing*) xíng 行

**expel** *person* kāichú 开除

**expend** *energy* huāfèi 花费

**expendable** *person* kě xiāofèi 可消耗

**expenditure** huāfèi 花费

**expense** xiāofèi 消费; **at the company's ~** yóu gōngsī fùfèi 由公司付费; **a joke at my ~** kāi wǒde wánxiào 开我的玩笑; **at the ~ of his health** zài sǔnhài tā shēntǐ de qíngkuàng xià 在损害他身体的情况下

**expense account** bàoxiāo zhànghù 报销帐户

**expenses** yòngfèi 用费

**expensive** ángguì 昂贵

**experience** 1 *n* (*event*) jīnglì 经历; (*in life*) tǐyàn 体验; (*in particular field*) jīngyàn 经验 2 *v/t* pain, pleasure gǎnjué 感觉; *problem, difficulty* yùdào 遇到

**experienced** yǒujīngyàn 有经验

**experiment** 1 *n* shìyàn 试验 2 *v/i* shíyàn 实验; **~ on X** (*on animals etc*) yòng X zuò shíyàn 用X做实验; **~ with** (*try out*) shìyàn 试验

**experimental** yòngyú shíyàn 用于实验

**expert** 1 *adj* shúliàn 熟练 2 *n* zhuānjiā 专家

**expert advice** zhuānjiā jiànyì 专家建议

**expertise** zhuānmén zhīshi 专门知识

**expire** dàoqī 到期

**expiry** qīmǎn 期满

**expiry date** zhōngzhǐ rìqī 终止日期

**explain** 1 *v/t* shuōmíng 说明 2 *v/i* jiěshì 解释

**explanation** jiěshì 解释

**explicit** *instructions* míngquè 明确

**explicitly** *state, forbid* míngquè 明确

**explode** *v/i* & *v/t bomb* bàozhà 爆炸

**exploit**[1] *n* yīngyǒng shìjì 英勇事迹

**exploit**[2] *v/t person* bōxuē 剥削; *resources* lìyòng 利用

**exploitation** (*of person*) bōxuē 剥削

**exploration** tànsuǒ 探索

**exploratory** *surgery* tànsuǒxìng 探索性

**explore** *country etc* kǎochá 考察;

*possibility* tàntǎo 探讨

explorer tànsuǒ zhě 探索者

explosion bàozhà 爆炸; (*in population*) jīzēng 激增

explosive *n* zhàyào 炸药

export **1** *n* (*action*) chūkǒu 出口; (*item*) chūkǒuwù 出口物 **2** *v/t* goods chūkǒu 出口; COMPUT dǎochū 导出

export campaign chūkǒu xuānchán 出口宣传

exporter chūkǒushāng 出口商

expose (*uncover*) lùchū 露出; *scandal* jiēlù 揭露; *person* jiēchuān 揭穿; **~ X to Y** ràng X shòudào Y 让 X 受到 Y

exposure bàolù 暴露; MED tǐwēn guòdī 体温过低; (*of dishonest behavior*) jiēchuān 揭穿; (*part of film*) bàoguāng 曝光

express **1** *adj* (*fast*) xùnsù 迅速; (*explicit*) míngquè 明确 **2** *n* (*train*) tèkuài 特快; (*bus*) kuàisù 快速 **3** *v/t* (*speak of, voice*) biǎoshì 表示; *feelings* biǎodá 表达; **~ oneself well** qīngchǔ biǎodá zìjǐde yìsi 清楚表达自己的意思; **~ oneself** (*emotionally*) zìwǒ biǎodá 自我表达

express elevator tèkuài diàntī 特快电梯

expression (*voiced*) biǎoshì 表示; (*on face*) biǎoqíng 表情; (*phrase*) biǎodáfǎ 表达法; (*expressiveness*) gǎnqíng 感情

expressive fùyǒu biǎoqíng 富有表情

expressly (*explicitly*) qīngchǔ biǎomíng 清楚表明; (*deliberately*) tèdì 特地

expressway gāosù gōnglù 高速公路

expulsion (*from school*) kāichú 开除; (*of diplomat*) qūzhú 驱逐

exquisite (*beautiful*) jīngměi 精美

extend **1** *v/t* kuòdà 扩大; *runway, path* yáncháng 延长; *contract, visa* yánqī 延期; *thanks, congratulations* biǎoshì 表示 **2** *v/i* (*of garden etc*) shēnzhǎn 伸展

extension (*to house*) kuòjiàn 扩建; (*of contract, visa*) yánqī 延期; TELEC fēnjī 分机

extension cable dǎoxiàn 导线

extensive guǎngfàn 广泛

extent chéngdù 程度; **to such an that** dàodá rúcǐ chéngdù yǐzhìyú 到达如此程度以致于; **to a certain ~** zài yídìng chéngdù shang 在一定程度上

exterior **1** *adj* wàibù 外部 **2** *n* (*of building*) wàiguān 外观; (*of person*) wàibiǎo 外表

exterminate *vermin* xiāomiè 消灭; *race* mièjué 灭绝

external (*outside*) wàimiàn 外面

extinct *species* juézhǒng 绝种

extinction juézhǒng 绝种

extinguish *fire* pūmiè 扑灭; *cigarette* xīmiè 熄灭

extinguisher mièhuǒqì 灭火器

extort: **~ money from X** lèsuǒ X de jīnqián 勒索 X 的金钱

extortion lèsuǒ 勒索

extortionate guògāo 过高

extra **1** *n* (*sth ~*) éwàide shìwù 额外的事物 **2** *adj* éwài 额外; **be ~** (*cost more*) lìngwài shōufèi 另外收费 **3** *adv* géwài 格外

extra charge fùjiāfèi 附加费

extract **1** *n* xuǎnlù 选录 **2** *v/t* qǔchū 取出; *oil, juice* zhàchū 榨出; *coal* wā 挖; *tooth* báchū 拔出; *information* huòqǔ 获取

extraction (*process*) zhàchū 榨出; (*of tooth*) báchū 拔出

extradite yǐndù 引渡

extradition yǐndù 引渡

extradition treaty yǐndù gōngyuē 引渡公约

extramarital hūnwài 婚外

extraordinarily yìcháng 异常

extraordinary bùpíngcháng 不平常

extravagance shēchǐ 奢侈

extravagant (*with money*) huīhuò 挥霍

extreme **1** *n* jíduān 极端 **2** *adj* jídù 极度; *views* piānjī 偏激

extremely jíqí 极其

extremist *n* jíduānzhǔyì zhě 极端主义者

**extricate** jiějiù 解救

**extrovert** *n* xìnggé wàixiàng de rén 性格外向的人

**exuberant** xìnggāocǎiliè 兴高采烈

**exult** kuángxǐ 狂喜

**eye 1** *n* yǎnjīng 眼睛; (*of needle*) zhēnbír 针鼻儿; *keep an ~ on* (*look after*) zhàokàn 照看; (*monitor*) guānchá 观察 **2** *v/t* qiáo 瞧

**eyeball** yǎnqiú 眼球; **eyebrow** méimao 眉毛; **eyeglasses** yǎnjìng 眼镜; **eyelash** jiémáo 睫毛; **eyelid** yǎnjiǎn 眼睑; **eyeliner** yǎnxiànyè 眼线液; **eyeshadow** yǎnyǐnggāo 眼影膏; **eyesight** shìlì 视力; **eyesore** bú shùnyǎn 不顺眼; **eye strain** yǎnjīng píláo 眼睛疲劳; **eyewitness** mùjīzhě 目击者

# F

F (= **Fahrenheit**) Huáshì 华氏
fabric bùliào 布料
fabulous jí hǎo 极好
façade (of building) zhèngmiàn 正面; (of person) wàibiǎo 外表
face 1 n liǎn 脸; *to ~* miàn duì miàn 面对面; *lose ~* diūliǎn 丢脸 2 v/t person, the sea miànduì 面对
facelift miànbù lāpí shǒushù 面部拉皮手术
face value piàomiàn jiàzhí 票面价值; *take X at ~* cóng biǎomiàn shang kàn X 从表面上看 X
facilitate shǐ … biànlì 使 … 便利
facilities shèshī 设施
fact shìshí 事实; *in ~*, *as a matter of ~* shíjì shang 实际上
factor yīnsù 因素
factory gōngchǎng 工厂
faculty (hearing etc) nénglì 能力; (at university) xì 系
fade v/i (of colors) xiāotuì 消退
faded color, jeans tuìsè 退色
fag F (homosexual) tóngxìngliàn 同性恋
Fahrenheit Huáshì 华氏
fail 1 v/i shībài 失败 2 v/t: *~ an exam* kǎoshì bù jígé 考试不及格
failure shībài 失败
faint 1 adj bù míngxiǎn 不明显 2 v/i hūndǎo 昏倒
fair[1] n COM jiāoyìhuì 交易会
fair[2] adj hair qiǎnsè 浅色; complexion báixī 白皙; (just) gōngzhèng 公正; *it's not ~* zhè bù gōngpíng 这不公平
fairly treat gōngzhèng 公正; (quite) xiāngdāng 相当
fairness (of treatment) gōngzhèng 公正
fairy xiānzǐ 仙子
fairy tale shénhuà gùshì 神话故事

faith xìnxīn 信心; REL xìnyǎng 信仰
faithful zhōngchéng 忠诚; *be ~ to one's partner* duì pèi'ǒu zhōngchéng 对配偶忠诚
fake 1 n yànpǐn 赝品 2 adj fǎngzhì 仿制
fall[1] (autumn) qiūtiān 秋天
fall[2] 1 v/i (of person) shuāidǎo 摔倒; (of government) kuǎtái 垮台; (of prices, temperature, exchange rate) xiàjiàng 下降; (of night) láilín 来临; *it ~s on a Tuesday* nà tiān shì xīngqī'èr 那天是星期二; *~ ill* shēngbìng 生病 2 n (of person) shuāijiāo 摔跤; (of government, minister) dǎotái 倒台; (in price, temperature) xiàjiàng 下降
◆fall back on yīkào 依靠
◆fall down dǎoxià 倒下
◆fall for person àishang 爱上; (be deceived by) xìnyǐwéizhēn 信以为真
◆fall out (of hair) diàoluò 掉落; (argue) nào bièniu 闹别扭
◆fall over dǎoxià 倒下
◆fall through (of plans) luòkōng 落空
fallout fàngshèchén 放射尘
false cuòwù 错误
false teeth jiǎyá 假牙
falsify wěizào 伪造
fame míngyù 名誉
familiar adj (intimate) qīnjìn 亲近; form of address qīnqiè 亲切; *be ~ with X* shúxī X 熟悉 X
familiarity (with subject etc) tóngxiǎo 通晓
familiarize shǐ shúxī 使熟悉; *~ oneself with X* shǐ zìjǐ shúxī yíxià X 使自己熟悉一下 X
family jiātíng 家庭
family doctor jiātíng yīshēng 家庭医生; family name xìng 姓;

**family planning** jìhuà shēngyù 计划生育

**famine** jīhuang 饥荒

**famous** zhùmíng 著名; **be ~ for X** yǐ X zhùmíng 以 X 著名

**fan**¹ *n* (*supporter*) mí 迷

**fan**² **1** *n* (*for cooling, electric*) diànshàn 电扇; (*handheld*) shànzi 扇子 **2** *v/t*: **~ oneself** gěi zìjǐ shānfēng 给自己扇风

**fanatic** kuángrè zhě 狂热者

**fanatical** kuángrè 狂热

**fan belt** MOT fēngshàn pídài 风扇皮带

**fancy** *adj design* jīngzhì 精致

**fancy dress** qítè fúzhuāng 奇特服装

**fancy-dress party** huàzhuāng wǎnhuì 化妆晚会

**fang** jiānyá 尖牙

**fanny pack** yāobāo 腰包

**fantastic** (*very good*) bàngjíle 棒极了; (*very big*) jùdà 巨大

**fantasy** huànxiǎng 幻想

**far** *adv* yuǎn 远; (*much*) fēicháng 非常; **~ away** yáoyuǎn 遥远; **how ~ is it to X?** dào X qù yǒu duōyuǎn? 到 X 去有多远？; **as ~ as the corner / hotel** dào jiǎoluò / bīnguǎn nàme yuǎn 到角落 / 宾馆那么远; **as ~ as I can see** yī wǒ kàn nǐ wǒ kàn 依我看; **as ~ as I know** jùwǒsuǒzhī 据我所知; **you've gone too ~** (*in behavior*) nǐzuòde guòfèn 你做得过分; **so ~ so good** dào mùqián wéizhǐ, yíqiè dōu hěn shùnlì 到目前为止，一切都很顺利

**farce** (*ridiculous goings-on*) nàojù 闹剧

**fare** *n* (*for travel*) piàojià 票价

**Far East** Yuǎndōng 远东

**farewell** *n* cíbié 辞别

**farewell party** sòngbié yànhuì 送别宴会

**farfetched** qiānqiáng 牵强

**farm** *n* nóngchǎng 农场

**farmer** nóngfū 农夫

**farmhouse** nóngshè 农舍

**farmworker** nóngchǎng gōngrén 农场工人

**farsighted** yǒu yuǎnjiàn 有远见; (*optically*) yuǎnshì 远视

**fart** F **1** *n* pì 屁 **2** *v/i* fàngpì 放屁

**farther** *adv* gèngyuǎn 更远

**farthest** *travel etc* zuìyuǎn 最远

**fascinate** *v/t* shǐ zháomí 使着迷; **be ~d by X** bèi X xīyǐnzhù 被 X 吸引住

**fascinating** mírén 迷人

**fascination** (*with subject*) chīmí 痴迷

**fascism** fǎxīsī zhǔyì 法西斯主义

**fascist 1** *n* fǎxīsī zhǔyì zhě 法西斯主义者 **2** *adj* fǎxīsī 法西斯

**fashion** *n* shíshàng 时尚; (*manner*) fāngshì 方式; **in ~** liúxíng 流行; **out of ~** guòshí 过时

**fashionable** *clothes, person, idea* shímáo 时髦

**fashion-conscious** yǒu shíshàng yìshí 有时尚意识

**fashion designer** shízhuāng shèjìshī 时装设计师

**fast**¹ **1** *adj* kuài 快; **be ~** (*of clock*) kuài 快 **2** *adv* kuài 快; **stuck ~** dùzhùle 堵住了; **~ asleep** shúshuì 熟睡

**fast**² *n* (*not eating*) jìnshí 禁食

**fasten** *v/t* shǐ gùdìng 使固定; **~ X onto Y** bǎ X gùdìng zài Y shang 把 X 固定在 Y 上 **2** *v/i* (*of dress etc*) jì xì 系

**fastener** (*for dress*) lālián 拉链; (*for lid*) jǐngqìqì 紧盖器

**fast food** kuàicān 快餐; **fast-food restaurant** kuàicāndiàn 快餐店; **fast forward 1** *n* (*on video etc*) kuàijìnjiàn 快进健 **2** *v/i* kuàijìn 快进; **fastlane** kuàisù chēdào 快速车道; **fast train** kuàichē 快车

**fat 1** *adj* pàng 胖 **2** *n* (*on meat*) zhīfáng 脂肪

**fatal** zhìmìng 致命; *error* wúkě wǎnjiù 无可挽救

**fatality** sǐwáng 死亡

**fatally**: **be ~ injured** shòu zhìmìng shāng 受致命伤

**fate** mìngyùn 命运

**father** *n* fùqīn 父亲

**fatherhood** shēnwéirénfù 身为人父

**father-in-law** (woman's) gōnggōng 公公; (man's) yuèfù 岳父

**fatherly** sì fùqīn 似父亲

**fathom** n NAUT yīngxún 英寻

**fatigue** n píjuàn 疲倦

**fatso** F pàngzi 胖子

**fatty 1** adj hán zhīfáng duo 含脂肪多 **2** n F (person) pàngzi 胖子

**faucet** lóngtóu 龙头

**fault** n (defect) máobìng 毛病; **it's your/my ~** shì nǐde/wǒde cuò 是你的/我的错; **find ~ with X** zhǎo X de cuò 找X的错

**faultless** wánměi 完美

**faulty** products yǒu máobìng 有毛病

**favor** n xǐ'ài 喜爱; **in ~ of X** (resign, withdraw) duì X yǒulì 对X有利; **be in ~ of ...** zhīchí ... 支持...; **do X a ~** bāng X ge máng 帮X个忙; **do me a ~!** (don't be stupid) bàituō! 拜托!

**favorable** reply etc zànchéng 赞成

**favorite 1** n zuì xǐhuān 最喜欢; (food) piān'ài 偏爱 **2** adj zuì xǐhuān 最喜欢

**fax 1** n chuánzhēn 传真; **send X by ~** bǎ X yòng chuánzhēn chuánsòng 把X用传真传送 **2** v/t yòng chuánzhēn chuán 用传真传; **~ X to Y** bǎ X chuánzhēn gěi Y 把X传真给Y

**FBI** (= **Federal Bureau of Investigation**) Liánbāng Diàochájú 联邦调查局

**fear 1** n kǒngjù 恐惧 **2** v/t hàipà 害怕

**fearless** wúwèi 无畏

**feasibility study** kěxíngxìng yánjiū 可行性研究

**feasible** qièshí kěxíng 切实可行

**feast** n shèngyàn 盛宴

**feat** jìyì 技艺

**feather** yǔmáo 羽毛

**feature 1** n (on face) róngmào 容貌; (of city, building, plan, style) tèsè 特色; (article in paper) zhuāntí 专题; (movie) zhèngpiàn 正片; **make a ~ of X** qiángdiào X 强调X **2** v/t (of movie) yóu ... 由...; zhǔyǎn 由...主演

**February** èryuè 二月

**federal** liánbāngzhì 联邦制

**federation** liánbāng 联邦

**fed up** adj F yànfán 厌烦; **be ~ with X** yīn X ér yànfán 因X而厌烦

**fee** fèiyòng 费用; (of lawyer, doctor, consultant) chóujīn 酬金; (for entrance) fèi 费; (for membership) huìfèi 会费

**feeble** person xūruò 虚弱; attempt wúlì 无力; laugh wēiruò 微弱

**feed** v/t gōngyǎng 供养; animal wèi 喂

**feedback** ⇩ fǎnkuì xìnxī 反馈信息

**feel 1** v/t (touch) chùmō 触摸; (sense) gǎndào 感到; pain, pleasure, sensation gǎnzhī 感知; (think) rènwéi 认为 **2** v/i (of cloth etc) gěirén gǎnjué 给人感觉; **it ~s like silk/cotton** mōqǐlái xiàng sī/miánhuā 摸起来像丝/棉花; **your hand ~s hot/cold** nǐde shǒu mōqǐlái rè/liáng 你的手摸起来热/凉; **I ~ hungry/tired** wǒ gǎnjué è/lèi le 我感觉饿/累了; **how are you ~ing today?** nǐ jīntiān gǎnjué zěnmeyàng? 你今天感觉怎么样?; **how does it ~ to be rich?** fùyǒu shì shénme gǎnjué? 富有是什么感觉?; **do you ~ like a drink/meal?** xiǎng bù xiǎng hē/chīdiǎn shénme? 想不想喝/吃点儿什么?; **I ~ like going/staying** wǒ xiǎng zǒu/dāi zài zhèr 我想走/呆在这儿; **I don't ~ like it** wǒ bù xiǎngyào 我不想要

♦**feel up to** rènwéi yǒu nénglì zuò 认为有能力做

**feeler** (of insect) chùjiǎo 触角

**feelgood factor** lèguān xīnlǐ 乐观心理

**feeling** (of happiness) gǎnjué 感觉; (emotion) gǎnqíng 感情; (sensation) zhījué 知觉; **what are your ~s about it?** nǐ shì zěnme xiǎng de? 你是怎么想的?; **I have mixed ~s about him** wǒ duì tā yǒu hěn máodùnde gǎnqíng 我对

对他有很矛盾的感情
**fellow** (*man*) jiāhuo 家伙
**fellow citizen** tóngbāo 同胞;
  **fellow countryman** tóngbāo 同
  胞; **fellow man** quánrénlèi 全人
  类
**felony** zhòngzuì 重罪
**felt** n máozhān 毛毡
**felt tip, felt-tip(ped) pen**
  zhāntóubǐ 毡头笔
**female 1** *adj animal, plant* cíxìng 雌
  性; (*referring to people*) nǚxìng 女
  性 **2** n (*of animals, plants*) cíxìng
  dòngzhíwù 雌性动植物;
  (*person*) nǚxìng 女性; *pej* (*woman*)
  nǚrén 女人
**feminine 1** *adj qualities* yǒu nǚxìng
  qìzhì 有女性气质; GRAM yīnxìng
  阴性; **she's very ~** tā hěn yǒu
  nǚrén wèidào 她很有女人味道
  **2** n GRAM yīnxìng 阴性
**feminism** ⇩ nǚquán zhǔyì 女权
  主义
**feminist** ⇩ **1** n nǚquán zhǔyì zhě
  女权主义者 **2** *adj* nǚquán 女权
**fen** (*Chinese money*) fēn 分
**fence** n zhàlán 栅栏
♦**fence in** *land* yòng zhàlán wéiqǐ
  用栅栏围起
**fencing** SP jíjiàn 击剑
**fend: ~ for oneself** dúlì shēnghuó
  独立生活
**fender** MOT yìzǐbǎn 翼子板
**ferment**[1] v/i (*of liquid*) fājiào 发酵
**ferment**[2] n (*unrest*) dòngdàng bù'ān
  动荡不安
**fermentation** fājiào 发酵
**fern** jué 蕨
**ferocious** cánrěn 残忍
**ferry** n dùchuán 渡船
**fertile** *soil* féiwò 肥沃; *woman,
  animal* néng shēngyù 能生育
**fertility** (*of soil*) féiwò 肥沃; (*of
  woman, animal*) fányù 繁育
**fertility drug** cùyùnyào 促孕药
**fertilize** v/t *ovum* shǐ shòujīng 使受
  精
**fertilizer** (*for soil*) féiliào 肥料
**fervent** *admirer* rèchéng 热诚
**fester** v/i (*of wound*) huànóng 化脓
**festival** jiérì 节日

**festive** jiérì 节日
**festivities** huānqìng 欢庆
**fetch** *person* jiē 接; *thing* ná 拿;
  *price* màidé 卖得
**fetus** tāi'ér 胎儿
**feud** n shìchóu 世仇
**fever** fāshāo 发烧
**feverish** fāshāo 发烧; *fig:
  excitement* jīdòng 激动
**few 1** *adj* (*not many*) hěnshǎo 很少;
  **a ~** (*things*) jǐgè 几个; **quite a ~, a
  good ~** (*a lot*) xiāngdāngduō 相当
  多 **2** *pron* (*not many*) shǎoshù jǐgè
  少数几个; **a ~** (*some*) yìxiē 一些;
  **quite a ~, a good ~** (*a lot*) xǔduō
  许多
**fewer** *adj* gèngshǎo 更少; **~ than
  ...** shǎoyú ... 少于 ...
**fiancé** wèihūnfū 未婚夫
**fiancée** wèihūnqī 未婚妻
**fiasco** chèdǐde shībài 彻底的失
  败
**fib** n xiǎohuǎng 小谎
**fiber** n xiānwéi 纤维
**fiberglass** bōlí xiānwéi 玻璃纤维;
  **fiber optic** guāng xiān 光纤; **fiber optics** guāngdǎo xiānwéi 光
  导纤维
**fickle** biànhuà wúcháng 变化无常
**fiction** (*novels*) xiǎoshuō 小说;
  (*made-up story*) biānzàode shì 编
  造的事
**fictitious** xūgòu 虚构
**fiddle 1** n F (*violin*) xiǎotíqín 小提
  琴 **2** v/i: **~ with** bǎinòng 摆弄; **~
  around with** húluàn bǎinòng 胡
  乱摆弄 **3** v/t *accounts, results*
  cuàngǎi 篡改
**fidelity** zhōngzhēn 忠贞
**fidget** v/i fánzào bù'ān 烦躁不安
**field** n tiándì 田地; (*for sport*)
  chǎng 场; (*competitors in race*)
  cānsài zhě 参赛者; (*of research,
  knowledge etc*) lǐngyù 领域; **that's
  not my ~** nà búzài wǒde fànwéi
  zhīnèi 那不在我的范围之内
**field events** tiánsài 田赛
**fierce** *animal* xiōngměng 凶猛;
  *wind, storm* qiángliè 强烈
**fiery** *personality* yìnù 易怒; *temper*
  bàozào 暴躁

fifteen shíwǔ 十五

fifteenth dìshíwǔ 第十五

fifth dìwǔ 第五

fiftieth dì wǔshí 第五十

fifty wǔshí 五十

fifty-fifty adv duìbàn 对半

fig wúhuāguǒ 无花果

fight 1 n zhàndòu 战斗; fig (for survival, championship) zhēngdòu 争斗; (in boxing) quánjī 拳击 2 v/t enemy, person yǔ ... dǎzhàng yǔ ... dǎzhàng 与 ... 打仗; (in boxing) jiāofēng 交锋; a disease, injustice zuò dòuzhēng 作斗争 3 v/i dǎjià 打架

◆fight for one's rights, cause zhēngqǔ 争取

fighter zhànshì 战士; (airplane) zhàndòujī 战斗机; (boxer) quánjīshǒu 拳击手; she's a ~ tāshìge fèndòu zhě 她是个奋斗者

figurative use of word bǐyù 比喻; art yòng túxíng biǎoxiàn 用图形表现

figure 1 n (digit) shùzì 数字; (of person) xíngtǐ 形体; (form, shape) túxíng 图形 2 v/t F (think) rènwéi 认为

◆figure on F (plan) jìhuà 计划

◆figure out (understand) lǐjiě 理解; calculation jìsuànchū 计算出

figure skating huāyàng huábīng 花样滑冰

file¹ 1 n (of documents) dàng'àn 档案; COMPUT wénjiàn 文件 2 v/t documents zhěnglǐ 整理

◆file away documents jiāng ... guīdàng 将 ... 归档

file² n (for wood, fingernails) cuòdāo 锉刀

file cabinet dàng'ànxiāng 档案箱

file manager COMPUT wénjiàn guǎnlǐ chéngxù 文件管理程序

Filipino 1 adj Fēilǜbīn 菲律宾 2 n (person) Fēilǜbīn rén 菲律宾人

fill 1 v/t zhùmǎn 注满 2 n: eat one's ~ chīgebǎo 吃个饱

◆fill in form tiánxiě 填写; hole tiánmǎn 填满

◆fill in for línshí tìdài 临时替代

◆fill out 1 v/t form tiánxiě 填写

2 v/i (get fatter) zhǎngpàng 长胖

◆fill up 1 v/t zhuāngmǎn 装满 2 v/i (of stadium, theater) chōngmǎn 充满

fillet n lǐjǐ 里脊

fillet steak lǐjǐ niúpái 里脊牛排

filling 1 n (in sandwich) xiàn 馅; (in tooth) bǔyá 补牙 2 adj food róngyì bǎorén 容易饱人

filling station jiāyóuzhàn 加油站

film 1 n (for camera) jiāojuǎn 胶卷; (movie) diànyǐng 电影 2 v/t person, event pāishè 拍摄

film-maker zhìpiàn rén 制片人

film star diànyǐng míngxīng 电影明星

filter 1 n guòlùqì 过滤器 2 v/t coffee, liquid guòlù 过滤

◆filter through (of news reports) mànmàn chuánkāi 慢慢传开

filter tip (cigarette) guòlùzuǐ 过滤嘴

filth huìwù 污物

filthy āngzāng 肮脏; language etc wěixiè 猥亵

fin (of fish) qí 鳍

final 1 adj (last) zuìhòu 最后; decision quèdìng 确定 2 n SP juésài 决赛

finalist cānjiā juésài zhě 参加决赛者

finalize plans, design quèdìng 确定

finally zuìhòu 最后; (at last) zhōngyú 终于

finance 1 n jīnróng 金融 2 v/t tígōng zījīn 提供资金

financial jīnróng 金融

financier jīnróngjiā 金融家

find v/t zhǎodào 找到; if you ~ it too hot / cold rúguǒ nǐ juéde tài rè / lěng 如果你觉得太热 / 冷; ~ X innocent / guilty LAW cáidìng X wúzuì / yǒuzuì 裁定 X 无罪 / 有罪

◆find out 1 v/t huòzhī 获知 2 v/i (inquire) cháxún 查询; (discover) liǎojiědào 了解到

fine¹ adj day, weather qínglǎng 晴朗; wine, performance, city hǎo 好; distinction xìwēi 细微; line xì 细; how's that? – that's ～ nǐ kàn zěnmeyàng? – hǎo 你看怎么样? –

好; *that's ~ by me* wǒ juédé kěyǐ
我觉得可以; *how are you? - ~*
nǐ hǎo ma? – hěn hǎo 你好吗？
–很好

**fine** 1 *n (penalty)* fájīn 罚金 2 *v/t*
fákuǎn 罚款

**finger** *n* shǒuzhǐ 手指

**fingernail** shǒuzhǐjiǎ 手指甲;
**fingerprint** shǒuyìn 手印; **fin-**
**gertip** zhǐjiān 指尖; *have X at*
*one's ~s* duì X liǎo rú zhǐzhǎng 对
X了如指掌

**finicky** *person* guòfèn tiāotì 过分
挑剔; *design, pattern* guòfèn
jiǎngjiū xìjié 过分讲究细节

**finish** 1 *v/t* jiéshù 结束; *~ doing X*
zuòwán X 做完 X 2 *v/i* jiéshù 结
束 3 *n (of product)* zuìhòu bùfen
最后部分; *(of race)* zhōngdiǎn 终
点

♦**finish off** *v/t: ~ a drink / meal /*
*one's work* bǎ shèngxiàde he /
chī / zuòwán 把剩下的喝/吃/
做完

**finish up** *v/t food* chīwán 吃完;
*he finished up liking it / living*
*there* tā hòulái xǐhuān tā le / zhù
zài nàr le 他后来喜欢它了/住
在那儿了

♦**finish with: ~ X with boyfriend etc**
yǔ X duànjué guānxì 与 X 断绝关
系

**finishing line** zhōngdiǎnxiàn 终点
线

**Finland** Fēnlán 芬兰

**Finn** Fēnlán rén 芬兰人

**Finnish** 1 *adj* Fēnlán 芬兰 2 *n*
*(language)* Fēnlán yǔ 芬兰语

**fir** lěngshān 冷杉

**fire** 1 *n* huǒ 火; *(electric, gas)* nuǎnlú
暖炉; *(blaze)* shīhuǒ 失火;
*(bonfire, campfire etc)* gōuhuǒ 篝
火; *be on ~* zháohuǒ 着火; *catch*
*~* shāocháo 烧着; *set X on ~, set*
*~ to X* gěi X fànghuǒ 给 X 放火
2 *v/i (shoot)* shèjī 射击 3 *v/t F*
*(dismiss)* jiěgù 解雇; *be ~d* bèi
chǎo yóuyú 被炒鱿鱼

**fire alarm** huǒjǐng jǐngbào 火警
警报; **firearm** qiāngzhī 枪支;
**firecracker** biānpào 鞭炮; **fire**

**department** xiāofángduì 消防
队; **fire escape** ānquán chūkǒu
安全出口; **fire extinguisher**
mièhuǒqì 灭火器; **firefighter**
xiāofángduìyuán 消防队员;
**fireplace** bìlú 壁炉; **fire truck**
xiāofángchē 消防车; **firewood**
mùchái 木柴; **fireworks** yānhuǒ
烟火; *(display)* yānhuǒ biǎoyǎn 烟
火表演

**firm** 1 *adj grip, handshake* wěn ér
yǒulì 稳而有力; *flesh, muscles*
jiēshi 结实; *voice, decision* jiāndìng
坚定; *a - deal* yíxiàng kěndìng de
xiéyì 一项肯定的协议

**firm** *n* COM gōngsī 公司

**first** 1 *adj* dìyī 第一; *who's*
*please?* shéi shì dìyīgè? 谁是第
一个？ 2 *n* dìyīgè 第一个 3 *adv*
*arrive, finish* dìyī 第一;
*(beforehand)* xiān 先; *~ of all (for*
*one reason)* shǒuxiān 首先; *at ~*
qǐchū 起初

**first aid** jíjiù 急救; **first-aid box**,
**first-aid kit** jíjiùxiāng 急救箱;
**first-born** *adj* zhǎngzǐ(nǚ) 长子
(女); **first class** 1 *adj ticket,*
*compartment* tóuděng 头等; *(very*
*good)* yīliú 一流 2 *adv travel*
tóuděng 头等; **first floor** yīlóu 一
楼; **first-hand** *adj* qīnshēn 亲身

**firstly** shǒuxiān 首先

**first name** míngzi 名字

**first-rate** yīliú 一流

**fiscal** cáizhèng 财政

**fiscal year** cáizhèng niándù 财政
年度

**fish** 1 *n* yú 鱼 2 *v/i* diàoyú 钓鱼

**fishbone** yúcì bùwèi 鱼刺

**fisherman** yúfū 渔夫

**fishing** bǔyú 捕鱼

**fishing boat** yúchuán 鱼船; **fish-**
**ing line** diàosī 钓丝; **fishing rod**
diàoyúgān 钓鱼杆

**fish stick** yútiáo 鱼条

**fishy** F *(suspicious)* kěyí 可疑

**fist** quán 拳

**fit** *n* MED hūnjué 昏厥; *a - of*
*rage / jealousy* yígǔ nùhuǒ / jídù
qíngxù 一股怒火／嫉妒情绪

**fit** *adj (physically)* jiànkāng 健康

(*morally*) qiàdàng 恰当; **keep ~** jiànshēn 健身

**fit**[3] **1** v/t (*of clothes*) héshì 合适; (*attach*) ānzhuāng 安装 **2** v/i (*of clothes*) héshì 合适; (*of piece of furniture etc*) róngdéxià 容得下 **3** n: **it is a good ~** hěn héshì 很合适; **it's a tight ~** yǒudiǎn jǐn 有点儿紧

◆**fit in** (*of person in group*) héqún 合群; **it fits in with our plans** zhè yǔ wǒmende jìhuà yízhì 这与我们的计划一致

**fitful** *sleep* bù wěndìng 不稳定

**fitness** (*physical*) jiànkāng 健康

**fitness center** jiànshēn zhōngxīn 健身中心

**fitted carpet** gùdìnghǎode dìtǎn 固定好的地毯

**fitted kitchen** yǒu gùdìng shèbèi de chúfáng 有固定设备的厨房

**fitter** n zhuāngpèigōng 装配工

**fitting** adj qiàdàng 恰当

**fittings** zhuāngzhì 装置

**five** wǔ 五

**Five Year Plan** Wǔnián Jìhuà 五年计划

**fix 1** n (*solution*) jiějué 解决; **be in a ~** F xiànrù kùnjìng 陷入困境 **2** v/t (*attach*) dìngláo 钉牢; (*repair*) xiūlǐ 修理; (*arrange: meeting etc*) ānpái 安排; *lunch* zhǔnbèi 准备; (*dishonestly: match etc*) zuòbì 作弊; **~ X onto Y** bǎ X gùdìng zài Y shang 把X固定在Y上; **I'll ~ you a drink** wǒ gěi nǐ nòng diǎn yǐnliào 我给你弄点饮料

◆**fix up** *meeting* ānpái 安排; **it's all fixed up** dōu shì ānpái hǎode dōu 都是安排好的

**fixed** (*in one position*) gùdìng 固定; *timescale, exchange rate* quèdìng búbiàn 确定不变

**fixture** (*in room*) gùdìng zhuāngzhì 固定装置

**flab** (*on body*) sōngchíde jīròu 松弛的肌肉

**flabbergast: be ~ed** F dàchīyìjīng 大吃一惊

**flabby** *muscles, stomach* sōngchí 松弛

**flag**[1] n qí 旗

**flag**[2] v/i (*tire*) píjuàn 疲倦

**flair** (*talent*) tiānfèn 天份; **have a natural ~ for X** duì X yǒu tiānfèn 对X有天份

**flake** n suìpiàn 碎片

◆**flake off** v/i bōluò 剥落

**flaky** yì bōluò 易剥落

**flaky pastry** sūbǐng 酥饼

**flamboyant** *personality* ài xuànyào 爱炫耀

**flame** n huǒyàn 火焰

**flammable** yì ránshāo 易燃烧

**flan** guǒxiànbǐng 果馅饼

**flank** n (*of horse etc*) lèibù 肋部; MIL cèyì 侧翼 **2** v/t zhìyú liǎngcè zhì yú liǎngcè 置于两侧; **be ~ed by X** liǎngcè yǒu X 两侧有 X

**flap 1** n (*of envelope, pocket*) kǒugài 口盖; (*of table*) huódòngbiān 活动边; **be in a ~** F jǐnzhāng huāngluàn 紧张慌乱 **2** v/t *wings* jīnyì 襟翼 **3** v/i (*of flag etc*) yáodòng 摇动

**flare 1** n (*distress signal*) shǎnguāng zhuāngzhì 闪光装置; (*in dress*) lǎbazhuàng 喇叭状 **2** v/t *nostrils* gǔqǐ 鼓起

◆**flare up** (*of violence*) tūqǐ 突起; (*of illness, rash*) fùfā 复发; (*of fire*) biànwàng 变旺; (*get very angry*) fānù 发怒

**flash 1** n (*of light*) shǎnshuò 闪烁; PHOT shǎnguāngdēng 闪光灯; **in a ~** F shǎndiànbān 闪电般; **have a ~ of inspiration** língjīyídòng 灵机一动; **~ of lightning** shǎndiàn 闪电 **2** v/i (*of light*) shǎnliàng 闪亮 **3** v/t *headlights* yòng guāng liánluò 用光联络

**flashback** (*in movie*) shǎnhuí 闪回

**flashbulb** shǎnguāng dēngpào 闪光灯泡

**flasher** MOT shǎnguāng zhǐshìdēng 闪光指示灯

**flashlight** shǒudiàntǒng 手电筒; PHOT shǎnguāngdēng 闪光灯

**flashy** pej huāshao 花哨

**flask** nuǎnpíng 暖瓶

**flat 1** adj *surface, land* píngtǎn 平坦; *beer* pǎoqì 跑气; *battery* yòngwán diàn 用完电; *tire* qì bùzú 气不足; *shoes* píngdǐ 平底; *sound, tone* píngdàn 平淡; **and that's ~** F shuōdìngle 说定了 **2** *adv* MUS yī dīdiào 以低调; **~ out** *work, run, drive* jiéjìnquánlì 竭尽全力

**flat-chested** píngxiōng 平胸

**flat rate** tǒngyī shōufèilǜ 统一收费率

**flatten** *v/t land, road* biànpíng 变平; *(by bombing, demolition)* jīdǎo 击倒

**flatter** *v/t* fèngcheng 奉承

**flattering** *comments* tǎohǎo 讨好; *color, clothes* shǐrén gèng piàoliàng 使人更漂亮

**flattery** fèngcheng 奉承

**flavor 1** *n* wèidào 味道 **2** *v/t:* **~ X** *food* gěi X tiáowèi 给 X 调味

**flavoring** tiáowèipǐn 调味品

**flaw** *n* xiácī 瑕疵

**flawless** wánměi 完美

**flea** tiàozao 跳蚤

**flee** *v/i* táopǎo 逃跑

**fleet** *n* NAUT jiànduì 舰队; *(of taxis, trucks)* chēduì 车队

**fleeting** *visit etc* duǎnzàn 短暂; **catch a ~ glimpse of** piējiàn 瞥见

**flesh** *n* ròutǐ 肉体; *(of fruit)* guǒròu 果肉; **meet/see X in the ~** jiàndào X běnrén 见到 X 本人

**flex** *v/t muscles* huódòng 活动

**flexible** línghuó 灵活; **I'm quite ~** *(about arrangements, timing)* wǒ kěyǐ jīdòng 我可以机动

**flick** *v/t tail* qīngtán 轻弹; **he ~ed a fly off his hand** tā gǎndiàole shǒushangde cángyíng 他赶掉了手上的苍蝇; **she ~ed her hair out of her eyes** tā bōkāi le yǎnqiánde tóufà 她拨开了眼前的头发

♦ **flick through** *book, magazine* liúlǎn 浏览

**flicker** *v/i (of light, candle, computer screen)* shǎndòng 闪动

**flies** *(on pants: zipper)* lāliànr 拉链儿; *(buttons)* kāikòu 开扣

**flight** *(in airplane)* hángbān 航班; *(flying)* fēixíng 飞行; *(fleeing)* táopǎo 逃跑; **~ (of stairs)** lóutīde

yíduàn 楼梯的一段

**flight crew** jīzǔ rényuán 机组人员; **flight deck** fēixíng jiǎbǎn 飞行甲板; **flight number** hángbānhào 航班号; **flight path** fēixíng lùxiàn 飞行路线; **flight recorder** fēixíng jìlùyí 飞行记录仪; **flight time** *(departure)* qǐfēi shíjiān 起飞时间; *(duration)* fēixíng shíjiān 飞行时间

**flighty** qīngfú 轻浮

**flimsy** *structure, furniture* bù jiēshi 不结实; *dress, material* qīng'érbó 轻而薄; *excuse* bù zúxìn 不足信

**flinch** tuìsuō 退缩

**fling** *v/t* rēng 扔; **~ oneself into a chair** zāidào yǐzi shang 栽到椅子上

♦ **flip through** *book, magazine* liúlǎn 浏览

**flipper** *(for swimming)* jiǎopǔ 脚蹼

**flirt 1** *v/i* tiáoqíng 调情 **2** *n* tiáoqíng zhě 调情者

**flirtatious** ài tiáoqíng 爱挑情

**float** *v/i* piāofú 漂浮; FIN fúdòng 浮动

**flock** *n (of sheep)* yìqún 一群

**flog** *v/t (whip)* biāndǎ 鞭打

**flood 1** *n* hóngshuǐ 洪水 **2** *v/t (of river)* yānmò 淹没; **~ its banks** *(of river)* yānmò tǐ'àn 淹没堤岸

**flooding** hóngshuǐ fànlàn 洪水泛滥

**floodlight** *n* fànguāngdēng 泛光灯

**floor** *n* dìbǎn 地板; *(story)* lóucéng 楼层

**floorboard** yíkuài dìbǎn 一块地板; **floor cloth** pū dìbǎn de hòubù 铺地板的厚布; **floor lamp** luòdìdēng 落地灯

**flop 1** *v/i* měngrán tǎngxià 猛然躺下; F *(fail)* chèdǐ shībài 彻底失败 **2** *n* F *(failure)* chèdǐ shībài 彻底失败

**floppy** *adj (not stiff)* sōngruǎn 松软; *(weak)* xūruò 虚弱

**floppy** *(disk)* ⇩ ruǎnpán 软盘

**floppy drive** COMPUT ruǎnqū 软驱

**florist** huāshāng 花商

**flour** miànfěn 面粉

**flourish** *v/i* fánróng 繁荣

**flourishing** *trade* xīngwàng 兴旺

**flow 1** *v/i* (*of river, electric current, traffic*) liúdòng 流动; (*of work*) jìnxíng 进行 **2** *n* (*of river*) liúdòng 流动; (*of information, ideas*) jiāoliú 交流

**flowchart** liúchéngtú 流程图

**flower 1** *n* huā 花 **2** *v/i* kāihuā 开花

**flowerbed** huātán 花坛

**flowerpot** huāpén 花盆

**flowery** *pattern* duōhuā 多花; *style of writing* cízǎo huálì 词藻华丽

**flu** liúgǎn 流感

**fluctuate** *v/i* bōdòng 波动

**fluctuation** bōdòng 波动

**fluency** (*in a language*) liúlì 流利

**fluent** *adj* liúlì 流利; **he speaks ~ Chinese** tā jiǎng yìkǒu liúlìde Hànyǔ 他讲一口流利的汉语

**fluently** *speak, write* liúlì 流利

**fluff**: *a bit of ~* (*material*) yìdiǎn róngmáo 一点绒毛

**fluffy** *adj material, hair* péngsōng 蓬松; *clouds* sōngruǎn 松软; **~ toy** sōngruǎnde wánjù 松软的玩具

**fluid** *n* liútǐ 流体

**flunk** *v/t* F *subject* bù jígé 不及格

**fluorescent** *light* fā yíngguāng 发荧光

**flush 1** *v/t toilet* chōngxǐ 冲洗; **~ X down the toilet** bǎ X chōngjìn cèsuǒ 把 X 冲进厕所 **2** *v/i* (*of toilet*) chōngxǐ 冲洗; (*go red in the face*) biànhóng 变红 **3** *adj* (*level*) qípíng 齐平; **be ~ with X** yǔ X wángquán qípíng 与 X 完全齐平

◆**flush away** (*down toilet*) chōngdiào 冲掉

◆**flush out** *rebels etc* gǎnchū 赶出

**fluster** *v/t* shǐ jǐnzhāng 使紧张; **get ~ed** jǐnzhāng 紧张

**flute** chángdí 长笛

**flutter** *v/i* (*of bird, wings*) bǎichì 摆翅; (*of flag*) piāodòng 飘动; (*of heart*) pūdòng 扑动

**fly¹** *n* (*insect*) cāngying 苍蝇

**fly²** *n* (*on pants: zipper*) lāliànr 拉链儿; (*buttons*) kāikòu 开扣

**fly³ 1** *v/i* (*of bird, airplane*) fēixíng 飞行; (*in airplane*) chéngjī 乘机; (*of flag*) piāoyáng 飘扬; (*rush*) fēipǎo 飞跑; **~ into a rage** bórán dànù 勃然大怒 **2** *v/t airplane* jiàshǐ 驾驶; *airline* dāchéng dāchéng 搭乘; (*transport by air*) kōngyùn 空运

◆**fly away** (*of bird, airplane*) fēizǒu 飞走

◆**fly back** *v/i* (*travel back*) fēihuí 飞回

◆**fly in** *v/i* (*of airplane, passengers*) fēidào 飞到 **2** *v/t supplies etc* kōngyùn 空运

◆**fly off** (*of hat etc*) fēituō 飞脱

◆**fly out** *v/i* chéng jī qù chéng jī qù 乘机去

◆**fly past** (*in formation*) fēixíng biānduì 编队飞行; (*of time*) fēishì 飞逝

**flying** *n* fēixíng 飞行

**foam** *n* (*on liquid*) pàomò 泡沫

**foam rubber** pàomò xiàngjiāo 泡沫橡胶

**FOB** (= *free on board*) lí'àn jiàgé 离岸价格

**fodder** sìliào 饲料

**fog** wù 雾

**foggy** duōwù 多雾

**foil¹** *n* (*silver ~ etc*) xīzhǐ 锡纸

**foil²** *v/t* (*thwart*) cuòbài 挫败

**fold¹** *v/t paper etc* zhédié 折叠; **~ one's arms** hébào shuāngbì 合抱双臂 **2** *v/i* (*of business*) tíngyè 停业 **3** *n* (*in cloth etc*) zhě 褶

◆**fold up 1** *v/t* zhé qǐlái 折起来 **2** *v/i* (*of chair, table*) néng zhédié 能折叠

**fold²** *n* (*for sheep etc*) yánglán 羊栏

**folder** *also* COMPUT wénjiànjiá 文件夹

**folding** zhédié 折叠; **~ chair** zhédiéyǐ 折叠椅

**foliage** yèzi 叶子

**folk** (*people*) rénmen 人们; **my ~** (*family*) wǒde jiārén 我的家人; **come in, ~s** F dàjiā qǐngjìn 大家

请进

**folk dance** ⇩ mínjiānwǔ 民间舞;
**folk music** mínyuè 民乐;**folk
singer** míngēshǒu 民歌手;**folk
song** míngē 民歌

**follow 1** v/t person gēnsuí 跟随;
road yánzhe ... qiánjìn 沿着 ... 前
进; guidelines, instructions zūnxún
遵循; TV series, news liánxù kàn
连续看; (understand) míngbái 明
白; ~ **me** gēn wǒ lái gēn wǒ lái 跟我来 **2** v/i
gēnzhe 跟着; (logically) bìrán
fāshēng 必然发生; **it ~s from
this that ...** yóucǐ fāshēng ... 由此
发生 ...; **as ~s** rúxià 如下
♦**follow up** v/t letter, inquiry hòuxù
后续

**follower** (of politician etc) zhuīsuí
zhě 追随者; (of football team)
zhīchí zhě 支持者; (of TV
program) zhōngshí guānzhòng 忠
实观众

**following 1** adj day, night jiēzhe 接
着; points xiàshù 下述; pages yǐxià
以下 **2** n (people) yìpī zhīchí zhě
一批支持者; **the ~** rúxià 如下

**follow-up meeting** gēnzōng huìyì
跟踪会议

**follow-up visit** (to doctor etc)
liánxùde bàifǎng 连续的拜访

**folly** (madness) yúchǔn 愚蠢

**fond** (loving) xǐ'ài 喜爱; memory
zhēn'ài 珍爱; **be ~ of** xǐhuan 喜
欢

**fondle** àifǔ 爱抚

**fondness** xǐ'ài 喜爱

**font** (for printing) zìtǐ 字体

**food** (formal word) shíwù 食物;
(informal word) chīde 吃的

**food freak** F dàchī 大吃;**food
mixer** shíwù jiǎobànqì 食物搅拌
器;**food poisoning** shíwù
zhòngdú 食物中毒

**fool** n chǔnrén 蠢人; **make a ~ of
oneself** shǐ zìjǐ chūchǒu 使自己
出丑
♦**fool around** húnào 胡闹;
(sexually) yǒu wàiyù 有外遇
♦**fool around with** knife, drill etc
bǎinòng 摆弄

**foolish** yúchǔn 愚蠢

**foolproof** búhuì chūcuò 不会出
错

**foot** jiǎo 脚; (measurement) yīngchǐ
英尺; **on ~** bùxíng 步行; **at the ~
of the page / hill** zài ~ shàng / shān jiǎo
xià 在页上 / 山角下; **put one's ~ in
it** F (by saying sth) lìngrénnánkān
说错话; (by doing sth) zuò cuòshì
做错事

**football** měishì zúqiú 美式足球;
(soccer) zúqiú 足球; (ball) zúqiú
足球;**football player** měishì
zúqiú duìyuán 美式足球队员;
(soccer) qiúyuán 球员;**foot-
bridge** bùxíngqiáo 步行桥

**footer** COMPUT jiǎozhù 脚注

**foothills** shānlù xiǎoqiū 山麓小丘

**footing** (basis) jīchǔ 基础; **lose
one's ~** shīzú diēdǎo 失足跌倒;
**be on the same / a different ~**
píngděng / bù píngděng de dìwèi
平等 / 不平等的地位; **be on a
friendly ~ with X** yǔ X guānxi
róngqià 与X关系融洽

**footlights** jiǎodēng xìxiàndēng灯;**footnote** jiǎozhù 脚注;**footpath**
xiǎolù 小路;**footprint** jiǎoyìn 脚
印;**footstep** jiǎobù 脚步; **follow
in X's ~s** xiàofǎng X 效仿X;
**footwear** xié 鞋

**for** ◊ (purpose, destination etc) wèile
为了; **save up ~ a vacation** wèile
dùjià zǎnqián 为了度假攒钱;
**study ~ an exam** wèile kǎoshì
xuéxí 为了考试学习; **a train ~ X**
qù X de huǒchē 去X的火车;
**clothes ~ children** tóngzhuāng 童
装; **it's too big / small ~ you** nǐ
chuān tài dà / xiǎo 你穿太大 / 小;
**here's a letter ~ you** zhè shì nǐde
xìn 这是你的信; **this is ~ you**
zhè shì gěi nǐde 这是给你的;
**what is there ~ lunch?** wǔcān chī
shénme? 午餐吃什么?; **the
steak is ~ me** niúpái shì wǒde 牛
排是我的; **what is this ~?** zhè
shì gàn shénme yòngde? 这是干
什么用的?; **what ~?**
wèishénme? 为什么?◊ (time):
**three days / two hours** sān
tiān / liǎnggè xiǎoshí 三天 / 两个

小时; *please get it done ~ Monday* qǐng zài xīngqīyī yǐqián zuòwán 请在星期一以前做完 ◊ (*distance*): *I walked ~ a mile* wǒ zǒule yīyīnglǐ 我走了一英里; *it stretches ~ 100 miles* liánmián yìbǎi yīnglǐ 连绵一百英里 ◊ (*in favor of*): *I am ~ the idea* wǒ tóngyì zhège xiǎngfǎ 我同意这个想法 ◊ (*instead of, in behalf of*): *let me do that ~ you* wǒ gěi nǐ zuò ba 我给你做吧; *we are agents ~ X* wǒmen shì X de dàilǐrén 我们是X的代理人 ◊ (*in exchange for*): *I bought it ~ $25* wǒ huāle èrshíwǔ měiyuán mǎide wǒ 花了二十五美元买的; *how much did you sell it ~?* nǐ duōshao qián màide? 你多少钱卖的?

**forbid** jìnzhǐ 禁止; *~ X to do Y* jìnzhǐ X zuò Y 禁止X做Y

**forbidden** yánjìn 严禁; *smoking / parking ~* jìnzhǐ xīyān/tíngchē 禁止吸烟/停车

**Forbidden City** Zǐjìnchéng 紫禁城

**forbidding** yánjùn 严峻

**force 1** *n* (*violence*) wǔlì 武力; (*of explosion, wind, punch*) lìliàng 力量; *come into ~* (*of law etc*) shēngxiào 生效; *the ~s* MIL bùduì 部队 **2** *v/t door, lock* yònglì dǎkāi 用力打开; *~ X to do Y* qiángpò X zuò Y 强迫X做Y; *~ X open* qiángxíng dǎkāi X 强行打开X

**forced** *laugh, smile* miǎnqiǎng 勉强; *confession* bèipò 被迫

**forced landing** pòjiàng 迫降

**forceful** *argument* qiángyǒulì 强有力; *speaker* yǒu shuōfúlì 有说服力; *character* jiānqiáng 坚强

**forceps** qiánzi 钳子

**forcible** *entry* yòng qiánglì 用强力; *argument* yǒu shuōfúlì 有说服力

**ford** *n* héliú qiǎnchù 河流浅处

**fore: come to the ~** tuō yǐng ér chū 脱颖而出

**foreboding** bùxiángde yùgǎn 不祥的预感; **forecast 1** *n* yùcè 预测; (*of weather*) yùbào 预报 **2** *v/t* yùbào 预报; **forecourt** (*of garage*) jiāyóuchù 加油处; **forefathers** zǔxiān 祖先; **forefinger** shízhǐ 食指; **foregone:** *that's a ~ conclusion* nà shì bìránde 那是必然的; **foreground** qiánbù 前部; **forehand** (*in tennis*) zhèngshǒu dǎo 正手打; **forehead** é 额

**foreign** wàiguó 外国

**foreign affairs** wàijiāo shìwù 外交事物

**foreign currency** wàibì 外币

**foreigner** wàiguórén 外国人

**foreign exchange** wàihuì 外汇; **foreign language** wàiyǔ 外语; **Foreign Office** *Br* Wàijiāobù 外交部; **foreign policy** wàijiāo zhèngcè 外交政策; **Foreign Secretary** *Br* Wàijiāobùzhǎng 外交部长

**foreman** língbān 领班; **foremost** zuì zhòngyào 最重要; **forerunner** xiānqū 先驱; **foresee** yùjiàn 预见; **foreseeable** kě yùjiàn 可预见; *in the ~ future* zài kě yùjiànde wèilái 在可预见的未来; **foresight** xiānjiàn zhī míng 先见之明

**forest** sēnlín 森林

**forestry** sēnlínxué 森林学

**foretaste** qiānchǎng 浅尝

**foretell** yùliào 预料

**forever** *adv* yǒngyuǎn 永远

**foreword** qiányán 前言

**forfeit** *v/t right, privilege etc* sàngshī 丧失

**forge** *v/t* (*counterfeit*) wěizào 伪造; *signature* mófǎng 模仿

**forger** wěizàorén 伪造人

**forgery** (*bank bill*) jiǎ chāopiào 假钞票; (*document*) wěizàopǐn 伪造品

**forget** wàngjì 忘记

**forgetful** jiànwàng 健忘

**forget-me-not** (*flower*) wùwàngwǒ 勿忘我

**forgive 1** *v/t* yuánliàng 原谅 **2** *v/i* liàngjiě 谅解

**forgiveness** yuánliàng 原谅

# fork

fork n chāzi 叉子; (in road) fēnchàchù 分岔处

♦fork out v/i F (pay) chūqián 出钱

forklift (truck) chāchē 叉车

form 1 n (shape) xíngzhuàng 形状; (document) biǎogé 表格 2 v/t (in clay etc) sùzào 塑造; friendship jiànlì 建立; opinion xíngchéng 形成; past tense etc xíngshì 形式 3 v/i (take shape, develop) xíngchéng 形成

formal zhèngshì 正式; recognition etc guānfāng 官方

formality guīfàn 规范; it's just a ~ zhè zhǐshì yìzhǒng xíngshì 这只是一种形式

formally adv speak, behave zhèngshì 正式; recognized guānfāng 官方

format v/t diskette shǐ géshìhuà 使格式化; document ānpái ... bǎnshì 安排... 版式 2 n (size: of magazine, paper etc) kāiběn 开本; (make-up: of program) fēnggé 风格

formation (act of forming) xíngchéng 形成; (of airplanes) biānduì 编队

formative lìyú chéngzhǎng 利于成长; in his ~ years zài tā xìnggé xíngchéng de shíqī 在他性格形成的时期

former yǐqián 以前; the ~ qiánzhě 前者

formerly yǐqián 以前

formidable kěpà 可怕

formula MATH gōngshì 公式; CHEM fēnzǐshì 分子式; (for success etc) mìjué 秘诀

formulate (express) biǎodá 表达

fort MIL yàosài 要塞

forth: back and ~ láihuí 来回; and so ~ děngděng 等等

forthcoming (future) jíjiāng fāshēng 即将发生; personality rèxīn 热心

fortieth dìsìshí 第四十

fortnight Br bàngèyuè 半个月

fortress MIL chéngbǎo 城堡

fortunate xìngyùn 幸运

fortunately xìngkuī 幸亏

fortune yùnqì 运气; (lot of money) dàbǐde qián 大笔的钱

fortune-teller suànmìng zhě 算命者

forty sìshí 四十

forward 1 adv xiàngqián 向前 2 adj pej zhíjiéliǎodàng 直截了当 3 n SP qiánfēng 前锋 4 v/t letter zhuǎndì 转递

forwarding agent COM zhuǎnyùnshāng 转运商

fossil huàshí 化石

foster child lǐngyǎngde háizi 领养的孩子

foster parents yǎngfùmǔ 养父母

foul 1 n SP fànguī 犯规; fànwéi 犯规行为 2 adj smell, taste nánwén 难闻; weather èluè 恶劣 3 v/t SP fànguī 犯规

found v/t school etc chuàngbàn 创办

foundation (of theory etc) jīchǔ 基础; (of organization) chénglì 成立; (organization) jījīnhuì 基金会

foundations (of building) dìjī 地基

founder n chuàngjiànrén 创建人

foundry zhùzàochǎng 铸造厂

fountain pēnquán 喷泉

four sì 四

four-star hotel etc sìxīngjí 四星级

fourteen shísì 十四

fourteenth dìshísì 第十四

fourth dìsì 第四

fowl qín 禽

fox n húli 狐狸

fraction xiǎobùfen 小部分; (decimal) fēnshù 分数

fracture 1 n gǔzhé 骨折 2 v/t zhéduàn 折断

fragile yìsuì 易碎

fragment n yíbùfen 一部分

fragmentary zhīlípòsuì 支离破碎

fragrance fāngxiāng 芳香

fragrant yǒu xiāngwèi 有香味

Fragrant Hills Xiāngshān 香山

frail xūruò 虚弱

frame 1 n kuàng 框; ~ of mind xīnqíng 心情 2 v/t picture gěi ... xiāngkuàng 给 ... 镶框; F person xiànhài 陷害

framework kuàngjià 框架

France Fǎguó 法国

**frank** tǎnshuài 坦率

**frankly** tǎnbái 坦白; *~, it's not worth it* tǎnbáide shuō, bù zhídé 坦白地说,不值得

**frantic** fāfēng 发疯

**fraternal** xiōngdìbān 兄弟般; *~ love* shǒuzú zhī qíng 手足之情

**fraud** qīpiàn 欺骗; (*person*) piànzi 骗子

**fraudulent** qīpiànxìng 欺骗性

**frayed** *cuffs* mósǔn 磨损

**freak** 1 *n* (*unusual event*) fǎncháng xiànxiàng 反常现象; (*two-headed person, animal etc*) jīxíng 畸形; F (*strange person*) guàirén 怪人; *movie / jazz ~* diànyǐng / juéshìyuè mí 电影 / 爵士乐迷 2 *adj wind, storm etc* yìcháng qiánglìè 异常强烈

**freckle** quèbān 雀斑

**free** 1 *adj* (*at liberty*) zìyóu 自由; (*no cost*) miǎnfèi 免费; *room, table* kòngyú 空余; *are you ~ this afternoon?* nǐ jīntiān xiàwǔ yǒukòng ma? 你今天下午有空吗？; *~ and easy* bùjū xíngshì 不拘形式; *for ~* (*travel, get something*) miǎnfèi 免费 2 *v/t prisoners* shìfàng 释放

**freebie** F zèngpǐn 赠品

**freedom** zìyóu 自由

**freedom of the press** xīnwén zìyóu 新闻自由

**free kick** (*in soccer*) rènyì qiú 任意球; **freelance** 1 *adj* gètǐ 个体 2 *adv*: *I work ~* wǒ shì gètǐhù 我是个体户; **freelancer** gètǐhù 个体户; **free market economy** zìyóu shìchǎng jīngjì 自由市场经济; **free sample** miǎnfèi yàngpǐn 免费样品; **free speech** yánlùn zìyóu 言论自由; **freeway** gāosù gōnglù 高速公路; **freewheel** *v/i* (*on bicycle*) guànxìng huáxíng 惯性滑行

**freeze** 1 *v/t food, river* lěngdòng 冷冻; *wages, bank account* dòngjié 冻结; *video* zàntíng 暂停 2 *v/i* (*of water*) nínggù 凝固

♦**freeze over** (*of river*) quánmiàn jiébīng 全面结冰

**freezer** lěngdòngshì 冷冻室

**freezing** 1 *adj* jílěng 极冷; *it's ~ out here* dòngsǐ rén le 冻死人了; *it's ~* (*cold*) (*of weather, water*) lěngjíle 冷极了; *I'm ~* (*cold*) wǒ dòngsǐle 我冻死了 2 *n* língdù 零度; *10 below ~* língxià shídù 零下十度

**freezing compartment** lěngdòngxiāng 冷冻箱

**freezing point** bīngdiǎn 冰点

**freight** *n* huòwù 货物; (*costs*) yùnfèi 运费

**freight car** (*on train*) huòchēxiāng 货车厢

**freighter** (*ship*) huòchuán 货船; (*airplane*) yùnshūjī 运输机

**freight train** huòyùn lièchē 货运列车

**French** 1 *adj* Fǎguó 法国 2 *n* (*language*) Fǎyǔ 法语; *the ~* Fǎguó rén 法国人

**French doors** luòdìchuāng 落地窗; **French fries** shǔtiáo 薯条; **Frenchman** Fǎguó nánrén 法国男人; **Frenchwoman** Fǎguó nǚrén 法国女人

**frequency** pínlǜ 频率; (*of radiowave*) bōduàn 波段

**frequent**[1] *adj* jīngcháng 经常

**frequent**[2] *v/t bar* chángqù 常去

**frequently** shícháng 时常

**fresh** *fruit, meat etc* xīnxiān 新鲜; (*cold*) liángshuǎng 凉爽; (*new*) xīn 新; (*impertinent*) cūlǔ 粗鲁 *~ start* chóngxīn kāishǐ 重新开始

♦**freshen up** 1 *v/i* shūxǐ 梳洗 2 *v/t room, paintwork* shǐ ... huànrán yì xīn 使 ... 焕然一新

**freshman** xīnshēng 新生

**freshness** (*of fruit, meat*) xīnxiān 新鲜; (*of style, approach*) xīnyǐng 新颖; (*of weather*) liángshuǎng 凉爽

**fresh orange** (*juice*) xīnxiānde júzizhī 新鲜的橘子汁

**freshwater** *adj* dànshuǐ 淡水

**fret** *v/i* fánzào 烦躁

**friction** PHYS mócā 摩擦; (*between people*) chōngtū 冲突

**friction tape** juéyuán jiāobù 绝缘

胶布

**Friday** xīngqīwǔ 星期五

**fridge** bīngxiāng 冰箱

**fried egg** jiāndàn 煎蛋; **fried noodles** chǎomiàn 炒面; **fried potatoes** shǔtiáo 薯条; **fried rice** chǎofàn 炒饭

**friend** péngyou 朋友; **make ~s** (*of one person*) jiāo péngyǒu 交朋友; (*of two people*) chéngwéi péngyǒu 成为朋友; **make ~s with X** yǔ X jiāo péngyǒu 与X交朋友

**friendly** *adj atmosphere* yǒuhǎo 友好; *person* héshàn 和善; (*easy to use*) qīnhéxíng 亲和性; **be ~ with X** (*be friends*) yǔ X guānxi róngqià 与X关系融洽

**friendship** yǒuyì 友谊

**Friendship Store** Yǒuyì Shāngdiàn 友谊商店

**fries** shǔtiáo 薯条

**fright** jīngxià 惊吓; **give X a ~** xià le X yítiào 吓了X一跳

**frighten** *v/t* jīngxià 惊吓; **be ~ed** hàipà 害怕; **don't be ~ed** bié hàipà 别害怕; **be ~ed of X** hàipà X 害怕X

**frightening** xiàrén 吓人

**frigid** (*sexually*) lěngdàn 冷淡

**frill** (*on dress etc*) shìbiān 饰边; (*fancy extra*) fùjiāwù 附加物

**fringe** (*on dress, curtains etc*) shìbiān 饰边; (*in hair*) liúhǎi 刘海儿; (*edge*) biānyuán 边缘

**frisk** *v/t* sōuchá 搜查

**frisky** *puppy etc* huópo yǒulì 活泼有力

♦ **fritter away** *time, fortune* xiāohào 消耗

**frivolous** *person, pleasures* fūqiǎn 肤浅

**frizzy** *hair* juǎn 卷

**frog** wā 蛙

**frogman** wārén 蛙人

**from** ◊ (*in time*): **~ 9 to 5** (*o'clock*) cóng jiǔdiǎn dào wǔdiǎn 从九点到五点; **~ the 18th century** cóng shíbā shìjì qǐ 从十八世纪起; **~ today on** cóng jīntiān qǐ 从今天起; **~ next Tuesday** cóng xiàge xīngqī èr qǐ 从下个星期二起

◊ (*in space*): **~ here to there** cóng zhèr dào nàr 从这儿到那儿; **we drove here ~ Shanghai** wǒmen cóng Shànghǎi kāichē láide 我们从上海开车来的 ◊ (*origin*): **a letter ~ Jo** Qiáo de láixìn 乔的来信; **a gift ~ the management** guǎnlǐ bùmén sòngde lǐwù 管理部门送的礼物; **it doesn't say who it's ~** méiyǒu shǔmíng 没有署名; **I am ~ New Jersey** wǒ láizì Xīn Zéxī zhōu 我来自新泽西州; **made ~ bananas** yòng xiāngjiāo zuòde 用香蕉做的 ◊ (*because of*): **tired ~ the journey** yīn lǚxíng ér pílǎo 因旅行而疲劳; **it's ~ overeating** shì yóu dàliàng jìnshí yǐnqǐde 是由大量进食引起的

**front 1** *n* (*of building, book*) zhèngmiàn 正面; (*cover organization*) huǎngzi 幌子; MIL qiánxiàn 前线; (*of weather*) fēngfēng 锋; **in ~** zài qiánmian 在前面; (*in a race*) lǐngxiān 领先; **in ~ of X** zài X de qiánmian 在X的前面; **at the ~ of X** zài X de qiánbù 在X的前部 **2** *adj wheel, seat* qiánmian 前面 **3** *v/t TV program* zhǔchí 主持

**front cover** fēngmiàn 封面

**front door** qiánmén 前门; **front entrance** zhèngmén 正门

**frontier** biānjiāng 边疆; *fig* (*of knowledge, science*) jíxiàn 极限

**front page** (*of newspaper*) tóubǎn 头版; **front page news** tóubǎn xīnwén 头版新闻; **front row** qiánpái 前排; **front seat passenger** (*in car*) qiánpáizuò chéngkè 前排座乘客; **front-wheel drive** qiánlún qūdòng 前轮驱动

**frost** *n* shuāng 霜

**frostbite** dòngshāng 冻伤

**frostbitten** dòngshāng 冻伤

**frosted glass** móshā bōlí 磨砂玻璃

**frosting** (*on cake*) tángshuāng 糖霜

**frosty** *weather* yánhán 严寒; *fig: welcome* lěngdàn 冷淡

**froth** n pàomò 泡沫

**frothy** cream etc qǐ pàomò 起泡沫

**frown** n & v/i zhòuméi 皱眉

**frozen** feet etc bīngliáng 冰凉; landscape bīngfēng 冰封; food lěngdòng 冷冻; **I'm ~** F wǒ dònghuài le 我冻坏了

**frozen food** lěngdòng shípǐn 冷冻食品

**fruit** shuǐguǒ 水果

**fruitful** talks etc chénggōng 成功

**fruit juice** guǒzhī 果汁

**fruit salad** shuǐguǒ sèlā 水果色拉

**frustrate** v/t person shǐ … jǔsàng 使 … 沮丧; plans zǔ'ài 阻碍

**frustrated** look, sigh jǔsàng 沮丧

**frustrating** shǐrén xīnfán 使人心烦

**frustratingly** slow, hard lìngrén huīxīn 令人灰心

**frustration** huīxīn 灰心; **sexual ~** xìng shēnghuó shīyì 性生活失意; **the ~s of modern life** xiàndài shēnghuó de bújìnrényì 现代生活的不尽人意

**fry** v/t (stir-~) chǎo 炒; (deep-~) yóuzhá 油炸

**fuck** v/t ∨ (screw) cào 操; **~!** māde! 妈的！; **~ him/that!** qù tāmāde! 去他妈的！

♦ **fuck off** ∨: **~!** gǔnkāi! 滚开！

**fucking** ∨ tāmāde 他妈的

**fuel** n ránliào 燃料

**fugitive** táofàn 逃犯

**fulfill** v/t shíxiàn 实现; **feel ~ed** gǎndào mǎnzú 感到满足

**fulfilling** job lìngrén mǎnyì 令人满意

**fulfillment** (of contract etc) lǚxíng 履行; (moral, spiritual) mǎnzú 满足

**full** bottle zhuāngmǎn 装满; hotel, bus mǎnyuán 满员; diskette mǎn 满; account, report xiángxì 详细; life chōngshí 充实; schedule, day fánmáng 繁忙; **~ of X** chōngmǎn X 充满 X; (of water etc) chōngmǎn X 充满 X; (of tourists etc) dàochù shì 到处是; (of errors) quánshì 全是; **~ up** hotel etc kèmǎn 客满; (with food) chī bǎo le 吃饱了; **pay in ~**

quánbù fùqīng 全部付清

**full coverage** (insurance) zǒngkuò bǎoxiǎn 总括保险; **full-grown** chéngshú 成熟; **full-length** dress quáncháng 全长; movie wèi shānjié 未删节; **full moon** mǎnyuè 满月; **full stop** jùhào 句号; **full-time 1** adj worker, job quánrìzhì 全日制 **2** adv work quánrì 全日

**fully** booked quánbù 全部; recovered wánquán 完全; understand, explain quánmiàn 全面; describe xiángxì 详细

**fumble** v/t catch, job bènzhuóde chǔlǐ 笨拙地处理

♦ **fumble around** mōsuǒde zhǎo 摸索地找

**fume**: **be fuming** F (be very angry) dànù 大怒

**fumes** fèiqì 废气

**fun** lèqù 乐趣; **it was great ~** hěn kāixīn 很开心; **bye, have ~!** zàijiàn, jìnqíng wánr ba! 再见，尽情玩儿吧！; **for ~** wèile wán 为了玩; **make ~ of X** qǔxiào X 取笑 X

**function 1** n zuòyòng 作用; (reception etc) jíhuì 集会 **2** v/i yùnzhuǎn 运转; **as X** qǐ X de zuòyòng 起 X 的作用

**fund 1** n jījīn 基金 **2** v/t project etc bōkuǎn 拨款

**fundamental** (basic) jīběn 基本; (substantial) běnzhì 本质; (crucial) shífēn zhòngyào 十分重要

**fundamentally** different, altered cóng gēnběn shang 从根本上

**funeral** zànglǐ 葬礼

**funeral home** bìnyíguǎn 殡仪馆

**funicular** (railway) lǎnsuǒ tiědào 缆索铁道

**funnel** n (of ship) yāncōng 烟囱

**funnily** (oddly) qíguài 奇怪; (comically) huájī 滑稽; **~ enough** qíguàide shì qíguài de 奇怪的是奇怪的

**funny** (comical) kěxiào 可笑; (odd) gǔguài 古怪

**fur** máopí 毛皮

**furious** (angry) fènnù 愤怒; **at a ~ pace** fēikuàide 飞快地

furnace lúzi 炉子

furnish *room* zhuāngbèi 装备; (*supply*) tígōng 提供

furniture jiāju 家具; *a piece of ~* yíjiàn jiāju 一件家具

furry *animal* máopí fùgài 毛皮覆盖

further 1 *adj* (*additional*) jìnyíbù 进一步; (*more distant*) gèngyuǎn 更远; *until ~ notice* lìngxíng tōngzhī 另行通知; *have you anything ~ to say?* nǐ hái yǒu shénme yào shuō de ma? 你还有什么要说的吗? 2 *adv walk, drive* gèngyuǎn 更远; *~, I want to say ...* cǐwài, wǒ yào shuō ... 此外, 我要说...; *2 miles ~ (on)* zài zǒu liǎng yīnglǐ zài zǒu 再走两英里 3 *v/t cause etc* cùjìn 促进

furthest *adj & adv* zuìyuǎn 最远

furtive *glance* tōutōu 偷偷

fury (*anger*) bàonù 暴怒

fuse ELEC 1 *n* bǎoxiǎnsī 保险丝 2 *v/i* bǎoxiǎnsī shǎoduàn 保险丝烧断 3 *v/t* shǎoduàn bǎoxiǎnsī 烧断保险丝

fusebox bǎoxiǎnsī hé 保险丝盒

fuselage jīshēn 机身

fuse wire bǎoxiǎnsī xiàn 保险丝线

fusion rónghé 熔合

fuss *n* dàjīng xiǎoguài 大惊小怪; *make a ~* (*complain*) tóusù 投诉; (*behave in exaggerated way*) xiǎotí dàzuò 小题大做; *make a ~ of* (*be very attentive to*) guòyú guānzhù 过于关注

fussy *person* tiāotī 挑剔; *design etc* tài duō zhuāngshì 太多装饰; *a ~ eater* tiāotī shíwù de rén 挑剔食物的人

futile wúxiào 无效

future *n* (*of person, company*) qiántú 前途; (*of humanity, earth*) wèilái 未来; GRAM jiānglái shí 将来时; *in ~* yǐhòu 以后

futures FIN qīhuò 期货

futures market FIN qīhuò shìchǎng 期货市场

futuristic *design* wèiláishì 未来式

fuzzy *hair* juǎn 卷; (*out of focus*) móhu 模糊

# G

gadget xiǎozhuāngzhì 小装置

gag 1 n dǔ zuǐ bù dǔzuǐbù 堵嘴布; (joke) xiàohua 笑话 2 v/t person sāizhù … de zuǐ 塞住 … 的嘴; the press yāzhì 压制

gain v/t (acquire) yíngdé 赢得; ~ **speed** jiāsù 加速; ~ **10 pounds** tǐzhòng zēngjiāle shí bàng 体重增加了十磅

gale dàfēng 大风

gallant yǒu shēnshì fēngdù 有绅士风度

gall bladder dǎnnáng 胆囊

gallery (for art) huàláng 画廊; (in theater) dǐngcéng lóuzuò 顶层楼座

galley (on ship) chuán shàng chúfáng 船上厨房

gallon jiālún 加仑; ~s of tea dàliàng de chá 大量的茶

gallop v/i fēipǎo 飞跑

gallows jiǎoxíngjià 绞刑架

gallstone dǎnjiéshí 胆结石

gamble dǔbó 赌博

gambler dǔtú 赌徒

gambling dǔbó 赌博

game n (match) bǐsài 比赛; (sport) yùndòng 运动; (children's) yóuxì 游戏; (in tennis) yìjú 一局

◆gang yìbāng 一帮

◆gang up on héhuǒ gōngjī 合伙攻击

Gang of Four Sìrénbāng 四人帮

gangster dǎitú 歹徒

gangway tiàobǎn 跳板

gap (in wall) lièfèng 裂缝; (for parking) kòngr 空儿; (in figures) chājù 差距; (in time, conversation) jiànxì 间隙; (between two people's characters) chāyì 差异

gape v/i (person) zhāngkǒu 张口; (hole) lièkāi 裂开

◆gape at mùdèng kǒudāi de níngshì 目瞪口呆地凝视

gaping adj hole lièkāi 裂开

garage for parking chēkù 车库; for gas jiāyóuzhàn 加油站; for repairs qìchē xiūlǐzhàn 汽车修理站

garbage ⇩ lājī 垃圾; fig (nonsense) fèihuà 废话

garbage can lājīxiāng 垃圾箱; garbage collection shōu lājī 收垃圾; garbage dump lājī zhàn 垃圾站

garden huāyuán 花园

gardener yuándīng 园丁; (professional) yuánlínshī 园林师

gardening yuányì 园艺

gargle v/i shùkǒu 漱口

garish súbùkěnài 俗不可耐

garland n huāhuán 花环

garlic dàsuàn 大蒜

garment fúzhuāng 服装

garnish v/t diǎnzhuì 点缀

garrison n (place) zhùdì 驻地; (troops) wèishù bùduì 卫戍部队

garter diàowàdài 吊袜带

gas n qìtǐ 气体; (gasoline) qìyóu 汽油

gash n qiēkǒu 切口

gasket diànpiàn 垫片

gasoline qìyóu 汽油

gasp 1 n chuǎnxì chuǎnxì 喘息 2 v/i qìchuǎn 气喘; ~ **for breath** chuǎnqì 喘气

gas pedal yóuménr 油门儿; gas pump yóubèng 油泵; gas station jiāyóuzhàn 加油站; gas works méiqìchǎng 煤气厂

gate (of house, castle) dàmén 大门; (at airport) dēngjīkǒu 登机口

gatecrash bùqǐngzìdào 不请自到

gateway ménkǒu 门口; fig tújìng 途径

gather 1 v/t facts, information sōují 搜集; am I to ~ that … ? wǒ yīnggāi lǐjiě wéi … ? 我应该理解为 … ?; ~ **speed** jiāsù 加速

2 v/i (*understand*) tuīxiǎng 推想

♦**gather up** *possessions* jīlěi 积累

**gathering** (*group of people*) jùhuì 聚会

**gaudy** huāshao 花哨

**gauge** 1 n jìliángqì 计量器 2 v/t cèdìng 测定

**gaunt** qiáocuì 憔悴

**gauze** bóshā 薄纱

**gay** n & adj (*homosexual*) tóngxìngliàn 同性恋

**gaze** 1 n zhùshì 注视 2 v/i níngshì 凝视

♦**gaze at** níngshì 凝视

**GB** (= *Great Britain*) Dà Bùlièdiān 大不列颠

**GDP** (= *gross domestic product*) guónèi shēngchǎn zǒngzhí 国内生产总值

**gear** n equipment yòngjù 用具; *in vehicles* chǐlún 齿轮; ~ **lever**, ~**shift** biànsùgǎnr 变速杆

**gel** (*for hair*) rǔ rǔ 乳乳; (*for shower*) yè yè 液

**gem** zhēnbǎo 珍宝; fig (*book etc*) zhēnpǐn 珍品; **you're a ~** (*person*) nǐ zhēn hǎo 你真好

**gender** xìngbié 性别

**gene** jīyīn 基因; **it's in his ~s** tā shēnglái rúcǐ 他生来如此

**general** 1 n (*in army*) jiāngjūn 将军; **in ~** dàtishang 大体上 2 adj (*overall, miscellaneous*) zǒngde 总的; (*widespread*) pǔbiàn 普遍

**general election** pǔxuǎn 普选

**generalization** gàikuò 概括; **that's a ~** nà shì gè gàikuò 那是个概括

**generalize** gàikuò 概括

**generally** yìbānde 一般地

**generate** (*create*) chǎnshēng 产生; (*in linguistics*) shēngchéng 生成; ~ **electricity** fādiàn 发电

**generation** dài dài 代; ~ **gap** dàigōu 代沟

**generator** fādiànjī 发电机

**generosity** dàfang 大方

**generous** (*with money*) dàfang 大方; (*not too critical*) kuānhóng dàliàng 宽宏大量; *portion etc* dàliàng 大量

**genetic** yíchuán 遗传

**genetically** yíchuán yīnzi shang 遗传因子上

**genetic engineering** yíchuán gōngchéng 遗传工程

**genetic fingerprint** gètǐ yíchuán xìngzhēng 个体遗传性征

**geneticist** yíchuánxuéjiā 遗传学家

**genetics** yíchuánxué 遗传学

**Genghis Khan** Chéngjísīhàn 成吉思汗

**genial** person, company qīnqiè 亲切

**genitals** shēngzhíqì 生殖器

**genius** tiāncái 天才

**gentle** wēnróu 温柔

**gentleman** shēnshì 绅士

**gents** (*toilet*) nányòngwèishēngjiān 男用卫生间

**genuine** zhēnpǐn 真品; (*sincere*) zhēnchéng 真诚

**geographical** features dìlǐ 地理

**geography** (*of area*) dìxíng 地形; (*subject*) dìlǐxué 地理学

**geological** dìzhì 地质

**geologist** dìzhìxué zhě 地质学者

**geology** (*of area*) dìzhì 地质; (*subject*) dìzhìxué 地质学

**geometric(al)** jíhéxué 几何学

**geometry** jǐhé 几何

**geriatric** 1 adj lǎonián 老年 2 n lǎoniánbìngxué 老年病学

**germ** bìngjūn 病菌; *of idea etc* méngyá 萌芽

**germ warfare** xìjūn zhànzhēng 细菌战争

**German** 1 adj Déguó 德国 2 n (*person*) Déguó rén 德国人; (*language*) Déyǔ 德语

**Germany** Déguó 德国

**gesticulate** zuò shǒushì 做手势

**gesture** n (*with hand*) shǒushì 手势; fig (*of friendship*) biǎoshì 表示

**get** (*obtain*) dédào 得到; (*fetch*) gěi … ná 给 … 拿; (*receive: letter*) shōudào 收到; (*receive: knowledge, respect etc*) huòdé 获得; (*catch: bus, train etc*) zuò 坐; (*arrive*) dào 到; (*understand*) míngbái 明白; **can I ~ you a**

**drink?** nǐ xiǎng hē shénme? 你想喝什么?; **~ going** (leave): **~** ◊ (become, grow): **~ tired / ~ old** lèi le/lǎo lē 累了/老了 ◊ (causative) bǎ ... bǎ ...; **~ one's hair cut** bǎ tóufa jiǎn le 把头发剪了; **~ the car fixed** bǎ chē xiūle 把车修了; **~ X ready** bǎ X zhǔnbèi hǎo 把 X 准备好; **~ X to do Y** jiào X zuò Y 叫 X 做 Y ◊ (have opportunity): **I got to meet him** wǒ yǒu jīhuì jiàndào tā 我有机会见到他; **did you ~ to go there?** nǐ yǒu jīhuì qù nàr le ma? 你有机会去那儿了吗 ? ◊: **~ to know** rènshi 认识: ◊: **have got** yǒu le: **have you got any children?** nǐ yǒu háizi ma? 你有孩子吗?; **I've got three tickets** wǒ yǒu sānzhāng piào 我有三张票; **I've got a headache** wǒ tóutòng 我头痛; **have you got time?** nǐ yǒu shíjiān ma? 你有时间吗? ◊: **have got to** (must) bìxū 必须: **I have got to study / see him** wǒ bìxū xuéxí/kàn tā 我必须学习/看他; **I don't want to, but I've got to** wǒ bùdébù 我不得不

♦ **get around** (travel) lǚxíng 旅行; (be mobile) zǒudòng 走动

♦ **get along** (progress) jìnzhǎn 进展; (come to party etc) dào 到; (with somebody) yú ... chùdelái 与 ... 处得来

♦ **get at** (criticize) pīpíng 批评; (imply, mean) yìzhǐ 意指

♦ **get away** 1 v/i (leave) líkāi 离开 2 v/t: **get X away from Y** bǎ X cóng Y názǒu 把 X 从 Y 拿走

♦ **get away with** táozuì 逃罪

♦ **get back 1** v/i (return) huídào 回到; **I'll ~ to you on that** wǒ yíhuìr zài huídá nǐde wèntí 我一会儿再回答你的问题 2 v/t (obtain again) chóngxīn dédào 重新得到

♦ **get by** (pass) tōngguò 通过; (financially) wéichí wéixng 维持

♦ **get down 1** v/i (from ladder etc) xiàlái 下来; (duck) wān yāo 弯腰 2 v/t (depress) jiào rén jǔsàng 叫人沮丧

♦ **get down to** (start: work) kāishǐ rènzhēn duìdài 开始认真对待; (reach: real facts) zhuījiū 追究

♦ **get in 1** v/i (arrive: of train, plane) dàodá 到达; (come home) dàojiā 到家; (to car) jìnrù 进入; **how did they ~?** (of thieves, snakes etc) tāmen zěnme jìnlaide? 他们怎麼进来的 ? (to suitcase etc) fàngjìnqù 放进去

♦ **get off 1** v/i (from bus etc) cóng ... xiàlái 从 ... 下来; (finish work) xià bān 下班; (not be punished) táotuō chéfen 逃脱处分 2 v/t (remove) nádiào 拿掉; **top, boots, clothes** tuō 脱; **~ the grass!** wùtà cǎopíng! 勿踏草坪!

♦ **get off with** (Br: sexually) yǔ ... jiéshí 与 ... 结识; **~ a small fine** jiāo diǎnr fájīn jiù liǎoshì le 交点儿罚金就了事了

♦ **get on 1** v/i (be friendly) chùdelái 处得来; (advance: of time) bù zǎo le 不早了; (become old) lǎo le 老了; (make progress) jìnzhǎn 进展; **~ to the train / bus / one's bike** shàng chē 上车; **~ to the airplane** shàng fēijī 上飞机; **it's getting on** tiānwǎn le 天晚了; **he's getting on** tā shàngle niánjì 他上了年纪; **he's getting on for 50** tā kuài wǔshí le 他快五十了 2 v/t: **~ the bus / one's bike** shàng chē 上车; **get one's hat on** dài shàng màozi 戴上帽子; **I can't get these pants on** wǒ chuān bú shàng kùzi 我穿不上裤子

♦ **get out 1** v/i (of car etc) chūlái 出来; **~ of prison** chūyù 出狱; **~!** gǔnchūqù! 滚出去!; **let's ~ of here** zánmen kuài zǒu ba 咱们快走吧; **I don't ~ much these days** jìnlái wǒ bú tài chūqù 近来我不太出去 2 v/t nail, something jammed nòngchū 弄出; stain chúqù 除去; gun, pen tāochū 掏出

♦ **get over fence** yuèguò 越过; lover etc wàngquè 忘却; disappointment kèfú 克服

♦ **get over with: let's get it over**

**with** zánmen kuàidiǎnr bǎ tā nòngwán ba 咱们快点儿把它弄完吧

♦**get through** (on telephone) dǎtōng 打通; (make self understood) ràng rén tīng dǒng 让人听懂

♦**get up 1** v/i (in morning) qǐchuáng 起床; (from chair etc) zhànqǐlái 站起来; (of wind) dà qǐlái 大起来 **2** v/t (climb: hill) pá 爬

♦**get up to**: *what have you been getting up to?* nǐ zuìjìn gànshénme? 你最近干什么？

**getaway** (from robbery) táopǎo 逃跑; **~ car** qiántáochē 潜逃车

**get-together** jùhuì 聚会

**ghastly** (horrible) kěpà 可怕

**gherkin** xiǎohuángguā 小黄瓜

**ghetto** shǎoshùmínzú jūzhùqū 少数民族居住区

**ghost** guǐ 鬼

**ghostly** guǐyíyàng 鬼一样

**giant 1** n jùrén 巨人 **2** adj pángdà 庞大

**gibberish** fèihuà 废话

**giblets** nèizàng 内脏

**giddiness** xuànyùn 眩晕

**giddy** tóuyūn 头晕

**gift** lǐwù 礼物

**gifted** yǒu tiānfù 有天赋

**giftwrap** bāozhuāng shāngpǐn 包装商品

**gigabyte** COMPUT qiānzhào zìjié 千兆字节

**gigantic** jùdà 巨大

**giggle 1** v/i gēgē de xiào 咯咯地笑 **2** n shǎxiào 傻笑

**gill** (of fish) sāi 鳃

**gilt** n dùjīn cáiliào 镀金材料; **~s** FIN jīnbiānr gǔpiào 金边儿股票

**gimmick** guǐbǎxì 鬼把戏

**gin** dùsōngzǐjiǔ 杜松子酒; **~ and tonic** kuíníng dùsōngzǐjiǔ 奎宁杜松子酒

**ginger** n (spice) jiāng 姜

**gingerbread** jiāngbǐng 姜饼

**ginseng** rénshēn 人参

**gipsy** jípǔsàirén 吉普赛人

**giraffe** chángjǐnglù 长颈鹿

**girder** n dàliáng 大梁

**girl** nǚhái 女孩

**girlfriend** (of boy) nǚ péngyou 女朋友; (of girl) nǚxìng péngyou 女性朋友

**girlie magazine** huángsè zázhì 黄色杂志

**girl scout** nǚ tóngzǐjūn 女童子军

**gist** yàozhǐ 要旨

**give** gěi sòng; (supply: electricity etc) gōngjǐ 供给; **~ a talk** zuò jiǎngzuò 作讲座; **~ a lecture** jiǎngkè 讲课; **~ a cry** dàshēng hūhǎn 大声呼喊; **~ her my love** xiàng tā wènhǎo 向她问好

♦**give away** (as present) sòng 送; (betray) xièlòu 泄露; *give oneself away* bàolù zìjǐ 暴露自己

♦**give back** huán 还

♦**give in 1** v/i surrender qūfú 屈服 **2** v/t (hand in) jiāochū 交出

♦**give off** smell, fumes fāchū 发出

♦**give onto** (open onto) tōngxiàng 通向

♦**give out 1** v/t leaflets etc fēnfā 分发; **~ a groan** shēnyín 呻吟 **2** v/i (of supplies, strength) yòngwán 用完

♦**give up 1** v/t smoking etc jiè 戒; *give oneself up* (to police etc) tóu'àn tóuàn 投案 **2** v/i (cease habit) jiè 戒; (stop making effort) fàngqì 放弃

♦**give way** (of bridge etc) bēngkuì 崩溃

**given name** míngzi 名字

**glacier** bīngchuān 冰川

**glad** gāoxìng 高兴

**gladly** yúkuài 愉快

**glamor** mèilì 魅力

**glamorous** yǒu mèilì 有魅力

**glance 1** n yìpiē 一瞥 **2** v/i sǎoshì 扫视

♦**glance at** sǎoshì 扫视

**gland** xiàn 腺

**glandular fever** línbāxiàn rè 淋巴腺炎

**glare 1** n (of sun, headlights) qiángliède guāng 强烈的光 **2** v/i (of sun, headlights) shǎnyào 闪耀

♦**glare at** nùmù ér shì 怒目而视

**glaring** adj mistake tūchū 突出

glass (*material*) bōli 玻璃; (*for drink*) bōlibēi 玻璃杯

glasses (*eye~*) yǎnjìng 眼镜

glasshouse nuǎnfáng 暖房

glaze n guānghuámiàn 光滑面

♦glaze over (*of eyes*) biànde móhu 变得模糊

glazed *expression* dāizhì 呆滞

glazier zhuāng bōli gōngrén 装玻璃工人

glazing chuāngyòngbōli 窗用玻璃

gleam 1 n wēiguāng 微光 2 v/i shǎnshuò 闪烁

glee kuàilè 快乐

gleeful lìngrén xīngfèn 令人兴奋

glib yóuzuǐhuáshé 油嘴滑舌

glide huáxiáng 滑行

glider huáxiáng jī 滑翔机

gliding n (*sport*) huáxiáng yùndòng 滑翔运动

glimmer 1 n (*of light*) wēiguāng 微光; a ~ of hope yíxiàn xīwàng 一线希望 2 v/i fāwēiguāng 发微光

glimpse 1 n yìpiē 一瞥; catch a ~ of piējiàn 瞥见 2 v/t piējiàn 瞥见

glint 1 n shǎnshuò 闪烁 2 v/i (*of light*) fāwēiguāng 发微光; (*of eyes*) shǎnxiàn mǒuzhǒng shénsè 闪现某种神色

glisten v/i shǎnguāng 闪光

glitter v/i shǎnshǎn fāguāng 闪闪发光

glitterati yǒu míngqì de ren 有名气的人

gloat v/i zhānzhānzìxǐ 沾沾自喜; ~ over xìngzāilèhuò de kǎolǜ ... 幸灾乐祸地考虑

global (*worldwide*) quánqiú 全球; (*without exceptions*) pǔbiàn 普遍

global economy quánqiú jīngjì 全球经济; global market quánqiú shìchǎng 全球市场; global warming quánqiú qìwēn shēnggāo 全球气温升高

globe (*the earth*) dìqiú 地球; (*model of earth*) dìqiúyí 地球仪

gloom (*darkness*) yīn'àn 阴暗; (*mood*) yōuyù 忧郁

gloomy *room* yīn'àn 阴暗; *mood, person* yōuchóu 忧愁

glorious *weather, day* qínglǎng 晴朗; *victory* guāngróng 光荣

glory n róngyù 荣誉

gloss n (*shine*) guāngzé 光泽; (*general explanation*) zhùshì 注释

glossary cíhuìbiǎo 词汇表

gloss paint yǒuguāng túliào 有光涂料

glossy 1 adj *paper* guānghuá 光滑 2 n (*magazine*) guāngmiàn 光面

glove shǒutào 手套

glow 1 n (*of light, fire*) guānghuī 光辉; (*in cheeks*) hóngrùn 红润 2 v/i (*of light, fire*) fāguāng 发光; (*of cheeks*) xiànchū hóngrùn 现出红润

glowing *description* rèqíng 热情

glue 1 n jiāo 胶 2 v/t zhān 粘; ~ X to Y bǎ X zhānzài Y shàng 把 X 粘在 Y 上

glum yōuyù 忧郁

glutinous rice nuòmǐ 糯米

glutton tānshí zhě 贪食者

gluttony tānshí tānshí 贪食

GMT (= Greenwich Mean Time) Gélínwēizhì biāozhǔn shíjiān 格林威治标准时间

gnarled *branch* niǔqū 扭曲; *hands* gǔjié línxún 骨节嶙峋

gnat ruì méng

gnaw v/t *bone* kěn 啃

GNP (= gross national product) guómín shēngchǎn zǒngzhí 国民生产总值

Go (*game*) wéiqí 围棋

go 1 n: on the ~ mánglù 忙碌 2 v/i qù 去; (*leave: of train, plane, of people*) líkāi 离开; (*work, function*) yùnzhuǎn 运转; (*become*) biànde 变锝; (*come out: of stain etc*) diào 掉; (*cease: of pain etc*) méi 没了; (*match: of colors etc*) pèi 配; ~ shopping / jogging qù mǎi dōngxi 去买东西 / 慢跑; I must be ~ing wǒ děi zǒule 我得走了; let's ~ zǒuba 走吧; ~ for a walk qù sànbù 去散步; ~ to bed shàngchuáng 上床; ~ to school shàngxué 上学; how's the work ~ing? gōngzuò jìnzhǎn rúhé? 工作进展如何 ? ;

**they're ~ing for $50** (*being sold at*) yǐ wǔshí měiyuán chūshòu 以五十美元出售; **hamburger to ~** hànbǎobāo, dàizǒu 汉堡包，带走; **be all gone** (*finished*) yòngwánle mǎi wán le 用完了; **be ~ing to do X** yàozuò X 要做 X

♦ **go ahead** (*and do something*) gàn(shuō)ba 干(说)吧; (*on you go*) qùba 去吧
♦ **go ahead with** *plans etc* àn ... jìnxíng 按 ... 进行
♦ **go along with** *suggestion* zàntóng 赞同
♦ **go at** (*attack*) gōngjī 攻击
♦ **go away** (*of person*) líkāi 离开; (*of rain*) tíng 停; (*of pain, clouds*) xiāoshī 消失
♦ **go back** (*return*) huíqù 回去; (*date back*) zhuīsù 追溯; **~ to sleep** zài shuì 再睡; **we ~ a long way** wǒmen xiāngshí duōnián le 我们相识多年了
♦ **go by** (*of car, people*) guòqù 过去; (*of time*) tuīyí 推移
♦ **go down** xiàqù 下去; (*of sun, ship*) luòxià 落下; (*of swelling*) xiāoqù 消去; **~ well / badly** (*of suggestion etc*) shòu / bùshòu huānyíng 受 / 不受欢迎
♦ **go for** (*attack*) xíjī 袭击; (*like*) xǐhuān 喜欢
♦ **go in** (*to room, house*) jìnqù 进去; (*of sun*) yǐnmò 隐没; (*fit: of part etc*) ān 安
♦ **go in for** *competition, race* cánjiā 参加; (*like, take part in*) kù'ài 酷爱
♦ **go off 1** *v/i* (*leave*) líkāi 离开; (*of bomb*) bàozhà 爆炸; (*of gun*) zǒuhuǒ 走火; (*of alarm*) xiǎngqǐ 响起; (*of milk etc*) huàile 坏了 **2** *v/t* (*stop liking*) bú zài xǐhuān 不再喜欢
♦ **go on** (*continue*) jìxù 继续; (*happen*) fāshēng 发生; **what's going on?** fāshēng shénme shì le? 发生什么事了?; **~, do it!** (*encouraging*) zuò ba! 做吧!
♦ **go on at** (*nag*) láodao 唠叨
♦ **go out** (*of person*) chūqù 出去;

(*of light, fire*) xīmiè 熄灭
♦ **go over** *v/t* (*check*) zǐxì jiǎnchá 仔细检查; (*do again*) zài guò yíbiàn 再过一遍
♦ **go through** *v/t illness, hard times* jīnglì 经历; (*check*) jiǎnchá 检查; (*read through*) liúlǎn 浏览
♦ **go under** (*sink*) chénmò 沉没; (*of company*) pòchǎn 破产
♦ **go up** (*climb*) shàngqù 上去; *mountain* pāndēng 攀登; (*of prices*) shàngzhǎng 上涨
♦ **go without 1** *v/t food etc* méiyǒu yě xíng 没有也行 **2** *v/i* rěnshòu méiyǒu 忍受没有
**goad** *v/t* cìjī 刺激
**go-ahead 1** *n* xǔkě 许可; **get the ~** dédào xǔkě 得到许可 **2** *adj* (*enterprising, dynamic*) yǒujìnqǔxīn 有进取心
**goal** (*sport: target*) mùbiāo 目标; (*sport: point*) bǐfēn 比分; (*objective*) mùbiāo 目标
**goalkeeper** shǒuményuán 守门员
**goalpost** ménzhù 门柱
**goat** shānyáng 山羊
♦ **gobble up** lángtūnhǔyàn 狼吞虎咽
**go-between** zhōngjiānrén 中间人
**Gobi Desert** ⇩ Gēbìtān 戈壁滩
**god** shén 神; **thank God!** xiètiānxièdì! 谢天谢地!; **oh God!** tiānna! 天哪!
**goddess** nǚshén 女神
**godfather** (*in mafia*) bāngtóu 帮头
**godforsaken** *place, town* dǎoméi 倒霉
**goggles** hùmùjìng 护目镜
**going** *adj price etc* xiànxíng 现行; **~ concern** xīngwàng de qǐyè 兴旺的企业
**goings-on** fāshēng de shìqíng 发生的事情
**gold 1** *n* huángjīn 黄金; (*~ medal*) jīnpái 金牌 **2** *adj* jīn 金
**golden** *sky, hair* jīnsè 金色; **~ handshake** wèiláojīn 慰劳金; **~ wedding anniversary** jīnhūn jìniàn 金婚纪念
**goldfish** jīnyú 金鱼
**goldsmith** jīnshǒushìshāng 金首

饰商

golf gāo'ěrfū 高尔夫

golf club (organization) gāo'ěrfū jùlèbù 高尔夫俱乐部; (stick) gāo'ěrfū qiúgùn 高尔夫球棍

golf course gāo'ěrfū qiúchǎng 高尔夫球场

golfer dǎ gāo'ěrfūqiúde ren 打高尔夫球的人

gong luó 锣; (in wrestling) mínglúo lìng 鸣锣令

good person, weather, movie, news, child hǎo 好; food hǎochī 好吃; a ~ many xǔduō 许多; be ~ at ... shànyú ... 善于 ...; be ~ for X duì X yǒuyǐng 对X有用

goodbye zàijiàn 再见; say ~ to X, wish X ~ gàobié X 告别X

good-for-nothing n méiyòng de rén 没用的人; Good Friday Fùhuójié Xīngqīwǔ 复活节星期五; good-humored xīnqínghǎo 心情好; good-looking woman, man hǎokàn 好看; good-natured píqi hǎo 脾气好

goodness (moral) shànxíng 善行; (of fruit etc) jīnghuá 精华; thank ~! xiètiānxièdì! 谢天谢地！

goods COM shāngpǐn 商品

goodwill yǒuhǎo 友好

goody-goody n chǎnmèi zhě 谄媚者

gooey nián 粘

goof v/i F nòngzāole 弄糟了

goose é 鹅

gooseberry cùlì 醋栗

gooseflesh jīpí gēda 鸡皮疙瘩

gorge 1 n xiágǔ 峡谷 2 v/t: ~ oneself on ... dàchī ... 大吃 ...

gorgeous weather fēnghé rìlì 风和日丽; dress, woman, hair piàoliang 漂亮; smell hěn xiāng 很香

gorilla dàxīngxing 大猩猩

go-slow dàigōng 怠工

Gospel (in Bible) Fúyīn 福音

gossip 1 n liúyán fēiyǔ 流言蜚语; (person) chángshé 长舌 2 v/i xiánliáo 闲聊

govern zhìlǐ 治理

government zhèngfǔ 政府

governor zhōuzhǎng 州长

gown (long dress) chángfú 长服; (wedding dress) jiéhūn lǐfú 结婚礼服; (of academic, judge, priest) lǐfúshì chángpáo 礼服式长袍; (of surgeon) dàguà 大褂

grab v/t zhuāzhù 抓住; ~ some food suíbiàn chīxiē kuàicān 随便吃些快餐; ~ some sleep xiǎoshuì 小睡

grace yōuměi 优美

graceful yōuyǎ 优雅

gracious person réncí 仁慈; style, living yǎzhì 雅致

grade 1 n (quality) děngjí 等级; EDU niánjí 年级 2 v/t gěi ... fēnlèi 给 ... 分类

grade crossing píngmiàn jiāochā 平面交叉

gradient xiépō 斜坡

gradual zhújiàn 逐渐

gradually zhújiàn 逐渐

graduate n bìyèshēng 毕业生

graduation bìyè 毕业

graffiti húluàn túmǒ 胡乱涂抹

graft n BOT jiàjiē 嫁接; MED yízhí 移植; F (hard work) xīnkǔ de huór 辛苦的活儿

grain lì 粒; (in wood) mùwén 木纹; go against the ~ gégé bú rù 格格不入

gram kè 克

grammar yǔfǎ 语法

grammatical héhū yǔfǎ 合乎语法

grand 1 adj zhuàngguān 壮观; F (very good) hǎojíle 好极了 2 n F ($1000) yìqiān 一千

grandad (paternal) yéye 爷爷; (maternal) wàigōng 外公

grandchild (son's son) sūnzi 孙子; (son's daughter) sūnnǚ 孙女; (daughter's son) wàisūnzi 外孙子; (daughter's daughter) wàisūnnǚ 外孙女

Grand Canal Dàyùnhé 大运河

granddaughter (son's daughter) sūnnǚ 孙女; (daughter's daughter) wàisūnnǚ 外孙女

grandeur hóngwěi 宏伟

grandfather (paternal) zǔfù 祖父; (maternal) wàizǔfù 外祖父;

grandma (*paternal*) nǎinai 奶奶; (*maternal*) lǎolao 姥姥; **grandmother** (*paternal*) zǔmǔ 祖母; (*maternal*) wàizǔmǔ 外祖母; **grandpa** (*paternal*) yéye 爷爷; (*maternal*) wàigōng 外公; **grandparents** (*paternal*) zǔfùmǔ 祖父母; (*maternal*) wàizǔfùmǔ 外祖父母; **grand piano** dàgāngqín 大钢琴; **grandson** (*son's son*) sūnzi 孙子; (*daughter's son*) wàisūnzi 外孙子; **grandstand** zhèngmiàn kàntái 正面看台

**granite** huāgāngshí 花岗石

**granny** (*paternal*) nǎinai 奶奶; (*maternal*) wàipó 外婆

**grant 1** *n money* bōkuǎn 拨款; (*money: for university, school*) zhùxuéjīn 助学金 **2** *v/t wish, peace* shòuyǔ 授予; *visa* zhǔnyǔ 准予; *request* tóngyì 同意; *take X for ~ed* (*assume to be true*) rènwéi X lǐ suǒ dāngrán 认为 X 理所当然; (*not appreciate fully*) bú gòu zhēnshì X 不够珍视 X

**granulated sugar** shātáng 砂糖

**granule** n xìlì 细粒

**grape** pútao 葡萄

**grapefruit** pútaoyòu 葡萄柚

**grapefruit juice** pútaoyòuzhī 葡萄柚汁; **grapevine**: *hear X through the ~* xiǎodào tīngláide X 小道听来的 X

**graph** túbiǎo 图表

**graphic 1** *adj description etc* shēngdòng 生动 **2** *n* COMPUT túxíng 图形

**graphics** COMPUT túxíngxué 图形学

**graphics card** COMPUT túxíngkǎ 图形卡

**graphics controller** COMPUT túxíng kòngzhìqì 图形控制器

♦ **grapple with** *attacker* yǔ ... gédòu 与 ... 格斗; *problem etc* jìnlì jiějué 尽力解决

**grasp 1** *n* (*physical*) zhuā 抓; (*mental*) zhǎngwò 掌握 **2** *v/t* (*physically*) zhuāzhù 抓住; (*understand*) lǐjiě 理解

**grass** cǎo 草

**grasshopper** zhàměng 蚱蜢;

**grasslands** cǎoyuán 草原;

**grass widow** yǔ zhàngfu chángqī fēnjū de nǚzi 与丈夫长期分居的女子

**grassy** duōcǎo 多草

**grate**[1] *n* (*metal*) lúgé 炉格

**grate**[2] **1** *v/t* (*in cooking*) mósuì 磨碎 **2** *v/i* (*of sounds*) cāxiǎng 擦响

**grateful** gǎnjī 感激; *be ~ to X* X xīncún gǎnjī 对 X 心存感激

**grater** cāzi 擦子

**gratification** mǎnzú 满足

**gratify** shǐmǎnzú 使满足

**grating 1** *n* (*on drain etc*) gé gé 格格 **2** *adj sound, voice* cì'ěr 刺耳

**gratitude** gǎn'ēn 感恩

**gratuity** xiǎofèi 小费

**grave**[1] *n* fénmù 坟墓

**grave**[2] *adj error* yánzhòng 严重; *face, voice* zhuāngzhòng 庄重

**gravel** n lìshí 砾石

**gravestone** mùbēi 墓碑

**graveyard** mùdì 墓地

**gravity** PHYS zhònglì 重力

**gravy** ròuzhī 肉汁

**gray** *adj* huīsè 灰色; *he / his hair is going ~* tóufa báile 头发白了

**gray-haired** tóufa huābái 头发花白

**graze**[1] *v/i* (*of cow, horse*) chīcǎo 吃草

**graze**[2] **1** *v/t arm etc* cāshāng 擦伤 **2** *n* mùcǎo 牧草

**grease** yóu 油

**greasy** *food* yóuzhī guòduō 油脂过多; *hair, skin, hands, plate* yóunì 油腻

**great** *mistake, misunderstanding, disappointment* hěndà 很大; *open space* guǎngkuò 广阔; *sum of money* dàliàng 大量; (*major: composer, writer*) wěidà 伟大; (*very good*) hěnbàng 很棒; *~ to see you!* jiàndào nǐ zhēn gāoxìng! 见到你真高兴!

**great-grandfather** (*paternal*) zēngzǔfù 曾祖父; (*maternal*) zēngwàizǔfù 曾外祖父; **great-grandmother** (*paternal*) zēngzǔmǔ 曾祖母; (*maternal*)

zēngwàizǔmǔ 曾 外 祖 母; **Great Hall of the People** Rénmín Dàhuìtáng 人民大会堂; **Great Leap Forward** Dàyuèjìn 大跃进
**greatly** fēicháng 非常
**greatness** wěidà 伟大
**Great Wall (of China)** (Wànlǐ) Chángchéng (万里) 长城
**greed** tānxīn 贪心
**greedy** tānlán 贪婪
**green** lǜsè 绿色; (*environmentally*) lǜsè 绿色
**greengrocer** shūcài shuǐguǒ shāng 蔬菜水果商; **greenhorn** shēngshǒu 生手; **greenhouse** wēnshì 温室; **greenhouse effect** wēnshì xiàoyìng 温室效应; **greenhouse gas** wēnshì qìtǐ 温室气体; **green tea** lǜchá 绿茶
**greet** yíngjiē 迎接
**greeting** wènhòu 问候
**grenade** shǒuliúdàn 手榴弹
**grid** wǎng 网
**gridiron** SP měishì zúqiúchǎng 美式足球场
**gridlock** (*in traffic*) jiāotōng dǔsè 交通堵塞
**grief** bēishāng 悲伤
**grievance** láosāo 牢骚
**grieve** bēitòng 悲痛; *~ for X* āidào X 哀悼 X
**grill 1** *n* (*for cooking*) kǎojià 烤架; (*window*) gézi 格子 **2** *v/t food* kǎo 烤; (*interrogate*) yánlì pánwèn 严厉盘问
**grille** gézi 格子
**grim** kèbù 可怖
**grimace** *n* guàixiàng 怪相
**grime** chéngòu 尘垢
**grimy** āngzāng 肮脏
**grin 1** *n* lièzuǐ 咧嘴 **2** *v/i* lòuchǐ'ěrxiào 露齿而笑
**grind** *v/t coffee, meat* niǎnsuì 碾碎
**grip 1** *n* (*on rope etc*) jǐnwò 紧握; *be losing one's ~* (*losing one's skills*) sàngshī néngli 丧失能力 **2** *v/t* zhuāzhù 抓住
**gristle** ruǎngǔ 软骨
**grit** *n* (*dirt*) cūshā 粗砂; (*for roads*) shāli 砂砾

**groan 1** *n* shēnyínshēng 呻吟声 **2** *v/i* shēnyín 呻吟
**grocer** záhuòshāng 杂货商
**groceries** záhuò 杂货
**grocery store** záhuòdiàn 杂货店
**groin** fùgǔgōu 腹股沟
**groom 1** *n* (*for bride*) xīnláng 新郎; (*for horse*) mǎfū 马夫 **2** *v/t horse* shuā 刷; (*train, prepare*) péixùn 培训; *well ~ed* (*in appearance*) xiūshì de hǎo 修饰得好
**groove** cáo 槽
**grope 1** *v/i* (*in the dark*) ànzhōng mōsuǒ 暗中摸索 **2** *v/t* (*sexually*) mōsuǒ 摸索
♦ **grope for** *door handle, the right word* xúnzhǎo 寻找
**gross** *adj* (*coarse, vulgar*) cūsú 粗俗; (*exaggeration*) shízú 十足; FIN zǒng 总; *~ domestic product* guónèi shēngchǎn zǒngzhí 国内生产总值; *~ national product* guómín shēngchǎn zǒngzhí 国民生产总值
**ground 1** *n* dìmiàn 地面; (*reason*) lǐyóu 理由; ELEC dìxiàn 地线; *on the ~* zài dìshang 在地上 **2** *v/t* ELEC shǐjiēdì 使接地
**ground control** dìmiàn kòngzhì 地面控制
**ground crew** dìqín rényuán 地勤人员
**groundless** wúgēnjù 无根据
**ground meat** suìròu 碎肉; **groundnut** luòhuāshēng 落花生; **ground plan** píngmiàntú 平面图; **ground staff** SP qiúchǎng guǎnlǐyuán 球场管理员; (*at airport*) dìqín rényuán 地勤人员; **groundwork** jīchǔ gōngzuò 基础工作
**group 1** *n* zǔ 组; *divide ... into ~s* bǎ ... fēnzǔ 把 ... 分组 **2** *v/t* (*put together*) zǔhé 组合; (*classify*) fēnlèi 分类
**grow** *v/i* (*of child, animal*) chéngzhǎng 成长; (*of plants*) shēngzhǎng 生长; (*of hair, beard*) liú 留; (*of number, amount*) zēngzhǎng 增长; (*of business*)

fāzhǎn 发展; ~ *old*/~ *tired* (become) lǎo le/lèi le 老了/累了 **2** v/t *flowers* zhòngzhí 种植

♦**grow up** (*of person*) zhǎngdà 长大; (*of city etc*) kuòdà 扩大; ~*!* bié xiàng háizi sìde! 别象孩子似的！

**growl 1** n páoxiàoshēng 咆哮声 **2** v/i páoxiào 咆哮

**grown-up 1** n chéngrén 成人 **2** adj chéngshú 成熟

**growth** (*of person*) chéngzhǎng 成长; (*of company*) fāzhǎn 发展; (*increase*) zēngzhǎng 增长; MED liú 瘤

**grub** (*of insect*) qícáo 蛴螬

**grubby** wūhuì 污秽

**grudge 1** n yuànhèn 怨恨; *bear a* ~ jìhèn 记恨 **2** v/t: ~ *a person* ... dùjì mǒurén de ... 妒忌某人的 ...

**grudging** miǎnqiǎng 勉强

**grueling** *climb, task* shǐ rén jīnpílìjìn 使人筋疲力尽

**gruff** cūbào 粗暴

**grumble** bàoyuàn 抱怨

**grumbler** ài fā láosāo de rén 爱发牢骚的人

**grunt 1** n hūlūshēng 呼噜声 **2** v/i zuò hūlūshēng 作呼噜声

**guarantee 1** n bǎozhèng 保证; ~ *period* bǎozhèngqī 保证期 **2** v/t dānbǎo 担保

**guarantor** dānbǎorén 担保人

**guard 1** n (*security* ~) jǐngwèi 警卫; MIL wèibīng 卫兵; (*in prison*) kānshǒu zhě 看守; *be on one's* ~ *against* dīfang tífáng 提防 **2** v/t shǒuwèi 守卫

♦**guard against** fángzhǐ 防止

**guarded** *reply* xiǎoxīn jǐnshèn 小心谨慎

**guardian** LAW jiānhùrén 监护人

**guerrilla** yóujīduì 游击队

**guess 1** n cāicè 猜测 **2** v/t *answer* cāixiǎng 猜想; *I* ~ *so*/*not* kěnéng kěnéng 可能/可能 **3** v/i cāi 猜

**guesswork** tuīcè 推测

**guest** kèrén 客人

**guesthouse** zhāodàisuǒ 招待所

**guestroom** kèfáng 客房

**guffaw** n & v/i kuángxiào 狂笑

**guidance** zhǐdǎo 指导

**guide 1** n (*person*) dǎoyóu 导游; (*book*) zhǐnán 指南 **2** v/t xiàngdǎo 向导

**guidebook** zhǐnán 指南

**guided missile** dǎodàn 导弹

**guided tour** (*in museum, art gallery*) yǒu dǎoyóu de cānguān 有导游的参观

**guidelines** fāngzhēn 方针

**guilt** (*legal, moral*) yǒukuì 有愧; (*guilty feeling*) nèijiù 内疚

**guilty** LAW yǒuzuì 有罪; (*responsible*) chéngdān zérèn 承担责任; *smile* nèijiù 内疚; *have a* ~ *conscience* wèn xīn yǒu kuì 问心有愧

**guinea pig** túnshǔ 豚鼠; *fig* gòng shìyàn yòng de rén 供试验用的人

**guitar** jítā 吉他

**guitarist** tán jítā de rén 弹吉他的人

**gulf** hǎiwān 海湾; *fig* fēnqí 分歧

**gull** ōu 鸥

**gullet** yānhóu 咽喉

**gullible** yì shòupiàn 易受骗

**gulp 1** n (*of water etc*) tūnyàn 吞咽 **2** v/i (*in surprise*) chījīng 吃惊

♦**gulp down** *drink* yìyǐn ér jìn 一饮而尽; *breakfast, food* lángtūnhǔyàn 狼吞虎咽

**gum**[1] (*in mouth*) chǐyín 齿龈

**gum**[2] n (*glue*) shùjiāo 树胶; (*chewing* ~) kǒuxiāngtáng 口香糖

**gun** qiāng 枪

♦**gun down** qiāngdǎ 枪打

**gun fire** pàohuǒ 炮火; **gunman** (*robber*) chíqiāng dǎitú 持枪歹徒; **gunshot** shèjī 射击; **gunshot wound** qiāngshāng 枪伤

**gurgle** v/i (*of baby*) gēgē de xiào 咯咯地笑; (*of drain*) gǔgǔ de liú 汨汨地流

**gush** v/i (*of liquid*) yǒngchū 涌出

**gushy** F (*very enthusiastic*) guòfèn duōqíng 过分多情

**gust** zhènfēng 阵风

**gusty** *weather* fēngdà 风大; ~ *wind* dàfēng 大风

**gut 1** *n* nèizàng 内脏；F (*stomach*)
dùzi 肚子；**-s** F (*courage*)
dǎnliàng 胆量 **2** *v/t* (*of fire*)
huǐhuài ... de nèibù 毁坏 ... 的内
部

**gutter** (*on sidewalk*) yáncáo 檐槽；
(*on roof*) tiāngōu 天沟

**guy** F jiāhuo 家伙；*hey, you ~s*
hèi, nǐmen 嘿，你们

**gym** (*sports club*) tǐyùguǎn 体育

馆；(*in school*) yùndòngshì 运动
室

**gym shoes** yùndòngxié 运动鞋
**gymnasium** tǐyùguǎn 体育馆；(*in
school*) yùndòngshì 运动室
**gymnast** tǐcāojiā 体操家
**gymnastics** tǐcāo 体操
**gynecologist** fùkē yīshēng 妇科医
生
**gypsy** jípǔsàiren 吉普赛人

# H

habit xíguàn 习惯
habitable shìyú jūzhù 适于居住
habitat qīxīdì 栖息地
habitual guàncháng 惯常; *smoker,*
*drinker* jīngcháng 经常
hack n *poor writer* wénqǐ 文乞
hacker COMPUT hēikè 黑客
hackneyed chénfǔ 陈腐
haddock hēixiànxuě 黑线鳕
haggard qiáocuì 憔悴
haggle tǎojià huánjià 讨价还价
hail n bīngbáo 冰雹
hailstorm báobào 雹暴
Hainan Island Hǎinán Dǎo 海南
岛
hair tóufa 头发; *(on body, animal)*
máo 毛
hairbrush shūzi 梳子; haircut lǐfà
理发; hairdo fàshì 发式; hairdresser lǐfàshī 理发师; *at the ~*
zài lǐfàdiàn 在理发店; hairdrier,
hairdryer chuīfēngqì 吹风器
hairless wúmáo 无毛
hairpin fàjiā 发夹; hairpin curve
jízhuǎnwān 急转弯; hair-raising
máogǔ sǒngrán 毛骨悚然; hair
remover chúmáojì 除毛剂; hair-
splitting n wúyì ěr suǒsuì de fēnxī
无益而琐碎的分析; hairstyle
fàxíng 发型
hairy *arm, animal* duōmáo 多毛; F
*(frightening)* jí rén 急人
half 1 n yíbàn 一半; *~ past ten, ~*
*after ten* shídiǎnbàn 十点半; *~*
*an hour* bànge xiǎoshí 半个小
时; *~ a pound* bànbàng 半磅
2 adj bàn 半 3 adv yíbàn 一半
half-hearted sānxīn'èryì 三心二
意; half term xuéqī zhōngxiū 学
期中休; half time 1 n SP
bànchǎng 半场 2 adj: *~ job* bànrì
gōngzuò 半日工作; halfway
1 adj *stage, point* bàntú 半途 2 adv
zhōngjiān 中间; *the bookstore is*

*~ down Zhongshan Avenue*
shūdiàn zài Zhōngshān dàjiē de
zhōngjiān shūdiàn zài Zhōngshān dàjiē de
中间;
hall *(large room)* dàtīng 大厅;
*(hallway in house)* zǒuláng 走廊
halo guānghuán 光环
halt 1 v/i tíngzhǐ 停止 2 v/t zhìzhù
止住 3 n: *come to a ~* tíngzhǐ bù
qián 停滞不前
halve v/t fēnchéng liǎngbàn 分成
两半
ham huǒtuǐ 火腿
hamburger ⇩ hànbǎobāo 汉堡包
hammer 1 n chuízi 锤子 2 v/i
chuídǎ 锤打; *~ at the door* zámén
砸门
hammock diàochuáng 吊床
hamper[1] n *(for food)* fànkuāng 饭
筐
hamper[2] v/t *(obstruct)* zǔ'ài 阻碍
hamster cāngshǔ 仓鼠
Han Hàn 汉; *(nationality)* Hànzú 汉
族
Han Dynasty Hàncháo 汉朝
hand 1 n shǒu 手; *(of clock)* zhēn
针; *(worker)* gōngrén 工人; *at ~,*
*to ~* zài shēnbiān 在身边; *at first*
*~* dìyīshǒu 第一手; *by ~* write
yòngshǒu 用手; *deliver* zhuānrén
专人; *on the one ~ ..., on the*
*other ...* yìfāngmiàn ...
lìngyìfāngmiàn ... 一方面 ... 另
一方面 ...; *in ~ (being done)* zài
chǔlǐ zhōng 在处理中; *on your*
*right ~* yòumiàn 右面; *~s off!* bié
pèng! 别碰! ; *~s up!* jǔqǐshǒulái!
举起手来! ; *change ~s*
zhuǎnshǒu 转手
♦ hand down chuánxiàlái 传下来
♦ hand in jiāochū 交出
♦ hand on chuánxiàqù 传下去
♦ hand out fēnfā 分发
♦ hand over yíjiāo 移交; *to*

*authorities* shàngjiāo 上交

**handbag** *Br* shǒutíbāo 手提包; **handbook** shǒucè 手册; **handbrake** *Br* shǒuzhá 手轧; **handcuffs** shǒukào 手铐

**handicap** *n* zhàng'ài 障碍

**handicapped** (*physically*) cánjí 残疾; *~ by lack of funds* yóuyú zījīn ér shòuzǔ 而受阻

**handicraft** shǒugōngyì 手工艺

**handiwork** shǒugōng 手工

**handkerchief** shǒujuàn 手绢

**handle 1** *n* bǎshou 把手 **2** *v/t goods* bānyùn 搬运; *case, deal* chǔlǐ 处理; *difficult person* duìfu 对付; *let me ~ this* wǒ lái chǔlǐ ba 我来处理吧

**handlebars** chēbǎ 车把

**hand luggage** shǒutí xínglǐ 手提行李; **handmade** shǒugōng zhìzuò 手工制作; **handrail** fúshǒu 扶手; **handshake** wòshǒu 握手

**hands-off** bùgānshè 不干涉

**handsome** shuài 帅

**hands-on** qīnzì dòngshǒu 亲自动手

**handwriting** zì字

**handwritten** shǒuxiě 手写

**handy** *tool, device* fāngbiàn 方便; *it might come in ~* yěxǔ huì yǒuyòng 也许会有用

**hang 1** *v/t picture* guà 挂; *person* diàosǐ 吊死 **2** *v/i* (*of dress, hair*) chuíxià 垂下 **3** *n*: *get the ~ of X* zhǎodào X de qiàomén 找到X的窍门

♦**hang around** xiánguàng 闲逛

♦**hang on** (*wait*) děngděng 等等

♦**hang on to** (*keep*) bǎoliú 保留

♦**hang up** TELEC guàduàn 挂断

**hangar** fēijīkù 飞机库

**hanger** *for clothes* yīfújià 衣服架

**hang glider** (*person*) xuánguà shì huáxiáng zhě 悬挂式滑翔者; (*device*) xuánguà shì huáxiángjī 悬挂式滑翔机

**hang gliding** xuánguà shì huáxiáng yùndòng 悬挂式滑翔运动

**hangover** (*jiǔhòu*) tóutòng (酒后)头痛

♦**hanker after** kěwàngyǒu 渴望有

**hankie, hanky** F shǒujuàn 手绢

**haphazard** ǒuránxìng 偶然性

**happen** fāshēng 发生; *if you ~ to see him* rúguǒ nǐ pèngqiǎo jiàndào tā 如果你碰巧见到他; *what has ~ed to you?* nǐ zěnme le? 你怎么了?

♦**happen across** ǒurán fāxiàn 偶然发现

**happening** shìjiàn 事件

**happily** gāoxìng 高兴; (*luckily*) xìngyùn 幸运

**happiness** xìngfú 幸福

**happy** kuàilè 快乐

**happy-go-lucky** wúyōuwúlǜ 无忧无虑

**happy hour** kuàilè shíjiān 快乐时间

**harass** sāorǎo 骚扰

**harassed** jiāozào 焦躁

**harassment** sāorǎo 骚扰; *sexual ~* xìngsāorǎo 性骚扰

**harbor 1** *n* gǎngwān 港湾 **2** *v/t criminal* bāobì 包庇; *grudge* huáiyuàn 怀有

**hard** yìng 硬; (*difficult*) nán 难; *facts, evidence* bùrónghuáiyí 不容怀疑; *~ of hearing* zhòngtīng 重听

**hardback** yìngpíshū 硬皮书; **hard-boiled** *egg* zhǔ de lǎo 煮得老; **hard copy** dǎyìn wénběn 打印文本; **hard core** POL zhōngjiān fènzǐ 中兼分子; **hard currency** ⇩ yìngtōnghuò 硬通货; **hard disk** ⇩ yìngpán 硬盘

**harden 1** *v/t* shǐbiànyìng 使变硬 **2** *v/i* (*glue*) biànyìng 变硬; (*attitude*) mánhèng 蛮横

**hardheaded** jiǎng shíjì 讲实际

**hardliner** qiángyìng lùxiàn zhě 强硬路线者

**hardly** jīhūbù 几乎不

**hardness** yìngdù 硬度; (*difficulty*) nándù 难度

**hard seat** (*on train*) yìngzuò 硬座

**hardsell** yìngxíng tuīxiāo 硬行推销

**hardship** jiānnán 艰难

**hard sleeper** (*on train*) yìngwò 硬卧；**hard up** quēqián 缺钱

**hardware** jīnshǔ qìjù 金属器具；COMPUT yìngjiàn 硬件；**hardware store** wǔjīn shāngdiàn 五金商店；**hard-working** qínmiǎn 勤勉

**hardy** qiángzhuàng 强壮

**hare** yětù 野兔

**harm 1** *n* sǔnhài 损害；*it wouldn't do any ~ to …* … méi shénme huàichù … 没什么坏处 **2** *v/t* sǔnhài 损害

**harmful** yǒuhài 有害

**harmless** wúhài 无害

**harmonious** héxié 和谐

**harmonize** shǐ héxié 使和谐

**harmony** MUS héshēng 和声；(*in relationship etc*) xiétiáo 协调

**harp** shùqín 竖琴

♦**harp on about** F xùdao 絮叨

**harpoon** *n* yúchā 鱼叉

**harsh** jiānkè 尖刻

**harvest** *n* shōuhuò 收获

**hash**: *make a ~ of X* F bǎ X nòngzāo 把X弄糟

**hash browns** shǔtiáo 薯条

**hashish** dàmá 大麻

**haste** cāngcù 仓促

**hasty** cǎoshuài 草率

**hat** màozi 帽子

**hatch** *n* (*for serving food*) chuāngkǒu 窗口；(*on ship*) cāngkǒu 舱口

♦**hatch out** (*of eggs*) fūchū 孵出

**hatchet** duǎnbǐng xiǎofǔ 短柄小斧

**hate** *n* & *v/t* zēnghèn 憎恨

**hatred** zēnghèn 憎恨

**haughty** àomàn 傲慢

**haul 1** *n*: *a ~ of fish* yīwǎngyú 一网鱼 **2** *v/t* (*pull*) tuōyè 托曳

**haulage** tuōyùn 托运

**haulage company** tuōyùn gōngsī 托运公司

**haulier** tuōyùn gōngsī 托运公司

**haunch** tuǐtúnbù 腿臀部

**haunt 1** *v/t* chángqù 常到；*this place is ~ed* zhè dìfang nàoguǐ 这地方闹鬼 **2** *n* cháng qù de dìfang 常去的地方

**haunting** *tune* yíngrào yú xīn 萦绕于心

**have** ◊ (*own*) yǒu 有；*I ~ three tickets* wǒ yǒu sānzhāng piào 我有三张票 ◊ *breakfast, lunch* chī 吃 ◊: *can I ~ a cup of coffee?* qǐng gěiwǒ yìbēi kāfēi? 请给我一杯咖啡?；*can I ~ more time?* qǐng zài gěiwǒ yìxiē shíjiān? 请再给我一些时间?；*do you ~ … ?* nǐ yǒu … ma? 你有 … 吗？◊ (*must*): ~ (*got*) *to* bìxū 必须 *I have to study* / *see him* wǒ bìxū xuéxí/kàn tā 我必须学习/看他；◊ (*causative*): *I had my hair cut* wǒ bǎ tóufa jiǎnle 我把头发剪了；*I'll ~ the car repaired* wǒ yào bǎ chē xiūle 我要把车修了 ◊ (*past tense*): *I ~ eaten* wǒ chīguò le 我吃过了；*~ you seen her?* nǐ jiàndào tā le ma? 你见到她了吗？

♦**have back**: *when can I have it back?* shénme shíhou huángěi wǒ? 什么时候还给我?；*it's good to have you back* nǐ huíláile zhēnhǎo 你回来了真好

♦**have on** (*wear*) chuān 穿；(*have planned*) yǒu shì 有事；*do you have anything on for tonight?* nǐ jīnwǎn yǒushì ma? 你今晚有事吗？

**haven** *fig* bìnànsuǒ 避难所

**havoc** hàojié 浩劫；*play ~ with X* jiāng X gǎodé yìtuán zāo 将X搞得一团糟

**haw** (*berry*) shānzhā 山楂

**hawk** yīngsǔn 鹰隼；*fig* qiángyìng pài rénwù 强硬派人物

**hay** gāncǎo 干草

**hay fever** huāfěnrè 花粉热

**hazard** *n* wēixiǎn 危险

**hazard lights** MOT xiǎnqíng zhíshìdēng 险情指示灯

**hazardous** màoxiǎn 冒险

**haze** bówù 薄雾

**hazel** (*tree*) zhēn 榛

**hazelnut** zhēnzi 榛子

**hazy** *view, image* wùméngméng 雾蒙蒙；*memories* móhu 模糊；*I'm a bit ~ about it* wǒ duìcǐ bú tài qīngchǔ 我对此不太清楚

he tā 他

head **1** n tóu 头; (boss, leader) lǐng-dǎo 领导; (of school) xiàozhǎng 校长; (on beer) pàomò 泡沫; (of nail) dīngmào 钉帽; (of queue, line) qiánmiàn 前面; **$15 a ~** měikè shíwǔ měiyuán 每客十五美元; **~s or tails?** zhèngmiàn hái-shì fǎnmiàn? 正面还是反面? ; **at the ~ of the list** míngdān shang dìyīwèi 名单上第一位; **~ over heels** fall tóu cháoxià 头朝下; **fall in love** shēnshēn 深深; **lose one's ~** (go crazy) fāfēng 发疯 **2** v/t (lead) lǐngdǎo 领导; **ball** yòng tóu dǐng 用头顶

headache tóutòng 头痛

header (in soccer) dǐngqiú 顶球; (in document) tóulán 头栏

headhunter COM wùsè réncái de rén 物色人才的人

heading (in list) biāotí 标题

headlamp qiándēng 前灯; head-light qiándēng 前灯; headline (in newspaper) dàzì biāotí 大字标题; **make the ~s** chéngwéi tóutiáo xīnwén 成为头条新闻; head-long adv fall tóu xiàng qián 头向前; headmaster xiàozhǎng 校长; headmistress xiàozhǎng 校长; head office (of company) zǒngbù 总部; head-on adv & adj crash tóudǐngtóu 头顶头; head-phones ěrjī 耳机; headquarters zǒng zhǐhuībù 总指挥部; headrest tóukào 头靠; head-room for vehicle under bridge jìngkōng gāodù 净空高度; in car tóushang kōngjiān 头上空间; headscarf tóujīn 头巾; head-strong rènxìng 任性; head teacher xiàozhǎng 校长; head waiter fúwùyuán zhǎng 服务员长; headwind nìfēng 逆风

heady drink, wine etc yìzuì 易醉

heal v/t & v/i yùhé 愈合

health jiànkāng 健康; **your ~!** zhù nǐ jiànkāng! 祝你健康!

health club jiànshēn jùlèbù 健身俱乐部; health food jiànkāng shípǐn 健康食品; **~ store**

jiànkāng shípǐndiàn 健康食品店; health insurance jiànkāng bǎoxiǎn 健康保险; health re-sort liáoyǎngdì 疗养地

healthy person jiànkāng 健康; food, lifestyle yǒuyì jiànkāng 有益健康; economy zhuàngdà 壮大

heap n duī 堆

♦heap up v/t duījī 堆积

hear tīngjiàn 听见

♦hear about tīngdào 听到

♦hear from (have news from) dédào xiāoxi 得到消息

hearing tīnglì 听力; LAW shěnxùn 审讯; **within ~** tīngjù 听距; **out of ~** tīngbúdào 听不到

hearing aid zhùtīngqì 助听器

hearsay: **by ~** chuánwén 传闻

hearse língchē 灵车

heart xīn 心; (of problem) shízhì 实质; (of city, organization) zhōngxīn 中心; **know X by ~** shóujì X 熟记 X

heart attack xīnzàngbìng 心脏病; heartbeat xīntiào 心跳; heart-breaking lìngrén xīnsuì 令人心碎; heartburn xīnkǒu zhuórè 心口灼热; heart failure xīnlì shuāijié 心力衰竭; heartfelt sympathy fāzì nèixīn 发自内心

hearth bìlú 壁炉

heartless wúqíng 无情

heartrending plea, sight shāngxīn 伤心

hearts (in cards) hóngtáo 红桃

heart throb F ǒuxiàng 偶像

heart transplant xīnzàng yízhí 心脏移植

hearty meal fēngshèng 丰盛; person rèchén 热忱; **~ appetite** hǎo wèikǒu 好胃口

heat rè 热

♦heat up v/t jiārè 加热

heated swimming pool jiā le rè 加了热; discussion rèliè 热烈

heater fārèqì 发热器

heath huāngdì 荒地

heathen n yìjiàotú 异教徒

heating nuǎnqì 暖气

heat-resistant kàngrè 抗热; heatstroke zhòngshǔ 中暑;

heatwave rèlàng 热浪

heave v/t (lift) yònglì jùqǐ 用力举起

heaven tiāntáng 天堂; **good ~s!** tiānna! 天哪！

heavy zhòng 重; rain dà 大; traffic yōngjǐ 拥挤; accent zhòng 重; food yóunì 油腻; financial loss chénzhòng 沉重; loss of life, bleeding dàliàng 大量; **~ smoker** yān chōu de duō de rén 烟抽得多的人; **~ drinker** jiǔ hē de duō de rén 酒喝得多的人

heavy-duty jìnyòng 禁用

heavyweight SP zhòngliàngjí 重量级

heckle v/t jiéwèn 诘问

hectic mánglù 忙碌

hedge n shùlí 树篱

hedgehog cìwei 刺猬

heed: **pay ~ to** zhùyì 注意

heel (of foot) jiǎohòugēn 脚后跟; (of shoe) xiégēn 鞋跟

heel bar xiūxiébù 修鞋部

hefty zhòng 重

height gāodù 高度; (of season) shèng 盛

heighten effect, tension zēngdà 增大

heir jìchéngrén 继承人

heiress nǚ jìchéngrén 女继承人

helicopter zhíshēngfēijī 直升飞机

hell dìyù 地狱; **what the ~ are you doing / do you want?** F nǐ jiūjìng zài gàn shénme / yào shénme? 你究竟在干什么 / 要什么？; **go to ~!** F qùnǐde! 去你的！; **a ~ of a lot** F duōde bùdéliǎo 多得不得了; **he's one ~ of a nice guy** F zhèi jiāhuo zhēn búcuò 这家伙真不错

hello nǐ hǎo 你好; TELEC wéi 喂

helm NAUT duò 舵

helmet tóukuī 头盔

help n & v/t bāngzhù 帮助; **~!** jiùmìng! 救命！; **can you ~ me?** jiègè shǒu, xíngma? 借个手，行吗？; **~ oneself** (to food) suíbiàn chī 随便吃; **I can't ~ it** wǒ rěnbúzhù 我忍不住; **I couldn't ~**

laughing wǒ jīnbúzhù xiàole 我禁不住笑了

helper zhùshǒu 助手

helpful yǒu bāngzhù 有帮助

helping (of food) yìfèn 一份

helpless (unable to cope) bùnéng zìzhù 不能自助; (powerless) wúzhù 无助

help screen COMPUT jiěyí píngmù 解疑屏幕

hem n (of dress etc) zhébiān 折边

hemisphere bànqiú 半球

hemorrhage n & v/i chūxiě 出血

hemp dàmá 大麻

hen mǔjī 母鸡

henchman pej púcóng 仆从

henpecked qīguǎnyán 妻管严; **~ husband** yǒu qīguǎnyán de zhàngfu 有妻管严的丈夫

hepatitis gānyán 肝炎

her 1 adj tāde 她的; **~ ticket** tāde piào 她的票 2 pron tā 她; **I know ~** wǒ rènshi tā 我认识她; **this is for ~** zhè shì gěi tā de 这是给她的

herb yàocǎo 药草

herb(al) tea yàocǎochá 药草茶

herbal medicine cǎoyào 草药

herd n shòuqún 兽群

here zhèr 这儿; **~'s to you!** (toast) wèi nǐ gānbēi! 为你干杯！; **~ you are** (giving sth) gěi nǐ 给你; **~ we are!** (finding sth) zài zhèr! 在这儿！

hereditary disease yíchuán 遗传

heritage shìxí yíchǎn 世袭遗产

hermit jūshì 居士

hernia MED shàn 疝

hero yīngxióng 英雄

heroic yīngyǒng 英勇

heroin hǎiluòyīn 海洛因

heroine nǚyīngxióng 女英雄

heron cānglù 苍鹭

herpes MED pàozhěn 疱疹

herring fēiyú 鲱鱼

hers tāde 她的; **a friend of ~** tāde péngyǒu 她的朋友

herself tā zìjǐ 她自己; **she hurt ~** tā nòngshāngle zìjǐ 她弄伤了自己; **by ~** tā dúzì 她独自

hesitate yóuyù 犹豫

hesitation yóuyù 犹豫

heterosexual adj yìxìng'ài 异性爱

heyday quánshèngqī 全盛期

hi nǐ hǎo 你好

hibernate dōngmián 冬眠

hiccup n dǎgér 嗝儿; (minor problem) xiǎowèntí 小问题; have the ~s dǎgér 打嗝儿

hick pej F xiāngxiàlǎo 乡下佬

hick town pej F qióngxiāng pìrǎng 穷乡僻壤

hidden meaning nèihán 内涵; treasure yǐncáng 隐藏

hide¹ v/t & v/i cáng 藏

hide² n (of animal) duǒcángchù 躲藏处

hide-and-seek zhuōmícáng 捉迷藏

hideaway pìjìngchù 僻静处

hideous kěpà 可怕; crime hài rén tīngwén 骇人听闻; face chǒulòu 丑陋

hiding¹ (beating) tòngdǎ 痛打

hiding² be in ~ duǒcángzhe 躲藏着; go into ~ duǒcáng qǐlái 躲藏起来

hiding place duǒcángchù 躲藏处

hierarchy děngjí zhìdù 等级制度

hi-fi gāo bǎozhēn diànqì 高保真电器

high 1 adj building, mountain, temperature, price, note, salary, speed gāo 高; quality gāojí 高级; society shàngliú 上流; (on drugs) táozuì 陶醉; ~ wind jìnfēng 劲风; have a very ~ opinion of duì ... yǒu hěn gāo píngjià 对 ... 有很高评价; it is ~ time ... gāi shì ... de shíhou le 该是 ... 的时候了 2 n MOT gāo 高; (in statistics) gāofēng 高峰; EDU zhōngxué 中学 3 adv gāo 高; ~ in the sky gāogāo zài kōng tiáo zhe 高高在空中; that's as ~ as we can go (in offer) zhè shì wǒmen chū de zuìgāo jià 这是我们出的最高价

highbrow adj gāodiào 高调;
highchair gāojiǎoyǐ 高脚椅;
highclass gāojí 高级; high diving gāokōng tiàoshuǐ 高空跳水;
high-frequency gāopín 高频;

high-grade yōuzhì 优质; high-handed zhuānhèng 专横; high-heeled gāogēn 高跟; high jump tiàogāo 跳高; high-level gāo jiēcéng 高阶层; high life háohuádé shēnghuó fāngshì 豪华的生活方式

highlight 1 n (main event) zuìjīngcǎi chǎngmiàn 最精采场面; (in hair) rǎnsè 染色 2 v/t (with pen) yòng sèbǐ huà 用色笔划; COMPUT xuǎn 选

highlighter (pen) ⇩ cǎibǐ 彩笔

highly desirable, likely fēicháng 非常; be ~ paid xīnshuǐ gāo 薪水高; think ~ of X duì X píngjià hěn gāo 对X评价很高

high performance drill dàgōnglǜ 高效率; battery gāonéng 高能; high-pitched gāoyīndiào 高音调; high point (of life, career) dǐngfēng 顶峰; high-powered engine dàgōnglǜ 大功率; intellectual yuānbó 渊博; salesman chíyǒu yàozhí 持有要职; high pressure 1 n (weather) gāoyā 高压 2 adj TECH gāoyā 高压; salesman qiángxíng tuīxiāo 强行推销; job, lifestyle yǒu hě ndà yālì 有很大压力; high priest dà jìsī 大祭司; high school zhōngxué 中学; high society shàngliú shèhuì 上流社会; high-speed train gāosù huǒchē 高速火车; high-strung shífēn mǐngǎn 十分敏感; high tech n & adj gāoxīn jìshù 高新技术; high technology gāoxīn jìshù 高新技术; high-tension cable gāoyā 高压; high tide gāocháo 高潮; high water gāocháo 高潮; highway gōnglù 公路; high wire (in circus) gāngsīshéng 钢丝绳

hijack v/t jiéchí 劫持; ~ a plane jiéjī 劫机; ~ a bus jiéchē 劫车

hijacker (of plane) jiéjī zhě 劫机者; (of bus) jiéchē zhě 劫车者

hike¹ 1 n yuǎnzú 远足 2 v/i bùxíng 步行

hike² n (in prices) jíjù táigāo 急遽抬高

**hiker** túbù lǚxíng zhě 徒步旅行者

**hilarious** fēicháng huájī 非常滑稽

**hill** xiǎoshānpō 小山坡; (*slope*) shānpō 山坡

**hillbilly** pej F xiāngxiàrén 乡下人

**hillside** shānpō 山坡

**hilltop** xiǎoshān shāndǐng 小山山顶

**hilly** yǒu pō 有坡

**hilt** jiànbǐng 剑柄

**him** tā 他

**Himalayas** Xǐmǎlāyǎshān 喜马拉雅山

**himself** tā zìjǐ 他自己; *he hurt ~* tā nòngshāngle zìjǐ 他弄伤了自己; *by ~* tā dúzì 他独自

**hinder** zǔzhǐ 阻止

**hindrance** zhàng'ài 障碍

**hindsight** *with ~* shìhòude rènshi 事后的认识

**hinge** zhéyè 折页

**hint** (*clue*) tíshì 提示; (*piece of advice*) tíyì 提议; (*implied suggestion*) ànshì 暗示; (*of red, sadness etc*) lùwēi 略微

**hip** túnbù 臀部

**hip pocket** pìdōur 屁兜儿

**hippopotamus** hémǎ 河马

**hire** vlt zū 租

**his 1** adj tāde 他的 **2** pron tāde 他的; *a friend of ~* tāde péngyǒu 他的朋友

**Hispanic 1** adj Lādīng Měizhōu 拉丁美洲 **2** n Lādīng Měizhōu rén 拉丁美洲人

**hiss** vli (*of snake*) fā sīsī shēng 发嘶嘶声; (*of audience*) fā xūshēng 发嘘声

**historian** lìshǐxuéjiā 历史学家

**historic** yǒu lìshǐ yìyì 有历史意义

**historical** yǒuguān lìshǐ 有关历史

**history** lìshǐ 历史

**hit 1** vlt person, ball dǎ jī 打击; (*collide with*) zhuàng 撞; *he was ~ by a bullet* tā bèi zǐdàn dǎzhòng le 他被子弹打中了; *it suddenly ~ me* (*I realized*) wǒ tūrán yìshí dào 我突然意识到 **2** n (*blow*) dǎjī 打击; MUS liúxíng chàngpiàn 流

行唱片; (*success*) jùdà chénggōng 巨大成功

♦**hit back** fǎnjī 反击

♦**hit on** *idea* pèngqiǎo zhǎodào 碰巧找到

♦**hit out at** (*criticize*) pēngjī 抨击

**hit-and-run**: *~ accident* zhàoshì zhě táopǎo shìgù 肇事者逃跑事故; *~ driver* zhàoshì zhě táopǎo sījī 肇事者逃跑司机

**hitch 1** n (*problem*) wèntí 问题; *without a ~* méiyǒu wèntí 没有问题 **2** vlt shuānzhù 拴住; *~ X to Y* bǎ X shuān zài Y shang 把X拴在Y上; *~ a ride* dā biànchē 搭便车 **3** vli (*hitchhike*) miǎnfèi dāchē 免费搭车

♦**hitch up** *wagon, trailer* lā 拉

**hitchhike** miǎnfèi dāchē 免费搭车; **hitchhiker** miǎnfèi dāchē de rén 免费搭车的人; **hitchhiking** miǎnfèi dāchē 免费搭车

**hi-tech** n & adj gāoxīn jìshù 高新技术

**hitlist** hēimíngdān 黑名单; **hitman** zhíyè shāshǒu 职业杀手; **hit-or-miss** pèng yùnqì 碰运气; **hit squad** tèshū rènwù zǔzhī 特殊任务组织

**HIV** rénlèi sàngshī miǎnyìlì bìngdú 人类丧失免疫力病毒

**hive** (*for bees*) fēngfáng 蜂房

♦**hive off** vlt (COM: *separate off*) chéngwéi dāndú tuántǐ 成为单独的团体

**HIV-positive** dàiyǒu rénlèi sàngshī miǎnyìlì bìngdú 带有人类丧失免疫力病毒

**hoard 1** n mìcángde qiáncái 密藏的钱财 **2** vlt jiàocáng 窖藏

**hoarse** sīyǎ 嘶哑

**hoax** n qīpiàn 欺骗

**hobble** vli pánshān 蹒跚

**hobby** shìhào 嗜好

**hobo** liúlànghàn 流浪汉

**hockey** (*ice ~*) bīngqiú 冰球

**hog** n (*pig*) zhū 猪

**hoist 1** n qǐzhòngjī 起重机 **2** vlt (*lift*) shēngqǐ 举起; *flag* shēng 升

**hokum** (*nonsense*) fèihuà 废话; (*sentimental stuff*) sútào qíngjié 俗

套情节
**hold 1** v/t (*in hands*) ná 拿; (*support, keep in place*) zhīchí 支持; *passport, license* chíyǒu 持有; *prisoner, suspect* guānyā 关押; (*contain*) chéngyǒu 盛有; *job, post* rèn 任; *course* bǎochí 保持; ~ **one's breath** bǐngzhù hūxī 屏住呼吸; **he can ~ his drink** tā hěn néng hē 他很能喝; ~ **X responsible** shǐ X fùzé 使 X 负责; **that ... (*believe, maintain*) rènwéi ... 认为...; ~ **the line** TELEC qǐng bié guàduàn 请别挂断 **2** n (*in ship, plane*) huòcāng 货舱; **catch or take ~ of X** zhuāzhù X 抓住 X; **lose one's ~ on X** (*on rope*) zhuābúzhù X 抓不住 X

♦ **hold against**: **hold X against Y** yīn X jìhèn Y 因 X 记恨 Y

♦ **hold back 1** v/t *crowds* lánzhù 拦住; *facts, information* yǐnmán 隐瞒 **2** v/i (*not tell all*) yǐnmán 隐瞒

♦ **hold on** (*wait*, TELEC) děngyíxià 等一下; **now ~ a minute!** biézháojí! 别着急!

♦ **hold on to** (*keep*) bǎoliú 保留; *belief* jiānchí 坚持

♦ **hold out 1** v/t *hand* shēnchū 伸出; *prospect* jùyǒu 具有 **2** v/i (*of supplies*) wéichí 维持; (*trapped miners etc*) zhīchēngzhù 支撑住

♦ **hold up** v/t *hand* shēnchū 伸出; *bank etc* qiǎngjié 抢劫; (*make late*) dāngē 耽搁; **hold X up as an example** bǎ X zuò lìzi 把 X 做例子

♦ **hold with** (*approve of*) zànchéng 赞成

**holder** (*container*) hé hé 盒; (*of passport, ticket, record etc*) chíyǒu zhě 持有者

**holding company** gǔdōng gōngsī 股东公司

**holdup** (*robbery*) qiǎngjié 抢劫; (*delay*) yánwù 延误

**hole** dòng 洞

**holiday** (*single day*) xiūxīrì 休息日; (*period*) jiàqī 假期; **take a ~** xiūjià 休假

**holidaymaker** dùjiàde rén 度假的人

**Holland** Hélán 荷兰
**hollow** *object* zhōngkōng 中空; *cheeks* āoxiàn 凹陷; *promise* xūjiǎ 虚假
**holly** dōngqīng 冬青
**holocaust** dà pòhuài 大破坏
**hologram** quánxītú 全息图
**holster** yāodài tào 腰带套
**holy** shénshèng 神圣
**Holy Spirit** Shènglíng 圣灵
**Holy Week** Fùhuójié qián yìzhōu 复活节前一周
**home 1** n jiā 家; (*native country*) zǔguó 祖国; (*town, part of country*) jiāxiāng jiāxiāng 家乡; (*for old people*) lǎorényuàn 老人院; **at ~** (*in my house*) zài jiā 在家; (*in my country*) zài guónèi 在国内; SP běnyíng 本营; **make yourself at ~** bié jūshù 别拘束; **at ~ and abroad** guónèiwài 国内外; **work from ~** zài jiā gōngzuò 在家工作 **2** adv jiā 家; **go ~** huíjiā 回家; (*to own country*) huíguó 回国
**home address** jiātíng zhùzhǐ 家庭住址; **homecoming** guījiā 归家; **home computer** jiāyòng diànnǎo 家用电脑
**homeless** adj wújiā 无家; **the ~** wújiāde rén 无家的人
**homeloving** liànjiā 恋家
**homepage** COMPUT zhǔyè 主页
**homely** (*homeloving*) yǒu jiā de qìfèn 有家的气氛; (*not goodlooking*) bù piàoliang 不漂亮
**homemade** zìzhì 自制; **home match** zài běndì dǎ de bǐsài 在本地打的比赛; **home movie** jiātíng lùxiàng 家庭录像
**homeopathy** shùnshì liáofǎ 顺势疗法
**homesick**: **be ~** xiǎngjiā 想家
**home town** jiāxiāng 家乡
**homeward** adv (*to own house*) xiàng jiā zǒu 向家走; (*to own country*) xiàng běnguó zǒu 向本国走
**homework** EDU zuòyè 作业
**homeworking** COM zài jiā gōngzuò 在家工作
**homicide** (*crime*) móushā 谋杀;

(*police department*) mìng'ànbù 命案部

**homograph** tóngxíngyìyìcí 同形异义词

**homophobia** tóngxìngliàn zèngwù gǎn 同性恋憎恶感

**homosexual** *n & adj* tóngxìngliàn 同性恋

**honest** chéngshí 诚实

**honestly** shuōzhēnde 说真的; *~!* zhēnshìde! 真是的！

**honesty** chéngshí 诚实

**honey** fēngmì 蜂蜜; F (*darling*) qīn'àide 亲爱的

**honeycomb** cháopí 巢脾

**honeymoon** *n* mìyuè 蜜月

**Hong Kong** Xiānggǎng 香港; *~ handover* Xiānggǎng huíguī 香港回归

**honk** *v/t horn* àn lǎba 按喇叭

**honor 1** *n* róngyù 荣誉 **2** *v/t* gěiyǐ róngyù 给以荣誉

**honorable** guāngróng 光荣

**hood** (*over head*) dōumào 兜帽; (*over cooker*) chōu yóuyān jī 抽油烟机; MOT qìchē yǐnqíng gàizi 汽车引擎盖子; F (*gangster*) huàidàn 坏蛋

**hoodlum** ègùn 恶棍

**hoof** tízhì 蹄

**hook** (*to hang clothes on*) guàgōu 挂钩; (*for fishing*) yúgōu 鱼钩; *off the ~* TELEC bú guà diànhuà 不挂电话

**hooked**: *be ~ on X* bèi X mízhù 被X迷住; *be ~ on drugs* xīdú chéngyǐn 吸毒成瘾

**hooker** F jìnǚ 妓女

**hookey**: *play ~* táoxué 逃学

**hooligan** liúmáng 流氓

**hooliganism** liúmáng xíngwéi 流氓行为

**hoop** gū 箍

**hoot** *v/t horn* àn lǎba 按喇叭; (*of owl*) māotóuyīngjiào 猫头鹰叫

**hop²** *n* (*plant*) shémácǎo 蛇麻草

**hop³** *v/i* (*of people*) dānjiǎotiào 单脚跳; (*of animals*) shuāngjiǎotiào 双脚跳

**hope 1** *n* xīwàng 希望; *there's no*

*~ of that* nà shì bùkěnéng de 那是不可能的 **2** *v/t* xīwàng 希望; *I ~ you like it* wǒ xīwàng nǐ xǐhuān tā 我希望你喜欢它; *~ for X* qīwàng X 期望 X; *I ~ so* xīwàng rúcǐ 希望如此; *I ~ not* wǒ bù xīwàng zhèyàng 我不希望这样

**hopeful** (*optimistic*) lèguān 乐观; (*promising*) yǒu xīwàng 有希望

**hopefully** *say* bàoyǒu xīwàng 抱有希望; (*I/we hope*) dànyuàn 但愿

**hopeless** *position, prospect* méiyǒu xīwàng 没有希望; (*useless*: *person*) méi qiántú 没前途

**horizon** dìpíngxiàn 地平线

**horizontal** shuǐpíng 水平

**hormone** hé'ěrméng 荷尔蒙

**horn** (*of animal*) jiǎo 角; MOT qìchē lǎba 汽车喇叭

**hornet** dàhuángfēng 大黄蜂

**horn-rimmed spectacles** yǒu jiǎozhìjià de yǎnjìng 有角质架的眼镜

**horny** F yǒu xìng chōngdòng 有性冲动

**horoscope** xīngzhàn bǔ 星占卜

**horrible** zāogāo 糟糕

**horrify**: *I was horrified* wǒ bèi xiàhuàile 我被吓坏了

**horrifying** *experience* kěpà 可怕; *idea, prices* lìngrén zhènjīng 令人震惊

**horror** kǒngbù 恐怖; *the ~s of war* zhànzhēngde kǒngbù 战争的恐怖

**horror movie** kǒngbù diànyǐng 恐怖电影

**hors d'œuvre** cānqiánde xiǎochī 餐前的小吃

**horse** mǎ 马

**horseback**: *on ~* qímǎ 骑马; **horse chestnut** qīyèshùshǔ zhíwù 七叶树属植物; **horsepower** mǎlì 马力; **horse race** sàimǎ 赛马; **horseshoe** mǎtítiě 马蹄铁

**horticulture** yuányì 园艺

**hose** ruǎnguǎn 软管

**hospice** jiùjìyuàn 救济院

**hospitable** hàokè 好客

**hospital** yīyuàn 医院; *go into the*

~ zhùyuàn 住院

hospitality rèqíng zhāodài 热情招待

host n (at party, reception) zhǔrén 主人; (of TV program) zhǔchírén 主持人

hostage rénzhì 人质; be taken ~ bèi kòuzuò rénzhì 被扣作人质

hostage taker kòuyā rénzhì de rén 扣押人质的人

hostel (for students) xiàowài jìsùshè 校外寄宿舍; (youth ~) lǚdiàn 旅店

hostess (at party, reception) nǚzhǔrén 女主人; (on airplane) kōngjiě 空姐; (in bar) nǚzhāodài 女招待

hostile dídui 敌对

hostility (of attitude) díyì 敌意; hostilities zhànzhēng 战争

hot weather, water, object, food rè 热; (spicy) là 辣; I'm ~ wǒ hěn rè 我很热; F (good) jíhǎo 极好

hot dog hóngcháng miànbāo 红肠面包

hotel bīnguǎn 宾馆

hot key COMPUT kuàijiéjiàn 快捷键; hotplate diànlú 电炉; hot spot (military, political) rèdiǎn 热点

hour xiǎoshí 小时

hourly adj měixiǎoshí 每小时

house n fángzi 房子; at your ~ zài nǐjiā 在你家

houseboat chuánwū 船屋; housebreaking rùshì qiǎngjié 入室抢劫; household jiāshǔ 家属; household name jiāyùhùxiǎo 家喻户晓; house husband jiātíng zhǔnán 家庭主男; housekeeper guǎnjiā 管家; housekeeping (activity) jiāwù guǎnlǐ 家务管理; (money) jiāwù kāixiāo 家务开消; House of Representatives Zhòngyìyuàn 众议院; housewarming (party) qìngzhù qiānjū de jùhuì 庆祝迁居的聚会; housewife jiātíng zhǔfù 家庭主妇; housework jiāwù 家务

housing zhùfáng 住房; TECH xiāng箱

housing conditions zhùfáng tiáojiàn 住房条件

hovel máoshè 茅舍

hover áoxiáng 翱翔

hovercraft qìdiànchuán 气垫船

how zěnme 怎么; ~ are you? nǐ hǎo ma? 你好吗? ; ~ about ... ? ... zěnmeyàng? ... 怎么样? ; ~ much? duōshao? 多少? ; ~ much is it? (cost) duōshao qián? 多少钱? ; ~ many? jǐgè? 几个? ; ~ often? duō jīngcháng? 多经常? ; ~ funny / sad! duō huáji / bēiāi! 多滑稽／悲哀！

however bùguò 不过; ~ big / rich / small they are bùguǎn tāmen duō dà/fù/xiǎo 不管他们多大/富/小

howl v/i (of dog) háojiào 嚎叫; (of person in pain) āiháo 哀号; (with laughter) kuángxiào 狂笑

hub (of wheel) lúngǔ 轮毂; COMPUT jíxiànqì 集线器

hubcap gǔgài 毂盖

◆ huddle together quánsuō zài yīqǐ 蜷缩在一起

hue yánsè 颜色

huff: be in a ~ fā píqì 发脾气

hug v/t yōngbào 拥抱

huge jùdà 巨大

hull wàiké 外壳

hullabaloo xuānxiāo 喧嚣

hum 1 v/t song, tune hēngchàng 哼唱 2 v/i (of person) fā hēnghēngshēng 发哼哼声; (of machine) fā wēngwēngshēng 发嗡嗡声

human 1 n rén 人 2 adj rénlèi 人类; strengths, weaknesses etc rénxíng 人性; ~ error rénwéide cuòwù 人为的错误

human being rén 人

humane réndào 人道

humanitarian réndàozhǔyì zhě 人道主义者

humanity (human beings) rénxìng 人性; (of attitude etc) réncí 仁慈

human race rénlèi 人类

human resources (department) rénlèi zīyuán 人类资源

humble attitude, person qiānbēi 谦

卑; *origins* dīwēi 低微; *meal* jiǎndān 简单; *house* jiǎnlòu 简陋
humdrum dāndiào 单调
humid shīrè 湿热
humidifier zēngshīqì 增湿器
humidity shīdù 湿度
humiliate xiūrǔ 羞辱
humiliating diūliǎn 丢脸
humiliation xiūrǔ 羞辱
humility qiāngōng 谦恭
humor (*comical*) yōumò 幽默; (*mood*) qíngxù 情绪; *sense of ~* yōumògǎn 幽默感
humorous huīxié 诙谐
hump 1 *n* (*of camel*) tuófēng 驼峰; (*of person*) tuóbèi 驼背; (*on road*) xiépō 斜坡 2 *v/t* (*carry*) bēizhe 背着
hunch (*idea*) yùgǎn 预感
hundred bǎi 百
hundredth dì yìbǎi 第一百
hundredweight yīngdàn 英担
Hungarian 1 *adj* Xiōngyálì 匈牙利 2 *n* (*person*) Xiōngyálì rén 匈牙利人; (*language*) Xiōngyálì yǔ 匈牙利语
Hungary Xiōngyálì 匈牙利
hunger jī'è 饥饿
hung-over jiǔhòu tóutòng 酒后头痛
hungry jī'è 饥饿; *I'm ~* wǒ è le 我饿了
hunk: *great ~* F (*man*) kuíwú 魁梧
hunky-dory F rúyì 如意
hunt 1 *n* (*for animals*) shòuliè 狩猎; (*for a new leader, actor*) wùsè 物色; (*for criminal, missing child*) xúnzhǎo 寻找 2 *v/t animal* lièqǔ 猎取
♦ hunt for sōuxú 搜寻
hunter (*as sport*) lièshǒu 猎手; (*for living*) lièrén 猎人
hunting dǎliè 打猎
hurdle SP tiàolán 跳栏; *fig* (*obstacle*) zhàng'ài 障碍
hurdler SP tiàolán yùndòngyuán 跳栏运动员
hurdles SP tiàolán 跳栏
hurl měngzhì 猛掷
hurray! hǎowa! 好哇！
hurricane jùfēng 飓风

hurried cōngcōng 匆匆
hurry 1 *n* cōngmáng 匆忙; *be in a ~* jímáng 急忙 2 *v/i* kuàidiǎnr 快点儿
♦ hurry up 1 *v/i* kuàidiǎnr 快点儿; *~!* gǎnjǐn! 赶紧！2 *v/t* cuīcù 催促
hurt 1 *v/i* tòng 痛; *does it ~?* tòng bútòng? 痛不痛？2 *v/t* shāng 伤; (*emotionally*) shānggǎnqíng 伤感情
husband zhàngfu 丈夫
hush *n* chénmò 沉默; *~!* biéchūshēng! 别出声！
♦ hush up *scandal etc* zhēyǎn 遮掩
husk (*of peanuts etc*) wàikè 外壳
husky *adj* shāyǎ 沙哑
hustle 1 *n* jǐ 挤; *~ and bustle* rènào 热闹 2 *v/t person* yìngjǐ 硬挤
hut péngwū 棚屋
hyacinth fēngxìnzǐ 风信子
hybrid *n* (*plant, animal*) zájiāo 杂交
hydrant xiāofáng lóngtóu 消防龙头
hydraulic yèyā 液压
hydro ... shuǐ 水
hydroelectric shuǐlì fādiàn 水力发电
hydrofoil (*boat*) shuǐyìtǐng 水翼艇
hydrogen qīng 氢; *~ bomb* qīngdàn 氢弹
hygiene wèishēng 卫生
hygienic wèishēng 卫生
hymn zànměishī 赞美诗
hype *n* dàchuī dàléi 大吹大擂
hyperactive huódòng guòdù 活动过度; hypermarket dàxíng chāojí shìchǎng 大型超级市场; hypersensitive guòmǐn 过敏; hypertension guòdù jǐnzhāng 过度紧张; MED gāoxuèyā 高血压; hypertext COMPUT chāowénběn 超文本
hyphen liánzìhào 连字号
hypnosis cuīmiánshù 催眠术
hypnotherapy cuīmián liáofǎ 催眠疗法
hypnotize: *~ X* shǐ X jìnrù cuīmián zhuàngtài 使 X 进入催眠状态
hypochondriac *n* yíbìngzhèng huàn zhě 疑病症患者
hypocrisy xūwěi 虚伪

**hypocrite** wěijūnzǐ 伪君子

**hypocritical** xūwěi 虚伪

**hypothermia** tǐwēn guòdī 体温过低

**hypothesis** jiǎshè 假设

**hypothetical** jiǎshè 假设

**hysterectomy** zǐgōng qiēchúshù 子宫切除术

**hysteria** xiēsīdǐlǐ 歇斯底里

**hysterical** *person, laugh* xiēsīdǐlǐ 歇斯底里; (*very funny*) huájī kěxiào 滑稽可笑; **become ~** biànde xiēsīdǐlǐ 变得歇斯底里

**hysterics** xiēsīdǐlǐde fāzuò 歇斯底里的发作; (*laughter*) kuángxiào 狂笑

# I

I wǒ 我

ice bīng 冰; **break the ~** fig dǎpò chénmò 打破沉默

◆ice up (of engine, wings) jiébīng 结冰

iceberg bīngshān 冰山

icebox bīngxiāng 冰箱; ice-breaker (ship) pòbīngchuán 破冰船; ice cream bīngqílín 冰淇淋; ice-cream parlor bīngqílín diàn 冰淇淋店; ice cube bīngkuài 冰块

iced drink jiābīng 加冰

iced coffee bīngkāfēi 冰咖啡

ice hockey bīngqiú 冰球

ice rink bīngchǎng 冰场

I-Ching Yìjīng 易经

icicle bīngzhù 冰柱

icon (cultural) shèngxiàng 圣像; COMPUT túbiāo 图标

icy road, surface huá 滑; welcome lěngdàn 冷淡

idea zhǔyì 主意; **good ~!** hǎo zhǔyì! 好主意！; **I have no ~** wǒ bù zhīdào 我不知道; **it's not a good ~ to do X** zuò X bú tài shìhé 做 X 不太适合

ideal (perfect) lǐxiǎng 理想

idealistic lǐxiǎnghuà 理想化

identical yìmúyíyàng 一模一样; **~ twins** tóngluǎn shuāngtāi 同卵双胎

identification yànzhèng 验证; (papers etc) shēnfen zhèngmíng 身分证明

identify jiànbié 鉴别

identity shēnfen 身分; **~ card** shēnfenzhèng 身分证

ideology sīxiǎng 思想

ideological yìshíxíngtài 意识形态

idiom (saying) xíyǔ 习语

idiomatic (natural) dìdào 地道; **she speaks quite ~ English** tā néng jiǎng yìkǒu dìdào de

yīngwén 她能讲一口地道的英文

idiosyncrasy píxìng 癖性

idiot báichī 白痴

idiotic yúchǔn 愚蠢

idle 1 adj person lǎnguǐ 懒鬼; threat shuōshuō ér yǐ 说说而已; machinery xiánzhì xián zhì 闲置; **in an ~ moment** xiánxiáshí 闲暇时 2 v/i (engine) kōngzhuàn 空转

◆idle away the time etc dǎfa 打发

idol ǒuxiàng 偶像

idolize chóngbài 崇拜

idyllic tiányuánshì 田园式

if rúguǒ 如果

igloo xuěwū 雪屋

ignite 1 v/t diǎnrán 点燃 2 v/i zháo着

ignition (in car) fādòng zhuāngzhì 发动装置; **~ key** dǎhuǒ yàoshi 打火钥匙

ignorance wúzhī 无知

ignorant wúzhī 无知; (rude) cūlǔ 粗鲁

ignore hūlüè 忽略

ill yǒubìng 有病; **fall ~, be taken ~** shēngbìng 生病; **feel ~ at ease** júcùbù'ān 局促不安

illegal fēifǎ 非法

illegible biànrèn bùqīng 辨认不清

illegitimate child sīshēng 私生

ill-fated búxìng 不幸

illicit wéifǎ 违法

illiterate wénmáng 文盲

ill-mannered jǔzhǐ cūlǔ 举止粗鲁

ill-natured píqi huài 脾气坏

illness jíbìng 疾病

illogical bù hé luójí 不合逻辑

ill-tempered píqi huài 脾气坏

ill-treat nüèdài 虐待

illuminate building etc zhàomíng 照明

illuminating remarks etc qǐfāxìng 启

发性

illusion huànxiàng 幻象

illustrate *book* chātú 插图; (*with examples*) shuōmíng 说明

illustration (*picture*) chātú 插图; (*with examples*) lìzhèng 例证

illustrator huìtúrén 绘图人

ill will èyì 恶意

image (*picture*) huàmiàn 画面; (*exact likeness*) xiāngxiàng 相象; (*of politician, company*) xíngxiàng 形象

image-conscious zhùyì xíngxiàng 注意形象

imaginable kěyǐ xiǎngxiàng 可以想象; *the biggest / smallest size* ~ kěyǐ xiǎngxiàngchū de zuìdà / zuìxiǎo chǐcùn 可以想象出的最大 / 最小尺寸

imaginary jiǎxiǎng 假想

imagination xiǎngxiàng 想象; *it's all in your* ~ dōu shì nǐ xiǎngxiàng de 都是你想象的

imaginative jùyǒu xiǎngxiànglì 具有想象力

imagine xiǎngxiàng 想象; *I can just* ~ *it* wǒ néng xiǎngxiàng chūlái 我能想象出来; *you're imagining things* nǐ shì zài húsīluànxiǎng 你是在胡思乱想

imbecile dīnéng'ér 低能儿

IMF (= *International Monetary Fund*) Guójì Huòbì Jījīn 国际货币基金

imitate mófǎng 模仿

imitation (*copying*) mófǎng 模仿; (*something copied*) fǎngzào 仿造

immaculate chúnjié 纯洁

immaterial (*not relevant*) wúguān jǐnyào 无关紧要

immature bù chéngshú 不成熟

immediate jíkè 即刻; *the ~ family* zhíxì qīnshǔ 直系亲属; *in the ~ neighborhood* jǐnlín 紧邻

immediately lìjí 立即; ~ *after the bank / church* yí guò yínháng / jiàotáng 一过银行 / 教堂

immense jùdà 巨大

immerse jìnpào 浸泡; ~ *oneself in studies etc* chénjìn 沉浸

immersion heater diàn rèshuǐqì

电热水器

immigrant *n* yímín 移民

immigrate yíjū 移居

immigration (*act*) yímín 移民; *Immigration* (*government office*) yímínjú 移民局

imminent pòjìn 迫近

immobilize *factory, person* shǐ ... tānhuàn 使 ... 瘫痪; *car* suǒzhù 锁住

immoderate wú jiézhì 无节制

immoral bú dàodé 不道德

immorality bú dàodé 不道德

immortal bùxiǔ 不朽

immortality bùxiǔ 不朽

immune (*to illness, infection*) miǎnyì 免疫; (*from ruling, requirement*) miǎnchú 免除

immune system MED miǎnyì xìtǒng 免疫系统

immunity (*to infection*) miǎnyì 免疫; (*from ruling*) tèmiǎn 特免; *diplomatic* ~ wàijiāo miǎnyì lì 外交免疫力

impact *n* (*of meteorite, vehicle*) zhuàngjī 撞击; (*of new manager etc*) yǐngxiǎnglì 影响力; (*effect*) yǐngxiǎng 影响

impair sǔnhài 损害

impaired xuēruò 削弱

impartial gōngzhèng 公正

impassable *road* bùtōng 不通

impasse (*in negotiations etc*) jiāngjú 僵局

impassioned *speech, plea* jīdòng 激动

impassive lěngdàn 冷淡

impatience bú nàixīn 不耐心

impatient bú nàixīn 不耐心

impatiently bú nàixīn 不耐心

impeccable *turnout* wúxièkějī 无懈可击; *English, Chinese* jīngtōng 精通

impeccably *dressed* wánměi 完美; *pronounce, speak* wánměi 完美

impede zǔ'ài 阻碍

impediment (*in speech*) kǒuchī 口吃

impending pò zài méijié 迫在眉睫

impenetrable cì bù chuān 刺不穿

**imperative 1** *adj* jǐnjí 紧急 **2** *n* GRAM qíshǐ 祈使

**imperceptible** nányǐ chájué 难以察觉

**imperfect 1** *adj* bù wánměi 不完美 **2** *n* GRAM bù wánzhěng 不完整

**imperial** huángdì 皇帝

**imperialism** dìguó zhǔyì 帝国主义

**impersonal** bú jù réngéxìng 不具人格性

**impersonate** (*as a joke*) jiǎbàn 假扮; (*illegally*) màochōng 冒充

**impertinence** wúlǐ 无礼

**impertinent** wúlǐ 无礼

**imperturbable** chéngzhuó lěngjìng 沉着冷静

**impervious**: **~ to X** duì X wúdòngyúzhōng 对 X 无动于衷

**impetuous** qīngshuài 轻率

**impetus** (*of campaign etc*) tuīdònglì 推动力

**implement 1** *n* gōngjù 工具 **2** *v/t measures etc* shíshī 实施

**implicate**: **~ X in Y** xiǎnshì X shèjí Y 显示 X 涉及 Y

**implication** ànshì 暗示

**implicit** hánxù 含蓄; *trust* juéduì 绝对

**implore** kěnqiú 恳求

**imply** ànzhǐ 暗指

**impolite** bù lǐmào 不礼貌

**import** *n & v/i* jìnkǒu 进口

**importance** zhòngyàoxìng 重要性

**important** zhòngyào 重要

**importer** jìnkǒushāng 进口商

**impose** *tax* zhēngshōu 征收; **~ oneself on X** yìng chánzhe X 硬缠着 X

**imposing** tūchū 突出

**impossibility** bù kěnéngxìng 不可能性

**impossible** bù kěnéng 不可能

**impostor** màomíng dǐngtì de rén 冒名顶替的人

**impotence** yángwěi 阳萎

**impotent** yángwěi 阳萎

**impoverished** pínkùn 贫困

**impractical** *person* bú xiànshí 不现实; *suggestion* bù shíjì 不实际

**impress**: **~ X** (*impress another person*) gěi X liúxià shēnkè yìnxiàng 给 X 留下深刻印象; **be ~ed by X** X gěi rén liúxià shēnkè yìnxiàng X 给人留下深刻印象; **I'm not ~ed** wǒ bù mǎnyì 我不满意

**impression** yìnxiàng 印象; (*impersonation*) huájī de mófǎng 滑稽的模仿; **make a good / bad ~ on X** gěi X liúxià hǎo / huài yìnxiàng 给 X 留下好 / 坏印象; **I get the ~ that ...** wǒ juéde ... 我觉得 ...

**impressionable** yì shòu yǐngxiǎng 易受影响

**impressive** gěi rén yǐ shēnkè yìnxiàng 给人以深刻印象

**imprint** *n* (*of credit card*) yāyìn 压印

**imprison** jiānjìn 监禁

**imprisonment** jiānjìn 监禁

**improbable** bú dà kěnéng 不大可能

**improper** *behavior* bú qiàdàng 不恰当

**improve 1** *v/t* gǎijìn 改进; *skills, Chinese* tígāo 提高; *relations* gǎishàn 改善 **2** *v/i* (*of health*) hǎozhuǎn 好转; (*of Chinese skills, life*) tígāo 提高

**improvement** gǎijìn 改进

**improvize** *v/i* jíxīng 即兴

**impudent** cūlǔ 粗鲁

**impulse** chōngdòng 冲动; **do X on an ~** yìshí chōngdòng zuò X 一时冲动做 X; **~ buy** chōngdòng gòuwù 冲动购物

**impulsive** yì chōngdòng 易冲动

**impunity**: **with ~** bú shòu chěngfá 不受惩罚

**impure** *thoughts* āngzāng 肮脏; *substance* bùchún 不纯

**in 1** *prep* ◊ zài lǐmiàn 在里面; **~ Washington / China** zài Huáshèngdùn / Zhōngguó 在华盛顿 / 中国; **~ the street** zài jiēshang 在街上; **~ the box** zài hézi lǐ 在盒子里; **put it ~ your pocket** bǎ tā fàng zài nǐde dōulǐ

把它放在你的兜里; **wounded ~ the leg / arm** tuǐ / gēbo shòu shāng 腿 / 胳膊受伤◇: **~ 1999** yījiǔjiǔjiǔ nián 19 99 年; **~ two hours** (*from now*) liǎng ge xiǎoshí yǐhòu 两个小时以后; (*over period of*) liǎng ge xiǎoshí nèi 两个小时内; **I haven't seen him ~ three years** wǒ sānnián méi kànjiàn tāle 我三年没看见他了; **~ the morning** zǎoshang zǎoshang 早上; **~ the summer** xiàtiān 夏天; **~ August** bāyuè 八月◇: **~ English / Chinese** yòng Yīngyǔ / Hànyǔ 用英语 / 汉语; **~ a loud voice** dàshēng 大声; **~ his style** yǐ tāde fāngshì 以他的方式; **dressed ~ yellow** chuān huángsè yīfu 穿黄色衣服◇: **~ crossing the road** (*while*) guò mǎlù shí 过马路时; **~ agreeing to this** (*by virtue of*) yídàn tóngyì zhège 一旦同意这个◇: **~ his novel** zài tāde xiǎoshuō lǐ 在他的小说里; **~ Confucius** zài Kǒngzǐde zhùzuò lǐ 在孔子的著作里◇: **three ~ all** yígòng sān gè 一共三个; **one ~ ten** shífēnzhīyī 十分之一 **2 adv** (*at home, in the building etc*) zài lǐmiàn 在里面; (*arrived: train*) dàodá 到达; (*in its position*) zài lǐtóu 在里头; **~ here** zài zhèr 在这儿 **3 adj** (*fashionable, popular*) liúxíng 流行

**inability** wúnéng 无能

**inaccessible** nán jiējìn 难接近

**inaccurate** bù jīngquè 不精确

**inactive** bù huóyuè 不活跃

**inadequate** búshì dàng 不适当

**inadvisable** bù míngzhì 不明智

**inanimate** wú shēngmìng 无生命

**inapplicable** bú shìyòng 不适用

**inappropriate** bú shìdàng 不适当

**inarticulate** kǒuchǐ bùqīng 口齿不清

**inattentive** bù jīngxīn 不经心

**inaudible** tīngbújiàn 听不见

**inaugural** *speech* jiùzhí 就职

**inaugurate** kāimù 开幕

**inborn** shēnglái 生来

**inbreeding** jìnqīn fánzhí 近亲繁殖

**inc.** (= *incorporated*) gōngsī 公司

**incalculable** *damage* shǔbuqīng 数不清

**incapable** wú nénglì 无能力; **be ~ of doing X** bùnéng zuò X 不能做 X

**incendiary device** ránshāodàn 燃烧弹

**incense**[1] *n* xiāng 香

**incense**[2] *v/t* jīnù 激怒

**incentive** dònglì 动力

**incessant** liánxù 连续

**incessantly** bùtíng 不停

**incest** luànlún 乱伦

**inch** *n* yīngcùn 英寸

**incident** shìjiàn 事件

**incidental** búchōng 补充; **~ expenses** záfèi 杂费

**incidentally** shùnbiàn shuō yíxià 顺便说一下

**incinerator** fénhuàlú 焚化炉

**incision** qiēkāi 切开

**incisive** *mind, analysis* jiānruì 尖锐

**incite** shāndòng 煽动; **~ X to do Y** shāndòng X zuò Y 煽动 X 做 Y

**inclement** *weather* èliè 恶劣

**inclination** *tendency, liking* yìyuàn 意愿

**incline: be ~d to do X** yǒu zuò X de qīngxiàng 有做 X 的倾向

**inclose → enclose**

**include** bāokuò 包括

**including** *prep* bāokuò 包括

**inclusive** *adj & prep price* bāokuò zàinèi 包括在内; **~ of X** bāokuò X zàinèi 包括 X 在内 **3 adv** yíqiè bāokuò zàinèi 一切包括在内; **from Monday to Thursday ~** cóng zhōuyī dào zhōusì 从周一到周四

**incoherent** bù liánguàn 不连贯

**income** shōurù 收入

**income tax** suǒdéshuì 所得税

**incoming** *flight* jídá 即达; *phonecall, mail* shōudào 收到; *president* xīnrèn 新任; **~ tide** zhǎngcháo 涨潮

**incomparable** bùkě bǐnǐ 不可比拟

**incompatibility** bù xiāngfú 不相符

incompatible bù xiāngfú 不相符

incompetence bú chènzhí 不称职

incompetent bú chènzhí 不称职

incomplete bù wánzhěng 不完整

incomprehensible bùkě lǐjiě 不可理解

inconceivable wúfǎ xiǎngxiàng 无法想象

inconclusive fēi jiélùnxìng 非结论性

incongruous bù xiétiáo 不协调

inconsiderate kǎolǜ bùzhōu 考虑不周

inconsistent bù yízhì 不一致

inconsolable wúfǎ wèijiè 无法慰藉

inconspicuous bù xiǎnyǎn 不显眼

inconvenience n bù fāngbiàn 不方便

inconvenient bù fāngbiàn 不方便

incorporate bāohán 包含

incorporated COM gōngsī 公司

incorrect bú zhèngquè 不正确

incorrectly bú zhèngquè 不正确

incorrigible bùkě jiùyào 不可救药

increase 1 v/t zēngjiā 增加 2 v/i tígāo 提高 3 n zēngjiā 增加

increasing zēngjiā 增加

increasingly yuèláiyuè 越来越

incredible (amazing, very good) lìngrén nányí zhìxìn 令人难以置信

incriminate xiànde yǒuzuì 显得有罪; ~ oneself shòuliánléi 受连累

incubator (for chicks) fūhuàqì 孵化器; (for babies) héngwēn yùyīng xiāng 恒温育婴箱

incur zhāozhì 招致

incurable bùkě zhìyù 不可治愈

indebted: be ~ to X qiàn X zhài 欠 X 债

indecent xiàliú 下流

indecisive yóuyù bù jué 犹豫不决

indecisiveness yóuyùbùjué 犹豫不决

indeed (in fact) shìshí shàng 事实上; (yes, agreeing) díquèshì 的确

是; very much ~ fēicháng 非常

indefinable nányí miáoshù 难以描述

indefinite bú quèdìng 不确定; ~ article GRAM búdìngguàncí 不定冠词

indefinitely wú xiànqī 无限期

indelicate bù jīngxì 不精细

indent 1 n (in text) suōjìn páiyìn 缩进排印 2 v/t line suōgé shūxiě 缩格书写

independence dúlì 独立

Independence Day Dúlìrì 独立日

independent dúlì 独立

independently deal with dúlì 独立; ~ of dāndú 单独

indescribable nányí xíngróng 难以形容; (very bad) zāo de wúfǎ xíngróng 糟得无法形容

indescribably wúfǎ xíngróng 无法形容; ~ bad zāo de wúfǎ xíngróng 糟得无法形容; ~ beautiful měi de wúfǎ xíngróng 美得无法形容

indestructible bùnéng sǔnhuài 不能损坏

indeterminate bú quèdìng 不确定

index (for book) suǒyǐn 索引

index card suǒyǐnkǎ 索引卡; index finger shízhǐ 食指; index-linked àn shēnghuó zhīshù tiáozhěng 按生活指数调整

India Yìndù 印度

Indian 1 adj Yìndù 印度 2 n Yìndù rén 印度人; (American) Yìndì'ān rén 印第安人

Indian summer xiǎoyángchūn 小阳春

indicate 1 v/t biǎomíng 表明 2 v/i (when driving) zhǐshì 指示

indication zhǐshì 指示

indicator (on car) fāngxiàng zhǐshìqì 方向指示器

indict kònggào 控告

indifference mò bù guānxīn 漠不关心

indifferent mò bù guānxīn 漠不关心; (mediocre) yìbān 一般

indigestible bùnéng xiāohuà 不能

消化 **indigestion** xiāohuà bùliáng 消化不良

**indignant** fènkǎi 愤慨

**indignation** fènkǎi 愤慨

**indirect** jiànjiē 间接

**indirectly** jiànjiē 间接

**indiscreet** qīngshuài 轻率

**indiscretion** (act) qīngshuài 轻率

**indiscriminate** rènyì ér wéi 任意而为

**indispensable** bùkě quēshǎo 不可缺少

**indisposed** (not well) xiǎobìng 小病

**indisputable** bùróng zhìyí 不容置疑

**indisputably** bùróng zhìyí 不容置疑

**indistinct** móhu 模糊

**indistinguishable** wúfǎ qūbié 无法区别

**individual 1** n gèrén 个人 **2** adj (separate) dāndú 单独; (personal) gèrén 个人

**individualist** gèrénzhǔyì zhě 个人主义者

**individually** gèzì 各自

**indivisible** bùkě fēngē 不可分割

**indoctrinate** guànshū 灌输

**indolence** lǎnduò 懒惰

**indolent** lǎnduò 懒惰

**Indochina** Yìndùzhīnà 印度支那

**Indochinese** adj Yìndùzhīnà 印度支那

**Indonesia** Yìndùníxīyà 印度尼西亚

**Indonesian 1** adj Yìndùníxīyà 印度尼西亚 **2** n (person) Yìndùníxīyà rén 印度尼西亚人

**indoor** shìnèi 室内

**indoors** zài shìnèi 在室内

**indorse** → endorse

**induction ceremony** jiùzhí yíshì 就职仪式

**indulge 1** v/t (oneself, one's tastes) fàngzòng zìjǐ 放纵自己 **2** v/i: ~ **in X** jìnqíng xiǎngshòu X 尽情享受 X

**indulgence** (of tastes, appetite etc) fàngzòng 放纵; (lax attitude) shūhū 疏忽

**indulgent** (not strict enough) bù yángé 不严格

**industrial** gōngyè 工业

**industrial action** gōngyè xíngdòng 工业行动

**industrial dispute** láozī jiūfēn 劳资纠纷

**industrialist** shíyèjiā 实业家

**industrialize 1** v/t shǐ gōngyèhuà 使工业化 **2** v/i gōngyèhuà 工业化

**industrial waste** gōngyè fèiliào 工业废料

**industrious** qínmiǎn 勤勉

**industry** gōngyè 工业

**ineffective** xiàoguǒ bùjiā 效果不佳

**ineffectual** person dīnéng 低能

**inefficient** wúxiàolǜ 无效率

**ineligible** wúzīgé 无资格

**inept** bùshúliàn 不熟练

**inequality** bùpíngděng 不平等

**inescapable** nánmiǎn 难免

**inestimable** nányí gūliàng 难以估量

**inevitable** xiǎn ér yìjiàn 显而易见

**inevitably** bùkě bìmiǎn 不可避免

**inexcusable** bùkě yuánliàng 不可原谅

**inexhaustible** person jīnglì chōngpèi 精力充沛; supply yuányuán búduàn 源源不断

**inexpensive** piányi 便宜

**inexperienced** méi jīngyàn 没经验

**inexplicable** fèijiě 费解

**inexpressible** joy nán yǐ biǎoshù 难以表述

**infallible** juéduì kěkào 绝对可靠

**infamous** chòumíng yuǎnyáng 臭名远扬

**infancy** (of person) yīng'érqī 婴儿期; (of state, institution) chūjí jiēduàn 初级阶段

**infant** yīng'ér 婴儿

**infantile** pej háiziqì 孩子气

**infantry** bùbīng 步兵

**infantry soldier** bùbīng 步兵

**infatuated**: be ~ **with X** míliàn X 迷恋 X

**infect** (*of person*) yǐngxiǎng 影响; *food, water* wūrǎn 污染; *become ~ed* gǎnrǎn 感染

**infected** *wound* gǎnrǎn 感染

**infection** chuánrǎn 传染

**infectious** *disease* chuánrǎn 传染; *fig: laughter* gǎnrǎn 感染

**infer**: ~ *X from Y* cóng Y tuīduànchū X 从 Y 推断出 X

**inferior** *quality* lièzhì 劣质; (*in rank, military*) dìwèidī 地位低; (*in company, workmanship*) zhíwèidī 职位低

**inferiority** (*in quality*) lièzhì 劣质

**inferiority complex** zìbēigǎn 自卑感

**infertile** bùnéng fányù 不能繁育

**infertility** wú shēngzhí nénglì 无生殖能力

**infidelity** bùzhōng 不忠

**infiltrate** v/t dǎrù 打入

**infinite** wúxiàn 无限

**infinitive** búdìngshì 不定式

**infinity** wúqióng 无穷

**infirm** tǐruò 体弱

**infirmary** yīyuàn 医院

**infirmity** tǐruò 体弱

**inflame** jīdòng 激动

**inflammable** yìrán 易燃

**inflammation** MED fāyán 发炎

**inflatable** *dinghy* kě chōngqì 可充气

**inflate** v/t *tire, dinghy* chōngqì 充气; *economy* péngzhàng 膨胀

**inflation** tōnghuò péngzhàng 通货膨胀

**inflationary** (*of inflation*) wùjià shàngzhǎng 物价上涨; (*causing inflation*) dǎozhì tōnghuò péngzhàng 导致通货膨胀

**inflection** (*of voice*) biànyīn 变音

**inflexible** *attitude, person* gùzhí 固执

**inflict**: ~ *X on Y* shǐ Y zāoshòu X 使 Y 遭受 X

**in-group** xiǎoquānzi 小圈子

**in-flight** fēixíngzhōng 飞行中; ~ *entertainment* fēixíngzhōng tígōng de yúlè huódòng 飞行中提供的娱乐活动

**influence** 1 *n* yǐngxiǎng 影响; (*power to influence*) yǐngxiǎnglì 影响力; *be a good / bad ~ on X* duì X yǒu hǎo / huài yǐngxiǎng 对 X 有好 / 坏影响 2 v/t yǐngxiǎng 影响

**influential** yǒu yǐngxiǎng 有影响

**influenza** liúxíngxìng gǎnmào 流行性感冒

**inform** 1 v/t tōngzhī 通知; ~ *X of Y* bǎ Y tōngzhī gěi X 把 Y 通知给 X; *please keep me ~ed* qǐng chuándá gěi wǒ 请传达给我 2 v/t gàofā 告发; ~ *on X* gàofā X 告发 X

**informal** fēi zhèngshì 非正式

**informality** fēi zhèngshì 非正式

**informant** tígōng xiāoxirén 提供消息人

**information** xìnxī 信息

**information science** xìnxīxué 信息学; **information scientist** xìnxīxuéjiā 信息学家; **information technology** xìnxī jìshù 信息技术

**informative** tígōng xìnxī 提供信息

**informer** gàofārén 告发人

**infra-red** *adj* hóngwàixiàn 红外线

**infrastructure** jīchǔ jiégòu 基础结构

**infrequent** shǎoyǒu 少有

**infuriate** jīnù 激怒

**infuriating** lìngrén shēngqì 令人生气

**infuse** v/i (*of tea*) pào 泡

**infusion** (*herb tea*) jìnpào 浸泡

**ingenious** jīngmíng 精明

**ingenuity** jīngmíng 精明

**ingot** dìng dìng 锭

**ingratiate**: ~ *oneself with X* qǔyuè X 取悦 X

**ingratitude** wàng'ēnfùyì 忘恩负义

**ingredient** (*for cooking*) yuánliào 原料; *fig* (*for success*) yīnsù 因素

**inhabit** jūzhù 居住

**inhabitable** shìyú jūzhù 适于居住

**inhabitant** jūmín 居民

**inhale** 1 v/t xīrù 吸入 2 v/i (*when smoking*) xīqì 吸气

**inhaler** xīrùqì 吸入器

**inherit** jìchéng 继承

inheritance jìchéng 继承

inhibit *growth, conversation etc* zǔzhǐ 阻止

inhibited yàyì 压抑

inhibition yāyì 压抑

inhospitable *(of people)* lěngdàn 冷淡; *(of place)* huāngliáng 荒凉

in-house *adj & adv* zài gōngsī nèi 在公司内

inhuman yěmán 野蛮

initial 1 *adj* zuìchū 最初 2 *n* xìngmíng shǒu zìmǔ 姓名首字母 3 *v/t (write initials on)* qiān xìngmíng shǒu zìmǔ 签姓名首字母

initially kāishǐ 开始

initiate *v/t* zhuóshǒu 着手

initiation kāichuàng 开创

initiative zhǔdòngxìng 主动性; *do X on one's own* ~ zhǔdòng zuò X 主动做 X

inject *medicine, drug* zhùshè 注射; *fuel* shūsòng 输送; *capital* tóurù 投入

injection MED zhùshè 注射; *(of fuel)* shūsòng 输送; *(of capital)* tóurù 投入

injure shānghài 伤害

injured 1 *adj leg* shòushāng 受伤; *feelings* shòushānghài 受伤害 2 *n: the* ~ shòushāng zhě 受伤者

injury shānghài 伤害

injustice fēizhèngyì 非正义

ink mòshuǐ 墨水

inkjet *(printer)* pēnmò (dǎyìnjī) 喷墨 (打印机)

inland nèilù 内陆

in-laws yīnqīn 姻亲

inlay *n* xiāngqiàn 镶嵌

inlet *(of sea)* hǎiwān 海湾; *(in machine)* rùkǒu 入口

inmate *(of prison)* fànrén 犯人; *(of mental hospital)* bìngyǒu 病友

inn xiǎolǚguǎn 小旅馆

innate tiānshēng 天生

inner nèibù 内部

inner city jiùchéngqū 旧城区

Inner Mongolia Nèi Ménggǔ 内蒙古

Inner Mongolian Grasslands Nèi Ménggǔ Dà Cǎo Yuán 内蒙古大草原

innermost zuìshēn 最深

inner tube nèitāi 内胎

innocence *(of child)* tiānzhēn 天真; LAW wúzuì 无罪

innocent *child* tiānzhēn 天真; LAW wúzuì 无罪

innovation géxīn 革新

innovative géxīn 革新

innovator géxīn zhě 革新者

innumerable shǔbuqīng 数不清

inoculate jiēzhòng 接种

inoculation jiēzhòng 接种

inoffensive bù chùfàn rén 不触犯人

inorganic wújī 无机

input *n & v/t (into project etc)* tóurù 投入; COMPUT shūrù 输入

input port COMPUT shūrù duānkǒu 输入端口

inquest shěnxùn 审讯

inquire xúnwèn 询问; ~ *into X* diàochá X 调查 X

inquiry xúnwèn 询问

inquisitive hàoqí 好奇

insane fēngkuáng 疯狂

insanitary bù wèishēng 不卫生

insanity fēngkuáng 疯狂

insatiable bùnéng mǎnzú 不能满足

inscription míngwén 铭文

inscrutable shénmì 神秘

insect kūnchóng 昆虫

insecticide shāchóngjì 杀虫剂

insect repellent fángchóngyào 防虫药

insecure bù ānquán 不安全

insecurity bù ānquángǎn 不安全感

insensitive bù mǐngǎn 不敏感

insensitivity bù língmǐnxìng 不灵敏性

inseparable *two issues* bùkě fēngē 不可分割; *two people* fēnbùkāi 分不开

insert 1 *n (in magazine etc)* fùjiāwù 附加物 2 *v/t* chārù 插入; ~ *X into Y* bǎ X chārù Y 把 X 插入 Y

insertion *(act)* chārù 插入

inside 1 *n (of house, box)* nèibù 内部; *(of road)* lícè 里侧; *somebody*

***on the*** ~ nèibùrén 内部人; ***~ out*** liámiàn fāndào wàimiàn 里面翻到外面; ***turn X ~ out*** bǎ X lǐ fān wài 把 X 里面翻外; ***know X ~ out*** chèdǐ liǎojiě X 彻底了解 X **2** *prep* zài … lǐ 在 … 里; ***~ the house*** zài wūlǐ 在屋里; ***~ of 2 hours*** bú dào liǎng xiǎoshí 不到两小时 **3** *adv stay, remain* zài lǐmiàn 在里面; ***go, carry*** lǐmiàn 里面; ***we went*** ~ wǒmen jìn lǐmiàn le 我们进里面了 **4** *adj* nèibù 内部; ***~ information*** nèibù xiāoxi 内部消息; ***~ lane*** SP lǐquān pǎodào 里圈跑道; (*on road*) lǐdào 里道; ***~ pocket*** lǐbiāndōu 里边兜

**insider** nèibùrén 内部人

**insider trading** FIN nèimù jiāoyì 内幕交易

**insides** lǐmiàn 里面

**insidious** yǐnfú 隐伏

**insight** dòngchá 洞察

**insignificant** wú jiàzhí 无价值

**insincere** bù zhēnchéng 不真诚

**insincerity** xūwěi 虚伪

**insinuate** (*imply*) ànshì 暗示

**insist** jiānchí 坚持; ***please keep it, I ~*** nǐ yídìng yào liúzhe 你一定要留着

♦**insist on** jiānjué yāoqiú 坚决要求

**insistent** jiānchí 坚持

**insolent** mánhèng 蛮横

**insoluble** *problem* bùnéng jiějué 不能解决; *substance* bù róngjiě 不溶解

**insolvent** wú chángzhài nénglì 无偿债能力

**insomnia** shīmián 失眠

**inspect** *work, tickets, baggage* jiǎnchá 检查; *building, factory, school* shìchá 视察

**inspection** (*of work, tickets, baggage*) jiǎnchá 检查; (*of building, factory, school*) shìchá 视察

**inspector** (*in factory*) jiǎncháyuán 检查员; (*on buses*) chápiàoyuán 查票员; (*of police*) xúnguān 巡官

**inspiration** línggǎn 灵感; (*very good idea*) hǎo zhǔyì 好主意

**inspire** (*cause: respect etc*) yǐnqǐ 引起; ***be ~d by X*** cóng X dédào línggǎn 从 X 得到灵感

**instability** (*of character, economy*) bù wěndìng 不稳定

**install** *computer, telephone, software* ānzhuāng 安装

**installation** (*of new equipment, software etc*) ānzhuāng 安装; ***military ~*** jūnshì zhuāngbèi 军事装备

**installment** (*of story, TV drama etc*) jí jí 集; (*payment*) yīqī fùkuǎn 一期付款

**installment plan** fēnqī fùkuǎn 分期付款

**instance** (*example*) lìzi 例子; ***for ~*** lìrú 例如

**instant 1** *adj* lìjí 立即 **2** *n* shànà 刹那; ***in an ~*** yíhuìr 一会儿

**instantaneous** jíkè 即刻

**instant coffee** sùróng kāfēi 速溶咖啡

**instantly** jíkè 即刻

**instant noodles** ⇩ fāngbiànmiàn 方便面

**instead** dàitì 代替; ***I'll take that one ~*** nà wǒ ná nèige ba 那我拿那个吧; ***I haven't got tea, would you like coffee ~?*** wǒ méiyǒu chá, nǐ hē kāfēi xíng ma? 我没有茶, 你喝咖啡行吗?; ***he didn't go home, he went to the bar ~*** tā méi huíjiā, tā qù jiǔbā le 他没回家, 他去酒吧了; ***~ of*** ér búshì 而不是

**instep** jiǎobèi 脚背

**instinct** běnnéng 本能

**instinctive** běnnéng 本能

**institute 1** *n* xiéhuì 协会; (*special home*) yuàn 院 **2** *v/t new law, inquiry* zhìdìng 制定

**institution** (*governmental*) jīgòu 机构; (*something traditional*) fēngsú xíguàn 风俗习惯; (*setting up*) jiànlì 建立

**instruct** (*order*) zhǐshì 指示; (*teach*) zhǐdǎo 指导; ***~ X to do Y*** (*order*) zhǐshì X zuò Y 指示 X 做 Y

**instruction** shuōmíng 说明; ***~s for use*** shǐyòng shuōmíngshū 使用

instruction manual shuōmíngshū 说明书

instructive yǒu zhǐdǎo yìyì 有指导意义

instructor zhǐdǎoyuán 指导员

instrument MUS yuèqì 乐器; (gadget, tool) qìjù 器具

insubordinate bùfúcóng 不服从

insufficient bùgòu 不够

insulate ELEC shǐ juéyuán 使绝缘; (against cold) shǐ gérè 使隔热

insulation ELEC juéyuán cáiliào 绝缘材料; (against cold) gérè 隔热

insulin yídǎosù 胰岛素

insult n & v/t wūrǔ 侮辱

insurance bǎoxiǎn 保险

insurance company bǎoxiǎn gōngsī 保险公司

insurance policy bǎoxiǎndān 保险单

insure v/t gěi ... bǎoxiǎn 给 ... 保险

insured: be ~ed cānjiā bǎoxiǎn 参加保险

insurmountable wúfǎ chāoyuè 无法超越

intact (not damaged) wèishòusǔn 未受损

intake (of college etc) zhāoshōu 招收

integrate v/t róngwéiyìtǐ 融为一体

integrated circuit jíchéng diànlù 集成电路

integrity (honesty) chéngshí 诚实

intellect zhìlì 智力

intellectual 1 adj zhìlì 智力 2 n zhīshífènzǐ 知识分子

intelligence zhìlì 智力; (news) qíngbào 情报

intelligence service qíngbàojú 情报局

intelligent cōngmíng 聪明

intelligible kě lǐjiě 可理解

intend dǎsuàn 打算; ~ to do X (do on purpose) zhìzài zuò X 旨在做 X; (plan to do) dǎsuàn zuò X 打算做 X; that's not what I ~ed nà bù shì wǒde yìtú 那不是我的意图

intense sensation, pleasure, heat,

---

pressure jùliè 剧烈; personality rèqíng 热情; concentration gāodù 高度

intensify 1 v/t effect, pressure jiāqiáng 加强 2 v/i (pain) jiājù 加剧; (fighting) biànqiángliè 变强烈

intensity (of sensation, heat, pain) qiángliè 强烈; (of fighting) jīliè 激烈

intensive study, training, treatment qiánghuà 强化

intensive care (unit) tèhù (bù) 特护 (部)

intensive course (of language study) jīngdúkè 精读课

intent: be ~ on doing X (determined to do) jiānjué zuò X 坚决做 X; (concentrating on) jízhōng jīnglì zuò X 集中精力做 X

intention yìtú 意图; I have no ~ of ... (refuse to) wǒ gēnběn bù xiǎng ... 我根本不想 ...

intentional yǒuyì 有意

intentionally yǒuyì 有意

interaction xiānghù zuòyòng 相互作用

interactive jiāohùshì 交互式

intercede tiáotíng 调停

intercept ball lánjié 拦截; message jiéchá 截查; missile jiéjī 截击

interchange n (of highways) jiāochādào 交叉道

interchangeable kěhùhuàn 可互换

intercom duìjiǎngjī 对讲机

intercourse (sexual) xìngjiāo 性交

interdependent xiānghù yīlài 相互依赖

interest 1 n xìngqù 兴趣; FIN lìxī 利息; take an ~ in X duì X yǒu xìngqù 对 X 有兴趣 2 v/t: ~ X yǐnqǐ X de xìngqù 引起 X 的兴趣; does that offer ~ you? nǐ zhèige tiáojiàn gǎn xìngqù ma? 你对这个条件感兴趣吗 ?

interested yǒu xìngqù 有兴趣; be ~ in X duì X yǒu xìngqù 对 X 有兴趣; thanks, but I'm not ~ xièxiè, dàn wǒ bù gǎn xìngqù 谢谢 , 但我不感兴趣

interesting yǒuqù 有趣

**interest rate** lìxīlù 利息率
**interface 1** n jièmiàn 界面 **2** v/i xiāngjiē 相接
**interfere** gānshè 干涉
♦ **interfere with** controls nònghuài 弄坏; plans gānrǎo 干扰
**interference** gānshè 干涉; (on radio) gānrǎo 干扰
**interior 1** adj nèibù 内部 **2** n (of house) nèibù 内部; (of country) nèilù 内陆; **Department of the Interior** Nèizhèngbù 内政部
**interior decoration** nèibù zhuāngxiū 内部装修; **interior design** shìnèi shèjì 室内设计; **interior designer** shìnèi shèjì zhě 室内设计者
**interlude** (at theater, concert) mùjiān 幕间; (period) shíjiān 时间
**intermediary** n zhōngrén 中人
**intermediate** adj zhōngjí 中级
**intermission** (in theater, movie theater) mùjiān xiūxī 幕间休息
**intern** v/t jūliú 拘留
**internal** nèibù 内部; trade guónèi 国内
**internal combustion engine** nèiránjī 内燃机
**internally** (in body) tǐnèi 体内; (within organization) nèibù 内部
**Internal Revenue (Service)** Guónèi Shuìshōu (bù) 国内税收 (部)
**international 1** adj guójì 国际 **2** n (match) guójì bǐsài 国际比赛; (player) guójì bǐsài xuǎnshǒu 国际比赛选手
**International Court of Justice** Guójì Fǎtíng 国际法庭
**International Labor Day** Guójì Láodòngjié 国际劳动节
**internationally** guójì 国际
**International Monetary Fund** Guójì Huòbì Jījīn Zǔzhī 国际货币基金组织
**Internet** yīntèwǎng 因特网, wǎngluò 网络; **on the** ~ zài wǎngluò shàng 在网络上
**Internet café** wǎngbā 网吧
**internist** nèikē yīshēng 内科医生

**interpret 1** v/t (linguistically) kǒuyì 口译; piece of music, comment etc jiěshì 解释 **2** v/i zuò fānyì 作翻译
**interpretation** (linguistic) kǒuyì 口译; (of piece of music, of meaning) lǐjiě 理解
**interpreter** kǒuyì zhě 口译者
**interrelated** facts xiānghù guānlián 相互关联
**interrogate** xúnwèn 询问
**interrogation** xúnwèn 询问
**interrogative** n GRAM yíwèn 疑问
**interrogator** shěnwèn zhě 审问者
**interrupt 1** v/t speaker dǎduàn 打断 **2** v/i chāhuà 插话
**interruption** zhōngduàn 中断
**intersect** v/t & v/i jiāochā 交叉
**intersection** (crossroads) shízì lùkǒu 十字路口
**interstate** n zhōujìjiān 州际间
**interval** jiàngé 间隔; (in theater, at concert) jiànxiē 间歇
**intervene** (of person, police etc) jièrù 介入
**intervention** jièrù 介入
**interview 1** n (on TV, in paper) cǎifǎng 采访; (for job) miànshì 面试 **2** v/t (on TV, for paper) cǎifǎng 采访; (for job) miànshì 面试
**interviewee** (on TV) bèi cǎifǎng zhě 被采访者; (for job) yìngshì zhě 应试者
**interviewer** (on TV, for paper) cǎifǎng zhě 采访者; (for job) miànshì zhě 面试者
**intestine** chángzi 肠子
**intimacy** (of friendship) qīnmì 亲密; (sexual) qīnnì 亲昵
**intimate** friend qīnmì 亲密; (sexually) qīnnì 亲昵; thoughts sīrén 私人
**intimidate** wēixié 威胁
**intimidation** wēixié 威胁
**into** dào ... lǐ 到 ... 里; **he walked** ~ **the store** tā zǒu dào diànlǐ tā走到店里; **he put it** ~ **his suitcase** tā bǎ tā fàngzài tāde yīxiāng lǐ 他把它放在他的衣箱里; **translate** ~ **English** fānyì chéng Yīngyǔ 翻译成英语; **turn** ~ biànchéng 变成

变成; *be ~ X* F (*like*) xǐhuān X 喜欢 X; (*be involved with*) chīmí X 痴迷 X; *when you're ~ the job* dāng nǐ shúxī zhè gōngzuò de shíhòu 当你熟悉这工作的时候

**intolerable** bùnéng rěnshòu 不能忍受

**intolerant** bù róngrěn 不容忍

**intoxicated** táozuì 陶醉

**intransitive** bù jíwù 不及物

**intravenous** jìngmàinèi 静脉内

**intrepid** wúwèi 无畏

**intricate** fùzá 复杂

**intrigue** 1 *n* cèhuà 策划 2 *v/t* yǐnqǐ hàoqíxīn 引起好奇心; *I would be ~d to know ...* wǒ huì yǒu xìngqù dézhī ... 我会有兴趣得知 ...

**intriguing** yǒu yìsi 有意思

**introduce** jièshào 介绍; *new technique etc* yǐnjìn 引进; *may I ~ ... ?* wǒ lái jièshào yíxià ... ... 我来介绍一下 ...

**introduction** (*to person, new food, sport etc*) jièshào 介绍; (*in book*) xùyán 序言; (*of new technique etc*) yǐnjìn 引进

**introvert** *n* nèixiàng xìnggé de rén 内向性格的人

**intrude** *v/i* qīnfàn 侵犯

**intruder** qīnfàn zhě 侵犯者

**intrusion** qīnfàn 侵犯

**intuition** zhíjué 直觉

**invade** qīnlüè 侵略

**invalid**[1] *adj* wúxiào 无效

**invalid**[2] *n* MED bìngruò 病弱

**invalidate** *claim, theory* shǐ wúxiào 使无效

**invaluable** *help, contributor* wújià 无价

**invariably** (*always*) búbiàn 不变

**invasion** qīnlüè 侵略

**invent** fāmíng 发明

**invention** fāmíng 发明

**inventive** yǒu fāmíng cáinéng 有发明才能

**inventor** fāmíng zhě 发明者

**inventory** mùlù 目录

**inverse** *adj order* xiāngfǎn 相反

**invert** dàozhì 倒置

**inverted commas** yǐnhào 引号

**invertebrate** *n* wú jízhuī dòngwù 无脊椎动物

**invest** *v/t & v/i* tóuzī 投资

**investigate** diàochá 调查

**investigation** diàochá 调查

**investigative journalism** diàochá bàodào 调查报道

**investment** tóuzī 投资

**investor** tóuzī zhě 投资者

**invigorating** *climate* shǐrén shuǎngkuài 使人爽快

**invincible** wúdí 无敌

**invisible** bùkějiàn 不可见

**invitation** yāoqǐng 邀请

**invite** yāoqǐng 邀请; *can I ~ you for a meal?* wǒ kěyǐ qǐng nǐ chī dùn fàn ma? 我可以请你吃顿饭吗?

**invoice** 1 *n* zhàngdān 帐单 2 *v/t customer* kāi zhàngdān 开帐单

**involuntary** fēiběnyì 非本意

**involve** *hard work, expense* xūyào 需要; (*concern*) shèjí 涉及; *what does it ~?* nà xūyào shénme? 那需要什么?; *get ~d with X* juànrù X 卷入 X; (*emotionally, romantically*) yǔ X yǒu gǎnqíng 与 X 有感情

**involved** (*complex*) fùzá 复杂

**involvement** (*in a project etc*) chāshǒu 插手; (*in a crime, accident*) juànrù 卷入

**invulnerable** búyì shòushāng 不易受伤

**inward** 1 *adj* nèibù 内部 2 *adv* xiàngnèi 向内

**inwardly** nèixīn 内心

**iodine** diǎn 碘

**IOU** (= *I owe you*) jièjù 借据

**IQ** (= *intelligence quotient*) zhìshāng 智商

**Iran** Yīlǎng 伊朗

**Iranian** 1 *adj* Yīlǎng 伊朗 2 *n* (*person*) Yīlǎng rén 伊朗人; (*language*) Yīlǎng yǔ 伊朗语

**Iraq** Yīlākè 伊拉克

**Iraqi** 1 *adj* Yīlākè 伊拉克 2 *n* (*person*) Yīlākè rén 伊拉克人

**Ireland** Ài'ěrlán 爱尔兰

**iris** (*of eye*) hóngmó 虹膜; (*flower*) yuānwěishǔ zhíwù 鸢尾属植物

Irish Ài'ěrlán 爱尔兰

Irishman Ài'ěrlán nánzǐ 爱尔兰男子

Irishwoman Ài'ěrlán nǔzǐ 爱尔兰女子

iron 1 n (substance) tiě 铁; (for clothes) yùndǒu 熨斗 2 v/t shirts etc yùn 熨

ironic(al) fěngcì 讽刺

ironing yùn 熨; do the ~ yùn yīfu 熨衣服

ironing board yùnyībǎn 熨衣板

ironworks gāngtiěchǎng 钢铁厂

iron rice bowl (job for life) tiě fànwǎn 铁饭碗

irony fěngcì 讽刺

irrational wúlǐxìng 无理性

irreconcilable wúfǎ héjiě 无法和解

irrecoverable wúfǎ wǎnhuí 无法挽回

irregular intervals bùguīlǜ 不规律; sizes bùguīzé 不规则; behavior bùguīfàn 不规范

irrelevant bùxiānggān 不相干

irreparable wúfǎ míbǔ 无法弥补

irreplaceable object, person bùkě tìdài 不可替代

irrepressible sense of humor bùnéng yìzhǐ 不能抑制; person bùjūshù 不拘束

irreproachable wúkě zhǐzé 无可指责

irresistible wúfǎ kàngjù 无法抗拒

irrespective: ~ of X búgù X 不顾 X

irresponsible búfùzérén 不负责任

irretrievable bùkě wǎnhuí 不可挽回

irreverent bùqiánchéng 不虔诚

irrevocable bùkě qǔxiāo 不可取消

irrigate guàngài 灌溉

irrigation guàngài 灌溉

irrigation canal guàngàiqú 灌溉渠

irritable fánzào 烦躁

irritate rěnù 惹怒

irritating fánrén 烦人

irritation fánzào 烦燥

Islam Yīsīlánjiào 伊斯兰教

Islamic Yīsīlánjiào 伊斯兰教

island dǎo 岛; (traffic) ~ ānquándǎo 安全岛

islander dǎoyǔrén 岛屿人

isolate (separate) gélí 隔离; (cut off) gūlì 孤立; (identify) fēngé 分隔

isolated house gūlì 孤立; occurrence dānyī 单一

isolation (of a region) gélí 隔离; in ~ dāndú 单独

isolation ward gélíjiān 隔离间

Israel Yǐsèliè 以色列

Israeli 1 adj Yǐsèliè 以色列 2 n (person) Yǐsèliè rén 以色列人

issue 1 n (matter) shìqíng 事情; (result) jiéguǒ 结果; (of magazine) qī 期; the point at ~ zhēnglùnde wèntí 争论的问题; take ~ with X yǔ X zhēngbiàn 与 X 争辩 2 v/t supplies, coins, passports, visa fāxíng 发行; warning fābiǎo 发表

IT (= information technology) xìnxī jìshù 信息技术

it tā 它 ◊ (not translated): ~'s on the table zài zhuōzi shang 在桌子上; ~'s raining xiàyǔ le 下雨了; ~'s me/him shì wǒ/tā 是我/他; ~'s yellow shì huángde 是黄的; ~'s Charlie here TELEC wǒ shì Chálí 我是查理; ~'s your turn gāi nǐ de le 该你的了; that's ~! (that's right) duìle! 对了！; (finished) wánle! 完了！

Italian 1 adj Yìdàlì 意大利 2 n (person) Yìdàlì rén 意大利人; (language) Yìdàlì yǔ 意大利语

italic xiétǐ 斜体

Italy Yìdàlì 意大利

itch 1 n yǎng 痒 2 v/i fāyǎng 发痒

item tiáo 条

itemize invoice fēnxiàng lièjǔ 分项列举

itinerary lǔxíng jìhuà 旅行计划

its tāde 它的

itself tā zìjǐ 它自己; by ~ (alone) dúzì 独自; (automatically) zìdòng 自动

ivory (substance) xiàngyá 象牙

ivy chángchūnténg 常春藤

# J

jab v/t chuō 戳

jack MOT qiānjīndǐng 千斤顶; (in cards) gōu 钩

♦jack up MOT yòng qiānjīndǐng dǐng 用千斤顶顶

jacket (coat) jiákè 茄克; (of book) hùfēng 护封

jacket potato kǎo tǔdòu 烤土豆

jack-knife v/i wānchéng V zì xíng 弯成V字形

jackpot lěijī de dǔzhù 累积的赌注; hit the ~ fā dàcái 发大财

jade n yù 玉

jagged cēncī bùqí 参差不齐

jail n jiānyù 监狱

jam¹ guǒjiàng 果酱

jam² 1 n MOT shīlíng 失灵; F (difficulty) kùnjìng 困境; be in a ~ xiànrù kùnjìng 陷入困境 2 v/t (ram) bǎ ... sāijìn 把 ... 塞进; (cause to stick) qiǎzhù 卡住; broadcast gānrǎo 干扰; be ~med (of roads) dǔsè 堵塞; (of door, window) qiǎzhù 卡住 3 v/i (stick) qiǎzhù 卡住; (squeeze) jǐjìn 挤进

jam-packed yōngjǐ 拥挤

janitor kānménrén 看门人

January yīyuè 一月

Japan Rìběn 日本

Japanese 1 adj Rìběn 日本 2 n (person) Rìběn rén 日本人; (language) Rìyǔ 日语

jar¹ n (container) guàn 罐

jar² v/i (of noise) cì'ěr 刺耳; ~ on cìjī 刺激

jargon hánghuà 行话

jasmine tea mòlìhuāchá 茉莉花茶

jaundice huángdǎn 黄疸

jaw n hé 颌

jaywalker luànchuǎng mǎlù de rén 乱闯马路的人

jaywalking luànchuǎng mǎlù 乱闯马路

jazz juéshìyuè 爵士乐

♦jazz up F diǎnzhuì 点缀

jealous dùjì 妒忌; be ~ of ... dùjì ... 妒忌

jealousy dùjì 妒忌

jeans niúzǎikù 牛仔裤

jeep jípǔchē 吉普车

jeer 1 n cháonòng 嘲弄 2 v/i qǐhōng 起哄; ~ at cháoxiào 嘲笑

jelly guǒdòng 果冻

jelly bean ruǎntáng 软糖

jellyfish hǎizhé 海蜇

jeopardize shǐ xiànyú kùnjìng 使陷于困境

jeopardy: be in ~ chǔyú wēixiǎn jìngdì 处于危险境地

jerk¹ n měngrán yídòng 猛然一动 2 v/t měnglā 猛拉

jerk² F chǔnrén 蠢人

jerky movement hūdònghūtíng 忽动忽停

jersey (sweater) jǐnshēn tàoshān 紧身套衫; (fabric) yōují xìmáoshā 优级细毛纱

jest 1 n xiàohuà 笑话; in ~ kāi wánxiào 开玩笑 2 v/i kāi wánxiào 开玩笑

Jesus Yēsū 耶稣

jet 1 n (of water) pēnshèliú 喷射流; (nozzle) guǎnzuǐ 管嘴; (airplane) pēnqìshì 喷气式 2 v/i (travel) fēi 飞

jet-black hēi yòu liàng 黑又亮

jet engine pēnqì fādòngjī 喷气发动机; jetlag shíchā fǎnyìng 时差反应

jettison tóuqì 投弃; fig fàngqì 放弃

jetty fángbōdī 防波堤

Jew Yóutàirén 犹太人

jewel zhūbǎo 珠宝; fig (person) shòu zhēnshì de rén 受珍视的人

jeweler zhūbǎoshāng 珠宝商

jewelry zhūbǎo 珠宝

**Jewish** Yóutài 犹太

**jiao** (*Chinese money*) jiǎo 角

**jiffy**: *in a ~* F yíhuìr 一会儿

**jigsaw** (*puzzle*) pīntú yóuxì 拼图游戏

**jilt** yíqì 遗弃

**jingle 1** *n* (*song*) shùnkǒuliū 顺口溜 **2** *v/i* (*of keys, coins*) fā dīngdāngshēng 发叮当声

**jinx** (*person*) zāixīng 灾星; (*bad luck*) èyùn 厄运; *there's a ~ on this project* zhèige xiàngmù yǒu fángrén de dōngxi 这个项目有妨人的东西

**jitters**: *get the ~* F gǎndào jǐnzhāng 感到紧张

**jittery** F jǐnzhāng 紧张

**job** (*employment*) gōngzuò 工作; (*task*) rènwù 任务; *out of a ~* shīyè 失业; *it's a good ~ you ...* xìngkuī nǐ ... 幸亏你...; *you'll have a ~* (*it'll be difficult*) nǐ yǒu huór gàn le 你有活儿干了

**job description** gōngzuò zhízé shuōmíng 工作职责说明; **job satisfaction** gōngzuò de mǎnzúgǎn 工作的满足感; **job hunt**: *be ~ing* zhǎo gōngzuò 找工作

**jobless** méi gōngzuò 没工作

**jockey** *n* qíshī 骑师

**jog 1** *n* mànpǎo 慢跑; *go for a ~* qù mànpǎo 去慢跑 **2** *v/i* (*as exercise*) mànpǎo 慢跑 **3** *v/t* elbow etc qīngtuī 轻推; *~ X's memory* yǐnqǐ X de huíyì 引起X的回忆

**jogger** (*person*) mànpǎo de rén 慢跑的人; (*shoe*) yùndòngxié 运动鞋

**jogging** mànpǎo 慢跑; *go ~* qù mànpǎo 去慢跑

**jogging suit** yùndòngyī 运动衣

**john** F (*toilet*) cèsuǒ 厕所

**join 1** *n* liánjiēchù 联结处 **2** *v/i* (*of roads, rivers*) huìhé 汇合; (*become a member*) cānjiā 参加 **3** *v/t* (*connect*) liánjiē 连接; *person* yǔ ... huìmiàn 与...会面; *club* cānjiā 参加; (*go to work for*) jiārù 加入; (*of road*) huìhé 汇合

♦**join in** cānjiā 参加

♦**join up** MIL cānjūn 参军

**joiner** mùgōng 木工

**joint 1** *n* ANAT guānjié 关节; (*in woodwork*) liánjiēchù 连接处; (*of meat*) dàkuài ròu 大块肉; F (*place*) dìfang 地方; (*of cannabis*) dàmáyān 大麻烟 **2** *adj* (*shared*) gòngtóng 共同

**joint account** liánhé zhànghù 联合帐户; **joint-stock company** gǔfèn gōngsī 股份公司; **joint venture** hézī qǐyè 合资企业

**joke 1** *n* (*story*) gùshì 故事; (*practical ~*) xiàohua 笑话; *play a ~ on X* kāi X de wánxiào 开X的玩笑; *it's no ~* bùshí nàozhe wánr de 不是闹着玩儿的 **2** *v/i* (*pretend*) shuō xiàohuà 说笑话; (*having a ~*) yīqǐ shuōxiào 一起说笑

**joker** (*person*) xiàoxīng 笑星; *pej* shǎguā 傻瓜; (*in cards*) bǎidā 百搭

**joking**: *~ apart* shuō zhèngjing de 说正经的

**jokingly** kāi wánxiào 开玩笑

**jolly** yúkuài 愉快

**jolt 1** *n* (*jerk*) diānbō 颠簸 **2** *v/t* (*push*) tuī 推

♦**jot down** cōngcōng jìxià 匆匆记下

**journal** (*magazine*) zázhì 杂志; (*diary*) rìjì 日记

**journalism** (*writing*) xīnwén xiězuò 新闻写作; (*trade*) xīnwényè 新闻业

**journalist** xīnwén gōngzuò zhě 新闻工作者

**journey** *n* lǚxíng 旅行

**joy** kuàilè 快乐

**jubilant** xīnxǐ 欣喜

**jubilation** huānxīn 欢欣

**judge 1** *n* LAW fǎguān 法官; (*in competition*) píngwěi 评委 **2** *v/t* pànduàn 判断; *competition* zuò píngwěi 作评委

**judgment** LAW cáijué 裁决; (*opinion*) kànfǎ 看法; (*good sense*) juéduànlì 决断力

**judicial** sīfǎ 司法

**judicious** míngzhì 明智
**judo** róudào 柔道
**jug** hú 壶
**juggle** wán záshuǎ 玩杂耍; *fig* bēnbō 奔波
**juggler** wán záshuǎ de rén 玩杂耍的人
**juice** zhī 汁
**juicy** duōzhī 多汁; *news, gossip* yǒuqù 有趣
**jukebox** zìdòng diǎnchàngjī 自动点唱机
**July** qīyuè 七月
**jumble** *n* yìtuán 一团
**jumble up** húluànde hùnzài yìqǐ 胡乱地混在一起
**jump 1** *n* tiào 跳; (*increase*) tūzēng 突增; (*of surprise*) xiàrényítiào 吓人一跳 **2** *v/i* tiào 跳; (*in surprise*) jīngtiào 惊跳; (*increase*) měngzēng 猛增; **~ to one's feet** zhàn qǐlái 站起来; **~ to conclusions** cōngcōng zuò juédìng 匆匆做决定 **3** *v/t fence etc* tiàoyuè 跳越; F (*attack*) tūrán gōngjī 突然攻击
♦**jump at** *opportunity* pòbùjídài de zhuāzhù 迫不及待地抓住
**jumper** (SP: *person*) tiàoyuè de rén 跳跃的人
**jumpy** jǐnzhāng 紧张
**junction** (*of roads*) jiāochā lùkǒu 交叉路口
**June** liùyuè 六月
**jungle** cónglín 丛林
**junior 1** *adj* (*subordinate*) dìwèi dī 地位低; (*younger*) dī 低 **2** *n* (*in rank*) dìwèi jiào dī zhě 地位较低者; **she is ten years my ~** tā bǐ wǒ xiǎo shísuì 她比我小十岁
**junk** fèipǐn 废品; (*boat*) fānchuán 帆船
**junk food** ⇩ kuàicān 快餐

**junkie** yǒu dúyǐn zhě 有毒瘾者
**junk mail** lājī yóujiàn 垃圾邮件
**junkyard** fèipǐnzhàn 废品站
**jurisdiction** LAW sīfǎquán 司法权
**juror** péishěnyuán 陪审员
**jury** péishěntuán 陪审团
**just 1** *adj law* gōngzhèng 公正; *war, cause* zhèngyì 正义 **2** *adv* (*barely*) gānggāng 刚刚; (*exactly*) qiàhǎo 恰好; (*only*) zhǐshì 只是; *I've ~ seen her* wǒ gānggāng kàndào tā 我刚刚看到她; **~ about** (*almost*) jīhū 几乎; *I was ~ about to leave when ...* wǒ zhèngyào líkāi, zhèishí ... 我正要离开，这时...; **~ like that** (*abruptly*) mòmíng qí miào 莫名其妙; (*exactly like that*) jiù nèiyàng 就那样; **~ now** (*a few moments ago*) gāngcái gāngcái 刚才; (*at the moment*) xiànzài xiànzài 现在; **~ you wait!** nǐ děngzhe ba! 你等着吧！; **~ be quiet!** bié chūshēng! 别出声！
**justice** gōngpíng 公平; (*of cause*) zhèngyì 正义
**justifiable** kě zhèngmíng wéi zhèngdāng 可证明为正当
**justifiably** yǒu lǐyóu 有理由
**justification** zhèngdāng lǐyóu 正当理由
**justify** zhèngmíng ... shì zhèngdāng 证明...是正当; *text* shēnmíng yuányóu 申明缘由
**justly** (*fairly*) gōngzhèng 公正; (*rightly*) zhèngquè 正确
♦**jut out** *v/i* shēnchū 伸出
**juvenile 1** *adj* wèi chéngnián 未成年; *pej* yòuzhì 幼稚 **2** *n fml* wèi chéngnián zhě 未成年者
**juvenile delinquency** shàonián fànzuì 少年犯罪
**juvenile delinquent** shàoniánfàn 少年犯

# K

**k** (= *kilobyte*) qiānzìjié 千字节; (= *thousand*) qiān 千

**karaoke** kǎlā O K 卡拉 OK

**karate** kōngshǒudào 空手道

**karate chop** kōngshǒudàode zhǎngcèpī 空手道的掌侧劈

**Kazakh 1** *adj* Hāsàkèsītǎn 哈萨克斯坦 **2** *n* (*person*) Hāsàkèsītǎn rén 哈萨克斯坦人

**Kazakhstan** Hāsàkèsītǎn 哈萨克斯坦

**keel** *n* NAUT lónggǔ 龙骨

**keen** rèqiè 热切; (*intense*) qiángliè 强烈

**keep 1** *n* (*maintenance*) shēngjì 生计; **for ~s** F yǒngyuǎn 永远 **2** *v/t* bǎoliú 保留; (*not give back*) yōngyǒu 拥有; (*not lose*) bǎozhù 保住; (*detain*) zǔdǎng 阻挡; (*in specific place*) cúnfàng 存放; *family* gōngyǎng 供养; *animals* yǎng 养; **~ a promise** bǎoshǒu chéngnuò 保守承诺; **~ ... company** péibàn ... 陪伴...; **~ X waiting** ràng X děng 让 X 等; **~ ... to oneself** (*not tell*) bǎ ... bǎozhù mìmì 把 ... 保住秘密; **~ X from Y** bùràng Y zhīdào X 不让 Y 知道 X; **~ on trying** jìxù chángshì 继续尝试; **~ on interrupting** zǒngshì gānrǎo 总是干扰 **3** *v/i* (*remain*) bǎochí bǎochí 保持; (*of food, milk*) bǎozhì bǎozhì 保质

♦ **keep away 1** *v/i* bú kàojìn 不靠近; **~ from X** bié kàojìn X 别靠近 X **2** *v/t* shǐ rén bú kàojìn 使人不靠近

♦ **keep back** *v/t* (*hold in check*) zǔzhǐ 阻止; *information* yǐnmán 隐瞒

♦ **keep down** *v/t voice, noise* yādī 压低; *costs, inflation etc* bǎochí dīshuǐpíng 保持低水平; *food* tūnxià 吞下

♦ **keep off** *v/t* (*avoid*) bìmiǎn 避免; **~ the grass!** wùtà cǎopíng! 勿踏草坪! **2** *v/i* (*of rain*) wèixià 未下

♦ **keep out** *v/i* bìkāi 避开; **~!** (*as sign*) xiánrén miǎnjìn! 闲人免进!

♦ **keep to** *path, rules* zūnxún 遵循

♦ **keep up 1** *v/i* (*when walking, running etc*) gēnshàng 跟上 **2** *v/t pace, payments* gēnshàng 跟上; *bridge* zhīchēng 支撑; *pants* tí 提

♦ **keep up with** tóngsù shàngshēng 同速上升; (*stay in touch with*) yǔ X liánxì 与 X 保持联系

**keeping: in ~ with** yízhì 一致

**keg** xiǎotǒng 小桶

**kennel** gǒuwō 狗窝

**kennels** yǎnggǒuchǎng 养狗场

**kernel** héxīn 核心

**kerosene** méiyóu 煤油

**ketchup** fānqiéjiàng 番茄酱

**kettle** hú 壶

**key 1** *n* (*to door, drawer*) yàoshi 钥匙; COMPUT, MUS jiàn 键 **2** *adj* (*vital*) guānjiàn 关键 **3** *v/t* COMPUT jiànrù 键入

♦ **key in** *data* yòng jiànpán shūrù 用键盘输入

**keyboard** COMPUT, MUS jiànpán 键盘; **keyboarder** COMPUT cāozuò jiànpán de rén 操作键盘的人; **keycard** yàoshi kǎ 钥匙卡

**keyed-up** jǐnzhāng 紧张

**keyhole** suǒkǒng 锁孔; **keynote speech** dìng diējiào de yǎnshuō 定基调的演说; **keyring** yàoshiquān 钥匙圈

**kick 1** *n* tī 踢; F (*thrill*) kuàigǎn 快感; (*just*) **for ~s** F wèile qǔlè 为了取乐 **2** *v/t* tī 踢; F *habit* jièchú 戒

除 3 v/i tī 踢

◆kick around v/t ball tīzhewánr 踢着玩儿; (treat harshly) shuǎnòng耍弄; F (discuss) shāngtán 商谈

◆kick in v/t F money gòngxiàn 贡献 2 v/i (of boiler etc) kāishǐ qǐdòng 开始启动

◆kick off v/i kāiqiú 开球; F (start) kāishǐ 开始

◆kick out qūzhú 驱逐; be kicked out of the company/army bèi qūzhúchū gōngsī/bùduì 被驱逐出公司/部队

◆kick up: ~ a fuss nàoshì 闹事

kickback F (bribe) huíkòu 回扣

kickoff kāiqiú 开球

kid F 1 n (child) xiǎoháir 小孩儿; ~ brother/sister dìdi/mèimei 弟弟/妹妹 2 v/t kāi wánxiào 开玩笑 3 v/i kāi wánxiào 开玩笑; I was only ~ding wǒ zhǐshì zài kāi wánxiào 我只是在开玩笑

kidder F huì kāi wánxiào de rén 会开玩笑的人

kidnap bǎngjià 绑架

kidnap(p)er bǎngjià zhě 绑架者

kidnap(p)ing bǎngjià 绑架

kidney ANAT shèn 肾; (food) yāozi 腰子

kill v/t shāsǐ 杀死; plant nòngsǐ 弄死; time xiāomó 消磨; be ~ed in an accident zài shìgù zhōng sàngshēng 在事故中丧生; ~ oneself zìshā 自杀

killer (murderer) xiōngshǒu 凶手; (cause of death) zhìmìngde dōngxi 致命的东西

killing móushā 谋杀; make a ~ (lots of money) dàzǒucáiyùn 大走财运

killingly: ~ funny F jíwéiyǒuqù 极为有趣

kiln yáo 窑

kilo gōngjīn 公斤

kilobyte qiānzìjié 千字节; kilogram gōngjīn 公斤; kilometer gōnglǐ 公里

kimono héfú 和服

kind¹ adj yǒuhǎo 友好

kind² n zhǒnglèi 种类; (make) pǐnpái 品牌; what ~ of ... ? shén-

meyàngde ... ? 什么样的 ...?; all ~s of people gèzhǒnggèyàngde rén 各种各样的人; nothing of the ~ háowú xiāngsi zhīchù 毫无相似之处; ~ of sad/strange F yǒudiǎn nánguò/qíguài 有点儿难过/奇怪

kindergarten yòu'éryuán 幼儿园

kind-hearted hǎoxīn 好心

kindly 1 adj yǒuhǎo 友好 2 adv réncí 仁慈; (please) qǐng 请

kindness hǎoyì 好意

king guówáng 国王

kingdom wángguó 王国

king-size(d) F tèdà 特大

kink (in hose etc) niǔjié 扭结

kinky F biàntài 变态

kiosk shòuhuòtíng 售货亭

kiss 1 n wěn 吻 2 v/t wěn 吻 3 v/i qīnwěn 亲吻

kit (equipment) chéngtào yòngpǐn 成套用品; (for assembly) zǔzhuāngjiàn 组装件

kitchen chúfáng 厨房

kitchenette xiǎochúfáng 小厨房

kitchen sink: everything but the ~ F chúle guōtái 除了锅台

kite fēngzheng 风筝; fly a ~ fàng fēngzheng 放风筝

kitten xiǎomāo 小猫

kitty (fund) gòngtóngde zījīn 共同的资金

klutz F (clumsy person) bènzhuóde rén 笨拙的人

KMT Guómíndǎng 国民党

knack juéqiào 诀窍

knead dough róu 揉

knee n xī 膝

kneecap xīgàigǔ 膝盖骨

kneel guìxià 跪下

knick-knacks xiǎoshìwù 小饰物

knife 1 n dāo 刀 2 v/t yòngdāocì 用刀刺

knit 1 v/t zhī 织 2 v/i biānzhī 编织

◆knit together (of broken bone) láogùde zhǎngzài yìqǐ 牢固地长在一起

**knitting** (*something being knitted*) biānzhīwù 编织物; (*activity*) biānzhī 编织

**knitwear** zhēnzhī yīfú 针织衣服

**knob** (*on door*) lāshǒu 拉手

**knock 1** *n* (*on door*) qiāo 敲; (*blow*) zhuàngjī 撞击 **2** *v/t* (*hit*) jī击; F (*criticize*) pīpíng 批评 **3** *v/i* (*on the door*) qiāo 敲

♦ **knock around 1** *v/t* (*beat*) cūbàode dǎ 粗暴地打 **2** *v/i* F (*travel*) mànyóu 漫游

♦ **knock down** (*of car*) zhuàngdǎo zài dìshang 撞倒在地上; *object, building etc* chāichú 拆除; F (*reduce the price of*) jiàngjià 降价

♦ **knock out** (*make unconscious*) shǐ hūnmí 使昏迷; (*of medicine*) mázuì 麻醉; *power lines etc* jīdǎo 击倒

♦ **knock over** bàndǎo 绊倒; (*of car*) zhuàngdǎo 撞倒

**knockdown**: *a ~ price* dīlián 低廉

**knockout** *n* (*in boxing*) jīdǎo 击倒; (*competition*) táotàisài 淘汰赛

**knot 1** *n* jié结 **2** *v/t* dǎjié 打结

**knotty** *problem* jíshǒu 棘手

**know** zhīdao 知道; *person* rènshi 认识; *place* shúxī 熟悉; *language* dǒng 懂; (*recognize*) rènchū 认出 **2** *v/i*: *I don't ~* wǒ bù zhīdào 我不知道; *yes, I ~* shì, wǒ zhīdào 是, 我知道 **3** *n*: *be in the ~* xiāoxī língtōng 消息灵通

**knowhow** jìnéng 技能

**knowing** xīnzhào bù xuān 心照不宣

**knowingly** (*wittingly*) zhīxī 知悉; *smile etc* xīnzhào bù xuān 心照不宣

**know-it-all** F zì yǐwéi wúsuǒbùzhī de rén 自以为无所不知的人

**knowledge** zhīshí 知识; *to the best of my ~* jùwǒsuǒzhī 据我所知; *have a good ~ of X* jīngtōng X 精通 X

**knowledgeable** zàiháng 在行

**knuckle** zhǐguānjié 指关节

♦ **knuckle down** kāishǐ rènzhēn gōngzuò 开始认真工作

♦ **knuckle under** qūfú 屈服

**KO** jīdǎo 击倒

**Korea** (*South*) Nán Hán 南韩; (*North*) Běi Cháoxiǎn 北朝鲜

**Korean 1** *adj* (*South*) Nán Hán 南韩; (*North*) Běi Cháoxiǎn 北朝鲜 **2** *n* (*South*) Nán Hán rén 南韩人; (*North*) Běi Cháoxiǎn rén 北朝鲜人; (*language*) Cháoxiǎn yǔ 朝鲜语

**kosher** REL hélǐ 合礼; F zhèngdāng 正当

**Kowloon** Jiǔlóng 九龙

**kudos** róngyù 荣誉

**kung-fu** gōngfu 功夫

**Kyrgyzstan** Jíěrjísī 吉尔吉斯斯

# L

lab shíyàn shì 实验室
label 1 n biāoqiān 标签 2 v/t
*baggage* tiē biāoqiān 贴标签
labor n (*work*) láodòng 劳动;
(*workers*) gōngrén 工人; (*in
pregnancy*) fēnmiǎn 分娩; **be in ~**
zài fēnmiǎn zhōng 在分娩中
laboratory shíyàn shì 实验室
laboratory technician shíyàn shì
jìshī 实验室技师
Labor Day Láodòngjié 劳动节
labored *style, speech* bú zìrán 不自
然
laborer láodòng zhě 劳动者
laborious (*difficult*) fèilì 费力
labor union gōnghuì 工会
labor ward chǎnfáng 产房
lace 1 n (*material*) huābiān 花边;
(*for shoe*) xiédài 鞋带
◆lace up *shoes* bǎngdài 绑带
lack 1 n quēshǎo 缺少 2 v/t quēfá
缺乏 3 v/i quēfá 缺乏; **be ~ing**
quēfá 缺乏
lacquer n (*for hair*) dìng fàjiāo 定
发胶
lacquerware qīqì 漆器
lad xiǎo huǒzi 小伙子
ladder tīzi 梯子
laden zhuāngmǎnle 装满了
ladies room nǚcè 女厕
ladle n cháng bǐngsháo 长柄勺
lady nǚshì 女士
ladybug piáochóng 瓢虫
lag v/t *pipes* zhuāng wàitào 装外套
◆lag behind luòhòu 落后
lager chénzhǔ píjiǔ 陈贮啤酒
lagoon huánjiāo hú 环礁湖
laidback yōuxián 悠闲
lake hú 湖
lamb (*animal*) gāoyáng 羔羊;
(*meat*) gāoyáng ròu 羔羊肉
lame *person* qué 瘸; *excuse* zhàn
búzhù jiǎo 站不住脚
lament 1 n (*speech*) dàocí 悼词;
(*song*) wǎngē 挽歌; (*music*) āiyuè
哀乐 2 v/t wèi ... ér bēitòng 为 ...
而悲痛
lamentable lìngrén wǎnxī 令人惋
惜
laminated yóu bópiàn diéchéng 由
薄片迭成; **~ glass** céngyā bōli
层压玻璃
lamp dēng 灯
lamppost lùdēng zhù 路灯柱
lampshade dēngzhào 灯罩
land 1 n tǔdì 土地; (*shore*) lùdì 陆
地; (*country*) guójiā 国家; **by ~**
yóu lùlù 由陆路; **on ~** zài lùdì 在
陆地; **work on the ~** (*as farmer*)
gàn nónghuó 干农活 2 v/t
*airplane* zhuólù 着陆; *job* dédào
得到 3 v/i (*airplane*) zhuólù 着陆;
(*ball, something thrown*) luò luò
落落
landing (*of airplane*) zhuólù 着陆;
(*top of staircase*) (lóutī) píngtái (楼
梯) 平台
landing field fēijī qǐjiàng chǎng 飞
机起降场; landing gear qǐluò
zhuāngzhì 起落装置; landing
strip jiǎnbiàn jīchǎng 简便机场
landlady (*of bar*) lǎobǎnniáng 老
板娘; (*of apartment etc*) fángdōng
房东; landlord (*of bar*) lǎobǎn 老
板; (*of apartment etc*) fángdōng 房
东; landmark lùbiāo 路标; *fig*
lǐchéng bēi 里程碑; land owner
dìzhǔ 地主; landscape 1 n
fēngjǐng 风景; (*painting*) fēngjǐng
huà 风景画 2 adv print héngpái
横排; landslide níshí liú 泥石
流; landslide victory yādào
duōshù de xuǎnpiào 压倒多数
的选票
lane (*in country*) xiǎoxiàng 小巷;
(*alley*) hútong 胡同; (*on freeway*)
hángdào 行道
language yǔyán 语言
lank *hair* píngzhí 平直

**lanky** *person* yòushòu yòugāo 又瘦又高

**lantern** dēnglóng 灯笼

**Lantern Festival** Yuánxiāojié 元宵节

**Lao** Lǎowō yǔ 老挝语

**Laos** ⇩ Lǎowō 老挝

**Laotian 1** *adj* Lǎowō 老挝 **2** *n* (*person*) Lǎowō rén 老挝人

**lap**[1] *n* (*of track*) quān 圈

**lap**[2] *n* (*of water*) pōlàng pāidǎ shēng 波浪拍打声

♦ **lap up** *drink, milk* tiǎn 舔; *flattery* xīnrán jiēshòu 欣然接受

**lap**[3] *n* (*of person*) dàtuǐ 大腿

**lapel** fānlǐng 翻领

**laptop** COMPUT ⇩ xiédài shì diànnǎo 携带式电脑

**larceny** tōuqiè 偷窃

**lard** zhūyóu 猪油

**larder** shípǐn chǔcáng shì 食品储藏室

**large** *building, country, hands, head* dà 大; *sum of money* duō 多; **at ~** (*of criminal*) xiāoyáo fǎwài 逍遥法外; (*of wild animal*) wèi bèibǔ 未被捕

**largely** (*mainly*) zhǔyào 主要

**lark** (*bird*) yúnquè 云雀

**larva** yòuchóng 幼虫

**laryngitis** hóuyán 喉炎

**larynx** yānhóu 咽喉

**laser** jīguāng 激光

**laser beam** jīguāng guāngshù 激光束

**laser printer** jīguāng dǎyìn jī 激光打印机

**lash**[1] *v/t* (*with whip*) biāndǎ 鞭打

♦ **lash down** (*with rope*) bǎngzhù 绑住

**lash**[2] *n* (*eyelash*) yǎn jiémáo 眼睫毛

**last**[1] *adj* (*in series*) zuìhòu 最后; (*preceding*) shàng yīcì 上一次; **~ but one** dàoshǔ dì'èrgè 倒数第二个; **~ night** zuówǎn 昨晚; **but not least** zuìhòu dàn bìngfēi zuì bú zhòngyào de 最后但并非最不重要的; **at ~** zhōngyú 终于; **Last Emperor** Mòdài Huángdì 末代皇帝

**last**[2] *v/i* chíxù 持续

**lastly** zuìhòu 最后

**latch** *n* ménshuān 门闩

**late** (*behind time*) chídào 迟到; (*in day*) wǎn 晚; **it's getting ~** yǐjīng wǎn le 已经晚了; **of ~** zuìjìn 最近; **the ~ 19th/20th century** shíjiǔ / èrshí shìjì mòqī 十九/二十世纪末期

**lately** zuìjìn 最近

**later** *adv* hòulái 后来; **see you ~!** yīhuǐr jiàn! 一会儿见！; **~ on** yǐhòu 以后, hòulái 后来

**latest** *news, girlfriend* zuìxīn 最新

**lathe** chēchuáng 车床

**lather** (*from soap*) pàomòr 泡沫儿; (*sweat*) hànmòr 汗沫儿

**Latin America** Lādīng Měizhōu 拉丁美洲

**Latin American 1** *adj* Lādīng Měizhōu 拉丁美洲 **2** *n* Lādīng Měizhōu rén 拉丁美洲人

**latitude** (*geographical*) wěidù 纬度; (*freedom to maneuver*) kuānróngdù 宽容度

**latter** hòuzhě 后者

**laugh 1** *n* xiàoshēng 笑声; **it was a ~** kāiwánxiào 开玩笑 **2** *v/i* xiào 笑

♦ **laugh at** cháoxiào 嘲笑

**laughing stock**: **make oneself a ~** shǐ zìjǐ chéngwéi xiàobǐng shǐ zìjǐ 成为笑柄; **become a ~** biànchéng xiàobǐng 变成笑柄

**laughter** xiàoshēng 笑声

**launch 1** *n* (*boat, without engine*) xiǎochuán 小船; (*with engine*) xiǎotǐng 小艇; (*of rocket*) fāshè 发射; (*of ship*) xiàshuǐ 下水; (*of product*) fāxíng 发行 **2** *v/t rocket* fāshè 发射; *ship* shǐchuán xiàshuǐ 使船下水; *new product* fāxíng 发行

**launch(ing) ceremony** (*for new product*) fāxíng qìngzhù 发行庆祝

**launch(ing) pad** fāshè tái 发射台

**launder** xǐ 洗

**laundromat** zìzhù xǐyī diàn 自助洗衣店

**laundry** (*place*) xǐyī diàn 洗衣店;

(*clothes*) yīwù 衣物; *get one's ~ done* xǐ yīfú 洗衣服
**laurel** yuèguì 月桂
**lavatory** (*place*) cèsuǒ 厕所; (*equipment*) mǎtǒng 马桶
**lavender** xūnyīcǎo 熏衣草
**lavish** *adj* huīhuò 挥霍
**law** fǎlìng 法令; (*as subject*) fǎlǜ 法律; *against the ~* fànfǎ 犯法; *forbidden by ~* fǎlǜ bùzhǔn 法律不准
**law court** fǎtíng 法庭
**lawful** héfǎ 合法
**lawless** méiyǒu fǎjì 没有法纪
**lawn** cǎopíng 草坪
**lawn mower** gécǎo jī 割草机
**lawsuit** sùsòng 诉讼
**lawyer** lǜshī 律师
**lax** sōngkuǎ 松垮
**laxative** *n* tōngxiè yào 通泄药
**lay** *v/t* (*put down*) fàngxià 放下; *eggs* xià 下; *v* (*sexually*) shuì 睡
♦ **lay into** (*attack*) tòngdǎ 痛打
♦ **lay off** *workers* jiěgù 解雇
♦ **lay on** (*provide*) zhǔnbèi 准备
♦ **lay out** *objects* ānpái 安排; *page* zhǎnkāi 展开
**lay-by** (*on road*) lùpáng tíngchē chù 路旁停车处
**layer** *n* céng 层
**layman** fēi zhuānyè rényuán 非专业人员
**layout** *n* bùjú 布局; COMPUT géshì 格式
♦ **laze around** lǎnsǎn 懒散
**lazy** *person* lǎn 懒; *day* língrén lǎnsǎn 令人懒散
**lb** (= *pound(s)*) bàng 磅
**LCD** (= *liquid crystal display*) yèjīngtǐ xiǎnshìqì 液晶体显示器
**lead**[1] *v/t procession, race* lǐngtóu 领头; *company, team* lǐngdǎo 领导; (*guide, take*) dàilǐng 带领 2 *v/i* (*in race, competition*) lǐngxiān 领先; (*provide leadership*) lǐngdǎo 领导; *a street ~ing off the square* cóng guǎngchǎng fāchū de yìtiáo jiē 从广场发出的一条街; *where is this ~ing?* zhè yǐndào nǎr? 这引到哪儿？3 *n* (*in race*)

lǐngxiān 领先; *be in the ~* lǐngxiān 领先; *take the ~* jū shǒuwèi 居首位; *lose the ~* luòhòu 落后
♦ **lead on** (*go in front*) zǒuzài qiánmiàn 走在前面
♦ **lead up to** yǐndào 引到
**lead**[2] *n* (*for dog*) jiāngsheng 缰绳
**lead**[3] *n* (*substance*) qiān 铅
**leader** lǐngxiù 领袖
**leadership** (*of party etc*) lǐngdǎo dìwèi 领导地位; *under his ~* zài tāde lǐngdǎo xià 在他的领导下; *skills of ~* lǐngdǎo jìqiǎo 领导技巧
**leadership contest** lǐngdǎo dìwèi jìngzhēng 领导地位竞争
**lead-free** *gas* bù hán qiān 不含铅
**leading** *adj runner* dìyī dì yī 第一; *company, product* lǐngxiān 领先
**leading-edge** *adj technology* lǐngxiān 领先
**leaf** yèzi 叶子
♦ **leaf through** fānyuè 翻阅
**leaflet** dānzhāng 单张
**league** (*group*) liánméng 联盟; (*in sport*) liánsài 联赛
**leak** 1 *n* lòu 漏; (*of information*) xièlòu 泄漏 2 *v/i* lòu 漏
♦ **leak out** (*of air, gas*) lòuqì 漏气; (*of news*) xièlòu 泄漏
**leaky** *pipe, boat* lòu 漏
**lean**[1] *v/i* (*be at an angle*) wāi 歪; ~ *against X* kàozhe X 靠着 X 2 *v/t* kàozhe 靠着; ~ *X against Y* bǎ X kàozài Y shàng 把 X 靠在 Y 上
**lean**[2] *adj meat* shòu 瘦; *style, prose* jiǎnjié 简洁
**leap** 1 *n* tiào 跳; *a great ~ forward* jìnle yī dàbù 进了一大步 2 *v/i* tiào 跳
**leap year** rùnnián 闰年
**learn** xuéxí 学习; ~ *how to do X* xuéxí zuò X 学习做 X
**learner** xuésheng 学生
**learning** *n* (*knowledge*) zhīshì 知识; (*act*) xuéxí 学习
**learning curve** xuéxí qǔxiàn 学习曲线; *be on the ~* zài xuéxí qǔxiàn shàng 在学习曲线上
**lease** 1 *n* zūqì 租契 2 *v/t apartment, equipment* zū 租

◆ **lease out** zūchū 租出

**lease purchase** zūjiè gòumǎi 租借购买

**leash** n (for dog) jiāngsheng 缰绳

**least 1** adj movement zuì qīngwēi 最轻微; reason zuìxiǎo 最小; amount zuìshǎo 最少 **2** adv zuìbù 最不 **3** n zuìshǎo 最少; **not in the ~** surprised/disappointed yìdiǎn yěbù qíguài/shīwàng 一点也不奇怪/失望; **at ~** zhìshǎo 至少

**leather** n & adj pí pí 皮

**leave 1** n (vacation) jiàqī 假期; **on ~** fàngjià 放假 **2** v/t city, place líkāi 离开; person yǔ ... fēnshǒu 与 ... 分手; husband, wife pāoqì 抛弃; food on plate shèngxia 剩下; scar, memory liúxià 留下; (forget, leave behind) wàngjì 忘记; **let's ~ things as they are** xiànzài jiù zhèyàng ba 现在就这样吧; **how did you ~ things with him?** nǐ zěnme hé tā jiāodài de 你怎么和他交待的？; **~ X alone** (not touch) biépèng X bié pèng X; (not interfere with) bù dǎjiǎo 不打搅; (not damage) bié nònghuài le 别弄坏了; **be left** shèngxia 剩下; **there is nothing left** méishèng shénme 没剩什么 **3** v/i (of person) líkāi 离开; (of airplane) qǐfēi 起飞; (of train, bus) chūfā 出发; (of ship) qǐháng 启航

◆ **leave behind** (intentionally) yíliú 遗留; (forget) yíwàng 遗忘

◆ **leave on** hat dàizhe 带着; coat chuānzhe 穿着; TV, computer biéguān 别关

◆ **leave out** word, figure shěnglüè 省略; (not put away) liúzhe 留着; **leave me out of this** bié suànwǒ 别算我

**leaving party** gàobié huì 告别会

**lecture 1** n jiǎngzuò 讲座 **2** v/i (at university) jiāo jiào 教

**lecture hall** jiǎngyǎn tīng 讲演厅

**lecturer** jiǎngshī 讲师

**LED** (= light-emitting diode) fāguāng èrjí guǎn 发光二极管

**ledge** (on rock face) yánjiāo 岩礁; (of window) chuāngtái 窗台

**ledger** COM zǒngzhàng 总帐

**leek** jiǔcōng 韭葱

**leer** n (sexual) xiéshì 邪视; (evil) hán èyìde yìpiē 含恶意的一瞥

**left 1** adj zuǒ 左 **2** n zuǒbiān 左边; POL zuǒpài 左派; **on the ~** zài zuǒbiān 在左边; **on the ~ of ...** zài ... de zuǒbiān 在 ... 的左边; **to the ~** turn, look zài zuǒcè 在左侧 **3** adv turn, look zài zuǒcè 在左侧

**left-hand** zài zuǒbiān 在左边; bend zuǒbiān 左边; **left-hand drive** zuǒbiān jiàshǐ chē 左边驾驶车; **left-handed** guànyòng zuǒshǒu 惯用左手; **left-overs** (food) shèngcài 剩菜; **left-wing** POL zuǒyì 左翼

**leg** tuǐ 腿; **pull X's ~** gēn X kāi wánxiào 跟X开玩笑

**legacy** yíchǎn 遗产

**legal** (allowed) héfǎ 合法; (relating to the law) fǎlǜ 法律

**legal adviser** fǎlǜ zīxún yuán 法律咨询员

**legalism** (philosophy) fǎjiā 法家

**legalist** philosophy fǎjiā 法家

**legality** héfǎ xìng 合法性

**legalize** shǐhéfǎ 使合法

**legend** chuánshuō 传说

**legendary** chūmíng 出名

**legible** yìbiànrèn 易辨认

**legislate** lìfǎ 立法

**legislation** (laws) fǎguī 法规; (passing of laws) lìfǎ guòchéng 立法过程

**legislative** powers lìfǎ 立法; assembly yǒu lìfǎ quán 有立法权

**legislature** POL lìfǎ jīgòu 立法机构

**legitimate** héfǎ 合法

**leg room** shēnjiǎo kōngjiān 伸脚空间

**leisure** kòngxián 空闲; **at your ~** yǒu kòng shí 有空时

**leisure center** yúlè zhōngxīn 娱乐中心

**leisurely** pace cóngróng 从容

**leisure time** kòngyú shíjiān 空余时间

**lemon** níngméng 柠檬

**lemonade** níngméng shuǐ 柠檬水

**lemon juice** níngméng zhī 柠檬汁儿

**lemon tea** níngméng chá 柠檬茶

**lend**: ~ *X to Y* jiègěi Y X 借给 Y X

**length** chángdù 长度; (*piece: of material etc*) yíduàn 一段; *at ~ describe, explain* xiángxì de 详细地; (*eventually*) zuìzhōng 最终

**lengthen** shǐ biàncháng 使变长

**lengthy** *speech* rǒngcháng 冗长; *stay* màncháng 漫长

**lenient** kuāndà 宽大

**Lenin** Lièníng 列宁

**lens** (*of camera*) jìngtóu 镜头; (*contact lens, of eyeglasses, of eye*) yǎnjìng 眼镜

**lens cover** (*of camera*) jìngtóu gài 镜头盖

**Lent** Dàzhāijié 大斋节

**lentil** bīngdòu 兵豆

**lentil soup** bīngdòutāng 兵豆汤

**leopard** bào 豹

**leotard** jǐnshēnyī 紧身衣

**lesbian** *n* nǚtóng xìngliàn zhě 女同性恋者

**less**: *eat / talk ~* shǎo chī / shuō 少吃 / 说; ~ *interesting / serious* méi nàme yǒuqù / rènzhēn 没那么有趣 / 认真; *it cost ~* bǐjiào piányi 比较便宜; ~ *than $200* shǎoyú liǎngbǎi měiyuán 少于两百美元

**lesson** kè 课

**let** *v/t* (*allow*) ràng 让; ~ *X do Y* ràng X zuò Y 让 X 做 Y; ~ *me go!* ràng wǒ zǒu! 让我走！; ~ *him come in* ràng tā jìnlái 让他进来; ~*'s go / stay* wǒmen zǒu ba / búzuò ba 我们走吧 / 不走吧; ~*'s not argue* wǒmen bié chǎole 我们别吵了; ~ *alone* gèng bù yòng shuō 更不用说; ~ *go of* (*of rope, handle*) fàngkāi 放开

♦ **let down** *hair* fàngsōng 放松; *blinds* fàngxià 放下; *skirt, pants* fàngcháng 放长; *let X down* (*disappoint*) ràng X shīwàng 让 X 失望

♦ **let in**: *let X in* (*to house*) ràng X jìnlái 让 X 进来

♦ **let off** (*not punish*) fàngguò 放过;

(*from car*) xiàchē 下车

♦ **let out** (*of room, building*) chūzū 出租; *jacket etc* fàngdà 放大; ~ *a cry* shīshēng 失声

♦ **let up** *v/i* (*stop*) tíngzhǐ 停止

**lethal** zhìmìng 致命

**lethargic** lǎnsǎn 懒散

**letter** (*of alphabet*) zìmǔ 字母; (*in mail*) xìnjiàn 信件

**letterhead** (*heading*) xìnzhǐ táitóu 信纸台头; (*headed paper*) táitóu xìnzhǐ 台头信纸

**letter of credit** COM shāngyè xìnyòng shū 商业信用书

**lettuce** shēngcài yè 生菜叶

**letup**: *without a ~* méiyǒu zhōngzhǐ 没有中止

**leukemia** báixuè bìng 白血病

**level 1** *adj field, surface* píngtǎn 平坦; (*in competition, scores*) bìngjìn 并进; *draw ~ with* ... hé ... lāpíng 和 ... 拉平 **2** *n* (*on scale*) shuǐpíng 水平; (*in hierarchy*) jíbié 级别; (*amount, quantity*) lǜ 率; (*of alcohol in blood etc*) nóngdù 浓度; *on the ~* (*on level ground*) zài píngmiàn shàng 在平面上; (*honest*) tǎnshuài 坦率

**level-headed** tóunǎo lěngjìng 头脑冷静

**lever 1** *n* gànggǎn 杠杆 **2** *v/t* yòng gànggǎn yídòng 用杠杆移动; ~ *X open* bǎ X qiàokāi 把 X 撬开

**leverage** gànggǎn lìliàng 杠杆力量; (*influence*) yǐngxiǎng 影响

**levy** *v/t taxes* zhēngshōu 征收

**lewd** yínwěi 淫猥

**Lhasa** Lāsà 拉萨

**liability** (*responsibility*) zérèn 责任; (*likeliness*) kěnéng xìng 可能性

**liability insurance** dìsān fāng bǎoxiǎn 第三方保险

**liable** (*answerable*) fùzé 负责; *be ~ to* (*likely*) yǒu kěnéng 有可能

♦ **liaise with** yǔ ... jiànlì liánxì 与 ... 建立联系

**liaison** (*contacts*) liánluò 联络

**liar** shuōhuǎng zhě 说谎者

**libel** *n* & *v/t* fěibàng 诽谤

**liberal** *adj* (*broad-minded*) dàfāng

大方; (generous: portion etc)
kāngkǎi 慷慨; POL zìyóu 自由
**liberate** jiěfàng 解放
**liberated** woman bèi jiěfàng 被解放
**liberty** zìyóu 自由; at ~ (prisoner etc) huòdé zìyóu 获得自由; be at ~ to do X yǒu quánlìzuò X 有权利做 X
**librarian** túshū guǎnyuán 图书馆员
**library** túshūguǎn 图书馆
**Libya** Lìbǐyà 利比亚
**Libyan** 1 adj Lìbǐyà 利比亚 2 n Lìbǐyà rén 利比亚人
**license** 1 n zhízhào 执照 2 v/t bar xǔkě 许可; ~ a company to produce ... xǔkě gōngsī shēngchǎn ... 许可公司生产...
**license number** zhízhào hàomǎ 执照号码
**license plate** (of car) chēpái 车牌
**lick** 1 n shétiǎn 舌舔 2 v/t tiǎn 舔; ~ one's lips chuíxián 垂涎
**licking**: get a ~ F (defeat) bèi dǎbài 被打败
**lid** gàizi 盖子
**lie**[1] 1 n (untruth) huǎnghuà 谎话 2 v/i shuō huǎnghuà 说谎话
**lie**[2] v/i (of person: on back) tǎng 躺; (on stomach) pā 趴; (of object) píng fàngzhe 平放着; (be situated) wèiyú 位于
♦ **lie down** tǎngxià 躺下
**lie-in**: have a ~ Br shuì lǎnjiào 睡懒觉
**lieutenant** zhōngwèi 中尉
**life** shēngmìng 生命; (of machine) shòumìng 寿命; all her ~ tā yī bèizi 她一辈子; that's ~! zhè jiùshì rénshēng! 这就是人生！
**life belt** jiùshēng quān 救生圈
**lifeboat** jiùshēng tǐng 救生艇
**life expectancy** yùqī shòumìng 预期寿命; **lifeguard** jiùshēng yuán 救生员; **life history** shēnghuó shǐ 生活史; **life insurance** rénshòu bǎoxiǎn 人寿保险; **life jacket** jiùshēng yī 救生衣
**lifeless** wú shēngmìng 无生命

**lifelike** shēngdòng 生动; **lifelong** zhōngshēn 终身; **life preserver** (for swimmer) shuǐshàng jiùshēng gōngjù 水上救生工具; **life-saving** adj medical equipment, drug jiùshēng 救生; **lifesized** yǔ yuánwù yìbān dàxiǎo 与原物一般大小; **life-threatening** shēngmìng wēixiǎn 有生命危险
**lifetime** shòumìng 寿命; in my ~ zài wǒ yìshēng zhōng 在我一生中
**lift** 1 v/t jǔqǐ 举起 2 v/i (fog) xiāosàn 消散 3 n (Br. elevator) diàntī 电梯; (in car) dā biànchē 搭便车; give X a ~ ràng X dāchē 让X搭车
♦ **lift off** v/i (of rocket) fāshè 发射
**ligament** rèndài 韧带
**light**[1] 1 n guāngxiàn 光线; (lamp) dēng 灯; in the ~ of jiànyú 鉴于; have you got a ~? kěyǐ jiège huǒ ma? 可以借个火吗？ 2 v/t fire, cigarette diǎnhuǒ 点火; (illuminate) zhàomíng 照明 3 adj (not dark) míngliàng 明亮
♦ **light up** 1 v/t (illuminate) zhàoliàng 照亮 2 v/i (start to smoke) diǎnyān 点烟
**light**[2] 1 adj (not heavy) qīng 轻 2 adv: travel ~ méi shénme xíngli 没什么行李
**light bulb** diàndēng pào 电灯泡
**lighten**[1] v/t color huǎnhé 缓和
**lighten**[2] v/t load shǐ biànqīng 使变轻
♦ **lighten up** (of person) fàngsōng 放松
**lighter** (for cigarettes) dǎhuǒ jī 火机
**light-headed** (dizzy) yūnxuàn 晕眩; **light-hearted** xiǎngdekāi 想得开; **lighthouse** dēngtǎ 灯塔
**lighting** zhàomíng 照明
**lightly** touch qīngqīng 轻轻; get off ~ táotuō chéngfá 轻易逃脱惩罚
**lightness**[1] (of room, color) yōuyǎ 优雅
**lightness**[2] (in weight) qīng 轻
**lightning** shǎndiàn 闪电

**lightning conductor** bìléi dǎoxiàn 避雷导线

**light pen** guāngbǐ 光笔

**lightweight** (*in boxing*) qīngliàng jí 轻量级

**light year** guāngnián 光年

**likable** kě'ài 可爱

**like¹ 1** *prep* xiàng 象; *be ~ X* (*in looks, character*) xiàng X 象X; *what is she ~?* (*in looks, character*) tā zhǎngde shénmeyàng? 她长得什么样？; *it's not ~ him* (*not his character*) bú xiàng tā 不象他 **2** *conj* F (*as*) rú 如; *~ I said* zhèngrú wǒyán 正如我言

**like² v/t** xǐhuan 喜欢; *I ~ it* wǒ xǐhuan 我喜欢; *I ~ her* wǒ xǐhuan tā 我喜欢她; *I would ~ ...* wǒ xiǎngyào ... 我想要...; *I would ~ to ...* wǒ xīwàng ... 我希望...; *would you ~ ...?* nǐyào ... ma? 你要 ... 吗？; *would you ~ to ...?* nǐyào ... ma? 你要 ... 吗？; *~ to do X* xǐhào X xǐhào X 喜好X; *if you* suíbiàn nǐ 随便你

**likeable** kě'ài 可爱

**likelihood** kěnéng xìng 可能性; *in all ~* duōbànr 多半儿

**likely** (*probable*) kěnéng 可能; *not ~!* méiménr! 没门儿！

**likeness** (*resemblance*) lèisì 类似

**liking:** *to your ~* hé nǐ kǒuwèir 合你口味儿; *take a ~ to X* kāishǐ xǐhuān X 开始喜欢X

**lilac** (*flower*) dīngxiāng huā 丁香花; (*color*) dàn zǐsè 淡紫色

**lily** bǎihé huā 百合花

**lily of the valley** línglán 铃兰

**limbs** sìzhī 四肢

**lime¹** (*fruit, tree*) suānchéng 酸橙

**lime²** (*substance*) shíhuī 石灰

**limegreen** lǜhuáng sè 绿黄色

**limelight:** *be in the ~* yǐnrén zhùmù 引人注目

**limit 1** *n* xiàndù 限度; *within ~s* zài yídìng fànwéi nèi 在一定范围内; *off ~s* jìnzhǐ rùnèi 禁止入内; *that's the ~!* shízài tài guòfèn le! 实在太过分了！ **2** *v/t* xiànzhì 限制

**limitation** júxiàn 局限

**limited company** yǒuxiàn gōngsī 有限公司

**limo, limousine** gāojí jiàochē 高级轿车

**limp¹** *adj material* róuruǎn 柔软; *body* ruò 弱

**limp²** *n* bǒxíng 跛行; *he has a ~* tā bǒxíng 他跛行

**line¹** *n* (*on paper, road*) xiàntiáo 线条; TELEC diànhuà xiàn 电话线; (*of people, trees*) pái 排; (*of text*) háng 行; (*of business*) zhíyè 职业; *the ~ is busy* zhànxiàn 占线; *hold the ~* qǐng shāoděng yíhuìr 请稍等一会儿; *draw the ~ at X* xiànzhì X 限制X; *~ of inquiry* diàochá fāngfǎ 调查方法; *~ of reasoning* sīlù 思路; *stand in ~* páiduì 排队; *in ~ with* (*conforming with*) fúhé ... 符合...; *he's out of ~* (*not doing the proper thing*) tā tài guòfènle 他太过分了

**line²** *v/t* (*with material*) ānchènlǐ 安里

♦ **line up** *v/i* páiduì 排队

**linen** (*material*) yàmá bù 亚麻布; (*sheets etc*) chuángshàng yòngpǐn 床上用品

**liner** (*ship*) bānchuán 班船

**linesman** SP xúnbiān yuán 巡边员

**linger** (*of person*) dòuliú 逗留; (*of pain*) áizhe 挨着

**lingerie** nǚ nèiyī 女内衣

**linguist** yǔyán xuéjiā 语言学家

**linguistic** yǔyán 语言

**lining** (*of clothes*) chènlǐ 衬里; (*of pipe*) chènliào 衬料; (*of brakes*) chèndiàn 衬垫

**link 1** *n* (*connection*) liánjiē 连接; (*in chain*) yìjié 一节 **2** *v/t* liánjiē 连接

♦ **link up** *v/i* huìhé 会合; TV liánjiē 联接

**lion** shīzi 狮子

**lip** zuǐchún 嘴唇

**lipread** *v/i* chúndú 唇读

**lipstick** kǒuhóng 口红

**liqueur** lìkǒu jiǔ 利口酒

**liquid 1** *n* yètǐ 液体 **2** *adj* yèzhuàng 液状

**liquidation** qīngsuàn 清算; *go into*

~ pòchǎn 破产

**liquidity** liúdòng chǎn 流动产

**liquor** jiǔjīng yǐnliào 酒精饮料

**liquorice** gāncǎo 甘草

**liquor store** mài jiǔdiàn 卖酒店

**lisp 1** n kǒuchǐ bùqīng 口齿不清 **2** v/i kǒuchǐ bùqīng de shuōhuà 口齿不清地说话

**list 1** n yīlán biǎo 一览表 **2** v/t biānliè 编列

**listen** tīng 听

◆ **listen in** pángtīng 旁听

◆ **listen to** radio, person tīng 听

**listener** (to radio) tīngzhòng 听众; **he's a good ~** tā hěn liúxīn tīng 他 很留心听

**listings magazine** jiémù biǎo 节 目表

**listless** wújīng dǎcǎi 无精打采

**liter** gōngshēng 公升

**literal** wánquán yīzhào yuánwén wánquán yīzhào yuánwén 完全依照原文; ~ **translation** zhíyì 直译

**literary** wénxué 文学

**literate**: **be** ~ yǒu wénhuà 有文化

**literature** wénxué 文学

**litter 1** adj xiǎo 小; **the ~ ones** xiǎo péngyǒu 小朋友 **2** n shǎoxǔ 少 许; **the ~ I know** wǒ suǒ zhīdào de nà yī diǎndiǎn 我所知道的那一点点; **a ~** yīdiǎn 一点; **a ~ bread / wine** yīdiǎn miànbāo / jiǔ 一点面包/酒; **a ~ is better than nothing** zǒng bǐ méiyǒu yào qiáng 总比没有要强 **3** adv shǎoxǔ 稍 许; ~ **by** zhújiàn de 逐渐地; **a ~ better / bigger** hǎo / dà yīdiǎn 好 /大一点; **a ~ before 6** bǐ liùdiǎn zǎo yīdiǎn 比六点早一点

**Little Red Book** Máo Zhǔxí Yǔlù 毛主席语录

**live¹** v/i (reside) zhùzài 住在; (be alive) shēnghuó 生活

◆ **live on 1** v/t rice, bread kào ... shēnghuó kào ... 生活 **2** v/i (continue living) huó xiàqù 活下去

◆ **live up**: **live it up** kuánghuān 狂 欢

◆ **live up to** bú kuìyú 不愧于

◆ **live with**: ~ **X** (with a person) hé X tóngjū 和 X 同居

**live²** adj broadcast shíkuàng 实况; ~ **ammunition** shídàn 实弹

**livelihood** shēngjì 生计

**lively** huópo 活泼

**liver** MED gānzàng 肝藏; (food) gān 肝

**livestock** shēngchù 牲畜

**livid** (angry) fēicháng shēngqì 非常 生气

**living 1** adj huóde 活的 **2** n móushēng 谋生; **earn one's** ~ móushēng 谋生; **standard of** ~ shēnghuó shuǐpíng 生活水平

**living room** kètīng 客厅

**lizard** xīyì 蜥蜴

**load 1** n fùdān 负担; ELEC fùzǎi 负 载; ~**s of** dàliàng 大量 **2** v/t car, truck zhuāng 装; camera zhuāng jiāojuǎn 装胶卷; gun zhuāng dànyào 装弹药; COMPUT: software zhuāng ruǎnjiàn 装软件; ~ **X onto Y** bǎ X zhuāngdào Y shàng 把 X 装到 Y 上

**loaded** F (very rich) hěn yǒuqián 很 有钱; (drunk) hēzuì le 喝醉了

**loaf** cháng miànbāo 长面包; **a ~ of bread** yīgē miànbāo 一个面包

◆ **loaf around** yóushǒu hàoxián 游 手好闲

**loafer** (shoe) píngdǐ píbiànxié 平底 皮便鞋

**loan 1** n dàikuǎn 贷款; **on** ~ jièyòng 借用 **2** v/t jiè 借; ~ **X Y** jiègěi X Y 借给 X Y

**loathe** tǎoyàn 讨厌

**lobby** (in hotel, theater) méntīng 门 厅; POL yuànwài huódòng jítuán 院外活动集团

**lobster** lóngxiā 龙虾

**local 1** adj dìfāng 地方; **I'm not** ~ wǒ búshì běndìde 我不是本地 的 **2** n (person) běndì rén 本地人

**local anesthetic** júmá 局麻; **local call** TELEC qūnèi diànhuà 区内电 话; **local government** dìfāng zhèngfǔ 地方政府

**locality** suǒzàiqū 所在区

**locally** live, work zài dāngdì 在当

地
**local produce** dāngdì tèchǎn 当地特产

**local time** dāngdì shíjiān 当地时间

**locate** *new factory etc* shèzhì 设置; (*identify position of*) zhǎochū 找出; **be ~d** zài mǒuchù 在某处

**location** (*siting*) dìngwèi 定位; (*identifying position of*) wèizhi 位置; **on ~** *movie* wàijǐng 外景

**lock**[1] (*of hair*) lǔ lǚ 缕

**lock**[2] **1** *n* (*on door*) suǒ 锁 **2** *v/t door* suǒ 锁; **~ X in position** bǎ X gùdìng 把 X 固定

◆ **lock away** suǒ qǐlái 锁起来

◆ **lock in** *person* suǒ zài lǐmiàn 锁在里面

◆ **lock out** (*of house*) suǒzài wàimiàn 锁在外面; **I've locked myself out** wǒ bǎ zìjǐ suǒ zài ménwài le 我把自己锁在门外了

◆ **lock up** (*in prison*) jūjìn 拘禁

**locker** yǒu suǒguì 有锁柜

**locket** xiǎo hé 小盒

**locksmith** suǒjiàng 锁匠

**locust** huángchóng 蝗虫

**lodge 1** *v/t complaint* shēnsù 申诉 **2** *v/i* (*of bullet, ball*) qiǎzhù 卡住

**lodger** fángkè 房客

**loft** gélóu 阁楼

**lofty** *heights* wēi'é 巍峨; *ideals* gāo'ào 高傲

**log** (*wood*) yuánmù 圆木; (*written record*) jìlù 记录

◆ **log off** (*from computer system*) xiàjī 下机; (*from network, database*) xiàwǎng 下网

◆ **log on** (*to computer system*) shàngjī 上机; (*to network, database*) shàngwǎng 上网

◆ **log on to** *computer system* shàngjī 上机; *network, database* shàngwǎng 上网

**logbook** rìzhì 日志

**log cabin** mùwū 木屋

**logic** luóji 逻辑

**logical** yǒu luóji 有逻辑

**logistics** hòuqín xué 后勤学

**logo** biāozhì 标志

**loiter** xiánguàng 闲逛

**London** Lúndūn 伦敦

**loneliness** (*of person*) gūdú gǎn 孤独感; (*of place*) jìmò gǎn 寂寞感

**lonely** *person* gūdú 孤独; *place* jìmò 寂寞

**loner** bù héqún de rén 不合群的人

**long**[1] **1** *adj road, leg time, wait* cháng 长; *journey* yuǎn 远; **it's a ~ way** hěnyuǎn a 很远啊 **2** *adv* chángjiǔ 长久; **don't be ~** kuàidiǎnr huílái 快点儿回来; **5 weeks is too ~** wǔge xīngqī tàicháng le 五个星期太长了; **will it take ~?** shìbúshì yào hěn cháng shíjiān? 是不是要很长时间?; **that was ~ ago** nàshì hěnjiǔ yǐqián le 那是很久以前了; **before then** láozǎo 老早; **before ~** bùjiǔ 不久; **we can't wait any ~er** wǒmen bùnéng zài děng le 我们不能再等了; **he no ~er works here** tā búzài zhèlǐ gōngzuò le 他不在这里工作了; **so ~ as** (*provided*) zhǐyào 只要; **so ~!** mànzǒu! 慢走!

**long**[2] *v/i*: **~ for X** pànwàng X 盼望 X; **be ~ing to do X** kěwàng zuò X 渴望做 X

**longing** *n* kěwàng 渴望

**longitude** jīngdù 经度

**long jump** tiàoyuǎn 跳远; **Long March** Chángzhēng 长征; **long-range** *missile* yuǎnchéng 远程; *forecast* chángyuǎn 长远; **long-sighted** yuǎnshì 远视; **long-sleeved** chángxiù 长袖; **long-standing** chángjiǔ chíxù 长久持续; **long-term** *adj* chángqī 长期; **long wave** chángpō 长波

**loo** *Br* cèsuǒ 厕所

**look 1** *n* (*appearance*) wàiguān 外观; (*glance*) kàn 看; **give X a ~** kàn X yìyǎn 看 X 一眼; **have a ~ at X** (*examine*) kànyíkàn X 看一看 X; **can I have a ~?** wǒ néng kàn yíxià ma? 我能看一下吗?; **can I**

*have a ~ around?* wǒ néng kànkan ma? 我能看看吗？; **~s** *(beauty)* měimào 美貌 **2** *v/i* kàn 看; *(search)* xúnzhǎo 寻找; *(seem)* sìhū 似乎; *you ~ tired / different* nǐ kànqǐlái hěn lèi / bù yíyàng 你看起来很累 / 不一样
♦**look after** zhàogù 照顾
♦**look around** *museum, city* guānguāng 观光
♦**look at** kàn 看; *(examine)* jiǎnchá 检查; *(consider)* kàn 看
♦**look back** huígù 回顾
♦**look down on** kànbùqǐ 看不起
♦**look for** zhǎo 找
♦**look forward to** qīdài 期待
♦**look in on** *(visit)* shùnbiàn kànwàng 顺便看望
♦**look into** *(investigate)* diàochá 调查
♦**look on 1** *v/i (watch)* pángguān 旁观 **2** *v/t:* **~ X as** *(consider)* bǎ X kànzuò 把 X 看作
♦**look onto** *garden, street* cháoxiàng 朝向
♦**look out** *v/i (of window etc)* cháo wàikàn 朝外看; *(pay attention)* liúshén 留神; **~!** xiǎoxīn! 小心！
♦**look out for** xúnzhǎo 寻找; *(be on guard against)* dāngxīn 当心
♦**look out of** *window* cháo wàikàn 朝外看
♦**look over** *house, translation* zǐxì jiǎnchá 仔细检查
♦**look through** *magazine, notes* liúlǎn 浏览
♦**look to** *(rely on)* yīkào 依靠
♦**look up 1** *v/i (from paper etc)* xiàng shàngkàn 向上看; *(improve)* hǎozhuǎn 好转; *things are looking up* yǒu hǎozhuǎn 有好转 **2** *v/t word, phone number* chákàn 查看; *(visit)* bàifǎng 拜访
♦**look up to** *(respect)* zūnjìng 尊敬
**lookout** *(person)* kānshǒu 看守; *be on the ~ for* xúnzhǎo 寻找
♦**loom up** yǐnyuē di chūxiàn 隐约地出现
**loony** F **1** *n* fēngzi 疯子 **2** *adj* fēngkuáng 疯狂
**loop** *n* quān 圈

**loophole** *(in law etc)* lòudòng 漏洞
**loose** *connection, wire, button* sōng 松; *clothes* kuānsōng 宽松; *morals* fàngdàng 放荡; *wording* bù yángé 不严格; **~ change** língqián 零钱; **~ ends** *(of problem, discussion)* shìqíng shàngwèi wánchéng de xìjié 事情尚未完成的细节
**loosely** *tied* sōng 松; *worded* bù yángé 不严格
**loosen** *collar, knot* jiěkāi 解开
**loot 1** *n* zāngwù 赃物 **2** *v/i* luèduó 掠夺
**looter** luèduó zhě 掠夺者
♦**lop off** kǎndiào 砍掉
**lop-sided** bù pínghéng 不平衡
**Lord** *(God)* Shàngdì 上帝; **~'s Prayer** Zhǔdǎo Wén 主祷文
**lorry** *Br* huòchē 货车
**lose 1** *v/t object* diūshī 丢失; *match* shū 输; *I'm lost* wǒ mílù le 我迷路了; *get lost!* gǔndàn! 滚蛋！ **2** *v/i SP* shūdiào 输掉; *(of clock)* zǒumàn 走慢
♦**lose out** shīlì 失利
**loser** *SP* shūzhě 输者; *(in life)* shībài zhě 失败者
**loss** *(of object)* sǔnshī 损失; *(of loved one)* sàngshī 丧失; *(in business)* kuīsǔn 亏损; *make a ~* kuīsǔn 亏损; *be at a ~* bù zhī suǒcuò 不知所措
**lost** shīqù 失去
**lost-and-found (office)** shīwù zhāolǐng chù 失物招领处
**lot:** *a ~, ~s* hěnduō 很多; *a ~ of, ~s of* hěnduō 很多; *a ~ better / a ~ easier* hǎo de duō / róngyì de duō 好得多 / 容易得多
**lotion** xǐjì 洗剂
**loud** *music, voice, noise* xiǎng 响; *color* súyàn 俗艳
**loudspeaker** yángshēng qì 扬声器
**lounge** qǐjū shì 起居室
♦**lounge around** xiánguàng 闲逛
**lounge suit** xīzhuāng 西装
**louse** shīzi 虱子
**lousy** *meal, weather, vacation* bù zěnme yàng 不怎么样; *thing to do* tǎoyàn 讨厌; *I feel ~* wǒ bù

shūfú 我不舒服

lout liúmáng 流氓

lovable kě'ài 可爱

love 1 n ài 爱; (*in tennis*) língfēn 零分; **be in ~** zài liàn'ài zhīzhōng 在恋爱之中; **fall in ~ with** àishàng 爱上; **make ~** zuò'ài 作爱; **yes, my ~** hǎode, wǒ qīn àide 好的,我亲爱的 2 v/t *person, country, wine* ài 爱; **~ to do X** xǐ ài zuò X 喜欢作 X

love affair fēngliú yùnshì 风流韵事; lovelife àiqíng shēnghuó 爱情生活; love letter qíngshū 情书

lovely *face, hair* měilì 美丽; *color* piàoliang 漂亮; *tune* yōuměi 优美; *person, meal* hěn hǎo 很好; *vacation, weather* lìngrén yúkuài 令人愉快; **we had a ~ time** wǒmén kě kāixīn le 我们可开心了

lover qíngrén 情人

loving *adj* zhōngqíng 钟情

low 1 *adj bridge, wall* ǎi 矮; *salary, price, voice* dī 低; *quality* chà 差; **be feeling ~** gǎndào qíngxù bùhǎo 感到情绪不好; **be ~ on gas/tea** méi duōshǎo méiqì/cháyè 没多少煤气/茶叶 2 n (*in weather*) dī qìyā qū 低气压区; (*in sales, statistics*) zuì dīdiǎn 最低点

lowbrow *adj* quēfá wénhuà sùyǎng 缺乏文化素养; low-calorie dī kǎlùlǐ 低卡路里; low-cut *dress* dī lǐngkǒu 低领口

lower *boat, something to the ground* fàngxià 放下; *flag* jiàng jiàng 降; *hemline* fàng 放; *pressure, price* jiàngdī 降低

low-fat dīzhīfáng 低脂肪; lowkey dīdiào 低调; lowlands dīdì 低地; low-pressure area dīyā dìqū 低压地区; low season dànjì 淡季; low tide dīcháo 低潮

loyal zhōngxīn 忠心

lozenge (*shape*) língxíng 菱形; (*tablet*) zhǐké táng 止咳糖

Ltd (= *limited*) yǒuxiàn gōngsī 有限公司

lubricant rùnhuá jì 润滑剂

lubricate rùnhuá 润滑

lubrication rùnhuá 润滑

lucid (*clear*) míngliǎo 明了; (*sane*) shénzhì qīngxǐng 神志清醒

luck yùnqì 运气; **bad ~** èyùn 恶运; **hard ~!** dǎoméi! 倒霉！; **good ~** xìngyùn 幸运; **good ~!** zhùnǐ 祝你走运！

♦luck out F jiǎoxìng chénggōng 侥幸成功

luckily xìngyùnde 幸运地

lucky *person* xìngyùn 幸运; *day, number* jíxiáng 吉祥; *coincidence* jiǎoxìng 侥幸; **you were ~** nǐ zhēn zǒuyùn 你真走运; **he's ~ to be alive** tā jiǎoxìng déyǐ táoshēng 他侥幸得以逃生; **that's ~!** zhēn zǒuyùn! 真走运!

ludicrous huāngtáng 荒唐

luggage xíngli 行李

lukewarm *water* wēiwēn 微温; *reception* bú rèqíng 不热情

lull 1 n (*in storm, fighting*) zànshí píngxī 暂时平息; (*in conversation*) jiānxiē 间歇; **~ X into a false sense of security** shǐ X chǎnshēng bù zhēnshíde ānquán gǎn 使 X 产生不真实的安全感

lullaby cuīmián qǔ 催眠曲

lumbago yāoténg 腰疼

lumber n (*timber*) mùcái 木材

luminous guāngmíng 光明

lump (*of sugar*) kuài 块; (*swelling*) zhǒngkuài 肿块

♦lump together bǎ ... guībìng zài yìqǐ 把 ... 归并在一起

lump sum zǒng'é 总额

lumpy āotū bùpíng 凹凸不平

lunacy jíduān yúchǔn 极端愚蠢

lunar yuèliang 月亮

lunatic n fēngzi 疯子

lunch wǔcān 午餐; **have ~** chī wǔcān 吃午餐

lunch box ⇩ wǔcān hé 午餐盒; lunch break wǔxiū 午休; lunch hour wǔxiū 午休; lunchtime wǔcān shíjiān 午餐时间

lung fèi 肺

lung cancer fèi'ái 肺癌

♦lunge at chōngjī 冲击

lurch v/i (*of person*) pánshān 蹒跚; (*of ship*) qīngxié 倾斜

**lure** *n & v/t* yòuhuò 诱惑

**lurid** *color* huǒhóng 火红; *details* sǒngrén tīngwén 耸人听闻

**lurk** *(of person)* qiáncáng 潜藏; *(of doubt)* qiánzài 潜在

**luscious** *fruit, dessert* gānměi 甘美; *woman, man* xìnggǎn 性感

**lust** *n* xìngyù 性欲

**luxurious** háohuá 豪华

**luxury** *n & adj* háohuá 豪华

**lychee** lìzhī 荔枝

**lymph gland** línbājié 淋巴结

**lynch** sīxíng chùsǐ 私刑处死

**lynx** shānmāo 山猫

**lyricist** cí zuòzhě 词作者

**lyrics** gēcí 歌词

# M

MA (= *Master of Arts*) wénkē shuòshì 文科硕士
ma'am nǚshì 女士
Macanese 1 *adj* Àomén 澳门 2 *n* (*person*) Àomén rén 澳门人
Macao Àomén 澳门
machine 1 *n* jīqì 机器 2 *v/t* (*on sewing machine*) féngrènjī 缝纫机; TECH jīzhì 机制
machine gun *n* jīqiāng 机枪
machine-readable kě jīdú 可机读
machinery (*machines*) jīqì 机器
machismo nánzǐ qìgài 男子气概
macho dànánzǐqì 大男子气
mackintosh yǔyī 雨衣
macro COMPUT hóng huìbiān 宏汇编
mad (*insane*) fēng疯; (*angry*) nǎohuǒ 恼火; **be ~ about** X (*keen on*) duì X zháomí 对 X 着迷; **drive** X **~** shǐ X fāfēng 使 X 发疯; **go ~** (*become insane*) fāfēng 发疯; (*with enthusiasm*) kuángrèqǐlái 狂热起来; **like ~ run, work** pīnmìng 拼命
madden (*infuriate*) shǐrén nǎohuǒ 使人恼火
maddening shǐrén nǎohuǒ 使人恼火
made-to-measure dìngzuò 定做
madhouse *fig* yí piàn hùnluàn 一片混乱
madly fēngkuáng 疯狂; **~ in love** rèliàn 热恋
madman fēngrén 疯人
madness jīngshén shīcháng 精神失常
Mafia: **the ~** hēishǒudǎng 黑手党
magazine (*printed*) zázhì 杂志
maggot qū 蛆
magic 1 *n* mófǎ 魔法; (*tricks*) móshù 魔术; **like ~** móshùbān 魔术般 2 *adj* juémiào 绝妙
magical *powers* mófǎ 魔法;

*moment* miàobùkěyán 妙不可言
magician (*performer*) móshùshī 魔术师
magic spell fúzhòu 符咒
magic trick móshù 魔术
magnanimous kāngkǎi 慷慨
magnet císhí 磁石
magnetic yǒucíxìng 有磁性; *fig: personality* yǒumèilì 有魅力
magnetism (*of person*) mèilì 魅力
magnificence zhuànglì 壮丽
magnificent zhuàngguān 壮观
magnify fàngdà 放大; *difficulties* kuādà 夸大
magnifying glass fàngdàjìng 放大镜
magnitude dàxiǎo 大小
magpie xǐque 喜鹊
mah-jong májiàng 麻将
maid nǚpú 女仆; (*in hotel*) fúwù-yuán 服务员
maiden name niángjiāxìng 娘家姓
maiden voyage shǒuháng 首航
mail 1 *n* yóuzhèng 邮政; **put** X **in the ~** yóujì X 邮寄 X 2 *v/t letter* yóujì 邮寄; *person* yóudìyuán 邮递员
mailbox (*in street*) yóutǒng 邮筒; (*for house, e-mail*) xìnxiāng 信箱
mailman yóudìyuán 邮递员
mail-order catalog yóugòu mùlù 邮购目录; mail-order firm yóugòu shāngpǐn gōngsī 邮购商品公司
maim zhìcán 致残
main *adj* zhǔyào 主要
mainboard COMPUT zhǔbǎn 主板; mainframe COMPUT zhǔjītǐ 主机体; mainland dàlù 大陆; **on the ~** zài dàlù shang 在大陆上; mainland China Zhōngguó dàlù 中国大陆
mainly zhǔyào 主要

**main road** dàlù 大路

**main street** zhǔjiē 主街

**maintain** *peace, law and order* wéichí 维持; *pace, speed, ship* bǎochí 保持; *machine, house* bǎoyǎng 保养; *family* gōngyǎng 供养; *innocence, guilt* jiānchí 坚持; **~ *that*** duànyán 断言

**maintenance** *(of machine, house)* bǎoyǎng 保养; *(money)* fǔyǎngfèi 抚养费; *(of law and order)* wéihù 维护

**majestic** wēiyán 威严

**major 1** *adj (significant)* zhǔyào 主要; **in C** – MUS C dàdiào C 大调 **2** *n* MIL shàoxiào 少校

♦**major in** zhǔxiū 主修

**majority** dàduōshù 大多数; POL duōdé piàoshù 多得的票数; **be in the ~** zhàn duōshù 占多数

**make 1** *n (brand)* páizi 牌子 **2** *v/t* zuò 做; *(earn)* zhèng 挣; MATH děngyú 等于; **~ *X do Y*** *(force to)* pòshǐ X zuò Y 迫使 X 做 Y; *(cause to)* cùshǐ X zuò Y 促使 X 做 Y; **you can't ~ me do it** wǒ bù néng pòshǐ wǒ zuò zhèijiànshì 你不能迫使我做这件事; **~ *X happy* / *angry*** shǐ X gāoxìng / shēngqì 使 X 高兴 / 生气; **~ *a decision*** zuò juédìng 做决定; **~ *a telephone call*** dǎ ge diànhuà 打个电话; **made in China** Zhōngguó zhìzào 中国制造; **~ *it*** *(catch bus, train)* gǎnshàng 赶上; *(succeed)* huòdé chénggōng 获得成功; *(survive)* cúnhuó 存活; **sorry, I can't ~ it tomorrow** *(come)* duìbùqǐ, wǒ míngr qùbùliǎo 对不起, 我明儿去不了; **what time do you ~ it?** nǐ biǎo jǐdiǎnle? 你表几点了?; **~ *believe*** jiǎzhuāng 假装; **~ *do with X*** yòng X jiāngjiù 用 X 将就; **what do you ~ it?** nǐ juédé zěnmeyàng? 你觉得怎么样?

♦**make for: ~ *X*** *(go toward)* cháo X yídòng 朝 X 移动

♦**make off** táozǒu 逃走

♦**make off with** *(steal)* tōuzǒu 偷走

♦**make out** *list* xiěchū 写出; *check*

♦**make over: make *X* over to *Y*** bǎ X zhuǎnràng gěi Y 把 X 转让给 Y

♦**make up 1** *v/i (of woman, actor)* huàzhuāng 化妆; *(after quarrel)* héjiě 和解 **2** *v/t story, excuse* biānzào 编造; *face* huàzhuāng 化妆; *(constitute)* zhàn 占; **be made up of *X*** yóu X zǔchéng 由 X 组成; **~ *one's mind*** xià juéxīn 下决心; **make it up** *(after quarrel)* héhǎo 和好

♦**make up for** míbǔ 弥补

**make-believe** *n* jiǎxiǎng 假想

**maker** zhìzào zhě 制造者

**makeshift** dàiyòngpǐn 代用品

**make-up** *(cosmetics)* huàzhuāngpǐn 化妆品

**maladjusted** xīnlǐ shītiáo 心理失调

**malaria** nüèjí 疟疾

**Malay** *(person)* Mǎláixīyà rén 马来西亚人; *(language)* Mǎlái yǔ 马来语

**Malaysia** Mǎláixīyà 马来西亚

**Malaysian** Mǎláixīyà 马来西亚

**male 1** *adj (masculine)* nánxìng 男性; *animal, bird, fish* xióng, gōng 雄, 公 **2** *n (man)* nánrén 男人; *(animal, bird, fish)* xióngxìng 雄性

**male chauvinist** *(pig)* dànánzǐ zhǔyì zhě 大男子主义者

**male nurse** nán hùshì 男护士

**malevolent** èdú 恶毒

**malfunction 1** *n* shīlíng 失灵 **2** *v/i* fāshēng gùzhàng 发生故障

**malice** èyì 恶意

**malicious** èyì 恶意

**malignant** *tumor* èxìng 恶性

**mall** *(shopping ~)* gòuwù zhōngxīn 购物中心

**malnutrition** yíngyǎng bùliáng 营养不良

**malpractice** wánhūzhíshǒu 玩忽职守

**maltreat** nüèdài 虐待

**maltreatment** nüèdài 虐待

**mammal** bǔrǔ dòngwù 哺乳动物

**mammoth** *adj (enormous)* jùdà 巨大

**man** *n* nánrén 男人; (*human being*) rén *n*; (*humanity*) rénlèi 人类; (*in checkers*) qízǐ 棋子

**manage 1** *v/t business* jīngyíng 经营; *money* guǎn 管; *suitcase* nádòng 拿动; ~ **to** ... zuòchéng ... 做成 ... **2** *v/i* (*cope*) yìngfù 应付; (*financially*) wéichí shēnghuó 维持生活; *can you* ~? nǐ néngxíng ma? 你能行吗？

**manageable** yì chǔlǐ 易处理

**management** (*managing*) guǎnlǐ 管理; (*managers*) zhǔguǎn rényuán 主管人员; *under his* ~ zài tāde guǎnlǐ xià 在他的管理下

**management buyout** guǎnlǐ rényuán shōumǎi 管理人员收买; **management consultant** jīngyíng gùwèn 经营顾问; **management studies** guǎnlǐxué 管理学; **management team** guǎnlǐ rényuán 管理人员

**manager** jīnglǐ 经理

**managerial** jīngyíng 经营

**managing director** zǒngjīnglǐ 总经理

**Manchu** (*nationality*) Mǎnzú 满族

**Manchuria** Mǎnzhōu 满洲

**Mandarin** (*language*) ⇩ Pǔtōnghuà 普通话

**mandarin** (*in China*) guānlì 官吏

**mandarin orange** júzi 橘子

**mandate** (*authority*) shòuquán 授权; (*task*) shǐmìng 使命

**mandatory** qiángzhì 强制

**mane** (*of horse*) zōng 鬃

**maneuver 1** *n* xíngdòng 行动 **2** *v/t* shèfǎ yídòng 设法移动

**mangle** *v/t* (*crush*) huǐhuài 毁坏

**manhandle** *person* cūbàode duìdài 粗暴地对待; *object* yònglì yídòng 用力移动

**manhood** (*maturity*) chéngnián 成年; (*virility*) nánzǐhànqì 男子汉气

**man-hour** gōngzuò shí 工作时

**manhunt** jīná 缉拿

**mania** (*craze*) pǐhào 癖好

**maniac** kuángrén 狂人

**manicure** *n* xiūjiǎn zhǐjiǎ 修剪指甲

**manifest 1** *adj* míngxiǎn 明显

**2** *v/t* xuānyán 宣言; ~ *itself* xiǎnlù 显露

**manipulate** *person* bǎibù 摆布; *bones* jiǎozhèng 矫正; *equipment* cāozòng 操纵

**manipulation** (*of person*) bǎibù 摆布; (*of bones*) jiǎozhèng 矫正

**manipulative** ài cāozòng rén 爱操纵人

**mankind** rénlèi 人类

**manly** yǒu nánzǐqì 有男子气

**man-made** rénzào 人造

**mannequin** (*for clothes*) réntǐ móxíng 人体模型

**manner** (*of doing sth*) fāngshì 方式; (*attitude*) tàidù 态度

**manners**: *good* / *bad* ~ yǒu / méiyǒu lǐmào 有 / 没有礼貌; *have no* ~ méilǐmào 没礼貌

**manpower** láodònglì 劳动力

**mansion** zháidì 宅第

**mantelpiece, mantelshelf** bìlútái 壁炉台

**manual 1** *adj* shǒugōng 手工 **2** *n* zhǐnán 指南

**manufacture 1** *n* zhìzào 制造 **2** *v/t equipment* zhìzào 制造

**manufacturer** zhìzàoshāng 制造商

**manufacturing** (*industry*) zhìzào 制造

**manure** féiliào 肥料

**manuscript** shǒugǎo 手稿

**many 1** *adj* xǔduō 许多; ~ *times* xǔduō cì 许多次; *not* ~ *people* taxis méiyǒu duōshao rén / chūzūchē 没有多少人 / 出租车; *too* ~ *problems* / *beers* tàiduō wèntí / píjiǔ 太多问题 / 啤酒 **2** *pron* xǔduō rén 许多人; *a great* ~, *a good* ~ xiāngdāng duō 相当多; *how* ~ *do you need?* nǐ xūyào duōshao? 你需要多少？

**mao** (*Chinese money*) máo 毛

**Mao badge** Máo zhǔxí xiàngzhāng 毛主席像章; **Mao jacket** Zhōngshānfú 中山服; **Mao Tse-tung, Mao Zedong** Máo Zédōng 毛泽东; **Mao Zedong thought** Máo Zédōng sīxiǎng 毛泽东思想

map 504

**map** *n* dìtú 地图
♦ **map out** chóuhuà 筹划
**maple** fēng 枫
**mar** pòhuài 破坏
**marathon** (*race*) mǎlāsōng 马拉松
**marble** (*material*) dàlǐshí 大理石
**March** sānyuè 三月
**march 1** *n* xíngjūn 行军; (*demonstration*) yóuxíng 游行 **2** *v/i* (*in protest*) yóuxíng 游行
**mare** mǔmǎ 母马
**margarine** rénzào huángyóu 人造黄油
**margin** (*of page*) kòngbái 空白; (COM: *profit margin*) yínglì 盈利; **by a narrow ~** hěnxiǎode chāshù 很小的差数
**marginal** (*slight*) hěnxiǎo 很小
**marginally** (*slightly*) shāowēi 稍微
**marihuana, marijuana** dàmá 大麻
**marina** yóutǐng tíngbó gǎng 游艇停泊港
**marinade** *n* yānpàozhī 腌泡汁
**marinate** yānpào 腌泡
**marine 1** *adj* hǎiyáng 海洋 **2** *n* MIL hǎilùbīng 海陆兵
**marital** hūnyīn 婚姻
**maritime** hǎishàng 海上
**mark 1** *n* (*stain*) wūdiǎn 污点; (*sign, token*) biāozhì 标志; (*trace*) jìxiàng 迹象; EDU fēnshù 分数; **leave one's ~** liúxià chíjiǔ yìnxiàng 留下持久印象 **2** *v/t* (*stain*) liú hénjì yú 留痕迹于; EDU pīgǎi 批改; (*indicate*) biāomíng 标明; (*commemorate*) jìniàn 纪念 **3** *v/i* (*of fabric*) liúyǒu wūjì 留有污迹
♦ **mark down** *goods* jiàngdī biāojià 降低标价
♦ **mark out** (*with a line etc*) huàxiàn biāochū 划线标出; **mark X out** *fig* (*set apart*) shǐ X yǔ zhòng bùtóng 使X与众不同
♦ **mark up** *price* tígāo biāojià 提高标价; *goods* zài chéngběn shang jiājià 在成本上加价
**marked** (*definite*) míngquè 明确
**marker** (*highlighter*) biāojìbǐ 标记笔
**market 1** *n* jíshì 集市; (*for particular commodity*) shìchǎng 市场; (*outlet*) xíngxiāo dìqū 行销地区; (*stock ~*) zhèngquàn shìchǎng 证券市场; **on the ~** shàngshì 上市 **2** *v/t* xiāoshòu 销售
**market economy** shìchǎng jīngjì 市场经济
**market forces** shìchǎng lìliàng 市场力量
**marketing** tuīxiāo 推销
**market leader** shìchǎng zhǔdǎo 市场主导; market-place shìchǎng 市场; market research shìchǎng diàochá 市场调查; market share shìchǎng zhànyǒulǜ 市场占有率
**mark-up** jiàgé tígāo 价格提高
**marmalade** chéngzijiàng 橙子酱
**marquee** dàzhàngpéng 大帐篷
**marriage** (*institution*) hūnyīnzhì 婚姻制; (*state of being married*) hūnyīn 婚姻; (*event*) hūnlǐ 婚礼
**marriage certificate** jiéhūn zhèngshū 结婚证书
**marriage counselor** hūnyīn gùwèn 婚姻顾问
**married** yǐhūn 已婚; **be ~ to X** yǔ X jiéhūn 与X结婚
**marry** jiéhūn 结婚; (*of priest*) zhǔchí hūnlǐ 主持婚礼; **get married** jiéhūn 结婚
**marsh** zhǎozé 沼泽
**marshal** *n* (*police officer*) jǐngchá 警察; (*official*) sīyí 司仪
**marshmallow** miánhuātáng 棉花糖
**marshy** yǒu zhǎozé 有沼泽
**martial arts** wǔshù 武术
**martial law** jièyánlìng 戒严令
**martyr** *n* xùndào zhě 殉道者
**martyred** miǎnqiǎng 勉强
**marvel** *n* qíyìde shìwù 奇异的事物
♦ **marvel at** dàwéijīngyà 大为惊讶
**marvelous** jíhǎo 极好
**Marx** Mǎkèsī 马克思
**Marxism** Mǎkèsīzhǔyì 马克思主义
**Marxist 1** *adj* Mǎkèsīzhǔyì 马克思主义 **2** *n* Mǎkèsīzhǔyì zhě 马

克思主义者

**Marxism-Leninism** Mǎlièzhǔyì 马列主义

**Marxist-Leninist** Mǎlièzhǔyì zhě 马列主义者

**mascara** jiémáogāo 睫毛膏

**mascot** jíxiángde rénwù 吉祥的人物

**masculine** *also* GRAM nánzǐqì 男子气

**masculinity** (*virility*) yángxìng 阳性

**mash** *v/t* dǎochénghúzhuàng 捣成糊状

**mashed potatoes** tǔdòuní 土豆泥

**mask** 1 *n* miànjù 面具 2 *v/t feelings* yǎngài 掩盖

**masochism** shòunüèkuáng 受虐狂

**masochist** shòunüèkuáng zhě 受虐狂者

**mason** níwǎjiàng 泥瓦匠

**masonry** (*stonework*) zhuānshí jiégòu 砖石结构; (*skill*) shígōng jiǎqiǎo 石工技巧

**masquerade** 1 *n fig* jiǎzhuāng 假装 2 *v/i*: ~ **as X** wěizhuāng wéi X 伪装为 X

**mass**[1] *n* (*great amount*) zhòngduō 众多; (*body*) tuán 团; **the ~es** qúnzhòng 群众; ~**es of** hěnduō 很多 2 *v/i* jíjié 集结

**mass**[2] REL zuò mísa 作弥撒

**massacre** 1 *n* dàtúshā 大屠杀; F (*in sport*) cánbài 惨败 2 *v/t* túshā 屠杀; F (*in sport*) yǐ xuánshū bǐfēn zhànshèng 以悬殊比分战胜

**massage** 1 *n* ànmó 按摩 2 *v/t* zuò ànmó 作按摩; *figures* tiáozhěng 调整

**massage parlor** ànmóyuàn 按摩院

**masseur** nán ànmóshī 男按摩师

**masseuse** ànmó xiǎojiě 按摩小姐

**massive** jùdà 巨大

**mass media** dàzhòng chuánméi 大众传媒; **mass-produce** dàliàng shēngchǎn 大量生产; **mass production** dàliàng

shēngchǎn 大量生产

**mast** (*of ship*) chuánwéi chángān 船樯; (*for radio signal*) tiānxiàntǎ 天线塔

**master** 1 *n* (*of dog*) zhǔrén 主人; (*of ship*) chuánzhǎng 船长; *be a ~ of X* zhǎngwò X 掌握 X 2 *v/t skill, language* jīngtōng 精通; *situation* kòngzhì 控制

**master bedroom** zhǔwòshì 主卧室

**master key** wànnéng yàoshi 万能钥匙

**masterly** gāomíng 高明

**mastermind** 1 *n* juécè zhě 决策者 2 *v/t* mùhòu cèhuà 幕后策划; **Master of Arts** wénkē shuòshì 文科硕士; **master of ceremonies** sīyí 司仪; **masterpiece** jiézuò 杰作; **master's (degree)** shuòshì 硕士

**mastery** jīngtōng 精通

**masturbate** shǒuyín 手淫

**mat** *n* (*for floor*) diàn 垫; (*for table*) gérèdiàn 隔热垫

**match**[1] (*for cigarette*) huǒchái 火柴

**match**[2] 1 *n* (*competition*) bǐsài 比赛; *be no ~ for X* bùnéng yǔ X pǐdí 不能与 X 匹敌; *meet one's ~* qígǔ xiāngdāng 旗鼓相当 2 *v/t* (*be the same as*) yǔ ... yīyàng 与 ... 一样; ~**X** (*equal*) yǔ X pǐdí yú X 匹敌 3 *v/i* (*of colors, patterns*) xiāngpèi 相配

**matchbox** huǒcháihé 火柴盒

**matching** *adj* xiétiáo 协调

**mate** 1 *n* (*of animal*) ǒu 偶; NAUT fùshǒu 副手 2 *v/i* jiāopèi 交配

**material** 1 *n* (*fabric*) bùliào 布料; (*substance*) cáiliào 材料 2 *adj* wùzhì 物质

**materialism** wéiwù zhǔyì 唯物主义

**materialist** wéiwù zhǔyì zhě 唯物主义者

**materialistic** wéiwùlùn 唯物论

**materialize** chéngxiàn 呈现

**materials** yuánliào 原料

**maternal** mǔqīn fāngmiàn 母亲方面

**maternity** mǔxìng 母性

**maternity dress** yùnfù fúzhuāng

孕妇服装; **maternity leave**
chǎnjià 产假; **maternity ward**
chǎnkē bìngfáng 产科病房
**math** shùxué 数学
**mathematical** *calculations, formula*
shùxué 数学; *mind, person* luójí
逻辑
**mathematician** shùxuéjiā 数学家
**mathematics** shùxué 数学
**matinée** xiàwǔchǎng 下午场
**matriarch** nǚzúzhǎng 女族长
**matrimony** hūnyīn 婚姻
**matt** cūmiàn 粗面
**matter** *(affair)* shìqing 事情; PHYS
wùzhì 物质; *as a ~ of course*
lǐsuǒdāngrán 理所当然; *as a ~*
*of fact* shìshí shang 事实上;
*what's the ~?* zěnmele? 怎么
了 ?; *no ~ what she says* bùguǎn
tā shuō shénme 不管她说什么
**2** *v/i* yàojǐn 要紧; *it doesn't ~*
méiguānxi 没关系
**matter-of-fact** búdònggǎnqíng 不
动感情
**mattress** chuángdiàn 床垫
**mature 1** *adj* chéngshú 成熟 **2** *v/i*
*(of person)* chéngshú 成熟; *(of*
*insurance policy etc)* dàoqī 到期
**maturity** chéngshú 成熟
**maximize** zēngzhì zuìdà xiàndù zēng
至最大限度
**maximum 1** *adj* zuìgāo/dà 最高/
大 **2** *n* zuìduō 最多
**May** wǔyuè 五月
**may ◊** *(possibility)* yěxǔ 也许; *it ~*
*rain* kěnéng huì xiàyǔ 可能会下
雨; *you ~ be right* nǐ yěxǔ duì 你
也许对; *it ~ not happen* zhèshìr
kěnéng búhuì fāshēng 这事儿可
能不会发生 ◊ *(permission)* kěyǐ
可以; *– I help/smoke?* wǒ kěyǐ
bāngmáng/xīyān ma? 我可以帮
忙/吸烟吗 ?; *you ~ if you like*
nǐ yuànyì de huà, kěyǐ 你愿意的
话, 可以
**maybe** kěnéng 可能
**May Day** Wǔyī Jié 五一节
**mayo, mayonnaise** –
dànhuángjiàng 蛋黄酱
**mayor** shìzhǎng 市长
**maze** mígōng 迷宫; *fig* qūjìng 曲

径
**MB** (= *megabyte*) zhàozìjié 兆字
节
**MBA** (= *Master of Business Ad-*
*ministration*) ↓ gōngshāng
guǎnlǐxué shuòshì 工商管理学
硕士
**MBO** (= *management buyout*)
guǎnlǐ rényuán shōumǎi 管理人
员收买
**MD** (= *Doctor of Medicine*) dàifū
大夫
**me** wǒ 我; *it's ~* shì wǒ 是我
**meadow** cǎopíng 草坪
**meager** shǎoliàng 少量
**meal** cān 餐
**mealtime** jìncān shíjiān 进餐时间
**mean¹** *(with money)* lìnsè 吝啬;
*(nasty)* bēibǐ 卑鄙
**mean² 1** *v/t (intend)* yìzhǐ 意指;
*(signify)* biǎoshì 表示; *~ to do X*
dǎsuàn zuò X 打算做 X; *be ~t for*
*(of remark)* zhǐdìng 指定; *be ~t*
*for X* yǒuyì wèi X zhǔnbèi 有意
为 X 准备; *doesn't it ~ anything*
*to you?* *(doesn't it matter?)* zhè
nándào yǔ nǐ wúguān ma? 这难
道与你无关吗 ? **2** *v/i*: *~ well*
huái hǎoyì 怀好意
**meaning** *(of word)* hányì 含义
**meaningful** *(comprehensible)* yǒu
yìyì 有意义; *(constructive)* jījí 积
极; *glance* yìwèi shēncháng 意味
深长
**meaningless** *sentence etc* wúyìyì 无
意义; *gesture* kōngdòng 空洞
**means** *(financial)* cáiyuán 财源;
*(way)* fāngfǎ 方法; *~ of transport*
jiāotōng gōngjù 交通工具; *by all*
*~ (certainly)* dāngrán kěyǐ 当然可
以; *by no ~ rich/poor* gēnběn bù
fù/qióng 根本不富/穷; *by ~ of*
yòng 用
**meantime**: *in the ~* tóngshí 同时
**measles** mázhěn 麻疹
**measure 1** *n (step)* cuòshī 措施;
*(certain amount)* chéngdù 程度
**2** *v/t* cèliáng 测量 **3** *v/i* yǒu ...
cháng/kuān 有 ... 长/宽; *it ~s 15*
*yards by 5 yards* cháng shíwǔ mǎ,
kuān wǔ mǎ 长十五码, 宽五码

◆**measure out** liángchū 量出

◆**measure up to:** ~ **X** dádào X de biāozhǔn 达到 X 的标准

**measurement** (*action*) cèliáng 测量; (*dimension*) chǐcun 尺寸; *system of* ~ dùliánghéng 度量衡

**meat** ròu 肉

**meatball** ròuwánzi 肉丸子

**meatloaf** ròugāo 肉糕

**mechanic** jìgōng 技工

**mechanical** *device* jīxiè 机械; *gesture* dāibǎn 呆板

**mechanically** jīxiè 机械; *do sth* dāibǎn 呆板

**mechanism** jīxiè zhuāngzhì 机械装置

**mechanize** shǐ jīxièhuà 使机械化

**medal** jiǎngzhāng 奖章

**medalist** jiǎngzhāng huòdé zhě 奖章获得者

**meddle** gānshè 干涉

**media:** *the* ~ dàzhòng chuánméi 大众传媒

**media hype** méitǐ xuànrǎn 媒体渲染

**median strip** zhōngyāng fēnchēdài 中央分车带

**mediate** tiáojiě 调解

**mediation** tiáojiě 调解

**mediator** tiáojiěrén 调解人

**medical 1** *adj* yīliáo 医疗 **2** *n* tǐgé jiǎnchá 体格检查

**medical certificate** jiànkāng zhèngshū 健康证书

**Medicare** yīliáo bǎozhàng fāng'àn 医疗保障方案

**medicated** hán yàowù 含药物

**medication** yào 药

**medicinal** yǒu yàoxìng 有药性

**medicine** (*science*) yīxué 医学; (*medication*) yào 药

**medieval** zhōngshìjì 中世纪

**mediocre** píngyōng 平庸

**mediocrity** (*of work etc*) píngyōng 平庸; (*person*) píngyōngde rén 平庸的人

**meditate** dǎzuò 打坐

**meditation** dǎzuò 打坐

**medium 1** *adj* (*average*) zhōngděng 中等; *steak* bāfēnshóu 八分熟 **2** *n* (*in size*) zhōnghào 中号;

(*vehicle*) méijiè 媒介; (*spiritualist*) língméi 灵媒

**medium-sized** zhōnghào 中号

**medium wave** RAD zhōngbō 中波

**medley** (*assortment*) hùnhé 混合

**meek** wēnshùn 温顺

**meet 1** *v/t* jiàn 见; (*collect*) jiē 接; (*of eyes*) xiāngyù 相遇; (*satisfy*) dádào 达到; ~ **X** (*in competition*) yǔ X bǐsài 与 X 比赛 **2** *v/i* jiànmiàn 见面; (*in competition*) bǐsài 比赛; (*of eyes*) xiāngyù 相遇; (*of committee etc*) jùhé 聚合 **3** *n* SP yùndònghuì 运动会

◆**meet with** *person* huìwù 会晤; *opposition, approval etc* zāodào 遭到

**meeting** huìyì 会议; *he's in a* ~ tā zài kāihuì 他在开会

**meeting place** huìchǎng 会场

**megabyte** COMPUT zhào 兆

**Mekong River** Méigōnghé 湄公河

**melancholy** *adj* yōuyù 忧郁

**mellow 1** *adj* róuhé 柔和 **2** *v/i* (*of person*) wēnhé 温和

**melodious** yuè'ěr 悦耳

**melodramatic** gǎnqíng kuāzhāng 感情夸张

**melody** xuánlù 旋律

**melon** guā 瓜

**melt** *v/t* & *v/i* rónghuà 融化

◆**melt away** *fig* xiāoshī 消失

◆**melt down** *v/t* metal rónghuì 熔毁

**melting pot** *fig* rónglú 熔炉

**member** chéngyuán 成员; ~ *of Congress* guóhuì yìyuán 国会议员

**membership** chéngyuán zīgé 成员资格; (*number of members*) chéngyuán rénshù 成员人数

**membership card** chéngyuánzhèng 成员证

**membrane** mó 膜

**memento** jìniànpǐn 纪念品

**memo** bèiwànglù 备忘录

**memoirs** huíyìlù 回忆录

**memorable** zhídé jìniàn 值得纪念

**memorial 1** *adj* jìniàn 纪念 **2** *n*

jìniànbēi 纪念碑
**Memorial Day** Zhènwáng Jiàngshì jìniànrì 阵亡将士纪念日
**memorize** jìzhù 记住
**memory** (*recollection*) jìyì 记忆; (*power of recollection*) jìyìlì 记忆力; (COMPUT: *device*) cúnchǔqì 存储器; (COMPUT: *capacity*) cúnchǔlì 存储力; *have a good / bad ~* jìyìlì hǎo / huài 记忆力好 / 坏; *in ~ of X* zuòwéi duì X de jìniàn 作为对X的纪念
**menace 1** *n* (*threat*) wēixié 威胁; (*person*) wēixiǎn zhě 危险者 **2** *v/t* wēixié 威胁
**menacing** wēixié 威胁
**mend 1** *v/t* xiūlǐ 修理 **2** *n* xiūlǐ 修理; *be on the ~* (*after illness*) zài hǎozhuǎn zhōng 在好转中
**menial** *adj* dīxià 低下
**meningitis** nǎomóyán 脑膜炎
**menopause** juéjīngqī 绝经期
**men's room** náncè 男厕
**menstruate** xíngjīng 行经
**menstruation** xíngjīngqī 行经期
**mental** jīngshén 精神; F (*crazy*) fēng 疯
**mental arithmetic** xīnsuàn 心算; **mental cruelty** jīngshén nüèdài 精神虐待; **mental hospital** jīngshénbìngyuàn 精神病院; **mental illness** jīngshénbìng 精神病
**mentality** xīnlǐ zhuàngtài 心理状态
**mentally** (*inwardly*) zài nè ixīn 在内心; *calculate etc* xīnlǐ 心里; *~ handicapped* dīnéng 低能; *~ ill* xīnlǐ jíbìng 心理疾病
**mention 1** *n* tíjí 提及 **2** *v/t* tídào 提到; *don't ~ it* búyòng kèqì 不用客气
**mentor** liángshīyìyǒu 良师益友
**menu** (*for food*, COMPUT) càidān 菜单
**mercenary 1** *adj* túlì 图利 **2** *n* MIL gùyōngbīng 雇佣兵
**merchandise** huòpǐn 货品
**merchant** shāngrén 商人
**merciful** réncí 仁慈

**mercifully** (*thankfully*) xìng'ér 幸而
**merciless** wúqíng 无情
**mercury** shuǐyín 水银
**mercy** réncí 仁慈; *be at X's ~* rènyóu X bǎibù 任由X摆布
**mere** *adj* zhǐbúguò 只不过
**merely** jǐnjǐn 仅仅
**merge** *v/i* (*of two lines etc*) héwéiyītǐ 合为一体; (*of companies*) hébìng 合并
**merger** COM hébìng 合并
**merit 1** *n* (*worth*) jiàzhí 价值; (*advantage*) yōudiǎn 优点 **2** *v/t* zhíde 值得
**merry** yúkuài 愉快; *Merry Christmas!* Shèngdàn kuàilè! 圣诞快乐！
**merry-go-round** xuánzhuàn mùmǎ 旋转木马
**mesh** *n* wǎngyǎn 网眼
**mess** *n* (*untidiness*) zāngluàn zāngluàn 脏乱; (*trouble*) kùnjìng 困境; *be a ~* (*of room, desk, hair*) záluàn 杂乱; (*of situation, life*) yītuánzāo 一团糟
♦ **mess around 1** *v/i* xiánkào 瞎闹 **2** *v/t person* hùnong 糊弄
♦ **mess around with** bǎinòng 摆弄; *s.o.'s wife* sītōng 私通
♦ **mess up** *room, papers* nòngluàn 弄乱; *task* gǎozāo 搞糟; *plans, marriage* gǎohuài 搞坏
**message** (*of movie, book*) qǐshì 启示; *can I leave a ~?* wǒ kěyǐ liúyán ma? 我可以留言吗？
**messenger** (*courier*) tōngxìnyuán 通信员
**messy** *room* língluàn 凌乱; *person* lāta 邋遢; *job* zāng zàng 脏; *divorce, situation* fùzá 复杂
**metabolism** xīnchéndàixiè 新陈代谢
**metal** *n & adj* jīnshǔ 金属
**metallic** (sì) jīnshǔ (似) 金属
**meteor** liúxīng 流星
**meteoric** *fig* fēisù 飞速
**meteorite** yǔnxīng 陨星
**meteorological** qìxiàng 气象
**meteorologist** qìxiàngxuéjiā 气象学家
**meteorology** qìxiàngxué 气象学

meter¹ (*for measuring*) biǎo 表; (*parking ~*) qì 器

meter² (*unit of length*) mǐ 米

method fāngfǎ 方法

methodical yǒutiáolǐ 有条理

methodically yǒutiáobùwěn 有条不紊

meticulous jíjīngxì 极精细

metric gōngzhì 公制

metropolis dà dūshì 大都市

metropolitan *adj* dà dūshì 大都市

mew → **miaow**

Mexican 1 *adj* Mòxīgē 墨西哥 2 *n* Mòxīgē rén 墨西哥人

Mexico Mòxīgē 墨西哥

mezzanine (*floor*) zhōngjiān lóucéng 中间楼层

miaow 1 *n* miāo 喵 2 *v/i* zuò miāomiāo shēng 作喵喵声

mickey mouse *adj* F *course, qualification* yějī 野鸡

microchip wēijīngpiàn 微晶片; microcosm wēiguān shìjiè 微观世界; microelectronics wēidiànzǐxué 微电子学; microfilm suōwēi jiāojuǎn 缩微胶卷; microphone màikèfēng 麦克风; microprocessor wēichǔlǐjī 微处理机; microscope xiǎnwēijìng 显微镜; microscopic jíwēixiǎo 极微小; microwave (*oven*) wēibōlú 微波炉

midair: *in ~* zài bànkōngzhōng 在半空中

midday zhōngwǔ 中午

middle 1 *adj* zhōngjiān 中间 2 *n* zhōngyāng 中央; *in the ~ of X* (*floor, room*) zài X zhōngyāng 在 X 中央; *in the ~ of* (*period of time*) zài ... zhōng 在 ... 中; *be in the ~ of doing X* zhèngzài zuò X dāngzhōng 正在做 X 当中

middle-aged zhōngnián 中年; Middle Ages Zhōngshìjì 中世纪; middle-class *adj* zhōngchǎn jiējí 中产阶级; middle classes zhōngchǎn jiējí 中产阶级; Middle East Zhōngdōng 中东; Middle Kingdom Zhōngguó 中国; middleman jīngjìrén 经纪人; middle name zhōngjiānmíng 中

间名; middleweight *n* (*boxer*) zhōngliàngjí 中量级

middling zhōngděng 中等

midget *adj* xiùzhēn 袖珍

midnight wǔyè 午夜; *at ~* wǔyèshí 午夜时; midsummer zhòngxià 仲夏; midway zhōngtú 中途; midweek *adv* lǐbài zhōng 礼拜中; Midwest Zhōngxībù 中西部; midwife zhùchǎnshì 助产士; midwinter zhòngdōng 仲冬

might¹ yěxǔ 也许; *I ~ be late* wǒ yěxǔ chídào 我也许迟到; *it ~ rain* tiān yěxǔ yào xiàyǔ 天也许要下雨; *it ~ never happen* zhè yěxǔ yǒngyuǎn bùhuì fāshēng 这也许永远不会发生; *I ~ have lost it* wǒ yěxǔ bǎ tā gěi diūle 我也许把它给丢了; *he ~ have left* tā yěxǔ yǐjīng zǒule 他也许已经走了; *you ~ as well spend the night here* nǐ háibùrú jiù zài zhèr guòyè 你还不如就在这儿过夜; *you ~ have told me!* nǐ zá méi gàosu wǒ! 你咋没告诉我!

might² (*power*) lìliàng 力量

mighty 1 *adj* qiángyǒulì 强有力 2 *adv* F (*extremely*) jíqí 极其

migraine piāntóutòng 偏头痛

migrant worker liúdòng gōngrén 流动工人

migrate qiānyí 迁移

migration qiānjū 迁居

mike màikèfēng 麦克风

mild wēnhé 温和

mildew méi 霉

mildly shìdù 适度

mildness wēnhé 温和

mile yīnglǐ 英里; *~s better / easier* hǎo / róngyì déduō 好 / 容易得多

mileage lǐchéng 里程

milestone *fig* lǐchéngbēi 里程碑

militant 1 *adj* yǒu zhàndòuxìng 有战斗性 2 *n* jījí fènzǐ 积极分子

military 1 *adj* jūnshì 军事 2 *n*: *the ~* jūnduì 军队

military academy jūnshì xuéyuàn 军事学院

militia mínbīng 民兵

milk 1 *n* nǎi 奶 2 *v/t* jǐnǎi 挤奶

milk chocolate niúnǎi qiǎokèlì 牛

奶巧克力

**milk shake** nǎixī 奶昔

**mill** *n* (*for grain*) mófáng 磨坊; (*for textiles*) máofǎngchǎng 毛纺厂
♦ **mill around** luànzhuàn 乱转

**millennium** yìqiānnián 一千年

**milligram(me)** háokè 毫克

**millimeter** háomǐ 毫米

**million** bǎiwàn 百万; **hundred ~** yì 亿

**millionaire** bǎiwànfùwēng 百万富翁

**mime** *v/t* dǎ yǎyǔ 打哑语

**mimic 1** *n* hào xuéyàng zhě 好学样者 **2** *v/t* mófǎng 模仿

**mince** *v/t* qièsuì 切碎

**mincemeat** ròuxiàn 肉馅

**mind 1** *n* tóunǎo 头脑; *it's all in your ~* dōu zài nǐde nǎohǎilǐ 都在你的脑海里; *be out of one's ~* fāfēng 发疯; *bear or keep X in ~* jìzhù X 记住 X; *I've a good ~ to ...* wǒ zhēn xiǎng ... 我真想...; *change one's ~* gǎibiàn zhǔyì 改变主意; *it didn't enter my ~* gēnběn méi xiǎngdào 根本没想到; *give X a piece of one's ~* zébèi X 责备 X; *make up one's ~* juédìng 决定; *have X on one's ~* guàlǜ X 挂虑; *keep one's ~ on X* zhuānxīnyú X 专心于 X **2** *v/t* (*look after*) zhàokàn 照看; (*object to*) jièyì 介意; (*heed*) liúxīn 留心; *I don't ~ what we do* wǒ bú zàihu zánmen zuò shénme 我不在乎咱们做什么; *do you ~ if I smoke?, do you ~ my smoking?* wǒ chōuyān nǐ bù fǎnduì ma? 我抽烟你不反对吗?; *would you ~ opening the window?* qǐng bǎ chuāngzi dǎkāi hǎoma? 请把窗子打开好吗?; *~ the step!* zhùyì jiǎoxià! 注意脚下!; *~ your own business!* bùguǎn nǐde shì! 不关你的事! **3** *v/i*: *~!* (*be careful*) dāngxīn 当心; *never ~!* méiguānxi! 没关系!; *I don't ~* wǒ wúsuǒwèi 我无所谓

**mind-boggling** jīngrén 惊人

**mindless** *violence* wútóunǎo 无头脑

**mine**[1] *pron* wǒde 我的; *a friend of ~* wǒde péngyǒu 我的朋友

**mine**[2] **1** *n* (*for coal etc*) kuàng 矿 **2** *v/i* (*for coal etc*) kāicǎi 开采; *~ for* kāicǎi 开采

**mine**[3] **1** *n* (*explosive*) dìléi 地雷 **2** *v/t* pūléi 铺雷

**minefield** MIL bùléiqū 布雷区; *fig* qiánzài kùnnánqū 潜在困难区

**miner** kuànggōng 矿工

**mineral** *n* kuàngwù 矿物

**mineral water** kuàngquánshuǐ 矿泉水

**minesweeper** NAUT sǎoléi tǐng 扫雷艇

**Ming Dynasty** Míngcháo 明朝

**mingle** *v/i* (*of sounds, smells*) hùnhé 混合; (*at party*) jiāowǎng 交往

**mini** (*skirt*) chāoduǎnqún 超短裙

**minibus** xiǎoxíng gōnggòngqìchē 小型公共汽车

**miniature** *adj* xiùzhēnxíng 袖珍型

**minimal** zuìxiǎo 最小

**minimize** jiǎnzhì zuìxiǎo 减至最小; (*downplay*) jìnkěnéng jiǎnshǎo 尽可能减少

**minimum 1** *adj* zuìshǎo 最少 **2** *n* zuìdī xiàndù 最低限度

**minimum wage** zuìdī gōngzī 最低工资

**mining** kuàngyè 矿业

**miniskirt** chāoduǎnqún 超短裙

**minister** POL bùzhǎng 部长; REL mùshī 牧师

**ministerial** bùzhǎng 部长

**ministry** POL bù 部

**mink** (*fur*) diāopí 貂皮; (*coat*) diāopí dàyī 貂皮大衣

**minor 1** *adj* cìyào 次要; *in D* MUS D xiǎodiào D 小调 **2** *n* LAW wèichéngniánrén 未成年人

**minority** shǎoshù 少数; *be in the ~* zhànshǎoshù 占少数

**mint** *n* (*herb*) bòhe 薄荷; (*chocolate*) bòhe diǎnxīn 薄荷点心; (*hard candy*) bòhe táng 薄荷糖

**minus 1** *n* (*~ sign*) jiǎnhào 减号 **2** *prep* jiǎnqù 减去

**minuscule** wēixiǎo 微小

**minute**[1] *n* (*of time*) fēnzhōng 分钟;

*in a ~ (soon)* yíhuìr 一会儿; *just a ~* děngyíxià 等一下

minute² *adj (tiny)* wēixiǎo 微小; *(detailed)* xiángxì 详细; *in ~ detail* jùtǐ xìzhì 具体细致

minutely *(in detail)* xiángxì 详细

minutes *(of meeting)* jìlù 记录

miracle qíjì 奇迹

miraculous qíjìbān 奇迹般

miraculously qíjì 奇迹

mirage hǎishì shènlóu 海市蜃楼

mirror 1 *n* jìngzi 镜子; MOT *(rearview)* hòushìjìng 后视镜; *(wing)* dàoguāngjìng 到光镜 2 *v/t* fǎnshè 反射

misanthropist yànwù rénlèi zhě 厌恶人类者

misapprehension: *be under a ~* zài wùjiě de qíngkuàng xià 在误解的情况下

misbehave jǔzhǐbúdàng 举止不当

misbehavior búdàngde jǔzhǐ 不当的举止

miscalculate *v/t & v/i* wùsuàn 误算

miscalculation wùsuàn 误算

miscarriage MED liúchǎn 流产; *~ of justice* wùpàn 误判

miscarry *(of plan)* shībài 失败

miscellaneous gèzhǒng gèyàng 各种各样

mischief *(naughtiness)* èzuòjù 恶作剧

mischievous *(naughty)* wánpí 顽皮; *(malicious)* yǒuhài 有害

misconception wùjiě 误解

misconduct wánhū zhíshǒu 玩忽职守

misconstrue wùhuì 误会

misdemeanor qīngzuì 轻罪

miser shǒucáinú 守财奴

miserable *(unhappy)* nánguò 难过; *weather, performance* lìngrén búkuài 令人不快

miserly *amount* shǎodékělián 少得可怜

misery *(unhappiness)* tòngkǔ 痛苦; *(wretchedness)* bēicǎn 悲惨

misfire *(of joke, scheme)* wèidé yùqīxiàoguǒ 未得预期效果

misfit *(in society)* yǔ shèhuì gégébúrù de rén 与社会格格不入的人

misfortune búxìng 不幸

misgivings gùlǜ 顾虑

misguided wùdǎo 误导

mishandle chǔlǐbúdàng 处理不当

mishap búxìng shìgù 不幸事故

misinterpret qūjiě 曲解

misinterpretation qūjiě 曲解

misjudge *person, situation* cuòwù gūjì 错误估计

mislay yíshī 遗失

mislead yǐndǎocuò 引导错

misleading shǐrén wùjiě 使人误解

mismanage guǎnlǐ búshàn 管理不善

mismanagement búdàngde guǎnlǐ 不当的管理

mismatch pèihé búdàng 配合不当

misplaced *loyalty, enthusiasm* cuòwùde fùchū 错误地付出

misprint *n* cuòyìn 错印

mispronounce fāwù 发错

mispronunciation fāyīn cuòwù 发音错误

misread *word, figures* dúcuò 读错; *situation* wùjiě 误解

misrepresent wāiqū 歪曲

miss¹: *Miss Wang* Wáng xiǎojiě 王小姐

miss¹ 1 *n* SP wèijīzhòng 未击中; *give X a ~ meeting, party etc* búqù X 不去 X 2 *v/t (not hit)* wèijīzhòng 未击中; *(emotionally)* xiǎngniàn 想念; *bus, train, plane* méigǎnshàng 没赶上; *(not notice, fail to see)* cuòguò 错过; *(not be present at)* bùchūxí 不出席; *you've just ~ed him (not met)* tā gāng zǒule 他刚走了 3 *v/i* wèijīzhòng 未击中

misshapen jīxíng 畸形

missile *(guided)* dǎodàn 导弹

missing diūshī 丢失; *be ~* xiàluòbùmíng 下落不明

mission *(task)* rènwù 任务; *(people)* shǐmìngtuán 使命团

missionary REL chuánjiàoshì 传教士

misspell pīnxiěcuò 拼写错

mist bówù 薄雾

♦ mist over (of eyes) móhu 模糊

♦ mist up (of window etc) méngshàng shuǐqì 蒙上水汽

mistake 1 n cuòwù 错误; make a ~ fàn cuòwù 犯错误; by ~ cuòwùde 错误地 2 v/t xuǎncuò 选错; ~ X for Y wùjiāng X rènzuò Y 误将 X 认作 Y

mistaken: be ~ nòngcuò 弄错

mister xiānsheng 先生

mistress (lover) qíngfù 情妇; (of servant, dog) nǚzhǔrén 女主人

mistrust 1 n búxìnrèn 不信任 2 v/t huáiyí 怀疑

misty weather bówù lǒngzhào 薄雾笼罩; eyes móhu 模糊; color méngménglónglóng 朦朦胧胧

misunderstand wùjiě 误解

misunderstanding (mistake) wùjiě 误解; (argument) zhēngzhí 争执

misuse 1 n wùyòng 误用 2 v/t yòngcuò 用错

mitigating circumstances jiǎnqīngde qíngjié 减轻的情节

mitt (in baseball) bàngqiú shǒutào 棒球手套

mitten liánzhǐ shǒutào 连指手套

mix 1 n (mixture) hùnhé 混合; (in cooking) hùnhéwù 混合物; (cooking: ready to use) hùnhé pèiliào 混合配料 2 v/t hùnhé 混合; cement jiǎohuo 搅和 3 v/i (socially) xiāngchǔ 相处

♦ mix up gǎoluàn 搞乱; mix X up with Y hùnxiáo X hé Y 混淆 X 和 Y; be mixed up (emotionally) míwǎng 迷惘; (of figures, papers) nòngluàn 弄乱; be mixed up in X yǔ X yǒu qiānlián 与 X 有牵连; get mixed up with X yǔ X sīhùn 与 X 厮混

♦ mix with (associate with) jiāowǎng 交往

mixed feelings fùzá 复杂; reactions, reviews gèzhǒng gèyàng 各种各样

mixed marriage yìzú tōnghūn 异族通婚

mixer (for food) jiǎobànqì 搅拌器; (drink) tiáopèi yǐnliào 调配饮料; she's a good ~ tā hěn héqún 她很合群

mixture hùnhé(wù) 混合(物); (medicine) fùfāngyào 复方药

mix-up hùnluàn 混乱

moan 1 n (of pain) shēnyín 呻吟; (complaint) láosao 牢骚 2 v/i (in pain) shēnyín 呻吟; (complain) bàoyuàn 抱怨

mob 1 n bàomín 暴民 2 v/t bāowéi 包围

mobile 1 adj person kě línghuó zǒudòng 可灵活走动; (that can be moved) kěyídòng 可移动 2 n (for decoration) fēngdòng shìwù 风动饰物; Br (phone) yídòng 移动, dàgēdà 大哥大

mobile home huódòng zhùfáng 活动住房

mobile phone Br yídòng 移动; (formal use) shǒutí diànhuà 手提电话

mobility yídòngxìng 移动性

mobster dàitú 歹徒

mock 1 adj mónǐ 摹拟 2 v/t qǔxiào 取笑

mockery (derision) cháonòng 嘲弄; (travesty) duì zhèngyì de wāiqū 对正义的歪曲

mock-up (model) dàmóxíng 大模型

mode (form) fāngshì 方式; COMPUT cāozuò fāngfǎ 操作方法

model 1 adj employee, husband mófàn 模范; boat, plane móxíng 模型 2 n (miniature) chúxíng 雏型; (pattern) móshì 模式; (fashion ~) mótèr 模特儿; male ~ nán mótèr 男模特儿 3 v/t zhǎnshì 展示 4 v/i (for designer, artist) zuò mótèr 作模特儿

modem tiáozhì jiětiáoqì 调制解调器

moderate 1 adj shìdù 适度; POL wēnhé 温和 2 n POL wēnhépài 温和派 3 v/t biànhéhuǎn 变和缓 4 v/i jiǎnruò 减弱

moderately shìdù 适度

moderation (*restraint*) jiézhì 节制; *in* ~ shìdù 适度

modern xiàndài 现代

modernization xiàndàihuà 现代化

modernize **1** *v/t* shǐxiàndàihuà 使现代化 **2** *v/i* (*of business, country*) xiàndàihuà 现代化

modest *house, apartment* pǔsù 朴素; (*small*) búdà 不大; (*not conceited*) qiānxùn 谦逊

modesty (*of house, apartment*) pǔsù 朴素; (*of wage, improvement*) shìdù 适度; (*lack of conceit*) qiānxùn 谦逊

modification xiūgǎi 修改

modify xiūgǎi 修改

modular *furniture* dāntǐ shèjì 单体设计

module dāntǐ 单体; (*space* ~) cāng 舱

moist cháoshī 潮湿

moisten nòngshī 弄湿

moisture shīrùn 湿润

moisturizer (*for skin*) rùnfūshuāng 润肤霜

molar móyá 磨牙

molasses tángjiāng 糖浆

mold¹ *n* (*on food*) méi 霉

mold² **1** *n* múzi 模子 **2** *v/t clay etc* jiāozhù 浇铸; *character, person* lèixíng 类型

moldy *food* fāméi 发霉

mole (*on skin*) zhì 痣

molecular fēnzǐ 分子

molecule fēnzǐ 分子

molest *child, woman* sāorǎo 骚扰

mollycoddle nì'ài 溺爱

molten rónghuà 熔化

mom F mā 妈

moment piànkè 片刻; *at the* ~ xiànzài 现在; *for the* ~ zànshí 暂时

momentarily (*for a moment*) shùnjiān 瞬间; (*in a moment*) jíkè 即刻

momentary duǎnzàn 短暂

momentous jízhòngyào 极重要

momentum dònglì 动力

monarch jūnzhǔ 君主

monastery xiūdàoyuàn 修道院

monastic xiūdào 修道

Monday xīngqīyī 星期一

monetary huòbì 货币

money qián 钱

money-lender fàngzhài zhě 放债者; **money market** jīnróng shìchǎng 金融市场; **money order** huìkuǎndān 汇款单

Mongolia Měnggǔ 蒙古

Mongolian **1** *adj* Měnggǔ 蒙古 **2** *n* (*person*) Měnggǔ rén 蒙古人

mongrel zázhǒnggǒu 杂种狗

monitor **1** *n* COMPUT jiānshìqì 监视器 **2** *v/t* chíxù guānchá 持续观察

monk héshàng 和尚; *become a* ~ chūjiā 出家

monkey hóu 猴; F (*child*) tiáopíguǐ 调皮鬼

♦monkey around with F bǎinòng 摆弄

monkey wrench huódòng bānshǒu 活动扳手

monogram *n* zìshǒu 字首

monogrammed zìshǒu 字首

monolog dúbái 独白

monopolize lǒngduàn 垄断

monopoly dúzhàn 独占

monosodium glutamate wèijīng 味精

monotonous dāndiào fáwèi 单调乏味

monotony wúliáo 无聊

monsoon jìfēng 季风

monsoon season jìfēng yǔjì 季风雨季

monster n yāoguài 妖怪

monstrosity jīxíng 畸形

monstrous jīxíng 畸形

month yuè 月

monthly **1** *adj* měiyuè 每月 **2** *adv* měiyuè yícì 每月一次 **3** *n* (*magazine*) yuèkān 月刊

monument jìniànbēi 纪念碑

mood (*frame of mind*) xīnqíng 心情; (*bad* ~) huàiqíngxù 坏情绪; (*of meeting, country*) qìfēn 气氛; *be in a good/bad* ~ qíngxù hǎo/huài 情绪好/坏; *be in the* ~ *for* yǒu xìngzhì 有兴致

moody xīnùwúcháng 喜怒无常

moon *n* yuèliang 月亮

moonlight **1** *n* yuèguāng 月光

**2** v/i F jiānzhí 兼职
**moonlit** yǒu yuèguāng 有月光
**moor** v/t boat tíngbó 停泊
**moorings** tíngbó qū 停泊区
**moose** tuólù 驼鹿
**mop 1** n tuōbǎ 拖布 **2** v/t floor tuōdì 拖地; eyes, face cā 擦
♦**mop up** cājìng 擦净; MIL sùqīng 肃清
**mope** yùyùbúlè 郁郁不乐
**moral 1** adj dàodé 道德; person, behavior jiǎngdàodé 讲道德 **2** n (of story) yùyì 寓意; ~s xíngwéide biāozhǔn 行为的标准
**morale** shìqì 士气
**morality** měidé 美德
**morbid** bìngtài 病态
**more 1** adj gèngduō 更多; we need ~ time wǒmen xūyao géngduo de shíjiān 我们需要更多的时间; some ~ tea? zài láidiǎnr chá ma? 再来点儿茶吗？; and ~ students / time yuèláiyuèduōde xuésheng / shíjiān 越来越多的学生 / 时间 **2** adv gèng(duō) 更（多）; ~ important gèng zhòngyào 更重要; ~ often gèng pínfán 更频繁; ~ and ~ yuèfā(duō) 越发（多）; ~ or less dàzhì 大致; once ~ zàiyícì 再一次; ~ than duōyú 多于; I don't live there any ~ wǒ búzài zhù nàrle 我不再住那儿了 **3** pron gèngduōde shùliàng 更多的数量; do you want some ~? hái yàodiǎnr ma? 你还要点儿吗？; a little ~ zài lái yìdiǎndiǎn 再来一点点
**moreover** érqiě 而且
**morgue** tíngshīfáng 停尸房
**morning** (before 10am) zǎochén 早晨; (between 10am and 12pm) shàngwǔ 上午; in the ~ (before 10am) zǎochén 早晨; (between 10am and 12pm) shàngwǔ 上午; (tomorrow: before 10am) míngtiān zǎochén 明天早晨; (tomorrow: between 10am and 12pm) míngtiān shàngwǔ 明天上午; this ~ (before 10am) jīntiān zǎochén 今天早晨; (usually between 10am

and 12pm) jīntiān shàngwǔ 今天上午; tomorrow ~ (before 10am) míngtiān zǎochén 明天早晨; (between 10am and 12pm) míngtiān shàngwǔ 明天上午; good ~ (before 10am) zǎochén hǎo 早晨好; (between 10am and 12pm) shàngwǔ hǎo 上午好
**moron** shǎguā 傻瓜
**morose** guāipì 乖僻
**morphine** mǎfēi 吗啡
**morsel**: a ~ of yīxiǎopiàn 一小片
**mortal 1** adj bìsǐ 必死; blow zhìmìng 致命; enemy búgòngdàitiān 不共戴天 **2** n rén 人
**mortality** bùmiǎnyìsǐ 不免一死, sǐwáng lǜ 死亡率
**mortar** MIL pǎijīpào 迫击炮
**mortar²** (cement) shājiāng 砂浆
**mortgage 1** n dǐyā 抵押 **2** v/t dǐyā jièkuǎn 抵押借款
**mortician** bìnyíyè zhě 殡仪业者
**mortuary** tàipíngjiān 太平间
**mosaic** mǎsàikè 马赛克
**Moscow** Mòsīkē 莫斯科
**mosquito** wénzi 蚊子
**mosquito coil** wénxiāng 蚊香
**mosquito net** wénzhàng 蚊帐
**moss** tái 苔
**mossy** zhǎngmǎn qīngtái 长满青苔
**most 1** adj duōshù 多数 **2** adv (very) hěn 很; the ~ beautiful / interesting zuì piàoliang / yǒuqù 最漂亮 / 有趣; that's the one I like zhè shì wǒ zuì xǐhuān de 那个是我最喜欢的; ~ of all zuì zhòngyào 最重要 **3** pron dàduōshù 大多数; at (the) ~ zhìduō 至多; make the ~ of jìnliàng lìyòng 尽量利用
**mostly** zhǔyào 主要
**motel** qìchē lǚguǎn 汽车旅馆
**moth** é 蛾
**mother 1** n mǔqīn 母亲 **2** v/t xiàng mǔqīnbān zhàogù 像母亲般照顾
**motherboard** COMPUT mǔbǎn 母板; **motherhood** mǔqīn shēnfèn 母亲身份; **mother-in-law** (of man) yuèmǔ 岳母; (of woman)

pópó 婆婆

motherly mǔxìng 母性

mother-of-pearl zhēnzhūmǔ 珍珠母; **Mother's Day** Mǔqīnjié 母亲节; **mother tongue** mǔyǔ 母语

motif zhuāngshì shìyàng 装饰式样

motion **1** n (*movement*) yùndòng 运动; (*proposal*) tíyì 提议; **put or set things in** n zuò bìyào de ānpái 作必要的安排 **2** v/t: **he ~ed me forward** tā shìyì wǒ qiánxíng 他示意我前行

motionless búdòng 不动

motivate *person* cùdòng 促动

motivation dònglì 动力

motive dòngjī 动机

motor fādòngjī 发动机

motorbike mótuōchē 摩托车; **motorboat** qìchuán 汽船; **motorcade** qìchē chángliè 汽车列; **motorcycle** mótuōchē 摩托车; **motorcyclist** qí mótuōchē de rén 骑摩托车的人; **motor home** zhùfáng qìchē 住房汽车

motorist sījī 司机

motor rickshaw bèngbèngchē 蹦蹦车; **motorscooter** xiǎoxíng mótuōchē 小型摩托车; **motor vehicle** jīdòngchē 机动车

motto zuòyòumíng 座右铭

mound (*hillock*) tǔqiū 土丘; (*in baseball*) tóushǒu chǎngdì 投手场地; (*pile*) duī 堆

mount **1** n (*mountain*) shān 山; (*horse*) zuòqí 坐骑 **2** v/t *steps* pá 爬; *horse, bicycle* qíshàng 骑上; *campaign* fāqǐ 发起; *photo, painting* biǎotiē 裱贴 **3** v/i zēngzhǎng 增长

♦mount up jīlěi 积累

mountain shān 山

mountain bike shāndìchē 山地车

mountaineer dēngshānjiā 登山家

mountaineering dēngshān yùndòng 登山运动

mountainous duōshān 多山

mourn **1** v/t dàoniàn 悼念 **2** v/i āidào 哀悼; **- for X** dàoniànX 悼念X

mourner āidào zhě 哀悼者

mournful bēi'āi 悲哀

mourning fúsāng 服丧; **be in** ~ zài fúsāng 在服丧; **wear** ~ chuān sāngfú 穿丧服

mouse shǔ 鼠; COMPUT ⇩ shǔbiāo 鼠标

mouse mat COMPUT shǔbiāodiàn 鼠标垫

mouth n (*of person*) zuǐ 嘴; (*of river*) hékǒu 河口

mouthful (*of food, drink*) yīkǒu 一口

mouthorgan kǒuqín 口琴; **mouthpiece** (*of instrument*) chuīkǒu 吹口; (*spokesperson*) hóushé 喉舌; **mouthwash** shùkǒují 漱口剂; **mouthwatering** lìngrén chuíxián 令人垂涎

move **1** n (*in chess, checkers*) yībù 一步; (*step, action*) jǔcuò 举措; (*change of house*) bānjiā 搬家; **get a ~ on!** gǎnkuài! 赶快！; **don't make a ~!** bùxǔdòng! 不许动！ **2** v/t *object* yídòng 移动; (*transfer*) zhuǎnyí 转移; (*emotionally*) gǎndòng 感动 **3** v/i dòng 动; (*transfer*) zhuǎn 转; **~ house** bānjiā 搬家

♦move around (*in room*) zǒudòng 走动; (*from place to place*) qiānyí 迁移

♦move away yíkāi 移开; (*move house*) bānzǒu 搬走

♦move in bānjìn 搬进

♦move on (*to another town*) jìxù xíngjìn 继续行进; (*to another job*) diào 调; (*to another subject*) zhuǎnxiàng 转向

♦move out (*of house*) bānchū 搬出; (*of area*) chèlí 撤离

♦move up (*in league*) tíshēng 提升; (*make room*) nuódòng 挪动

movement dòngzuò 动作; (*organization*) yùndòng 运动; MUS yuèzhāng 乐章

movers bānyùn gōngrén 搬运工人

movie diànyǐng 电影; **go to a ~** / **the ~s** qù kàn diànyǐng 去看电影

moviegoer guānzhòng 观众

movie theater diànyǐngyuàn 电影
院

moving (which can move) huódòng
活动; (emotionally) gǎnrén 感人

mow grass gē 割

♦mow down sǎomiè 扫灭

mower yìcǎojī 刈草机

moxibustion jiǔshù 灸术

MP (= Military Policeman) jūnjǐng
军警

mph (= miles per hour) yīnglǐ shísù
英里时速

Mr xiānsheng 先生; ~ Wang Wáng
xiānsheng 王先生

Mrs tàitai 太太; ~ Wang Wáng
tàitai 王太太

Ms nǚshì 女士; ~ Wang
Wáng nǚshì 王女士

much 1 adj xǔduō 许多; ~ money
xǔduō qián 许多钱; there's not
~ difference méiyǒu duōshao
chābié 没有多少差别; as ~ X
as Y (same amount as) hé Y yíyàng
duō de X 和Y一样多的X 2 adv
hěn 很; he is ~ admired tā hěn
lìngrén xiànmù 他很讨人羡慕;
I don't like him ~ wǒ bútài xǐhuan
tā 我不太喜欢他; ~ better hǎo
de duō 好得多; ~ cheaper piányi
de duō 偏宜得多; very ~
fēicháng 非常; thank you very ~
fēicháng gǎnxiè 非常感谢; too ~
guòduō 过多; you talk too ~ nǐ
shuōde guòduō 你说得过多
3 pron duōshǎo 多少; nothing ~
méi shénme 没什么; as ~ as ...
gēn ... yíyàng (duō) 跟 ... 一样(
多 ); I lost as ~ as you did wǒ gēn
nǐ shūde yíyàng duō 我跟你输
的一样多; do as ~ as you can
jìnliàng zuò ba 尽量做吧; take
as ~ as you want suíbiàn ná 随便
拿; as ~ as ten thousand dollars
duōdá yíwàn měiyuán 多达一万
美元; I thought as ~ wǒ jiùshì
zhème xiǎngde 我就是这么想
的

muck (dirt) zāngwù 脏物

mucus niányè 粘液

mud ní 泥

muddle 1 n hùnluàn 混乱 2 v/t

nòng hútu 弄糊涂

♦muddle up gǎoluàn 搞乱

muddy adj nínìng 泥泞

muffin sōngbǐng 松饼

muffle yāyì 压抑

♦muffle up v/i chuān hòu yīdiǎn
穿厚一点

muffler MOT páiqì xiāoshēngqì 排
汽消声器

mug n (for tea, coffee) dàbēi 大杯;
F (face) liǎndànr liǎn 脸儿

mug² v/t (attack) xíngxiōng qiǎngjié
行凶抢劫

mugger xíngxiōng qiǎngjié zhě 行
凶抢劫者

mugging xíngxiōng qiǎngjié 行凶
抢劫

muggy mēnrè 闷热

mule (animal) luó luo 骡; (slipper)
tuōxié 拖鞋

♦mull over zìxì kǎolù 仔细考虑

multilingual shǐyòng duōzhǒng
yǔyán 使用多种语言

multimedia n duōméitǐ 多媒体

multinational 1 adj guójì 国际 2 n
COM duōguó 多国

multiple adj duōgè 多个

multiplication zēngduō 增多

multiply 1 v/t chéng 乘 2 v/i
zēngjiā 增加

mumble 1 n gūnong 咕哝 2 v/t
gūnong 咕哝 3 v/i hánhude shuō
含糊地说

mumps sāixiànyán 腮腺炎

munch 1 v/t yònglì jǔjué 用力咀
嚼 2 v/i dàjǔdàjué 大咀大嚼

municipal shìzhèng 市政

mural n bìhuà 壁画

murder 1 n móushā 谋杀 2 v/t
person móushā 谋杀; song zāotà
糟蹋

murderer xiōngshǒu 凶手

murderous rage, look shāqì téngténg 杀气腾腾

murmur 1 n dīyǔshēng 低语声
2 v/t dīyǔ 低语

muscle jīròu 肌肉

muscular pain, strain jīròu 肌肉;
person jīròu fādá 肌肉发达

muse v/i chénsī 沉思

museum bówùguǎn 博物馆

mushroom **1** *n* mógū 蘑菇 **2** *v/i* xùnsù zēngzhǎng 迅速增长

music yīnyuè 音乐; (*in written form*) yuèpǔ 乐谱

musical **1** *adj* yīnyuè 音乐; *person* yǒu yuègǎn 有乐感; *voice* yuè'ěr 悦耳 **2** *n* (*movie*) yīnyuèpiān 音乐片; (*on stage*) gēwǔjù 歌舞剧

musical instrument yuèqì 乐器

musician yīnyuèjiā 音乐家

mussel yíbèi 贻贝

must ◊ (*necessity*): *I ~ be on time* wǒ bìxū zhǔnshí 我必须准时; *I ~n't be late ...* 我必须得...; *I ~n't be late* wǒ bùnéng chídào 我不能迟到 ◊ (*probability*): *it ~ be about 6 o'clock* dàgài liùdiǎnzhōng le 大概六点钟了; *they ~ have arrived by now* tāmen xiànzài kěndìng dàole 他们现在肯定到了

mustache bāzì hú 八字胡

mustard jièmò 芥末

musty yǒu méiwèir 有霉味儿

mute *adj animal* wúshēng 无声

muted jiǎnruò 减弱

mutilate sǔnshāng 损伤

mutiny **1** *n* pànluàn 叛乱 **2** *v/i* fǎnpàn 反叛

mutter **1** *v/i* gūnong 咕哝 **2** *v/t* dīshēng shuō 低声说

mutton yángròu 羊肉

mutual xiānghù 相互

muzzle **1** *n* (*of animal*) bíkǒu bùfēn 鼻口部分; (*for dog*) kǒutào 口套 **2** *v/t*: *~ the press* qiánzhì xīnwén 钳制新闻

my wǒde 我的

myopic jìnshì 近视

myself wǒzìjǐ 我自己; *by ~* dúzì 独自

mysterious shénmì 神秘

mysteriously bùkě sīyì 不可思议

mystery mí 谜

mystify míhuo 迷惑

myth shénhuà 神话; *fig* xūhuà 虚话

mythical cúnzài yú shénhuà zhōng 存在于神话中

mythology shénhuàxué 神话学

# N

nab (*take for oneself*) qiǎng qiǎng 抢

nag 1 v/i (*of person*) láodao bùtíng 唠叨不停 2 v/t fán fàn; **~ X to do Y** méiwán méiliǎo de yào X qùzuò Y 没完没了地要X去做Y

nagging *person* hào láodao 好唠叨; *doubt* kùnrǎo 困扰; *pain* lìngrén fánnǎo 令人烦恼

nail (*for wood*) dīng 钉; (*on finger, toe*) zhǐjia 指甲

nail clippers zhǐjia dāo 指甲刀; nail file zhǐjia cuò 指甲锉; nail polish zhǐjia yóu 指甲油; nail polish remover zhǐjia yóu qùchú jì 指甲油去除剂; nail scissors zhǐjia jiǎn 指甲剪; nail varnish zhǐjia yóu 指甲油

naive tiānzhēn 天真

naked luǒtǐ 裸体; **to the ~ eye** yòng ròuyǎn láikàn 用肉眼来看

name 1 n míngzi 名字; **what's your ~?** nǐ jiào shénme míngzi? 你叫什么名字？; (*formal use*) qǐngwèn guìxìng? 请问贵姓？; **call X ~s** jiào X wàihào 叫X外号; **make a ~ for oneself** chéngmíng 成名 2 v/t qǐmíng 起名

♦name for: **name X for Y** yǐ Y de míngzi wèi X qǐmíng 以Y的名字为X起名

namely jí 即

namesake tóngmíng rén 同名人

nametag (*on clothing etc*) biāoqiān 标签

nanny n bǎomǔ 保姆

nap n xiǎoshuì 小睡; **have a ~** dǎdǔnr 打盹儿

nape: **~ of the neck** hòu bójǐng 后脖颈

napkin (*table ~*) cānjīn 餐巾; (*sanitary*) wèishēngjīn 卫生巾

narcotic n mázuì pǐn 麻醉品

narcotics agent fǎndú jǐng 反毒警

narrate xùshù 叙述

narration (*telling*) xùshù 叙述

narrative 1 n (*story*) gùshì 故事 2 adj *poem, style* xùshì tǐ 叙事体

narrator xùshì zhě 叙事者

narrow *street, bed etc* xiázhǎi 狭窄; *views, mind* xiáyì 狭隘; *victory* miǎnqiáng 勉强

narrowly *win* miǎnqiángde 勉强地; **~ escape X** miǎnqiáng de táotuō X 勉强地逃脱X

narrow-minded xīnxiōng xiázǎi 心胸狭窄

nasal *voice* bíyīn zhòng 鼻音重

nasty *person, thing to say* xiàbēi bǐ bǐ 卑鄙; *smell, weather* èliè 恶劣; *cut, wound, disease* yánzhòng 严重

nation guójiā 国家

national 1 adj *currency, identity, issues* guólì 国立; *newspaper, security* guójiā 国家; *economic indicators* guómín 国民; *pride* àiguó 爱国 2 n guómín 国民

national anthem guógē 国歌

National Day Guóqìngjié 国庆节

national debt guózhài 国债

nationalism mínzú zhǔyì 民族主义

Nationalist Party (*KMT*) Guómíndǎng 国民党

nationality guójí 国籍

nationalize *industry etc* shǐ guóyǒu huà 使国有化

national park guójiā gōngyuán 国家公园

National People's Congress Quánguó Rénmín Dàibiǎo Dàhuì 全国人民代表大会

native 1 adj (*of a country*) běnguó běnlì 本国; (*of a place*) běndì 本地; **~ language** (*of a nation*) běnguó yǔ 本国语; (*mother tongue*) mǔyǔ 母语 2 n dāngdì rén 当地人; (*tribesman*) tǔrén 土人

native country zǔguó 祖国

**native speaker** jiǎng běnguóyǔ de rén 讲本国语的人

**NATO** (= *North Atlantic Treaty Organization*) Běiyuē 北约

**natural** zìrán 自然; *resources, forces* zìrán jiè 自然界; *death* zìrán 自然; *flavor* fēi rénzào 非人造; *a ~ blonde* tiānshēng jīn tóufà rén 天生金头发人

**natural gas** tiānrán qì 天然气

**naturalist** bówù xuéjiā 博物学家

**naturalize**: *become ~d* jiārù guójí 加入国籍

**naturally** (*of course*) dāngrán 当然; *behave, speak* zìrán de 自然地; (*by nature*) tiānshēng 天生

**natural science** zìrán kēxué 自然科学

**natural scientist** zìrán kēxué jiā 自然科学家

**nature** zìrán 自然; (*of person*) xìnggé 性格; (*of problem*) běnzhì 本质

**nature reserve** zìrán bǎohùqū 自然保护区

**naughty** táoqì 淘气; *photograph, word etc* bùdétǐ 不得体

**nausea** ěxin 恶心

**nauseate** *fig* (*disgust*) shǐ ěxin 使恶心

**nauseating** *smell, taste* lìngrén zuò'ǒu 令人作呕; *person* ròumá 肉麻

**nauseous**: *feel ~* juéde ěxin 觉得恶心

**nautical** hánghǎi 航海

**nautical mile** hǎilǐ 海里

**naval** hǎijūn 海军

**naval base** hǎijūn jīdì 海军基地

**navel** dùqí 肚脐

**navigable** *river* kě tōngháng 可通航

**navigate** *v/i* (*in ship, airplane*) cèháng 测航; (*in car*) zhǐlù 指路; COMPUT zǒu 走

**navigation** (*nautical, in airplane*) hángxíngxué 航行学; (*in car*) lǐnglù 领路; (*skills*) yǐndǎo 引导

**navigator** (*on ship*) hánghǎi jiā 航海家; (*in airplane*) jiàshǐ yuán 驾驶员; (*in car*) zhǐlùrén 指路人

**navy** hǎijūn 海军

**navy blue** *n & adj* hǎijūn lán 海军蓝

**near 1** *adv* jìn 近 **2** *prep* jiējìn 接近; *~ the bank* jìn yínháng 近银行; *do you go ~ the bank?* nǐ huìbuhuì zǒu yínháng nàbian? 你会不会走银行那边? **3** *adj* jìn 近; *the ~est bus stop* zuìjìnde gōnggòng qìchē zhàn 最近的公共汽车站; *in the ~ future* bùyuǎnde jiānglái 不远的将来

**nearby** *adv* *live* zài fùjìn 在附近

**nearly** jīhū 几乎

**near-sighted** jìnshì 近视

**neat** *room, desk* zhěngjié 整洁; *person* zhěngqí 整齐; *whiskey* chún 纯; *solution* qiǎomiào 巧妙; F (*terrific*) tǐnghǎo 挺好

**necessarily** yídìng 一定

**necessary** bìbù kěshǎo 必不可少; *it is ~ to X* yǒu bìyào zuò X 有必要做 X

**necessitate** xūyào 需要

**necessity** (*being necessary*) bìyào xìng 必要性; (*sth necessary*) bìxū pǐn 必需品

**neck** bózi 脖子

**necklace** xiàngliàn 项链; **neckline** (*of dress*) lǐngkǒu 领口; **necktie** lǐngdài 领带

**née** mǔjiā xìng 母家姓

**need 1** *n* xūyào 需要; *if ~ be* rǔguǒ yǒu xūyào dehuà 如果有需要的话; *in ~* yǒu kùnnán 有困难; *be in ~ of X* xūyào X 需要 X; *there's no ~ to be rude / upset* méi bìyào zhème cūlǔ / shāngxīn 没必要这么粗鲁 / 伤心 **2** *v/t* xūyào 需要; *you'll ~ to buy one* nǐ yǒu bìyào mǎi yígè 你有必要买一个; *you don't ~ to wait* nǐ bùbì děngzhe 你不必等着; *I ~ to talk to you* wǒ yào hé nǐ tánhuà 我要和你谈话; *~ I say more?* wǒ háiyǒu shénme kě-shuōde? 我还有什么可说的？

**needle** (*for sewing*) zhēn 针; (*for injection*) zhēntóu 针头; (*on dial*) zhǐzhēn 指针

**needlework** zhēnxiàn huór 针线

活儿
needy qióng 穷
negative 1 adj verb, sentence
fǒudìng 否定；attitude, person
xiāojí 消极；ELEC fùdiàn 负电
2 n: answer in the ~ jǐyǔ fǒudìngde huídá 给予否定的回答
neglect 1 n hūlüè 忽略 2 v/t
garden, one's health zhàogù bùzhōu
照顾不周；~ to do X méiyǒu zuò
X 没有做 X
neglected gardens, author búshòu
zhòngshì 不受重视；feel ~
gǎndào búshòu zhòngshì 感到不
受重视
negligence wánhū zhíshǒu 玩忽
职守
negligent cūxīn dàyì 粗心大意
negligible quantity, amount kěyǐ
hūlüè 可以忽略
negotiable salary, contract kě
xiéshāng 可协商
negotiate 1 v/i xiéshāng 协商
2 v/t deal, settlement xiéshāng 协
商；obstacles jiějué 解决；bend in
road tōngguò 通过
negotiation xiéshāng 协商
negotiator tánpàn yuán 谈判员
Negro (person) Hēi rén 黑人
neigh v/i sī 嘶
neighbor línjū 邻居
neighborhood (in town) dìqū 地
区；in the ~ of ... fig dàyuē ... 大
约 ...
neighboring house, state fùjìn 附近
neighborly yǒuhǎo 友好
neither 1 adj liǎngzhě dōubù 两者
都不；~ answer was correct liǎng
ge dá'àn dōu búduì 两个答案都
不对 2 pron něige dōu bù 哪个
都不；in the end I bought ~
zuìhòu wǒ něige dōu mǎi 最
后我哪个都买；~ of them
recognized me tāmenliǎ shéi dōu
méi rènchū wǒ lai 他们俩谁都
没认出我来 3 adv: ~ ... nor ...
jìbù ... yěbù ... 既不 ... 也不 ...
4 conj yěbù 也不；~ do I wǒ yě bù
我也不
neon light níhóng dēng 霓虹灯
Nepal Níbó'ěr 尼泊尔

Nepalese 1 adj Níbó'ěr 尼泊尔
2 n (person) Níbó'ěr rén 尼泊尔
人；(language) Níbó'ěr yǔ 尼泊尔
语
nephew (brother's son) zhízi 侄子；
(sister's son) wàisheng 外甥
nerd F guàirén 怪人
nerve n shénjīng 神经；(courage)
yǒngqì 勇气；(impudence) dǎliàng
胆量；it's bad for my ~s duì wǒde
shénjīng bùhǎo 对我的神经不
好；get on X's ~s shǐ X xīnfán
yiluàn 使 X 心烦意乱
nerve-racking shǐrén xīnfán 使人
心烦
nervous person jǐnzhāng 紧张；
twitch shénjīng xìng 神经性；be ~
about doing X hàipà zuò X 害怕
做 X
nervous breakdown jīngshén
bēngkuì 精神崩溃
nervous energy jīnglì chōngpèi 精
力充沛
nervousness jǐnzhāng 紧张
nervous wreck hěn jǐnzhāng
derén 很紧张的人
nervy (fresh) dàdǎn 大胆
nest n cháo 巢
nestle shūshìde āndùn xiàlái 舒适
地安顿下来
net¹ (for fishing) yúwǎng 鱼网；(for
tennis) wǎngqiú wǎng 网球网
net² adj price, amount chún 纯；
weight jìng 净
net curtain shā chuānglián 纱窗
帘
net profit jìnglì 净利
nettle xúnmá 荨麻
network (of contacts, cells) liánluò
wǎng 联络网；COMPUT wǎngluò
网络
neurologist shénjīngbìng xuéjiā 神
经病学家
neurosis shénjīng jīnéng bìng 神经
机能病
neurotic adj shénjīng zhì 神经质
neuter v/t animal yāngē 阉割
neutral 1 adj country zhōnglì 中立；
color fēi cǎisè 非彩色 2 n (gear)
kōngdǎng 空档；in ~ zài kōngdǎng 在空档

**neutrality** zhōnglì dìwèi 中立地位

**neutralize** *effect of drug etc* shǐ zhōnghé shǐ 中和; *argument* shǐ wúxiào 使无效

**never** ◊ (*in past*) cónglái méi 从来没; *I've ~ eaten this* wǒ cónglái méi chīguo zhège 我从来没吃过这个 ◊ (*in present*) cónglái bù 从来不; *she ~ goes to the movies* tā cónglái búqù kàn diànyǐng 她从来不去看电影 ◊ (*in future tenses*) juébúhuì 绝不会; *she will ~ marry him* tā juébúhuì gēn tā jiéhūn 她绝不会跟他结婚 ◊ (*in disbelief*) bùkěnéng 不可能; *you're ~ going to believe this* nǐ búhuì xiāngxìn zhè jiàn shì 你不会相信这件事; *you ~ promised, did you?* nǐ cónglái méiyǒu xǔnuòguò, shì ba? 你从来没有许诺过, 是吧？

**never-ending** méiwán 没完

**nevertheless** dànshì 但是

**new** xīn 新; *this system is still ~ to me* wǒ duì zhège xìtǒng háishì bù shúxī 我对这个系统还是不熟悉; *I'm ~ to the job* wǒ shì xīnlái de 我是新来的; *that's nothing ~* méiyǒu shénme kě qíguàide 没有什么可奇怪的

**newborn** *adj* xīnshēng 新生

**newcomer** xīnlái derén 新来的人

**newly** (*recently*) zuìjìn 最近

**newly-weds** xīnhūn rén 新婚人

**new moon** xīnyuè 新月

**news** xīnwén 新闻; (*on TV, radio*) xīnwén bàodào 新闻报导; *that's ~ to me* wǒ méi tīngshuō guò zhèjiànshì 我没听说过这件事

**news agency** tōngxùnshè 通讯社; **newscast** TV xīnwén guǎngbō 新闻广播; **newscaster** TV xīnwén guǎngbōyuán 新闻广播员; **newsdealer** bàokān jīngshòu rén bào kān jīngshòu rén 报刊经售人; **news flash** jǐnjí xīnwén bàodào 紧急新闻报道

**newspaper** bàozhǐ 报纸

**newsreader** TV *etc* xīnwén bōyīn yuán 新闻播音员; **news report**

xīnwén bàodào 新闻报道; **newsstand** bàotānr 报摊儿; **newsvendor** bàofàn 报贩

**New Territories** (*in Hong Kong*) Xīnjiè 新界

**New Year** Xīnnián 新年; (*Chinese*) Chūnjié 春节; *Happy ~!* Xīnnián kuàilè! 新年快乐!

**New Year's Day** (*Jan 1*) Yuándàn 元旦; (*Chinese*) Chūyī 初一

**New Year's Eve** (*Dec 31*) Yuándàn Qiányè 元旦前夜; (*Chinese*) Chúxī 除夕

**New York** Niǔyuè 纽约

**New Zealand** ⇩ Xīnxīlán 新西兰

**New Zealander** ⇩ Xīnxīlán rén 新西兰人

**next 1** *adj* (*in time, space*) xià yīgè 下一个; *the ~ week / month he came back again* xiàgè xīngqī / xiàgè yuè tā zàilái 下个星期 / 下个月他再来; *who's ~?* shuí shì xià yīgè? 谁是下一个？ **2** *adv* xià yībù 下一步; *to X* (*beside*) zài X de pángbiān 在X的旁边; (*in comparison with*) yǔ X xiāngbǐ 与X相比

**next door** *adj & adv* gébì 隔壁

**next of kin** zuìjìnde qīnshǔ 最近的亲属

**nibble** *v/t* kěn 啃

**nice** *person* tǐtiē 体贴; *day, weather, meal, food, party, trip, vacation* lìngrén yúkuài 令人愉快; *house, hair* piàoliang 漂亮; *be ~ to your sisters* duì nǐ jiěmèi hǎodiǎnr 对你姐妹好点儿; *that's very ~ of you* nǐ tàihǎole 你太好了

**nicely** *presented etc* jīngxīn de 精心地; (*pleasantly*) héyí di 合宜地

**niceties**: *social ~* shèjiāo lǐjié 社交礼节

**niche** (*in market*) quēkǒu 缺口; (*special position*) héshìde wèizhì 合适的位置

**nick** *n* (*cut*) kèhén 刻痕; *in the ~ of time* qiàhǎo 恰好

**nickel** niè 镍

**nickname** *n* wàihào 外号

**niece** (*brother's daughter*) zhínǚ 侄女; (*sister's daughter*) wài shengnǚ

外甥女

**niggardly** *adj amount, person* xiǎoqì 小气

**night** yè 夜; *tomorrow ~* míngyè 明夜; *(evening)* míngwǎn 明晚; *11 o'clock at ~* wǎnshàng shíyī diǎn 晚上十一点; *travel by ~* yèjiān lǚxíng 夜间旅行; *during the ~* yèjiān 夜间; *stay the night* guòyè 过夜; *a room for 2/3 ~s* yīgè fángjiān, liǎngsān yè 一个房间, 两三夜; *work ~s* shàng yèbān 上夜班; *good ~* wǎn'ān 晚安; *in the middle of the ~* bànyè sāngēng 半夜三更

**nightcap** *(drink)* shuìqián jiǔ 睡前酒; **nightclub** yèzǒnghuì 夜总会; **nightdress** shuìyī 睡衣; **nightfall**: *at ~* huánghūn 黄昏; **night flight** yèjiān fēixíng 夜间飞行; **nightgown** shuìyī 睡衣

**nightingale** yèyīng 夜莺
**nightlife** yè shēnghuó 夜生活
**nightly 1** *adj* yèjiān 夜间 **2** *adv* zài yèjiān 在夜间

**nightmare** èmèng 恶梦; *fig* kěpàde jīngyàn 可怕的经验; **night-market** yèshì 夜市; **night porter** yèbān fúwùyuán 夜班服务员; **night school** yèxiào 夜校; **night shift** yèbān 夜班; **nightshirt** shuìyī 睡衣; **nightspot** yèzǒnghuì 夜总会; **nighttime**: *at ~, in the ~* zài yèjiān 在夜间

**nil** líng 零
**nimble** jílíng 机灵
**nine** jiǔ 九
**nineteen** shíjiǔ 十九
**nineteenth** dìshíjiǔ 第十九
**ninetieth** dìjiǔshí 第九十
**ninety** jiǔshí 九十
**ninth** dìjiǔ 第九
**nip** *n (pinch)* qiā qiā 掐; *(bite)* yǎo 咬
**nipple** rǔtóu 乳头
**nitrogen** dàn 氮
**no 1** *adv* bù 不; *do you understand? ~ ~* nǐ dǒng ma? – bùdǒng 你懂吗? – 不懂; *does he agree? ~ ~* tā tóngyì ma? – bù tóngyì 他同意吗? – 不同意 **2** *adj* méiyǒu 没有; *there's ~*

*coffee / tea left* méiyǒu kāfēi / chá le 没有咖啡 / 茶了; *I have ~ family / money* wǒ méiyǒu jiātíng / qián 我没有家庭 / 钱; *I'm ~ linguist / expert* wǒ bùshì yǔyán xuéjiā / zhuānjiā 我不是语言学家 / 专家; *~ smoking / parking* jìnzhǐ xīyān / tíngchē 禁止吸烟 / 停车

**nobility** guìzú 贵族
**noble** *adj* gāoguì 高贵
**nobody** méirén 没人; *~ knows* méirén zhīdào 没人知道; *there was ~ at home* méirén zàijiā 没人在家

**nod** *n & v/i* diǎntóu 点头
♦**nod off** *(fall asleep)* dǎ kēshuì 打瞌睡

**no-hoper** bù zhōngyòng derén 不中用的人
**noise** shēngyīn 声音; *(loud, unpleasant)* zàoyīn 噪音
**noisy** xuānhuá 喧哗
**nominal** *amount* míngyì shàng 名义上
**nominate** *(appoint)* tímíng 提名; *~ X for a post (propose)* tuījiàn X rèn mǒugè zhíwèi 推荐X任某个职位
**nomination** *(appointment)* rènmìng 任命; *(proposal)* tímíng 提名; *(person proposed)* bèi tímíng rén 被提名人
**nominee** bèi tímíng rén 被提名人
**non ...** bù ... 不...
**nonalcoholic** bù hán jiǔjīng 不含酒精
**nonaligned** bù jiéméng 不结盟
**nonchalant** mòbù guānxīn 漠不关心
**noncommissioned officer** fēi shòumìng guānyuán 非受命官员
**noncommittal** *person, response* bù mínglǎng 不明朗
**nondescript** méiyǒu tèzhēng 没有特征
**none** méi yīgè 没一个; *~ of the students* méi yīgè xuéshēng 没一个学生; *~ of the chocolate* méi yìzhǒng qiǎokèlì 没一种巧克

力; **there is / are ~ left**
méishèngde 没剩的
**nonentity** wúzú qīngzhòng 无足
轻重
**nonetheless** rán'ér 然而
**nonexistent** bù cúnzài 不存在
**nonfiction** fēi xiǎoshuō 非小说;
**non(in)flammable** bùrán 不燃;
**noninterference, nonintervention** bù gānyù 不干预; **non-iron**
*shirt* miǎnyùntàng 免熨烫
**no-no: that's a ~** bùxíngde 不行
的
**no-nonsense** *approach* rènzhēn 认
真
**nonpayment** wèifù 未付; **non-polluting** fēi wūrǎn 非污染;
**nonresident** *n* kèrén 客人; **nonreturnable** bù kětuì 不可退
**nonsense** húshuō 胡说; **don't talk ~** bié húshuō 别胡说; **~, it's easy!** húshuō, zhèhěn róngyì! 胡
说, 这很容易！
**nonskid** *tires* fánghuá 防滑; **nonslip** *surface* bùhuá 不滑; **nonsmoker** (*person*) bù xīyān zhě 不
吸烟者; **nonstandard** fēi
chángguī 非常规; **nonstick** *pan*
bùzhān 不粘; **nonstop 1** *adj*
*flight, train* zhídá 直达; *chatter*
bùtíng 不停 **2** *adv fly, travel* zhídá
直达; *chatter, argue* bùtíng 不停;
**nonswimmer** búhuì yóuyǒng zhě
不会游泳者; **nonunion** *adj*
bùshǔ gōnghuì 不属工会; **nonviolence** fēi bàolì 非暴力; **nonviolent** fēi bàolì 非暴力
**noodles** miàntiáo 面条
**noodle soup** tāngmiàn 汤面
**nook** jiǎoluò 角落
**noon** zhōngwǔ 中午; **at ~** zài
zhōngwǔ 在中午
**noose** quāntào 圈套
**nor** yòubù 又不; **~ do I** wǒ yěbù 我
也不
**norm** zhǔnzé 准则
**normal** zhèngcháng 正常
**normality** zhèngcháng 正常
**normalize** *relationships* zhèngcháng
huà 正常化
**normally** (*usually*) yìbān de 一般

地; (*in a normal way*) zhèngcháng
de 正常地
**north 1** *n* běibù 北部; **to the ~ of**
*X* X yǐběi X 以北 **2** *adj* běibù 北
部 **3** *adv travel* xiàngběi 向北; **~
of X** X běibù X 北部
**North America** Běiměi 北美
**North American 1** *adj*
Běiměizhōu 北美洲 **2** *n*
Běiměizhōu rén 北美洲人
**northeast** *n* dōngběi bù 东北部
**northerly** *adj* běi 北
**northern** běifāng 北方
**northerner** běifāng rén 北方人
**North Korea** ⇩ Běicháoxiān 北朝
鲜
**North Korean** ⇩ **1** *adj* Běicháoxiān 北朝鲜 **2** *n* Běicháoxiān rén
北朝鲜人
**North Pole** Běijí 北极
**northward** *travel* xiàngběi 向北
**northwest** *n* xīběi bù 西北部
**Norway** Nuówēi 挪威
**Norwegian 1** *adj* Nuówēi 挪威
**2** *n* (*person*) Nuówēi rén 挪威人;
(*language*) Nuówēi yǔ 挪威语
**nose** bízi 鼻子; **it was right under
my ~** jiù zài wǒ yǎnqián 就在我
眼前
♦ **nose around** tàntīng 探听
**nosebleed** liú bíxuè 流鼻血
**nostalgia** huáijiù 怀旧
**nostalgic** huáijiù 怀旧
**nostril** bíkǒng 鼻孔
**nosy** hàoguǎn xiánshì 好管闲事
**not** ◊ (*present and future*) bù 不; **~
this one, that one** búshì zhège,
shì nèige 不是这个, 是那个; **~
now** xiànzài bùxíng 现在不行; **~
there** nàr bùxíng 那儿不行; **~
like that** bùnéng nàyàng 不能那
样; **~ before Tuesday / next week**
xīngqī èr / xià xīngqī qián bùxíng
星期二 / 下星期前不行; **~ for
me, thanks** bù wǒbù, xièxiè bù
不要, 谢谢; **~ a lot** yìdiǎndian
一点点; **it's ~ allowed** bù yúnxǔ
没成呢 / 不允许; **I don't know**
wǒ bù zhīdào 我不知道; **I am ~
American** wǒ búshì Měiguó rén
我不是美国人; **I'm ~ going** wǒ

búqù 我不去; *it won't be cold tomorrow* míngtiān bùnéng lěng 明天不能冷 ◊ *(past tense, and with you)* méi 没; *he didn't help* tā méi bāngmáng 他没帮忙; *he wasn't there* tā méi zài 他没在; *I haven't told him yet* wǒ hái méi gàosu tā 我还没告诉他; *I don't have that book* wǒ méiyǒu nèi běn shū 我没有那本书; *we don't have a car* wǒmen méiyǒu chē 我们没有车

**notable** zhuóyuè 卓越

**notary** gōngzhèng rén 公证人

**notch** āokǒu 凹口

**note** n *(short letter)* biàntiáo 便条; MUS yīndiào 音调; *(memo to self)* jìlù 记录; *(comment on text)* zhùshì 注释; *take ~s* jì bǐjì 记笔记; *take ~ of X* zhùyì dào X 注意到 X

♦**note down** jìlù xiàlái 记录下来

**notebook** *also* COMPUT bǐjìběn 笔记本

**noted** zhùmíng 著名

**notepad** biàntiáo běn 便条本

**notepaper** biàntiáo zhǐ 便条纸

**nothing** méiyǒu shénme 没有什么; ~ *for me thanks* wǒ shēnme yě búyào xièxie 我什么也不要谢谢; *there was ~ to eat* méiyǒu shénme chīde 没有什么吃的; *there's ~ left* méiyǒu shénme le 没有什么了; ~ *works in this office* bàngōngshì lǐ shénme dōu huài le 办公室里什么都坏了; ~ *but* zhǐ 只; *there's ~ but work in his life* tā shēnghuó zhōng zhǐyǒu gōngzuò 他生活中只有工作; *he wants ~ but the best* tā zhǐ yào zuìhǎo de 他只要最好的; ~ *much* méi duōshǎo 没多少; *for ~ (for free)* miǎnfèi 免费; *(for no reason)* wúyuán wúgù 无缘无故; *I'd like ~ better* zuì hǎole 最好了

**notice 1** n *(on bulletin board, in street, in newspaper)* tōnggào 通告; *(advance warning)* yùxiān tōngzhī 预先通知; *(to leave job)* cízhí tōngzhī 辞职通知; *(to leave house)* zūpíng tōngzhī 租凭通知;

*at short ~* tūrán 突然; *until further ~* zài lìngxíng tōngzhī zhīqián 在另行通知之前; *give X his / her ~ (to quit job)* xiàng X tíchū cízhí tōngzhī 向 X 提出辞职通知; *(to leave house)* xiàng X tíchū tuìfáng tōngzhī 向 X 提出退房通知; *hand in one's ~ (to employer)* tíchū cízhí tōngzhī 提出辞职通知; *four weeks' ~* sìge xīngqī de yùxiān tōngzhī 四个星期的预先通知; *take ~ of X* zhùyì X 注意 X; *take no ~ of X* búyào guǎn X 不要管 X **2** v/t zhùyì 注意

**noticeable** míngxiǎn 明显

**notify** tōngzhī 通知

**notion** kànfǎ 看法

**notions** zhēnxiàn 针线

**notorious** shēngmíng lángjí 声名狼籍

**nougat** jiā jiānguǒ táng 夹坚果糖

**nought** Br líng 零

**noun** míngcí 名词

**nourishing** yǒu yíngyǎng 有营养

**nourishment** yíngyǎng 营养

**novel** n xiǎoshuō 小说

**novelist** xiǎoshuō jiā 小说家

**novelty** *(being novel)* xīnyǐng 新颖; *(sth novel)* xīnyǐng shìwù 新颖事物

**November** shíyī yuè 十一月

**novice** xuétú 学徒

**now** xiànzài 现在; ~ *and again*, ~ *and then* yǒushí 有时; *by ~* zhèshí 这时; *from ~ on* cóng xiànzài kāishǐ 从现在开始; *right ~* cǐkè cǐkè 此刻此刻; *just ~ (at this moment)* xiànzài 现在; *(a little while ago)* gāngcái 刚才; ~, ~! déla, déla! 得啦，得啦！; ~, *where did I put it?* nàme, wǒ bǎ tā fàng zài nǎr le? 那么，我把它放在哪儿了？

**nowadays** xiànjīn 现今

**nowhere** wúchù 无处; *it's ~ near finished* lí wánchéng hái zǎozhe ne 离完成还早着呢

**nozzle** pēnzuǐ 喷嘴

**nuclear** yuánzǐhé 原子核

**nuclear energy** hénéng 核能;

nuclear fission hé lièbiàn 核裂变; nuclear-free wúhé 无核; nuclear physics yuánzíhé wùlǐ 原子核物理; nuclear power hénéng 核能; nuclear power station hénéng zhàn 核能站; nuclear reactor hé fǎnyìng duī 核反应堆; nuclear waste hé fèiwù 核废物; nuclear weapons hé wǔqì 核武器

nude 1 adj luǒtǐ 裸体 2 n (painting) luǒtǐ huà 裸体画; in the ~ chì luǒluo 赤裸裸

nudge v/t qīngtuī 轻推

nudist n luǒtǐ zhǔyì zhě 裸体主义者

nuisance fánrén 烦人; make a ~ of oneself lìngrén tǎoyàn 令人讨厌; what a ~! tǎoyàn! 讨厌！

nuke v/t yòng hé wǔqì gōngjī 用核武器攻击

null and void wúxiào 无效

numb mámù 麻木; (emotionally) chídùn 迟钝

number 1 n (figure) shùmù 数目; (quantity) ruògàn 若干; (of hotel room, house, phone number etc) shùzì 数字 2 v/t (put a number on) biānhào 编号

numeral shùmù 数目

numerate jìshù nénglì qiáng 计数能力强

numerous xǔduō 许多

nun nígū 尼姑; become a ~ chūjiā 出家

nurse hùshi 护士

nursery tuō'érsuǒ 托儿所; (for plants) miáopǔ 苗圃

nursery rhyme tóngyáo 童谣; nursery school yòu'éryuán 幼儿园; nursery school teacher yòu'éryuán lǎoshī 幼儿园老师

nursing hùlǐ 护理

nursing home (for old people) lǎorén yuàn 老人院

nut jiānguǒ 坚果; (for bolt) luómǔ 螺母; ~s F (testicles) dàn dàn 蛋蛋

nutcrackers jiānguǒ qián 坚果钳

nutrient n yíngyǎng pǐn 营养品

nutrition yíngyǎng 营养

nutritious yǒu yíngyǎng 有营养

nuts adj F (crazy) fēng 疯; be ~ about X míliàn X 迷恋 X

nutshell: in a ~ yìyán yǐ bìzhī 一言以蔽之

nutty taste jiānguǒ wèir 坚果味儿; F (crazy) fēngkuáng 疯狂

nylon nílóng 尼龙

# O

oak (*tree*) xiàngshù 橡树; (*wood*) xiàngmù 橡木

oar jiǎng 桨

oasis lǜzhōu 绿洲; *fig* shìwài táoyuán 世外桃源

oath LAW shìyán 誓言; (*swearword*) zǔzhòu 诅咒; *on ~* zài shìyán de yuēshù xià 在誓言的约束下

oatmeal yànmàipiàn 燕麦片

oats yànmàipiàn 燕麦片

obedience fúcóng 服从

obedient fúcóng 服从

obey fúcóng 服从

obituary *n* fùgào 讣告

object¹ *n* (*thing*) wùtǐ 物体; (*aim*) mùdì 目的; GRAM bīnyǔ 宾语

object² *v/i* fǎnduì 反对

♦ object to fǎnduì 反对

objection fǎnduì 反对

objectionable (*unpleasant*) tǎoyàn 讨厌

objective 1 *adj* kèguān 客观 2 *n* mùbiāo 目标

obligation yìwù 义务; *be under an ~ to X* duì X yǒu yìwù 对 X 有义务

obligatory bìxū 必须

oblige: *much ~d!* duōxièle! 多谢了!

obliging lèyú zhùrén 乐于助人

oblique 1 *adj* reference hánhu qící 含糊其辞 2 *n* (*in punctuation*) xiéxiàn 斜线

obliterate city huǐmiè 毁灭; memory chúqù 除去

oblivion (*being forgotten*) yíwàng 遗忘; *fall into ~* jiànbèi wàngquè 渐被忘却

oblivious: *be ~ of ...* yìshí búdào ... 意识不到 ...

oblong *adj* chángfāngxíng 长方形

obnoxious yǐnrén fǎngǎn 引人反感

obscene yínhuì 淫秽; salary, poverty guòfèn 过分

obscure (*hard to see*) hūn'àn 昏暗; (*hard to understand*) nánjiě 难解; (*little known*) wúmíng 无名

observance (*of festival*) zūnshǒu 遵守

observant liúxīn 留心

observation (*of nature, stars*) guānchá 观察; (*comment*) yìjiàn 意见

observatory tiānwén tái 天文台

observe behavior zhùyì 注意; people kàndào 看到; nature guāncè 观测

observer (*of human nature etc*) guānchá zhě 观察者; (*at conference, elections*) guāncháyuán 观察员

obsess: *be ~ed with X* duì X zháomí 对 X 着迷

obsession pǐ pì 癖; (*with a person, hobby*) zháomí 著迷

obsessive behavior guòfèn 过分

obsolete yǐ fèiqì 已废弃

obstacle (*physical*) zhàng'ài wù 障碍物; (*to progress etc*) zhàng'ài 障碍

obstetrician chǎnkē yīshī 产科医师

obstinacy wángù 顽固

obstinate wángù 顽固

obstruct road, passage zǔsè 阻塞; investigation, police zǔdǎng 阻挡

obstruction (*on road etc*) zhàng'ài wù 障碍物

obstructive behavior fáng'ài fáng'ài 妨碍

obtain dédào 得到

obtainable products kě huòdé 可获得

obvious (*evident, not subtle*) míngxiǎn 明显

obviously míngxiǎnde 明显地; *~!* dāngránle! 当然了!

occasion jīhuì 机会

occasional ǒu'ěr 偶尔

**occasionally** ŏurán 偶然

**occult 1** adj shénmì 神秘 **2** n: the ~ mìshù 秘术

**occupant** (of vehicle) chéngkè 乘客; (of house) jūzhù zhě 居住者

**occupation** (job) zhíyè 职业; (of country) zhànlǐng 占领

**occupy** one's time, mind zhànyòng 占用; position in company chōngrèn 充任; country zhànlǐng 占领

**occur** fāshēng 发生; **it ~red to me that ...** wŏ xiǎngdào ... 我想到 ...

**occurrence** chūxiàn 出现

**ocean** hǎiyáng 海洋

**o'clock: at five / six ~** wŭ / liù diǎn-zhōng 五 / 六点钟

**October** shíyuè 十月

**octopus** zhāngyú 章鱼

**odd** (strange) qíguài 奇怪; (not even) jīshù 奇数; **the ~ one out** yŭzhòng bùtóng 与众不同; **50 ~** dàgài wŭshí 大概五十

**odds: be at ~ with X** yŭ X duìlì 与 X 对立

**odds and ends** (objects) língxīng cánwù 零星残物; (things to do) suŏsuì shì 琐碎事

**odometer** lǐchéng biǎo 里程表

**odor** qìwèi 气味

**of: the name ~ the street / hotel** jiē / lǚguǎn de míngzi 街 / 旅馆的名字; **the color ~ the car** qìchē yánsè 汽车颜色; **the works ~ Dickens** Díqěngsī zhùzuò 狄更斯著作; **five / ten minutes ~ twelve** shí'èr diǎn chà wŭ / shí fēn 十二点差五 / 十分; **die ~ cancer / a stroke** sĭyú áizhèng / zhòngfēng 死于癌症 / 中风; **love ~ money / adventure** duì qián / màoxiǎn de xǐ'ài 对钱 / 冒险的喜爱; **~ the three this is ...** sāngè zhīzhōng zhèshì ... 三个之中这是 ...

**off 1** prep: **~ the main road** (away from) líkāi dà mǎlù 离开大马路; (leading off) cóng dà mǎlù fēnchà chūlái 从大马路分岔出来; **$20 ~ the price** jiǎnjià èrshí měiyuán 减价二十美元; **he's ~ his food** tā bùchī dōngxi 他不吃东西

**2** adv: **be ~** (of light) méi kāidēng 没开灯; (of TV, machine) méikāi 没开; (of brake) méi shàng zhá 没上闸; (of lid, top) méi gàizhe gàir 没盖着盖儿; (not at work) méi shàngbān 没上班; (canceled) qŭxiāo 取消; **we're ~ tomorrow** (leaving) wŏmen míngtiān líkāi 我们明天离开; **I'm ~ to New York** wŏ qù Niŭyuē 我去纽约; **with his pants ~** tā bù chuān kùzi 他不穿裤子; **with his hat ~** tā bù dài màozi 他不戴帽子; **take a day ~** xiūjià yītiān 休假一天; **it's 3 miles ~** sān yīnglǐ yuǎn 三英里远; **it's a long way ~** (in the distance) hái yuǎn zhene 还远着呢; (in future) hái qiě zhene 还且着呢; **drive / walk ~** kāizŏu / zŏukāi 开走 / 走开 **3** adj: **the ~ switch** guānbì jiàn 关闭键

**offend** v/t (insult) màofàn 冒犯

**offender** LAW zuìfàn 罪犯

**offense** LAW zuìxíng 罪行

**offensive 1** adj behavior, remark, smell tǎoyàn 讨厌 **2** n MIL (attack) gōngjī 攻击; **go onto the ~** cǎiqŭ gōngjī 采取攻击

**offer 1** n tígōng 提供 **2** v/t tígōng 提供; **~ X Y** gěi X Y 给 X Y

**offhand** adj attitude bùjū lǐjié 不拘礼节

**office** (building) bàngōnglóu 办公楼; (room) bàngōngshì 办公室; (position) zhíwèi 职位

**office block** bàngōng dàlóu 办公大楼

**office hours** bàngōng shíjiān 办公时间

**officer** MIL jūnguān 军官; (in police) jǐngguān 警官

**official 1** adj organization, statement view, theory guānfāng 官方; (confirmed) zhèngshì 正式 **2** n guānyuán 官员

**officially** (strictly speaking) zhèng-guī láishuō 正规来说

**off-line** adj working, input xiàwǎng 下网; **go ~** líxiàn 离线; **off-peak rates, season** dīfēng shíjiān 低峰时间; **~ electricity** dīfēng shíjiān gōngdiàn 低峰时间供电; **off-season 1** *adj rates, vacation* dànjì 淡季 **2** *n* dànjì 淡季; **offset** *v/t losses, disadvantage* dǐxiāo 抵消; **offside 1** *adj wheel etc* wàibiān 外边 **2** *adv* SP yuèwèi 越位; **offspring** hòudài 后代; **off-white** *adj* huībái sè 灰白色

**often** jīngcháng 经常

**oil 1** *n* (*for machine, food, skin*) yóu 油; (*as resource*) shíyóu 石油 **2** *v/t hinges, bearings* jiāyóu 加油

**oil company** shíyóu gōngsī 石油公司; **oil painting** yóuhuà 油画; **oil rig** yóujǐng 油井; **oil tanker** yóuchuán 油船; **oil well** yóujǐng 油井

**oily** yǒuyóu 有油; *food* yóunì 油腻

**ointment** ruǎngāo 软膏

**ok** kěyǐ 可以; *can I?* – ~ kěyǐ ma? – kěyǐ 可以 可以; *is it ~ with you if ...?* nǐ bù jièyì ba? ... 你不介意吧?; *that's ~ by me* wǒ tóngyì 我同意; *are you ~?* (*well, not hurt*) nǐ méishìr ba? 你没事儿吧?; *are you ~ for Friday?* xīngqī wǔ xíngma? 星期五行吗?; *he's ~* (*is a good guy*) tā tǐnghǎo 他挺好; *is this bus for ...?* zhè gōnggòng qìchē qù ... ma? 这公共汽车去...吗?

**old** lǎo 老; (*previous*) jiù 旧; *how are you / is he?* nǐ / tā duōdà niánji le? 你 / 他多大年纪了?; *he's getting ~* tā shàng niánji le 他上年纪了

**old age** lǎonián 老年

**old-fashioned** guòshí 过时

**Old Summer Palace** Yuánmíngyuán 圆明园

**olive** gǎnlǎn 橄榄

**olive oil** gǎnlǎn yóu 橄榄油

**Olympic Games** Àoyùnhuì 奥运会

**omelet** jiān dànjuǎn 煎蛋卷

**ominous** yùzhào 预兆

**omission** yílòu 遗漏

**omit** yílòu 遗漏; *to do X* wàngjì zuò X 忘记做 X

**on 1** *prep*: ~ *the table / wall* zài zhuō / qiáng shàng 在桌 / 墙上; ~

*the bus / train* gōnggòng qìchē / huǒchē lǐ 公共汽车 / 火车里; ~ *TV / the radio* diànshì shàng / guǎngbō lǐ 电视上 / 广播里; ~ *Sunday* xīngqī tiān 星期天; ~ *the 1st of ...* dìyī tiān ... 第一天; *this is ~ me* (*I'm paying*) wǒ lái fùqián 我来付钱; ~ *his arrival / departure* tā dàodá / líkāi shí 他到达 / 离开时 **2** *adv*: *be ~* (*of light*) kāidēng 开灯; (*of TV, computer etc*) kāi 开; (*of brake*) shàngzhá 上闸; (*of lid, top*) gàizhe gàir 盖着盖儿; (*of program: being broadcast*) kāiyǎn 开演; (*of meeting etc: be scheduled to happen*) jìnxíng 进行; *what's ~ tonight?* (*on TV etc*) jīnwǎn yǒu shénme jiémù? 今晚有什么节目?; (*what's planned?*) jīnwǎn gàn shénme? 今晚干什么?; *with his jacket ~* tā chuānzhe wàiyī tā chuān 着外衣; *with his hat ~* tā dàizhe màozi 他戴着帽子; *you're ~* (*I accept your offer etc*) xíng 行; ~ *you go* (*go ahead*) nǐ gànba 你干吧; *walk / talk ~* zǒu / tán xiàqù 走 / 谈下去; *and so ~* děngdeng 等等; ~ *and ~* talk etc méiwán méiliǎo 没完没了 **3** *adj*: *the ~ switch* kāiqí jiàn 开启键

**once 1** *adv* (*one time*) yīcì 一次; (*formerly*) céngjīng 曾经; ~ *again*, ~ *more* yòu yīcì 又一次; *at ~* (*immediately*) lìjí 立即; *all at ~* (*suddenly*) tūrán 突然; (*all*) *at ~* (*together*) yīqǐ 一起; ~ *upon a time there was ...* cóngqián yǒu ... 从前有 ... 了; *you have finished* nǐ yī wánle yǐhòu nǐ yī完了以后

**one 1** *n* (*number*) yī 一; (*in numbers*) yāo 幺 **2** *adj* yīgè 一个; ~ *day* yītiān 一天; *country, two systems* yīguó liǎngzhì 一国两制 **3** *pron* yīgè 一个; *which ~?* nǎ yīgè? 哪一个?; ~ *by* ~ enter, deal with yīyī 一一; ~ *another* hùxiāng 互相; *the little ~s* xiǎo péngyǒu mén 小朋友们 **4** *personal pron*: *what can ~ say?*

háiyǒu shénme kě shuō de? 还有什么可说的？

one child policy jìhuà shēngyù 计划生育; one-off n (*unique event, person*) yīcì xìng 一次性; (*exception*) tèshū qíngkuàng 特殊情况; one-parent family dānshēn fùmǔ jiātíng 单身父母家庭

oneself zìjǐ 自己; do X by ~ zìjǐ zuò X 自己做 X

one-sided discussion, fight yībiān dǎo 一边倒; one-way street dānxíng dào 单行道; one-way ticket dānchéng piào 单程票

onion yángcōng 洋葱

on-line adj shàngwǎng 上网; be ~ zài wǎngshang 在网上; go ~ (to) shàngwǎng 上网

on-line service COMPUT wǎngluò fúwù 网络服务

onlooker pánguān zhě 旁观者

only 1 adv zhǐ 只; not ~ X but also Y bù jǐnjǐn X, Y yěshì 不仅仅 X, Y 也是; ~ just gānggang 刚刚 2 adj wéiyī 唯一; ~ son / daughter dúzǐ / nǚ 独子/女

onset jiànglín 降临

onside adv SP wèi yuèwèi 未越位

onto: put X ~ Y bǎ X fàngdào Y shàng 把 X 放到 Y 上

onward xiàngqián 向前; from ... ~ ... zhīhòu ... 之后

oolong tea wūlóngchá 乌龙茶

ooze 1 v/i (*of liquid, mud*) shènchū 渗出 2 v/t: he ~s charm tā xiǎnde hěnyǒu mèilì 他显得很有魅力

opaque glass bù tòumíng 不透明

OPEC (= *Organization of Petroleum Exporting Countries*) Shíyóu Shūchūguó Zǔzhī 石油输出国组织

open 1 adj door, store, file kāizhe 开着; (*honest, frank*) tǎnbái tǎbái 坦白; relationship wú zhàng'ài 无障碍; countryside kōngkuàng 空旷; in the ~ air lùtiān 露天 2 v/t door, store, window, bottle kāi 开; book, paper tānkāi 摊开; COMPUT: file dǎkāi 打开; meeting kāishǐ 开始; ~ a bank account kāi hù 开户 3 v/i (*of door, store, flower*) kāi 开

open up v/i (*of person*) fàngkāi 放开

open-air adj meeting, concert lùtiān 露天; ~ pool shìwài yóuyǒng chí 室外游泳池; open-door policy kāifàng zhèngcè 开放政策; open-ended contract etc bú gùdìng 不固定

opening (*in wall etc*) kòngxì 空隙; (*beginning: of movie, novel etc*) kāishǐ 开始; (*job going*) kòngquē 空缺

openly (*honestly, frankly*) tǎnshuài 坦率

open-minded xūxīn 虚心; open plan office tǒngyī bàngōngshì 统一办公室; open ticket fēi gùdìng piào 非固定票

opera gējù 歌剧; Peking Opera Jīngjù 京剧

opera glasses xiǎo wàngyuǎnjìng 小望远镜; opera house gējù yuàn 歌剧院; Peking Opera House Jīngjù Yuàn 京剧院; opera singer gējù jiā 歌剧家

operate 1 v/i (*of company*) jīngyíng 经营; (*of airline, bus service*) guǎnlǐ 管理; (*of machine*) yùnzhuàn 运转; shǒushù 动手术 2 v/t machine cāozuò 操作

◆operate on MED gěi ... kāidāo 给 ... 开刀

operating instructions cāozuò shǒuzé 操作手则; operating room MED shǒushù shì 手术室; operating system COMPUT cāozuò xìtǒng 操作系统

operation MED shǒushù 手术; (*of machine*) cāozuò 操作; ~s (*of company*) jīngyíng 经营; have an ~ MED zuò shǒushù 做手术

operator TELEC jiēxiàn shēng 接线生; (*of machine*) cāozuò zhě 操作者; (*tour ~*) lǚxíng dàiyíng zhě 旅行代营者

ophthalmologist yǎnkē yīshēng 眼科医生

opinion (*view*) kànfǎ 看法; what's your ~? nǐ yǒu shénme yìjiàn? 你有什么意见？; in my ~ zài wǒ kànlái 在我看来

**opium** yāpiàn 鸦片

**Opium War** Yāpiàn Zhànzhēng 鸦片战争

**opponent** duìshǒu 对手

**opportunity** jīhuì 机会

**oppose** fǎnduì 反对; *be ~d to ...* fǎnduì ... 反对 ...; *as ~d to X* yǔ X xiāngfǎn 与X相反

**opposite 1** *adj side of road, end of town* duìmiàn 对面; *direction, meaning* xiāngfǎn 相反; *views, characters* duìkàng 对抗; *the ~ sex* yìxìng 异性 **2** *n* fǎnmiàn 反面

**opposition** (*to plan*) fǎnduì 反对; *Br POL* zàiyědǎng 在野党

**oppress** *the people* yāpò 压迫

**oppressive** *rule, dictator* bàonüè 暴虐; *weather* chénzhòng 沉重

**optical illusion** cuòshì 错视

**optician** yǎnjìng diàn 眼镜店

**optimism** lèguān 乐观

**optimist** lèguān zhě 乐观者

**optimistic** lèguān 乐观

**optimum 1** *adj* zuì shìyí 最适宜 **2** *n* zuìjiā tiáojiàn 最佳条件

**option** xuǎnzé 选择, xuǎnxiàng 选项

**optional** kě xuǎnzé 可选择

**optional extras** kě xuǎnzé de fùjiā jiàn 可选择的附加件

**or** huò 或; *~ else!* bùrán dehuà děngzhe qiáo! 不然的话等着瞧！

**oral exam** kǒushì 口试; **oral hygiene** kǒuqiāng wèishēng 口腔卫生; **oral sex** kǒuyín 口淫

**orange 1** *adj* (*color*) chéng chéng 橙橙 **2** *n* (*fruit*) chéng chéng 橙橙; (*color*) chéngsè 橙色

**orangeade** chéngzhīr 橙汁儿

**orange juice** ⇩ chéngzhīr 橙汁儿

**orator** yǎnshuōjiā 演说家

**orbit 1** *n* (*of earth*) tiāntǐ yùnxíng guǐdào 天体运行轨道; *send X into ~* jiāng X sòngrù guǐdào 将X送入轨道 **2** *v/t the earth* rào guǐdào yùnxíng 绕轨道运行

**orchard** guǒyuán 果园

**orchestra** guǎnxián yuèduì 管弦乐队

**orchid** lánhuā 兰花

**ordeal** kǔnànde jīnglì 苦难的经历

**order 1** *n* (*command*) mìnglìng 命令; (*sequence*) cìxù 次序; (*being well arranged*) zhìxù 秩序; (*for goods*) dìnggòu 定购; (*in restaurant*) dìng càidān 定菜单; *in ~ to* wèile ... 为了 ...; *out of ~* (*not functioning*) shīlíng 失灵; (*not in sequence*) cìxù diāndǎo 次序颠倒 **2** *v/t* (*put in sequence etc*) ānpái 安排; *goods* dìnghuò 定货; *meal* jiàocài 叫菜; *~ X to do Y* mìnglìng X qù zuò Y 命令X去做Y **3** *v/i* (*in restaurant*) diǎncài 点菜

**orderly 1** *adj* yǒu zhìxù 有秩序 **2** *n* (*in hospital*) qínzá gōng 勤杂工

**ordinary** pǔtōng 普通

**ore** kuàngshí 矿石

**organ** ANAT qìguān 器官; MUS fēngqín 风琴

**organic** *food, fertilizer* zìrán 自然

**organism** shēngwù 生物

**organization** jīgòu 机构; (*organizing*) zǔzhī 组织

**organize** zǔzhī 组织

**organizer** (*person*) zǔzhī zhě 组织者

**orgasm** xìngyù gāocháo 性欲高潮

**Orient** Dōngfāng 东方

**orient** *v/t* (*direct*) cháo X de fāngxiàng 朝X的方向; *~ oneself* (*get bearings*) rènqīng xíngshì 认清形势

**Oriental 1** *adj* Dōngfāng 东方 **2** *n* Dōngfāng rén 东方人

**origin** qǐyuán 起源; *person of Chinese ~* Huáyì 华裔; *idea of Chinese ~* qǐyuán yú Zhōngguóde sīxiǎng 起源于中国的思想

**original 1** *adj* (*not copied*) yuánzuò 原作; (*first*) zuìchū 最初 **2** *n* (*painting etc*) yuán zuòpǐn 原作品

**originality** dúchuànglì 独创力

**originally** yuánxiān 原先

**originate 1** *v/t scheme, idea* fāmíng

发明 2 v/i (of idea, belief) fāqǐ 发起; (of family) láizì yú wěi zì yú

**originator** (of scheme etc) fāqǐrén 发起人; **he's not an ~** tā bùshì gè fāmíngjiā 他不是个发明家

**ornament** zhuāngshì wù 装饰物

**ornamental** zhuāngshì 装饰

**ornate** style huá ér bùshì 华而不实

**orphan** gū ér 孤儿

**orphanage** gū ér yuàn 孤儿院

**orthopedic** adj jiǎoxíng wàikē 矫形外科

**ostentatious** style, behavior zìgāo zìdà 自高自大; clothes kuāzhāng 夸张

**other 1** adj (referring to people) qítā 其他; (referring to things, animals) qítā 其它; **the ~ day** (recently) nàtiān 那天; **every ~ day / person** měi liǎngtiān / gèrén zhōng de yīgè 每两天 / 个人中的一个 **2** n lìng yīgè 另一个; **the ~s** (people) qítāde 其他的; (things, animals) qítāde 其它的

**otherwise** bùrán dehuà 不然的话; (differently) bùtóng 不同

**otter** shuǐtǎ 水獭

**ought**: **I / you ~ to know** wǒ / nǐ yīnggāi zhīdào 我 / 你应该知道; **you ~ to have done it** nǐ zǎo yīnggāi zuòle 你早应该做了

**ounce** àngsī 盎司

**our** wǒmen 我们

**ours** wǒménde 我们的; **a friend of ~** wǒménde péngyǒu 我们的朋友

**ourselves** wǒmen zìjǐ 我们自己; **by ~** wǒmen zìjǐ 我们自己

**oust** (from office) miǎnzhí 免职

**out**: **be ~** (of light) guāndiào 关掉; (of fire) xīmiè 熄灭; (of flower) shèngkāi 盛开; (of sun) chūlái 出来; (not at home, not in building) búzài 不在; (of calculations) cuò 错; (be published) chūbǎn 出版; (of secret) xiǎnlòu 显露; (no longer in competition) táotài 淘汰; (no longer in fashion) guòshí 过时; **~ here in Dallas** zài zhèlǐ Dálāsī 在这里达拉斯; **he's ~ in the gar-**

den tā zài huāyuán lǐ 他在花园里; **(get) ~!** chūqù! 出去！; **(get) ~ of my room!** gǔnchū wǒ fángjiān! 滚出我房间！; **that's ~** (out of the question) bùxíng 不行; **he's ~ to win** (fully intending to) tā fēi yíng bùkě 他非赢不可

**outboard motor** chuánwěi diàndòngjī 船尾电动机

**outbreak** (of violence, war) bàofā 爆发

**outburst** (emotional) bèngfā 迸发

**outcast** n bèi yíqì zhě 被遗弃者

**outcome** jiéguǒ 结果

**outcry** qiángliè kàngyì 强烈抗议

**outdated** guòshí 过时

**outdo** shèngguò 胜过

**outdoor** toilet, activities, life shìwài 室外

**outdoors** adv shìwài 室外

**outer** wall etc wàibù 外部

**outer space** tàikōng 太空

**outfit** (clothes) tàozhuāng 套装; (company, organization) zǔzhī 组织

**outgoing** flight chūháng 出航; personality kāilǎng 开朗

**outgrow** old ideas chāoguò 超过

**outing** (trip) chūyóu 出游

**outlet** (of pipe) chūkǒu 出口; (for sales) xiāoshòu diǎn 销售点; ELEC chāzuò 插座

**outline 1** n (of person, building etc) lúnkuò 轮廓; (of plan, novel) cǎotú 草图 **2** v/t plans etc dǎ cǎotú 打草图

**outlive** bǐ ... gèngjiǔ 活得比 ... 更长

**outlook** (prospects) zhǎnwàng 展望

**outlying** areas biānyuǎn 边远

**outnumber**: **X ~s Y by ... times** X bǐ Y dà ... bèi X 比 Y 大 ... 倍

**out of** ◊ (motion): **run ~ the house** pǎochū wūwài 跑出屋外 ◊ (position): **20 miles ~ Nanjing** Nánjīng yǐwài èrshí yīnglǐ 南京以外二十英里 ◊ (cause): ◊ **jealousy / curiosity** yóuyú jídù / hàoqí 由于嫉妒 / 好奇 ◊ (without): **we're ~ gas** wǒmen chē méi

yóu le 我们车没油了◊ (*from a group*): **5 ~ 10** shífēn zhīwǔ 十分 之五
**out-of-date** guòshí 过时
**out-of-the-way** huāngpì 荒僻
**outperform** bǐ ... hǎo bǐ ... 好
**output 1** *n* (*of factory*) chǎnliàng 产 量; COMPUT: shūchū 输出 **2** *v/t* (*produce*) shēngchǎn 生产; COMPUT: *signal* fāchū 发出
**outrage 1** *n* (*feeling*) gōngfèn 公 愤; (*act*) bàoxíng 暴行 **2** *v/t* yǐnqǐ fènkǎi 引起愤慨; *I was ~d to hear X* dāng wǒ tīngdào X shí gǎndào shífèn fènnù 当我听到 X 时感到十分愤怒
**outrageous** *acts* wúchǐ 无耻; *prices* guòfèn 过分
**outright 1** *adj winner* chèdǐ 彻底 **2** *adv win* chèdǐ 彻底; *kill ~* jísǐ 即 死
**outrun** (*run faster than*) pǎode gèngkuài 跑得更快; (*run for longer than*) pǎode gèngjiǔ 跑得 更久
**outset** kāishǐ 开始; *from the ~* yī kāitóu 一开头
**outside 1** *adj surface, wall, lane* wàibù 外部 **2** *adv sit, go* wàimiàn 外面 **3** *prep* zài ... yǐwài 在 ... 以 外; (*apart from*) chúle 除了 **4** *n* (*of building, case etc*) wàimiàn 外 面; *at the ~* zuìduō 最多
**outside broadcast** lùyīn shìwài bōyīn 录音室外播音
**outsider** lěngmén 冷门
**outsize** *adj clothing* tè dàhào 特大 号
**outskirts** jiāoqū 郊区
**outspoken** zhíyán bùhuì 直言不 讳
**outstanding** *success, quality* xiǎn- zhù 显著; *writer, athlete* jiéchū 杰 出; FIN: *invoice, sums* wèifù 未付
**outward** *adj appearance* wàibiǎo 外 表; *~ journey* wàichū lǚchéng 外 出旅程
**outward-going** kāilǎng 开朗
**outwardly** xiàngwàide 向外地
**outweigh** bǐ ... zhòngyào 比 ... 重 要

**outwit** zhìshèng 智胜
**oval** *adj* tuǒyuán 椭圆
**ovary** luǎncháo 卵巢
**oven** kǎoxiāng 烤箱
**over 1** *prep* (*across*) guò 过; (*more than*) chāoguò 超过; (*above*) zài ... shàngfāng 在 ... 上方; (*during*) zài ... qījiān 在 ... 期间; *travel all ~ China* yóulǎn quán Zhōngguó 游览全中国; *you find them all ~ China* tāmén biànbù Zhōngguó 它们遍布中国; *let's talk ~ a drink / meal* wǒmen biān hē / chī biān tán 我们边喝／吃边谈; *we're ~ the worst* wǒmen yǐjīng dùguòle zuì kùnnán de shíkè 我 们已经度过了最困难的时刻 **2** *adv*: *be ~* (*finished*) wánjié 完 结; (*left*) shèngyú shèng 剩余; *~ to you* (*your turn*) gāi nǐ le 该你了; *~ in Europe* zài Ōuzhōu 在欧洲; *~ here* zài zhèlǐ 在这里; *~ there* zài nàlǐ 在那里; *it hurts all ~* wǒ húnshēn dōu téng 我浑身都疼; *painted white all ~* quánbù shuā báisè 全部刷白色; *it's all ~* quánwánle 全完了; *~ and again* lǚcì 屡次; *do X ~* (*again*) zàicì zuò X 再次做 X
**overall 1** *adj length* zǒngtǐ 总体 **2** *adv* cóng tóu zhì wěi 从头至尾
**overawe**: *be ~d by X* bèi X xiàzhù 被 X 吓住
**overboard**: *man ~!* yǒurén luò- shuǐ! 有人落水！; *go ~ for X* duì X kuángrè zhuīqiú 对 X 狂热 追求
**overcast** *day, sky* duōyún 多云
**overcharge** *v/t customer* guògāo yàojià 过高要价
**overcoat** dàyī 大衣
**overcome** *difficulties, shyness* zhēngfú 征服; *be ~ by emotion* bùnéng zìzhì 不能自制
**overcrowded** yōngjǐ 拥挤
**overdo** (*exaggerate*) kuāzhāng 夸 张; (*in cooking*) zhǔ guóhuǒ 煮过 火儿; *you're ~ing things* guòyú láolèi 过于劳累
**overdone** *meat* guòhuǒ 过火
**overdose** *n* guòliàng 过量

overdraft chāozhī 超支; *have an ~* yǒu chāozhī 有超支

overdraw *account* chāozhī 超支; *be $800 ~n* chāozhī bābǎi měiyuán 超支八百美元

overdrive MOT chāosù 超速

overdue *apology, alteration* qīdài yǐjiǔ 期待以久

overestimate *abilities, value* guògāo gūjì 过高估计

overexpose *photograph* guòdù gǎnguāng 过度感光

overflow 1 *n (pipe)* fànlàn 泛滥 2 *v/i (of water)* shǐ yìchū 使溢出

overgrown *garden* cùyè cóngshēng 簇叶丛生; *he's an ~ baby* tā shuǎ xiǎohái píqì 他耍小孩脾气

overhaul *v/t engine* dàxiū 大修; *plans* chèdǐ jiǎnchá 彻底检查

overhead 1 *adj lights* tóudǐng shàng 头顶上; *railroad* jiàkōng 架空 2 *n* FIN tōngcháng kāizhī 通常开支

overhear tōutīng 偷听

overjoyed kuángxǐ 狂喜

overland *adj & adv* jīngguò lùdì 经过陆地

overlap *v/i (of tiles, periods of time etc)* chóngdié 重迭; *(of theories)* fùhé 复合; ELEC fùhé guòzhòng 负荷过重

overlook *(of tall building etc)* fǔshì 俯视; *(not see)* hūlüè 忽略

overly guòdùde 过度地; *not ~ ...* méi guòdùde ... 没过度地 ...

overnight *adv* yèjiān 夜间

overnight bag guòyè dài 过夜袋

overpaid fùqián guòduō 付钱过多

overpass lìtǐ jiāochā 立体交叉

overpower *v/t (physically)* jíbài jíbài 击败

overpowering *smell* nónglie 浓裂; *sense of guilt* qiánglie 强烈

overpriced yàojià guògāo 要价过高

overrated guògāo gūjì 过高估计

overrule *decision* fǒujué 否决

overrun *country* qīnzhàn 侵占; *time* chāoshí 超时; *be ~ with* mànyán 蔓延

overseas *adj & adv* hǎiwài 海外

overseas Chinese Huáqiáo 华侨

oversee jiānshì 监视

oversight shūhū 疏忽

oversleep shuì guòtóu 睡过头

overtake *(in work, development)* chāoguò 超过; *Br* MOT chāochē 超车

overthrow tuīfān 推翻

overtime *work* jiābān 加班

overture MUS xùqǔ 序曲; *make ~s to* tíchū jiànyì 提出建议

overturn 1 *v/t vehicle, object* fānzhuàn 翻转; *government* tuīfān 推翻 2 *v/i (of vehicle)* fān fānzhuàn 翻

overweight chāozhòng 超重

overwhelm *(with work)* bèi gōngzuò yāde chuǎnbù guòqì 被工作压得喘不过气; *(with emotion)* bùzhī suǒcuò 不知所措; *be ~ed by (by response)* jīngxǐ jiāojí 惊喜交集

overwork 1 *n* guòdù gōngzuò 过度工作 2 *v/i* gōngzuò guòdù 工作过度 3 *v/t*: *~ X* shǐ X píláo guòdù 使 X 疲劳过度

owe *v/t* qiàn 欠; *~ X $500* qiàn X wǔbǎi měiyuán 欠 X 五百美元; *~ X an apology* yīng xiàng dàoqiàn 应向 X 道歉; *how much do I ~ you?* wǒ qiàn nǐ duōshǎo? 我欠你多少？

owing to yóuyú 由于

owl māotóuyīng 猫头鹰

own[1] *v/t* yǒngyǒu 拥有

own[2] 1 *adj* zìjǐ 自己 2 *pron*: *an apartment of my ~* wǒ zìjǐde gōngyù 我自己的公寓; *on my / his ~* wǒ / tā zìjǐ 我 / 他自己

♦ own up tǎnbái de chéngrèn 坦白地承认

owner yǒngyǒu zhě 拥有者

ownership suǒyǒu quán 所有权

ox niú 牛

oxide yǎnghuà wù 氧化物

oxygen yǎngqì 氧气

oyster háo 蚝

oyster sauce háoyóu 蚝油

ozone chòuyǎng 臭氧

ozone layer chòuyǎng céng 臭氧层

# P

**pace 1** *n* (*step*) bù bù 步; (*speed*) sùdù 速度 **2** *v/i*: **~ up and down** duóbù 踱步

**pacemaker** MED qǐbóqì 起搏器; SP dìng sùdù zhě 定速度者

**Pacific: the ~ (Ocean)** Tàipíngyáng 太平洋

**Pacific Rim: the ~** Tàipíngyáng àn 太平洋岸; **~ countries** Tàipíngyáng guójiā 太平洋岸国家

**pacifier** (*for baby*) xiàngpí nǎitóu 橡皮奶头

**pacifism** hépíng zhǔyì 和平主义

**pacifist** *n* hépíng zhǔyì zhě 和平主义者

**pacify** ānfǔ 安抚

**pack 1** *n* (*back~*) bēibāo 背包; (*of cereal, food*) dài dài 袋; (*of cigarettes*) bāo bāo 包; (*of cards*) fù 副 **2** *v/t* bag jiāng dōngxi zhuāngrù 将东西装入; *item of clothing etc* fàngrù xínglǐ 放入行李; *goods* bāozhuāng 包装; *groceries* zhuāngrù kǒudài 装入口袋 **3** *v/i* zhěnglǐ xíngzhuāng 整理行装

**package 1** *n* (*parcel*) bāoguǒ 包裹; (*of offers etc*) zhěngdài cáiliào 整袋材料 **2** *v/t* (*in packs*) dǎbāo 打包; (*for promotion*) bāozhuāng 包装

**package deal** (*for vacation*) bāobàn lǚxíng 包办旅行

**package tour** bāobàn lǚxíng 包办旅行

**packaging** (*of product*) bāozhuāng 包装; (*of rock star etc*) xíngxiàng bāozhuāng 形象包装

**packed** (*crowded*) mǎnyuán 满员

**packet** bāo 包

**pact** xiéyì 协议

**pad¹ 1** *n* (*piece of cloth etc*) diànliào 垫料; (*for writing*) biànjiānběn 便笺本 **2** *v/t* (*with material*) diànchèn 垫衬; *speech, report* pīncòu 拼凑

**pad²** *v/i* (*move quietly*) qīngqīng zǒu 轻轻走

**padded** *jacket, shoulders* dài chèndiàn 带衬垫

**padding** (*material*) chènliào 衬料; (*in speech etc*) fèihuà 废话

**paddle¹ 1** *n* (*for canoe*) lǚ 橹 **2** *v/i* (*in canoe*) yáolǔ 摇橹

**paddle²** *v/i* (*in water*) tāngshuǐ 趟水

**paddock** xiǎowéichǎng 小围场

**paddy** dàozi 稻子

**paddy field** dàotián 稻田

**padlock 1** *n* guàsuǒ 挂锁 **2** *v/t* gate yòng guàsuǒ suǒ 用挂锁锁; **~ X to Y** yòng guàsuǒ bǎ X suǒ zài Y shàng 用挂锁把 X 锁在 Y 上

**page¹ 1** *n* (*of book etc*) yè 页; **~ number** yèmǎ 页码

**page²** *v/t* (*call*) ⇩ chuánhū 传呼

**pager** ⇩ chuánhūjī 传呼机

**pagoda** bǎotǎ 宝塔

**paid employment** yǒuchángu gùyòng 有偿雇佣

**pail** tǒng 桶

**pain** téngtòng 疼痛; **be in ~** tòng tòng 痛; **take ~s to ...** fèi kǔxīn ... 费苦心 ...; **X is a ~ in the neck** F X zhēn fánrén X 真烦人

**painful** *arm, leg etc* téngtòng 疼痛; (*distressing*) lìngrén tòngkǔ 令人痛苦; (*laborious*) fèishì 费事

**painfully** (*extremely, acutely*) tèbié 特别

**painkiller** zhǐtòngpiàn 止痛片

**painless** wútòng 无痛

**painstaking** zǐxì 仔细

**paint 1** *n* (*for wall, car*) túliào 涂料; (*for artist*) yánliào 颜料 **2** *v/t* wall etc shàng túliào 上涂料; *picture* yòng yánliào huà 用颜料画 **3** *v/i* (*as art form*) huìhuà 绘画

**paintbrush** (*for wall, ceiling*) qīshuā 漆刷; (*of artist*) huàbǐ 画笔

painter (*decorator*) fěnshuāgōng 粉刷工; (*artist*) huàjiā 画家

painting (*activity*) huìhuà 绘画; (*picture*) túhuà 图画

paintwork (*in room*) fěnshuā 粉刷; (*of car*) qī 漆

pair duì 对; *a ~ of shoes / sandals* yìshuāng xié / liángxié 一双鞋 / 凉鞋

pajama jacket shuìyī 睡衣

pajama pants shuìkù 睡裤

pajamas shuìyīkù 睡衣裤

Pakistan Bājīsītǎn 巴基斯坦

Pakistani 1 *adj* Bājīsītǎn 巴基斯坦 2 *n* Bājīsītǎn rén 巴基斯坦人

pal F (*friend*) gēmenr 哥们儿; *hey ~, got a light?* lǎoxiōng, jiège huǒr? 老兄,借个火儿?

palace gōngdiàn 宫殿

palate è 腭

palatial fùlì 富丽

pale *person* cāngbái 苍白; *~ pink / blue* dànfěn / lánsè 淡粉 / 蓝色

pallet huòbǎn 货板

pallor liǎnsè cāngbái 脸色苍白

palm[1] (*of hand*) shǒuzhǎng 手掌

palm[2] (*tree*) zōnglǘshù 棕榈树

palpitations MED xīnjì 心悸

paltry wēibùzúdào 微不足道

pamper fàngzòng 放纵

pamphlet xiǎocèzi 小册子

pan 1 *n* (*for cooking*) guō 锅 2 *v/t* F (*criticize severely*) yánlì pīpíng 严厉批评

♦pan out (*develop*) fāzhǎn 发展

pancake bóbǐng 薄饼

panda xióngmāo 熊猫

pandemonium dà hùnluàn 大混乱

pane (*of glass*) kuài kuài 块

panel (*section*) xiāngbǎn 镶板; (*people*) xiǎozǔ 小组

paneling xiāngqiàn 镶嵌

panhandle v/i F xíngqǐ 行乞

panic 1 *n* kǒnghuāng 恐慌 2 *v/i* shòujīng 受惊; *don't ~* biéhuāng 别慌

panic buying FIN kǒnghuāng gòumǎi 恐慌购买; panic selling FIN kǒnghuāng pāoshòu 恐慌抛售; panic-stricken jīnghuāng

shīcuò 惊惶失措

panorama quánjǐng 全景

panoramic *view* quánjǐng 全景

pansy (*flower*) sānsèjǐn 三色堇; F jiǎxiǎozi 假小子

pant v/i chuánxī 喘息

panties nèikù 内裤

pants kùzi 裤子

pantyhose liánkùwà 连裤袜

paper 1 *n* (*material*) zhǐ 纸; (*news~*) bàozhǐ 报纸; (*wall~*) bìzhǐ 壁纸; (*academic*) lùnwén 论文; (*examination ~*) kǎoshìjuàn 考试卷; *~s* (*documents*) wénjiàn 文件; (*identity ~s*) zhèngjiàn 证件; *a piece of ~* yìzhāng zhǐ 一张纸 2 *adj* zhǐzhì 纸制 3 *v/t room, walls* biǎohú 裱糊

paperback píngzhuāngshū 平装书; paper bag zhǐdài 纸袋; paper clip huíxíngzhēn 回形针; paper cup zhǐ bēizi 纸杯子; paperwork wénshū gōngzuò 文书工作

par (*in golf*) biāozhǔn gānshù 标准杆数; *be on a ~ with X* yǔ X tóngděng zhòngyào 与 X 同等重要; *feel below ~* gǎnjué bú tài hǎo 感觉不太好

parachute 1 *n* jiàngluòsǎn 降落伞 2 *v/i* tiàosǎn 跳伞 3 *v/t troops, supplies* (yòng jiàngluòsǎn) kōngtóu (用降落伞) 空投

parachutist tiàosǎn zhě 跳伞者

parade 1 *n* (*procession*) yuèbīng 阅兵 2 *v/i* xíngzǒu 行走 3 *v/t knowledge, new car* xuànyào 炫耀

paradise Biblical lèyuán 乐园; fig tiāntáng 天堂

paradox zìxiāng máodùn 自相矛盾

paradoxical sì fēi ér shì 似非而是

paradoxically sì fēi ér shì 似非而是

paragraph duànluò 段落

parallel 1 *n* (*line*) píngxíngxiàn 平行线; (*of latitude*) wěidùxiàn 纬度线; fig xiāngsì zhī chù 相似之处; *do two things in ~* tóngshí zuò liǎngjiàn shì 同时做两件事

**2** adj line píngxíng 平行; fig tóngshí fāshēng 同时发生 **3** v/t (match) xiāngdāng 相当

**paralysis** tānhuàn 瘫痪

**paralyze** tānhuàn 瘫痪; fig bù zhī suǒ cuò 不知所措

**paramedic** hùlǐ rényuán 护理人员

**parameter** jièxiàn 界限

**paramilitary 1** adj zhǔn jūnshì 准军事 **2** n zhǔn jūnshì bùduì chéngyuán 准军事部队成员

**paramount** zuì zhòngyào 最重要; be ~ tóuděng dàshì 头等大事

**paranoia** wàngxiǎngkuáng 妄想狂

**paranoid** adj duōyí 多疑

**paraphernalia** záqīzábāde dōngxi 杂七杂八的东西

**paraphrase** shìyì 释义

**paraplegic** n xiàshēn tānhuàn de rén 下身瘫痪的人

**parasite** jìshēngchóng 寄生虫; fig kào jiùjì wéishēng kào救济为生

**parasol** yángsǎn 阳伞

**paratrooper** sǎnbīng 伞兵

**parcel** n bāoguǒ 包裹

♦**parcel up** bāoqǐ 包起

**parch** v/t shǐ jiāogān 使焦干; be ~ed (of person) kě jíle 渴极了

**pardon 1** n LAW shèmiǎn 赦免; I beg your ~? (what did you say) nǐ shuō shénme? 你说什么？; I beg your ~ (I'm sorry) qǐng yuánliàng 请原谅 **2** v/t yuánliàng yuánliàng 原谅; LAW shèmiǎn 赦免; ~ me? nǐ shuō shénme? 你说什么？

**pare** (peel) xiāopí 削皮

**parent** jiāzhǎng 家长

**parental** fùmǔ 父母

**parent company** zǒnggōngsī 总公司

**parent-teacher association** jiāzhǎng jiàoshī liányìhuì 家长教师联谊会

**park**[1] (area) gōngyuán 公园

**park**[2] MOT **1** v/t tíngfàng 停放 **2** v/i tíngchē 停车

**parka** fēngxuě dàyī 风雪大衣

**parking** MOT tíngchē 停车; no ~ jìnzhǐ tíngchē 禁止停车

**parking brake** shǒuzhá 手刹;

**parking garage** shìnèi tíng-chēchǎng 室内停车场; **parking lot** tíngchēchǎng 停车场; **parking meter** tíngchē jìshí shōufèiqì 停车计时收费器; **parking place** tíngchēchù 停车处; **parking ticket** wéizhāng tíngchē fákuǎndān 违章停车罚款单

**parliament** yìhuì 议会

**parliamentary** yìhuì 议会

**parole 1** n jiǎshì 假释; be on ~ huòdé jiǎshì 获得假释 **2** v/t zhǔnxǔ jiǎshì 准许假释

**parrot** yīngwǔ 鹦鹉

**parsley** ōuqín 欧芹

**part 1** n yíbùfen 一部分; (section, area) bùfen 部分; (of machine) língjiàn 零件; (in play, movie) juésè 角色; MUS shēngbù 声部; (in hair) fèng 缝; take ~ in cānjiā 参加 **2** adv (partly) bùfen 部分 **3** v/i fēnkāi 分开 **4** v/t: ~ one's hair jiāng tóufa fēnkāi 将头发分开

♦**part with** things chūràng 出让

**part exchange** bùfen dǐjià jiāoyìfǎ 部分抵价交易法; **take X in ~** yǐ bùfen dǐjià jiāoyìfǎ gòumǎi X 以部分抵价交易法购买X

**partial** (incomplete) bù wánquán 不完全; **be ~ to** piān'ài 偏爱

**partially** bùfen 部分

**participant** cānjiā zhě 参加者

**participate** cānjiā 参加; ~ in X cānjiā X 参加X

**participation** cānjiā 参加

**particle** PHYS lìzǐ 粒子; (small amount) yìdiǎnr 一点儿

**particular** (specific) tèbié 特别; (special) tèshū 特殊; (fussy) tiāoti 挑剔; in ~ yóuqí 尤其

**particularly** tèbié 特别

**parting** (of people) líbié 离别

**partition 1** n (screen) píngfēng 屏风; (of country) fēnliè 分裂 **2** v/t country fēnliè 分裂

♦**partition off** gékāi 隔开

**partly** bùfen 部分

**partner** COM héhuǒrén 合伙人; (in relationship) tóngbàn 同伴; (in particular activity) dādàng 搭档

**partnership** COM héhuǒ jīngyíng 合伙经营; (*in particular activity*) dādàng guānxi 搭档关系

**part of speech** cíxìng 词性; **part owner** gòngyǒu zhě 共有者; **part-time 1** *adj* jiānzhí 兼职 **2** *adv work* jiānzhí 兼职

**party 1** *n* (*celebration*) qìngzhùhuì 庆祝会; POL dǎng 党; (*group of people*) zǔ 组; *be a ~ to* cānyù 参与 **2** *v/i* F wánr 玩儿

**party member** dǎngyuán 党员

**pass 1** *n* (*for getting into a place*) tōngxíngzhèng 通行证; SP chuánqiú 传球; (*in mountains*) guān'ài 关隘; *make a ~ at X* xiàng X tiáoqíng 向 X 调情 **2** *v/t* (*hand*) dì 递; (*go past*) yuèguò 经过; (*overtake*) yuèguò 越过; (*go beyond*) chāoguò 超过; (*approve*) biǎojué tōngguò 表决通过; SP chuánqiú 传球; *~ an exam* tōngguò kǎoshì 通过考试; *~ sentence* LAW pànxíng 判刑; *~ the time* xiāomó shíjiān 消磨时间 **3** *v/i* (*of time*) tuīyí 推移; (*in exam*) jígé 及格; SP chuándì 传递; (*go away*) xiāoshī 消失

♦ **pass around** hùxiāng chuán 互相传

♦ **pass away** (*die*) qùshì 去世

♦ **pass by** *v/t* & *v/i* (*go past*) jīngguò 经过

♦ **pass on 1** *v/t information, book* chuándì 传递 **2** *v/i* (*die*) qùshì 去世

♦ **pass out** (*faint*) hūnjué 昏厥

♦ **pass through** *town* tújīng 途经

♦ **pass up** *opportunity* fàngguò 放过

**passable** *road* kě tōngguò 可通过; (*acceptable*) guòdéqù 过得去

**passage** (*corridor*) tōngdào 通道; (*from poem, book*) yíduàn 一段; (*of time*) tuīyí 推移

**passageway** zǒuláng 走廊

**passenger** chéngkè 乘客

**passenger seat** chéngkè zuòwèi 乘客座位

**passer-by** guòlùrén 过路人

**passion** (*emotion*) qínggǎn 情感; (*sexual desire*) xìng'ài 性爱; (*fervor*) rèqíng 热情

**passionate** *lover* rèliàn 热恋; (*fervent*) rèqíng 热情

**passive 1** *adj* bèidòng 被动 **2** *n* GRAM bèidòng yǔtài 被动语态; *in the ~* bèidòng xíngshì 被动形式

**pass mark** jígéfēn 及格分

**passport** hùzhào 护照

**passport control** hùzhào jiǎnchàchù 护照检查处

**password** kǒulìng 口令

**past 1** *adj* (*former*) yǐqián 以前; *the ~ few days* jìnjǐtiān 近几天; *that's all ~ now* nà dōu yǐjīng guòqù le 那都已经过去了 **2** *n* guòqù 过去; *in the ~* zài guòqù 在过去 **3** *prep* (*in time*) chíyú 迟于; (*in position*) jīngguò 经过; *it's half ~ two* xiànzài liǎngdiǎnbàn 现在两点半 **4** *adv*: *run/walk ~* pǎo/zǒuguò 跑/走过

**paste 1** *n* (*adhesive*) jiànghú 糨糊 **2** *v/t* (*stick*), COMPUT zhāntiē 粘贴

**pastel** *n* (*color*) qīngdànsè 清淡色 **2** *adj* qīngdàn 清淡

**pastime** xiāoqiǎn 消遣

**pastor** jiàoqū mùshī 教区牧师

**past participle** guòqù fēncí 过去分词

**pastrami** wǔxiāng xūnniúròu 五香熏牛肉

**pastry** (*for pie*) yóusū miàntuán 油酥面团; (*small cake*) sūpí gāodiǎn 酥皮糕点

**past tense** guòqùshí 过去时

**pasty** *adj complexion* cāngbái 苍白

**pat 1** *n* qīngpāi 轻拍; *give X a ~ on the back* fig xiàng X biǎoshì zhùhè 向 X 表示祝贺 **2** *v/t* pāipāi 拍拍

**patch 1** *n* (*on clothing*) bǔdīng 补丁; (*period of time*) yíduàn shíqī 一段时期; (*area*) bùfen 部分; *be not a ~ on* F yuǎnyuǎn bùrú 远远不如 **2** *v/t clothing* dǎ bǔdīng 打补丁

♦ **patch up** (*repair temporarily*) línshí xiūlǐ 临时修理; *quarrel* jiějué 解决

**patchwork 1** n (needlework) zápǐn huābù 杂拼花布 **2** adj quilt zápǐn huābèi miánbèi 杂拼花布棉被

**patchy** quality bùyīzhì 不一致; work, performance xiáyúhùjiàn 瑕瑜互见

**patent 1** adj míngxiǎn 明显 **2** n (for invention) zhuānlì 专利 **3** v/t invention qǔdé zhuānlìquán 取得专利权

**patent leather** qīpí 漆皮

**patently** (clearly) míngxiǎn 明显

**paternal** relative fùxì 父系; pride, love fùqīnbān 父亲般

**paternalism** jiāzhǎng zhǔyì 家长主义

**paternalistic** jiāzhǎng zuòfēng 家长作风

**paternity** fùqīn shēnfèn 父亲身分

**path** xiǎolù 小路; fig tújìng 途径, lùjìng 路径

**pathetic** (invoking pity) zhāorén liánmǐn 招人怜悯; F (very bad) kěbēi 可悲

**pathological** bìngtài 病态

**pathologist** bìnglǐxuéjiā 病理学家

**pathology** bìnglǐxué 病理学

**patience** nàixīn 耐心

**patient 1** n bìngrén 病人 **2** adj yǒu nàixīn 有耐心; just be ~! nàixīn diǎnr! 耐心点儿！

**patiently** nàixīn 耐心

**patio** píngtái 平台

**patriot** àiguó zhě 爱国者

**patriotic** àiguó 爱国

**patriotism** àiguó zhǔyì 爱国主义

**patrol 1** n xúnluóduì 巡逻队; be on ~ zài xúnluó zhōng 在巡逻中 **2** v/t streets, border xúnluó 巡逻

**patrol car** xúnluóchē 巡逻车; **patrolman** xúnjǐng 巡警; **patrol wagon** qiúchē 囚车

**patron** (of store, movie house) gùkè 顾客; (of artist, charity etc) zànzhùrén 赞助人

**patronage** (of artist, charity etc) zànzhùyìng 赞助

**patronize** person gāorén yīděngde duìdài 高人一等地对待

**patronizing** gāorén yīděng 高人一等

**patter 1** n (of rain etc) pādāshēng 啪嗒声; F (of salesman) xuétóu 噱头 **2** v/i pāidǎ 拍打

**pattern** n (on wallpaper, fabric) tú'àn 图案; (for knitting, sewing) yàngshì 样式; (model) móxíng 模型; (in behavior, events) fāngshì 方式

**patterned** yǒu tú'àn 有图案

**paunch** dà dùzi 大肚子

**pause 1** n tíngdùn 停顿 **2** v/i tíngdùn 停顿 **3** v/t tape zàntíng 暂停

**pave** pū 铺; ~ the way for X fig wèi X chuàngzào tiáojiàn 为 X 创造条件

**pavement** (roadway) lùmiàn 路面

**paving stone** pūlù shíbǎn 铺路石板

**paw 1** n (of animal) zhuǎzi 爪子; (hand) shǒuzhuǎzi 手爪子 **2** v/t F yòng shǒu luànmō 用手乱摸

**pawn** n (in chess) zú 卒; fig xiǎozú 小卒

**pawn** v/t diǎndàng 典当

**pawnbroker** dàngpù lǎobǎn 当铺老板

**pawnshop** dàngpù 当铺

**pay 1** n xīnjīn 薪金; in the ~ of X shòugù yú X 受雇于 X **2** v/t employee fùqián gěi fù qián gěi 付钱给; sum, bill fù 付; ~ attention zhùyì 注意; ~ X a compliment biǎoyáng X 表扬 X **3** v/i fùzhàng 付帐; (be profitable) yǒu lìrùn 有利润; it doesn't ~ to do X zuò X débùchángshī 做 X 得不偿失; ~ for X (purchase) fù X fèi 付 X 费; you'll ~ for this! fig nǐ děngzhe qiáoba! 你等着瞧吧！

♦ **pay back** person huánqián 还钱; loan chánghuán 偿还; (get revenge on) bàofù 报复

♦ **pay in** (to bank) cúnrù 存入

♦ **pay off 1** v/t debt chángqīng 偿清; corrupt official huìlù 贿赂 **2** v/i (be profitable) yǒu bàocháng 有报偿

♦ **pay up** quánbù fùqīng 全部付清

**payable** yīng zhīfù 应支付

pay check xīnjīn zhīpiào 薪金支票

payday fāxīnrì 发薪日

payee shōukuǎnrén 收款人

pay envelope gōngzīdài 工资袋

payer fùkuǎnrén 付款人

payment (of bill) fùkuǎn 付款; (money) fùchūde kuǎnxiàng 付出的款项

pay phone gōngyòng diànhuà 公用电话

payroll (money) xīnshuǐ zǒng'é 薪水总额; (employees) xīnshuǐ míngcè 薪水名册; **be on the ~** shì gùyuán 是雇员

PC (= **personal computer**) gèrén diànnǎo 个人电脑; (= **politically correct**) wú zhèngzhì cuòwù 无政治错误

pea wāndòu 豌豆

peace (as opposed to war) hépíng 和平; (quietness) níngjìng 宁静

peaceable person héqì 和气

Peace Corps Hépíngduì 和平队

peaceful píngjìng 平静

peacefully ānjìng 安静

peach táozi 桃子

peacock kǒngquè 孔雀

peak 1 n (of mountain) shāndǐng 山顶; (mountain) shānfēng 山峰; fig dǐngfēng 顶峰 2 v/i dádào dǐngfēng 达到顶峰

peak consumption gāofēng xiāohào 高峰消耗

peak hours gāofēng shíjiān 高峰时间

peanut huāshēng 花生; **get paid ~s** F zhèng bù liǎo jǐfēn qián 挣不了几分钱; **that's ~s to him** F nà duì tā láishuō búsuàn shénme 那对他来说不算什么

peanut butter huāshēngjiàng 花生酱

pear lí 梨

pearl zhēnzhū 珍珠

Pearl River Zhūjiāng 珠江

Pearl River Delta Zhūjiāng sānjiǎozhōu 珠江三角洲

peasant nóngmín 农民

pebble luǎnshí 卵石

pecan měizhōu shānhétáo 美洲山核桃

peck 1 n (bite) zhuó 啄; (kiss) cōngcōngyīwěn 匆匆一吻 2 v/t (bite) zhuó 啄; (kiss) cōngcōngde wěn 匆匆地吻

peculiar (strange) qíguài 奇怪; **~ to** (special) tèyǒu 特有

peculiarity (strangeness) guàiyì 怪异; (special feature) dútèxìng 独特性

pedal 1 n (of bike) tàbǎn 踏板 2 v/i (turn ~s) cǎi tàbǎn 踩踏板; (cycle) qí 骑

pedal rickshaw dàoqílú 倒骑驴

pedantic shūdāiziqì 书呆子气

pedestal (for statue) jīzuò 基座

pedestrian n xíngrén 行人

pedestrian crosswalk rénxíng héngdào 人行横道

pedestrian precinct xíngrénqū 行人区

pediatrician érkēxuéjiā 儿科学家

pediatrics érkēxué 儿科学

pedicab sānlúnchē 三轮车

pedigree 1 n (of dog, racehorse) chúnzhǒng 纯种; (of person) xuètǒng 血统 2 adj chúnzhǒng 纯种

pee v/i F sāniào 撒尿

peek 1 n yīyǎn 一眼 2 v/i piējiàn 瞥见

peel 1 n guǒpí 果皮 2 v/t fruit, vegetables xiāopí 削皮 3 v/i (of nose, shoulders) tuōluò 脱落; (of paint) bōluò 剥落

peep → **peek**

peephole kuīkǒng 窥孔

peer[1] n (equal) tóngděngrén 同等人

peer[2] v/i níngshì 凝视; **~ through the mist** xiàng wùzhōng zhāngwàng 向雾中张望; **~ at** zǐxìkàn 仔细看

peeved F nǎonù 恼怒

peg n (for hat, coat) guàgōu 挂钩; (for tent) zhuāng 桩; **off the ~** xiànchéng 现成

pejorative biǎnyì biǎnyì 贬抑

Peking Běijīng 北京

Peking duck Běijīng kǎoyā 北京烤鸭

Peking Opera Jīngjù 京剧

pellet xiǎotuán 小团; (bullet) zǐdàn 子弹

pelt 1 v/t: ~ **X with Y** jiāng Y tóuxiàng X 将 Y 投向 X 2 v/i: **they ~ed along the road** tāmen yánlù xùnsù qiánjìn 他们沿路迅速前进; **it's ~ing down** dàyǔ piáopō 大雨飘泼

pelvis gúpén 骨盆

pen¹ n (ballpoint) yuánzhūbǐ 圆珠笔; (fountain ~) zìláishuǐbǐ 自来水笔

pen² (enclosure) juàn 圈

pen³ F (penitentiary) láo láo 牢

penalize búlìyú 不利于

penalty chéngfá 惩罚; SP fáqiú 罚球

penalty area SP fáqiúqū 罚球区

penalty clause wéiyuē fákuǎn de guīdìng 违约罚款的规定

pencil qiānbǐ 铅笔

pencil sharpener xiāoqiānbǐ dāo 削铅笔刀

pendant (necklace) chuíshì 垂饰

pending 1 prep zhídào 直到 2 adj: **be ~** (awaiting a decision) xuán ér wèi jué 悬而未决; (about to happen) pòjìn 迫近

penetrate chuāntòu 穿透; market dǎrù 打入

penetrating stare shēnmíng zhēnxiàng 深明真相; scream jiānruì 尖锐; analysis yǒu dòngchálì 有洞察力

penetration tūpò 突破

pen friend bǐyǒu 笔友

penicillin qīngméisù 青霉素

peninsula bàndǎo 半岛

penis yīnjīng 阴茎

penitence chànhuǐ 忏悔

penitent adj hòuhuǐ 后悔

penitentiary jiānyù 监狱

pen name bǐmíng 笔名

pennant jǐnbiāoqí 锦标旗

penniless yīwénbùmíng 一文不名

penpal bǐyǒu 笔友

pension yǎnglǎojīn 养老金

♦pension off bèipò tuìxiū 被迫退休

pension fund yǎnglǎo jījīn 养老基金

pension scheme yǎnglǎojīn fāng'àn 养老金方案

pensive chénsī 沉思

Pentagon: **the ~** Wǔjiǎo Dàlóu 五角大楼

penthouse dǐngcéng gōngyù 顶层公寓

pent-up yāyì 压抑

penultimate dàoshù dì'èr 倒数第二

peony mǔdān 牡丹

people rén 人; (race, tribe) mínzú 民族; **the ~** rénmín 人民; **the American ~** Měiguó rénmín 美国人民; **~ say that ...** tīngshuō ...听说 ...

People's Commune Rénmín Gōngshè 人民公社; People's Congress Rénmín Dàibiǎo Dàhuì 人民代表大会; People's Daily Rénmín Rìbào 人民日报; People's Liberation Army Jiěfàngjūn 解放军; People's Republic of China Zhōnghuá Rénmín Gònghéguó 中华人民共和国

pepper (spice) hújiāofěn 胡椒粉; (vegetable) làjiāo 辣椒

peppermint (candy) bòhetáng 薄荷糖; (flavoring) hújiāo bòhe 胡椒薄荷

pep talk gǔlì de huà 鼓励的话

per měi 每

per annum měinián 每年

perceive (with senses) juéchá 觉察; (view, interpret) lǐjiě 理解

percent bǎifēnzhī 百分之; **one hundred ~** bǎifēnzhī bǎi 百分之百

percentage bǎifēnbǐ 百分比

perceptible kě juéchá 可觉察

perceptibly kàndechū 看得出

perception (through senses) gǎnzhī nénglì 感知能力; (of situation) kànfǎ 看法; (insight) dòngchálì 洞察力

perceptive person, remark yǒu dòngchálì 有洞察力

perch 1 n (for bird) qīxīchù 栖息处 2 v/i (of bird) qīxī 栖息; (of *person*) dāzuò 搭坐

**percolate** v/i (*of coffee*) guòlǜ 过滤

**percolator** guòlǜshì kāfēihú 过滤式咖啡壶

**percussion** dǎjīyuè 打击乐

**percussion instrument** dǎjī yuèqì 打击乐器

**perfect 1** n GRAM wánchéngshì 完成式 **2** adj wánměi 完美 **3** v/t wánshàn 完善

**perfection** wánměi 完美; **to ~** qiàdào hǎochù 恰到好处

**perfectionist** wánměi zhǔyì zhě 完美主义者

**perfectly** jíjiā 极佳; (*totally*) wánquán 完全

**perforated** dǎkǒng 打孔

**perforated line** xūxiàn 虚线

**perforations** chǐkǒng 齿孔

**perform 1** v/t (*carry out*) zuò 做; (*of actor, musician etc*) biǎoyǎn 表演 **2** v/i (*of actor, musician, dancer*) biǎoyǎn 表演; (*of machine*) yùnzhuǎn 运转

**performance** (*by actor, musician etc*) biǎoyǎn 表演; (*of employee, company etc*) biǎoxiàn 表现; (*by machine*) xìngnéng 性能

**performance car** gāonéng qìchē 高能汽车

**performer** biǎoyǎn zhě 表演者

**perfume** (*for woman*) xiāngshuǐ 香水; (*of flower*) xiāngwèi 香味

**perfunctory** fūyǎn 敷衍

**perhaps** yěxǔ 也许

**peril** wēixiǎn 危险

**perilous** duōxiǎn 多险

**perimeter** zhōubiān 周边

**perimeter fence** zhōubiān zhàlan 周边栅栏

**period** (*time*) yíduàn 一段; (*menstruation*) yuèjīng 月经; (*punctuation mark*) jùhào 句号; **I don't want to, ~!** wǒ bùxiǎng zuò, jiù zhèiyàng! 我不想做，就这样！

**periodic** zhōuqīxìng 周期性

**periodical** n qīkān 期刊

**periodically** dìngqī 定期

**peripheral 1** adj (*not crucial*) cìyào 次要 **2** n COMPUT wàiwéi zhuāngzhì 外围装置

**periphery** biānyuán 边缘

**perish** (*of rubber*) fǔlàn 腐烂; (*of person*) mò yù 殁殒

**perishable** adj food yìhuài 易坏

**perjure: ~ oneself** zuò wěizhèng 作伪证

**perjury** zuò wěizhèng 作伪证

**perk** n (*of job*) dàiyù 待遇

♦**perk up 1** v/t shǐ ... kuàihuó 使 ... 快活 **2** v/i huóyuè qǐlái 活跃起来

**perky** (*cheerful*) yǒu huólì 有活力

**perm** n & v/t tàngfà 烫发

**permanent** adj yǒngjiǔ 永久

**permanently** chángqī 长期

**permissible** róngxǔ 容许

**permission** xǔkě 许可

**permissive** fàngrèn 放任

**permit** n xǔkězhèng 许可证 **2** v/t róngxǔ 容许; **~ X to do Y** zhǔnxǔ X zuò Y 准许 X 做 Y

**perpendicular** adj chuízhí 垂直

**perpetual** chíxù 持续

**perpetually** búduàn 不断

**perpetuate** shǐ yǒngcún 使永存

**perplex** shǐ kùnhuò 使困惑

**perplexed** kùnhuò 困惑

**perplexity** kùnhuò 困惑

**persecute** *oppress* pòhài 迫害

**persecution** pòhài 迫害

**perseverance** jiānchíbúxiè 坚持不懈

**persevere** jiānchí zuò 坚持做

**persist** chíxù 持续; **~ in** zhíyì zuò 执意做

**persistence** (*perseverance*) jiānchíbúxiè 坚持不懈; (*continuation*) jìxù cúnzài 继续存在

**persistent** *person* gùzhí 固执; *questions, rain, unemployment etc* chíxù búduàn 持续不断

**persistently** (*continually*) liánxù búduàn 连续不断

**person** rén 人; **in ~** qīnzì 亲自

**personal** (*private*) sīrén 私人; (*relating to a particular individual*) gèrén 个人; **don't make ~ remarks** bié tánlùn biérén 别谈论别人

**personal assistant** sīrén zhùlǐ 私人助理; **personal computer**

gèrén diànnǎo 个人电脑; **personal hygiene** gèrén wèishēng 个人卫生

**personality** gèxìng 个性; (*celebrity*) míngrén 名人

**personally** (*for my part*) jiù wǒ láishuō 就我来说; (*in person*) qīnzì 亲自; *don't take it* ~ bié wèicǐ fánnǎo 别为此烦恼

**personal pronoun** rénchēng dàicí 人称代词

**personal stereo** suíshēntīng 随身听

**personnel** (*employees*) zhíyuán 职员; (*department*) rénshì bùmén 人事部门

**personnel manager** rénshìbù zhǔrèn 人事部主任

**perspiration** hànshuǐ 汗水

**perspire** chūhàn 出汗

**persuade** *person* shuōfú 说服; ~ *X to do Y* shuōfú X zuò Y 说服 X 做 Y

**persuasion** quànshuō 劝说

**persuasive** yǒu shuōfúlì 有说服力

**pertinent** yǒuguān 有关

**perturb** shǐ bù'ān 使不安

**perturbing** lìngrén bù'ān 令人不安

**pervasive** *influence, ideas* pǔbiàn cúnzài 普遍存在

**perverse** (*awkward*) bèilǐ 背理

**perversion** (*sexual*) biàntài xīnlǐ 变态心理

**pervert** *n* (*sexual*) xìngbiàntài 性变态

**pessimism** bēiguān 悲观

**pessimist** bēiguān zhě 悲观者

**pessimistic** bēiguān 悲观

**pest** (*bird*) hàiniǎo 害鸟; (*insect*) hàichóng 害虫; (*animal*) hàishòu 害兽; F tǎoyànguǐ 讨厌鬼

**pest control** xiāomiè yǒuhài dòngwù 消灭有害动物

**pester** jiūchán jiūchán 纠缠; ~ *X to do Y* chánzhe X zuò Y 缠着 X 做 Y

**pesticide** shāchóngjì 杀虫剂

**pet 1** *n* (*animal*) chǒngwù 宠物; (*favorite*) chǒng'ér 宠儿 **2** *adj* (*favorite*) zuì xǐhuān 最喜欢 **3** *v/t*

*animal* fǔmō 抚摸 **4** *v/i* (*of couple*) àifǔ 爱抚

**petal** huābàn 花瓣

♦ **peter out** jiànjiàn xiāoshī 渐渐消失

**petite** jiāoxiǎo 娇小

**petition** *n* qǐngyuànshū 请愿书

**petrified** shòujīngxià 受惊吓

**petrify** xiàdāi 吓呆

**petrochemical** shíyóu huàxué chǎnpǐn 石油化学产品

**petroleum** shíyóu 石油

**petty** *person, behavior* xiǎoqì 小气; *details, problem* suǒsuì 琐碎

**petty cash** língyòng xiànjīn 零用现金

**petulant** xìngjí 性急

**pew** jiàotáng chángyǐ 教堂长椅

**pewter** xīqiān héjīn 锡铅合金

**pharmaceutical** zhìyào 制药

**pharmaceuticals** zhìyào gōngsī 制药公司

**pharmacist** (*in store*) yàoshāng 药商

**pharmacy** (*store*) yàofáng 药房

**phase** jiēduàn 阶段

♦ **phase in** zhúbù yǐnjìn 逐步引进

♦ **phase out** zhúbù zhōngzhǐ 逐步中止

**PhD** (= *Doctor of Philosophy*) bóshì 博士

**phenomenal** fēifán 非凡

**phenomenally** jīngrén 惊人

**phenomenon** xiànxiàng 现象

**philanthropic** réncí 仁慈

**philanthropist** císhànjiā 慈善家

**philanthropy** réncí 仁慈

**Philippines:** *the* ~ Fēilǜbīn 菲律宾

**philistine** *n* yìmáng 艺盲

**philosopher** zhéxuéjiā 哲学家

**philosophical** yǒu zhélǐ 有哲理

**philosophy** zhéxué 哲学

**phobia** kǒngbùzhèng 恐怖症

**phoenix** fènghuáng 凤凰

**phone 1** *n* diànhuàjī 电话机 **2** *v/t & v/i* dǎ diànhuà 打电话

**phone book** diànhuàbù 电话簿; **phone booth** diànhuàtíng 电话亭; **phonecall** diànhuà 电话; **phone number** diànhuà hàomǎ 电话号码

phon(e)y *adj* wěizhuāng 伪装

photo *n* xiàngpiàn 相片

photo album xiàngcè 相册

photocopier yǐngyìnjī 影印机

photocopy **1** *n* yǐngyìnběn 影印本 **2** *v/t* yǐngyìn 影印

photogenic shàngxiàng 上相

photograph **1** *n* zhàopiàn 照片 **2** *v/t* pāishè 拍摄

photographer shèyǐngshī 摄影师

photography shèyǐng 摄影

phrase **1** *n* piànyǔ 片语 **2** *v/t* cuòcí 措词

phrasebook duǎnyǔ shǒucè 短语手册

physical **1** *adj* (*relating to the body*) shēntǐ 身体 **2** *n* MED tǐgé jiǎnchá 体格检查

physical handicap cánjí 残疾

physically shēntǐ shang 身体上

physician yīshēng 医生

physicist wùlǐxuéjiā 物理学家

physics wùlǐ 物理

physiotherapist lǐliáo yīshēng 理疗医生

physiotherapy lǐliáo 理疗

physique tǐgé 体格

pianist gāngqínjiā 钢琴家

piano gāngqín 钢琴

pick **1** *n*: take your ~ xuǎnba 选吧 **2** *v/t* (*choose*) xuǎn 选; *flowers, fruit* cǎi 采; ~ one's nose wā bíkǒng 挖鼻孔 **3** *v/i*: ~ and choose tiāotiāojiǎnjiǎn 挑挑拣拣

◆pick at: ~ one's food xiǎokǒu chī dōngxi 小口吃东西

◆pick on (*treat unfairly*) qīfu 欺负; (*select*) xuǎn 选

◆pick out (*identify*) rènchū 认出

◆pick up **1** *v/t* náqǐ 拿起; (*from ground*) jiǎnqǐ 拣起; (*collect*) qǔhuí 取回; (*from airport etc*) jiē接; (*in car*) ràngrén dā biànchē 让人搭便车; (*in sexual sense*) gōuyǐn 勾引; *language, skill* xuéhuì 学会; *habit* yǎngchéng 养成; *illness* gǎnrǎn 感染; (*buy*) mǎi买; *criminal* dàibǔ 逮捕; ~ the tab mǎidān 买单 **2** *v/i* (*improve*) hǎozhuǎn 好转

picket **1** *n* (*of strikers*) jiūcháduì 纠察队 **2** *v/t* shèzhì jiūchá 设置纠察

picket fence jiānbǎntiáo zhàlan 尖板条栅栏

picket line jiūcháxiàn 纠察线

pickle *v/t* yānzì 腌渍

pickles pàocài 泡菜

pickpocket páshǒu 扒手

pick-up (truck) qīngxíng xiǎohuòchē 轻型小货车

picky F tiāotì 挑剔

picnic **1** *n* yěcān 野餐

picture **1** *n* (*photo*) zhàopiàn 照片; (*painting*) huìhuà 绘画; (*illustration*) chātú 插图; (*movie*) diànyǐng 电影; keep X in the ~ shǐ X liǎojiě shíqíng 使 X 了解实情 **2** *v/t* xiǎngxiàng 想象

picture book túhuàshū 图画书

picture postcard míngxìnpiàn 明信片

picturesque rúhuà 如画

pie pài 派

piece (*fragment*) suìpiàn 碎片; (*component*) bùfen 部分; (*in board game*) zǐr 子儿; a ~ of pie / bread yíkuài pài / miànbāo 一块派 / 面包; a ~ of advice yíxiàng jiànyì 一项建议; go to ~s jīngshén bēngkuì 精神崩溃; take to ~s chāikāi 拆开

◆piece together *broken plate* zǔzhuāng 组装; *facts, evidence* pīncòu 拼凑

piecemeal *adv* yíbùfen yíbùfen 一部分一部分

piecework *n* jìjiàn gōngzuò 计件工作

pierce (*penetrate*) cìtòu 刺透; *ears* zhāyǎn 扎眼

piercing *noise* jiānlì 尖利; *eyes* ruìlì 锐利; *wind* cìgǔ 刺骨

pig zhū 猪; (*unpleasant person*) húndàn 混蛋

pigeon gēzi 鸽子

pigheaded wángù 顽固

pigpen (*also fig*) zhūjuàn 猪圈

pigskin zhūpí 猪皮

pigtail mǎwěibiàn 马尾辫

pile duī 堆; a ~ of work xǔduō 许多

♦ pile up **1** *v/i (of work, bills)* jījù 积聚 **2** *v/t* duīchéngduī 堆成堆

piles MED zhìchuāng 痔疮

pile-up MOT liánhuán pèngzhuàng 连环碰撞

pilfering xiǎotōu xiǎomō 小偷小摸

pilgrim cháoshèng zhě 朝圣者

pilgrimage cháoshèng zhī xíng 朝圣之行

pill yào 药; *the* ~ kǒufú bìyùnyào 口服避孕药; *be on the* ~ chī bìyùnyào 吃避孕药

pillar zhùzi 柱子

pillion *(of motor bike)* mótuōchē hòuzuò 摩托车后座

pillow *n* zhěntou 枕头

pillowcase, pillowslip zhěntào 枕套

pilot **1** *n (of airplane)* fēixíngyuán 飞行员 **2** *v/t airplane* jiàshǐ 驾驶

pilot plant shìyàn qū 试验区

pilot scheme shìyàn fāng'àn 试验方案

pimp *n* lāpítiáode nánrén 拉皮条的男人

pimple fěncì 粉刺

PIN (= *personal identification number*) mìmǎ 密码

pin **1** *n (for sewing)* dàtóuzhēn 大头针; *(in bowling)* mùzhù 木柱; *(badge)* huīzhāng 徽章; ELEC chātóu chāzuò 插头插座 **2** *v/t (hold down)* ànzhù 按住; *(attach)* yòng zhēn gùdìng 用针固定

♦ pin down: *pin X down to a date* jiào X dìngge shíjiān 叫 X 定个时间

♦ pin up *notice* zhāngtiē 张贴

pincers áo 螯; *a pair of* ~ yìbǎ qiánzi 一把钳子

pinch **1** *n* niē 捏; *(of salt, sugar etc)* yìniē 一捏; *at a* ~ bìyàoshí 必要时 **2** *v/t* niē 捏 **3** *v/i (of shoes)* jiājiǎo 夹脚

pine *n (tree)* sōngshù 松树; *(wood)* sōngmù 松木

♦ pine for sīniàn 思念

pineapple ⇩ bōluó 菠萝

ping **1** *n* pēngde yìshēng 砰的一声 **2** *v/i* fāchū pēngde yìshēng 发

出砰的一声

ping-pong pīngpāngqiú 乒乓球

pink *(color)* fěnhóngsè 粉红色

pinnacle *fig* dǐngfēng 顶峰

pinpoint míngquè zhǐchū 明确指出

pins and needles fāmá 发麻

pinstripe *adj* xìtiáowén 细条纹

pint pǐntuō 品脱

pin-up *(girl)* měinǚ 美女

pinyin pīnyīn 拼音

pioneer **1** *n fig* chuàngshǐrén 创始人 **2** *v/t* shǒuchàng 首倡

pioneering *adj work* kāituò 开拓

pious qiánchéng 虔诚

pip *n (of fruit)* zhǒngzi 种子

pipe **1** *n (for smoking)* yāndǒu 烟斗; *(for water, gas, sewage)* guǎnzi 管子 **2** *v/t yòng* guǎndào shūsòng 用管道输送

♦ pipe down ānjìng 安静

piped music bèijǐng yīnyuè 背景音乐

pipeline guǎndào 管道; *in the* ~ jíjiāng fāshēng 即将发生

piping hot gǔntàng 滚烫

pirate *v/t software etc* dàobǎn 盗版

piss **1** *v/i* F *(urinate)* sāniào 撒尿 **2** *n* F niào 尿

pissed F *(annoyed)* nǎonù 恼怒; *Br (drunk)* hēzuìle 喝醉了

pistol shǒuqiāng 手枪

piston huósāi 活塞

pit *n (hole)* kēng 坑; *(coal mine)* kuàngkēng 矿坑

pitch[1] *n* MUS yīndiào 音调

pitch[2] **1** *v/i (in baseball)* tóuqiú 投球 **2** *v/t tent* dā 搭; *ball* tóu 投

pitch black qīhēi 漆黑

pitcher[1] *(baseball player)* tóushǒu 投手

pitcher[2] *(container)* guàn 罐

piteous kělián 可怜

pitfall xiànjǐng 陷阱

pith *(of citrus fruit)* suí 髓

pitiful *sight* lìngrén liánmǐn 令人怜悯; *excuse, attempt* kěbǐ 可鄙

pitiless wúqíng 无情

pittance wēibóde gōngzī 微薄的工资

pity **1** *n* tóngqíng 同情; *it's a* ~

*that* ... yíhàn ... 遗憾 ...; *what a ~!* zhēn yíhàn! 真遗憾！; *take ~ on* chūyú tóngqíng ér bāngzhù 出于同情而帮助 **2** *v/t person* tóngqíng 同情

**pivot 1** *v/i* zài zhīdiǎn shang zhuàndòng 在支点上转动 **2** *n* zhīdiǎn 支点

**pizza** bǐsà 比萨

**PLA** (= *People's Liberation Army*) Jiěfàngjūn 解放军

**PLA soldier** Jiěfàngjūn 解放军

**placard** biāoyǔpái 标语牌

**place 1** *n* dìfang 地方; (*bar, restaurant*) cānyǐnchù 餐饮处; (*apartment, house*) jiā 家; (*in book*) yè 页; (*in race, competition*) míngcì 名次; (*seat*) zuòwèi 座位; *at my/his ~* zài wǒ/tā nàr de 在我/他那儿; *in ~ of* dàitì 代替; *feel out of ~* gǎndào bù xiāngchèn 感到不相称; *take ~* fāshēng 发生; *in the first ~* (*firstly*) shǒuxiān 首先; (*in the beginning*) kāishǐ 开始 **2** *v/t* (*put*) fàng 放; (*identify*) wánquán rèndìng 完全认定; *~ an order* dìnghuò 订货

**place mat** cānjù diàn 餐具垫

**placid** ānjìng 安静

**plague 1** *n* wēnyì 瘟疫 **2** *v/t* (*bother*) fánrǎo 烦扰

**plain**[1] *n* píngyuán 平原

**plain**[2] **1** *adj* (*clear, obvious*) qīngchǔ 清楚; (*not fancy*) qīngdàn 清淡; (*not pretty*) pǔtōng 普通; (*not patterned*) méiyǒu tú'àn 没有图案; (*blunt*) shuàizhí 率直; *~ chocolate* chún qiǎokèlì 纯巧克力 **2** *adv* xiǎnrán 显然; *it's ~ crazy* zhēnshì fēngkuáng 真是疯狂

**plain clothes:** *in ~* chuān biànyī 穿便衣

**plainly** (*clearly*) qīngchǔ 清楚; (*bluntly*) zhíshuài 直率; (*simply*) pǔsù 朴素

**plain-spoken** zhíyánbúhuì 直言不讳

**plaintiff** yuángào 原告

**plaintive** āishāng 哀伤

**plait 1** *n* (*in hair*) biànzi 辫子 **2** *v/t hair* biān biànzi 编辫子

**plan 1** *n* (*project, intention*) jìhuà 计划; (*drawing*) shèjìtú 设计图 **2** *v/t* (*prepare*) zhǔnbèi 准备; (*design*) shèjì 设计; *~ to do X, ~ on doing X* dǎsuàn zuò X 打算做 X **3** *v/i* dìng jìhuà 订计划

**plane**[1] (*airplane*) fēijī 飞机

**plane**[2] (*tool*) bàozi 刨子

**planet** xíngxīng 行星

**plank** (*of wood*) mùbǎn 木板; *fig* (*of policy*) zhèngcè zhǔnzé 政策准则

**planning** jìhuà 计划; *at the ~ stage* zài chóuhuà zhōng 在筹划中

**plant**[1] **1** *n* zhíwù 植物 **2** *v/t* zhòng 种

**plant**[2] *n* (*factory*) chǎng 厂; (*equipment*) shèbèi 设备

**plantation** dà zhòngzhíyuán 大种植园

**plaque** (*on wall*) shìbǎn 饰板; (*on teeth*) yábān 牙斑

**plaster 1** *n* (*on wall, ceiling*) huīní 灰泥 **2** *v/t wall, ceiling* yòng huīní túmǒ 用灰泥涂抹; *be ~ed with* túmǎn 涂满

**plaster cast** shígāo bēngdài 石膏绷带

**plastic 1** *n* sùliào 塑料 **2** *adj* (*made of ~*) sùliào 塑料

**plastic bag** sùliàodài 塑料袋; **plastic money** xìnyòngkǎ 信用卡; **plastic surgeon** zhěngxíng wàikē yīshēng 整形外科医生; **plastic surgery** zhěngxíng wàikē 整形外科

**plate** *n* (*for food*) pánzi 盘子; (*sheet of metal*) bóbǎncái 薄板材

**plateau** gāoyuán 高原

**platform** (*stage*) wǔtái 舞台; (*of railroad station*) ⬇ zhàntái 站台; *fig* (*political*) zhènggāng 政纲

**platinum** *n* & *adj* bó 铂

**platitude** chéncí làndiào 陈词滥调

**platonic** *relationship* chún yǒuyì 纯友谊

**platoon** (*of soldiers*) pái 排

**platter** (*for meat, fish*) dà qiǎnpán 大浅盘

**plausible** sìhū yǒu dàolǐ 似乎有道理

**play 1** n (*in theater, on TV*) jù jù 剧; (*of children*) yóuxì 游戏; TECH huódòng 活动; SP bǐsàide biǎoxiàn 比赛的表现 **2** v/i (*of children*) wánr 玩儿; (*of musician*) tánzòu 弹奏; (SP: *perform*) dǎ 打; (SP: *take part*) cānsài 参赛 **3** v/t *musical instrument* tán 弹; *piece of music* yǎnzòu 演奏; *game* wánr 玩儿; *opponent* yǔ … bǐsài 与 … 比赛; (*perform: Macbeth etc*) biǎoyǎn 表演; *particular role* bànyǎn 扮演; ~ *a joke on X* kāi X de wánxiào 开X的玩笑

**play around** (*be unfaithful*) sīhùn 厮混

♦ **play down** dànhuà 淡化

♦ **play up** (*of machine*) chū gùzhàng 出故障; (*of child*) rě máfan 惹麻烦; (*of tooth, bad back etc*) gěi rén tòngkǔ 给人痛苦

**playact** (*pretend*) jiǎzhuāng 假装

**playback** huífàng 回放

**playboy** huāhuāgōngzǐ 花花公子

**player** SP yùndòng yuán 运动员; (*musician*) yǎnzòu zhě 演奏者; (*actor*) yǎnyuán 演员

**playful** *punch etc* nàozhe wánr 闹着玩儿

**playground** yóuxìchǎng 游戏场

**playing card** zhǐpái 纸牌

**playing field** yùndòngchǎng 运动场

**playmate** yóuxìde huǒbàn 游戏的伙伴

**playwright** jùzuòjiā 剧作家

**plaza** (*for shopping*) gòuwù zhōngxīn 购物中心

**plea** n kěnqiú 恳求

**plead** v/i qǐngqiú 请求; ~ *for* kěnqiú 恳求; ~ *guilty / not guilty* fú / bùfú zuì shíe 服/不服罪; ~ *with X* qǐngqiú X 请求X

**pleasant** lìngrén yúkuài 令人愉快

**please 1** adv qǐng 请; *more tea? – yes,* – hái yào chá ma? – hǎode, xièxiè 还要茶吗? - 好的，谢谢; ~ *do* méiwèntí 没问题 **2** v/t shǐ gāoxìng 使高兴; ~ *yourself*

qǐngbiàn 请便

**pleased** gāoxìng 高兴; ~ *to meet you* hěn gāoxìng rènshí nǐ 很高兴认识你

**pleasing** shǐrén yúkuài 使人愉快

**pleasure** (*happiness, satisfaction*) kuàilè 快乐; (*as opposed to work*) yúlè 娱乐; (*delight*) lèqù 乐趣; *it's a* ~ (*you're welcome*) méiguānxi 没关系; *with* ~ dāngrán 当然

**pleat** n (*in skirt*) zhě 褶

**pledge 1** n (*promise*) bǎozhèng 保证; *Pledge of Allegiance* Zhōngchéng Xuānshì 忠诚宣誓 **2** v/t (*promise*) chéngnuò 承诺

**plentiful** dàliàng 大量

**plenty** (*abundance*) fùzú 富足; ~ *of* xǔduō 许多; *that's* ~ zúgòu duō le 足够多了; *there's* ~ *for everyone* yǒudeshì gěi dàjiā 有的是给大家

**pliable** kěsù 可塑

**pliers** qiánzi 钳子; *a pair of* ~ yìbǎ qiánzi 一把钳子

**plight** kùnjìng 困境

**plod** v/i (*walk*) jiānnán xíngzǒu 艰难行走

♦ **plod along** (*with a job*) huǎnmàn jìnxíng 缓慢进行

**plodder** (*at work, school*) chénmèn kǔgàn de rén 沉闷苦干的人

**plot** n (*land*) xiǎokuài tǔdì 小块土地

**plot²** **1** n (*conspiracy*) yīnmóu 阴谋; (*of novel*) qíngjié 情节 **2** v/t mìmóu 密谋 **3** v/i mìmóu 密谋

**plotter** yīnmóu zhě 阴谋者; COMPUT huìtúyí 绘图仪

**plow 1** n lí 犁 **2** v/t & v/i gēngdì 耕地

♦ **plow back** *profits* fǎn tóuzī 反投资

**pluck** v/t *eyebrows* zhāichú 摘除; *chicken* bámáo 拔毛

♦ **pluck up:** ~ *courage* gǔqǐ yǒngqì 鼓起勇气

**plug 1** n (*for sink, bath*) sāizi 塞子; (*electrical*) chātóu 插头; (*spark* ~) huǒhuāsāi 火花塞; (*for new book etc*) xuānchuán 宣传 **2** v/t *hole* yòng sāizi dǔ 用塞子堵; *new book etc* tuīxiāo 推销

♦ **plug away** F nǔlì búxiè 努力不懈

♦ **plug in** v/t jiētōng diànyuán 接通电源

**plum 1** n lǐzi 李子 **2** adj *job* yōuyuè 优越

**plumage** yǔyī 羽衣

**plumb** adj chuízhí 垂直

**plumber** shuǐnuǎngōng 水暖工

**plumbing** (*pipes*) guǎndào zhuāngzhì 管道装置

**plume** n yǔmáo 羽毛

**plummet** (*of airplane*) kuàisù luòxià 快速落下; (*of share prices*) dàdiē 大跌

**plump** adj féipàng 肥胖

♦ **plump for** xuǎnzé 选择

**plunge 1** n měngrán diēluò 猛然跌落; (*in prices*) xiàdiē 下跌; *take the* ~ cǎiqǔ dàdàn cuòshī 采取大胆措施 **2** v/i tūrán diērù 突然跌落; (*of prices*) xiàdiē 下跌 **3** v/t tóurù 投入; *the city was* ~*d into darkness* zhèi chéngshì xiànrù yípiàn hēi'àn zhōng 这城市陷入一片黑暗中; *the news* ~*d him into despair* tā tīngdào nà xiāoxi jiù xiànrùle juéwàng 他听到那消息就陷入了绝望

**plunging:** ~ *neckline* shēn V zì lǐng 深 V 字领

**plural 1** adj fùshù xíngshì 复数形式 **2** n fùshù 复数

**plus 1** prep jiāshàng 加上 **2** adj duō 多; *$500* ~ wǔbǎiduō měiyuán 五百多美元 **3** n (*symbol*) jiāhào 加号; (*advantage*) hǎochù 好处 **4** conj (*moreover, in addition*) érqiě 而且

**plush** háohuá 豪华

**plywood** jiāohébǎn 胶合板

**p.m.** xiàwǔ 下午

**pneumatic** chōngqì 充气

**pneumatic drill** fēngzuàn 风钻

**pneumonia** fèiyán 肺炎

**poach**¹ v/t (*cook*) wēi wēi 煨

**poach**² **1** v/i tōubǔ 偷捕 **2** v/t *salmon etc* tōubǔ 偷捕

**poached egg** wò jīdàn 卧鸡蛋

**P.O. Box** yóuzhèng xìnxiāng 邮政信箱

**pocket 1** n kǒudài 口袋; *line one's own* ~*s* fā wāicái 发歪财; *be out of* ~ péiqián 赔钱 **2** adj (*miniature*) wēixíng 微型 **3** v/t jùwéijǐyǒu 据为己有

**pocketbook** (*woman's*) xiǎo shǒutíbāo 小手提包; (*wallet*) qiánbāo 钱包; (*book*) píngzhuāngshū 平装书; **pocket calculator** xiǎo jìsuànqì 小计算器; **pocketknife** xiǎo zhédāo 小折刀

**podium** zhǐhuītái 指挥台

**poem** shī 诗

**poet** shīrén 诗人

**poetic** *person, description* yǒu shīyì 有诗意

**poetic justice** yīngdéde jiǎngchéng 应得的奖惩

**poetry** shīgē 诗歌

**poignant** tòngqiè 痛切

**point 1** n (*of pencil, knife*) jiānduān 尖端; (*in competition, exam*) fēnfēn 分; (*purpose*) yìyì 意义; (*moment*) shíkè 时刻; (*in argument, discussion*) guāndiǎn 观点; (*in decimals*) diǎn 点; *beside the* ~ lítí 离题; *be on the* ~ *of* zhèngyào ... 正要 ...; *get to the* ~ shuō zhèngshì 说正事; *the* ~ *is* ... wèntí shì ... 问题是 ...; *there's no* ~ *in waiting / trying* děng / shì gēnběn méiyòng 等 / 试根本没用 **2** v/i zhǐ 指 **3** v/t *gun* duìzhǔn 对准

♦ **point at** (*with finger*) zhǐxiàng 指向

♦ **point out** *sights* shǐ zhùyì 使注意; *advantages etc* zhǐchū 指出

♦ **point to** (*with finger*) yòngshǒu zhǐ 用手指; *fig* (*indicate*) ànshì 暗示

**point-blank 1** adj *refusal, denial* zhíjiēliǎodàng 直截了当; *at* ~ *range* zài jìnjùlí nèi 在近距离内 **2** adv *refuse, deny* duànrán 断然

**pointed** jiānruì 尖锐

**pointer** (*for teacher*) jiàobiān 教鞭; (*hint*) diǎnzi 点子; (*sign, indication*) jìxiàng 迹象

**pointless** wúyìyì 无意义; *it's* ~

***trying to do X*** chángshì zuò X gēnběn méiyòng 尝试做 X 根本没用

**point of sale** (*place*) xiāohòudiǎn 销货点; (*promotional material*) cùxiāo zīliào 促销资料

**point of view** guāndiǎn 观点

**poise** zìzhì 自制

**poised** *person* tàiránzìruò 泰然自若

**poison 1** *n* dúyào 毒药 **2** *v/t* dúhài 毒害

**poisonous** yǒudú 有毒

**poke 1** *n* tǒng 捅 **2** *v/t* (*prod*) tǒng 捅; (*stick*) shēnchū 伸出; ~ **fun at** cháoxiào 嘲笑; ~ **one's nose into** gānyù 干预

♦**poke around** xúnzhǎo 寻找

**poker** (*card game*) pūkèpái 扑克牌

**poky** (*cramped*) xiáxiǎo 狭小

**Poland** Bōlán 波兰

**polar** dìjí 地极

**polar bear** běijíxióng 北极熊

**polarize** *v/t* liǎngjí fēnhuà 两极分化

**Pole** Bōlán rén 波兰人

**pole**[1] (*of wood, metal*) gān gǎn 杆杆

**pole**[2] (*of earth*) dìjí 地极

**polevault** chēnggān tiàogāo 撑竿跳高

**police** *n* jǐngfāng 警方

**policeman** jǐngchá 警察; **police state** jǐngchá guójiā 警察国家; **police station** jǐngchájú 警察局; **policewoman** nǚjǐngchá 女警察

**policy**[1] zhèngcè 政策

**policy**[2]: ***insurance*** ~ bǎoxiǎndān 保险单

**polio** xiǎo'ér mábìzhèng 小儿麻痹症

**Polish 1** *adj* Bōlán 波兰 **2** *n* (*language*) Bōlán yǔ 波兰语

**polish 1** *n* (*product*) cāguāngjì 擦光剂 **2** *v/t* cāliàng 擦亮; *speech* rùnsè 润色

♦**polish off** *food* chīguāng 吃光

♦**polish up** *skill* tígāo 提高

**polished** *performance* xùnliàn-yǒusù 训练有素

**Politbureau** Zhèngzhìjú 政治局

**polite** yǒu lǐmào 有礼貌

**politely** lǐmào 礼貌

**politeness** lǐmào 礼貌

**political** zhèngzhì 政治

**politically correct** wú zhèngzhì cuòwù 无政治错误

**politician** zhèngzhìjiā 政治家

**politics** zhèngzhì 政治; ***what are his*** ~? tā yǒu shénme zhèngzhì xìnyǎng? 他有什么政治信仰？

**poll 1** *n* (*survey*) mínyì cèyàn 民意测验; ***the*** ~ (*election*) xuǎnjǔ 选举; ***go to the*** ~**s** (*vote*) xuǎnjǔ tóupiào 选举投票 **2** *v/t people* diàochá 调查; *votes* huòdé 获得

**pollen** huāfěn 花粉

**pollen count** huāfěn jìshù 花粉计数

**polling booth** tóupiàozhàn 投票站

**pollster** mínyì cèyàn zhě 民意测验者

**pollutant** wūrǎn wùzhì 污染物质

**pollute** wūrǎn 污染

**pollution** wūrǎn 污染

**polo neck** (*sweater*) yuán gāo fān-lǐng 圆高翻领

**polo shirt** gāolǐngshān 高领衫

**polyethylene** jùyǐxī 聚乙烯

**polyester** jùzhǐxiānwéi 聚酯纤维

**polystyrene** jùběnyǐxī 聚苯乙烯

**polyunsaturated** hányǒu duō-chóng bùbǎohé huàhéwù 含有多重不饱和化合物

**pompous** zìfù 自负

**pond** chítáng 池塘

**ponder** *v/i* shēnsī 深思

**pony** xiǎomǎ 小马

**ponytail** mǎwěifà 马尾发

**poodle** juǎnmáo xiǎogǒu 卷毛小狗

**pool**[1] (*swimming* ~) chí 池; (*of water, blood*) tān 摊

**pool**[2] (*game*) ⇩ pǔ'ěrdànzǐxì 普尔弹子戏

**pool**[3] **1** *n* (*common fund*) gòngtóng chǔjīn 共同储金 **2** *v/t resources* jíhé 集合

**pool hall** pǔ'ěrdànzǐxì tīng 普尔弹子戏厅

**pool table** pǔ'ěrdànzǐxì zhuō 普尔弹子戏桌

pooped F jīnpílìjìn 筋疲力尽

poor 1 adj (not wealthy) pínqióng 贫穷; (not good) bùhǎo 不好; (unfortunate) búxìng 不幸; **be in ~ health** shēntǐ bùhǎo 身体不好; ~ **old Tony!** kěliánde Tuōní! 可怜 的托尼! 2 n: **the ~** qióngrén 穷人

poorly 1 adv hěnzāo 很糟 2 adj (unwell) bùshūfu 不舒服

pop¹ 1 n (noise) pēngde yīshēng 砰的一声 2 v/i (of balloon etc) fāchū pēngde yīshēng 发出砰的一声 3 v/t cork báchū 拔出; balloon bàopò 爆破

pop² 1 n MUS liúxíng yīnyuè 流行音乐 2 adj liúxíng 流行

pop³ (father) bà ba 爸爸

pop⁴ v/t (put) fàng 放

♦pop up v/i (appear suddenly) tūrán chūxiàn 突然出现

popcorn yùmǐhuā 玉米花

pope jiàohuáng 教皇

poplar yángshù 杨树

poppy yīngsù 罂粟

Popsicle® bàngbàngbīng 棒棒冰

pop song liúxíng gēqǔ 流行歌曲

popular shòu huānyíng 受欢迎; belief, support pǔbiàn 普遍

popularity (of person) shēngwàng 声望

populate jūzhù 居住

population rénkǒu 人口

porcelain n & adj cí 瓷

porch ménláng 门廊

porcupine háozhū 豪猪

pore (of skin) máokǒng 毛孔

♦pore over xìkàn 细看

pork zhūròu 猪肉

porn n huángsè zuòpǐn 黄色作品

porn(o) adj huángsè 黄色

pornographic huángsè 黄色

pornography sèqíng zuòpǐn 色情作品

porous tòu shuǐqì 透水汽

port¹ 1 n (town) gǎngshì 港市; (area) gǎngkǒu 港口; COMPUT duānkǒu 端口

port² adj (left-hand) zuǒxián 左舷

portable 1 adj shǒutíshì 手提式 2 n COMPUT bǐjìběn 笔记本; ~ **TV**

wēixíng diànshì 微型电视

porter (at railroad station) bānyùngōng 搬运工; (doorman in hotel) ménwèi 门卫

porthole NAUT xiánchuāng 舷窗

portion n yíbùfen 一部分; (of food) fèn 份

portrait 1 n (painting, photograph) xiàoxiàng 肖像; (depiction) miáoxiě 描写 2 adv print shùpái 竖排

portray (of artist) huà huà 画; (of photographer) pāi pāi 拍; (of actor) bànyǎn 扮演; (of author) miáoshù 描述

portrayal (by actor) bànyǎn 扮演; (by author) miáoshù 描述

Portugal Pútáoyá 葡萄牙

Portuguese 1 adj Pútáoyá 葡萄牙 2 n (person) Pútáoyá rén 葡萄牙人; (language) Pútáoyá yǔ 葡萄牙语

pose 1 n (pretense) zhuāngqiāng zuòshì 装腔作势 2 v/i (for artist, photographer) bǎi zīshì 摆姿势; ~ **as** zhuāngzuò 装作 3 v/t: ~ **a problem / a threat** zàochéng kùnnán / wēixié zàochéng 困难 / 威胁

position 1 n (location) wèizhi 位置; (stance) zīshì 姿势; (in race, competition) wèi 位; (occupied by soldiers) zhèndì 阵地; (point of view) lìchǎng 立场; (situation) chǔjìng 处境; (job) zhíwèi 职位; (status) dìwèi 地位 2 v/t ānfàng 安放

positive attitude lèguān 乐观; response biǎoshì tóngyì 表示同意; medical test yángxìng 阳性; GRAM kěndìng 肯定; ELEC zhèngjí 正极; **be ~** (sure) quèdìng 确定

positively (decidedly) shífēn kěndìng 十分肯定; (definitely) juéduì 绝对

possess chíyǒu 持有

possession (ownership) chíyǒu 持有; (thing owned) cáichǎn 财产; ~s suǒyǒuwù 所有物

possessive person xiǎnshì zhànyǒuyù 显示占有欲

possessive pronoun GRAM wùzhǔ dàicí 物主代词

possibility kěnéng xìng 可能性

possible kěnéng 可能; **the short-est / quickest ~ ...** jìn kěnéng zuìduǎn/zuìkuài ... 尽可能最短/最快 ...; **the best ~ ...** jìn kěnéng zuìhǎo ... 尽可能最好 ...

possibly kěnéng 可能; (*perhaps*) yěxǔ 也许; **that can't ~ be right** nà bù kěnéng duì 那不可能对; **could you ~ tell me ...?** nǐ néngbùnéng gàosù wǒ ...? 你能不能告诉我 ...?

post¹ **1** n (*of wood, metal*) gānzi 杆子 **2** v/t notice zhāngtiē zhāng tiē; profits gōngbù 公布; **keep X ~ed** ràng X zhīdào 让 X 知道

post² **1** n (*place of duty*) zhíwèi zhíwèi 职位 **2** v/t soldier, employee pàiwǎng 派往; guards bùzhì 布置

postage yóuzī 邮资

postal yóudí 邮递

postcard míngxìnpiàn 明信片

postdate tiánwǎn rìqī 填晚日期

poster hǎibào 海报

posterior n hum (*buttocks*) pìgu 屁股

posterity hòudài 后代

postgraduate **1** n yánjiūshēng 研究生 **2** adj dàxué bìyèhòu 大学毕业后

posthumous novel zuòzhě sǐhòu chūbǎn 作者死后出版; award sǐhòu huòdé 死后获得; baby yífù 遗腹

posthumously sǐhòu fāshēng 死后发生

posting (*assignment*) wěipài 委派

postmark yóuchuō yóu chuō 邮戳

postmortem yànshī 验尸

post office yóujú 邮局

postpone tuīchí 推迟

postponement yánqī 延期

posture zīshì 姿势

postwar zhànhòu 战后

pot¹ (*for cooking in*) guō guō 锅; (*for coffee, tea*) hú hú 壶; (*for plant*) pén pén 盆

pot² F (*marijuana*) dàmá 大麻

potato tǔdòu 土豆

potato chips ⇩ zháshǔpiàn 炸薯片

potent drug, medicine xiàolì dà xiào 效

力大; ruler qiángyǒulì 强有力

potential **1** adj kěnéng chūxiàn 可能出现 **2** n qiánlì 潜力

potentially yǒu kěnéng 有可能

pothole (*in road*) kēngwā 坑洼

potter n táogōng 陶工

pottery (*activity*) zhìtáoshù 制陶术; (*items*) táoqì 陶器; (*place*) táojú zuòfang 陶器作坊

potty n (*for baby*) biànpén 便盆

pouch (*bag*) xiǎodài 小袋

poultry (*birds*) jiāqín 家禽; (*meat*) jiāqínròu 家禽肉

pounce v/i (*of animal*) měngpǔ 猛扑; fig túrán xíjí 突然袭击

pound¹ n (*weight*) bàng 磅

pound² (*for strays*) wéichǎng 围场; (*for cars*) mòshōu chēliàng chù 没收车辆处

pound³ v/i (*of heart*) jùliè tiàodòng 剧烈跳动; **~ on** (*hammer on*) zhòngjī 重击

pound sterling yīngbàng 英镑

pour **1** v/t liquid dào 倒 **2** v/i yǒngchū 涌出; **it's ~ing (with rain)** dàyǔqīngpén 大雨倾盆

♦ **pour out** liquid dàochū 倒出; troubles qīngsù 倾诉

pout v/i juězuǐ 撅嘴

poverty pínkùn 贫困

poverty-stricken pínkùn bùkān 贫困不堪

powder **1** n fěnmò 粉末; (*for face*) fěn 粉 **2** v/t face chāfěn 搽粉

powder room nǚcèsuǒ 女厕所

power **1** n (*strength*) lì 力; (*authority*) quánlì 权力; (*energy*) nénglliàng 能量; (*electricity*) diàn 电; **in ~** POL zhízhèng 执政; **fall from ~** POL shīshì 失势 **2** v/t: **be ~ed by X** yóu X zuò dònglì 由 X 作动力

power-assisted yǒu dònglì yuánzhù 有动力援助; power cable diànyuán diànlǎn 电源电缆; power cut tíngdiàn 停电

powerful qiángyǒulì 强有力

powerless wúlìliàng 无力量; **be ~ to ...** wúnéngwéilì ... 无能为力 ...

power line diànxiàn 电线; power outage tíngdiàn 停电; power

station fādiànzhàn 发电站;
power steering gāonéng zhuǎnxiàng 高能转向; power unit
néngliàng dānwèi 能量单位
PR (= *public relations*) gōngguān
公关
practical *experience* shíjì 实际;
*person* xiànshí 现实; (*functional*)
shíyòng 实用
practical joke èzuòjù 恶作剧
practically *behave, think* shíshìqiú-
shì 实事求是; (*almost*) jīhū 几乎
practice 1 *n* shíjiàn 实践, liànxí
练习; (*rehearsal*) páiliàn 排练;
(*custom*) chángguī 常规; *in ~* (*in
reality*) shíjì shang 实际上; *be out
of ~* shūyúliànxí 疏于练习 2 *v/i*
xùnliàn 训练 3 *v/t* liànxí 练习;
*law, medicine* zhíyè 执业
pragmatic wùshí 务实
pragmatism shíyòngzhǔyì 实用主
义
prairie dàcǎoyuán 大草原
praise 1 *n* zànyù 赞誉 2 *v/t*
chēngzàn 称赞
praiseworthy zhídé chēngzàn 值
得称赞
prank *n* èzuòjù 恶作剧
prattle *v/i* xiánliáo 闲聊
pray qídǎo 祈祷
prayer dǎogào 祷告
PRC (= *People's Republic of
China*) Zhōnghuá Rénmín Gònghéguó 中华人民共和国
preach 1 *v/i* (*in church*) bùdào 布
道; (*moralize*) shuōjiào 说教 2 *v/t*:
*~ a sermon* bùdào 布道
preacher chuándàorén 传道人
precarious bù wěndìng 不稳定
precariously bù wěngù 不稳固
precaution yùfáng cuòshī 预防措
施
precautionary *measure* yùfáng 预
防
precede *v/t* (*in time*) xiānyú 先于;
(*walk in front of*) lǐngxiān zǒu 领
先走
precedence: *take ~* yōuxiān 优
先; *take ~ over ...* lǐngxiānyú ...
领先于 ...
precedent *n* xiānlì 先例

preceding *week* qiányī 前一;
*chapter* shàngyī 上一
precinct (*district*) qūyù 区域
precious bǎoguì 宝贵
precipitate *v/t crisis* jiāsù 加速
précis *n* zhāiyào 摘要
precise zhǔnquè 准确
precisely jīngquè 精确
precision jīngquè 精确
precocious *child* zǎoshú 早熟
preconceived *idea* shìxiān xíngchéng 事先形成
precondition bìbèi 必备
predator (*animal*) shíròu dòngwù
食肉动物
predecessor (*in job*) qiánrènzhě
前任者; (*machine*) qiányī xínghào
前一型号
predestination sùmìng 宿命
predicament jiǒngkuàng 窘况
predict yùyán 预言
predictable kě yùyán 可预言
prediction yùyán 预言
predominant zhàn yōushì 占优势
predominantly zhǔyào 主要
predominate zhàn yōushì 占优势
prefabricated yùzhì 预制
preface *n* qiányán 前言
prefecture (*in ancient China*) zhōu
州
prefer gèng xǐhuān 更喜欢; *~ X to
Y* yǔ Y xiāngbǐ gèng xǐhuān X 与
Y 相比更喜欢 X; *~ to do*
nìngyuàn zuò 宁愿做
preferable gèng chènxīn 更称心;
*be ~ to* gèng shìyí 更适宜
preferably gèng kěqǔ 更可取
preference piān'ài 偏爱
preferential yōuxiān 优先
prefix qiánzhuì 前缀
pregnancy yùnqī 孕期
pregnant huáiyùn 怀孕
prehistoric shǐqián 史前
prejudice 1 *n* piānjiàn 偏见 2 *v/t
person* yǐngxiǎng 影响; *chances*
xuēruò 削弱
prejudiced piānxīn 偏心
preliminary *adj* yùbèixìng 预备性
premarital hūnqián 婚前
premature: *~ birth* zǎochǎn 早产
premeditated yùmóu 预谋

premier n (*prime minister*) zǒnglǐ 总理

première n shǒucì gōngyǎn 首次公演

premises dìfang 地方

premium n (*in insurance*) bǎoxiǎnfèi 保险费

premonition yùgǎn 预感

prenatal chǎnqián 产前

preoccupied xīnbúzàiyān 心不在焉

preparation (*act*) zhǔnbèi 准备; **in ~ for X** wèi X zuòhǎo zhǔnbèi 为 X 作好准备; **~s** zhǔnbèi gōngzuò 准备工作

prepare 1 v/t zhǔnbèi 准备; **be ~d to do X** (*willing*) yuànyì zuò X 愿意做 X 2 v/i zhǔnbèi 准备

preposition jiècí 介词

preposterous huāngmiù 荒谬

prerequisite bìbèi 必备

prescribe (*of doctor*) kāi yàofāng 开药方

prescription MED yàofāng 药方

presence zàichǎng 在场; **in the ~ of X** zài X miànqián 在 X 面前

presence of mind yùshì bùhuāng 遇事不慌

present[1] 1 adj (*current*) mùqián 目前; (*in attendance*) zàichǎng 在场 2 n dāngqián 当前; **the ~** xiànzài 现在; GRAM xiànzàishí 现在时; **at ~** cǐkè cǐkè 此刻

present[2] 1 n (*gift*) lǐwù 礼物 2 v/t award, bouquet shòuyǔ 授予; program zhǔchí 主持; **~ X with Y, ~ Y to X** bǎ Y zèngsònggěi X 把 Y 赠送给 X

presentation (*to audience*) bàogào 报告

present-day dāngjīn 当今

presently (*at the moment*) xiànzài 现在; (*soon*) bùjiǔ 不久

preservation bǎochí 保持

preservative n fángfǔjì 防腐剂

preserve 1 n (*domain*) lǐngyù 领域 2 v/t standards, peace etc wéihù 维护; wood etc bǎohù 保护; food bǎocún 保存

preside v/i (*at meeting*) zhǔchí 主持

presidency zǒngtǒng zhíwèi 总统职位

president POL zǒngtǒng 总统; (*of company*) dǒngshìzhǎng 董事长

presidential zǒngtǒng 总统

press 1 n: **the ~** xīnwénjiè 新闻界 2 v/t button àn 按; (*urge*) dūncù 敦促; (*squeeze*) jǐyā 挤压; clothes yùn 熨 3 v/i: **~ for** cuīcù 催促

press conference jìzhě zhāodàihuì 记者招待会

pressing adj pòqiè 迫切

pressure 1 n yālì 压力; **be under ~** chéngshòu yālì 承受压力; **be under ~ to do X** pòyú yālì zuò X 迫于压力做 X 2 v/t qiǎngpò 强迫

prestige wēiwàng 威望

prestigious yǒu wēiwàng 有威望

presumably dàgài 大概

presume tuīcè 推测; **~ to do** màomèi zuò 冒昧做

presumption (*of innocence, guilt*) tuīdìng 推定

presumptuous màoshī 冒失

pre-tax nàshuì qián 纳税前

pretend 1 v/t zhuāngzuò 装作 2 v/i jiǎzhuāng 假装

pretense xūjiǎ 虚假

pretentious xuànyào 炫耀

pretext jièkǒu 借口

pretty 1 adj piàoliang 漂亮 2 adv (*quite*) xiāngdāng 相当

prevail (*triumph*) zhànshèng 战胜

prevailing shèngxíng 盛行

prevent fángzhǐ 防止; **~ X (from) doing Y** zǔzhǐ X zuò Y 阻止 X 做 Y

prevention yùfáng 预防

preventive yùfángxìng 预防性

preview n (*of movie, exhibition*) yùzhǎn 预展

previous qiányī 前一

previously yǐqián 以前

prewar zhànqián 战前

prey n lièwù 猎物

♦prey on bǔshí 捕食; fig (*of conman etc*) lièqǔ 猎取

price 1 n jiàgé 价格 2 v/t COM dìngjià 定价

priceless wújià 无价

price war jiàgézhàn 价格战

pricey ángguì 昂贵

prick¹ **1** n (pain) cì 刺 **2** v/t (jab) chuō 戳

prick² n ∨ (penis) jība 鸡巴; (person) chǔnrén 蠢人

♦ **prick up**: ~ **one's ears** (of dog) shùqǐ ěrduo 竖起耳朵; (of person) tūrán kāishǐ zhùyì tīng 突然开始注意听

prickle (on plant) cì 刺

prickly beard, plant duōcì 多刺; (irritable) yìnù 易怒

prickly heat fèizi pèizi 痱子

pride **1** n (in person, achievement) zìháo 自豪; (self-respect) zìzūn 自尊; **take ~ on X** yǐ X wéi zìháo 以 X 为自豪

priest mùshi 牧师

primarily yuánxiān 主要

primary **1** adj zhǔyào 主要 **2** n POL chūxuǎn 初选

prime **1** n: **be in one's ~** zhèngzhí shèngnián 正值盛年 **2** adj example, reason zhǔyào 主要; **of ~ importance** zhìguān zhòngyào 至关重要

prime minister shǒuxiàng 首相

prime time TV huángjīn shíjiān 黄金时间

primitive yuánshǐ 原始; conditions jiǎnlòu 简陋

prince wángzǐ 王子

princess gōngzhǔ 公主

principal **1** adj zhǔyào 主要 **2** n (of school) xiàozhǎng 校长

principally zhǔyào 主要

principle (in moral sense) zhǔnzé 准则; (rule) yuánzé 原则; **on ~** yījù zìjǐ de yuánzé 依据自己的原则; **in ~** yuánzé shang 原则上

print **1** n (in book etc) yìnshuā zìtǐ 印刷字体; PHOT zhàopiàn 照片; **out of ~** juébǎn 绝版 **2** v/t yìnshuā 印刷; COMPUT dǎyìn 打印; (in block capitals) dàxiě 大写

♦ **print out** yìnchū 印出

printed matter yìnshuāpǐn 印刷品

printer (person) yìnshuāshāng 印刷商; (machine) ⇩ dǎyìnjī 打印机

printing press yìnshuājī 印刷机

printout dǎyìnchū de zīliào 打印出的资料

prior **1** adj shìxiān 事先 **2** prep: ~ **to** zài ...yǐqián zài ... 以前

prioritize (put in order of priority) huàfēn qīngzhònghuǎnjí 划分轻重缓急; (give priority to) jǐyǔ yōuxiān 给予优先

priority yàowèi 要位; **have ~** yǒu yōuxiānquán 有优先权

prison jiānyù 监狱

prisoner qiúfàn 囚犯; **take X ~** fúlǔ X 俘虏 X

prisoner of war zhànfú 战俘

privacy sīrén kōngjiān 私人空间

private **1** adj sīrén 私人 **2** n MIL shìbīng 士兵; **in ~** sīxià 私下

privately (in private) sīxià 私下; funded, owned gèrén 个人; (inwardly) nèixīn 内心

private sector mínyíng qǐyè 民营企业

privilege (special treatment) tèquán 特权; (honor) róngxìng 荣幸

privileged xiángyǒu tèquán xiǎngyǒu 享有特权; (honored) róngxìng 荣幸

prize **1** n jiǎngshǎng 奖赏 **2** v/t zhēnshì 珍视

prizewinner huòjiǎng zhě 获奖者

prizewinning huòjiǎng 获奖

pro¹ n: **the ~s and cons** yōushì hé lièshì 优势和劣势

pro² → **professional**

pro³: **be ~ ...** (in favor of) zànchéng ... 赞成 ...

probability kěnéng xìng 可能性

probable hěn kěnéng 很可能

probably yěxǔ 也许

probation (in job) shìyòng 试用; LAW huǎnxíng 缓刑

probation officer huǎnxíng jiāndūguǎn 缓刑监督官

probation period (in job) shìyòngqī 试用期

probe **1** n (investigation) diàochá 调查; (scientific) tàncè 探测 **2** v/t tànchá 探查; (investigate) diàochá 调查

problem wèntí 问题; **no ~** méi

wèntí 没问题
**procedure** bùzhòu 步骤
**proceed 1** v/i (go: of people) qiánxíng 前行; (of work etc) jìnzhǎn 进
展 **2** v/t: **~ to do X** jìxù zuò X 继
续做 X
**proceedings** (events) jìnchéng 进
程
**proceeds** shōurù 收入
**process 1** n guòchéng 过程; **in
the ~** (while doing it) zài … de
guòchéng zhōng 在 … 的过程中
**2** v/t food, raw materials jiāgōng 加
工; data chǔlǐ 处理; application etc
shěnchá 审查
**procession** hángliè 行列
**processor** COMPUT chǔlǐqì 处理器
**proclaim** xuānbù 宣布
**prod** n & v/t tǒng 捅
**prodigy:** (infant) ~ shéntóng 神童
**produce 1** n chǎnpǐn 产品 **2** v/t
commodity shēngchǎn 生产;
(bring about) yǐnqǐ 引起; (bring
out) náchū 拿出; play, movie, TV
program zhìzuò 制作
**producer** (of commodity) zhìzào
chǎngjiā 制造厂家; (of play,
movie, TV program) zhìpiānrén 制
片人
**product** chǎnpǐn 产品; (result)
jiéguǒ 结果
**production** chǎnliàng 产量; (of
play, movie, TV program) zhìzuò 制
作; (play, movie, TV program)
zuòpǐn 作品
**production capacity** shēngchǎn
nénglì 生产能力
**production costs** shēngchǎn
chéngběn 生产成本
**productive** duōchǎn 多产; meeting
yǒu chéngxiào 有成效
**productivity** shēngchǎnlì 生产力
**profane** language xiàliú 下流
**profess** shēngchēng 声称
**profession** zhíyè 职业
**professional 1** adj (not amateur),
advice, help zhuānyè 专业; piece of
work yǒu jìqiǎo 有技巧; **turn ~**
biànchéng zhuānyè 变成专业
**2** n (doctor, lawyer etc, expert)
zhuānyè rénshì 专业人士; (not

an amateur) zhíyè rényuán 职业
人员
**professionally** play sport zuòwéi
zhuānyè 作为专业; (well,
skillfully) zhuānyè 专业
**professor** jiàoshòu 教授
**proficiency** jīngtōng 精通
**proficient** jīngtōng 精通
**profile** (of face) cèmiàn 侧面;
(description) jièshào 介绍
**profit 1** n lìrùn 利润 **2** v/i: **~ by**, **~
from** cóngzhōng xīqǔ yìchù 从中
吸取益处
**profitability** yǒulìkětú 有利可图
**profitable** kěhuò lìrùn 可获利润
**profit margin** lìrùnlǜ 利润率
**profound** shēnqiè 深切
**profoundly** shēnshēn 深深
**prognosis** yùhòu 预后
**program 1** n jìhuà 计划; (on radio,
TV) jiémù 节目; COMPUT chéngxù
程序; (in theater) jiémùdān 节目
单 **2** v/t COMPUT biān chéngxù 编
程序
**programmer** COMPUT chéngxùyuán 程序员
**progress 1** n jìnbù 进步; **make ~**
yǒu jìnbù 有进步; **in ~** jìnxíngzhōng 进行中 **2** v/i (advance in
time) jìnzhǎn 进展; (move on) jìnxíng 进行; (make progress) qǔdé
jìnbù 取得进步; **how is the work
~ing?** gōngzuò jìnzhǎnde zěnmeyàng? 工作进展得怎么样?
**progressive** adj (enlightened) kāimíng 开明; (which progresses)
zhúbù fāzhǎn 逐步发展
**progressively** zhúbù 逐步
**prohibit** jìnzhǐ 禁止
**prohibition** jìnzhǐ 禁止; **Prohibition** jìnjiǔ shíqí 禁酒时期
**prohibitive** prices gāode mǎibùqǐ
高得买不起
**project¹** n (plan) jìhuà 计划;
(undertaking) xiàngmù 项目; EDU
kètí 课题; (housing area) ⇩
tǒngjiàn zhùzháiqū 统建住宅区
**project²** 1 v/t figures, sales jìhuà 计
划; movie fàngyìng 放映 **2** v/i
(stick out) tūchū 突出
**projection** (forecast) yùcè 预测

**projector** (*for slides*) fàngyìngjī 放映机

**proletariat** wúchǎn jiējí 无产阶级

**prolific** *writer, artist* duōchǎn 多产

**prolong** yáncháng 延长

**prom** (*school dance*) wǔhuì 舞会

**prominent** *nose, chin* tūchū 突出; (*significant*) xiǎnzhù 显著

**promiscuity** xìng luànjiāo 性乱交

**promiscuous** xìngluàn 性乱

**promise 1** *n* chéngnuò 承诺 **2** *v/t* xǔnuò 许诺; **~ to ...** xǔnuò zuò ... 许诺做 ...; **~ X to Y** xǔnuò gěi Y X 许诺给 Y X **3** *v/i* bǎozhèng 保证

**promising** yǒu qiántú 有前途

**promote** *employee* jìnshēng 晋升; (*encourage, foster*) zēngjìn 增进; COM xuānchuán 宣传

**promoter** (*of sports event*) chuàngbànrén 创办人

**promotion** (*of employee*) jìnjí 晋级; (*of scheme, idea*) xuānchuán 宣传; COM cùxiāo 促销

**prompt 1** *adj* (*on time*) zhǔnshí 准时; (*speedy*) jíshí 及时 **2** *adv*: **at two o'clock ~** liǎngdiǎnzhěng 两点正 **3** *v/t* (*cause*) jīqǐ 激起; *actor* tící 提词 **4** *n* COMPUT tíshìfú 提示符

**promptly** (*on time*) jíshí 及时; (*immediately*) lìjí 立即

**prone**: **be ~ to** yìyú zuò 易于做

**pronoun** dàicí 代词

**pronounce** *word* fāyīn 发音; (*declare*) xuānbù 宣布

**pronounced** *accent* míngxiǎn 明显; *views* míngquè 明确

**pronunciation** fāyīn 发音

**proof** *n* zhèngjù 证据; (*of book*) jiàoyàng 校样

**prop 1** *v/t* xiékào 斜靠 **2** *n* (*in theater*) dàojù 道具

♦**prop up** zhīchēngqǐ 支撑起; *regime* zhīchí 支持

**propaganda** xuānchuán 宣传

**propel** tuījìn 推进

**propellant** (*in aerosol*) qì tuījìn zuòyòng 起推进作用

**propeller** (*of boat*) luóxuánjiǎng 螺旋桨

**proper** (*real*) zhēnzhèng 真正; (*correct*) qiàdàng 恰当; (*fitting*) shìdàng 适当

**properly** (*correctly*) zhèngquè 正确; (*fittingly*) shìdàng 适当

**property** cáichǎn 财产; (*land*) fángdìchǎn 房地产

**property developer** fángdìchǎn kāifārén 房地产开发人

**prophecy** yùyán 预言

**prophesy** zuò yùyán 作预言

**proportion** bǐlì 比例, bùfen bùfen 部分; **~s** (*dimensions*) miànjī 面积

**proportional** chéng bǐlì 成比例

**proposal** (*suggestion*) tíyì 提议; (*of marriage*) qiúhūn 求婚

**propose 1** *v/t* (*suggest*) jiànyì 建议; (*plan*) jìhuà 计划 **2** *v/i* (*make offer of marriage*) qiúhūn 求婚

**proposition 1** *n* jiànyì 建议 **2** *v/t* *woman* tíchū xìngyàoqiú 提出性要求

**proprietor** yèzhǔ 业主

**proprietress** nǚ yèzhǔ 女业主

**prose** sǎnwén 散文

**prosecute** *v/t* LAW tíqǐ gōngsù 提起公诉

**prosecution** LAW qǐsù 起诉; (*lawyers*) yuángàofāng 原告方

**prosecutor** gōngsùrén 公诉人

**prospect 1** *n* (*chance, likelihood*) kěnéng 可能; (*thought of sth in the future*) qīwàng 期望; **~s** qiánjǐng 前景 **2** *v/i*: **~ for** *gold* kāntàn 勘探

**prospective** kěnéng 可能

**prosper** chénggōng 成功

**prosperity** xīngshèng 兴盛

**prosperous** xīngwàng 兴旺

**prostitute** *n* jìnǚ 妓女; **male ~** nánjì 男妓

**prostitution** màiyín 卖淫

**prostrate**: **be ~ with grief** bēitòngyùjué 悲痛欲绝

**protect** *v/t* bǎohù 保护

**protection** bǎohù 保护

**protection money** bǎohùfèi 保护费

**protective** yǒu bǎohùxìng 有保护性

**protector** bǎohù zhě 保护者

**protein** dànbáizhì 蛋白质

**protest 1** n kàngyì 抗议; (*demonstration*) shìwēi 示威 **2** v/t shēnmíng 申明; (*object to*) fǎnduì 反对 **3** v/i shēngbiàn 声辩; (*demonstrate*) shìwēi 示威

**Protestant 1** n Xīnjiàotú 新教徒 **2** adj Xīnjiào 新教

**protester** shìwēi zhě 示威者

**protocol** lǐyí 礼仪

**prototype** móxíng 模型

**protracted** yáncháng 延长

**protrude** v/i tūchū 凸出

**proud** jiāo'ào 骄傲; (*independent*) zìzūn 自尊; **be ~ of** yǐ ... wéi zìháo 以 ... 为自豪

**proudly** zìháo 自豪

**prove** zhèngmíng 证明

**proverb** yànyǔ 谚语

**provide** tígōng 提供; **~ Y to X, ~ X with Y** wèi X tígōng Y 为 X 提供 Y; **~d (that)** (*on condition that*) zhǐyào 只要

♦**provide for** *family* gōngyǎng 供养; **~ X** (*of law etc*) guīdìng X 规定 X

**province** shěng 省

**provincial** *city* shěng 省; *pej* (*attitude*) shǒujiù 守旧

**provision** (*supply*) gōngyìng 供应; (*of law, contract*) tiáokuǎn 条款

**provisional** línshí 临时

**proviso** fùdài tiáojiàn 附带条件

**provocation** tiǎoxìn 挑衅

**provocative** tiǎoxìn 挑衅; (*sexually*) tiǎodòu 挑逗

**provoke** (*cause*) yǐnqǐ 引起; (*annoy*) jīnù 激怒

**prow** NAUT chuánshǒu 船首

**prowess** zhuāncháng 专长

**prowl** v/i (*of tiger etc*) qīngqīng yídòng 轻轻移动; (*of burglar*) qiánxíng 潜行

**prowler** guǐguǐsuìsuìde rén 鬼鬼祟祟的人

**proximity** línjìn 邻近

**proxy** (*authority*) dàilǐ quán 代理权; (*person*) dàilǐ rén 代理人

**prude** jiǎzhèngjīng 假正经

**prudence** shěnshèn 审慎

**prudent** shěnshèn 审慎

**prudish** jiǎzhèngjīng 假正经

**prune**[1] n xīméifú 西梅脯

**prune**[2] v/t *plant* xiūjiǎn 修剪; *fig* xuējiǎn 削减

**pry** dǎtīng 打听

♦**pry into** cìtàn 刺探

**PS** (= **postscript**) dùjí 又及

**PSB** (= **Public Security Bureau**) Gōng'ān Jú 公安局

**pseudonym** huàmíng 化名

**psychiatric** jīngshénbìng 精神病

**psychiatrist** jīngshénkē yīshēng 精神科医生

**psychiatry** jīngshénbìngxué 精神病学

**psychic** adj yǒu tèyì gōngnéng 有特异功能

**psychoanalysis** jīngshén fēnxī 精神分析

**psychoanalyst** jīngshén fēnxīxuéjiā 精神分析学家

**psychoanalyze** zuò jīngshén fēnxī 作精神分析

**psychological** xīnlǐ 心理

**psychologically** xīnlǐ 心理

**psychologist** xīnlǐxuéjiā 心理学家

**psychology** xīnlǐxué 心理学

**psychopath** jīngshén biàntài zhě 精神变态者

**puberty** qīngchūnqī 青春期

**pubic hair** yīnmáo 阴毛

**public 1** adj gōngzhòng 公众 **2** n: **the ~** mínzhòng 民众; **in ~** dāngzhòng 当众

**publication** (*of book, report*) chūbǎn 出版; (*by newspaper*) kānchū 刊出; (*book, newspaper*) chūbǎnwù 出版物

**publicity** xuānchuán 宣传

**publicize** (*make known*) xuānchuán 宣传; COM zuò guǎnggào 作广告

**publicly** dāngzhòng 当众

**public minibus** xiǎo gōnggòng 小公共; **public prosecutor** gōngsùrén 公诉人; **public relations** gōngguān 公关; **public school** gōngxué 公学; **public sector** zhèngfǔ jīgòu 政府机构; **Public Security Bureau** Gōng'ān Jú 公安局

**publish** chūbǎn 出版

publisher chūbǎnshè 出版社
publishing chūbǎnyè 出版业
publishing company chūbǎn gōngsī 出版公司
puddle n shuǐkēng 水坑
puff **1** n (of wind, smoke) yīgǔ 一股 **2** v/i (pant) chuǎnxī 喘息; *~ on a cigarette* yīkǒuyīkǒude chōuyān 一口一口地抽烟
puffy eyes, face péngzhàng 膨胀
pull **1** n (on rope) lā 拉; F (appeal) xīyǐnlì 吸引力; F (influence) yǐngxiǎnglì 影响力 **2** v/t (drag) lā 拉; (tug) chě 扯; tooth bá 拔; muscle lāshāng 拉伤 **3** v/i zhuài 拽
♦ pull apart (separate) lākāi 拉开
♦ pull away v/t chōukāi 抽开
♦ pull down (lower) làxià 拉下; (demolish) chāihuǐ 拆毁
♦ pull in v/i (of bus, train) jìn zhàn 进站
♦ pull off leaves etc lādiào 拉掉; F deal zuòchéng shì 做成事
♦ pull out **1** v/t chōuchū 抽出; troops chèlí 撤离 **2** v/i (of an agreement, a competition) tuìchū 退出; (of troops) chèlí 撤离; (of ship) shǐchū 驶出
♦ pull through (from an illness) kāngfù 康复
♦ pull together **1** v/i (cooperate) tōnglìhézuò 通力合作 **2** v/t: *pull oneself together* kòngzhì zìjǐ 控制自己
♦ pull up **1** v/t (raise) tíqǐ 提起; plant, weeds báqǐ 拔起 **2** v/i (of car etc) tíng 停
pulley huálún 滑轮
pullover jǐnshēn tàoshān 紧身套衫
pulp guǒròu 果肉; (for paper-making) zhǐjiāng 纸浆
pulpit bùdàotán 布道坛
pulsate (of heart, blood) bódòng 搏动; (of rhythm) chàndòng 颤动
pulse màibó 脉搏
pump **1** n (machine) ⇩ bèng 泵; (gas ~) qìyóubèng 汽油泵 **2** v/t yòng bèng chōuyà 用泵抽压
♦ pump up gěi … chōngqì 给 … 充气

pumpkin nánguā 南瓜
pun shuāngguānyǔ 双关语
punch **1** n (blow) jīdǎ 击打; (implement) dǎkǒngjī 打孔机 **2** v/t (with fist) yòng quán jī 用拳击; hole, ticket dǎ kǒng 打孔
punch line miàoyǔ 妙语
punctual zhǔnshí 准时
punctuality shǒushí 守时
punctually zhǔnshí 准时
punctuate jiā biāodiǎn 加标点
punctuation biāodiǎn fúhào yòngfǎ 标点符号用法
punctuation mark biāodiǎn fúhào 标点符号
puncture **1** n xiǎokǒng 小孔 **2** v/t chuān kǒng 穿孔
pungent cìbí 刺鼻
punish person chéngfá 惩罚
punishing pace, schedule chīlì 吃力
punishment chéngfá 惩罚
puny person ruòxiǎo 弱小
pup yòuxiǎo dòngwù 幼小动物
pupil[1] (of eye) tóngkǒng 瞳孔
pupil[2] (student) xuésheng 学生
puppet mù'ǒu 木偶
puppet government kuǐlěi zhèngfǔ 傀儡政府
puppet show mù'ǒuxì 木偶戏
puppy xiǎogǒu 小狗
purchase[1] n & v/t gòumǎi 购买
purchase[2] (grip) jǐnwò 紧握
purchaser mǎizhǔ 买主
pure silk, wool chún 纯; air, water jiéjìng 洁净; white etc chúncuì 纯粹; sound chúnzhèng 纯正; (morally) chúnjié 纯洁
purely wánquán 完全
purge **1** n (of political party) zhěngsù 整肃 **2** v/t qīngchú 清除
purify water jìnghuà 净化
puritan qīngjiàotú 清教徒
puritanical qīngjiàotúshì 清教徒式
purity chúndù 纯度; (moral) chúnjié 纯洁
purple adj zǐsè 紫色
Purple Heart MIL Zǐxīn Xúnzhāng 紫心勋章
purpose (aim, object) mùdì 目的;

*on* ~ gùyì 故意
**purposeful** jiāndìng 坚定
**purposely** yǒuyì 有意
**purr** *v/i* (*of cat*) hūlushēng 呼噜声
**purse** *n* (*pocketbook*) shǒudài 手袋
**pursue** *v/t person* zhuīzhú 追逐;
*career* zhuīqiú 追求; *course of action* jìxù jìnxíng 继续进行
**pursuer** zhuīgǎn zhě 追赶者
**pursuit** (*chase*) zhuīgǎn 追赶; (*of happiness etc*) zhuīqiú 追求;
(*activity*) huódòng 活动; *those in* ~ nàxiē zhuībǔ de rén 那些追捕的人
**pus** nóng 脓
**push 1** *n* (*shove*) tuī 推; (*of button*) àn 按 **2** *v/t* (*shove*) tuī 推; *button* àn 按; (*pressurize*) bīpò 逼迫;
*drugs* fànmài 贩卖; *be ~ed for X* (*be short of*) X jǐn 紧; *be ~ing 40* kuài sìshí le 快四十了 **3** *v/i* tuī 推
◆**push along** *cart etc* xiàng qián tuī 向前推
◆**push away** tuīkāi 推开
◆**push off 1** *v/t lid* tuīdiào 推掉 **2** *v/i* (*leave*) líkāi 离开; ~! zǒukāi! 走开!
◆**push on** *v/i* (*continue*) jìxù qiánjìn 继续前进
◆**push up** *prices* shàngtiáo 上调
**push-button** yòng ànniǔ cāozòng 用按纽操纵
**pusher** (*of drugs*) dúpǐn fànzi 毒品贩子
**push-up** fǔ wòchēng 俯卧撑
**pushy** kěyǐ cǐ 苛求
**puss, pussy** (*cat*) māomī 猫咪
**put** fàng 放; *question* wèn 问; ~ *the cost at ...* gūjià ... 估价 ...
◆**put aside** *money* chǔcún 储存; *work* fàngzài yībiān 放在一边
◆**put away** (*in closet etc*) shōuqǐlái 收起来; (*in institution*) guānjìn 关进; (*consume*) hē 喝; *money* chǔcún 储存; *animal* jiéguǒ 结果
◆**put back** (*replace*) fànghuí yuánchù 放回原处
◆**put by** *money* chǔcún 储存
◆**put down** fàngxià 放下; *deposit* fù dìngjīn 付定金; *rebellion*

zhènyā 镇压; (*belittle: person*) qīngshì 轻视; (*in writing*) xièxià 写下; *put one's foot down* (*in car*) cǎi yóuménr 踩油门儿; (*be firm*) jiāndìng 坚定; *put X down to Y* (*attribute*) bǎ X guīyīn yú Y 把 X 归因于 Y
◆**put forward** *idea etc* jiànyì 建议
◆**put in** fàngjìnqù 放进去; *time* fùchū 付出; *request, claim* chéngjiāo 呈交
◆**put in for** shēnqǐng 申请
◆**put off** *light, radio, TV* guāndiào 关掉; (*postpone*) tuīchí 推迟; (*deter*) shǐ rén búzuò 使人不做; (*repel*) gǎndào fǎngǎn 感到反感; *put X off Y* shǐ X bù xǐhuān Y 使 X 不喜欢 Y
◆**put on** *light, radio, TV* dǎkāi 打开; *tape, music* fàng 放; *jacket, shoes* chuān 穿; *make-up* cháyòng 搽用; *brake* shā 刹; (*perform*) yǎnchū 演出; (*assume*) jiǎzhuāng 假装; ~ *weight* zēngjiā tǐzhòng 增加体重; *she's just putting it on* tā zhǐshì zhuāng de 她只是装底
◆**put out** *hand* shēnchū 伸出; *fire* xīmiè 熄灭; *light* guāndiào 关掉
◆**put through** (*on phone*) jiētōng 接通
◆**put together** (*assemble*) zǔhéchéng yītǐ 组合成一体; (*organize*) zǔzhī 组织
◆**put up** *v/t hand* jǔqǐ 举起; (*give a bed to*) gōngyìng shísù 供应食宿; (*erect*) shùqǐ 竖起; *prices* tígāo 提高; *poster, notice* zhāngtiē 张贴; *money* tígōng 提供; ~ *for sale* chūshòu 出售
◆**put up with** (*tolerate*) rěnshòu 忍受
**putty** yóuhuī 油灰
**puzzle 1** *n* (*mystery*) mí 谜; (*game*) zhìlì yóuxì 智力游戏; (*jigsaw* ~) pīntú wánjù 拼图玩具; (*crossword* ~) zònghéng zìmí 纵横字谜 **2** *v/t* shǐkùnhuò 使困惑
**puzzling** lìngrén fèijiě 令人费解
**PVC** jùlǜyǐxī 聚氯乙烯
**pylon** diànlǎntǎ 电缆塔
**pyramid selling** chuánxiāo 传销

# Q

Qin Dynasty Qín Cháo 秦朝
Qing Dynasty Qīng Cháo 清朝
quack¹ 1 n (of duck) guāgua yīshēng 呱呱一声 2 v/i guāgua jiào 呱呱叫
quack² F (bad doctor) jiānghú yīshēng 江湖医生
quadrangle (figure) sìbiān xíng 四边形; (courtyard) sìfāng yuàn 四方院
quadruped sìzú dòngwù 四足动物
quadruple v/i chéng sìbèi 成四倍
quadruplets sì bāotāi 四胞胎
quaint little cottage gǔyǎ xiǎoqiǎo 古雅小巧; (slightly eccentric: ideas etc) gǔguài 古怪
quake 1 n (earthquake) dìzhèn 地震 2 v/i (of earth) dìzhèn 地震; (with fear) duōsuo 哆嗦
qualification (from university etc) wénpíng 文凭; (of remark etc) xiànjué tiáojiàn 先决条件; have the right ~s for a job yǒu zuò yīfèn gōngzuò de zīgé 有做一份工作的资格
qualified doctor, engineer etc hégé 合格; (restricted) yǒu xiàndù 有限度; I am not ~ to judge wǒ bùgòu zīgé lái juédìng 我不够资格来决定
qualify 1 v/t (of degree, course etc) shǐ jùyǒu zīgé 使具有资格; remark etc xiànzhì 限制 2 v/i (get degree etc) qǔdé zīgé 取得资格; (in competition) qǔdé bǐsài zīgé 取得比赛资格; our team has qualified for the semi-final wǒmen duì huòdé cānjiā bànjuésài de zīgé 我们队获得参加半决赛的资格; that doesn't ~ as ... nà bùsuàn ... 那不算 ...
quality zhìliàng 质量; (characteristic) tèxìng 特性

quality control (activity) zhìliàng kòngzhì 质量控制; (department) zhìliàng guǎnlǐ 质量管理
qualm dānyōu 担忧; have no ~s about ... bù dānyōu ... 不担忧 ...
quantify yòng shùliàng biǎoshì 用数量表示
quantity liàng liàng 量
quarantine gélí 隔离
quarrel n & v/i chǎozuǐ 吵嘴
quarrelsome ài chǎojià 爱吵架
quarry (for mining) cǎishíchǎng 采石场
quart kuātuō 夸脱
quarter 1 n sìfēn zhīyī 四分之一; (part of town) dìqū 地区; a ~ of an hour yīkèzhōng 一刻钟; a ~ to 5 chà yīkè wǔdiǎn 差一刻五点; ~ past 5 wǔdiǎn yīkè 五点一刻 2 v/t fēnchéng sìfèn 分成四份
quarterback SP sìfēnwèi 四分卫; quarterfinal sìfēn zhīyī juésài 四分之一决赛; quarterfinalist jìnrù sìfēn zhīyī juésài zhě 进入四分之一决赛者
quarterly adj & adv jìdù 季度
quarternote MUS sìfēn yīnfú 四分音符
quarters MIL yíngfáng 营房
quartet (instrumentalists) sì chóngzòu 四重奏; (singers) sì chóngchàng 四重唱
quartz shíyīng 石英
quaver 1 n (in voice) chàndǒu 颤抖 2 v/i (of voice) chàndǒu 颤抖
queen nǚwáng 女王; (monarch's wife) wánghòu 王后
queen bee fēngwáng 蜂王
queer (peculiar) gǔguài 古怪
quench flames xīmiè 熄灭; ~ one's thirst zhǐkě 止渴
query 1 n yíwèn 疑问 2 v/t (express doubt about) duì ... biǎoshì yíwèn 对 ... 表示疑问;

(*check*) wèn 问; **~ X with Y** wèn Y yǒuguān X 问 Y 有关 X

**question 1** *n* wèntí 问题; **in ~** (*being talked about*) suǒtán 所谈; (*in doubt*) bèi huáiyí 被怀疑; **it's a ~ of money / time** shì qián / shíjiān de wèntí 是钱 / 时间的问题; **that's out of the ~** bù kěnéng 不可能 **2** *v/t person* wèn 问; LAW shěnwèn 审问; (*doubt*) huáiyí 怀疑

**questionable** *honesty* kě huáiyí 可怀疑; *figures, statement* bù kěxìn 不可信

**questioning** *look, tone* cháwèn 查问

**question mark** yídiǎn 疑点

**questionnaire** wèndá juàn 问答卷

**quick** kuài 快; **be ~!** kuàidiǎnr! 快点儿!; **let's have a ~ drink** wǒmen kuàizhe hē diǎnr ba 我们快着喝点儿吧; **can I have a ~ look?** wǒ néngbùnéng kàn yīyàn? 我能不能看一眼?; **that was ~!** zhème kuài! 这么快!

**quicksand** liúshā 流沙; **quicksilver** shuǐyín 水银; **quickwitted** jīmǐn 机敏

**quiet** *voice, music* xiǎoshēng 小声; *engine* dī zàoyīn 低噪音; *street* ānjìng 安静; *life, town* píngjìng 平静; **keep ~ about X** bù tí X de shì 不提X的事; **~!** bìzuǐ! 闭嘴!
♦ **quieten down 1** *v/t children, class* shǐ ānjìng 使安静 **2** *v/i* (*of children*) ānjìng xiàlái 安静下来; (*of political situation*) píngjìng xiàlái 平静下来

**quilt** (*on bed*) bèizi 被子

**quinine** kuíníng 奎宁

**quip 1** *n* qiàopí huà 俏皮话 **2** *v/i* shuō qiàopí huà 说俏皮话

**quirky** gǔguài 古怪; *machine* bù wěndìng 不稳定

**quit 1** *v/t job* cízhí 辞职; **~ doing X** fàngqì zuò X 放弃做 X **2** *v/i* (*leave job*) cízhí 辞职; COMPUT tuìchū 退出

**quite** (*fairly*) xiāngdāng 相当; (*completely*) wánquán 完全; **not ~ ready** méi wánquán zhǔnbèi hǎo 没完全准备好; **I didn't ~ understand** wǒ bū tài míngbái 我不太明白; **is that right? – not ~** duìma? – bù wánquán duì ma ? – 不完全; **~!** zhèngshì zhèyàng! 正是这样!; **~ a lot** hěn duō 很多; **it was ~ a surprise / change** zhēn jīngrén / biànhuà xiāngdāng dà 真惊人 / 变化相当大

**quits: be ~ with X** (*person*) yǔ X liǎngqīng 与X两清

**quiver** *v/i* chàndǒu 颤抖

**quiz 1** *n* wèndá bǐsài 问答比赛 **2** *v/t* pánwèn 盘问

**quiz program** wèndá bǐsài jiémù 问答比赛节目

**quota** dìngliàng 定量

**quotation** (*from author*) yǐnwén 引文; (*price*) bàojià 报价; **give X a ~ for Y** gěi X tígōng yīgè Y de bàojià 给X提供一个Y的报价

**quotation marks** yǐnhào 引号

**quote 1** *n* (*from author*) yǐnwén 引文; (*price*) bàojià 报价; (*quotation mark*) yǐnhào 引号 **2** *v/t text* yǐnyòng 引用; *price* bàojià 报价 **3** *v/i*: **~ from an author** yǐnyòng yīgè zuòjiā de zuòpǐn 引用一个作家的作品

# R

rabbit tùzi 兔子

rabies kuángquǎn bìng 狂犬病

raccoon huànxióng 浣熊

race² n (of people) zhǒngzú 种族

race² 1 n SP jìngsài 竞赛; **the ~s** (horse ~s) pǎomǎ 跑马 2 v/i (run fast) jíxíng 疾行; SP cānjiā jìngsài 参加竞赛; **he ~d through his meal / work** tā xùnsù chīwánle fàn / zuòwánle gōngzuò 他迅速吃完了饭 / 做完了工作 3 v/t: **I'll ~ you** wǒ hé nǐ bǐsài 我和你比赛

racecourse pǎomǎ dào 跑马道

racehorse bǐsài yòng mǎ 比赛用马; racetrack pǎodào 跑道

racial zhǒngzú 种族; **~ equality** zhǒngzú píngděng 种族平等

racing jìngsài 竞赛

racing car sàichē 赛车

racing driver sàichē yùndòngyuán 赛车运动员

racism zhǒngzú qíshì 种族歧视

racist 1 n zhǒngzú qíshì zhě 种族歧视者 2 adj zhǒngzú qíshì 种族歧视

rack 1 n (for parking bikes) zìxíngchē jià 自行车架; (for bags on train) xínglì jià 行李架; (for CDs) chàngpiān jià 唱片架 2 v/t: **~ one's brains** jiǎojìn nǎozhī 绞尽脑汁

racket¹ SP qiúpāi 球拍

racket² (noise) xuānnào 喧闹; (criminal activity) piànjú 骗局

radar léidá 雷达

radiant smile, appearance hóngguāng mǎnmiàn 红光满面

radiate v/i (of heat, light) guāngmáng sìshè 光芒四射

radiation PHYS fàngshè 放射

radiator (in room) nuǎnqì 暖气; (in car) qūnuǎn qì 取暖器

radical 1 adj chèdǐ 彻底; POL views

jījìn 激进 2 n POL jījìn zhǔyì zhě 激进主义者

radicalism POL jījìn zhǔyì 激进主义

radically chèdǐ 彻底

radio shōuyīnjī 收音机; **on the ~** shōuyīnjī lǐ 收音机里; **by ~** yòng wúxiàndiàn 用无线电

radioactive fàngshè xìng 放射性

radioactivity fàngshè xìng 放射性; radio alarm shōuyīnjī nàozhōng 收音机闹钟; radio station guǎngbō diàntái 广播电台; radio taxi wúxiàn chūzūchē 无线出租车; radio telephone wúxiàn diànhuà 无线电话; radiotherapy fàngshè liáofǎ 放射疗法

radish xiǎoluóbo 小萝卜

radius bànjìng 半径

raffle n chōujiǎng 抽奖

raft mùpái 木排

rafter chuánzi 椽子

rag (for cleaning etc) mābù 抹布

rage 1 n kuángnù 狂怒; **be in a ~** fānù fāxíng 发怒; **all the ~** fēngxíng yīshí 风行一时 2 v/i (of person) fānù fāxíng 发怒; (of storm) kuángbào 狂暴

ragged edge pòlàn 破烂; appearance luàn péngpeng 乱蓬蓬; clothes lánlǚ 褴褛

raid 1 n (by troops, police) tūxí 突袭; (by robbers) qiǎngjié 抢劫; FIN jítǐ pāoshòu 集体抛售 2 v/t (of troops, police) tūrán sōuchá 突然搜查; (of robbers) tūrán xíjī 突然袭击

raider (on bank etc) qiǎngjié fàn 抢劫犯

rail (on track) tiěguǐ 铁轨; (hand~) fúshǒu 扶手; (for towel) máojīn jià 毛巾架; **by ~** (of people) zuò huǒchē 坐火车; (of goods) yòng tiělù 用铁路

**railings** *(around park etc)* lángān 栏杆

**railroad** tiělù 铁路

**railroad station** huǒchē zhàn 火车站

**rain 1** *n* yǔ 雨; *in the* ~ yǔzhōng 雨中; *the* ~s yǔjì 雨季 **2** *v/i* xiàyǔ 下雨; *it's* ~*ing* xià zhe yǔ ne 下着雨呢

**rainbow** cǎihóng 彩虹; **rain-check**: *can I take a* ~ *on that?* *(take up offer later)* shìfǒu kěyǐ tuīchí? 是否可以推迟？; **rain-coat** yǔyī 雨衣; **raindrop** yǔdiǎnr 雨点儿; **rainfall** jiàngyǔ liàng 降雨量; **rain forest** yǔlín 雨林; **rainstorm** bàofēngyǔ 暴风雨

**rainy** duōyǔ 多雨; *it's* ~ lǎo xiàyǔ 老下雨

**rainy season** yǔjì 雨季

**raise 1** *n (in salary)* zēngjiā 增加 **2** *v/t shelf etc* shēnggāo 升高; *offer* tígāo 提高; *children* fǔyǎng 抚养; *question* tíchū 提出; *money* chóují 筹集

**raisin** pútáo gān 葡萄干

**rake** *n (for garden)* pázi 耙子

**rally round 1** *v/i* jíhuì jíhé集会; MOT gōnglù sàichē 公路赛车; *(in tennis)* liánxù duìdǎ 连续对打

♦**rally round 1** *v/i* jíhé qǐlái jíhé qǐlái 集合起来 **2** *v/t*: ~ *X* tuánjié zài X de zhōuwéi 团结在 X 的周围

**RAM** (= *random access memory*) nèicún 内存

**ram 1** *n* gōngyáng 公羊 **2** *v/t ship, car* zhuàng 撞

**ramble 1** *n (walk)* mànbù 漫步 **2** *v/i (walk)* mànbù 漫步; *(when speaking)* dōnglā xīchě 东拉西扯; *(talk incoherently)* màntán 漫谈

**rambler** *(walker)* mànbù zhě 漫步者

**rambling** *n (walking)* mànbù 漫步; *(in speech)* dōnglā xīchě 东拉西扯 **2** *adj speech* màntán 漫谈

**ramp** pōdào 坡道; *(for raising vehicle)* xiépō 斜坡; *(unevenness in road)* qīngxié lùmiàn 倾斜路面

**rampage 1** *v/i* héngchōng zhízhuàng 横冲直撞 **2** *n*: *go on the* ~ bàotiào rúléi 暴跳如雷

**rampart** bìlěi 壁垒

**ramshackle** yáoyao yùzhuì 摇摇欲坠

**ranch** dà mùchǎng 大牧场

**rancher** mùchǎng zhǔ 牧场主

**rancid** hāla 哈喇

**rancor** jīyuàn 积怨

**R & D** (= *research and development*) yánfā 研发

**random 1** *adj* suíjī 随机; ~ *sample* suíjī chōuyàng 随机抽样 **2** *n*: *at* ~ suíbiàn 随便

**range 1** *n (of products)* xìliè 系列; *(of gun)* shèchéng 射程; *(of airplane)* zuìdà chángxíng 最大行程; *(of voice)* yīnyù 音域; *(of mountains)* shānmài 山脉 **2** *v/i*: ~ *from X to Y* zài X yǔ Y zhījiān 在 X 与 Y 之间

**ranger** *(for park and forest)* hùlínyuán 护林员; *(police in thinly populated area)* qíjǐng 骑警

**rank 1** *n* MIL jūnxián 军衔; *(in society)* děngjí 等级; *the* ~s MIL shìbīng 士兵 **2** *v/t* pái pái 排

♦**rank among** zài ... zhī liè 在 ... 之列

**ransack** xǐjié 洗劫

**ransom** *n* shújīn 赎金; *hold X to* ~ bǎngpiào 绑票

**rant** *v/i*: ~ *and rave* kǒutǔ kuángyán 口吐狂言

**rap 1** *n (at door etc)* kòujī shēng 叩击声; MUS shuōchàng yīnyuè 说唱音乐 **2** *v/t table etc* kòujī 叩击

♦**rap** *at window etc* qiāo 敲

**rape** *n & v/t* qiángjiān 强奸

**rape victim** qiángjiān shòuhài zhě 强奸受害者

**rapid** kuài 快

**rapidity** kuàisù 快速

**rapids** jíliú 急流

**rapist** qiángjiān fàn 强奸犯

**rapture** xīnxǐ ruòkuáng 欣喜若狂

**rapturous** huānxǐ 欢喜

**rare** hǎnjiàn 罕见; *steak* chūshú 初熟

**rarely** hěnshǎo 很少

**rarity** xīshǎo 稀少

**rascal** xiǎo táoqì 小淘气

**rash**[1] MED pízhěn 皮疹

**rash**[2] *action, behavior* lǔmǎng 鲁莽

**raspberry** xuángōuzi 悬钩子

**rat** lǎoshǔ 老鼠

**rate 1** n (*of exchange*) bǐlǜ 比率; (*of pay*) lǜ 率; (*price*) jiàgé 价格; (*speed*) sùdù 速度; ~ *of interest* FIN lìxī lǜ 利息率; *at this* ~ (*at this speed*) zhào zhèyàng de sùdù 照这样的速度; (*carrying on like this*) zhào zhèyàng 照这样 **2** v/t (*consider, rank*) rènwéi 认为

**rather** xiāngdāng 相当; *I would* ~ *stay here* wǒ qíngyuàn zài zhèr zhù 我情愿在这儿住; *or would you* ~ ... ? nǐ shìfǒu gèng xǐhuān ...? 你是否更喜欢 ... ?

**ration 1** n pèijǐ liàng 配给量 **2** v/t *supplies* dìngliàng gōngyìng 定量供应

**rational** hélǐ 合理

**rationality** hélǐ xìng 合理性

**rationalization** (*of production etc*) hélǐ huà 合理化

**rationalize 1** v/t *production etc* shǐ hélǐ huà 使合理化; *emotions, one's actions etc* jiěshì 解释 **2** v/i zhǎo jièkǒu 找借口

**rat race** shǔpīn 鼠拼

**rattle 1** n (*noise*) gāga shēng 嘎嘎声; (*toy*) bōlàng gǔ 拨浪鼓 **2** v/t *chains etc* shǐ fāchū gāga shēng 使发出嘎嘎声 **3** v/i (*of chains etc*) fāchū gāga shēng 发出嘎嘎声; (*of crates*) fāchū gāla gāla shēng 发出嘎拉嘎拉声

♦**rattle off** *poem, list of names* yìkǒuqìde shuō 一口气地说

**rattlesnake** xiǎngwěishé 响尾蛇

**ravage:** ~*d by war* shòudào zhànzhēng de chuàngshāng 受到战争的创伤

**rave** v/i (*talk deliriously*) jiǎng húhuà 讲胡话; (*talk wildly*) húchě 胡扯; ~ *about X* (*be very enthusiastic*) kuángrè de tánlùn X 狂热地谈论 X

**raven** dà wūyā 大乌鸦

**ravenous** *appetite* èhuàile 饿坏了

**rave review** jiàokǒu chēngzàn 交口称赞

**ravine** shēngǔ 深谷

**raving:** ~ *mad* fēngle 疯了

**ravishing** mírén 迷人

**raw** *meat, vegetable* shēng 生; *sugar, iron* wèijīng jiāgōng 未经加工

**raw materials** yuán cáiliào 原材料

**ray** guāngxiàn 光线; *a* ~ *of hope* yīxiàn xīwàng 一线希望

**razor** tìxū dāo 剃须刀

**razor blade** tìxū dāo dāopiàn 剃须刀刀片

**re** COM yǒuguān 有关

**reach 1** n: *within* ~ zài fùjìn 在附近; *out of* ~ ná bùdào 拿不到 **2** v/t *city etc* dàodá 到达; (*go as far as*) dào 到; *decision, agreement, conclusion* dédào 得到

♦**reach out** shēnchū shǒu 伸出手

**react** fǎnyìng 反应

**reaction** fǎnyìng 反应

**reactionary** n & adj POL fǎndòng pài 反动派

**reactor** (*nuclear*) fǎnyìng duī 反应堆

**read 1** v/t *book. disk* dú 读; *Chinese* rènshi 认识 **2** v/i yuèdú 阅读; ~ *to X* dúgěi X tīng 读给 X 听

♦**read out** (*aloud*) lǎngsòng 朗诵

♦**read up on** yuèdú xuéxí 阅读学习

**readable** *handwriting* yìdú 易读

**reader** (*person*) dúzhě 读者

**readily** *admit, agree* xīnrán 欣然

**readiness** (*for action*) zhǔnbèi jiùxù 准备就绪; (*to agree*) yuànyì 愿意

**reading** (*activity*) yuèdú 阅读; (*from meter etc*) dúshù 读数

**reading matter** yuèdú cáiliào 阅读材料

**readjust 1** v/t *equipment, controls* tiáozhěng 调整 **2** v/i (*to conditions*) shìyìng 适应

**read-only file** COMPUT zhǐdú dǎng'àn 只读档案

**read-only memory** COMPUT zhǐdú cúnchǔ qì 只读存储器

**ready** (*prepared*) zhǔnbèi hǎo 准备好; (*willing*) yuànyì 愿意; **get** (*oneself*) ~ zhǔnbèi hǎo 准备好; **get X** ~ bǎ X zhǔnbèi hǎo 把 X 准备好

**ready-made** *stew, solution etc* xiànchéng 现成

**ready-to-wear** xiànchéng yīfu 现成衣服

**real** *adj* zhēn 真

**real estate** fángdì chǎn 房地产

**realism** xiànshí zhǔyì 现实主义

**realist** xiànshí zhǔyì zhě 现实主义者

**realistic** xiànshí 现实

**reality** xiànshí 现实

**realization** (*of ideal, hope*) shíxiàn 实现

**realize** *v/t truth, importance* yìshí dào 意识到; *ideal, hope* shíxiàn 实现; FIN zhuàndé 赚得; **I ~ now that ...** wǒ xiànzài cái yìshí dào ... 我现在才意识到 ...

**really** zhēnzhèng 真正; (*very*) hěn 很; **~?** zhēnde ma? 真的吗 ? ; **not ~** (*not much*) bù zěnme yàng 不怎么样

**real time** COMPUT shíshí 实时

**realtor** búdòng chǎn zhōngjiān shāng 不动产中间商

**reap** shōugē 收割

**reappear** chóngxiàn 重现

**rear** 1 *n* hòumiàn 后面 2 *adj legs* hòu 后; *seats, wheels, lights* hòumiàn 后面

**rearm** *v/t & v/i* chóngxīn wǔzhuāng 重新武装

**rearmost** zuìhòu 最后

**rearrange** *flowers, furniture* chóngxīn bǎifàng 重新摆放; *schedule, meetings* chóngxīn ānpái 重新安排

**rear-view mirror** hòushì jìng 后视镜

**reason** 1 *n* (*faculty*) lǐzhì 理智; (*cause*) yuányīn 原因 2 *v/i*: **~ with** hé ... jiǎnglǐ hé ... 讲理

**reasonable** *person, behavior* hélǐ 合理; *price* gōngpíng 公平; **a ~ number of people** bùshǎo rén 不少人

**reasonably** *act, behave* hélǐ de 合理地; (*quite*) jīhū 几乎

**reassure** dǎxiāo yílǜ 打消疑虑

**reassuring** lìngrén yǒu xìnxīn 令人有信心

**rebate** (*money back*) zhékòu 折扣

**rebel** *n* fǎnpàn zhě 反叛者; **~ troops** fǎnpàn jūnduì 反叛军队

**rebellion** fǎnpàn 反叛

**rebellious** bù fúguǎn 不服管

**rebound** *v/i* (*of ball etc*) tán huìlái 弹回来

**rebuff** *n* cuòzhé 挫折

**rebuild** chóngjiàn 重建

**rebuke** *v/t* zhǐzé 指责

**recall** *v/t ambassador* zhàohuí 召回; (*remember*) jìqǐ 记起

**recapture** MIL duóhuí 夺回; *criminal* zàicì zhuāhuò 再次抓获

**receding**: **~ hair** kāishǐ tūtóu 开始秃头

**receipt** shōujù 收据; **acknowledge ~ of X** quèrèn shōudào X 确认收到 X; **~s** FIN shōurù 收入

**receive** shōudào 收到

**receiver** (*of letter*) shōuxìn rén 收信人; TELEC tīngtǒng 听筒; (*for radio*) shōuyīnjī 收音机

**receivership**: **be in ~** pòchǎn 破产

**recent** zuìjìn 最近

**recently** zuìjìn 最近

**reception** (*in hotel, company*) jiēdài chù 接待处; (*party*) zhāodài huì 招待会; (*welcome*) huānyíng 欢迎; (*for radio, mobile phone*) jiēshōu lì 接收力

**reception desk** jiēdài chù 接待处

**receptionist** jiēdài yuán 接待员

**receptive**: **be ~ to X** yì jiēshòu X 易接受 X

**recess** (*in wall etc*) āochù 凹处; EDU xiūxi 休息; (*of parliament*) xiūjià 休假

**recession** (*economic*) bù jǐngqì 不景气

**recharge** *battery* chōngdiàn 充电

**recipe** càipǔ 菜谱

**recipient** (*of parcel etc*) jiēshōu rén 接收人; (*of payment*) shōukuǎn rén 收款人

**reciprocal** hùhuì 互惠

recital MUS yǎnzòu huì 演奏会

recite poem bèisòng 背诵; details, facts xùshù 叙述

reckless búgù hòuguǒ 不顾后果

reckon (think, consider) rènwéi 认为

♦reckon with: have X to ~ duìfu X 对付 X

reclaim land from sea shōuhuí 收回

recline v/i xiéyǐ 斜倚

recluse yǐnshì 隐士

recognition (of state, achievements) chéngrèn 承认; changed beyond ~ biànde rènbùchū 变得认不出

recognizable rèndechū 认得出

recognize person, voice, tune rènde 认得; symptoms biànrèn chū 辨认出; POL: state chéngrèn 承认; it can be ~d by … píng … biànrèn chū píng … 辨认出

recollect huíyì 回忆

recollection huíyì 回忆

recommend tuījiàn 推荐

recommendation tuījiàn 推荐

recompense n bǔcháng 补偿; LAW péicháng 赔偿

reconcile people, differences tiáojiě 调解; facts shǐ yīzhì 使一致; ~ oneself to … gānxīn yú … 甘心于…; be ~d (of two people) héhǎo 和好

reconciliation (of people, differences) tiáojiě 调解; (of facts) yīzhì 一致

recondition xiūfù 修复

reconnaissance MIL zhēnchá 侦察

reconsider 1 v/t offer, one's position chóngxīn kǎolǜ 重新考虑 2 v/i chóngxīn kǎolǜ 重新考虑

reconstruct city, one's life chóngjiàn 重建; crime xiànchǎng shìfàn 现场示范

record 1 n MUS chàngpiān 唱片; SP jìlù 纪录; (written document, in database) jìlù 记录; (file) dǎngàn 档案; ~s jìlù 记录; say sth off the ~ fēi guānfāng de shuō 非官方地说; have a criminal ~ yǒu xíngshì jìlù 有刑事记录; have a good ~ for punctuality yíxiàng zhǔnshì 一向

准时 2 v/t (on tape etc) lù lù 录

record-breaking dǎpò jìlù 打破纪录

recorder MUS shùdí 竖笛

record holder jìlù bǎochí zhě 纪录保持者

recording lùyīn 录音

recording studio lùyīn shì 录音室

record player diànchàngjī 电唱机

recoup financial losses míbǔ 弥补

recover 1 v/t sth lost, stolen goods zhǎohuí 找回; composure huīfù 恢复 2 v/i (from illness) huīfù 恢复

recovery (of sth lost, stolen goods) zhǎohuí 找回; (from illness) huīfù 恢复; he has made a good ~ tā huīfù de hěnhǎo 他恢复得很好

recreation yúlè yóuxì 娱乐

recruit 1 n MIL xīnbīng 新兵; (to company) xīnlái de 新来的 2 v/t new staff zhāopìn 招聘; MIL zhēngmù 征募

recruitment zhāopìn 招聘

recruitment drive dà guīmó zhāopìn 大规模招聘

rectangle chángfāng xíng 长方形

rectangular chángfāng xíng 长方形

recuperate huīfù yuánqì 恢复元气

recur zàicì chūxiàn 再次出现

recurrent zàifā 再发

recycle huíshōu 回收

recycling huíshōu 回收

red hóng 红; in the ~ yǒu chìzì 有赤字

Red Army Hóngjūn 红军; Red China Hóngsè Zhōngguó 红色中国; Red Cross Hóngshízì 红十字

redden v/i (blush) biànhóng 变红

redecorate v/t chóngxīn zhuāngxiū 重新装修

redeem debt fùqīng 付清; sinners miǎnzuì 免罪

redeeming adj: ~ feature wéiyī kěqǔ zhīchù 唯一可取之处

redevelop part of town chóngxīn fāzhǎn 重新发展

Red Guard Hóngwèibīng 红卫兵;

red-handed: *catch X ~* dāngchǎng bǔhuò X 当场捕获 X;
redhead yǒu hóng tóufà de rén 有红头发的人; red-hot rè téngteng 热腾腾; red light (*at traffic light*) hóngdēng 红灯; red light district hóngdēng qū 红灯区; red meat niú yáng ròu 牛羊肉; redneck xiāngbālǎo 乡巴佬; red pepper làjiāo 辣椒; red tape guānliáo chéngxù 官僚程序

reduce jiàngdī 降低

reduction jiǎnshǎo 减少

redundant (*unnecessary*) duōyú 多余

reed BOT lúwěi 芦苇

reef (*in sea*) jiāo 礁

reef knot suǒfān jié 缩帆结

reek v/i fā chòuqì 发臭气; *~ of ...* yǒu ... wèir 有 ... 味儿

reel n (*of film, thread*) juǎn 卷

refer 1 v/t: *~ a decision / problem to s.o.* bǎ juédìng / wèntí jiāogěi mǒurén 把决定 / 问题交给某人 2 v/i: *~ to* (*allude to*) tídào ... 提到 ...; (*to dictionary etc*) cānkǎo ... 参考 ...

referee SP cáipàn 裁判; (*for job*) tuījiàn rén 推荐人

reference (*allusion*) shèjí 涉及; (*for job*) tuījiàn 推荐; (*~ number*) cānkǎo hàomǎ 参考号码; *with ~ to* guānyú 关于

reference book cānkǎo shū 参考书

referendum gōngmín tóupiào 公民投票

refill v/t tank, glass zài zhuāngmǎn 再装满

refine oil, sugar tíliàn 提炼; technique shǐ jīngměi 使精美

refined manners, language wényǎ 文雅

refinery tíliàn chǎng 提炼厂

reflation tōnghuò zài péngzhàng 通货再膨胀

reflect 1 v/t light fǎnshè 反射; *be ~ed in ...* fǎnshè zài ... zhīzhōng 反射在 ... 之中 2 v/i (*think*) fǎnxǐng 反省

reflection (*in water, glass etc*) fǎnshè 反射; (*consideration*) fǎnxǐng 反省

reflex (*in body*) fǎnyìng nénglì 反应能力

reflex reaction zìdòng fǎnyìng 自动反应

reform n & v/t gǎigé 改革

refrain[1] v/i yìzhì 抑制; *please ~ from smoking* qǐngwù xīyān 请勿吸烟

refrain[2] n (*in song*) fùgē 副歌; (*in poem*) diéjù 迭句

refresh person shǐ jīngshén zhènzuò 使精神振作; *feel ~ed* gǎndào jīngshén zhènzuò 感到精神振作

refresher course fùxí kèchéng 复习课程

refreshing drink qīngshuǎng 清爽; experience qīngxīn yuèmù 清新悦目

refreshments chádiǎn 茶点

refrigerate lěngcáng 冷藏

refrigerator bīngxiāng 冰箱

refuel v/t & v/i jiā ránliào 加燃料

refuge bìhù 庇护; *take ~* (*from storm etc*) duǒbì 躲避

refugee nànmín 难民

refund n & v/t tuìkuǎn 退款

refusal jùjué 拒绝

refuse: *~ to do X* jùjué zuò X 拒绝做 X

regain control, lost territory, the lead chónghuò 重获

regard 1 n: *have great ~ for* zūnzhòng 尊重; *in this ~* zài zhèi fāngmiàn 在这方面; *with ~ to* guānyú 关于; (*kind*) *~s* wènhòu 问候; *give my ~s to X* dài wǒ wènhòu X 代我问候 X; *with no ~ for ...* bù kǎolù ... 不考虑 ... 2 v/t: *~ X as Y* bǎ X kànzuò Y 把 X 看作 Y; *as ~ X* guānyú X 关于 X

regarding guānyú 关于

regardless háowú gùjì 毫无顾忌; *~ of* búgù 不顾

regime (*government*) zhèngquán 政权

regiment n tuán 团

region dìqū 地区; *in the ~ of* dàyuē

大约

**regional** dìqū 地区

**register 1** n dēngjì bú 登记簿
**2** v/t birth, death dēngjì 登记;
vehicle shàngpái 上牌; letter
guàhào 挂号; emotion xiǎnshì 显
示; **send a ~ed letter** jì guàhào
xìn 寄挂号信 **3** v/i (for a course,
with police) dēngjì 登记

**registered letter** guàhào xìn 挂号
信

**registrar** (of births etc) dēngjì rén
登记人

**registration** (for a course) zhùcè 注
册; (with police) dēngjì 登记

**regret 1** v/t hòuhuǐ 后悔 **2** n yíhàn
遗憾

**regrettable** búxìng 不幸

**regrettably** búxìng 不幸

**regular 1** adj flights dìngqī 定期;
intervals, habits yǒu guīlǜ 有规律;
pattern, shape yúnchèn 匀称;
(normal, ordinary) pǔtōng 普通
**2** n (at bar etc) chángkè 常客

**regulate** kòngzhì 控制

**regulation** (rule) guīzhāng 规章

**rehabilitate** ex-criminal gǎixiéguīzhèng 改邪归正

**rehearsal** páiyǎn 排演

**rehearse** v/t & v/i páiyǎn 排演

**reign** n & v/i tǒngzhì 统治

**reimburse** bǔcháng 补偿

**rein** jiāngshéng 缰绳

**reincarnation** línghún zhuǎnshì 灵
魂转世

**reinforce** structure xiūbǔ 修补;
beliefs jiāqiáng 加强

**reinforced concrete** gāngjīn hùnníng tǔ 钢筋混凝土

**reinforcements** MIL yuánjūn 援军

**reinstate** person in office shǐ fùzhí
使复职; paragraph in text chóng-
xīn bǔshàng 重新补上

**reject** v/t jùjué 拒绝

**rejection** jùjué 拒绝

**relapse** MED jiùbìng fùfā 旧病复
发; **have a ~** jiùbìng fùfā 旧病复
发

**relate 1** v/t story xùshù 叙述; **~ X
to Y** jiāng X yǔ Y liánxì qǐlái 将X
与Y联系起来 **2** v/i: **~ to ...** (be

connected with) yǔ ... yǒu guānlián
与 ... 有关联; **he doesn't ~ to
people** tā hé rén xiāngchǔ bùhǎo
他和人相处不好

**related** (by family) yǒu qīnshǔ
guānxi 有亲属关系; events, ideas
etc xiāngguān 相关

**relation** (in family) qīnshǔ 亲属;
(connection) guānxi 关系; busi-
ness/diplomatic ~s shāngyè/
wàijiāo guānxi 商业/外交关系

**relationship** guānxi 关系; **have a
~** (sexual) fāshēng guānxi 发生关
系

**relative 1** n qīnqi 亲戚 **2** adj
xiāngduì 相对; **X is ~ to Y** X yǔ Y
yǒuguān 有关

**relatively** xiāngduì 相对

**relax 1** v/i fàngsōng 放松; **~!,
don't get angry** xiǎng kāi diǎnr,
bié shēngqì! 想开点儿, 别生
气! **2** v/t muscle fàngsōng 放松;
pace of work sōngxiè 松懈

**relaxation** fàngsōng 放松

**relay 1** v/t message zhuǎngào 转告;
radio, TV signals zhuǎnbō 转播
**2** n: **~ (race)** jiēlì sài 接力赛

**release 1** n (from prison) shìfàng
释放; (of CD etc) fāxíng 发行
**2** v/t prisoner shìfàng 释放;
parking brake sōngkāi 松开;
information gōngbù 公布

**relent** ràngbù 让步

**relentless** (determined) búxiè 不
懈; rain etc wúqíng 无情

**relevance** guānlián 关联

**relevant** yǒuguān 有关

**reliability** kěkào xìng 可靠性

**reliable** kěkào 可靠

**reliably** kěndìng 肯定; **I am ~
informed that ...** wǒ dédào kěkào
xiāoxi shuō ... 我得到可靠消息
说 ...

**reliance** yīkào 依靠; **~ on ...** yīkào
... 依靠 ...

**relic** (object) yíwù 遗物; (of tradition) yísú 遗俗

**relief** kuānwèi 宽慰; **that's a ~**
tàihǎole 太好了; **in ~** (in art)
fúdiāo 浮雕

**relieve** pressure, pain jiǎnqīng 减

轻; (take over from) jiētì 接替; **be ~d** (at news etc) kuānwèi 宽慰

**religion** zōngjiào 宗教

**religious** zōngjiào 宗教

**religiously** (conscientiously) rènzhēn 认真

**relish 1** n (sauce) bàncài zhīr 伴菜汁儿 **2** v/t idea, prospect xīhuan 喜欢

**relive** the past, an event zài tǐyàn 再体验

**relocate** v/i (of business, employee) bānqiān 搬迁

**reluctance** miǎnqiǎng 勉强

**reluctant** miǎnqiǎng 勉强; **be ~ to do X** bù qíngyuàn zuò X 不情愿做 X

**reluctantly** miǎnqiǎng 勉强

♦ **rely on** yīkào 依靠; **~ X to do Y** yīkào X qùzuò Y 依靠 X 去做 Y

**remain** (be left) shèngxia 剩下; (stay) dāizài 呆在; (continue) réngrán 仍然; **~ silent / loyal** bǎochí chénmò / zhōngchéng 保持沉默 / 忠诚

**remainder** (rest) yúxià 余下; MATH yúshù 余数

**remains** (of body) yítǐ 遗体

**remand 1** v/t: **~ X in custody** jūliú X 拘留 X **2** n: **be on ~** huányā 还押

**remark 1** n huà 话 **2** v/t pínglùn 评论

**remarkable** fēifán 非凡

**remarkably** fēifán 非凡

**remarry** v/i zàihūn 再婚

**remedy** n MED liáofǎ 疗法; fig bǔjiù 补救

**remember 1** v/t s.o., sth jìde 记得; **~ to lock the door** jìzhù suǒmén 记住锁门; **~ me to her** tì wǒ wèn tā hǎo 替我问她好 **2** v/i jìde 记得; **I don't ~** wǒ bú jìde 我不记得

**remind** v/t: **~ X to do Y** tíxǐng X zuò Y 提醒 X 做 Y; **~ X of Y** (call to mind) shǐ X xiǎngqǐ Y 使 X 想起 Y

**reminder** tíxǐng wù 提醒物; (COM: for payment) cuīzhàng dān 催账单

**reminisce** huáijiù 怀旧

**reminiscent: be ~ of X** huíyì qǐ X 回忆起 X

**remnant** cánjì 残迹

**remorse** àohuǐ 懊悔

**remorseless** person, pace, demands wúqíng 无情

**remote** village piānpì 偏僻; possibility, connection jíxiǎo 极小; (aloof) lěngmò 冷漠; ancestor jiǔyuǎn 久远

**remote access** COMPUT yuǎnchéng tōnglù 远程通路

**remote control** yáokòng 遥控

**remotely** related, connected shūyuǎn 疏远; **just ~ possible** yǒu jíxiǎo kěnéng xìng 有极小可能性

**removal** (of garbage, demonstrators) yídòng 移动; (of doubt) páichú 排除; (from home) qiānjū 迁居

**remove** yídòng 移动; top, lid nákāi 拿开; growth, tumor qùchú 去除; coat etc tuō 脱; doubt, suspicion jiěchú 解除

**remuneration** bàochóu 报酬

**remunerative** yǒu lìrùn 有利润

**rename** chóngxīn mìngmíng 重新命名

**render** service jǐyǔ 给予; **~ X helpless / unconscious** shǐ X gūlì wúyuán / hūnmí 使 X 孤立无援 / 昏迷

**rendering** (of piece of music) yǎnzòu 演奏

**rendez-vous** (romantic) yuēhuì 约会; MIL zhǐdìng jíhé diǎn 指定集合点

**renew** contract, license zhǎnqī 展期; discussions chóngxīn kāishǐ 重新开始; **feel ~ed** gǎndào jīnglì chōngpèi 感到精力充沛

**renewal** (of contract etc) zhǎnqī 展期; (of discussions) chóngxīn kāishǐ 重新开始

**renminbi** FIN rénmínbì 人民币

**renounce** v/t title, rights xuānbù fàngqì 宣布放弃

**renovate** zhěngxiū 整修

**renovation** zhěngxiū 整修

**renown** shēngyù 声誉

**renowned** zhùmíng 著名

**rent 1** n zūjīn 租金; **for ~** chūzū 出租 **2** v/t apartment, car, equipment zū 租; (~ **out**) chūzū 出租

**rental** (for apartment, for TV etc) zūjīn 租金

**rental agreement** zūyuē 租约

**rental car** zūyòng chē 租用车

**rent-free** adv miǎnzū 免租

**reopen 1** v/t business, store chóngxīn kāizhāng 重新开张; negotiations zài jìnxíng 再进行; LAW: case chóngshěn 重审 **2** v/i (of theater etc) chóngxīn kāizhāng 重新开张

**reorganization** (of business) gǎizǔ 改组; (of room, schedule) chóngxīn ānpái 重新安排

**reorganize** business gǎizǔ 改组; room, schedule chóngxīn ānpái 重新安排; chapter gǎibiān 改编

**rep** COM dàilǐ shāng 代理商

**repaint** chóngxīn shuā yóuqī 重新刷油漆

**repair 1** v/t xiūlǐ 修理 **2** n xiūlǐ 修理; **in a good / bad state of ~** wánhǎo wúsǔn / pòsǔn 完好无损／破损

**repairman** xiūlǐ gōng 修理工

**repatriate** sòng huíguó 送回国

**repay** money chánghuán 偿还; person bàodá 报答

**repayment** fùhuíkuǎn 付回款

**repeal** v/t law fèichú 废除

**repeat 1** v/t sth said, performance, experience chóngfù 重复; **am I ~ing myself?** wǒ shìbùshì chóngfù le? 我是不是重复了？ **2** v/i chóngfù 重复; **I ~, do not touch it** wǒ zàishuō yīcì, biépéng zhè gè 我再说一次，别碰 **3** n (TV program etc) chóngbō 重播

**repeat business** COM huítóu shēngyì 回头生意

**repeated** fǎnfù 反复

**repeat order** COM chóngfù dìnghuò 重复定货

**repel** v/t invaders, attack jītuì 击退; insects qūgǎn 驱赶; (disgust) shǐ yànwù 使厌恶

**repellent 1** n (insect ~) qūchóng jì 驱虫剂 **2** adj lìngrén yànwù 令人厌恶

**repent** v/i hòuhuǐ 后悔

**repercussions** yǐngxiǎng 影响

**repetition** chóngfù 重复

**repetitive** chóngfù 重复

**replace** (put back) fànghuí 放回; (take the place of) tìdài 替代

**replacement** (person) dàitì rén 代替人; (thing) dàitì wù 代替物

**replacement part** tìjiàn 替件

**replay 1** n (recording) chóngfàng 重放; (match) chóngsài 重赛 **2** v/t match chóngsài 重赛

**replica** fùzhì pǐn 复制品

**reply** n, v/t & v/i huídá 回答

**report 1** n (account) bàogào 报告; (by journalist) bàodào 报道 **2** v/t facts bàodào 报道; (to authorities) tōngzhī 通知; **~ one's findings to X** jiāng diàochá jiéguǒ huìbào gěi X 将调查结果汇报给X; **~ X to the police** xiàng jǐngfāng gàofā X 向警方告发X; **he is ~ed to be in Hong Kong** jùshuō tā zài Xiānggǎng 据说他在香港 **3** v/i (of journalist) bàodào 报道; (present oneself) bàodào 报到; **who do you ~ to?** (in business) shuí shì nǐde shàngjí? 谁是你的上级？

**report card** huìbào 汇报

**reporter** jìzhě 记者

**repossess** COM shōuhuí 收回

**reprehensible** yīngshòu zhǐzhāi 应受指摘

**represent** (act for) dàibiǎo 代表; (stand for) zhǔzhāng 主张; (of images in painting etc) miáohuì 描绘

**representative 1** n dàibiǎo rén 代表人; COM dàilǐ shāng 代理商; POL zhòngyìyuán 众议员 **2** adj (typical) diǎnxíng 典型

**repress** revolt zhènyā 镇压; feelings, natural urges yāyì 压抑; laugh rěnzhe 忍着

**repression** POL zhènyā 镇压

**repressive** POL yāzhì 压制

**reprieve** n & v/t also fig huǎnxíng 缓刑

reprimand *v/t* shēnchì 申斥

reprint 1 *n* zàibǎn 再版 2 *v/t* chóngyìn 重印

reprisal bàofù xíngwéi 报复行为; **take ~s** jìnxíng bàofù xíngwéi 进行报复行为

reproach 1 *n* zébèi 备备; **be beyond ~** wúkě zhǐzé 无可指责 2 *v/t* zhǐzé 指责

reproachful zhǐzé 指责

reproduce 1 *v/t atmosphere, mood* zàixiàn 再现 2 *v/i* BIO fánzhí 繁殖

reproduction BIO fánzhí 繁殖; *(of sound, images)* fùzhì 复制; *(piece of furniture)* fùzhì pín 复制品

reproductive BIO fánzhí 繁殖

reptile páxíng dòngwù 爬行动物

republic gònghé guó 共和国

republican 1 *n* gònghé zhǔyì zhě 共和主义者; POL **Republican** Gònghé dàngrén 共和党人 2 *adj* gònghé zhǔyì 共和主义

Republic of China Zhōnghuá Mínguó 中华民国

repudiate *(deny)* fǒudìng 否定

repulsive lìngrén yànwù 令人厌恶

reputable yǒu míngshēng 有名声

reputation míngyù 名誉; **have a good/bad ~** yǒuhǎo/huài míngshēng 有好／坏名声

request 1 *n* yāoqiú 要求; **on ~** yìjīng yāoqiú 一经要求 2 *v/t* yāoqiú 要求

require *(need)* xūyào 需要; **it ~s great care** yào hěn xiǎoxīn 要很小心; **as ~d by law** àn fǎlǜ guīdìng 按法律规定; **guests are ~d to ...** kèrénmen bìxū ... 客人们必须 ...

required *(necessary)* bìyào 必要

requirement *(need)* xūyào 需要; *(condition)* tiáojiàn 条件

reroute *airplane etc* gēnggǎi xiànlù 更改线路

rerun *tape* fùyìng 复映

rescue 1 *n* yuánjiù 援救; **come to X's ~** yuánjiù X 援救 X 2 *v/t* yuánjiù 援救

rescue party yuánjiù duì 援救队

research *n* yánjiū 研究

♦research into yánjiū 研究

research and development yánjiū yǔ fāzhǎn 研究与发展

research assistant zhùlǐ yánjiū yuán 助理研究员

researcher yánjiū yuán 研究员

research project yánjiū kètí 研究课题

resemblance xiāngsì chù 相似处

resemble xiàng 像

resent bùmǎn 不满

resentful bùmǎn 不满

resentment bùmǎn 不满

reservation *(of room, table)* yùdìng 预定; *(mental)* bǎoliú 保留; *(special area)* bǎohù dìqū 保护地区; **I have a ~** wǒ yǒugè yùdìng 我有个预定

reserve 1 *n (store)* chǔbèi 储备; *(aloofness)* hánxù 含蓄; SP yùbèi duìyuán 预备队员; **~s** FIN chǔbèi jīn 储备金; **keep X in ~** chǔbèi X dàiyòng 储备 X 待用 2 *v/t seat, table* yùdìng 预定; *judgment* bǎoliú 保留

reserved *person, manner* nèixiàng 内向; *table, seat* bèi yùdìng 被预定

reservoir *(for water)* shuǐkù 水库

reside zhù 住

residence *(house etc)* zhùsuǒ 住所; *(stay)* jūzhù 居住

residence permit jūliúzhèng 居留证

resident 1 *n* jūmín 居民 2 *adj (living in a building)* zhùdì 驻地

residential district zhùzhái qū 住宅区

residue cánzhā 残渣

resign 1 *v/t position* cízhí 辞职; **~ oneself to** tīngqí zìrán 听其自然 2 *v/i (from job)* cízhí 辞职

resignation *(from job)* cízhí 辞职; *(mental)* wúkě nàihé 无可奈何

resigned tīngtiān yóumìng 听天由命; **we have become ~ to the fact that ...** wǒmen yǐjīng jiēshòu ... 我们已经接受 ...

resilient *personality* dáguān 达观; *material* nàiyòng 耐用

resin sōngxiāng 松香

**resist 1** v/t *enemy, s.o.'s advances* dǐkàng 抵抗; *new measures* dǐzhì 抵制; **~ temptation** bùshòu yòuhuò 不受诱惑 **2** v/i dǐkàng 抵抗

**resistance** (*to enemy, advances*) dǐkàng 抵抗; (*to new measures*) zǔlù 阻力; (*to disease, heat etc*) dǐkàng lì 抵抗力

**resistant** *material* jiāngù 坚固; **~ to heat / rust** fángrè / xiù 防热 / 锈

**resolute** jiānjué 坚决

**resolution** (*decision*) juéyì 决议; (*made at New Year etc*) juédìng 决定; (*determination*) juéxīn 决心; (*of problem*) jiějué fāngfǎ 解决方法; (*of image*) qīngxī dù 清晰度

**resolve** *problem, mystery* jiějué 解决; **~ to do X** juédìng zuò X 决定做 X

**resort 1** n (*place*) dùjià shèngdì 度假胜地; **as a last ~** zuòwéi zuìhòu yìzhāo 作为最后一招

**resounding** *success, victory* chèdǐ 彻底

**resource** zīyuán 资源; **we don't have the ~s for such a big contract** wǒmen méiyǒu zuò zhème dà hétóng de zīyuán 我们没有做这么大合同的资源

**resourceful** zúzhì duōmóu 足智多谋

**respect 1** n zūnjìng 尊敬; (*consideration*) zūnzhòng 尊重; **show ~ to** duì … biǎoshì zūnzhòng 对 … 表示尊重; **with ~ to** guānyú 关于; **in this / that ~** zài zhè / nà fāngmiàn 在这 / 那方面; **in many ~s** zài xǔduō fāngmiàn 在许多方面; **pay one's last ~s to s.o.** xiàng sǐzhě gàobié 向死者告别 **2** v/t *person, s.o.'s opinion, privacy* zūnzhòng 尊重; *law* zūnshǒu 遵守

**respectable** *person* tǐmiàn 体面; *bar* xiàngyàng 象样

**respectful** yǒu lǐmào 有礼貌

**respectfully** yǒu lǐmào 有礼貌

**respective** gèzì 各自

**respectively** fēnbié 分别

**respiration** hūxī 呼吸

**respirator** MED réngōng hūxī qì 人工呼吸器

**respite** huǎnhé 缓和; **without ~** bùtíng 不停

**respond** (*answer*) dáfù 答复; (*react*) zuòchū fǎnyìng 做出反应; (*to treatment*) fǎnyìng 反应

**response** (*answer*) dáfù 答复; (*reaction*) fǎnyìng 反应

**responsibility** zérèn 责任; **accept ~ for** fù zé 负责; (*duty*) zérèn 责任; **a job with more ~** yǒu gèngduō zérèn de gōngzuò 有更多责任的工作

**responsible** (*to blame*) fùzé 负责; (*liable, for children, production etc*) fùzé 负责; (*trustworthy, showing seriousness*) kěkào 可靠; (*involving responsibility: job*) xūyào fùzé 需要负责

**responsive** *audience* yì shòu gǎndòng 易受感动; *brakes* mǐngǎn 敏感

**rest**[1] **1** n xiūxi 休息 **2** v/i xiūxi 休息; **~ on …** (*be based on*) yǐ … wéi jīchǔ 以 … 为基础; (*lean against*) gē zài … shàng 搁在 … 上; **it all ~s with him** dōu zàiyú tāle 都在于他了 **3** v/t (*lean, balance etc*) kào 靠

**rest**[2] n: **the ~** yúxià 余下

**restaurant** cānguǎn 餐馆

**restaurant car** cānchē 餐车

**rest cure** xiūyǎng liáofǎ 休养疗法

**rest home** yǎnglǎo yuàn 养老院

**restless** bù ānfēn 不安分; **have a ~ night** méi shuì hǎo 没睡好

**restoration** xiūfù 修复

**restore** *building etc* xiūfù 修复

**restrain** *dog, troops* yuēshù 约束; *emotions* yìzhì 抑制; **~ oneself** kòngzhì zìjǐ 控制自己

**restraint** (*moderation*) jiézhì 节制

**restrict** xiànzhì 限制; **I'll ~ myself to …** (*in speech, book*) wǒ jǐn tán … zhǐ jǐn tán …

**restricted** *view* shòu xiànzhì 受限制

**restricted area** MIL jìndì 禁地

**restriction** xiànzhì 限制

**rest room** wèishēngjiān 卫生间

**result** n jiéguǒ 结果; *as a ~ of this*
yīncǐ 因此

◆**result from** qǐyú 起于

◆**result in** dǎozhì 导致

**resume** v/t huīfù 恢复

**résumé** lǚlì 履历

**resurface 1** v/t roads lìng pū
lùmiàn 另铺路面 **2** v/i (reappear)
chóngxīn chūxiàn 重新出现

**resurrection** REL fùhuó 复活

**resuscitate** shǐ sūxǐng 使苏醒

**retail 1** adv yǐ língshòu fāngshì 以
零售方式 **2** v/i: *~ at ...* língshòu
jià wéi ... 零售价为...

**retail price** língshòu jià 零售价

**retailer** língshòu shāng 零售商

**retain** bǎoliú 保留

**retainer** FIN pìnjīn 聘金

**retaliate** bàofù 报复

**retaliation** bàofù 报复

**retarded** (mentally) zhìlì chídùn 智
力迟钝

**retire** v/i (from work) tuìxiū 退休

**retired** tuìxiū 退休

**retirement** tuìxiū 退休

**retirement age** tuìxiū niánlíng 退
休年龄

**retiring** miǎntiǎn 腼腆

**retort** n & v/i fǎnbó 反驳

**retrace** footsteps shùn yuánlù fǎnhuí 顺原路返回

**retract** v/t claws suōjìn 缩进;
undercarriage shōusuō 收缩; statement shōuhuí 收回

**retreat 1** v/i MIL chètuì 撤退; (in
discussion etc) tuìràng 退让 **2** n
MIL chètuì 撤退; (place) yǐnjū chù
隐居处

**retrieve** v/t wǎnjiù 挽救

**retriever** (dog) lièquǎn 猎犬

**retroactive** law etc zhuīsù 追溯

**retrograde** move, decision hòutuì
后退

**retrospect** n: *in ~* xiànzài kànlái 现
在看来

**retrospective** huígù 回顾

**return 1** n (coming back, going
back) fǎnhuí 返回; (giving back)
tuìhuán 退还; COMPUT fǎnhuí 返
回; (in tennis) huíqiú 回球; *by ~*

(of post) lìjí huífù 立即回复; *~s*
(profit) lìrùn 利润; *many happy
~s (of the day)* zhù nǐ chángshòu
祝你长寿 **2** v/t (give back)
tuìhuán 退还; (put back) fànghuí
放回; favor, invitation huíbào 回
报 **3** v/i (go back, come back)
fǎnhuí 返回; (of good times, doubts
etc) huífù 回复

**return flight** huíchéng fēijī 回程
飞机

**return journey** huíchéng 回程

**reunification** tǒngyī 统一

**reunion** tuánjù 团聚

**reunite** v/t tǒngyī 统一

**reusable** kě zài yòng 可再用

**reuse** zàiyòng 再用

**rev** n huízhuǎn 回转; *~s per minute* měi fēnzhōng huízhuǎn cìshù
每分钟回转次数

◆**rev up** v/t engine cǎi yóuménr 踩
油门儿

**revaluation** chóngxīn píngjià 重新
评价

**reveal** (make visible) xiǎnshì 显示;
secret, truth jiēlù 揭露; feelings
lùchū 露出

**revealing** remark tòulù zhēnxiàng
透露真相; dress lùtǐ 露体

**revelation** xièlù 泄露

**revenge** n bàofù 报复; *take one's
~* wèi zìjǐ bàochóu 为自己报仇

**revenue** shōurù 收入

**reverberate** (of sound) huíxiǎng 回
响

**revere** chóngjìng 崇敬

**Reverend** mùshī 牧师

**reverent** qiánchéng 虔诚

**reverse 1** adj sequence diāndǎo 颠
倒 **2** n (opposite) xiāngfǎn 相反;
(back) bèimiàn 背面; MOT dàodǎng 倒档 **3** v/t sequence diāndǎo
颠倒; vehicle dàochē 倒车 **4** v/i
MOT dàochē 倒车

**review 1** n (of book, movie) pínglùn
评论; (of troops) jiǎnyuè 检阅;
(of situation etc) shěnchá 审查
**2** v/t book, movie pínglùn 评论;
troops jiǎnyuè 检阅; situation etc
shěnchá 审查; EDU fùxí 复习

**reviewer** (of book, movie) pínglùn

jiā 评论家

revise v/t opinion xiūzhèng 修正；text jiàozhèng 校正

revision (of opinion) xiūzhèng 修正；(of text) jiàozhèng 校正

revisionism POL xiūzhèng zhǔyì 修正主义

revival (of custom, old style etc) fùxīng 复兴；(of patient) sūxīng 苏醒

revive 1 v/t custom, old style etc fùxīng 复兴；patient shǐ sūxīng 使苏醒 2 v/i (of business, exchange rate etc) shǐ shàngshēng 使上升

revoke law fèichú 废除；license qǔxiāo 取消

revolt 1 n fānkàng 反抗 2 v/i zàofǎn 造反

revolting (disgusting) ěxin 恶心

revolution POL etc gémìng 革命；(turn) xuánzhuǎn 旋转；1911 Revolution Xīnhài Gémìng 辛亥革命；1949 Revolution Jiěfàng 解放

revolutionary 1 n POL gémìng jiā 革命家 2 adj spirit, forces gémìng 革命；new ideas chuàngxīn 创新

revolutionize chèdǐ biàngé 彻底变革

revolve v/i xuánzhuǎn 旋转

revolver zuǒlún shǒuqiāng 左轮手枪

revolving door xuánzhuǎn mén 旋转门

revue THEA shíshì fěngcì jù 时事讽刺剧

revulsion fǎngǎn 反感

reward 1 n (financial) shǎngjīn 赏金；(benefit derived) bàochóu 报酬 2 v/t (financially) jiǎnglì 奖励

rewarding experience zhíde zuò 值得做

rewind v/t film, tape dǎo 倒

rewrite v/t chóngxiě 重写

rhetoric huálìde cízǎo 华丽的词藻

rhetorical question fǎnwèn 反问

rheumatism fēngshī bìng 风湿病

rhinoceros xīniú 犀牛

rhubarb cài yòng dàhuáng 菜用大黄

rhyme 1 n yùn 韵 2 v/i yāyùn 压韵；~ with ... yǐ ... yāyùn 以 ... 压韵

rhythm jiézòu 节奏

rib lèigǔ 肋骨

ribbon sīdài 丝带

rice mǐ 米

rice bowl fànwǎn 饭碗；rice cooker diànfànguō 电饭锅；ricefield dàotián 稻田；rice noodles mǐfěn 米粉；rice porridge zhōu 粥；rice wine mǐjiǔ 米酒

rich 1 adj (wealthy) yǒuqián 有钱；food yóunì 油腻 2 n: the ~ fùrén 富人

rickshaw rénlìchē 人力车

rid: get ~ of garbage, unwanted furniture rēngdiào 扔掉；foreign accent, excess weight, illusions bǎituō 摆脱

riddle míyǔ 谜语

ride 1 n (on horse) qímǎ 骑马；(in vehicle) chèngchē jīhuì 乘车机会；(journey) lǚtú 旅途；do you want a ~ into town? xiǎng dāchē jìnchéng ma? 想搭车进城吗？；thanks for the ~ xièxie nǐ jiào wǒ dāchē 谢谢你叫我搭车 2 v/t horse, bicycle qímǎ 骑马 3 v/i (on horse) qímǎ 骑马；(on bike) qí zìxíngchē 骑自行车；(in vehicle) chèngchē 乘车

rider (on horse) qímǎ rén 骑马人；(on bike) qí zìxíngchē rén 骑自行车人

ridge (raised strip) jǐ 脊；(of mountain) shānjǐ 山脊；(of roof) wūjǐ 屋脊

ridicule 1 n xīluò 奚落 2 v/t fěngcì 讽刺

ridiculous huāngmiù 荒谬

ridiculously huāngmiù 荒谬

riding (on horseback) qímǎ 骑马

rifle n láifù qiāng 来复枪

rift (in earth) lièxì 裂隙；(in party etc) fēnliè 分裂

rig 1 n (oil ~) yóujǐng 油井；(truck) qiānyǐn tuōchē 牵引拖车 2 v/t elections cāozòng 操纵

right 1 adj (correct) zhèngquè 正

确; (*proper, just*) zhèngdāng 正当; (*suitable*) héshì 合适; (*not left*) yòu 右; *be ~* (*of answer*) zhèngquè 正确; (*of person*) zhèngzhí 正直; (*of clock*) zhǔnquè 准确; *that's ~!* duì a! 对 啊！; *put things ~* jiūzhèng cuòwù 纠正错误; *that's not ~* (*not allowed, not fair*) nà bùxíng 那不行; → *alright*
**2** *adv* (*directly*) jiù 就; (*correctly*) zhèngquè 正确; (*completely*) chèdǐ 彻底; (*not left*) yòu 右; *now* (*immediately*) mǎshàng 马上; (*at the moment*) xiànzài 现在 **3** *n* (*civil, legal etc*) quánlì 权利; (*not left*) yòu 右; POL yòupài 右派; *on the ~* zài yòubiān 在右边; POL zài yòuyì nàbiān 在右翼那边; *turn to the ~, take a ~* xiàng yòu guǎi 向右拐; *be in the ~* yǒulǐ 有理; *know ~ from wrong* qūbié hǎohuài 区别好坏

**right-angle** zhíjiǎo 直角; *at ~s to …* chéng zhíjiǎo … 成直角…

**rightful** *heir, owner etc* héfǎ 合法

**right-hand** *adj* yòubiān 右边; *on the ~ side* zài yòubiān 在右边

**right-hand drive** MOT yòuzuò fāngxiàngpán 右座方向盘; **right-handed** yòu piězi 右撇子; **right-hand man** délì zhùshǒu 得力助手; **right of way** (*in traffic*) yōuxiān xíngshǐ quán 优先行驶权; (*across land*) tōngxíng quán 通行权; **right wing** *n* POL, SP yòuyì 右翼; **right-wing** *adj* POL yòuyì 右翼; **~ extremism** POL jíyòu zhǔyì 极右主义; **right-winger** POL yòupài 右派

**rigid** *material* jiānyìng 坚硬; *principles* wěngù wěngù 稳固; *attitude* kèbǎn 刻板

**rigor** (*of discipline*) yángé 严格; *the ~s of the winter* dōngrì de jiānxīn 冬日的艰辛

**rigorous** *discipline* yángé 严格; *tests, analysis* jīngquè 精确

**rim** (*of wheel*) lúnyuán 轮缘; (*of cup*) biān 边; (*of eyeglasses*) jìngkuàng 镜框

**ring¹** (*circle*) yuánquān 圆圈; (*on finger*) jièzhi 戒指; (*in boxing*) quánjí chǎng 拳击场; (*at circus*) mǎxì quān 马戏圈

**ring²** **1** *n* (*of bell*) zhōngshēng 钟声; (*of voice*) shēngdiào 声调 **2** *v/t bell* qiāozhōng 敲钟 **3** *v/i* (*of bell*) míng 鸣; *please ~ for attention* ànlíng zhāohuàn fúwù 按铃召唤服务

**ringleader** tóumù 头目

**ring-pull** lāhuán 拉环

**rink** liūbīng chǎng 溜冰场

**rinse** **1** *n* (*for hair color*) rǎnsè 染色 **2** *v/t clothes, dishes, hair* piǎoxǐ 漂洗

**riot** **1** *n* bàoluàn 暴乱 **2** *v/i* nàoshì 闹事

**rioter** nàoshì zhě 闹事者

**riot police** píngluàn jǐngchá 平乱警察

**rip** **1** *n* (*in cloth etc*) sīliè 撕裂 **2** *v/t cloth etc* sīliè 撕裂; *~ X open* sīkái X 撕开 X

♦ **rip off** F *customers* shōufèi guògāo 收费过高; (*cheat*) qiāo zhúgàng 敲竹杠

**ripe** *fruit* shóu 熟

**ripen** *v/i* (*of fruit*) chéngshóu 成熟

**ripeness** (*of fruit*) shóu 熟

**rip-off** *n* F bōxuē 剥削

**ripple** (*on water*) xìlàng 细浪

**rise** **1** *v/i* (*from chair etc*) qǐlái 起来; (*of sun*) shēngqǐ 升起; (*of rocket*) fāshè 发射; (*of price, temperature*) shàngzhǎng 上涨; (*of water level*) shàngshēng 上升 **2** *n* (*in price, temperature*) shàngzhǎng 上涨; (*in water level*) shàngshēng 上升; (*in salary*) tígāo 提高

**risk** **1** *n* fēngxiǎn 风险; *take a ~* màoxiǎn 冒险 **2** *v/t* mào … fēngxiǎn 冒…风险; *let's ~ it* wǒmen shìshìba 我们试试吧

**risky** màoxiǎn 冒险

**ritual** *n & adj* yíshì 仪式

**rival** **1** *n* duìshǒu 对手 **2** *v/t* yǔ … jìngzhēng 与…竞争; *I can't ~ that* wǒ bǐ bú guò 我比不过

**rivalry** jìngzhēng 竞争

**river** héliú 河流

**riverbed** héchuáng 河床

riverside hébiān 河边

rivet 1 n mǎodīng 铆钉 2 v/t mǎo-jiē 铆接; **~ X to Y** bǎ X dīngláo dào Y shàng 把 X 钉牢到 Y 上

RMB (= **renminbi**) rénmínbì 人民币

road lù 路; **it's just down the ~** jiù zài nàbiān 就在那边

roadblock lùzhàng 路障; **road hog** kāichē zài lù zhōngjiān 开车在路中间; (of vehicle) gāosù jiàshǐ nénglì 高速驾驶能力; **road map** xiànlù tú 线路图; **roadside: at the ~** zài lùbiān 在路边; **roadsign** lùbiāo 路标; **roadway** gōnglù 公路; **roadworthy** shìyú gōnglù xíngshǐ 适于公路行驶

roam mànyóu 漫游

roar 1 n (of traffic, engine) hōng-míng shēng 轰鸣声; (of lion) páoxiào 咆哮; (of person) dàshēng chǎo 大声吵 2 v/i (of engine) hōngmíng 轰鸣; (of lion) páoxiào 咆哮; (of person) dàshēng chǎo 大声吵; **~ with laughter** dàshēng xiào 大声笑

roast 1 n (of beef etc) kǎoròu 烤肉 2 v/t kǎo 烤 3 v/i (of person) kǎo 烤; **we're ~ing** F wǒmen rèsǐle 我们热死了

roast beef kǎo niúròu 烤牛肉

roast pork kǎo zhūròu 烤猪肉

rob person, bank qiǎngjié 抢劫; **I've been ~bed** wǒ bèi qiǎngjié le 我被抢劫了

robber qiǎngjié zhě 抢劫者

robbery qiǎngjié 抢劫

robe (of judge) guānfú 官服; (of priest) fǎyī 法衣; (bath~) yùyī 浴衣

robin dōng jú 冬鹟

robot jīqìrén 机器人

robust person, health jiànzhuàng 健壮; material, structure jiāngù 坚固

ROC (= **Republic of China**) Zhōnghuá Mínguó 中华民国

rock 1 n yánshí 岩石; MUS yáogǔn yuè 摇滚乐; **on the ~s** drink chānbīng 掺冰; marriage jíjiāng pòliè 即将破裂 2 v/t baby, cradle

qīngyáo 轻摇; (surprise) shǐ zhènjīng 使震惊 3 v/i (on chair) yáodòng 摇动; (of boat) yáo-huáng 摇晃

rock bottom: **reach ~** zǒurù zuìdīdiǎn 走入最低点

rock-bottom adj prices zuìdī 最低

rocket 1 n huǒjiàn 火箭 2 v/i (of prices etc) jùzēng 剧增

rocking chair yáoyǐ 摇椅

rock'n'roll yáogǔn yuè 摇滚乐

rock star yáogǔn yuè gēxīng 摇滚乐歌星

rocky beach, path duō yánshí 多岩石

rod gùn 棍; (for fishing) gān 竿

rodent nièchǐmù dòngwù 啮齿目动物

rogue táoqìbāo 淘气包

role juésè 角色

role model bǎngyàng 榜样

roll 1 n (bread) xiǎo yuán miànbāo 小圆面包; (of film) juǎn 卷; (of thunder) lónglong shēng 隆隆声; (list, register) míngcè 名册 2 v/i (of ball etc) gǔn 滚; (of boat) yáobǎi 摇摆 3 v/t: **~ X into a ball** bǎ X juǎn chéngqiú 把 X 卷成球

◆roll over 1 v/i fānshēn 翻身 2 v/t person, object fān 翻; (renew, extend) yánxù 延续

◆roll up 1 v/t sleeves juǎnqǐ 卷起 2 v/i (arrive) chūxiàn 出现

roll call diǎnmíng 点名

roller (for hair) juǎnfà juǎn 卷发卷

roller blade n sìlún hànbīng xié 四轮旱冰鞋; **roller blind** juǎnlián 卷帘; **roller coaster** guò shān chē 过山车; **roller skate** n hànbīng xié 旱冰鞋

rolling pin gǎnmiànzhàng 擀面杖

ROM (= **read only memory**) zhǐ dú cúnchǔ qì 只读存储器

Roman Catholic 1 n Tiānzhǔjiào tú 天主教徒 2 adj Tiānzhǔjiào 天主教

romance (affair) fēngliú yùnshì 风流韵事; (novel, movie) chuánqí 传奇

romantic làngmàn 浪漫

**roof** wūdǐng 屋顶

**roof rack** MOT chēdǐng jià 车顶架

**room** fángjiān 房间; (space) kōngjiān 空间; **there's no ~ for X** méi yǒu X de dìfang 没有 X 的地方

**room clerk** jiēdài yuán 接待员; **roommate** shìyǒu 室友; **room service** fángjiān fúwù 房间服务

**roomy** house etc dàchǎng kuānchǎng 宽敞; clothes dà 大

**root** gēn bèi; (of word) cígēn 词根; **~s** (of person) gēnjī 根基

♦**root out** (get rid of) sǎochú 扫除; (find) zhǎodào 找到

**rope** shéng 绳

♦**rope off** yòng shéngzi gékāi 用绳子隔开

**rose** BOT méigui 玫瑰

**rosy** cheeks hóngrùn 红润; future guāngmíng 光明

**rot 1** n (in wood, teeth) fǔlàn 腐烂 **2** v/i (of food, wood, teeth) fǔlàn 腐烂

**rota** lúnzhí biǎo 轮值表

**rotate** v/i (of blades, earth) xuánzhuǎn 旋转

**rotation** (around the sun etc) xuánzhuǎn 旋转; **do in ~** lúnliú zuò 轮流做

**rotten** food, wood etc fǔlàn 腐烂; trick, thing to do lìngrén tǎoyàn 令人讨厌; weather, luck jíhuài 极坏

**rough 1** adj surface bùpíng 不平; hands, skin cūcāo 粗糙; voice shāyǎ 沙哑; (violent) cūbào 粗暴; crossing, seas jiānnán 艰难; (approximate) dàgài 大概; **~ draft** cǎogǎo 草稿 **2** adv: **sleep ~** lùsù 露宿 jiētóu 露宿街头 **3** n (in golf) zhàng'ài qūyù 障碍区域 **4** v/t: **~ it** cùhē còujù 凑合

**roughage** (in food) cū sìliào 粗饲料

**roughly** (approximately) dàyuē 大约

**roulette** lúnpán dǔ 轮盘赌

**round 1** adj yuán 圆; **in ~ figures** zhěngshù 整数 **2** n (of postman, doctor) xúnhuí 巡回; (of toast) piàn 片; (of drinks) lún 轮; (of competition) chǎng chǎng 场; (in boxing match) huíhé 回合 **3** v/t the corner ràoxíng 绕行 **4** adv & prep → **around**

♦**round off** edges bǎ ... xiūyuán 把 ... 修圆; meeting, night out jiéshù 结束

♦**round up** figure bǎ ... tiáogāo chéng zhěngshù 把 ... 调高成整数; suspects, criminals dōubǔ 兜捕

**roundabout** adj route, way of saying sth jiànjiē 间接

**round trip** láihuí lǚxíng 来回旅行

**round trip ticket** láihuí piào 来回票

**round-up** (of cattle) gǎnlǒng 赶拢; (of suspects, criminals) dōubǔ 兜捕; (of news) zōnghé bàodào 综合报道

**rouse** (from sleep) xǐng 醒; interest, emotions shāndòng 煽动

**rousing** speech, finale lìngrén zhènfèn 令人振奋

**route** lùxiàn 路线

**routine 1** adj chángguī 常规 **2** n chángguī 常规; **as a matter of ~** zuòwéi chángguī 作为常规

**row**[1] (line) pái 排; (in spreadsheet etc) háng 行; **5 days in a ~** jiēlián wǔ tiān 接连五天

**row**[2] **1** v/t boat huá 划 **2** v/i huáchuán 划船

**rowboat** huátǐng 划艇

**rowdy** hào chǎonào 好吵闹

**row house** páifáng 排房

**royal** adj huángjiā 皇家

**royalty** (royal persons) huángzú 皇族; (on book, recording) chōubǎn fèi 筹办费

**rub** v/t cuō 搓

♦**rub down** (to clean) cāshuā 擦刷

♦**rub off 1** v/t dirt cādiào 擦掉; paint etc módiào 磨掉 **2** v/i: **it rubs off on you** duì nǐ yǒu yǐngxiǎng 对你有影响

♦**rub out** (with eraser) móqù 磨去

**rubber 1** n (material) xiàngpí 橡皮 **2** adj xiàngjiāo 橡胶

**rubbish** Br lājī 垃圾; (poor quality item) pòlàn 破烂; (nonsense) húshuō 胡说

**rubble** cūshí 粗石
**ruby** (*jewel*) hóng bǎoshí 红宝石
**rucksack** bèibāo 背包
**rudder** duò 舵
**ruddy** *complexion* hóngrùn 红润
**rude** cūlǔ 粗鲁; *it is ~ to ...* ... shì cūlǔ de ... 是粗鲁的; *I didn't mean to be ~* wǒ bìngbùshì gùyì wúlǐ 我并不是故意无礼
**rudeness** wúlǐ 无礼
**rudimentary** jīběn 基本
**rudiments** jīběn yuánlǐ 基本原理
**ruffian** ègùn 恶棍
**ruffle 1** *n* (*on dress*) zhě褶 **2** *v/t hair* nòngluàn 弄乱; *clothes* nòngzhòu 弄皱; *person* shǐ xīnfán yìluàn 使心烦意乱; *get ~d* xīnfán yìluàn 心烦意乱
**rug** xiǎo dìtǎn 小地毯; (*blanket*) tǎnzi 毯子
**rugged** *scenery, cliffs* qíqū 崎岖; *face* cūguǎng 粗犷; *resistance* jiānqiáng 坚强
**ruin 1** *n:* ~**s** fèixū 废墟; *in* ~**s** (*of city, building*) chéng fèixū 成废墟; (*of marriage*) pòliè 破裂; (*of plans*) pòchǎn 破产 **2** *v/t party, birthday, vacation, plans* pòhuài 破坏; *reputation* huǐhuài 毁坏; *be ~ed* (*financially*) pòchǎn 破产
**rule 1** *n* (*of club, game*) guīzé 规则; (*of monarch*) tǒngzhì 统治; (*for measuring*) chǐdù 尺度; *as a ~* tōngcháng 通常 **2** *v/t country* tǒngzhì 统治; *the judge ~d that ...* fǎguān pàndìng ... 法官判定 ... **3** *v/i* (*of monarch*) tǒngzhì 统治
**♦rule out** páichú 排除
**ruler** (*for measuring*) chǐzi 尺子; (*of state*) tǒngzhìzhě 统治者
**ruling 1** *n* cáijué 裁决 **2** *adj party* dāngquán 当权
**rum** (*drink*) lǎngmǔ jiǔ 朗姆酒
**rumble** *v/i* (*of stomach*) lónglong zuòxiǎng 隆隆作响; (*of train in tunnel*) lùlu shǐguò 辘辘驶过
**♦rummage around** fānxún 翻寻
**rummage sale** jiùwù chūshòu 旧物出售
**rumor 1** *n* yáoyán 谣言 **2** *v/t: it is ~ed that ...* yǒu yáoyán shuō ...

有谣言说...
**rump** (*of animal*) túnbù 臀部
**rumple** *clothes, paper* nòngzhòu 弄皱
**rumpsteak** túnbù niúpái 臀部牛排
**run 1** *n* (*on foot*) pǎobù 跑步; (*in car*) xíngchéng 行程; (*in tights*) chōusī 抽丝; (THEA: *of play*) liánxù yǎnchū 连续演出; *go for a ~* pǎobù 跑步; *go for a ~ in the car* zuòchē qù dōu gè quān 坐车去兜个圈; *make a ~ for it* táopǎo 逃跑; *a criminal on the ~* zàitáo zuìfàn 在逃罪犯; *in the short / long ~* cóng duǎnqī / chángyuǎn láikàn 从短期 / 长远来看; *a ~ on the dollar* měiyuán jǐduì 美元挤兑 **2** *v/i* (*of person, animal*) pǎo 跑; (*of river*) liú 流; (*of trains etc*) xíngshǐ 行驶; (*of paint, makeup*) tǎngliú 淌流; (*of nose, eyes*) tǎng 淌; (*of tap*) kāi 开; (*of play*) liánxù yǎnchū 连续演出; (*of engine, machine, software*) yùnzhuǎn 运转; (*in election*) jìngxuǎn 竞选; *~ for President* jìngxuǎn zǒngtǒng 竞选总统 **3** *v/t race* jìngsài 竞赛; *3 miles etc* pǎo 跑; *business, hotel, project etc* guǎnlǐ 管理; *software* yùnzhuǎn 运转; *car* yōngyǒu 拥有; *can I ~ you to the station?* wǒ kěyǐ kāichē sòng nǐ qù chēzhàn ma? 我可以开车送你去车站吗？; *he ran his eye down the page* tā liúlǎn le zhè yīyè 他浏览了这一页
**♦run across** (*meet*) pèngjiàn 碰见
**♦run away** táopǎo 逃跑
**♦run down 1** *v/t* (*knock down*) zhuàngdǎo chuàngdǎo 撞倒; (*criticize*) biǎndī 贬低; *stocks* jiǎnshǎo 减少 **2** *v/i* (*of battery*) hàojìn 耗尽
**♦run into** (*meet*) pèngjiàn 碰见; *difficulties* yùdào 遇到
**♦run off 1** *v/i* táopǎo 逃跑 **2** *v/t* (*print off*) dǎyìn 打印
**♦run out** (*of contract*) qīmǎn 期满; (*of time*) yòngwán 用完; (*of*

supplies) hàojìn 耗尽
♦ **run out of** *time* yòngwán 用完;
*patience* shīqù 失去; *supplies*
yòngguāng 用光; *I ran out of gas*
wǒ chē méi yóu le 我车没油了
♦ **run over** 1 *v/t (knock down)*
zhuàngdǎo 撞倒; *can we ~ the
details again?* wǒmen zàikàn
yībiàn xiángqíng hǎoma? 我们再
看一遍详情好吗？ 2 *v/i (of
water etc)* yìchū 溢出
♦ **run through** *(rehearse)* páiliàn 排
练; *(go over)* liúlǎn 浏览
♦ **run up** *v/t debts, large bill* lěijī 累
积; *clothes* gǎnzhì 赶制
**run-down** *person* píjuàn 疲倦; *part
of town* pòjiù 破旧; *building* shīxiū
失修
**rung** *(of ladder)* tījí 梯级
**runner** *(athlete)* sàipǎo zhě 赛跑者
**runner-up** yàjūn 亚军
**running** 1 *n* SP sàipǎo 赛跑; *(of
business)* jīngyíng 经营; *for
two days* ~ liánxù liǎngtiān 连续
两天
**running dog** *pej* zǒugǒu 走狗
**running water** *(from tap)* zìláishuǐ
自来水; *(flowing)* liúshuǐ 流水
**runny** *liquid* liúdòng 流动; ~ *nose*
liú bítì 流鼻涕
**run-up** SP yùbèi jiēduàn 预备阶
段; *in the ~ to* zài yùbèi jiēduàn
qíjiān 在预备阶段期间
**runway** pǎodào 跑道
**rupture** 1 *n* pòliè 破裂 2 *v/i (of
pipe etc)* pòliè 破裂

**rural** nóngcūn 农村
**rush** 1 *n* tūjī 突击; *do ... in a ~*
cōngmáng zuò ... 匆忙做...; *be
in a ~* máng 忙; *what's the big ~?*
máng shénme? 忙什么？ 2 *v/t*
*person* cuī 催; *meal* kuàichī 快吃;
~ *X to the hospital* bǎ X huǒsù
sòngjìn yīyuàn 把X火速送进医
院 3 *v/i* gǎn 赶
**rush hour** gāofēng shíjiān 高峰时
间
**Russia** Éluósī 俄罗斯
**Russian** 1 *adj* Éluósī 俄罗斯 2 *n*
*(person)* Éluósī rén 俄罗斯人;
*(language)* Éyǔ 俄语
**rust** 1 *n* xiù 锈 2 *v/i* shēngxiù 生锈
**rustle** 1 *n (of silk, leaves)* shāsha-
shēng 沙沙声 2 *v/i (of silk, leaves)*
shāsha zuòxiǎng 沙沙作响
♦ **rustle up** F *meal* cōngcōng zuò 匆
匆做
**rust-proof** *adj* fángxiù 防锈
**rust remover** chúxiùjì 除锈剂
**rusty** shēngxiù 生锈; *French, math
etc* shēngshū 生疏; *I'm a little ~*
wǒ yǒudiǎnr shēng le 我有点儿
生了
**rut** *(in road)* chēzhé 车辙; *fig*
chángguī 常规; *be in a ~* guò
kèbǎnde shēnghuó 过刻板的生
活
**ruthless** wúqíng 无情
**ruthlessness** wúqíng 无情
**rye** hēimài 黑麦
**rye bread** hēimài miànbāo 黑麦
面包

# S

sabbatical n (of academic) xiūjiànián 休假年
sabotage n & v/t pòhuài 破坏
saccharin n tángjīng 糖精
sachet (of shampoo, cream etc) yīxiǎodài 一小袋
sack 1 n dà kǒudài 大口袋 2 v/t jiěgù 解雇
sacred shénshèng 神圣
sacrifice 1 n (act) xīshēng 牺牲; (person, animal sacrificed) jìpǐn 祭品; make ~s fig zuòchū xīshēng 作出牺牲 2 v/t xiànjì 献祭; one's freedom etc xīshēng 牺牲
sad person, face, song bēishāng 悲伤; state of affairs yíhàn 遗憾
saddle n ānzi 鞍子
sadism shīnüèkuáng 施虐狂
sadist nüèdàikuáng zhě 虐待狂者
sadistic yǒu shīnüèkuáng 有施虐狂
sadly look, sing etc yōuchóu 忧愁; (regrettably) lìngrén yíhàn 令人遗憾
sadness yōuchóu 忧愁
safe 1 adj (not dangerous) ānquán 安全; (not in danger) wúwēixiǎn 无危险; investment, prediction wúfēngxiǎn 无风险; bǎoxiǎnguì 保险柜 2 n bǎoxiǎnguì 保险柜
safeguard 1 n ānquán zhuāngzhì 安全装置; as a ~ against X zuòwéi fángzhǐ X de bǎohù cuòshī 作为防止 X 的保护措施 2 v/t bǎohù 保护
safekeeping: give X to Y for ~ bǎ X gěi Y tuǒshàn bǎoguǎn 把 X 给 Y 妥善保管
safely arrive píng'ān 平安; complete tests etc yǒu bǎwò 有把握; drive ānquán 安全; assume kěndìng 肯定
safety ānquán 安全; (of investment, prediction) bǎoxiǎn 保险; be in ~ chùyú ānquán zhuàngtài 处于安全状态
safety belt ānquándài 安全带; safety-conscious yǒu ānquán yìshí 有安全意识; safety first ānquán dìyī 安全第一; safety pin biézhēn 别针
sag 1 n (in ceiling etc) xiàchuí 下垂 2 v/i (of ceiling, rope) xiàchuí 下垂; (of output, tempo) xiàjiàng 下降
sage (herb) shǔwěicǎo 鼠尾草
sail 1 n fān 帆; (trip) hángchéng 航程; go for a ~ chéngchuán yóulǎn 乘船游览 2 v/t yacht jiàshǐ 驾驶 3 v/i jiàshǐchuán 驾驶船; (depart) qǐháng 启航
sailboard 1 n fānbǎn 帆板 2 v/i zuò fānbǎn yùndòng 作帆板运动
sailboarding fānbǎn yùndòng 帆板运动
sailboat fānchuán 帆船
sailing SP fānchuán yùndòng 帆船运动
sailing ship fānchuán 帆船
sailor (in the navy) hǎiyuán 海员; SP shuǐshǒu 水手; be a good/bad ~ bùcháng/chángcháng yùnchuán de rén 不常/常常晕船的人
saint shèngtú 圣徒
sake: for my/your ~ wèile wǒ/nǐ 为了我/你; for the ~ of X wèile X 为了 X
salad ⇩ sèlā 色拉
salad dressing ⇩ sèlā tiáowèizhī 色拉调味汁
salary xīnshuǐ 薪水
salary scale xīnshuǐ jíbié 薪水级别
sale xiāoshòu 销售; (reduced prices) liánshòu 廉售; for ~ (sign) dàishòu 待售; be on ~ yǒushòu 有售; (at reduced prices) liánjià

chūshòu 廉价出售

**sales** (*department*) xiāoshòu 销售

**sales clerk** (*in store*) shòuhuòyuán 售货员; **sales figures** xiāoshòu'é 销售额; **salesman** tuīxiāoyuán 推销员; **sales manager** yíngyè jīnglǐ 营业经理; **sales meeting** xiāoshòu huìyì 销售会议

**saliva** tuòyè 唾液

**salmon** dàmǎhāyú 大马哈鱼

**saloon** MOT xiǎojiàochē 小轿车; (*bar*) jiǔbā 酒吧

**salt** yán 盐

**saltcellar** yánpíng 盐瓶

**salty** xián 咸

**salutary** *experience* yǒuyì 有益

**salute 1** *n* MIL jìnglǐ 敬礼 **2** *v/t & v/i* zhìjìng 致敬

**salvage** *v/t* (*from wreck*) qiǎngjiù 抢救

**salvation** zhěngjiù 拯救

**Salvation Army** Jiùshìjūn 救世军

**same 1** *adj* tóngyàng 同样 **2** *pron*: *I'll have the ~ as you* hé nǐ yīyàng 和你一样; *Happy New Year – the ~ to you* Xīnnián kuàilè – Xīnnián kuàilè 新年快乐 – 新年快乐; *he's not the ~ any more* tā búzài hé yǐqián yíyàng le tā bùzài 不再和以前一样了; *all the ~* jǐnguǎn rúcǐ 尽管如此; *men are all the ~* nánrén dōu yíyàng 男人都一样; *it's all the ~ to me* duì wǒ láishuō dōu yíyàng 对我来说都一样 **3** *adv*: *look / sound the ~* kànqǐlái / tīngqǐlái yíyàng 看起来 / 听起来一样

**sample** *n* yàngběn 样本

**sanatorium** liáoyǎngyuàn 疗养院

**sanction 1** *n* (*approval*) pīzhǔn 批准; (*penalty*) zhìcái 制裁 **2** *v/t* (*approve*) tóngyì 同意

**sanctity** shénshèng 神圣

**sanctuary** REL shèngdì 圣地; (*for wild animals*) yěshēng dòngwù bǎohù qū 野生动物保护区

**sand 1** *n* shā 沙 **2** *v/t* (*with sandpaper*) yòng shāzhǐ móguāng 用砂纸磨光

**sandal** liángxié 凉鞋

**sandbag** shādài 沙袋; **sandblast** pēnshā qīngxǐ 喷沙清洗; **sand dune** shāqiū 沙丘

**sander** (*tool*) dǎmójī 打磨机

**sandpaper 1** *n* shāzhǐ 砂纸 **2** *v/t* yòng shāzhǐ móguāng 用砂纸磨光; **sandpit** shākēng 沙坑; **sandstone** shāyán 沙岩

**sandwich 1** *n* sānmíngzhì 三明治 **2** *v/t*: *be ~ed between two ...* shòujiáyú liǎng ... zhījiān 受夹于两 ... 之间

**sandy** *beach, soil* duōshā 多沙; *hair* shāsè 沙色

**sane** shénzhì zhèngcháng 神志正常

**sanitarium** liáoyǎngyuàn 疗养院

**sanitary** *conditions* wèishēng 卫生; *installations* qīngjié 清洁

**sanitary napkin** wèishēngjīn 卫生巾

**sanitation** (*sanitary installations*) wèishēng shèbèi 卫生设备; (*removal of waste*) xiàshuǐ xìtǒng 下水系统

**sanitation department** huánjìng wèishēng bùmén 环境卫生部门

**sanity** shénzhì zhèngcháng 神志正常

**Santa Claus** Shèngdàn Lǎorén 圣诞老人

**sap 1** *n* (*in tree*) shùyè 树液 **2** *v/t s.o.'s energy* xuēruò 削弱

**sapphire** *n* (*jewel*) lánbǎoshí 蓝宝石

**sarcasm** jīfèng 讥讽

**sarcastic** jīfèng 讥讽

**sardine** shādīngyú 沙丁鱼

**sash** (*on dress, uniform*) jiāndài 肩带; (*in window*) chuānkuàng 窗框

**Satan** Sādàn 撒旦

**satellite** wèixīng 卫星

**satellite dish** wèixīng diànshì pán 卫星电视盘

**satellite TV** wèixīng diànshì 卫星电视

**satin** duànzi 缎子

**satire** fěngcì 讽刺

**satirical** hán fěngcì yìwèi 含讽刺意味

**satirist** fěngcì zhě 讽刺者

**satisfaction** mǎnzú 满足; *get ~ out of X* cóng X zhōng dédào mǎnzú 从 X 中得到满足; *a feeling of ~* mǎnyìde gǎnjué 满意的感觉; *is that to your ~?* nǐ duìcǐ mǎnyì ma? 你对此满意吗?

**satisfactory** lìngrén mǎnyì 令人满意; (*just good enough*) fúhé yāoqiú 符合要求; *this is not ~* zhè hái bùgòu hǎo 这还不够好

**satisfy** *customers* shǐ mǎnyì 使满意; *needs, hunger, sexual desires* mǎnzú 满足; *conditions* fúhé 符合; *I am satisfied that he ...* (*convinced*) wǒ xiāngxìn tā ... 我相信他 ...; *I hope you're satisfied!* wǒ xiǎng nǐ gāi mǎnyì le ba! 我想你该满意了吧!

**Saturday** xīngqīliù 星期六

**sauce** jiàng 酱

**saucepan** píngdǐguō 平底锅

**saucer** chábēidié 茶杯碟

**saucy** *person* wúlǐ 无礼; *dress* tòuguāng 透光

**Saudi (Arabia)** Shātè Ālābó 沙特阿拉伯

**Saudi (Arabian) 1** *adj* Shātè Ālābó 沙特阿拉伯 **2** *n* (*person*) Shātè Ālābó rén 沙特阿拉伯人

**sauna** zhēngqìyù 蒸汽浴

**saunter** mànbù 漫步

**sausage** xiāngcháng 香肠

**savage 1** *adj* yěxìng 野性; *attack* cánkù 残酷; *criticism* èdú 恶毒 **2** *n* yěrén 野人

**save 1** *v/t* (*rescue*) jiù 救; *money* chǔcún 存储; *time* jiéshěng 节省; (*collect*) sōují 搜集; COMPUT cúnpán 存盘; *goal* jiùqiú 救球; *~ as* COMPUT cúnwéi 存为; *you could ~ yourself a lot of effort* nǐ kěyǐ jiéshěng hěnduō jīnglì 你可以节省很多精力 **2** *v/i* (*put money aside*) zǎnqián 攒钱; SP jiùqiú 救球 **3** *n* SP jiùqiú 救球

♦ **save up for** wèi ... zǎnqián 为 ... 攒钱

**saving** (*amount saved*) jiéshěng 节省; (*activity*) cúnqián 存钱

**savings** cúnkuǎn 存款

**savings account** chǔxù zhànghù

储蓄帐户

**savings bank** chǔxū yínháng 储蓄银行

**savior** REL jiùshìzhǔ 救世主

**savor 1** *n* fēngwèi 风味 **2** *v/t* pǐncháng 品尝

**savory** *adj* (*not sweet*) xián 咸

**saw 1** *n* (*tool*) jù 锯 **2** *v/t* jùkāi 锯开

♦ **saw off** jùdiào 锯掉

**sawdust** jùmò 锯末

**saxophone** sàkèsīguǎn 萨克斯管

**say 1** *v/t* shuō 说; *can I ~ something?* wǒ kěyǐ fābiǎo yīxià wǒde yìjiàn ma? 我可以发表一下我的意见吗?; *that is to ~* jiùshì shuō 那就是说; *what do you ~ to that?* nǐ juédé nàyàng rúhé? 你觉得那样如何? **2** *n: have one's ~* biǎodá yìjiàn 表达意见

**saying** yànyǔ 谚语

**scab** jiā jiā 痂

**scaffold(ing)** jiǎoshǒujià 脚手架

**scald** *v/t* tàngshāng 烫伤

**scale**[1] (*on fish*) línpiàn 鳞片

**scale**[2] **1** *n* (*size*) guīmó 规模; (*on thermometer etc*) kèdù 刻度; (*of map*) bǐlì 比例; MUS yīnjiē 音阶; *on a larger/smaller ~* gèngdà/gèngxiǎo guīmó 更大/更小规模 **2** *v/t cliffs etc* pāndēng 攀登

**scale drawing** bǐlì huìtú 比例绘图

**scales** (*for weighing*) tiānpíng 天平

**scalp** *n* tóupí 头皮

**scalpel** shǒushùdāo 手术刀

**scalper** ⇩ piàofànzi 票贩子

**scan 1** *v/t horizon, page* sǎoshì 扫视; MED sǎomiáo 扫描; COMPUT sōusuǒ 搜索 **2** *n* MED sǎomiáo 扫描

♦ **scan in** COMPUT sōusuǒ jìnrù 搜索进入

**scandal** liúyán fēiyǔ 流言蜚语

**scandalous** *affair* diūliǎn 丢脸; *prices* lìngrén zhènjīng 令人震惊

**scanner** MED sǎomiáoyí 扫描器; COMPUT sǎomiáoyí 扫描仪

**scantily** *adv: ~ clad* chuānzhuó dānbó 穿着单薄

scanty *clothes* dānbó 单薄
scapegoat tìzuìyáng 替罪羊
scar **1** *n* shāngbā 伤疤 **2** *v/t* liúxià shānghén 留下伤痕
scarce (*in short supply*) duǎnquē 短缺; **be ~** bìkāi 避开
scarcely jīhūbù 几乎不
scarcity quēfá 缺乏
scare **1** *v/t* jīngxià 惊吓; **be ~d of X** hàipà X 害怕 X **2** *n* (*panic, alarm*) jīngkǒng 惊恐; **give X a ~** gěi X xiàle yī tiào 给 X 吓了一跳
♦ **scare away** xiàpǎo 吓跑
scarecrow dàocǎorén 稻草人
scarf (*around neck*) wéijīn 围巾; (*over head*) tóujīn 头巾
scarlet xiānhóng 鲜红
scarlet fever xīnghóngrè 猩红热
scary *music, movie* hěn kǒngbù 很恐怖
scathing kèbó 刻薄
scatter **1** *v/t leaflets, seeds* sǎ 撒; **be ~ed all over the room** fángjiānlǐ dàochù dōushì 房间里到处都是 **2** *v/i* (*of crowd etc*) sànkāi 散开
scatterbrained jiànwàng 健忘
scattered *showers* língxīng 零星; *family, villages* fēnsàn 分散
scenario qíngkuàng 情况
scene THEA chǎng 场; (*view, sight*) qíngjǐng 情景; (*of accident, crime etc*) shìfā dìdiǎn 事发地点; (*of novel, movie*) chǎngjǐng 场景; (*argument*) chǎonào 吵闹; **make a ~** dàchǎo dànào 大吵大闹; **~s** THEA bùjǐng 布景; **jazz / rock ~** juéshìyuè / yáogǔnyuè lǐngyù 爵士乐 / 摇滚乐领域; **behind the ~s** zài mùhòu 在幕后
scenery jǐngsè 景色; THEA wǔtái bùjǐng 舞台布景
scent *n* (*smell*) xiāngwèi 香味; (*perfume*) xiāngjīng 香精; (*of animal*) xiùjì 臭迹
schedule **1** *n* (*of events*) chéngxùbiǎo 程序表; (*of work*) jìhuàbiǎo 计划表; (*for trains*) shíkèbiǎo 时刻表; (*of lessons*) kèchéngbiǎo 课程表; **be on ~** (*of work, of workers, of train etc*) àn yùdìng shíjiān 按预定时间; **be**

behind ~ (*of work, of workers, of train etc*) luòhòuyú yùdìng jìhuà 落后于预定计划 **2** *v/t* (*put on schedule*) lièrù jìhuà 列入计划; **it's ~d for completion next month** dìngyú xiàgèyuè wánchéng 定于下个月完成
scheduled flight dìngqī hángbān 定期航班
scheme **1** *n* (*plan*) jìhuà 计划; (*plot*) yīnmóu 阴谋 **2** *v/i* (*plot*) túmóu 图谋
scheming *adj* guǐjì duōduān 诡计多端
schizophrenia jīngshén fēnlièzhèng 精神分裂症
schizophrenic **1** *n* jīngshén fēnlièzhèng huànzhě 精神分裂症患者 **2** *adj* jīngshén fēnliè 精神分裂
scholar xuézhě 学者
scholarship (*work*) xuéshù chéngjiù 学术成就; (*financial award*) jiǎngxuéjīn 奖学金
school xuéxiào 学校; (*university*) xuéyuàn 学院
schoolbag xiǎoshūbāo 小书包; schoolboy zhōngxiǎoxué nánshēng 中小学男生; schoolchildren zhōngxiǎoxué xuéshēng 中小学学生; school days xuésheng shídài 学生时代; schoolgirl zhōngxiǎoxué nǚ xuésheng 中小学女生; schoolmate xiàoyǒu 校友; schoolteacher zhōngxiǎoxué jiàoshī 中小学教师
sciatica zuògǔ shénjīngtòng 坐骨神经痛
science kēxué 科学
science fiction kēhuàn 科幻
scientific kēxué 科学
scientist kēxuéjiā 科学家
scissors jiǎnzi 剪子
scoff[1] *v/t* (*eat fast*) tānlánde chī 贪婪地吃; (*eat whole lot*) chīguāng 吃光
scoff[2] *v/i* jīxiào 讥笑
♦ **scoff at** cháoxiào 嘲笑
scold *v/t child, husband* zémà 责骂
scoop **1** *n* (*implement*) chǎnzi 铲子; (*story*) qiǎngxiān bàodào 抢先

报道 2 v/t (pick up) yǎochū 舀出
♦ scoop up pěngqǐ 捧起
scooter (with motor) xiǎoxíng mótuōchē 小型摩托车; (child's) tàbǎnchē 踏板车
scope fànwéi 范围; (freedom, opportunity) jīhuì 机会
scorch v/t tàngjiāo 烫焦
scorching hot rèsǐle 热死了
score 1 n SP bǐfēn 比分; (written music) yuèpǔ 乐谱; (of movie etc) pèiyuè 配乐; what's the ~? bǐfēn shì duōshǎo? 比分是多少?; have a ~ to settle with X gēn X suàn jiùzhàng 跟 X 算旧账; (of goal, point défēn 得分; (cut: line) huāhén 划痕 3 v/i défēn 得分; (keep the score) jìfēn 记分; that's where he ~s nà shì tāde qiángxiàng 那是他的强项
scorer (of goal, point) défēn yùndòngyuán 得分运动员; (scorekeeper) jìfēnyuán 记分员
scorn 1 n bǐshì 鄙视; pour ~ on X yòng qīngmiède kǒuwěn tán X 用轻蔑的口吻谈 X 2 v/t idea, suggestion àomànde jùjué 傲慢地拒绝
scornful qīngmiè 轻蔑
Scot Sūgélán rén 苏格兰人
Scotch (whiskey) wēishìjì 威士忌
Scotland Sūgélán 苏格兰
Scottish Sūgélán 苏格兰
scot-free: get off ~ xiāoyáo fǎwài 逍遥法外
scoundrel wúlài 无赖
scour¹ (search) sōuxún 搜寻
scour² pans shuājìng 刷净
scout n (boy ~) tóngzǐjūn 童子军
scowl 1 n nùróng 怒容 2 v/i nùshì 怒视
scram F pǎo 跑
scramble 1 n (rush) mángluàn 忙乱 2 v/t message rǎopín 扰频 3 v/i (climb) pāndēng 攀登; he ~d to his feet tā téngde zhàn qǐlái 他腾地站起来
scrap 1 n (metal) fèijīnshǔ 废金属; (fight) dǎjià 打架; (little bit) shǎoliàng 少量 2 v/t plan, project, paragraph etc fèidiào 废掉

scrapbook jiǎntiēbù 剪贴簿
scrape 1 n (on paintwork) guācā 刮擦 2 v/t paintwork guādiào 刮掉; one's arm cāshāng 擦伤; vegetables yòng dāo xiāojìng 用刀削净; ~ a living miǎnqiǎng wéichí shēnghuó 勉强维持生活
♦ scrape through (in exam etc) miǎnqiǎng jígé qǔdé 勉强及格
scrap heap fèiliàoduī 废料堆; good for the ~ háowúyòngchù 毫无用处
scrap metal fèijīnshǔ 废金属
scrappy work záluànwúzhāng 杂乱无章
scratch 1 n (mark) huāhén 划痕; have a ~ (to stop itching) sāoyǎng 搔痒; start from ~ cónglíng kāishǐ 从零开始; not up to ~ búgòuhǎo 不够好
scratch 2 v/t (mark: skin, paint) zhuāshāng 抓伤; (because of itch) sāoyǎng 搔痒 3 v/i (of cat, nails) zhuā 抓
scrawl 1 n liáocǎode zìjì 潦草的字迹 2 v/t luànxiě 乱写
scream 1 n jiānjiàoshēng 尖叫声 2 v/i jiānjiào 尖叫
screech 1 n (of tires) jiānlìshēng 尖利声; (scream) jiānjiàoshēng 尖叫声 2 v/i (of tires) fāchū jiānlìshēng 发出尖利声; (scream) fāchū jiānjiàoshēng 发出尖叫声
screen 1 n (in room, hospital) gélián 隔帘; (protective) yǎnbìwù 掩避物; (in movie theater) yínmù 银幕; COMPUT píngmù 屏幕; on the ~ (in movie theater) zài yínmùshang 在银幕上; on (the) ~ COMPUT zài píngmùshang 在屏幕上 2 v/t (protect, hide) zhēbì 遮蔽; movie fàngyìng 放映; (for security reasons) shěnchá 审查
screenplay diànyǐng jùběn 电影剧本; screen saver COMPUT píngmù bǎohùqì 屏幕保护器; screen test shìjìng 试镜
screw 1 n luósīdīng 螺丝钉; ∨ (sex) xìngjiāo 性交 2 v/t ∨ gēn ... shuìjiào 跟 ... 睡觉; F (cheat)

qīpiàn 欺骗; **~ X to Y** yòng luósīdīng bǎ X nīngzài Y shàng yòng 螺丝钉把 X 拧在 Y 上

◆**screw up 1** v/t eyes niǔqū 扭曲; piece of paper róuchéntuán 揉成团; F (make a mess of) dǎluàn 打乱 **2** v/i F (make a bad mistake) nòngzāo 弄糟

screwdriver luósīdāo 螺丝刀

screwed up F (psychologically) shénjīng 神经

screw top (on bottle) xuángài 旋盖

scribble **1** n liáocǎode zìjì liáocǎo de zìjì 潦草的字迹 **2** v/t (write quickly) cǎocǎo shūxiě 草草书写 **3** v/i luànxiě 乱写

script (for play etc) jiǎoběn 脚本; (form of writing) shūxiětǐ 书写体

scripture: the (Holy) Scriptures Shèngjīng 圣经

scriptwriter zhuàngǎorén 撰稿人

scroll n (manuscript) zhǐjuàn 纸卷

◆scroll down v/i COMPUT chuízhí xiàyí 垂直下移

◆scroll up v/i COMPUT chuízhí shàngyí 垂直上移

scrounger wúlài 无赖

scrub v/t floors, hands cāxǐ 擦洗

scrubbing brush (for floor) yìngshuāzi 硬刷子; (for hands) xǐshǒushuā 洗手刷

scruffy lātà 邋遢

◆scrunch up plastic cup etc niǎnsuì 捻碎

scruples gùlù 顾虑; **have no ~ about doing X** duì zuò X wúsuǒ gùjì 对做 X 无所顾忌

scrupulous (with moral principles) shènshèn 审慎; (thorough) zǐxì chèdǐ 仔细彻底; attention to detail yìsībùgǒu 一丝不苟

scrutinize (examine closely) xìchá xìchá 细察

scrutiny xìchá xìchá 细察; **come under ~** bèishěnchá 被审查

scuba diving dài shuǐfèi qiánshuǐ 戴水肺潜水

scuffle n niùdǎ 扭打

sculptor diāokè (sù) jiā 雕刻 (塑) 家

sculpture n (art) diāokè (sù) 雕刻

(塑); (sth sculpted) diāosù 雕塑

scum (on liquid) fúgòu 浮垢; pej (people) zhāzi 渣子

scythe n chángbǐng dàliándāo 长柄大廉刀

sea dàhǎi 大海; **by the ~** zài hǎibiān 在海边

seafaring nation hǎishàng 海上; seafood hǎiwèi 海味; seafront bīnhǎiqū 滨海区; seagoing vessel shìyú yuǎnháng 适于远航; seagull hǎi'ōu 海鸥

seal[1] n (animal) hǎibào 海豹

seal[2] n (on document) yìnzhāng 印章; TECH mìfēng 密封 **2** v/t container mìfēng 密封

◆seal off area fēngsuǒ 封锁

sea level: **above / below ~** hǎibá / dīyú hǎipíngmiàn 海拔 / 低于海平面

seam n (on garment) fèng fèng 缝缝; (of ore) kuàngcéng 矿层

seaman shuǐshǒu 水手

seamstress nǚcáiféng 女裁缝

seaport hǎigǎng 海港

sea power (nation) hǎijūn qiángguó 海军强国

search **1** n sōuxún 搜寻 **2** v/t city, files sōuchá 搜查

◆search for xúnzhǎo 寻找

searching adj look, question jiānruì ér shēnkè 尖锐而深刻

searchlight tànzhàodēng 探照灯; search party sōusuǒduì 搜索队; search warrant sōucházhèng 搜查证

seasick yùnchuán 晕船; **get ~** yùnchuán 晕船; seaside hǎibīn 海滨; **at the ~** zài hǎibīn 在海滨; **go to the ~** qù hǎibīn 去海滨

seaside resort hǎibīn shèngdì 海滨胜地

season n (winter etc) jìjié 季节; (for tourism etc) wàngjì 旺季

seasoned wood fēnggān 风干; traveler etc yǒu jīngyàn 有经验

seasoning zuóliào 作料

season ticket chángqīpiào 长期票

seat **1** n zuòwèi 座位; (of pants) túnbù 臀部; POL xíwèi 席位;

***please take a* ~** qǐng luòzuò 请落坐 **2** *v/t* (*have seating for*) zuòdexià 坐得下; ***please remain ~ed*** jiùzuò wùdòng 就座勿动

**seat belt** ānquándài 安全带

**sea urchin** hǎidǎn 海胆

**seaweed** hǎidài 海带

**secluded** rénjìhǎnzhì 人际罕至

**seclusion** yǔshìgéjué 与世隔绝

**second 1** *n* (*of time*) yī miǎozhōng 一秒钟; ***just a* ~** děngyíxià 等一下 **2** *adj* dì'èr 第二 **3** *adv come in* yǐ dì'èrwèi 以第二位 **4** *v/t motion* fùyì 附议

**secondary** cìyào 次要; ***of* ~ *importance*** cìyào 次要

**secondary education** zhōngděng jiàoyù 中等教育

**second best** *adj* dì'èr hǎo 第二好; **second biggest** dì'èr dà 第二大; **second class** *adj ticket* èrděng 二等; **second gear** MOT èrdǎng 二档; **second hand** (*on clock*) miǎozhēn 秒针 **second-hand** èrshǒu 二手

**secondly** qícì 其次

**second-rate** èrliú 二流

**second thoughts: *I've had* ~** wǒ gǎibiàn zhǔyì le 我改变主意了

**secrecy** bǎomì 保密

**secret 1** *n* mìmì 秘密; ***do X in* ~** mìmì zuò X 秘密做 X **2** *adj garden, passage* mìmì 秘密; *work, department* bǎomì 保密

**secret agent** tègōng rényuán 特工人员

**secretarial** *tasks, job* mìshū 秘书

**secretary** mìshū 秘书; POL bùzhǎng 部长

**Secretary of State** Guówùqīng 国务卿

**secrete** (*give off*) fēnmì 分泌; (*hide away*) yǐncáng 隐藏

**secretion** (*of liquid*) fēnmì 分泌; (*liquid secreted*) fēnmìwù 分泌物; (*hiding*) cángnì 藏匿

**secretive** ài bǎomì 爱保密

**secretly** mìmì 秘密

**secret police** mìmì jǐngchá 秘密警察

**secret service** tèwù jīguān 特务

机关

**sect** pàibié 派别

**section** bùfen 部份

**sector** bùmén 部门

**secular** shìsú 世俗

**secure 1** *adj shelf etc* láogù 牢固; *feeling* wú yōulù 无忧虑; *job, contract* yǒu bǎozhèng 有保证 **2** *v/t shelf etc* gùdìngzhù 固定住; *s.o.'s help, finances* dédào 得到

**security** (*in job*) bǎozhàng 保障; (*for investment*) bǎozhèng 保证; (*at airport etc*) ānquán 安全; (*department responsible for* ~) bǎo'ānbù 保安部; (*of beliefs etc*) wěngù 稳固; **securities** FIN zhèngquàn 证券; **securities market** FIN zhèngquàn shìchǎng 证券市场

**security alert** ānquán jǐngtì 安全警惕; **security check** ānquán jiǎnchá 安全检查; **security-conscious** yǒu ānquán yìshí 有安全意识; **security forces** bǎo'ān bùduì 保安部队; **security guard** bǎo'ān rényuán 保安人员; **security risk** (*person*) wēixiǎn rénwù 危险人物

**sedan** xiǎo jiàochē 小轿车

**sedative** *n* zhènjìngyào 镇静药

**sediment** chéndiànwù 沉淀物

**seduce** (*sexually*) gōuyǐn 勾引

**seduction** (*sexual*) yǐnyòu 引诱

**seductive** *dress* yòurén 诱人; *offer* yǒu xīyǐnlì 有吸引力

**see** kànjiàn 看见; (*understand*) míngbái 明白; *I* ~ wǒ míngbái le 我明白了; *can I* ~ *the manager?* wǒ kěyǐ jiàn jīnglǐ ma? 我可以见经理吗？; *you should* ~ *a doctor* nǐ yīnggāi qù kàn yīshēng 你应该去看医生; ~ *X home* sòng X huíjiā 送 X 回家; *I'll* ~ *you to the door* wǒ sòng nǐ dào ménkǒu 我送你到门口; ~ *you!* zàijiàn! 再见！

♦**see about** (*look into*) chǔlǐ 处理

♦**see off** (*at airport etc*) sòngxíng 送行; (*chase away*) gǎnpǎo 赶跑

♦**see out**: *see X out* (*to the door*) sòngsòng X 送送 X

♦see to (deal with) chǔlǐ 处理；~ it that X gets done wùbì bǎozhèng zuòwán X 务必保证做完X

seed zhǒngzi 种子；(in tennis) zhǒngzi xuǎnshǒu 种子选手；go to ~ (of person, district) shuāibài 衰败

seedling yòumiáo 幼苗

seedy bar, district pòjiù 破旧

seeing (that) jìrán 既然

seek 1 v/t employment xúnzhǎo 寻找；truth zhuīqiú 追求 2 v/i tànsuǒ 探索

seem kànqǐlái 看起来；it ~s that ... kànqǐlái sìhū ... 看起来似乎 ...

seemingly kànshàngqu 看上去

seep (of liquid) lòuchū 漏出

♦seep out (of liquid) shènlòu 渗漏

seesaw qiāoqiāobǎn 跷跷板

see-through dress, material tòumíng 透明

segment bàn 瓣

segmented língsuì 零碎

segregate gélí 隔离

segregation gélí 隔离

seismology dìzhènxué 地震学

seize person, arm zhuāzhù 抓住；opportunity bǎwò 把握；(of customs, police etc) kòuyā 扣押

♦seize up (of engine) qiǎzhù 卡住

seizure MED fāzuò 发作；(of drugs etc) kòuyā 扣押

seldom hǎnjiàn 罕见

select 1 v/t xuǎnzé 选择 2 adj (exclusive) gāojí 高级

selection (choosing) xuǎnzé 选择；(that / those chosen) xuǎnchūde 选出的；(assortment) kě gōng tiāoxuǎn 可供挑选

selection process xuǎnzé guòchéng 选择过程

selective tiāojiǎn 挑拣

self zìjǐ 自己

self-addressed envelope xiě yǒu zìjǐ dìzhǐ de xìnfēng 写有自己地址的信封；self-assured yǒu bǎwò 有把握；self-catering apartment zìchuī gōngyù 自炊公寓；self-centered yǐ zìwǒ wéi zhōngxīn 以自我为中心；self-

confessed zìjǐ tǎnbái 自己坦白；self-confidence zìxìn 自信；self-confident zìxìn 自信；self-conscious búzìrán 不自然；self-contained apartment shèbèi qíquán shèbèi 设备齐全；self control zìzhìlì 自制力；self-criticism zìwǒ pīpíng 自我批评；self-defense zìwèi 自卫；self-discipline zìwǒ yuēshù 自我约束；self-doubt zìwǒ kùnhuò 自我困惑；self-employed gètǐ 个体；self-evident bùyán'éryù 不言而喻；self-interest sìlì 私利

selfish zìsī 自私

selfless wúsī 无私

self-made man báishǒuqǐjiāde rén 白手起家的人；self-possessed chénzhuó 沉着；self-reliant yīkào zìjǐ 依靠自己；self-respect zìzūn 自尊；self-righteous pej zìyǐwéishì 自以为是；self-satisfied pej zìmíngdéyì 自鸣得意；self-service adj zìzhùshì 自助式；self-service restaurant zìzhù cānguǎn 自助餐馆；self-study zìxué 自学

sell 1 v/t mài 卖；you have to ~ yourself nǐ děi tuīxiāo zìjǐ 你得推销自己 2 v/i (of products) xiāoshòu 销售

seller màifāng 卖方

selling n COM xiāoshòu 销售

selling point COM shāngpǐn tèsè 商品特色

semen jīngyè 精液

semester xuéqí 学期

semi (truck) jiǎojiēchē 铰接车

semicircle bànyuánxíng 半圆形

semicircular bànyuánxíng 半圆形；semiconductor ELEC bàndǎotǐ 半导体；semifinal bànjuésài 半决赛

seminar yántǎohuì 研讨会

semiskilled bànshúliàn 半熟练

senate cānyìyuàn 参议院

senator cānyìyuán 参议员

send v/t (by mail) yóujì 邮寄；(by mail, e-mail, fax etc) fā 发；~ X to Y bǎ X yóu fāgěi Y 把X邮发给Y；~ X to see Y jiào X qù jiàn Y 叫X

去见 Y; *~ her my best wishes*
xiàng tā wènhǎo 向她问好
♦ **send back** sònghuí 送回; *food in restaurant* tuìhuán 退还
♦ **send for** *doctor, help* pàirén qùzhǎo 派人去找
♦ **send in** *troops* pàiqiǎn 派遣; *next interviewee* jiào … jìnqù 叫 … 进去; *application form* jìqù 寄去
♦ **send off** *letter, fax etc* fāchū 发出
♦ **send up** (*mock*) qǔxiào 取笑
**sender** (*of letter*) yóujìrén 邮寄人
**senile** shuāilǎo 衰老
**senility** shuāilǎo zhuàngtài 衰老状态
**senior** (*older*) niánzhǎng 年长; (*in rank*) gāojí 高级; *be ~ to X* (*in rank*) bǐ X zīgé lǎo 比 X 资格老
**senior citizen** lǎorén 老人
**sensation** (*feeling*) gǎnjué 感觉; (*surprise event*) hōngdòng 轰动; *be a ~* (*very good*) hěn bàng 很棒
**sensational** *news, discovery* hōngdòng 轰动; (*very good*) juémiào 绝妙
**sense 1** *n* (*meaning*) yìyì 意义; (*purpose, point*) yìsi 意思; (*common ~*) jiànshi 见识; (*of sight, smell etc*) guānnéng 官能; (*feeling*) gǎnjué 感觉; *in a ~* zài mǒuzhǒng yìyì shang 在某种意义上; *talk ~, man!* hēi, shuōdiǎnr yǒu dàolǐ de huà! 嘿，说点儿有道理的话！; *it doesn't make ~* zhè méi dàolǐ 这没道理; *there's no ~ in trying / waiting* chángshì / děngdài méiyǒu yòng 尝试 / 等待没有用
**2** *v/t s.o.'s presence* yìshídào 意识到
**senseless** (*pointless*) wú yìyì 无意义
**sensible** *person, decision* míngzhì 明智; *advice* hélǐ 合理
**sensitive** *skin* jiāonèn 娇嫩; *person* mǐngǎn 敏感
**sensitivity** (*of skin, person*) mǐngǎnxìng 敏感性
**sensual** xìnggǎn 性感
**sensuality** ròuyù 肉欲
**sensuous** cìjī gǎnguān 刺激感官
**sentence 1** *n* GRAM jùzi 句子;

LAW túxíng 徒刑 **2** *v/t* LAW pànxíng 判刑
**sentiment** (*sentimentality*) róunuò qínggǎn 柔懦情感; (*opinion*) yìjiàn 意见
**sentimental** shānggǎn 伤感
**sentimentality** róunuò qíngdiào 柔懦情调
**sentry** shàobīng 哨兵
**separate 1** *adj* dúlì 独立; *keep X ~ from Y* fēnkāi X hé Y 分开 X 和 Y **2** *v/t* fēnkāi 分开; *~ X from Y* bǎ X yǔ Y fēnkāi 把 X 与 Y 分开 **3** *v/i* (*of couple*) fēnjū 分居
**separated** *couple* fēnshǒu 分手
**separately** *pay* fēnzhe 分着; *treat, deal with* fēnbié 分别
**separation** fēnlí 分离; (*of couple*) fēnshǒu 分手
**September** jiǔyuè 九月
**septic** gǎnrǎn 感染; *go ~* (*of wound*) shòu gǎnrǎn 受感染
**sequel** xùjí 续集
**sequence** *n* shùnxù 顺序; *in ~* àn shùnxù 按顺序; *out of ~* bú àn shùnxù 不按顺序; *the ~ of events* shìqíng fāshēng de xiānhòu shùnxù 事情发生的先后顺序
**serene** níngjìng 宁静
**sergeant** zhōngshì 中士
**serial** *n* liánxù gùshì 连续故事
**serialize** *novel on TV* liánbō 连播
**serial killer** liánxù shārénfàn 连续杀人犯; **serial number** (*of product*) biānhào 编号; **serial port** COMPUT chuànxíng duānkǒu 串行端口
**series** (*of numbers, events, errors*) xìliè 系列
**serious** *illness, situation, damage* yánzhòng 严重; (*person: earnest*) rènzhēn 认真; *company* zhèngshì 正式; *I'm ~* wǒ zài shuō zhèngjīngde 我在说正经的; *listen, this is ~* tīngzhe, zhè shì zhèngshìr 听着，这是正事儿; *we'd better take a ~ look at it* wǒmen zuì hǎo hǎohǎo kànyíxià 我们最好好好看一下
**seriously** *injured, understaffed*

yánzhòng 严重; ~ *intend to ...*
zhēnde xiǎng 真的想...; ~*?*
shuōzhēnde ma? 说真的吗？;
*take X* ~ rènzhēn duìdài X 认真
对待 X

**sermon** jiǎngdào 讲道

**servant** púrén 仆人

**serve 1** *n* (*in tennis*) fāqiú 发球
**2** *v/t food, meal* duānshang 端上;
*customer in store* zhāodài 招待;
*one's country, the people* fúwù 服
务; *it ~s you / him right* nǐ / tā zuì
yǒu yīngdé bào / 他罪有应得
**3** *v/i* (*give out food*) shàng cài 上
菜; (*as politician etc*) gòngzhí 供
职; (*in tennis*) fāqiú 发球
♦ **serve up** *meal* tígōng 提供

**server** (*in tennis*) fāqiúrén 发球人;
COMPUT fúwùqì 服务器

**service 1** *n* (*to customers, community*) fúwù 服务; (*for vehicle,
machine*) wéixiū 维修; (*in tennis*)
fāqiú 发球; *the* ~*s* jūnduì 军队
**2** *v/t vehicle, machine* wéixiū 维修

**service area** fúwùqū 服务区;
**service charge** (*in restaurant,
club*) fúwùfèi 服务费; **service
industry** fúwù hángyè 服务行
业; **serviceman** MIL jūnrén 军人;
**service provider** COMPUT fúwù
tígōng zhě 服务提供者; **service
sector** fúwù hángyè 服务行业;
**service station** jiāyóuzhàn 加油
站

**sesame oil** xiāngyóu 香油

**session** (*of Congress etc*) huìyì 会
议; (*with psychiatrist, consultant etc*)
yíduàn shíjiān 一段时间

**set 1** *n* (*of tools, books etc*) tào 套;
(*group of people*) yìhuǒrén 一伙
人; THEA: *scenery*
bùjǐng 布景; (*where a movie is
made*) pāishè chǎngdì 拍摄场地;
(*in tennis*) pán 盘; *television* ~
diànshì jī 电视机 **2** *v/t* (*place*)
fàng 放; *movie, novel etc* yǐ ... wéi
bèijǐng 以 ... 为背景; *date, time,
limit* dìng 定; *mechanism* tiáozhěng
调整; *alarm clock* tiáohé 调合;
*broken limb* jiēhǎo 接好; *jewel*
xiāngqiàn 镶嵌; (*type~*) páibǎn 排

版; ~ *the table* bǎifàng cānjù 摆
放餐具; *a task for X* gěi X yígè
rènwù 给 X 一个任务 **3** *v/i* (*of
sun*) luò 落; (*of glue*) níngjié 凝结
**4** *adj views, ideas* wángù 顽固; *be
dead ~ on X* jiānjué zuò X 坚决
做 X; *be very ~ in one's ways* yì
chéng búbiàn 一成不变; ~
*book / reading* (*in course*) zhǐdìng
jiàocái / yuèdú cáiliào 指定教材 /
阅读材料; ~ *meal* dìngcān 定餐
♦ **set apart**: *set X apart from Y* shǐ
X yǔ Y bùtóng 使 X 与 Y 不同
♦ **set aside** (*for future use*) bōchū
拨出
♦ **set back** (*in plans etc*) zǔ'ài
jìnchéng 阻碍进程; *it set me
back $400* huāle wǒ sìbǎi
měiyuán 花了我四百美元
♦ **set off 1** *v/i* (*on journey*) chūfā 出
发 **2** *v/t explosion, chain reaction*
dǎozhì 导致
♦ **set out 1** *v/i* (*on journey*) chūfā
出发; ~ *to do X* (*intend*) yǒu mùdì
de zuò X 有目的地做 X **2** *v/t
ideas, proposal* chénshù 陈述;
*goods* bǎifàng 摆放
♦ **set to** (*start on a task*) kāishǐ gàn
开始干
♦ **set up 1** *v/t new company* chénglì
成立; *system* jiànlì 建立;
*equipment, machine* zhuāngpèi 装
配; *market stall* shèlì 设立; F
(*frame*) shè quāntào 设圈套 **2** *v/i*
(*in business*) chénglì 成立

**setback** zǔ'ài 阻碍

**setting** (*of novel etc*) bèijǐng 背景;
(*of house*) huánjìng 环境

**settle 1** *v/i* (*of liquid*) chéngqīng 澄
清; (*of dust*) xiàchén 下沉; (*to
live*) dìngjū 定居; (*of bird*) tíngxiē
停歇 **2** *v/t dispute, issue* jiějué 解
决; *s.o.'s debts* chánghuán 偿还;
*check* jiésuàn 结算; *that's it!* nà
jiù dìng le! 那就定了！
♦ **settle down** *v/i* (*stop being noisy*)
ānjìng 安静; (*stop wild living*)
āndìng xiàlái 安定下来; (*in an
area*) dìngjū 定居
♦ **settle for** (*take, accept*) miǎnqiǎng
rènkě 勉强认可

settlement (*of claim, debt*) qīngcháng 清偿; (*of dispute*) jiějué解决; (*payment*) chángfù 偿付

settler (*in new country*) zhímín zhě 殖民者

set-up (*structure*) xìtǒng 系统; (*relationship*) guānxì 关系; F (*frameup*) kēnghài 坑害

seven qī 七

seventeen shíqī 十七

seventeenth dìshíqī 第十七

seventh dìqī 第七

seventieth dìqīshí 第七十

seventy qīshí 七十

sever v/t arm, cable etc qiēduàn 切断; relations zhōngduàn 中断

several adj & pron jǐge 几个

severe illness, penalty yánzhòng 严重; teacher, face yánlì 严厉; winter, weather èliè 恶劣

severely punish yánlì 严厉; speak, stare kēkè 苛刻; injured, disrupted yánzhòng 严重

severity (*of illness, penalty*) yánzhòng 严重; (*of look etc*) yánsù 严肃

sew 1 v/t féng 缝 2 v/i féngrèn 缝纫

♦ sew on button féngshang 缝上

sewage wūwù 污物

sewage plant wūwù chǔlíchǎng 污物处理场

sewer wūshuǐguǎn 污水管

sewing (*skill*) féngrèn 缝纫; (*that being sewn*) xiànhuózhēn 针线活

sewing machine féngrènjī 缝纫机

sex (*act*) xìngjiāo 性交; (*gender*) xìngbié 性别; **have ~ with X** yǔ X xìngjiāo 与X性交

sexual xìng fāngmiàn 性方面

sexual intercourse xìngjiāo 性交

sexually transmitted disease xìng chuánbō jíbìng 性传播疾病

sexy xìnggǎn 性感

SEZ (= **special economic zone**) jīngjì tèqū 经济特区

shabby coat etc hánsuān 寒酸; treatment bù gōngpíng 不公平

shack péngzi 棚子

shade 1 n (*for lamp*) dēngzhào 灯罩; (*of color*) sèdù 色度; (*on window*) liánzi 帘子; **in the ~** yīnliángchù 阴凉处 2 v/t (*from sun, light*) zhēbì 遮蔽

shadow n yǐngzi 影子

shady spot yīnliáng 阴凉; character, dealings kàobúzhù 靠不住

shaft (*of axle*) zhóu 轴; (*of mine*) kuàngjǐng 矿井

shaggy hair, dog cūnóng péngsōng 粗浓蓬松

shake 1 n: give X a good ~ bǎ X hǎohǎo yáohuàng yíxià 把X好好摇晃一下 2 v/t yáo 摇; ~ hands wòshǒu 握手; ~ hands with X yǔ X wòshǒu 与X握手; ~ one's head yáotóu 摇头 3 v/i (*of hands, voice*) chàndǒu 颤抖; (*of building*) huàngdòng 晃动

shaken (*emotionally*) fādǒu 发抖

shake-up chóngzǔ 重组

shaky table etc yáohuàng 摇晃; (*after illness, shock*) ruò 弱; grasp of sth, grammar etc bù zhāshí 不扎实

shall: I ~ do my best wǒ jiāng jìnwǒsuǒnéng 我将尽我所能; ~ we go now? wǒmen xiànzài zǒuba? 我们现在走吧？

shallow water qiǎn 浅; person qiǎnbó 浅薄

shallow fry jiān 煎

shame 1 n xiūchǐ 羞耻; bring ~ on X gěi X dàilái chǐrǔ 给X带来耻辱; what a ~! zhēn yíhàn! 真遗憾！; ~ on you! zhēn kěchǐ! 真可耻！ 2 v/t shǐ diūliǎn 使丢脸; X into doing Y shǐ X gǎndào xiūkuì ér zuò Y 使X感到羞愧而做Y

shameful bù tǐmiàn 不体面

shameless bú yào liǎn 不要脸

shampoo 1 n xǐfàjīng 洗发精; a ~ and set xǐ tóufa bìng zuò tóufa 洗头发并做头发 2 v/t gěirén xǐtóufa 给人洗头发

Shandong Peninsula Shāndōng Bàndǎo 山东半岛

Shanghai Shànghǎi 上海

shape 1 n xíngzhuàng 形状 2 v/t clay, s.o.'s life sùzào 塑造; the *future* cùchéng 促成

**shapeless** *dress etc* wú dìngxíng 无定形

**shapely** *figure* yúnchèn 匀称

**share 1** *n* yífèn 一份; FIN gǔfèn 股份; *do one's ~ of the work* zuò yīngzuòde gōngzuò 做应做的工作 **2** *v/t* fēnxiǎng 分享; *s.o.'s feelings, opinions* gòngtóng jùyǒu 共同具有 **3** *v/i* fēnxiǎng 分享; *do you mind sharing with Patrick?* (bed, room, table) nǐ yǔ Pàtèlǐkè gòngyòng hǎoma? 你与帕特里克共用好吗？

♦ **share out** píngfēn 平分

**shareholder** gǔdōng 股东

**shark** shā 鲨

**sharp 1** *adj knife* fēnglì 锋利; *mind* língmǐn 灵敏; *pain* jùliè 剧烈; *taste* xīnlà 辛辣 **2** *adv* MUS piāngāo 偏高; *at 3 o'clock ~* sāndiǎn zhěng 三点整

**sharpen** *knife* shǐ fēnglì 使锋利; *skills* tígāo 提高

**sharp practise** bēibǐ jiāoyì 卑鄙交易

**shatter 1** *v/t glass* fěnsuì 粉碎; *illusions* pòmiè 破灭 **2** *v/i* (of glass) dǎsuì 打碎

**shattered** F (exhausted) jīnpílìjìn 筋疲力尽; (very upset) fēicháng nánguò 非常难过

**shattering** *news, experience* lìngrén zhènjīng 令人震惊; *effect* lìngrén jīngtàn 令人惊叹

**shave 1** *v/t* guā 刮 **2** *v/i* guāliǎn 刮脸 **3** *n*: *have a ~* guāliǎn 刮脸; *that was a close ~* nà zhēnshì jiǎoxìng tuōxiǎn 那真是侥幸脱险

♦ **shave off** *beard* guādiào 刮掉; (from piece of wood) bàoqù yìcéng 刨去一层

**shaven** *head* tìguāng 剃光

**shaver** (electric) tìdāo 剃刀

**shaving brush** húshuā 胡刷

**shaving soap** tìxūgāo 剃须膏

**shawl** pījiān 披肩

**she** tā 她

**shears** dàjiǎndāo 大剪刀

**sheath** *n* (for knife) qiào 鞘;

(contraceptive) bìyùntào 避孕套

**shed¹** *v/t blood, tears* liú 流; *leaves* tuōluò 脱落; *~ light on X* fig shǐ X gèng qīngchǔ xiē 使 X 更清楚些

**shed²** *n* péng 棚

**sheep** miányáng 绵羊

**sheepdog** mùyángquǎn 牧羊犬

**sheepish** xiūqiè 羞怯

**sheepskin** *adj lining* yángpí 羊皮

**sheer** *adj madness, luxury* shízú 十足; *drop, cliffs* jìnhū chuízhí 近乎垂直

**sheet** (for bed) chuángdān 床单; (of paper) zhāng 张; (of metal, glass) bǎn 板

**shelf** jià 架; *shelves* jià 架

**shell 1** *n* (of mussel, egg, tortoise etc) ké 壳; MIL pàodàn 炮弹; *come out of one's ~* fig búzài xiūqiè 不再羞怯 **2** *v/t peas* bāoké 剥壳; MIL pàojī 炮击

**shellfire** pàohuǒ 炮火; *come under ~* zāodào pàohuǒ xíjī 遭到炮火袭击

**shellfish** bèilèi 贝类

**shelter 1** *n* (refuge) bìhù 庇护; (construction) yǎnbìwù 掩蔽物 **2** *v/i* (from rain, bombing etc) duǒbì 躲避 **3** *v/t* (protect) bǎohù 保护

**sheltered** *place* kě bì fēngyǔ 可避风雨; *lead a ~ life* guòzhe wúyōuwúlǜde shēnghuó 过着无忧无虑的生活

**shepherd** *n* mùyángrén 牧羊人

**sherry** xuělìjiǔ 雪利酒

**shield 1** *n* dùn 盾; (sports trophy) dùnxíng jǐnbiāo 盾形锦标; TECH hùbǎn 护板 **2** *v/t* (protect) bǎohù 保护

**shift 1** *n* (in attitude, thinking) gǎibiàn 改变; (switchover) zhuǎnbiàn 转变; (in direction of wind etc) zhuǎnxiàng 转向; (period of work) bān 班 **2** *v/t* (move) yídòng 移动; *stains etc* nòngdiào 弄掉; *~ the emphasis onto* bǎ zhòngdiǎn zhuǎnyídào 把重点转移到 **3** *v/i* (move) nuódòng 挪动; (in attitude, opinion) gǎibiàn 改变; (of wind) zhuǎnbiàn 转变; *that's ~ing!* F tàikuàile! 太快了！

**shift key** COMPUT huàndǎngjiàn 换档键

**shift work** lúnbānde gōngzuò 轮班的工作

**shifty** pej bù duì jìnr 不对劲儿

**shifty-looking** pej guǐguǐ suìsui 鬼鬼祟祟

**shimmer** v/i fā shǎnshuò de wēiguāng 发闪烁的微光

**shin** n jìngbù 胫部

**shine 1** v/i (of sun, moon) zhàoyào 照耀; (of shoes, polish) fāguāng 发光; fig (of student etc) chūzhòng chūzhòng 出众 **2** v/t flashlight etc zhàoyīzhào 照一照 **3** n (on shoes etc) guāngzé 光泽

**shingle** (on beach) hǎibīn shāshí 海滨砂石

**shingles** MED dàizhuàng pàozhěn 带状疱疹

**shiny** surface fāliàng 发亮

**ship 1** n chuán 船 **2** v/t (send) yùnsòng 运送; (send by sea) hǎiyùn 海运

**shipment** (consignment) huòwù 货物

**shipowner** chuánzhǔ 船主

**shipping** (sea traffic) chuánbó 船舶; (sending) yùnsòng 运送; (sending by sea) hǎiyùn 海运

**shipping company** yùnshū gōngsī 运输公司

**shipshape** adj zhěngqí 整齐

**shipwreck 1** n hǎinàn 海难 **2** v/t shǐ rén zāoyù hǎinàn 使人遭遇海难; **be ~ed** yù hǎinàn 遇海难; **shipyard** zàochuánchǎng 造船厂

**shirk** táobì 逃避

**shirt** chènshān 衬衫; **in his ~ sleeves** tā chuānzhe chènshān, méi chuān wàiyī 他穿着衬衫，没穿外衣

**shit F 1** n shǐ 屎; (bad quality goods, work) gǒushǐ bùrú 狗屎不如; **I need a ~** wǒ děi qù lāshǐ 我得去拉屎 **2** v/i lāshǐ 拉屎 **3** interj māde 妈的

**shitty** F zāogāo 糟糕

**shiver** v/i chàndǒu 颤抖

**shock 1** n zhènjīng 震惊; ELEC chùdiàn 触电; **be in ~** MED chǔyú xiūkè zhuàngtài 处于休克状态 **2** v/t shǐrén zhènjīng 使人震惊; **be ~ed by X** bèi X xià le yítiào 被X吓了一跳

**shock absorber** MOT jiǎnzhènqì 减震器

**shocking** behavior, poverty lìngrén zhènjīng 令人震惊; F (very bad) hěn zāo 很糟

**shoddy** goods lièzhì 劣质; behavior bēiliè 卑劣

**shoe** xié 鞋

**shoelace** xiédài 鞋带; **shoestore** xiédiàn 鞋店; **shoestring: do X on a ~** yòng jíshǎo de qián zuò X 用极少的钱做X

◆ **shoo away** children, chicken fā xūshēng gǎnzǒu 发嘘声赶走

**shoot 1** n BOT nènyá 嫩芽 **2** v/t shèzhòng 射中; (and kill) qiāngbì 枪毙; movie pāishè 拍摄; **~ X in the leg** X tuǐshang zhòngle yídàn X腿上中了一弹

◆ **shoot down** airplane jīluò 击落; suggestion bódǎo 驳倒

◆ **shoot off** (rush off) pǎodiào 跑掉

◆ **shoot up** (of prices) xùnsù shàngshēng 迅速上升; (of children) zhǎnggāo cháng gāo 长高; (of new suburbs, buildings etc) xùnsù jiànqǐ 迅速建起

**shooting star** liúxīng 流星

**shop 1** n shāngdiàn 商店; **talk ~** shuō hánghuà 说行话 **2** v/i mǎi dōngxi 买东西; **go ~ping** qù mǎi dōngxi 去买东西

**shopkeeper** diànzhǔ 店主

**shoplifter** rùdiàn xíngqiè 入店行窃

**shopper** gòuwùrén 购物人

**shopping** (activity) gòuwù 购物; (items) mǎidào de dōngxi 买到的东西; **do one's ~** gòuwù 购物

**shopping mall** gòuwù zhōngxīn 购物中心

**shop steward** gōnghuì fāyánrén 工会发言人

**shore** àn 岸; **on ~** (not at sea) ànshang 岸上

**short 1** adj (in height) ǎi 矮; road,

*distance, time* duǎn 短; *be ~ of* quēfá 缺乏 **2** *adv*: *cut a vacation / meeting ~* suōduǎn jiàqī / huìyì 缩短假期 / 会议; *stop a person ~* shǐrén de tánhuà gānàn ér zhǐ 使人的谈话嘎然而止; *go ~* qiànquē 欠缺; *in ~* jiǎn ér yánzhī 简而言之

**shortage** quēfá 缺乏

**short circuit** *n* duǎnlù 短路;

**shortcoming** quēdiǎn 缺点;

**short cut** jiéjìng 捷径

**shorten** *v/t dress, hair etc* nòngduǎn 弄短; *chapter, article* biànduǎn 变短; *vacation, work day* suōduǎn 缩短

**shortfall** chìzì 赤字; **shorthand** *n* sùjì 速记; **shortlist** *n (of candidates)* juéxuǎn 决选; **short-lived** duǎnzàn 短暂;

**shortly** *(soon)* bùjiǔ 不久; *~ before that* jiù zài nà yǐqián 就在那以前

**shorts** duǎnkù 短裤; *(underwear for men)* sānjiǎo kù 三角裤

**shortsighted** jìnshì 近视; *fig* wú yuǎnjiàn 无远见; **short-sleeved** duǎnxiù 短袖; **short-staffed** rényuán bùzú 人员不足; **short story** duǎnpiān xiǎoshuō 短篇小说; **short-tempered** ài fā píqì 爱发脾气; **short-term** duǎnqī 短期; **short time**: *be on ~ (of workers)* chǔyú duǎngōng shíqī 处于短工时期; **short wave** duǎnbō 短波

**shot** *(from gun)* shèjīshēng 射击声; *(photograph)* jìngtóu 镜头; *(injection)* zhùshè 注射; *be a good / poor ~* hǎo / chàjìn de shèshǒu 好 / 差劲的射手; *like a ~ accept, run off* háobùyóuyù 毫不犹豫; *in one ~ drink, write etc* yíxiàzi 一下子

**shotgun** lièqiāng 猎枪

**should** yīnggāi 应该; *what ~ I do?* wǒ gāi zuò shénme? 我该做什么?; *you ~n't do that* nǐ bù yīnggāi nàme zuò 你不应该那么做; *that ~ be long enough* nà yīnggāi gòucháng le 那应该够长

了; *you ~ have heard him!* nǐ zhēn yīnggāi tīngtīng tā shuōde! 你真应该听听他说的!

**shoulder** *n* jiānbǎng 肩膀

**shoulder blade** jiānjiǎgǔ 肩胛骨

**shout 1** *n* hǎnshēng 喊声 **2** *v/i* jiàohǎn 叫喊 **3** *v/t order* mìnglìng 命令

◆**shout at** duì ... hǎn 对 ... 喊

**shouting** hǎnjiào 喊叫

**shove 1** *n* zhuàng 撞 **2** *v/t* bān 搬 **3** *v/i* jǐ 挤

◆**shove in** *v/i (in line-up)* jiāxiēr 加楔儿

◆**shove off** *v/i* F *(go away)* zǒukāi 走开

**shovel** *n* tiěqiāo 铁锹

**show 1** *n* THEA, TV jiémù 节目; *(display)* biǎolù 表露; *on ~ (at exhibition)* zài zhǎnlǎn 在展览; *it's all done for ~* pej dōu shì wèi gěi biérén kàn de 都是为给别人看的 **2** *v/t passport, ticket* chūshì 出示; *interest, emotion* biǎodá 表达; *(at exhibition)* zhǎnshì 展示; *movie* diànyǐng 电影; *~ X to Y* bǎ X gěi Y kàn 把 X 给 Y 看 **3** *v/i (be visible)* kàndejiàn 看得见; *(of movie)* shàngyìng 上映; *does it ~?* néng kànchūlái ma? 能看出来吗?

◆**show off 1** *v/t skills* zhǎnshì 展示 **2** *v/i pej* xuányào 炫耀

◆**show up 1** *v/t s.o.'s shortcomings etc* xiǎnxiànchū 显现出; *don't show me up in public (embarrass)* bié dāngzhòng ràng wǒ chūchǒu 别当众让我出丑 **2** *v/i (arrive, turn up)* dàolái 到来; *(be visible)* kàndejiàn 看得见

**show business** yǎnyìjiè 演艺界

**showdown** zuìhòu jiàoliàng 最后较量

**shower 1** *n (of rain)* zhènyǔ 阵雨; *(to wash)* línyù 淋; *take a ~* línyù 淋浴 **2** *v/i* línyù 淋浴 **3** *v/t*: *~ X with compliments / praise* jiélì zànshǎng / biǎoyáng X 竭力赞赏 / 表扬 X

**shower bath** línyù 淋浴; **shower cap** yùmào 浴帽; **shower**

curtain línyùlián 淋浴帘;
showerproof *adj* fángyǔ 防雨
show jumping mǎpǐ zhàng'ài
yùndòng 马匹障碍运动
show-off ài xuányào de rén 爱炫
耀的人
showroom shāngpǐn chénlièshì 商
品陈列室
showy *jacket, behavior* kuāyào 夸
耀
shred 1 *n (of paper etc)* suìpiàn 碎
片; *(of evidence etc)* sīháo 丝毫
2 *v/t paper* sīchéng suìpiàn 撕成
碎片; *(in cooking)* qiēchéng
xiǎotiáo 切成小条
shredder *(for documents)* qiēsuìjī
切碎机
shrewd jīngmíng 精明
shriek 1 *n* jiānjiào 尖叫 2 *v/i*
jiānshēng shuōchū 尖声说出
shrimp xiǎoxiā 小虾
shrine shénkān 神龛
shrink *v/i (of material)* suōshuǐ 缩
水; *(of level of support etc)* jiǎnruò
减弱
shrink-wrap sùmó bāozhuāng 塑
膜包装
shrink-wrapping *(process)* sùmó
bāozhuāng 塑膜包装; *(material)*
sùmó 塑膜
shrivel wěisuō 萎缩
shrub guànmù 灌木
shrubbery guànmùcóng 灌木丛
shrug 1 *n* sǒngjiān 耸肩; *he gave
a ~ and left* tā sǒnglesǒng jiān jiù
zǒule 他耸了耸肩就走了 2 *v/i*
sǒngjiān 耸肩 3 *v/t*: *~ one's
shoulders* sǒngjiān 耸肩
shudder 1 *n (of fear, disgust)* fādǒu
发抖; *(of earth etc)* zhèndòng 震
动 2 *v/i (with fear, disgust)* fādǒu
发抖; *(of earth, building)*
zhèndòng 震动
shuffle 1 *v/t cards* xǐ 洗 *v/i (in
walking)* jiǎo cèng dì 脚蹭地
shun duǒbì 躲避
shut 1 *v/t* guān 关 2 *v/i* guān 关;
*they were ~* tāmen yǐjīng guānle
他们已经关了
♦ shut down 1 *v/t business* tíngyè
停业; *computer* guānjī 关机 2 *v/i*

*(of business)* guānbì 关闭; *(of
computer)* guānjī 关机
♦ shut up *v/i (be quiet)* ānjìng 安
静; *~!* zhùzuǐ! 住嘴!
shutter *(on window)* chuāngbǎn 窗
板; PHOT kuàiménr 快门儿
shuttle *v/i* chuānsuō 穿梭
shuttlebus *(at airport)* chuānsuō
yíngyùn 穿梭营运; **shuttlecock**
SP yǔmáo qiú 羽毛球; **shuttle
service** chuānsuō yèwù 穿梭业
务
shy hàixiū 害羞
shyness miǎntiǎn 腼腆
Siamese twins liántǐ shuāngbāotāi 连体双胞胎
Sichuan Basin Sìchuān Péndì 四
川盆地
sick shēngbìng 生病; *sense of
humor* cánkù 残酷; *society* bìngtài
病态; *I feel ~ (about to vomit)* wǒ
gǎndào ěxīn 我感到恶心; *I'm
going to be ~ (vomit)* wǒ yào tù wǒ
要吐; *be ~ of (fed up with)*
gǎndào yànwù 感到厌恶
sicken *v/t (disgust)* shǐrén gǎndào
yànwù 使人感到厌恶 2 *v/i: be
~ing for* déle ... bìng 得了 ...病
sickening *adj* lìngrén yànwù 令人
厌恶
sickle liándāo 镰刀
sick leave bìngjià 病假; *be on ~*
xiū bìngjià 休病假
sickly *person* duōbìng 多病; *color*
bú jiànkāng 不健康
sickness jíbìng 疾病; *(vomiting)*
ǒutù 呕吐
side *n (of box, house)* cèmiàn 侧面;
*(of room, field)* biān 边; *(of
mountain)* miàn 面; *(of person)* lèi
肋; SP yìfāng 一方; *take ~s (favor
one side)* piānxiàng 偏向; *take ~s
with* zhīchí 支持; *I'm on your ~*
wǒ zhīchí nǐ 我支持你; *~ by ~*
bìngpái 并排; *at the ~ of the
road* zài lùbiān 在路边; *on the
big / small ~* piān dà / xiǎo 偏大 /
小
♦ side with zhīchí 支持
sideboard *(furniture)* cānjùguì 餐
具柜; **sideburns** liánbìn húzi 连

鬓胡子；**side dish** xiǎocài 小菜；
**side effect** fùzuòyòng 副作用；
**sidelight** MOT cèdēng 侧灯；
**sideline 1** n fùyè 副业 **2** v/t: **feel ~d** gǎndào bèi hūshì 感到被忽视；**side street** xiǎoxiàng 小巷；
**sidetrack** v/t chàkāi 岔开；**get ~ed** bèi chàkāi 被岔开；**sidewalk** xíngréndào 人行道；**sidewalk café** lùbiān kāfēiguǎn 路边咖啡馆；**sideways** adv xiézhe 斜着

**siege** wéikùn 围困；**lay ~ to** bāowéi 包围

**sieve** n shāizi 筛子

**sift** v/t corn, ore shāi 筛

♦ **sift through** details, data xìshěn 细审

**sigh 1** n tànxī 叹息；**heave a ~ of relief** sōng yìkǒu qì 松一口气 **2** v/i tànqì 叹气

**sight** n qíngjǐng 情景；(power of seeing) shìlì 视力；**~s** (of city) míngshèng 名胜；**catch ~ of** kànjiàn 看见；**know by ~** miànshú 面熟；**within ~ of X** zài X shìyě zhī nèi 在 X 视野之内；**out of ~** zài shìchéng zhī wài 在视程之外；fig F gàilemàole 盖了帽了；**what a ~ you are!** kàn nǐ shì shénme xíngxiàng! 看你是什么形象！；**lose ~ of** objective etc hūlüè 忽略

**sightseeing** guānguāng 观光；**go ~** qù guānguāng 去观光

**sightseeing tour** guānguāng lǚyóu 观光旅游

**sightseer** guānguāngkè 观光客

**sign 1** n (indication) jìxiàng 迹象；(road ~) zhǐshìpái 指示牌；(outside store, on building) zhāopai 招牌；**it's a ~ of the times** shídài de biāozhì 时代的标志 **2** v/t & v/i qiānzì 签字

♦ **sign up** v/i (join the army) yìngzhēng 应征

**signal 1** n xìnhào 信号；**be sending out all the right / wrong ~s** fāchū zhèngquè / cuòwù de ànshì 发出正确 / 错误的暗示 **2** v/i (of driver) zhǐshì 指示

**signatory** qiānyuēfāng 签约方

**signature** qiānmíng 签名

**signature tune** kāishǐqǔ 开始曲

**significance** (importance) zhòngyàoxìng 重要性；(meaning) yìyì 意义

**significant** event etc zhòngyào 重要；(quite large) dàliàng 大量

**signify** yìwèi 意味

**sign language** shǒushì yǔyán 手势语言

**signpost** lùbiāo 路标

**silence 1** n chénmò 沉默；**in ~** work, march ānjìng 安静；**~!** sùjìng! 肃静！ **2** v/t yāzhì 压制

**silencer** (on gun) xiāoyīnqì 消音器

**silent** ānjìng 安静；movie wúshēng 无声；**stay ~** (not comment) yìshēng bùkēng 一声不吭

**silent partner** búrù shíyè de gǔdōng 不入实业的股东

**silhouette** n lúnkuò 轮廓

**silicon** ⇩ guī 硅

**silicon chip** ⇩ guīpiàn 硅片

**silk 1** n sīchóu 丝绸 **2** adj shirt etc sīzhì 丝制

**Silk Road** Sīchóu zhī lù 丝绸之路

**silly** shǎ 傻

**silver 1** n yín 银；(~ medal) yínpái 银牌 **2** adj ring yínzhì 银制；hair huībái 灰白

**silver-plated** dùyín 镀银

**similar** xiāngsì 相似

**similarity** xiāngsì 相似

**simmer** v/i (in cooking) dùn 炖；(with rage) yíchùjífā 一触即发

♦ **simmer down** ānjìngxiàlái 安静下来

**simple** (easy) jiǎndān 简单；person tóunǎo jiǎndān 头脑简单

**simplicity** jiǎndān 简单

**simplified characters** jiǎntǐzì 简体字

**simplify** shǐ jiǎndān 使简单

**simplistic** guòyú jiǎndānhuà 过于简单化

**simply** (absolutely) juéduì 绝对；(in a simple way) jiǎndān 简单；**it is ~ the best** jiǎnzhí shì zuìhǎode 简直是最好的

**simulate** móní 摹拟

**simultaneous** tóngshí 同时

**simultaneously** tóngshí 同时

**sin 1** *n* zuì'è 罪恶 **2** *v/i* fànyǒu zuì'è 犯有罪恶

**since 1** *prep* zìcóng 自从; *~ last week* zìcóng shàngzhōu yǐlái 自从上周以来 **2** *adv* zìnà yǐhòu 自那以后; *I haven't seen him ~* zìnà yǐhòu, wǒ zài méi jiànguò tā 自那以后，我再没见过他 **3** *conj* (*expressions of time*) cóng ... yǐlái 从 ... 以来; (*seeing that*) jìrán 既然; *~ you left* zìcóng nǐ zǒu yǐhòu 自从你走以后; *~ you don't like it* jìrán nǐ bù xǐhuān 既然你不喜欢

**sincere** chéngzhì 诚挚

**sincerely** chéngzhì 诚挚; *hope* zhēnchéng 真诚; *Yours ~* jǐnqí 谨启

**sincerity** zhēnchéng 真诚

**sinful** xié'è 邪恶

**sing** chàng 唱

**Singapore** Xīnjiāpō 新加坡

**Singaporean 1** *adj* Xīnjiāpō 新加坡 **2** *n* (*person*) Xīnjiāpō rén 新加坡人

**singe** *v/t* shāojiāo 烧焦

**singer** gēshǒu 歌手

**single 1** *n* (*sole*) wéiyī 唯一; (*not double*) yígè 一个; (*not married*) dúshēn 独身; *there wasn't a ~ ...* yígè ... dōu méiyǒu 一个 ... 都没有; *in ~ file* chéngdānháng 成单行 **2** *n* MUS dānqǔ chàngpiàn 单曲唱片; *~s* (*in tennis*) dāndǎ 单打
♦ **single out** (*choose*) tiāochū 挑出; (*distinguish*) shírén chūzhòng 使人出众

**single-breasted** dānpáikòu 单排扣; **single-handed 1** *adj* dānqiāng pīmǎ 单枪匹马 **2** *adv* dúzì 独自; **single-minded** zhuānxīnzhìzhì 专心致志; **single mother** dānshēn mǔqīn 单身母亲; **single parent** dānqīn 单亲; **single parent family** dānqīn jiātíng 单亲家庭

**singular** GRAM **1** *adj* dānshù 单数 **2** *n* dānshù xíngshì 单数形式; *in the ~* dānshù xíngshì 单数形式

**sinister** xié'è 邪恶

**sink 1** *n* xǐdícáo 洗涤槽 **2** *v/i* (*of ship, object*) chénmò 沉没; (*of sun*) luòxià 落下; (*of interest rates, pressure etc*) xiàjiàng 下降; *he sank onto the bed* tā zāidǎo zài chuáng shàng 他栽倒在床上 **3** *v/t ship* chénmò 沉没; *funds* xiàjiàng 下降
♦ **sink in** *v/i* (*of liquid*) shènrù 渗入; *it still hasn't really sunk in* (*of realization*) háishì méiyǒu zhēnzhèng yìshí dào 还是没有真正意识到

**sinner** zuìrén 罪人

**Sino-** Zhōng- 中

**Sino-Japanese war** Zhōng Rì Zhànzhēng 中日战争

**sinologist** Hànxuéjiā 汉学家

**sinology** Hànxué 汉学

**Sino-Tibetan** Hàn Zàng 汉藏

**sinusitis** MED dòuyán 窦炎

**sip 1** *n* yìxiǎokǒu 一小口 **2** *v/t* xiǎokǒu hē 小口喝

**sir** xiānsheng 先生

**siren** bàojǐngqì 报警器

**sirloin** niúyāoròu 牛腰肉

**sister** (*older*) jiějie 姐姐; (*younger*) mèimei 妹妹

**sister-in-law** (*wife's elder sister*) qīzǐ 妻姊; (*wife's younger sister*) qīmèi 妻妹; (*husband's elder sister*) dàgūjiě 大姑姐; (*husband's younger sister*) xiǎogū 小姑; (*younger brother's wife*) dìmèi 弟妹; (*older brother's wife*) sǎozi 嫂子

**sit** *v/i* zuò 坐
♦ **sit down** zuòxià 坐下
♦ **sit up** (*in bed*) zuòqǐlái 坐起来; (*straighten back*) zuòzhí 坐直; (*wait up at night*) áoyè 熬夜

**sitcom** TV qíngjǐng xǐjù 情景喜剧

**site 1** *n* chǎngdì 场地 **2** *v/t new offices etc* zédìng wèizhi 择定位置

**sitting** (*of committee, court*) kāitíng 开庭; (*for artist*) gōngrén huàxiàng huò pāizhào de shíjiān 供人

画像或拍照的时间；(for meals) shíjiānduàn 时间段

**sitting room** kètīng 客厅

**situated**: be ~ zuòluòzài 坐落在

**situation** xíngshì 形势；(of building etc) wèizhi 位置

**six** liù 六

**sixteen** shíliù 十六

**sixteenth** dìshíliù 第十六

**sixth** dìliù 第六

**sixtieth** dìliùshí 第六十

**sixty** liùshí 六十

**size** dàxiǎo 大小；(of jacket, shoes) hàomǎ 号码

♦**size up** gūliáng 估量

**sizeable** xiāngdāng dà 相当大

**sizzle** fā sīsī shēng 发咝咝声

**skate 1** n (for ice) huábīng 滑冰；(roller skate) huá hànbīng 滑旱冰 **2** v/i (on ice) huábīng 滑冰；(roller skating) huá hànbīng 滑旱冰

**skateboard** n huábǎn 滑板

**skater** huábīngrén 滑冰人

**skating** huábīng 滑冰

**skeleton** kūlóu 骷髅

**skeleton key** wànnéng yàoshi 万能钥匙

**skeptic** huáiyílùn zhě 怀疑论者

**skeptical** huáiyí 怀疑

**skepticism** huáiyí tàidù 怀疑态度

**sketch 1** n cǎotú 草图；THEA huájī duǎnjù 滑稽短剧 **2** v/t xiěshēng 写生

**sketchbook** sùmiáobù 素描簿

**sketchy** knowledge etc fúqiǎn 肤浅

**ski** n & v/i huáxuě 滑雪

**skid 1** n shāchē 刹车 **2** v/i dǎhuá 打滑

**skier** huáxuě zhě 滑雪者

**skiing** huáxuě 滑雪

**ski lift** diàosuǒ yùnshūchē 吊索运输车

**skill** jìqiǎo 技巧

**skilled** yǒujìnéng 有技能

**skilled worker** jìgōng 技工

**skillful** shúliàn 熟练

**skim** surface lüèguò 掠过；milk piēqù 撇去

♦**skim off** the best tíqǔ 提取

♦**skim through** text liúlǎn 浏览

**skimmed milk** tuōzhīrǔ 脱脂乳

**skimpy** account etc qūfá 缺乏；little dress bàolù 暴露

**skin 1** n pífū 皮肤 **2** v/t qùpí 去皮

**skin diving** qiányóu yùndòng 潜游运动

**skinny** píbāogǔ 皮包骨

**skin-tight** jǐnshēn 紧身

**skip 1** n (little jump) bèng 蹦 **2** v/t (omit) lüèguò 略过

**ski pole** huáxuězhàng 滑雪杖

**skipper** NAUT chuánzhǎng 船长；(of team) duìzhǎng 队长

**skirt** n qúnzi 裙子

**ski run** huáxuědào 滑雪道

**ski tow** diàosuǒ yùnshūchē 吊索运输车

**skull** tóulúgǔ 头颅骨

**sky** tiānkōng 天空

**skylight** tiānchuāng 天窗；**skyline** kōngzhōng lúnkuò xiàn 空中轮廓线；**skyscraper** mótiāndàlóu 摩天大楼

**slab** (of stone) hòubǎn 厚板；(of cake etc) yídàkuài 一大块

**slack** rope sōngchí 松弛；discipline xièdài 懈怠；person búrènzhēn 不认真；work cūxīn 粗心；period qīngdàn 清淡

**slacken** rope sōngchí 松弛；pace fàngmàn 放慢

♦**slacken off** v/i (of trading) jiǎnhuǎn 减缓；(of pace) fàngmàn 放慢

**slacks** kuānsōng kù 宽松裤

**slam 1** v/t door pēngde guānshang 砰地关上 **2** v/i (of door etc) fāchū pēngshēng 发出砰声

♦**slam down** shuāi 摔

**slander** n & v/t fěibàng 诽谤

**slang** lǐyǔ 俚语；(of a specific group) hánghuà 行话

**slant** v/i qīngxié 倾斜 **2** n xiépō 斜坡；(given to a story) guāndiǎn 观点

**slanting** qīngxié 倾斜

**slap** n & v/t zhǎngjī 掌击

**slash 1** n (cut) kǎnhén 砍痕；(in punctuation) xiéxiàn 斜线 **2** v/t skin etc luànkǎn 乱砍；prices, costs dà xùjiǎn 大削减；~ one's wrists gēwàn 割腕

slate n (type of rock) bǎnyán 板岩; (for writing on) shíbǎn 石板

slaughter 1 n (of animals) túshā 屠杀; (of people, troops) shālù 杀戮 2 v/t animals túshā 屠杀; people, troops shālù 杀戮

slave n núlì 奴隶

slay shā 杀

slaying (murder) móushā 谋杀

sleazy bar, characters xiàliú 下流

sled(ge) n xuěqiāo 雪橇

sledge hammer dàchuí 大锤

sleep 1 n shuìjiào 睡觉; go to ~ qù shuìjiào 去睡觉; I need a good ~ wǒ xūyào hǎohāo shuìyíjiào 我需要好好睡一觉; I couldn't get to ~ wǒ shuìbùzháo 我睡不着 2 v/i shuì 睡
♦ sleep in (sleep late) shuìge lǎnjiào 睡个懒觉
♦ sleep on v/t proposal, decision dài cìrì juédìng 待次日决定
♦ sleep with (have sex with) yǔ ... shuìjiào 与 ... 睡觉

sleeping bag shuìdài 睡袋; sleeping car wòchē 卧车; sleeping pill ānmiányào 安眠药

sleepless night bùmián 不眠

sleep walker mèngyóu zhě 梦游者

sleepy yawn kùnjuàn 困倦; town yōujìng 幽静; I'm ~ wǒ kùn le 我困了

sleet n yǔjiáxuě 雨夹雪

sleeve (of jacket etc) xiùzi 袖子

sleeveless wúxiù 无袖

sleigh n xuěqiāo 雪橇

sleight of hand qiǎomiàode shǒufǎ 巧妙的手法

slender figure, arms xiānxì 纤细; chance wēixiǎo 微小; income, margin wēibó 微薄

slice 1 n (of bread, tart) piàn 片; fig (of profits etc) fènr 份儿 2 v/t loaf etc qiēchéng báopiàn 切成薄片

sliced bread qiēpiàn miànbāo 切片面包

slick 1 adj performance búfèilì 不费力; pej (cunning) yuánhuá 圆滑 2 n (of oil) fúyóu 浮油

slide 1 n (for kids) huátī 滑梯; PHOT huàndēngpiàn 幻灯片 2 v/i huá 滑; (drop: of exchange rate etc) xiàjiàng 下降 3 v/t nuó 挪

sliding door lāmén 拉门

slight 1 adj person, figure miáotiáo 苗条; (small) xiǎo 小; no, not in the ~est bù, yìdiǎnr yě bù 不，一点儿也不 2 n (insult) wǔrǔ 侮辱

slightly shāowēi 稍微

slim 1 adj miáotiáo 苗条; chance wēixiǎo 微小 2 v/i jiǎnféi 减肥

slime níjiāng 泥浆

slimy liquid yǒu níjiāng 有泥浆

sling 1 n (for arm) xuándài 悬带 2 v/t (throw) rēng 扔

slip 1 n (on ice etc) shuāijiāo 摔跤; (mistake) cuòwù 错误; a ~ of paper yìxiǎokuài zhǐ 一小块纸; a ~ of the tongue zǒuzuǐ 走嘴; give X the ~ bǎituō X bǎituō X 2 v/i (on ice etc) huá 滑; (decline: of quality etc) xiàjiàng 下降; he ~ped out of the room tā liūchūle fángjiān 他溜出了房间 3 v/t (put) qīngfàng 轻放; he ~ped it into his briefcase tā qīngqīngde bǎ tā fàng jìng wénjiànbāo lǐ 他轻轻地把它放进文件包里
♦ slip away (of time) liúshì 流逝; (of opportunity) shīqù 逝去; (die quietly) qiāorán qùshì 悄然去世
♦ slip off v/t jacket etc tuōdiào 脱掉
♦ slip out v/i (go out) liūchūqù 溜出去
♦ slip up (make mistake) chū chācuò 出差错

slipped disc tūchūde zhuījiānpán 突出的椎间盘

slipper tuōxié 拖鞋

slippery huá 滑

slipshod cūxīn 粗心

slit 1 n (tear) kǒuzi 口子; (hole) lièfèng 裂缝; (in skirt) kāichà 开叉 2 v/t sīkāi 撕开

slither v/i huálái huáqù 滑来滑去

slobber v/i liú kǒushuǐ 流口水

slogan kǒuhào 口号

slop v/t yìchū 溢出

slope 1 n pō 坡; (of mountain) xiépō 斜坡; built on a ~ zài

pōshang jiàn de 在坡上建的 **2** v/i qīngxié 倾斜; **the road ~s down to the sea** dàolù xiàng hǎimiàn qīngxié 道路向海面倾斜

**sloppy** work cǎoshuài 草率; (in dress) yīzhuó bùzhěng 衣着不整; (too sentimental) yōngsú shānggǎn 庸俗伤感

**slot** n fèngxì 缝隙; (in schedule) ānpáide shíjiān 安排的时间

♦ **slot in 1** v/t shǐ chārù 使插入 **2** v/i chārù 插入

**slot machine** (for vending) ⇩ tóubìshòuhuòjī 投币售货机

**slouch** v/i lǎnsàn 懒散

**slovenly** lātà 邋遢

**slow** màn 慢; **be ~** (of clock) mànle 慢了

♦ **slow down 1** v/t jiǎnmàn 减慢 **2** v/i mànxiàlái 慢下来

**slowdown** (in production) xiàjiàng 下降

**slow motion: in ~** màndòngzuò 慢动作

**slug** n (animal) kuòyú 蛞蝓

**sluggish** xíngdòng chíhuǎn 行动迟缓

**slum** n pínmínkū 贫民窟

**slump 1** n (in trade) xiāotiáoqī 萧条期 **2** v/i (economically) zhòurán xiàdiē 骤然下跌; (collapse: of person) chénzhòngde dǎoxià 沉重地倒下

**slur 1** n (on s.o.'s character) dǐhuǐ 诋毁 **2** v/t words hánhubùqīngde shuōhuà 含糊不清地说话

**slurred** speech hánhubùqīng 含糊不清

**slush** bànróngxuě 半融雪; pej (sentimental stuff) gǎnshāngde dōngxi 感伤的东西

**slush fund** hēiqián 黑钱

**slut** fàngdàng nǚzǐ 放荡女子

**sly** jiǎohuá 狡猾; **on the ~** mìmì 秘密

**smack 1** n zhǎngjī 掌击 **2** v/t child zhǎngjī 掌击; bottom pāidǎ 拍打

**small 1** adj xiǎo 小 **2** n: **the ~ of the back** hòuyāo 后腰

**small change** língqián 零钱;

**small hours** língchén shífēn 凌晨时分; **smallpox** tiānhuā 天花; **small print** xiǎozì 小字; **small talk** liáotiān 聊天

**smart 1** adj (elegant) piàoliang 漂亮; (intelligent) cōngmín 聪敏; pace mǐnjié 敏捷; **get ~ with X** gēn X shuǎ huátóu 跟 X 要滑头 **2** v/i (hurt) cìtòng 刺痛

**smart card** ⇩ shuākǎ 刷卡

♦ **smarten up** v/t shǐ gèng yǒu tiáolǐ 使更有条理

**smash 1** n (noise) huālā yīshēng 哗啦一声; (car crash) zhuàngsuì 撞碎; (in tennis) kòuqiú 扣球 **2** v/t (break) dǎsuì 打碎; (hit hard) zhàngjī 撞击; **~ X to pieces** bǎ X zhuàngsuì 把 X 撞碎 **3** v/i (break) pòsuì 破碎; **the driver ~ed into ...** sījī bǎ chē zhuàngdào ... 司机把车撞到 ...

**smash hit** F jīwéi hōngdòng 极为轰动

**smattering** (of a language) yīzhībànjiě 一知半解

**smear 1** n (of ink etc) wūjì 污迹; MED túpiàn 涂片; (on character) wūmiè 污蔑 **2** v/t paint etc túmǒ 涂抹; character fěibàng 诽谤

**smear campaign** fěibàng huódòng 诽谤活动

**smell 1** n (noise) qìwèi 气味; **it has no ~** tā méiyǒu qìwèi 它没有气味; **sense of ~** xiùjué 嗅觉 **2** v/i (unpleasantly) yǒu chòuwèi 有臭味; (sniff) wén 闻; **what does it ~ of?** tā yǒu shénme wèir? 它有什么味儿？; **you ~ of beer** nǐ yǒu píjiǔwèi 你有啤酒味

**smelly** yǒu chòuwèi 有臭味

**smile** n & v/i wēixiào 微笑

♦ **smile at** duì ... wēixiào 对 ... 微笑

**smirk** n &v/i jiānxiào 尖笑

**smog** yānwù 烟雾

**smoke 1** n yān 烟; **have a ~** xīyān 吸烟 **2** v/t cigarettes xī 吸; bacon yòng yānxūn 用烟熏 **3** v/i xīyān 吸烟; **I don't ~** wǒ bù xīyān 我不吸烟

**smoker** (*person*) xīyānde rén 吸烟的人

**smoking** xīyān 吸烟；*no ~* jìnzhǐ xīyān 禁止吸烟

**smoking compartment** RAIL xīyān chēxiāng 吸烟车厢

**smoky** *room, air* duōyān 多烟

**smolder** (*of fire*) huǎnmàn ránshāo 缓慢燃烧；*fig* (*with anger*) yùjī yùjī 郁积；(*with desire*) yùhuǒzhōngshāo 欲火中烧

**smooth 1** *adj surface, skin, sea* guānghuá 光滑；*ride* píngwěn 平稳；*transition* shùnlì 顺利；*pej* (*person*) yuánhuá 圆滑 **2** *v/t hair* shǐ guānghuá 使光滑

♦ **smooth down** (*with sandpaper etc*) móguāng 磨光

♦ **smooth out** *paper, cloth* lāpíng 拉平

♦ **smooth over**: **smooth things over** shǐ shìqíng huǎnjiě 使事情缓解

**smother** *flames* mēnzhù 闷住；*person* shǐ zhìxī 使窒息；*~ X with kisses* bùtíngde qīnwěn X 不停地亲吻 X；*~ bread with jam* guǒjiàng hòuhòude fàngzài miànbāo shang 把果酱厚厚地放在面包上

**smudge 1** *n* wūjì 污迹 **2** *v/t* nòngzāng 弄脏

**smug** zìmǎn 自满

**smuggle** *v/t* zǒusī 走私

**smuggler** zǒusī zhě 走私者

**smuggling** zǒusī 走私

**smutty** *joke, sense of humor* xiàliú 下流

**snack** *n* xiǎochī 小吃

**snack bar** xiǎochīdiàn 小吃店

**snag** (*problem*) xiǎo wèntí 小问题

**snail** wōniú 蜗牛

**snake** *n* shé 蛇

**snap 1** *n* kāchāshēng 喀嚓声；PHOT zhàopiàn 照片；(*break*) duànliè 断裂；(*say sharply*) lìshēng shuō 厉声说 **3** *v/i* (*break*) pāde zhéduàn 啪地折断 **4** *adj decision, judgment* kuàisù 快速

♦ **snap up** *bargains* qiǎnggòu 抢购

**snappy** *person, mood* yìnù 易怒；

*decision, response* lìluò 利落；(*elegant*) shímáo 时髦

**snapshot** zhàopiàn 照片

**snarl 1** *n* (*of dog*) nùhǒu 怒吼 **2** *v/i* chánjié 缠结

**snatch 1** *v/t* duódé 夺得；(*steal*) tōuzǒu 偷走；(*kidnap*) bǎngjià 绑架 **2** *v/i* zhuāqǔ 抓取

**snazzy** shuài 帅

**sneak 1** *v/t* (*remove, steal*) tōuná 偷拿；*~ a glance at* tōukàn yīyǎn 偷看一眼 **2** *v/i*: *~ into the room* / *out of the room* tōutōu liūjìn / liūchū fángjiān 偷偷溜进 / 溜出房间

**sneakers** fānbùxié 帆布鞋

**sneaking** *adj*: *have a ~ suspicion that ...* xīnzhōng yǒu nányǐ xiāochú de cāiyí ... 心中有难以消除的猜疑 ...

**sneaky** F (*crafty*) guǐguǐsuìsuì 鬼鬼祟祟

**sneer** *n & v/i* lěngxiào 冷笑

**sneeze 1** *n* pēntì 喷嚏 **2** *v/i* dǎ pēntì 打喷嚏

**sniff 1** *v/i* (*to clear nose*) yòng bí xīqì bíqiāng 用鼻吸鼻气；(*of dog*) xiù xiù 嗅 **2** *v/t* (*smell*) wén 闻

**sniper** jūjīshǒu 狙击手

**snitch 1** *n* (*telltale*) bānnòngshìfēi de rén 搬弄是非的人 **2** *v/i* (*tell tales*) gàomì 告密

**snob** shìlìyǎn 势利眼

**snobbish** shìlì 势利

**snooker** ⇩ táiqiú 台球

♦ **snoop around** kuīchá 窥察

**snooty** mùzhōngwúrén 目中无人

**snooze 1** *n* kēshuì 瞌睡；*have a ~* xiǎoshuì 小睡 **2** *v/i* dǎ kēshuì 打瞌睡

**snore** *v/i* dǎ hān 打鼾

**snoring** *n* hānshēng 鼾声

**snorkel** *n* tōngqìguǎn 通气管

**snort** *v/i* (*of bull, horse*) pēnbíxī 喷鼻息；(*of person: disdainfully*) fāhēngshēng 发哼声

**snout** (*of pig, dog*) kǒubíbù 口鼻部

**snow 1** *n* xuě 雪 **2** *v/i* xià xuě 下雪

♦ **snow under**: *be snowed under with work* gōngzuò mángbùguòlái

工作忙不过来

**snowball** n xuěqiú 雪球；**snow-bound** bèi xuě kùnzhù 被雪困住；**snow chains** MOT fáng huá liàn 防滑链；**snowdrift** xuěduī 雪堆；**snowdrop** xuělián 雪莲；**snowflake** xuěhuā 雪花；**snowman** xuěrén 雪人；**snowplow** xuělí 雪犁；**snowstorm** bàofēngxuě 暴风雪

**snowy** *weather* duōxuě 多雪；*roads, hills* jīxuě 积雪

**snub** n & v/t dàimàn 怠慢

**snub-nosed** tābí 塌鼻

**snug** nuǎnhuo 暖和；(*tight-fitting*) jǐnshēn 紧身

♦**snuggle down** quánfú 蜷伏

♦**snuggle up to** wēiyīzhe 偎依着

**so 1** adv: ~ *hot* / *cold* tàirè / lěng 太热 / 冷；*not ~ much* búnàme 不那么；~ *much better* / *easier* hǎo / róngyì duōle 好 / 容易多了；*eat* / *drink ~ much* chī / hē hěnduō 吃 / 喝很多；*I miss you ~* wǒ hěn xiǎng nǐ 我很想你；~ *am I* / *do I* wǒ yě shì 我也是；~ *is she* / *does she* tā yě shì 她也是；*and ~ on* děngděng 等等 **2** pron: *I hope* ~ wǒ xīwàng rúcǐ / wǒ rènwéi shì zhèiyàng 我希望如此 / 我认为是这样；*you didn't tell me ~* nǐ méi gàosù wǒ – wǒ gàosù nǐ le 你没告诉我 – 我告诉你了；*50 or ~* dàyù wǔshí 大约五十 **3** conj (*for that reason*) yīncǐ 因此；(*in order that*) shǐde 使得；*and ~ I missed the train* jiùzhèiyàng wǒ méi gǎnshang huǒchē 就这样我没赶上火车；~ (*that*) *I could come too* wǒ jiùshì shuō wǒ yě néng qù 我就是说我也能去；~ *what?* nà yòu zěnmeyàng? 那又怎么样？

**soak** v/t (*steep*) pào pào 泡泡；(*of water, rain*) jìnshī 浸湿

♦**soak up** *liquid* xīshōu 吸收

**soaked** shītòu 湿透

**so-and-so** F (*unknown person*) mǒumǒu rén 某某人；(*annoying person*) tǎoyànguǐ 讨厌鬼

**soap** n (*for washing*) féizào 肥皂

**soap** (*opera*) féizào jù 肥皂剧

**soapy** *water* hán féizào 含肥皂

**soar** (*of rocket*) shēngrù 升入；(*of bird, plane*) áoxiáng 翱翔；(*of prices*) měngzēng 猛增

**sob 1** n wūyān 呜咽 **2** v/i chōuqì 抽泣

**sober** (*not drunk*) qīngxǐng 清醒；(*serious*) yánsù 严肃

♦**sober up** xǐngjiǔ 醒酒

**so-called** suǒwèi 所谓

**soccer** zúqiú 足球

**sociable** héqún 合群

**social** adj shèhuì 社会；(*recreational*) shèjiāo 社交

**socialism** shèhuì zhǔyì 社会主义

**socialist 1** adj shèhuì zhǔyì 社会主义 **2** n shèhuì zhǔyì zhě 社会主义者

**socialize** shèjiāo 社交

**social work** shèhuì gōngzuò 社会工作

**social worker** shègōng 社工

**society** shèhuì 社会；(*organization*) shètuán 社团

**sociology** shèhuì xué 社会学

**sock**[1] (*for wearing*) wàzi 袜子

**sock**[2] **1** n (*punch*) quán 拳 **2** v/t (*punch*) zòu 揍

**socket** (*electrical*) chāzuò 插座；(*of arm, eye*) wō 窝

**soda** (~ *water*) sūdá 苏打；(*ice-cream*) bīngqílíng sūdá shuǐ 冰淇淋苏打水；(*soft drink*) ruǎnxìng yǐnliào 软性饮料

**sofa** shāfā 沙发

**sofa bed** shāfā chuáng 沙发床

**soft** *pillow, chair* ruǎn 软；*voice* wēnróu 温柔；*music* yuè'ěr 悦耳；*light, color* róuhé 柔和；*skin* róuhuá 柔滑；(*lenient*) kuānhòu 宽厚；*have a ~ spot for X* piān'ài X piān'ài X

**soft drink** ruǎnxìng yǐnliào 软性饮料

**soften 1** v/t position huǎnhé 缓和；*impact, blow* jiǎnqīng 减轻 **2** v/i (*of butter, ice cream*) biànruǎn 变软

**softly** (*quietly*) dīshēng 低声

**soft seat** (*on train*) ruǎnzuò 软座

**soft sleeper** (*on train*) ruǎnwò 软卧

**software** ruǎnjiàn 软件

**soggy** shīrùn 湿润

**soil 1** *n* (*earth*) tǔrǎng 土壤 **2** *v/t* nòngzāng 弄脏

**solar energy** tàiyáng néng 太阳能

**solar panel** tàiyáng diànchí bǎn 太阳电池板

**soldier** shìbīng 士兵

**sole**[1] *n* (*of foot*) jiǎodǐ bǎn 脚底板; (*of shoe*) xiédǐ 鞋底

**sole**[2] *adj* wéiyī 唯一; ~ **responsibility** dāndú fùzé 单独负责

**solely** jǐnjǐn 仅仅

**solemn** (*serious*) yánsù 严肃; *promise* zhèngzhòng 郑重

**solid** *adj* (*hard*) yìng bāngbang 硬梆梆; (*without holes*) wú kòngxì 无空隙; *gold, silver* chún 纯; (*sturdy*) láogù 牢固; *evidence* chōngfèn 充分; *support* chèdǐ 彻底

**solidarity** tuánjié yīzhì 团结一致

**solidify** *v/i* gùhuà 固化

**solitaire** (*card game*) ⇩ dānrén zhǐpái xì 单人纸牌戏

**solitary** *life, activity* gūdú 孤独; (*single*) gū línglíng 孤零零

**solitude** dúzì yīrén 独自一人

**solo 1** *n* (*of instrumentalist*) dúzòu qǔ 独奏曲; (*of singer*) dúchàng qǔ 独唱曲 **2** *adj* dānrén 单人

**soloist** (*instrumentalist*) dúzòu yǎnyuán 独奏演员; (*singer*) dúchàng yǎnyuán 独唱演员

**soluble** *substance* kěróng 可溶; *problem* kě jiějué 可解决

**solution** jiědá 解答; (*mixture*) róngyè 溶液

**solve** jiějué 解决

**solvent** *adj* (*financially*) wú zhàiwù 无债务

**somber** *dark* huī'àn 灰暗; (*serious*) yánjùn 严峻

**some 1** *adj* yīxiē 一些; ~ **people say that** ... yǒuxiē rén shuō ... 有些人说...; *would you like* ~ **water / cookies?** nǐ yào diǎn shuǐ /

qǔqíbǐng ma? 你要点水 / 曲奇饼吗？**2** *pron* yīxiē 一些; ~ **of the group** zǔlǐ de yīxiē rén 组里的一些人; *would you like* ~? nǐ yào diǎnrma? 你要点儿吗？*give me* ~ gěiwǒ diǎnr 给我点儿 **3** *adv* (*a bit*) shāowēi 稍微; *we'll have to wait* ~ wǒmen yào děnghuìr 我们要等会儿

**somebody** yǒurén 有人

**someday** yǒuzhāo yīrì 有朝一日

**somehow** (*by some means*) xiǎng bànfǎ 想办法; (*for some unknown reason*) bùzhī zěnde 不知怎的

**someone** yǒurén 有人

**someplace** → **somewhere**

**somersault 1** *n* jīndǒu 筋斗 **2** *v/i* fān jīndǒu 翻筋斗

**something** dōngxi 东西; *would you like* ~ *to drink* / *eat?* nǐ yàobúyào hē / chī diǎn dōngxi? 你要不要喝 / 吃点东西？*is* ~ *wrong?* zěnme le? 怎么了？

**sometime** gǎirì 改日; ~ *last year* qùnián mǒugè shíhòu 去年某个时候

**sometimes** yǒushí 有时

**somewhere 1** *adv* mǒugè dìfāng 某个地方 **2** *pron* mǒuchù 某处

**son** érzi 儿子

**song** gēqǔ 歌曲

**Song Dynasty** Sòng Cháo 宋朝

**Song Dynasty lyrics** Sòngcí 宋词

**songwriter** cíqǔ zuòjiā 词曲作者

**son-in-law** nǚxù 女婿

**son of a bitch** *n* F húndàn 混蛋

**soon** (*in no time*) hěnkuài 很快; (*early*) zǎo 早; *soon after* bùjiǔ zhīhòu 不久之后; *as* ~ *as* ... yī ... jiù ... 一...就...; *as* ~ *as possible* jǐnkuài 尽快; ~*er or later* chízǎo 迟早; *the* ~*er the better* yuèkuài yuèhǎo 越快越好

**soot** yóuyān 油烟

**soothe** *pain* jiǎnqīng 减轻; *person* ānwèi 安慰

**sophisticated** *person* jīngtōng shìgù 精通世故; *tastes, lifestyle* bùluò sútào 不落俗套; *machine* jīngmì 精密

**sophomore** èrniánjí 二年级

**soprano** *n* gāoyīn 高音

**sordid** *affair, business* bēibǐ 卑鄙

**sore 1** *adj (painful)* téng 疼；F
(*angry*) nǎohuǒ 恼火；*is it ~?* téng
bùténg? 疼不疼？ **2** *n* chuāng 疮

**sorghum** gāoliáng 高粱

**sorrow** *n (sad things)* shāngxīn shì
伤心事；(*sadness*) yōushāng 忧伤

**sorry** *adj (regretful)* hòuhuǐ 后悔；(*sad*)
nánguò 难过；*I'm ~ that ...*
(*apology*) duìbuqǐ ... 对不起 ...；
(*expressing sympathy*) hěn yíhàn ...
很遗憾 ...；(*I'm*) ~! duìbuqǐ! 对不
起！；*I feel ~ for her* wǒ wèi tā
gǎndào nánguò 我为她感到难
过

**sort 1** *n* zhǒng 种；*~ of ...* F yǒu
nàme diǎnr ... 有那么点儿 ...；*is
it finished?* – *~ of* F wánle ma? –
chàbùduō wánle ma? – 差不多
**2** *v/t* fēnlèi 分类；COMPUT páiliè 排
列

♦ **sort out** *papers* zhěnglǐ 整理；
*problem* jiějué 解决

**so-so** *adv* còuhe 凑和

**soul** REL línghún 灵魂；*fig (of a
nation etc)* jīngshén 精神；(*character*) shēngqì 生气；(*person*) rén
人

**sound¹** *adj (sensible)* hélǐ 合理；
(*healthy*) jiànkāng 健康；*business*
qiángzhuàng 强壮；(*strong, not
damaged*) wánhǎo wúsǔn 完好无
损；*a ~ sleep* hānshuì 酣睡

**sound²** **1** *n* shēngyīn 声音；(*noise*)
shēng 声 **2** *v/t (pronounce)* fāyīn
发音；MED tīngzhěn 听诊；*~
one's horn* àn lǎba 按喇叭 **3** *v/i:
that ~s interesting* tīngqǐlái hěn
yǒuqù 听起来很有趣；*that ~s
like a good idea* tīngqǐlái xiàng
hǎo zhǔyì 听起来象好主意；
*she ~ed unhappy* tā hǎoxiàng bù
gāoxìng 她好像不高兴

**sound card** COMPUT shēngkǎ 声卡

**soundly** *sleep* shóu 熟；*beaten* chèdǐ
彻底

**soundproof** *adj* géyīn 隔音

**soundtrack** pèiyuè 配乐

**soup** tāng 汤

**soup bowl** tāngwǎn 汤碗

**sour** *adj apple, orange* suān 酸；*milk*
sōu 馊；*expression, comment* jiānsuān kèbó 尖酸刻薄

**source** *n* láiyuán 来源；(*of river*)
yuántóu 源头；(*person*) xiāoxirén
消息人

**south 1** *adj* nán 南 **2** *n* nánbù 南
部；*to the ~ of X* zài X de nánbiān
在X的南边 **3** *adv* wǎngnán 往南

**South Africa** Nánfēi 南非；**South
African 1** *adj* Nánfēi 南非 **2** *n*
Nánfēi rén 南非人；**South
America** Nánměi 南美；**South
American 1** *adj* Nánměi 南美
**2** *n* Nánměi rén 南美人；**South
China Sea** Nánhǎi 南海；**South
Korea** Nánhán 南韩；**South
Korean 1** *adj* Nánhán 南韩 **2** *n*
Nánhán rén 南韩人；**southeast
1** *n* dōngnán bù 东南部 **2** *adj*
dōngnán 东南 **3** *adv* wǎng
dōngnán 往东南；*it's ~ of X* zài X
de dōngnán fāng 在X的东南方；
**Southeast Asia** Dōngnán yà 东
南亚；**Southeast Asian** *adj*
Dōngnán yà 东南亚；**south-
eastern** dōngnán 东南

**southerly** *adj* nán 南

**southern** nán 南

**southward** *adv* xiàng nán 向南

**southwest 1** *n* xīnán bù 西南部
**2** *adj* xīnán 西南 **3** *adv* wǎng
xīnán 往西南；*it's ~ of X* zài X de
xīnán fāng 在X的西南方

**southwestern** xīnán 西南

**souvenir** jìniàn pǐn 纪念品

**sovereign** *adj state* zhǔquán 主权

**sovereignty** (*of state*) zhǔquán 主
权

**Soviet Union** Sūlián 苏联

**sow¹** *n (female pig)* mǔzhū 母猪

**sow²** *v/t seeds* bōzhǒng 播种

**soy bean** huángdòu 黄豆；**soy
bean oil** dòu yóu 豆油；**soy milk**
dòujiāng 豆浆；**soy sauce** jiàngyóu 酱油

**space** *n (beyond earth)* tàikōng 太
空；(*area*) kòngbái 空白；(*room*)
kōngjiān 空间

♦ **space out** bǎ ... jiàngé kāi 把 ...
间隔开

space bar COMPUT kònggé jiàn 空
隔键; spacecraft yǔzhòu fēichuán 宇宙飞船; spaceship
yǔzhòu fēichuán 宇宙飞船;
space shuttle ↓ hángtiān fēijī
航天飞机; space station
yǔzhòu kōngjiān zhàn 宇宙空间
站; spacesuit yǔháng fú 宇航服

spacious kuānchǎng 宽敞

spade (for digging) qiāo qiū; ~s (in
card game) hēitáo 黑桃

Spain Xībānyá 西班牙

span v/t kuà 跨; (of bridge) héngkuà 横跨

Spaniard Xībānyá rén 西班牙人

Spanish 1 adj Xībānyá 西班牙
2 n (language) Xībānyá yǔ 西班牙
语

spank dǎ pìgǔ 打屁股

spare 1 v/t time, money yúnchū 匀
出; (do without) shěngdiào 省掉;
can you ~ the time? yǒukōngma?
有空吗?; there were five to ~
(left over, in excess) yǒu wǔgè
shèngxià 有五个剩下 2 adj
money duōyú 多余; (extra)
bèiyòng 备用 3 n (part) língjiàn
零件

spare ribs páigǔ 排骨; spare
room kèfáng 客房; spare time
yèyú shíjiān 业余时间; spare
tire MOT bèiyòng lúntāi 备用轮
胎; spare wheel bèiyòng chēlún
备用车轮

spark n huǒxīng 火星

sparkle v/i shǎnyào 闪耀

sparkling wine qìjiǔ 汽酒

spark plug huǒhuāsāi 火花塞

sparrow máquè 麻雀

sparse vegetation xīshū 稀疏

sparsely: ~ populated rényān
xīshǎo 人烟稀少

spatter of mud, paint jiàn 溅

speak 1 v/i shuōhuà 说话; we're
not ~ing (to each other) (we've
quarreled) wǒmen nào bièniu 我
们闹别扭; ~ing TELEC wǒshì 我
是 2 v/t foreign language huìjiǎng
会讲; ~ one's mind zhíshuō 直说
♦ speak to yǔ ... tánhuà 与 ... 谈
话; (make a speech) fāyán 发言

♦ speak for dàibiǎo ... jiǎnghuà 代
表 ... 讲话; speaking for myself
jù wǒ lái kàn 据我来看

♦ speak out dàdǎn di shuō 大胆
地说

♦ speak up (speak louder) dàshēng
diǎn 大声点

♦ speak with yǔ ... tánhuà 与 ...
谈话

speaker (at conference) yǎnjiǎng
zhě 演讲者; (orator) yǎnshuō jiā
演说家; (of sound system)
yīnxiāng 音箱

spearmint bòhe 薄荷

special tèshū 特殊; (particular)
tèbié 特别

special economic zone jīngjì
tèqū 经济特区

specialist zhuānjiā 专家

specialize zhuānmén cóngshì 专
门从事; ~ in ... zhuānmén
cóngshì ... 专门从事 ...

specially tèbié 特别

specialty (of company etc) zhuāncháng 专长; (of restaurant) náshǒu
hǎocài 拿手好菜

species zhǒnglèi 种类

specific tèbié 特别

specifically tèbié 特别

specifications (of machine etc)
guīgé 规格

specify zhǐdìng 指定

specimen yàngpǐn 样品

speck (of dust, soot) lì粒 粒

spectacle (impressive sight)
zhuàngguān 壮观; (a pair of) ~s
(yīfú) yǎnjìng (一副) 眼镜

spectacular adj (stunning)
zhuàngguān 壮观; (impressive)
yǐnrén zhùmù 引人注目

spectator guānzhòng 观众

spectrum fig fànwéi 范围

speculate v/i cāicè 猜测; FIN zuò
tóujī mǎimài 做投机买卖

speculation cāicè 猜测; FIN tóujī
mǎimài 投机买卖

speculator FIN tóujī shāng 投机商

speech (address) jiǎnghuà 讲话;
(in play) táicí 台词; (ability to
speak) shuōhuà nénglì 说话能力;
(way of speaking) shuōhuà fāngshì

说话方式

speechless (with shock, surprise)
yīshí jiǎng bùchū huà lái 一时讲
不出话来
speech defect yányǔ quēxiàn 言语
缺陷; speech therapist yányǔ
jiǎozhì shī 言语矫治师; speech
writer yǎnjiǎnggǎo zhuànxiě rén
演讲稿撰写人
speed 1 n sùdù 速度; at a ~ of
150 mph sùdù měi xiǎoshí yībǎi
wǔshí yīnglǐ 速度每小时一百
五十英里 2 v/i (drive quickly)
jíshǐ jíshǐ 疾驶; (walk quickly) kuàizǒu
快走; (drive too quickly) chāosù 超
速
♦speed by fēiguò 飞过
♦speed up v/t & v/i jiākuài sùdù 加
快速度
speedboat kuàitǐng 快艇
speedily xùnsù 迅速
speeding n (when driving) chāosù
超速
speeding fine chāosù xíngshǐ
fákuǎn 超速行驶罚款
speed limit ⇩ sùdù jíxiàn 速度极
限
speedometer lǐchéng jì 里程计
speedy xùnsù 迅速
spell¹ v/t & v/i pīn 拼
spell² n (period of time) yīduàn
shíjiān 一段时间
spellbound rùmí 入迷; spellcheck COMPUT pīnxiě chácuò 拼
写查错; do a ~ on ... jiǎnchá ...
de pīnxiě jiǎnchá ... 的拼写;
spellchecker COMPUT pīnxiě
chácuò chéngxù 拼写查错程序
spelling pīnxiě 拼写
spend money huāqián 花钱; time
dùguò 度过
spendthrift n pej dàshǒu dàjiǎo de
rén 大手大脚的人
sperm jīngzǐ 精子; (semen) jīngyè
精液
sperm bank jīngzǐ kù 精子库
sphere qiútǐ 球体; fig lǐngyù 领
域; ~ of influence shìlì fànwéi 势
力范围
spice n (seasoning) xiāngliào 香料
spicy food duō xiāngliào 多香料

spider zhīzhū 蜘蛛
spiderweb zhīzhū wǎng 蜘蛛网
spike n jiāntóu 尖头; (on shoes)
xiédīng 鞋钉
spill v/t & v/i sǎ 洒
spin¹ 1 n (turn) xuánzhuǎn 旋转
2 v/t xuánzhuǎn 旋转 3 v/i (of
wheel) xuánzhuǎn 旋转; my head
is ~ning wǒ tóuhūn nǎozhàng 我
头昏脑胀
spin² v/t wool, cotton fǎng 纺; web
jiéwǎng 结网
♦spin around (of person) zhuǎnshēn 转身
♦spin out tuōcháng 拖长
spinach bōcài 菠菜
spinal jízhù 脊柱
spinal column jízhù 脊柱
spin doctor xuānchuán jiā 宣传
家; spin-dry v/t shuǎigān 甩干;
spin-dryer shuǎigān jī 甩干机
spine (of person, animal) jízhù 脊
柱; (of book) shūjí 书脊; (on plant,
hedgehog) cì 刺
spineless (cowardly) méi gǔqì 没
骨气
spin-off pàishēng chǎnpǐn 派生产
品
spiral 1 n luóxuán 螺旋 2 v/i (rise
quickly) jíjù shàngshēng 急剧上
升
spiral staircase luóxuán shì lóutī
螺旋式楼梯
spire jiāntǎ 尖塔
spirit n (as opposed to body)
jīngshén 精神; (of dead person)
línghún 灵魂; (energy) huólì 活
力; (courage) yǒngqì 勇气;
(attitude) tàidù 态度; we did it in
a ~ of cooperation / friendliness
wǒmen yǐ hézuò / yǒuhǎo de
jīngshén chūfā 我们以合作 / 友
好的精神出发
spirited (energetic) shēngqì bóbo 生
气勃勃
spirit level shuǐzhǔn yí 水准仪
spirits¹ (alcohol) lièjiǔ 烈酒
spirits² (morale) qíngxù 情绪; be
in good / poor ~ jīngshén hǎo /
huài 精神好 / 坏
spiritual adj shén 神

spiritualism wéilíng lùn 唯灵论

spiritualist n zhāohúnshù zhě 招魂术者

spit v/i (of person) tǔtán 吐痰; it's ~ting with rain xià xiǎoyǔ 下小雨

♦ spit out food, liquid tǔchū 吐出

spite n èyì 恶意; in ~ of jǐnguǎn 尽管

spiteful huáiyǒu èyì 怀有恶意

spitting image: be the ~ of X hě X jiānzhí yīmó yīyàng 和 X 简直一模一样

splash 1 n (noise) pūtōng 扑通; (small amount of liquid) yīdiǎnr 一点儿; (of color) bāndiǎn 斑点 2 v/t person jiàn 溅; water, mud pō 泼 3 v/i xīshuǐ 嬉水; (of water) fēijiàn 飞溅

♦ splash down (of spacecraft) jiànluò 溅落

♦ splash out (in spending) dàshǒu dàjiǎo de huāqián 大手大脚地花钱; I splashed out on a round the world trip wǒ dàshǒu dàjiǎo de huāqián zài yīgé huánqiú lǚxíng shàng 我大手大脚地花钱在一个环球旅行上

splendid jíhǎo 极好

splendor (of achievement) guānghuī cànlàn 光辉灿烂; (of building, ceremony) zhuàngguān 壮观

splint n MED jiábǎn jiá 夹板夹

splinter 1 n cì 刺 2 v/i fēnliè 分裂

splinter group xiǎo pàibié 小派别

split 1 n (damage) lièkǒu 裂口; (disagreement) fēnliè 分裂; (division, share) fēngē 分割 2 v/t (damage) lièkāi 裂开; logs pī 劈; (cause disagreement in) fēnliè 分裂; (divide) fēn 分 3 v/i (tear) lièkāi 裂开; (disagree) fēnliè 分裂

♦ split up v/i (of couple) fēnshǒu 分手

split personality PSYCH fēnliè réngé 分裂人格

splitting headache jùliè de tóutòng 剧烈的头痛

spoil v/t child chǒnghuài 宠坏; party, fun pòhuài ... de xìngzhì 破坏 ... 的兴致; cooking, essay etc nòngzāo 弄糟

spoilsport F bàixìng zhě 败兴者

spoilt adj child chǒnghuài 宠坏; be ~ for choice tàiduō xuǎnzé le 太多选择了

spoke (of wheel) chētiáo 车条

spokesman fāyánrén 发言人

spokesperson fāyánrén 发言人

spokeswoman fāyánrén 发言人

sponge n hǎimián hǎimián 海绵

♦ sponge off, sponge on F kào ... báichī shí kào ... 白吃食

sponger F jìshēng chóng 寄生虫

sponsor 1 n dānbǎo rén 担保人 2 v/t dānbǎo 担保

sponsorship dānbǎo 担保

spontaneous zìfā 自发; person zìrán 自然

spooky F yīn sēnsēn 阴森森

spool n (for film) juǎnpán 卷盘; (for thread) xiànzhóu 线轴

spoon n sháo 勺

spoonfeed fig tiányā shì guànshū 填鸭式灌输

spoonful: two ~s of sugar liǎng sháo táng 两勺糖

sporadic língsàn 零散

sport n tǐyù yùndòng 体育运动

sporting event tǐyù yùndòng 体育运动; (fair, generous) dàfang 大方; a ~ gesture dàfang de jǔdòng 大方的举动

sportscar pǎochē 跑车; sportscoat yùndòng shàngyī 运动上衣; sports journalist tǐyù jìzhě 体育记者; sportsman yùndòng yuán 运动员; sports news tǐyù xīnwén tǐyù xīnwén 体育新闻; sports page tǐyù bǎn 体育版; sportswoman yùndòng yuán 运动员

sporty person àihào yùndòng 爱好运动; clothes huāshao 花哨

spot¹ (pimple) fěncì 粉刺; (caused by measles etc) qiūzhěn 丘疹; (part of pattern) bāndiǎn 斑点儿

spot² (place) dìdiǎn 地点; on the ~ (in the place in question) zài xiànchǎng 在现场; (immediately) dāngchǎng 当场; put X on the ~ shǐ X nánkān 使 X 难堪

spot³ v/t (notice) zhǎodào 找到; (identify) biànrèn 辨认

**spot check** chōuyàng jiǎnchá 抽样检查; *carry out spot checks* jìnxíng chōuyàng jiǎnchá 进行抽样检查

**spotless** yīchén bùrǎn 一尘不染

**spotlight** *n* jùguāng dēng 聚光灯

**spotted** *fabric* huādiǎn 花点

**spotty** (*with pimples*) duō fěncì 多粉刺

**spouse** *fml* pèi'ǒu 配偶

**spout 1** *n* zuǐ 嘴 **2** *v/i* (*of liquid*) pēnchū 喷出

**sprain** *n & v/t* niǔshāng 扭伤

**Spratley Islands** Nánshā Qúndǎo 南沙群岛

**sprawl** *v/i* shēnkāi sìzhī 伸开四肢; (*of city*) mànyán 蔓延; *send X ~ing* (*of punch*) bǎ X shuāi pā zài dìshàng 把X摔趴在地上

**sprawling** *city*, *suburbs* mànyán 蔓延

**spray 1** *n* (*of sea water*) lànghuā 浪花; (*from fountain*) shuǐhuā 水花; (*paint*) pēnqī 喷漆; (*for hair*) pēnfà jiāo 喷发胶; (*container*) pēnwù qì 喷雾器 **2** *v/t* pēn 喷; ~ *X with Y* gěi X pēn Y 给X喷Y

**spraygun** pēnqiāng 喷枪

**spread** *v/i* **1** *n* (*of disease, religion etc*) mànyán 蔓延; F (*big meal*) shèngyàn 盛宴 **2** *v/t* (*lay*) tānkāi 摊开; *butter* mǒ 抹; *news, rumor, disease* chuánbō 传播; *arms, legs* shēnzhǎn 伸展 **3** *v/i* (*of fire*) mànyán 蔓延; (*of rumor, news, disease*) chuánbō 传播; (*of butter*) mǒ 抹

**spreadsheet** COMPUT biǎogé 表格

**spree**: *go* (*out*) *on a ~* F tòngkuài yīfān 痛快一番; *go on a shopping ~* dàmǎi tèmǎi yīfān 大买特买一番

**sprightly** huópo 活泼

**spring**[1] *n* (*season*) chūntiān 春天

**spring**[2] *n* (*device*) tánhuáng 弹簧

**spring**[3] *n* (*stream*) quánshuǐ 泉水

**spring**[4] *n & v/i* (*jump*) tiàoyuè 跳跃
♦**spring from** láizì 来自

**springboard** tiàobǎn 跳板;
**spring chicken**: *she's no ~* hum tā shàngle niánjì 她上了年纪;
**spring-cleaning** dà sǎochú 大扫

除; **Spring Festival** Chūnjié 春节; **springtime** chūntiān 春天

**springy** *mattress, ground* yǒu tánxìng 有弹性; *walk* qīngkuài 轻快

**sprinkle** *v/t* sǎ 撒; ~ *X with Y* jiāng X sǎzài Y shàng 将X撒在Y上

**sprinkler** (*for garden*) pēnsǎ qì 喷撒器; (*in ceiling*) pēnshuǐ zhuāngzhì 喷水装置

**sprint** *n & v/i* bēnpǎo 奔跑

**sprinter** SP duǎnpǎo yùndòng yuán 短跑运动员

**sprout 1** *v/i* (*of seed*) fāyá 发芽 **2** *n* xīnyá 新芽; (*Brussels*) ~*s* qiúzhuàng gānlán 球状甘蓝

**spruce** *adj* zhěngjié piàoliàng 整洁漂亮

**spur** *n* fig jīlì 激励; *on the ~ of the moment* píng yīshíde chōngdòng 凭一时的冲动
♦**spur on** (*encourage*) jīlì ... qiánjìn 激励 ... 前进

**spurt 1** *n* (*in race*) chōngcì 冲刺; *put on a ~* jiāsù fēibēn 加速飞奔 **2** *v/i* (*of liquid*) pēnshè 喷射

**spy 1** *n* jiàndié 间谍 **2** *v/i* cóngshì jiàndié huódòng 从事间谍活动 **3** *v/t* F fāxiàn 发现
♦**spy on** ànzhōng jiānshì 暗中监视

**squabble** *n & v/i* zhēngchǎo 争吵

**squalid** āngzāng 肮脏

**squalor** wūhuì 污秽

**squander** *money* huīhuò 挥霍

**square 1** *adj* (*in shape*) fāng 方; ~ *mile / yard* píngfāng yīnglǐ / mǎ 平方英里/码 **2** *n* (*shape*) sìfāng xíng 四方形; (*in town*) guǎngchǎng 广场; (*in board game*) gé 格; MATH píngfāng 平方; *we're back to ~ one* wǒmen yòu huídào qǐdiǎn le 我们又回到起点了

**square root** píngfāng gēn 平方根

**squash**[1] *n* (*vegetable*) nánguā 南瓜

**squash**[2] *n* (*game*) bìqiú 壁球

**squash**[3] *v/t* (*crush*) yālàn 压烂

**squat 1** *adj* (*in shape*) ǎi 矮 **2** *v/i* (*sit*) dūn 蹲; (*illegally*) shànzì zhànyòng 擅自占用

**squatter** shànzì zhàndì zhě 擅自占地者

**squeak 1** n (of mouse) zhīzhī shēng 吱吱声; (of hinge) zhīgā shēng 吱嘎声 **2** v/i (of mouse) zhīzhī jiào 吱吱叫; (of hinge, shoes) zhīgā zuòxiǎng 吱嘎作响

**squeal 1** n cháng ér jiān de jiào-shēng 长而尖的叫声 **2** v/i fāchū cháng ér jiān de jiàoshēng 发出长而尖的叫声

**squeamish** jiāoqì 娇气

**squeeze 1** n (of hand, shoulder) jǐnwò 紧握 **2** v/t (press) jǐ 挤; package etc yònglì niē 用力捏; shoulder, hand jǐnwò 紧握; (remove juice from) zhà 榨

♦ **squeeze in 1** v/i (to a car etc) jǐ jǐ 挤挤 **2** v/t sāi 塞

♦ **squeeze up** v/i (to make space) jǐjǐn 挤紧

**squid** yóuyú 鱿鱼

**squint** n xiéyǎn 斜眼

**squirm** (wriggle) niúdòng 扭动; (in embarrassment) jùcù bù'ān 局促不安

**squirrel** n sōngshǔ 松鼠

**squirt 1** v/t pēnshè 喷射 **2** n pej F wàngzì zūndà de rén 妄自尊大的人

**stab 1** n F chángshì 尝试 **2** v/t person cì 刺

**stability** wěndìng 稳定

**stabilize 1** v/t prices, currency wěndìng 稳定; boat pínghéng 平衡 **2** v/i (of prices etc) wěndìng 稳定

**stable**[1] n (for horses) mǎjiù 马厩

**stable**[2] adj wěndìng 稳定

**stack 1** n (pile) dié 叠; (smoke-stack) dà yāncōng 大烟囱 **2** v/t bǎ ... diéchéng duī 把 ... 叠成堆

**stadium** tǐyùchǎng 体育场

**staff** n (employees) gùyuán 雇员; (teachers) jiàoyuán 教员

**staffroom** (in school) jiàoyuán shì 教员室

**stage**[1] (in life, project etc) jiēduàn 阶段; (of journey) duàn lù 段路

**stage**[2] **1** n THEA wǔtái 舞台; go on the ~ dāng yǎnyuán 当演员 **2** v/t play biǎoyǎn 表演; demonstration, strike jǔxíng 举行

**stage door** jùchǎng hòumén 剧场后门

**stagger 1** v/i diēdiē zhuàngzhuang 跌跌撞撞 **2** v/t (amaze) shǐ chījīng 使吃惊; coffee breaks etc cuòkāi 错开

**staggering** lìngrén chījīng 令人吃惊

**stagnant** water bù liúdòng 不流动; economy tíngzhì 停滞

**stagnate** fig (of person, mind) bù fāzhǎn 不发展

**stag party** hūnqián nánzi jùhuì 婚前男子聚会

**stain 1** n (dirty mark) wūjì 污迹; (for wood) rǎnsè jì 染色剂 **2** v/t (dirty) zhānwū 沾污; wood rǎnsè 染色 **3** v/i (of wine etc) chǎnshēng wūjì 产生污迹; (of fabric) yìcún wūjì 易存污迹

**stained-glass window** cǎisè bōlí chuāng 彩色玻璃窗

**stainless steel** n búxiùgāng 不锈钢

**stain remover** qùwū jì 去污剂

**stair** tījí 梯级; the ~s lóutī 楼梯

**staircase** lóutī 楼梯

**stake 1** n (of wood) zhuāng 桩; (when gambling) dǔzhù 赌注; (investment) gǔfèn 股份; be at ~ zài wēixiǎn zhōng 在危险中 **2** v/t tree yòng zhuāng zhīchēng 用桩支撑; money xià dǔzhù 下赌注; person zīzhù 资助

**stale** bread zǒuwèir 走味儿; air mēn 闷; fig: news guòshí 过时

**stalemate** (in chess) jiāngjú 僵局; fig jiāngjú 僵局

**Stalin** Sīdàlín 斯大林

**stalk**[1] n (of fruit, plant) gěng 梗

**stalk**[2] v/t (follow) gēnzōng 跟踪

**stalker** (of person) gēnzōng zhě 跟踪者

**stall**[1] n (at market) tānzi 摊子; (for cow, horse) péng 棚

**stall**[2] **1** v/i (of engine) xīhuǒ 熄火; (of vehicle, plane) pāomáo 抛锚; (play for time) tuōyán 拖延 **2** v/t engine xīhuǒ 熄火; people fūyǎn 敷衍

**stallion** mǔmǎ 牡马

**stalwart** adj support, supporter jiāndìng 坚定

**stamina** nàilì 耐力

**stammer** n & v/i jiēba 结巴

**stamp**¹ **1** n (for letter) yóupiào 邮票; (device) yìnchuō 印戳; (mark made with device) yìn yìn 印; **2** v/t letter tiē yóupiào 贴邮票; document, passport gàizhāng 盖章

**stamp**² v/t: ~ one's feet duòjiǎo 跺脚

♦ **stamp out** (eradicate) xiāomiè 消灭

**stampede** n (of cattle etc) jīngpǎo 惊跑; (of people) fēngyōng 蜂拥

**stance** (position) tàidù 态度

**stand 1** n (at exhibition) tānzi 摊子; (witness ~) zhèngrén xí 证人席; (support, base) zuò 座; take the ~ LAW zuòzhèng 作证 **2** v/i (be situated: of person) zhànlì 站立; (of object) bèi fàngzhì 被放置; (of building) sǒnglì 耸立; (as opposed to sit) zhànzhe 站着; (rise) qǐlì 起立; ~ still yídòng bùdòng 一动不动; where do I ~ with you? wǒmen jiūjìng shì shénme guānxi? 我们究竟是什么关系? **3** v/t (tolerate) rěnshòu 忍受; (put) shùfàng 竖放; you don't ~ a chance nǐ gēnběn méi jīhuì 你根本没机会; ~ one's ground jiānchí zìjǐ de lìchǎng 坚持自己的立场

♦ **stand back** hòutuì 后退

♦ **stand by 1** v/i (not take action) xiùshǒu pángguān 袖手旁观; (be ready) zuò hǎo zhǔnbèi 作好准备 **2** v/t person zhīchí 支持; decision jiānchí 坚持

♦ **stand down** (withdraw) tuìchū 退出

♦ **stand for** (tolerate) róngrěn 容忍; (represent) dàibiǎo 代表

♦ **stand in for** dàitì 代替

♦ **stand out** yǐnrén zhùmù 引人注目

♦ **stand up 1** v/i zhàn qǐlái 站起来 **2** v/t: **stand X up** F (on date) ràng X báiděng 让 X 白等

♦ **stand up for** wéihù 维护

♦ **stand up to** miànduì 面对

**standard 1** adj (usual) chángguī 常规 **2** n (level of excellence) shuǐzhǔn 水准; (expectation), TECH biāozhǔn 标准; be up to ~ fúhé biāozhǔn 符合标准; not be up to ~ bù fúhé biāozhǔn 不符合标准

**standard of living** shēnghuó shuǐzhǔn 生活水准

**standardize** v/t shǐ biāozhǔn huà 使标准化

**standby: on ~** (for flight) hòubǔ 候补

**standby passenger** hòubǔ lǚkè 候补旅客

**standing** n (in society etc) dìwèi 地位; (repute) shēngyù 声誉; a musician / politician of some ~ zhuóyuè de yīnyuèjiā / zhèngzhìjiā 卓越的音乐家 / 政治家

**standing room** zhànlì kōngjiān 站立空间

**standoffish** lěngmò 冷漠; **standpoint** guāndiǎn 观点; **standstill: be at a ~** tíngdùn 停顿; **bring ... to a ~** shǐ ... tíngdùn shǐ ... 停顿

**staple**¹ n (foodstuff) zhǔshí 主食

**staple**² **1** n (fastener) dìngshūdīng 订书钉 **2** v/t dìng 钉

**staple diet** zhǔshí 主食

**staple gun** tiěsī dìngshūjī 铁丝订书机

**stapler** dìngshūjī 订书机

**star 1** n (in sky) xīng 星; fig míngxīng 明星 **2** v/t (of movie) zhǔyǎn 主演 **3** v/i (in movie) zhǔyǎn 主演

**starboard** adj yòuxián 右舷

**stare 1** n níngshì 凝视 **2** v/i mùbù zhuǎnjīng de kàn 目不转睛地看; ~ at dīngzhe 盯着

**starfish** hǎixīng 海星

**stark 1** adj landscape huāngliáng 荒凉; room, surroundings kōng luòluo 空落落; reminder, etc yánkù 严酷; contrast xiānmíng 鲜明 **2** adv: ~ naked yīsī bùguà 一丝不挂

**starling** liángniǎo 椋鸟

**Stars and Stripes** Xīngtiáo qí 星

条旗

**start 1** *n* (*beginning*) kāitóu 开头；
***get off to a good / bad ~*** (*in race,
marriage, career*) yīkāishǐ hěnhǎo /
zāo 一开始很好 / 糟；*from the ~*
yīkāishǐ 一开始；*well, it's a ~!*
qǐmǎ kāigètóu! 起码开个头！
**2** *v/i* kāishǐ 开始；(*of engine, car*)
fādòng 发动；***~ing from tomor-
row*** cóng míngtiān kāishǐ 从明天
开始 **3** *v/t* kāishǐ 开始；*engine, car*
fādòng 发动；*business* chuàngbàn
创办；***to do X, ~ doing X*** kāishǐ
zuò X 开始做X

**starter** (*part of meal*) tóupán 头盘；
(*of car*) qǐdòng zhuāngzhì 起动装
置

**starting point** (*for walk, discussion,
thesis*) chūfā diǎn 出发点

**starting salary** qǐshǐ gōngzī 起始
工资

**startle**: ~ *X* shǐ X xià yītiào 使X吓
一跳

**startling** jīngrén 惊人

**starvation** jī'è jī'è 饥饿

**starve** *v/i* ái'è āi'è 挨饿；***to death*** èsǐ
饿死；*I'm starving* F wǒ èsǐ le 我
饿死了

**state¹ 1** *n* (*of car, house etc*)
zhuàngkuàng 状况；(*part of
country*) zhōu 州；(*country*) guójiā
国家；***the States*** Měiguó 美国
**2** *adj capital etc* zhōu 州；
(*ceremonial*) zhèngshì 正式；*~
banquet* guóyàn 国宴

**state²** *v/t* shēngmíng 声明

**State Department** Guówù Yuàn
国务院

**statement** (*to police*) kǒugōng 口
供；(*announcement*) shēngmíng 声
明；(*bank ~*) jiésuàn dān 结算单

**state of emergency** jǐnjí
zhuàngtài 紧急状态

**state-of-the-art** *adj* zuì yōuliáng
最优良

**statesman** zhèngzhì jiā 政治家

**state trooper** zhōu jǐngchá 州警
察

**state visit** guówù fǎngwèn 国务访
问

**static (electricity)** jìngdiàn 静电

**station 1** *n* RAIL huǒchē zhàn 火车
站；RAD, TV diàntái 电台 **2** *v/t
guard etc* zhùzhā 驻扎；*be ~ed at*
(*of soldier*) zhùzhā zài 驻扎在

**stationary** jìngzhǐ 静止

**stationery** wénjù 文具

**station wagon** kèhuò liǎngyòng
jiàochē 客货两用轿车

**statistical** tǒngjì 统计

**statistically** cóng tǒngjìxué jiǎodù
láishuō 从统计学角度来说

**statistics** (*science*) tǒngjì xué 统计
学；(*figures*) tǒngjì zīliào 统计资
料

**statue** sùxiàng 塑像

**Statue of Liberty** Zìyóu Nǚshén
Xiàng 自由女神像

**status** dìwèi 地位

**status symbol** shēnfènde xiàngzhēng 身份的象征

**statute** fǎlìng 法令

**staunch** *adj* jiāndìng 坚定

**stay 1** *n* dòuliú 逗留 **2** *v/i* (*in a
place*) dòuliú 逗留；(*in a condition*)
bǎochí 保持；*~ at home* dāi zài
jiā lǐ 呆在家里；*~ in a hotel* dāi
zài lǚguǎn 呆在旅馆；*~ right
there!* biédòng! 别动！；*~ put*
(*don't move*) bié zǒukāi 别走开；*~
put in* (*job, city*) yǒngyuǎn
dāizài 永远呆在
♦ **stay away** líkāi 离开
♦ **stay away from** bù jiējìn 不接
近
♦ **stay behind** wǎnzǒu 晚走
♦ **stay up** (*not go to bed*) bù qùshuì
不去睡

**steadily** *improve etc* zhújiàn 逐渐

**steady 1** *adj* (*not shaking*) píngwěn
平稳；(*regular*) yǒu guīlǜ 有规律；
(*continuous*) chíxù 持续 **2** *adv*: ***be
going ~*** zuò qínglǚ 做情侣；*~ on!*
yōu zhe diǎnr! 悠着点儿！**3** *v/t
wēnzhù* 稳住

**steak** niúpái 牛排

**steal 1** *v/t money etc* tōu 偷 **2** *v/i*
(*be a thief*) tōu dōngxi 偷东西；
(*move quietly*) qiāoqiāode xíngzǒu
悄悄地行走

**stealthy** qiāoqiāo 悄悄

**steam 1** *n* zhēngqì 蒸汽 **2** *v/t food*

zhēng 蒸

♦ **steam up 1** v/i (of window etc) méngshàng shuǐqì 蒙上水汽 **2** v/t: **be steamed up** F nǎohuǒ 恼火

**steamed bread** mántou 馒头

**steamer** (for cooking) zhēngguō 蒸锅

**steam iron** zhēngqì diàn yùndǒu 蒸汽电熨斗

**steel** n & adj gāng 钢

**steep**¹ adj hill etc dǒu 陡; F prices guì 贵

**steep**² v/t (soak) pào 泡

**steeple** jiāntǎ 尖塔

**steeplechase** (in athletics) yuèyě sài 越野赛

**steer**¹ n (animal) yān gōngniú 阉公牛

**steer**² v/t car, boat jiàshǐ 驾驶; person yǐndǎo 引导; conversation diàozhuǎn 掉转

**steering** (of motor vehicle) jiàshǐ jīgòu 驾驶机构

**steering wheel** fāngxiàng pán 方向盘

**stem**¹ n (of plant) gàn 干; (of glass) jīng 茎; (of pipe) bǐng 柄; (of word) cígàn 词干

♦ **stem from** qǐyuán yú 起源于

**stem**² v/t (block) zhìzhǐ 制止

**stemware** bōlí qìmǐn 玻璃器皿

**stench** èchòu 恶臭

**step 1** n (pace) bù 步; (stair) jiētī 阶梯; (measure) cuòshī 措施; (decision) juédìng 决定; **~ by ~** zhúbùde 逐步地 **2** v/i (put feet in/on sth) cǎi 踩; (walk forward) zǒu 走

♦ **step down** (from post etc) ràngwèi 让位

♦ **step out** (go out for a short time) chūqù yīhuìr 出去一会儿

♦ **step up** v/t (increase) jiākuài 加快

**stepbrother** jìxiōngdì 继兄弟; **stepdaughter** jìnǚ 继女; **stepfather** jìfù 继父; **stepladder** zhétī 折梯; **stepmother** jìmǔ 继母

**stepping stone** tàjiǎo shí 踏脚石; fig jìnshēn zhījiē 进身之阶

**stepsister** (same father different mother) tóngfù yìmǔ jiěmèi 同父异母姐妹; (same mother different father) tóngmǔ yìfù jiěmèi 同母异父姐妹

**stepson** jìzǐ 继子

**stereo** n (sound system) yīnxiǎng 音响

**stereotype** n chéngjiàn 成见

**sterile** woman, man bùyù 不育; MED xiāodú 消毒

**sterilize** woman jiézhá 结扎; equipment xiāodú 消毒

**sterling** n FIN yīngbàng 英镑

**stern** adj yánsù 严肃

**steroids** jīsù 激素

**stethoscope** tīngzhěnqì 听诊器

**Stetson®** Sītàisēn Zhānmào 斯泰森毡帽

**stevedore** zhuāngxiè gōng 装卸工

**stew** n dùn shípǐn 炖食品

**steward** (on plane, ship) chéngwùyuán 乘务员

**stewardess** (on plane, ship) chéngwùyuán 乘务员

**stick**¹ n (wood) mùgùn 木棍; (of policeman) jǐnggùn 警棍; (walking ~) guǎizhàng 拐杖; **the ~s** F xiāngxià 乡下

**stick**² **1** v/t (with adhesive) niánzhù 粘住; F (put) fàng 放 **2** v/i (jam) qiǎ zhù le 卡住了; (adhere) niánzhù 粘住

♦ **stick around** F dāi yīhuìr 呆一会儿

♦ **stick by**: **~ X** F zhōngyú X 忠于X

♦ **stick out** v/i (protrude) tūchū 突出; (be noticeable) xiǎnyǎn 显眼

♦ **stick to** (adhere to) niánzài … shàngmiàn 粘在 … 上面; F (keep to) jiānchí 坚持; path, road yánzhe 沿着; F (follow) jǐnsuí 紧随

♦ **stick together** F dāi zài yīqǐ 呆在一起

♦ **stick up** poster, leaflet shùqǐ 竖起

♦ **stick up for** F wèi … biànhù 为 … 辩护

♦ **stick with** F jiānchí 坚持

**sticker** biāoqiān 标签

**sticking plaster** hùchuànggāo 护

创膏
**stick-in-the-mud** mòshǒu chéng-guī zhě 墨守成规者
**sticky** *hands, surface* nián hūhū 黏糊糊; *a ~ label* tiēqiān 贴签
**stiff 1** *adj brush, cardboard, leather* yìng bāngbang 硬邦邦; *muscle, body* jiāngyìng 僵硬; *mixture, paste* chóu mì 稠密; *(in manner)* jūjín 拘谨; *drink* nóngliè 浓裂; *fine, penalty* yánlì 严厉; *competition* jīliè 激烈 **2** *adv*: **be scared ~** F hěn hàipà 很害怕; **be bored ~** F mènsǐle 闷死了
♦**stiffen** *v/i* biànde jǐnzhāng 变得紧张
♦**stiffen up** *(of muscle)* biàn jiāngyìng 变僵硬
**stifle** *v/t yawn, laugh* rěnzhe 忍着; *criticism, debate* èshā 扼杀
**stifling** lìngrén zhìxī 令人窒息
**stigma** chǐrǔ 耻辱
**stilettos** *(shoes)* xì gāo gēnxié 细高跟鞋
**still**[1] **1** *adj* píngjìng 平静 **2** *adv*: **keep ~!** bié dòngláidòngqù! 别动来动去!; **stand ~!** biédòng! 别动!
**still**[2] *adv (yet)* hái 还; *(nevertheless)* wúlùn rúhé 无论如何; *do you ~ want it?* nǐ háiyào ma? 你还要吗?; *she ~ hasn't finished* tā hái méiwán ne 她还没完呢; *she might ~ come* tā kěnéng réngrán huìlái 她可能仍然会来; *they are ~ my parents* tāmén zǒng háishì wǒde fùmǔ a 他们总还是我的父母啊; *~ more (even more)* gèngduō 更多
**stillborn**: **be ~** sǐchǎn 死产
**stilted** bú zìrán 不自然
**stilts** *(under house)* chēngzhù 撑柱
**stimulant** xīngfèn jì 兴奋剂
**stimulate** *person* cìjī 刺激; *growth, demand* cùjìn 促进
**stimulating** zhènfèn rénxīn 振奋人心
**stimulation** jīlì 激励
**stimulus** *(incentive)* dònglì 动力
**sting 1** *n (from bee, jellyfish)* zhēcì 螫刺 **2** *v/t (of bee, jellyfish)* zhē 螫

**3** *v/i (of eyes)* fātòng 发痛; *(of scratch)* gǎndào cìtòng 感到刺痛
**stinging** *remark, criticism* kèbó 刻薄
**stingy** F kōuménr 抠门儿
**stink 1** *n (bad smell)* chòuwèir 臭味儿; F *(fuss)* xuānrán dàbō 轩然大波; *make a ~* F dànào yīchǎng 大闹一场 **2** *v/i (smell bad)* dài chòuwèir 带臭味儿; F *(be very bad)* zāotòule 糟透了
**stint** *n* guīdìng de rènqī 规定的任期; *do a ~ in the army* fú bīngyì 服兵役
♦**stint on** jiéshěng 节省
**stipulate** guīdìng 规定
**stipulation** tiáojiàn 条件
**stir 1** *n*: *give the soup a ~* jiǎo yī jiǎo tāng 搅一搅汤; *cause a ~ fig* yǐnqǐ yīchǎng fēngbō 引起一场风波 **2** *v/t* jiǎobàn 搅拌 **3** *v/i (of sleeping person)* nuódòng 挪动
♦**stir up** *crowd* shāndòng 煽动; *bad memories* huíyì qǐ 回忆起
**stir-crazy**: **be ~** F juànhuàile 圈坏了
**stir-fry** *v/t* wànghuǒ biānchǎo 旺火煸炒
**stirring** *music, speech* jīdòng rénxīn 激动人心
**stitch 1** *n (in sewing)* zhēnjiǎo 针脚; *(in knitting)* yīzhēn 一针; *~es* MED féngzhēn 缝针; *have a ~* tūrán jùtòng 突然剧痛 **2** *v/t sew* féng 缝
♦**stitch up** *wound* féng qǐlái 缝起来
**stitching** *(stitches)* xiàn xiàn 线线
**stock 1** *n (reserves)* chǔcún 储存; COM: *of store* huò 货; *(animals)* shēngchù 牲畜; FIN gǔpiào 股票; *(food)* tāng 汤; *in ~/out of ~* yǒu/wúhuò 有/无货; *take ~* pínggū 评估 **2** *v/t* COM bèiyǒu 备有
♦**stock up on** chǔbèi 储备
**stockbroker** gǔpiào jīngjìrén 股票经纪人; *stock exchange* gǔpiào jiāoyìsuǒ 股票交易所; **stockholder** gǔdōng 股东
**stocking** chángtǒngwà 长统袜

**stock market** gǔpiào shìchǎng 股票市场; **stockmarket crash** gǔpiào shìchǎng bàodiē 股票市场暴跌; **stockpile 1** n (of food, weapons) chǔbèi wùzī 储备物资 **2** v/t chǔbèi 储备; **stockroom** cāngkù 仓库; **stocktaking** pándiǎn 盘点

**stocky** ǎizhuàng 矮壮

**stock-still** *stand ~* yīdòng búdòng 一动不动

**stodgy** *food* yìbǎo 易饱

**stomach 1** n (inside) dùzi 肚子; (abdomen) fùbù 腹部 **2** v/t (tolerate) rěnshòu 忍受

**stomach-ache** dùzi téng 肚子疼

**stone** n (material, pebble) shítou 石头; (precious ~) bǎoshí 宝石

**stoned** F (on drugs) mázuì 麻醉

**stone-deaf** wánquán lóng 完全聋

**stonewall** v/i F tángsè 搪塞

**stony** ground, path duōshí 多石

**stool** (seat) dèngzi 凳子

**stoop**[1] **1** n wānyāo qūbèi 弯腰曲背 **2** v/i (bend down) wānyāo 弯腰; (have bent back) hāyāo 哈腰

**stoop**[2] n (porch) ménláng 门廊

**stop 1** n (for train, bus) zhàn 站; *come to a ~* tíngle 停了; *put a ~ to* tíngzhǐ 停止 **2** v/t (put an end to, cease) tíngzhǐ 停止; (prevent) zǔzhǐ 阻止; person in street lánzhù 拦住; car, bus, train, etc v/t driver tíng tíng 停; of pedestrian lánzhù 拦住; *~ talking immediately!* mǎshàng zhùzuǐ! 马上住嘴!; *I ~ped her from leaving* wǒ bùràng tā zǒu 我不让她走; *it has ~ped raining* yǔtíngle 雨停了; *~ a check* tíngzhǐ duìfù zhīpiào 停止兑付支票 **3** v/i tíng tíng 停

♦**stop by** (visit) shùnbiàn guòfǎng 顺便过访

♦**stop off** zhōngtú tíngliú 中途停留

♦**stop over** zhōngtú tíngliú 中途停留

♦**stop up** sink dǔsāi 堵塞

**stopgap** línshí tìdài 临时替代; **stoplight** (traffic light) hónglǜdēng 红绿灯; (brake light) shāchē

dēng shāchē dēng 刹车灯; **stopover** dòuliú 逗留; (in air travel) zhōngtú tíngliú 中途停留

**stopper** (for bath, basin) sāizi 塞子; (for bottle) píngsāi 瓶塞

**stopping:** *no ~* (sign) bùzhǔn tíngchē 不准停车

**stop sign** tíngchē biāozhì 停车标志

**stopwatch** miǎobiǎo 秒表

**storage** zhùcáng 贮藏; *put X in ~* bǎ X zhùcáng qǐlái bǎ 把X贮藏起来; *be in ~* zài zhùcáng kù 在贮藏库

**storage capacity** COMPUT cúnchǔ róngliàng 存储容量

**storage space** zhùcún kōngjiān 贮存空间

**store 1** n shāngdiàn 商店; (stock) chǔbèi 储备; (storehouse) cāngkù 仓库 **2** v/t cúnfàng 存放; COMPUT chǔcún 储存

**storefront** línjiē diànpù 临街店铺; **storehouse** cāngkù 仓库; **storekeeper** diànzhǔ 店主; **storeroom** cāngkù 仓库; **store window** shāngdiàn chúchuāng 商店橱窗

**storm** n bàofēngyǔ 暴风雨

**storm drain** yǔshuǐ dào 雨水道

**storm window** wàicéng chuāng 外层窗; **storm warning** fēngbào jǐngbào 风暴警报

**stormy** weather yǒu bàofēngyǔ 有暴风雨; relationship yībō sānzhé 一波三折

**story**[1] (tale) gùshì 故事; (account) xùshù 叙述; (newspaper article) bàodào 报道; F (lie) huǎnghuà 谎话

**story**[2] (of building) céng 层

**stout** adj person féipàng 肥胖; boots nàichuān 耐穿

**stove** (for cooking) lúzi 炉子; (for heating) jiārè qì 加热器

**stow** chǔcáng 储藏

♦**stow away** v/i (on ship) wúpiào tōuchéng 无票偷乘

**stowaway** wúpiào tōuchéng zhě 无票偷乘者

**straight 1** adj line, hair zhí 直; back

bǐzhí 笔直; (honest, direct) tǎnshuài 坦率; (not criminal) zhèngpài 正派; (whiskey etc) chún 纯; (tidy) zhěngqí 整齐; (conservative) bǎoshǒu 保守; (not homosexual) fēi tóngxìngliàn 非同性恋; *be a ~ A student* chéngjì yōuxiùde xuéshēng 成绩优秀的学生 2 *adv* (in a straight line) jìngzhí 径直; (directly, immediately) zhíjiē 直接; (clearly) zhèngquè 正确; *stand up ~!* zhànzhíle! 站直了！; *look X ~ in the eye* dīngzhe X de yǎnjīng 盯着 X 的眼睛; *go ~* F (of criminal) gǎixié guīzhèng 改邪归正; *give it to me ~* F tǎnbái gàosù wǒ 坦白告诉我; *~ ahead be situated* jiùzài qiánmiàn 就在前面; *walk, drive* zhíxiàn zǒu zhí zǒu 直着走; *look* xiàngqián kàn 向前看; *carry ~ on* (of driver etc) zhízhe zǒu 直着走; *~away, ~off* mǎshàng Tú 马上了; *~ out* zhíjiēliǎodàng 直截了当; *~ up* (without ice) bù jiābīng 不加冰

**straighten** v/t nòngzhí 弄直

♦**straighten out 1** v/t situation jiěshì qīng 解释清 **2** v/i (of road) biànzhí 变直

♦**straighten up** tǐngzhí 挺直

**straightforward** (honest, direct) zhíjiéliǎodàng 直截了当; (simple) jiǎndān 简单

**strain**[1] n (on rope, engine, heart) zuòyòng lì 作用力; (on person) zhòngfù 重负 **2** v/t (injure) shāng 伤; fig: finances, budget shījiā yālì 施加压力

**strain**[2] v/t vegetables lùgàn 滤干; oil, fat etc guòlù 过滤

**strainer** (for vegetables etc) guòlù qì 过滤器

**strait** hǎixiá 海峡

**straitlaced** gǔbǎn 古板

**strand**[1] n (of hair, wool, thread) lǚlǚ 缕缕

**strand**[2] v/t shǐ chǔyú kùnjìng 使处于困境; *be ~ed* chǔyú kùnjìng 处于困境

**strange** (odd, curious) qíguài 奇怪; (unknown, foreign) mòshēng 陌生

**strangely** (oddly) qíguài 奇怪; *~ enough* chūhū yìliào 出乎意料

**stranger** (person you don't know) mòshēng rén 陌生人; *I'm a ~ here myself* wǒ duì zhèlǐ yě hěn mòshēng 我对这里也很陌生

**strangle** person èsǐ 扼死

**strap** n (of schoolbag) shūbāo dài 书包带; (of bra, dress) jiāndài 肩带; (of watch) biǎodài 表带; (of shoe) xiédài 鞋带

♦**strap in** jìhǎo ānquándài 系好安全带

**strapless** wúdài 无带

**strategic** zhànlüè 战略

**strategy** zhànlüè 战略

**straw**[1] cǎo 草; *that's the last ~!* zuìzhōng shǐrén wúfǎ rěnshòu! 最终使人无法忍受！

**straw**[2] (for drink) xīguǎn 吸管

**strawberry** cǎoméi 草莓

**stray 1** adj animal shīsàn 失散; bullet liúdàn 流弹 **2** n (dog) zǒushī de gǒu 走失的狗; (cat) zǒushī de māo 走失的猫 **3** v/i (of animal, child) zǒushī 走失; fig (of eyes, thoughts) bùyóu zìzhǔ 不由自主

**streak** (of dirt, paint) tiáowén 条纹; fig (of nastiness etc) gèxìngde yímiàn 个性的一面; *he's got a cruel ~* tā yǒudiǎn cánrěn 他有点儿残忍 **2** v/i (move quickly) fēibēn 飞奔 **3** v/t: *be ~ed with ...* yǒu ... de hénjì 有 ... 的痕迹

**stream 1** n fig (of people, complaints) yīliánchuàn 一连串; *come on ~* kāishǐ shēngchǎn 开始生产 **2** v/i yuányuán búduàn 源源不断; *sunlight ~ed into the room* yángguāng zhàoshè rù fángjiān 阳光照射入房间

**streamer** héngfú 横幅

**streamline** v/t fig tígāo xiàolù 提高效率

**streamlined** car, plane liúxiànxíng 流线型; fig: organization gāo xiàolù 高效率

**street** jiēdào 街道

**streetcar** yǒuguǐ diànchē 有轨电车; **streetlight** jiēdēng 街灯

**streetpeople** piāobó jiētóu rén-shì 漂泊街头人士; **street-walker** jìnǚ妓女; **streetwise** *adj* yǒu chéngshì shēnghuó nénglì 有城市生活能力

**strength** (*of person: physical*) lìqì 力气; *fig* (*strong point*) yōudiǎn 优点; (*of wind, current*) qiángdù 强度; (*of emotion, friendship etc*) lìliàng 力量; (*of organization, country, currency*) shílì 实力

**strengthen 1** *v/t* jiāqiáng 加强 **2** *v/i* biànqiáng 变强

**strenuous** jiānkǔ 艰苦

**stress 1** *n* (*emphasis*) zhòngdiǎn 重点; (*tension*) yālì 压力; *be under ~* shòudào yālì 受到压力 **2** *v/t* syllable zhòngdú 重读; *importance etc* qiángdiào 强调; *I must ~ that ... * wǒ bìxū qiángdiào ... 我必须强调 ...

**stressed out** F jiāotóulàn'é 焦头烂额

**stressful** jǐnzhāng 紧张

**stretch 1** *n* (*of land, water*) piàn piàn 片片; *at a ~* (*non-stop*) liánxù 连续 **2** *adj* fabric kě shēnsuō 可伸缩 **3** *v/t* material shēnzhǎn 伸展; *small income* jiéyuē 节约; F *rules* hūlüè 忽略; *he ~ed out his hand* tā shēnchū shǒu lái 他伸出手来; *a job that ~es me* yīfèn yǒu tiǎozhàn xìng de gōngzuò 一份有挑战性的工作 **4** *v/i* (*to relax muscles*) shēn lányāo 伸懒腰; (*to reach sth*) shēnshǒu 伸手; (*spread*) yánshēn 延伸; (*of fabric: give*) shēnsuō 伸缩; (*of fabric: sag*) chēngcháng 撑长; *~ from X to Y* (*extend*) cóng X yánshēn zhì Y 从 X 延伸至 Y

**stretcher** dānjià 担架

**strict** *person instructions, rules* yángé 严格

**strictly** yángé 严格; *it is ~ forbidden* juéduì bù yǔnxǔ 绝对不允许

**stride 1** *n* dàbù 大步; *take ... in one's ~* cóngróngzìrúde chǔlǐ ... 从容自如地处理 ... **2** *v/i* dàbù zǒu 大步走

**strident** jiānruì cì'ěr 尖锐刺耳; *fig: demands* shēngsīlìjié 声嘶力竭

**strike 1** *n* (*of workers*) bàgōng 罢工; (*in baseball*) hǎoqiú 好球; (*of oil*) fāxiàn 发现; *be on ~* zài bàgōng 在罢工; *go on ~* jǔxíng bàgōng 举行罢工 **2** *v/i* (*of workers*) bàgōng 罢工; (*attack*) xíjí 袭击; (*of disaster*) jiànglín 降临; (*of clock*) qiāoxiǎng 敲响 **3** *v/t* (*hit*) zhuàng 撞; *fig* (*of disaster, illness*) qīnxí 侵袭; (*match*) huá huá 划; (*of idea, thought*) chūxiànyú nǎozhōng 出现于脑中; *oil* fāxiàn 发现; *she struck me as being ... * tā gěi wǒde yìnxiàng shì ... 她给我的印象是 ...

♦ **strike out** *v/t* huàdiào 划掉

**strikebreaker** pòhuài bàgōng zhě 破坏罢工者

**striker** (*person on strike*) bàgōng zhě 罢工者

**striking** (*marked*) xiǎnzhù 显著; (*eye-catching*) yǐnrén zhùmù 引人注目

**string** *n* (*cord*) xìshéng 细绳; (*of violin, cello etc*) xián 弦; (*of tennis racket*) bēngshéng 绷绳; *~s* (*musicians*) xiányuèqì yǎnzòu zhě 弦乐器演奏者; *pull ~s* lā guānxi 拉关系; *a ~ of* (*series*) yīliánchuàn 一连串

♦ **string along 1** *v/i* gēnsuí 跟随 **2** *v/t: string X along* yǒuyì wùdǎo X 有意误导 X

♦ **string up** F diàosǐ 吊死

**stringed instrument** xiányuèqì 弦乐器

**stringent** yángé 严格

**string player** xiányuèqì yǎnzòu zhě 弦乐器演奏者

**strip 1** *n* chángtiáo 长条; (*comic ~*) liánhuánhuà 连环画 **2** *v/t* (*remove*) chúqù 除去; (*undress*) bōguāng yīfu 剥光衣服; *~ X of Y* bōduó X de Y 剥夺 X 的 Y **3** *v/i* (*undress*) tuōquāng yīfu 脱去衣服; (*of stripper*) tuōguāng yīfu 脱光衣服

**strip club** tuōyīwǔ yèzǒnghuì 脱

衣舞夜总会

stripe tiáowén 条纹; (*indicating rank*) jíbié tiáowén 级别条纹

striped yǒu tiáowén 有条纹

stripper tuōyīwǔ biǎoyǎn zhě 脱衣舞表演者

strip show tuōyīwǔ biǎoyǎn 脱衣舞表演

striptease tuōyīwǔ 脱衣舞

strive 1 *v/t*: ~ *to do X* nǔlì zuò X 努力做 X 2 *v/i* fèndòu 奋斗; ~ *for* lìzhēng 力争

stroke 1 *n* MED zhòngfēng 中风; (*when writing*) bǐhuà 笔画; (*when painting*) yìbǐ 一笔; (*style of swimming*) yóufǎ 游法; ~ *of luck* zǒuyùn 走运; *she never does a* ~ (*of work*) tā cónglái bù gōngzuò 她从来不工作 2 *v/t* fǔmō 抚摸

stroll 1 *n* sànbù 散步 2 *v/i* xiánzǒu 闲走

stroller (*for baby*) yīng'érchē 婴儿车

strong *person* qiángzhuàng 强壮; *structure* jiāngù 坚固; *candidate* qiáng 强; *supporter, supporter* jiāndìng 坚定; *wind* qiángjìn 强劲; *drink* lièxìng 烈性; *tea, coffee* nóng 浓; *taste, smell* wèinóng 味浓; *views, objections* jiānjué 坚决; *currency* jiāntǐng 坚挺

stronghold *fig* gēnjùdì 根据地

strongly qiángliè 强烈

strong-minded yìzhì jiānqiáng 意志坚强

strong-willed yìzhì jiānjué 意志坚决

structural gòujià 构架

structure 1 *n* (*sth built*) jiànzhùwù 建筑物; (*way in which sth has been put together*) jiégòu 结构 2 *v/t* jìhuà 计划

struggle 1 *n* (*fight*) zhēngdòu 争斗; (*hard time*) jiānnán jiānnán 艰难 2 *v/i* (*with a person*) gédòu 格斗; (*have a hard time*) nǔlì 努力 3 *v/t*: ~ *to do X* zhēngzhá zuò X 挣扎做 X

strum luàntán 乱弹

strut *v/i* dàyáodàbǎide zǒu 大摇大摆地走

stub 1 *n* (*of cigarette*) yāndì 烟蒂;

(*of check, ticket*) cúngēn 存根 2 *v/t*: *I* ~ *bed my toe* wǒ cǎidào wǒde jiǎozhǐ 我踩到我的脚趾

♦stub out niǎnmiè 碾灭

stubble (*on man's face*) húcházi 胡茬子

stubborn gùzhí 固执; *defense* wánqiáng 顽强

stubby cū'ér duǎn 粗而短

stuck: *be* ~ *on X* F duì X yǒu xìngqu 对 X 有兴趣

stuck-up F bǎi jiàzi 摆架子

student xuésheng 学生; (*at college, university*) dàxuéshēng 大学生

student nurse shíxí hùshì 实习护士

student teacher shíxí jiàoshī 实习教师

studio (*of artist, sculptor*) gōngzuòshì 工作室; (*recording* ~) lùyīnpéng 录音棚; (*film* ~) shèyǐngpéng 摄影棚; (*TV* ~) yǎnbōshì 演播室

studious hàoxué 好学

study 1 *n* (*room*) shūfáng 书房; (*learning*) xuéxí 学习; (*investigation*) yánjiū 研究 2 *v/t* (*at school, university*) gōngdú 攻读; (*examine*) zǐxì chákàn 仔细察看 3 *v/i* xuéxí 学习

stuff 1 *n* (*objects, things*) dōngxi 东西; (*belongings*) suǒyǒuwù 所有物 2 *v/t* *turkey* tiánchōng 填充; ~ *X into Y* bǎ X sāijìn Y 把 X 塞进 Y

stuffed toy tiánliào wánjù 填料玩具

stuffing (*for turkey, in chair etc*) tiánliào 填料

stuffy *room* mèn 闷; *person* gǔbǎn 古板

stumble *v/i* bànjiǎo 绊脚

stumble across *v/t* yìwài fāxiàn 意外发现

stumble over *v/t* bàndào 绊到; *words* chūcuò 出错

stumbling block zhàng'ài 障碍

stump 1 *n* (*of tree*) shùzhuāng 树桩 2 *v/t* (*of question, questioner*) nánzhù 难住

♦stump up F fùchū 付出

stun (*of blow*) dǎhūn 打昏; (*of

news) dàchīyìjīng 大吃一惊

**stunning** (*amazing*) lìngrén jīngyì 令人惊异; (*very beautiful*) jí piàoliàng 极漂亮

**stunt** n (*for publicity*) xuétóu 噱头; (*in movie*) tèjì 特技

**stuntman** (*in movie*) tìshēn yǎnyuán 替身演员

**stupefy** mùdèngkǒudāi 目瞪口呆

**stupendous** jíhǎo 极好

**stupid** yúchǔn 愚蠢

**stupidity** yúchǔn 愚蠢

**stupor** shénzhì bùqīng 神志不清

**sturdy** jiēshi 结实

**stutter** v/i jiēbā 结巴

**sty** (*for pig*) zhūjuàn 猪圈

**style** n (*method, manner*) fēnggé 风格; (*fashion*) liúxíng kuǎnshì 流行款式; (*fashionable elegance*) gédiào 格调; **go out of ~** búzài liúxíng 不再流行

**stylish** yǒu gédiào 有格调

**subcommittee** xiǎozǔ wěiyuánhuì 小组委员会

**subcompact** (**car**) chāoxiǎoxíng qìchē 超小型汽车

**subconscious: the ~** (**mind**) qiányìshí 潜意识

**subcontract** v/t fēnbāo hétóng 分包合同

**subcontractor** fēnbāorén 分包人

**subdivide** v/t xìfēn 细分

**subdued** lighting róuhé 柔和; voice dīluò 低落

**subheading** fùbiāotí 副标题

**subject 1** n (*of country*) gōngmín 公民; (*topic*) zhǔtí 主题; (*branch of learning*) kēmù 科目; GRAM zhǔyǔ 主语; **change the ~** gǎibiàn huàtí 改变话题 **2** adj: **be ~ to X** yǒu X de qīngxiàng 有X的倾向; **~ to availability** shòuwán wéizhǐ 售完为止 **3** v/t shǐ ... zāoshòu shǐ ... 遭受

**subjective** zhǔguān 主观

**sublet** v/t zhuǎnzū 转租

**submachine gun** chōngfēngqiāng 冲锋枪

**submarine** qiántǐng 潜艇

**submerge 1** v/t yānmò 淹没 **2** v/i (*of submarine*) qiánrù 潜入

**submission** (*surrender*) tóuxiáng 投降; (*to committee etc*) chéngwén 呈文

**submissive** shùncóng 顺从

**submit** v/t plan, proposal chéngjiāo 呈交

**subordinate 1** adj employee, role etc xiàjí 下级 **2** n xiàshǔ 下属

**subpoena 1** n chuánpiào 传票 **2** v/t person chuánhuàn 传唤

♦**subscribe to** magazine etc dìngyuè 订阅; theory zànchéng 赞成

**subscriber** (*to magazine*) dìngyuè zhě 订阅者

**subscription** dìng dìng 订订

**subsequent** suíhòu 随后

**subsequently** hòulái 后来

**subside** (*of flood waters*) tuìqù 退去; (*of high winds*) píngxī 平息; (*of building*) xiàxiàn 下陷; (*of fears, panic*) jiǎnruò 减弱

**subsidiary** n fùshǔ gōngsī 附属公司

**subsidize** zīzhù 资助

**subsidy** bǔzhù 补助

♦**subsist on** kào ... shēnghuó 靠 ... 生活

**subsistence farmer** zìjǐ nóngchǎngzhǔ 自给农场主

**subsistence level** pínkùn shuǐzhǔn 贫困水准

**substance** (*matter*) wùzhì 物质

**substandard** dīyú biāozhǔn 低于标准

**substantial** xiāngdāng dà 相当大

**substantially** (*considerably*) kěguān 可观; (*in essence*) shízhì shang 实质上

**substantiate** adj zhèngmíng 证明

**substantive** adj shíjì 实际

**substitute 1** n dàitìpǐn 代替品; SP tìhuàn zhě 替换者 **2** v/t: **X for Y** yòng X qǔdài Y 用X取代Y **3** v/i: **~ for X** dàitì X 代替X

**substitution** (*act*) qǔdài 取代; **make a ~** SP tìhuàn duìyuán 替换队员

**subtitle 1** n zìmù 字幕 **2** v/t movie gěi ... jiā zìmù 给 ... 加字幕

**subtle** qiǎomiào 巧妙

**subtract** v/t number jiǎnqù 减去; **~**

**X from Y** cóng Y zhōng jiǎnqù X 从 Y 中减去 X

**suburb** jiāoqū 郊区; **the ~s** shìjiāo 市郊

**suburban** jiāoqū 郊区

**subversive 1** adj yǒu diānfùxìng 有颠覆性 **2** n diānfù fènzǐ 颠覆分子

**subway** dìtiě 地铁

**subzero** adj xiàlíngqí 零下

**succeed 1** v/i (be successful) chénggōng 成功; (to throne) jíwèi 即位; **~ in doing X** chénggōngde zuò X 成功地做 X **2** v/t (come after, monarch) jìrèn 继任

**succeeding** jiēxiàlái 接下来

**success** chénggōng 成功; **be a ~** chénggōng 成功

**successful** chénggōng 成功

**successfully** chénggōng 成功

**succession** (sequence) yíxìliè 一系列; (to the throne) jíwèi 即位; **in ~** yígè jiē yígè 一个接一个

**successive** jiēlián búduàn 接连不断

**successor** jìrènrén 继任人

**succinct** jiǎnyào 简要

**succulent** meat, fruit xiānměi 鲜美

**succumb** (give in) qūfú 屈服; **~ to temptation** qūcóngyú yòuhuò 屈从于诱惑

**such 1** adj (of that kind) zhèyàng 这样; **~ a** (so much of a) nàme 那么; **~ as** xiàng ... yíyàng 像 ... 一样; **there is no ~ word as ...** méiyǒu rú ... zhèmege cí 没有如 ... 这么个词 **2** adv zhème 这么; **as ~** an qí běnshēn yìyì 按其本身意义

**suck** lollipop, hard candy shǔnxī 吮吸; **~ a** thumb shǔnxī mǔzhǐ 吮吸拇指; **~ X from Y** cóng Y xīchū X 从 Y 吸出 X

♦ **suck up** moisture xīshōu 吸收

♦ **suck up to** F fèngchéng 奉承

**sucker** F (person) qīngxìn zhě 轻信者; F (lollipop) bàngbàngtáng 棒棒糖

**sucking pig** rǔzhū 乳猪

**suction** chōuxī 抽吸

**sudden** yìwài 意外; **all of a ~** tūrán 突然

**suddenly** tūrán 突然

**suds** (soap ~) pàomò 泡沫

**sue** v/t kònggào 控告

**suede** n róngmiàngé 绒面革

**suffer 1** v/i (be in great pain) shòukǔ 受苦; (deteriorate) biànchà 变差; **be ~ing from** huànyǒu 患有 **2** v/t loss zāoshòu 遭受; setback jīngshòu 经受

**suffering** n tòngkǔ 痛苦

**sufficient** zúgòu 足够

**sufficiently** chōngzú 充足

**suffocate 1** v/i zhìxī ér sǐ 窒息而死 **2** v/t shǐ ... zhìxī 使 ... 窒息

**suffocation** zhìxī 窒息

**sugar 1** n shítáng 食糖 **2** v/t jiātáng 加糖

**sugar bowl** tángguàn 糖罐

**sugar cane** gānzhè 甘蔗

**suggest** v/t jiànyì 建议; **I ~ that we stop now** wǒ jiànyì wǒmen xiànzài tíngxià 我建议我们现在停下

**suggestion** jiànyì 建议

**suicide** zìshā 自杀; **commit ~** zìshā 自杀

**suit 1** n xīzhuāng 西装; (in cards) huāsè pái 花色牌 **2** v/t (of clothes, color) shìhé 适合; **~ yourself!** suí nǐde biàn! 随你的便!; **be ~ed for X** shìhé X 适合 X

**suitable** shìyí 适宜

**suitcase** shǒutí xiāng 手提衣箱

**suite** (of rooms) tàojiān 套间; (furniture) yītào jiājù 一套家具; MUS zǔqǔ 组曲

**sulfur** liúhuáng 硫磺

**sulk** v/i shēng mènqì 生闷气

**sulky** shēng mènqì 生闷气

**sullen** mènmènbúlè 闷闷不乐

**sultry** climate mēnrè 闷热; (sexually) xìnggǎn 性感

**sum** (total) zǒngshù 总数; (amount) shùmù 数目; (in arithmetic) suànshù 算术; **a large ~ of money** amount yí dà bǐ qián 一大笔钱; **insured amount** bǎoxiǎn jīn'é 保险金额; **the ~ total of his efforts** tā yíqiè nǔlìde jiéguǒ 他一切努力的结果

♦ **sum up 1** v/t (summarize) gàikuò

概括; (assess) píngjià 评价 2 v/i
LAW gàishù 概述

summarize v/t gàikuò 概括

summary n zǒngjié 总结

summer xiàtiān 夏天

Summer Palace Yíhéyuán 颐和园

summit (of mountain) shāndǐng 山顶; fig zhìgāodiǎn 至高点; POL zuì gāojí huìyì 最高级会议

summon staff, ministers zhàojí 召集; meeting zhàokāi 召开

♦summon up strength fāhuī 发挥

summons LAW chuánpiào 传票

sump (for oil) rùnhuáyóuxiāng 润滑油箱

sun tàiyáng 太阳; in the ~ zài yángguāng xià 在阳光下; out of the ~ zài bèiyīnchù 在背阴处; he has had too much ~ tā zhòngshǔ le 他中暑了

sunbathe shài tàiyáng 晒太阳

sunblock fángshàigāo 防晒膏; sunburn shàibān 晒斑; sunburnt shàishāng 晒伤

Sunday xīngqīrì 星期日

sundial rìguī 日晷

sundries záxiàng 杂项

sunglasses mòjìng 墨镜

sunken cheeks āoxiàn 凹陷

sunny day yángguāng chōngzú 阳光充足; disposition kāilǎng 开朗; it is ~ tiānqì qínglǎng 天气晴朗

sunrise rìchū 日出; sunset rìluò 日落; sunshade yángsǎn 阳伞; sunshine yángguāng 阳光; sunstroke zhòngshǔ 中暑; suntan shàihēi 晒黑; get a ~ shàichéng gǔtóngsè 晒成古铜色

Sun Yat-sen Sūn Zhōngshān 孙中山

super 1 adj F jíhǎo 极好 2 n (janitor) guǎnlǐyuán 管理员

superb bàngjíle 棒极了

superficial comments, analysis fúqiǎn 肤浅; person qiǎnbó 浅薄; wounds biǎopí 表皮

superfluous duōyú 多余

superhuman efforts chāohūchángrén 超乎常人

superintendent (of apartment

block) guǎnlǐyuán 管理员

superior 1 adj (better) gènghǎo 更好; pej (attitude) yǒu yōuyuègǎn 有优越感 2 n (in organization, society) shàngjí 上级

supermarket chāojí shìchǎng 超级市场

supernatural 1 adj powers chāozìrán 超自然 2 n: the ~ chāozìrán de shìwù 超自然的事物

superpower POL chāojí dàguó 超级大国

supersonic flight, aircraft chāoyīnsù 超音速

superstition míxìn sīxiǎng 迷信思想

superstitious person míxìn 迷信

supervise jiāndū 监督

supervisor (at work) zhǐdǎo zhě 指导者

supper wǎnfàn 晚饭

supple róuruǎn 柔软

supplement (extra payment) fùjiāfèi 附加费

supplier COM gōngyìngshāng 供应商

supply 1 n gōngyìng 供应; ~ and demand gōngyìng yǔ xūqiú 供应与需求; supplies gōngyìngpǐn 供应品 2 v/t goods tígōng 提供; ~ X with Y xiàng X tígōng Y 向 X 提供 Y; be supplied with ... zhuāngyǒu ... 装有 ...

support 1 n (for structure) zhīzhù 支柱; (backing) zhīchí 支持 2 v/t building, structure zhīchēng 支撑; (financially) yuánzhù 援助; (back) zhīchí 支持

supporter yǒnghù zhě 拥护者; (of football team etc) zhīchí zhě 支持者

supportive zhīchí 支持

suppose (imagine) liàoxiǎng 料想; I - so wǒ kàn shì zhèyàng 我看是这样; be ~d to ... (be meant to) yīnggāi ... 应该 ...; (be said to be) jùshuō ... 据说 ...; you are not ~d to ... (not allowed to) nǐ bùgāi ... 你不该 ...

suppository MED shuānjì 栓剂

**suppress** *rebellion etc* zhènyā 镇压

**suppression** zhènyā 镇压

**supremacy** zuìgāo quánwēi 最高权威

**supreme** *being, commander* zhìgāo-wúshàng 至高无上; *effort, courage, delight* jídà 极大

**Supreme Court** Gāojí Fǎtíng 高级法庭

**surcharge** fùjiāfèi 附加费

**sure 1** *adj:* **I'm ~** wǒ néng quèdìng 我能确定; **I'm not ~** wǒ bú quèdìng 我不确定; **be ~ about X** duì X néng quèdìng 对 X 能确定; **make ~ that …** chámíng … 查明 … **2** *adv:* **~ enough** guǒrán rúcǐ 果然如此; **it ~ is hot today** F jīntiān quèshí rè 今天确实热; **~!** dāngrán! 当然!

**surely** yídìng 一定; *(gladly)* dāng-rán 当然

**surf 1** *n (on sea)* jùlàng 激浪 **2** *v/t the Net* sōuxún 搜寻

**surface 1** *n (of table, object)* biǎomiàn 表面; *(of water)* shuǐmiàn 水面; **on the ~** *fig* biǎomiàn shang 表面上 **2** *v/i (of swimmer, submarine)* fúdào shuǐmiàn 浮到水面; *(appear)* chóngxīn chūxiàn 重新出现

**surface mail** pǔtōng yóujiàn 普通邮件

**surfboard** chōnglàngbǎn 冲浪板

**surfer** *(on sea)* chōnglàng zhě 冲浪者

**surfing** chōnglàng yùndòng 冲浪运动; **go ~** zuò chōnglàng yùndòng 做冲浪运动

**surge** *n (in electric current)* diànliú jíchéng 电流急冲; *(in demand, interest, growth etc)* jīzēng 激增

♦ **surge forward** *(of crowd)* yǒngjìn 涌进

**surgeon** wàikē yīshī 外科医师

**surgery** shǒushù 手术; **undergo ~** jiēshòu shǒushù zhìliáo 接受手术治疗

**surgical** wàikē 外科

**surly** guāilì 乖戾

**surmount** *difficulties* kèfú 克服

**surname** xìng 姓

**surpass** chāoguò 超过

**surplus 1** *n* guòshèng 过剩 **2** *adj* shèngyú 剩余

**surprise 1** *n* jīngqí 惊奇; **it'll come as no ~ to hear that …** tīngdào … bùzú wéiqí 听到 … 不足为奇 **2** *v/t shǐ … chījīng* 使 … 吃惊; **be/look ~d** chīle yìjīng/kànqǐlái chīle yìjīng 吃了一惊/看起来吃了一惊

**surprising** lìngrén jīngyà 令人惊讶

**surprisingly** chūrényìwài 出人意外

**surrender 1** *v/i (of army)* tóuxiáng 投降 **2** *v/t (hand in: weapons etc)* jiāochū 交出 **3** *n* tóuxiáng 投降; *(handing in)* jiāochū 交出

**surrogate mother** dàimǔ 代母

**surround 1** *v/t* bāowéi 包围; **be ~ed by X** bèi X bāowéi 被 X 包围 **2** *n (of picture etc)* biānyuán 边缘

**surrounding** *adj* zhōuwéi 周围

**surroundings** huánjìng 环境

**survey 1** *n (of modern literature etc)* gàikuàng 概况; *(of consumer habits)* diàochá 调查; *(of building)* jiàndìng 鉴定 **2** *v/t (look at)* shěnshì 审视; *building* jiàndìng 鉴定

**surveyor** jiàndìngrén 鉴定人

**survival** xìngcún 幸存

**survive** *v/i (of species)* cúnhuó 存活; *(of patient)* yǒuxìng cúnhuó 有幸存活; **how are you? – I'm surviving** nǐ hǎo ma?- wǒ miǎnqiǎng huózhe 你好吗？- 我勉强活着; **his two surviving daughters** tāde liǎnggè huózhede nǚ'ér 他的两个活着的女儿 **2** *v/t accident, operation* cúncún 幸存; *(outlive)* bǐ … chángmìng 比 … 长命

**survivor** xìngcún zhě 幸存者; **he's a ~** *fig* tā shì yígè jīngdeqǐ fēngshuāng de rén 他是一个经得起风霜的人

**susceptible** *(emotionally)* yìshòu gǎndòng 易受感动; **be ~ to the cold/heat** duì lěng/rè mǐngǎn 对冷/热敏感

**suspect 1** *n* xiányífàn 嫌疑犯

**2** v/t person huáiyí 怀疑; (suppose) juéde 觉得

suspected murderer xiányí 嫌疑; the ~ cause bèi huáiyí de yuányīn 被怀疑的 原因

suspend (hang) xuánguà 悬挂; (from office, duties) lèlìng tíngzhí 勒令停职

suspenders (for pants) diàokùdài 吊裤带

suspense jǐnzhānggǎn 紧张感

suspension (in vehicle) jiǎnzhèn zhuāngzhì 减震装置; (from duty) tíngzhí 停职

suspension bridge diàoqiáo 吊桥

suspicion huáiyí 怀疑

suspicious (causing suspicion) kěyí 可疑; (feeling suspicion) yǒu yíxīn 有疑心; be ~ of X duì X yǒu yíxīn 对X有疑心

sustain zhīcheng 支撑

swab **1** n yàoqiān 药签 **2** v/t yòng yàoqiān cā yòng 药签擦

swagger n zhǐgāoqìyáng 趾高气扬

swallow¹ **1** v/t liquid, food yàn 咽 **2** v/i yànshí 咽食

swallow² (bird) yànzi 燕子

swamp **1** n zhǎozé 沼泽 **2** v/t yānmò 淹没; be ~ed with X X yìngjiēbùxiá X 应接不暇

swampy ground shīruǎn 湿软

swan tiān'é 天鹅

swap **1** v/t jiāohuàn 交换; ~ X for Y yòng X huàn Y 用X换Y **2** v/i huàn 换

swarm **1** n (of bees) dàqún 大群 **2** v/i (of ants, tourists etc) mìjí 密集; the town was ~ing with X chéngshìlǐ dàochù dōu shì X 城市 里到处都是X

swarthy face, complexion yǒuhēi 黝黑

swat v/t insect, fly zhòngpāi 重拍

sway **1** n (influence, power) yǐngxiǎng 影响 **2** v/i yáobǎi 摇摆

swear v/i (use swearword) zhòumà 咒骂; (promise) fāshì 发誓; LAW xuānshì 宣誓; ~ at X zhòumà X 咒骂X

♦swear in witness shì ... xuānshì 使 ... 宣誓

swearword màrénhuà 骂人话

sweat **1** n hànshuǐ 汗水; covered in ~ dàhànlínlí 大汗淋漓 **2** v/i chūhàn 出汗

sweater máoyī 毛衣

sweatshirt wúlǐng chángxiùshān 无领长袖衫

sweaty hands, smell hànlínlín 汗淋 淋

Swede Ruìdiǎn rén 瑞典人

Sweden Ruìdiǎn 瑞典

Swedish **1** adj Ruìdiǎn 瑞典 **2** n (language) Ruìdiǎn yǔ 瑞典语

sweep **1** v/t floor, leaves sǎo 扫 **2** n (long curve) wānqū 蜿蜒

♦sweep up v/t mess, crumbs sǎolǒng 扫拢

sweeping adj generalization, statement lǒngtǒng 笼统; changes yǒu guǎngfàn yǐngxiǎng 有广泛影响

sweet adj taste, tea tián 甜; F (kind) hǎoxīn 好心; F (cute) rěrén xǐ'ài 惹人喜爱

sweet and sour adj tángcù 糖醋

sweetcorn tián yùmǐ 甜玉米

sweeten v/t drink, food shǐ ... biàntián 使 ... 变甜

sweetener (for drink) tiánwèijì 甜味剂

sweetheart xīnshàng rén 心上人

swell **1** v/i (of limb etc) zhǒngzhàng 肿胀 **2** adj F (good) jíhǎo jíle 极好 **3** n (of the sea) qǐfú 起伏

swelling n MED zhǒngkuài 肿块

sweltering heat, day kùrè 酷热

swerve v/i (of driver, car) tūrán zhuǎnxiàng 突然转向

swift adj xùnsù 迅速

swim **1** v/i yóuyǒng 游泳; go ~ming qù yóuyǒng 去游泳; my head is ~ming wǒ tóuyūnmùxuàn 我头晕目眩 **2** n yóuyǒng 游泳; go for a ~ qù yóuyǒng 去游泳

swimmer yóuyǒng zhě 游泳者

swimming yóuyǒng 游泳

swimming pool yóuyǒngchí 游泳池

swimsuit yóuyǒngyī 游泳衣

swindle **1** n piànjú 骗局 **2** v/t: ~ X

***out of Y*** cóng Y piàndé X 从 Y 骗得 X

**swine** F (*person*) xiàliúpī 下流坯

**swing 1** *n* zhuǎnbiàn 转变; (*for child*) qiūqiān 秋千; **~ *to the Democrats*** zhuǎn ér zhīchí Mínzhǔdǎng 转而支持民主党 **2** *v/i* huīdòng 挥动; *hips* yáobǎi 摇摆 **3** *v/i* bǎidòng 摆动; (*turn*) zhuǎndòng 转动; (*of public opinion etc*) biàndòng 变动

**swing-door** tuīhémén 推合门

**Swiss 1** *adj* Ruìshì 瑞士 **2** *n* (*person*) Ruìshì rén 瑞士人

**switch 1** *n* (*for light*) kāiguān 开关; (*change*) biànhuà 变化 **2** *v/t* (*change*) huàn 换 **3** *v/i* (*change*) gǎihuàn 改换

♦**switch off** *v/t & v/i lights, engine, PC, TV* guāndiào 关掉

♦**switch on 1** *v/t lights, engine, PC, TV* kāi 开 **2** *v/i* kāijī 开机

**switchboard** diànhuà jiāohuàntái 电话交换台

**switchover** (*to new system*) zhuǎnbiàn 转变

**Switzerland** Ruìshì 瑞士

**swivel** *v/i* (*of chair, monitor etc*) xuánzhuàn 旋转

**swollen** zhǒngzhàng 肿胀

**swoop** *v/i* (*of bird*) měngpū 猛扑

♦**swoop down on** *prey* měngpū xiàng 猛扑向

♦**swoop on** (*of police etc*) tūrán sōuchá 突然搜查

**sword** jiàn 剑

**sycamore** xīkèmò shù 西克莫树

**syllable** yīnjié 音节

**syllabus** dàgāng 大纲

**symbol** (*character*) fúhào 符号; (*in poetry etc*) xiàngzhēng 象征

**symbolic** yǒu xiàngzhēngxìng 有象征性

**symbolism** (*in poetry, art*) xiàngzhēng shǒufǎ 象征手法

**symbolize** xiàngzhēng 象征

**symmetric(al)** duìchèn 对称

**symmetry** duìchèn 对称

**sympathetic** (*showing pity*) biǎoshì tóngqíng 表示同情; (*understanding*) lǐjiě rén 理解人; ***be ~ toward a person / an idea*** duì rén / xiǎngfǎ biǎoshì tóngqíng, zhīchí 对人 / 想法表示同情、支持

♦**sympathize with** *person, views* tóngqíng 同情

**sympathizer** POL yōnghù zhě 拥护者

**sympathy** (*pity*) tóngqíngxīn 同情心; (*understanding*) lǐjiě 理解; ***don't expect any ~ from me!*** bié zhǐwàng wǒ kělián nǐ! 别指望我可怜你!

**symphony** jiāoxiǎngyuè 交响乐

**symptom** MED zhèngzhuàng 症状; *fig* zhēngzhào 征兆

**symptomatic:** ***be ~ of X*** MED shì Xde zhèngzhuàng 是 X 的症状; *fig* shì Xde zhēngzhào 是 X 的征兆

**synchronize** *watches* shǐ ... tóngshí 使 ... 同时; *operations* shǐ ... tóngbù 使 ... 同步

**synonym** tóngyìcí 同义词

**syntax** jùfǎ 句法

**synthetic** rénzào 人造

**syphilis** méidú 梅毒

**syringe** zhùshèqì 注射器

**syrup** tángjiāng 糖浆

**system** (*method*) xìtǒng 系统; (*orderliness*) chéngxù 程序; (*computer*) zǔhé zhuāngzhì 组合装置; ***the braking / fuel injection / digestive ~*** shāchē / ránliào shūrù / xiāohuà xìtǒng 刹车 / 燃料输入 / 消化系统

**systematic** *approach, person* yǒu tiáolǐ 有条理

**systematically** *analyze, study* yǒu tiáolǐ 有条理; *destroy* xùyì 蓄意

**system crash** xìtǒng bēngkuì 系统崩溃

**systems analyst** COMPUT xìtǒng fēnxī zhě 系统分析者

**Szechuan** Sìchuān 四川

# T

tab *n* lāshé 拉舌; (*in text*) fáng-mǒshé 防抹舌
table *n* zhuōzi 桌子; (*of figures*) biǎo 表
tablecloth zhuōbù 桌布
tablespoon cānsháor 餐勺儿
tablet yàopiànr 药片儿
table tennis pīngpāngqiú 乒乓球
tabloid *n* (*newspaper*) xiǎobào 小报
taboo *adj* bìhuì 避讳
tacit xīnzhào bù xuān 心照不宣
tack 1 *n* (*nail*) píngtóudīng 平头钉 2 *v/t* (*sew*) bēng 绷 3 *v/i* (*of yacht*) zhuǎnháng 转航
tackle 1 *n* (*equipment*) yòngjù 用具; SP zǔdǎng 阻挡 2 *v/t* SP jiéqiú 截球; *problem* chǔlǐ 处理; *intruder* zhuāzhù 抓住
tacky *paint, glue* nián 粘; (*cheap, poor quality*) súqì 俗气; *behavior* bù yǎguān 不雅观
tact jīzhì 机智
tactful détǐ 得体
tactical zhànshù 战术
tactics cèlüè 策略
tactless bù détǐ 不得体
tadpole kēdǒu 蝌蚪
tag (*label*) biāoqiān 标签
Tai: Mount ~ Tàishān 泰山
tai chi tàijíquán 太极拳
tail *n* wěiba 尾巴
tail coat yànwěifú 燕尾服
tail light wěidēng 尾灯
tailor cáiféng 裁缝
tailor-made *suit* dìngzuò 定做; *solution* shìdàng 适当
tail wind shùnfēng 顺风
tainted *food* wūrǎn 污染
Taipei Táiběi 台北
Taiwan Táiwān 台湾
Taiwanese 1 *adj* Táiwān 台湾 2 *n* (*person*) Táiwān rén 台湾人; (*dialect*) Táiwān huà 台湾话

Taiwan Straits Táiwān Hǎixiá 台湾海峡
Tajik Tǎjíkè rén 塔吉克人
Tajiki 1 *adj* Tǎjíkè 塔吉克 2 *n* (*language*) Tǎjíkè yǔ 塔吉克语
Tajikistan Tǎjíkè 塔吉克
take *v/t* (*remove*) ná 拿; (*steal*) tōu 偷; (*transport*) sòng 送; (*accompany*) péi 陪; (*accept: money, gift, credit cards*) jiēshòu 接受; (*study: math, French*) xué 学; *photograph* zhàoxiàng 照相; *exam, degree* kǎo 考; *shower* línyù 淋浴; *stroll* sànbù 散步; *s.o.'s temperature* liáng 量; (*endure*) rěnshòu 忍受; (*require*) xūyào 需要; *how long does it ~?* yào duōcháng shíjiān? 要多长时间？; *I'll ~ it* (*when shopping*) wǒ mǎi le 我买了
◆take after xiàng 像
◆take away *pain* jiěchú 解除; *object* názǒu 拿走; MATH jiǎn 减; *take X away from Y* cóng Y nàlǐ názǒu X 从 Y 那里拿走 X
◆take back (*return: object*) tuìdiào 退掉; *person* sòng 送; (*accept back: husband etc*) jiēshòu 接受; *that takes me back* (*of music, thought etc*) shǐ wǒ huíyìqǐ 使我回忆起
◆take down (*from shelf*) qǔxià 取下; *scaffolding* chāidiào 拆掉; *pants* tuō 脱; (*write down*) xiěxià 写下
◆take in (*take indoors*) ná jìnlái 拿进来; (*give accommodation*) shōuliú 收留; (*make narrower*) gǎixiǎo 改小; (*deceive*) qīpiàn 欺骗; (*include*) bāokuò 包括
◆take off *v/t clothes, hat* qǔxià 取下; *10% etc* jiàngjià 降价; (*mimic*) mófǎng 模仿; *can you take a bit off here?* (*to barber*) néngbùnéng zài zhèlǐ jiǎn yìdiǎnr? 能不能在

这里剪一点儿？；*take a day / week off* fàngjià yītiān / yīxīngqī 放假一天／一星期 **2** *v/i* (*of airplane*) qǐfēi 起飞；(*become popular*) fēiyuè 飞跃

♦ **take on** *job* dānrèn 担任；*staff* pìnyòng 聘用

♦ **take out** (*from bag, pocket*) náchū 拿出；*stain* qùdiào 去掉；*tooth* qǔchū 取出；*appendix, word from text* shānchú 删除；*money from bank* qǔ 取；(*to dinner etc*) dài ... chūqù 带 ... 出去；*insurance policy* bànlǐ 办理；*take it out on X* (*s.o.*) zài X de shēnshàng bàofù 在X的身上报复

♦ **take over 1** *v/t company etc* jiānbìng 兼并；*tourists ~ the town* dōushì lǚkè 满镇都是旅客 **2** *v/i* (*of new management etc*) jiēguǎn 接管；(*do sth in s.o.'s place*) jiēshǒu 接手

♦ **take to** (*like*) xǐhuan 喜欢；(*form habit of*) yǎngchéng ... xíguàn 养成 ... 习惯

♦ **take up** *carpet etc* jiēqǐ 揭起；(*carry up*) ná shàngqù 拿上去；(*shorten: dress etc*) shōuduǎn 收短；*hobby* kāishǐ 开始；*judo, new language* kāishǐ xuéxí 开始学习；*offer* jiēshòu 接受；*new job* kāishǐ cóngshì 开始从事；*space, time* zhànqù 占去；*I'll take you up on your offer* wǒ jiēshòu nǐde tíyì 我接受你的提议

**take-home pay** shídé gōngzī 实得工资

**takeoff** (*of airplane*) qǐfēi 起飞；(*impersonation*) mófǎng 模仿

**takeover** COM jiānbìng 兼并；**takeover bid** jiānbìng tóubiāo 兼并投标

**takings** shōurù 收入

**talcum powder** shuǎngshēnfěn 爽身粉

**tale** gùshi 故事

**talent** tiāncái 天才

**talented** yǒu tiāncái 有天才

**talk 1** *v/i* tánhuà 谈话；*can I ~ with ...?* qǐngzhǎo ...? 请找 ... ？；*I'll ~ to him about it* wǒ huì hé tā

tán wǒ huì hé tā tán 我会和他谈 **2** *v/t English etc* shuō 说；*business, politics* tán 谈；*~ X into doing Y* shuōfú X zuò Y 说服X做Y **3** *n* (*conversation*) jiāotán 交谈；(*lecture*) yǎnjiǎng 演讲；*he's all ~ pej* tā zhǐshì kōngtán 他只是空谈

♦ **talk over** tǎolùn 讨论

**talkative** jiàntán 健谈

**talk show** tánhuà jiémù 谈话节目

**tall** gāo 高

**tall order** gāo yāoqiú 高要求

**tall story** kuādàde gùshi 夸大的故事

**tame** *animal* xùnfú 驯服；*joke etc* píngdàn 平淡

♦ **tamper with** sǔnhuài 损坏

**tampon** ⇩ yuèjīng shuān 月经栓

**tan 1** *n* (*from sun*) rì shài fūsè 日晒肤色；(*color*) zōnghè sè 棕褐色 **2** *v/i* (*in sun*) shài hēi 晒黑 **3** *v/t leather* róu 鞣

**tandem** (*bike*) qiánhòu shuāngzuò zìxíngchē 前后双座自行车

**Tang Dynasty** Táng Cháo 唐朝

**tangerine** gānjú 柑桔

**tangle** *n* yītuánzāo 一团糟

♦ **tangle up:** *get tangled up* (*of string etc*) chán zài yìqǐ 缠在一起

**tango** *n* tángē wǔ 探戈舞

**Tang poetry** Tángshī 唐诗

**tank** chúshuǐ chí 储水池；MOT xiāng 箱；MIL tǎnkè 坦克；(*for skin diver*) shuǐfèi 水肺

**tanker** (*ship*) yóuchuán 油船；(*truck*) guànchē 罐车

**tanned** shài hēi 晒黑

**tantalizing** yòurén 诱人

**tantamount:** *be ~ to* xiāngdāngyú 相当于

**tantrum** fā píqí 发脾气

**Tao** Dào 道

**Taoism** (*philosophy*) Dàojiā 道家；(*religion*) Dàojiào 道教

**Taoist priest** Dàoshì 道士

**tap 1** *n* lóngtóu 龙头 **2** *v/t* (*knock*) qīngqiāo 轻敲；*phone* qiètīng 窃听

♦ **tap into** *resources* lìyòng 利用

**tap dance** *n* tǐdǎ wǔ 踢踏舞

**tape 1** n (for recording) cídài 磁带; (sticky) jiāodài 胶带 **2** v/t conversation etc lùyīn 录音; (with sticky tape) zhān 粘

**tape deck** lùyīnzuò 录音座; **tape drive** COMPUT cídài qūdòngqì 磁带驱动器; **tape measure** juǎnchǐ 卷尺

**taper** v/i jiǎnxiǎo 减小

♦**taper off** (of production) zhújiàn tíngzhǐ 逐渐停止; (of figures) zhújiàn jiǎnshǎo 逐渐减少

**tape recorder** lùyīnjī 录音机

**tape recording** lùyīn 录音

**tapestry** zhījǐn 织锦

**tapeworm** tāochóng 绦虫

**tar** n bǎiyóu 柏油

**tardy** huǎnmàn 缓慢

**target 1** n (in shooting, for sales, production) mùbiāo 目标 **2** v/t market bǎ … zuòwéi mùbiāo 把 … 作为目标

**target date** mùbiāo rìqī 目标日期; **target group** COM duìxiàng zǔ 对象组; **target market** duìxiàng shìchǎng 对象市场

**tariff** (price) jiàmùbiǎo 价目表; (tax) shuì 税

**tarmac** (at airport) pǎodào 跑道

**tarnish** v/t metal shǐ … shīqù guāngzé 使 … 失去光泽; reputation sǔnhuài 损坏

**tarpaulin** yóubù 油布

**tart** n guǒxiànr bǐng 果馅儿饼

**task** rènwù 任务

**task button** rènwùniǔ 任务钮

**task force** tèbié gōngzuòzǔ 特别工作组

**tassel** liúsū 流苏

**taste 1** n (sense, of food etc) wèidao 味道; (in clothes, art etc) pǐnwèi pǐn味; **he has no ~** tā méiyǒu shěnměi yǎnguāng 他没有审美眼光 **2** v/t food cháng 尝; (experience: freedom etc) chángshì 尝试

**tasteful** yǒu shěnměi yǎnguāng 有审美眼光

**tasteless** food méiwèir 没味儿; remark, person cūsú 粗俗

**tasty** xiāng 香

**tattered** clothes, book pòlàn 破烂

**tatters: in ~** (of clothes) pòpo lànlàn 破破烂烂; (of reputation, career) chèdǐ cuīhuǐ 彻底摧毁

**tattoo** wénshēn 纹身

**taunt** n & v/t cháoxiào 嘲笑

**taut** jǐn 紧

**tax 1** n shuì 税; **before / after ~** shuì qián/hòu 税前/后 **2** v/t people, product chōushuì 抽税

**taxation** (act of taxing) zhēngshuì 征税; (taxes) shuìshōu 税收

**tax code** shuìwù hàomǎ 税务号码; **tax-deductible** kě jiǎnshuì 可减税; **tax-free** miǎnshuì 免税

**taxi** ⇩ chūzūchē 出租车

**taxidriver** chūzūchē sījī 出租车司机

**taxi rank, taxi stand** chūzūchē tíngchēchù 出租车停车处

**tax inspector** shuìwù diàocháyuán 税务调查员; **tax payer** nàshuì rén 纳税人; **tax return** (form) nàshuì dān 纳税单

**tea** (drink) chá 茶; (meal) chádiǎn 茶点; **black ~** hóngchá 红茶; **green ~** lǜchá 绿茶

**teabag** chábāo 茶包

**teach 1** v/t person, subject jiāo 教; **~ X to do Y** jiāo X zuò Y 教 X 做 Y **2** v/i jiāoshū 教书

**teacher** lǎoshī 老师

**teacher training** jiàoshī péixùn 教师培训

**teaching** (profession) jiāoxué 教学

**teaching aid** jiàojù 教具

**teaching assistant** zhùjiào 助教

**tea cloth** chájīn 茶巾

**teacup** chábēi 茶杯; **tea drinker** hēchárén 喝茶人; **tea house** cháguǎnr 茶馆儿

**teak** yòumù 柚木

**tea leaf** cháyè 茶叶

**team** zǔ 组

**team spirit** jítǐ jīngshén 集体精神

**teamster** kǎchē sījī 卡车司机

**teamwork** ⇩ pèihé 配合

**teapot** cháhú 茶壶

**tear¹ 1** n (in cloth etc) lièkǒu 裂口 **2** v/t paper, cloth sī 撕; **be torn between two alternatives** yóuyù bùjué 犹豫不决 **3** v/i (run fast,

*drive fast*) jí bēn 急奔
♦ **tear up** *paper* sī 撕; *agreement* sīhuǐ 撕毁
**tear²** (*in eye*) lèi 泪; *burst into ~* fàngshēng dàkū 放声大哭; *be in ~s* kū 哭
**teardrop** yǎnlèi 眼泪
**tearful** yǎnlèi wāngwāng 眼泪汪汪
**tear gas** cuīlèi qì 催泪气
**tearoom** cháshì 茶室
**tease** v/t dòunòng 逗弄
**tea service, tea set** chájù 茶具
**teaspoon** cháchí 茶匙
**teat** rǔtóu 乳头
**tea towel** cā wǎn bù 擦碗布
**technical** jìshù xìng 技术性
**technicality** (*technical nature*) zhuānmén xìng 专门性; LAW sùsòng xìjié 诉讼细节; *that's just a ~* nà zhǐshì xìjié éryǐ 那只是细节而已
**technically** (*strictly speaking*) yángé láishuō 严格来说
**technician** jìshùyuán 技术员
**technique** fāngfǎ 方法
**technological** jìshù 技术
**technology** jìshù 技术
**technophobia** kǒng jìshù bìng 恐技术病
**tedious** shǐrén yànfán 使人厌烦
**tee** n (*in golf*) qiúzuò 球座
**teem**: *be ~ing with rain* qīngpén dàyǔ 倾盆大雨; *be ~ing with tourists* / *ants* chōngmǎn yóukè / mǎyǐ 充满游客 / 蚂蚁
**teenage** *fashions* qīngshàonián 青少年; *~ boy* / *girl* shàonán / nǚ 少男 / 女
**teenager** qīngshàonián 青少年
**teens**: *be in one's ~* shíjǐsuì 十几岁; *reach one's ~* jìnrù qīngshàonián shíqí 进入青少年时期
**telecommunications** diànxìn 电信
**telegram** diànbào 电报
**telegraph pole** diànxiàn gān 电线杆
**telepathic** xīnlíng gǎnyìng 心灵感应; *you must be ~!* nǐ kěndìng shì xīnlíng gǎnyìng! 你肯定是心灵感应!
**telepathy** xīnlíng gǎnyìng 心灵感应
**telephone 1** n diànhuà 电话; *be on the ~* (*be speaking*) jiǎng diànhuà 讲电话; (*possess a phone*) yǒu diànhuà 有电话 **2** v/t & v/i dǎ diànhuà 打电话
**telephone booth** diànhuà tíng 电话亭; **telephone call** diànhuà 电话; **telephone directory** diànhuà běn 电话本; **telephone exchange** zǒngjī 总机; **telephone number** diànhuà hàomǎ 电话号码
**telephoto lens** shèyuǎn jìngtóu 摄远镜头
**telesales** diànhuà tuīxiāo 电话推销
**telescope** wàngyuǎnjìng 望远镜
**televise** diànshì bōfàng 电视播放
**television** diànshì 电视; (*set*) diànshì jī 电视机; *on ~* diànshì shang 电视上; *watch ~* kàn diànshì 看电视
**television program** diànshì jiémù 电视节目; **television set** diànshì jī 电视机; **television studio** diànshì shèyǐng shì 电视摄影室
**tell 1** v/t *story, lie* jiǎng 讲; *the difference* qūfēn 区分; *~ X Y* gàosù X Y 告诉 X Y; *don't ~ Mom* bié gàosù māma 别告诉妈妈; *could you ~ me the way to ...?* qǐng gàosù wǒ zěnme qù ...? 请告诉我怎么去...?; *~ X to do Y* jiào X zuò Y 叫 X 做 Y; *you're ~ing me!* háiyòng nǐ shuō! 还用你说! **2** v/i (*have effect*) chǎnshēng xiàoguǒ 产生效果; *the heat is ~ing on him* gāowēn duì tā chǎnshēng yǐngxiǎng 气温对他产生影响; *time will ~* shíjiān zì huì dìnglùn 时间自会定论
♦ **tell off** (*reprimand*) shǔluò 数落
**teller** (*in bank*) chūnàyuán 出纳员
**telltale 1** adj *signs* xièlòu 泄露 **2** n xièmìzhě 泄密者
**temp 1** n (*employee*) línshígōng 临

时工 2 *v/i* dǎ línshígōng 打临时工

temper (*bad ~*) píqi 脾气; *be in a ~* fā píqi 发脾气; *keep one's ~* nàzhe xìngzi 捺着性子; *lose one's ~* fā píqi 发脾气

temperament xìnggé 性格

temperamental (*moody*) yì jīdòng 易激动

temperature wēndù 温度; (*fever*) fāshāo 发烧; *have a ~* fāshāo 发烧

temple¹ REL miàoyǔ 庙宇

temple² ANAT tàiyángxuè 太阳穴

Temple of Heaven Tiāntán 天坛

tempo sùdù 速度

temporarily zànshí 暂时

temporary zànshí 暂时

tempt xīyǐn 吸引

temptation yòuhuò 诱惑

tempting yǒu xīyǐnlì 有吸引力

ten shí 十

tenacious jiānrèn 坚韧

tenant (*of building*) fángkè 房客; (*of farm, land*) diànhù 佃户

tend¹ *v/t* (*look after*) zhàogù 照顾

tend² - *to do* ... qīngxiàng yú zuò ... 倾向于做...; *~ toward* ... qīngxiàng yú ... 倾向于...

tendency qīngxiàng 倾向

tender¹ *adj* (*sore*) xūruò 虚弱; (*affectionate*) wēnróu 温柔; *steak* ruǎn 软

tender² *n* COM tóubiāo 投标

tenderness (*soreness*) xūruò 虚弱; (*of kiss etc*) wēnróu gǎn 温柔感; (*of steak*) ruǎn 软

tendon jiàn 腱

tennis wǎngqiú 网球

tennis ball wǎngqiú 网球; tennis court wǎngqiú chǎng 网球场; tennis player wǎngqiú shǒu 网球手; tennis racket wǎngqiú pāi 网球拍

tenor *n* MUS nángāoyīn 男高音

tense¹ *n* GRAM shítài 时态

tense² *adj muscle* jǐn 紧; *voice, person, moment* jǐnzhāng 紧张

♦tense up *v/i* (*of muscles*) bēngjǐn 绷紧; (*of person*) jǐnzhāng 紧张

tension (*of rope*) lālì 拉力; (*in atmosphere, voice*) jǐnzhāng 紧张; (*in movie, novel*) jǐnyào guāntóu 紧要关头

tent zhàngpeng 帐篷

tentacle chùshǒu 触手

tentative yóuyù 犹豫

tenterhooks: *be on ~* tíxīn diàodǎn 提心吊胆

tenth dìshí 第十

tepid *water, reaction* wēiwēn 微温

term (*period of time*) shíqī 时期; EDU xuéqí 学期; (*condition*) tiáojiàn 条件; (*word*) cí 词; *be on good / bad ~s with X* yǔ X guānxi hǎo / huài 与 X 关系 好 / 坏; *in the long / short* ~ cháng / duǎnqī 长 / 短期; *come to ~s with X* duì X cǎiqǔ jiāngjiù tàidù 对 X 采取将就态度

terminal 1 *n* (*at airport*) chūrùjìng kǒu 出入境口; (*for buses*) zhōngdiǎnzhàn zhōngdiǎn zhàn 终点站; (*for containers*) yùnshū zhōngdiǎnzhàn 运输终点站; ELEC xiàn jiētóu 线接头; COMPUT diànnǎo zhàn 电脑站 2 *adj illness* wánqī 晚期

terminally *adv* wǎnqī 晚期; *~ ill* bìngzhèng wǎnqī 病症晚期

terminate 1 *v/t* zhōngzhǐ 终止; *pregnancy* liúchǎn 流产 2 *v/i* zhōngzhǐ 终止

termination (*of contract*) zhōngzhǐ 终止; (*of pregnancy*) réngōng liúchǎn 人工流产

terminology shùyǔ 术语

terminus (*for buses, trains*) zhōngdiǎn zhàn 终点站

terrace (*of houses*) páifáng 排房; (*on hillside*) tītián 梯田; (*patio*) yángtái 阳台

terracotta chìtáo 赤陶

terracotta warriors bīngmǎyǒng 兵马俑

terrain dìshì 地势

terrestrial 1 *n* dìqiú jūmín 地球居民 2 *adj television* wúxiàn diànshì 无线电视; (*of the earth*) lùdì 陆地

terrible kěpà 可怕

terribly (*very*) hěn 很

terrific liǎobuqǐ 了不起

**terrifically** (*very*) hěn 很

**terrify** kǒnghè 恐吓; *be terrified* hàipà 害怕

**terrifying** kěpà 可怕

**territorial** lǐngtǔ 领土

**territorial waters** lǐnghǎi 领海

**territory** lǐngtǔ 领土; *fig* lǐngyù 领域

**terror** kǒngjù 恐惧

**terrorism** kǒngbù zhǔyì 恐怖主义

**terrorist** kǒngbù fènzi 恐怖分子

**terrorist organization** kǒngbù jīgòu 恐怖机构

**terrorize** kǒnghè 恐吓

**test 1** *n* (*of equipment, scientific*) cèyàn 测验; (*exam*) kǎoyàn 考验 **2** *v/t machine, theory* cèyàn 测验; *student* kǎo 考

**testament** (*to s.o.*) shízhèng 实证; *Old / New Testament* REL Jiù / Xīnyuē Quánshū 旧 / 新约全书

**testicle** gāowán 睾丸

**testify** *v/i* LAW zuòzhèng 作证

**testimonial** jièshào xìn 介绍信

**test tube** shìguǎn 试管

**test-tube baby** shìguǎn yīng'ér 试管婴儿

**testy** bàozào 暴躁

**tetanus** pòshāngfēng 破伤风

**tether 1** *v/t horse* shuān 拴 **2** *n* xìshéng 系绳; *be at the end of one's* ~ shānqióng shuǐjìn 山穷水尽

**text** yuánwén 原文

**textbook** kèběn 课本

**textile** fǎngzhī 纺织

**texture** zhìdì 质地

**Thai 1** *adj* Tàiguó 泰国 **2** *n* (*person*) Tàiguó rén 泰国人; (*language*) Tàiguó yǔ 泰国语

**Thailand** Tàiguó 泰国

**than** bǐ 比; *bigger / faster ~ me* bǐ wǒ dà / kuài 比我大 / 快

**thank** *v/t* xiè 谢; ~ *you* xièxie 谢谢; *no - you* búyòng, xièxie 不用, 谢谢

**thanks** gǎnxiè 感谢; ~! xièxie 谢谢; ~ *to* guīgōng yú 归功于

**thankful** gǎnjī 感激

**thankfully** gǎnjī 感激; (*luckily*) xìngkuī 幸亏

**thankless** *task* túláo 徒劳

**Thanksgiving (Day)** Gǎn'ēn jié 感恩节

**that 1** *adj* nàge 那个; ~ *one* nàge 那个 **2** *pron* nà 那; *what's ~?* nàshì shénme? 那是什么 ?; *who's ~?* nàshì shuí? 那是谁 ?; ~*'s mine* nàshì wǒde 那是我的; ~*'s tea* nàshì chá 那是茶; ~*'s very kind* nǐ tài hǎo le 你太好了; *I think ~ ...* wǒ xiǎng ... 我想 ...; *the person / car ~ you see* nǐ kànjiàde nàge rén / nà liàng chē 你看见的那个人 / 那辆车 **4** *adv* (*so*) nàme 那么; ~ *big / expensive* nàme dà / guì 那么大 / 贵

**thaw** *v/i* huà 化

**the** ◊ (*no translation*): ~ *border* biānjiè 边界; ~ *embassy* dàshǐguǎn 大使馆; *is that ~ ring he gave you?* nà shì tā gěi nǐ de jièzhi ma? 那是他给你的戒指吗 ?; ~ *capital of France* Fǎguó de shǒudū 法国的首都 ◊ (*when previous reference has been made*) zhè 这, nèi 那; ~ *old man* nèige lǎotóu 那个老头; ~ *blue bag is mine* zhè lánsè de bāo shì wǒde 这蓝色的包是我的 ◊ ~ *sooner ~ better* yuèkuài yuèhǎo 越快越好

**theater** jùchǎng 剧场

**theatrical** xìjù 戏剧; (*overdone*) zuòzuò 做作

**theft** tōuqiè 偷窃

**their** tāmende 他们的; (*his or her*) tā / tāde 他 / 她的

**theirs** tāmende 他们的; *a friend of ~* tāmende péngyǒu 他们的朋友

**them** tāmen 他们; (*him or her*) tā / tā 他 / 她

**theme** zhǔtí 主题

**theme park** yóulè yuán 游乐园

**theme song** zhǔtí gē 主题歌

**themselves** *by ~* (*alone*) tāmen zìjǐ 他们自己

**then** (*at that time*) nàshí 那时; (*after that*) érhòu 而后; (*deducing*) nàme

那么; *by* ~ dào nàshí 到那时
**theology** shénxué 神学
**theoretical** lǐlùn 理论
**theory** lǐlùn 理论; *in* ~ lǐlùn shàng láishuō 理论上来说
**therapeutic** yīliáo 医疗
**therapist** zhìliáo xuéjiā 治疗学家
**therapy** liáofǎ 疗法
**there** nàr 那儿; *over*/*down* ~ zài nàr/xiàmiàn nàr 在那儿/下面那儿; ~ *is*/*are* ... yǒu ... 有 ...; *is*/*are* ~ ...? yǒu ... ma? 有 ... 吗 ?; ~ *is*/*are not* ... méiyǒu ... 没有 ...; ~ *you are* (*giving sth*) gěinǐ zhèzhè 给你这这; (*finding sth*) yuánlái nǐ zài zhèr 原来你在这儿; (*completing sth*) wánle wán le 完了; ~ *and back* láihuí lái huí 来回; ~ *he is!* tā zài nàr! 他在那儿!; ~, ~! hǎole, hǎole! 好了, 好了!
**thereabouts** dàyù 大约
**therefore** yīncǐ 因此
**thermometer** wēndùjì 温度计
**thermos flask** bǎowēnpíng 保温瓶
**thermostat** héngwēnqì 恒温器
**these** *adj* & *pron* zhèxie 这些
**thesis** lùnwén 论文
**they** tāmen 他们; (*he or she*) tā 他/她; ~ *say that* ... tīngshuō ... 听说 ...; ~ *are going to change the law* tāmen yào xiūgǎi fǎlǜ 他们要修改法律
**thick** *hair* mì 密; *soup* chóu 稠; *crowd* chóumì 稠密; *fog* duō 多; *wall*, *book* hòu 厚; F (*stupid*) bèn 笨
**thicken** *sauce* shǐ biànchóu 使变稠
**thickset** ǎizhuàng 矮壮
**thickskinned** *fig* liǎnpí hòu 脸皮厚
**thief** xiǎotōu 小偷
**thigh** dàtuǐ 大腿
**thimble** dǐngzhēn 顶针
**thin** *hair*, *soup* xī 稀; *coat* báo 薄; *line* xì 细; *person* shòu 瘦
**thing** dōngxi 东西; ~*s* (*belongings*) suǒyǒuwù 所有物; *how are* ~*s*? zuìjìn zěnyàng? 最近怎样?; *good* ~ *you told me* xìngkuī nǐ gàosù wǒle 幸亏你告诉我了;

*what a* ~ *to do*/*say!* zěnme néng nàme zuò/shuō ne! 怎么能那么做/说呢!
**thingumajig** F (*item*) dōngxi 东西; (*person*) nèirén 那人
**think** xiǎng 想; *I* ~ *so* wǒ rènwéi rúcǐ 我认为如此; *I don't* ~ *so* wǒ bú rènwéi rúcǐ 我不认为如此; *I* ~ *so too* wǒ yě shì zhème xiǎng de 我也是这么想的; *what do you* ~? nǐ shuō ne? 你说呢?; *what do you* ~ *of it?* nǐ duì cǐ yǒu hé xiǎngfǎ? 你对此有何想法?; *I can't* ~ *of anything more* wǒ xiǎngbùchū qítādele 我想不出其它的了; ~ *hard!* hǎohao xiǎngxiang! 好好想想!; *I'm my* ~*ing about emigrating* wǒ yǒuyì yímín 我有意移民
♦ **think over** kǎolù 考虑
♦ **think through** kǎolù 考虑
♦ **think up** *plan* xiǎngchū 想出
**third** 1 *adj* dìsān 第三 2 *n* dìsān gè 第三个; (*fraction*) sānfēnzhīyī 三分之一
**thirdly** dìsān 第三
**third-party insurance** dìsān fāng bǎoxiǎn 第三方保险; **third-rate** xiàděng 下等; **Third World** Dìsān Shìjiè 第三世界
**thirst** kě 渴
**thirsty**: *be* ~ kě 渴
**thirteen** shísān 十三
**thirteenth** dìshísān 第十三
**thirtieth** dìsānshí 第三十
**thirty** sānshí 三十
**this** 1 *adj* zhège 这个; ~ *one* zhège 这个 2 *pron* zhège 这个; ~ *is good* zhè hǎo 这好; ~ *is* ... (*introducing s.o.*) zhèshì ... 这是 ...; TELEC wǒshì ... 我是 ... 3 *adv* zhème 这么; ~ *big*/*high* zhème dà/gāo 这么大/高
**thorn** cì 刺
**thorough** *search* chèdǐ 彻底; *knowledge* wánzhěng 完整; *person* búyànqífán 不厌其烦
**thoroughbred** (*horse*) chúnzhǒng 纯种
**those** *adj* & *pron* nàxiē 那些
**though** 1 *conj* (*although*) jǐnguǎn

尽管; ~ *it might fail* jǐnguǎn kěnéng shībài 尽管可能失败; *as* ~ hǎoxiàng 好像 2 *adv* rán'ér 然而; *it's not finished* ~ hái méi wánne 还没完呢

**thought** (*single*) xiǎngfa 想法; (*collective*) sīxiǎng 思想

**thoughtful** *look, face, person* chénsī 沉思; *book* jīng rènzhēn tuīqiāo 经认真推敲; (*considerate*) xìxīn 细心

**thoughtless** cūxīn 粗心

**thousand** qiān 千; *~s of* wúshù 无数; *ten* ~ wàn 万

**thousandth** 1 *n* dì yī qiān gè 第一千个; (*fraction*) qiānfēnzhīyī 千分之一 2 *adj* dì yī qiān gè 第一千个

**thrash** *v/t* chōu 抽; SP dǎbài 打败
♦ **thrash around** (*with arms etc*) fánzào bù'ān de dònglái dòngqù 烦躁不安地动来动去
♦ **thrash out** *solution* jiějué wèntí 解决问题

**thrashing** tòngdǎ 痛打; SP cǎnbài 惨败

**thread** 1 *n* xiàn 线; (*of screw*) luówén 螺纹 2 *v/t needle* chuānxiàn 穿线; *beads* chuān 穿

**threadbare** lánlǚ 褴褛

**threat** wēixié 威胁

**threaten** wēixié 威胁

**threatening** *gesture, tone* yǒu wēixié xìng 有威胁性; *sky* yīnchén 阴沉

**three** sān 三

**Three Gorges** Sānxiá 三峡

**Three Kingdoms** Sānguó 三国

**three-quarters** *n* sì fēn zhī sān 四分之三

**thresh** *v/t corn* tuōlì 脱粒

**threshold** (*of house*) ménkǎn 门槛; (*of new age*) kāiduān 开端; *on the* ~ *of* zài ... de kāiduān 在 ... 的开端

**thrift** jiéyù 节约

**thrifty** jiéyù 节约

**thrill** 1 *n* xìngfèn 兴奋 2 *v/t* shǐ ... xìngfèn 使 ... 兴奋; *be ~ed* gāoxìng 高兴

**thriller** (*movie*) jīngxiǎn diànyǐng 惊险电影; (*novel*) jīngxiǎn xiǎoshuō 惊险小说

**thrilling** lìngrén máogǔ sǒngrán 令人毛骨悚然

**thrive** (*of plant*) zhuózhuàng shēngzhǎng 茁壮生长; (*of business, economy*) fánróng 繁荣

**throat** hóulóng 喉咙

**throat lozenges** rùnhóu táng 润喉糖

**throb** 1 *n* (*of heart*) tiàodòng 跳动; (*of music*) zhènchàn 震颤 2 *v/i* (*of heart*) tiàodòng 跳动; (*of music*) zhènchàn 震颤

**thrombosis** xuěshuān xíngchéng 血栓形成

**throne** wángwèi 王位

**throng** *n* rénqún 人群

**throttle** 1 *n* (*on motorbike, boat*) jiéliú fá 节流阀 2 *v/t* (*strangle*) qiā zhù bózi 掐住脖子
♦ **throttle back** *v/i* guānxiǎo yóumén jiǎnsù 关小油门减速

**through** 1 *prep* (*across*) chuānguò 穿过; (*during*) zài ... qījiān 在 ... 期间; (*thanks to*) yóuyú 由于; *go* ~ *the city* chuānguò shìqū 穿过市区; ~ *the winter* / *summer* dōng / xiàjì qījiān 冬 / 夏季期间; *Monday* ~ *Friday* xīngqī yī zhì wǔ 星期一至五; *arranged* ~ *him* tōngguò tā ānpái 通过他安排 2 *adv*: *wet* ~ shī tòule 湿透了; *watch a movie* ~ cóngtóu dàowěi kànwán yìchǎng diànyǐng 从头到尾看完一场电影; *read a book* ~ cóngtóu dàowěi dúwán yìběn shū 从头到尾读完一本书 3 *adj*: *be* ~ (*of couple*) wánle 完了; (*have arrived: of news etc*) dàodá 到达; *you're* ~ TELEC tōngle 通了; *I'm* ~ *with X* (*finished with a person*) wǒ yǔ X juéjiāo 我与X绝交; (*finished with a task*) wǒ wánchéng le X 我完成了X

**through flight** zhíháng fēijī 直航飞机

**throughout** 1 *prep* guànchuān 贯穿 2 *adv* (*in all parts*) dàochù 到处

**through train** zhítōng huǒchē 直通火车

**throw** 1 v/t rēng 扔; (of horse) shuāidào 摔倒; (disconcert) shǐ … cānghuáng shīcuò 使 … 仓皇失措; party jǔxíng 举行 2 n tóuzhì 投掷

♦**throw away** rēngdiào 扔掉

♦**throw out** old things rēngdiào 扔掉; husband, drunk etc niǎnzǒu 撵走; plan fǒujué 否决

♦**throw up 1** v/t ball pāoqǐ 抛起 **2** v/i (vomit) ǒutù 呕吐

**throw-away** remark suíyì 随意; (disposable) yīcì xìng 一次性

**throw-in** SP zhì jiè wài qiú 掷界外球

**thru → through**

**thrush** (bird) dōngniǎo 鸫鸟

**thrust** v/t (push hard) měngtuī 猛推; ~ X into Y's hands bǎ X sāirù Y shǒu zhōng 把 X 塞入 Y 手中; ~ one's way through the crowd chuǎngguò rénqún 闯过人群

**thud** n péng de yìshēng pēng de yìshēng 砰的一声

**thug** ègùn 恶棍

**thumb 1** n mǔzhǐ 拇指 **2** v/t: ~ a ride dāchē 搭车

**thumbtack** túdīng 图钉

**thump 1** n (blow) zhòngjī 重击; (noise) pēng pēng 砰 **2** v/t person zhòngjī 重击; ~ one's fist on the table yòng quántóu chuí zhuōzi 用拳头捶桌子 **3** v/i (of heart) měngtiào 猛跳; ~ on the door pāimén 拍门

**thunder** n dǎléi 打雷

**thunderstorm** léiyǔ 雷雨

**thundery** weather yào dǎléi 要打雷

**Thursday** xīngqī sì 星期四

**thus** yīncǐ 因此

**thwart** person, plans héngxiàng 横向

**thyroid** (gland) jiǎzhuàngxiàn 甲状腺

**Tiananmen** (incident) liùsì 六四; (square) Tiān'ānmén 天安门

**Tiananmen Square** Tiān'ānmén Guǎngchǎng 天安门广场

**Tibet** Xīzàng 西藏

**Tibetan 1** adj Xīzàng 西藏 **2** n (person) Xīzàng rén 西藏人;

(language) Xīzàng yǔ 西藏语

**Tibetan Plateau** Qīng Zàng Gāoyuán 青藏高原

**tick 1** n (of clock) dīdā 滴答; (checkmark) dǎgōu 打勾 **2** v/i (of clock) dīdā dīdā xiǎng 滴答滴答响

♦**tick off** (reprimand) xùnchì 训斥

**ticket** piào 票

**ticket collector** shòupiào yuán 售票员; **ticket inspector** chápiào yuán 查票员; **ticket machine** shòupiàojī 售票机; **ticket office** (at station, theater) shòupiàochù 售票处

**tickle 1** v/t person gēzhī 胳肢 **2** v/i (of material) fāyǎng 发痒; (of person) shǐ fāyǎng 使发痒

**ticklish** person fāyǎng 怕痒

**tidal wave** làngcháo 浪潮

**tide** cháo 潮; high ~ gāocháo 高潮; low ~ dīcháo 低潮; the ~ is in / out zhǎngcháo / luòcháo 涨潮 / 落潮

**tidy** person, habits zhěngjié 整洁; room, house zhěngqí 整齐

♦**tidy up 1** v/t room, shelves shōushi 收拾; tidy oneself up bǎ zìjǐ shōushi yīxià 把自己收拾一下 **2** v/i shōushi 收拾

**tie 1** n (necktie) lǐngdài 领带; (SP: even result) píngjú 平局; he doesn't have any ~s tā méiyǒu rènhé liánxi 他没有任何联系 **2** v/t knot dǎjié 打结; hands jì 系; ~ two ropes together bǎ liǎngtiáo shéngzi jì zài yìqǐ 把两条绳子系在一起 **3** v/i SP chéng píngjú 成平局

♦**tie down** (with rope) kǔnzhù 捆住; (restrict) yùshù 约束

♦**tie up** person bǎngzhù 绑住; laces jìzhù 系住; boat bó pō 泊; hair xì qǐlái xì qǐlái 系起来; I'm tied up tomorrow (busy) míngtiān wǒ yǒushì 明天我有事

**tier** (of hierarchy) céng 层; (in stadium) pái pái 排

**tiger** lǎohǔ 老虎

**tight 1** adj clothes, (hard to move) jǐn 紧; security yán 严; (properly shut)

yán 严; (*not leaving much time*)
jǐncòu 紧凑; F (*drunk*) zuì 醉
**2** *adv hold* jǐn 紧; *shut* yán 严

**tighten** *screw* shǐ … biànjǐn 使 …
变紧; *control* shǐ … yángé 使 …
严格; *security* shǐ … yánjǐn 使 …
严谨; **~ one's grip on …** zhuā láo
… 抓牢 …

♦ **tighten up** *v/i* (*in discipline,
security*) yánjǐn qǐlái 严谨起来

**tight-fisted** kōumén'r 抠门儿

**tightrope** bēngsuǒ 绷索

**tile** cízhuān 瓷砖

**till**[1] → **until**

**till**[2] (*cash register*) shōukuǎn tái 收
款台

**till** *v/t soil* gēngzhòng 耕种

**tilt 1** *v/t* shǐ qīngxié 使倾斜 **2** *v/i*
qīngxié 倾斜

**timber** mùcái 木材

**time** shíjiān 时间; (*occasion*) cì 次;
**~ is up** dào shíjiān le 到时间了;
**for the ~ being** zànshí 暂时; **have
a good ~** kāixīn 开心; **have a
good ~!** wánr kāixīn diǎnr! 玩儿
开心点儿！; **what's the ~?,
what ~ is it?** jǐdiǎnle? 几点了？;
**the first ~** dìyīcì 第一次; **four ~s**
sìcì 四次; **~ and again** duōcì duō
次; **all the ~** yīzhí 一直; **two /
three at a ~** yīcì liǎng / sāngè yīcì
两 / 三个; **at the same ~** speak,
reply etc tóngshí 同时; (*however*)
dànshì 但是; **in ~** jíshí 及时; **on ~**
ànshí 按时; **in no ~** lìkè 立刻

**time bomb** dìngshí zhàdàn 定时
炸弹; **time clock** (*in factory*)
jìshízhōng 计时钟; **time-
consuming** huā shíjiān 花时间;
**time-lag** shíjiān jiàngé 时间间
隔; **time limit** qīxiàn 期限

**timely** jíshí 及时

**time out** SP zàntíng 暂停

**timer** dìngshíqì 定时器

**timesaving** *n* jiéshěng shíjiān 节省
时间; **timescale** (*of project*)
shíjiān fànwéi 时间范围; **time
switch** dìngshíqì 定时器; **timetable** shíjiān biǎo 时间表;
**timewarp** (kēhuàn zhōng)
zhuǎnshí (科幻中) 转时; **time
zone** shíqū 时区

**timid** miǎntiǎn 腼腆

**timing** (*choosing a time*) shíjiān
xuǎnzé 时间选择; (*of actor,
dancer*) shíjiān fēncùn 时间分寸

**tin** (*metal*) xī 锡

**tinfoil** xīpó 锡箔

**tinge** *n* (*of color*) wēirǎn 微染; (*of
sadness*) dài … qìxī 带 … 气息

**tingle** *v/i* yǒu cìtòng gǎn 有刺痛
感

♦ **tinker with** bǎinòng 摆弄

**tinkle** *n* (*of bell*) dīngdāng shēng 丁
当声

**tinsel** jīnyín sī 金银丝

**tint 1** *n* (*of color*) dànsè 淡色; (*in
hair*) rǎnsè 染色 **2** *v/t hair* rǎnsè
染色

**tinted** *eyeglasses* fǎnguāng 反光;
*paper* zháosè 着色

**tiny** jíxiǎo 极小

**tip**[1] *n* (*of stick, finger*) jiān 尖; (*of
mountain*) shāntóu 山头; (*of
cigarette*) yānzuǐ 烟嘴

**tip**[2] *n* (*piece of advice*) quàngào 劝
告; (*money*) xiǎofèi 小费 **2** *v/t
waiter etc* gěi xiǎofèi 给小费

♦ **tip off** tōngfēng bàoxìn 通风报
信

♦ **tip over** *jug, liquid* dào 倒; **he
tipped water all over me** tā dào
de wǒ shēn dōu shì shuǐ 他
倒得我满身都是水

**tipped** *cigarettes* yǒu yānzuǐ 有烟
嘴

**tippy-toe: on ~** yòng jiǎojiān 用脚
尖

**tipsy** shāozuì 稍醉

**tire**[2] (*on wheel*) chētāi 车胎

**tire**[2] **1** *v/t* láolèi 劳累 **2** *v/i* láolèi 劳
累; **he never ~s of it** ta yǒngyuǎn
búhuì yànjuàn 他永远不会厌
倦

**tired** lèi 累; **be ~ of X** duì X
yànjuàn 对 X 厌倦

**tireless** *efforts* zīzī bùjuàn 孜孜不
倦

**tiresome** (*annoying*) tǎoyàn 讨厌

**tiring** pífá 疲乏

**tissue** ANAT zǔzhī 组织; (*handkerchief*) zhǐjīn 纸巾

tissue paper ⇩ báozhǐ 薄纸

tit¹ (*bird*) shānquè 山雀

tit²: ~ *for tat* yǐyá huányá 以牙还牙

tit³ V (*breast*) nǎizi 奶子

title (*of novel etc*) piānmíng 篇名; (*of person*) tóuxiánr 头衔儿; LAW suǒyǒu quán 所有权

titter v/i shǎxiào 傻笑

to 1 *prep* dào 到; ~ *China* dào Zhōngguó 到中国; ~ *Hangzhou* dào Hángzhōu 到杭州; *let's go - my place* zánmen dào wǒ nàr qù ba 咱们到我那儿去吧; *walk - the station* zǒu dào chēzhàn 走到车站; *the north / south of X* dào X de běi / nánbiān 到X的北／南边; *give X ~ Y* jiāng X gěi Y 将X给Y; *from Monday ~ Wednesday* cóng xīngqīyī dào xīngqīsān 从星期一到星期三; *from 10 ~ 15 people* shí zhì shíwǔ rén 十至十五人 2 *with verbs*: ~ *speak*, ~ *shout* jiǎnghuà, hǎnjiào 讲话，喊叫; *learn ~ drive* xuéxí jiàshǐ 学习驾驶; *nice ~ eat* hǎochī 好吃; *too heavy ~ carry* tàizhòng 太重; ~ *be honest with you* hé nǐ shíshuō le ba 和你实说了吧 3 *adv*: ~ *and fro* láihuí 来回

toad làiháma 癞蛤蟆

toadstool sǎnjūn 伞菌

toast 1 *n* kǎo miànbāo 烤面包; (*drinking*) gānbēi 干杯; *propose a ~ to* wèi ... gānbēi 为 ... 干杯 2 *v/t* (*when drinking*) wèi ... gānbēi 为 ... 干杯

tobacco yāncǎo 烟草

toboggan *n* píngdǐ xuěqiāo 平底雪橇

today jīntiān 今天

toddle (*of child*) xiǎoháir xíngzǒu 小孩儿行走

toddler xiǎoháir 小孩儿

toe 1 *n* jiǎozhǐ 脚指 2 *v/t*: ~ *the line* fúcóng mìnglìng 服从命令

toffee tàifēi táng 太妃糖

tofu dòufu 豆腐

together yìqǐ 一起; (*at the same time*) tóngshí 同时

toil *n* kǔgàn 苦干

toilet cèsuǒ 厕所; *go to the ~* qù cèsuǒ 去厕所

toilet paper cèzhǐ 厕纸

toiletries wèishēngjiān yòngpǐn 卫生间用品

token (*sign*) xiàngzhēng 象征; (*for gambling*) fúbì 辅币; (*gift ~*) shāngpǐn quàn 商品券

tolerable *pain etc* kěyǐ rěnshòu 可以忍受; (*quite good*) guòdéqù 过得去

tolerance kuānróng 宽容

tolerant kuānróng 宽容

tolerate *noise* róngxǔ 容许; *person* róngrěn 容忍; *I won't ~ it!* wǒ bùnéng róngrěn! 我不能容忍！

toll¹ v/i (*of bell*) míng 鸣

toll² (*deaths*) sǐwáng rénshù 死亡人数

toll (*for bridge, road*) tōngxíng fèi 通行费; TELEC diànhuà fèi 电话费

toll booth shōufèichù 收费处; toll-free TELEC miǎnfèi diànhuà 免费电话; toll road shōufèi gōnglù 收费公路

tomato (*in northern China*) xīhóngshì 西红柿; (*in southern China*) fānqié 蕃茄

tomato ketchup fānqiéjiàng 蕃茄酱

tomb fénmù 坟墓

tomboy yěyátóu 野丫头

tombstone mùbēi 墓碑

tomcat gōngmāo 公猫

tomorrow míngtiān 明天; *the day after ~* hòutiān 后天; ~ *morning* míngchén 明晨

ton dūn 吨

tone (*of color*) fēnggé 风格; (*of musical instrument*) yuèyīn 乐音; (*of conversation etc*) yǔqì 语气; (*of neighborhood*) qìfēn 气氛; ~ *of voice* shēngdiào 声调

♦tone down *demands, criticism* huǎnhé 缓和

toner tiáosè jì 调色剂

tongs qiánzi 钳子; (*for hair*) juǎnfǎ qián 卷发钳

tongue *n* shétou 舌头

tonic MED yàoshuǐ 药水

**tonic** (**water**) ⇩ tānglìshuǐ 汤力水

**tonight** jīnwǎn 今晚

**tonsil** biǎntáotǐ 扁桃体

**tonsillitis** biǎntáoxiàn yán 扁桃腺炎

**too** (*also*) yě 也; (*excessively*) tài 太; ~ *me* ~ wǒ yě shì 我也是; ~ *big/hot* tài dà/rè 太大/热; ~ *much rice* tàiduō fàn 太多饭; *eat* ~ *much* chī tàiduō 吃太多

**tool** gōngjù 工具

**toolbar** COMPUT gōngjùgé 工具格

**tooth** yáchǐ 牙齿

**toothache** yáténg 牙疼

**toothbrush** yáshuā 牙刷

**toothless** méiyá 没牙

**toothpaste** yágāo 牙膏

**toothpick** yáqiān 牙签

**top 1** *n* (*of mountain, tree*) dǐng 顶; (*upper part*) shàngbù 上部; (*lid: of bottle etc, pen*) gài 盖; (*of the class, league*) zuì yōuxiù 最优秀; (*clothing*) shàngyī 上衣; (MOT: *gear*) zuìgāodǎng 最高档; *on* ~ *of* zài ... zhī shàng 在 ... 之上; *at the* ~ *of* zài ... zuìshàng 在 ... 最上; *at the* ~ *of the mountain* zài shāndǐng 在山顶; *get to the* ~ (*of company etc*) shēng zhì zuìgāo zhíwèi 升至最高职位; *be over the* ~ (*exaggerated*) guòhuǒ 过火 **2** *adj branches* zuìdǐng 最顶; *floor* zuìgāo yīcéng 最高一层; *management, official* gāojí 高级; *player* jiānzi 尖子; *speed, note* zuìgāo 最高 **3** *v/t:* ~*ped with cream* shàng jiā nǎiyóu 上加奶油

**top hat** gāodǐngmào 高顶帽

**topheavy** tóuzhòng jiǎoqīng 头重脚轻

♦ **top up** glass, tank zhuāng mǎn 装满

**topic** tímù 题目

**topical** zhǔtí 主题

**topless** adj luǒxiōng 裸胸

**topmost** branches, floor zuìgāo 最高

**topping** (*on pizza*) dǐngcéng fùjiā wù 顶层附加物

**topple 1** v/i dǎo 倒 **2** v/t government tuīfān 推翻

**top secret** adj juémì 绝密

**topsy-turvy** adj (*in disorder*) luànqī bāzāo 乱七八糟; *world* diāndǎo hēibái 颠倒黑白

**torch** (*with flame*) huǒbǎ 火把

**torment 1** *n* zhémo 折磨 **2** *v/t person, animal* zhémo 折磨; ~*ed by doubt* yílù chóngchong 疑虑重重

**tornado** lóngjuǎn fēng 龙卷风

**torrent** jīliú 激流; (*of lava*) róngliú 熔流; (*of abuse, words*) tāotao bùjué 滔滔不绝

**torrential:** ~ *rain* bàoyǔ 暴雨

**tortoise** wūguī 乌龟

**torture** *n & v/t* zhémo 折磨

**toss 1** *v/t ball* zhì 掷; *rider* shuāidǎo 摔倒; *salad* bànyún 拌匀; ~ *a coin* zhìbì 掷币 **2** *v/i:* ~ *and turn* zhǎnzhuǎn fǎncè 辗转反侧

**total 1** *n* zǒngshù 总数 **2** adj *sum, amount* zǒng 总; *disaster, idiot* juéduì 绝对; *stranger* wánquán 完全 **3** *v/t F car* zálàn 砸烂

**totalitarian** jíquán zhǔyì 极权主义

**totally** wánquán 完全

**tote bag** dà shǒutí bāo 大手提包

**totter** (*of person*) pánshān 蹒跚

**touch 1** *n* (*act of touching*) chùmō 触摸; (*sense*) chùjué 触觉; (*little bit*) shǎoxǔ 少许; SP biānxiàn wài 边线外; *lose* ~ *with X* (*s.o.*) yǔ X shīqù liánxì 与 X 失去联系; *keep in* ~ *with X* (*s.o.*) yǔ X bǎochí liánxì 与 X 保持联系; *we kept in* ~ wǒmen bǎochí liánxì 我们保持联系; *be out of* ~ tuōjié 脱节 **2** *v/t* chùmō 触摸; (*emotionally*) shǐ gǎndòng 使感动 **3** *v/i* mō 摸; (*of two lines etc*) chùchù 接触

♦ **touch down** v/i (*of airplane*) zháolù 着陆; SP chùdì 触地

♦ **touch on** (*mention*) tídào 提到

♦ **touch up** *photo* xiūshì 修饰; (*sexually*) dòngshǒu dòngjiǎo 动手动脚

**touchdown** (*of airplane*) zháolù 着陆; SP chùdì 触地

**touching** adj gǎnrén 感人

**touch judge** SP biānxiàn cáipàn-yuán 边线裁判员

**touchline** SP biānxiàn 边线

**touchy** person míngǎn 敏感

**tough** person jiānqiáng 坚强; meat bú yì jǔjiáo 不易咀嚼; question, exam nán 难; material jiānrèn 坚韧; punishment wúqíng 无情

**tough guy** yǒngshì 勇士

**tour** 1 n lǚyóu 旅游 2 v/t area cānguān 参观

**tourism** lǚyóu yè 旅游业

**tourist** lǚyóu zhě 旅游者

**tourist (information) office** lǚyóu zīliào chù 旅游资料处

**tournament** jǐnbiāo sài 锦标赛

**tour operator** lǚyóu gōngsī 旅游公司

**tousled** hair péngluàn 蓬乱

**tow** 1 v/t car, boat zhuài 拽 2 n zhuài 拽; give X a ~ bāng X zhuài 帮 X 拽

♦ **tow away** car tuōzǒu 拖走

**toward** prep xiàng 向

**towel** máojīn 毛巾

**tower** n tǎ 塔

**town** zhèn 镇

**town council** zhèn zhèngfǔ 镇政府

**town hall** zhèn zhèngfǔ dàlóu 镇政府大楼

**towrope** tuōlǎn 拖缆

**toxic** yǒudú 有毒

**toy** wánjù 玩具

♦ **toy with** object bǎinòng 摆弄; idea bú dà rènzhēnde kǎolǜ 不大认真地考虑

**trace** 1 n (of substance) wēiliàng 微量 2 v/t (find) xúnzhǎo 寻找; (follow: footsteps) gēnzōng 跟踪; (draw) miáohuì 描绘

**track** n (path) xiǎojìng 小径; (for racing) pǎodào 跑道; RAIL guǐdào 轨道; ~ **10** RAIL dì shí zhàntái 第十站台; keep ~ of X jìlù X 记录 X

♦ **track down** criminal gēnzōng zhuībǔ 跟踪追捕; copy of a book cházhǎo dào 查找到

**tracksuit** chángxiù yùndòngfú 长袖运动服

**tractor** ⇩ tuōlājī 拖拉机

**trade** 1 n (commerce) màoyì 贸易; (profession, craft) hángyè 行业 2 v/i (do business) jīngyíng 经营; ~ **in X** zuò X de mǎimài 做 X 的买卖 3 v/t (exchange) jiāohuàn 交换; ~ **X for Y** yòng X huàn Y 用 X 换 Y

♦ **trade in** v/t (when buying) yǐ jiù huàn xīn 以旧换新

**trade fair** miàoyìhuì 贸易会

**trademark** shāngbiāo 商标

**trade mission** màoyì dàibiǎo-tuán 贸易代表团

**trader** shāngrén 商人

**trade secret** shāngyè mìmì 商业秘密

**tradesman** (plumber etc) shǒu-gōngyì zhě 手工艺者

**trade(s) union** gōnghuì 工会

**tradition** chuántǒng 传统

**traditional** chuántǒng 传统

**traditional characters** fántǐzì 繁体字

**traditionally** chuántǒng 传统

**traffic** n (on roads) jiāotōng 交通; (at airport) jiāoliú liàng 交流量; (in drugs) fànmài 贩卖

♦ **traffic in** drugs fànmài 贩卖

**traffic circle** huánxíng jiāochā 环形交叉; **traffic cop** F jiāotōng jǐng 交通警; **traffic island** jiāotōng dǎo 交通岛; **traffic jam** jiāotōng dǔsè 交通堵塞; **traffic light** hónglǜdēng 红绿灯; **traffic police** jiāotōng jǐng 交通警; **traffic sign** jiāotōng biāozhì 交通标志

**tragedy** bēijù 悲剧

**tragic** búxìng 不幸

**trail** 1 n (path) xiǎojìng 小径; (of blood) hénjì 痕迹 2 v/t (follow) gēnzōng 跟踪; (tow) tuōlā 拖拉 3 v/i (lag behind) luòhòu 落后

**trailer** (pulled by vehicle) tuōchē 拖车; (mobile home) péngchē 篷车; (of movie) diànyǐng yùgào piān 电影预告片

**train** n huǒchē 火车; go by ~ zuò huǒchē 坐火车

**train²** v/t team, athlete, dog xùnliàn

训练; *employee* péixùn 培训 **2** *v/i*
(*of team, athlete*) xùnliàn 训练; (*of
teacher etc*) péixùn 培训

**trainee** shíxí shēng 实习生

**trainer** SP jiàolián yuán 教练员;
(*of dog*) xùnshòu zhě 训兽者

**trainers** *Br* (*shoes*) yùndòng xié 运
动鞋

**training** (*of new staff*) péixùn 培训;
SP xùnliàn 训练; **be in ~** SP
xùnliàn zhōng 训练中; **be out of
~** SP jìngjì zhuàngtài bùjiā 竞技状
态不佳

**training course** péixùn kèchéng
培训课程

**training scheme** péixùn jìhuà 培
训计划

**train station** huǒchē zhàn 火车站

**trait** tèxìng 特性

**traitor** pàntú 叛徒

**tramp 1** *n* (*Br. hobo*) yóumín 游民
**2** *v/i* chénzhòng de zǒu 沉重地走

**trample** *v/t*: **be ~d to death** zhòng
cǎi zhì sǐ 重踩至死; **be ~d under-
foot** zhòngcǎi jiàn 重踩

♦ **trample on** *person, object* cǎi 踩

**trampoline** bēngchuáng 绷床

**trance** huǎnghū 恍惚; **go into a ~**
chūshénr 出神儿

**tranquil** níngjìng 宁静

**tranquility** níngjìng 宁静

**tranquilizer** zhènjìngjì 镇静剂

**transact** *deal, business* jiāoyì 交易

**transaction** jiāoyì 交易

**transatlantic** héngkuà Dàxīyáng
横跨大西洋

**transcendental** xiānyàn 先验

**transcript** jìlù 纪录

**transfer 1** *v/t* diàodòng 调动;
*passengers* zhuǎnjī 转机; *one's
custom to another company etc*
zhuǎnyí 转移 **2** *v/i* (*when
traveling*) qiānyí 迁移; (*from one
language to another*) zhuǎnhuàn 转
换 **3** *n* (*move, of money*) diàodòng
调动; (*in travel*) diàohuàn 调换

**transferable** *ticket* kě diàohuàn 可
调换

**transform** *v/t* gǎibiàn 改变

**transformation** gǎibiàn 改变

**transformer** ELEC biànyāqì 变压
器

**transfusion** shūxuè 输血

**transistor** jīngtǐguǎn 晶体管;
(*radio*) jīngtǐguǎn shōuyīnjī 晶体
管收音机

**transit**: **in ~** zài yùnshū zhōng 在运
输中

**transition** guòdù 过渡

**transitional** guòdù 过渡

**transit lounge** (*at airport*) zhuǎnjī
tīng 转机厅

**translate** fānyì 翻译

**translation** fānyì 翻译

**translator** fānyì 翻译

**transliterate** yīnyì 音译

**transmission** (*of news, program*)
bōfàng 播放; (*of disease*) chuánrǎn 传染; MOT biànsùqì 变速器

**transmit** *news, program* bōfàng 播
放; *disease* chuánrǎn 传染

**transmitter** (*for radio, TV*)
chuándáqì 传达器

**transpacific** kuàyuè Tàipíngyáng
跨越太平洋

**transparency** PHOT huàndēngpiān
幻灯片

**transparent** tòumíng 透明;
(*obvious*) míngxiǎn 明显

**transplant** *v/t & n* MED yízhí 遗植

**transport** *v/t & n* yùnshū 运输

**transportation** (*of goods, people*)
yùnshū 运输; **means of ~**
jiāotōng gōngjù 交通工具; **public ~** gōngzhòng jiāotōng yùnshū
gōngjù 公众交通运输工具;
**Department of Transportation**
Jiāotōng Bù 交通部

**transvestite** yì zhuāng pì zhě 易装
癖者

**trap 1** *n* (*for animal*) bǔshòu jīguān
捕兽机关; (*question, set-up etc*)
quāntào 圈套; **set a ~ for X** gěi X
shè quāntào 给 X 设圈套 **2** *v/t*
*animal* shèlì bǔshòu jīguān 设立
捕兽机关; *person* shè quāntào 设
圈套; **be ~ped** (*by enemy, flames,
landslide etc*) xiànrù quāntào 陷入
圈套

**trapdoor** huóbǎnmén 活板门

**trapeze** diàojià 吊架

**trappings** (*of power*) wàizài

biāozhì 外在标志

**trash** (*garbage*) lājī 垃圾; (*poor product*) fèipǐn 废品; (*despicable person*) wúnéng de rén 无能的人

**trashcan** lājītǒng 垃圾桶

**trashy** *goods, novel* lièzhì 劣质

**traumatic** chuàngshāng xìng 创伤性

**travel 1** *n* lǚxíng 旅行; ~s lǚtú 旅途 **2** *v/i & v/t* lǚxíng 旅行

**travel agency** lǚxíng shè 旅行社

**travel bag** lǚxíng dài 旅行袋

**traveler** lǚxíng zhě 旅行者

**traveler's check** lǚxíng zhīpiào 旅行支票

**travel expenses** jiāotōng fèiyòng 交通费用; **travel insurance** lǚxíng bǎoxiǎn 旅行保险; **travelsick** lǚxíng jíbìng 旅行疾病

**trawler** tuōwǎng yúchuán 拖网鱼船

**tray** tuōpán 拖盘

**treacherous** *person* bùzhōng 不忠; *currents, roads* àncáng wēixiǎn 暗藏危险

**treachery** pànnì 叛逆

**tread 1** *n* zúyīn 足音; (*of staircase*) tīmiàn 梯面; (*of tire*) tāimiàn 胎面 **2** *v/i* zǒuguò 走过

♦**tread on** cǎi 踩

**treason** pànguó zuì 叛国罪

**treasure 1** *n* cáifù 财富; (*person*) bùkě duōdé de réncái 不可多得的人材 **2** *v/t gift etc* zhēnxī 珍惜

**treasurer** sīkù 司库

**Treasury Department** Cáiwù Bù 财务部

**treat 1** *n* kuǎndài 款待; *it was a real ~* fēicháng lìngrén mǎnyì 非常令人满意; *I have a ~ for you* wǒ yǒu yàng hǎo dōngxi gěi nǐ 我有样好东西给你; *it's my ~* (*I'm paying*) wǒ qǐngkè 我请客 **2** *v/t materials* chǔlǐ 处理; *illness* zhìliáo 治疗; (*behave toward*) duìdài 对待; *~ X to Y* yòng Y kuǎndài X 用 Y 款待 X

**treatment** (*of materials*) chǔlǐ 处理; (*of illness*) zhìliáo 治疗; (*of people*) duìdài 对待

**treaty** tiáoyuē 条约

**treble**[1] MUS zuì gāoyīn bù 最高音部

**treble**[2] **1** *adv* sānbèi 三倍; *~ the price* jiàgé zhǎng sānbèi 价格涨三倍 **2** *v/i* fānle sān fān 翻了三番

**tree** shù 树

**tremble** (*of person, hand, voice*) fādǒu 发抖; (*of building*) yáohuàng 摇晃

**tremendous** (*very good*) juémiào 绝妙; (*enormous*) jùdà 巨大

**tremendously** (*very*) hěn 很; (*a lot*) hěnduō 很多

**tremor** (*of earth*) zhèndòng 震动

**trench** gōu 沟

**trend** qūxiàng 趋向; (*fashion*) cháoliú 潮流

**trendy** xīncháo 新潮

**trespass** fēifǎ qīnrù 非法侵入; *no ~ing* bùdé rùnèi 不得入内

♦**trespass on** *land* fēifǎ qīnrù 非法侵入; *privacy* dǎrǎo 打扰

**trespasser** fēifǎ qīnrù zhě 非法侵入者

**trial** LAW shěnpàn 审判; (*of equipment*) shìyàn 试验; *on ~* LAW shòushěn 受审; *have X on ~ equipment etc* shìyàn X 试验 X

**trial period** (*for employee*) shíxí qī 实习期; (*for equipment*) shìyàn qī 试验期

**triangle** sānjiǎo xíng 三角形

**triangular** sānjiǎo xíng 三角形

**tribe** bùluò 部落

**tribunal** cáipàn yuàn 裁判院

**tributary** zhīliú 支流

**trick 1** *n* (*to deceive*) jìmóu 计谋; (*knack*) jiǎoláo 技巧; *play a ~ on X* zhuōnòng X 捉弄 X **2** *v/t* qīpiàn 欺骗; *~ X into doing Y* piàn X zuò Y 骗 X 做 Y

**trickery** qīpiàn 欺骗

**trickle** *n & v/i* dī 滴

**trickster** piànzi 骗子

**tricky** (*difficult*) jíshǒu 棘手

**tricycle** sānlúnchē 三轮车

**trifle** (*triviality*) suǒshì 琐事

**trifling** suǒsuì 琐碎

**trigger** *n* bānjī 扳机; (*on camcorder*) qǐdòng zhuāngzhì 起

动装置
♦ **trigger off** chùfā 触发

**trim 1** adj (neat) zhěngqí 整齐; figure miáotiáo 苗条 **2** v/t hair, hedge xiāo 削; budget, costs xùjiǎn 削减; (decorate: dress) zhuāngshì 装饰 **3** n (light cut) xiāobiānr 削边儿; just a ~, please (to hairdresser) qǐng zhǐ xiāobiānr 请只削边儿; in good ~ jīngjìng yǒutiáo 井井有条

**trimming** (on clothes) xiūshì pǐn 修饰品; with all the ~s yǒu suǒyǒu dāpèi 有所有搭配

**trinket** wányìr 玩意儿

**trio** MUS sān chóng chàng 三重唱

**trip 1** n (journey) lǚxíng 旅行 **2** v/t & v/i (~ up) bàndǎo 绊倒

♦ **trip up 1** v/t (make fall) bàndǎo 绊倒; (cause to go wrong) shǐ ... fàn cuòwù 使 ... 犯错误 **2** v/i (stumble) bàndǎo 绊倒; (make a mistake) fàn cuòwù 犯错误

**tripe** (food) niúdǔ 牛肚

**triple** → treble

**triplets** sānbāotāi 三胞胎

**tripod** PHOT sānjiǎojià 三脚架

**trite** chénjiù 陈旧

**triumph** n shènglì de xǐyuè 胜利的喜悦

**trivial** suǒsuì 琐碎

**triviality** suǒshì 琐事

**trombone** chánghào 长号

**troops** jūnduì 军队

**trophy** jiǎngbēi 奖杯

**tropic** huíguīxiàn 回归线

**tropical** rèdài 热带

**tropics** rèdài dìqū 热带地区

**trot** v/i xiǎopǎo 小跑

**trouble 1** n (difficulties) kùnnan 困难; (illness) bìngtòng 病痛; (inconvenience) máfan 麻烦; (disturbance) sāoluàn 骚乱; go to a lot of ~ to do X búcì xīnkǔ qù zuò X 不辞辛苦去做 X; no ~ méi wèntí 没问题; get into ~ zhāozhì máfán 招致麻烦 **2** v/t (worry) dānyōu 担忧; (bother, disturb) máfán 麻烦; (of back, liver etc) shǐ bù shūfu 使不舒服

**trouble-free** wú gùzhàng 无故障

**troublemaker** dǎoluàn zhě 捣乱者

**troubleshooter** (mediator) tiáojiěrén 调解人

**troubleshooting** páichú gùzhàng 排除故障

**troublesome** fánrén 烦人

**trousers** Br kùzi 裤子; a pair of ~ yītiáo kùzi 一条裤子

**trout** zūnyú 鳟鱼

**truce** xiūzhàn 休战

**truck** kǎchē 卡车

**truck driver** kǎchē sījī 卡车司机; **truck farm** shūcài nóngchǎng 蔬菜农场; **truck farmer** càinóng 菜农; **truck stop** kǎchē sījī kuàicāndiàn 卡车司机快餐店

**trudge** v/i & n báshè 跋涉

**true** zhēn 真; friend gòu wéi 够; come ~ (of hopes, dream) shíxiàn 实现

**truly** zhēnde 真地; Yours ~ cǐzhì cǐ zhì 此致

**trumpet** lǎba 喇叭

**trunk** (of tree) shùgàn 树干; (of body) qūgàn 躯干; (of elephant) xiàngbí xiàng bí 象鼻; (large case) dà píxiāng 大皮箱; (of car) xínglǐ xiāng 行李箱

**trust 1** n xìnrèn 信任; FIN shòutuō jítuán 受托集团 **2** v/t xiāngxìn 相信; I ~ you wǒ xìnrèn nǐ 我信任你

**trusted** kěxìn 可信

**trustee** lǐshì 理事

**trustful, trusting** xìnrèn 信任

**trustworthy** zhíde xìnrèn 值得信任

**truth** shìshí 事实

**truthful** chéngshí 诚实

**try 1** v/t chángshì 尝试; LAW shěnpàn 审判; ~ to do X chángshì qùzuò X 尝试去做 X **2** v/i shìshì 试试; you must ~ harder nǐ yīdìng yào gèngjiā nǔlì 你一定要更加努力 **3** n chángshì 尝试; can I have a ~? (of food) ràng wǒ shìshì 让我试试; (at doing sth) ràng wǒ shìshì 让我试试; give X a ~ shìzuò X 试做 X

♦ **try on** clothes shìchuān 试穿

♦ **try out** new machine, new method

shìyòng 试用

**trying** (*annoying*) nányǐ róngrěn 难以容忍

**T-shirt** ⇩ yuánlǐng shān 圆领衫

**tub** (*bath*) yùgāng 浴缸; (*of liquid*) tǒng 桶; (*for yoghurt, ice cream*) hé 盒

**tubby** *adj* ǎipàng 矮胖

**tube** (*pipe*) guǎndào 管道; (*of toothpaste, ointment*) guǎn 管

**tubeless** *tire* wú nèitāi 无内胎

**tuberculosis** jiéhé bìng 结核病

**tuck 1** *n* (*in dress*) zhě 褶 **2** *v/t* (*put*) sāijìn 塞进

♦**tuck away** (*put away*) shōucáng 收藏; (*eat quickly*) dàchī 大吃

♦**tuck in 1** *v/t children* gàihǎo bèizi 盖好被子; *sheets* sāihǎo guǒjǐn 塞好裹紧 **2** *v/i* (*start eating*) kāishǐ chī 开始吃

♦**tuck up** *sleeves etc* juǎnqǐ 卷起; **tuck X up in bed** gěi X gàihǎo bèizi ānshuì 给 X 盖好被子安睡

**Tuesday** xīngqī èr 星期二

**tuft** cóng 丛

**tug 1** *n* (*pull*) lā 拉; NAUT tuōchuán 拖船 **2** *v/t* (*pull*) lā 拉

**tuition** fǔdǎo 辅导

**tulip** xiāngxìng yùjīnxiāng 郁金香

**tumble** *v/i* dǎo 倒

**tumbledown** yáoyáo yùzhuì 摇摇欲坠

**tumble-dryer** shuǎigān jī 甩干机

**tumbler** (*for drink*) wújiǎo bōlíbēi 无脚玻璃杯; (*in circus*) fān jīdǒu zhě 翻筋斗者

**tummy** dùzi 肚子

**tummy ache** dùzi téng 肚子疼

**tumor** zhǒngliú 肿瘤

**tumult** xuānnào 喧哗

**tumultuous** xuānnào 喧闹

**tuna** jīnqiāng yú 金枪鱼

**tune 1** *n* qǔdiào 曲调; **in ~** hédiào 合调; **out of ~** zǒudiào 走调 **2** *v/t instrument* tiáo zhǔn yīndiào 调准音调

♦**tune in** *v/i* RAD shōutīng 收听; TV shōukàn 收看

♦**tune in to** RAD shōutīng 收听; TV shōukàn 收看

♦**tune up 1** *v/i* (*of orchestra,*

players) tiáoyīn 调音 **2** *v/t engine* tiáozhěng 调整

**tuneful** yīndiào yuè'ěr 音调悦耳

**tuner** (*hi-fi*) tiáoxié qì 调谐器

**tunic** EDU duǎnpáo 短袍

**tunnel** *n* suìdào 隧道

**turbine** (*operated by air*) qìlún jī 气轮机; (*operated by water*) wōlún jī 涡轮机; (*operated by steam*) yèlún jī 叶轮机

**turbot** dàlíngpíng 大菱鲆

**turbulence** (*in air travel*) tuānliú 湍流

**turbulent** *meeting, life, love affair* hǔnluàn 混乱; *weather* kuángbào 狂暴

**turf** cǎopí 草皮

**Turk** Tǔ'ěrqí rén 土耳其人

**Turkey** Tǔ'ěrqí 土耳其

**turkey** huǒjī 火鸡

**Turkish 1** *adj* Tǔ'ěrqí 土耳其 **2** *n* (*language*) Tǔ'ěrqí yǔ 土耳其语

**turmoil** dòngluàn 动乱

**turn 1** *n* (*rotation*) zhuǎndòng 转动; (*in road*) zhuǎn 转; (*in vaudeville*) jiémù 节目; **take ~s doing X** lúnliú zuò X 轮流做X; **it's my ~** gāi wǒ le 该我了; **it's not your ~ yet** méi dào nǐ ne 没到你呢; **take a ~ at the wheel** kāi yíhuìr chē 开一会儿车; **do X a good ~** wèi X zuò hǎoshì 为X做好事 **2** *v/t wheel* zhuǎn 转; *corner* guǎiwānr 拐弯儿; **~ one's back on X** rēngxià X bùguǎn 扔下 X 不管 **3** *v/i* (*of driver, car, wheel*) zhuǎn 转; **~ right / left here** zhuànyòu / zuǒ 转右 / 左; **it has ~ed sour / cold** biànsuān / lěng le 变酸 / 冷了; **he has ~ed 40** tā sìshí le 他四十了

♦**turn around 1** *v/t object, company* niǔzhuàn 扭转; (COM: *deal with*) wánchéng 完成 **2** *v/i* (*of person*) zhuǎnshēn 转身; (*of driver*) diàotóu 调头

♦**turn away 1** *v/t* (*send away*) jùjué 拒绝 **2** *v/i* (*walk away*) zǒule 走了; (*look away*) zhuǎnliǎn 转脸

♦**turn back 1** *v/t edges, sheets* fānhuí 翻回 **2** *v/i* (*of walkers, in*

*course of action*) huítóu 回头
♦ **turn down** v/t *offer, invitation* jùjué 拒绝; *volume, TV, heating* guānxiǎo 关小; *edge, collar* fānxià 翻下
♦ **turn in 1** v/i (*go to bed*) shàngchuáng 上床 **2** v/t (*to police*) zìshǒu 自首
♦ **turn off 1** v/t *TV, faucet, heater, engine* guān 关; F (*sexually*) shǐ shīqù xìngqù 使失去兴趣 **2** v/i (*of car, driver*) xià 下
♦ **turn on 1** v/t *TV, faucet, heater, engine* kāi 开; F (*sexually*) cìjī 刺激 **2** v/i (*of machine*) kāi 开
♦ **turn out 1** v/t *lights* guān 关 **2** v/i: *as it turned out* jiéguǒ shì 结果是
♦ **turn over 1** v/i (*in bed*) fānshēn 翻身; (*of vehicle*) fān guòlái 翻过来 **2** v/t (*put upside down*) fān guòlái 翻过来; *page* fān piānr 翻篇儿; FIN zhōuzhuǎn 周转
♦ **turn up 1** v/t *collar* fānqǐ 翻起; *volume, heating* kāidà 开大 **2** v/i (*arrive*) lòumiàn 露面
**turning** guǎijiǎo 拐角
**turning point** zhuǎnzhé diǎn 转折点
**turnip** luóbo 萝卜
**turnout** (*people*) cānjiā zhě 参加者
**turnover** FIN chéngjiāo liàng 成交量
**turnpike** gāosù gōnglù 高速公路
**turnstile** ràogān 绕杆
**turntable** (*of record player*) diànchàng pán 电唱盘
**turquoise** adj qīnglǜsè 青绿色
**turret** (*of castle*) jiǎolóu 角楼; (*of tank*) xuánzhuǎn pàotǎ 旋转炮塔
**turtle** wūguī 乌龟
**turtleneck** (*sweater*) gāolǐng tàoshān 高领套衫
**tusk** xiàngyá 象牙
**tutor**: (*private*) ~ sīrén jiàoshī 私人教师
**tuxedo** lǐfú 礼服
**TV** diànshì 电视; *on* ~ diànshì shang 电视上
**TV program** diànshì jiémù 电视节目

**twang 1** n (*in voice*) bíyīn 鼻音 **2** v/t *guitar string* shǐ fā xián shēng 使发弦声
**tweezers** nièzi 镊子
**twelfth** dìshí'èr 第十二
**twelve** shí'èr 十二
**twentieth** dìèrshí 第二十
**twenty** èrshí 二十
**twice** liǎngcì 两次; ~ *as much* liǎngbèi nàme duō 两倍那么多
**twiddle** bǎinòng 摆弄; ~ *one's thumbs* fig xiánzhe 闲着
**twig** n xìzhī 细枝
**twilight** huánghūn 黄昏
**twin** shuāng bāo tāi 双胞胎
**twin beds** liǎng zhāng chuáng 两张床
**twinge** (*of pain*) cìtòng 刺痛
**twinkle** v/i (*of stars*) shǎnyào 闪耀; (*of eyes*) fāguāng 发光
**twin town** yǒuyì shì 友谊市
**twirl 1** v/t shǐ xuánzhuǎn 使旋转 **2** n (*of cream etc*) zhuāngshì 装饰
**twist 1** v/t cuō 搓; ~ *one's ankle* niǔle jiǎohuái 扭了脚踝 **2** v/i (*of road, river*) pánxuán 盘旋 **3** n (*in rope*) nǐng 拧; (*in road*) guǎiwānr 拐弯儿; (*in plot, story*) qūzhé 曲折
**twisty** *road* wānwan qūqu 弯弯曲曲
**twit** bèndàn 笨蛋
**twitch 1** n (*nervous*) chōuchù 抽搐 **2** v/i (*jerk*) chōuchù 抽搐
**twitter** v/i (*of birds*) zhīzhī de jiào 吱吱地叫
**two** èr 二; (*with measure words*) liǎng 两; *the ~ of them* tāmen liǎng 他们俩
**two-faced** liǎngmiànpài 两面派; **two-piece** n (*woman's suit*) tàofú 套服; **two-stroke** adj engine èrchōngchéng 二冲程; **two-way** traffic shuāngxiàng jiāotōng 双向交通
**tycoon** jùtóu 巨头
**type 1** n (*sort*) zhǒnglèi 种类; *what ~ of ...?* nǎ yīzhǒng ...? 那一种 ...? **2** v/t & v/i (*with a keyboard*) dǎzì 打字

typhoid (fever) shānghán 伤寒
typhoon táifēng 台风
typhus bānzhěn shānghán 斑疹伤寒
typical diǎnxíng 典型; *that's ~ of him* tā jiù shì nàyàng 他就是那样
typically diǎnxíng 典型; ~

*American* diǎnxíng Měiguórén 典型美国人
typist dǎzìyuán 打字员
tyrannical bàonüè 暴虐
tyrannize shī bàonüè 施暴虐
tyranny (*behavior*) bàonüè 暴虐; (*regime*) bàozhèng 暴政
tyrant bàojūn 暴君

# U

ugly chǒulòu 丑陋

UK (= **United Kingdom**) Yīngguó 英国; (*formal use*) Liánhé Wángguó 联合王国

ulcer kuìyáng 溃疡

ultimate (*best, definitive*) zuìhǎo 最好; (*final*) zuìhòu 最后; (*fundamental*) gēnběn 根本

ultimately (*in the end*) zuìzhōng 最终

ultimatum zuìhòu tōngdié 最后通牒

ultrasound MED chāoshēngbō 超声波

ultraviolet *adj* zǐwài 紫外

umbilical cord qídài 脐带

umbrella sǎn 伞

umpire *n* cáipànyuán 裁判员

umpteen F wúshù 无数

UN (= **United Nations**) Liánhéguó 联合国

un ... (*with adjs*) bù, fēi (qiánzhuì) 不, 非 (前缀)

unable: **be ~ to X** (*not know how to*) bùhuì zuò X 不会做 X; (*not be in a position to*) méiyǒu nénglì zuò X 没有能力做 X

unacceptable bùnéng jiēshòu 不能接受; **it is ~ that ...** ... shì lìngrén bùnéng jiēshòu de ... 是令人不能接受的

unaccountable wúfǎ jiěshì 无法解释

unaccustomed: **be ~ to X** bù xíguànyú X 不习惯于 X

unadulterated *fig* (*absolute*) shízú 十足

un-American (*not fitting*) fēi Měiguó 非美国

unanimous *verdict* yīzhì tóngyì 一致同意; **get X dáchéng yīzhì** 对 X 达成一致

unanimously *vote, decide* yīzhì 一致

unapproachable *person* nányǐ jiējìn 难以接近

unarmed *person* wú wǔqì 无武器; **~ combat** túshǒu gédòu 徒手格斗

unassuming qiānxùn 谦逊

unattached (*without a partner*) wú gùdìng bànlǚ 无固定伴侣

unattended wúzhǔ 无主; **leave X ~** diūxià X bùguǎn 丢下 X 不管

unauthorized shànzì shànzì 擅自

unavoidable bùkě bìmiǎn 不可避免

unavoidably: **be ~ detained** chōu bù kāi shēn 抽不开身

unaware: **be ~ of** méiyǒu chájué-dào 没有察觉到

unawares: **catch X ~** shǐ X chījīng 使 X 吃惊

unbalanced bù pínghéng 不平衡; PSYCH shīcháng 失常

unbearable nányǐ rěnshòu 难以忍受

unbeatable *team, quality* bùkě zhànshèng 不可战胜

unbeaten *team* wèi bèi jībài 未被击败

unbeknownst: **~ to X** X bù zhīdào X 不知道

unbelievable nányǐzhìxìn 难以置信; F *heat, value* jíduān 极端; **he's ~ F** (*very good/bad*) tā zhēn búshì yìbān rén 他真不是一般人

unbias(s)ed bù piāntǎn 不偏袒

unblock *pipe* qīngchú dǔsè 清除堵塞

unborn wèi chūshēng 未出生

unbreakable *plate* dǎbúpò 打不碎; *world's record* bùkě dǎpò 不可打破

unbutton jiěkāi niǔkòu 解开纽扣

uncalled-for wú lǐyóu 无理由

uncanny *resemblance* yìhūxún-cháng 异乎寻常; *skill* bùkě sīyì

不可思议; (*worrying: feeling*) líqí 离奇

**unceasing** búduàn 不断

**uncertain** *future, weather* kěnéng gǎibiàn 可能改变; *origins* bú quèdìng 不确定; *be ~ about X* duì X bú quèdìng 对 X 不确定

**uncertainty** (*of the future*) bú quèdìng 不确定; *there is still ~ about X* duì X háiyǒu bú quèdìngxìng 对 X 还有不确定性

**unchecked:** *let X go ~* rèn X zìyóu fāzhǎn 任 X 自由发展

**uncle** (*mother's brother*) jiùjiu 舅舅; (*father's elder brother*) bóbo 伯伯; (*father's younger brother*) shūshu 叔叔; (*mother's sister's husband*) yífu 姨父; (*father's sister's husband*) gūfù 姑父; (*to older non-related men*) shūshu 叔叔

**uncomfortable** *chair* bù shūshì 不舒适; *sitting position* bù shūfu 不舒服; *feel ~ about X* (*about decision etc*) duì X yǒu zhíyí 对 X 有质疑; *I feel ~ with him* wǒ gēn tā zài yìqǐ gǎndào bú zìzai 我跟他在一起感到不自在

**uncommon** bù xúncháng 不寻常; *it's not ~* zhè bù hǎnjiàn 这不罕见

**uncompromising** bú ràngbù 不让步

**unconcerned** lěngmò 冷漠; *be ~ about X* bù bǎ X fàngzài xīn shang 不把 X 放在心上

**unconditional** wú tiáojiàn 无条件

**unconscious** MED shīqù zhíjué 失去知觉; PSYCH xiàyìshí 下意识; *knock X ~* dǎde X bùxíngrénshì 打得 X 不醒人事; *be ~ of X* (*not aware*) wèi chájué chū X 未察觉出

**uncontrollable** *anger, desire, children* kòngzhì bùliǎo 控制不了

**unconventional** bùxún xísú 不循习俗

**uncooperative** búyuàn hézuò 不愿合作

**uncork** *bottle* báchū ... sāizi 拔出 ... 塞子

**uncover** (*remove cover from*) jiēkāi 揭开; *plot* jiēlù 揭露; *ancient remains* fājué 发掘

**undamaged** wèishòu sǔnshāng 未受损伤

**undaunted:** *carry on ~* yǒng wǎng zhí qián 勇往直前

**undecided** *question* xuán ér wèijué 悬而未决; *be ~ about X* duì X yóuyù bú dìng 对 X 犹豫不定

**undeniable** bùkě fǒurèn 不可否认

**undeniably** díquè 的确

**under 1** *prep* (*beneath*) zài ... xiàmian 在 ... 下面; (*less than*) bú dào 不到 **2** *adv* (*anesthetized*) shīqù zhíjué 失去知觉

**underage** *drinking etc* wèi dào chéngnián 未成年; *be ~* wèi dào fǎdìng niánlíng 未到法定年龄

**undercarriage** qǐluòjià 起落架

**undercover** *adj agent* mìmì 秘密

**undercut** *v/t* COM xùjià qiǎng ... shēngyì 削价抢 ... 生意

**underdog** chǔyú lièshì de yìfāng 处于劣势的一方

**underdone** *meat* bù shútòu 不熟透

**underestimate** *v/t person, skills, task* guòfèn dīgū 过分低估

**underexposed** PHOT bàoguāng bù zú 曝光不足

**underfed** yíngyǎng bùliáng 营养不良

**undergo** *surgery, treatment* jiēshòu 接受; *experiences* jīngshòu 经受

**underground 1** *adj also* POL dìxià 地下 **2** *adv work* mìmì 秘密; *go ~* POL zhuǎnrù dìxià 转入地下

**undergrowth** guànmùcóng 灌木丛

**underhand** *adj* (*devious*) guǐzhà 诡诈

**underlie** *v/t:* *~ the theory* gòuchéng zhè yī lǐlùn de jīchǔ 构成这一理论的基础

**underline** *v/t text* xià huàxiàn 下划线

**underlying** *causes, problems* gēnběn 根本

**undermine** *v/t s.o.'s position* xùruò 削弱

削弱; *theory* chèdǐ jīkuǎ 彻底击垮

**underneath 1** *prep* zài ... dǐxià 在 ... 底下 **2** *adv* xiàngxià 向下

**underpants** nèikù 内裤

**underpass** (*for pedestrians*) dìxià tōngdào 地下通道

**underprivileged** dìwèi dīxià 地位低下

**underrate** *v/t* guòdī píngjià 过低评价

**undershirt** bèixīn 背心

**undersized** tàixiǎo 太小

**underskirt** chènqún 衬裙

**understaffed** rényuán bùzú 人员不足

**understand 1** *v/t* lǐjiě 理解; *I ~ that you ...* wǒ tīngshuō nǐ ... 我听说你...; *they are understood to be in Canada* jù liǎojiě tāmen zài Jiānádà 据了解他们在加拿大 **2** *v/i* míngbái 明白

**understandable** kě lǐjiě 可理解

**understandably** kě lǐjiě 可理解

**understanding 1** *adj person* tōngqíng dálǐ 通情达理 **2** *n* (*of problem, situation*) lǐjiě 理解; (*agreement*) xiéyì 协议; *on the ~ that ...* (*condition*) zài ... tiáojiàn xià 在 ... 条件下

**understatement** zhòngshì qīngshuō 重事轻说

**undertake** *task* chéngdān 承担; *~ to do X* (*agree to*) tóngyì zuò X 同意做 X

**undertaking** (*enterprise*) shìyè 事业; (*promise*) xǔnuò 许诺

**undervalue** *v/t* dīgū 低估

**underwear** nèiyī 内衣

**underweight** *adj* biāozhǔn zhòngliàng yǐxià 标准重量以下

**underworld** (*criminal*) hēi shèhuì 黑社会; (*in mythology*) yīnjiān 阴间

**underwrite** *v/t* FIN tóngyì zīzhù 同意资助

**undeserved** bú qiàdàng 不恰当

**undesirable** *features, changes* búshòu huānyíng 不受欢迎; *person* tǎoyàn 讨厌; *~ element* (*person*) dǎoluàn fènzǐ 捣乱分子

**undisputed** *champion, leader* wúkě zhēngbiàn 无可争辩

**undo** *parcel, wrapping* dǎkāi 打开; *buttons, shirt, shoelaces* jiěkāi 解开; *s.o. else's work* fèichú 废除; COMPUT chèxiāo 撤销

**undoubtedly** wúyí 无疑

**undreamt-of** *riches* zuòmèng yě xiǎng bú dào 做梦也想不到

**undress 1** *v/t* gěi ... tuō yīfu 给 ... 脱衣服; *get ~ed* tuō yīfu 脱衣服 **2** *v/i* tuō yīfu 脱衣服

**undue** (*excessive*) guòdù 过度

**unduly** *punished, blamed* bú shìdàng 不适当; (*excessively*) guòfèn 过分

**unearth** *ancient remains* fājué 发掘; *fig* (*find*) fāxiàn 发现; *secret* jiēkāi 揭开

**unearthly**: *at this ~ hour* zài zhè gè huāngmiù de shíhou 在这个荒谬的时候

**uneasy** *relationship, peace* lìngrén bù'ān 令人不安; *feel ~ about X* wèi X gǎndào bù'ān 为 X 感到不安

**uneatable** bùnéng chī 不能吃

**uneconomic** bù jīngjì 不经济

**uneducated** wèi shòu liánghǎo jiàoyù 未受良好教育

**unemployed** shīyè 失业; (*laid off from state enterprise*) xiàgǎng 下岗; *the ~* shīyèzhě 失业者; (*from state enterprise*) xiàgǎng gōngrén 下岗工人

**unemployment** shīyè 失业

**unending** wú zhǐjìng 无止境

**unequal** bù píngděng 不平等; *be ~ to the task* nányǐ shèngrèn zhèxiàng gōngzuò 难以胜任这项工作

**unerring** *judgment, instinct* wànwúyīshī 万无一失

**uneven** *quality* bù yìzhì 不一致; *surface, ground* bù píng 不平

**unevenly** *distributed, applied* bù jūnyún 不均匀; *~ matched* (*of two contestants*) bú shìjūnlìdí 不势均力敌

**uneventful** *day, journey* píngdàn 平淡

**unexpected** chūhū yìliào 出乎意料

**unexpectedly** yìwài 意外

**unfair** bù gōngpíng 不公平

**unfaithful** husband, wife bù zhōng 不忠; be ~ to X duì X bù zhōng 对 X 不忠

**unfamiliar** bù shúxī 不熟悉; be ~ with X bù shúxī X 不熟悉 X

**unfasten** belt jiěkāi 解开

**unfavorable** report, review fùmiàn 负面; weather conditions búlì 不利

**unfeeling** person wúqíng 无情

**unfinished** wèi wánchéng 未完成; leave X ~ bàntú rēngxià X 半途扔下 X

**unfit** (physically) bú jiànkāng 不健康; (not morally suited) bú shìhé 不适合; be ~ to eat / drink bùyí shíyòng / yǐnyòng 不宜食用 / 饮用

**unfix** part chāixià 拆下; screw nǐngxià 拧下

**unflappable** zhèndìng zìruò 镇定自若

**unfold** 1 v/t sheets, letter tānkāi 摊开; one's arms zhāngkāi 张开 2 v/i (of story etc) zhǎnkāi 展开; (of view) xiànxiàn 显现

**unforeseen** wèi yùjiàn dào 未预见到

**unforgettable** nánwàng 难忘

**unforgivable** bù kě ráoshù 不可饶恕; that was ~ of you bùnéng yuánliàng nǐ 不能原谅你

**unfortunate** people, event búxìng 不幸; choice of words bú qiàdàng 不恰当; that's ~ for you nǐ bù zǒuyùn 你不走运

**unfortunately** búxìng de shì 不幸的是

**unfounded** wúduān 无端

**unfriendly** lěngmò 冷漠; software bú yì shǐyòng 不易使用

**unfurnished** wú jiājù shèbèi 无家具设备

**ungodly**: at this ~ hour zài zhème ge huāngmiù shíhòu 在这么个荒谬时候

**ungrateful** bù lǐngqíng 不领情

**unhappiness** bù yúkuài 不愉快

**unhappy** bù yúkuài 不愉快; (not content: customers etc) bù mǎnyì 不满意; be ~ with X duì X bù mǎnyì 对 X 不满意

**unharmed** píng'ān wúyàng 平安无恙

**unhealthy** person bú jiànkāng 不健康; conditions, food, atmosphere yǒuhài yú jiànkāng 有害于健康; economy, balance sheet bù jǐngqì 不景气

**unheard-of** qián suǒ wèi wén 前所未闻

**unhurt** wèi shòu shānghài 未受伤害

**unhygienic** bú wèishēng 不卫生

**unification** tǒngyī 统一

**uniform** 1 n zhìfú 制服 2 adj yízhì 一致

**unify** tǒngyī 统一

**unilateral** dān fāngmiàn 单方面

**unimaginable** nányǐ xiǎngxiàng 难以想象

**unimaginative** qùfá xiǎngxiànglì 缺乏想象力

**unimportant** bú zhòngyào 不重要

**uninhabitable** bú shìyú jūzhù 不适于居住

**uninhabited** building, region huāng wú rényān 荒无人烟

**uninjured** wèi shòu sǔnshāng 未受损伤

**unintelligible** nán lǐjiě 难理解

**unintentional** fēi gùyì 非故意

**unintentionally** wúxīn 无心

**uninteresting** wúliáo 无聊

**uninterrupted** sleep, work bù jiānduàn 不间断

**union** POL liánméng 联盟; (labor ~) gōnghuì 工会

**unique** dúyīwú'èr 独一无二; F (very good) biéjùyígé 别具一格; with his own ~ humor / style yǐ tā dútè de yōumò / fēnggé 以他独特的幽默 / 风格

**unit** (of measurement) dānwèi 单位; (section: of machine, structure) bùjiàn 部件; (part with separate function) yuánjiàn 元件; (department) bù 部; MIL bùduì 部队; work ~ dānwèi 单位; we

**unpredictable**

*must work together as a ~*
wǒmen bìxū zuòwéi yígè zhěngtǐ
yìqǐ gōngzuò 我们必须作为一
个整体一起工作

**unit cost** COM dānjià 单价
**unite 1** *v/t* tǒngyī 统一; *family
members* tuánjù 团聚 **2** *v/i* tuánjié
团结
**united** tuánjié 团结
**United Kingdom** Yīngguó 英国;
*(formal use)* Liánhé Wángguó 联
合王国
**United Nations** Liánhéguó 联合
国
**United States (of America)**
Měiguó 美国; *(formal use)*
Měilìjiān Hézhòngguó 美利坚合
众国
**unity** tǒngyī 统一
**universal** pǔbiàn 普遍
**universally** yízhì 一致
**universe** yǔzhòu 宇宙
**university 1** *n* dàxué 大学; *he is
at ~* tā zài dú dàxué 他在读大学
**2** *adj* dàxué 大学
**unjust** *adj* wúqián 不公正
**unkempt** bù zhěngjié 不整洁
**unkind** kèbó 刻薄
**unknown 1** *adj* wèizhī 未知 **2** *n: a
journey into the ~* qiántú wèibǔ
前途未卜
**unleaded** *adj* wúqiān 无铅
**unless** chúfēi 除非
**unlike** *prep* búxiàng 不像; *it's ~
him to drink so much* tā hē
zhèmeduō jiǔ búxiàng tā píngshí
de yàngzi 他喝这么多酒不像
他平时的样子; *the photograph
was completely ~ her* zhàopiàn
yìdiǎnr yě bú xiàng tā běnrén 照
片一点儿也不像她本人
**unlikely** bú dà kěnéng 不大可能;
*he is ~ to win* tā bú dà kěnéng
yíng 他不大可能赢; *it is ~ that
... ...* bú dà kěnéng ... 不大可能
**unlimited** wúxiàn 无限
**unload** *truck, goods* xiè 卸
**unlock** dǎkāi 打开
**unluckily** yíhànde shì 遗憾的是
**unlucky** *day, choice* dǎoméi 倒霉;
*person* búxìng 不幸; *that was so*

*~ for you!* nà nǐ tài dǎoméi le! 那
你太倒霉了！
**unmade-up** *face* méi huàzhuāng
没化妆
**unmanned** *spacecraft* wúrén cāozòng 无人操纵
**unmarried** wèihūn 未婚
**unmistakable** juéwú jǐnyǒu 绝无
仅有
**unmoved** *(emotionally)* wèi bèi
gǎndòng 未被感动
**unmusical** *person* méiyǒu yīnyuè
tiānfù 没有音乐天赋; *sounds*
cì'ěr 刺耳
**unnatural** fǎncháng 反常; *it's not
~ to be annoyed* gǎndào fánnǎo
shì zhèngcháng de 感到烦恼是
正常的
**unnecessary** bú biyào 不必要
**unnerving** lìngrén qìněi 令人气
馁
**unnoticed:** *it went ~* bèi hūlüè 被
忽略
**unobtainable** *goods* mǎi bú dào 买
不到; TELEC chábúdào 查不到
**unobtrusive** bù yǐnrén zhùmù 不
引人注目
**unoccupied** *building, house* wúrén
zhù 无人住; *room* kōngzhe 空
着; *post* wúrén chéngdān 无人承
担; *person* kòngxián 空闲
**unofficial** fēi zhèngshì 非正式
**unofficially** fēi zhèngshì 非正式
**unpack 1** *v/t* dǎkāi 打开 **2** *v/i*
dǎkāi bāoguǒ 打开包裹
**unpaid** *work* wúcháng 无偿
**unpleasant** shǐ rén bù yúkuài 使
人不愉快; *he was very ~ to her*
tā dài tā hěn cūlǔ 他待她很粗
鲁
**unplug** *v/t* TV, computer báchū
chātóu 拔出插头
**unpopular** *person* bú shòu
huānyíng 不受欢迎; *decision*
bùdé rénxīn 不得人心
**unprecedented** kōngqián 空前; *it
was ~ for a woman to X* dāngshí,
nǚxìng X shì shǐwúqiánlì de 当
时，女性X是史无前例的
**unpredictable** *person, weather*
fǎnfù wúcháng 反复无常

**unprincipled** *pej* bú dàodé 不道德

**unpretentious** *person, style, hotel* bù xuànyào 不炫耀

**unproductive** *meeting, discussion* méiyǒu jiéguǒ 没有结果; *soil* bù féiwò 不肥沃

**unprofessional** *person, behavior* bú jìngyè 不敬业; *workmanship* zāogāo 糟糕

**unprofitable** bù yínglì 不盈利

**unpronounceable** nányǐ zhèngquè fāyīn 难以正确发音

**unprotected** *borders* wèi shèfáng 未设防; *machine* méiyǒu ānquán zhuāngzhì 没有安全装置; ~ *sex* wèi jīng bǎohù de xìng xíngwéi 未经保护的性行为

**unprovoked** *attack* wúduān 无端

**unqualified** *worker, doctor etc* bù hégé 不合格

**unquestionably** *(without doubt)* wúkě zhēngbiàn 无可争辩

**unquestioning** *attitude, loyalty* wú yìyì 无异议

**unravel** *v/t string, knitting* chāikāi 拆开; *mystery, complexities* chéngqīng 澄清

**unreadable** *book* bùzhíyìdú 不值一读

**unreal** bù zhēnshí 不真实; *this is* ~*!* F xiàng mèng yíyàng! 像梦一样!

**unrealistic** bú xiànshí 不现实

**unreasonable** *person* chāoyuè qínglǐ 超越情理; *demand, expectation* guòfèn 过分

**unrelated** *issues* bù xiāngguān 不相关; *people* wú qīnqī guānxi 无亲戚关系

**unrelenting** búxiè 不懈

**unreliable** bù kěkào 不可靠

**unrest** dòngluàn 动乱

**unrestrained** *emotions* wú jūshù 无拘束

**unroadworthy** búyí zài gōnglù shang xíngshǐ 不宜在公路上行使

**unroll** *v/t carpet, scroll* zhǎnkāi 展开

**unruly** bù guījù 不规矩

**unsafe** *bridge, vehicle, wiring* wēixiǎn 危险; *district, beach* bù

ānquán 不安全; ~ *to drink / eat* bùyí hē / chī 不宜喝 / 吃; *it is* ~ *to X* X bù ānquán X 不安全

**unsanitary** *conditions, drains* bú wèishēng 不卫生

**unsatisfactory** bùnéng lìngrén mǎnyì 不能令人满意

**unsavory** *person, reputation* lìngrén tǎoyàn 令人讨厌; *district* lìngrén búkuài 令人不快

**unscathed** *(not injured)* wèi shòu sǔnshāng 未受损伤; *(not damaged)* wèi shòu sǔnhuài 未受损坏

**unscrew** *sth screwed on* xuánsōng 旋松; *top* nǐngkāi 拧开

**unscrupulous** bù jiǎng dàodé 不讲道德

**unselfish** wúsī 无私

**unsettled** *issue* wèi jiějué 未解决; *weather, stock market* yìbiàn 易变; *lifestyle* bù wěndìng 不稳定; *bills* wèi zhīfù 未支付

**unshaven** méi xiūmiàn 没修面

**unsightly** bù yǎguān 不雅观

**unskilled** wú tèshū jìnéng 无特殊技能

**unsociable** bù héqún 不合群

**unsophisticated** *person* zhìpǔ 质朴; *equipment* jiǎndān 简单

**unstable** *person* fǎnfù wúcháng 反复无常; *structure* bù jiāngù 不坚固; *area, economy* dòngdàng bù'ān 动荡不定

**unsteady** *(on one's feet)* bùwěn 不稳; *ladder* yáobǎi yáobǎi 摇摆摇摆

**unstinting** *be* ~ *in one's efforts* búyíyúlì 不遗余力

**unstuck** *come* ~ *(of notice etc)* méi zhānzhù 没粘住; *(of plan etc)* shībài 失败

**unsuccessful** *writer, party* bù chénggōng 不成功; *candidate, attempt* shībài 失败; *he tried but was* ~ tā chángshìle kěshì méi chénggōng 他尝试了可是没成功

**unsuccessfully** *try, apply* shībài 失败

**unsuitable** bù héshì 不合适

**unsuspecting** wú jièxīn 无戒心

**unswerving** *loyalty, devotion* búbiàn 不变

**unthinkable** bùkě sīyì 不可思议

**untidy** *room, desk, hair* língluàn 凌乱

**untie** *knot, laces, prisoner* jiěkāi 解开

**until 1** *prep* zhídào 直到; *from Monday ~ Friday* cóng zhōuyī dào zhōuwǔ 从周一到周五; *I can wait ~ tomorrow* wǒ kěyǐ děngdào míngtiān 我可以等到明天; *not ~ Friday* děi zhōuwǔ 得周五; *it won't be finished ~ July* zhídào qīyuè cái néng wánchéng 直到七月才能完成 **2** *conj*: *can you wait ~ I'm ready?* nǐ kěyǐ děng wǒ zhǔnbèi hǎo ma? 你可以等我准备好吗? *they won't do anything ~ you say so* nǐ shuōle tāmen cái néng zuò 你说了他们才能做

**untimely** *death* guòzǎo 过早

**untiring** *efforts* bújuàn 不倦

**untold** *riches, suffering* wúxiàn 无限; *story* wèi tòulù 未透露

**untranslatable** bùnéng fānyì 不能翻译

**untrue** bù zhēnshí 不真实

**unused¹** *goods* xīn 新

**unused²**: *be ~ to X* bù xíguàn X 不习惯 X; *be ~ to doing X* bù xíguàn zuò X 不习惯做 X

**unusual** bùtóng xúncháng 不同寻常

**unusually** yìcháng 异常

**unveil** *memorial, statue etc* jiēmù 揭幕

**unwell** bù shūfu 不舒服

**unwilling**: *be ~ to do X* búyuàn zuò X 不愿做 X

**unwind 1** *v/t tape* jiěkāi 解开 **2** *v/i (of tape, story)* zhǎnkāi 展开; *(relax)* fàngsōng 放松

**unwise** bù míngzhì 不明智

**unwrap** *gift* dǎkāi 打开

**unwritten** *law, rule* wèi chéngwén 未成文

**unzip** *v/t dress etc* lākāi lāliàn 拉开拉链; COMPUT jiě yāsuō 解压缩

**up 1** *adv* xiàngshàng 向上; *look ~* xiàngshàng kàn 向上看; *~ in the sky / ~ on the roof* zài gāokōng / zài wūdǐng shang 在高空 / 在屋顶上; *~ here / there* zài zhè / nà shang 在这 / 那上; *be ~ (out of bed)* qǐchuáng 起床; *(of sun)* shēngqǐ 升起; *(be built)* jiànchéng 建成; *(of shelves)* ānhǎo 安好; *(of prices, temperature)* shàngshēng 上升; *(have expired)* dàoqī 到期; *what's ~?* zěnmele? 怎么了?; *to the year 1989* zhídào yījiǔbājiǔ nián 直到 1989 年; *he came ~ to me* tā xiàng wǒ zǒuguòlái 他向我走过来; *what are you ~ to these days?* zuìjìn zài mángxiē shénme? 最近在忙些什么?; *what are those kids ~ to?* nàxiē háizimen zài gǎo shénme guǐ? 那些孩子们在搞什么鬼?; *be ~ to something (bad)* méi zuò shénme hǎoshì 没做什么好事; *I don't feel ~ to it* wǒ juéde zìjǐ bùnéng shèngrèn 我觉得自己不能胜任; *it's ~ to you* nǐ lái juédìng 你来决定; *it is ~ to them to solve it (their duty)* jiějué zhèijiànshì shì tāmende zhízé 解决这件事是他们的职责; *be ~ and about (after illness)* qǐchuáng zǒudòng 起床走动 **2** *prep*: *further ~ the mountain* zài wǎng shānshàng yìxiē 再往山上一些; *he climbed ~ a tree* tā pádào shùshang qù le 他爬到树上去了; *they ran ~ the street* tāmen yánzhe jiē pǎo 他们沿着街跑; *the water goes ~ this pipe* shuǐ shùnzhe zhèitiáo guǎndào xiàngshàng xíng 水顺着这条管道向上行; *we traveled ~ to Shanghai* wǒmen lǚxíng zhì Shànghǎi 我们旅行至上海 **3** *n*: *~s and downs* gānkǔ 甘苦

**upbringing** jiàoyǎng 教养

**upcoming** *adj (forthcoming)* jíjiāng láilín 即将来临

**update 1** *v/t file, records* xiūdìng 修订; *~ X on Y* xiàng X tígōng zuìxīn yǒuguān Y de xìnxī 向 X 提供最新有关 Y 的信息 **2** *n (of files,* *records*) xiūdìng 修订; (*software version*) zuìxīn bǎnběn 最新版本; *can you give me an ~ on the situation?* nǐ néng gàosù wǒ júshìde zuìxīn xìnxī ma? 你能告诉我局势的最新信息吗？

**upgrade** *v/t* computers etc gǎijìn 改进; (*replace with new versions*) gēngxīn 更新; *ticket* tígāo ... děngjí 提高 ... 等级

**upheaval** (*emotional*) jùbiàn 剧变; (*physical*) biàndòng 变动; (*political, social*) dòngluàn 动乱

**uphill 1** *adv walk* shàngpō 上坡 **2** *adj struggle* jiānnán 艰难

**uphold** *traditions, rights* wéihù 维护; (*vindicate*) zhèngshí 证实

**upholstery** (*coverings*) jiājù zhuāngshì cáiliào 家具装饰材料; (*padding*) diànliào 垫料

**upkeep** *n* (*of old buildings, parks etc*) bǎoyǎng 保养

**upload** *v/t* COMPUT jiāzài 加载

**upmarket** *adj restaurant, hotel* gāojí 高级

**upon** → **on**

**upper** *part of sth* shàngbù 上部; *stretches of a river* shàngyóu 上游; *deck* shàngcéng 上层

**upper atmosphere** dàqì wàicéng 大气外层; **upper-class** *adj accent, family* shàngcéng shèhuì 上层社会; **upper classes** shàngděng jiēcéng 上等阶层

**upright 1** *adj citizen* zhèngzhí 正直 **2** *adv* sit bǐzhí 笔直

**upright** (**piano**) shùshì (gāngqín) 竖式 (钢琴)

**uprising** qǐyì 起义

**uproar** (*loud noise*) xuānxiāo 喧嚣; (*protest*) kàngyì 抗议

**upset 1** *v/t drink, glass* nòngfān 弄翻; (*emotionally*) shǐrén nánguò 使人难过 **2** *adj* (*emotionally*) nánguò 难过; *get ~ about X* yīn X ér nánguò 因 X 而难过; *have an ~ stomach* gǎndào cháng wèi bùshì 感到肠胃不适

**upsetting** lìngrén nánguò 令人难过

**upshot** (*result, outcome*) zuìhòu

jiéguǒ 最后结果

**upside down** *adv* dǐ cháo shàng dǐ cháo shàng 朝上; *turn X ~ box etc* bǎ X shàngxià diāndǎo guòlái 把 X 上下颠倒过来

**upstairs 1** *adv* zài lóushàng 在楼上 **2** *adj room* lóushàng 楼上

**upstart** xīnguì 新贵

**upstream** *adv* xiàng shàngyóu 向上游

**uptight** F (*nervous*) jǐnzhāng 紧张; (*inhibited*) jūjǐn 拘谨

**up-to-date** *information* zuìxīn 最新; *fashions* xīnshì 新式

**upturn** (*in economy*) hǎozhuǎn 好转

**upward** *adv fly, move* xiàngshàng 向上; *~ of 10,000* yíwàn duō 一万多

**uranium** yóu 铀

**urban** dūshì 都市

**urbanization** chéngshìhuà 城市化

**urchin** wántóng 顽童

**urge 1** *n* yùwàng 欲望 **2** *v/t*: *~ X to do Y* jiélì cuīcù X zuò Y 竭力催促 X 做 Y

♦ **urge on** (*encourage*) gǔlì 鼓励

**urgency** (*of situation*) jǐnjí 紧急

**urgent** *job* jí gè 急; *letter* jǐnjí 紧急; *be in ~ need of X* jíxū X 急需 X; *is it ~?* shì jíshì ma? 是急事吗？

**urinate** páiniào 排尿

**urine** niào 尿

**urn** (*for ashes*) gǔhuīwèng 骨灰瓮

**us** wǒmen 我们

**US(A)** (= *United States* (*of America*)) Měiguó 美国; (*formal use*) Měilìjiān Héhòngguó 美利坚合众国

**usable** kě shǐyòng 可使用

**usage** (*linguistic*) guànyòngfǎ 惯用法

**use 1** *v/t* shǐyòng 使用; *skills, knowledge* yùnyòng 运用; *car* yòng 用; *a lot of gas* xiāohào 消耗; *pej: person* lìyòng 利用; *I could ~ a drink* F wǒ zhēn xiǎng hē dōngxi 我真想喝东西 **2** *n* shǐyòng 使用; *be of great ~ to X* duì X dàyǒu yòngchù 对 X 大有

用处; *be of no ~ to X* duì X méiyǒuyòng 对 X 没有用; *is that of any ~?* nà yǒuyòng ma? 那有用吗？; *it's no ~* méiyòng 没用; *it's no ~ trying / waiting* shì / děng yě méiyòng 试 / 等也没用
♦ **use up** yòngguāng 用光

**used**[1] *car etc* yòngguò 用过

**used**[2]: *be ~ to X* duì X xíguàn 对 X 习惯; *get ~ to X* duì X zhújiàn shìyìng 对 X 逐渐适应; *be ~ to doing X* xíguàn zuò X 习惯做 X; *get ~ to doing X* zhújiàn xíguàn zuò X 逐渐习惯做 X

**used**[3]: *I ~ to like him* wǒ céng xǐhuānguò tā 我曾喜欢过他; *I don't work there now, but I ~ to* wǒ yǐqián zài nàlǐ gōngzuò, xiànzài bù le 我以前在那里工作，现在不了

**useful** *person, information, gadget* yǒuyòng 有用

**usefulness** yòngchù 用处

**useless** *information* méiyòng 没用; F *person* chàjìn 差劲; *machine, computer* bùnéng yòng 不能用; *it's ~ trying* shì yě méiyòng 试也

没用

**user** (*of product*) yònghù 用户

**user-friendly** *software, device* yònghù yǒuhǎo 用户友好

**usher** *n* (*at wedding*) yíngbīnyuán 迎宾员
♦ **usher in** *new era* yùshì 预示

**usherette** nǚ yǐnzuòyuán 女引座员

**usual** tōngcháng 通常; *as ~* xiàng wǎngcháng yíyàng 像往常一样; *the ~, please* gēn píngcháng yíyàng 跟平常一样

**usually** tōngcháng 通常

**utensil** yòngjù 用具

**uterus** zǐgōng 子宫

**utility** (*usefulness*) shíyòngxìng 实用性; *public utilities* gōngyòng shíyè 公用实业

**utilize** yìngyòng 应用

**utmost 1** *adj* jídù 极度 **2** *n*: *do one's ~* jiéjìn suǒnéng 竭尽所能

**utter 1** *adj* wánquán 完全 **2** *v/t sound* fāchū 发出

**utterly** jiānzhí 简直

**U-turn** U xíngwān U 形弯; *fig* (*in policy*) zhuǎnxiàng 转向

# V

**vacant** *building, position* kōng 空;
*look, expression* mángrán 茫然
**vacate** *room* téngchū 腾出
**vacation** *n* xiūjià 休假; **be on ~**
dùjià 度假; **go to X on ~** qù X
dùjià 去X度假
**vacationer** dùjià zhě 度假者
**vaccinate** jiēzhòng yìmiáo 接种
疫苗; **be ~d against X** jiēzhòng X
yìmiáo 接种X疫苗
**vaccination** jiēzhòng 接种
**vaccine** yìmiáo 疫苗
**vacuum 1** *n* PHYS zhēnkōng 真空;
*leave a ~ in one's life* shǐ rénde
shēnghuó biànde kōngrán 茫然使人的
生活变得空虚 **2** *v/t floors*
xīchén 吸尘
**vacuum cleaner** xīchén qì 吸尘
器; **vacuum flask** bǎowēn píng
保温瓶; **vacuum-packed** zhēnkōng bāozhuāng 真空包装
**vagabond** nǚ liúláng zhě 流浪者
**vagina** yīndào 阴道
**vaginal** yīndào 阴道
**vague** *answer, wording* bù mínglǎng
不明朗; *feeling, resemblance*
móhu 模糊; *taste of sth* yīdiǎndian
一点点; *he was very ~ about it*
tā hánhú qící他含糊其辞
**vaguely** *answer* bù mínglǎng 不明
朗; *(slightly)* yǒudiǎn 有点; **~**
*possible* bú tài kěnéng 不太可能
**vain 1** *adj person* zìfù 自负; *hope*
túláo 徒劳 **2** *n:* **in ~** bái fèilì 白费
力; *their efforts were in ~* tāmen
báigànle yīchǎng 他们白干了一
场
**valet** *(person)* nán púcóng 男仆从
**valet service** *(for clothes)* xǐyī
fúwù 洗衣服务; *(for cars)* xǐchē
fúwù 洗车服务
**valiant** yǒnggǎn 勇敢
**valid** *passport, document* yǒuxiào 有
效; *reason, argument* yǒu gēnjù 有

根据
**validate** *(with official stamp)* shǐ
shēngxiào 使生效; *(prove)*
quèzhèng 确证
**validity** *(of reason, argument)* zhèngquè xìng 正确性
**valley** shāngǔ 山谷
**valuable 1** *adj* yǒu jiàzhí 有价值
**2** *n:* **~s** guìzhòng wùpǐn 贵重物
品
**valuation** gūjià 估价; *at his ~* jù tā
gūjià 据他估价
**value 1** *n* jiàzhí 价值; *be good ~*
zhídàng 值当; *~ for money* qián
huāde zhídé qiánhuā de zhídé 钱花的值得; *rise/*
*fall in ~* jiàzhí shàngshēng / xiàjiàng 价值上升 / 下降 **2** *v/t s.o.'s*
*friendship, one's freedom* zhēnshì
珍视; *I ~ your advice* wǒ duì nǐde
quàngào shífēn zhòngshì 我对你
的劝告十分重视; *have an ob-*
*ject ~d* jiào rén gūjià mǒuwù 叫
人估价某物
**valve** fá 阀
**van** huòchē 货车
**vandal** pòhuài gōnggòng cáichǎn
zhě 破坏公共财产者
**vandalism** pòhuài gōnggòng
cáichǎn xíngwéi 破坏公共财产
行为
**vandalize** sìyì pòhuài 肆意破坏
**vanilla** *n & adj* xiāngcǎo 香草
**vanish** xiāoshī 消失
**vanity** *(of person)* xūróng 虚荣; *(of*
*hopes)* kōngxū 空虚
**vanity case** xiǎo shūzhuāng hé 小
梳妆盒
**vantage point** *(on hill etc)*
guānwàng diǎn 观望点
**vapor** qì 汽
**vaporize** *v/t* qìhuà 汽化
**vapor trail** *(of airplane)* wùhuà
wěijī 雾化尾迹
**variable 1** *adj amount* kěbiàn 可

变; *moods, weather* duōbiàn 多变 **2** *n* MATH, COMPUT biànliàng 变量

**variation** biànhuà 变化

**varicose vein** jìngmài qūzhāng 静脉曲张

**varied** *quality* bùtóng 不同; *range* gèzhǒng gèyàng 各种各样; *diet* fēngfù 丰富

**variety** duōyàng huà 多样化; (*type*) zhǒnglèi zhǒnglèi 种类; *a ~ of things to do* fēngfù duōcǎi de huódòng 丰富多彩的活动

**various** (*several*) jǐgè 几个; (*different*) bùtóng 不同

**varnish** **1** *n* (*for wood*) qīngqī 清漆; (*for fingernails*) zhǐjiǎ yóu 指甲油 **2** *v/t* tú 涂

**vary 1** *v/i* biànhuà 变化; *it varies* bù yīyàng 不一样 **2** *v/t* gǎibiàn 改变

**vase** huāpíng 花瓶

**vast** *desert, city, subject* jùdà 巨大; *collection of books* dàliàng 大量; *knowledge* yuānbó 渊博

**vaudeville** záshuǎ 杂耍

**vault**[1] *n* (*in roof*) gǒngdǐng 拱顶; *~s* (*cellar*) dìjiào 地窖

**vault**[2] **1** *n* (*in athletics*) chēnggān tiào 撑杆跳 **2** *v/t beam etc* yòngshǒu zhīchēng yuèguò 用手支撑跃过

**VCR** (= *video cassette recorder*) lùxiàng jī 录像机

**veal** xiǎo niúròu 小牛肉

**vegan 1** *n* sùshí zhǔyì zhě 素食主义者 **2** *adj* sùshí zhǔyì 素食主义

**vegetable** shūcài 蔬菜

**vegetarian 1** *n* sùshí zhě 素食者 **2** *adj* sùshí 素食

**vehicle** chēliàng 车辆; (*for information etc*) gōngjù 工具

**veil 1** *n* miànshā 面纱 **2** *v/t* yǐ miànshā zhēyǎn 以面纱遮掩

**vein** (*in body*) jìngmài 静脉

**Velcro®** ⇩ zhānkòu 粘扣

**velocity** sùdù 速度

**velvet** sīróng 丝绒

**vending machine** zìdòng shòuhuò jī 自动售货机

**vendor** LAW màizhǔ 卖主

**veneer** (*on wood*) shìmiàn bóbǎn

饰面薄板; (*of politeness etc*) wàibiǎo 外表

**venereal disease** xìngbìng 性病

**venetian blind** bǎiyè lián 百叶帘

**vengeance** bàofù 报复; *with a ~* měngliè 猛烈; *raining with a ~* dàyǔ pāngtuó 大雨滂沱

**venison** lùròu 鹿肉

**venom** (*of snake*) dúyè 毒液

**vent** *n* (*for air*) tōngfēng kǒng 通风孔; *give ~ to* feelings, emotions fāxiè 发泄

**ventilate** *room, building* shǐ tōngfēng 使通风

**ventilation** tōngfēng 通风

**ventilation shaft** tōngfēng jǐng 通风井

**ventilator** tōngfēng shèbèi 通风设备

**ventriloquist** kǒujì yìrén 口技艺人

**venture 1** *n* (*undertaking*) màoxiǎn 冒险; COM tóujī huódòng 投机活动 **2** *v/i* màoxiǎn 冒险

**venture park** chuàngyèyuán 创业园

**venue** (*for meeting, concert etc*) dìdiǎn 地点

**veranda** yóuláng 游廊

**verb** dòngcí 动词

**verdict** LAW cáijué 裁决; (*opinion, judgment*) dìnglùn 定论

**verge** *n* (*of road*) lùbiān 路边; *be on the ~ of ...* (*of ruin, collapse*) bīnyú ... 濒于 ...; *be on the ~ of tears* jīhū yào kūchūlái le 几乎要哭出来了

♦**verge on** jiējìn 接近

**verification** héshí 核实; (*confirmation*) zhèngmíng 证明

**verify** (*check out*) héshí 核实; (*confirm*) zhèngmíng 证明

**vermicelli** mǐfěn 米粉

**vermin** hàichóng 害虫

**vermouth** wèiměisī jiǔ 味美思酒

**vernacular** *n* fāngyán 方言

**versatile** *person* duōcái duōyì 多才多艺; *gadget* duō gōngnéng 多功能; *mind* fǎnfù wúcháng 反复无常

**versatility** (*of person*) duōcái duōyì

多才多艺; (of gadget) duō gōngnéng 多功能; (of mind) fǎnfù wúcháng 反复无常

**verse** (poetry) shī 诗; (part of poem, song) jié 节

**versed**: *be well ~ in X* jīngtōng X 精通 X

**version** (of book) bǎnběn 版本; (of song, story) gǎibiān běn 改编本; (of events) shuōfǎ 说法

**versus**: *X ~ Y* SP, LAW X duì Y X 对 Y

**vertebra** jǐzhuī 脊椎

**vertebrate** n yǒu jǐzhuī dòngwù 有脊椎动物

**vertical** chuízhí 垂直

**vertigo** xuànyùn 眩晕

**very 1** adv hěn 很; *was it cold? ~ not* - lěngbùlěng? – bù zěnme lěng 冷不冷？–不怎么冷; *the ~ best* zuìhǎo 最好 **2** adj: *caught in the ~ act* dāngchǎng zhuāhuò 当场抓获; *that's the ~ thing I need* zhèngshì wǒ suǒ xūyào de 正是我所需要的; *the ~ thought* (merely) yī xiǎngdào 一想到; *right at the ~ top / bottom* zài zuì shàngmiàn / dǐxià 在最上面 / 底下

**vessel** NAUT chuán 船

**vest** bèixīn 背心

**vestige** (of previous civilization etc) yíjì 遗迹; (of truth) sīháo 丝毫

**vet**[1] n shòuyī 兽医

**vet**[2] v/t applicants etc shēnchá 审查

**veteran 1** n tuìwǔ jūnrén 退伍军人 **2** adj (old) lǎoshì 老式; (old and experienced) lǎoliàn 老练

**veterinarian** shòuyī 兽医

**veto 1** n fǒujué quán 否决权 **2** v/t fǒujué 否决

**vex** (concern, worry) shǐ shāng nǎojīn 使伤脑筋

**vexed** (worried) kǔnǎo 苦恼; *the ~ question of ...* zhēnglùn bùxiū de ... wèntí 争论不休的 ... 问题

**via** jīngguò 经过; (by means of) tōngguò 通过

**viable** life form néng yǎnghuó 能养活; company néng dúlì shēngcún 能独立生存; alternative, plan

qièshí kěxíng 切实可行

**vibrate** v/i zhèndòng 振动

**vibration** zhèndòng 振动

**vice** èxí 恶习; *the problem of ~* dàodé bàihuài de wèntí 道德败坏的问题

**vice president** fù zǒngtǒng 副总统

**vice squad** jǐngchá jiūbǔ duì 警察纠捕队

**vice versa** fǎnzhī yìrán 反之亦然

**vicinity** dìdiǎn 地点; *in the ~ of* (the church etc) zài ... fùjìn 在 ... 附近; *$500 etc ...* zuǒyòu ... 左右

**vicious** dog xiōnghěn 凶狠; attack, temper, criticism èdú 恶毒

**victim** shòuhài zhě 受害者

**victimize** shǐ shòuhài 使受害

**victor** shènglì zhě 胜利者

**victorious** zhànshèng 战胜

**victory** shènglì 胜利; *win a ~ over X* zhànshèng X 战胜 X

**video 1** n lùxiàng 录像; COMPUT shìpín 视频; *have X on ~* lùle X dexiàng 录了 X 的像 **2** v/t lùxiàng 录像

**video camera** shèxiàng jī 摄像机;
**video cassette** lùxiàng dài 录像带;
**video conference** TELEC diànshì huìyì 电视会议;
**video game** diànshì yóuxì 电视游戏;
**videophone** kěshì diànhuà 可视电话;
**video recorder** lùxiàng jī 录像机;
**video recording** lùxiàng 录像;
**videotape** lùxiàng dài 录像带

**Vietnam** Yuènán 越南

**Vietnamese 1** adj Yuènán 越南 **2** n (person) Yuènán rén 越南人; (language) Yuènán yǔ 越南语

**view 1** n fēngjǐng 风景; (of situation) guāndiǎn 观点; *in ~ of* jiànyú 鉴于; *be on ~* (of paintings) zài zhǎnchū 在展出; *with a ~ to X* yǐ X wéi mùbiāo 以 X 为目标 **2** v/t events, situation kàndài 看待; TV program, house for sale shōukàn 收看 **3** v/i (watch TV) kàn kàn 看看

**viewer** TV guānzhòng 观众

**viewfinder** PHOT qǔjǐng qì 取景器

**viewpoint** guāndiǎn 观点

vigor (*energy*) huólì 活力

vigorous *person* jīnglì chōngpèi 精力充沛; *shake* yònglì 用力; *denial* qiánglìe 强烈

vile *thing to do* èliè 恶劣; *a ~ smell* èchòu 恶臭

village cūnzhuāng 村庄

villager cūnlǐ rén 村里人

villain huàidàn 坏蛋

vindicate (*prove correct*) zhèngmíng zhèngquè 证明正确; (*prove innocent*) zhèngmíng wúgū 证明无辜; *I feel ~d* wǒ gǎndào bèi zhèngshí le 我感到被证实了

vindictive yǒu bàofù xīn 有报复心

vine pútáo 葡萄

vinegar cù 醋

vineyard pútáo yuán 葡萄园

vintage 1 *n* (*of wine*) shēngchǎn niánfèn 生产年份 2 *adj* (*classic*) jīngdiǎn 经典

violate *rules, sanctity of a place* wéifǎn 违犯; *treaty* wéibèi 违背

violation (*of rules, sanctity*) wéifǎn 违犯; (*of treaty*) wéibèi 违背; *traffic ~* wéifǎn jiāotōng fǎguī 违反交通法规

violence (*of person, movie*) bàolì 暴力; (*of emotion, reaction*) kuángrè 狂热; (*of gale*) měngliè 猛烈; *outbreak of ~* bàodòng 暴动

violent *person, movie* bàolì 暴力; *emotion, reaction* kuángrè 狂热; *gale* měngliè 猛烈; *have a ~ temper* píqì bùhǎo 脾气不好

violently *react* qiángbào 强暴; *object* jīliè 激烈; *fall ~ in love with X* shēnshen de àishàng X 深深地爱上 X

violet (*color*) zǐ luólán sè 紫罗兰色; (*plant*) zǐ luólán 紫罗兰

violin xiǎo tíqín 小提琴

violinist xiǎo tíqín jiā 小提琴家

VIP (= *very important person*) yàorén 要人

viral *infection* bìngdú 病毒

virgin (*female*) chǔnǚ 处女; (*male*) chǔnán 处男

virginity zhēnjié 贞洁; *lose one's ~* shīshēn 失身

virile *man* qiángjìn 强劲; *prose* yǒulì 有力

virility nánzi qìgài 男子气概; (*sexual*) nánxìng shēngzhí lì 男性生殖力

virtual shízhì 实质

virtual reality xūnǐ xiànshí 虚拟现实

virtually (*almost*) jīhū 几乎

virtue pǐndé 品德; *in ~ of* yīnwèi 因为

virtuoso MUS yuèqì yǎnzòu míngshǒu 乐器演奏名手

virtuous dàodé gāoshàng 道德高尚

virulent *disease* èxìng 恶性

virus MED, COMPUT bìngdú 病毒

visa qiānzhèng 签证

visibility néngjiàn dù 能见度

visible *object* yìjiàn 易见; *difference* míngxiǎn 明显; *anger* yì chájué 易察觉; *not ~ to the naked eye* ròuyǎn kànbújiàn 肉眼看不见

visibly *different* míngxiǎn 明显; *he was ~ moved* kěyǐ kànchū tā hěnshòu gǎndòng 可以看出他很受感动

vision (*eyesight*) shìlì 视力; REL *etc* yōulíng 幽灵

visit 1 *n* bàifǎng 拜访; (*to place, country*) yóulǎn 游览; *pay a ~ to the doctor / dentist* qù kàn yīshēng / yáyī 去看医生 / 牙医; *pay X a ~* bàifǎng X 拜访 X 2 *v/t person* bàifǎng 拜访; *place, country, city* yóulǎn 游览; *doctor, dentist* kàn *be*

visiting card míngpiàn 名片

visiting hours (*at hospital*) tànwàng shíjiān 探望时间

visitor (*guest*) kèrén 客人; (*to museum etc*) cānguān zhě 参观者; (*tourist*) yóukè 游客

visor màozhē 帽舌

visual shìjué 视觉; *arts* zhíguān 直观

visual aid zhíguān jiàojù 直观教具

visual display unit zhíguān xiǎnshì bùjiàn 直观显示部件

visualize xiǎngxiàng 想象; (*foresee*) shèxiǎng 设想

visually shìjué 视觉

visually impaired shìjué qùxiàn 视觉缺陷

vital (*essential*) bìbù kěshǎo 必不可少; *it is ~ that …* … shì hěn zhòngyào de … 是很重要的 …

vitality (*of person, city etc*) huólì 活力

vitally: *~ important* fēicháng zhòngyào 非常重要

vital organs wéichí shēngmìngde zhòngyào qìguān 维持生命的重要器官

vital statistics (*of woman*) nǚzǐ sānwéi 女子三围

vitamin wéitāmìng 维他命

vitamin pill wéitāmìng yàopiàn 维他命药片

vivacious huópo 活泼

vivacity huópo 活泼

vivid *color* xiānyàn 鲜艳; *memory* qīngxī 清晰; *imagination* huóyuè 活跃

V-neck jīxīn lǐng 鸡心领

vocabulary cíhuì 词汇; (*list of words*) cíhuì biǎo 词汇表

vocal (*to do with the voice*) sǎngyīn 嗓音; (*expressing opinions*) chàngsuǒ yùyán chàng suǒ yù yán 畅所欲言

vocal cords shēngdài 声带

vocal group MUS gēchàng tuán 歌唱团

vocalist MUS gēchàng jiā 歌唱家

vocation (*calling*) shǐmìng 使命; . (*profession*) zhíyè 职业

vocational *guidance* zhíyè 职业

vodka fútèjiā 伏特加

vogue liúxíng 流行; *be in ~* zhèngzài liúxíng 正在流行

voice 1 *n* shēngyīn 声音 2 *v/t opinions* biǎodá 表达

voicemail diànhuà dàlù jī 电话答录机

void 1 *n* kōngjiān 空间 2 *adj: ~ of* qùfá 缺乏

volatile *personality, moods* biànhuà wúcháng 变化无常

volcano huǒshān 火山

volley *n* (*of shots*) páiqiāng shèjī 排枪射击; (*in tennis*) jiéjī kōngzhōng qiú 截击空中球

volleyball páiqiú 排球

volt fútè 伏特

voltage diànyā 电压

volume (*of container*) róngliàng 容量; (*of work, liquid etc*) liàng 量; (*of business*) é é 额; (*of book*) cè 册; (*of radio etc*) yīnliàng 音量

volume control yīnliàng tiáokòng 音量调控

voluntary *adj helper* zhìyuàn 志愿; *work* yìwù 义务

volunteer 1 *n* yìgōng 义工 2 *v/i* zhìyuàn 志愿

voluptuous *woman, figure* fēngmǎn 丰满

vomit 1 *n* ǒutù wù 呕吐物 2 *v/i* ǒutù 呕吐

♦vomit up ǒutù 呕吐

voracious *appetite* lángtūn hǔyàn 狼吞虎咽

vote 1 *n* xuǎnpiào 选票; *have the ~* (*be entitled to vote*) yǒu xuǎnjǔ quán 有选举权 2 *v/i* POL tóupiào 投票; *~ for / against …* tóu zànchéng piào / fǎnduì piào 投赞成票 / 反对票 3 *v/t: they ~d him President* tāmen xuǎn tā dāng zǒngtǒng 他们选他当总统; *they ~d to stay behind* tāmen juédìng bùqù 他们决定不去

♦vote in *new member* xuǎnrù 选入

♦vote on *issue* tóupiào juédìng 投票决定

♦vote out (*of office*) tóupiào shǐ luòxuǎn 投票使落选

voter POL yǒu tóupiào quán zhě 有投票权者

voting POL tóupiào 投票

voting booth tóupiào jiān 投票间

♦vouch for *truth of sth* bǎozhèng 保证; *person* dānbǎo 担保

voucher piàoquàn 票券

vow 1 *n* shìyuè shěyuè 誓约 2 *v/t: ~ to do X* lìshì yàozuò X 立誓要做 X

vowel yuányīn 元音

voyage (*by sea*) hánghǎi 航海; (*in space*) hángkōng 航空

vulgar *person, language* cūsú 粗俗

vulnerable (*to attack*) bóruò 薄弱; (*to criticism etc*) mǐngǎn 敏感

vulture měizhōu jiù 美洲鹫

# W

**wad** n (*of paper, absorbent wool etc*) tuán 团; *a ~ of $100 bills* yīdá yībǎiměiyuán de chāopiào 一沓一百美元的钞票

**waddle** v/i yáobǎide xíngzǒu 摇摆地行走

**wade** báshè 跋涉

♦**wade through** book, documents fèilìde yuèdú 费力地阅读

**wafer** (*cookie*) wēifú bǐnggān 威佛饼干

**waffle**¹ n (*to eat*) wǎfūbǐng 瓦夫饼

**waffle**² v/i hánhude tánhuà 含糊地谈话

**wag 1** v/t tail, finger yáodòng 摇动 **2** v/i (*of tail*) bǎidòng 摆动

**wage**¹ v/t war zuòzhàn 作战

**wage**² n gōngzī 工资

**wage earner** yǐ gōngzī wéishēng de rén 以工资为生的人

**waggle** v/t hips, ears láihuí yáodòng 来回摇动; loose screw, tooth etc huàngdòng 晃动

**wagon** RAIL chǎngpéng huòchē 敞篷货车; **be on the ~** F jièjiǔ 戒酒

**wail 1** n (*of person, baby*) tòng-kūshēng 恸哭声; (*of siren*) jiānxiàoshēng 尖啸声 **2** v/i (*of person, baby*) tòngkū 恸哭; (*of siren*) jiānxiào 尖啸

**waist** yāobù 腰部

**waistline** yāowéi 腰围

**wait 1** n děngdài 等待 **2** v/i děng 等; *we'll ~ until he's ready* wǒmen děng tā zhǔnbèihǎo 我们等他准备好 **3** v/t meal zànhuǎn 暂缓; *~ table* zuò fúwùyuán 作服务员

♦**wait for** děngdài 等待; *~ me!* děng wǒ! 等我!

♦**wait on** person cìhou 伺候

♦**wait up** děngzhe búshuì 等着不睡

**waiter** nán fúwùyuán 男服务员;

*~!* fúwùyuán! 服务员!

**waiting** n děngdài 等待; *no ~ sign* bùzhǔntíngchēde biāopái 不准停车的标牌

**waiting list** děnghòuzhě míngdān 等候者名单

**waiting room** děnghòushì 等候室

**waitress** nǚ fúwùyuán 女服务员

**wake**¹ v/i: *~ (up)* xīnglái 醒来 **2** v/t huànxíng 唤醒

**wake**² (*of ship*) chuán hángguòhòu de bōlàng 船航过后的波浪; *in the ~ of* fig jǐnjiēzhe 紧接着; *follow in the ~ of X* zhuīsuí X yǐhòu 追随 X 以后

**wake-up call** huànxíng diànhuà 唤醒电话

**walk 1** n bùxíng 步行; (*path*) xiǎolù 小路; *it's a long / short ~ to the office* zǒudào bàngōngshì yào hěncháng / hěnduǎn shíjiān 走到办公室要很长/很短时间; *go for a ~* qù sànbù 去散步 **2** v/i zǒu 走; (*as opposed to taking the car / bus etc*) zǒulù 走路; (*hike*) chángtú túbù lǚxíng 长途徒步旅行 **3** v/t dog liù 遛; *~ the streets* (*walk around*) zài jiēshang zǒu 在街上走

♦**walk out** (*of spouse*) zǒule 走了; (*of room etc*) tuìchǎng 退场; (*go on strike*) bàgōng 罢工

♦**walk out on** spouse, family yíqì 遗弃

**walker** (*hiker*) túbù lǚxíngzhě 徒步旅行者; (*for baby, old person*) fúchē 扶车; *be a slow / fast ~* zǒulù màn / kuài de rén 走路慢/快的人

**walkie-talkie** bùhuàjī 步话机

**walk-in closet** dàxíng yīguì 大型衣柜

**walking** (*as opposed to driving*) zǒulù 走路; (*hiking*) chángtú xíngzǒu 长途行走; **be within ~ distance** zài bùxíng jùlí zhīnèi 在步行距离之内

**walking stick** shǒuzhàng 手杖

**walking tour** túbù lǚxíng dùjià 徒步旅行度假

**Walkman®** suíshēntīng 随身听; **walkout** (*strike*) bàgōng 罢工; **walkover** (*easy win*) qīngyì huòdé de shènglì 轻易获得的胜利; **walk-up** n wú diàntī gōngyù 无电梯公寓

**wall** qiáng 墙; *fig* (*of silence etc*) sì qiángbì zhīwù 似墙壁之物; **go to the ~** (*of company*) pòchǎn 破产

**wallet** qiánbāo 钱包

**wallop** F 1 n (*blow*) zhòngjī 重击 2 v/t měngdǎ 猛打; *opponent* dǎbài 打败

**wallpaper** 1 n bìzhǐ 壁纸 2 v/t tiē bìzhǐ 贴壁纸

**Wall Street** Huá'ěrjiē 华尔街

**walnut** hétáo 核桃

**waltz** n huá'ěrzīwǔ 华尔兹舞

**wan** *face* cāngbái 苍白

**wander** v/i (*roam*) mànbù 漫步; (*stray*) zǒusàn 走散; (*of attention*) zǒushén 走神

♦**wander around** mànyóu 漫游

**wane** (*of interest, enthusiasm*) jiǎnruò 减弱

**wangle** v/t yòng guǐjì huòdé 用诡计获得

**want** 1 n (*need*) xūyào 需要; **for ~ of** yīn quēfá 因缺乏 2 v/t yào 要; (*need*) xūyào 需要; **~ to do X** xiǎngzuò X 想做 X; **I ~ to stay here** wǒ xiǎng dāi zài zhèr 我想待在这儿; **do you want to come too? – no, I don't ~ to** nǐ yě xiǎnglái ma? – bù, wǒ bù xiǎng 你也想来吗？– 不，我不想; **you can have whatever you ~** nǐ yào shénme dōu xíng 你要什么都行; **it's not what I ~ed** zhè búshì wǒ xiǎngyàode 这不是我想要的; **she ~s you to go back** tā yào nǐ huíqù 她要你回去; **he ~s a haircut** tā děi jiǎn tóufa 他得剪发 3 v/i: **~ for nothing** shénme

yě bùquē 什么也不缺

**want ad** suǒqiú guǎnggào 索求广告

**wanted** (*by police*) bèi tōngjī 被通缉

**wanting: be ~ in** qiànqù 欠缺

**wanton** adj zìyì 恣意

**war** n zhànzhēng 战争; **be at ~** chǔyú jiāozhàn zhuàngtài 处于交战状态

**warble** v/i (*of bird*) wǎnzhuǎnde jiào 婉转地叫

**ward** (*in hospital*) bìngfáng 病房; (*child*) shòu jiānhù de rén 受监护的人

♦**ward off** bìkāi 避开

**warden** (*of prison*) jiānguǎnrén 监管人

**wardrobe** (*for clothes*) yīguì 衣柜; (*clothes*) yīwù 衣物

**warehouse** cāngkù 仓库

**warfare** zhànzhēng 战争; **warhead** dàntóu 弹头; **warlord** jūnfá 军阀

**warily** jǐngtì 警惕

**warm** 1 adj nuǎnhuo 暖和; *welcome, smile* rèqíng 热情 2 v/t shǐ nuǎnrè 使暖热

♦**warm up** 1 v/t rè 热 2 v/i (*of person*) rèshēn 热身; (*of room, soup*) rèqǐlái 热起来; (*of athlete etc*) zhǔnbèi liànxí 准备练习

**warmhearted** rèxīncháng rèxīn cháng 热心肠

**warmly** *dressed* nuǎnhuo 暖和; *welcome, smile* rèqíng 热情

**warmth** wēnnuǎn 温暖; (*of welcome, smile*) rèqíng 热情

**warn** jǐnggào 警告

**warning** n jǐnggào 警告; **without ~** méiyǒu jǐnggào 没有警告

**warp** 1 v/t *wood* shǐ wānqū 使弯曲; *character* shǐ fǎncháng 使反常 2 v/i (*of wood*) qiáoléng 翘棱

**warped** *fig* fǎncháng 反常

**warplane** zhàndòujī 战斗机

**warrant** 1 n xǔkězhèng 许可证 2 v/t (*deserve, call for*) shòuquán 授权

**warranty** (*guarantee*) bǎodān 保单; **be under ~** zài bǎoxiūqī nèi 在保修期内

warrior wǔshì 武士

warship jūnjiàn 军舰

wart yóu 疣

wartime zhànshí 战时

wary jǐnshèn 谨慎; *be ~ of* jǐnfáng 谨防

wash 1 *n* xǐdí 洗涤; *have a ~* xǐ/yīxǐ 洗一洗; *that jacket / shirt needs a ~* děi xǐyīxià nàjiàn jiākè/chènshān 得洗一下那件夹克/衬衫 2 *v/t & v/i* xǐ 洗

♦wash up (*wash one's hands and face*) xǐyīxǐ 洗一洗

washable kěxǐ 可洗

washbasin, washbowl liǎnpén 脸盆

washcloth máojīn 毛巾

washed out jīnpílìjìn 筋疲力尽

washer (*for faucet etc*) diànquānquān 垫圈; (*washing machine*) xǐyījī 洗衣机

washing xǐde yīwù 洗的衣物; *do the ~* xǐ yīfú 洗衣服

washing machine xǐyījī 洗衣机

Washington Huáshèngdùn 华盛顿

washroom guànxǐshì 盥洗室

wasp (*insect*) huángfēng 黄蜂

waste 1 *n* làngfèi 浪费; (*from industrial process*) fèiwù 废物; *it's a ~ of time / money* zhēnshì làngfèi shíjiān/jīnqián 真是浪费时间/金钱 2 *adj* fèiqì 废弃 3 *v/t* làngfèi 浪费

♦waste away shuāiruò 衰弱

wasteful huīhuò 挥霍

wasteland fèixū 废墟; wastepaper fèizhǐ 废纸; wastepaper basket fèizhǐlǒu 废纸篓; waste product fèipǐn 废品

watch 1 *n* (*timepiece*) shǒubiǎo 手表; *keep ~* fàngshào 放哨 2 *v/t* movie, TV kàn 看; (*spy on*) jiānshì 监视; (*look after*) zhàokàn 照看 3 *v/i* kàn 看

♦watch for shǒuhòu 守候

♦watch out xiǎoxīn 小心; *~!* xiǎoxīn! 小心！

♦watch out for (*be careful of*) dāngxīn 当心

watchful jǐngtì 警惕

watchmaker zhōngbiǎo jiàng 钟表匠

water 1 *n* shuǐ 水; *~s* NAUT lǐnghǎi 领海 2 *v/t plant* jiāo 浇 3 *v/i* (*of eyes*) liúlèi 流泪; *my mouth is ~ing* wǒ zài liú kǒushuǐ 我在流口水

♦water down *drink* xīshì 稀释

water chestnut gāncǎo lìzi 甘草栗子; watercolor shuǐcǎi 水彩; waterfall pùbù 瀑布

watering can jiāoshuǐtǒng 浇水筒

water level shuǐwèi 水位; waterlogged jìnmǎnshuǐ 浸满水; watermelon xīguā 西瓜; waterproof *adj* fángshuǐ 防水; waterside *n* shuǐbiān 水边; *at the ~* zài shuǐbiān 在水边; waterskiing huáshuǐ 滑水; watertight *compartment* búlòushuǐ 不漏水; waterway shuǐlù 水路; watery duōshuǐ 多水

watt wǎtè 瓦特

wave[1] *n* (*in sea*) bōlàng 波浪

wave[2] 1 *n* (*of hand*) zhìyì 致意 2 *v/i* (*with hand*) huīshǒu 挥手; *~ to X* xiàng X huīshǒu 向 X 挥手 3 *v/t flag etc* huīwǔ 挥舞

wavelength RAD bōcháng 波长; *be on the same ~* fig yìqù xiāngtóu 意趣相投

waver dòngyáo 动摇

wavy *hair, line* bōfú 波状

wax *n* (*for floor, furniture*) là 蜡; (*in ear*) ěrgòu 耳垢

way 1 *n* (*method*) fāngfǎ 方法; (*of behaving etc*) fāngshì 方式; (*route*) lùxiàn 路线; *this ~* (*in this direction*) zhèyàng 这样; (*in this direction*) zhètiáolù 这条路; *by the ~* (*incidentally*) shùnbiàn wènyīxià 顺便问一下; *~ by ~ of* (*via*) jīngyóu 经由; (*in the form of*) zuòwéi 作为; *in a ~* (*in certain respects*) zài yídìng chéngdùshang 在一定程度上; *be under ~* zài jìnxíngzhōng 在进行中; *give ~* MOT rànglù 让路; (*collapse*) tāntā 坍塌; *give ~ to X* (*be replaced by*) yóu X dàitì 由 X 代替; *have one's* (*own*) ~ zìzhǔ xíngshì 自主行事; *OK, we'll do it your* ~ hǎoba, wǒmen àn nǐde fāngfǎ zuò 好吧，我们按你的方法做; *lead the* ~ yǐnlù 引路; *lose one's* ~ mílù 迷路; *be in the* ~ (*be an obstruction*) dǎnglù 挡路; *it's on the* ~ *to the station* tā zài qù chēzhàn de lùshang 它就在去车站的路上; *I was on my* ~ *to the station* wǒ zhèng zài qù chēzhàn de lù shang 我正在去车站的路上; *no* ~! juéduì bù! 绝对不！; *there's no* ~ *he can do it* tā gēnběn bùnéng zuò 他根本不能做 2 *adv* ~ (*much*) yuǎnyuǎn 远远; *it's* ~ *too soon to decide* xiànzài zuò juédìng háishí tàizǎo 现在作决定还是太早; *they are* ~ *behind with their work* tāmende gōngzuò yuǎnyuǎnde làzài hòumiàn 他们的工作远远地落在后面

**way in** rùkǒu 入口; **way of life** shēnghuó fāngshì 生活方式; **way out** *n* chūkǒu 出口; *fig* (*from situation*) chūlù 出路

**we** wǒmen 我们

**weak** *tea, coffee* dàn 淡; *government, currency* bóruò 薄弱; (*physically*) xūruò 虚弱; (*morally*) ruǎnruò 软弱

**weaken 1** *v/t* xuēruò 削弱 **2** *v/i* biànruò 变弱

**weakling** (*morally*) ruòzhě 弱者; (*physically*) tǐruò de rén 体弱的人

**weakness** ruòdiǎn 弱点; *have a ~ for X* (*liking*) piān'ài X 偏爱 X

**wealth** cáifù 财富; *a ~ of* dàliàng 大量

**wealthy** fùyǒu 富有

**weapon** wǔqì 武器

**wear 1** *n*: ~ *(and tear)* sǔnhào 损耗; *clothes for everyday / evening* ~ rìjiān / wǎnyànfú 日间/晚宴服 **2** *v/t* (*have on*) chuān 穿; (*damage*) yònghuài 用坏 **3** *v/t* (*of carpet, fabric: wear out*) mósǔn 磨损; (*last*) nàiyòng 耐用

♦**wear away 1** *v/i* mósǔn 磨损 **2** *v/t* chōngshí 冲蚀

♦**wear off** (*of effect, feeling*) xiāoshī 消失

♦**wear out 1** *v/t* (*tire*) shǐ pífá 使疲乏; *shoes* yònghuài 用坏 **2** *v/i* (*of shoes, carpet*) yòngjiù 用旧

**wearing** (*tiring*) shǐrén kùnfá 使人困乏

**weary** kùnfá 困乏

**weather 1** *n* tiānqì 天气; *be feeling under the* ~ gǎndào bùshūfu 感到不舒服 **2** *v/t crisis* jīnglì 经历

**weather-beaten** bǎo jīng fēng-shuāng 饱经风霜; **weather forecast** tiānqì yùbào 天气预报; **weatherman** qìxiàng yùbào-yuán 气象预报员

**weave 1** *v/t* biānzhī 编织 **2** *v/i* (*move*) yūhuí xíngjìn 迂回行进

**web** (COMPUT, *of spider*) wǎng 网

**webbed feet** yǒu pǔ de jiǎo 有蹼的脚

**web page** wǎngzhǐ 网址

**web site** wǎngzhǐ 网址, zhàndiǎn 站点

**wedding** hūnlǐ 婚礼

**wedding anniversary** jiéhūn zhōunián 结婚周年; **wedding cake** hūnlǐ dàngāo 婚礼蛋糕; **wedding day** hūnlǐrì 婚礼日; **wedding dress** hūnshā 婚纱; **wedding ring** jiéhūn jièzhǐ 结婚戒指

**wedge** *n* (*to hold sth in place*) xiēzi 楔子; (*of cheese etc*) yījiǎo 一角

**Wednesday** xīngqīsān 星期三

**weed 1** *n* zácǎo 杂草 **2** *v/t* chúqù zácǎo 除去杂草

♦**weed out** (*remove*) táotài 淘汰

**weedkiller** chúcǎojì 除草剂

**week** xīngqī 星期; *a ~ tomorrow* xiàyīzhōude míngtiān 下一周的明天

**weekday** xīngqī yī dào wǔ 星期一到五

**weekend** zhōumò 周末; *on the* ~ zhōumò 周末

**weekly 1** *adj* měizhōu yīcì 每周一次 **2** *n* (*magazine*) zhōukān 周刊 **3** *adv* měizhōu yīcì 每周一次

**weep** kūqì 哭泣

weigh 1 v/t chēng ... de zhòngliàng 称...的重量 2 v/i cèchū zhòngliàng 测出重量

♦weigh down: be weighed down with (with bags) bèi ... yāwān 被...压弯; (with worries) shǐrén jǔsàng 使人沮丧

♦weigh up (assess) gūliàng 估量

weight (of person, object) zhòngliàng 重量

weightlifter jǔzhòng yùndòngyuán 举重运动员

weightlifting jǔzhòng 举重

weir yàn 堰

weird guàiyì 怪异

weirdo n F gǔguàide rén 古怪的人

welcome 1 adj shòu huānyíng 受欢迎; you're ~! biékèqì! 别客气！; you're ~ to try some suíbiàn chángcháng 随便尝尝 2 n (for guests etc) huānyíng 欢迎; fig (to news, proposal) yōnghù 拥护 3 v/t guests etc yíngjiē 迎接; fig: decision etc duì ... gǎndào yúkuài 对...感到愉快

weld v/t hànjiē 焊接

welder hànjiē gōngrén 焊接工人

welfare jiànkāng 健康; (financial assistance) fúlì jiùjì 福利救济; be on ~ jiēshòu fúlì jiùjìjīn 接收福利救济金

welfare check fúlì zhīpiào 福利支票; welfare state fúlì guójiā 福利国家; welfare work fúlì gōngzuò 福利工作; welfare worker fúlì gōngzuò zhě 福利工作者

well² n (for water, oil) jǐng 井

well² 1 adv hǎo 好; (too) yě 也; as ~ as (in addition to) hái hái 还; it's just as ~ you told me nǐ gàosù wǒ, shì jiàn hǎoshì 你告诉我，是件好事; very ~ (when acknowledging an order) shì 是; (signifying you don't agree with sth but are doing it anyway) hǎoba 好吧; ~, ~! (surprise) yōu, yōu! 呦，呦！; ~ ... (uncertainty, thinking) āi ... 哎... 2 adj: be ~ jiànkāng 健康; feel ~ gǎndào jiànkāng 感到

健康; get ~ soon! zǎorì kāngfù! 早日康复！

well-balanced person qíngxù wěndìng 情绪稳定; meal, diet yíngyǎng dāpèihǎo 营养搭配好; well-behaved xíngwéi guījù 行为规矩; well-being jiànkāng 健康; well-done meat shútòu 熟透; well-dressed yīzhuó zhěngjié 衣着整洁; well-earned yīngdé 应得; well-known zhòngsǒ zhōuzhī 众所周知; well-made zuògōnghǎo 做工好; well-mannered bīnbīn yǒu lǐ 彬彬有礼; well-off fùyù 富裕; well-read bóxué 博学; well-timed shìshí 适时; well-to-do fùyǒu 富有; well-worn yòngjiù 用旧

west 1 n xībiān 西面; the West (western nations) Xīfāng Guójiā 西方国家; (western part of a country) xībù 西部 2 adj xī 西 3 adv xiàngxī 向西; ~ of X de xībù X 的西部

West Coast (of USA) Xī Hǎi'àn 西海岸

westerly xīfēng 西风

western 1 adj zài xībù 在西部; Western xīfāng guójiā 西方国家 2 n (movie) xībùpiàn 西部片

Westerner Xīfāngrén 西方人

westernized xīfānghuà 西方化

Western medicine xīyī Xīyī 西医; (drugs etc) xīyào 西药

West Lake Xīhú 西湖

westward xiàngxī 向西

wet adj shī 湿; (rainy) duōyǔ 多雨; "~ paint" "yóuqīwèigān" "油漆未干"; be ~ through shītòu 湿透

whack F 1 n (blow) zhòngjī 重击 2 v/t jīdǎ 击打

whale jīng 鲸

whaling bǔjīng 捕鲸

wharf mǎtóu 码头

what 1 pron shénme 什么; ~ is that? nà shì shénme? 那是什么？; ~ is it? (what do you want?) zěnmele? 怎么了？; ~? (what you want?) shénme shì? 什么事？; (what did you say?) shénme? 什么？

什么？; (*astonishment*) nǐ shuō shénme? 你说什么？; **~ about some dinner?** chī diǎnr fàn zěnmeyàng? 吃点儿饭怎么样？; **~ about heading home?** huíjiāba? 回家吧？; **~ for?** (*why?*) wèishénme? 为什么？; **so ~?** nà yòu zěnmeyàng? 那又怎么样？; **2 adj** shénme 什么; **~ color is the car?** chē shì shénme yánsè? 车是什么颜色？; **~ university are you at?** nǐ zài nǎge dàxué? 你在哪个大学？

**whatever 1** *pron* búlùn shénme 不论什么; (*regardless of*) bùguǎn shénme 不管什么 **2** *adj* rènhé rènhé 任何; **you have no reason ~ to worry** nǐ gēnběn búyòng dānxīn 你根本不用担心

**wheat** xiǎomài 小麦

**wheedle: ~ X out of Y** hǒng Y yǐ dédào X 哄 Y 以得到 X

**wheel 1** *n* lúnzi 轮子; (*steering ~*) fāngxiàngpán 方向盘 **2** *v/t bicycle* tuī 推 **3** *v/i* (*of birds*) xuánzhuǎn 旋转

◆**wheel around** zhuǎnshēn 转身

**wheelbarrow** shǒutuīchē 手推车; **wheelchair** lúnyǐ 轮椅; **wheel clamp** chēlún jiájù 车轮夹具

**wheeze** *v/i* hūxīshí yǒu shēngxiǎng 呼吸时有声响

**when 1** *adv* shénme shíhòu 什么时候; **~ do you go on vacation?** nǐ shénme shíhòu qù dùjià? 你什么时候去度假？; **do you remember ~ you saw him last?** nǐ jì bu jìde shàngcì jiàndào tā shì shénme shíhòu? 你记不记得上次见到他是什么时候？ **2** *conj* dāng ... de shíhòu 当 ... 的时候; **~ I was a child** dāng wǒ shì ge háizi de shíhòu 当我是个孩子的时候; **I'll tell her ~ I see her** wǒ kànjiàn tā jiù gàosu tā 我看见她就告诉她; **don't interrupt ~ I'm talking** wǒ shuōhuà de shíhou, bié dǎduàn wǒ 我说话的时候，别打断我

**whenever** wúlùn shénme shíhòu 无论什么时候

**where 1** *adv* nǎr 哪儿; **~ should I put this?** wǒ bǎ zhège fàng nǎr? 我把这个放哪儿？; **I can't remember ~ I put my glasses** wǒ bújìde bǎ yǎnjìng fàng nǎr le 我不记得把眼镜放哪儿了 **2** *conj*: **the hotel ~ Chairman Mao stayed** Máo Zhǔxí zhùguòde bīnguǎn 毛主席住过的宾馆; **this is ~ I used to live** zhè shì wǒ céngjīng zhùguò de dìfang 这是我曾经住过的地方

**whereabouts** *adv* nǎli 哪里; **~ in ... do you live?** nǐjiā zài ... nǎli? 你家在 ... 哪里?

**wherever 1** *conj* wúlùn nǎli 无论哪里 **2** *adv* dàodǐ zài nǎli 到底在哪里

**whet** *appetite* yǐnqǐ 引起

**whether** shìfǒu 是否

**which 1** *adj* nǎyíge 哪一个; **~ one is yours?** nǎge shì nǐde? 哪个是你的？ **2** *pron* (*interrogative*) nǎge 哪个; (*relative*): **the book ~ I bought** wǒ mǎide nèiběn shū 我买的那本书; **the flight ~ I missed** wǒ méi gǎnshang de fēijī 我没赶上的飞机; **take one, it doesn't matter** ná yíge, nǎ yíge dōu kěyǐ 拿一个，哪一个都可以

**whichever 1** *adj* rènhé rènhé 无论任何 **2** *pron* wúlùn nǎge 无论哪个

**whiff** (*smell*) yígǔ qìwèi 一股气味

**while 1** *conj*: **~ ... zài ... shíqī** 在 ... 时期; (*although*) suīrán 虽然 **2** *n* shíjiān 时间; **a long ~** hěncháng shíjiān 很长时间; **for a ~** yíduàn shíjiān 一段时间; **I'll wait a ~ longer** wǒ zài děng yíhuìr 我再等一会儿

◆**while away** xiāoyáode dùguò 逍遥地度过

**whim** tūfā qíxiǎng 突发奇想

**whimper 1** *n* wūyèshēng 呜咽声 **2** *v/i* wūyè 呜咽

**whine** *v/i* (*of dog*) fāchū chángjiàoshēng 发出长叫声; F (*complain*) bàoyuàn 抱怨

**whip 1** *n* biānzi 鞭子 **2** *v/t* (*beat*) biāndǎ 鞭打; *cream* jiǎodǎ 搅打;

F (defeat) dǎbài 打败

♦ **whip out** F (take out) xùnsù náchū 迅速拿出

♦ **whip up** (arouse) huànqǐ 唤起

**whipping** (beating) biāndǎ 鞭打; F (defeat) dǎbài 打败

**whirl 1** n: *my mind is in a ~* wǒde sīxù yípiàn hùnluàn 我的思绪一片混乱 **2** v/i xuánzhuǎn 旋转

**whirlpool** (in river) xuánwō 旋涡; (for relaxation) ànmó yùgāng 按摩浴缸

**whirlwind** xuànfēng 旋风

**whir(r)** v/i zuò hūhūshēng 作呼呼声

**whisk 1** n (kitchen implement) jiǎodànqì 搅蛋器 **2** v/t eggs jiǎobàn 搅拌

♦ **whisk away** chúqù 除去

**whiskers** (of man) húzi 胡子; (of animal) xū 须

**whiskey, whisky** wēishìjìjiǔ 威士忌酒

**whisper 1** n ěryǔ 耳语 **2** v/i qièqièsīyǔ 窃窃私语 **3** v/t dīshēng shuō 低声说

**whistle 1** n (sound) kǒushàoshēng 口哨声; (device) shàozi 哨子 **2** v/i fā xūxūshēng 发嘘嘘声 **3** v/t yòng kǒushào chuī 用口哨吹

**white 1** n (color) báisè 白色; (of egg) dànbái 蛋白; (person) báirén 白人 **2** adj cāngbái 苍白; person báirén 白人

**white-collar worker** báilǐng gōngrén 白领工人; **White House** Bái Gōng 白宫; **white lie** wú èyì de huǎngyán 无恶意的谎言; **white meat** báiròu 白肉; **whiteout** (for text) túgǎiyè 涂改液; **whitewash 1** n bái túliào 白涂料; fig yǎngài zhēnxiàng 掩盖真相 **2** v/t fěnshuā 粉刷; **white wine** bái pútaojiǔ 白葡萄酒

**whittle** wood xùchéngxíng 削成形

♦ **whittle down** xùjiǎn 削减

**whiz(z)** n: *be a ~ at ..* F zài ... fāngmiàn chūsè 在 ... 方面出色

♦ **whizz by, whizz past** (of time, car) fēiguò 飞过

**whizzkid** F jiāozi 骄子

**who ◊** (interrogative) shéi 谁; *~'s that?* nà shì shéi? 那是谁？; *~ were you speaking to?* nǐ gēn shéi shuōhuà? 你跟谁说话 ◊ (relative): *the man ~ taught me* jiāoguò wǒ de nèige rén 教过我的那个人; *those ~ can speak Chinese* huì jiǎng Zhōngwén de rén 会讲中文的人

**whoever** wúlùn shì shéi 无论是谁

**whole 1** adj zhěnggè 整个; *the ~ town / country* zhěnggè chéngshì / guójiā 整个城市 / 国家; *it's a ~ lot easier / better* zhèyàng róngyì / hǎo duō le 这样容易 / 好多了 **2** n zhěngtǐ 整体; *the ~ of the United States* zhěnggè Měiguó 整个美国; *on the ~* zǒngde kànlái 总的看来

**whole-hearted** quánxīn quányì 全心全意; **wholesale 1** adj pīfā 批发; fig dàguīmó 大规模 **2** adv yǐ pīfājià 以批发价; **wholesaler** pīfāshāng 批发商; **wholesome** cùjìn jiànkāng 促进健康

**wholly** wánquán 完全

**whom:** *~ did you see?* fml nǐ jiàndè shì nǎwèi? 你见的是哪位？

**whooping cough** bǎirìké 百日咳

**whore** n jìnǚ 妓女

**whose 1** pron (interrogative) shéide 谁的; (relative): *~ is this?* zhè shì shéide? 这是谁的？; *a country ~ economy is booming* yígè jīngjì zhèngzài péngbó fāzhǎn de guójiā 一个经济正在蓬勃发展的国家 **2** adj shéide 谁的; *~ bike is that?* nà liàng zìxíngchē shì shéide? 那辆自行车是谁的？

**why** wèishénme 为什么; *that's ~* nà jiùshì yuányīn 那就是原因; *~ not?* wèishénme bù? 为什么不？; *I don't know ~ I said that* wǒ bù zhīdào wèishénme nàyàng shuō 我不知道为什么那样说

**wicked** xié'è 邪恶

**wicker** téngtiáo 藤条

**wicker chair** téngyǐ 藤椅

**wicket** (in station, bank etc) guìtái

柜台

**wide** adj kuānkuò 宽阔; experience fēngfù 丰富; range guǎngfàn 广泛; be 12 yards ~ shí'èr mǎ kuān 十二码宽

**wide awake** wánquán qīngxǐng 完全清醒

**widely** used, known guǎngfàn 广泛

**widen 1** v/t jiākuān 加宽 **2** v/i biànkuān 变宽

**wide-open** dàkāi 大开

**widespread** biànbù 遍布

**widow** guǎfu 寡妇

**widower** guānfu 鳏夫

**width** kuāndù 宽度

**wield** weapon huīdòng 挥动; power xíngshǐ 行使

**wife** ⇩ qīzi 妻子

**wig** jiǎfà 假发

**wiggle** v/t hips bǎidòng 摆动; loose screw etc niǔdòng 扭动

**wild 1** adj animal, flowers yěshēng 野生; teenager, party yěxìng 野性; (crazy: scheme) mángmù 盲目; applause rèliè 热烈; be ~ about (keen on) rèzhōng yú 热衷于; go ~ fēngkuáng huānhū 疯狂欢呼; (become angry) biàndé fènnù 变得愤怒; run ~ (of children) zìyóu fàngdàng 自由放荡; (of plants) sìchù mànyán 四处蔓延 **2** n: the ~s huāngyě 荒野

**wilderness** (empty place) huāngyuán 荒原; (garden) zhíwù cóngshēng de dìfang 植物丛生的地方

**wildfire: spread like ~** fēisù chuánkāi 飞速传开; **wildgoose chase** háowú xīwàng de zhuīxún 毫无希望的追寻; **wildlife** yěshēng niǎoshòu 野生鸟兽

**willful** person gùzhí 固执; action gùyì 故意

**will¹** n LAW yízhǔ 遗嘱

**will²** n (willpower) yìzhì 意志

**will³**: I ~ let you know tomorrow míngtiān wǒ huì gàosù nǐ 明天我会告诉你; ~ you be there? nǐ huì zài nàr ma? 你会在那儿吗？; I won't be back until late wǒ hěn wǎn cái néng huílái 我很

晚才能回来; you ~ call me, won't you? nǐ huì gěi wǒ dǎ diànhuà, shì ba? 你会给我打电话，是吧？; I'll pay for this – no you won't wǒ lái fùkuǎn – nǐ bú yòng fù 我来付款 – 你不用付; the car won't start chē qǐdòng bù liǎo 车启动不了; ~ you tell her that ...? nǐ kěyǐ gàosù tā ... ma? 你可以告诉她 ... 吗？; ~ you have some more tea? nǐ yào-bùyào zài hē yìdiǎn chá? 你要不要再喝一点茶？; ~ you stop that! déleba! 得了吧！

**willing** lèyú 乐于

**willingly** gānxīn qíngyuàn 甘心情愿

**willingness** yuànyì 愿意

**willow** liǔshù 柳树

**willpower** yìzhìlì 意志力

**wilt** v/i (of plant) kūwěi 枯萎

**wily** jiǎohuá 狡猾

**wimp** F jiāoqìbāo 娇气包

**win 1** n shènglì 胜利 **2** v/t huòshèng 获胜 **3** v/i yíngdé 赢得

**wince** v/i tuìsuō 退缩

**wind¹** n fēng 风; (flatulence) wèichángzhōng de qì 胃肠中的气; get ~ of ... dédào ... de fēngshēng 得到 ... 的风声 **2** v/t be ~ed qìchuǎnxūxū 气喘嘘嘘

**wind²** v/i (of path etc) wānyán 蜿蜒 **2** v/t cloth etc chánrào 缠绕

♦ **wind down 1** v/i (of party etc) píngjìng 平静 **2** v/t car window yáoxià 摇下; business jiǎnchǎn 减产

♦ **wind up 1** v/t clock shàng fātiáo 上发条; car window yáoshàng 摇上; speech, presentation, affairs jiéshù 结束; company guānbì 关闭 **2** v/i (finish) jiéshù 结束; ~ in hospital zuìzhōng zhùjìn yīyuàn 最终住进医院

**windfall** fig yìwài huòdé 意外获得

**winding** wānyán 蜿蜒

**wind instrument** guǎnyuèqì 管乐器

**windmill** fēngchē 风车

**window** chuānghu 窗户; COMPUT

shìchuāng 视窗; **in the ~** (of store) chúchuāng 橱窗

**windowpane** chuāng bōli 窗玻璃; **window-shop: go ~ping** liúlǎn chúchuāng 浏览橱窗; **windowsill** chuāngtái 窗台

**windshield** dǎngfēng bōli 挡风玻璃; **windshield wiper** ⇩ guāshuǐqì 刮水器; **windsurfer** (person) fānbǎn yùndòngyuán 帆板运动员; (board) fānbǎn 帆板); **windsurfing** fānbǎn yùndòng 帆板运动

**windy** weather, day duōfēng 多风; **it's getting ~** qǐ fēng le 起风了

**wine** pútaojiǔ 葡萄酒

**wine list** pútaojiǔ dān 葡萄酒单

**wing** n chìbǎng 翅膀; SP biāncè 边侧

**wink 1** n zhǎyǎn 眨眼 **2** v/i (of person) shǐ yǎnsè 使眼色; **~ at** xiàng ... zhǎyǎn 向 ... 眨眼

**winner** huòshèng zhě 获胜者

**winning** adj huòshèng 获胜

**winning post** zhōngdiǎn biāozhù 终点标柱

**winnings** yíngdéde qián 赢得的钱

**winter** n dōngtiān 冬天

**winter sports** dōngjì yùndòng 冬季运动

**wintry** hánlěng 寒冷

**wipe** v/t cā 擦; tape mǒdiào 抹掉

♦ **wipe out** (kill, destroy) cuīhuǐ 摧毁; debt huánqīng 还清

**wire** (made of metal) jīnshǔsī 金属丝; ELEC diànxiàn 电线

**wire netting** jīnshǔwǎng 金属网

**wiring** ELEC xiànlù 线路

**wiry** person shòu ér jiēshí 瘦而结实

**wisdom** zhìhuì 智慧

**wisdom tooth** zhìyá 智牙

**wise** yīngmíng 英明

**wisecrack** n fēngliánghuà 风凉话

**wise guy** pej néngnàiàigmen 能耐梗

**wisely** act míngzhì 明智

**wish 1** n yuànwàng 愿望; **best ~es** zhùhǎo 祝好 **2** v/t xiǎngyào 想要; **I ~ that ...** yàoshì ... jiù hǎo le 要是 ... 就好了; **~ X well** zhù

X zǒuyùn 祝 X 走运; **I ~ed him good luck** wǒ zhù tā hǎoyùn 我祝他好运 **3** v/i: **~ for** qídǎo 祈祷

**wishful thinking** zhǔguān yuànwàng 主观愿望

**wishy-washy** person kōngdòng wúwù 空洞无物; color dàn ér wúwèi 淡而无味

**wistful** kěwàng 渴望

**wit** (humor) jīzhì yōumò 机智幽默; (person) jīzhì yōumò de rén 机智幽默的人; **be at one's ~s' end** zhìqióngjìjìn 智穷计尽

**witch** nǚwū 女巫

**with** ◊ (accompanied by, proximity) hé ... yìqǐ 和 ... 一起; **she came ~ her sister** tā hé tāde mèimei yìqǐ láide 她和她的妹妹一起来的; **I work ~ some very nice people** hé wǒ yìqǐ gōngzuò de rén dōu hěn hǎo 和我一起工作的人都很好; **I live ~ my daughter** wǒ hé wǒ nǚ'ér zhù zài yìqǐ 我和我女儿住在一起; **a meeting ~ the President** yǔ zǒngtǒng huìmiàn 与总统会面; **~ no money** méiyǒu qián 没有钱; **are you ~ me?** (do you understand?) nǐ dǒng wǒde yìsi ma? 你懂我的意思吗? ◊ (agency) yòng 用; decorated **~ flowers** yòng huā zhuāngshì 用花装饰; write **~** brush yòng máobǐ xiězì 用毛笔写字 ◊ (cause) yóuyú 由于; **shivering ~ fear** yóuyú kǒngjù ér chàndǒu 由于恐惧而颤抖; **~ a smile / a wave** wēixiàozhe / huīzheshǒu 微笑着 / 挥着手 ◊ (possession) yǒu 有; **the house ~ the red door** yǒu hóng mén de nèige fángzi 有红门的那个房子; **a girl ~ blue eyes** lán yǎnjīng de gūniang 蓝眼睛的姑娘; **we need someone ~ experience** wǒmen xūyào yǒu jīngyàn de rén 我们需要有经验的人

**withdraw** v/t complaint, application chèxiāo 撤消; money from bank tíqǔ 提取; troops chèhuí 撤回 **2** v/i (of competitor) tuìchū 退出; (of troops) chètuì 撤退

**withdrawal** (*of complaint, application*) chèxiāo 撤消; (*of money*) tíkuǎn 提款; (*of troops*) chètuì 撤退; (*from drugs*) jièdú 戒毒

**withdrawal symptoms** jièdú shí de zhèngzhuàng 戒毒时的症状

**withdrawn** *adj person* gūpì 孤僻

**wither** diāoxiè 凋谢

**withhold** bù gěi 不给

**within** *prep* (*in expressions of distance*) bù chāoguò 不超过; (*inside*) zài ... lǐmiàn 在 ... 里面; (*in expressions of time*) zài ... zhīnèi 在 ... 之内; *we kept ~ the budget* wǒmen bǎochí zài yùsuàn zhīnèi 我们保持在预算之内; *~ my power / my capabilities* zài wǒde quánlì / nénglì zhīnèi 在我的权力 / 能力之内; *~ reach* zài shǒubiān 在手边

**without** méiyǒu 没有; *~ looking / asking* méi kàn / wèn 没看 / 问

**withstand** jīndezhù 禁得住

**witness 1** *n* (*at trial*) zhèngrén 证人; (*of accident, crime*) mùjīzhě 目击者; (*to signature*) jiànzhèngrén 见证人 **2** *v/t accident, crime* mùjī 目击; *signature* zuò liánshǔrén 作连署人

**witness stand** zhèngrénxí 证人席

**witticism** miàoyǔ 妙语

**witty** jīzhì 机智

**wobble** *v/i* yáohuàng 摇晃

**wobbly** bùwěn 不稳

**wok** guō 锅

**wolf** *n* (*animal*) láng 狼; *fig* (*womanizer*) sèláng 色狼 **2** *v/t: ~* (*down*) lángtūn hǔyàn 狼吞虎咽

**wolf whistle** *n* tiǎodòu hūshào 挑逗嘘哨

**woman** nǚrén 女人

**woman doctor** nǚ yīshēng 女医生

**womanizer** sèguǐ 色鬼

**woman priest** nǚ mùshī 女牧师

**womb** zǐgōng 子宫

**Women's Day** Sānbā Fùnǚjié 三八妇女节; **women's lib** fùnǚ jiěfàng 妇女解放; **women's libber** gǔchuī fùnǚ jiěfàng de rén 鼓吹妇女解放的人

**wonder 1** *n* (*amazement*) jīngqí 惊奇; *no ~!* nánguài! 难怪！; *it's a ~ that ...* qíguàide shì ... 奇怪的是 ... **2** *v/i* gǎndào jīngyà 感到惊讶 **3** *v/t* xiǎng zhīdào 想知道; *I ~ if you could help* wǒ xiǎng zhīdào nǐ néngbùnéng bāngmáng 我想知道你能不能帮忙

**wonderful** jíhǎo 极好

**wood** mù 木; (*forest*) shùlín 树林

**wooded** zhǎngmǎn shùmù 长满树木

**wooden** (*made of wood*) mùzhì 木制

**woodwind** MUS mùzhì guānyuèqì 木制管乐器

**woodwork** (*parts made of wood*) mùzhìpǐn 木制品; (*activity*) mùgōnghuó 木工活

**wool** yángmáo 羊毛

**woolen 1** *adj* yángmáozhì 羊毛制 **2** *n* yángmáo yīwù 羊毛衣物

**word 1** *n* cí 词; (*news*) xiāoxi 消息; (*promise*) nuòyán 诺言; *is there any ~ from X?* yǒuméiyǒu X de xiāoxi? 有没有 X 的消息？; *you have my ~* wǒ xiàng nǐ bǎozhèng 我向你保证; *have ~s* (*argue*) zhēngchǎo 争吵; *have a ~ with X* yǔ X sīxià tántán 与 X 私下谈谈 **2** *v/t article, letter* xuǎncí 选词

**wording** cuòcí 措辞

**word processing** wénzì chǔlǐ 文字处理

**word processor** (*software*) wénzì chǔlǐjī 文字处理机

**work 1** *n* gōngzuò 工作; *out of ~* shīyè 失业; *be at ~* shàngbān 上班; *I go to ~ by bus* wǒ zuò gōngchē qù shàngbān 我坐公车去上班 **2** *v/i* (*of person*) gōngzuò 工作; (*of machine*) yùnzhuǎn 运转; (*succeed*) zòuxiào 奏效; *I used to ~ with him* wǒ céng hé tā yìqǐ gōngzuò 我曾和他一起工作; *how does it ~?* zhè dōngxi zěnme yùnzhuǎn? 这东西怎么运转？ **3** *v/t employee* shǐ gōngzuò 使工作; *machine* kāidòng 开动

♦ **work off** *bad mood, anger* xiāochú

消除; *flab* chúqù 除去
♦ **work out 1** *v/t* nòng míngbái 弄明白; *solution* zhǎochū 找出 **2** *v/i* (*at gym*) dàliàng yùndòng 大量运动; (*of relationship etc*) qǔdé chénggōng 取得成功
♦ **work out to** (*add up to*) zǒngjìwéi 总计为
♦ **work up** *enthusiasm* jīqǐ 激起; *appetite* jīfā 激发; *get worked up* (*get angry*) shēngqì 生气; (*get nervous*) jīnghuāng 惊慌
**workable** *solution* kěxíng 可行
**workaholic** *n* F gōngzuòkuáng 工作狂
**worker** gōngrén 工人; *she's a good ~* (*of student*) tā hěn huì gōngzuò 她很会工作
**work day** (*hours of work*) gōngzuòrì 工作日; (*not a holiday*) fēi xiūxīrì 非休息日; *workforce* láodònglì 劳动力; **work hours** gōngzuò qījiān 工作期间
**working class** *n* gōngrén jiējí 工人阶级
**working-class** *adj* gōngrén jiējí 工人阶级
**working knowledge** jīběn zhīshí 基本知识
**workload** gōngzuòliàng 工作量; **workman** gōngrén 工人; **workmanlike** jìshù xiánshú 技术娴熟; **workmanship** jìyì 技艺
**work of art** jīngzhìde wùpǐn 精致的物品; **workout** duànliàn 锻炼; **work permit** gōngzuò xǔkě 工作许可; **workshop** gōngchǎng 工场; (*seminar*) jiǎngxíbān 讲习班; **work station** gōngzuòzhàn 工作站; **work unit** (gōngzuò) dānwèi (工作) 单位
**world** shìjiè 世界; *the ~ of computers / the theater* diànnǎo / xìjù lǐngyù 电脑 / 戏剧领域; *out of this ~* F hǎo dé bùdéliǎo 好得不得了
**worldly** shìsú 世俗; *person* lǎochéng liàndá 老成练达
**world power** shìjiè qiángguó 世界强国; **world war** shìjiè dàzhàn 世界大战; **worldwide 1** *adj* biànjí shìjiè 遍及世界 **2** *adv* quánshìjiè 全世界
**worm** *n* chóngzi 虫子
**worn-out** *shoes, carpet, part* pòjiù 破旧; *person* jīnpílìjìn 筋疲力尽
**worried** dānyōu 担忧
**worry 1** *n* dānyōu 担忧 **2** *v/t* dānyōu 担心; (*upset*) shǐrén yōuchóu 使人忧愁 **3** *v/i* dānyōu 担忧; *it will be alright, don't ~!* méiyǒushì, bié dānxīn! 没有事, 别担心!
**worrying** lìngrén dānxīn 令人担心
**worse 1** *adj* gènghuài 更坏 **2** *adv* gèng bùhǎo 更不好
**worsen** *v/i* biàndé gènghuài 变得更坏
**worship 1** *n* chóngbài 崇拜 **2** *v/t* chóngbài 崇拜; *fig* àimù 爱慕
**worst 1** *adj* zuìhuài 最坏 **2** *adv* zuìzāo 最糟 **3** *n: the ~* zuìhuài 最坏; *if the ~ comes to the ~* rúguǒ zuì zāogāo de shì fāshēng 如果最糟糕的事发生
**worth** *adj*: *$20 ~ of gas* jiàzhí wéi èrshí měiyuán de qìyóu 价值为二十美元的汽油; *be ~ ...* (*in monetary terms*) zhí ... 值 ...; *be ~ reading / seeing* zhíde dú / kàn 值得读 / 看; *be ~ it* hěn zhíde 很值得
**worthless** *object* wú jiàzhí 无价值; *person* méiyòng 没用
**worthwhile** *cause* zhíde zuò 值得做; *be ~* zhíde 值得
**worthy** kějìng 可敬; *cause* zhíchí 值得支持; *be ~ of* (*deserve*) zhíde 值得
**would**: *I ~ help if I could* rúguǒ wǒ néng de huà, wǒ huì bāngmángde 如果我能的话, 我会帮忙的; *I said that I ~ go* wǒ shuōguò wǒ huì qù 我说过我会去; *I told him I ~ not leave unless ...* wǒ gàosù tā, chúfēi ... bùrán wǒ bùhuì zǒu 我告诉他, 除非 ... 不然我不会走; *~ you like to go to the movies?* nǐ xiǎng qù kàn diànyǐng ma? 你想去看电影

吗？；*~ you mind if I smoked?*
wǒ chōuyān nǐ jièyì ma? 我抽烟
你介意吗？；*~ you tell her that
...?* qǐng nǐ gàosù tā ... hǎoma? 请
你告诉她 ... 好吗？；*~ you
close the door?* qǐng guānshang
mén, hǎoma? 请关上门，好
吗？；*I ~ have told you but ...* wǒ
běn yīnggāi gàosù nǐ, dànshì ... wǒ
本应该告诉你，但是 ...；*I ~
not have been so angry if ...* rúguǒ ... wǒ jiù búhuì nàme shēngqì
如果 ... 我就不会那么生气
**wound** 1 *n* shāng 伤 2 *v/t* (*with
weapon*) dǎshāng 打伤; (*with
remark*) shānghài 伤害
**wow!** *interj* āiya! 哎呀！
**wrap** *v/t parcel, gift* bāo 包; (*wind*)
chánrào 缠绕; (*cover*) bāozhù 包
住
♦ **wrap up** *v/i* (*against the cold*)
chuān nuǎnhuo de yīwù 穿暖和
的衣物
**wrapper** bāozhuāng zhǐdài 包装
纸袋
**wrapping** bāozhuāng cáiliào 包装
材料
**wrapping paper** bāozhuāngzhǐ 包
装纸
**wreath** huāquān 花圈
**wreck** 1 *n* cánhái 残骸; *be a
nervous ~* shìge shénjīngzhì 是个
神经质 2 *v/t car, marriage* huǐmiè 毁灭
**wreckage** (*of car, plane*) cánhái 残
骸; (*of marriage, career*) cánhuǐ
zhuàngtài 残毁状态
**wrecker** tuōchē 拖车
**wrecking company** gùzhàng qìchē fúwù gōngsī 故障汽车服务
公司
**wrench** 1 *n* (*tool*) bānzi 扳子;
(*injury*) niǔshāng 扭伤 2 *v/t*
(*injure*) niǔshāng 扭伤; (*pull*)
měnglā 猛拉
**wrestle** shuāijiāo 摔跤
♦ **wrestle with** *problems* nǔlì duìfu
努力对付
**wrestler** shuāijiāo yùndòngyuán
摔跤运动员

**wrestling** shuāijiāo yùndòng 摔跤
运动
**wrestling match** shuāijiāo bǐsài 摔
跤比赛
**wriggle** *v/i* (*squirm*) niǔdòng 扭动;
(*along the ground*) wānyán xíngjìn
蜿蜒行进
♦ **wriggle out of** zhǎo jièkǒu
bìmiǎn 找借口避免
♦ **wring out** *cloth* níngchū 拧出
**wrinkle** 1 *n* zhòuwén 皱纹 2 *v/t
clothes* shǐ qǐ zhòuzhě 使起皱褶
3 *v/i* (*of clothes*) chū zhòuzhě 出皱
褶
**wrist** shǒuwàn 手腕
**wristwatch** shǒubiǎo 手表
**write** 1 *v/t* xiě 写; *check* kāi 开 2 *v/i*
xiě 写; (*of author*) xiězuò 写作;
(*send a letter*) xiěxìn 写信
♦ **write down** xiěxià 写下
♦ **write off** *debt* gōuxiāo 勾销; *car
in crash* shǐ chéng fèipǐn 使成废
品
**writer** zuòzhě 作者
**write-up** pínglùn 评论
**writhe** niǔdòng 扭动
**writing** (*as career*) xiězuò 写作;
(*hand-writing*) zìjì 字迹; (*words*)
wénzì 文字; (*script*) shūxiě tǐxì 书
写体系; *in ~* yǐ shūmiàn xíngshì
以书面形式
**writing brush** máobǐ 毛笔
**writing paper** xìnzhǐ 信纸
**wrong** 1 *adj* cuòwù 错误; *be ~* (*of
person*) cuòle 错了; (*morally*) bú
duì 不对; *what's ~?* zěnmele? 怎
么了？; *there is something ~
with the car* chē yǒu diǎn máobìng 车有点毛病 2 *adv* cuòwù
错误; *go ~* (*of person*) fàn cuòwù
犯错误; (*of marriage, plan etc*)
chūxiàn wèntí 出现问题 3 *n* bù
gōngzhèng de shì 不公正的事;
*be in the ~* yīngshòu zébèi 应受
责备
**wrongful** bù héfǎ 不合法
**wrongly** cuòwù 错误
**wrong number** bōcuòle hàomǎ 拨
错了号码
**wry** *~ smile* kúxiào 苦笑

# XYZ

xenophobia kǒngwài zhèng 恐外症

X-ray 1 n X guāng zhàopiān X 光照片 2 v/t zhào X guāng 照 X 光

yacht yóutǐng 游艇

yachting chèng yóutǐng 乘游艇

yachtsman yóutǐng jiàshǐ yuán 游艇驾驶员

yak máoniú 牦牛

Yangtze River Chángjiāng 长江

Yank F Měiguó Lǎo 美国佬

yank v/t měnglā 猛拉

yap v/i (of small dog) wāngwang jiào 汪汪叫; F (talk a lot) guālā guālā 呱啦呱啦

yard¹ (of prison, institution etc) fàngfēng chǎng 放风场; (behind house) yuànzi 院子; (for storage) duīchǎng 堆场

yard² (measurement) mǎ mǎ 码

yardstick fig héngliáng biāozhǔn 衡量标准

yarn n (thread) shāxiàn 纱线; F (story) qítán 奇谈

yawn 1 n hēqiàn 呵欠 2 v/i dǎ hēqiàn 打呵欠

year nián 年; for ~s F xǔduō nián 许多年; we were in the same ~ (at school) wǒmen shì tóngjí de 我们是同级的; ~ of the tiger / dog hǔ / gǒu nián 虎 / 狗年; be born in the ~ of the ... shǔ ...年; I was born in the ~ of the dragon wǒ shǔ lóng 我属龙

yearly adj & adv měinián 每年

♦yearn for kěwàng 渴望

yearning n xiàngwǎng 向往

yeast xiàomǔ 酵母

yell 1 n jiàohǎn 叫喊 2 v/i rāngrang 嚷嚷 3 v/t dàjiào 大叫

yellow 1 n huángsè 黄色 2 adj huáng 黄

Yellow Emperor Huángdì 黄帝; yellow pages Huángyè 黄页; Yellow River Huánghé 黄河; Yellow Sea Huánghǎi 黄海

yelp n & v/i jiānjiào 尖叫

yen FIN rìyuán 日元

yes shìde 是的; are you Mr Wang? – ~ nín shì Wáng xiānsheng ma? – shìde 您是王先生吗? – 是的 ◊ (repetition of verb etc): are you cold? – ~ nǐ lěng bu lěng? – lěng 你冷不冷? – 冷; do you like it here? – ~ nǐ xǐhuan zhèr ma? – xǐhuan 你喜欢这儿吗? – 喜欢 ◊ (showing agreement) duì 对; he should go – ~ tā yīnggāi qù – duì 他应该去 – 对 ◊ (accepting suggestion) xíng 行; let's go see a movie – ~ zánmen qù kàn diànyǐng ba – xíng 咱们去看电影吧 – 行

yesman pej zǒugǒu 走狗

yesterday zuótiān 昨天; the day before ~ qiántián 前天

yet 1 adv qìjīn 迄今; as ~ dàocǐ wéizhǐ 到此为止; have you finished ~? nǐ wánle méiyǒu? 你完了没有? ; he hasn't arrived ~ tā hái méidào ne 他还没到呢; is he here ~? – not ~ tā láile ma? – méine 他来了吗? – 没呢 2 conj: ~ I'm not sure kěshì wǒ háishí bù kěndìng 可是我还是不肯定

yield 1 n (from fields etc) chǎnliàng 产量; (from investment) lìrùn 利润 2 v/t fruit, good harvest chūchǎn 出产; interest shēngxī 生息 3 v/i (to enemy) tóuxiáng 投降; (to wish) dāyìng 答应; (of traffic) rànglù 让路

yogurt suānnǎi 酸奶

yoke (for carrying) biǎndan 扁担; (for oxen) è 轭

**yolk** dànhuáng 蛋黄

**you** (*singular*) nǐ 你; (*plural*) nǐmen 你们; (*polite*) nín 您 (*polite plural, rare*) nínmen 您们; *never know* shéi zhīdào 谁知道; *it's good for* ~ duì nǐ yǒu hǎochù 对你有好处

**young** *person* niánqīng 年青; *wine* wèi chéngshóu 未成熟

**youngster** qīngshàonián 青少年

**your** (*singular*) nǐde 你的; (*plural*) nǐmende 你们的; (*polite singular*) nínde 您的; (*polite plural*) nínmende 您们的

**yours** (*singular*) nǐde 你的; (*plural*) nǐmende 你们的; (*polite singular*) nínde 您的; (*polite plural*) nínmende 您们的; (*at end of letter*) yǒngyuǎn shì nǐde 永远是你的; *a friend of* ~ nǐde péngyǒu 你的朋友

**yourself** nǐ zìjǐ 你自己; *by* ~ nǐ zìjǐ dúzì 你自己独自

**yourselves** nǐmen zìjǐ 你们自己; *by* ~ nǐmen zìjǐ 你们自己

**youth** (*age*) qīngchūn niándài 青春年代; (*young man*) xiǎo huǒzi 小伙子; (*young people*) qīngshào nián 青少年

**youthful** *fashion, ideas* shìyù qīngnián 适于青年; *person* zhāoqì péngbó 朝气蓬勃

**youth hostel** qīngnián zhāodàisuǒ 青年招待所

**yuan** (*Chinese money*) yuán 元

**Yuan Dynasty** Yuán Cháo 元朝

**zap** *v/t* COMPUT (*delete*) xiāochú 消除; F (*kill*) shāsǐ 杀死; F (*hit*) kuàijī 快击

♦**zap along** F (*move fast*) kuàisù jìnxíng 快速进行

**zapped** F (*exhausted*) jīngpí lìjìn 筋疲力尽

**zappy** F *car, pace* kuài 快; (*lively,*

*energetic*) jīnglì chōngpèi 精力充沛

**zeal** rèxīn 热心

**zebra** bānmǎ 斑马

**Zen** Chán 禅

**Zen Buddhism** Chánzōng Fójiào 禅宗佛教

**zero** líng 零; *10 below* ~ língxià shídù 零下十度

**zero growth** wú zēngzhǎng 无增长

♦**zero in on** (*identify*) xiàng … jízhōng zhùyì lì 向 … 集中注意力

**zest** rèqíng 热情

**zigzag 1** *n* qūzhé xiàntiáo 曲折线条 **2** *v/i* qūzhé xíngjìn 曲折行进

**zilch** F yīwú suǒyǒu 一无所有

**zinc** xīn 锌

♦**zip up** *v/t dress, jacket* lā lāliàn 拉拉链; COMPUT yāsuō 压缩

**zip code** yóuzhèng biānmǎ 邮政编码

**zip drive** COMPUT yāsuō qūdòngqì 压缩驱动器

**zipper** lāliàn 拉链

**zodiac** huángdào dài 黄道带; *signs of the* ~ huángdào shí'èr gōngtú 黄道十二宫图

**zombie** F (*idiot*) mùdāidai de rén 木呆呆的人; *feel like a* ~ (*exhausted*) kuǎle 垮了

**zone** qū 区

**zoo** dòngwù yuán 动物园

**zoological** dòngwù xué 动物学

**zoology** dòngwù xué 动物学

**zoom** F (*move fast*) jísù xíngshǐ 急速行驶

♦**zoom in** COMPUT fàngdà 放大

♦**zoom in on** PHOT lājìn 拉近

♦**zoom out** COMPUT suōxiǎo 缩小

**zoom lens** kěbiàn jiāojù jìngtóu 可变焦距镜头

# Taiwanese equivalents

This list contains a selection of mainland Chinese words in the first Chinese column and, in the second Chinese column, equivalents which are more likely to be used in Taiwan. The Taiwanese words are written in traditional characters. It should be said that there is a good deal of linguistic interaction between the two language groups.

| | | |
|---|---|---|
| ace (in cards) | jiānr 尖儿 | A A |
| adhesive plaster | chuàngkětiě 创可贴 | OK bèng OK绷 |
| aerobics | zēng yǎng jiànshēn fǎ 增氧健身法 | yǒuyǎng wǔdào 有氧舞蹈 |
| afternoon: good afternoon | xiàwǔ hǎo 下午好 | wǔ'ān 午安 |
| air conditioning | kōngtiáo 空调 | lěngqì 冷气 |
| ankle | jiǎowàn 脚腕 | jiǎohuái 脚踝 |
| answerphone | lùyīn diànhuà 录音电话 | diànhuà dálùjī 电话答录机 |
| awesome F | gàilemàole 盖了帽了 | kùbìle 酷毙了 |
| ballpoint (pen) | yuánzhū bǐ 圆珠笔 | yuánzǐbǐ 原子笔 |
| Band-Aid® | chuàngkětiě 创可贴 | OK bèng OK绷 |
| bar code | tiáoxíng mǎ 条形码 | tiáomǎ 条码 |
| barbecue n | shāokǎo huì 烧烤会 | kǎoròu 烤肉 |
| bicycle n | zìxíng chē 自行车 | jiǎotàchē 脚踏车 |
| blood donor | xiànxuè zhě 献血者 | juānxiěrén 捐血人 |
| burglar alarm | fángqiè jǐngbào qì 防窃警报器 | fángdàoqì 防盗器 防窃警报器 |
| butter n | huángyóu 黄油 | nǎiyóu 奶油 |
| cell phone | shǒutí diànhuà 手提电话 | xíngdòng diànhuà 行动电话 |
| check out (of hotel) | jiézhàng 结账 | tuìfáng 退房 |
| checkout time | jiézhàng shíjiān 结账时间 | tuìfáng shíjiān 退房时间 |
| cheese | nǎilào 奶酪 | rǔluò 乳酪, qǐshì 黄鹗 |
| cheesecake | nǎilào nàngāo 奶酪蛋糕 | qǐshì dàngāo 起士蛋糕 |
| chips | shǔpiàn 薯片 | yángyùpiàn 洋芋片 |
| college exam | gāokǎo 高考 | liánkǎo 联考 |
| condom | bìyùn tào 避孕套 | bǎoxiǎntào 保险套 |
| connecting flight | liányùn fēijī 联运飞机 | zhuǎnjiē bānjī 转接班机 |
| container COM | jízhuāng xiāng 集装箱 | huòguì 货柜 |
| container ship | jízhuāng xiāng chuán 集装箱船 | huòguìchuán 货柜船 |
| corkscrew | luósī qǐzi 螺丝起子 | luósī kāijiǔqì 螺丝开酒器 |
| crosswalk | rénxíng héngdào 人行横道 | xíngrén chuānyuèdào 行人穿越道 |
| cursor | guāngbiāo 光标 | yóubiāo 游标 |

| | | |
|---|---|---|
| deodorant | chúxiù jì 除臭剂 | fángchòujì 防臭剂 |
| desktop computer | táishìjì 台式机 | zhuōshàngxíng diànnǎo 桌上型电脑 |
| disco(theque) (*place*) | dítīng 迪厅 | díshìkè 迪士可 |
| disk COMPUT | cípán 磁盘 | cídiépiàn 磁碟片 |
| disk drive | cípán dàijī 磁盘带机 | cídiéjī 磁碟机 |
| diskette | ruǎn cípán 软磁盘 | cídiépiàn 磁碟片 |
| donut | zhá miànbǐngquān 炸面饼圈 | tiántiánquān 甜甜圈 |
| dress *n* (*for woman*) | liányīqún 连衣裙 | yángzhuāng 洋装 |
| driving school | jiàshǐ xuéxiào 驾驶学校 | jiàxùn zhōngxīn 驾训中心 |
| duplex (apartment) | èrliánshì gōngyù 二连式公寓 | shuāngpīn gōngyù 双拼公寓 |
| DVD | shùzì shìpín guāngpán 数字视频光盘 | shùwèi xiǎnshì guāngdié 数位显示光碟 |
| epicenter | zhènzhōng 震中 | zhènyāng 震央 |
| feedback | fǎnkuì xìnxī 反馈信息 | huíkuì 回馈 |
| feminism | nǚquán zhǔyì 女权主义 | nǚxìngzhǔyì 女性主义 |
| feminist | nǚquán zhǔyì zhě 女权主义者 | nǚxìngzhǔyì zhě 女性主义者 |
| floppy (disk) | ruǎnpán 软盘 | cídiépiàn 磁碟片 |
| folk dance | mínjiānwǔ 民间舞 | mínsú wǔdào 民俗舞蹈 |
| garbage | lājī 垃圾 | lèsè 垃圾 |
| gin and tonic | kuíníng dùsōngzǐjiǔ 奎宁杜松子酒 | qínjiǔ jiā kuíníngshuǐ 琴酒加一燠 |
| Gobi Desert | Gēbìtān 戈壁滩 | Gēbì dàshāmò 戈壁大沙漠 |
| hamburger | hànbǎobāo 汉堡包 | hànbǎo 汉堡 |
| hard currency | yìngtōnghuò 硬通货 | qiángshì huòbì 强势货币 |
| hard disk | yìngpán 硬盘 | yìngdié 硬碟 |
| highlighter (*pen*) | cǎibǐ 彩笔 | yíngguāngbǐ 萤光笔 |
| instant noodles | fāngbiànmiàn 方便面 | pàomiàn 泡麵 |
| junk food | kuàicān 快餐 | lèsè shíwù 垃圾食物 |
| Laos | Lǎowō 老挝 | Liáoguó 寮国 |
| laptop COMPUT | xiédài shì diànnǎo 携带式电脑 | bǐjìxíng diànnǎo 笔计型电脑 |
| Mandarin (*language*) | Pǔtōnghuà 普通话 | Guóyǔ 国语 |
| mayo, mayonnaise | dànhuángjiàng 蛋黄酱 | měinǎizī 美奶滋 |
| MBA | gōngshāng guǎnlǐxué shuòshì 工商管理学硕士 | qǐguǎn shuòshì 企管硕士 |
| Mount Everest | Zhūmùlǎngmǎfēng 珠穆朗玛峰 | Shèngmǔfēng 圣母峰 |
| mouse COMPUT | shǔbiāo 鼠标 | huáshǔ 滑鼠 |

| New Zealand | Xīnxīlán 新西兰 | Nǔxīlán 纽西兰 |
|---|---|---|
| North Korea | Běicháoxiān 北朝鲜 | Běi Hán 北韩 |
| orange juice | chéngzhīr 橙汁儿 | liǔchéngzhī 柳橙汁 |
| page (call) | chuánhū 传呼 | dǎ hūjiàoqì 打呼叫器 |
| pager | chuánhūjī 传呼机 | hūjiàoqì 呼叫器 |
| pineapple | bōluó 菠萝 | fènglí 凤梨 |
| platform RAIL | zhàntái 站台 | yuètái 月台 |
| pool (game) | pǔ'ěrdànzǐxì 普尔弹子戏 | zhuàngqiú 撞球 |
| potato chips | zháshǔpiàn 炸薯片 | yángyùpiàn 洋芋片 |
| printer (machine) | dǎyìnjī 打印机 | yìnbiǎojī 印表机 |
| project | tǒngjiàn zhùzháiqū | guózhái 国宅 |
| (housing area) | 统建住宅区 | |
| pump n | bèng 泵 | (for water) chōushuǐjī |
| | | 抽水机; (for air) |
| | | dǎqìtǒng 打气筒 |
| salad | sèlā 色拉 | shālā 沙拉 |
| salad dressing | sèlā tiáowèizhī 色拉调味汁 | shālājiàng 沙拉酱 |
| sauna | zhēngqìyù 蒸汽浴 | sānwēnnuǎn 三温暖 |
| scalper | piàofànzi 票贩子 | mài huángniúpiàode rén |
| | | 卖黄牛票的人 |
| silicon | guī 硅 | xì 矽 |
| silicon chip | guīpiàn 硅片 | xìpiàn 矽片 |
| slot machine | tóubìshòuhuòjī 投币售货机 | zìdòng fànmàijī |
| (for vending) | | 自动贩卖机 |
| smart card | shuākǎ 刷卡 | cōngmíngkǎ 聪明卡 |
| snooker | táiqiú 台球 | sīnuòkè 斯诺克 |
| solitaire | dānrén zhǐpái xì | jiēlóng 接龙 |
| (card game) | 单人纸牌戏 | |
| space shuttle | hángtiān fēijī 航天飞机 | tàikōngsuō 太空梭 |
| speed limit | sùdù jíxiàn 速度极限 | sùdù xiànzhì 速度限制 |
| tampon | yuèjīng shuān 月经栓 | wèishēngmiántiáo |
| | | 卫生棉条 |
| taxi | chūzūchē 出租车 | jìchéngchē 计程车 |
| teamwork | pèihé 配合 | tuánduì jīngshén |
| | | 团队精神 |
| tissue paper | báozhǐ 薄纸 | miànzhǐ 面纸 |
| tonic (water) | tānglìshuǐ 汤力水 | kuíníngshuǐ 奎宁水 |
| tractor | tuōlājī 拖拉机 | qiānyǐnjī 牵引机 |
| T-shirt | yuánlǐng shān 圆领衫 | T xuè T恤 |
| Velcro® | zhānkòu 粘扣 | móshùtiē 魔术贴 |
| wife | qīzi 妻子 | tàitai 太太, lǎopó 老婆 |
| windshield wiper | guāshuǐqì 刮水器 | yǔshuā 雨刷 |

# Numbers

| | | | | |
|---|---|---|---|---|
| 0 | 〇 líng | | 1,000,000 | 百万 bǎiwàn |
| 1 | 一 yī | | 10,000,000 | 千万 qiānwàn |
| 2 | 二 èr *or* liǎng* | | 100,000,000 | 万万 wànwàn |
| 3 | 三 sān | | 100,000,000 | 亿 yì |
| 4 | 四 sì | | | |

The following more complex characters are also used on bills, checks etc.

| | |
|---|---|
| 5 | 五 wǔ |
| 6 | 六 liù |
| 7 | 七 qī |
| 8 | 八 bā |
| 9 | 九 jiǔ |
| 10 | 十 shí |
| 11 | 十一 shíyī |
| 12 | 十二 shí'ér |
| 13 | 十三 shísān *etc* |
| 20 | 二十 èrshì |
| 30 | 三十 sānshí |
| 40 | 四十 sìshí *etc* |
| 21 | 二十一 èrshíyī |
| 35 | 三十五 sānshíwǔ |
| 99 | 九十九 jiǔshíjiǔ |
| 100 | 百 bǎi |
| 105 | 一百零五 yìbǎi líng wǔ |
| 300 | 三百 sānbǎi |
| 350 | 三百五十 sānbǎi wǔshí |
| 356 | 三百五十六 sānbǎi wǔshíliù |
| 1,000 | 千 qiān |
| 1,005 | 一千零五 yìqiān líng wǔ |
| 1,050 | 一千零五十 yìqiān líng wǔshí |
| 5,300 | 五千三百 wǔqiān sānbǎi |
| 10,000 | 万 wàn |
| 65,300 | 六万五千三百 liùwàn wǔqiān sānbǎi |
| 100,000 | 十万 shíwàn |

| | | |
|---|---|---|
| 0 | 零 líng |
| 1 | 壹 yī |
| 2 | 贰 èr |
| 3 | 叁 sān |
| 4 | 肆 sì |
| 5 | 伍 wǔ |
| 6 | 陆 liù |
| 7 | 柒 qī |
| 8 | 捌 bā |
| 9 | 玖 jiǔ |
| 10 | 拾 shí |
| 100 | 佰 bǎi |
| 1,000 | 仟 qiān |

## Ordinal numbers

Ordinal numbers are formed by putting **dì** in front of the cardinal numbers:

| | | |
|---|---|---|
| 1 | 一 yī |
| 1st | 第一 dìyī |
| 2 | 二 èr |
| 2nd | 第二 dì'èr |
| 3 | 三 sān |
| 3rd | 第三 dìsān |
| | *etc* |

\* **liǎng** is used when the number two is used in combination with a measure word.